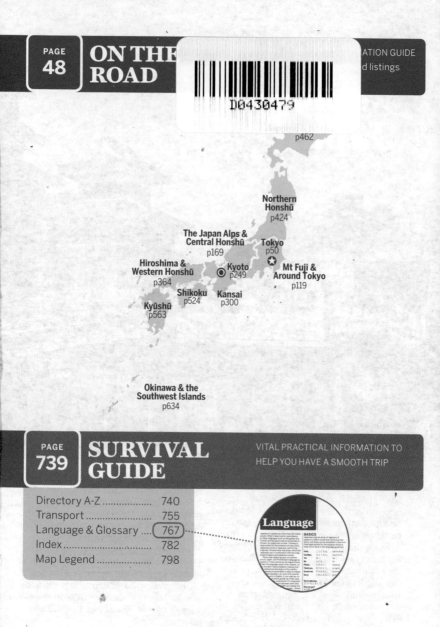

p462

Northern Honshū
p424

The Japan Alps & Central Honshū
p169

Tokyo
p50

Hiroshima & Western Honshū
p364

Kyoto
p249

Mt Fuji & Around Tokyo
p119

Shikoku
p524

Kansai
p300

Kyūshū
p563

Okinawa & the Southwest Islands
p634

PAGE 739

SURVIVAL GUIDE

VITAL PRACTICAL INFORMATION TO HELP YOU HAVE A SMOOTH TRIP

Language

BASICS

THIS EDITION WRITTEN AND RESEARCHED BY

Chris Rowthorn,

Andrew Bender, Laura Crawford, Matthew D Firestone,

Timothy Hornyak, Rebecca Milner, Brandon Presser, Tom Spurling

OCT 0 7 2011

welcome to Japan

Japan Is Open for Travel

Since 11 March 2011, one cannot talk about or consider visiting Japan without the devastating earthquake and tsunami that struck northeast Japan coming up. Yet, rather than focus on the immediate horrors and lingering fears of the tragedy, one should focus on the beauty and accessibility of Japan today. One should note how the Japanese people, resilient and steadfast, behaved after the waters receded: they gathered calmly in evacuation shelters, set off bravely on rescue missions, began the task of rebuilding.

Every image from those first weeks reflects some of the culture's highest virtues: the ability to *gambaru* (do their best) and to *gaman* (bear suffering without complaint). They also capture the famous Japanese thoroughness and civility. This spirit will allow the Japanese people to rebuild northern Japan faster than anyone expects. And it is this very same spirit that makes travelling in Japan such a joy.

Do not avoid Japan because of fear. The March 2011 disaster was of once-in-a-lifetime proportions, and even at the height of the crisis most of Japan was perfectly safe for travel. At the time of writing, only a small area of Fukushima Prefecture was off limits.

Japan is wide open for travel. If you have been considering your first visit to Japan or returning to re-experience the unique magic of the country, the perfect time to go – and to celebrate Japan and its people – is now.

Japan is a world apart – a cultural Galápagos where a unique civilisation blossomed, and thrives today in delicious contrasts of traditional and modern. The Japanese spirit is strong, warm and incredibly welcoming.

(left) Japan's oldest wooden castle, the graceful Matsumoto-jō (p216).

(below) Models displaying traditional style and elegance in a modern Kyoto shopping mall.

Japan Is Approachably Exotic

Japan hits the travel sweet spot. It's unique enough to give you regular doses of 'Wow!' without any downside. Indeed, travelling in Japan is remarkably comfortable, even with the language barrier thrown in – but it's *never* familiar. Staying in a ryokan (traditional Japanese inn) is marvellously different from staying in a chain hotel. Soaking naked in an onsen (hot spring) with a bunch of strangers might be a little odd at first, but it is beyond relaxing. Sitting in a robe on tatami mats eating raw fish and mountain vegetables may not be how you dine back home, but it is unforgettably delicious.

Japan Makes You Think

Perhaps more than any country on earth, Japan makes you think. It is a country that took a good, hard look at the West and said 'We'll take your technology, but we're keeping our culture'. It was never extensively missionised or colonised. It practises an ancient animist/pantheist religion while pushing the boundaries of modern technology. It is a country where tens of millions of people can cram into crowded cities without ever losing their temper. And while you explore Japan, you will regularly find yourself awed by how the Japanese do things – and perhaps, just as often, wondering 'Why don't we do it that way back home?'

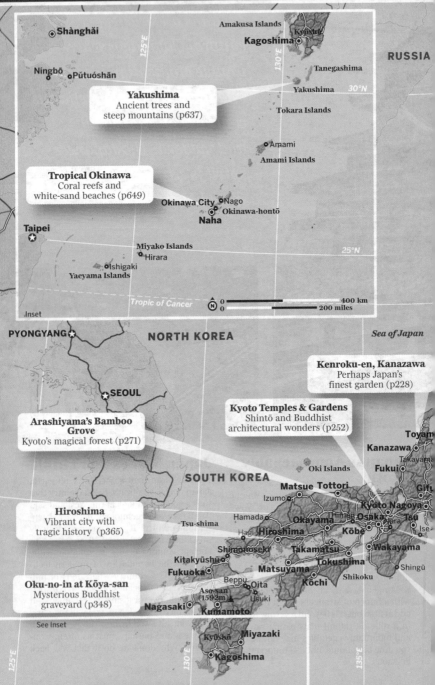

› Japan

Yakushima
Ancient trees and
steep mountains (p637)

Tropical Okinawa
Coral reefs and
white-sand beaches (p649)

Kenroku-en, Kanazawa
Perhaps Japan's
finest garden (p228)

Kyoto Temples & Gardens
Shintō and Buddhist
architectural wonders (p252)

Arashiyama's Bamboo Grove
Kyoto's magical forest (p271)

Hiroshima
Vibrant city with
tragic history (p365)

Oku-no-in at Kōya-san
Mysterious Buddhist
graveyard (p348)

RUSSIA

Shànghǎi

Níngbō Pǔtuóshān

Taipei

Amakusa Islands

Kagoshima

Kyūshū

Tanegashima

Yakushima

30°N

Tokara Islands

Amami

Amami Islands

Okinawa City Nago

Okinawa-hontō

Naha

Miyako Islands

Hirara

25°N

Ishigaki

Yaeyama Islands

Tropic of Cancer

0   400 km
0   200 miles

Inset

125°E

130°E

PYONGYANG

NORTH KOREA

Sea of Japan

SEOUL

SOUTH KOREA

Oki Islands

Toyam

Kanazawa Takayama

Fukui

Matsue Tottori

Izumo

Kyoto Nagoya

Hamada

Okayama Himeji Osaka Tsu

Tsu-shima

Hagi Hiroshima Kōbe Nara Ise

Shimonoseki Takamatsu Wakayama

Kitakyūshū Tokushima

Fukuoka Matsuyama Shingū

Beppu Kōchi Shikoku

Aso-san Ōita

(1592m) Usuki

Nagasaki

Kumamoto

See Inset

Kyūshū Miyazaki

Kagoshima

125°E

130°E

135°E

Gifu

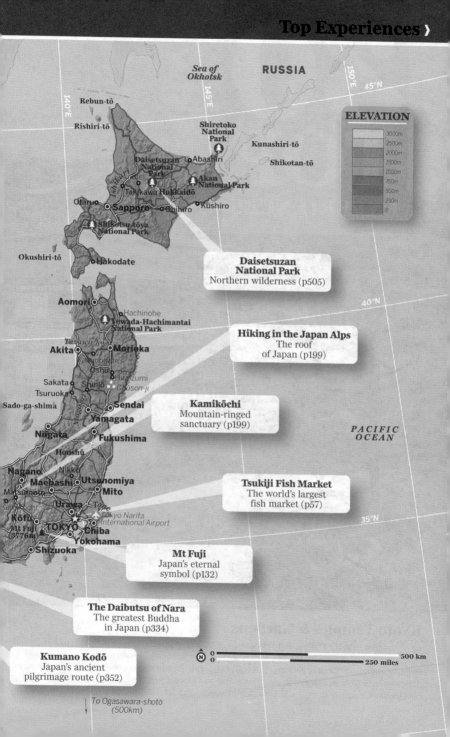

ELEVATION

3000m
2500m
2000m
1500m
1000m
750m
500m
250m
0

Sea of
Okhotsk

RUSSIA

150°E

45°N

140°E

145°E

Rebun-tō

Rishiri-tō

Shiretoko
National
Park

Kunashiri-tō

Shikotan-tō

Daisetsuzan
National
Park

Abashiri

Akan
National Park

Hokkaidō

Takikawa

Otaru

Sapporo

Obihiro

Kushiro

Shikotsu-tōya
National Park

Okushiri-tō

Hakodate

**Daisetsuzan
National Park**
Northern wilderness (p505)

40°N

Aomori

Hachinohe

Towada-Hachimantai
National Park

Tazawa-ko

Hiking in the Japan Alps
The roof
of Japan (p199)

Akita

Morioka

Kakunodate

Ōshū

Sakata

Shinjō

Hiraizumi

Chūson-ji

Tsuruoka

Sado-ga-shima

Sendai

Yamagata

Kamikōchi
Mountain-ringed
sanctuary (p199)

Niigata

Fukushima

Honshū

*PACIFIC
OCEAN*

Nagano

Nikkō

Maebashi

Utsunomiya

Matsumoto

Mito

Urawa

Tone

Tsukiji Fish Market
The world's largest
fish market (p57)

35°N

Kamikōchi

Kōfu

*Tokyo Narita
International Airport*

Mt Fuji
(3776m)

TOKYO

Chiba

Yokohama

Shizuoka

Mt Fuji
Japan's eternal
symbol (p132)

The Daibutsu of Nara
The greatest Buddha
in Japan (p334)

Kumano Kodō
Japan's ancient
pilgrimage route (p352)

Ⓝ 0 _____ 500 km
    0 _____ 250 miles

*To Ogasawara-shotō
(500km)*

30 TOP EXPERIENCES

Kyoto Temples & Gardens

1 With more than 1000 temples to choose from, you're spoiled for choice in Kyoto (p249). Spend your time finding one that suits your taste. If you like things gaudy and grand, you'll love the retina-burning splendour of Kinkaku-ji. If you prefer *wabi-sabi* to rococo, you'll find the tranquillity of Hōnen-in or Shōren-in more to your liking. And don't forget that temples are where you'll find the best gardens: some of them are at Ginkaku-ji, Ryōan-ji and Tōfuku-ji. Kinkaku-ji, above.

Japanese Cuisine

2 Japan is a food lover's paradise and the cuisine (p699) is incredibly varied, running the gamut from simple *soba* noodles to multi-course *kaiseki* banquets. In a city such as Tokyo or Kyoto, you could eat a different Japanese speciality cuisine every night for a month without repeating yourself. There's no doubt that a food tour of Japan will be memorable, but there's just one problem: once you try the real thing in Japan, the restaurants back home will pale in comparison. The only solution is another trip to Japan!

Onsen

3 There's nothing like lowering yourself into the tub at a classic Japanese onsen (p728). You can feel your muscles relax and the 'ahhh' that you emit is just an easy way of saying 'Damn, I'm glad I came to Japan!' If you're lucky, the tub is outside and there's a nice stream running nearby. The Japanese have turned the simple act of bathing into a folk religion, and the country is dotted with temples and shrines to this most relaxing of faiths. Takaragawa Onsen, above.

Staying in a Ryokan

4 Eat in your bedroom. Spend the day lounging about in a robe. Soak in a bath while looking at a garden. Don't lift a finger except to bring food to your mouth. Sounds relaxing? Then we highly recommend a night in a good ryokan (p725). The Japanese had the whole spa thing figured out long before they ever heard the word 'spa'. From first-class place to the most humble ryokan, they will all give you a taste of how the Japanese used to live. Tawaraya ryokan, below.

Hiking in the Japan Alps

5 Close your eyes and picture Japan. If all you see are geisha, Zen gardens, bullet trains and hyper-modern cities, you might be in for a real surprise when you get into the Japan Alps (p199). Hike right into the heart of the high peaks here and you'll be in awe of so much mountain splendour. You can go hut-to-hut among the peaks for a week with nothing on your back but a solid day pack.

Castles

6 Japan's castles have about as much in common with their European counterparts as kimonos have in common with Western dinner dresses. Their graceful contours belie the grim military realities behind their construction. Towering above the plains, they seem designed more to please the eye than to protect their lords. If you have an interest in the world of samurai, shōguns and military history, you'll love Japan's castles. Now that the castle at Himeji is under wraps, try the one at Matsuyama (p550) or Hikone (p329). Hikone-jō, above.

Tokyo's Modern Architecture

7 Japan may be known for its traditional temples, but Tokyo's cityscape is a veritable open-air museum of contemporary structures. The capital has come a long way from copying the Eiffel Tower – these days you'll find dozens of inspired and original works by a pantheon of the world's greatest designers. Fill up on such architectural eye-candy as the chic boutiques in Omote-sandō (p70), the quirky postmodern projects on Odaiba (p82), or even the new army of office towers in Marunouchi (p54). See also p723. Tokyo International Forum, above.

Tropical Okinawa

8 Home to 160 islands – less than half of which are inhabited – Okinawa (p634) is a subtropical playground sandwiched between southern Japan and Taiwan. Stretch out on white-sand beaches, snorkel through rainbow-coloured corals and sail up rivers through thick mangrove jungles while island-hopping. Divers can rub shoulders with manta rays, hammerhead sharks and a zillion tropical fish off the Yaeyama and Kerama Islands. Back on land, refuel with a typically Okinawan dish of stir-fried pork, bitter melon and tofu, and don't forget to wash it down with some fiery *awamori* liquor.

Sumō

9 Sitting ringside when two *yoko-zuna* (sumō grand champions) clash is like watching two mountains get into a shoving match. You can just about feel the earth shake. Even if you're up in the nosebleed seats, catching a sumō match is a highlight of any Japan trip. It's just so different from any other sport we know of: the salt-throwing ritual, the otherworldly calls of the referee, the drawn-out staring matches before the bout, the whole thing just screams 'only in Japan!'

Mt Fuji

10 Even from a distance Mt Fuji (p132) will take your breath away. Close up, the perfectly symmetrical cone of Japan's highest peak is nothing short of awesome. Dawn from the summit? Pure magic. Fuji-san is Japan's most revered and timeless attraction. Hundreds of thousands of people climb it every year, continuing a centuries-old tradition of pilgrimages up this sacred volcano. Those who'd rather search for picture-perfect views from the less daunting peaks nearby can follow in the steps of Japan's most famous painters and poets.

Tsumago–Magome Hike

11 A beautifully preserved post town in southern Nagano Prefecture, Tsumago is home to traditional wooden inns including Tsumago Honjin, which hosted travelling samurai lords. From Tsumago, follow the old Nakasendō post road up through sleepy alpine hamlets, old-growth cedar forests and waterfalls to the mountain pass of Magome-tōge. Here you can rest at a teahouse before continuing to Magome, where fantastic mountain views are a backdrop to old inns and shops. The 8km hike (see p221) winds through a world of farmhouses, waterwheels and rice paddies that time seems to have passed by.

Hiroshima

12 Seeing the city's leafy boulevards, it's hard to picture Hiroshima (p365) as the devastated victim of an atomic bomb. It's not until you walk through the Peace Memorial Museum that the terrible reality becomes clear – the displays of battered personal effects say it all. But outside the quiet of the Peace Memorial Park, energetic Hiroshima rolls on. A visit here is a heartbreaking, important history lesson, but the modern city and its people ensure that's not the only memory you leave with.

Arashiyama's Bamboo Grove

13 Western Kyoto is home to one of the most magical places in all of Japan: the famed bamboo grove in Arashiyama (p271). The visual effect of the seemingly infinite stalks of bamboo is quite different from any forest we've ever encountered – there's a palpable presence to the place that is utterly impossible to capture in pictures, but don't let that stop you from trying. If you've seen *Crouching Tiger, Hidden Dragon*, you'll have some idea of what this place is about.

Ogasawara Archipelago

14 This Pacific island chain (p165), located some 1000km south of Tokyo, is one of Japan's best-kept secrets. Inhabited only within the last 180 years, these subtropical islands boast white-sand beaches, warm blue waters and dozens of rare plant and animal species. Divers and snorkellers can swim with the likes of dolphins, mantas and sea turtles. Hiking, kayaking, whale-watching and stargazing are also on the bill. The catch? The most accessible main island of Chichi-jima is a 25-hour ferry ride away from Tokyo.

Kabuki

15 For sheer otherworldly bizarre-ness, few theatrical spectacles come close to kabuki (p716). It's not a drama if you don't understand the words, for this amps up the 'alien beings who've come down to earth to flummox and mind-boggle the earthlings' factor that makes kabuki one of the most entertaining ways to lose yourself in Japan. While your kids might feel differently, we're pretty sure that you'll find kabuki to be one of those things that resonate long after leaving these islands.

Skiing

16 Travellers the world over are finally savvy about one of Japan's greatest secrets: skiing and snowboarding (p39). From the Japan Alps in Central Honshū to the Siberi-an-blasted Hokkaidō highlands, this is one country where it pays to pack a few extra layers. Well-priced equip-ment rental shops will have you up on the slopes in no time at all, while onsen are waiting to receive you for a unique après-ski experience. Indeed, there is nothing quite like a hot bath and a cold sake after an adrenaline-fuelled day of black diamonds.

Tsukiji Fish Market, Tokyo

17 If it swims in the sea, it's probably on sale at Tokyo's Tsukiji Fish Market (p57). The mother of all fish markets, Tsukiji is a sprawling monument to the Japanese love of seafood. It's a must for sushi fans and anyone who loves a good market tour. Just watch out for those evil electric carts – they don't have it in for you personally, but it might feel that way! Even if you don't wake up early to see the tuna auction, if Tokyo is in your Japan itinerary, you've got to make the pilgrimage to Tsukiji.

EVERETT KENNEDY BROWN / CORBIS ©

Oku-no-in at Kōya-san

RACHEL LEWIS / LONELY PLANET IMAGES ©

19 Riding the funicular up to the sacred Buddhist monastic complex of Kōya-san (p348), you almost feel like you're ascending to another world. The place is permeated with a kind of august spiritual grandeur, and nowhere is this feeling stronger than in the vast Oku-no-in cemetery. Trails weave their way among towering cryptomeria trees and by the time you arrive at the main hall, a sudden appearance of a Buddha would seem like the most natural thing in the world.

Nishiki Market, Kyoto

18 There's something strangely enjoyable about touring a food market where more than half of the goods on display are utterly baffling (is it a food, a spice or some sort of Christmas tree decoration?). Even after years in Japan, you'd be forgiven for not being sure about some of the things on sale here, but you'll love wandering Kyoto's Nishiki Market (p254). The place positively oozes 'old Japan' atmosphere, and you can imagine what it was like here before some decided to attach the word 'super' to the word 'market'.

GREG ELMS / LONELY PLANET IMAGES ©

YAMANASHI SHASHIN JINJUSHO / PHOTOLIBRARY ©

Yakushima

20 A Unesco World Heritage Site, the island of Yakushima (p637) in southern Japan has a staggeringly wild interior that's full of giant Japanese cedar trees, endemic flora and fauna subspecies and mountain peaks of more than 1800m. Some cedars, like the massive Jōmon Sugi, are thought to be more than 3000 years old. To hike into the interior of Yakushima is to enter another world, with every surface glistening with thick, emerald moss and streaming rivulets, products of the 4000mm of annual rainfall on the island.

Osaka by Night

21 Osaka's Dōtombori district (p305) is what Lady Gaga would look like if she were a city. It's an over-the-top neon madhouse where human peacocks prowl beneath giant plastic crabs and *fugu* (pufferfish) the size of small dirigibles (don't worry, it's not a hallucination – you'll see what we mean when you get there). Allow yourself to be carried along by the human tide that rushes through the endless arcades here, and be sure to stop for some octopus balls or automatic sushi.

Kyoto's Geisha Dances

22 It can't be stressed enough: if you find yourself in Kyoto when the geisha dances are on (p293) – usually in the spring – do everything in your power to see one. It's hard to think of a more colourful, charming and diverting stage spectacle. You might find that the whole thing takes on the appearance of a particularly vivid dream. When the curtain falls after the final burst of colour and song, the geisha might continue to dance in your mind for hours afterwards.

GAVIN HELLER / PHOTOLIBRARY ©

Daisetsuzan National Park

23 'Big Snow Mountain' (p505) is Japan's largest national park, covering more than 2300 sq km of pristine wilderness at the heart of Hokkaidō. Serious survivalists set out to tackle the Daisetsuzan Grand Traverse, a multiday hike that crosses rugged mountain chains and penetrates deep patches of forest. But even casual hikers can find adventure and inspiration by basing themselves in any of the park's picturesque onsen villages, and scaling a mountain or two in time for an epic sunrise or sunset.

OCEAN / CORBIS ©

Kanazawa's Kenroku-en

24 This magnificent example of Japanese landscaping is one of the country's top three gardens. Developed over 200 years by the Maeda clan as part of Kanazawa-jō (Kanazawa Castle), Kenroku-en (p228) is said to incorporate the six attributes of a perfect landscape. Stroll the meandering paths past arching bridges, gurgling fountains, plum and pine groves and savour the garden's highlights – the unique Kenroku-en Kikuzakura cherry tree, and the iconic Kotoji-tōrō stone lantern by the Kasumiga-ike pond. Kenroku-en is a delight in any season.

Shopping in Tokyo

RACHEL LEWIS / LONELY PLANET IMAGES ©

25 If you want to see some incredible shops, you've got to come to a country that's been running a multibillion-dollar trade surplus for the last several decades. If it's available to humanity, you can buy it in Japan. Whether it's US$100 melons or curios from ¥100 shops (where everything goes for about US$1), you'll be amazed at the sheer variety of the goods on offer in Tokyo (see p107). Head to the boutiques of Ginza to see the glitterati do their shopping, or join the mere mortals in Shibuya and Shinjuku.

The Daibutsu (Great Buddha) of Nara

BRENT WINEBRENNER / LONELY PLANET IMAGES ©

26 Here's the drill: go to the temple of Tōdai-ji in Nara (p334) and stop for a moment outside the main hall. Then, without looking up, step into the hall. Calm your thoughts. Now raise your eyes to behold the Great Buddha. This is probably the closest one can come to enlightenment without years of meditation. Perhaps no other sight in Japan has as much impact as this cosmic Buddha – you can almost feel the energy radiating from its bulk.

Kamikōchi

27 One of the most stunning natural vistas in Japan, Kamikōchi (p199) is a highland valley surrounded by the eye-popping summits of the Northern Japan Alps. Trails start from the photogenic bridge, Kappa-bashi, and follow the pristine Azusa-gawa through tranquil forests of willow, larch and elm trees. The birthplace of Japanese alpinism, Kamikōchi can be the gateway for ascending Yariga-take (3180m) or for a simple one-hour stroll along the river to the local hot springs. In winter, you can trek in through the access tunnel and have the entire valley to yourself for a snowshoe jaunt.

Shinkansen

28 Sort of like low-flying rocket ships, Japan's *shinkansen* (bullet trains; p762) are probably the coolest trains on earth (apologies to the great trains of Europe and China). If there's a little kid in your heart that still thrills when a train goes by, you can spend hours on the platforms watching the *shinkansen* zip past. And for getting around the country, they are even better than aeroplanes: they're smooth, comfortable and quiet, and you might find yourself wanting to skip your station and just keep going.

Kumano Kodō

29 On southern Kansai's ancient pilgrimage route, the Kumano Kodō (see the box, p352), you can just about imagine the old days when most goods were transported along winding mountain trails on someone's back. If you like the idea of a few days spent wandering through cedar forests, visiting shrines, staying at comfortable lodges and finishing up with a good soak in some of the area's best onsen, this old pilgrims' path might be for you.

Cherry-Blossom Viewing

30 If you think of the Japanese as sober, staid and serious people, you owe it to yourself to join them under a cherry tree laden with blossoms in the springtime. It's as if the cherries release some sort of narcotic that renders all inhibition meaningless. They'll drench you in sake and beer, stuff you with snacks, pull out portable karaoke systems and perhaps even get up and dance. Japan is a happy place when the cherry blossoms are out, and you're more than welcome to join the party.

need to know

Currency
» Yen (¥)

Language
» Japanese

When to Go

Hot summers, mild winters
Warm summers, cold winters

Sapporo
GO Apr–Oct

Takayama
GO Apr–Oct

Tokyo
GO any time

Kyoto
GO Mar–Jun or Sep–Nov

Naha
GO Mar–Nov

High Season
(Apr & May, Aug)

» Flights are pricey around the Golden Week (early May), O-Bon (mid-August) and New Year.

» Honshū cities are busy in the cherry blossom (late March to early April) and autumn foliage (November) seasons.

Shoulder
(Jun & Jul, Sep–Dec)

» June and July is rainy season in most of Japan (except Hokkaidō) – it doesn't rain every day but it can be pretty humid.

» Autumn (September to mid-December) is usually cool and clear.

Low Season
(Jan–Mar)

» Winter is cool or cold in most of Honshū, but it's fine for travel.

» Be ready for snow in the mountains.

Your Daily Budget

Budget less than ¥8000

» Guesthouse room: ¥2800

» Two meals: ¥2000

» Train/bus tickets: ¥1500

» Temple/museum entry: ¥500

» Sundries: ¥1000

Midrange ¥15,000–20,000

» Business hotel room: ¥9000

» Two meals: ¥4000

» Train/bus tickets: ¥1500

» Two temple/museum entries: ¥1000

» Sundries: ¥2000

Top end over ¥20,000

» First-class hotel room: ¥20,000

» Two meals: ¥6000

» Train/bus/taxi: ¥4500

» Two temple/museum entries: ¥1000

» Sundries: ¥2000

Money

» ATMs in post offices and some convenience stores accept foreign cards. Most hotels and department stores, but only some restaurants and ryokan, accept credit cards.

Visas

» Visas are issued on arrival for most nationalities for stays of up to 90 days.

Mobile Phones

» Only 3G phones work in Japan. SIM cards are very hard to find. Mobile phone rental is common and easy.

Transport

» Brilliant public transport system: trains, buses, ferries and planes are all widely available and efficient.

Websites

» **Lonely Planet** (www .lonelyplanet.com) Destination information, hotel bookings, traveller forum and more.

» **Japan Ministry of Foreign Affairs** (MOFA; www.infojapan.org) Links to embassies and consulates.

» **Japan National Tourist Organization** (JNTO; www.jnto.go.jp) Official tourist site.

» **Kōchi University Weather Home Page** (weather.is.kochi-u .ac.jp/index-e.html) Up-to-date weather satellite images.

» **Tokyo Sights** (www .tokyotojp.com) Hours, costs, phone numbers etc for major sights.

» **Rikai** (www.rikai .com/perl/home.pl) Japanese to English translations.

Exchange Rates

Australia	A$1	¥87
Canada	C$1	¥86
Europe	€1	¥117
New Zealand	NZ$1	¥65
UK	£1	¥134
USA	US$1	¥83

For current exchange rates, see www.xe.com.

Important Numbers

Drop the 0 when dialling an area code from abroad.

Ambulance & fire	☏119
Police	☏110
Country code	☏81
International access code	☏001
International operator	☏0051
Local directory	☏104

Arriving in Japan

» **Narita International Airport**
Narita Express – ¥2940; 53 minutes to Tokyo station
Limousine bus – ¥3000; two hours to the city
Taxi – around ¥30,000 to the city

» **Haneda Airport**
Monorail – ¥470; 25 minutes to Tokyo
Limousine bus – ¥1000; 45 minutes to the city
Taxi – around ¥6000 to the city

» **Kansai International Airport**
Express trains – ¥2980; 78 minutes to Kyoto
Limousine bus – ¥2500; 90 minutes to the city
Shared taxi – ¥3500; about 90 minutes to the city

Safe Travel

The Great East Japan Earthquake of March 2011 and the resulting tsunami wrought incredible devastation on parts of northeast Honshū (the main island of Japan). To learn more about the quake and tsunami, see the box on p435. For more information about the nuclear crisis that followed the earthquake and tsunami, see the box on p736.

While the vast majority of Japan was safe for travel at the time of writing, we recommend that you check your government's warnings or restrictions when planning your trip; for more details, see p748. To find out about relief efforts following the Great East Japan Earthquake, see the box, p752.

what's new

For this edition of Japan, our authors have hunted down the fresh, the revamped, the transformed, the hot and the happening. These are some of our favourites. For up-to-the-minute recommendations, see lonelyplanet.com/japan.

Haneda Goes International

1 Tokyo has just become a whole lot more convenient: Haneda Airport (p755) is once again serving international routes. Only 30 minutes out of downtown Tokyo and within reasonable taxi distance, Haneda is much closer to the city than Narita, which remains Tokyo's main international entry point.

Setouchi International Art Festival
2 First held in 2010, this festival is slated to be held every three years, with the next one coming in 2013 (July to October). Events are centred on the island-cum-art-museum of Naoshima (see the box, p397).

Extended Shinkansen Lines
3 *Shinkansen* (bullet train) lines have been extended north to the city of Aomori (p429), at the northern tip of Honshū, and south to the city of Kagoshima (p613), in Kyūshū. You can now cross almost all of Kyūshū and Honshū by bullet train.

Jetstar Opens Japan Routes
4 Jetstar, Australia's budget airline, launched service to Japan (Kansai and Narita) in 2007. This makes Japan a much more reasonable destination for Australian backpackers, skiers and families.

Local Food Movement
5 Local food is all the rage in Japan and locavores can sample the fare in cities and villages across the archipelago (see the box, p708).

Lee Ufan Museum
6 Designed by Andō Tadao, this new museum (named after Korean-born artist Lee Ufan) is a great new addition to the museums and galleries on Naoshima (p397).

Hip Capsule Hotels
7 Capsule hotels used to be the refuge of sozzled salarymen who missed the last train home. Not anymore. A wave of cool designer capsule hotels has swept the country. A good example of this is the Capsule Ryokan Kyoto (p283).

Sky Tree Blooms in Tokyo
8 Scheduled to open in spring 2012, the Tokyo Sky Tree will soar to 634m and feature two observation decks (p81).

New Bus Routes on Mt Fuji
9 New bus routes and more frequent departures make climbing Mt Fuji easier (p134).

Kumano Kodō Development
10 Local tourism authorities have been working hard to open the Kumano Kodō pilgrimage trails to foreign tourists and their work has paid off in a big way (see the box, p352).

if you like...

Temples, Shrines & Gardens

You'll find the Japan of your imagination – immaculately raked gardens, quiet Buddhist temples and mysterious Shintō shrines – waiting for you all across the archipelago, even in the ultra-modern capital of Tokyo.

Kyoto You could stay in Kyoto for a month and see a different garden, temple and shrine each day. If you're after traditional Japan, you could spend your whole trip here and not get bored (p252).

Nara A short hop, skip and jump from Kyoto, Nara is a compact wonder of a city that some consider the birthplace of Japanese culture. It has some of our favourite gardens, temples and shrines (p333).

Kanazawa Some call this small city on the Sea of Japan coast a 'mini-Kyoto', but Kanazawa isn't a 'mini' anything – it's big on temples and has one of the best gardens in Japan: Kenroku-en (p228).

Tokyo That's right: amid all that concrete and neon there are some wonderful hints of traditional culture. If you can't make it to Kyoto, the capital has enough to satisfy the craving for 'old Japan' (p51).

Culinary Adventure

Who doesn't come to Japan to eat? And we don't just mean 'extreme eating'; we mean some of the food you might have tried back home, only much better versions. Then there's all the new stuff to try – and did we mention really good sake?

Tokyo With more Michelin stars than any city on earth, this is the place for the best Japanese food in the country. And, if you need a break from local cuisine, some of the best French and Italian food you'll find anywhere (p91).

Tsukiji Tokyo's fish market deserves its own entry. Simply pointing out that it's the biggest in the world doesn't begin to convey the size, variety and excitement of the place. If you enjoy eating or cooking, you'll enjoy Tsukiji (p57).

Kyoto If you want to sample *kaiseki* (haute cuisine) in traditional surroundings, or dine with a geisha, this is the place. And don't forget the Japanese sweet shops and the wonderful old Nishiki food market (p286).

Depachika Department-store food halls in Tokyo and Kyoto are the best food shops on the planet. Be prepared to get hungry, get overwhelmed and get lost (p108 and p287).

Hiking

When you think of going overseas to hike, Japan probably doesn't rank near the top of your list. But Japan has some *brilliant* hiking and a reasonably priced hut system that rivals anything you'll find elsewhere. Whether you fancy a week-long hike across the peaks with nothing but a daypack or just a few good strolls in the hills between bouts of temple-hopping, Japan will definitely satisfy.

Japan Alps The Japan Alps in Central Honshū form the roof of Japan. If you like big peaks, grand scenery and long walks, this is the place (p199).

Hokkaidō You'll find some seriously rugged hiking on Japan's northern island. From incredible coastal treks to the famed Daisetsuzan Grand Traverse, Hokkaidō is a destination for nature lovers (p462).

Kyūshū If the whiff of volcanic gases and the threat of an occasional eruption adds a certain frisson to your hiking, you'll love the volcanoes of Japan's southern island of Kyūshū (p563).

Kumano Kodō Head down to the wooded wilds of southern Kansai to follow the ancient pilgrimage path to the shrines and hot springs of Hongū (p352).

» Serious shoppers can find just about anything in Tokyo (p107)

Castles

For anyone with an interest in Japan's feudal era (think samurai, shōguns and *daimyō*), a visit to a Japanese castle is sure to get the imagination working. Kids, in particular, find them fascinating. The Japanese word for 'castle', by the way, is *jō*.

Himeji-jō The queen of all Japanese castles, the 'White Heron' is presently undergoing a multiyear renovation and the main keep is under wraps, but it's still an interesting stop for castle fans (p325).

Hikone-jō Within easy day-trip distance of Kyoto, Hikone-jō is a beautiful castle that makes up for its lack of size with a fine view and graceful lines (p329).

Osaka-jō It's not original and it's not subtle, but it sure looks good from a distance or when the cherries in the surrounding park are in bloom (p304).

Matsuyama-jō Dominating the city of Matsuyama on the island of Shikoku, this is easily one of Japan's finest original castles (p550).

Shuri-jō Way down in Okinawa, this rebuilt castle is a completely different kettle of fish from its mainland cousins – the Chinese influence is clear (p651).

Onsen (Hot Springs)

If you're tired of coming home from a vacation and feeling like you need a vacation, you should try a Japanese onsen holiday. Spend some time soaking in a few of Japan's great onsen or, better yet, in an onsen ryokan (a traditional inn built around a private hot spring) and you'll arrive home recharged.

Kinosaki Japan's classic onsen town is everything an onsen town ought to be: quaint, friendly and packed with homey ryokan. Walk from one great bath to another in your *yukata* (robe) and don't miss the crab cuisine in the winter (p360).

Kayōtei We're going to single this onsen ryokan out for special mention. If your finances run to a night or two here, you will surely be glad you made the trip. It's sublime in every way and it's the perfect way to round out a trip to Japan – there are even fairly convenient flights right back to Tokyo (p238).

Hongū Trek for a few days along Japan's ancient pilgrimage route, the Kumano Kodō, then soak your sore muscles in the three great onsen near the village of Hongū. There's even a river that turns into a giant hot pool in the winter (p356).

Shopping

Forget sumō and judo – Japan's national sport is shopping. And the Japanese go at it with a real passion. Whether your taste runs to expensive boutiques or ¥100 shops, if you're a shopper you have to come to Japan.

Tokyo If it can't be found in a store somewhere in Tokyo, it probably doesn't exist. The capital of Japan has the widest selection of stores on the planet – everything from gadgets to Gucci bags (p107).

Kyoto Sure, the old capital has a brilliant selection of traditional goods (think ceramics, antiques, scrolls, tea-ceremony articles and kimonos), but you might be surprised to find that it's also got heaps of trendy boutiques and well-stocked department stores, not to mention the two best flea markets in the country (p294).

Osaka The Osakans come in for quite a ribbing from their fellow Japanese: they're famed for driving a hard bargain and shopping with abandon. And you know what? They work hard every day to earn this reputation. Osaka is a city of merchants and you better believe the shopping's good here (p316).

If you like... installations in stunning natural settings, you'll positively love Naoshima – this island-cum-art-museum is quickly becoming Japan's most exciting destination (p396)

Modern Architecture

Japan is where the world's architects come to play. During the heady years of the economic bubble, wild and wonderful buildings sprouted up and down the archipelago.

Tokyo If Japan is an architect's playground, Tokyo is an architect's Disneyland. Sure, it's got the architectural consistency of, say, Las Vegas, but what a madly inspired clutter it all is! Take a stroll and enjoy the nuggets of genius scattered among the concrete afterthoughts (p51).

Naoshima This island-cum-art-museum is graced with several Andō Tadao creations and lots of other fantastic buildings besides (p396).

Kanazawa While it's more famous for its temples and gardens, the Central Honshū city of Kanazawa gets a lot of visits from architecture buffs who come to see the 21st Century Museum of Contemporary Art (p227).

Skiing

It started as a well-kept secret among expats living in Hong Kong and Singapore, and now the word is out: Japan has the best skiing in Asia and some of the most reliable powder snow on earth. If you want to combine a bit of culture with some snow time, Japan is the perfect place.

Niseko You could be forgiven for thinking that the Japanese word for 'powder snow' is 'Niseko': this Hokkaidō ski area is just about synonymous with the stuff (p485).

Hakuba Up in Central Honshū's Japan Alps, Hakuba hosted some of the downhill events during the 1998 Nagano Winter Olympics. With some excellent advanced runs and a stunning alpine backdrop, this is a consistent favourite among Japan's expat skiers (p213).

Nozawa Onsen No place in Japan does the ski-onsen combination better than Nozawa Onsen. With 14 free onsen in which to soak after your day on the slopes, it's a must for hot spring fans who also happen to enjoy skiing (p212).

Festivals

Perhaps you imagine the Japanese to be a serious and staid people. If so, check out one of the country's wilder *matsuri* (festivals) to see these people bust loose, and join the fun!

Gion Matsuri OK, the main event here (the parade of floats) is pretty tame, but the evenings leading up to this great Kyoto summer festival get pretty wild. Put on a *yukata* (robe) and stroll through town, stopping for beer and snacks as you go (p280).

Hanami Strictly speaking, the Japanese cherry-blossom-viewing parties *(hanami)* that take place up and down the archipelago in March and April aren't *matsuri*, but they sure feel like festivals.

Hatsumōde Again, the first shrine visit of the year *(hatsu-mōde)* is not a *matsuri* in the strict sense, but if you find yourself at a popular Shintō shrine on New Year's Eve or New Year's Day, you'll see why we've included it here.

Kishiwada Danjiri Matsuri This *matsuri*, which takes place in southern Osaka in September, is one of the wilder events in Japan. Basically, the local haul floats through the streets, sometimes at surprising speeds. Join the fun, but stand well back when those things go by (p310).

WILL ROBB / LONELY PLANET IMAGES ©

» Lockers in Akihabara (p76) painted with distinctive anime characters.

Pop Culture

The folks who brought you Godzilla, Pokémon and Shonen Knife are still hard at work. While the Japanese today are worried about a shrinking population, there still seem to be a zillion kids out there hungry to leap on the latest craze – whether it be *cosplay* (costume play), manga (comics) or 'maid cafes' – not to mention the 100 new ones that will erupt by the time you finish reading this sentence. Tokyo is all about pop culture, so it really deserves its own entry here!

Akihabara Better known as 'Akiba', Tokyo's main electronics district is alive with the pulse of *otaku* (geek) trends (p76).

Shibuya Shibuya is the shopping mecca at the centre of Tokyo's youth universe. Keep your eyes peeled and you'll see several trends coming into being as you walk down the street (p66).

Ghibli Museum If you know the name Miyazaki Hayao (the king of Japanese anime), or if your kids do, you'll want to make a half-day trip out of Tokyo to see his museum (p73).

Beaches

Beaches may not be the first thing you associate with Japan, but the archipelago has some real stunners, many of them on the islands of Okinawa. But you don't have to head all the way south to hit the sand: you'll find good beaches on all the main islands of Japan. Here are some of our favourites.

Sakibaru Kaigan This lovely stretch of white sand and clear water on Amami-Ōshima is a winner by any definition (p644).

Kerama islands It's impossible to pick a favourite beach on these three charming islands – the fun is in exploring each one and finding your own white-sand paradise (p657).

Hoshisuna-no-hama While the beach here is nothing to sneeze at, it's the drop-off at the edge of the coral reef that really gets our motor running (p668).

Shirara-hama This blinding-white stretch of sand in Kansai's Wakayama Prefecture is backed by one of the worst tourist circuses in the country, but swim a few hundred metres offshore and it's all a distant memory (p352).

month by month

Top Events

1 **Gion Matsuri**, July

2 **Cherry-Blossom Viewing**, March–April

3 **Takayama Matsuri**, April

4 **Awa-odori**, August

5 **Yuki Matsuri**, February

January

Japan comes to life after the lull of the New Year holiday (things open on 3 or 4 January). Winter grips the country in the mountains and in the north, but travel is still possible in most places.

Shōgatsu (New Year)

New Year (31 December to 3 January) is one of the most important celebrations in Japan and includes plenty of eating and drinking. The central ritual, *hatsu-mōde,* involves the first visit to the local shrine to pray for health, happiness and prosperity during the coming year.

Skiing

While many ski areas open in December, the ski season really gets rolling in January. For more details, see the Skiing in Japan chapter (p39).

Seijin-no-hi (Coming-of-Age Day)

On the second Monday in January, ceremonies are held for boys and girls who have reached the age of 20. A good place to see the action is at large shrines, where you'll find crowds of girls in kimonos and boys in suits or kimonos.

February

It's still cold in February in most of Japan (with the exception of Okinawa). Skiing is in full swing and this is a good time to soak in onsen.

Setsubun Matsuri

On 3 or 4 February, to celebrate the end of winter and drive out evil spirits, the Japanese engage in throwing roasted beans while chanting '*oni wa soto, fuku wa uchi*' (meaning 'out with the demons, in with good luck'). Check local shrines for events.

Yuki Matsuri

Drawing over two million annual visitors, Sapporo's famous snow festival (p471) really warms up winter in Hokkaidō from 7 to 13 February. Teams from around the world compete to create the most impressive ice and snow sculptures. After touring the sculptures, head to one of the city's friendly pubs and eateries to warm up with sake and great local food.

March

By March it's starting to warm up in the main islands of Japan. Plums start the annual procession of blossoms across the archipelago. This is a pleasant time to travel in Honshū, Kyūshū and Shikoku.

Plum-Blossom Viewing

Not as famous as the cherries, but quite lovely in their own right, Japan's plum trees bloom from late February into early March. Strolling among the plum orchards at places like Kyoto's Kitano Tenman-gū (p270) is a fine way to spend an early spring day in Japan.

April

Spring is in full swing by April. The cherry blossoms usually peak early in April in most of Honshū. Japan is beautiful at this time, but places like Kyoto can be crowded.

Cherry-Blossom Viewing

When the cherry blossoms burst into bloom, the Japanese hold rollicking *hanami* (cherry-blossom viewing) parties. It's hard to time the blossoms: to hit them at their peak in Tokyo or Kyoto, you have to be in the country from around 25 March to 5 April.

Takayama Matsuri

Held on 14 and 15 April, the Takayama Matsuri (p191) is one of the best festivals in the Japan Alps region. The festival floats here are truly spectacular. Book well in advance if you want to spend the night.

May

May is one of the best months to visit Japan. It's warm and sunny in most of the country. Book accommodation well in advance during the April/ May Golden Week holidays.

Golden Week

Most Japanese are on holiday from 29 April to 5 May, when a series of national holidays coincide. This is one of the busiest times for domestic travel, so be prepared for crowded transport and accommodation.

June

June is generally a lovely time to travel in Japan – it's warm but not sweltering. Keep in mind that the rainy season generally starts in Kyūshū and Honshū sometime in June. It doesn't rain every day but it can be humid.

Japan Alps Hiking Season

Most of the snow has melted off the high peaks of the Japan Alps (p199) by June and hikers flock to the trails. You should check conditions before going, however, as big snow years can mean difficult conditions for skiers.

July

The rainy season ends in Honshū sometime in July and, once it does, the heat cranks up and it can be very hot and humid. Head to Hokkaidō or the Japan Alps to escape the heat.

Mt Fuji Climbing Season

Mt Fuji officially opens to climbing on 1 July, and the months of July and August are ideal for climbing the peak (see p132).

Gion Matsuri

Held on 17 July, this is the mother of all Japanese festivals (p280). Dozens of huge floats are pulled through the streets of Kyoto by teams of chanting citizens. On the three evenings preceding the parade, people stroll through Shijō-dōri's street stalls dressed in beautiful *yukata* (light cotton kimonos).

August

August is hot and humid across most of Japan. Once again, Hokkaidō and the Japan Alps can provide some relief. Several interesting festivals happen in Japan in August.

Nebuta Matsuri

Held in Aomori, at the northern tip of Honshū (p427), for several days in early August, this is one of Japan's more colourful festivals. On the final day of the festival enormous parade floats are pulled through the city by teams of chanting dancers.

Awa-odori Matsuri

The city of Tokushima, on the southern island of Shikoku, comes alive from 12 to 15 August for the nation's largest and most famous *bon* dance (p530). Teams of dancers take to the streets to perform sake-inspired *bon* dances, and the best troupes are awarded prizes. *Bon* dances are performed to welcome the souls of the departed back to this world (and this is usually considered a good excuse to consume vast quantities of sake).

O-Bon (Festival of the Dead)

The Buddhist festival of the dead occurs in mid-August (it is one of the high-season travel periods). This is a time when ancestors return to earth to visit their descendents. Lanterns are lit and floated on rivers, lakes or the sea to help guide them on their journey. See also Daimon-ji Gozan Okuribi (below).

Daimon-ji Gozan Okuribi

Huge fires in the shape of Chinese characters and other symbols are set alight in Kyoto (p281) during this festival, which forms part of the O-Bon (festival of the dead). It's one of Japan's most impressive spectacles.

★☆★ Summer Fireworks Festivals

Cities and towns across Japan hold spectacular summer fireworks festivals in August. You'll be amazed at the quality and duration of some of these incredible displays.

☆ Earth Celebration

The island of Sado-ga-shima, off the coast of Northern Honshū, is the scene of this internationally famous festival of dance, art and music. The festival (p454) is held in the third week of August.

September

Sometime in early to mid-September, the heat breaks and temperatures become very pleasant in the main islands. Skies are generally clear at this time, making it a great time to travel.

★★★ Kishiwada Danjiri Matsuri

Huge *danjiri* (festival floats) are pulled through the narrow streets in the south of Osaka during this lively festival (p310) on 14 and 15 September. Much alcohol is consumed and occasionally the *danjiri* go off course and crash into houses.

(Above) Catch an eyeful of the spectacular floats at Takayama Matsuri (p191), in the Japan Alps region.

(Below) Osaka's Kishiwada Danjiri Matsuri (p310) is a party for young and old; dress up and enjoy the fanfare, but watch out for wayward floats!

October

October is one of the best months to visit Japan: the weather can be warm or cool and it's usually sunny. The fall foliage peaks in the Japan Alps at this time.

★ Kurama-no-hi Matsuri

On 22 October, huge flaming torches are carried through the streets of the tiny hamlet of Kurama (p277) in the mountains north of Kyoto. This is one of Japan's more primeval festivals.

November

November is also beautiful for travel in most of Japan. Skies are reliably clear and temperatures are pleasantly cool. Snow starts to fall in the mountains and foliage peaks in places like Kyoto and Nara. Expect crowds.

★ Shichi-Go-San (7-5-3 Festival)

This is a festival in honour of girls aged three and seven and boys aged five. On 15 November, children are dressed in their finest clothes and taken to shrines or temples, where prayers are offered for good fortune.

December

December is cool to cold across most of Japan. The Japanese are busy preparing for the New Year. Most things shut down from 29 or 30 December, making travel difficult (but transport runs and accommodation is open).

★ Shōgatsu (New Year)

The country shuts down on the last two or three days of the year. Transport is busy as people head back to their hometowns. On New Year's Eve, people visit temples to ring bells and shrines to wish for a lucky New Year.

(Above) Dressed to the nines for Shichi-Go-San, which celebrates girls aged three and seven and boys aged five.

(Below) Fire is a central element of the primeval Kurama-no-hi Matsuri (p281), held in tiny Kurama.

itineraries

Whether you've got six days or 60, these itineraries provide a starting point for the trip of a lifetime. Want more inspiration? Head online to lonelyplanet. com/thorntree to chat with other travellers.

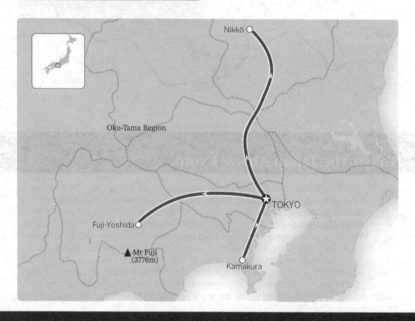

One Week
Tokyo & Around

> If your time in Japan is limited, don't try to do too much. Fly into Narita or Haneda (the latter is closer to the city). Stay in a convenient transport hub like **Shinjuku**, **Shibuya**, **Ginza** or the **Tokyo Station area**. Visit **Tsukiji fish market** your first morning (a good idea if you've got jetlag). Next, head up to **Asakusa** to visit the temple of **Sensō-ji**, then over to nearby **Ueno** for the **Tokyo National Museum**. The next day, take the loop line to **Harajuku** and walk to **Meiji-jingū**, the city's finest Shintō shrine, then take a stroll down chic **Omote-sandō**. From there, head up to **Shibuya** to soak up some of modern Tokyo. Make sure you spend an evening wandering east **Shinjuku**, since this is where you'll get the full experience of Tokyo's neon madness. Other urban areas to check out include **Ginza**, for high-end shopping; **Akihabara**, for electronics and geek culture; and **Roppongi**, for international nightlife.

Break up your time in Tokyo with day trips to nearby attractions like the fantastic shrines at **Nikkō** and the temples at **Kamakura**; if you're a hiker and it's summertime, you could even climb **Mt Fuji**.

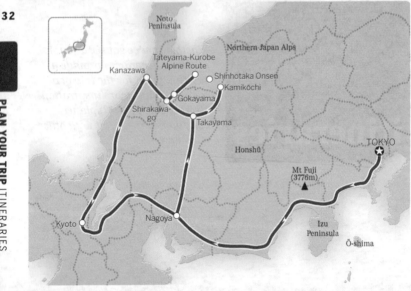

Tokyo, the Japan Alps & Kyoto

The Tokyo–Japan Alps–Kyoto route is *the* classic Japan journey and the best way to get a quick taste of the country. You'll experience three faces of Japan: the modern wonders of **Tokyo**, the traditional culture of **Kyoto**, and the natural beauty of the **Japan Alps**. While you can do this itinerary in any season, keep in mind that the Japan Alps can be snow covered any time from early November to late March – this rules out hiking unless you're an experienced winter mountaineer – but you can visit the attractive cities of Takayama and Kanazawa any time of year.

Let's assume that you'll fly into **Tokyo**. Follow the preceding Tokyo & Around itinerary, which will give you a taste of things in the capital. Don't worry about skipping some of the traditional sights in that itinerary, because you'll be heading to **Kyoto**, and you'll get your fill of shrines and temples there.

From Tokyo, take the *shinkansen* (bullet train) to Nagoya, then an express to **Takayama**. Spend a day here checking out the restored **Sanmachi-suji** district, then head into the **Japan Alps** via **Shinhotaka Onsen** or nearby **Kamikōchi**.

Return to Takayama and rent a car so you can visit the nearby thatched-roof villages of **Shirakawa-go** and **Gokayama**. From there, if you feel like some more alpine scenery, drive northeast and head back into the Japan Alps via the **Tateyama–Kurobe Alpine Route** (the route is open from late spring to early fall). Next, drive to **Kanazawa** (some rental agencies will allow you to drop the car in Kanazawa). Note that you can also go from Takayama to Kanazawa by bus, with a stop in Shirakawa-go en route. In Kanazawa, check out the famous garden of **Kenroku-en**, the **21st Century Museum of Contemporary Art** and the **Nagamachi** district.

From Kanazawa, there are several daily express trains that will get you to **Kyoto** in a little over two hours. In Kyoto, follow the Kansai in Depth itinerary, then jump on the *shinkansen* and get yourself back to Tokyo in time for your flight home.

» (above) A young maiko (apprentice geisha) is pretty as a picture on a Kyoto street (p249).
» (left) Tokyo's Shinjuku district (p71) is pulsing with life.

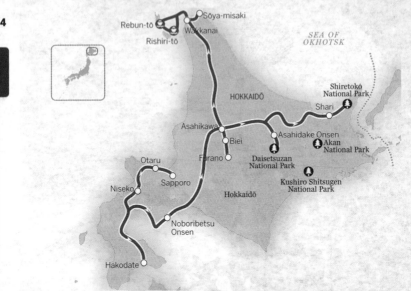

Three Weeks
The Wilds of Hokkaidō

Whether you're on a JR Pass or flying directly, **Sapporo** makes a good hub for Hokkaidō excursions. If you're here in February, your prize for enduring the arctic cold is a front-row seat at the **Sapporo Snow Festival**, highlighted by life-size carvings of everything from European cityscapes to elaborate ice mazes. But any time of year is perfect for a visit to the **Sapporo Bīru-en**, birthplace of Hokkaidō's golden lager.

On a day trip from Sapporo, see romantic **Otaru**, with its Victorian brick warehouses and unbelievably fresh sushi spreads. If you have a little more time to spare, a couple of nights in **Hakodate** transports you back to the era of European colonisation. On the way back to Sapporo, hot-springs fans can take a healing dip in the famed waters of **Noboribetsu Onsen**.

In the winter months, **Niseko** is an absolute must for powder fiends. Whether you're partial to parabolic skis or a waxed-up snowboard, this alpine village is nothing short of a carver's paradise. The burgeoning expat population also ensures fine cosmopolitan eating and a boisterous nightlife.

In the summer months, make a brief stop in **Asahikawa** for a few rounds of Otokoyama sake before pressing on to the northern outpost of **Wakkanai**. From here, take the ferry to the islands of **Rishiri-tō** and **Rebun-tō** in search of the annual wildflower blooms. On the return, see **Sōya-misaki**, Japan's northernmost point.

From there, jump to **Asahidake Onsen**, and hike around **Daisetsuzan National Park**. As a complement to burning shoe leather, jump behind the wheel of a rental car and explore the lavender fields and gourmet attractions in the countryside around **Furano** and **Biei**. Although smaller than Niseko, Furano is an impressive skiing and snowboarding destination in its own right.

If you really want to leave it all behind, head east to **Shari**, the jumping-off point for **Shiretoko National Park**. But don't forget your bear bell, as humans aren't the only creatures that call this remote peninsula home. For more passive encounters, you can watch cranes and deer in **Kushiro Shitsugen National Park**. And don't forget about *marimo*, the anthropogenic balls of algae that inhabit **Akan National Park**. This is also a top spot to learn more about the island's traditional **Ainu culture**.

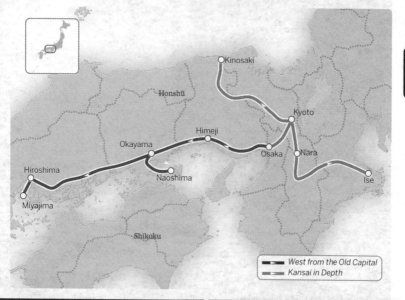

West from the Old Capital
Kansai in Depth

Two Weeks
Kansai in Depth

Kansai contains the thickest concentration of must-sees in all of Japan. If you want to see a lot of traditional Japanese sights without spending a lot of time in transit, then spending your entire trip in Kansai is a great idea.

Kyoto is the obvious place to base yourself: it's central and it's got a wide range of excellent accommodation, not to mention the nation's finest temples, gardens and shrines. Spend a day exploring the **Higashiyama area** (both southern and northern), followed by another day strolling through the bamboo groves of **Arashiyama**. Then, hop on a train for a day trip to **Nara** to see the sights of **Nara-kōen**, including **Tōdai-ji**, with its enormous Buddha figure. Another day trip to see **Ise-jingū**, in the town of **Ise**, is highly recommended – the ride is scenic and the shrine is awe-inspiring.

If you've got the urge to see the modern side of Japan, **Osaka** is only about 30 minutes by train from Kyoto. And if you really want to wind down and relax, an overnight trip up to the onsen town of **Kinosaki** will be the perfect way to round off your Kansai experience.

Two to Three Weeks
West from the Old Capital

This route can be done with a start in **Tokyo** (Haneda or Narita Airports), **Nagoya** (Centrair), or **Kansai** (KIX).

If you fly into Tokyo or Nagoya, check out those cities, then jump on the *shinkansen* for the quick trip to **Kyoto**, which is worth as many days as you can give it – see the Kansai in Depth itinerary for some ideas of what to see there.

After soaking up Kyoto's traditional culture, consider a day and night in **Osaka** (especially if you won't be visiting Tokyo). This will give you a dose of the modern urban Japanese phenomenon, with all that it entails.

From Osaka, head west to **Himeji**. The famous castle here, Himeji-jō, is presently 'under wraps' while it's being restored, but you can see enough to make it interesting. Then, travel to the island of **Naoshima**, in the Inland Sea, near the city of Okayama. The entire island has been converted into a giant art museum and it's a must for culture vultures.

Return to the mainland and travel west to visit **Hiroshima** and learn about its tragic history (consider spending the night on **Miyajima**), then head east to catch your return flight.

» (above) A tranquil tableau on the trail to Jōmon Sugi (p639), Yakushima.
» (left) Beckoned by an inviting sea on Miyako-Jima (p660).

JTB PHOTO / PHOTOLIBRARY ©

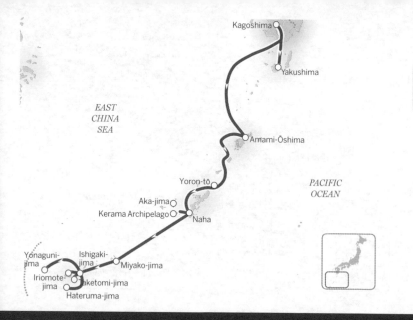

Three Weeks
Island-Hopping Through the Southwest Islands

> If you fancy beaches, jungles and coral reefs, island-hopping through the Southwest Islands is a unique adventure. Start in the city of **Kagoshima**, on the southern island of Kyūshū, and catch a ferry to **Yakushima**, a wild island of eons-old Japanese cedar trees including **Jōmon Sugi**, hikable in a day. Return to Kagoshima and board an overnight ferry to the island of **Amami-Ōshima**, which has some great beaches and subtropical jungles. From there, board another ferry and head south to tiny **Yoron-tō**. This little gem is fringed by beaches on all sides, and has some great snorkelling and windsurfing spots. After a few days kicking back on Yoron's sands, hop on another ferry for the short ride to **Naha**, on the island of Okinawa-hontō. Check out the city for a day or two, and then take the short ferry trip out to **Kerama Archipelago**. Here, the tiny island of **Aka-jima** has some of the best beaches in the entire archipelago.

If you're out of time, you can fly back to the mainland from Naha; otherwise, take a flight from Naha to **Miyako-jima** and spend a couple of days experiencing its long, golden beaches and outlying islets.

A short flight will then take you to **Ishigaki-jima**. If you've got scuba certification and you're there between June and October, you'll want to dive amid swarms of manta rays offshore. If not, just chill out along the fabulous bay beaches around Ishigaki's Kabira-wan.

Next, grab a short-haul ferry to neighbouring, jungle-covered **Iriomote-jima**, which has some incredible coral reefs around its shores, as well as river cruises along mangrove forests and some very wild hikes through the interior.

Back on Ishigaki-jima, a variety of ferries can whisk you to some minor but fascinating outlying islands: pancake-flat **Taketomi-jima** hosts a small community of wonderfully preserved Okinawan houses with heavy tile roofs and *shīsā* (protective lion statues); laid-back and covered with sugarcane fields, **Hateruma-jima** is Japan's southernmost inhabited island and has beaches with pristine turquoise waters; **Yonaguni-jima**, Japan's westernmost island and some 100km from Taiwan, is a hot spot for hammerhead sharks in winter. At all times of the year, visitors come to see a collection of bizarre undersea blocks that some say are the ruins of a lost civilisation. Return to Ishigaki-jima for the flight back to the mainland.

10 Days
Kyūshū & Yakushima

Sunny **Kagoshima** offers an instant change of pace from the rest of Japan. **Sengan-en** garden and **Sakurajima** volcano are must-sees before going south for a sand bath in the seaside town of **Ibusuki** or testing your chopstick skills fishing noodles from a tank near **Ikeda-ko**. Then catch the *shinkansen* north to plunge into samurai history at the fabulous **Kumamoto-jō**, and head inland to **Aso-san**, the world's largest volcanic caldera.

If you have time and enjoy hiking, take a ferry south from Kagoshima to the island of **Yakushima** for some hiking and onsens.

Nagasaki is known for tragedy, and visiting the atomic-bombing sights offers a lesson that can never be learned too often, but this welcoming city also bubbles with colourful East-West history and unique fusion cuisine. From here, train it to **Arita** for immersion in Japan's heralded ceramics history at **Kyūshū Ceramic Museum** (and nearby galleries!).

Crowning the island is worldly, river-crossed **Fukuoka**, Kyūshū's largest city, crammed with spirited dining and nightlife in the lanes of **Tenjin** and **Daimyō**. Shoot across the island's northeast to finish your adventure with a relaxing soak in one of the eight hot-spring enclaves of seaside **Beppu**.

One Week
Inland Sea

Start day one in the city of **Okayama**, allowing enough time to stroll the fetted garden **Kōraku-en** before finding lodgings. On day two it's a morning train and ferry ride to **Naoshima**, artsy star of the Inland Sea, where you can lose yourself among installations and subterranean museums. Take your time and spend two nights here. On day four, head back to the mainland and onwards to Kasaoka to catch the afternoon boat for **Manabe-shima**. A seafood dinner and a soak in the open-air tub at **Santora**, on the island, should see you feeling refreshed on day five – go for a morning wander around this quiet, feline-friendly island. If you haven't decided to throw it all in and move here, return to Kasaoka and catch a train down the coast to **Onomichi**. Squeeze in a temple walk or learn about Onomichi's literary history, but eat plenty of the local *rāmen* to prepare for day six – cycling the **Shimanami Kaidō**. You could go flat out to Shikoku, but it's better to stop at **Ikuchi-jima**, see colourful **Kōsan-ji**, and rest up for the night. Day seven, get back on the bike, or turn in your wheels and take the ferry back to port.

Skiing in Japan

What to Bring

Almost everything you need is available in Japan. However, due to prices or difficulty in finding some items, it's best to bring the following things from abroad:

Lift pass chip case Look for the 'around the arm'–type case to hold your pass. You will be scanning this at every lift, and the case attached to your arm is easily the best place to keep it.

Goggles They're very expensive in Japan, so it's best to bring your own.

Essential toiletries Sunblock, aspirin and other pharmacy items you're used to may be hard to track down, so it's best to bring your own favourites.

Large-sized ski boots Rental places at most resorts have boots of up to 30cm (which is equivalent to men's size 12 in the USA, UK or Australia). Resorts such as Niseko, which attract strong international followings, typically stock larger sizes. But if you have very large feet, play it safe and bring your own boots.

Mobile phones Many of Japan's ski areas are covered by one or more mobile-phone networks, and these are a great way to keep in touch with others in your party. Mobile phones are easy to rent in Japan (see p749).

Japan is home to more than 600 ski resorts, all of which offer regular snowfall, stunning mountain vistas, well-groomed runs, friendly locals, excellent food and an incredible variety of onsen (hot springs) for that all-important après-ski soak. Quite simply, Japan may be one of the skiing world's best-kept secrets. As an added bonus, skiing in Japan is remarkably reasonable: it generally costs less to ski here than in comparable areas in North America or Europe. Finally, if you plan your itinerary accordingly, it's possible to head from powdery slope to Zen garden with relative ease, allowing for one of the most exotic ski holidays imaginable.

The ski season officially starts in December, though conditions are highly variable. During this time, resorts will intermittently open runs depending on the quality and quantity of snowfall. January and February are peak months across the country. Things begin to warm up in March, heralding the close of the ski season before the start of April.

Costs

Many people unfamiliar with skiing in Japan often assume that it will cost an arm and a leg to ski here. But, even after factoring in the international air ticket, it might actually be cheaper to ski for a week in Japan than in your home country. Are we mad? Well, let's check the numbers.

» Lift tickets and equipment rental A full-day lift ticket at most ski areas in Japan costs between ¥4000 and ¥5500. This is significantly less than

DID YOU KNOW?

» Hokkaidō's Niseko ski area receives a whopping 15m of snow every year.

» More than two-thirds of foreign skiers at Niseko come from Australia.

» The first Winter Olympics held outside Europe or North America was at Sapporo in 1972.

» Snowboarding first debuted as an Olympic sport at the 1998 Nagano Winter Olympics.

» Naeba is home to the world's longest ski lift, the 'Dragondola' (5.5km).

a full day at large resorts in North America or Europe. Many resorts also offer packages including lunch or even a dip in an onsen. Even if you don't have your own equipment, full equipment rental is typically no more than ¥5000 per day (both ski and snowboard sets are available). The Japanese tend to be connoisseurs of quality, which means that you need not worry about getting stuck with shabby and/or outdated gear.

» **Accommodation** You can find plenty of upmarket accommodation in the ¥6500 to ¥10,000 range at major ski areas in Japan, and this price will often include one or two meals. This is often less than half of what you'd expect to pay for similar accommodation in the USA or Europe. The budget traveller will find a variety of backpacker-type hostels near most resorts, and families will be glad to know that young children (under six years of age) can usually stay for free or at a significant discount.

» **Food** On-slope meals top out at around ¥1000, which is slightly less than what you'd pay in North America or Europe. The restaurant selection anywhere you go is also varied, including the likes of *rāmen* (egg noodles), *udon* (wheat noodles), curry-rice and beef bowls, as well as more familiar fast-food options including sandwiches, pizza, burgers and kebabs. Beer and snacks, however, can be quite expensive – better to bring your own rather than buy from one of the ubiquitous convenience stores.

» **Transport** Airport-to-resort transport in Japan costs no more than in other countries, and is usually faster and more efficient (and, unlike in North America, you don't need to rent a car).

Where to Ski

Japan's best ski resorts are found in the Japan Alps region of Central Honshū, and on the northern island of Hokkaidō. The former lays claim to the highest mountains, while the latter boasts the deepest and most regular snowfall in the country. Although the ski resorts of Northern Honshū were not directly affected by the Great East Japan Earthquake, it remains to be seen whether or not they will open to full capacity during the life cycle of this edition.

If you're planning on doing a bit of sight-seeing in Tokyo, Kyoto and Hiroshima, the ski resorts in the Japan Alps are a quick and convenient add-on. Niseko and Furano on the island of Hokkaidō might be the way to go if your main goal is Sapporo. To be fair, however, Japan's small size and excellent infrastructure means that the difference is really only one quick internal flight. What follows is our overview of the five best ski areas in Japan. This is just to whet your appetite, of course, as there are over 600 more that we don't mention here!

» **Happō-one** (p213) Happō-one (pronounced 'hah-poh-oh-nay') is the quintessential Japan Alps ski resort. With the sprawling Hakuba mountain range as a backdrop, it offers eye-popping views in addition to excellent and varied skiing. The layout is pretty straightforward here, with plenty of good wide burners heading straight down the fall line from the top of the area.

» **Shiga Kōgen** (p211) Also in the Japan Alps, Shiga Kōgen is one of the largest ski resorts in the world, with an incredible 21 different areas, all interconnected by trails and lifts and accessible with one lift ticket. With such a variety of terrain on offer, there is something for everyone here, including skier-only areas and family-fun runs.

» **Nozawa Onsen** (p212) This quaint little Swiss-style village is tucked high up in the Japan Alps. Despite its small size, it has a good variety of runs, including some challenging mogul courses. Snowboarders will enjoy the terrain park and half-pipe, and there's even a cross-country skiing course that traverses the peaks.

» **Niseko** (p485) As far as most foreign skiers are concerned, Niseko is how you say 'powder' in Japanese. This is understandable, as Niseko

» (above) A snowboarder enjoys the characteristic fresh powder of Niseko (p485).
» (left) The ever-popular Hakuba offers Olympic-standard runs (p213).

SKIING LESSONS IN ENGLISH

The following outfits offer skiing lessons in English for both children and adults (usually with foreign instructors).

» **Canyons Japan** (www.canyons.jp/index_E.html) With a base at Hakuba (p213), close to Happō-one, Canyons offers skiing, backcountry skiing and snowboarding lessons, as well as snowshoeing tours.

» **Evergreen Outdoor Center** (www.evergreen-hakuba.com) Also in Hakuba, Evergreen offers skiing, snowboarding, powder skiing and telemark lessons.

» **Myōkō Backcountry Ski School** (www.myokobackcountry.com/english/index.html) Headquartered in Myōkō Kōgen (p460), this outfit specialises in telemark tours through the backwoods.

receives an average snowfall of 15m annually. Located on Hokkaidō, Niseko is actually four interconnected ski areas: Hirafu, Higashiyama, Annupuri and Hanazono.

» **Furano** (p503) Also located on the island of Hokkaidō, Furano shot to world fame after hosting 10 FIS World Ski Cup and two FIS World Snowboarding Cup events. Relatively undiscovered in comparison to Niseko, Furano rewards savvy powder fiends with polished runs through pristine birch forests.

Can You Say 'Ski' in Japanese?

That's right: it's 'ski' (all right, it's pronounced more like 'sukee'). But the point is that communication won't be much of a problem on your Japan ski trip. Tackling the language barrier has never been easier: most resorts employ a number of English-speaking foreigners on working-holiday visas. They work the lifts and in the cafeterias, and often find employment in the hotels or guesthouses that are most popular with foreign guests. All major signs and maps are translated into English, and provided you have some experience at large resorts back home, you'll find the layout and organisation of Japanese resorts to be pretty intuitive. The information counter at the base of the mountain always has helpful and polite staff available to answer questions.

The Japanese Way of Skiing

Snow is snow, skis are skis, right? How different can it be to ski in Japan? Not very much, but it's the little differences that will keep reminding you that you're not in, say, Colorado or the Swiss Alps. For example:

» Lift-line management is surprisingly poor in Japan. Skiers are often left to jostle and fend for themselves, and even when it's crowded, singles are allowed to ride triple and quad lifts alone.

» Not all resorts use the green/blue/black coding system for difficulty. Some have red, purple, orange, dotted lines, or black-numbered runs on the map.

» The majority of Japanese skiers start skiing at 9am, have lunch exactly at noon, and get off the hill by 3pm. If you work on a slightly different schedule, you will avoid a lot of the crowds.

» The signposting is inconsistent and irregular, something you may not expect in Japan. It's a good idea to study the map carefully and plan a central meeting point and/or time at the beginning of the day.

» Off-piste and out-of-bounds skiing is often high quality but also highly illegal and potentially dangerous, resulting in the confiscation of your lift pass if you're caught by the ski patrol. Cut the ropes at your own risk.

» Pop music – often really annoying pop music – is played along ski lifts and in restaurants. Bring an MP3 player if you prefer real music to the latest girl/boy band.

Travel with Children

Best Regions for Kids

Tokyo
Tokyo Disneyland and the youth meccas of Shibuya and Harajuku are only the start of the list of attractions here.

Kansai
A giant park filled with friendly deer and eye-popping sights like the Great Buddha in Nara has the makings of a kids' paradise. There's even a restaurant where they can eat lunch while operating a giant train set.

Okinawa & the Southwest Islands
What kid doesn't like the beach? Especially if the sand is white, the water warm and the coral good. If the weather's bad for snorkelling, take the kids to one of the world's best aquariums.

Kyoto
Cycling the backstreets, wandering the shopping arcades, picnics by the river and hikes in the hills will please the kids. And Kiyomizu-dera is as close to child-friendly as temples come, with the underground of Tainai-meguri.

Sapporo & Hokkaidō
If your kids ski or snowboard, they'll *love* the powder snow up in Hokkaidō.

Japan for Kids

Japan is a great place to travel with kids. The usual concerns that parents have about safety and food are simply not concerns in ultrasafe and spotless Japan. Instead, your biggest challenge will probably be keeping your kids entertained, as the very things that many adults come to Japan to see often bore kids silly. Use your imagination and balance your diet of temples with a few kid-friendly highlights.

Visiting Japan with children requires minimal planning, unless your child suffers from allergies or has other dietary restrictions, or requires specific medicine that may not be available in Japan. The following is an overview of things to bring and preparations to make.

Infants & Toddlers
Most supermarkets stock a good selection of baby food, but you may need to ask a clerk to help you read the contents. Organic baby food is hard to find outside Tokyo, so consider bringing a supply from home.

Cots are available in most hotels (but not usually in ryokan) and can be booked in advance. High chairs are available in lots of restaurants (though in many restaurants everyone simply sits on the floor).

Nappies (diapers) are readily available. A picture on the package usually indicates if they are for boys or girls, but you may have to ask a clerk to help you choose. The package also usually indicates (in numbers and

WHEN THE KIDS GET TEMPLED OUT

Let's face it: even the most precocious kid will eventually get tired of temples, gardens and shrines. Here are a few hints to keep the little ones entertained in Japan.

» Rent a bicycle, do some walking or climb a hill. After burning off those calories, even the most restless kid will appreciate a few moments quietly observing a rock garden.

» Japanese kids on school excursions always make a beeline for the downtown *shōtengai* shopping streets – between the ¥100 shops and the game centres, there's enough to keep them occupied for hours.

» Kids, especially boys, love to watch the *shinkansen* (bullet trains) roll in and out of the stations. You can by a platform ticket for ¥100 to watch them for as long as you want.

» Hollywood films are usually screened in English in Japan, so why not spend a few hours checking out the latest release.

» Even if they can't eat what they pull off the conveyor belt, most kids get a big kick out of Japan's famous 'sushi trains'.

» Kids seem to have a natural ability to understand video games, whatever the language, so try arming them with some funds and letting them try the latest in Japanese virtual-reality game centres.

» Japanese zoos can be depressing – animal pens are small and conditions are dire – but if you're desperate to keep the young ones happy, it might be worth swallowing your ethical qualms for a while.

» Many companies in towns like Kyoto will dress your kids in samurai and geisha garb for a small fee, then photograph them in scenic spots around town.

'kgs') the weight range of the nappies. Bottles, wipes and medications are also available at large pharmacies.

There are nappy-changing facilities in some public places, eg department stores and some larger train stations. Breastfeeding is generally not done in public.

Child seats in taxis are generally not available, but most car-rental agencies will provide one if you ask in advance.

There are child-care agencies in larger cities, although outside Tokyo there are few agencies with English-speaking staff.

Most cities are fairly accessible to those with strollers. Most train stations and many large buildings have elevators. However, many attractions such as temples and shrines do not have ramps. An issue, particularly in Kyoto, is the relative lack of pavements away from the main streets (luckily, the Japanese tend to be safe drivers!).

Finally, you'll find that the Japanese love kids and will fawn over the young ones, declaring them to be *kawaii* (cute). Unfortunately, this doesn't always extend to people giving up seats on trains or buses to those with children in tow. That said, most trains and buses do have *yūsen zaseki* (priority seating for elderly, handicapped, pregnant women and those with young children).

Older Children

Food can be an issue if your child is a picky or unadventurous eater. Even adults can be put off by some of the things in Japanese cuisine – sea urchin or squid might simply be too much for a kid. With this in mind, choose your restaurants carefully. If you're going to a *kaiseki* (haute cuisine) place, have your lodgings call ahead to ask for some kid-friendly dishes. Ditto if you'll be dining at your ryokan. If necessary, have your lodgings write your child's dietary restrictions or allergies for you in Japanese.

You'll find a lot of so-called 'family restaurants' in Japan, which usually serve food that even finicky kids can stomach (pizza, fried chicken, French fries), or offer special kids' meals (sometimes called *o-ko-sama ranchii*). *Shokudō* (all-round eateries) also tend to serve something that children will eat.

Finally, if your child simply will not eat Japanese food, don't worry: the big cities are chock-a-block with international restaurants, while fast-food joints can be found even in smaller towns. For rural areas, where only Japanese food may be available, you can stock up on food your child likes at a supermarket before heading into the hinterlands.

Regions at a Glance

Tokyo

Food ✓✓✓
Shopping ✓✓✓
Museums ✓✓✓

Dining & Shopping
There's a very good reason why more than 35 million people live in the capital's greater metropolitan area – in Tokyo you're spoilt for choice on just about everything. Over 140,000 restaurants (more than anywhere else in the world) and a seemingly equal amount of stores can make a local feel like a stranger in their own town.

Museum-Hopping
An entire trip of dining and shopping would undoubtedly be time well spent, but there's so much more to the city. Dozens of dynamic neighbourhoods are begging to be explored on foot, and when you're done poking your head down all of the little backstreets, a collection of world-class museums awaits.

p50

Mt Fuji & Around Tokyo

Ryokan ✓✓
Hiking ✓✓
Temples ✓✓

Country Inns
Some of Japan's best ryokan and hotels are just a few hours from Tokyo. Each direction offers a distinct flavour: rugged onsen towns to the north, lakeside resorts to the west and laid-back coastal villages to the south.

Natural Attractions
From iconic Mt Fuji to the little-known Ogasawara Islands, there is a range of outdoor activities: hiking among cedar groves, scrambling up volcanoes, swimming with dolphins or lounging in beachside onsen.

Cultural Sights
The cultural legacies of different eras come to life in the World Heritage–listed shrines and temples of Nikkō and the more austere ones of medieval Kamakura.

p119

The Japan Alps & Central Honshū

Onsen ✓✓✓
Villages ✓✓
Skiing ✓✓✓

Ultimate Onsen
The mountainous heart of Japan bubbles over with exquisite hot springs and fantastic inns to enjoy them. Gaze up at snowy peaks while steam rises from your body.

Thatched Roofs
Travel to the remote village of Shirakawa-gō (or, even remoter, Ainokura) and fall asleep to the sound of chirping frogs in a centuries-old thatched-roof farmhouse.

Powder Peaks
Ski some of Asia's best slopes, commanding breathtaking views of the northern Japan Alps. Après-ski soaking in hot springs is mandatory.

p169

Kyoto

Temples ✓✓✓
Culture ✓✓✓
Food ✓✓✓

Shintō & Buddhist Masterpieces

With over 1000 Buddhist temples and more than 400 Shintō shrines, Kyoto is *the* place to savour Japanese religious architecture and garden design. Find a quiet temple to call your own for the morning or join the throngs at a popular shrine.

Japan's Cultural Storehouse

Whether it's geisha, tea ceremony, painting, theatre performances or textiles, Kyoto is Japan's cultural capital.

Cuisine: Refined & Otherwise

If you're after *kaiseki* (haute cuisine) in sublime surroundings, go to Kyoto. But if a steaming bowl of *rāmen* is more your speed, you'll find endless choices here too.

p249

Kansai

Culture ✓✓✓
Nature ✓✓
Onsen ✓✓

Where It All Started

Southern Kansai is where Japanese culture came into being. Trace the history of the Yamato people (modern Japanese) from their roots in Asuka, through Nara and up to Kyoto.

Deep Mountains & Pilgrimage Routes

Southern Kansai (Wakayama and southern Nara) is a world of mountains, winding rivers and Shintō shrines. Pilgrims have been communing with the gods here for thousands of years.

Seaside & Riverside Onsen

From the quaint town of Kinosaki in the north to the riverside Hongū in the south, Kansai has plenty of hot springs to soak in after a day of soaking up the culture.

p300

Hiroshima & Western Honshū

Islands ✓✓✓
Food ✓✓
Onsen ✓

Island Adventures

An art-filled weekend, a mountain hike, a beachside frolic or an escape to slow-paced solitude – you can take your pick on one of the countless islands of the glittering Inland Sea.

Seafood Heaven

Seafood is king along the salty coasts of Western Honshū, and every seaside town has its speciality. Don't miss the chance to risk your life for a plate of fish in *fugu*-mad Shimonoseki.

Onsen Side Trips

Sure, they're not all superstars, and you have to seek them out, but that's what makes the quiet onsen towns here so inviting.

p364

Northern Honshū (Tōhoku)

Outdoors ✓✓✓
Food ✓✓
People ✓✓✓

Parks & Peaks

Temperate summers lure in hikers by the droves, while snowy winters attract powder fiends and snow bunnies.

Regional Delicacies

Restaurants pay homage to the region's agricultural and fishing roots. Supporting these industries helps to generate income and rebuild local livelihoods.

The Road Ahead

Residents of Tōhoku have endured tremendous suffering and loss due to the March 2011 earthquake and tsunami, but their determination to move forward is a testament to the strength of the Japanese spirit.

p424

Sapporo & Hokkaidō

Outdoors ✓✓✓
Food ✓✓
Weather ✓

Pristine Wilderness
Hokkaidō is where all your preconceived notions of Japan will be shattered. Walks in the park span days on end. Ocean voyages navigate precarious ice floes. Skiers carve snow drifts reaching several metres in depth.

Unique Cuisine
Flash-frozen salmon sashimi, soup curries, massive crabs and Sapporo lager are just some of Hokkaidō's much-revered culinary specialities.

Battling the Elements
In the short but splendid summer, Hokkaidō erupts in wildflower blooms. In the veritable Siberian winter, bring plenty of warm clothes.

p462

Shikoku

Nature ✓✓✓
Temples ✓✓✓
Surfing ✓✓✓

Ain't No Valley Wide Enough
A short drive from the mainland madness, Iya Valley has dramatic gorges, ancient vine bridges and a hint of sustainable living. Raft, hike or holler along the pristine Yoshino-gawa.

Good Buddha
The 88-temple pilgrimage is a rite of passage for many Japanese who, dressed in white and armed with a walking stick, lower the pulse, raise the gaze and seek to honour the great Buddhist saint, Kobo Daishi.

Surfin' Shikoku!
From the fishing villages of Tokushima Prefecture to the wild bluffs at Ashizuri-misaki, hidden banks and huge swells make consistent, crowd-free waves. Ohkihama Beach should be legendary.

p524

Kyūshū

History ✓✓
Nature ✓✓
Onsen ✓✓✓

Saints & Samurai
Christian rebellions led to over two centuries of seclusion from the rest of the world – the only contact was on Nagasaki's island of Dejima. Isolation ended as Kyūshū rebels led the Meiji Restoration.

Kaboom!
The active volcanoes Aso-san and Sakurajima are only the most famous of Kyūshū's mountains, with fantastic hiking in between. The ever-present chance of eruption gives residents a unique *joie de vivre.*

Ahhhh!
Soak away riverside in intimate Kurokawa Onsen or in one of Beppu's onsen, or get buried in a sand bath in Ibusuki. Even Kyūshū's biggest city, Fukuoka, has natural onsen.

p563

Okinawa & the Southwest Islands

Beaches ✓✓✓
Hiking ✓✓
Food ✓

Sun-Soaked
Splash out on the gorgeous golden beaches of the Kerama Archipelago, where you can whale-watch in winter and have the sand all to yourself.

Super Cedars
Climb into the green, pulsing heart of Yakushima, where ancient cedar trees grow really, really big. Looking more like a *Star Wars* set than Earth, this is the closest we've come to an otherworldly experience.

Goin' Goya
Tuck into a plateful of *gōya champurū,* Okinawa's signature stir-fry with bitter melon. Add some *awamori,* the local firewater, and you'll be ready to grab the *sanshin* (banjo) and party.

p634

Look out for these icons:

 TOP CHOICE Our author's recommendation **A green or sustainable option **FREE** No payment required

See the Index for a full list of destinations covered in this book.

On the Road

Tokyo

🎵 03 / POP 13,010,000

Best Places to Eat

» Beige (p91)
» Ukai Tofu-ya (p93)
» Ippūdō (p97)
» Ninja Akasaka (p93)

Best Places to Stay

» Claska (p88)
» Sukeroku No Yado Sadachiyo (p90)

Why Go?

Chaotic yet organised, hyper-modern yet utterly classic, garish yet demure, unique yet unquestionably Japanese, Tokyo (東京) is a paradox that – like a pop star – seems smug in its greatness yet obsessed with reinvention.

It's a city bent on collecting superlatives, and since the early days of Edo, Tokyo has done everything in its power to stay ahead of the pack, from reclaiming miles of swampland to transforming war-torn moonscapes into shimmering skyscraper districts.

Today that constant hunger for improvement and change has created a tapestry of sensorial madness unlike anywhere else in the world. In sheer size and scope alone, Tokyo far outweighs other major global centres.

And although Tokyo already seems like some sort of future city, it will undoubtedly continue to push forward, further securing its reputation as the most beautiful ugly city in the world.

When to Go
Tokyo

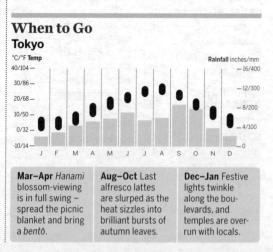

Mar–Apr Hanami blossom-viewing is in full swing – spread the picnic blanket and bring a bentō.

Aug–Oct Last alfresco lattes are slurped as the heat sizzles into brilliant bursts of autumn leaves.

Dec–Jan Festive lights twinkle along the boulevards, and temples are overrun with locals.

History

Tokyo's humble beginnings could not have foreshadowed its bright future as one of the world's great cities. Originally called Edo (literally 'Gate of the River') due to its location at the mouth of the Sumida-gawa, this small farming village rose from obscurity in 1603 when Tokugawa Ieyasu established his shōgunate (military government) among Edo's swampy lands. As the Tokugawa clan grew to govern the whole of Japan, Edo quickly transformed into a bustling city and de facto capital.

In fact, by the late 18th century, Edo had become the most populous city in the world, and was ages ahead of its contemporaries, having already mastered civic waste removal, recycling and eco-sensitive land reclamation. When the authority of the emperor was reinstated in 1868, the capital was officially moved from Kyoto to Edo, which was then renamed Tokyo, meaning Eastern Capital.

After more than 250 years of self-prescribed isolation, Tokyo suddenly welcomed foreign influence with open arms during the Meiji Restoration. Western fashion and ideas were swiftly incorporated into the fabric of society as the city eagerly sought to take its place among the pantheon of the world's great cities.

Nothing could hold Tokyo back – not even the Great Kantō Earthquake and ensuing fires, which levelled the city in 1923. It was once again torn to shreds during the devastating Ally air raids during the final years of WWII.

Emerging from the rubble after the US occupation, Tokyo quickly propelled itself towards modernity when it won the bid to host the 1964 Olympic Games. All eyes were on the city as it proudly showed lookers-on that it was indeed ready for its time in the spotlight. A soaring economic crescendo followed, culminating in the giddy heights of the 1980s Bubble Economy. After the 'burst' in the '90s, the city has failed to hold its ground amid recession, but it undeniably remains the beating heart of its island nation, never ceasing to reinvent itself while holding significant global influence over fashion, design and technology.

⊙ Sights & Activities

The first thing you should know about touring Tokyo is that there's no such thing as a complete list of attractions. Endless in size and scope, Japan's illustrious capital has countless must-sees to fill your itinerary. Perhaps more fascinating than expertly curated museums and eye-catching architecture, however, are Tokyo's forgotten backstreets. The city's no-named roads are begging to reveal their secrets, and a wrong turn down an unknown alley could end up being the most interesting and rewarding experience you have during your visit. Unknown noodle shops, hidden gardens and obscurely themed museums await your perusal, and the best part is that everything's always in flux, rewarding repeat visitors just as much as Nihon novices. Nothing should discourage you from hopping on the subway and alighting at a random station to explore; just make sure to carry your hotel's *meishi* (business card) in case you can't find your way back.

But Tokyo isn't just a wild cityscape – it's also very much about the people who fill it. Every day is like a subculture safari – you'll spot packs of suit-clad businessmen toting their briefcases around town, *otaku* (geeks) furiously thumbing manga digests, *hime gal* (think Marie Antoinette after a Hollywood makeover) holding court – pooch in hand – in the trendier neighbourhoods, and *goth loli* (think Marie Antoinette after the guillotine) angstfully loitering in parks or at subway stops. At the end of the day, all stripes and colours unite for the train ride back to the suburbs, dozing in unison and perking up suddenly just as they reach their station.

Despite the seemingly chaotic nature of the city, Tokyo isn't as hard to navigate as one might expect. An above-ground rail loop known as the JR Yamanote line unofficially marks the extent of central Tokyo, with the imperial palace or 'empty centre' acting as

HAVE YOUR SAY

Found a fantastic restaurant that you're longing to share with the world? Disagree with our recommendations? Or just want to talk about your most recent trip?

Whatever your reason, head to lonelyplanet.com, where you can post a review, ask or answer a question on the Thorntree forum, comment on a blog, or share your photos and tips on Groups. Or you can simply spend time chatting with like-minded travellers. So go on, have your say.

Tokyo Highlights

1 Strut your stuff down the concrete catwalks of **Harajuku** (p70) alongside faithful legions of fashion-hungry teens

2 Wander through the vast *depachika* food halls tucked below opulent department stores in **Ginza** (p108)

3 Don colourful robes and soak in steamy mineral baths at the wonderfully time-warped **Ō-edo Onsen Monogatari** (p82)

4 Attend the seasonal spectacle of sumō in **Ryōgoku** (p107) for salt-slinging, belly-slapping and solemn ritual

5 Dodge flying fish on the floor of **Tsukiji Fish Market** (p57) and sip savoury teas in the manicured gardens of **Hama-rikyū-teien** (p58) next door

6 Raise a glass in the colourful nightlife neighbourhoods of **Shinjuku** (p103), be it with the *yakuza* in Kabuki-chō or among drag queens in Ni-chōme

7 Lose yourself amid the vestiges of *shitamachi* culture in **Ueno** (p77)

8 Root for the home team during a furious baseball match at **Tokyo Dome City** (p74), then amble through the cobbled alleys of **Kagurazaka** (p75) in search of a tasty local meal

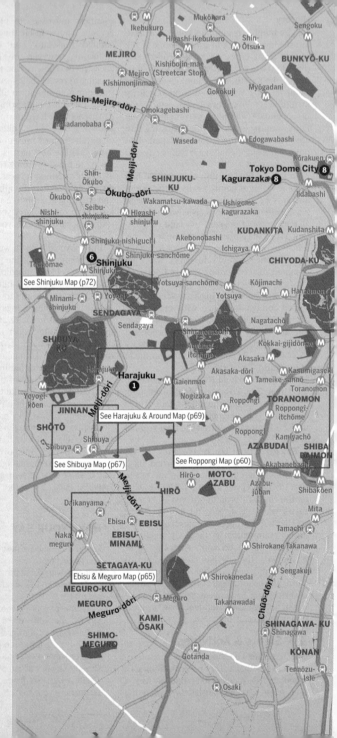

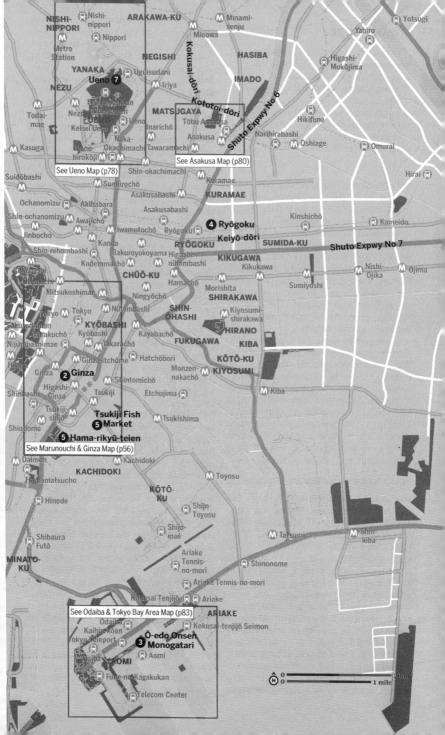

WANT MORE?

For in-depth information, reviews and recommendations at your fingertips, head to the Apple App Store to purchase Lonely Planet's *Tokyo City Guide* iPhone app.

Alternatively, head to **Lonely Planet** (www.lonelyplanet.com/japan/tokyo) for planning advice, author recommendations, traveller reviews and insider tips.

the city's incongruously verdant core. A trip around the JR Yamanote line makes a good introduction to the city, as it links most of Tokyo's major neighbourhoods.

The following sights are presented in a clockwise fashion starting around Marunouchi (Tokyo Station) and Ginza, looping west through Roppongi and Ebisu towards Shibuya, then up to Shinjuku, into northwest Tokyo and over to *shitamachi* ('lowtown'; Ueno and Asakusa). The chapter's sleeping, eating and shopping sections are laid out in a similar order.

If you plan on sticking around for a while, the best way to dig below the glowing neon lights and copper-topped temples is to choose a hobby – be it anything from manga to tango dancing – and follow it down the rabbit hole. When you emerge on the other side, you'll find a fascinating world of fanaticism, from speciality boutiques to thematic discussion bars. But best of all is the opportunity to connect with locals through those commonalities, as offbeat as they may be.

MARUNOUCHI & GINZA   丸の内・銀座

MARUNOUCHI (TOKYO STATION AREA) 丸の内（東京駅）
Just east of the imperial palace you'll find **Tokyo Station** and the bustling business district of Marunouchi. Unlike many of the city's great neighbourhoods, this area is just starting to come into its own as Tokyo Station receives an extended refurbishment and facelift (to be completed in 2013). Once a district of tired, almost Soviet-style structures, Marunouchi's architectural renaissance has spawned several postcard-worthy endeavours, like the **Tokyo International Forum** (東京国際フォーラム; Map p56; www.t-i-forum.co.jp, www.marunouchi.com/marubiru; 3-5-1 Marunouchi), which features a prominent glass wing that looks like a transparent ship plying the city's urban waters. Also worth

a look is the **Marunouchi Building** (Maru Biru; Map p56; 2-4-1 Marunouchi), towering high above the city and offering up restaurants, elegant shopping and privileged views of the imperial grounds. Its sister structure, **Shin Marunouchi** (Shin Maru; www.marunouchi.com/shinmaru), soars over the skyline next door.

Although the area can easily be explored on foot, tourists can make use of the free **Marunouchi shuttle bus** (http://marunouchi.bus-location.com/bloc/tm), which transports passengers up Daimyōkoji and down Hibiyadōri every 15 to 20 minutes. Another option (geared more towards businessfolk) is the **Metro Link Nihonbashi** (www.busnav.net/nihonbashi), which links Kyōbashi and Mitsukoshimae metro stations with Tokyo Station.

Marunouchi Cafe (p114) offers a handy free brochure of the evolving district, featuring a neat little guide to the area's street sculpture and recommending different walking routes depending on your mood.

TOP CHOICE **Imperial Palace**   HISTORICAL BUILDING
(皇居; Kōkyo; Map p56; 3213-1111; www.sankan.kunaicho.go.jp; Tokyo, exit D2) Japan's Imperial Palace is an appropriate place to start the city's laundry list of interesting sights, as it is – geographically, at least – the centre of Tokyo. The leafy grounds occupy the site of the original Edo-jō, the Tokugawa shōgunate's castle when they ruled the land. In its heyday the castle was the largest in the world, though little remains of it today apart from the moat and walls. The present palace, completed in 1968, replaced the one built in 1888, which was destroyed during WWII.

As it's the home of Japan's emperor and imperial family, the palace itself is closed to the public for all but two days of the year, 2 January and 23 December (the Emperor's birthday). It is possible, however, to take a tour of the imperial grounds, but you must book ahead through the Imperial Household Agency's website. Reserve well in advance – slots become available on the first day of each month. Tours run twice daily from Monday to Friday (10am and 1.30pm), but not on weekends, public holidays and afternoons from late July through to the end of August.

The main park of the palace grounds is the **Imperial Palace East Garden** (皇居東御苑; Kōkyo Higashi-gyoen; Map p56; 9am-4.30pm Tue-Thu; Ōtemachi, exit C10), which is open to the public without reservations. You must take a token upon arrival and return it at the end of your visit.

TOP CHOICE Mitsubishi Ichigokan MUSEUM

(Map p56; http://mimt.jp/english; 2-6-2 Marunou-chi; 10am-8pm Wed-Fri, to 6pm Tue, Sat & Sun; Hibiya, exit B7, or Nijūbashimae, exit 1) The Mitsubishi Ichigokan was the area's first office building, designed shortly after the Meiji Restoration by controversial architect Josiah Conder. Though the first structure was destroyed long ago, the current structure (completed in 2009) is an exact replica of the original. Today, the building is one of Tokyo's most inviting gallery spaces. The concept behind the museum is simple: to create a convivial place where local businessfolk can stop by on their lunch break to unwind and enjoy the exhibits. Thus, the museum doesn't overload you with art – the gorgeous galleries take only around 45 minutes to explore. International exhibitions rotate regularly, meaning that the area's workforce could ostensibly stop by several times a year. Admission fees vary.

Consider visiting around lunchtime and check out the in-house **Café 1894**, which, like the rest of the building, has been reproduced inch by inch from the original floor plans. The space used to be the central bank – you'll notice dark wood teller windows near the entrance. The cafe is one of the new favourite spots for the ladies who lunch in nearby Ginza.

Kite Museum MUSEUM

(Map p56; 3271-2465; www.tako.gr.jp; 5th fl, Taimeiken Bldg 1-12-10 Nihonbashi; admission ¥200; 11am-5pm Mon-Sat; Nihonbashi, exit C5) An explosion of eye-popping graphics and blazing colours, this friendly little place features over 2000 kites in its crammed-to-the-ceiling showroom. On the benches at the back you'll find laminated cards detailing the fascinating history of kites in China and Japan. From late spring to early autumn you can even build your own kite with help from an expert (¥300 to ¥600; call at least 24 hours in advance). The museum can be a bit tricky to find – if you get lost on the street, ask for 'Taimeiken'.

National Film Center MUSEUM

(Map p56; www.momat.go.jp/fc.html; 3-7-6 Kyōbashi; admission/film ¥200/500; gallery 11am-6.30pm Tue-Sun; Kyōbashi, exit 1) Under the auspices of the National Museum of Modern Art, the National Film Centre is an archive of films, books, periodicals, posters and other ancillary materials related to Japanese film. There are two or three screenings al-most every day of the year – most films are in Japanese only, but the ¥500 admission price can't be beaten. On the 7th floor you'll find a permanent exhibit dedicated to the history of Japanese cinema. Excellent English captions provide interesting historical insight, and the collection of retro posters and video clips offer at least an hour's worth of fun. If the location of this museum seems a bit random (lost in a modern business district), know that this is where some of Japan's first cinemas were constructed in the Meiji period.

Bridgestone Museum of Art MUSEUM

(Map p56; www.bridgestone-museum.gr.jp; 1-10-1 Kyōbashi; admission ¥800; 10am-8pm Tue-Sat, to 6pm Sun; JR Tokyo, Yaesuguchi exit) Tokyo has a love affair with all things French, so it shouldn't come as too much of a surprise that French impressionist art looms large in the civic imagination. The Bridgestone Tyre Company's collection, which was previously kept as a private collection by Bridgestone founder Ishibashi Shōjiro, features all the big names – Renoir, Ingres, Monet, Matisse, Picasso – and an interesting selection of works by Japanese impressionists as well.

Mitsui Museum MUSEUM

(Map p56; www.mitsui-museum.jp; 2-1-1 Nihonbashi-muromachi; admission ¥1000; 10am-5pm; Mitsukoshimae) Stately wood panelling surrounds a small collection of traditional Japanese art and artefacts.

GINZA & AROUND 銀座

Ginza is Tokyo's answer to New York's Fifth Ave or London's Oxford St. In the 1870s the area was one of the first neighbourhoods in Tokyo to modernise, welcoming Western-style brick buildings, the city's first department stores, gas lamps and other harbingers of globalisation.

Today, other shopping districts rival Ginza in opulence, vitality and popularity, but it retains a distinct snob value – conspicuous consumption remains big here. It's therefore a superb place to window-shop and people-watch – especially on weekends when bustling **Chūō-dōri** (Ginza dōri) and several smaller streets are closed to vehicular traffic, allowing gaggles of 'ladies who lunch' to gambol down the middle of the boulevard with sass and style. Climb to the 2nd floor of **Le Cafe Doutor Ginza** (Map p56; 1st & 2nd fl, San'ai Bldg 5-7-2) for impressive views of the action at Ginza Crossing.

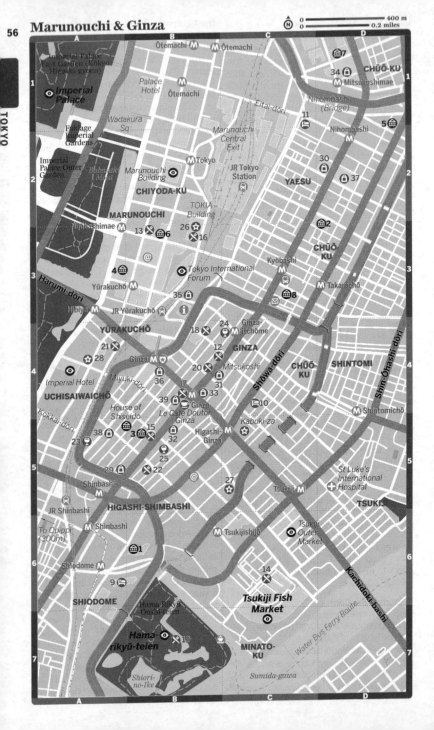

Tsukiji Fish Market MARKET
(築地市場; Map p56; ☏3547-8011; www.tsukiji-market.or.jp; 5-2 Tsukiji; ⓢTsukijishijō, exits A1 & A2) Tsukiji Fish Market has the distinct honour of being the world's biggest seafood market. 'Japan's kitchen' moves at a frenetic pace as thousands upon thousands of fish are processed, purchased and carted off to different corners of the country. The infamous **tuna auction** starts at 5am and peters out by 8am, when the day's catch has been purchased by middlemen and sold off to gawking retailers. By 11am the crowds have dwindled and the sprinkler trucks plough through to prep the empty market for tomorrow's sale.

To access the tuna auction, arrive at 4.30am and queue in front of the Fish Information Center (Osakana Fukyū Center) located at the Kachidoki Gate in the northwest corner of the market (when facing the Main Gate, head left, round the block at the second traffic light and head down Harumi-dōri again turning right at the second traf-

fic light). The first 140 individuals will be granted admission to the auction – the first shift of 70 visitors takes place from 5am to 5.40am, the second shift begins at 5.40am and ends at 6.15am. Note that if you plan on arriving around 4.30am, you must take a taxi to the market, as public transport does not start running until around 5am.

If you aren't keen to wake up before dawn, you can indeed show up later in the morning and still get a flavour of the frenetic atmosphere of the other parts of the market. The intermediate wholesalers area opens up to visitors at 9am, while other areas of the market including the Jogai Shijō are open even earlier.

Perhaps the most confusing thing about the market is the rather convoluted calendar. In general, it's closed on Sundays, most Wednesdays and all public holidays – check the website for details, or call directly for the most up-to-date info. Please exercise caution and respect when visiting any part of the market so as not to spoil the opportunity for future visitors to sneak a peek at the goings-on. Large groups, babies and young children are prohibited. And finally, don't fret if you can't watch the auction – the outer market is just as interesting, if not moreso.

For the last few years, rumours have been flying about Tsukiji's uncertain future – it is expected to move to Toyosu at the end of 2012. There has been, however, some grumbling about the market's fate, especially since the matter falls under the jurisdiction of the Tokyo Metropolitan Government and not the Tsukiji Market Association. Although the decree is considered definitive, it is possible that things could change – keep your ears open for the latest updates.

Hama-rikyū-teien PARK
(浜離宮恩賜庭園; Detached Palace Garden; Map p56; www.tokyo-park.or.jp/park/format/index028.html; 1-1 Hama-rikyu-teien; admission ¥300; ◎9am-5pm; 🚇Shiodome, exit 5) Once the horse stables and hunting ground of the Tokugawas, this gorgeous garden features perfectly manicured hills set below the imposing towers of Shiodome next door. Trees are dutifully pruned and the water level is monitored electronically, but the most impressive thing about the Hama-rikyu is the complimentary audio guide that uses modern satellite technology to detect your location within the garden and automatically narrates interesting facts and stories about your surroundings.

The park is within walking distance from Ginza and is also accessible via river cruise from Asakusa (see p117).

Shiodome NEIGHBOURHOOD
(汐留; Map p56; www.caretta.jp; 🚇Shiodome) Built with similar aspirations as Roppongi Hills, Shiodome is a complex of multipurpose towers stuffed with the usual spread of offices and restaurants. Unlike its Roppongi counterpart, this 'future-city' hasn't quite hit its stride, which means it's thankfully never too crowded, but there also isn't a whole lot to see or do.

FREE **Advertising Museum Tokyo** (ア ド・ミュージアム東京; www.admt.jp; B1-B2 fl, Caretta Shiodome Bldg 1-8-2 Higashi-shinbashi; ◎11am-6.30pm Tue-Fri, to 4.30pm Sat; 🚇Shiodome, JR Shinbashi exit) recounts the history of product marketing in Japan. None of the displays have English signage, but the appealing visuals (both images and video) offer plenty of stimuli for a short visit.

Take the elevator to the Caretta Building's 'Sky Restaurants' on the 46th and 47th floors and you'll find a small **observation area** boasting excellent views of the city's east end – especially Hama-rikyū-teien and Odaiba. It's free to stare out the windows, and the nook is rarely cluttered with people.

Idemitsu Museum of Arts MUSEUM
(出光美術館; Map p56; www.idemitsu.co.jp; 9th fl, Teigeki Bldg 3-1-1 Marunouchi; admission ¥1000; ◎10am-5pm Tue-Sun; 🚇Yūrakuchō, Teigeki exit) This museum contains the private collection of Idemitsu Savo, founder of the Idemitsu Kosan Co. Objects on display include Japanese and Chinese art and artefacts – most notably the works of Zen monk Sengai. It's next door to the Imperial Theatre and affords excellent views of the imperial grounds.

FREE **Ginza Graphic Gallery** ART GALLERY
(Map p56; www.dnp.co.jp/gallery; 7-7-2 Ginza, exit A2; ◎11am-6pm Mon-Fri, to 7pm Sat; 🚇Ginza, exit A2) An interesting graphic design showcase funded by one of the country's biggest printing conglomerates. The gallery hosts workshops and talks by visiting artists, covering everything from tiny typography to monumental architecture.

FREE **House of Shiseido** ART GALLERY
(Map p56; www.shiseido.co.jp/house-of-shiseido; 7-5-5 Ginza; ◎10am-6pm Mon-Sat; 🚇Ginza, exit B5) Often showcases modern decorative objects and artfully crafted items of consumer consumption.

ROPPONGI 六本木
Exiting the subway station at Roppongi Crossing is like entering the world of *Bladerunner* or *Star Wars,* where throngs of the galaxy's most unscrupulous citizens gather to engage in a host of unsavoury activities under the sizzling neon lights. Club music thumps, and the streets are filled with catcalls and other shady offers.

Over the last decade, however, Roppongi has really started to clean up its act – and it shows. Perhaps just as famous as Roppongi itself is the enormous complex of **Roppongi Hills** (六本木ヒルズ; Map p60; www.roppongihills.com; 6-10 Roppongi; 🚇Roppongi, exits 1c & 3). It took developer Mori Minoru no fewer than 17 years to acquire the land and construct his labyrinthine kingdom. He envisioned improving the quality of urban life by centralising home, work and leisure into a utopic microcosm of a city. A grand vision realised? It's a matter of opinion. But the overflow of restaurants, shops and entertainment consistently draws crowds (largely of the *gaijin* variety).

Roppongi's other anchor is the newer **Tokyo Midtown** (東京ミッドタウン; Map p60; www.tokyo-midtown.com; 9-7 Akasaka; ℝRoppongi 1-chome, exit 1) with its own set of intriguing dining and shopping options.

The area's three major museums – the Mori Art Museum, the Suntory Art Museum and the National Art Center Tokyo – are collectively known as the **Roppongi Art Triangle**. It's well worth spending the day connecting the dots – finish with the Mori Art Museum and take in the morphing cityscapes during sunset.

Tokyo Tower   NOTABLE BUILDING
(東京タワー; Map p60; www.tokyotower.co.jp; 4-2-8 Shiba-kōen; main observation deck ¥820, special observation deck ¥1400; ⊙9am-10pm; ℝKamiyachō, exits 1 & 2) Tokyo Tower proves that Japan always has to one-up the competition. Tokyo's first TV broadcasting tower is a duplicate of Paris' Eiffel Tower; however, the orange-and-white behemoth stands at 333m – 13m higher than the icon of modernity in the City of Light. In the 1890s, Paris' steel tower was an emblem of the incoming age of machines and international progress, but Tokyo Tower, constructed over 60 years later, lacks the 'wow' impact that Eiffel achieved. Instead, the retro spire provides a strange old-school counterpoint to the ultramodern developments of Roppongi Hills and Tokyo Midtown nearby. Tokyo Tower is, however, quite the sight for sore eyes after dark – the light shows change every day; check the website for details about the significance and meaning of each display.

Mori Art Museum   ART GALLERY
(森美術館; Map p60; www.mori.art.museum; 53rd floor, Roppongi Hills Mori Tower 6-10-1 Roppongi; admission ¥1500; ⊙10am-10pm Wed-Mon, to 5pm Tue; ℝRoppongi, exits 1c & 3) Enviably ensconced atop Mori Tower is the Mori Art Museum, forming one corner of the Roppongi Art Triangle. Exhibitions at this contemporary-art space tend towards the (mind-bogglingly myriad) multimedia variety and are of a consistently high calibre.

Admission to the museum also gets you into **Tokyo City View** (東京シティビュー; www.tokyocityview.com; 52nd floor, Roppongi Hills Mori Tower 6-10-1 Roppongi; adult/child ¥1500/500; ⊙9am-1am; ℝRoppongi, exits 1c & 3), with 360-degrees' worth of Tokyo. If the floor-to-ceiling windows aren't enough of an eyeful, a roof deck (which doubles as an emergency heli-pad – think *Inception*) is open when weather permits. It costs an additional ¥300.

 SIGHTSEEING IN TOKYO

Tokyo's endless cityscape plays host to thousands of incredible sights and sounds. The following are among hundreds of web resources designed to enrich a traveller's experience in the city. Use these in conjunction with our detailed coverage found throughout the chapter.

» **Grutt Pass** (www.rekibun.or.jp/grutto) If you're planning on sticking around Tokyo for a week or more, then consider investing in a Grutt Pass – a booklet of discount coupons to over 70 museums in greater Tokyo, including the Tokyo National Museum, the Museum of Contemporary Art Tokyo and the Mori Art Museum.

» **Tokyo Tourist Information** (www.tourism.metro.tokyo.jp) Municipally run website detailing what to see, do and eat in greater Tokyo. Walking tour ideas are also on offer.

» **JNTO** (www.jnto.go.jp) The national tourism board's website featuring heaps of useful info for visitors including itinerary builders.

» **Tokyo Pocket Guide** (www.tokyopocketguide.com/tokyo) A web library of English pdf maps detailing most major neighbourhoods in the city centre.

» **Tokyo Parks** (www.tokyo-park.or.jp) Resource of picturesque places to unwind in the capital.

» **Tokyo Art Beat** (www.tokyoartbeat.com) Bilingual art and design guide with regularly updated list of events.

» **Super Sentos** (www.sunnypages.jp/search/tokyo_sightseeing/super_sentos) A good list of places to scrub down around town.

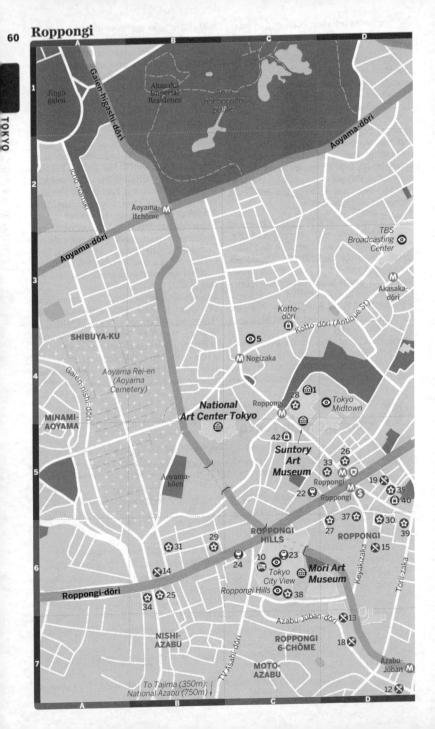

Jingū-gaien

Gaien-higashi-dōri

Ichiōmannriki

Akasaka Imperial Residence

Area not open to public

Aoyama-dōri

Aoyama-dōri

Aoyama-itchōme

TBS Broadcasting Center

Akasaka-dōri

SHIBUYA-KU

Kottō-dōri

Kottō-dōri (Antique St)

⊙5

Nogizaka

Gaien-nishi-dōri

Aoyama Rei-en (Aoyama Cemetery)

28 ☆1

National Art Center Tokyo

Roppongi

Tokyo Midtown

MINAMI-AOYAMA

Aoyama-kōen

42

Suntory Art Museum

26
33
Roppongi
22
Roppongi

19 35
40

37 30
27 ROPPONGI 39

15

31 29

ROPPONGI HILLS

24 10 23

14

Tokyo City View

Mori Art Museum

Roppongi Hills 38

25
34

Roppongi-dōri

Azabu-Jūban-dōri 13

NISHI-AZABU

18

ROPPONGI 6-CHŌME

MOTO-AZABU

Azabu-Jūban

TV Asahi-dōri

To Tajima (350m); National Azabu (750m)

12

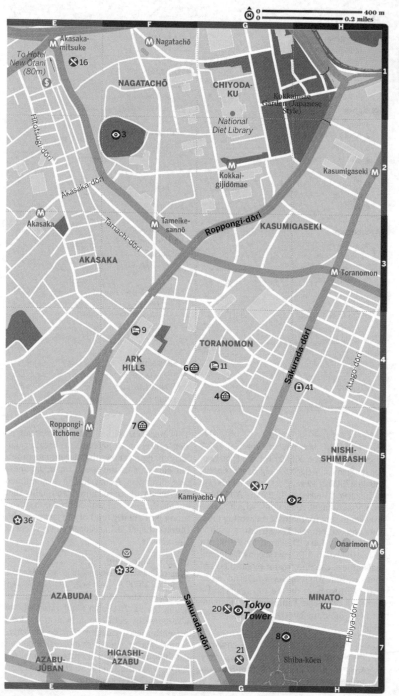

N

0 ——— 400 m
0 ——— 0.2 miles

E
F
G
H

Akasaka-mitsuke
Nagatachō Ⓜ
🅼

To Hotel New Otani (80m)
✕ 16
$
NAGATACHŌ
CHIYODA-KU
Kokkaman Garden (Japanese Style)

National Diet Library

◉ 3

Kasumigaseki Ⓜ

Akasaka-dōri

Kokkai-gijidōmae Ⓜ

Ⓜ Akasaka

Tamachi-dōri
Ⓜ Tameike-sannō
Roppongi-dōri
KASUMIGASEKI

AKASAKA

Ⓜ Toranomon

📂 9

TORANOMON

🏛 6 📂 11
ARK HILLS
🏛 4

🔒 41

Atago-dōri

🏛 7
Roppongi-itchōme Ⓜ
NISHI-SHIMBASHI

✕ 17

😵 36
Kamiyachō Ⓜ
◉ 2

Onarimon Ⓜ

✉
★ 32

Sakurada-dōri

AZABUDAI
MINATO-KU

Hibiya-dōri

20 ✕ ◉ *Tokyo Tower*

8 ◉

AZABU-JŪBAN
HIGASHI-AZABU
21 ✕
Shiba-kōen

E
F
G
H

1
2
3
4
5
6
7

National Art Center Tokyo ART GALLERY
(国立新美術館; Map p60; www.nact.jp; 7-22-2 Roppongi; admission ¥1500; ⏰10am-6pm Wed-Mon, to 8pm Fri; 🚇Nogizaka, exit 6, or Roppongi, exits 4a & 7) With 42 gallery spaces, this is one of the largest museums in Japan. And there are no permanent collections, which makes it the go-to spot for many of the world's most engaging exhibitions. The structure itself is also a work of art. Designed by Kurokawa Kisho, the beautifully curvaceous facade reveals an eye-catching realm of cantilevered cones within. You'll find a wonderful **art library** (⏰11am-6pm) on the top floor, and a branch of celeb-chef Paul Bocuse's Michelin-starred restaurant hovering over the grand lobby.

Suntory Art Museum ART GALLERY
(サントリー美術館; Map p60; www.suntory.co.jp/sma; 4th fl, 9-7 Akasaka; ⏰10am-6pm Sun-Mon, to 8pm Wed-Sat; 🚇Roppongi 1-chome, exit 1) This regal exhibition hall draws from its rich collection of artefacts to create regularly changing shows that accentuate different elements of the spectrum of Japanese arts. Architect Kuma Kengō has imbued the space with an uncanny Zen quality that should definitely be experienced even if you aren't particularly fond of the current exhibition's theme. Admission fees vary; check the website.

21_21 Design Sight MUSEUM
(Map p60; www.2121designsight.jp; 9-7-6 Akasaka; admission ¥1000; ⏰11am-8pm Wed-Sun; 🚇Nogizaka, exit 3) More of a workshop than a museum, the 21_21 Design Sight raises design awareness by acting as a beacon for local art enthusiasts, whether they be designers themselves or simply onlookers. Frequent exhibits and group discussions are the norm. Visit the iTunes store to download 21_21's curious iPhone app.

Musée Tomo
MUSEUM

(Map p60; www.musee-tomo.or.jp; 4-1-35 Torano-mon; admission ¥1300; ⊙11am-6pm Tue-Sun; ℝKamiyachō, exit 4b) Part of Roppongi's 'Small Triangle', Musée Tomo should not be overlooked due to its steep price and small size – this is one of the most elegant and best curated museums in the city. The collection features a stunning assortment of ceramics displayed in spaces that are themselves a work of art – the walls are coated in *washi* paper; even the crystalline banister leading down to the galleries is an original commission. Note the giant painting at the entrance – it says 'welcome' (*ume*) in thick coats of kanji brushstrokes.

Ōkura Museum of Art
MUSEUM

(大倉集古館; Map p60; www.hotelokura.co.jp/tokyo/shukan; 2-10-3 Toranomon; adult/child ¥800/free; ⊙10am-4.30pm Tue-Sun; ℝTameike-sannō, exit 13, or Kamiyachō, exit 4B) On the grounds of the venerable Ōkura Hotel, this two-storey museum displays a rotating collection of sculpture, hand-painted dishware, lacquer writing boxes and no fewer than three national treasures, all surrounded by a small but well-populated sculpture garden.

It's free for hotel guests, and also forms part of Roppongi's 'Small Triangle'.

Sen-oku Hakuko Kan
MUSEUM

(Map p60; ☑5777-8600; www.sen-oku.or.jp; 1-5-1 Roppongi; admission ¥520; ⊙10am-4.30pm Wed-Mon, closed Jul-Aug & Dec-Feb; ℝRoppongi 1-chome, exit 2) This small museum abutting the Izumi Gardens complex features a diverse collection of decorative arts. It's part of Roppongi's 'Small Triangle' of galleries.

Zōjō-ji
TEMPLE

(増上寺; Map p60; 4-7-35 Shiba-kōen; ⊙dawn-dusk; ℝAkabanebashi, Akabanebashi exit) Behind Tokyo Tower, Zōjō-ji was the family temple of the Tokugawas. Visit in the evening, when you can admire the bizarre juxtaposition of the illuminated tower leaping skyward above the dark shape of the main hall.

Nogi-jinja
SHRINE

(Map p60; 8-11-27 Akasaka; ⊙8.30am-5pm; ℝNogizaka, exit 1) This shrine honours General Nogi, hero of the Russo-Japanese War. Hours after Emperor Meiji's funerary processional, Nogi and his faithful wife committed ritual suicide (Nogi disembowelled himself; his wife slit her throat), following

---

TOKYO IN FOUR DAYS

Something Old

Savour that old *shitamachi* feel in **Ueno** and **Asakusa**, then head down to **Ginza** to visit the district's collection of grand department stores – relics of a bygone era. Book ahead to tour the stately grounds of the **Imperial Palace**, and in the evening uncover the cluster of well-worn hovel-bars in Shinjuku's **Golden Gai** district.

Something New

Scout out the latest designer trends in **Harajuku**, peek at **Meiji-jingū**, then march between the luxury boutique monuments on **Omote-sandō-dōri**. Walk down to **Shibuya** to find Tokyo's teens – the city's freshly minted fashion victims – frenetically bouncing between shops.

Something Borrowed

Rummage through other people's closets at some of the city's top secondhand shops in the trendy satellite districts of **Shimokitazawa** and **Jiyūgaoka**. Later in the day, head to **Tokyo Dome City** to witness Japan's favourite American import – baseball. Afterwards, wander the backstreets of **Kagurazaka** and choose between traditional eats or exceptional French fare.

Something Blue

Start the day early with a trip to **Tsukiji Fish Market**, then walk off your sushi breakfast at the manicured grounds of **Hama-rikyū-teien**. Hop on a **river bus** bound for **Ryōgoku** to check out the **Edo-Tokyo Museum**, or a rousing **sumō match** if a tournament is in session. Then sail over to the artificial island of **Odaiba** for a Vegas-like shopping experience and a quick trip back in time at the Edo-themed **Ō-edo Onsen Monogatari**.

their master into death. Their blood spatter can still be seen on the tatami floors if you peek through the window.

Atago-jinja
SHRINE

(Map p60; www.atago-jinja.com; 1-5-3 Atago; Kamiyachō, exit 3) Originally constructed at the behest of Tokugawa Ieyasu, Atago's main feature is its giant stone stairway at the entrance. The shrine itself sits at the top – a welcome reward for huffing visitors. In Edo times it doubled as a fire watchtower, and thus *Homusubi no Mikoto*, the Shintō fire god, is worshiped here.

Hie-jinja
SHRINE

(日枝神社; Map p60; 2-10-5 Nagatachō; Akasaka-mitsuke, Belle Vie exit) The highlight of this modern shrine is the long 'tunnel' of orange *torii* (shrine gates) at the entrance – a spectacular sight during cherry-blossom season.

EBISU & MEGURO
恵比寿・目黒

EBISU & AROUND
恵比寿

Named for the prominent beer manufacturer that once provided a lifeline for most of the neighbourhood's residents, Ebisu has morphed into a rather upscale neighbourhood with a generous smattering of excellent restaurants and bars.

A short zip along the 'Skywalk' from Ebisu Station takes you to **Yebisu Garden Place** (恵比寿ガーデンプレイス; Map p65; www.gardenplace.jp; 4-20 Ebisu), another one of Tokyo's 'micro-cities' with a string of shops and restaurants, a luxury hotel, hundreds of offices and two museums. In the sprawl around Ebisu you'll find a couple of the city's hippest neighbourhoods.

Daikanyama
NEIGHBOURHOOD

(代官山; Map p65; Tōkyū Tōyoko line to Daikanyama) The geometric wonderland of Daikanyama is a shopper's paradise set on a series of small rolling hills. There's little to do here besides swiping your plastic and sitting in cafes – but we're not saying that's a bad thing... The neighbourhood eschews big brands in favour of unique boutiques, which means prices are high, but there are some wonderful treasures to be uncovered. Although the area is quite spread out compared to Tokyo's other nooks, the district's core is located around **Daikanyama Address**, a commercial complex known throughout the city for its special evening illuminations.

Naka-meguro
NEIGHBOURHOOD

(中目黒; Map p65; Naka-meguro) To the untrained eye, Nakame – as it's often known – may seem like nothing more than another unholy mishmash of offices, shops and apartments clustered around a convenient train station. But insiders know better. In fact, over the last few years this vibrant community has grown to become one of the most sought-after areas to live in – real-estate prices have boomed, and gaggles of trendy cafes and restaurants have set up shop along the concreted banks of the picturesque **Meguro-gawa**. You'll be spoilt for choice come dinnertime; stroll along the canal and choose a spot that tickles your fancy.

Tokyo Metropolitan Museum of Photography
MUSEUM

(東京都写真美術館; Map p65; www.syabi.com; 1-13-3 Mita; admission ¥500-1700; 10am-6pm Tue-Sun, to 8pm Thu & Fri) In a corner of Yebisu Garden Place, this large museum chronicles the history and contemporary use of still and moving images, and holds 23,000 works, roughly 70% of them Japanese. Displays often comprise exceptional work by photographers from both Japan and abroad, and there's an extensive library of photographic literature from throughout the world. Ticket prices are generally based on how many exhibits you see.

FREE Yebisu Beer Museum
MUSEUM

(エビスビール記念館; Map p65; www.sapporobeer.jp; 4-20-1 Ebisu; tour ¥500; Ebisu) This freshly renovated museum details the colourful 120-year history of Yebisu Beer through a series of photographs, artefacts and panels. Samples of four different ales are available for ¥400 each. The museum is free, and guided tours (currently in Japanese only) include a drink and an intense beer-drinking education session at the Communication Stage. Yes, you read that right – the guide will show you the correct posture for drinking a cold one as well as teach you the rules of holding a beer glass (finger positioning, glass angle etc) while sipping. The museum also serves full German-style meals if you're so inclined.

MEGURO & AROUND
目黒

South of Ebisu, **Meguro** (off Map p65; www.meguroku.com) has a prosperous residential vibe mixed with a few corporate towers in the vicinity of the JR station. Although

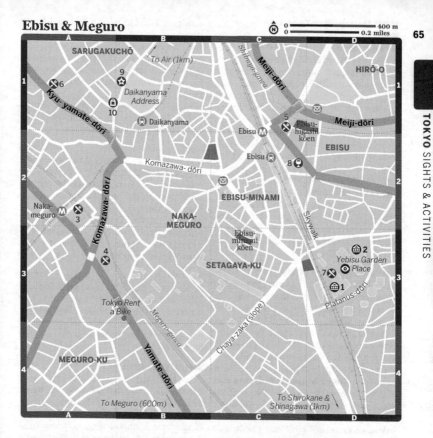

TOKYO SIGHTS & ACTIVITIES

there isn't a lot for tourists to experience here, you'll find a couple of noteworthy museums as well as MISC (see p109), an entire sub-district of fantastic furniture boutiques and bric-a-brac shops.

FREE Meguro Parasitological Museum

MUSEUM

(目黒寄生虫館; http://kiseichu.org; 4-1-1 Shimo-meguro; ⊙10am-5pm Tue-Sun; 🚇Meguro, West exit) A fun, offbeat retreat – although it's a bit of a buzz-kill for foodies – this veritable parasite safari will probably encourage you to cut back on your sushi intake. Although there isn't much English signage, you'll still get a kick out of the rows of formaldehyde-preserved critters, which are labelled with their Latin names (don't miss the 8.8m-long tapeworm!). Upstairs, the lab-coat-donning staff also sell various parasite-themed trinkets and T-shirts to guffawing Japanese girls.

Ebisu & Meguro

Tokyo Metropolitan Teien Art Museum
MUSEUM

(www.teien-art-museum.com; 5-21-9 Shirokanedai; ⊙10am-6pm, closed 2nd & 4th Wed each month; ®Meguro, East exit) Although the Teien museum hosts regular art exhibitions – like Meissen porcelain, or pottery by important Japanese artists – its appeal lies principally in the building itself: it's an art deco structure built in 1933, designed by French architect Henri Rapin. The interior details remain alluring, including etched tile trim, light fixtures sculpted to look like peaches and pumpkins, and the 'perfume fountain', sort of an early aromatherapy device. The house was originally home to Prince Asaka (1887–1981), Emperor Hirohito's uncle, who was pardoned for his part in the Rape of Nanjing. It became a museum in 1983; admission fees vary.

Institute for Nature Study
PARK

(附属自然教育園; www.ins.kahaku.go.jp; 5-21-5 Shirokanedai; adult/child ¥300/free; ⊙9am-5pm Tue-Sun; ®Shirokanedai, exit 1) These 200,000 sq metres of land were part of the estate of a *daimyō* (regional lord under the shōgun) some six centuries ago, and during the Meiji period it was the site of several gunpowder warehouses. Since 1949 the garden has been part of the **Tokyo National Museum** and aims to preserve the local flora in undisciplined profusion. There are wonderful walks through its forests, marshes and ponds, making this one of Tokyo's least known and most appealing getaways. Bonus: admission is limited to 300 people at a time.

SHIROKANE & SHINAGAWA
白金・品川

Beyond Meguro in the southern part of the city centre, Shirokane is another picturesque residential area with a sprinkling of interesting attractions. Shinagawa bustles with the flow of commuters who come from far and wide using the country's hyper-efficient *shinkansen* (bullet trains).

TOP CHOICE Hara Museum
MUSEUM

(www.haramuseum.or.jp; 4-7-25 Kitashinagawa; admission ¥1000; ⊙11am-5pm Tue-Sun, to 8pm Wed; ®JR Shinagawa, Takanawa exit) A hipster's museum dream, the Hara is a mansion turned unconventional art space, with regularly rotating exhibits and a clutch of permanent wonders (including a gender-bending bathroom installation by Morimura Yasumasa). In addition to the fascinating architecture and exhibits, the building itself has had a colourful history – in a former life, the structure housed the Sri Lankan Embassy and American soldiers during the occupation. Figure around an hour to explore all of the nooks and crannies, and afterwards hit up the fantastic cafe and inspired gift shop.

At the time of research, a free bus shuttles visitors between the museum and Shinagawa every 30 minutes on Sundays.

Hatakeyama Collection
MUSEUM

(畠山記念館; www.ebara.co.jp/csr/hatakeyama/index.html; 2-20-12 Shirokanedai; admission ¥500; ⊙10am-5pm Tue-Sun; ®Takanawadai, exit A2) Glide through the exhibition space in borrowed slippers while perusing earthenware dedicated to the elaborate yet austere tea ceremony. Ponder the elusive *wabi-sabi* aesthetic in the grounds, which cloaks the museum with its army of gnarled trees.

Sengaku-ji
TEMPLE

(www.sengakuji.or.jp; 2-11-1 Takanawa; ⊙7am-6pm; ®Sengakuji, exit A2) Follow the steps up to find the tombs of the famous 47 *rōnin* – soldiers without a samurai – who followed their master Ako to death after he pulled a sword on a rival.

SHIBUYA & AROUND
渋谷

Considered the centre of the city's teen culture, Shibuya isn't shy when it comes to living loud. Each day, legions of determined youth flock to the neighbourhood to consume a vibrant array of wares from fierce fashion to fruity drinks. Their castle is **Shibuya 109** (渋谷１０９; Map p67; www.shibuya109.jp; 2-29-1 Dōgenzaka) – a tower of trash and trends.

The first thing you'll notice when you arrive in Shibuya is the astonishing amount of human traffic. Swarms of locals mill about at all times of day – **Shibuya Crossing** (Map p67), the area's centrepiece, is one of the world's busiest intersections, with an estimated 100,000 people passing through every hour! It's worth pausing for a moment to take in a bird's eye view of the crowds from the **Starbucks** (Map p67) perched above the easily spotted Tsutaya bookshop. Fun fact – it's the highest grossing Starbucks in the world and only 'tall' sizes are served, to discourage patrons from lingering.

If a local friend asks to meet you at Shibuya, you'll probably gather at **Hachikō** (忠犬ハチ公; Map p67), a statue erected in honour of the eponymous akita. The dog's master was professor Ueno, who lived in the

Shibuya

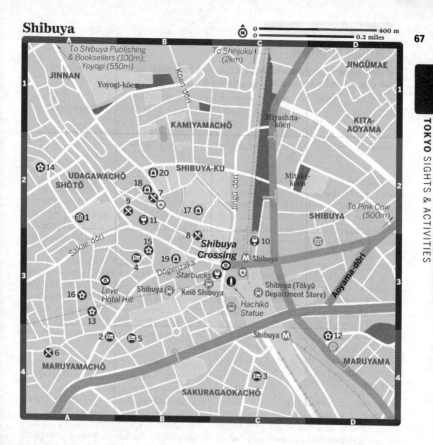

Shibuya

KIKUCHI RINKO: ACTRESS

If a movie were being made about Tokyo, and each neighbourhood was a character, which neighbourhood would you want to play?

I'd want to be Shibuya. There's an amazing overflow of spirit and vigour that the neighbourhood cannot digest! It's seedy, sloppy and reckless – it's filled with tonnes of energy to waste. Seems like it could be a very colourful role.

Kikuchi Rinko is an internationally recognised actress and Tokyo native. She was nominated for an Academy Award for her performance in Babel *(2006).*

neighbourhood in the 1920s. Every afternoon Hachikō would come to the station to await his master's return. The professor died suddenly in 1925, but Hachikō continued to show up and wait each day until his own death 11 years later. The poor dog's faithfulness was not lost on the locals, who built the statue in his honour.

Up the slope slightly removed from the throngs of pedestrians, Dōgenzaka's **Love Hotel Hill** (Map p67) is another of Shibuya's trademark destinations. With the highest concentration of these so-called 'boutique inns', the area sees quite a diverse array of clientele, from amorous sweethearts and club kids needing a cheap crash pad to less savoury characters… See the box on p89 for more info.

Japan Folk Crafts Museum MUSEUM
(日本民藝館; Mingeikan; http://mingeikan.x0.com; 4-3-33 Komaba; admission ¥1000; ⏰10am-5pm Tue-Sun; 🚉Komaba-Todaimae, West exit) Set in an old mansion from the early Shōwa era, this wonderful museum is dedicated to the nameless artists in Japanese history who produced publicly consumed items, including everything from kitchenware to dolls. It's two stations west of Shibuya.

Bunkamura MUSEUM
(Map p67; www.bunkamura.co.jp; 2-24-1 Dōgenzaka; admission ¥1400; 🚉Shibuya, exit 3a) Bunkamura (*boon*-camera) – meaning 'culture village' – provides a beacon for the arts, where Shibuya's seedier streets suddenly morph into a posh residential district. Inside you'll find a slew of performance spaces and galleries. The museum is closed until December 2011.

BEYOND SHIBUYA

TOP CHOICE **Shimokitazawa** NEIGHBOURHOOD
(下北沢; www.shimokitazawa.org; 🚉Odakyū line to Shimokitazawa) Safely removed from Shibuya

one express-train stop away, Shimokita, as it's casually known, is a trendy alternative to the city's overexposed neighbourhoods like Harajuku. The area has long been known for its edginess, which is slowly fading away as chain retailers and restaurants gobble up the commercial spaces. But if you look hard enough you'll still find some hipster treasures hidden down crooked alleyways and in crammed basements. Take the North exit, loosely follow the Odakyū tracks and once you pass the Mos Burger, head left – here you'll find scores of vintage shops, and several fun bars for a bit of vino.

Jiyūgaoka NEIGHBOURHOOD
(自由が丘; www.jiyugaoka.or.jp; 🚉Tōkyū Tōyoko line to Jiyūgaoka) Already a stomping ground for well-heeled locals and boho expats, Jiyūgaoka is shaping up to be Tokyo's next *it* neighbourhood. Orbiting the city's central core slightly further out than Shimokita, this garden suburb has a solid following of lunching Tokyoites who come in droves (usually with their dogs in tow) to hit up the hippest cafes around. You should go before the area officially takes its place on the tourist trail; it's only 15 minutes from Shibuya Station on the express train towards Yokohama.

HARAJUKU 原宿
International superstar Harajuku is virtually a name brand in its own right. Famed for its fashion – from Gucci to *goth-loli* girls (think zombie Little Bo Peep) – this vibrant neighbourhood is a veritable outdoor shopping mall with hundreds upon hundreds of shops lining every street and tucked down every alley. Shopping must-sees include the hoards of trendsetters on **Takeshita-dōri** and the more chilled out **Cat Street**, which runs perpendicular to Omote-sandō-dōri (see p110).

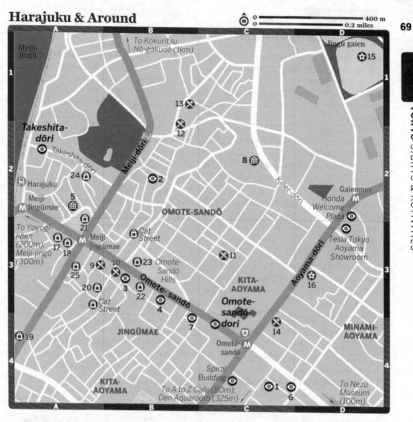

Harajuku & Around

DON'T MISS

RETAIL ARCHITECTURE IN OMOTE-SANDŌ

Pop icon Gwen Stefani once described Tokyo's fashion-hungry vibe as 'a pedestrian paradise where the catwalk got its claws', and her observation pretty much holds true. Shopping is a national pastime – a competitive sport, even – where Gucci purses and Chanel sunglasses are both a snazzy accessory and a souvenir from a whirlwind day of high-speed purchasing. Chaotic as they may seem, outfits are assembled with the utmost seriousness, from the pattern of safety pins in one's Catholic schoolgirl tartan to the zig-zagging streak of fuchsia accenting a Mohawk coiffure. The result of this fashion fixation is a magnificent parade of sculpture-like stores – monuments to the brand names that inhabit them.

Start from Meiji-jingūmae Station, and as you make your way down linden-lined Omote-sandō-dōri you'll pass the following boutique superstars:

Louis Vuitton BOUTIQUE
(Map p69; 5-7-5 Jingūmae) The first powerhouse boutique plunked down along Omote-sandō-dōri, Louis Vuitton's flagship store was designed by noted Japanese architect Jun Aoki. The shop sold over US$1 million dollars of merchandise on the day of its grand opening.

Dior Omote-sandō BOUTIQUE
(Map p69; 5-9-11 Jingūmae) Any architecture buff will recognise Dior Omote-sandō's trademark white-box facade designed by SANAA's leading Japanese architects Sejima Kazuyo and Nishizawa Ryūe. The exterior is made entirely of glass and a thin grey sheath acts as a semipermeable veil protecting the refined interior from the urban tangle outside.

Tod's Omote-sandō BOUTIQUE
(Map p69; 5-1-15 Jingūmae) Designed by local architect Toyo Ito, Tod's secured its spot in Tokyo's retail pantheon with its mesmerising glass facade covered in opaque ribbons that wend their way skyward like the branches of a tree.

Prada Aoyama BOUTIQUE
(プラダ青山店; Map p69; 5-2-6 Minami-aoyama) The brainchild of the Pritzker Prize–winning design firm Herzog & de Meuron, this beehivelike concoction has become Tokyo's second-most visited 'attraction' after Tokyo Disneyland.

Bapexclusive Aoyama BOUTIQUE
(ベイプエクスクルーシヴ 青山店; Map p69; 5-5-8 Minami-aoyama) Although not as ostentatious as the other superstore slam-dunks, the Bape-iest of the Bathing Ape boutiques, designed by Wonderwall, makes the list for its sterile-yet-swish ambience, which feels like hospital for fashion victims.

TOP CHOICE Omote-sandō-dōri STREET
(Map p69; ⓡOmote-sandō) The Champs-Élysées of Tokyo, Omote-sandō-dōri is a regal boulevard lined with shady trees and an endless parade of upscale fashion houses. As Christmas approaches, it's here that you'll find the city's most elaborate showcase of festive lights and ornaments. See the box on p70 to learn more about the street's many treasures.

FREE Meiji-jingū SHRINE
(明治神宮; off Map p69; www.meijijingu.or.jp; 1-1 Yoyogi Kamizonochō; ☉dawn-dusk; ⓡJR Harajuku, Omote-sandō exit) Completed in 1920, the shrine was built in memory of Emperor Meiji and Empress Shōken, though the current structure dates from 1958, as the original was destroyed in WWII. Meiji-jingū is the largest Shintō shrine in Tokyo and boasts the nation's largest *torii* (shrine gates), made from Japanese cypress. The shrine swells with over a million visitors during the New Year festivities. It's well worth visiting at any time, however; if you're lucky you'll catch a surprisingly sombre Shintō wedding processional, which makes a wonderful photo op.

The shrine's inner garden, **Meiji-jingū-gyoen** (admission ¥500; ☉9am-5pm), is almost deserted on weekdays. It's especially beautiful in June, when the irises are in bloom, but it is not by any means the most attractive garden in the city.

FREE Yoyogi-kōen
PARK

(代々木公園; off Map p69; 2-1 Yoyogi-Kaminzonochō; ◉dawn-dusk; ◎JR Harajuku, Omote-sandō exit) Weekend picnics in Yoyogi-kōen are the perfect way to stumble upon the cool and unusual, from *shamisen* (three-stringed lute) players to practising punk rockers and everything in between. The area was once home to the American headquarters during the occupation after WWII. Later, Tange Kenzō gave the area a new vibe when he created the swirling **Yoyogi National Stadium** for the 1964 Olympics. Today, this 53-hectare woodland is at its best on a sunny Sunday in spring or autumn when it teems with local families and friends.

Watari-Um
ART GALLERY

(ワタリウム美術館; Watari Museum of Contemporary Art; Map p69; www.watarium.co.jp; 3-7-6 Jingūmae; admission ¥1000; ◉11am-7pm Tue-Sun, to 9pm Wed; ◎Gaienmae, exit 3) This alternative art space is squeezed into a four-storey building in Harajuku's outer orbit. Regularly changing shows explore a variety of fascinating topics ranging from the conceptual and cultural to the architectural and industrial. Even if the current exhibit isn't your cup of tea, it's worth stopping by to check out the killer bookstore on the ground and basement levels.

Nezu Museum
MUSEUM

(off Map p69; www.nezu-muse.or.jp; 6-5-1 Minami-aoyama; admission ¥1000; ◉10am-5pm Tue-Sun; ◎Omote-sandō, exit A5) Past the Prada Aoyama building when walking from Omote-sandō, the Nezu is a welcome refuge from the shopping scene outside. Slatted planks of wood mark the demure entrance, and once inside visitors will discover a gorgeous collection of artefacts including a brilliant gallery of Chinese bronzes. The biggest draw, however, is the lush garden out back – overgrown trees shelter four hidden teahouses.

Ōta Memorial Art Museum
MUSEUM

(太田記念美術館; Map p69; www.ukiyoe-ota-muse.jp; 1-10-10 Jingūmae, Shibuya-ku; adult/student ¥1000/700; ◉10.30am-5.30pm Tue-Sun, closed 27th to end of month; ◎Meiji-jingūmae, exit 5) Pad quietly in slippers through the Ōta Museum to view its first-rate collection of *ukiyo-e* (woodblock prints), including works by masters of the art such as Hiroshige.

Also in the neighbourhood are several product showrooms where visitors can test out new gadgets and watch strange promotional videos for free, including the **Tesla Tokyo Aoyama Showroom** (Map p69; www.teslamotors.com; 2-23-8 Minami-aoyama; ◉10am-6pm Mon-Fri, to 7pm Sat & Sun; ◎Gaienmae, exit 1B) and **Honda Welcome Plaza** (Map p69; www.honda.co.jp; 2-2-1 Minami-aoyama; ◉10am-6pm Mon-Fri, to 7pm Sat & Sun; ◎Gaienmae, exit 1B).

SHINJUKU & WEST TOKYO 新宿

SHINJUKU 新宿

Here in Shinjuku, much of what makes Tokyo tick is crammed into one busy district: upscale department stores, anachronistic shanty bars, buttoned-up government offices, swarming crowds, streetside video screens, hostess clubs, hidden shrines and soaring skyscrapers.

At the heart of Shinjuku is the sprawling train station, which acts as a nexus for over three million commuters each day, making it one of the busiest in the world. The west side of the station (Nishi-shinjuku) is a perfectly planned expanse of gridded streets and soaring corporate towers. Tokyo's municipal government is located here, housed in Tange Kenzō's Tokyo Metropolitan Government Offices. Also worth a look – from the outside, at least – is the photogenic **Mode Gakuen Cocoon Tower** (Map p72; 1-7-3 Nishi-shinjuku).

While the west side of Shinjuku houses the straight-laced government towers, it's a different world on the other side of the tracks. East Shinjuku (or Higashi-shinjuku) is where you'll find the red-light district of **Kabuki-chō**, home of the notorious *yakuza* (mafia) and myriad fetish clubs. Just beyond Kabuki-chō is **Golden Gai** (Map p72), an almost-forgotten district of hovel-like bars.

FREE Tokyo Metropolitan Government Offices
NOTABLE BUILDING

(東京都庁; Tokyo Tochō; Map p72; www.metro.tokyo.jp; 2-8-1 Nishi-shinjuku; ◉observatories 9.30am-11.30pm, North Tower closed 2nd & 4th Mon, South Tower closed 1st & 3rd Tue; ◎Tochōmae, exits A3 & A4) Considered the crown jewel of Shinjuku's stuffy government district, these two towers are the headquarters for most of the city's officials – visitors should stop by to check out the great views from the **twin observation floors** (www.metro.tokyo.jp/ENGLISH/TMG/observat.htm). On really clear days, you might even spot Mt Fuji to the west. To reach the observation decks, take one of the two 1st-floor lifts.

Shinjuku

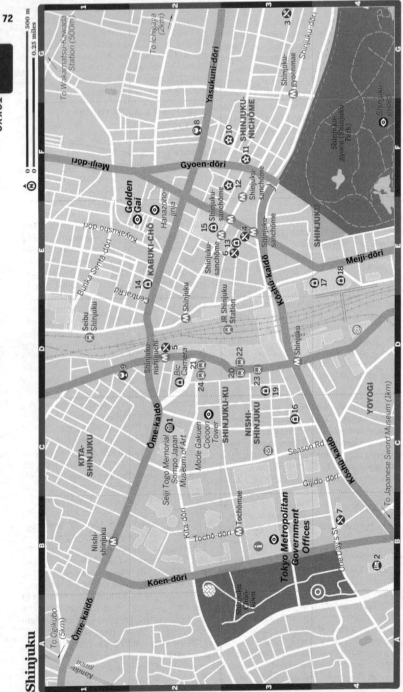

To Oglikubo
(5km)

Ôme-kaidô

KITA-
SHINJUKU

Nishi-
shinjuku

Kôen-dôri

Ôme-kaidô

Seibu
Shinjuku

Shinjuku-
nishiguchi

Bunka Senta-dôri

Kuyakusho-dôri

Meiji-dôri

KABUKI-CHÔ

Golden
Gai

Hanazono-
jinja

Central Rd

Shinjuku

Shinjuku
sanchôme

Yasukuni-dôri

Gyoen-dôri

SHINJUKU-
NICHÔME

Shinjuku-
gyoenmae

Shinjuku-
dôri

Shinjuku-
sanchôme

Shinjuku-
sanchôme

Shinjuku-
sanchôme

Shinjuku

JR Shinjuku
Station

Kôshû-kaidô

Meiji-dôri

SHINJUKU

Shinjuku-
gyoen

Shinjukugyoen (Shinjuku
Park)

To Wakamatsu-Kawada
Station (500m)

To Ichigaya
(2km)

Seiji Togo Memorial
Sompo Japan
Museum of Art

Mode Gakuen
Cocoon
Tower

SHINJUKU-KU

Bic
Camera

Kita-dôri

Tochô-dôri

NISHI-
SHINJUKU

Season Rd

Gijido-dôri

Tochômae

Tokyo Metropolitan
Government
Offices

YOYOGI

Kôshû-kaidô

To Japanese Sword Museum (1km)

Shinjuku
Chûô-gyoen

One Day's St

Kanda-Bôrai

1 2 3 4

A B C D E F G

Shinjuku

Shinjuku-gyoen   PARK

(新宿御苑; Map p72; www.env.go.jp/garden/
shinjukugyoen; Naitochō; adult/child ¥200/50;
☺9am-4pm Tue-Sun; ⓡShinjuku-gyoenmae, exit 1)
One of the city's best escapes and top cherry-
blossom-viewing spots, Shinjuku-gyoen is
also one of Tokyo's largest parks at 57.6 hectares. It dates back to 1906 and was designed
as a European-style park, though it also has
a Japanese garden, a hothouse containing
tropical plants and a pond with giant carp.

Seiji Togo Memorial Sompo Japan
Museum of Art   MUSEUM

(Map p72; www.sompo-japan.co.jp/museum; 42nd
fl, 1-26-1 Nishi-shinjuku; admission ¥1000; ☺10am-
6pm Tue-Sun; ⓡShinjuku, West exit) Art buffs will
appreciate this modest museum devoted to
the works of Seiji Togo, a Japanese painter
who was admired early on for his hypnotic
depictions of the female figure. The views
from the museum's vestibule are worth the
admission alone.

Japanese Sword Museum   MUSEUM

(刀剣博物館; off Map p72; www.touken.or.jp; 2nd
fl, 4-25-10 Yoyogi; admission ¥600; ☺10am-4.30pm
Tue-Sun; ⓡOdakyū line to Hakadai Sangubashi) Set
on the outskirts of Shinjuku, this museum
is for sword enthusiasts only, displaying a
small collection of weapons including three

national treasures. There's a small exhibit on
the ground floor (before you reach the gallery) detailing the intricate sword-making
process.

WEST OF SHINJUKU (THE CHŪŌ LINE)

Heading west along the JR Chūō line, you'll
pass several neighbourhoods of note including **Nakano** (中野), best known for its
sprawling shopping mall, and **Kōenji** (高
円寺), a younger district with an emerging music scene. Further out you'll find the
charming suburb of Kichijōji, and the Ghibli
Museum just beyond. It's best to avoid the
Chūō line during the morning and evening
rush-hour commutes (around 7am to 10am
inbound and 6pm to 10pm outbound), lest
you be crushed betwixt snoozing salarymen.
Masochists who are keen to experience this
quintessential cramming should be aware
that the novelty wears off after 12 seconds.

Ghibli Museum   MUSEUM

(三鷹の森ジブリ美術館; www.ghibli-museum
.jp; 1-1-83 Shimo-renjaku; admission ¥1000;
☺10am-5pm; ⓡJR Mitaka, South exit) Anime
master Miyazaki Hayao designed the Ghibli
Museum with children in mind, though anyone who fell in love with *Princess Mononoke* or *Spirited Away* should consider visiting. Miyazaki's animations come to life as

soon as you walk in – swirling stairs, ambient boops and bonks, and kooky ornaments give the mansion a fairy-tale feel, and the artist's studio replica is papered with hand-drawn sketches. Don't miss the original 20-minute movie playing on the 1st floor – if you weren't a Miyazaki fanatic before visiting, you'll be instantly converted.

Getting to the Ghibli (incorrectly pronounced *jiburi*) is part of the adventure. Tickets must be purchased in advance, and you must choose the exact date and time of your visit – check the website for details. The kiosks at Lawson's superettes dispense tickets as well, though a mastery of Japanese is required to work the machine. When you arrive at the museum, you'll exchange your voucher for a ticket – an original animation cell from a Studio Ghibli film.

Take the South exit when you reach Mitaka Station. A minibus (round trip/one way ¥300/200) shuttles passengers to the museum, or you can walk the 1250m (around 15 minutes) by following the ravine and turning right when you reach the parkland.

Kichijōji NEIGHBOURHOOD

(吉祥寺; 🚇Chūō line to Kichijōji, South exit) This wonderful neighbourhood in Tokyo's far west corner is a sanctuary for families with its open spaces and almost European vibe. The area's highlight is **Inokashira-kōen** (井の頭恩賜公園), a gorgeous greenbelt with tucked-away cafes, plenty of space to roam and an inviting lake peppered with the occasional swan boat. In spring, this is one of the most scenic spots to snap photos of the electric cherry blossoms.

There are many roads leading down to the park from the train station, the best being **Nanabashi-dōri** (found just to the right of Marui – 'OIOI' – when coming from the station's South exit). Teeming with skewer shops, cat cafes and boutiques selling oddities like Nepalese crafts, this largely pedestrian thoroughfare is a great place to pause for an espresso and some people-watching. On the back side of the station you'll find neon lights and gaudy shopping – also worth a look as it sharply contrasts with the hippie-hipster vibe near the park.

A trip to Kichijōji (combined with the Ghibli Museum) makes the perfect half-day getaway from the hustle of central Tokyo.

IKEBUKURO & NORTHWEST TOKYO 池袋

This giant swath of urban sprawl radiates out into the suburbs from the edge of the imperial grounds. Though largely overlooked by tourists who prefer the city's big-name neighbourhoods, Tokyo's northwest has far more to offer than you might think. It's here that you'll find the city's major baseball stadium, a controversial shrine and several charming pockets that often dodge the tourist radar.

Tokyo Dome City STADIUM

(東京ドームシティ; Big Egg; Map p52; 1-3-61 Kōraku; 🚇Kōrakuen, Kōrakuen exit) Tokyo Dome is home to Japan's favourite baseball team, the Yomiuri Giants, and its surrounding 'city' features a wide variety of attractions, including **Kōrakuen Amusement Park** (Tokyo Dome City, 1-3-61 Kōraku; rides ¥200-1000; unlimited rides adult/child ¥3300/2600; ⏰10am-10.30pm Mon-Sat, 9am-10.30pm Sun; 🚇Kōrakuen, Kōrakuen exit), known for its old-school roller-coaster, which thunders through Tokyo's core.

Also on the grounds is **Spa LaQua** (スパラクーア; www.laqua.jp; 5th-9th fl, Tokyo Dome City, 1-1-1 Kasuga; admission ¥2565, with healing baden ¥3090; ⏰Kasuga), which offers an inner-city onsen experience, where you can bathe in spacious luxury while gazing out over the infinite expanse of concrete and neon. Of particular interest are the colour therapy suites (which supposedly help with rejuvenation) and the trippy aquarium

TOKYO BY NUMBERS

» **13** Subway lines in the city centre

» **300** Price (US$) of a prized cantaloupe at Takashimaya department store

» **21,000** *Rāmen* restaurants in greater Tokyo

» **400,000** Vending machines spread across the city

» **3,750,000** Commuters passing through Shinjuku Station each day

» **35,676,000** Citizens of Tokyo's greater metropolitan area

» **5,500,000,000** Annual total sales (US$) at Tsukiji Fish Market

When it comes to cherry-blossom viewing, everyone knows that Ueno-kōen is the big cheese. Here are three spots known only by locals that blissfully fly under the radar in spring:

Meguro-gawa RIVERBANK
(Map p65; 🚉Meguro or Naka-meguro) Though the riverbank is lined with thick sheets of concrete (as they all are in Japan), the gnarled trunks above curl high over the stream, as though they were reaching for the other side. This creates a scenic gauntlet of colour.

Aoyama-reien CEMETERY
(Map p60; 🚉Gaienmae) This sprawling, stunning cemetery overflows with radiant blooms. Superstitious locals dare not enter in the evening when the spirits run wild.

Seijo NEIGHBOURHOOD
(🚉Odakyū line to Seijoenmae) A garden suburb in Setagaya-ku offering some of the best blossom-viewing in Tokyo, especially near the river.

room where you can sit and gaze at alienlike jellyfish pulsing around their blue-tinted world. Just remember – no tattoos allowed (though you could probably get away with covering a small one).

Tokyo Dome City is best on Sundays – stop by to see some *cosplay* freaks (it's the new favourite hang-out for the costume play gangs), watch a rousing baseball match, swoosh around on the rollercoaster and relax at the onsen.

Kagurazaka NEIGHBOURHOOD
(神楽坂; Map p52; 🚉Kagurazaka, exit 1) Mention the name Kagurazaka to a Tokyoite, and it will likely conjure up visions of geisha, winding cobbled alleys and tucked-away *ryōtei* (traditional Japanese restaurants). Fortunately, this romantic atmosphere still very much exists today, despite Tokyo's penchant for hyper-modernity. The best way to explore the neighbourhood is to simply lose yourself in some of the backstreets – **Kakurenbo-yokochō** ('hide and seek' alley) is particularly charming and features several high-end dining options that are worth checking out. Be sure to stop by **Akagi-jinja** (http://akagi-jinja.jp), which puts an interesting spin on the traditional shrine with mod decor that feels undeniably sleek. There's a welcoming cafe on the grounds, or continue down the hill and pause at **Canal Café** for a snack along the river.

Kitanomaru-kōen PARK
(北の丸公園; 🚉Kudanshita, exit 2, or Takebashi, exit 1a) Rounding out the northern edge of the imperial palace grounds, Kitanomaru-kōen makes a pleasant picnicking locale and is good for a leisurely stroll.

The sprawling park contains the **Nihon Budōkan** (日本武道館; 2-3 Kitanomaru-kōen), where you may witness a variety of martial arts. South of the Budōkan is the **Science Museum** (科学技術館; Kagaku Gijutsukan; www.jsf.or.jp; 2-1 Kitanomaru-kōen; adult/child ¥600/250; ⊘9am-4.50pm; 🚻), a decent rainy-day stop for those with children in tow, especially since most exhibits are interactive. An English booklet is included with entry.

Continuing south from the Science Museum brings you to the **National Museum of Modern Art** (東京国立近代美術館; Kokuritsu Kindai Bijutsukan; www.momat.go.jp/english; 3-1 Kitanomaru-kōen; adult ¥420; ⊘10am-5pm Tue-Sun, to 8pm Fri). The permanent exhibition features Japanese art from the Meiji period onwards, but check the website for special exhibitions. Hold on to your ticket stub, which gives you free admission to the nearby **Crafts Gallery** (東京国立近代美術館工芸館; Bijutsukan Kōgeikan; 1-1 Kitanomaru-kōen; admission ¥200; ⊘2-5pm Tue-Fri), housing a good display of crafts such as ceramics, lacquerware and dolls.

Yasukuni-jinja SHRINE
(靖国神社; www.yasukuni.or.jp; 3-1-1 Kudankita; ⊘9am-5pm Nov-Feb, 9am-6pm Mar, Apr, Sep & Oct, 9am-7pm May-Aug; 🚉Kudanshita, exit 1) Known as the Shrine for Establishing Peace in the Empire, Yasukuni-jinja is dedicated to the 2.4 million Japanese war-dead since 1853, and is considered the most controversial shrine in Japan. One of the biggest controversies associated with Yasukini was its enshrinement of a group of convicted Class-A war criminals in 1979; Emperor Hirohito refused to visit the shrine thereafter because of it.

The **Yūshūkan** (遊就館; www.yasukuni .or.jp; adult ¥800; ⊙9am-5pm; ℝKudanshita, exit 1), next to Yasukuni-jinja, commemorates the Japanese war-dead through detailed displays. There are limited English explanations, but an English pamphlet is available. Exhibits detail Japan's modern military history with a variety of interesting photographs, diagrams and artefacts. Much of the museum is subject to interpretation; local historians seem to have their own take on major wartime events...

Showa-kan   MUSEUM

(www.showakan.go.jp; 1-6-1 Kudan-minami; admission ¥300; ⊙10am-5.30pm Tue-Sun; ℝKudanshita, exit 4) Providing an interesting counterpoint to the museum at Yasukuni-jinja up the street, this small museum, encased in a striking tooth-shaped structure, offers insights into the daily lives of those who suffered before, during and after the atrocities of WWII. Curated artefacts, detailed captions and a bottomless computer database of photographs and magazines give the museum an engaging, interactive quality.

Ikebukuro   NEIGHBOURHOOD

(池袋; Map p52; ℝIkebukuro) Though Ikebukuro once boasted the world's largest department store, tallest building and longest escalator, these former glories have since been outshone elsewhere. But Ikebukuro's **Sunshine City** (サンシャインシティ) is still perfect for rainy weather, since you could spend 40 days roaming the humongous mall, visiting the **aquarium** (サンシャイン国際水族館 10th fl, World Import Mart Bldg 3-1-3 Higashi-ikebukuro; adult/child ¥1800/900; ⊙10am-6pm Mon-Fri, to 6.30pm Sat & Sun) – the highest in the world – and sampling enough ice cream and *gyōza* to last you a biblical deluge. The neighbourhood shouldn't rate high on a busy schedule unless you're looking for manga and girl-geek culture, in which case you'll want to walk down **Otome Road** (乙女ロード), the female version of the overwhelmingly male-centric *otaku* zone in Akihabara.

AKIHABARA & AROUND   秋葉原

Akihabara (Map p52) began its evolution into 'Denki-gai' (**Electric Town**) post-WWII, when the area around the station became a black market for radio parts. In more recent decades, Akihabara has been widely known as *the* place to hunt for bargains on new and used electronics in general. Nowadays, you're more likely to hear it referred to as **Akiba** (http://akiba-guide.com), which is the more common nickname among the manga and anime fans who are drawn by its gravitational pull, as Akihabara has morphed into the centre of the known *otaku* (geek) universe.

Geographically, Akihabara and its neighbours sit at the Tokyo's crossroads, where the towers of Marunouchi and the low-lying world of *shitamachi* collide, thus you'll find a true hodgepodge of architectural styles in the area. Not to be missed is **Jinbocho**, which is home to hundreds of secondhand booksellers.

AKB48 Theatre   NOTABLE BUILDING

(www.akb48.co.jp; 8th fl, Don Quijote 4-3-3 Sotokanda; ℝAkihabara, main exit) Tokyo's biggest pop phenomenon takes the girl-group prototype and expands it far beyond the five-girl quorum that proved successful for the Spice Girls. AKB48 has not 10, not 20, but over 50 members in the lot, and they perform in shifts at their very own workhouse...er...theatre in the heart of Akihabara. Shows run almost every day, offering audience members the chance to interact with the stars. Stop by the theatre to pick up tickets, or check the website for details.

TOYLETS

From singing johns to heated commodes, Japan has long been number one when it comes to number two. And now Sega is taking things to a new level in the men's WC with a unique gaming console that partners peeing and points. These so-called 'toylets' are making a splash with four different programs, including one that lifts a woman's skirt à la Marilyn Monroe. It's fairly straightforward – the faster and longer you pee, the higher your score goes; and there's a port for your USB key if you're keen on keeping a running tally.

The best place to test these out is at the Sega Mega-store in Akihabara's Electric Town. Free gaming urinals have been installed on the 2nd, 3rd and 4th floors. At the moment, the displays are only in kanji – if you can read Japanese, then urine luck.

UENO 上野

In Edo times, Yamanote referred to 'Uptown': the estates and residences of feudal barons, military aristocracy and other Edo elite, in the hilly regions of the city. *Shitamachi* or 'Downtown' ('Lowtown') was home to the working classes, merchants and artisans. Even today this distinction persists – and Ueno retains that old *shitamachi* feeling. The neighbourhood's ageing but spry shopping arcade, **Ameya-yokochō**, remains a bustling market that feels worlds away from the monumental marketplace of Roppongi Hills. But Ueno has no need for fancy shopping malls; it instead boasts two drawcards: **Ueno-kōen** (上野公園), which has the highest concentration of museums and galleries anywhere in Japan; and **Yanese**, a sprawling neighbourhood riddled with antique merchants' houses and gorgeous, garden-shrouded shrines.

UENO-KŌEN 上野公園

Ueno Hill is known as the site of a last-ditch defence of the Tokugawa shōgunate by 2000 loyalists in 1868. They were duly dispatched by the imperial army, and the new Meiji government decreed that Ueno Hill would be transformed into Tokyo's first public park. Today, Ueno-kōen may not be the sexiest of Tokyo's green spaces, but it certainly packs the biggest cultural punch. Like a sprawling Ivy League campus, the area is home to a wonderful conglomeration of museums, each housed in stately colonial-esque structures.

The park is famous as Tokyo's most popular site for *hanami* (blossom-viewing) in early to mid-April (which isn't to say it's the *best* place – see the box on p75). At the southern end of the park, in all seasons, enormous round lotus leaves blanket Shinobazu-ike (Shinobazu Pond).

Large maps showing the park's layout can be found throughout the area – there's even one when you emerge from Ueno Station at the Park exit.

Note that at the time of research, the **Tokyo Metropolitan Museum of Art** (東京都美術館; Map p78; www.tobikan.jp; 8-36 Ueno-kōen; 9am-5pm Tue-Sun; Ueno, Park exit) was closed for renovations. It is expected to reopen in April 2012.

TOP CHOICE Tokyo National Museum MUSEUM
(東京国立博物館; Tokyo Kokuritsu Hakubutsukan; Map p78; www.tnm.jp; 13-9 Ueno-kōen, Taitō-ku; adult ¥600; 10am-4pm Tue-Fri, to 6pm Sat & Sun; Ueno, Park exit) If you visit only one museum in Tokyo, make it this one. Considered the Louvre of Japan, the Tokyo National Museum's grand buildings hold the world's largest collection of Japanese art, and you could easily spend half a day perusing the galleries here. The building dates from 1939 and is in the imperial style, which fuses Western and Japanese architectural motifs.

There are four galleries, the most important of which is the **Honkan** (Main Gallery). For an introduction to Japanese art history from Jōmon to Edo in one fell swoop, head to the 2nd floor to find the Highlights of Japanese Art exhibition (and be sure to snag one of the detailed brochures). Other galleries include ancient pottery, religious sculpture, arms and armour, exquisite lacquerware and calligraphy.

The **Gallery of Hōryū-ji Treasures** displays masks, scrolls and gilt Buddhas from Hōryū-ji – located in Nara Prefecture, and said to be the first Buddhist temple in Japan (founded in 607) – in a spare, elegant box of a contemporary building (1999) by Taniguchi Yoshio, who also designed New York's Museum of Modern Art (MoMA). The **Heiseikan** (Heisei Hall) opened in 1993 to commemorate the marriage of Crown Prince Naruhito, and is used for exhibitions of Japanese archaeology as well as special exhibits.

Hyōkeikan (Hyōkei Hall) was built in 1909, with Western-style architecture that is reminiscent of a museum you might find in Paris, though inside it shows works from across East and South Asia and the Middle East. Normally these are in a fifth building, **Tōyōkan** (Gallery of Eastern Antiquities), which is closed for earthquake retrofitting and due to reopen in 2012.

Shitamachi Museum MUSEUM

(下町風俗資料館; Map p78; 2-1 Ueno-kōen; admission ¥300; 9.30am-4.30pm Tue-Sun; Ueno, Hirokōji exit) This museum re-creates life in *shitamachi* – the plebeian 'lowtown' quarter of old Tokyo – during the 1900s. Exhibits include a sweet shop, the home and business of a copper boilermaker and a tenement house. Docents are on hand to teach games or help you try on the clothes, making for an engaging hands-on visit. There's a list of local onsen (with accompanying photographs) on the 2nd floor of the museum, where you'll also find home furnishing from the 1960s.

Ueno

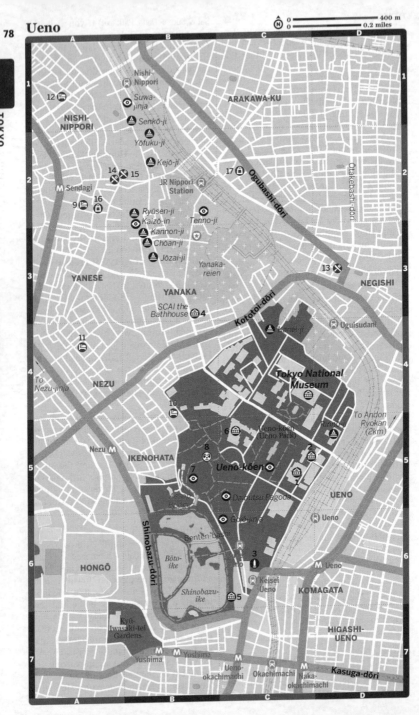

N

0 ————— 400 m
0 ————— 0.2 miles

ARAKAWA-KU

Nishi-Nippori

12

NISHI-NIPPORI

Suwa-jinja

Senkō-ji

Yōfuku-ji

Kejō-ji

17

Ogubashi-dōri

Otakebashi-dōri

14 15

Sendagi

JR Nippori Station

9 16

Ryūsen-ji

Kaizō-in

Tenno-ji

Kannon-ji

Chōan-ji

Jōzai-ji

YANESE

YANAKA

Yanaka-reien

13

NEGISHI

Kototoi-dōri

SCAI the Bathhouse 4

11

Kan'ei-ji

Oguisudani

NEZU

To Nezu-jinja

Tokyo National Museum

10

To Andon Ryokan (2km)

Nezu

6

Ueno-kōen Ueno Park

Rinnō-ji

8

2

IKENOHATA

7

Ueno-kōen

1

Shinobazu-dōri

Daibutsu Pagoda

UENO

Gojō-jinja

Ueno

Benten-bashi

Bōto-ike

3

Keisei Ueno

Ueno

KOMAGATA

Shinobazu-ike

5

HONGŌ

Kyū-Iwasaki-tei Gardens

HIGASHI-UENO

Yushima

Yushima

Ueno-okachimachi

Okachimachi

Naka-okachimachi

Kasuga-dōri

Ueno

National Science Museum MUSEUM
(国立科学博物館; Kokuritsu Kagaku Hakubutsu-kan; Map p78; www.kahaku.go.jp/english; 7-20 Ueno-kōen, Taitō-ku; adult/child ¥600/free; ⊙9am-5pm Tue-Sun, to 8pm Fri; ℝUeno, Park exit) Though there's limited interpretive signage in English, this enormous museum has beautiful hi-tech displays recounting the history of the earth and its inhabitants. The interactive exhibits make it a good place to bring kids, especially combined with a trip to the Ueno Zoo.

National Museum of Western Art MUSEUM
(国立西洋美術館; Kokuritsu Seiyō Bijutsukan; Map p78; www.nmwa.go.jp; 7-7 Ueno-kōen; admission ¥420; ⊙9.30am-5.30pm Tue-Sun, to 8pm Fri; ℝUeno, Park exit) Yes, we know, it might seem counterintuitive to come all the way to Japan and visit a museum of Western art, but the collection is actually quite impressive. The museum also often hosts special exhibits on loan from other institutions of international repute. Sculpture enthusiasts can appreciate the wind and passion in Rodin's body of work – he has several pieces sprinkled around the museum. There's also a full gallery dedicated to the paintings of Monet. And the museum itself is wonder – it was designed by legendary architect Le Corbusier.

Ueno Zoo ZOO
(上野動物園; Map p78; www.tokyo-zoo.net; 9-83 Ueno-kōen; adult/child ¥600/free; ⊙9.30am-5pm Tue-Sun; ℝUeno, Park exit) Established in 1892, this is Japan's oldest zoo. It shouldn't feature on your Tokyo to-do list, but the little ones might enjoy cavorting with the veritable cast of the *Lion King*. Photographers will get a kick out of shooting giraffes with a skyscraper backdrop.

Tōshōgū SHRINE
(東照宮; Map p78; 9-88 Ueno-kōen, Taitō-ku; admission ¥200; ⊙9am-5.30pm; ℝUeno, Shinobazu exit) Tōshōgū, like its counterpart in Nikkō, is dedicated to Tokugawa Ieyasu, who unified Japan. The shrine, resplendent in gold leaf and ornate details, dates from 1651 and is one of the few extant early-Edo structures, having fortuitously survived Tokyo's innumerable disasters.

Saigō Takamori Statue STATUE
(西郷隆盛銅像; Map p78; ℝUeno, Shinobazu exit) Near the southern entrance to the park is this unconventional statue of a samurai walking his dog. Saigō Takamori started out supporting the Meiji Restoration but ended up ritually disembowelling himself in defeated opposition to it.

YANAKA, NEZU & SENDAGI (YANESE) 谷中
If you aren't planning on visiting Kyoto during your time in Japan, you should head directly to Yanaka and its neighbouring districts for your fill of wondrous temples. If you happen to be in Asakusa beforehand, swing by the tourist information office and pick up its handy Yanaka brochure that details a suggested walking tour and plots the location of several of the district's temples and shrines, including **Nezu-jinja** with its radiant *torii,* and **Tenno-ji** (7-14-8 Yanaka), a relic from the 13th century with a giant Buddha and perfectly kept gardens. There are more than 70 places of worship in the district.

Hemming Sendagi and Nippori stations, **Yanaka Ginza** is a bustling pedestrian strip with countless vendors peddling delicious street snacks.

Yanaka-reien
CEMETERY

(Map p78; 7 Yanaka; ⓇNippori) One of Tokyo's largest graveyards, Yanaka-reien is the final resting place of over 7000 souls, many of whom were quite well known in their day, like Meiji-era novelist Soseki Natsume (you'll find his portrait on the ¥1000 bill). In spring, the cemetery comes alive with trillions of cherry blossoms blanketing the tombs and statues.

CAI the Bathhouse
MUSEUM

(Map p78; www.scaithebathhouse.com; 6-1-23 Yanaka; ⊙noon-7pm Tue-Sat; ⓇNippori, South exit) A converted 200-year-old bathhouse, SCAI showcases scores of Japanese and international artists in its austere vaulted space.

ASAKUSA & AROUND
浅草・両国

If you aren't staying in the area, the city's **river buses** provide a scenic transportation alternative to the subway. Within the neighbourhood you'll also find the **Panda Bus** (http://sg-elem.co.jp/esta/pandabus.html) offering its services for free from 10am to 5pm

ASAKUSA
浅草

Like Ueno next door, Asakusa is one of the few areas of Tokyo to have retained the old-fashioned spirit of *shitamachi*. Though more a tourist quarter than pleasure district, Asakusa continues to attract crowds

not only with the Sensō-ji complex, but also with its bustling marketplaces of Nakamise-dōri and Kappabashi-dōri, famous for its plastic food. Also worth a camera snap is the **Asahi Flame**, said to be an artistic interpretation of the foam at the top of a glass of beer (though most locals lovingly refer to it as the Golden Turd).

FREE Sensō-ji
TEMPLE

(浅草寺; Map p80; 2-3-1 Asakusa; ⊙24hr; ⓇAsakusa, exits 1 & A5) This temple enshrines a golden image of Kannon (the Buddhist Goddess of Mercy), which, according to legend, was miraculously pulled out of the nearby Sumida-gawa by two fishermen in AD 628. The image has remained on the spot ever since; the present structure dates from 1950.

When approaching Sensō-ji from Asakusa subway station, the entrance is via **Kaminarimon** (Thunder Gate). The gate's protector gods are Fūjin, the god of wind, on the right; and Raijin, the god of thunder, on the left.

Straight ahead is **Nakamise-dōri**, the temple precinct's shopping street, where everything from tourist trinkets to genuine Edo-style crafts is sold. Need a formal wig to wear with your kimono? Here's where to shop.

Walk down Nakamise-dōri to reach the temple entrance – to your left you'll spot the **Five-Storeyed Pagoda** (55m) almost

Asakusa

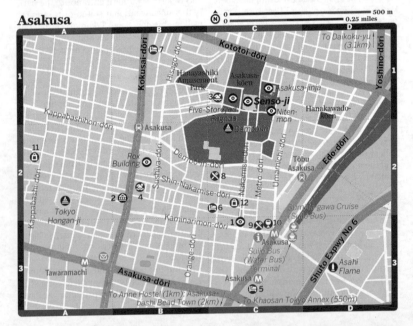

begging you to take its photo. It's even more picturesque at night, all lit up.

It remains to be seen if the ancient image of Kannon actually exists, as it's not on public display. This doesn't stop a steady stream of worshippers from travelling to the top of the stairs to bow and clap. In front of the temple is a large incense cauldron: the smoke is said to bestow health and you'll see visitors rubbing it into their bodies through their clothes.

Taiko Drum Museum
MUSEUM

(Map p80; 2-1-1 Nishi-asakusa; adult/child ¥300/150; ⏱10am-5pm Wed-Sun; ⊞; ⓇTarawachō, exit 3) Buy your tickets on the 1st floor then hop on the elevator to reach this one-room shine to all things percussion. Five continents and dozens of countries are represented in the collection, from large kabuki gongs to the Senufo drums of Côte d'Ivoire. The instructions are simple: drums with a red dot are off limits, blue dots mean play gently, and you have free reign over the drums sans dots. Plenty of English captions make it fun for the whole family.

Daikoku-yu
PUBLIC BATH

(大黒湯; off Map p80; 32-6 Senju-kotobukichō; admission ¥450; ⏱3pm-midnight Tue-Sun; ⓇKitasenju, West exit 3) With an impressive wing-

like roof befitting an elegant temple, Daikokuyu – constructed in 1929 – is known as the 'king of public bathhouses'. Inside, the beautiful murals of Mt Fuji require repainting every 30 months due to steam damage. When this *sentō* (public bath) first opened, the walls were covered in paper advertisements.

Jakotsu-yu
ONSEN

(Map p80; www.jakotsuyu.co.jp; 1-11-11 Asakusa; admission ¥450; ⏱1pm-midnight Wed-Mon; ⓇTawaramachi, exit 3) One of the hottest onsen in town, with mineral-rich dark water at 45°C.

Asakusa Kannon Onsen
ONSEN

(浅草観音温泉; Map p80; 2-7-6 Asakusa; admission ¥700; ⏱6.30am-6pm Thu-Tue; ⓇAsakusa, exits 1, 3 & 6) A large, old-school bathhouse – look for its ivy-covered exterior near Sensō-ji.

RYŌGOKU & EAST SUMIDA
両国

Just over the river from Asakusa, Ryōgoku and the surrounding neighbourhoods continue the area's old *shitamachi* feel. The district's centrepiece is the imposing **sumō stadium** (see p107) – you'll often see chubby wrestlers waddling around Ryōguku Station.

Tokyo Sky Tree
NOTABLE BUILDING

(東京スカイツリー; www.tokyo-skytree.jp; ⓇOshiage, exit A2) Tokyo's at it again, trying to insert itself into yet another one of the world's superlative lists. After trumping the Eiffel Tower in the late 1950s, the city's newest challenge is taking things to new heights, so to speak. At 634m, the Sky Tree will be one of the world's highest towers – it opens in the spring of 2012, and will feature two observation decks (at 350m and 450m). Plans are also under way to create a commercial complex at its base that will include dozens of shops, an aquarium and a planetarium.

Edo-Tokyo Museum
MUSEUM

(江戸東京博物館; ☎3626-9974; www.edo-tokyo-museum.or.jp; 1-4-1 Yokoami; admission ¥600; ⏱9.30am-5.30pm Tue-Sun, to 7.30pm Sat; ⓇRyōgoku, West exit) A soaring replica of Nihonbashi (Tokyo's first bridge, still alive and kickin' in its namesake neighbourhood, though hardly noticeable due to its unfortunate position under a concrete highway) immediately sets the tone at this larger-than-life homage to bygone eras. Carefully crafted exhibits document heaps of fascinating facts about life in Tokyo before it evolved into its modern avatar. Exhibits range from examples of actual Edo infrastructure – a wooden sewage pipe, for one – to exquisite scale models of markets and shops, including such meticulous details as period costumes and stray cats scavenging fish scraps. If you plan on having a thorough look around, figure around 90 minutes for the 'Edo Zone' and an additional hour for the 'Tokyo Zone'.

The museum really comes to life with the help of a volunteer guide (free) – available between 10am and 3pm on a first-come basis. You can usually grab a guide at 10am or at around 2pm when they return from their lunch break. Call ahead to double check that an English-speaking staff member will be present on the day you'd like to visit.

Museum of Contemporary Art
Tokyo
MUSEUM

(www.mot-art-museum.jp; 4-1-1 Miyoshi; admission ¥500; ◎10am-6pm Tue-Sun; ⊞Kiyosumi-shirakawa, exits B2 & A3, or Kiba, exit 3) Dedicated to showcasing modern artists and designers from Japan and abroad, MOT also holds some 3800 pieces in its permanent collection, by the likes of David Hockney and Andy Warhol, and several Japanese artists such as Yokō Tadanori. The building's stunning stone-steel-wood architecture (by Yanagisawa Takahiko) is a work of art in its own right. The museum is in Metropolitan Kiba Park – it takes about 15 minutes on foot to reach the museum from any of the nearby subway stations.

Fukugawa Edo Museum
MUSEUM

(深川江戸資料館; ☑3630-8625; 1-3-28 Shirakawa; admission ¥300; ◎9.30am-5pm Tue-Sun; ⊞Kiyosumi-shirakawa, exit A3) If you haven't the time to make the rounds at the expansive Edo-Tokyo Museum, this quaint exhibition does an admirable job of depicting the life and times of locals during the Edo period, through life-sized replicas of merchants' shops and commoners' houses. Most of the volunteers speak English and can walk you through the museum pointing out interesting tidbits about Tokyo's history. Call ahead if you want to be sure that an English-speaking staff member is on duty.

Kiyosumi-teien
GARDEN

(http://teien.tokyo-park.or.jp/contents/index033 .html; 3-9-9 Kiyosumi; admission ¥150; ◎9am-5pm; ⊞Kiyosumi-shirakawa) This marvellous garden was the first place to be named a 'site of scenic beauty' by the Tokyo Metropolitan Government – and it's easy to see why. Kiyosumi started as a *daimyō*'s estates in the 1700s, and after the 1923 earthquake it was purchased by Iwasaki Yatarō, founder of the Mitsubishi Corporation. He was able to use company ships to haul prize stones from all over Japan onto the garden grounds – count all 50 (they're numbered). They're set around a carp-filled pond that's ringed with Japanese black pine, hydrangeas, Taiwan cherries and other plants designed to bloom at different times of the year – especially during *hanami* and *kōyō* (autumn colours).

Arashio Stable
SUMŌ

(www.arashio.net; 2-47-2 Nihonbashi-hamamchi; ◎6.30-10.30am; ⊞Ningyōchō) Back over the river on the west side of the Sumida-gawa, Arashio is one of the more welcoming sumō stables. Complete silence is expected during the practice session, but afterwards guests are invited to eat *chanko* (the sumō protein-rich diet) and chat with the wrestlers. Visit the website for additional information and pricing.

ODAIBA & TOKYO BAY　お台場・東京湾
Only in Tokyo can you find the Eiffel Tower, the Statue of Liberty and the Golden Gate Bridge, and they can all be seen from Odaiba. If you hadn't already guessed, this synthetic marvel is a manmade island created from zillions of pounds of refuse. On the surface you'll find a smattering of architectural oddities and two giant malls – **Venus Fort** and **Decks Tokyo**.

To reach Odaiba, use the driverless Yurikamome monorail, which departs from Shinbashi Station. Ride around the island on **Tokyo Bay Shuttle Bus Navi** (www.bus navi.net/odaiba).

TOP CHOICE **Ōedo Onsen Monogatari**
ONSEN

(大江戸温泉物語; Map p83; ☑5500-1126; www .ooedoonsen.jp/english; 2-6-3 Aomi; adult/child ¥2900/1600; ◎11am-9am; ⊞Yurikamome line to Telecom Center) Modelled after a town from Edo times, this honest-to-goodness onsen actually pipes in sourced mineral waters from 1400m beneath Tokyo Bay. Enjoy comedians and a noodle-stocked food court between soaks in the various tubs (separated by gender, of course). Couples can relax at the co-ed footbath/stream outside. Be sure to grab a brochure when you walk in – it explains how to properly wear your *yukata* (light cotton kimono). If you arrive after 6pm, admission is slashed to ¥2000 (¥1600 for children). There's a ¥1700 surcharge if you stay the night.

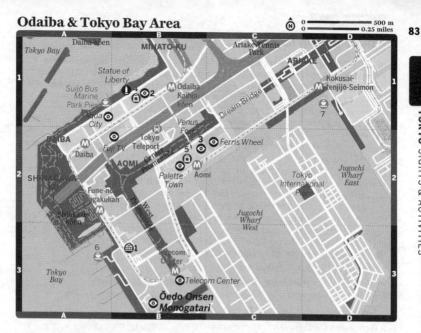

Odaiba & Tokyo Bay Area

◎ Top Sights

◎ Sights

🄐 Shopping

Transport

National Museum of Emerging Science and Innovation
MUSEUM

(日本科学未来館; Miraikan; Map p83; www.miraikan.jst.go.jp; 2-3-6 Aomi; adult/child ¥600/200; ⊙10am-5pm Wed-Mon; 🄬Yurikamome line to Fune-no-Kagakukan) Kids will love the engaging exhibits at this science museum, where most displays have excellent explanations in English and friendly staff can fill in the blanks. There are the spectacular planetarium (buy

tickets for a show upon arrival), opportunities to interact with robots, and tonnes of exhibits about space, medicine and the environment.

Sega Joypolis
AMUSEMENT PARK

(Map p83; http://tokyo-joypolis.com; 3rd-5th fl, Decks Tokyo 1-6-1 Daiba; passport ¥3500; 🄬Odaiba Kaihin-kōen) Unleash your inner child at this three-storey indoor amusement park, operated by game-maker Sega. You'll find a mix of virtual reality and action rides, of which the Spin Bullet (part whirling dervish, part roller-coaster) and the snowboardlike Halfpipe Canyon are the most popular. Lines are shortest on weekdays when kids are in school. Separate admission and individual ride tickets (most from ¥500) are available, but if you plan to go on more than six attractions the unlimited 'passport' makes sense.

FREE Toyota Mega Web
AMUSEMENT PARK

(メガウェブ; Map p83; www.megaweb.gr.jp; Palette Town 1 Aomi; ⊙11am-9pm; 🄬Yurikamome line to Aomi) Car fiends and kids can get behind the wheel of hybrid and electric cars at Toyota Mega Web, one of Toyota's company showrooms. Consult the website before cruising by, as opening hours can vary.

SHICHIFUKUJIN MEGURI

At the beginning of each year, locals flock to the city's shrines and temples to make wishes for the upcoming seasons. While big-name places like Senso-ji and Meiji-jingū get millions of luck-seekers, many Tokyoites opt to perform a *meguri* (pilgrimage) instead, visiting some of the city's smaller places of worship. Of particular interest are the Shichifukujin, or the Seven Deities of Good Fortune – a coin toss, a few claps and a bow at a shrine devoted to each god ensures a year full of wishes granted, or so they say.

One of Tokyo's most popular Shichifukujin Meguri (or pilgrimage of the Seven Deities of Good Fortune) is in the quiet neighbourhood of **Monzennakachō**, near Ryōgoku on the east side of the Sumida-gawa. Though it may not be New Year's Eve when you're in town, completing this *meguri* is a great way to get acquainted with a neighbourhood that is squarely off the tourist trail – the shrines themselves are quite charming too.

Below you'll find the names and addresses of the seven lucky gods in Monzennakachō. Plot them (in order) into Google Maps to find the way, or check out www.mediatinker .com/blog/shichifukujin/fukagawa-map.gif for a ready-made plan created by local expat Kristin McQuillin. Start at Morishita Station on the Ōedo line and you'll finish near Monzennakachō Station, also on the Ōedo line.

» **Jurojin** (1-3-17 Morishita) Bearded god of longevity.

» **Hotei** (2-12-12 Kiyosumi) Pot-bellied deity of prosperity and happiness.

» **Daikokuten** (1-13-6 Hirano) Purveyor of good fortune and bountiful harvests.

» **Bishamonten** (2-7-5 Miyoshi) Protector of the righteous.

» **Benzaiten** (22-31 Fuyuki) Female deity of the arts, virtue and happiness.

» **Fukurokuju** (2-16-7 Fukagawa) God of wisdom and prosperity, usually depicted with a large, cone-shaped head.

» **Ebisu** (1-20-3 Tomioka) Offers good fortune in one's occupation. Usually seen toting a sea bream.

Tokyo Disney Resort   AMUSEMENT PARK
(www.tokyodisneyresort.co.jp; 1-1 Maihama, Urayasu-shi, Chiba; 1-day ticket adult/child ¥5800/3900; 🚻; 🚃 JR Keiyō line to Maihama) Pop quiz: what's the most visited sight in Japan? Kyoto's temples? Nope. Harajuku? Not quite. Ten points go to the person who guessed Tokyo Disney. As tragic (or as telling) as it may be, Tokyo Disney is a smashing success, offering visitors two theme parks – Tokyo Disney, modelled after the California original, and Tokyo DisneySea, a clever add-on that caters more to adults. Invest in a Fast Pass to cut down on time lost waiting in lines; it's also worth packing a *bentō*, as onsite restaurants are almost always overrun with diners.

🍢 Courses

Learning almost any traditional Japanese art is a bit like producing a fine wine – it takes a whole lotta time. Thus, it can be tricky finding one-off classes for many popular pastimes. The **Institute for Japa-nese Cultural Exchange and Experience** (www.ijcee.com/e.html) offers a wide variety of course/tour hybrids (like visiting Tsukiji Fish Market and learning how to make sushi), as does **HIS Experience** (http://hisexperience.jp/culturalactivities). Check the websites for additional details. Several upscale hotels – including Hotel Ōkura (p87) and Hotel New Ōtani (p88) – hold interactive tea ceremonies. Check with the concierge for more information – participation fees are upwards of ¥1000.

A Taste of Culture   COOKING
(www.tasteofculture.com) Established by noted Japanese culinary expert Elizabeth Andoh, these courses encompass everything from market tours to culinary classes, all imbued with deep cultural knowledge. Consult the website for current offerings.

Sōgetsu Kaikan   FLOWERS
(草月会館; www.sogetsu.or.jp/english/index. html) If you're interested in the art of ikebana (flower arranging), this avant-

garde school offers classes that are taught in English. The school was founded on the idea that there are no limits to when, where or in what style ikebana can be practised.

Tours

The best way to get under the skin of any city is to have a local show you around, and in Tokyo you can meet up with someone to do just that, even gratis.

According to legend, when Donald Ritchie (noted Japanophile, author and Kurosawa subtitler) arrived in Tokyo, the first thing he did was ride the **Yamanote line** all the way around the loop. Not a bad idea – it's a quick (and cheap) way to take in little chunks of the city's deepest urban pockets, as most of Tokyo's major nexuses congregate along the looped track.

Walking Tours

Mr Oka SIGHTSEEING
(www.homestead.com/mroka) A wonderful, well-informed English-speaking guide who conducts walking tours around the city.

Haunted Tokyo Tours OFFBEAT
(www.meetup.com/Haunted-Tokyo-Tours) Fun and friendly Lilly takes amblers on a tour of a variety of offbeat sites around the city, particularly around Asakusa. Try the late-night visit to Aoyama-reien and you might spot a ghost!

Bus Tours

All of the following companies offer a variety of reliable bus tours and provide English-speaking guides.

SkyBus SIGHTSEEING
(www.skybus.jp) Double-decker bus tours explore different neighbourhoods of the city, including a new 'Sky Tree' route that trundles through Asakusa and beyond (adult/child ¥1800/900).

Hato Bus Tours SIGHTSEEING
(はとバス; www.hatobus.com) Among its variety of tours, the Panoramic Tour (adult/child ¥9900/6600) takes in most of Tokyo's major sights and also includes lunch and a Tokyo Bay cruise.

Japan Gray Line SIGHTSEEING
(www.jgl.co.jp/inbound/traveler/traveler.htm) The full-day Grand Tour (adult/child ¥9700/6600) includes lunch, pick-up and drop-off.

✺ Festivals & Events

Seems like there's a festival or a day off from work almost every week in Tokyo. Check with the JNTO (see p115) for up-to-date information. Some major celebrations:

Ganjitsu TRADITIONAL
At New Year, Tokyoites head to the city's myriad shrines and temples – many also complete the Shichifukujin Meguri.

Hanami CHERRY BLOSSOM
Cherry-bloossom viewing obsession takes over as locals flock to the city's parks and cemeteries from late March to mid-April.

Design Festa ARTS
(www.designfesta.com) In mid-May a wide showcase of work from budding designers and artists is displayed at Tokyo Big Sight. A second showing takes place in November.

Sanja Matsuri MIKOSHI
A massive festival held in mid-May featuring hundreds of *mikoshi* (portable shrines) paraded through Asakusa.

Emperor's Birthday HOLIDAY
On 23 December, this is one of only two days a year that the Imperial Palace is open to the public; the other is 2 January.

ⓘ TOURING TOKYO FOR FREE

Although the language barrier is immediately apparent upon arriving in Tokyo, you might be surprised to learn there are a wealth of tour groups in the city dedicated to showing visitors around. And the best part is they're free! These teams of so-called Systemised Goodwill Guides offer an endless array of prepared or customised tours – advanced booking is a must. You'll have to pay for any admission, transport fees and meal, but no tips are expected.

» **Tokyo SGG Club** (www2.ocn.ne.jp/~sgg)

» **Shinagawa SGG Club** (www1.cts.ne.jp/~koasa/SGG)

» **Volunteer Walking Tour Blog** (http://volunteerfreewalking.blogspot.com)

» **Edo Tokyo Guides** (http://blog.goo.ne.jp/edo_tokyo_int)

» **Free Walking Tour** (http://freewalkingtour.org)

🛌 Sleeping

When travellers talk about Tokyo's high prices, they're usually referring to the city's accommodation. You'll find cheap eats and free sights all over the metropolis, but when it comes to sleeping, get ready to widen your wallet a bit more. That said, there's a whole spectrum of price tags to choose from – even backpackers will find a place to nest – but remember one thing: book ahead!

Tokyo naturally has Japan's most diverse selection of accommodation, from capsule coffins to luxurious suites with city views. Quick internet searches will yield hundreds of accommodation options as well as thousands of traveller comments. The following are some of the top spots around town in all the different budget categories. See p87 for some tips on booking beds in the city, and turn to p740 for information about the different types of accommodation on offer in Japan.

It should be noted that some midrange and budget options do not accept credit cards – come prepared with cash.

MARUNOUCHI & GINZA 丸の内・銀座

Ginza is smack dab in the middle of things, which makes staying here very convenient, but you'll be paying for a prime slice of real estate.

Conrad Hotel   HOTEL $$$

(コンラッド東京; Map p56; ☑6388-8000; www.conradtokyo.co.jp; 1-9-1 Higashi-Shimbashi; s/d from ¥74,000/79,000; @ 🛜 🆒; 🚇Shiodome, exit 10) One of the gigantic, glittery gems comprising the Shiodome development, the Conrad Hotel is definitely a new contender for the attentions of upmarket travellers looking for that central, super-sophisticated base in Tokyo. The garden or city views are equally spectacular, as are the varnished hardwood interiors and floor-to-ceiling glassed bathrooms.

Ginza Yoshimizu   RYOKAN $$$

(銀座吉水; Map p56; ☑3248-4432; www.yoshimizu.com; 3-11-3 Ginza; s/tw/tr ¥17,000/27,500/31,800; @ 🆒; 🚇Higashi-Ginza, exit 3) Stepping through the bamboo doors of the Yoshimizu means leaving behind phones,

---

GAY & LESBIAN TOKYO

Tokyo's gay and lesbian enclave is **Shinjuku-nichōme** ('Ni-chōme'), found just east of Shinjuku-sanchōme Station's C8 exit. You'll find a diverse array of establishments here and in other little nooks around the city: hole-in-wall bars, dance clubs, sex shops, sex clubs, host clubs and love hotels. It should be noted that not all bars and clubs welcome foreigners, so it's best to ask around ahead of time before getting the cold shoulder at the door.

If you're in Tokyo during the summer, the **Tokyo International Lesbian & Gay Film Festival** (www.tokyo-lgff.org) hits screens in mid-July.

Click on www.utopia-asia.com/japntoky.htm to find a list of gay-friendly places (including a small map of Ni-chōme). The following venues are mainstays in Tokyo's LGBT scene.

Advocates Bar   BAR

(アドボケイツカフェ; Map p72; 7th Tenka Bldg 2-18-1 Shinjuku; 🚇Shinjuku-sanchōme, exit C8) Advocates Bar is so small that as the crowd gets bigger during the course of an evening, it becomes more like a block party and takes to the streets. Anyone and everyone is welcome.

Arty Farty   NIGHTCLUB

(アーティー・ファーティ; Map p72; www.arty-farty.net; 2nd fl, 2-11-7 Shinjuku; 🚇Shinjuku-sanchōme, exit C8) Arty Farty has been around forever, and it's a popular spot to tune into the local gay scene (be it Japanese or international). There's a dance floor for weekend revelry – 'hags' are welcome when accompanied by their male friends.

Chestnut & Squirrel   BAR

(Map p67; 3rd fl, Ooishi Bldg 3-7 Shibuya; 🕙Wed; 🚇Shibuya, East exit) This is a hugely popular lesbian hang-out with an international flavour and an English-speaking mama-san. The name is a tricky li'l play on words – 'Chestnut and Squirrel' is *kuri to risu* in Japanese (try saying it a few times fast, with your best attempt at a Japanese accent, to recognise the homophone).

TVs, internet access and city din in favour of more natural living. This elegantly simple ryokan features earth walls, bamboo and tatami flooring, organic cotton bedding and a *sentō* made from immaculate granite and *hinoki* (Japanese cypress). Organic meals are served in a peaceful, communal dining room – breakfast is included in room rates, but dinner reservations are a must. Rooms with shared toilet and shower are considerably cheaper.

Hotel Ryumeikan HOTEL $$$
(Map p56; ☎3271-0971; www.ryumeikan-tokyo.jp; 1-3-22 Yaesu; d ¥19,600; ⊖@; ⓡTokyo, Yaesu North exit) Mixing subtle Japanese details with modern design, Ryumeikan strikes the right balance between comfortable amenities, polite service and a winning location close to Tokyo Station. It's a fantastic alternative to the cookie-cutter business digs found in the same budget category – several rooms here could even be considered spacious.

ROPPONGI 六本木
The Akasaka area is known for its high concentration of luxury hotels. If nightlife features prominently on your agenda, Roppongi is a good place to hang your hat.

Grand Hyatt Tokyo HOTEL $$$
(グランドハイアット東京; Map p60; ☎4333-1234; www.tokyo.grand.hyatt.com; 6-10-3 Roppongi; d from ¥63,500; @✈; ⓡRoppongi, exits 1c & 3) Set in uber-desirable Roppongi Hills, the Grand Hyatt gleams with polished refinement. Though the look is decidedly urban, the interior makes liberal use of natural materials, lending an earthy and comfortable feel to this modern hotel with details like rain-shower fixtures and mahogany walls. Hi-tech luxuries include DVD players and flat-screen TVs in the bathrooms, while in-house hotel facilities encompass a spa with wet and dry saunas, large indoor pool and gym, some of Tokyo's best dining and a number of bars. Book the west side for views of Mt Fuji (if the weather cooperates).

ANA Intercontinental Tokyo HOTEL $$$
(ANAインターコンチネンタルホテル東京; Map p60; ☎3505-1111; www.anaintercontinental-tokyo.jp; 1-12-33 Akasaka; d from ¥36,000; @✈; ⓡTameike-sannō, exit 13) Midway between Akasaka and Roppongi, the ANA caters to discerning travelling professionals, and gleams with businesslike glam. Essential oils waft through the air, and the 'Club Rooms' have exclusive access to lounges, private concierg-

ⓘ SLEEPING IN TOKYO 87

When it comes to booking beds in Japan's biggest city, we suggest planning ahead. If you're counting your yen, it's worth checking out the small hotel groups within Tokyo, like **Tokyu Hotels** (www.tokyuhotels.co.jp), **Villa Fontaine** (ホテルヴィラ フォンテーヌ汐留; www.hvf.jp/eng) and the **Ishin Hotels Group** (www.ishinhotels.com).

» **Tocoo!** (www.tocoo.jp) Japanese hotel search engine and booker with fantastic discounts.

» **Welcome Inn Reservation Center** (www.itcj.jp/eng/tokyo_met) Handy reservation centre listing scores of sleeping options for all budget sizes. Even if you don't book on the site, it still provides a good up-to-date list of choices.

» **Ryokan Collection** (www.ryokancollection.com) Long list of ryokan options.

» **Japanese Guest Houses** (www.japaneseguesthouses.com) Similar to Ryokan Collection.

» **Sakura House** (www.sakurahouse.com) Old-school *gaijin* (foreign) house stalwart offering cheap places to call home for longer stays in the city.

» **Duplex** (www.duplexcs.jp) Higher-end and high-quality fully furnished apartments for those looking to stick around a while.

es and myriad other perks. Even if you're not staying at the hotel, it's worth stopping by to sample the exquisite restaurants and bars serving top-notch sushi, steak, champagne and cigars.

Hotel Ōkura HOTEL $$$
(ホテルオークラ; Map p60; ☎3582-0111, 3582-3707; www.okura.com/tokyo; 2-10-4 Toranomon; d from ¥42,000; @✈; ⓡTameike-sannō, exit 13) A preferred landing place for visiting dignitaries and businesspeople, the unpretentious but graceful Hotel Ōkura exudes old-school elegance. The inviting feel of the hotel's retro decor and low-lying architecture is complemented by a beautiful Japanese garden. Personable staff, excellent business facilities and top-notch restaurants complete the picture. The hotel grounds also house a lovely museum (see p63).

Hotel New Ōtani
HOTEL $$$

(ホテルニューオータニ; off Map p60; ☎3265-1111; www.newotani.co.jp; 4-1 Kioi-chō; d from ¥37,800; ❺Akasaka-mitsuke, exit D) There's a whiff of pretension about this classic choice, but it's justified. The New Ōtani is stuffed to the gills with large, luxurious rooms, upmarket restaurants, boutiques and gift shops. This landmark has its own art museum and an immaculate 400-year-old garden.

EBISU & MEGURO
恵比寿・目黒

Ebisu and Meguro aren't overflowing with accommodation options, but you'll find a cluster of options near Shinagawa Station catching commuters and Japanese families.

TOP
CHOICE Claska
HOTEL $$$

(クラスカ; ☎3719-8121; www.claska.com/en/hotel; 1-3-18 Chūō-chō; d from ¥12,600; ❺Tōkyū Tōyoko line to Gakugei-daigaku, East exit) With an intriguing selection of rooms, including 'Japanese Modern', 'Tatami' and 'D.I.Y.' (you'll see), the Claska is a dream of contemporary design. Gorgeously appointed furnishings, and prim tooth-white walls make the rooms feel like staged spreads from a trendy architectural magazine. With neat shops and a hip lobby cafe, the Claska sits among a cluster of design and interior stores on Meguro-dōri.

Strings Hotel Tokyo
HOTEL $$$

(☎5783-1111; www.intercontinental-strings.jp; 2-16-1 Kōnan; r from ¥48,000; ❺JR Shinagawa, Kōnan exit) Take in the views of Tokyo Tower and the Rainbow Bridge in this serene, lofty space designed by award-winning architect Terry McGinnity. The Premier corner rooms offer the most spectacular panoramas, also visible from the gym on the 26th floor. Deluxe bath view rooms have tubs right by the windows.

SHIBUYA & AROUND
渋谷

Around the top of Dōgenzaka is the highest concentration of **love hotels** (also referred to as 'boutique' hotels; see p89) in Japan. Tokyo's love hotels are not as wacky as elsewhere in the country, but you'll find a theme to suit your tastes – from pink and girly to bondage-ready. Wander into the lobbies and take a look at the screens picturing the available rooms. Check-in is usually around 10pm to midnight for a full-night's stay, but prices are pretty budget-friendly.

Granbell Hotel
HOTEL $$$

(渋谷グランベルホテル; Map p67; ☎5457-2681; www.granbellhotel.jp; 15-17 Sakuragaokachō; s/d/ste from ¥13,100/21,400/55,400; @; ❺JR Shibuya, South exit) Though most of the Granbell's rooms are Tokyo-tiny, the glass-walled bathrooms and bright tropical colour schemes give the illusion of spaciousness. In addition to the usual mod-cons, rooms in the main building feature curtains with fun Lichtenstein-esque designs. Suites, such as the two-storey View Bath, are uniquely well appointed with luxuries like record players and open-air terraces.

Capsule & Sauna Century Shibuya
CAPSULE HOTEL $

(Map p67; ☎3464-1777; 1-19-14 Dōgenzaka; standard/deluxe ¥3700/4000; ❺JR Shibuya, South exit) Freshly refurbished, this capsule contender isn't just for folks who missed their last train; services are now geared towards foreign tourists and a few down-on-their-luck locals. Multinight stays are allowed.

SHINJUKU & WEST TOKYO
新宿

Shinjuku is full of business hotels and chain hotels accustomed to foreign guests, and the competition keeps prices reasonable.

Park Hyatt Tokyo
HOTEL $$$

(パークハイアット東京; Map p72; ☎5322-1234; www.tokyo.park.hyatt.com; 3-7-1 Nishi-shinjuku; r from ¥38,500; @❻; ❺JR Shinjuku, South exit) Views are stunning, day and night, and appear to be part of another world from these serene heights. Dignified but relaxed, the stylishly understated rooms are done in naturally finished wood, fabric and marble. Staff are gracefully, discreetly attentive and the restaurants are some of Tokyo's best – check out the panorama from the top-level New York Grill.

IKEBUKURO & NORTHWEST TOKYO
池袋

It may not be the most intuitive place to stay – and it's definitely not one of Tokyo's sexiest areas – but the city's northwest neighbourhoods offer reasonable prices and several well-established ryokan.

There are innumerable business, love and capsule hotels in the Ikebukuro area. Be aware that the local capsule hotels here are not as accustomed to foreign guests as their counterparts in Asakusa and Shinjuku.

Hōmeikan
RYOKAN $$

(鳳明館; ☎3811-1181; www.homeikan.com; 5-10-5 Hongō; r from ¥11,600; @; ❺Kasuga, exit A6) The venerable Hōmeikan is a beautifully crafted wooden ryokan, with its main Honkan wing dating all the way back to the Meiji era –

LOVE HOTELS

A place to get a little peace and quiet with your significant other, Tokyo's love hotels are scattered through the city, but the best are in Shibuya's **Dōgenzaka** area and in Shinjuku's **Kabuki-chō** neighbourhood.

Prices generally start around ¥4000 for a 'rest' and ¥10,000 for a 'stay', but expect to pay double that and more if you're keen on testing out some of the swankier options. The following options are a safe bet for a memorable love hotel experience.

P&A Plaza   LOVE HOTEL
(Map p67; 1-17-9 Dōgenzaka; 圓Shibuya, South exit) Jacuzzis come standard with each room, or splash out on a private, full-sized swimming pool tucked into your oversized suite.

Meguro Club Sekitei   LOVE HOTEL
(2-1-6 Shimo-meguro; 圓Meguro, West exit) The 'emperor' is considered to be Tokyo's first love hotel. The facade takes a lazy stab at Cinderella's castle.

Hotel Art   LOVE HOTEL
(Map p67; 2-26-2 Dōgenzaka; 圓Shibuya, South exit) Like little art galleries, each room has an assortment of art adorning the walls. Wildly popular.

it's also registered as an important cultural property. The Daimachi Bekkan wing is equally inviting, equipped with 31 tatami rooms as well as a large downstairs communal bath. This oasis in the middle of Tokyo is a real treasure.

Kimi Ryokan   RYOKAN **$$**
(貴美旅館; ☎3971-3766; www.kimi-ryokan.jp; 2-36-8 Ikebukuro; s ¥4500, d ¥6500-7500, all with shared bathroom; @; 圓Ikebukuro, exit C6) Easily one of the best budget ryokan in Tokyo, this convivial inn provides a welcoming base for travellers discovering the city. Fragrant tatami rooms are small but not cramped, and the large wood-floored lounge area is a comfortable place to meet fellow travellers over green tea. There's a lovely Japanese cypress bath. Book well in advance.

Hotel Niwa Tokyo   RYOKAN **$$$**
(☎3293-0028; www.hotelniwa.jp; 1-1-16 Misakichō; d ¥25,610; @; 圓Suidōbashi) Niwa aspires to a minimal Japanese design aesthetic without sacrificing quality or forfeiting the modcons. And it succeeds. The hotel is easily accessible from Narita via the Tokyo Dome Hotel limousine bus.

UENO   上野
Ueno and the surrounding neighbourhoods may be a bit removed from the bright lights, but they make a great sightseeing base, especially for museum buffs. Additionally, the many budget ryokan in the area are not only inexpensive but also more interesting than bland business hotels.

Ueno is one of the more convenient areas for Narita Airport.

Andon Ryokan   RYOKAN **$$**
(行燈旅館; off Map p78; ☎3873-8611; www.andon .co.jp; 2-34-10 Nihonzutsumi; r per person ¥8190; @; 圓Minowa, exit 3) Fabulously designed in form and function, the minimalist and modern Andon Ryokan has tiny but immaculate tatami rooms. Pluses include free internet access, DVD players, cheap breakfast and laundry facilities.

Sawanoya Ryokan   RYOKAN **$$**
(旅館澤の屋; Map p78; ☎3822-2251; www.sawa noya.com; 2-3-11 Yanaka; d/tr ¥10,080/14,490, s without bathroom ¥5040-5355; @; 圓Nezu, exit 1) The Sawanoya is a budget gem in quiet Yanaka, with very friendly staff and all the traditional hospitality you would expect of a ryokan – even origami paper cranes perched on your futon pillow in welcome. The shared cypress and earthenware baths are the perfect balm after a long day of walking.

TokHouse   GUESTHOUSE **$$**
(Map p78; www.tokhouse.com; 3-52-9 Sendagi; s/d/q ¥11,000/11,000/12,000; ☎; 圓Nishi-Nippori, West exit) Go one better than staying at a guesthouse and rent an entire one out. For the price of a room in a crammed business hotel you'll get your very own house in the heart of *shitamachi*. Amenities are basic, but there's a kitchen and plenty of room to stretch out. Richard, the American owner, has been living in Tokyo for well over a decade and is a font of knowledge about the city's northern neighbourhoods.

MISSING THE MIDNIGHT TRAIN

Cinderellas who've stayed out partying past midnight and found that their last train has turned into a *kabocha* (pumpkin) needn't fret. If dancing the night away doesn't appeal, and an astronomically priced taxi ride doesn't compute, give the capsule hotel a miss and try a *manga kissa* instead.

Kissaten (coffee shops) have long been mainstays for socialising away from home, but the next-generation versions offer a place for watching DVDs, getting some PlayStation action, catching up on email or catching some Zs. *Manga kissa* have libraries of DVDs and manga, bottomless cups of coffee and cola, and inexpensive food. The staff make regular rounds to ensure safe surfing and sleeping.

Overnight rates – typically around ¥2500 for eight hours – are a bargain. Check in at the reception desk, prepay for your stay and while away the wee hours in a cosy private cubicle. Both **Aprecio** (アプレシオ; www.aprecio.co.jp) and **Bagus Gran Cyber Cafe** (グランサイバーカフェバグース; www.bagus-99.com/netcafe) have branches all over town – check the websites for detailed location lists.

Annex Katsutarō Ryokan HOTEL $$
(アネックス勝太郎旅館; Map p78; ☑3828-2500; www.katsutaro.com; 3-8-4 Yanaka; s/d/tr from ¥6300/10,500/14,700; @; ℝSendagi, exit 2) Opened in 2001, this spotless, efficient establishment seems more like a modern hotel than a traditional ryokan. Though far from Ueno Station, it's ideal for exploring the old Yanaka district. The tatami rooms, while rather small, have attached Western bathrooms.

Ryokan Katsutarō RYOKAN $$
(旅館勝太郎; Map p78; ☑3821-9808; www.katsutaro.com; 4-16-8 Ikenohata; s/d/tr from ¥5200/8400/14,700; @; ℝNezu, exit 2) This older, more homey sister inn to Annex Katsutarō Ryokan has a more quiet and family-like atmosphere, with very affable managers. Though the building may be aged, the tatami rooms here have been renovated without ruining the inn's character.

ASAKUSA & AROUND 浅草
If you don't mind sacrificing central location for unpretentious *shitamachi* atmosphere, Asakusa is a fine place to stay, crammed with some of Tokyo's best budget ryokan and hostels.

TOP CHOICE Sukeroku No Yado
Sadachiyo RYOKAN $$$
(助六の宿千代; Map p80; ☑3842-6431; www.sadachiyo.co.jp; 2-20-1 Asakusa; d ¥19,000; ℝAsakusa, exit 1) This stunning ryokan virtually transports its guests to old Edo. Gorgeously maintained tatami rooms are spacious for two people, and all come with modern, Western-style bathrooms. Splurge on an exquisite

meal here, and make time for the *o-furo* (traditional baths), one made of fragrant Japanese cypress and the other of black granite. Look for the rickshaw parked outside.

Khaosan Tokyo Guesthouse HOSTEL $
(カオサン東京ゲストハウス; Map p80; ☑3842-8286; www.khaosan-tokyo.com; 2-1-5 Kaminarimon; dm/s/tw ¥2200/3700/5000; @; ℝAsakusa, exits 4 & A2b) Very friendly, remarkably inexpensive and homey, the Khaosan is a warm intro to Tokyo. Located on the bank of the Sumida-gawa, it has a tiny but cheery kitchen and pleasant rooftop terrace. Khaosan has several comfortable annex locations as well.

K's House GUESTHOUSE $$
(バックパッカーズホステルケイズハウス東京; ☑5833-0555; http://kshouse.jp/tokyo-e/index.html; 3-20-10 Kuramae; dm/s/d from ¥2800/3400/6800; @; ℝKuramae, exits A2 & A6) This homey, modern hostel has quickly become a backpacker favourite. Just steps from the Sumida-gawa and Sensō-ji, K's feels more like someone's apartment, with comfy sofas in the living room and a tatami common space. Another branch – the family-oriented K's House Tokyo Oasis – has opened closer to Sensō-ji; see website for details.

Anne Hostel HOSTEL $
(浅草橋旅荘庵; off Map p80; ☑5829-9090; http://j-hostel.com; 2-21-14 Yanagibashi; dm/tw from ¥2400/6400; @; ℝAsakusabashi (East or A6 exit)) Located in a former corporate space, laid-back Anne has standard wooden bunk beds, modern toilets and showers, and a homey, cosy atmosphere overall. Look for the traditional wooden lantern on the street outside.

Khaosan Tokyo Annex

HOSTEL $

(カオサン東京アネックス; off Map p80; ☑5856-6560; www.khaosan-tokyo.com; 2-2-5 Higashi-komagata; dm/tw ¥2300/5000; @; ℞Asakusa, exits 4 & A2b) Run by Khaosan Tokyo Guesthouse, regular rack rate discounts make this the cheapest hostel in Tokyo.

Khaosan Tokyo Kabuki

HOSTEL $

(Map p80; ☑3842-8286; www.khaosan-tokyo. com; 1-17-2 Asakusa; dm/s & tw ¥3000/6800; @; ℞Asakusa, exits 4 & A2b) Well maintained, and one of Khaosan Tokyo's best. All rooms are en suite.

ODAIBA & TOKYO BAY　お台場・東京湾

There's no good reason to stay on Odaiba unless you're coming to Tokyo for a conference, or visiting family who live in the area. The man-made island is barely tethered to the city centre, making transportation to various attractions a bit of a headache, especially in the evening when the trains start to shut down.

🍴 Eating

When it comes to Tokyo superlatives, the city's eating scene takes the cake. There are more restaurants, cafes and bars in this pulsing megalopolis than in any other city around the world. And the quality is unparalleled too – you'll have to look pretty hard to find a bad meal.

So, where does one begin when trying to dig in? As the capital of Japan, it's only natural to want to sample every type of Japanese dish, but Tokyo's victual vocabulary extends far beyond fish and noodles. The cosmopolitan city boasts some of the best international cuisine on the planet. Thus, the best plan of attack is to try a little of everything, and be savvy about your selections. Lunch, for example, is a great time to try those upmarket eats, as most restaurants offer huge discounts during the noontime hours. For dinner, plan ahead – a reservation is almost always a must if your culinary aspirations are higher than, say, a bowl of *rāmen* (egg noodles).

The following restaurants represent a wide range of cuisines and budgets, and everything's under ¥10,000, proving you don't need a rock star's budget to have a memorable meal in the city. We've even provided a list of useful websites to help with the search.

Now go forth and enjoy – Tokyo's incredible dining scene is yours for the taking.

MARUNOUCHI & GINZA　丸の内・銀座

The sprawling, tower-clad districts of Marunouchi and Ginza cater to swarms of businessmen with speedy set menu lunches during the day, and sociable, smoke-filled venues in the evening for when work's through. You'll be spoilt for choice at many of the glitzy office buildings, including the **Marunouchi Building** (Maru Biru; 2-4-1 Marunouchi) and **Shin Marunouchi** (Shin Maru; www .marunouchi.com/shinmaru) next door. Also a popular option are the hovel-like joints crammed under the JR tracks at Yūrakuchō and Shinbashi stations.

Further south, in the business district of Shiodome, you'll find the towering **Caretta Building** with its own clutch of sky-high restaurants. The options here are often good value as this business district is noticeably quieter than the corporate hubs of Roppongi Hills and Marunouchi.

In Japan's world of finance there is a sanctioned break on the trading floor between 11am and 12.30pm – if you're planning on hitting up some of the cheap lunch deals in the Marunouchi and Ōtemachi districts, consider dining outside of those times lest you be ensnared by the legions of queuing businessmen.

Beyond the infinite corporate lunch options, these neighbourhoods also play host to most of Tokyo's illustrious *depachikas* (see p108), upscale grocery stores tucked away in the basements of high-end department stores.

TOP CHOICE Beige

FUSION $$$

(Map p56; ☑5159-5500; www.beige-tokyo.com; 3-5-3 Ginza; lunch/dinner from ¥5000/13,000; ▣; ℞Ginza, exits A9 & A13) Beige is the love child of fashion headliner Chanel and celebrity chef Alain Ducasse, and the menu is decadence defined: locally raised beef, fresh-from-the-sea lobster, hand-selected vegetables and expertly blended marinades. This is complemented by a wine list of encyclopaedic proportions and swish, East-meets-West decor to round out the perfect top-end Tokyo experience. The **Jardin de Tweed** (lunch ¥2500), nesting on the building's rooftop, offers something a bit more affordable to those with luxe aspirations.

Kiji

OKONOMIYAKI $$

(きじ; Map p56; ☑3216-3123; www.o-kizi.jp; B1 fl, Tokia Bldg 2-7-3 Marunouchi; mains ¥1000; ⊙lunch & dinner; ℞Tokyo, Marunouchi South exit) Fresh off the bullet train from Osaka, Kiji brings

EATING IN TOKYO

With over 140,000 restaurants in greater Tokyo, it seems almost impossible to make a restaurant decision come mealtime. Fortunately for you, the Japanese like to rank things almost as much as they love their food, so you'll find dozens of websites devoted to decoding the city's infinite dining scene. Many of these sites are in Japanese only – we recommend using a browser with built-in translation capabilities, like Google Chrome.

» **Tabelog** (http://r.tabelog.com/tokyo) The 'eating log' is the ultimate ranking database that breaks options down by neighbourhood and/or food type. The annual 'top' lists have a great selection of establishments around town. And remember – the local critics are harsh. A score of four out of five should be considered top honours.

» **Time Out** (www.timeout.jp/en/tokyo/restaurants-cafes) Excellent resource with regularly updated articles on restaurants, cafes and bars.

» **Tokyo Food Page** (www.bento.com/tokyofood.html) Foreigner-friendly food page with to-the-point reviews detailing over 1000 dining options.

» **Gournavi** (www.gnavi.co.jp/en) A self-proclaimed gourmet navigator with hundreds of eating options and reviews. The Japanese version (delete the 'en' in the URL) is far more comprehensive.

» **Rāmen Database** (http://rāmendb.supleks.jp) A vast database of *rāmen* (egg noodle) restaurants.

» **Metropolis** (www.metropolis.co.jp) The articles may be rather misinformed, but rumour has it that an interactive restaurant database is starting up soon. Check the website for updates.

expertly crafted *okonomiyaki* to the legions of businessmen in the bustling office district of Marunouchi. Slide down the escalator to sample some seriously scrumptious soul food. Perfect for neophytes, these pancake/omelette/noodle mash-ups come ready to serve (rather than DIY).

Robata Honten IZAKAYA $$$
(爐端本店; Map p56; ☎3591-1905; 1-3-8 Yūrakuchō; meals ¥4500, dishes ¥1300-1500; ☾dinner; 🚇Hibiya, exit A4 & A11) Along the alley paralleling the JR tracks, this is one of Tokyo's most celebrated *izakaya* (pub-eatery). A little Japanese ability is helpful here, but the point-and-eat method works fine, as the country-style dishes are piled invitingly on the counter in gorgeous ceramic pots. Look for the rustic black shop, huge sign on the 2nd floor, and vegetables displayed at the door.

Rengatei WESTERN $$
(煉瓦亭; Map p56; www.ginza-rengatei.com; 3-5-16 Ginza; mains ¥1300; 🔄; 🚇Ginza, exit A13) Dating back to the early days of the Meiji period, Rengatei is credited with inventing the *katsu* cutlet and the omelette – Japan's first stab at Western cuisine, which quickly became its own culinary category called *yōshoku*. Wonderfully outdated decor (think clanging

cash register, faded waitress uniforms and well-worn chequered tablecloths) hint at the restaurant's lengthy history.

Daiwa Sushi SUSHI & SASHIMI $$
(大和寿司; Map p56; ☎3547-6807; Bldg 6 5-2-1 Tsukiji; meals ¥3500; ☾lunch Mon-Sat; 🚇Tsukijishijō) Waits of over one hour are commonplace at Tsukiji's most famous sushi bar, but it's all worth it once you're past the *noren* (curtains) and your first piece of sushi hits the counter. Unless you're comfortable ordering in Japanese, the standard set (seven *nigiri*, plus *maki* and miso soup) is a good bet; there's a picture menu. Though the staff may be too polite to say so, you're expected to eat and run so others can partake in this quintessential Tsukiji experience.

Sushi Kanesaka SUSHI & SASHIMI $$$
(Map p56; ☎5568-4411; B1 fl, 8-10-3 Ginza; lunch/dinner from ¥10,00/20,000; 🚇Shinbashi, exit 5) Tucked away below street level, this sushi superstar is the workshop of the eponymous master chef – a prodigy by culinary standards – who slices through premium pieces of fresh fish with a surgeon's precision. If you're contemplating a sushi splurge during your time in Tokyo, this is the place to do it. But book ahead – there's only a dozen seats.

Mikimoto Lounge
CAFE **$$**

(Map p56; www.mikimoto.co.jp; 3rd fl, 2-4-12 Ginza; dessert ¥1200; 🍴; 🚉Ginza, exit B2) Elegantly positioned behind the futuristic pastel webbing of the pearl magnate's flagship boutique, Mikimoto Lounge is one of Ginza's premier dessert parlours. Tuck into your artisanal treat – made from fairy-tale ingredients like cloud-ear compote and wolfberry – while dining upon ivory-smooth tabletops.

Meal MUJI
SANDWICH SHOP **$**

(Map p56; www.muji.net; 2nd fl, 3-8-3 Marunouchi; mains ¥500-1000; 🍴; 🚉Yūrakuchō, exit D9) Those who subscribe to the Muji lifestyle will be delighted to know that the 'no name brand' experience goes beyond neutral-toned notebooks, containers and linens. Meal MUJI follows the 'simpler is better' mantra with fresh deli fare uncluttered by chemicals and unpronounceable ingredients.

Opippi
RĀMEN **$**

(おぴっぴ; off Map p56; 1-20-11 Shinbashi; mains ¥750-1350; 🚉Shinbashi, exit 8) Quietly lost amid Shinbashi's urban grid, this mom-and-pop soup shop whips up slurp-worthy udon noodles with a twist – instead of factory-line fare and vats of broth, each bowl is individually assembled from fresh ingredients.

Manneken
BAKERY **$**

(Map p56; www.manneken.co.jp; 5-7-19 Ginza; waffles from ¥150; 🍴; 🚉Ginza, exit B3) Participate in Tokyoites' favourite pastime – waiting in line – at this bustling Belgian waffle stand. They taste as good as they smell, and adventurous types can try the seasonal specials that blend rather incongruous savoury-sweet ingredients.

Nakajima no Ochaya
TEAHOUSE **$**

(Map p56; 1-1 Hama-rikyu-teien; admission ¥300; 🕐9am-4pm; 🚉Shiodome, exit 5) Hama-rikyū-teien's elegant teahouse nestled among the perfectly manicured hills.

Ginza Bairin
TONKATSU **$**

(銀座梅林; Map p56; www.ginzabairin.com; 7-8-1 Ginza; meals from ¥980; 🍴; 🚉Ginza, exit A2) Cheap and cheerful *tonkatsu* (deep-fried pork cutlets) are the name of the game at this no-frills joint in the heart of Ginza.

ROPPONGI
六本木

It's only logical that there's an abundance of international options in Tokyo's capital of *gaijin*-dom. In general, however, the prices are skewed a bit higher here, as they are largely geared towards tourists and moneyed expats. Stacks of restaurants can be found in the modern complexes of **Roppongi Hills** and **Tokyo Midtown**.

Further north, the district of Akasaka acts like a buffer between raucous Roppongi and the quiet garden-scapes of the imperial palace. Once a prominent geisha area, Akasaka is now a bustling business centre – great lunch deals and after-work *izakaya* can be scouted here.

TOP CHOICE Ukai Tofu-ya
KAISEKI **$$$**

(Map p60; 📞3436-1028; www.ukai.co.jp; 4-4-13 Shiba-kōen; meals ¥8400-12,600; 🍴; 🚉Kamiyachō, exit 4) Make your reservations when you book your flights. You'll be glad you did; this is perhaps Tokyo's most gracious restaurant, in a former sake brewery moved from northern Japan and plunked down in an exquisite garden in the shadow of Tokyo Tower. Seasonal preparations of the namesake tofu and accompanying dishes are served in more ways than you may have thought possible.

Ninja Akasaka
FUSION **$$$**

(Map p60; 📞5157-3936; www.ninjaakasaka.com; 2-14-3 Nagatachō; meals from ¥5500; 🕐dinner; 🍴; 🚉Akasaka-mitsuke, Belle Vie exit) Super-stealth staff, trained in the deadly art of catering, escort you through a maze of trap doors and trick drawbridges before seating you at your private table. Savour tasty Japanese fare, like 'cloaked chicken' or 'crouching salmon', and at the end of the meal, a saucy senior ninja swings by to perform some impressive close magic. But perhaps the biggest trick of all is the food's swift disappearing act – portions are extremely small, so if you're sharing, make sure to order more plates than there are people (if you're dining à la carte). Reservations are a must.

Gonpachi
FUSION **$$$**

(権八; Map p60; 📞5771-0170; www.gonpachi.jp; 1-13-11 Nishi-azabu; meals ¥4500, dishes ¥750-1950; 🕐11.30am-5am; 🍴; 🚉Roppongi, exit 2) If the screen shots of Uma Thurman in a yellow jumpsuit didn't clue you in, Gonpachi is the place that inspired the Lucy Liu sequence in *Kill Bill* (think Charlie Brown and the Crazy 88). Though the menu isn't authentically Japanese (camembert tempura – yum!), the decor is undeniably Edo. Reserve early for a booth on the 2nd floor overlooking the crowd below. There's a sushi room on the 3rd level, which is separate from the rest of the restaurant.

Jomon

YAKINIKU $$

(ジョウモン; Map p60; ☑3405-2585; www
.teyandei.com; 5-9-17 Roppongi; meals ¥1750,
skewers ¥200-1200; ⊙dinner; ⓘ; ⓡRoppongi,
exit 3) Slide the stable door open to find a
wonderfully cosy kitchen with bar seating
and rows of ornate *shochu* (liquor) jugs lin-
ing the wall. Hundreds of freshly prepared
skewers lie splayed in front of the patrons –
don't miss the heavenly *zabuton* beef stick
(¥400). Jomon can be a bit hard to find,
even though it is on a main street – it's al-
most directly across from the Family Mart
as you walk down the slope towards Rop-
pongi Hills – look for the name in Japanese
on the door.

Eat More Greens

VEGETARIAN $

(イートモアグリーンズ; Map p60; www.eat
moregreens.jp; 2-2-5 Azabu-Jūban; mains from
¥950; ⊙@☎ⓘ; ⓡAzabu-Jūban, exit 4 & 5a) In-
spired, interestingly, by the greengrocers
and farmers markets of NYC, this shop
holds its own farmers market on Saturdays.
Choose the airy interior or outdoor patio
to enjoy a delicious assortment of vegetar-
ian and vegan dishes – the mushroom rice
is divine.

Tajima

SOBA $$

(蕎麦たじま; off Map p60; ☑3445-6617; www
.sobatajima.com; 3-8-6 Nishi-azabu; meals ¥2500-
3500; ⓡHirō-o, exit 3) Slip behind the polished
white wall to find Tajima – one of Tokyo's
best *soba* (buckwheat noodle) houses. The
understated decor lets senses focus exclusively on the flavours and aromas emanat-
ing from the freshly prepared dishes. Tease your
tastebuds with a few appetisers, like daintily
fried sweet-potato wedges, then slurp your
scrumptious soup and noodles.

Nirvanam

INDIAN $$

(Map p60; ☑3433-1217; www.nirvanam.jp; 2nd fl,
3-19-7 Toranomon; lunch ¥1200, dinner ¥3000-
4000; ☎ⓘ; ⓡKamiyachō, exit 3) Skip the pomp
and circumstance of the city's celebrity-run
dhabas and head to Nirvanam, the culinary
sweetheart of Tokyo's expat Indian commu-
nity. Although dinner can feel slightly over-
priced, the all-you-can-eat lunch – loaded up
with spicy curries and pillowy *naan* bread –
is undoubtedly the city's best deal from the
subcontinent.

Tokyo Curry Lab

CURRY $$

(Map p60; 4-2-8 Shiba-kōen; meals ¥1000-1350;
ⓘ; ⓡKamiyachō, exit 1) The brainchild of local
design powerhouse Wonderwall, this curry-
wielding space station tucked under the
soaring spires of Tokyo Tower sports personal TVs at each barstool. The hilariously
illustrated placemats (you'll see) make the
perfect 'Tokyo is weird' souvenir.

Seryna

STEAKHOUSE $$$

(瀬里奈; Map p60; ☑3402-1051; www.seryna
.co.jp; 3-12-2 Roppongi; lunch/dinner ¥6000/15,000;
ⓡRoppongi, exits 3 & 5) Seryna is the go-to stal-
wart for those wishing to try Kōbe (Wagyū)
beef. With several eateries under its roof, you
can try *shabu-shabu* (pieces of thinly sliced
beef cooked quickly with vegetables in boil-
ing water and then dipped in sauce) and
sukiyaki (sliced meat simmered with vegeta-
bles and sauce), or opt for a slab of steak and
teppan-yaki (table-top grilling). The restau-
rant surrounds a pretty rock garden. It has
an English sign and menu.

Savoy

PIZZA $$

(Map p60; www.savoy.vc; 201 3-10-1 Moto-azabu;
mains from ¥1000; ⓘ; ⓡAzabu-Jūban, exit 4) Seriously delicious personal pizzas are made to
order and baked right in front of you.

Like any good *gaijin* neighbourhood, Roppongi has several international grocery
stores, including the following:

Food Magazine

SUPERMARKET $

(Map p60; 6-11-1; ⊙24hr; ⓡRoppongi, exit 3)
Never-closing grocery with a well-priced
assortment of international and local
choices.

National Azabu

SUPERMARKET $$

(off Map p60; 4-5-2 Minami-azabu; ⊙9am-8pm;
ⓡHiro-o, exits 1 & 2) Go-to spot for embassy
staff picking up produce for important
banquets. Great wine selection. English-
speaking pharmacy inside.

EBISU & MEGURO

恵比寿・目黒

EBISU TO NAKA-MEGURO

恵比寿・中目黒

In Ebisu, snoop around the **Atré** building
above Ebisu Station for dozens of yummy
bakeries and scores of standard Japanese
standbys, or you could venture forth into
the neighbourhood for more variety and
worthwhile eating establishments serving
international food. **Yebisu Garden Place**
(恵比寿ガーデンプレイス), tethered to
Ebisu Station by a 'Skywalk', has an assort-
ment of restaurants as well, including sev-
eral options on the 38th and 39th floors of
the **Yebisu Garden Place Tower**, offering
expansive city views.

Rivalling Harajuku and Aoyama as the centre of Tokyo's cafe society, Daikanyama is a chic destination to sip a cappuccino and engage in serious people-watching before perusing the local designer boutiques.

Tonki   TONKATSU $$
(とんき; ☎3491-9928; 1-1-2 Shimo-Meguro; meals ¥1800; ☺dinner Wed-Mon, closed 3rd Mon each month; 🚇JR Meguro, West exit) You know a place is doing something right when it only offers three choices – all different types of *tonkatsu*. The service is practically a science: the cooks have the seating order memorised, so hunker down on any of the benches behind the bar stools. After a wait, your perfectly prepared meal will arrive with rice, cabbage and miso soup. From the station walk westward down the hill on Meguro-dōri, take a left at the first alley and look for a white sign and *noren* across the sliding doors. If you'd like to reserve ahead, there's restaurant-style seating on the 2nd floor.

Ebisu-yokochō   STREET FOOD $$
(Map p65; www.ebisu-yokocho.com; 1-7-4 Ebisu; meals ¥1600-3000; 🚇Ebisu) Ebisu is full of upscale options, so this covered cluster of street food stalls comes as a very welcome surprise. Inside you'll find everything from raw horsemeat to *okonomiyaki* – and it's all served up in quaint, sociable pods that overflow amid clanging pots and billowy smoke.

Maison Paul Bocuse   FRENCH $$$
(Map p65; ☎5468-6324; www.paulbocuse.jp; B1 fl, Daikanyama Forum 17-16 Sarugakuchō; lunch/dinner ¥2860/8400; 📷; 🚇Tōkyū Tōyoko line to Daikanyama, main exit) Celebrity chef and Michelin-star collector Paul Bocuse makes a splash in the heart of Daikanyama with his classic French fare. Try the truffle soup, said to have launched chef Bocuse's career. There's a second branch at the National Art Center in Roppongi.

Naka-meguro is practically bursting at the seams with trendy cafes and restaurants. From the station, walk towards the river and take your pick. Up the road from MISC in Meguro, snack stalls are perfect for an afternoon break while perusing furniture. The following are recommended:

Combine   CAFE $
(Map p65; www.combine.jp; 1-10 Naka-meguro; lunch ¥800, dinner mains ¥500-1000; 📷; 🚇Naka-meguro) Cool, could-be-anywhere decor

attracts flannel-clad hipster kids who pull books from the floor-to-ceiling shelves or recline in tattered couches to listen to DJ beats.

Chano-ma   CAFE $$
(Map p65; 6th fl, 1-22-4 Kami-meguro; lunch ¥880; 📶📷; 🚇Naka-meguro) Pearly white cafe with cosy daybed seating stretched along the windows. Keep an eye out for the microscopic sign out front.

Ganko Dako   FAST FOOD $
(3-11-6; snacks ¥500; 🚇Meguro, West exit) Despite the rather unfortunate location directly across from the parasite museum, Ganko Dako's octopus balls have something of a cult following (check out the framed celebrity signatures on the walls).

Meguro Gojuuban   FAST FOOD $
(4-13-5 Meguro; buns from ¥400; 🚇Meguro, West exit) These freshly made hot cakes sell like...well, hot cakes. The pillowy *nikuman* (meat bun) is the most popular.

SHIROKANE & SHINAGAWA   白金・品川
You'll be spoilt for choice in the area surrounding bustling Shinagawa Station. There's a New York–themed dining complex at the **Atré** building near the tracks.

Maruichi Bagel   BAKERY $
(www.maruichibagel.com; 1-15-22 Shirokane; bagel/half-sandwich from ¥200/600; ☺Wed-Sun; 📷; 🚇Shirokane Takanawa, exit 3) The Japanese have mastered almost all of the world's recipes, but when it comes to bagels, no one's quite found the perfect ratio of dough and Jewish guilt like Maruichi. A simple strand of masking tape marks the bagelry's name on the glass facade – it would be near impossible to find if it weren't for the line of lunchtime pilgrims.

TY Harbor Brewery   BURGERS $$
(www.tyharborbrewing.co.jp; 2-1-3 Higashi-Shinagawa; mains ¥1700-3800; 📷; 🚇Shinagawa, Kōnan East exit) This American-style brew pub boasts an eclectic menu (pan-roasted scallops with curry and couscous anyone?), beer tanks on the premises and a huge, loyal following. It's a gathering place for Tokyo's moneyed expat community, especially for weekend brunch.

Café d'Art   CAFE $$
(www.haramuseum.or.jp; 4-7-25 Kitashinagawa; lunch/mains ¥2100/1050; ☺lunch; 📷; 🚇JR Shinagawa, Takanawa exit) Arcing along a tranquil sculpture garden in the Hara Museum (p66),

Café d'Art serves tasty international fare in an inviting setting. Don't miss the regularly changing 'image cake' (¥735) – a uniquely crafted confection inspired by a piece in the gallery (thus making the dessert itself a work of art!).

SHIBUYA & AROUND   渋谷

SHIBUYA   渋谷

Tsukiji Honten   SUSHI & SASHIMI $

(築地本店; Map p67; 24-8 Udagawachō; meals from ¥840; ℝShibuya, Hachikō exit) When it comes to *kaiten-sushi* (conveyor-belt sushi restaurants), it's hard to beat this local stalwart situated smack dab in the middle of the Shibuya chaos. After a hearty welcome yell, you'll be escorted to the benches on the right while waiting for a stool to open up. There's a seven-plate minimum (which is often enough for most diners), and you can order directly from the chefs if you don't see what you like.

Kaikaya   SEAFOOD $$

(開花屋; Map p67; ☎3770-0878; www.kaikaya .com; 23-7 Maruyama-chō; meals around ¥3000; ☻lunch Mon-Fri, dinner daily; ⓓ; ℝShibuya, Hachikō exit) There are plenty of fish in the sea and Kaikaya knows plenty of ways to prepare 'em. Hugely popular with both locals and foreigners, this cheery *izakaya* flexes its culinary muscles with scrumptious dishes like carpaccio and melt-off-the-bone tuna steak.

Viron   BAKERY $

(Map p67; ☎5458-1770; 33-8 Udagawachō; mains ¥500-1200; ℝShibuya, Hachikō exit) A fantastic French bakery (it apparently imports the flour from the motherland), Viron serves up sandwiches and quiches to take away – or you can take 'em upstairs to the pleasant cafe.

Nabezo   SHABU-SHABU $$

(Map p67; ☎3461-2941; http://nabezo.jp; Beams, 6th fl, 31-2 Udagawachō; meals ¥1990; ℝShibuya, Hachikō exit) The Shibuya branch of this all-you-can-eat chain is a great spot for first-timers to try *shabu-shabu*. Diners are given two hours to dunk as many slices of raw pork and beef as they can into the gurgling pot at the centre of the table.

SHIMOKITAZAWA   下北沢

Magic Spice   CURRY $$

(1-40-15 Kitazawa; soup ¥950-1150; ☻Thu-Mon; ⓓ; ℝOdakyū line to Shimokitazawa, South exit) Like an acid trip in India, Magic Spice's loud decor mirrors the menu of flavour-ful curries (which taste more like Southeast Asian *soto* than the usual Japanese definition).

Village Vanguard Diner   BURGERS $$

(www.village-v.co.jp/diner; 6-3-1 Shirota; mains ¥1200; ⓓ; ℝOdakyū line to Shimokitazawa, North exit) Hugely popular home-spun burgers brought to you by the same folks that do funky knickknack shops.

Bear Pond   CAFE $

(www.bear-pond.com; 2-36-12 Kitazawa; espresso ¥300-700; ☻Wed-Mon; ⓓ; ℝOdakyū line to Shimokitazawa, North exit) A quaint cottage serving up some of the best espresso in Tokyo. Nab a doughnut from across the street and enjoy.

Nikku 'n Roll   FAST FOOD $

(R29; www.nikkunroll.com; 2-14-15 Kitazawa; meat rolls from ¥290; ℝOdakyū line to Shimokitazawa, South exit) Flip an *onigiri* (rice ball) inside out and you've got Nikku 'n Roll – rice covered in meat. It's the perfect pit stop for an afternoon of secondhand shopping.

JIYŪGAOKA   自由が丘

If there were a Japanese version of *Sex and the City*, Carrie and her clique would 'do brunch' in Jiyūgaoka every weekend. Scores of cool cafes lure a variety of Tokyoites, from families to pooch-toting socialites.

Nazeya   BAKERY $

(www.nazeya.com; 2-16-19 Jiyūgaoka; taiyaki from ¥230; ⓓ; ℝTōkyū Tōyoko line to Jiyūgaoka, main exit) Easily worth the trip down the Tōyoko line, Nazeya takes *taiyaki* (stuffed, fish-shaped pancakes) to the next level with rich, creamy fillings like vanilla cream and maple nut. You won't be able to eat just one. Trust us...

Table Modern Service   CAFE $$

(http://tms.cibone.com; 2-17-8 Jiyūgaoka; lunch ¥1000; ☻lunch; ℝTōkyū Tōyoko line to Jiyūgaoka, main exit) A concrete hang-out above a trendy housewares boutique. You'll find gaggles of dog-toting brunchers lounging on bright Eames-inspired furniture. And it's not just about appearances – the food's pretty darn good too.

Kosoan   TEAHOUSE $$

(古桑庵; www.kosoan.co.jp; 1-24-23 Jiyūgaoka; tea ¥500-800; ℝTōkyū Tōyoko line to Jiyūgaoka, main exit) Gorgeous traditional-looking teahouse set in a tree-shrouded grove. Sharply contrasts with the strange Venice-like complex across the street, complete with actual gondola.

THE CHAIN GANG

When it comes to restaurants, the term 'chain' has a very different meaning in Tokyo compared to countries like America, Australia or the UK. Sure, they're still low-cost places to grab a bite, but the evolution from the singular to the plural is often related to quality recipes rather than corporate aspirations.

So skip the trip to McDonald's and try one of the following Tokyo chains when you're on the run. You'll find them almost all over town – check the relevant websites for store locators, or leave it up to chance as you wander around the city.

Ippūdō
JAPANESE

(一風堂; www.ippudo.com; 🈳) We're not surprised that Ippūdō has transformed into an internationally recognised chain. The Kyūshū-style *rāmen* evokes visceral 'yums' and deafening slurps – crack some fresh garlic over the slow-roasted pork and you've got yourself the perfect meal.

Goemon
FUSION

(洋麺屋五右衛門; www.yomenya-goemon.com; 🖉🈳) A genius fusion option for penny pinchers – it's Japanese-style Italian. Think pasta mixed with local ingredients and served with chopsticks.

Kua 'Aina
BURGERS

(クアアイナ; www.kua-aina.com; 🈳) This burger superstar started on the big island (of Hawai'i, that is) as a beachside barbecue shack. In Tokyo it's the top spot for all-beef patties – the 'avocado burger' is divine.

Unatoto
UNAGI

(宇奈とと; www.unatoto.com) Why are some *unagi* (eel) restaurants priced for royalty, while other shops serve it up for pennies? We haven't quite figured it out, especially since an undiscerning palate will have a hard time telling the difference between the two. This makes Unatoto a great choice if you're keen to try eel, but don't want to dent your wallet.

Sukiya
GYŪDON

(www.sukiya.jp) This hugely popular purveyor of *gyūdon* (beef bowls) has over a thousand chains around Japan, and most are open all night.

Freshness Burger
BURGERS

(www.freshnessburger.co.jp; 🖉🈳) Despite the name, you'll be surprised to learn that this popular American-style chain serves up several tried-and-true vegetarian options in addition to the usual fast-food fare.

Gindaco
TEKOYAKI

(www.gindaco.com) Octopus balls – or *tekoyaki* – is the game of the game at the Gindaco. There are heaps of similar chains around town, but this one is the big daddy.

Mos Burger
BURGERS

(www.mos.co.jp; 🖉🈳) Pioneers of the 'rice burger', with buns made from a mix of rice, millet and barley. It's the second most popular fast-food franchise after McDonald's.

HARAJUKU
原宿

Nid Cafe
FRENCH $$

(Map p69; ☎5772-7639; www.ctn139.com; 3rd fl, 3-13-23 Minami-aoyama; mains ¥800-2000; 🈳; 🚈Omote-sandō, exit A3) With the quaintness of a charming Parisian brasserie, the 'nest' features mouthwatering French fare and perfect, unobstructed views of Tokyo Tower (at least until something's built in the lot across the street). In the evening, after a glass of wine, you really could trick yourself into thinking you were dining in the City of Light.

A to Z Cafe
CAFE $$

(off Map p69; http://atozcafe.exblog.jp; 5th fl, 5-8-3 Minami-aoyama; mains ¥500-1500; 🚈Omote-sandō, exit B3) A fortuitous partnership between a local design agency and celebrity artist Yoshitomo Nara, A to Z mixes country-style wooden slatting (there's a freestanding cottage within the cafe) with white-washed industrial piping overhead. Seemingly effortless yet undeniably inviting, this is one of Aoyama's best chill-out spots, and the food is delicious too.

Harajuku Gyoza Rō
GYŌZA **$**

(原宿餃子楼; Map p69; 6-4-2 Jingūmae; gyōza ¥400; ❿Omote-sandō, exit A2) This unassuming dumpling station is tucked behind regal Omote-sandō on a quiet backstreet that begins to bustle at mealtime when hordes of lip-lickers line up for the cheap and tasty grub. Look for the kanji on a glowing red sign if you don't see the dozens of people making the queue first. If you're in a rush, consider the tasty Thai options at **Kaffir Lime** (Map p69; 2nd fl, 6-1-5 Jingūmae; meals around ¥1800; ☺Mon-Sat; ❿) across the alley.

Honoji
SHOKUDŌ **$$**

(ほの字; Map p69; http://harajuku.honoji.com; 4th fl, 5-10-1 Jingūmae; lunch ¥900-1000, dinner ¥4700; ❿Meiji-jingūmae, exit 4) Sharing a building with the likes of Chanel and Bulgari hasn't given Honoji a big head. In fact, this was once an expensive *kaiseki* (Japanese haute cuisine) restaurant that has since been transformed into a more modest place. Enjoy fish and croquettes for lunch and skewers for dinner while taking in the amazing views of the city from the floor-to-ceiling windows. You'll find Honoji on the 4th floor of the GYRE building – there's no English signage, so keep an eye out for the kanji.

Mominoki House
VEGETARIAN **$$**

(モミノキハウス; Map p69; ☎3405-9144; www2.odn.ne.jp/mominoki_house; 2-18-5 Jingūmae; lunch/dinner from ¥800/3200; ☎❿; ❿JR Harajuku, Takeshita exit) Those seeking some relief from too much *tonkatsu* can stop into Mominoki House, which turns out excellent macrobiotic food. In this rambling little warren of a space, corners are filled with jazz and happy plants, and the proprietor will stop and chat about Stevie Wonder, pottery and holistic living.

mother kurkku
CAFE **$$**

(Map p69; www.kurkku.jp; 2-18-15 Jingūmae; mains ¥800-1500; ❿; ❿JR Harajuku, Takeshita exit) Our pick of the kurkku restaurant trifecta, mother kurkku is a sleek space with sky-high ceilings and giant windows. It's popular with the local design crowd who come to scribble in their Moleskines and down glasses of house wine.

Maisen
TONKATSU **$$**

(まい泉; Map p69; ☎3470-0071; 4-8-5 Jingūmae; lunch/dinner ¥1500/2100; ☺11am-10pm; ❿; ❿Omote-sandō, exit A2) Maisen turns out righteous, crisp *tonkatsu* that draws consistent queues. Thankfully, the place is housed in a converted bathhouse, so there's plenty of room for the many souls craving Kagoshima *kurobuta* pork. If you're on the run, pick up a *bentō* at the takeaway window – the *katsu* sandwiches are particularly delicious.

SHINJUKU & WEST TOKYO
新宿

If you can't find anything to your liking on the streets, try the *resutoran-gai* (restaurant 'towns') of the big department stores like **Isetan** (伊勢丹; Map p72; 8th fl, 3-14-1 Shinjuku) or **Takashimaya Times Square** (高島屋タイムズスクエア; Map p72; 12th-14th fl, 5-24-2 Sendagaya). Both places also have huge, sparkly *depachika* (see the box on p108).

Omoide-yokochō
YAKITORI **$**

(思い出横丁; Memory Lane; Map p72; 1 Nishi-shinjuku; skewers from ¥100; ❿Shinjuku-nishiguchi, exit D3) Since the postwar days, smoke has been billowing nightly from the little shacks lining this alley by the train tracks, purveying *yakitori* (skewers of grilled chicken) and cold beers to long-time regulars. Literally translated as 'Memory Lane' (and less politely known as Shoben-yokochō, 'Piss Alley'), Omoide-yokochō may actually be just a memory someday; there's been on-again, off-again talk of razing it to make way for new development. Stop by around 7pm to indulge in a few skewers and pre-emptive nostalgia.

Nakajima
KAISEKI **$$**

(中嶋; Map p72; ☎3356-7962; http://shinjyuku-nakajima.com, in Japanese; 3-32-5 Shinjuku; lunch/dinner from ¥800/12,500; ☺Mon-Sat; ❿Shinjuku-sanchōme, exit A1) The speciality of this warmly lit, immaculate basement restaurant is the *iwashi* (sardines) – simmered in sweet broth with egg, served as sashimi, or delicately fried and laid on a bed of rice. Though there's no English menu, the hostess will explain the options to you in flawless English. Dinners are *kaiseki*, but lunches are fabulously inexpensive. Down the alley next to the Beams building, look for an outside stairwell leading down to this one-Michelin-star shop. Small sign with calligraphic kanji marks the name.

Zauo
SEAFOOD **$$**

(ざうお; Map p72; ☎3343-6622; www.zauo.com; 1st fl, Shinjuku Washington Hotel, 3-2-9 Nishi-shinjuku; meals ¥2500-4500; ❿❿; ❿Shinjuku, South exit) The idea may sound gimmicky in theory

– a boat-shaped restaurant where guests fish from the aquarium below – but in practice, Zauo is a riot for any age. Toss the line in from your table and wait for a tug; when you catch a critter you're met with praise from the waitstaff in the form a chant-y cheer and a clap. If you have a craving for a specific dish, you can order it from the kitchen rather than plucking it out of the 'sea', though, surprisingly, it's about ¥1000 cheaper if you catch it.

Tsunahachi
TEMPURA $$

(つな八; Map p72; ☎3352-1012; www.tunahachi .co.jp; 3-31-8 Shinjuku; meals from ¥1800; ®Shinjuku, East exit) Tsunahachi keeps them coming with its reasonably priced, tasty tempura. Sit at the counter for the pleasure of watching the efficient chefs fry each course of your dinner and place it on your dish.

Armwood Cottage
CAFE $$

(Map p72; ☎5935-8897; www.atticroom.jp/arm; 2nd fl, 1-10-5 Shinjuku; mains ¥700-1200; @; ®Shinjuku-gyoenmae) Bright blue scaffolding holds this inviting wooden structure up over a two-car parking lot near Shinjuku-gyoen. Log beams and comfy furnishings welcome customers with a cosy, chalet-like atmosphere.

WEST OF SHINJUKU (THE CHŪŌ LINE)

Las Meninas
FUSION $$

(2nd fl, Plaza Koenju 3-22-7 Koenji-kita; meals ¥3000; ⊙dinner Tue-Sun; @; ®Koenji, North exit) Though technically a bar, this favourite expat haunt is well worth tracking down for its tasty home-cooked fare, made by the affable owner Johnny. There's a great wine list with a heavy emphasis on Spanish imports.

Pepacafe Forest
THAI $$

(www.peppermintcafe.com; 4-1-5 Inokashira; meals ¥1200; ®Kichijōji, South exit) Brilliant Thai fare served in airy, bistro-style surrounds amid Inokashira's greenery.

IKEBUKURO & NORTHWEST TOKYO
池袋

At lunchtime, check out the *depachika* and restaurant floors in Ikebukuro's **Seibu** (西武) and **Tōbu** (東武) department stores. The eastern side of Ikebukuro Station is crammed with *rāmen* shops and *kaiten-sushi* restaurants.

Lugdunum Bouchon Lyonnais
FRENCH $$

(☎6426-1201; www.lyondelyon.com; 4-3-7 Kagurazaka; lunch/dinner from ¥1850/3850; @;

®Kagurazaka, exit 1) Bringing the proud culinary heritage of Lyon to the backstreets of Kagurazaka, this welcoming outpost of French fare does everything imaginable to transport the senses across continents. The emphasis here is on simple, back-to-nature recipes accompanied by one of the best wine lists in town.

Shin-Ōkubo
KOREAN $$

(新大久保; ®JR Shin-Ōkubo) Tokyo's Korean community thrives in Shin-Ōkubo, just north of Shinjuku. Dozens of joints serve up delicious dishes spiced with chilli and garnished with *kimchi* – a jolt for the palate when compared to the more demure flavours of Japanese cuisine. One recommendation in the neighbourhood is **Kankiku Shokudō** (1-12-3 Ōkubo; meals around ¥1800).

Namco Namjatown
SHOKUDŌ $

(ナムコ・ナンジャタウン; 2nd fl, World Import Mart Bldg 3-1-3 Higashi-ikebukuro; adult/child ¥300/200) Namco Namjatown houses three food 'theme parks', specialising in *gyōza*, desserts and ice cream. Admission only gets you in; you'll have to pay extra for the treats you want to sample.

norari:kurari
CAFE $

(2nd fl, 14-6 Babashitachō; dishes from ¥600; ®Waseda) Join the lounging Waseda students at this homely cafe decorated like a university dorm (ripped couches and amateur art on the walls). Tuck into a 'moffle' (*mochi*-waffle) and wash it down with an espresso.

Due Italian
FUSION $$

(http://dueitalian.media-sp.jp; 4-5-11 Kudan-minami; rāmen ¥1000-1200; ®Ichigaya) Plunk your coin in the slot and choose from a curious array of Italian *rāmen*. The 'golden bowl' is a big hit, but tomato *rāmen* – filled with dozens of cherry tomatoes – is the most intriguing. English is thin on the ground, but there are pictures on the ordering machine.

Fire House
BURGERS $$

(www.firehouse.co.jp; 4-5-10 Hongo; burgers ¥900-2000; ®Hongo-sanchōme) Thick juicy patties, gooey cheese and a freshly baked bun – these are the best burgers in Tokyo, bar none.

AKIHABARA & AROUND
秋葉原

Edokko (江戸っ子寿司; www.edokko.co.jp) has a handful of low-cost sushi bars scattered around Kanda Station. You'll also find several quaint cafes in Jinbocho's secondhand booksellers' district.

Marugo TONKATSU $$
(丸五; ☎3255-6595; 1-8-14 Soto Kanda; meals from ¥1400; ®Jinbocho, exit A6) Marugo's succulent slices of slow-cooked pork and chicken cutlets are served with generous mounds of shredded cabbage, miso soup and pickled vegies. Dine among a cast of regulars who tuck into their meals amid old clocks upstairs or sit side-by-side at the bar on the ground level. Marugo's been around for over 35 years, so you know they're doin' something right.

@Home CAFE $$
(@ほぉ～むカフェ; www.cafe-athome.com; 4th-7th fl, 1-11-4 Soto-kanda; drinks/mains from ¥500/1000; ◙; ®Akihabara, main exit) Although it has the design aesthetic of a McDonald's, @Home is Tokyo's number one 'maid cafe', where costumed hostesses draw ketchup pictures on omelettes across four floors of seating. There's usually one English-speaking maid on duty – check the poster near the elevator to see which level she's on.

UENO 上野
In addition to the following options, you'll find dozens of choices in and around the **Ameya-yokochō** shopping street.

Yanaka Ginza STREET FOOD $
(Map p78; snacks from ¥60; ®Nippori, West exit) Toto, I don't think we're in Tokyo any more. Like a yellow brick road unfurling down the hill, Yanaka Ginza's cluttered cluster of street stalls feels more like a bustling village thoroughfare than a Tokyo backstreet. Amblers will be treated to a variety of cheap eats from *yakitori* skewers to crunchy croquettes. Hunker down on a milk carton with the other locals and wash it all down with a beer.

Sasa-no-Yuki TOFU $$
(笹乃雪; Map p78; ☎3873-1145; www.sasanoyuki.com; 2-15-10 Negishi; meals from ¥1800; ◓Tue-Sun; ◙; ®JR Uguisudani, North exit) Sasa-no-Yuki opened its doors in Edo times, serving beautifully presented *tōfu-ryōri* (multicourse, tofu-based meals). To find it, turn right out the station exit, cross the big intersection at Kototoi-dōri and look for the black-walled restaurant on your left about 200m up, past the pedestrian overpass.

Zakuro PERSIAN $$
(Map p78; ☎5685-5313; 3-14-13 Nishi-Nippori; lunch/dinner from ¥600/1550; ◙; ®Nippori, West exit) Meaning 'pomegranate', Zakuro sits at the top of the hill near Yanaka Ginza and is run by a wonderfully eccentric expat owner, who invites guests to take a seat among the sea of pillows.

ASAKUSA & AROUND 浅草・両国

Kappo Yoshiba SHOKUDŌ $$$
(☎3623-4480; 2-14-5 Yokoami; lunch/dinner around ¥900/7000; ◓Mon-Sat; ®Ryōgoku, West exit) If you're curious about a sumō wrestler's diet, then Yoshiba is the place for you. Set in a converted sumō stable, this large, welcoming joint serves *chanko-nabe* – a key part of a wrestler's weight-gain diet – in addition to a variety of other fare (including fish direct from Tsujiki). Sumō demonstrations often take place on weekday evenings.

Hana no Mae SHOKUDŌ $
(1-3 Ryōgoku; mains ¥800-2000; ®Ryōgoku) If you're visiting Ryōgoku and aren't too keen on chomping down on *chanko*, Hana no Mae is a relaxed, tourist-friendly alternative near the station. Cheap eats – including sushi platters – are on offer, but the setting is the biggest draw. The restaurant is located in an old building that miraculously survived both WWII and the Great Kanto earthquake (though just barely). There's a faux sumō ring inside providing an extra bit of atmosphere.

Daikokuya TEMPURA $$
(大黒家天麩羅; Map p80; 1-38-10 Asakusa; mains ¥1500-3000; ◙; ®Asakusa, exit 1) Near Nakamise-dōri, this is the place to get down-home tempura, an Asakusa speciality. The line out the door usually snakes around the corner at lunchtime, but if it looks unbearably long, try your luck at the branch on the next block. If there's no queue, look for the bench in front of this small, traditional building.

Ef CAFE $
(Map p80; www.gallery-ef.com; 2-19-18 Kaminari-mon; mains ¥900; ◙; ®Asakusa, exit 2) Set in a wobbly wooden house that beat the 1923 earthquake and WWII, this wonderfully unpretentious space serves simple bites and doubles as a small gallery showcasing local artists.

ODAIBA & TOKYO BAY お台場・東京湾
The shopping malls of Odaiba are filled to the brim with secondary branches of some of Tokyo's famous restaurants and restaurant chains.

🍷 Drinking

Bar and club life being what it is, the venue of the moment might be passé come tomorrow morning. The following is a rundown on bars and clubs that have shown some staying power and were going strong at the time of writing.

For a true Japanese drinking experience, round up a few people and check out an *izakaya;* chains like **Tsubohachi** (つぼ八; www.tsubohachi.co.jp) have branches all over Tokyo and huge picture menus to choose what to eat with your *nama-biiru* (draught beer). During the summer, many of the large department stores like Keiō in Shinjuku or Matsuya in Ginza open up their rooftop beer gardens, a treat on hot summer evenings. Join the salarymen after work and hoist a few on these open-air terraces.

For something more high-end, your best bet is to hit up one of the city's high-rise hotels, where you'll find stupendous views over Tokyo. The best ones are in Roppongi and Shinjuku.

If you're looking for karaoke bars (c'mon, don't be shy), see p104.

MARUNOUCHI & GINZA   丸の内・銀座

Ginza is a pricier drinking destination than Roppongi unless you stick to the *yakitori* joints under the JR tracks. There are plenty of upscale *izakaya* and European-style bars to clink glasses in here.

Aux Amis des Vins   BAR

(銀座オザミデヴァン本店; Map p56; www .auxamis.com/desvins; 2-5-6 Ginza; ⊙Mon-Sat; 🚇Ginza itchōme, exits 5 & 8) Both the informal indoor and small outdoor seating area at this wine bar feel welcoming in all seasons. A solid selection of mostly French wines comes by the glass or the bottle. You can also order small plates or full prix-fixe dinners.

300 Bar   BAR

(銀座300バー; Map p56; www.300bar-8chome .com; B1 fl, No 2 Column Bldg 8-3-12 Ginza; 🚇Shinbashi, Ginza exit) One of the few places in Ginza that can truthfully say it offers a bargain, this bar charges ¥300 for every drink or snack (tax not included). There's no cover at this friendly standing spot.

Ginza Lion   BAR

(Map p56; www.ginzalion.jp; 7-9-20 Ginza; 🚇Ginza, exit A4) An institution, the Lion was one of Japan's first beer halls when Yebisu rose to

ℹ CLUBBING IN TOKYO

With a seemingly endless assortment of venues appealing to every whim and fetish, partying in Tokyo is undoubtedly one of the city's highlights. Here are a few websites to get you sorted:

» Clubberia (www.clubberia.com) Although it may sound like something you catch after one too many nights out, Clubberia has a detailed list of clubbing events around town.

» Nonjatta (http://nonjatta.blogspot .com) Detailed guide to all things whisky in Japan.

» iFlyer (www.iflyer.tv) Event listings all over Japan but mainly in Tokyo. Lots of DJ-ed parties and live acts.

» Higher Frequency (www.higher -frequency.com) More live music and club listings.

» Tokyo Dandy (www.tokyodandy .com) Fashion-oriented club kids tend to toss up links to a few good parties around town.

popularity during the early Meiji period. Come for the atmosphere – skip the food.

ROPPONGI   六本木

Roppongi is a separate entity from the rest of Tokyo – it's like an Asian Mardi Gras where *gaijin* and locals mix it up and boozily schmooze until the first trains at dawn. The city's nightlife is most intensely concentrated here. There are loads of shot bars and cheap dives for getting wasted, but plenty of spots offer style as well as stiff drinks.

eleven   NIGHTCLUB

(Map p60; www.go-to-eleven.com; Thesaurus Nishi-azabu, B1-B2 fl, 1-10-11 Nishi-azabu; 🚇Roppongi, exit 2) Notorious party box 'Yellow' is back with a vengeance as 'eleven' and it's still as hot as ever. Dive down to the lower basement and dance the night away to mostly house and techno beats.

New Lex-Edo   NIGHTCLUB

(六本木 ニューレックス エドゥ; Map p60; www.newlex-edo.com; B1 fl, Gotō Bldg 3-13-14 Roppongi; 🚇Roppongi, exit 3) The Lex was one of Roppongi's first discos and recently had a facelift. It's still the place where visiting celebrities – who get in for free – end up, but even noncelebs get three free drinks.

Vanity   NIGHTCLUB

(Map p60; www.vanitylounge.com; 13th fl, 5-5-1 Roppongi; Roppongi, exit 3) Perched high above the chaos, Vanity is a new name in Roppongi, blasting top 40 tunes with amped-up bass tracks. Co-ed gogo dancer teams take to the bar tops, encouraging club-goers to drop their drinks and get down. There are great views of the city when the windows aren't fogged up.

328   NIGHTCLUB

(Map p60; www.3-2-8.jp; B1 fl, Kotsu Anzen Center Bldg 3-24-20 Nishi-azabu; Roppongi, exits 1b & 3) DJs at San-ni-pa (Japanese for the numbers three-two-eight) spin a quality mix, from funk to reggae to R&B. With its refreshing un-Roppongi feel and a cool crowd of Japanese and *gaijin*, 328 is a good place to party until daybreak. Admission includes two drinks. It's on Roppongi-dōri just off Nishi-azabu Crossing.

Muse   NIGHTCLUB

(ミューズ; Map p60; www.muse-web.com; 4-1-1 Nishi-azabu; Roppongi, exits 1b & 3) With a friendly, international crowd, multilevel Muse has something for everyone – packed dance floor, several bar areas, cosy alcoves big enough for two – but also pool tables, darts and karaoke. Women usually don't pay a cover, which includes a drink or two. It's near the Hobson's on the corner of Nishi-azabu Crossing; there's a neon 'Bar' sign marking the entrance.

BuL-Let's   NIGHTCLUB

(ブレッツ; Map p60; www.bul-lets.com; B1 fl, Kasumi Bldg 1-7-11 Nishi-azabu; Roppongi, exit 2) This mellow basement space plays worldwide trance and ambient sounds for barefoot patrons. Beds and sofas furnish this carpeted club, but don't get the wrong idea – it's not all tranquillity and deadbeats.

Agave   BAR

(アガヴェ; Map p60; B1 fl, 7-15-10 Roppongi; Mon-Sat; Roppongi, exit 2) This amiable spot, all dolled up in warm Mexican hues and design, is more about savouring the subtleties of its 400-plus types of tequila rather than tossing back shots of Cuervo. Walking west from Roppongi Crossing, find it on the small alley on the north side of the street.

Mado Lounge   BAR

(マドラウンジ; Map p60; www.ma-do.jp; 52nd fl, Mori Tower Roppongi Hills 6-10-1 Roppongi; Roppongi, exits 1c & 3) On the 52nd floor of Mori Tower, the views are indeed stunning from this very cool lounge bar. To get in, you must first pay admission to the Mori Art Museum and/or Tokyo City View, so it's only worth the additional cover if you're here anyway.

SuperDeluxe   LOUNGE

(スーパー・デラックス; Map p60; www.super-deluxe.com; B1 fl, 3-1-25 Nishi-azabu; Mon-Sat; Roppongi, exits 1b & 3) SuperDeluxe morphs from lounge to gallery to club to performance space from night to night, so admission varies. Check the website for current events to see what's on, but you're guaranteed to run into an interesting mix of creative types from Tokyo and beyond.

EBISU & MEGURO   恵比寿・目黒

Air   NIGHTCLUB

(エアー; off Map p65; www.air-tokyo.com; B1-B2 fl, Hikawa Bldg 2-11 Sarugakuchō; Mon, Thu-Sat; Tōkyū Tōyoko line to Daikanyama, main exit) DJs spin mostly house here, and the crowd tends to be happy and friendly – though not huge on dancing. Keep an eye out for Frames (フレイムス) – the entrance to the basement is inside. Bring your ID.

Tableux Lounge   BAR

(Map p65; www.lounge.tableux.jp; B1 fl, 11-6 Sarugakuchō; Tōkyū Tōyoko line to Daikanyama) If you love jazz, wine and cigars, Tableaux is the perfect spot to mix all three under chandeliers and stuffed bookshelves. Drinks start at ¥1000 and the band from 9.30pm. Oysters and Cohiba cigars are also on offer. It's next door to the popular Tableaux restaurant.

Footnik   BAR

(Map p65; www.footnik; 1-11-2 Ebisu; Ebisu, East exit) Football...er, soccer is always on the big screen at this international joint. The fish and chips are surprisingly delicious.

SHIBUYA & AROUND   渋谷

SHIBUYA   渋谷

Although Shibuya mainly caters to teens and 20-somethings, you'll find an eclectic assortment of pubs and lounges scattered around. Check out **Nonbei-yokochō** – northeast of Shibuya Station near the JR tracks – it's Shibuya's version of Golden Gai, with a gaggle of cramped bars each seating but a handful of people.

Womb   NIGHTCLUB

(ウーム; Map p67; www.womb.co.jp; 2-16 Maruya machō; Shibuya, Hachikō exit) A perennial favourite, 'Oomu' (as pronounced in Japanese) has DJs spinning house, techno and drum 'n' bass, and the four floors get packed on weekends. Picture ID required at the door.

Pink Cow
CAFE

(off Map p67; www.thepinkcow.com; B1 fl, 1-3-18 Shibuya; ⊙Tue-Sun; ℝOmote-sandō, exit B2) With its animal-print decor, rotating display of local artwork and terrific all-you-can-eat buffet every Friday and Saturday, the Pink Cow is a funky, friendly place to hang out. Also host to stitch-and-bitch evenings, writers' salons and indie film screenings, it's a good bet if you seek some artistic stimulation.

Beat Café
BAR

(Map p67; 33-13-3 Udagawachō; ℝShibuya, Hachikō exit) It's all about the music at this shabby bar in the centre of the action. Join an eclectic mix of local and international regulars who swig beers and chat beats under the watchful eyes of taxidermic elk.

Harlem
NIGHTCLUB

(ハーレム; Map p67; www.harlem.co.jp; 2nd-3rd fl, Dr Jeekahn's Bldg 2-4 Maruyamachō; ⊙Tue-Sat; ℝShibuya, Hachikō exit) Bust a few hip-hop moves with Tokyo B-boys and B-girls. Be aware that Harlem maintains a (questionable) policy of not admitting groups of foreign males, so guys, come with a girlfriend.

Ruby Room
NIGHTCLUB

(ルビールーム; Map p67; www.rubyroomtokyo.com; 2nd fl, Kasumi Bldg 2-25-17 Dōgenzaka; ℝShibuya, Hachikō exit) This dark, sparkly cocktail lounge is on a hill behind the Shibuya 109 building. The Ruby Room hosts both DJs and live music, and is a fun place for older kids hanging in Shibuya. If you dine at Sonoma (ソノマ), the restaurant downstairs, you get in for free.

SHIMOKITAZAWA 下北沢

Gardena
BAR

(Flower Bar; ☎6638-8714; flkawashima@yahoo.co.jp; 2-34-6 Kitazawa; ℝShimokitazawa, North exit) Shimokita is known for its inventive bar and cafe concepts, and Gardena is undoubtedly one of the most original. A flower shop by trade, this veritable greenhouse gets the wine flowing in the early evening. Flower-arranging classes are also available.

1Bangai
BAR

(www.shisha-tokyo.com; 3-30-3 Kitazawa; ℝShimokitazawa, North exit) Fragrant puffs of fruity hookah smoke waft through this cramped, cubby-like hang-out. Grab a business card to find the super-secret location of the second branch on a nondescript residential block up the street.

HARAJUKU 原宿

Den Aquaroom
BAR

(デンアクアルーム青山; off Map p69; B1 fl, 5-13-3 Minami-aoyama; ℝOmote-sandō, exit B1) Darting fish within the walls of back-lit, blue aquariums make a visual counterpoint to the bop of jazz basslines.

Le Baron
NIGHTCLUB

(Map p69; www.lebaron.jp; 3-8-40 Minami-aoyama; ⊙Wed-Sun; ℝOmote-sandō, exit A4) A swank import from Paris, Le Baron is Tokyo's new *it* venue for the partying jet set.

SHINJUKU & WEST TOKYO 新宿

Shinjuku is one of Tokyo's best neighbourhoods for a night out on the town, featuring the most diverse array of drinking options. If you're looking for something more high-end, you can try the **New York Bar** (www.tokyo.park.hyatt.com; 52nd fl, Park Hyatt Tokyo, 3-7-1-2 Nishi-shinjuku; ℝTochōmae, exit A4), famously featured in *Lost in Translation*. The views alone are worth the ¥2000 evening cover charge.

TOP CHOICE Golden Gai
NEIGHBOURHOOD

(Map p72; ℝShinjuku, exit B10-13) Golden Gai is a neighbourhood unlike anywhere else in Tokyo. Over 300 bars – each one smaller than the next – are crammed into the miniature backstreets of this seemingly neglected district. Although there are myriad options to choose from, Golden Gai isn't the place for a pub crawl. It's more about choosing a seat for the night, hunkering down and chatting with the other patrons until sunrise. In fact, many of these hovel-like bars have themes – not so much in the decor but more in conversation – you'll find dens dedicated to all stripes of people, from tango fanatics to French film connoisseurs. This is why most places have a seating fee (anywhere from ¥300 to ¥2500) – you're essentially renting real estate for the night, especially since most joints only have six or eight stools. **Araku** (2nd fl, 1-1-9 G2) and **Albatross** (アルバトロス; www.alba-s.com; 2nd fl, 5th Avenue) are among the dozen or so bars that accept foreigners.

Kabuki-chō
NEIGHBOURHOOD

(歌舞伎町; Map p72; www.kabukicho.or.jp; ℝShinjuku, exit B10-13) Tokyo's most notorious red-light district lies east of Seibu

Shinjuku Station. This is one of the world's more imaginative red-light districts, with 'soaplands' (massage parlours), love hotels, pink cabarets ('pink' is the Japanese equivalent of 'blue' in English) and strip shows. Cracking neon lights shine above drunken salarymen and shady-looking *yakuza* in sharkskin suits, while *freeters* (part-time workers) earn some yen passing out tissue-pack advertisements. Kabuki-chō isn't just wall-to-wall sex; you'll also find some great restaurants here, and lounges catering to nonsexual fetishes like cats (we hope) and punk rock.

Ni-chōme   NEIGHBOURHOOD
(歌舞伎町; Map p72; 🚇Shinjuku-sanchōme, exit C8) 'Ni-chōme' is Tokyo's gay neighbourhood, offering over 200 venues from sociable everyone's-welcome bars to sex clubs with strict face control. For information, check out the box on p86.

Zoetrope   BAR
(ゾートロープ; Map p72; http://homepage2 .nifty.com/zoetrope; 3rd fl, Gaia Bldg 7-10-14 Nishi-shinjuku; ⊙Mon-Sat; 🚇Shinjuku-nishiguchi, exit D5) Spend a sociable, relaxed evening at this cosy spot, which features more than 300 kinds of Japanese whisky and screens silent films on the wall.

phonic:hoop   BAR
(Map p72; www.ph-hp.jp; 5-10-1 Shinjuku; 🚇Shinjuku-sanchōme, exit C7) Too-cool-for-school surrounds and effortlessly hip in its casual positioning of potted plants and outmoded pieces of machinery.

IKEBUKURO & NORTHWEST TOKYO   池袋
Nekobukuro   CAFE
(ねこぶくろ; 8th fl, Tōkyū Hands 1-28-10 Higashi-ikebukuro; 🚇Ikebukuro, East exit) For Tokyoites who may not have the time or space to keep their own pets, Nekobukuro provides a venue for short-term cuddling with surrogate cats. Creep up to the 8th floor of the Ikebukuro branch of Tōkyū Hands department store, opposite, to get in on the kitten action.

Sasashū   IZAKAYA
(笹周; 2-2-6 Ikebukuro; ⊙Mon-Sat; 🚇Ikebukuro, exit C5) Sasashū is a highly respected sake specialist maintaining a dignified old facade amid west Ikebukuro's strip joints. If you lack Japanese-language ability, ask for *omakase* (chef's choice).

ASAKUSA & AROUND   浅草・両国
Kamiya Bar   BAR
(神谷バー; Map p80; www.kamiya-bar.com; 1-1-1 Asakusa; ⊙Wed-Mon; 🚇Asakusa, exit C5) Kamiya holds the title of Tokyo's oldest Western-style bar, and it remains perennially popular among locals despite the rather faded atmosphere, which feels somewhat like an outdated hotel lobby.

Popeye   BAR
(www.40beersontap.com; 2-18-7 Ryōgoku; 🚇Ryōgoku, West exit) Ignore the URL, Popeye's has a whopping 70 beers on tap – most were brewed in Japan.

☆ Entertainment
Cinemas
Going to the cinema in Tokyo can be surprisingly expensive. You can save several hundred yen by buying discounted tickets at convenience stores, but most theatres offer steep discounts on admission on the first day of the month (¥1000 rather than ¥1800, for example), and a similar 'ladies' day' discount on Wednesdays. Check the *Japan Times, Metropolis* or the *Tokyo Journal* to see what's playing while you're in town. Imported films are usually subtitled in Japanese, so the sound tends to be in the original language.

National Film Center   CINEMA
(Map p56; www.momat.go.jp/fc.html; 3-7-6 Kyōbashi; admission/film ¥200/500; 🚇Kyōbashi, exit 1) Screens two or three Japanese movies a day at bargain basement prices.

Tōhō Cinemas Roppongi Hills   CINEMA
(TOHOシネマズ六本木ヒルズ; Map p60; www .tohotheater.jp 6-10-2 Roppongi; admission ¥1800; 🚇Roppongi, exit 3) Nine-screen mainstream multiplex with luxurious reclining seats and all-night weekend screenings.

Karaoke
Karaoke is ever popular in the land of its birth, and Tokyoites love belting out a few tunes at their local karaoke bars. There's no shortage of them in Tokyo, and most offer a sizeable selection of songs in English (with even a few in Spanish, French and Chinese). Oh, by the way, it's not 'carry-okie' in this country, so watch your pronunciation if you're asking the way to 'kah-rah-oh-kay'.

The following options are some of the best bets geared towards international singers; or try karaoke mega-chain **Big Echo** (www.clubdam.com), with branches all over the city and an impressive selection of songs.

TOP CHOICE Festa Iikura
KARAOKE

(Map p60; www.festa-iikura.com; 1st-2nd fl, Amerex Bldg 3-5-7 Azabudai; 3hr room & set meal ¥4515-7350; ⊙5pm-5am Mon-Sat; ℝAzabudai) Kill two *tori* with one stone and savour some sushi while singing your heart out. Excellent service and complimentary costume rentals make this one of the best places to perfect your rendition of 'My Sharona' – we know you've been practising...

Lovenet
KARAOKE

(ラブネット; Map p60; www.lovenet-jp.com; 3rd fl, Hotel Ibis 7-14-4 Roppongi; ⊙6pm-5am; ℝRoppongi, exit 4a) If you're going for a more unique, upmarket experience, you can try one of the themed rooms at Lovenet – one even has a hot tub from which you can warble (don't worry, the microphones are waterproof).

Smash Hits
KARAOKE

(スマッシュヒッツ; www.smashhits.jp; B1 fl, M2 Bldg 5-2-26 Hiro-o; ⊙7pm-3am Mon-Sat; ℝHiro-o, exit B2) You're spoilt for choice at Smash Hits, with thousands of international songs to choose from. There's no time limit, and entry includes two drinks.

Pasela
KARAOKE

(Map p60; www.pasela.co.jp; 5-16-3 Roppongi; ℝRoppongi, exit 3) Pasela boasts decor that is a cut above the other yodelling parlours, as well as six floors of karaoke rooms including swanky VIP suites. There's an extensive selection of Western songs, wine and sweets on the menu, and a decent Mexican bar-restaurant in the basement. From 5pm to 7pm it's karaoke happy hour – ¥400, including one drink.

Live Music

Tokyo's home-grown live music scene has turned out some good live acts, often found playing around Shibuya and Ebisu. If you're willing to wander a bit further, tiny bars and clubs in Shimokitazawa and Kichijōji often have live shows featuring local talent as well.

Abbey Road
ROCK

(Map p60; www.abbeyroad.ne.jp; B1 fl, 4-11-5 Roppongi; ⊙Mon-Sat; ℝRoppongi, exits 4a & 7) Abbey Road is, appropriately, the home of the Parrots, who reproduce a variety of Beatles hits with uncanny accuracy. They perform several nights a week – check the website for their schedule and set list. Advance bookings are recommended.

Alfie
JAZZ

(Map p60; http://homepage1.nifty.com/live/alfie; 5th fl, 6-2-35 Roppongi; ℝRoppongi, exit 1) Not to be confused with Alife, this is one of Roppongi's finest jazz venues. Soft amber lighting melts over the lounge singers, and patrons nurse their cocktails.

Billboard Live
ROCK

(Map p60; www.billboard-live.com; 4th fl, Tokyo Midtown 9-7-4 Akasaka; ℝRoppongi, exit 7) This glitzy amphitheatre-like space in Tokyo Midtown plays host to major foreign talent like Steely Dan, the Beach Boys and Arrested Development. Japanese jazz, soul and rock groups also shake the rafters. The service is excellent and the drinks are reasonably priced.

Blue Note Tokyo
JAZZ

(ブルーノート東京; www.bluenote.co.jp; Raika Bldg 6-3-16 Minami-aoyama; ℝOmote-sandō, exit B3) Tokyo's marquee jazz venue in Minami-aoyama allows aficionados the opportunity to listen up close and personal to world-class talent like Chick Corea and Maceo Parker. You can print out an English map from its website. Entry will set you back ¥7000 to ¥10,000.

Blues Alley
LIVE MUSIC

(www.bluesalley.co.jp; B1 fl, 1-3-14 Meguro; ℝMeguro, West exit) A mix of international and local music across a variety of genres. And yes, there's blues music too.

Cavern Club
ROCK

(キャヴァンクラブ; Map p60; www.cavernclub.jp; 1st fl, Saito Bldg 5-3-2 Roppongi; ℝRoppongi, exit 3) Eerily flawless renditions of Beatles covers have to be heard to be believed, sung by four Japanese mop-heads at this club named for the place the originals appeared at in Liverpool. It's best to reserve a table.

Cotton Club
JAZZ

(Map p56; www.cottonclubjapan.co.jp; 2nd fl, Tokia Bldg 2-7-3 Marunouchi; ℝTokyo, Marunouchi South exit) Inspired by New York's Cotton Club, where the likes of Duke Ellington would croon for jazz enthusiasts, this classic Golden Age venue hides among office towers in Marunouchi.

Satin Doll
JAZZ

(Map p60; www.leglant.com/satindoll; 4th fl, 4-11-5 Roppongi; ℝRoppongi, exits 4a & 7) Satin Doll began in Kobe in the mid-1970s, and its Tokyo location continues the tradition of smooth, Euro-style jazz accompanied by tasty French cuisine.

Shinjuku Pit Inn
JAZZ

(新宿ピットイン; Map p72; www.pit-inn.com; B1 fl, Accord Shinjuku Bldg 2-12-4 Shinjuku; ⍟Shinjuku-sanchōme, exit C8) This club has been going strong for around 40 years now. It's an intimate space hosting day and evening performances by mostly Japanese jazz musicians.

TB 139
JAZZ

(スイートベイジル139; Sweet Basil; Map p60; http://stb139.co.jp; 6-7-11 Roppongi; ⍟Mon-Sat; ⍟Roppongi, exit 3) This is a large, comfortable space that draws big-name domestic and international acts, with performances covering the gamut of jazz genres. Call for reservations between 11am and 8pm.

Theatre & Dance

Tokyo is very much the heart of the country's traditional and modern arts scenes. Check with the TIC or the appropriate theatre for performance information. If you're looking for the **Kabuki-za** (歌舞伎座) theatre, you won't find it – it's undergoing a massive renovation, and will likely see the light of day sometime during 2013.

Shinbashi Enbujyō
KABUKI

(Map p56; www.shochiku.co.jp/play/enbujyo; 6-18-2 Ginza; ⍟Shinbashi) While Tokyo's famous Kabuki-za theatre hides under rubble, Shinbashi Enbujyō returns to its roots to act as the city's main venue for kabuki (stylised Japanese theatre). A full performance of traditional kabuki comprises three or four acts (usually from different plays) over an afternoon or an evening (typically 11am to 3.30pm or 4.30pm to 9pm), with long intervals between the acts. If four-plus hours sounds too long, you can usually purchase last-minute tickets for a single act. Since some acts tend to be more popular than others, enquire ahead as to which to catch, and arrive well in advance. See website for details.

Kokuritsu Nō-gakudō
NŌ

(国立能楽堂; National Nō Theatre; off Map p69; ⍟3423-1331; www.ntj.jac.go.jp/nou/index.html; 4-18-1 Sendagaya; ⍟reservations 10am-6pm; ⍟Sendagaya, main exit) The National Nō Theatre stages its own productions (for which written English synopses are provided), but also hosts privately sponsored performances of nō (stylised dance-drama). To get there, exit Sendagaya Station with Shinjuku to your left and follow the road that hugs the railway tracks. The theatre is on the left.

Kanze Nō-gakudō
NŌ

(観世能楽堂; Map p67; ⍟3469-5241; www.kanze .net; 1-16-4 Shōtō; ⍟Shibuya, Hachikō exit) One of the oldest and most highly respected schools of nō in Tokyo, Kanze Nō-gakudō is about a 15-minute walk west from Shibuya Station.

Bunkamura Theatre Cocoon
DANCE

(Bunkamura シアターコクーン; Map p67; ⍟3477-9111; www.bunkamura.co.jp/english; 2-24-1 Dōgenzaka; ⍟Shibuya, exit 3a) This behemoth of an arts centre houses a cinema, theatre, concert hall and art gallery. The Theatre Cocoon hosts innovative, offbeat and traditional musical and theatrical performances; check the website for information on current productions.

Session House
DANCE

(セッションハウス; ⍟3266-0461; 158 Yaraichō; ⍟performances 7pm; ⍟Kagurazaka, exit 1) Dance aficionados consider Session House one of the best traditional, folk and modern dance spaces in the city. The theatre seats only 100 people, ensuring an intimate and memorable performance. Exit right from Kagurazaka Station, make a right into the first narrow alley, and turn left where it dead-ends. Session House will be a few metres on your right.

Kokuritsu Gekijō
PUPPET THEATRE

(国立劇場; National Theatre; ⍟3230-3000; www .ntj.jac.go.jp/english/index.html; 4-1 Hayabusachō; ⍟reservations 10am-6pm; ⍟Nagatachō, exit 4) Performances are staged several times a year here, even though Osaka is the home of *bunraku* (classical puppet theatre). Check the English-language website for a performance schedule.

Honda Theatre
THEATRE

(www.honda-geki.com; 2-10-15 Kitazawa; ⍟Keio line to Shimokitazawa, South exit) The Honda Theatre Group has several theatres in the area – this is the largest. The troupe is one of Tokyo's most highly respected performing groups, and visiting performers are also showcased in the space.

Shinjuku Suehirotei
RAKUGO

(Map p72; www.suehirotei.com; 3-6-12 Shinjuku; noon-4pm & 5-9pm) Popular performances include late-night *rakugō* (*shinya yose*) – a monologue style of storytelling in which the actor uses props and remains seated – which is only performed at five places in Japan. The casual atmosphere means that no advance booking is required and you can come and go as you please.

Takarazuka Theatre THEATRE
(宝塚劇場; Takarazuka Revue; Map p56; ☎5251-2001; http://kageki.hankyu.co.jp/english; 1-1-3 Yūrakuchō; ⊗Hibiya, exits A5 & A13) Kabuki kicked women out of the tradition, but the ladies have taken the ball and run with it at the Takarazuke Gekijō, founded in 1913. The extensively trained, all-female cast puts on an equally grand – if drastically different – show, with women in drag playing the male roles. These musical productions tend towards the soap-operatic and attract a disproportionate percentage of swooning female fans.

Sport
BASEBALL
Baseball is more of an obsession than a sport in Japan, and it's worth getting tickets to a game if only to watch as the rabid fans go wild at each play, sing songs in perfect unison, and slurp lagers served by manic beer girls. Within Tokyo, the Yomiuri Giants and Yakult Swallows are crosstown rivals. Baseball season runs from April through to the end of October. Check the *Japan Times* to see who's playing while you're in town. The cheapest unreserved outfield seats start at ¥1000.

Tokyo Dome SPORTS
(Big Egg; Map p52; ☎5800-9999; 1-3-61 Kōraku; ⊗Suidōbashi, West exit, or Kōrakuen, Kōrakuen exit) Home to Japan's favourite baseball team, the Yomiuri Giants.

Jingū Kyūjo SPORTS
(神宮球場; Jingū Baseball Stadium; Map p69; ☎3404-8999; 13 Kasumigaokamachi; ⊗Gaienmae, North exit) Jingū Baseball Stadium was originally built to host the 1964 Olympics, and today it's where the Yakult Swallows are based.

SUMŌ
Sumō is a fascinating, highly ritualised activity steeped in Shintō tradition. Perhaps sumō's continuing claim on the national imagination lies in its ancient origins and elaborate rites; it's the only traditional Japanese sport that still has enough clout to draw big crowds and dominate primetime TV.

Ryōgoku Kokugikan SPORTS
(両国国技館; Ryōgoku Sumō Stadium; ☎3623-5111; www.sumo.or.jp; 1-3-28 Yokoami; ⊗tournaments Jan, May & Sep; ⊗Ryōgoku, exit A4) Travellers who visit Tokyo in January, May or September should not miss the opportunity to attend a Grand Tournament at Tokyo's Kokugikan. Ringside tickets cost ¥14,300, boxes cost between ¥9200 and ¥11,300 per person, and arena tickets will set you back between ¥2100 and ¥8200. Tickets can be purchased up to a month prior to the tournament, or you can simply turn up on the day (you'll have to arrive very early, say 6am, to snag seats during the last days of a tournament). If you need additional assistance booking tickets, particularly from abroad, check out www.buysumotickets .com; it charges a ¥1200 service fee per ticket purchased.

During the rest of the year, you can swing by the Kokugikan's small **Sumō Museum**, or visit one of the neighbourhood stables and watch the wrestlers practise (see p82).

🔒 Shopping
Eat, sleep, work, shop, lather, rinse, repeat – so goes the everyday life of your average local.

With cramped quarters at home, Tokyoites tend to spend most of their free time in public spaces – shopping is, in essence, a social device that allows friends to catch up and hang out without dropping too much cash (unless you're actually buying things – browsing is commonplace). Thus, items purchased on a fun day of scouring boutiques are often considered souvenirs of the shopping experience rather than must-have treasures to take home.

Once you hop on the bandwagon (trust us, it's inevitable – even for self-professed nonshoppers), you'll quickly find that not everything is wildly overpriced. In fact, there are some great deals to be scouted around town on all sorts of products, from hand-me-down fashion to electronics hot off the conveyor belt.

It's worth checking out www.frma.jp, which features a regularly updated list of **flea markets** around the city. They are definitely worth visiting, as thousands of people gather to sell forgotten treasures found at the back of their closets. It's a great way to strike up a conversation with a local and gain an interesting perspective on the city's bygone trends.

MARUNOUCHI & GINZA 丸の内・銀座
Ginza is Tokyo's original shopping neighbourhood, and although other areas have risen in power, it is still the benchmark to which all of the other boutique-filled districts are compared. Don't miss the grandiose department stores, vestiges of the 1950s and '60s when ceremony and much ado were wrapped up in the shopping experience.

DEPACHIKA DECODED

Department stores, or *depāto*, have long been a staple of Japan's modern consumerism. Popularised in the early boom years, these capitalist bastions offered elegant one-stop shopping for the hurried Tokyoite. Tucked in the basement, the *depachika* (デパ地下) was the department store's supermarket avatar, where locals could tick-off a wide array of items on their grocery list. Today, the *depachika* has evolved into a destination in its own right, boasting a veritable library of domestic and international products.

For the uninitiated, a trip to the vast, bustling *depachika* can be overwhelming. So, we've compiled a short list of picnic-prone items to help you navigate the seemingly endless array of stalls. Oh, and don't forget to pick up disposable chopsticks or *waribashi* (割り箸).

» Cakes and pastries (スイーツ) Be prepared to spend around ¥500 on a slice of cake (ケーキ); don't worry – it's worth it. The best and most popular stalls sell out quickly, especially the 'strawberry shortcake', a Japanese favourite made with whipped cream, sponge cake and fresh strawberries. Keep an eye out for signs touting 'limited time only' confections (期間限定); they usually incorporate seasonal fruits and flavours. Dried ice is included gratis with refrigerated cakes.

» Souvenirs (お土産) *Depachika* are busiest during the perfunctory holiday gift-giving season, but stalls sell meticulously packaged cookies, rice crackers, teas and traditional Japanese desserts all throughout the year. Be on the lookout for rare products from the distant regions within Japan.

» Sashimi (刺身) The best place to snag some of the freshest and most affordable sashimi is at the *depachika* after 6pm, when prices are slashed and the crowds begin to dwindle. Platters of sashimi come with packets of wasabi (Japanese horseradish), but rarely with soy sauce. '解凍' indicates previously frozen, while '天然' indicates fresh (never frozen). Adventurous types can taste-test plates of *fugu* (ふぐ; globefish or pufferfish) – don't worry, they've been sliced by licensed fishmongers.

» Souzai (総菜) Multiple stalls offer *souzai* – side dishes inspired by diverse cuisines (stick to the Japanese preparations). While rubbing elbows with the older folks ordering items for dinner, take note of their selections to get your hands on the tastiest items. 'Delica' (デリカ), short for delicatessen, refers to all Western-style fare.

» Bentō (弁当) Look for artfully crafted *bentō* (boxed meals) with a mix of meat, fish, flavoured rice and seasonal vegetables (stay away from anything fried; they are inevitably soggy). Some booths steam giant vats of traditional sticky rice with vegetables, or *okowa* (おこわ). Pair these up with various *souzai* to create a personalised *bentō*.

Researched and written in collaboration with Marissa Seamans.

Mitsukoshi
DEPARTMENT STORE

(三越; Map p56; www.mitsukoshi.co.jp; 4-6-16 Ginza; 🚇Ginza, exits A7 & A11) One of Ginza's grande dames, Mitsukoshi embodies the essence of the Tokyo department store, and it gleams after a recent renovation. You'll find a variety of exciting treasures tucked inside, such as the 2nd-floor's outpost of Ladurée – the Parisian *macaron* monolith – decked out like a giant pastel Easter egg. A crown of restaurants are lofted on the building's top floors, ensuring you get some heady views of pulsing neon signs. The original Mitsukoshi department store is located north of Ginza's main drag near Mitsukoshimae Station.

Takashimaya
DEPARTMENT STORE

(高島屋; Map p56; www.takashimaya.co.jp; 2-4-1 Nihonbashi; 🚇Nihonbashi) Step into the luxe marble entrance and you'll feel like you've walked onto the set of *Mad Men*. Uniformed docents operate the old-fashioned lifts and bow demurely with a geisha grin as you arrive and depart on each level. You'll find the ultimate pantheon of high-end brands upstairs, and a bustling *depachika* in the basement.

MUJI
ACCESSORIES

(無印良品; Map p56; 2nd-3rd fl, 3-8-3 Marunouchi; 🚇Yūrakuchō, exit A4b) Mujirushi Ryōhin – literally, 'no-name brand' – has taken the world by storm with its signature line of simple lifestyle goods. At the flagship store, things are taken to the next level – customers can tour a full-sized 'MUJI House' fully constructed within the shop. It's on the 1st level to the left of the escalator, and yes, this do-it-yourself abode is for sale (available in in three different sizes). If you happen to have an empty plot of land at home, why not take home the ultimate souvenir – a Japanese house!

Sony Building
ELECTRONICS

(ソニービル; Map p56; www.sonybuilding.jp; 5-3-1 Ginza; ☒Ginza, exit B9) Although essentially a Sony showroom, this place has hands-on displays of Sony's latest gizmos and gadgets – some of which have yet to be released. It's a good place to test-drive Sony's latest digital cameras, laptops and idiosyncratic electronic 'pets'.

Mikimoto
ACCESSORIES

(Map p56; www.mikimoto.co.jp; 2-4-12 Ginza; ☒Ginza, exit B2) No one can touch Mikimoto when it comes to pearls, so it's no surprise that this luxury slugger has joined its fellow name brands and created a memorable boutique facade. This eye-catching endeavour looks like the work of a futuristic spider that has woven trapezoidal crystals into its elaborate, pastel web. Check out the trendy cafe on the 3rd floor (see p93).

Uniqlo
CLOTHING

(ユニクロ; Map p56; www.uniqlo.jp; 5-7-7 Ginza; ☒Ginza, exit A2) Qlothe yourself in brilliant basics at this low-cost chain. There are dozens of branches around the city, but the Ginza location is the flagship behemoth with an entire building devoted to each gender.

Takumi Handicrafts
JAPANESE CRAFTS

(たくみ; Map p56; www.ginza-takumi.co.jp; 8-4-2 Ginza; ☒Shinbashi, Ginza exit) Takumi offers an elegant selection of toys, textiles, ceramics and other traditional folk crafts from around Japan. The shop also provides information detailing the origin and background of pieces you purchase.

Hakuhinkan Toy Park
KIDS

(博品館; Map p56; www.hakuhinkan.co.jp; 8-8-11 Ginza; ☒Shinbashi, Ginza exit) This multilevel toy shop along Chūō-dōri in Ginza is full of distractions and objects of desire, with an 8th-floor theatre and two floors of child-friendly restaurants.

Maruzen
BOOKSHOP

(丸善; Map p56; www.maruzen.co.jp; 1st-4th fl, Oazo Bldg 1-6-4 Marunouchi; ☒Tokyo, Marunouchi North exit) Based in the curvy Oazo Building just across from Tokyo Station's Marunouchi exit, Maruzen boasts a satisfyingly wide selection of English-language books and local guides. Foreign-language material can be found on the 4th floor alongside a cafe and stationery shop.

Matsuya
DEPARTMENT STORE

(松屋; Map p56; www.matsuya.com; 3-6-1 Ginza; ☒Ginza, exits A12 & A13) Also opens its beer garden during the summer and has a good *depachika*.

Matsuzakaya
DEPARTMENT STORE

(松坂屋; Map p56; www.matsuzakaya.co.jp; 6-10-1 Ginza; ☒Ginza, exit A3) How many department stores besides this one can say they've been around for almost 400 years?

ROPPONGI
六本木

Souvenir hunters will be surprised to find a worthy selection of knickknacks clustered on the 3rd floor of **Tokyo Midtown** (東京ミッドタウン; Map p60; www.tokyo-midtown.com; 9-7 Akasaka; ☒Roppongi 1-chome, exit 1).

Kurofune
JAPANESE CRAFTS

(黒船; Map p60; www.kurofuneantiques.com; 7-7-4 Roppongi; ☒Roppongi, exits 4a & 7) Kurofune, run for the past quarter-century by a friendly American collector, carries an awesome treasure-trove of Japanese antiques. Correspondingly impressive amounts of cash are necessary to acquire such items, like painstakingly constructed antique *tansu* (Japanese chests of drawers), but it's a nice place to window-shop.

Japan Sword
JAPANESE CRAFTS

(Map p60; www.japansword.co.jp; 3-8-1 Toranomon; ☒Toranomon, exit 2) Hattori Hanzō would be proud – this highly respected dealer has a beautiful showroom and lots of experience helping foreigners choose the right *katana* for their taste and budget. Priciest are the macabre *tameshi-giri* blades that have been 'used on humans'.

EBISU & MEGURO
恵比寿・目黒

TOP CHOICE MISC
NEIGHBOURHOOD

(Meguro Interior Shops Community; www.misc .co.jp; Meguro-dōri; ☒JR Meguro, West exit) Imagine not just one cool boutique, but an entire district filled with funky furniture shops, car-boot-sale bric-a-brac and hand-me-down treasures. Welcome to MISC – an inviting stretch of pavement linking dozens of interesting storefronts. Favourites include **Moody's** (www.moody-s.net; 4-26-3 Meguro), **Claska** (www.claska.com; 1-3-18 Nakatachō) and **Brunch** (http://brunchone.com; 3-12-7 Meguro). Several quaint cafes lurk about – perfect for your furniture-shopping snack break.

Kamawanu   JAPANESE CRAFTS
(かまわぬ; Map p65; www.kama wanu.co.jp; 23-1 Sarugakuchō; 🚇Ebisu, West exit) In Daikanyama, this shop specialises in beautifully dyed *tenugui*, those ubiquitous Japanese handtowels used for everything from *bentō* carriers to handkerchiefs. Designs come in a spectrum of colours, incorporating traditional abstract patterns and representations of natural elements.

Hara Museum Gift Shop   SOUVENIRS
(www.haramuseum.or.jp; 4-7-25 Kitashinagawa; 🚇JR Shinagawa, Takanawa exit) The cherry on top of a perfect Sunday afternoon, Hara Museum's eclectic gift shop is stocked with a fascinating assortment of unique collectables – perfect for your friends back home. Most of the store's items are created in cooperation with the artist currently exhibiting, which means that everything's original – from the silk-screened T-shirts to curiously ergonomic bric-a-brac.

SHIBUYA & AROUND   渋谷
Before Tokyo's *joshikōsei* (fashionista teens) graduate to Harajuku, they first swamp the shops in Shibuya. For tourists, **Shibuya 109** (www.shibuya109.jp; 2-29-1 Dōgenzaka) isn't so much of a department store as it is a study in rabid, gotta-have-it consumerism.

There are also great shopping spots in **Shimokitazawa** – you'll find everything from used clothes and costumes to quirky and questionable trinkets.

Cïbone   ACCESSORIES
(www.cibone.com; 2-14-6 Jiyūgaoka; 🚇Jiyūgaoka, main exit) Cïbone trumps the competition when it comes to cool designer home furnishings. The kitchenware is sublime, but you might have to stock your pantry with Cup Noodle, as the prices are quite high. Don't miss the fun cafe on the 3rd floor. There's a second location in Aoyama near Gaienmae Station.

Loft   DEPARTMENT STORE
(ロフト; Map p67; www.loft.co.jp; 21-1 Udagawachō; 🚇Shibuya, Hachikō exit) Insert expendable income here. Loft offers an enormous range of goodies, from colourful kitchenware to sleek furnishings – but the best merchandise is the goofier stuff, like wigs, psychedelic stationery and animal-shaped soap.

Shibuya Publishing & Booksellers   BOOKSHOP
(off Map p67; www.shibuyabooks.net; 17-3 Kami yamachō; 🚇Tomigaya) The ultimate neighbourhood bookstore offering those unfindable treasures, this eclectic bookseller also publishes its own volumes, offers editing and design workshops, and holds monthly thematic exhibits.

Shimokita Garage Department   FLEA MARKET
(Toyo Hyakkatten; 2-25-8 Kitazawa) Near the train station, this unconventional space puts an interesting spin on the Tokyo department store by offering up rentable cubbies for local artisans to display and sell their wares, be it anything from jewellery to scarfs. Secondhand clothes are also up for grabs.

Haight & Ashbury   CLOTHING
(2-37-2 Kitazawa) Like the forgotten closet of a chain-smoking drag queen, H&A – not H&M – provides all the props and costumes you'd need to re-enact almost any theatrical number, from the goatherd scene in *The Sound of Music* to the opening act of *Cabaret*.

Also recommended:

Village Vanguard   ACCESSORIES
(2-10-15 Kitazawa) The hipster's answer to Don Quijote. It's crammed just as tight, but the collection is more offbeat and playful. There are a few locations, including one in Jiyūgaoka.

New York Joe Exchange   CLOTHING
(http://newyorkjoeexchange.com; 3-26-4 Kitazawa) Racks and racks of quality hand-me-downs line this converted *sentō*.

HARAJUKU   原宿
Harajuku has reached iconic proportions internationally, having become synonymous with Tokyo street fashion. While established houses of haute couture such as Vuitton, Comme les Garçons and Prada line Omotesandō, **Ura-Hara** (the Harajuku backstreets) is where the small boutiques and studios represent the indie spirit. Wander the alleys snaking off either side of Omotesandō and check out the boutiques and secondhand shops. Further south, Aoyama caters to more sophisticated mainstream (and expensive) tastes.

(Map p69; ®Harajuku, Takeshita exit) Nippon neophytes will chuckle at the name, but the local brigade of Harajuku girls strut down Takeshita-dōri with the utmost seriousness. The human gridlock is bewildering as eager youngsters bounce between boutiques while trying on the latest fashion trends. Crepe stalls, faux hip-hop hagglers and tonnes of camera-clicking tourists come standard.

Cat Street   STREET

(Map p69; ®Meiji-jingūmae) A welcome alternative to Takeshita-dōri, this Omote-sandō backstreet is filled with an ever-changing assortment of designer boutiques, many with names that sound like Swedish swear words. The retail architecture is also quite a spectacle, as this is where smaller brands strike their monuments to consumerism if they couldn't afford to do so on the main drag.

On Sundays   BOOKSHOP

(Map p69; www.watarium.co.jp; 3-7-6 Jingūmae; ®Gaienmae, exit 3) This might just be the coolest store ever. Attached to the Watari-Um (p71), this incredible bookshop and cafe carries an eclectic collection of avant-garde art, retro postcards, Scandi-style office accoutrements and a wide selection of colourful coffee-table books.

Pass the Baton   ACCESSORIES

(Map p69; www.pass-the-baton.com; B2 fl, Omote-sandō Hills 4-12-10 Jingūmae; ®Omote-sandō, exit A3) Representing the new wave in secondhand shopping, Pass the Baton isn't just a shop, it's a museum. Self-described as the 'new recycle', this fascinating space is a veritable treasure trove of once-loved possessions ranging from handmade T-shirts to ornate candelabras. Everything's been meticulously catalogued, so when you purchase your (rather overpriced) item, you'll also inherit its colourful history.

Condomania   ACCESSORIES

(Map p69; www.cowbooks.jp.com; 3-13-14 Minami-aoyama; ®Meiji-jingūmae,exit 4) Inside this tiny shop you'll find more condoms than you can poke a...stick at. For your love-hotel expeditions or footloose friends back home, Condomania's colourful shrine to planned parenthood offers up everything from enigmatic prophylactics like the 'Masturbator's Condom' to the more conservative glow-in-the-dark variety. Rubbers are available for all sizes...

Hysteric Glamour   CLOTHING

(Map p69; www.hystericglamour.jp; 6-23-2 Jingūmae; ®Meiji-jingūmae, exit 4) It's more attitudinal tongue-in-cheek than hysterical or glamorous, but whatever you want to call it, it's fun stuff spiked generously with that trademark Tokyo flavour. There's even a toddler line, the ultimate in designer punk for your diapered rocker.

Kiddyland   KIDS

(キデイランド; Map p69; www.kiddyland.co.jp; 6-14-2 Jingūmae; ®Meiji-jingūmae, exit 4) Just as the name suggests – Kiddyland is *kawaii* (cute) overdose in the heart of Harajuku. Not just for tots, you'll find droves of teenagers playing around on weekends. The flagship store along Omote-sandō-dōri is under construction until the end of 2012 – the address above is for the smaller location on Cat St.

Oriental Bazaar   SOUVENIRS

(オリエンタルバザー; Map p69; 5-9-13 Jingūmae; ⊗closed Wed; ®Omote-sandō, exit 4) Set right along the main thoroughfare and noticeably out of place with its gaudy Disney-meets-temple facade, Oriental Bazaar is a decent spot for one-stop shopping if you're looking to buy a variety of different souvenirs. Though the collection of fans, sake sets, *yukata* and pottery can feel a bit uninspired, the prices are surprisingly low considering the store's location.

Laforet   DEPARTMENT STORE

(ラフォーレ原宿; Map p69; 1-11-6 Jingūmae; ®Meiji-jingūmae, exit 5) Laforet is to Harajuku as 109 is to Shibuya. Gentlemen beware: this is where the colour pink was invented, and ambient giggles confirm the patrons' predilections for anything frilly, furry, fuzzy or cutesy.

Chicago   CLOTHING

(Map p69; www.chicago.co.jp; 6-31-21 Jingūmae; ®Meiji-jingūmae, exit 1) Classic American secondhand never seems to go out of fashion in Tokyo, and Chicago has been the reseller of choice ever since belly shirts were in fashion. Dig through the racks to find everything from tweed coats to Harvard varsity jerseys.

Ragtag   CLOTHING

(Map p69; www.ragtag.jp; 1-7-2 Jingūmae; ®JR Harajuku, Takeshita exit) The clear winner for those who are serious about scouting out secondhand high-end brands. Only clothes in excellent condition are resold.

WE GO CLOTHING
(Map p69; www.wego.jp; 1st & 2nd fl, Iberia Biru 6-5-3 Jingūmae; Ⓜ Meiji-jingūmae, exit 1) A popular chain with a mixed bag of new and vintage clothing. This multistorey outpost features everything from lensless nerd glasses to furry purses.

SHINJUKU & WEST TOKYO 新宿

Music lovers will run wild through the area's backstreets hunting down their favourite hard-to-find tracks in the gaggles of used-CD shops. **Disk Union** (ディスクユニオン; Map p72; http://diskunion.net) is the place to go, with over a dozen shops in Shinjuku alone – check the website for location details.

Photographers should head to Shinjuku as well. The area behind the Keiō department store on the west side of the station is home to the city's largest camera stores, **Yodobashi** (ヨドバシカメラ; Map p72; www.yodobashi.co.jp; 1-11-1 Nishi-shinjuku; Ⓜ Shinjuku, West exit) and **Sakuraya** (さくらや; Map p72; www.sakuraya.co.jp; 1-16-4 Nishi-shinjuku; Ⓜ Shinjuku, West exit). They carry practically everything photography-related that you could possibly want, including computers and electronics, all at quite reasonable prices. Be sure to shop around for the best deals.

Don Quijote DEPARTMENT STORE
(ドンキホーテ; Map p72; www.donki.com; 1-16-5 Kabuki-chō; ⊙ 24hr; Ⓜ Shinjuku, East exit) This fluorescent-lit, trashy cousin of Tōkyū Hands is filled to the gills with weird loot: knock-off designer goods, packaged snacks, gimmicky seasonal rubbish and sex toys. There are branches of 'the donkey' all over Tokyo – the one in Roppongi has a weird horseshoe-shaped roller-coaster track on the roof (a clear zoning violation – it's not in use).

Tōkyū Hands DEPARTMENT STORE
(東急ハンズ; Map p72; Takashimaya Times Square 5-24-2 Sendagaya; Ⓜ Shinjuku, New South exit) Ostensibly a do-it-yourself store, Tōkyū Hands carries a comprehensive collection of everything you didn't know you needed, from blown-glass pens and chainsaws to tofu tongs and party supplies. There are a few branches all over town – browsing through the Takashimaya Times Square location is probably the least maddening.

Nakano Broadway MALL
(http://bwy.jp; 5-52-15 Nakano; Ⓜ Nakano, North exit) A resplendently retro shopping arcade on the outskirts of the city centre, Nakano Broadway is another place of pilgrimage for fanatical *otaku* who scour the land for obscure action figures and collectable comics. **Mandarake** (まんだらけ; 2nd-4th fl, Nakano Broadway), the manga and anime behemoth, has its flagship store here.

Bingoya SOUVENIRS
(備後屋; www.quasar.nu/bingoya; 10-6 Wakamatsuchō; Ⓜ Wakamatsu-Kawada, Kawadachō exit) Regional ceramics, vibrant batik textiles, richly dyed *washi* (handmade paper), handmade glassware and tatami mats fill up several floors of this wonderful handicrafts shop. It's quite off the grid, making it better for buyers than browsers.

IKEBUKURO & NORTHWEST TOKYO 池袋

Tobu DEPARTMENT STORE
(www.tobu-dept.jp; 1-1-25 Nishi-ikebukuro; Ⓜ Ikebukuro) Although most of Tokyo's *depāto* are located in and around Ginza, you'll find a few shopping behemoths in Ikebukuro, including Tobu. In general, the prices here are noticeably lower than in Ginza since the real estate is cheaper. Tobu's worth a visit for its vast basement *depachika*, boasting the cheapest sashimi in town (come at 7pm when prices are halved).

Animate BOOKSHOP
(www.animate.co.jp; 3-2-1 Higashi-ikebukuro; Ⓜ Ikebukuro, East exit) Across from the western street-level entrance to Sunshine City, Animate marks the first stop for girl geeks and manga freaks when they reach Omote Rd.

Japan Traditional Crafts Center JAPANESE CRAFTS
(全国伝統的工芸品センター; www.kougei.or.jp /english/center.html; 1st-3rd fl, Metropolitan Plaza Bldg 1-11-1 Nishi-ikebukuro; Ⓜ Ikebukuro, Metropolitan exit) Demonstrations and temporary exhibitions of handmade crafts, such as weavings, mosaics, ceramics and *washi,* are held on the 3rd floor of this centre. High-quality folk arts and handicrafts are available for purchase on the 1st and 2nd floors.

Blue Parrot BOOKSHOP
(ブルーパロット; www.blueparrottokyo.com; 3rd fl, Obayashi Bldg 2-14-10 Takadanobaba. Ⓜ Takadanobaba, Waseda-dōri exit) One of the best selections of used English-language books in Tokyo.

AKIHABARA & AROUND 秋葉原

'Akihabara' might as well be the Japanese word for electronics. Wander through the area's **Electric Town** (秋葉原電気街), popping in and out of gadget shops in search of the best deals. Bring your passport and ask about tax exemptions if you're planning on dropping some serious cash.

Jinbocho Secondhand
Bookstores
NEIGHBOURHOOD

(⊠Jinbocho, exits A1, A6 or A7) Definitely worth a visit if only to witness the incredible feats of hoarding, Jinbocho's fascinating neighbourhood of over 170 secondhand booksellers stretches far across Yasukuni-dōri. Amid the clutter you'll find everything from antique guidebooks of the Yoshiwara pleasure district to obscure sheet music from your favourite symphony. Start with **Isseido Books** (www.isseido-books.co.jp; 1-7 Kanda-jinbocho) to pick up a copy of the neighbourhood booksellers' map, then wander down the main drag and up into the backstreets north of Yasukuni-dōri for more. Keep an eye out for **Ohya-Shobo** (www.ohya-shobo.com; 1-1 Kanda-jinobcho), purveyor of rare books and *ukiyo-e* prints.

Akihabara Gachapon Kaikan
KIDS

(www.akibagacha.com; MN Bldg 3-15-5 Sotokanda; ⊠Akihabara, West exit) Come with pockets full of 100-yen coins, as this shop houses hundreds of *gachapon* (capsule-vending machines) dispensing manga character toys, keychain trinkets and assembly-required figurines – perfect prepackaged Tokyo souvenirs.

UENO
上野

[TOP CHOICE] **Ameya-yokochō**
MARKET

(アメ横; Ameyoko Arcade; ⊠JR Okachimachi, North exit, or Ueno, Hirokōji exit) This market has a flavour unlike any other in Tokyo, resembling noisy, pungent bazaars elsewhere in Asia. It was famous as a black-market district after WWII, and is still a lively outdoor shopping arcade where bargains abound. There are sneakers, dried squid and shirts emblazoned with Japanese motifs. Look for its big archway sign opposite Ueno Station's south side.

Isetatsu
JAPANESE CRAFTS

(いせ辰; Map p78; www.norenkai.net/shop/isetatsu; 2-18-9 Yanaka; ⊠Yanaka) Tokyo's last maker of *chiyogami* (Edo-style woodblock-printed paper with bright colours; ¥2625), Isetatsu sells vibrant floral prints that have attracted many discerning eyes, including those of van Gogh.

Nippori Fabric Town
NEIGHBOURHOOD

(Map p78; www.netlaputa.ne.jp/~nippori; ⊠JR Nippori, South exit) After exiting the train station, pass the Mos Burger and you'll know you're heading in the right direction to uncover more than 85 storefronts selling all sorts of textiles. The **Tomato** group of shops, in particular – there are five of them, and most of these are located about halfway across the area – have great deals on inexpensive fabric, weird cotton prints and end-of-spool cuts. Leather goods and strange ribbons can be scouted in the neighbourhood too.

ASAKUSA & AROUND
浅草・両国

Kappabashi-dōri
STREET

(かっぱ橋道具街; Map p80; ⊠Tawaramachi, exit 1) Imagine a market full of food, yet none of it is edible...welcome to Kappabashi-dōri! Located on the west side of Asakusa, this kitchenware shopping strip supplies restaurants as well as locals with a variety of items – most notably masses of plastic food. Sadly, we found the faux-noodles and synthetic pizzas to be shockingly expensive – even a teeny sushi key chain will set you back ¥1000.

Yoshitoku
SOUVENIRS

(吉德大光; 1-9-14 Asakusabashi; ⊠Asakusabashi, exit A2) Dollmaker to the emperor, Yoshitoku is the most famous of the many traditional *ningyō* shops lining Edo-dōri. Yoshitoku has been crafting exquisite *ningyō* since 1711 and is now owned by its 11th-generation descendant.

Nakamise-dōri
STREET

(Map p80; www.asakusa-nakamise.jp; ⊠Asakusa, exit 1) This lively pedestrian street leading up to Sensō-ji is chock-a-block with shops selling tourist wares like *geta* (wooden sandals worn with kimonos) and Edo-style toys and trinkets. Keep an eye out for stalls selling *sembei* (savoury rice crackers), *anko* (azuki-bean paste) and freshly made *mochi* (sticky-rice cakes).

Asakusa-bashi Bead Town
NEIGHBOURHOOD

(off Map p80; ⊠JR Asakusabashi) Tokyo has a street for every other fashion accessory, so why not an entire neighbourhood devoted to beadwork! Alight at Asakusabashi Station (one stop west of Akihabara) and lose yourself amid blocks of bead makers, vendors and craftsfolk. Check out www.bel-art.co.jp/shop_shop/map_color.html for a handy map.

Venus Fort   MALL

(ヴィーナスフォート; Map p83; www.venus
fort.co.jp; Palette Town 1 Aomi; 🚇Rinkai line to Tokyo
Teleport) Venus Fort embodies a Japanese
vision of a young woman's shopping paradise, in a building that mimics 17th-century
Venice with ceilings that simulate the sky (it
even shifts from day to night). With around
170 boutiques and restaurants all aimed at
young ladies, this kitschy shopping centre
also boasts the distinction of having Japan's
biggest lavatory (64 stalls).

Decks Tokyo   MALL

(デックス東京ビーチ; Map p83; www.odaiba
-decks.com; 1-6-1 Daiba; 🚇Yurikamome line to
Odaiba Kaihin-kōen) Fashioned after a beachside boardwalk, Decks Tokyo is split into
two sides: the Seaside Mall and Island Mall.
Both house myriad shopping and dining
options, including an over-the-top Hong
Kong–themed floor.

ℹ Information

Dangers & Annoyances

For a megalopolis with over 35,000,000 people,
Tokyo is a surprisingly safe place. See p748 for
information about earthquake safety.

Over-stuffed train cars can be a novelty at
first, but it's best to avoid the city's rail network
during prime commuting hours (around 8am
to 9.30am and 5pm to 8pm) – especially the JR
Chuo and Yamanote lines.

Smokers should note that although it's OK to
smoke in most restaurants, clubs and hotels (at
least at the time of research), each *ku* (ward) has
its own laws regarding smoking outdoors. Seek
out sanctioned smoking areas (easily spotted by
the oversized ashtray bins) to avoid municipal
fines.

Emergency

Ambulance & fire (☎119)
Emergency interpretation (☎5285-8185)
Police (警察; ☎110)
Tokyo English Life Line (☎5774-0992)

Internet Access

It may come as a surprise, but sometimes it can
be rather challenging to track down an internet
hook-up in some of the city's neighbourhoods.
If your accommodation doesn't have a connection, try hitting up a local **manga kissa** (see
the box on p90), or stop by one of the many
FedEx Kinko's (フェデックスキンコーズ; http://
english-fedexkinkos-cojp.presencehost.net/
companyinfo/locations.html) sprinkled around
town. Check the website for a complete list of

locations. As a general rule, there's one near
every major rail station in the city centre.

Marunouchi Cafe (丸の内カフェ; Map p56;
www.marunouchicafe.com; Shin Tokyo Bldg
3-3-1 Marunouchi; ⊙8am-9pm Mon-Fri,11am-
8pm Sat & Sun; 🚇Yūrakuchō, exit 6) offers free
internet access for 30 minutes.

Visit **Freespot** (www.freespot.com/users/
map_e.html) for a list of free wireless hotspots
around the city.

Left Luggage

You'll find luggage lockers at almost every train
station in Tokyo. Prices range from ¥300 to
¥600 per day depending on the size of the locker. In general, you're allowed to store luggage in
these lockers for a maximum of three days.

If you've misplaced your luggage contact the
relevant agency:

Haneda Airport (☎5757-8107)
Narita Airport (☎0476-32-2105,
0476-34-5220)
Toei Transportation Lost & Found
(☎3812-2011)
Tokyo Metro Lost & Found (☎3834-5577)
Tokyo Taxi Center (☎3648-0300)

Media

These days you'll find almost everything online,
including internet-friendly versions of the local
English-language newspapers: **Japan Times**
(www.japantimes.co.jp), **Daily Yomiuri** (www
.yomiuri.co.jp/dy) and **Asahi Shimbun** (www
.asahi.com/english).

It's worth picking up the free weekly *Metropolis*
magazine.

Medical Services

For a comprehensive list of medical services with
English-speaking staff, check out http://japan
.usembassy.gov/e/acs/tacs-tokyodoctors.html.

Keiō University Hospital (慶應義塾大学病院;
www.hosp.med.keio.ac.jp; 35 Shinanomachi;
⊙24hr; 🚇JR Sobu line to Shinanomachi)

St Luke's International Hospital (聖路加国際
病院; Map p56; Seiroka Byōin; www.luke
.or.jp/eng/index.html; 9-1 Akashichō; 🚇Tsukiji,
exit 3)

Money

Although Tokyo is one of the largest and most
modern metropolises in the world, credit cards
and ATMs are less abundant than one might
think (see p746). You'll find 24-hour machines
(with English consoles) at most 7-Elevens – cash
dispensers at banks are sometimes offline during nonbusiness hours. **Citibank** (シティバン
ク; www.citibank.co.jp/en) is the only place that
accepts cards from every country. Check the
website for a list of locations.

Banks are generally open from 9am to 3pm on weekdays. Most post offices also offer convenient foreign-exchange services, and have English-language ATMs.

Post

Japan's postal system has its headquarters near Kasumigaseki Station (1-3-2 Kasumigaseki) – there is no need for tourists to drop by as there are hundreds of post offices scattered around town. The **Azabu post office** (Map p60; 1-6-19 Azabudai; ◎9am-7pm Mon-Fri; ⓇKamiyachō, exit 2) is accustomed to foreigners and can hold post restante mail for 30 days.

Telephone

For information about using coin- and card-friendly public phones, check out p749.

If you're interested in snagging a prepaid SIM card, head to the Roppongi branch of SoftBank. There are native English speakers on staff who can help you get sorted. You must pay in cash. See p749 for information about using mobiles phones in Japan.

Tourist Information

The Japan National Tourism Organization (JNTO) runs two **tourist information centres** (TIC; ◎8am-8pm) on the arrival floors of both terminals at Narita Airport. Staffed by knowledgeable folks who speak English, this centre is a good place to get oriented or to make a hotel booking if you haven't yet figured out where to stay.

In town, you'll find a variety of information centres including a national authority and a municipal body. Also, several *ku* have opened tourist offices offering brochures about the sites nearby.

JNTO Tourist Information Center (日本政府観光局ツーリスト・インフォメーション・センター; TIC; www.jnto.go.jp; 10th fl, Kōtsu Kaikan Bldg 2-10-1 Yūrakuchō; ◎9am-5pm; ⓇYūrakuchō) The main JNTO-operated TIC is just outside Yūrakuchō Station. It has the most comprehensive information on travel in Tokyo and Japan, and is an essential port of call. The Kōtsu Kaikan Building is just opposite the station as you exit to the right.

Tokyo Tourist Information Center (東京観光情報センター; Map p72; www.tourism.metro.tokyo.jp; 1st fl, Tokyo Metropolitan Government Bldg 1 2-8-1 Nishi-shinjuku; ◎9.30am-6.30pm; ⓇTōchōmae, exit A4) Run by the municipal government, this is a handy stop for visitors looking for local info only. The staff aren't too helpful, but there are enough brochures to wallpaper your house. Internet access is available. There's also a branch at the entrance to the Keisei tracks in Ueno Station.

Asakusa Tourist Information Center (浅草文化観光センター; Map p80; 2-18-9 Kaminari-mon, Taitō-ku; ◎9.30am-8pm; ⓇAsakusa, exit

2) Free neighbourhood tours can be arranged here. English-speaking staff work from 10am to 5pm. At the time of research, the centre was under construction – the temporary location is 50m up the street closer to the river.

Websites

Throughout this chapter you'll find Practical Tip boxes showcasing a variety of useful websites. Many of these sites only offer information in Japanese, so we advise you to download a browser with a built-in translator, like Google Chrome. For an interesting look into the city's latest trends and headlines, check out **CNNGo** (www.cnngo.com/tokyo).

ⓘ Getting There & Away

Air

Tokyo has two major airports: **Narita Airport** (www.narita-airport.jp.en) and **Haneda Airport** (www.tokyo-airport-bldg.co.jp/en). Traditionally, most international flights operate through the former while domestic travel is usually funnelled through the latter. However, Haneda opened an international wing in October 2010, offering an assortment of late-night flights to a variety of international destinations. In general, flights to Narita are cheaper, but on the other hand Narita is considerably further from the city centre than Haneda.

Immigration and customs procedures are usually straightforward, but they can be time-consuming. Note that Japanese customs officials are very scrupulous; backpackers arriving from anywhere even remotely considered as a developing country (the Philippines, Thailand etc) can expect some questions and perhaps a thorough search.

It is important to note that there are two distinct terminals at Narita, separated by a five-minute train ride. Be sure to check which terminal your flight departs from, and give yourself plenty of time to get out to Narita. Airport officials recommend leaving four hours before your flight.

Bus

Far less convenient than trains (and far more cramped), long-distance buses are managed by the regional branches of Japan Rail and several private rail companies, including **Keio** (www.keio-bus.com). Check out www.highwaybus.com for discounted rates on major bus routes (you'll need a translating function on your browser), or flip to the page of your desired destination to learn more about travelling there by bus.

Train

The following information pertains to cross-country travel from Tokyo – see p762 for general information about Japan's trains.

TRANSPORT IN TOKYO

Getting around Tokyo may seem daunting at first, but after a couple of days you'll undoubtedly start to appreciate the efficiency and layout of the city's massive transportation network. Check out the following websites to help you get sorted.

» **Hyperdia** (www.hyperdia.com) Plug in your starting point and terminus and let this handy website calculate the cheapest and/or quickest journey between points A and B.

» **Tokyo Transfer Guide** (www.tokyo-subway.net) Similar to Hyperdia.

» **Yahoo** (http://transit.map.yahoo.co.jp) The favoured train schedule website for Tokyoites sans iPhone, this transportation calculator one-ups the other sites with a handy 'last train' display. You'll need a browser with a translator to use this site if you can't read Japanese.

» **Diddlefinger** (www.diddlefinger.com) Excellent resource for those needing to check English names on Japanese maps.

» **Bad Japanese Words** (www.intercom.net/user/logan1/jap.htm) A handy little website with a directory of bad words in Japanese. Perfect for when you miss a train or take the subway in the wrong direction!

JR LINES

There are several *shinkansen* (bullet train) lines that connect Tokyo with the rest of Japan – they are the fastest way to move around the country. The Nozomi trains are the fastest, but cost additional money if you are travelling on a JR Rail Pass.

Tōkaidō line Zips through Central Honshū, stopping in Osaka and Kyoto, then changing its name along the way to the Sanyō line before terminating in Kyūshū.

Tōhoku line Runs northeast through Sendai all the way to Shin-Aomori, from where you can continue on to Hokkaidō.

Akita line Branches off from the Tōhoku line at Morioka, heading to Akita.

Yamagata line Splinters off from the Tōhoku line at Fukushima, bound for Yamagata.

Jōetsu line Northbound for Niigata.

Nakano line Splinters off from the Jōetsu line, bound for Nagano.

All lines pass through Tokyo Station, though you can ride the Tōkaidō line to Shinagawa Station and the Jōetsu or Tōhoku lines to Ueno Station. Shinagawa and Ueno are both on the JR Yamanote line, like Tokyo Station.

There is also a local Tōkaidō service that shadows the bullet train, making regular stops throughout Central Honshū as it trundles towards Nagoya, Kyoto and Osaka. The local Takasaki line follows in the footsteps of the Tōhoku line. For those intent on saving the expense of a night's accommodation, there are also overnight services.

PRIVATE LINES

Tokyo's private train lines generally service the city's sprawling suburbia, but you can also travel on these lines to reach several interesting destinations near the capital that make for a worthwhile day trip or weekend excursion. All private lines depart from a major station along the JR Yamanote line, with the exception of the Tobu Nikkō line.

Tōkyū Tōyoko line Runs south from Shibuya and Naka-meguro stations to Yokohama, passing through Jiyūgaoka.

Tobu Nikkō line Connects Asakusa and Nikkō, and links up to the Tobu Isesaki line.

Odakyū Odawara line Heads west from Shinjuku to Odawara, which services the Hakone region.

Keio Inokashira line Services the popular suburb of Kichijōji from Shibuya Station.

Getting Around

To/From the Airport

TO/FROM NARITA AIRPORT

Narita Airport is 66km from central Tokyo, and is used by most international airlines. Depending on where you're headed, it's generally cheaper and faster to travel into Tokyo by train than by limousine bus. However, rail users will probably need to change trains somewhere, and this can be frustrating on a jetlagged first visit. Bus services provide a hassle-free direct route to a number of Tokyo's top hotels, and you don't have to be a hotel guest to use them. We don't recommend taking a taxi to Narita – it'll set you back around ¥30,000. Figure one to two hours into your itinerary to get to/from Narita.

Narita Express (N'EX; www.jreast.co.jp/e/nex/index.html) Narita Express links the airport to Tokyo Station (¥2940, 53 minutes), Shinjuku Station (¥3110, 1½ hours), Ikebukuro Station (¥3110, one hour and 40 minutes; limited service) and Yokohama Station (¥4180, 1½ hours). N'EX runs approximately half-hourly between 7am and 10pm. Seats are reserved, but can be bought immediately before departure if they are available. The local 'Airport Narita' trains cost ¥1280 and take 1½ hours to or from Tokyo.

Keisei Skyliner (www.keisei.co.jp) The Sky Access express train (¥2400, 45 minutes) zips you to the airport in comfort and style. The Keisei Main Line (¥1000, 1½ hours) is its local (read: turtle speed) counterpart. If you're transferring to/from the JR Yamanote line, access the train from Nippori Station; metro passengers should use Ueno Station.

Limousine Bus (www.limousinebus.co.jp/en) Convenient airport shuttle buses connect Narita to a vast array of major hotels and metro stations (¥3000, 1½ hours to two hours). Service is usually hourly.

Keikyu line Runs between Narita and Haneda airports (¥1560, two hours), though you'll have to transfer to/from the Keisei line at Aoto Station.

Cab-Station Co (www.cab-station.co.jp) Cab-Station Co has recently announced a plan to offer discounted bus rides between Narita and the Asakusa area – the ¥1000 fare is geared towards backpackers.

TO/FROM HANEDA AIRPORT

From the city centre, it takes far less time to reach Haneda Airport than Narita. There's a transfer bus service between the two major airports (¥3000, 1¼ hours). Taxis to the city centre cost around ¥6000.

Tokyo Monorail A direct link to Haneda from Hamamatsuchō Station on the JR Yamanote line (¥470, 25 minutes).

Keikyu line Departs from Shinagawa Station. Alight at Keikyu Haneda Station (¥400, 16 minutes).

Limousine Bus (www.limousinebus.co.jp/en) More of a coach bus than a limousine, this service connects major centres like Shibuya (¥1000), Shinjuku (¥1200) and Tokyo Station (¥900) to the airport.

Bicycle

Bicycles are still a common mode of transport in Tokyo for many locals – especially those who stay out past midnight (when the trains close down). Almost all hotels and hostels can help arrange bicycle rentals for around ¥500 per day. Several accommodation options (especially the ones in Asakusa) have their own wheels to lend out. You can also stop by the water cruise terminal located just across from Asakusa Station and ask about wheels – when they have bikes available they only charge ¥200 for 24 hours of use. Also check out http://cycle-tokyo.cycling.jp for more information.

Tokyo Rent a Bike (Map p65; www.tokyorent abike.com; 8th fl, 3-5-11 Naka-meguro; per day ¥1000) City bike tours also available.

Boat

Often overlooked as a simple tourist attraction, **river buses** (http://suijobus.co.jp) are a convenient and scenic way to move around the eastern part of the city, including Asakusa, Shiodome (through Hama-rikyū-teien) and Odaiba. See the website for details.

Bus

Tokyo's bus system has limited English in comparison to the city's network of trains and subways. Most routes are of limited use to short-stay tourists, with the exception of the uber-convenient Roppongi-to-Shibuya service. You'll find English signs posted at the East exit of Shibuya Station. One-way tickets cost ¥210. For more information about buses, pick up the handy *TOEI BUS Route Guide* brochure at the tourist bureau in Shinjuku.

Car & Motorcycle

It's common knowledge that riding a bike through Tokyo can actually be faster than driving a car, and with the city's chaotic network of curling streets, we do not recommend renting a vehicle to get around – especially since the public transportation network is so efficient and advanced.

Outside the metropolis, highway tolls can also be discouraging for DIY drivers – if you're keen on using a car to explore, consider taking a train away from central Tokyo and renting a car from there.

If you must rent a car from the city centre, your accommodation can help you get sorted; also, all major brands are represented in Tokyo and/or at Narita Airport.

Taxi

Tokyo's trains are so clean and efficient that it's hardly necessary to use a taxi unless you're trying to hoof across town in the late evening. The meter starts at ¥710, which gives you 2km of travel. After that, the meter starts to clock an additional ¥100 for every 350m (and up to ¥100 for every two minutes you sit idly in traffic). Figure around ¥1500 for a ride from Roppongi to Ginza. It's best to have cash on you, as not all taxis take credit cards.

Train

As far as public transportation networks go, no city can touch Tokyo's awesome network of trains and subway lines. It's clean, quick, efficient and convenient, but night owls beware: the system shuts down at around midnight every day, starting up again between 5am and 6am. You might also want to plan your schedule to avoid rush hour, unless you like being crushed among hundreds of hurried businessmen. The quietest block of the day is between 10.30am and 4pm.

Discounted day-pass tickets are available for those who plan on using a lot of public transportation (¥710 to ride the central subway system all day), but in general it's more cost-effective to purchase one ticket at a time.

Beyond the central sphere of JR lines and subways, several private lines service Tokyo's suburban sprawl (including a few noteworthy attractions) – see p116 for details.

JR LINES

Carving out the city's central ring, the JR Yamanote line does a 35km-long loop around the metropolis, taking in most of the important areas. Another useful aboveground JR route is the Chūō line, which cuts across the city centre between Shinjuku and Akihabara. Tickets are transferable on all JR lines.

The major JR stations are massive junctions with thronging crowds and an overwhelming amount of signage (often without enough English translation). Just working out how to buy a ticket can be an exercise in patience for a newcomer. For JR trains, look for the appropriate sign (usually green). You'll find rows of vending machines near the turnstiles. If you don't know the fare to your destination, simply purchase a ¥130 ticket – when you get to your destination you can pay the balance at a fare adjustment machine, found near the ticket gates.

Travellers planning to spend an extended period of time in Tokyo might consider getting a

Suica card – the Suica card can be swiped without being removed from a wallet, and they can be recharged at any JR vending machine. They can be used on most other metropolitan railway lines in addition to JR lines, and can even be used as debit cards at convenience stores and restaurants in the stations. Suica cards require a ¥500 deposit, refundable when you return it to a JR window.

SUBWAY LINES

There are a total of 13 subway lines zigzagging through Tokyo. Four are operated by TOEI; nine belong to Tokyo Metro. Ticket prices on the Tokyo Metro start at ¥160; it's ¥170 to ride the TOEI lines. Tickets are priced according to distance, so if you ride the subway for around eight stops or more, the fare goes up to ¥190 (¥210 for TOEI). As with the JR system, if you're confused about the ticket price to your destination, simply buy the cheapest ticket and do a fare adjustment at your destination.

Transfers between lines are seamless; if you plan to switch between TOEI trains and Tokyo Metro trains, you'll need to purchase a transfer ticket at the start of your journey. Or, even simpler, consider buying a **Pasmo card**, which works in the same way as a Suica card but is sold by the Tokyo Metro system. The Pasmo card can be used on Tokyo Metro, JR and most other metropolitan lines, saving you time, money and confusion when switching between the various systems.

Mt Fuji & Around Tokyo

Why Go?

With ancient sanctuaries, hot springs, mountains and beaches, the region surrounding Tokyo is a natural foil for the dizzying capital. Really, you couldn't design it any better if you tried.

Authentic country ryokan, regional cuisines and cedar-lined trails are all within two hours of central Tokyo. There's history here too, including an old medieval capital and ports that were among the first to open to the West. These are, for better or for worse, well-visited places and you'll find transport and communication to be a comparative breeze.

The Izu-shotō and Ogasawara-shotō, island chains that trickle some 1000km south from Tokyo, are the exception. Though they're technically still part of the capital, you'll find many Tokyoites only vaguely familiar with them – so much the better for those looking for total escape.

Best Places to Eat

» Gorosaya (p147)
» Gyōshintei (p126)
» Matsubara-an (p159)
» Yamaji (p130)
» Ryōzanpaku (p165)

Best Places to Stay

» Hōshi Onsen Chōjūkan (p130)
» Arai Ryokan (p150)
» K's House Itō Onsen (p144)
» Fukuzumirō (p139)
» Tetsuya (p167)

When to Go
Kawaguchi-ko

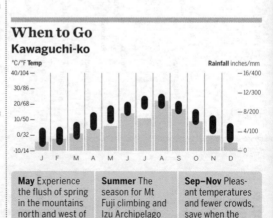

| **May** Experience the flush of spring in the mountains north and west of Tokyo. | **Summer** The season for Mt Fuji climbing and Izu Archipelago island-hopping. | **Sep–Nov** Pleasant temperatures and fewer crowds, save when the autumn leaves blaze red. |

Mt Fuji & Around Tokyo Highlights

1 Watching the sunrise from the summit of majestic **Mt Fuji** (p132), Japan's highest mountain and national symbol

2 Taking in the grandeur of old Edo at the dazzling shrines and temples of **Nikkō** (p122)

3 Dipping into onsen culture in the mountains of **Gunma Prefecture** (Gunmaken; p128)

4 Flip-flopping between sandy beaches and seaside hot springs in the **Izu Peninsula** (p143) and **Izu Archipelago** (p161)

5 Resetting your senses in the Zen temples and sylvan hills of the medieval

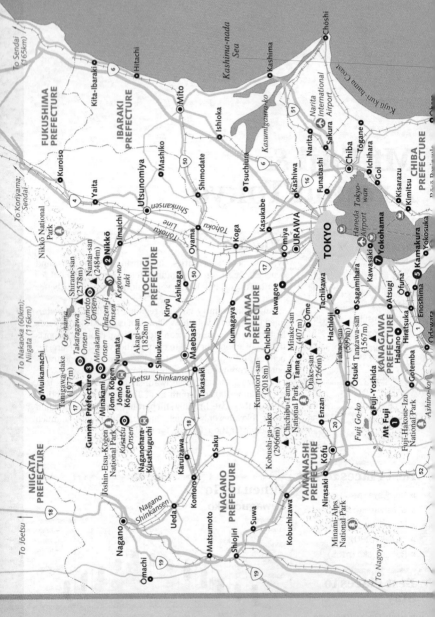

PACIFIC OCEAN

PACIFIC OCEAN

SHIZUOKA
PREFECTURE

Kakegawa

Tōkaidō Line
Tōkaidō Shinkansen

Yaizu

Shizuoka

Shimizu

To Hamamatsu (20km);
Nagoya (120km)

Suruga-wan

Tōi

Dogashima

Matsuzaki

Irozaki

Numazu

Mishima

Fuji-Hakone-Izu
National Park

Shuzen-ji

Atami

Itō

Atagawa

Inatori

Izu Peninsula

Shimoda

Ferries to Shikoku,
Kyūshū, Okinawa

To-shima

Shikine-jima

Nii-jima

Kōzu-shima

Fuji-Hakone-Izu
National Park

O-shima

Sagami-wan

Miura
Peninsula

Miura

Kamogawa

Tateyama

Shirahama

Miyake-jima

Mikura-jima

Izu Archipelago

50 km
30 miles

N

Ferries to
Ogasawara Archipelago
(700km)

Hachijō-jima

Urami-ga-
taki Onsen

Chichi-jima

capital of **Kamakura**
(p156)

6 Getting the
Japanese resort
experience in timeless
Hakone (p138)

7 Sampling
vintage fusion tastes
and sounds in the
cosmopolitan port
city of **Yokohama**
(p151)

8 Truly getting away
from it all (except the
dolphins) on pristine,
subtropical **Chichi-
jima** (p66)

NORTH OF TOKYO

North of Tokyo, the Kantō plain gives way to mountain country. This rugged landscape makes a fine backdrop for the spectacular shrines of Nikkō and the bubbling hot springs of Gunma-ken.

Nikkō 日光

📞 0288 / POP 90,000

Ancient moss clinging to a stone wall, rows of perfectly aligned stone lanterns, vermillion gates and towering cedars: this is only a pathway in Nikkō, a sanctuary that enshrines the glories of the Edo period (1600–1868). Scattered among hilly woodlands, Nikkō is one of Japan's major attractions. If there's any drawback, it's that plenty of other people have discovered it too; peak season (summer and autumn) and weekends can be extremely crowded. Nikkō is certainly possible as a day trip from Tokyo, though spending at least one night allows for an early start before the crowds arrive. Gorgeous natural scenery west of the city merits another night.

History

Nikkō's religious history dates back to the middle of the 8th century, when the Buddhist priest Shōdō Shōnin (735–817) established a hermitage here. For centuries the mountains served as a training ground for Buddhist monks, though the area fell gradually into obscurity. Nikkō became famous when chosen as the site for the mausoleum of Tokugawa Ieyasu, the warlord who took control of Japan and established the shōgunate that ruled for more than 250 years, until the Meiji Restoration ended the feudal era.

Ieyasu was laid to rest among Nikkō's towering cedars in 1617, and in 1634 his grandson, Tokugawa Iemitsu, commenced work on the shrine that can be seen today. The original shrine, Tōshō-gū, was completely rebuilt using an army of some 15,000 artisans from across Japan, who took two years to complete the shrine and mausoleum. Whatever one's opinion of Ieyasu, the grandeur at Nikkō is awesome, a display of wealth and power by a family that for two and a half centuries was Japan's supreme arbiter of power.

⊙ Sights

The World Heritage Sites around Tōshō-gū are Nikkō's centrepiece. A ¥1000 'combination ticket', valid for two days and available at booths in the area, covers entry to Rinnō-ji, Tōshō-gū and Futarasan-jinja. The Nemuri-Neko (Sleeping Cat) and Ieyasu's tomb in Tōshō-gū require a separate admission ticket (¥520).

Most sites are open from 8am to 4.30pm (until 3.30pm from November to March). To avoid the hordes, visit early on a weekday. Be sure to pick up a map, as finding the English signposts to the shrines and temples can be tricky.

Shin-kyō   HISTORICAL SITE
(神橋; crossing fee ¥300) This much-photographed red bridge over the Daiya-gawa is located at the sacred spot where Shōdō Shōnin was said to have been carried across the river on the backs of two giant serpents. It's a reconstruction of the 17th-century original.

Rinnō-ji   TEMPLE
(輪王寺) This Tendai-sect temple was founded 1200 years ago by Shōdō Shōnin. The **Sambutsu-dō** (三仏堂; Three-Buddha Hall), constructed from some 360m of zelkova trees, is the main attraction. It's undergoing construction until 2020, though it is still possible to enter. Inside are three 8m gilded wooden Buddha statues. The central image is Amida Nyorai (one of the primal deities in the Mahayana Buddhist canon), flanked by Senjū (1000-armed Kannon, deity of mercy and compassion) and Batō (a horse-headed Kannon), whose special domain is the animal kingdom.

Rinnō-ji's **Hōmotsu-den** (宝物殿; Treasure Hall; admission ¥300) houses some 6000 treasures associated with the temple; the separate admission ticket includes entrance to the **Shōyō-en** (逍遥園) strolling garden.

Tōshō-gū   SHRINE
(東照宮) The entrance to the main shrine is through the torii (shrine gate) at **Omotemon** (表門), a gate protected on either side by Deva kings.

Just inside are the **Sanjinko** (三神庫; Three Sacred Storehouses). On the upper storey of the last storehouse are imaginative relief carvings of elephants by an artist who famously had never seen the real thing. To the left of the entrance is **Shinkyūsha** (神厩舎; Sacred Stable), adorned with allegorical relief carvings of monkeys. The famous 'hear no evil, see no evil, speak no evil' monkeys demonstrate three principles of Tendai Buddhism.

Just beyond the stable is a granite font at which, in accordance with Shintō practice, worshippers cleanse themselves by washing their hands and rinsing their mouths. Next to the gate is a sacred library containing 7000 Buddhist scrolls and books; it's closed to the public.

Pass through another torii, climb another flight of stairs, and on the left and right are a drum tower and a belfry. To the left of the drum tower is **Honji-dō** (本地堂). This hall is best known for the painting on its ceiling of the Nakiryū (Crying Dragon). Monks demonstrate the acoustical properties of this hall by clapping two sticks together. The dragon 'roars' (a bit of a stretch) when the sticks are clapped beneath the dragon's mouth, but not elsewhere.

Next comes **Yōmei-mon** (陽明門; Sunset Gate), dazzlingly decorated with glimmering gold leaf and intricate, coloured carvings and paintings of flowers, dancing girls, mythical beasts and Chinese sages. Worrying that its perfection might arouse envy in the gods, those responsible for its construction had the final supporting pillar placed upside down as a deliberate error. Although the style is more Chinese than Japanese and some critics deride it as gaudy, it's a grand spectacle.

To the left of Yōmei-mon is **Jin-yōsha** (神輿舎), the storage for the *mikoshi* (portable shrines) used during festivals.

Tōshō-gū's **Honden** (本殿; Main Hall) and **Haiden** (拝殿; Hall of Worship) are across the enclosure. Inside – open only to *daimyō* (domain lords) during the Edo period – are paintings of the 36 immortal poets of Kyoto, and a ceiling-painting pattern from the Momoyama period; note the 100 dragons, each different. *Fusuma* (sliding door) paintings depict a *kirin* (a mythical beast that's part giraffe and part dragon). It's said that it will appear only when the world is at peace.

Through Yōmei-mon and to the right is **Nemuri-Neko** (眠り猫), a small wooden sculpture of a sleeping cat that's famous throughout Japan for its life-like appearance (though admittedly the attraction is lost on some visitors). From here, **Sakashita-mon** (坂下門) opens onto an uphill path through towering cedars to the appropriately solemn **tomb of Ieyasu** (奥社（徳川家康の墓）).

Futarasan-jinja
SHRINE

(二荒山神社) Shōdō Shōnin founded this shrine; the current building dates from 1619, making it Nikkō's oldest. It's the protector shrine of Nikkō itself, dedicated to the nearby mountain, Nantai-san (2484m), the mountain's consort, Nyotai-san, and their mountainous progeny, Tarō. There are other shrine branches on Nantai-san and by Chūzenji-ko (p127).

Taiyūin-byō
TEMPLE

(大猷院廟) Enshrining Ieyasu's grandson Iemitsu (1604–51) is Taiyūin-byō. Though it houses many of the same elements as Tōshō-gū (storehouses, drum tower, Chinese-style gates etc), its smaller, more intimate scale and setting in a cryptomeria forest make it very appealing.

Among Taiyūin-byō's many structures, look for dozens of lanterns donated by *daimyō*, and the gate Niō-mon, whose guardian deities have a hand up (to welcome those with pure hearts) and a hand down (to suppress those with impure hearts). Inside the main hall, 140 dragons painted on the ceiling are said to carry prayers to the heavens; those holding pearls are on their way up, and those without are returning to gather more prayers.

Takinō-jinja
SHRINE

(滝尾神社) In between Futarasan-jinja and Taiyūin-byō a stone-paved path leads to Takinō-jinja (25 minutes), less grand than the main attractions and thus delightfully less crowded. The stone torii gate, called **Unmeshi-no-torii**, dates back to Iemitsu's time (1696). Before entering, it's customary to try your luck tossing three stones through the small hole near the top. Head back down to the fork in the path and take the trail to the left to pass a handful of small temples and the tomb of Shōdō Shōnin before coming out behind Rinnō-ji.

Kanman-ga-Fuchi Abyss
PARK

(憾満ガ淵) Another quiet alternative is the 20-minute walk to Kanman-ga-Fuchi Abyss, a collection of *jizō* statues (the small stone statues of the Buddhist protector of travellers and children) set along a wooded path. It's said that if you try to count them there and back you'll end up with a different number, hence the nickname 'Bake-jizō' (ghost *jizō*). Take a left after passing the Shin-kyo bridge and follow the river for about 800m, crossing another bridge en route.

FREE Nikkō Woodcarving Center
MUSEUM

(日光木彫りの里 工芸センター; ☎53-0070; fax 53-0310; 2848 Tokorono; ☺9am-5pm) You've seen Nikkō-bori, the traditional local woodcraft, all over temples and gift shops. Here

Nikkō

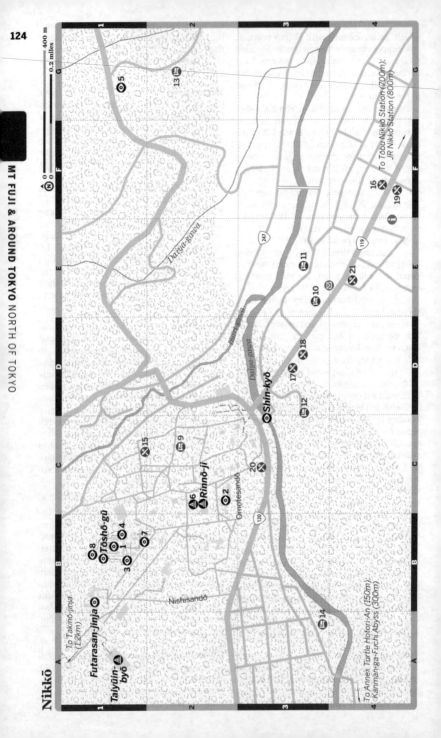

0 0
0.2 miles
400 m

To Takino-jinja
(1.2km)

Futarasan-jinja

Taiyūin-
byō

To Takino-jinja
(1.2km)

Tōshō-gū

Rinnō-ji

Omotesandō

Nishisandō

Shin-kyō

Daiya-gawa

Daiya-gawa

To Tobu Nikkō Station (700m);
JR Nikkō Station (800m)

To Annex Turtle Hotori-An (150m);
Kanman-ga-Fuchi Abyss (300m)

Nikkō

◎ Top Sights

◎ Sights

◎ Sleeping

◎ Eating

you can try your hand at making your own, daily from 9am to 11am and 1pm to 3pm (from ¥900). Groups of five and over should reserve in advance. There's also a shop and on the 2nd floor a collection of museum-grade showpieces.

✪ Festivals & Events

Yayoi Matsuri　　　　　　　　　　MIKOSHI
Procession of *mikoshi* held at Futarasan-jinja on 16 and 17 April.

Tōshō-gū Grand Festival　　　HISTORICAL
Nikkō's most important annual festival is held on 17 and 18 May and features horseback archery on the first day and a 1000-strong costumed re-enactment of the delivery of Ieyasu's remains to Nikkō on the second.

Tōshō-gū Autumn Festival　　HISTORICAL
Autumnal repeat on 16 and 17 October of the May festival.

🛏 Sleeping

Nikkō Kanaya Hotel　　　　　HOTEL $$$
(日光金谷ホテル; ☎54-0001; www.kanayahotel.co.jp; fax 53-2487; 1300 Kamihatsu-ishimachi; tw from ¥17,325; @) This grand lady from 1893 wears her history like a well-loved, if not slightly worn, dress. The best rooms have excellent vistas, spacious quarters and private bathrooms; the cheaper rooms by contrast are rather ordinary. The lobby bar, open to visitors as well, is deliciously dark and amenable to drinking whisky. Rates do not include meals and rise steeply in peak seasons.

Jōhsyū-ya Ryokan　　　　　　RYOKAN $
(上州屋旅館; ☎54-0155; www.johsyu-ya.co.jp; fax 53-2000; 911 Nakahatsu-ishimachi; r per person ¥4500) This very tidy inn on the main road beside the post office is just good honest value. There are no private facilities and there's little English spoken, but there's a hot-spring bath. Breakfast/dinner from ¥800/2000.

Nikkō Park Lodge　　　　GUESTHOUSE $$
(日光パークロッジ; ☎53-1201; www.nikkoparklodge.com; fax 53-4332; 28285 Tokorono; dm/d from ¥2990/7980; ⊜@🛜) In the wooded hills north of town, this cute, well-kept guesthouse has Western-style rooms and English-speaking staff. Take advantage of the afternoon pickup service. Breakfast/dinner from ¥395/650; vegan dinners (¥1800) available on request.

Turtle Inn Nikkō　　　　　　　INN $$
(タートル・イン・日光; ☎53-3168; www.turtle-nikko.com; fax 53-3883; 2-16 Takumi-chō; s/tw without bathroom ¥4950/9300, with bathroom ¥5750/10,900; ⊜@🛜) This long-time favourite is still in the running with recently touched-up rooms, both Japanese- and Western-style. Take a bus to Sōgō-kaikan-mae, backtrack about 50m, turn right along the river and walk for about five minutes; you'll see the turtle sign on the left. Breakfast/dinner is ¥1050/2100.

Annex Turtle Hotori-An　　　　INN $$
(☎53-3663; www.turtle-nikko.com; fax 53-3883; 8-28 Takumi-chō; s/tw ¥6650/12,700; ⊜@🛜) The Turtle Inn's newer annexe is more modern, with Japanese- and Western-style rooms plus river views from the onsen bath. Breakfast/dinner is ¥1050/2100.

NIKKO INN

Located just 30 minutes from Nikkō in positively pastoral Shimogoshiro, **Nikkō Inn** (☎0288-27-0008; www.nikko-inn.jp; 333 Koshiro; r per person ¥4500; ⊜) offers an antidote to the concrete boxes of modern Japan. Creative unit Nikko Design reworked three old-style Japanese homes into guest cottages that sleep four to seven people. Each vintage wooden structure features tatami sleeping rooms and traditional verandahs, plus modern kitchen and bathroom facilities. Beyond is little more than rice fields, a village of 1000 people and the mountains of Nikkō. Shimogoshiro is on the Tōbu line from Asakusa (2¼ hours; ¥1160), four stops before Nikkō.

Rindō-no-Ie   MINSHUKU **$**
(りんどうの家; ☎/fax 53-0131; www3.ocn
.ne.jp/~garrr/Rindou.html; 1462 Tokorono; r
per person with shared bathroom from ¥3500;
⊜@☎) Small but thoughtfully arranged
tatami rooms; tasty meals and pick-up
service. Breakfast/dinner is ¥700/1800. It's
across the river, a 15-minute walk northwest of the train station; see the website
for a map.

Hotel Seikōen   HOTEL **$$**
(ホテル清晃苑; ☎53-5555; www.hotel-seikoen
.com; fax 53-5554; 2350 Sannai; r per person with
2 meals from ¥10,650; ⊜@☎) A little dated
but conveniently located near the main
sites, with neat (mostly Japanese-style)
rooms and onsen baths.

Nikkō Daiyagawa Youth Hostel   HOSTEL **$**
(日光大谷川ユースホステル; ☎/fax 54-1974;
www5.ocn.ne.jp/~daiyayh; 1075 Nakahatsu-
ishimachi; dm ¥2730; ⊜) A little shabby after
all these years, but still the cheapest bed
in town. It's a four-minute walk from the
Nikkō Shishō-mae bus stop, behind the
post office and overlooking the river.

🍴 Eating & Drinking

A local speciality is *yuba* (the skin that
forms when making tofu) cut into strips;
better than it sounds, it's a staple of *shōjin
ryōri* (Buddhist vegetarian cuisine). You'll
see it all over town, in everything from
noodles (*yuba soba*) to fried bean buns
(*age yuba manju*). Nikkō's award-winning
local beer is available at many shops and
restaurants.

TOP CHOICE Gyōshintei   KAISEKI **$$$**
(尭心亭; ☎53-3751; www.meiji-yakata.com/gyou
shin, in Japanese; 2339-1 Sannai; set courses
¥3150-8400; ⊙lunch & dinner Fri-Wed; 🚗📶)
Splurge here on deluxe spreads of *shōjin
ryōri*, featuring local bean curd and veg-

etables served half a dozen delectable ways.
The elegant tatami dining room overlooks a
carefully tended garden. It's directly north
of the Shin-kyō bridge (about 250m) and
there's a three-peaked emblem on the door
curtain.

Yuba Yūzen   KAISEKI **$$**
(日光ゆば遊膳; 1-22 Yasukawachō; sets ¥2700-
3200; ⊙lunch Thu-Tue) This *yuba* speciality
house serves it sashimi-style, with tofu and
soy milk, and with the addition of a variety
of seasonal side dishes. There's no English
menu, but there are only two choices for
sets: ¥2700 if you're hungry and ¥3200 if
you're really hungry. Look for the two-storey
tan building across from the first left turn
after Shin-kyō.

Hippari Dako   YAKITORI **$**
(ひっぱり凧; 1011 Kamihatsu-ishimachi; meals
¥500-850; ⊙lunch & dinner; 🚗📶) This three-
table shop is an institution among foreign
travellers, as years of business cards tacked
to the walls testify. It serves filling sets, in-
cluding *tsukune* (chicken meatballs) and
yaki udon (fried noodles). It's on Rte 119 and
has an English sign.

Shokudō Suzuki   SHOKUDŌ **$$**
(食堂すゞき; 581-2 Gokō-machi; mains from
¥1000; ⊙lunch & dinner Thu-Tue) This tiny joint
is strewn with wine bottles, comic books,
and autographs from celebrity diners.
Equally eclectic is the menu of pasta (get the
tarioriini; it's fresh tagliolini) and inventive
yuba dishes. Look for the beige building
with the giant pasta picture; there are pictures on the menu too.

Yuzawaya   CAFE **$**
(湯沢屋; 946 Kamihatsu-ishimachi; tea sets from
¥450; ⊙11am-5pm) A 200-year-old teahouse
specialising in *manju* (bean-jam buns)
and other traditional sweets; look for the
green and white banners.

Meiji-no-Yakata INTERNATIONAL $$

(明治の館; 2339-1 Sannai; mains from ¥1785; ⊙lunch & dinner; 🖬) Upscale meat and veg in a classic western-style mansion, next to Gyōshintei.

Kiko KOREAN $

(希光; 1007 Kamihatsu-ishimachi; mains from ¥800; ⊙lunch & dinner; 🖉🖬) Korean home cooking, a few doors downhill from Hippari Dako.

Hi no Kuruma OKONOMIYAKI $

(ひの車; 597-2 Gokō-machi; mains ¥500-1500; ⊙lunch & dinner Thu-Tue; 🖬) A popular choice for cheap and easy grill-your-own meals. Look for the small parking lot and red-black-and-white Japanese sign.

ⓘ Information

Kyōdo Center Tourist Information Office (📋54-2496; www.nikko-jp.org; internet access per 15min ¥50; ⊙9am-5pm) Has English speakers and maps for sightseeing and hiking. There are several computers available for internet use.

Post office There's one on the main road, three blocks past the Kyōdo Center, and another across the street from Tōbu Nikkō Station on Rte 119; both have international ATMs.

Tōbu Nikkō Station Tourist Information Desk (📋53-4511; ⊙8.30am-5pm)

Tochigi Volunteer Interpreters & Guides Association (NikkoTVIGA@hotmail.co.jp) Offers free guided tours.

ⓘ Getting There & Away

Nikkō is best reached from Tokyo via the Tōbu Nikkō line from Asakusa Station. You can usually get last-minute seats on the hourly reserved *tokkyū* (limited-express) trains (¥2620, 1¾ hours). *Kaisoku* (rapid) trains (¥1320, 2½ hours, hourly from 6.20am to 4.30pm) require no reservation. For either train, you may have to change at Shimo-imaichi. Be sure to ride in the last two cars to reach Nikkō (some cars may separate at an intermediate stop).

JR Pass holders can take the Tohoku *shinkansen* from Tokyo to Utsunomiya (¥4800, 54 minutes) and change there for an ordinary train to Nikkō (¥740, 45 minutes).

Both JR Nikkō Station (designed by Frank Lloyd Wright) and the nearby Tōbu Nikkō Station lie southeast of the shrine area within a block of Nikkō's main road (Rte 119, the old Nikkō-kaidō). Follow this road uphill for 30 minutes to the shrine area, past restaurants, souvenir shops and the main tourist information centre, or take a bus to the Shin-kyō bus stop (¥190). Bus stops are announced in English. Buses leave from both JR and Tōbu Nikkō station; buses bound for both Chūzen-ji Onsen and Yumoto Onsen stop at Shin-kyō and other stops around the World Heritage Sites.

Train/Bus Passes

Tōbu Railway (www.tobu.co.jp/foreign) Offers two passes covering rail transport from Asakusa to Nikkō (though not the *tokkyū* surcharge, from ¥1040) and unlimited hop-on-hop-off bus services around Nikkō. Purchase these passes at the **Tōbu Sightseeing Service Center** (⊙7.45am-5pm) in Asakusa Station.

All Nikko Pass (adult/child ¥4400/2210) Valid for four days and includes buses to Chūzenji Onsen and Yumoto Onsen.

World Heritage Pass (adult/child ¥3600/1700) Valid for two days and includes buses to the World Heritage Sites, plus admission to Tōshō-gū, Rinnō-ji and Futarasan-jinja.

Tōbu Nikkō Bus Free Pass

If you've already got your rail ticket, two-day bus-only passes allow unlimited rides between Nikkō and Chūzenji Onsen (adult/child ¥2000/1000) or Yumoto Onsen (adult/child ¥3000/1500), including the World Heritage Site area. The **Sekai-isan-meguri** (World Heritage Bus Pass; adult/child ¥500/250) covers the area between the stations and the shrine precincts. Buy these at Tōbu Nikkō Station.

Around Nikkō 日光周辺

Nikkō is part of Nikkō National Park, 1400 sq km sprawling over Fukushima, Tochigi, Gunma and Niigata Prefectures. This mountainous region features extinct volcanoes, lakes, waterfalls and marshlands. There are good hiking opportunities and some remote hot-spring resorts.

CHŪZEN-JI ONSEN 中禅寺温泉

This highland area 11.5km west of Nikkō offers some natural seclusion and striking views of Nantai-san from Chūzen-ji's lake, Chuzenji-ko. The big-ticket attraction is the billowing, 97m-high **Kegon-no-taki** (華厳ノ滝; Kegon Falls; 2479-2 Chūgushi; adult/child ¥530/320; ⊙8am-5pm). Take the elevator down to a platform to observe the full force of the plunging water. **Futarasan-jinja** (二荒山神社; 2484 Chūgushi; ⊙8am-4.30pm) complements the shrines at Tōshō-gū and is the starting point for pilgrimages up Nantai-san. The shrine is about 1km west of the falls, along the lake's north shore. The eponymous temple **Chūzen-ji Tachiki-kannon** (中禅寺立木観音; 2578 Chūgushi; adult/child ¥500/200; ⊙8am-4.30pm), located on the lake's eastern shore, was founded in the 8th century and houses a 6m-tall Kannon statue from that time.

Beyond the temple, the former summer residence of Italy's ambassadors (from 1928 to 1997), now the **Italian Embassy Villa Memorial Park** (イタリアン大使館別荘記念公園; 2482 Chūgūshi; admission ¥100; ⏰9am-4pm Tue-Sun), has a pleasant sun terrace with excellent lake views.

Chūzenji-ko has the usual flotilla of sightseeing boats at the dock (prices vary). The lake (161m deep) is a fabulous shade of deep blue in good weather.

🛏 Sleeping

Chūzenji Pension   INN $$
(中禅寺ペンション; ☎0288-55-0888; chuzen ji-pension.com, in Japanese; fax 55-0721; 2482 Chūgūshi; r per person with/without 2 meals from ¥8925/5250; ⏰@) This pink hostelry set back from the lake's eastern shore has nine mostly Western-style rooms that feel a bit like grandma's house. There's a cosy fireplace and two onsen baths; bike rental (per day ¥3000) is available.

Nikkō Lakeside Hotel   HOTEL $$$
(日光レークサイドホテル; ☎0288-55-0321; www.tobuhotel.co.jp/nikkolake, in Japanese; fax 55-0771; 2482 Chūgūshi; s/tw with 2 meals from ¥17,650/27,300; ☎) The rooms at this Meiji-era hotel (1894) are a little worn, but the classy dining room still carries an old-time resort feel. The wooden bathhouse with milky onsen water is also open to day trippers (admission ¥1000).

ℹ Getting There & Away

Buses run from Tōbu Nikkō Station to Chūzen-ji Onsen (¥1100, 45 minutes) or use the economical Tōbu Nikkō Bus Free Pass (see p127).

YUMOTO ONSEN   湯元温泉

From Chūzen-ji Onsen, you might continue on to the quieter hot-springs resort of Yumoto Onsen by bus (¥840, 30 minutes) or reach it by a rewarding three-hour hike on the **Senjōgahara Shizen-kenkyu-rō** (戦場ヶ原自然研究路; Senjōgahara Plain Nature Trail).

For the latter option, take a Yumoto-bound bus and get off at Ryūzu-no-taki (竜頭ノ滝; ¥410, 20 minutes), a waterfall that marks the start of the trail. The hike follows the Yu-gawa across the picturesque marshland of Senjōgahara (partly on wooden plank paths), alongside the 75m-high falls of Yu-daki (湯滝) to the lake Yu-no-ko (湯の湖), then around the lake to Yumoto Onsen.

Towards the back of the town, the hot-spring temple **Onsen-ji** (温泉時; adult/child ¥500/300; ⏰9am-4pm late Apr-Nov) has a humble bathhouse (with extremely hot water) and a tatami lounge for resting weary muscles.

From Yumoto Onsen you can return to Nikkō by bus (¥1650, 1½ hours).

Gunma Prefecture   群馬県

The Japanese archipelago is filled with onsen, but the star in the Kantō-area hot-spring firmament is Gunma Prefecture (Gunma-ken). Mineral baths seem to bubble out of the ground at every turn in this mountainous landscape, and some small towns feel delightfully traditional. Here's just a small selection.

KUSATSU ONSEN   草津温泉
☎0279 / POP 7300

Kusatsu has been voted Japan's favourite onsen year after year since the Edo period – apparently shōgun Tokugawa Ieyasu himself was a fan. The pungent, emerald-coloured waters are relatively heavy in sulphuric acid, which has an anti-bacterial effect. Their source is **Yubatake** (湯畑, 'hot-water field') in the town centre, flowing at 4000L per minute and topped with wooden tanks from which Kusatsu's ryokan fill their baths.

Stop in at or phone the **City Hall Tourist Section** (☎88-0001; ⏰8.30am-5.30pm Mon-Fri), next to the bus station (there's an English speaker on hand). For more town info, see www.kusatsu-onsen.ne.jp/foreign/index.html.

There are plenty of onsen open to the public, including **Ōtakinoyu** (大瀧乃湯; 596-13 Ōaza Kusatsu; adult/child ¥800/400; ⏰9am-9pm), known for its tubs at a variety of temperatures; try different ones for an experience known as *awase-yu* (mix-and-match waters). West of town in Sai-no-kawara kōen is **Sai-no-kawara** (西の河露天風呂; 521-2 Ōaza Kusatsu; adult/child ¥500/300; ⏰7am-8pm), a 500-sq-metre *rotemburo* (outdoor bath) that can fit 100 people. It's a 15-minute walk from the town centre or a 20-minute ride (¥100) on the 'A course' bus from Kusatsu bus terminal.

From 1 April to 30 November Kusatsu also offers a touristy but unique opportunity to see *yumomi*, in which local women stir the waters to cool them while singing folk songs. It's next to Yubatake at the bathhouse **Netsu-no-Yu** (熱の湯; 414 Kusatsu-machi; adult/child ¥500/250); there are four to five shows daily.

🛏 Sleeping & Eating

Hotel Ichii HOTEL $$

(ホテル一井; ☎88-0011; www.hotel-ichii.co.jp; fax 88-0111; 411 Kusatsu-machi; r per person with 2 meals from ¥14,000) Though you might not know from looking at its tower next to Yubatake, this hotel has been a Kusatsu institution for over 300 years. It's a rambling, retro-decor place featuring Japanese-style rooms, plus indoor and outdoor onsen baths. In winter, ask about discounted lift tickets for Kusatsu Kokusai ski resort.

Pension Segawa INN $$

(ペンションセガワ; ☎88-1288; http://scty.net/segawa/, in Japanese; fax 88-1377; 543 Kusatsu-machi; r per person with 2 meals from ¥8025) Inns in the town centre are pretty expensive, but this alpine-vibe lodging is an affordable option, a 10-minute walk from the bus terminal (or call for pick-up). There are Western- or Japanese-style rooms, three bathtubs and fresh-baked bread.

Mikuniya NOODLES $

(三国家; 386 Ōaza Kusatsu; dishes from ¥650; ⏱lunch; 🚭) Fill up on tasty bowls of *sansai soba* (buckwheat noodles with mountain vegetables; ¥800) at this popular place on the shopping street that runs behind Yubatake towards Sai-no-kawara Rotemburo. Look for the renovated wooden building with the black door curtains, or the line out the front.

ⓘ Getting There & Away

Buses connect Kusatsu Onsen to Naganohara-Kusatsuguchi train station (¥670, 25 minutes). *Tokkyū* Kusatsu trains run from Ueno to Nagano-Kusatsuguchi Station (¥4620, 2½ hours) three times a day. Alternatively, take the Joetsu *shinkansen* to Takasaki (¥4600, one hour) and transfer to the JR Agatsuma line (¥1110, 1½ hours). **JR Bus Kantō** (☎03-3844-1950; www.jrbuskanto.co.jp) offers direct service to Kusatsu Onsen (¥3200, four hours) from Shinjuku Station's New South exit; reservations required.

MINAKAMI & TAKARAGAWA ONSEN 水上温泉・宝川温泉

☎0278 / POP 21,000

Minakami is a sprawling onsen town. It's home to Takaragawa Onsen (about 30 minutes away by road), a riverside spa ranked among the nation's best, and a growing outdoor-adventure scene.

The train station is in the village of Minakami Onsen, as are most of Minakami's lodgings. **Minakami Tourist Information**

» Most dramatic: Jinata Onsen (p164)

» Prettiest bathhouse: Hōshi Onsen Chōjūkan (p130)

» Strongest waters: Kusatsu Onsen (p128)

» Best view: Urami-ga-taki Onsen (p164)

» Most unconventional waters: Yunessun (p141)

Center (水上観光協会; ☎62-0401; www.enjoy-minakami.jp/eng; ⏱8.30am-5.30pm), across from the station, has English pamphlets and bus schedules and can make accommodation reservations. Ask which inns in town have *higaeri nyuuyoku* (day-use baths) open when you visit.

Takaragawa Onsen (adult/child ¥1500/1000; ⏱9am-5pm) is idyllic and rangy. All of the bathing pools – save one just for women – are mixed bathing. Women are allowed to take modesty towels (rental is ¥100) into the mixed baths. The curious junk and gems you'll pass on your way to the baths are decades' worth of gifts from local villagers. The bears in cages on the same path will upset some visitors. Buses run hourly between Minakami Station and Takaragawa Onsen (¥1100) or Takaragawa Iriguchi (¥1000), from where it's a short walk to the onsen.

Tanigawadake Ropeway (谷川岳ロープウェイ; return ¥2000; ⏱8am-5pm) takes you via gondola to the peak of Tenjin-daira, from where hiking trips, ranging from a couple of hours to all day, are available from May to November. There's skiing and snowboarding in winter. From Minakami Station, take a 20-minute bus to Ropeway-Eki-mae bus stop (¥650, about hourly).

A number of operators lead rafting and kayaking trips in warmer months, and winter expeditions such as snowshoeing, from about ¥6000 for a half-day. **Canyons Minakami** (キャニオンズみなかみ; ☎72-2811; http://canyons.jp), a leader in the sustainable development of the local outdoor scene, is run by a professional, English-speaking team. It offers four-season packages and budget accommodations at its sister operation, **Alpine Lodge** (アルパイン・ロッジ; ☎72-2811; http://lodge.canyons.jp; 45 Yubiso; dm from ¥4000).

TOP
CHOICE **Hōshi Onsen Chōjūkan** RYOKAN $$
(法師温泉長寿館; 📞66-0005; www.houshi
-onsen.jp, in Japanese; fax 66-0003; 650 Nagai; r per
person with 2 meals from ¥13,800) This perfectly
rustic, supremely photogenic lodging is one
of Japan's finest onsen ryokan. The main
bathhouse is a stunning wooden structure
from 1896, with rows of individual bathing
pools. It's mixed bathing, with an additional
modern bathhouse just for women; baths
are open to day trippers from 10.30am to
1.30pm (admission is ¥1000). The inn is on
the southwestern fringes of Minakami. To
get there, take a bus from Gokan Station
(two stops before Minakami on the Jōetsu
line) or from the Jōmō Kōgen *shinkansen*
station to Sarugakyō (¥860, about 40 min-
utes); at the last stop, take another bus for
Hōshi Onsen (¥590, 15 minutes). Check bus
schedules at the tourist information centre.

Ōsenkaku RYOKAN $$
(汪泉閣; 📞75-2121; www.takaragawa.com; fax 75-
2038; 1899 Fujiwara; r per person with 2 meals from
¥11,700) Across the river from Takaragawa
Onsen, this inn has gorgeous river-front
rooms over several buildings and a mighty
old-style feel. It also has 24-hour use of the
Takaragawa baths. Prices rise steeply for
nicer rooms with better views and private
baths, but aim for the 1930s-vintage No 1 annexe. Note that dinner includes bear-meat
soup; if you'd prefer not to eat this, ask for
no kuma-jiru (熊汁) when reserving.

🍜 **Yamaji** NOODLES $$
(山路; 15 Fujiwara; meals from ¥1050; ⊙11am-
4pm Wed-Mon) The place to sample authentic
mountain cuisine. The chef forages daily for
the wild mushrooms and shoots that top
the huge cast-iron bowls of *hōtō* udon (thick
noodles; ¥1050) served here. The miso-
flavoured ice cream (¥370) is a treat, too.
It's halfway between Minakami Station and
Takaragawa Onsen, a short walk from the
Okutone Ski-jō bus stop. Take the side road
towards the ski park, turn left at the dead
end and look for the log cabin on your right.

ℹ️ **Getting There & Away**
From Ueno, take the Joetsu *shinkansen* (¥4600,
50 minutes) or JR Takasaki line (¥1890, two
hours) to Takasaki and transfer to the Jōetsu line
(¥950, one hour). You can also catch the Joetsu
shinkansen to Jōmō Kōgen from Tokyo/Ueno
(¥5750/5550, 1¼ hours), from where buses run
to Minakami (¥600, 25 minutes).

Mito 水戸
📍029 / POP 264,000
Capital of Ibaraki Prefecture and a one-
time castle town, Mito is best known for
Kairaku-en (偕楽園; 1-3-3 Tokwachō; admission
free; ⊙6am-7pm). It's one of the three most
celebrated landscape gardens in Japan; the
other two are Kenroku-en (p228) in Kanaza-
wa and Kōraku-en in Okayama (p383).

Kairaku-en dates back to 1842 when it
was built by the *daimyō* of the Mito *han* (do-
main), a member of the clan of the Tokugawa
shōgun. 'Kairaku-en' means 'the garden to
enjoy with people', and it was one of the first
gardens in the nation to open to the public.

The 32-acre gardens are popular for their
3000 *ume* (plum-blossom) trees; some 100
varieties bloom in late February or early
March. A **plum-blossom festival** happens
around this time; check at the **Kairaku-en
Park Center** (📞244-5454; www.koen.pref.ibara
ki.jp/park/kairakuen01.html) for dates. Other
flowering trees (azaleas, camellias, cherries
etc) make for impressive viewing in other
seasons, and the hillside setting allows broad
views. The three-storey pavilion **Kobun-tei**
(好文亭; admission ¥190; ⊙9am-4.30pm) is a
1950s reproduction of the *daimyō's* villa
(the original was destroyed in WWII).

From Tokyo, JR Jōban line trains depart
from Ueno Station for Mito (*tokkyū*; ¥3510,
75 minutes). During the plum-blossom fes-
tival, connect by local train to Kairaku-en
Station (¥180, five minutes); otherwise take
a bus to Kairaku-en bus stop (¥230, 15 min-
utes) or walk (about 30 minutes) from the
station's south exit along the lake Senba-ko.

WEST OF TOKYO

Nature reasserts herself at the western edge
of Tokyo, spreading green through the sce-
nic Fuji Go-ko lake region towards Mt Fuji.
To the southwest are the classic hot-spring
resorts of Hakone and the seaside onsen and
beach towns of the Izu Peninsula.

Takao-san 高尾山
📍042
Easily reached from Shinjuku Station, gentle
Takao-san is one of Tokyo's most popular day
trips. Although it's often busy on weekends
and holidays and rather built up compared
to other regional hikes, it can make for a
perfect family outing.

One of the chief attractions on this 599m mountain is the temple **Yaku-ō-in** (薬王院; ☏661-1115; ⏱24hr), best known for the **Hiwatari Matsuri** (fire-crossing ceremony), which takes place on the second Sunday in March, at 1pm near Takaosanguchi Station. Priests walk across hot coals with bare feet amid the ceremonial blowing of conch shells. The public is also welcome to participate.

Year-round, Takao-san offers **nature hikes**. Keio-line offices have free trail maps in English, or check www.takaotozan.co.jp.

The most popular trail (No 1) leads you past the temple; allow about 3¼ hours return for the 400m ascent. Alternatively, a cable car and a chair lift can take you part of the way up (adult/child one way ¥470/230, return ¥900/450).

From Shinjuku Station, take the Keio line (*jun-tokkyū*; ¥370, 47 minutes) to Takaosanguchi. The tourist village (with snack and souvenir shops), trail entrances, cable car and chairlift are a few minutes away to the right. JR Pass holders can travel to Takao Station on the JR Chūō line (48 minutes) and transfer to the Keio line to Takaosanguchi (¥120, two minutes).

Oku-Tama Region
奥多摩周辺

Oku-Tama is Tokyo's best spot for hiking getaways. Here, the Tama-gawa runs through magnificent mountains with waterfalls, woodlands and hiking trails, ideal for day trips or overnight stays.

Mitake-san (御岳山; elevation 831m) is a charming old-world mountain hamlet that seems light years from Tokyo's bustle. Access is easiest by cable car, and about 20 minutes on foot from the terminus, up dozens of steps, is **Musashi Mitake-jinja** (武蔵御嶽神社; 176 Mitake-san; ⏱24hr), a Shintō shrine and pilgrimage site said to date back some 1200 years. The site commands stunning views of the surrounding mountains. Pick up maps at the **Mitake Visitors Centre** (御岳ビジターセンター; ☏0428-78-9363; 38-5 Mitake-san; ⏱9am-4.30pm Tue-Sun), 250m beyond the cable car, near the start of the village.

If you've got time, the five-hour round-trip **hike** from Musashi Mitake-jinja to the summit of **Ōtake-san** (大岳山; 1266m) is highly recommended. Although there's some climbing involved, it's a fairly easy hike and the views from the summit are excellent – Mt Fuji is visible on clear days. On the way, you can detour to Nanayo-no-taki falls, Ganseki-en rock garden and Ayahiro-no-taki falls.

If you're not spending the night on Mitake-san, note before you set out that the cable car operates 7.30am to 6.30pm only.

🛏 Sleeping & Eating

The following places are all near Musashi Mitake-jinja.

Komadori San-sō   MINSHUKU $
(駒鳥山荘; ☏0428-78-8472; www.hkr.ne.jp/~komadori; fax 78-8472; 155 Mitake-san; r per person with shared bathroom from ¥4500; @) Below the shrine near the back end of the village, this former pilgrims' inn brims with bric-a-brac and history – it's been in the same family for 17 generations. The friendly, English-speaking owners will happily tell you all about it. Rooms and the verandah have excellent views.

Mitake Youth Hostel   HOSTEL $
(御嶽ユースホステル; ☏0428-78-8501; www.jyh.or.jp; fax 78-8774; 57 Mitake-san; dm with/without 2 meals ¥4800/2880, nonmembers extra ¥600) This comfortable hostel has fine tatami rooms inside a handsome old building that used to be a pilgrims' lodge. It's midway between the top of the cable car and Musashi Mitake-jinja, about a minute beyond the visitors centre.

Reiunso   RYOKAN $$
(嶺雲荘; ☏0428-78-8501; www.reiunsou.com, in Japanese; fax 78-8774; 57 Mitake-san; r per person with 2 meals from ¥8400) In the same building as the Mitake Youth Hostel, Reiunso has upgraded facilities and more elaborate meals featuring seasonal mountain vegetables.

Momiji-ya   NOODLES $
(紅葉屋; 151 Mitake-san; mains ¥735-1155; ⏱10am-5pm; 🚭) This cosy shop near the shrine gate has mountain views out the back windows and dishes like *kamonanban soba* (noodles in hearty duck broth; ¥1155). Look for the brown-and-white curtain outside.

ⓘ Getting There & Away

Take the JR Chūō line from Shinjuku Station, changing to the JR Ōme line at Tachikawa Station or Ōme Station depending on the service, and get off at Mitake (¥890, 90 minutes). Buses (¥270, 10 minutes) run from Mitake Station to Takimoto, where a cable car takes you near Mitake village (one way/return ¥570/1090, six minutes, 7.30am to 6.30pm); on foot, the climb takes about one hour.

Mt Fuji Area 富士山周辺

Mt Fuji (Fuji-san; 3776m), Japan's highest and most famous peak, is obviously this region's natural draw. In addition to climbing Fuji-san, visitors can hunt for precious views of the sacred volcano from around the Fuji Go-ko (Fuji Five Lakes). Winter and spring months are your best bets for Fuji-spotting; however, even during these times the snowcapped peak may be visible only in the morning before it retreats behind its cloud curtain. Its elusiveness, of course, is part of the appeal.

MT FUJI 富士山

Of all the iconic images of Japan, Mt Fuji is the real deal. Admiration for the mountain appears in Japan's earliest recorded literature, dating from the 8th century. Back then the now dormant volcano was prone to spewing smoke, making it all the more revered. Mt Fuji continues to captivate both Japanese and international visitors; in 2010, some 320,000 people climbed it.

Climbing Mt Fuji

The mountain is divided into 10 'stations' from base (first station) to summit (10th), but most climbers start from one of the four fifth

Mt Fuji Area

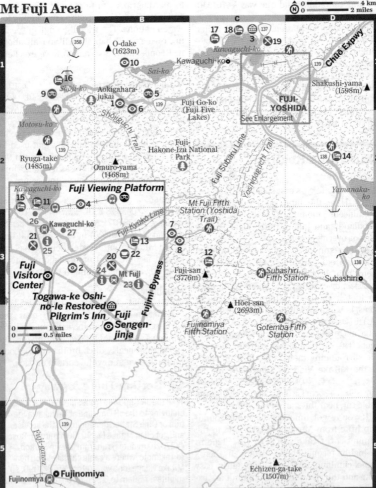

stations, reachable by road. From the fifth stations, allow five to six hours to reach the top and about three hours to descend, plus 1½ hours for circling the crater at the top.

North of Mt Fuji is Mt Fuji fifth station (2305m), the gateway to the **Yoshida Trail**, and reachable from the town of Kawaguchi-ko. This station is particularly popular with climbers starting from Tokyo. Other fifth stations are at Subashiri (1980m), Gotemba (1440m; allow seven to eight hours to reach the summit) and Fujinomiya (2380m), which is best for climbers coming from the west (Nagoya, Kyoto and beyond).

To time your arrival for dawn you can either start up in the afternoon, stay overnight in a mountain hut and continue early in the morning, or climb the whole way at night. You do not want to arrive on the top too long before dawn, as it's likely to be very cold and windy.

Trails below the fifth stations are now used mainly as short hiking routes, but you might consider the challenging but rewarding hike from base to summit on the **Yoshidaguchi Trail** (see the box, p135) from Fuji-Yoshida or on the **Shōjiguchi Trail** from near Shōji-ko. There are alternative trails on the Yoshida, Subashiri and Gotemba routes, which, assum-

ing strong knees and expendable clothing, you can descend rapidly by running, schussing and sliding down loose, clay-red sand.

MOUNTAIN HUTS

From the fifth stations and up, dozens of mountain huts offer hikers simple hot meals and a place to sleep (with/without meals from ¥7350/5250). Though much maligned for their spartan conditions (a blanket on the floor sandwiched between other climbers), they can fill up fast – reservations are recommended and are essential on weekends. **Taishikan** (太子館; ☎0555-22-1947) and **Fujisan Hotel** (富士山ホテル; ☎0555-22-0237) at the eighth station (Yoshida trail) usually have an English speaker on hand. Most huts allow you to rest inside as long as you order something. Camping on the mountain is not permitted.

Mt Fuji Fifth Station

The road to the fifth station from Kawaguchi-ko, the Fuji Subaru Line, stays open as long as the weather permits. Even when hiking is off-limits, it's still possible to take the bus here just to stand in awesome proximity to the snow-capped summit.

From roughly mid-May to late October, you can hike from here along a flat trail that

Mt Fuji Area

MT FUJI: KNOW BEFORE YOU GO

Although children and grandparents regularly reach the summit of Fuji-san, this is a serious mountain. It's high enough for altitude sickness, and as on any mountain, the weather can be volatile. On the summit it can go from sunny and warm to wet, windy and cold remarkably quickly. Even if conditions are fine, you can count on it being close to freezing in the morning, even in summer.

At a minimum, bring clothing appropriate for cold and wet weather, including a hat and gloves. If you're climbing at night, bring a torch (flashlight) or headlamp, and spare batteries. Descending the mountain is much harder on the knees than ascending; hiking poles can really help.

The official **climbing season** is from 1 July to 31 August. It's a busy mountain during these two months, with occasional nighttime queues. To get around the crowds, consider heading up on a weekday or starting earlier during the day and spending a night in a mountain hut. Authorities strongly caution against climbing outside the regular season, when the weather is highly unpredictable and first-aid stations on the mountain are closed. Many mountain huts on the Yoshida Trail do stay open through mid-September, when conditions may still be good for climbing; none open before July, when snow still blankets the upper stations.

Outside of the climbing season, check weather conditions carefully before setting out (see www.snow-forecast.com/resorts/Mount-Fuji/6day/top), bring appropriate equipment, do not climb alone, and be prepared to retreat at any time. A guide (see p134) can be invaluable. Once snow or ice is on the mountain, Fuji becomes a very serious and dangerous undertaking and should only be attempted by those with winter mountaineering equipment and plenty of experience. Off-season climbers must register with the local police department; fill out the form at the Kawaguchi-ko or Fuji-Yoshida information center (p134).

The Shobunsha Yama-to-kōgen Mt Fuji Map (山と高原地図・富士山; in Japanese), available at major book stores, is the most comprehensive map of the area.

hugs the mountain at the tree line. The trail stretches 4km past **Oniwa** (御庭) to **Okuniwa** (奥庭), where you'll have to double back. At either end of the climbing season, check conditions before setting out.

ℹ Information

All of the following have English-speaking staff and brochures in English on climbing and area sights.

Fuji-Yoshida City Hall (☎0555-24-1236; www.city.fujiyoshida.yamanashi.jp; iadfuji@city.fujiyoshida.lg.jp; ◷8.30am-5.15pm Mon-Fri) Has a must-read website.

Fuji-Yoshida Tourist Information Center (☎0555-22-7000; ◷9am-5.30pm) Inside Mt Fuji Station.

Kawaguchi-ko Tourist Information Center (☎0555-72-6700; ◷9am-5.30pm Sun-Fri, 8.30am-7pm Sat & holidays) Next to Kawaguchi-ko Station.

JNTO Tourist Information Center In Tokyo (see p115).

Shin-Fuji Station Tourist Information Center (☎0545-64-2430; ◷8.45am-5.30pm) On the 1st floor of the *shinkansen* station.

TOURS Discover Japan Tours (www.discover-japan-tours.com/en) Makes logistics a breeze with tours (from ¥10,000 per person) up the less-crowded Subashiri Trail that include some equipment rental and private transport to and from Shinjuku.

Fujiyama Guides (☎0555-23-7554; www.fujiyamaguides.com) Delve into the rich cultural history of the mountain with two-day pilgrim tours (from ¥22,000 per person). It also offers one-day off-season guided ascents (June to October, weather permitting; from ¥31,000 per person).

WEBSITES For summit weather conditions, see www.snow-forecast.com/resorts/Mount-Fuji/6day/top.

Climbing Mt Fuji (www17.plala.or.jp/climb_fujiyama/index.html) is an excellent resource.

ℹ Getting There & Away

The Mt Fuji area is most easily reached from Tokyo by bus. The two main towns on the north side of the mountain, Fuji-Yoshida and Kawaguchi-ko, are the principal gateways. See Fuji Go-ko (p135) for more.

From 1 July to 31 August, **Keiō Dentetsu Bus** (✆03-5376-2222; www.highwaybus.com, in Japanese) runs **direct buses** (¥2600, 2½ hours; reservations necessary) from the **Shinjuku Highway Bus Terminal** (Map p72) to Mt Fuji fifth station. From roughly mid-April to early December, buses run between Kawaguchi-ko and Mt Fuji fifth station (one way/return ¥1500/2000, 50 minutes). The schedule is highly seasonal; call **Fujikyū Yamanashi bus** (✆0555-72-6877) for details. At the height of the climbing season there are buses until 9.15pm – ideal for climbers intending to make an overnight ascent.

A taxi from either Kawaguchi-ko or Fuji-Yoshida to Mt Fuji fifth station should cost around ¥12,000, plus tolls.

Coming from western Japan, buses connect the Shin-Fuji *shinkansen* station and Fujinomiya fifth station (one way/return ¥2310/3000, two hours) from July to September.

For detailed schedules and route information, see transportation.fujikyu.co.jp/english.

FUJI GO-KO 富士五湖
✆555

The Fuji Go-ko (Fuji Five Lakes) region is a postcard-like area around Fuji's northern foothills; its lakes act as natural reflecting pools for the mountain's perfect cone. Yamanaka-ko is the largest and easternmost lake, followed by Kawaguchi-ko, Sai-ko, Shōji-ko (the smallest) and Motosu-ko, the deepest and least visited of the lakes. Particularly during the autumn *kōyō* (foliage) season, the lakes make a good overnight trip out of Tokyo, for leisurely strolling and for hiking in the nearby mountains.

⊙ Sights & Activities
FUJI-YOSHIDA 富士吉田

Togawa-ke Oshi-no-Ie Restored Pilgrim's Inn HISTORICAL BUILDING
(御師旧外川家住宅; 3-14-8 Kami-Yoshida; adult/child ¥100/50; ⊙9.30am-4.30pm Wed-Mon) Fuji-Yoshida's *oshi-no-ie* (pilgrims' inns) have served visitors to the mountain since the days when climbing Mt Fuji was a pilgrimage rather than a tourist event. *Shide* (paper streamers) still mark their entrances, though very few still function as inns. Togawa-ke Oshi-no-Ie, on Honchō dōri, offers some insight into the fascinating Edo-era practice of Mt Fuji worship.

Fuji Sengen-jinja TEMPLE
(5558 Kami-Yoshida) A necessary preliminary to the ascent was a visit to this deeply wooded, atmospheric temple, built in 1615 but thought to have been the site of a shrine as early as 788. It is worth a visit for its 1000-year-old cedar; its main gate, which is rebuilt every 60 years (slightly larger each time); and its two one-tonne *mikoshi* used in the annual Yoshida no Himatsuri (Yoshida Fire Festival). From Mt Fuji Station you can walk (15 minutes) or take a bus to Sengen-jinja-mae (¥150, five minutes).

Gekkō-ji NEIGHBOURHOOD
(月江寺) This central Fuji-Yoshida district feels like the little town that time forgot, with original mid-20th-century facades. Inside are some surprisingly hip cafes and shops, and it's worthwhile getting a little lost here.

Fuji-Q Highland AMUSEMENT PARK
(www.fuji-q.com; 5-6-1 Shin-Nishihara; admission only adult/child ¥1200/600, day pass ¥4800/3500; ⊙9am-5pm Mon-Fri, to 8pm most Sat & Sun) One stop west of Mt Fuji Station, this amusement park has roller coasters, bumper cars, Gundam and Thomas the Tank Engine attractions, and more.

KAWAGUCHI-KO 河口湖
On the lake of the same name, the sleepy town of Kawaguchi-ko is the closest town to four of the five lakes and a popular departure point for climbing Mt Fuji.

THE YOSHIDAGUCHI TRAIL UP MT FUJI

The completion in 1964 of the road to Mt Fuji fifth station dramatically changed the culture of climbing Mt Fuji, allowing busy Tokyoites to bus in after work and bus out the next morning. Historically, Fuji pilgrims began at Sengen-jinja near present-day Fuji-Yoshida, paying their homage to the shrine gods before beginning their 19km ascent up Japan's most sacred mountain. Today, the **Yoshidaguchi Trail**, the oldest up the mountain, offers climbers a chance to participate in this centuries-old tradition. Purists will tell you this is the only way to climb, saying that the lower reaches are the most beautiful, through lush forests along an isolated path.

It takes about five hours to reach the old Yoshidaguchi fifth station; the trail meets up with the one leaving from the new Mt Fuji fifth station at the sixth station. The *Climbing Mt Fuji* brochure, available at the Fuji-Yoshida Tourist Information Center (p134), is invaluable.

Kachi Kachi Yama Ropeway
ROPEWAY

(カチカチ山ロープウェイ; 1163-1 Azagawa; 1 way/return ¥400/700) Around 600m north of Kawaguchi-ko Station, on the lower eastern edge of the lake, this ropeway runs to the **Fuji Viewing Platform** (1104m). If you have time, there is a 3½-hour hike from here to **Mitsutōge-yama** (三つ峠山; 1785m); it's an old trail with excellent Fuji views. Ask at Kawaguchi-ko Tourist Information Center (p134) for a map.

Itchiku Kubota Art Museum
MUSEUM

(久保田一竹美術館; 2255 Kawaguchi; admission ¥1300; ⊙10am-5pm) Near the north shore of the lake, this unique museum presents lavishly dyed kimonos by Itchiku Kubota, whose life's work of continuous landscapes is displayed in a grand hall made of cypress.

Fuji Visitor Center
VISITOR CENTRE

(富士ビジターセンター; 6663-1 Funatsu; ⊙8.30am-10pm late Jul-late Aug, to 5pm Dec-Feb, sliding hr rest of yr) If Mt Fuji isn't visible, this visitor centre shows you what you've missed. An English video gives a great summary of the mountain and its geological history.

SAI-KO

Sai-ko Iyashi-no-Sato Nenba
CULTURAL CENTRE

(西湖いやしの里根場; 2710 Nenba; adult/child ¥350/150; ⊙9am-5pm) This complex opened in 2006 on the site of some historic thatched-roof houses, washed away in a typhoon 40 years earlier. Inside these dozen reconstructed frames are demonstrations of silk and paper crafts; restaurants specialise in *soba* and *konyakku* (arrowroot starch).

Kōyō-dai
LOOKOUT

There are good views of Mt Fuji from this lookout, near the main road, and from the western end of the lake.

Narusawa Ice Cave
CAVE

(adult/child ¥280/130; ⊙8am-5pm) Close to the road, this cave was formed by lava flows from a prehistoric eruption of Mt Fuji.

Fugaku Wind Cave
CAVE

(adult/child ¥280/130; ⊙8am-5pm) Also formed by prehistoric lava flows from Mt Fuji.

SHŌJI-KO & MOTOSU-KO

Further west from Sai-ko, tiny **Shōji-ko** is said to be the prettiest of the Fuji Go-ko. From here, you can continue toward **Motosu-ko**, famous as the image on the ¥1000 bill.

Panorama-dai
HIKING

(パノラマ台) This trail ends in a spectacular, spot-on view of Mt Fuji. It's a one-hour hike from the trailhead, a 20-minute walk beyond the Motosu-Iriguchi bus stop (¥1240, 45 minutes from Kawaguchi-ko).

✹✹ Festivals & Events

Yoshida no Himatsuri
FIRE

This annual festival (26 to 27 August) is held to mark the end of the climbing season and to offer thanks for the safety of the year's climbers. The first day involves a *mikoshi* procession and the lighting of bonfires on the town's main street. On the second day, festivals are held at Sengen-jinja.

🛏 Sleeping

If you're not overnighting in a mountain hut, Fuji-Yoshida and Kawaguchi-ko make good bases. Their respective tourist information offices (see p134) can make reservations for you. Most inns far from the station offer free pick-up.

K's House Mt Fuji
HOSTEL $

(☑83-5556; http://kshouse.jp; fax 83-5557; 6713-108 Funatsu; dm/d from ¥2500/7800; ⊜@⊜) This clean, modern hostel in Kawaguchi-ko has a welcoming atmosphere and helpful, English-speaking staff. It has a fully loaded kitchen, mountain bikes for hire and no curfew. Rooms fill up fast during the climbing season.

Fuji-Yoshida Youth Hostel
HOSTEL $

(☑22-0533; www.jyh.or.jp; 2-339 Honchō; member/nonmember dm ¥2900/3500; ⊜) This is a popular old lodging in Fuji-Yoshida's old town. Some of these Japanese-style rooms have mountain views. The hostel is around 600m south of Shimo-Yoshida Station; walk down the main street, go through three sets of lights and turn down the small alley on the right.

Sunnide Resort
HOTEL $$

(サニーデリゾート; ☑76-6004; www.sunnide.com, in Japanese; fax 76-7706; 2549-1 Ōishi; r per person ¥6300, cottages from ¥16,000; @⊜) Offering views of Mt Fuji from the far side of Kawaguchi-ko, friendly Sunnide has hotel rooms and rental cottages with a delicious outdoor bath. You can splash out in the stylish premium suites with private balcony bathrooms or ask for the discounted 'backpacker' rates (¥4200) if same-day rooms are available. Breakfast/dinner costs ¥1050/1575.

Fuji Lake Hotel
HOTEL $$

(☏72-2209; www.fujilake.co.jp; fax 73-2700; 1 Funatsu; r per person with 2 meals from ¥10,500; @☎) Near the Kawaguchi-ko town centre and right on the lakefront, this seven-storey historic (1935) hostelry offers mountain and lake views from its Japanese-Western combo rooms. In addition to private facilities (some rooms have their own *rotemburo*), there are common onsen, too.

Inn Fujitomita
RYOKAN $$

(☏84-3359; www.tim.hi-ho.ne.jp/innfuji; 3235 Shibokusa, Oshino-mura; r per person with 2 meals from ¥8400) Spacious tatami rooms (with and without bath) and generous meals, in the nearby woodsy hamlet of Oshino on the way to Yamanaka-ko.

Murahamasō
MINSHUKU $$

(村浜荘; ☏87-2436, in English 83-2375; www .murahamasou.com; 807 Shōji; r per person with 2 meals ¥7000; ☎) Traditional lodgings on quiet Shōji-ko, with a helpful English speaker in the family.

Sakuya
GUESTHOUSE $$

(咲耶; ☏/fax 76-7887; www.justmystage .com/home/sakuya; 2526 Ōishi; s/tw from ¥7500/12,000; ⊝@☎) Run by an English-speaking mountain guide in a village overlooking Kawaguchi-ko, with Fuji views from the bathhouse; vegetarian meals available.

Mt Fuji Hostel Michael's
HOSTEL $

(☏72-9139; www.mfi.or.jp/mtfujihostel; 2nd fl, 795-1 Shimo-Yoshida; dm ¥2800; ⊝@☎) New, no-frills Western-style hostel above Michael's American Pub in Gekkō-ji.

✖ Eating & Drinking

Fuji-Yoshida is known for its *teuchi udon* (homemade, white-wheat noodles); some 60 shops sell it! Try yours with tempura, *kitsune* (fried tofu) or *niku* (beef). The Fuji-Yoshida Tourist Information Center (p134) has a map and a list of restaurants (dishes are around ¥500).

Kawaguchi-ko's local noodles are *hōtō*, sturdy, hand-cut and served in a thick miso stew with pumpkin, sweet potato and other vegetables.

Sanrokuen
TEPPANYAKI $$

(3370-1 Funatsu; set meals ¥2100-4200; ☼10am-7.30pm Fri-Wed) Here diners sit on the floor around traditional *irori* charcoal pits grilling their own meals – skewers of choice fish, meat, tofu and vegies. There's a picture menu. From Kawaguchi-ko Station, turn left, left again after the 7-Eleven and after 600m you'll see the thatched roof on the right.

Hōtō Fudō
NOODLES $$

(ほうとう不動; 707 Kawaguchi; hōtō ¥1050; ☼11am-7pm) Three branches around town serve this massive stew bubbling in its own cast-iron pot. The *honten* (main branch) is a brown-and-white barn of a restaurant north of the lake, near the Kawaguchi-ko Art Museum via the Retro-bus.

Matsuya
CAFE

(まつや茶房; 294-3 Shimo-Yoshida; ☼10am-7pm Tue-Sun; @☎✎⌨) Stop by for well-brewed coffee (¥450), grilled-cheese sandwiches and a chat with the savvy, English-speaking owner. It's in a wooden merchant's house from the 1930s on the main drag in Gekkō-ji; look for an old hanging wooden sign.

M2
INTERNATIONAL $$

(319 Shimo-Yoshida; mains ¥700-1350; ☼11.30am-10pm; @⌨) This kitschy place around the corner from the Fuji-Yoshida Youth Hostel serves Western and Japanese diner food, like fried shrimp and curry rice; look for the orange awning.

Michael's American Pub
BURGERS $$

(マイケルズアメリカンパブ; 795-1 Shimo-Yoshida; meals ¥800-1100; ☼7pm-2am Fri-Wed, lunch Sun-Fri; ⌨) For traditional Americana (burgers, pizzas and brew), drop by this expat and local favourite in Gekkō-ji.

❶ Getting There & Away

Frequent buses (¥1700, 1¾ hours) operate directly to Kawaguchi-ko and Fuji-Yoshida (Mt Fuji Station) from the **Shinjuku Highway Bus Terminal** (Map p72; ☏03-5376-2222). Some continue on to Yamanaka-ko (¥2000, 2¼ hours) or Motosu-ko (¥2150, 2½ hours; via Shōji-ko). In Kawaguchi-ko, contact **Fujikyū Kōsoku Bus** (☏72-5111) for reservations and schedule info.

JR Chūō line trains go from Shinjuku to Ōtsuki (*tokkyū* ¥2980, one hour; *futsū* ¥1280, 1½ hours), where you transfer to the Fuji Kyūkō line for Mt Fuji (¥990, 45 minutes) and Kawaguchi-ko (¥1110, 50 minutes).

❶ MT FUJI STATION

In 2011, Fuji-Yoshida Station changed its name to Mt Fuji Station. This is not to be confused with the Mt Fuji fifth station, which is on the mountain and the starting point for the Yoshida Trail to the summit.

Getting Around

City buses run from Kawaguchi-ko to Fujinomiya (¥2040, 75 minutes), via the three smaller lakes, and to the shinkansen stop of Mishima (¥2130, two to 2½ hours), via Mt Fuji Station.

The **'Retro-bus'** has hop-on-hop-off service from Kawaguchi-ko Station to all of the sightseeing spots around the western lakes. One route (two-day passes adult/child ¥1000/500) follows Kawaguchi-ko's northern shore, and the other (¥1300/650) heads south and around Sai-ko and Aokigahara.

There is a **Toyota Rent-a-Car** (☑72-1100, in English 0800-7000-815) a few minutes' walk from Kawaguchi-ko Station; head right from the station, turning right at the next intersection. **Sazanami** (☉9am-6pm), on Kawaguchi-ko's southeast shore, rents bicycles (¥400/1500 per hour/day) and rowboats (¥1000 per hour).

Hakone   箱根

☑0460 / POP 13,300

If you only have a day or two outside Tokyo, Hakone can give you almost everything you could desire from the Japanese countryside – spectacular mountain scenery crowned by Mt Fuji, onsen and traditional inns.

During holidays, Hakone can be quite busy and feel highly packaged. To beat the crowds, plan your trip during the week. For more information, try www.hakone.or.jp/english.

★ Festivals & Events

Ashino-ko Kosui Matsuri   FIREWORKS

At Hakone-jinja near Moto-Hakone, this festival on 31 July features fireworks displays over Hakone's landmark lake.

Hakone Daimonji-yaki Matsuri   SUMMER

During this summer festival on 16 August, the torches are lit on Myojoga-take so that they form the shape of the Chinese character for 'big' or 'great'.

Hakone Daimyō Gyoretsu Parade   HISTORICAL

On the national Bunka-no-hi (Culture Day) holiday on 3 November, 450 costumed locals re-enact a feudal lord's procession.

Getting There & Away

The private **Odakyū line** (www.odakyu.jp) from Shinjuku Station goes directly into Hakone-Yumoto, the region's transit hub. Use either the convenient Romance Car (¥2020, 85 minutes) or kyūkō (regular-express) service (¥1150, two hours); the latter may require a transfer at Odawara.

JR Pass holders can take the Kodama shinkansen (¥3130, 35 minutes) or the JR Tōkaidō line (futsū ¥1450, 1¼ hours; tokkyū ¥2350, one hour) from Tokyo Station or the Shōnan-Shinjuku line from Shinjuku (¥1450, 80 minutes) to Odawara and change there for trains or buses for Hakone-Yumoto.

The narrow-gauge, switchback Hakone-Tōzan line runs from Odawara via Hakone-Yumoto to Gōra (¥650, one hour).

Odakyū's **Hakone Freepass** (箱根フリーパス), available at Odakyū stations and Odakyū Travel branches, is an excellent deal, covering the return fare to Hakone and unlimited use of most modes of transport within the region, plus other discounts. It's available as a two-day pass (adult/child from Shinjuku ¥5000/1500, from Odawara ¥3900/1000) or a three-day pass (adult/child from Shinjuku ¥5500/1750, from Odawara ¥4400/1250). Freepass holders need to pay an additional limited-express surcharge (¥870 each way) to ride the Romance Car.

Getting Around

Part of Hakone's popularity comes from the chance to ride assorted norimono (modes of transport): switchback train (from Hakone-Yumoto to Gōra), cable car (funicular), ropeway (gondola), ship and bus. Check out www.odakyu.jp, which describes this circuit.

BOAT From Tōgendai, sightseeing boats crisscross Ashino-ko to Hakone-machi and Moto-Hakone (¥970, 30 minutes).

BUS The Hakone-Tōzan and Izu Hakone bus companies service the Hakone area, linking most of the sights. Hakone-Tōzan buses, included in the Hakone Freepass, run between Hakone-machi and Odawara (¥1150, 55 minutes) and between Moto-Hakone and Hakone-Yumoto (¥930, 35 minutes).

CABLE CAR & ROPEWAY Gōra is the terminus of the Hakone-Tōzan railway and the beginning of the cable car to Sōun-zan, from where you can catch the Hakone Ropeway line to Ōwakudani and Tōgendai.

LUGGAGE FORWARDING At Hakone-Yumoto Station, deposit your luggage with **Hakone Baggage Service** (箱根キャリーサービス; ☑86-4140; per piece from ¥700; ☉8.30am-7pm) by noon, and it will be delivered to your inn within Hakone from 3pm. From inns, pick-up is at 10am for a 1pm delivery at Hakone-Yumoto. Hakone Freepass holders get a discount of ¥100 per bag.

HAKONE-YUMOTO ONSEN 箱根湯元温泉
Hakone-Yumoto is the starting place for most visits to Hakone. Though heavily visited, it's an ambient riverside resort town with a high concentration of onsen. If the weath-

er looks dodgy, it makes sense to spend the day soaking in the baths. You can also approach the town on foot from Moto-Hakone via the Old Hakone Hwy (see p143).

Pick up maps and info at the excellent **Tourist Information Center** (☎85-5700; ⊙9am-5.45pm), by the bus stops across the main road from the train station.

Onsen are the main attraction of Hakone-Yumoto. **Kappa Tengoku Rotemburo** (かっぱ天国; 777 Yumoto; adult/child ¥750/400; ⊙10am-10pm), behind and above the station, is a popular outdoor bath, though it's a bit seedy. More upmarket are the fantastic onsen of **Tenzan Tōji-kyō** (天山湯治郷; 208 Yumoto-chaya; admission ¥1200; ⊙9am-10pm), which has a larger selection of indoor and outdoor baths. To get here, take the B Course shuttle bus from the bridge outside the station.

For a something unexpected, visit the **Key Hiraga Museum** (平賀敬美術館; 613 Yumoto; admission ¥500; ⊙10am-5pm Fri-Tue), dedicated to the bold, Pigalle-inspired paintings of Key Hiraga (1936–2000). It's run by the late artist's elegant wife in their old-style villa. Cross the Haya-kawa at Yumoto-bashi and take the first right; the museum is down a small lane.

🛏 Sleeping

TOP CHOICE **Fukuzumirō**   RYOKAN $$$
(福住楼; ☎85-5301; www.fukuzumi-ro.com; fax 85-5911; 74 Tōnozawa; r per person with 2 meals from ¥18,000) No two rooms are alike at this 100-year-old inn, though all have exquisite original woodwork. Most have sun terraces that rub up against the Haya-kawa; the small, quiet room overlooking the garden was a favourite of author Kawabata Yasunori. There are onsen baths but no private facilities. The inn is just below Tōnozawa Station on the Hakone-Tōzan railway, on the river side of the road, or a short taxi ride from Hakone-Yumoto.

Hotel Okada   HOTEL $$$
(ホテルおかだ; ☎85-6000; www.hotel-okada.co.jp; fax 85-5774; 191 Yumoto-chaya; r per person with 2 meals from ¥17,000; ⊝◉⌨) This rambling hotel on the edge of the Sukumogawa has excellent Japanese- and Western-style rooms and baths including the large Yu-no-Sato complex (open to day trippers, for ¥1600). Take bus A from the train station (¥100, 10 minutes).

Hakone-no-Mori Okada   HOTEL $
(箱根の森おかだ; ☎85-6711; www.hakoneno mori-okada.jp; 191 Yumoto-chaya; r per person from ¥5930) Adjacent to the Hotel Okada, this cheaper option also includes access to the onsen at Yu-no-Sato.

MIYANOSHITA   宮ノ下
The first worthwhile stop on the Hakone-Tōzan railway towards Gōra, this village has antique shops along the main road (head down the hill from the station), some splendid ryokan, and a pleasant hiking trail skirting up 800m Sengen-yama (浅間山). The trailhead is just below Fujiya Hotel, marked by a shrine.

On the slope from the station, **Naraya Cafe** (ナラヤカフェ; 404-13 Miyanoshita; drinks from ¥250; ⊙10.30am-6pm; 📶) opened recently in a derelict structure that was once part of the grand, 300-year-old Naraya Hotel (closed in 2001). More importantly, you can take your espresso while soaking in the free footbath on the terrace.

TOP CHOICE **Fujiya Hotel** (富士屋ホテル; ☎82-2211; www.fujiyahotel.jp; fax 82-2210; 359 Miyanoshita; d from ¥19,830; ⊝◉⌨🏊) is one of Japan's finest Western-heritage hotels, opened in 1878. Now sprawled across several wings, it remains dreamily elegant due to its old-world lounge areas and hillside garden. It's worth a visit to soak up the atmosphere and have tea in the lounge. Guest rooms show their age, but that counts as part of the charm; all have hot-spring water and there are shared onsen, too. Foreign travellers should enquire about the weekday special of roughly US$135 for a twin room (you can pay the equivalent sum in yen).

If you don't fancy paying resort prices for dinners at the Fujiya, a short walk up the street is the friendly sushi shop **Miyafuji** (鮨みやふじ; 310 Miyanoshita; meals from ¥1260; ⊙lunch & dinner Wed-Mon; 📶), known for its *aji-don* (brook trout over rice). Look for the English sign.

CHŌKOKU-NO-MORI & GŌRA   彫刻の森・強羅
Located two stops beyond Miyanoshita, the **Hakone Open-Air Museum** (彫刻の森美術館; www.hakone-oam.or.jp; 1121 Ninotaira; adult/child ¥1600/800; ⊙9am-4.30pm; 📶) has an impressive selection of 19th- and 20th-century Japanese and Western sculptures (including works by such famous names as Henry Moore, Rodin, Maillol and Miró) in a soaring hillside setting. It also has a Picasso pavilion, a children's play area as well as restaurants. Hakone Freepass holders get ¥200 off the admission price.

Hakone Region

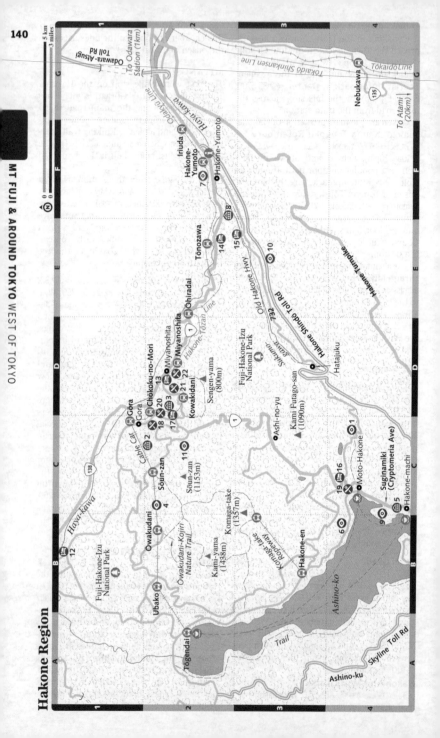

Hakone Region

Yunessun (箱根小涌園ユネッサン; www.yunessun.com; 1297 Ninotaira; adult/child ¥3500/1700; ⊙9am-7pm; ♿), which is probably best described as an onsen amusement park, is your rainy-day option. Here you can soak in everything from green tea to red wine, and ride waterslides too. Note that it's mixed bathing here, so you'll need to bring a swimsuit. Buses running to Hakone-machi from Gōra or Hakone-Yumoto (via Chōkoku-no-mori or Miyanoshita, respectively) stop at Yunessun.

Gōra, one stop after Chōkoku-no-mori, is the terminus of the Hakone-Tōzan line and the starting point for the funicular and cable-car trip to Tōgendai on Ashino-ko. There are a handful of minor attractions here, the best of which is the **Hakone Museum of Art** (箱根美術館; 1300 Gōra; adult/child ¥900/free; ⊙9.30am-4pm Fri-Wed). Set in a velvety moss garden, this small museum has a collection of Japanese pottery dating from as far back as the Jōmon period (ie some 5000 years ago).

🛏 Sleeping & Eating

Yudokoro Chōraku   RYOKAN $
(湯処長楽; ☎82-2192; fax 82-4533; 525 Kowaku-dani; r per person from ¥5150) This simple, modern ryokan has surprisingly spacious tatami rooms with kitchenettes and onsen bath (available for day use for ¥550). It's a 10-minute walk uphill from the Hakone Open-Air Museum, on the left.

Gyōza Center   JAPANESE $
(餃子センター; www.gyozacenter.com; 1300 Gōra; mains from ¥735; ⊙lunch & dinner Fri-Wed; 🖃) The humble *gyōza* (dumpling) stars here in a dozen different roles, from plain pan-fried (*nōmaru*) to boiled in soup with kimchi (*kimchi sui-gyōza*). The restaurant is between Gōra and Chōkoku-no-mori Stations, with an English sign.

Kappeizushi   SUSHI $
(かっ平寿し; 1143-49 Ni-no-taira; meals from ¥980; ⊙10am-9pm Wed-Mon; 🖉🖃) *Chirashi-zushi* (rice topped with assorted sashimi), uphill from Chōkoku-no-mori Station. Look for the blue door curtain.

SŌUN-ZAN & ŌWAKUDANI   早雲山・大桶谷

From Gōra, continue to near the 1153m-high summit of Sōun-zan by cable car (¥410, 10 minutes).

From Sōun-zan, there are several hiking trails including one to Kami-yama (1¾ hours) and another up to Ōwakudani (1¼ hours). The latter is sometimes closed due to the mountain's toxic gases. Check at the tourist information office.

Sōun-zan is the starting point for the Hakone Ropeway, a 30-minute, 4km gondola ride to Tōgendai (one way/return ¥1330/2340), stopping at Ōwakudani en route. In fine weather Mt Fuji looks fabulous from here.

Ōwakudani is a volcanic cauldron of steam, bubbling mud and mysterious smells. The **Ōwakudani-Kojiri Nature Trail** (大涌谷湖尻自然探勝歩道; Ōwakudani Kojiri Shizen Tanshō Hodō) leads uphill through the charred, somewhat apocalyptic landscape to some of the boiling pits. Here you can buy *onsen tamago*, eggs boiled and blackened in the sulphurous waters. Don't linger, as the gases are poisonous.

🛏 Sleeping

In addition to places listed in other individual destination sections there are these long-time favourites.

ROAD-TRIPPING, EDO STYLE

You know that old chestnut about all roads leading to Rome? Well, in Edo-era Japan all of the important roads literally led to the shōgun's capital.

Under a system called *sankin-kotai*, *daimyō* were required to maintain residences in Edo as well as in their home provinces and go back and forth to attend to affairs in both places. Their families, meanwhile, remained in Edo in order to suppress the temptation towards insurrection.

Travel to the provinces was via main 'trunk' roads, including the Tōkaidō ('Eastern Sea road', connecting Edo to Heian-kyō, now Kyoto), the Nikkō-kaidō (Nikkō road) and the Nakasendō ('Central Mountain road' through Nagano Prefecture). These roads became celebrated, notably through Hiroshige's series of *ukiyo-e* (wood-block prints) entitled *53 Stations of the Tōkaidō*.

At these strategically located 'stations', inns thrived, while checkpoints, called *sekisho*, maintained order. Travelling commoners had to present a *tegata* (a wooden plaque that served as a passport) and subject themselves to inspection for contraband. Violation of these rules – including trying to circumnavigate the *sekisho* – could bring severe penalties including a particularly ghastly form of crucifixion.

The *sekisho* at Hakone and at Kiso-Fukushima were among the most important and remain the best preserved. Other atmospheric station towns are Arimatsu on the Tōkaidō, and Tsumago (p221) on the Nakasendō.

Fuji Hakone Guest House   GUESTHOUSE **$**
(富士箱根ゲストハウス; 📞84-6577; www
.fujihakone.com; fax 84-6578; 912 Sengokuhara;
r per person ¥5400-6450; ⊜@⬤📶) Run by a
welcoming English-speaking family, this
guesthouse has handsome tatami rooms, a
cosy onsen and a wealth of information on
sights and hiking in the area. Rates may rise
by ¥1000 to ¥2000 per person during peak
seasons. Take the bus to Senkyōrō-mae from
Odawara Station (stop 4; ¥1020, 50 minutes)
or Tōgendai (¥370, 10 minutes). There's an
English sign close by.

**Hakone Sengokuhara Youth
Hostel**   HOSTEL **$**
(箱根仙石原ユースホステル; 📞84-8966;
www.theyh.com; fax 84-6578; members/nonmem-
bers dm ¥3510/4140, r per person ¥5190/5400;
⊜@📶) Directly behind the Fuji Hakone
Guest House and run by the same family,
this hostel has Japanese-style shared and
private rooms plus hot-spring baths.

ASHINO-KO   芦ノ湖
Between Tōgendai, Hakone-machi and
Moto-Hakone, this leg-shaped lake is touted
as the primary attraction of the Hakone
region; but it's Mt Fuji, with its snow-clad
slopes glimmering in reflection on the water, that lends the lake its poetry. If the venerable mountain is hidden behind clouds (as
often happens), you have the consolation of
a trip across the lake with recorded com-

mentary in English about the history and
natural surroundings. See p138 for details
about lake transport.

**HAKONE-MACHI &
MOTO-HAKONE**   箱根町・元箱根
The sightseeing boats across Ashino-ko deposit you at either of these two towns, both
well touristed and with sights of historical
interest. The main attraction in Hakone-
machi is the **Hakone Sekisho** (箱根関所; Hakone Checkpoint Museum; 1 Hakone-machi; adult/
child ¥500/250; ⏰9am-5pm), a recent reconstruction of the feudal-era checkpoint on the
Old Tōkaidō Hwy. The museum has Darth
Vader–like armour and grisly implements
used on lawbreakers but unfortunately no
English explanations. On a small peninsula
nearby is a scenic park, **Onshi Hakone Kōen**
(恩賜箱根公園; 171 Moto-Hakone; admission
free; ⏰9am-4.30pm). Its elegant Western-style
building was once used by the imperial family, and has Fuji views across the lake.

Suginamiki (杉並木; Cryptomeria Ave) is
a 2km stone path beside the busy lakeside
road connecting Hakone-machi and Moto-
Hakone, lined with some 400 cryptomeria
cedars that were planted nearly 400 years
ago. It is impossible to miss Moto-Hakone's
Hakone-jinja (箱根神社; treasure hall ¥500;
⏰9am-4pm) with its signature red torii rising
from the lake. A pleasant stroll around the
lake to the torii follows another cedar-lined
path. A wooded grove surrounds the shrine.

Just up the hill from the lakeside Moto-Hakone bus stop is the entrance to the stone-paved **Old Hakone Hwy** (箱根旧街道), part of the Edo-era Tokkaidō Hwy, which leads back to Hakone-Yumoto (about 3½ hours). Along the way you'll pass the 350-year-old **Amazake-jaya** (甘酒茶屋; ⊙7am-5.30pm), an isolated, traditional-looking teahouse where you can enjoy a cup of *amazake* (warm, sweet sake; ¥400). The wooded trail intersects with the paved road in **Hatajuku** (畑宿), a small village with a high concentration of work-shops producing *yosegi*, the local woodcraft. From here, you can hop on a bus or continue walking to Hakone-Yumoto Station.

🛏 Sleeping & Eating

Moto-Hakone Guesthouse   MINSHUKU **$**
(元箱根ゲストハウス; ☑83-7880; www.fujihakone.com; fax 84-6578; 103 Moto-Hakone; r per person without bathroom ¥5250; ⊖◉⊚) A popular spot with foreign tourists, this place offers simple but pleasant Japanese-style rooms. From Odawara Station, take the stop 3 bus to Hakone-machi or Moto-Hakone and get off at Ōshiba (¥1100, one hour); the guest-house is a one-minute walk away.

Ieyasu   YAKITORI **$**
(家康; 107-1 Moto-Hakone; meals from ¥690; lunch & dinner Thu-Tue; ◉) You won't pay tourist prices at this casual, counter restaurant. The lunch set – try the *shōga yaki* (grilled pork and ginger) – is a steal and in the evening *yakitori* (skewers from ¥130) is served until midnight. It's on a side street, one block past the Moto-Hakone bus stop; look for the white lanterns.

Izu Peninsula   伊豆半島

The Izu Peninsula (Izu-hantō), about 100km southwest of Tokyo in Shizuoka Prefecture, has a cool surfer vibe backed by plenty of history, particularly the famed *Kurofune* (Black Ships) of US Commodore Perry (p688). It also packs lush greenery, rugged coastlines, abundant onsen, and foods such as *himono* (sun-dried fish) and *mikan* (mandarin oranges). Weekends and holidays can be very crowded on the east coast, particularly in summer. It's always quieter on the west coast, which has Mt Fuji views over Suruga-wan.

An easy loop takes you by train to Itō on the east coast (reachable by JR from Tokyo), from where you can enjoy drop-dead coastal views on the train to historic Shimoda. Then journey by bus across a landscape of hilly countryside, farms and rural townships to Matsuzaki and Dōgashima on Izu's west coast. Finish at the intimate onsen village of Shuzenji before catching the Izu-Hakone Tetsudō line to Mishima to connect back to the JR.

ATAMI   熱海
☑0557 / POP 40,000

Atami may be the gateway to Izu, but this overdeveloped hot-springs resort has little charm aside from its museum. Overlooking the coastline, the sleek **MOA Museum of Art** (MOA美術館; www.moaart.or.jp; 26-2 Momoyama-chō; adult/student ¥1600/800; ⊙9.30am-4pm Fri-Wed, closed 4-14 Jan & 25-31 Dec) has an excellent collection of Japanese and Chinese pottery and paintings, spanning over 1000 years and including national treasures. Take the bus from stop 4 outside Atami Station to the last stop (¥160, eight minutes).

Discount tickets to the museum (¥1400) and town information are available at the **tourist office** (☑81-5297; ⊙9.30am-5.30pm), at the station building.

ⓘ Getting There & Away
JR trains run from Tokyo Station to Atami on the Tōkaidō line (Kodama *shinkansen* ¥4080, 50 minutes; Odoriko ¥3700, 1¼ hours; Acty *kaisoku* ¥1890, 1½ hours).

ITŌ & JŌGASAKI   伊東・城ヶ崎
☑0557

Itō is a hot-springs resort famous for being the place where Anjin-san (William Adams), the hero of James Clavell's book *Shogun*, built a ship for the Tokugawa shōgunate. It is said that this resort town was so popular that 100 geisha entertained here a century ago, although these days it's a commendably relaxed place. The **Tourist Information Center** (☑37-6105; ⊙9am-5pm) across the street from Itō Station has helpful, English-speaking staff.

A seven-minute walk south of the station is the **Tōkaikan** (東海館; 12-10 Higashi Matsubara-chō; adult/child ¥200/100; ⊙9am-9pm), a 1920s inn and now a national monument for its elegant woodwork, each of its three storeys designed by a different architect. Its large **bath** (adult/child ¥500/300; ⊙11am-7pm Sat & Sun) is still open to bathers.

South of Itō is the striking Jōgasaki coast, with its windswept cliffs formed by lava. A harrowing 48m-long suspension bridge leads over **Kadowaki Point** (Kadowaki-zaki) with waves crashing 23m below. It's a popular location for film and TV shoots, particularly suicide scenes. A moderately strenuous cliff-side hike, with volcanic rock and pine forests,

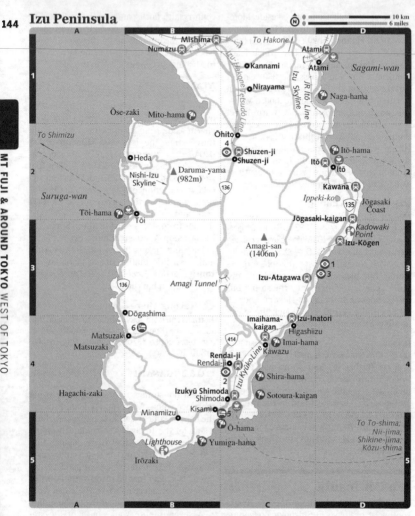

Izu Peninsula

winds south of the lighthouse to Izu Kōgen Station (about 6.5km). It's a 1.5km walk from Jōgasaki-kaigan Station to the coast.

🛏 Sleeping & Eating

K's House Itō Onsen HOSTEL **$**

TOP
CHOICE

(ケイズハウス伊東温泉; ☎35-9444; http:// kshouse.jp/ito-e/index.html; fax 35-9440; 12-13 Higashi Matsubara-chō; dm/s from ¥2990/3990; ➡@🛜) This newly opened hostel in a 100-year-old former ryokan might be the best deal in Japan. The beautifully maintained Japanese-style dorms and private rooms

WORTH A TRIP

BEACHSIDE BATHING

Izu's coastline is studded with onsen. Some are enclosed in expensive resorts, others are brazenly out in the open, right on the beach. You'll find two of the latter in the neighbouring towns of Izu-Ōkawa and Izu-Hokkawa, in between Itō and Shimoda on the Izukyū line. **Iso-no-yu** (磯の湯; admission ¥500; ⊙11am-6pm Mon-Fri, to 8pm Sat & Sun) in Izu-Ōkawa has two small *rotemburo*, one each for men and women, with a stone wall for coverage. **Kuroneiwa-buro** (黒根岩風呂; admission ¥600; ⊙6.30-9.30am & 4-11pm, women only 7-9pm), in Izu-Hokkawa, is for pure exhibitionists – mixed bathing at the edge of the water with unobstructed views of the Pacific. Neither have amenities; both are a 10-minute walk from their respective train stations, downhill towards the coast. Look for the wooden huts on the rocky beach. Hint: to get to Iso-no-yu you'll need to pass through a drainage tunnel under the road.

have river views and a classic feel. There's an onsen bath, spotless kitchen and inviting lounge. It's next door to the Tōkaikan.

Yamaki Ryokan
RYOKAN **$$**
(山喜旅館; ☎37-4123; www.ito-yamaki.co.jp; fax 38-8123; 4-7 Higashi Matsubara-chō; r per person with 2 meals ¥8550) A block east of the Tōkaikan, this is a charming wooden inn from the 1940s with an onsen bath. The owner is very friendly but has limited English. Ask for reservations at the Tourist Information Center.

Fuji Ichi
SUSHI **$$**
(ふじいち; 7-6 Shizumi-chō; sets from ¥1100; ⊙10am-3pm Fri-Wed) The coastal road is lined with restaurants and fishmongers – this is both. The casual upstairs eatery (enter through the shop) is noted for its grilled squid (*ika maruyaki teishoku*, ¥1100), but you can't miss with the sashimi set (*sashimi teishoku*, ¥1100). Heading south, it's a block past the Aoki supermarket; look for the vertical blue signs on the right.

ⓘ Getting There & Away
Itō is connected to Atami by the JR Itō line (¥320, 25 minutes). The JR limited-express Odoriko service also runs from Tokyo Station to Itō (¥4020, 1¾ hours).

From Itō, the Izukyūkō (aka Izukyū) line goes to Shimoda, stopping at Jōgasaki-kaigan (¥560, 18 minutes). There are six buses daily to Shuzen-ji (¥1100, one hour).

SHIMODA
下田
☎0558 / POP 25,000
Shimoda's laid-back vibe is perfectly suited to an exploration of its beaches and history. It holds a pivotal place in Japan's evolution as the spot where the nation officially

opened to the outside world after centuries of isolation. Following the opening of Japan by the *Kurofune* under Commodore Matthew Perry, the American Townsend Harris opened the first Western consulate here.

◉ Sights & Activities

Ryōsen-ji & Chōraku-ji
TEMPLES
(了仙寺・長楽寺) A 25-minute walk south of Shimoda Station is **Ryōsen-ji**, site of the treaty that opened Shimoda, signed by Commodore Perry and representatives of the Tokugawa shōgunate. The temple's **Black Ship Art Gallery** (了仙寺宝物館; Hōmotsukan; 3-12-12 Shichiken-chō; adult/child ¥500/150; ⊙8.30am-5pm) displays artefacts relating to Perry, the Black Ships, and Japan as seen through foreign eyes and vice versa.

Behind and up the steps from Ryōsen-ji is **Chōraku-ji**, where a Russo-Japanese treaty was signed in 1854; look for the cemetery and *namako-kabe* (black-and-white lattice-patterned) walls.

Hōfuku-ji
TEMPLE
(宝福寺; 1-18-26 Shimoda; admission ¥300; ⊙8am-5pm) In the centre of town is Hōfuku-ji, a temple that is chiefly a museum memorialising the life of Okichi (see the box, p148).

The museum is filled with scenes and artefacts from the various movie adaptations of her life on stage and screen. Okichi's grave is also here, in the far corner of the back garden, next to a faded copper statue. Other stones in this garden are dedicated to her, with the names of actors who played her.

FREE Gyokusenji
TEMPLE
(玉泉寺; 31-6 Kakizaki; ⊙8am-5pm) Founded in 1590, this Zen temple is most famous as the first Western consulate in Japan,

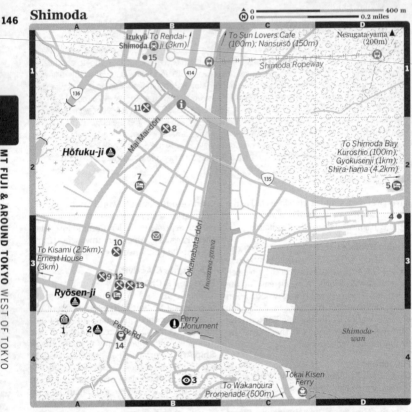

established in 1856. A small **museum** (adult/child ¥400/200) has artefacts of the life of Townsend Harris, the first consul general. The bas-relief of a cow in front of the temple depicts the serving of the first glass of milk in Japan, which Harris requested during an illness. It's a 25-minute walk from Shimoda Station, or take bus 9 to Kakizaki-jinja-mae (¥160, five minutes).

Shimoda Kōen & Wakanoura Promenade

PARK

(下田公園・和歌の浦遊歩道) If you keep walking east from Perry Rd, you'll reach the pleasant hillside park of Shimoda Kōen, which overlooks the bay. It's loveliest in June, when the hydrangeas are in bloom. The coastal road is also a fine place to walk. If you have an hour or so, keep following it around the bay, passing an overpriced aquarium, and eventually you'll meet up with the 2km-long Wakanoura Promenade, a stone path along a peaceful stretch of beach.

BEACHES

The beaches in **Kisami**, just south of Shimoda, are among the best in Japan. Ōhama (大浜) has the largest stretch of sand and Tatado (多々戸) is particularly popular with surfers. Irōzaki-bound buses (buses 3 and 4; ¥340, 10 minutes) stop at Kisami, from where it's a 10-minute walk to the coast. North of Shimoda, **Shira-hama** (bus 9; ¥320, 10 minutes) isn't bad either – its name means 'white-sand beach'. For young Kantō-area surfers it is a popular place to spend the summer (yes, it gets packed). Board and wetsuit rentals are available at Tatado and Shira-hama for about ¥4000 per day. Camping is not permitted on any of the beaches.

BAY CRUISES

Izu Cruise (伊豆クルーズ; ☏22-1151) runs a 20-minute *Kurofune* loop around the bay, departing from a dock on the east edge of town approximately every 30 minutes from 9.10am to 3.30pm (¥1000/500 per adult/child).

Shimoda

⊙ Top Sights

⊙ Sights

Activities, Courses & Tours

🛌 Sleeping

🍴 Eating

🍷 Drinking

Transport

🎎 Festivals & Events

Kurofune Matsuri   BLACK SHIPS

Shimoda commemorates the first landing of Commodore Perry on the third weekend in May, with parades by the US Navy Marine band and fireworks displays.

Shimoda Taiko Matsuri   DRUMS

A spectacular parade of *dashi* floats and some serious Japanese-style drumming on 14 and 15 August.

🛌 Sleeping

The **Shimoda Tourist Association** (下田市観光協会; ☎22-1531; ⊙10am-5pm) can help with reservations.

Ōizu Ryokan   RYOKAN $

(大伊豆旅館; ☎22-0123; 3-3-25 Shimoda; r per person ¥3500) Popular with international travellers for its excellent prices, Ōizu has plain but comfy Japanese-style rooms with TV, and a two-seater onsen. It's at the southern end of town, two blocks north of Perry Rd. Check-in is from 3pm. It's often closed on weekdays, so phone ahead.

Yamane Ryokan   RYOKAN $$

(やまね旅館; ☎22-0482; 1-19-15 Shimoda; s/d ¥5000/9000) You wouldn't guess this place has been running for 50 years from its tidy, well-maintained Japanese-style rooms. The owner speaks little English but is very friendly and the central location is excellent. Facilities are shared; breakfast is available for ¥1000.

Kurofune Hotel   HOTEL $$$

(黒船ホテル; ☎22-1234; www.kurofune-hotel.com, in Japanese; fax 22-1801; 3-8 Kakizaki; r per person with 2 meals from ¥15,000; @🏊) This glitzy old-line hotel has bay views, seafood dinners, palm trees by the *rotemburo* and a heated swimming pool. Rooms are Japanese style except for the suites, some of which have their own *rotemburo* (from ¥37,000 per person).

Ernest House   B&B $$

(アーネストハウス; ☎22-5880; www.ernest-house.com; fax 23-3906; 1893-1 Kisami; s/tw from ¥6300/10,500; ⊙@🏊) A great escape, two minutes' walk from the beach in Kisami Ō-hama, down the coast from Shimoda. In a Western-style house named after Hemingway, this 13-room pension has a restaurant (dinner ¥2625) and a youthful vibe. Reservations are recommended; note that rates can more than double at peak times. From Izukyū Shimoda Station, take an Irōzaki-bound bus (stop 3 or 4; ¥360) to Kisami, from where it's a 15-minute walk towards the coast.

Nansuisō   RYOKAN $

(南水荘; ☎22-2039; fax 22-4027; 1-21-17 Higashi Hongo; r per person ¥4000) A quiet old inn along the river with simple rooms and a shared onsen bath; it's pretty in the spring when the cherry trees bloom.

Shimoda Bay Kuroshio   HOTEL $$$

(下田ベイクロシオ; ☎27-2111; www.baykuro.co.jp; fax 27-2115; 4-1 Kakizaki; s/tw from ¥12,180/18,060; @) This uniquely modern hotel gleams white and chrome above the bay. Most rooms are Japanese style; upgrade to a Western-style suite for an extra ¥5250. Follow the main road along the bay and you'll see the hotel on your left, set on the hill.

🍴 Eating & Drinking

Seafood is the speciality in Shimoda.

TOP CHOICE / Gorosaya   JAPANESE $$

(ごろさや; 1-5-25 Shimoda; lunch/dinner ¥1575/3150; ⊙lunch & dinner Fri-Wed; 📖) Elegant, understated ambience and fantastic seafood.

THE LEGEND OF OKICHI

Although Shimoda is famous in international affairs, it is an affair of the heart that remains this town's most enduring claim to fame. As with all good stories, there are many versions.

Saito Kichi (the 'O' was later added as an honorific) was born a carpenter's daughter in Shimoda. Some accounts say that her exceptional beauty and talent for music led her poor family to sell her to a geisha house at age seven. Others skip directly to 1854, when the Black Ships arrived in Shimoda and a devastating earthquake destroyed Okichi's home and possessions.

Okichi's home was rebuilt by a long-time admirer named Tsurumatsu, and the two fell in love. But in 1856, when Townsend Harris became America's first consul in Shimoda, he needed a maid, and local authorities assigned the task to Okichi, then in her late teens. Despite her initial refusal, authorities prevailed on her to sacrifice her love of Tsurumatsu for the good of the nation. Tsurumatsu received a position with the shōgunate in Edo (now Tokyo).

Okichi gradually developed respect for Harris, even reportedly protecting him from an assassination attempt. Some versions of the story say that Harris forced her to fulfil his needs as well, and locals began taunting her as 'tōjin Okichi' (the foreigner's concubine), driving her to drink.

Following Harris's departure in 1858, Okichi and Tsurumatsu were reunited briefly; however, drink had taken its hold of Okichi and she ended up penniless and alone before eventually drowning herself in a river.

Okichi's story has been told in just about every form of Japanese drama. Outside Japan, the best-known version of it is The Barbarian and the Geisha, the 1958 film starring John Wayne, which – no surprise – tells the story its own way.

Try the simmered fish, usually a whole red snapper (*kinmedai*) in a delicate, sweet and salty broth. The *Isōjiru* soup is made from over a dozen varieties of shellfish and looks like a tide pool in a bowl. Look for the wooden fish decorating the entrance and come early for lunch.

Mimatsu SUSHI **$$**
(美松寿司; 2-12-8 Shimoda; sets ¥1400-2500; ⊙11am-10pm) No matter that there's no English menu, everyone orders the same thing anyway – the *kurofune* sushi set (¥2000), a selection of the freshest local catch. With a crisp interior and seating for no more than 15, there's little to distract you from the pleasure of eating it. Look for the white sign and black door curtains.

Nami Nami IZAKAYA **$$**
(開国厨房なみなみ; 3-3-26 Shimoda; skewers/small plates from ¥120/550; ⊙5pm-midnight) This friendly counter bar has a retro vibe and an inventive menu. Local fish (*honjitsu no sakana*) and assorted delicacies, like quail eggs (*uzura no tamago*) and camembert (*kamanbēru chīzu*), are served *yakitori* style or breaded and fried. It's right next door to Ōizu Ryokan, with a yellow sign.

Tosaya BAR
(土佐屋; 3-14-30 Shimoda; drinks & snacks from ¥600; ⊙6pm-midnight; 🏠) One of the oddest mash-ups we've seen: a traditional residence from the era of the Black Ships that's now a soul-music bar complete with disco ball. It's actually wicked fun. Just look for the lattice-pattern walls and twinkling lights.

Musashi NOODLES **$**
(むさし; 1-13-1 Shimoda; mains ¥630-1000; ⊙lunch Wed-Mon) In business since 1916, serving hearty comfort food like *kamo nabeyaki* udon (duck hotpot; ¥1000); there's a big badger out the front.

Porto Caro ITALIAN **$$**
(ポルトカーロ; 3-3-7 Shimoda; mains from ¥1260; ⊙lunch & dinner Thu-Tue; 🖊️🏠) Colourful, 2nd-floor trattoria specialising in pasta dishes with local seafood, and pizzas; look for the English sign two blocks down from the post office.

Hiranoya INTERNATIONAL **$$**
(平野屋; 3-1-4 Shimoda; meals ¥1260-3500; ⊙9.30am-8pm Wed-Mon; 🏠) A vintage residence filled with antiques, history and slightly overpriced burgers, cakes and coffee.

ℹ Information

Shimoda information can be found online at www.shimoda-city.info.

Post office A few blocks north of Perry Rd, with an international ATM.

Sun Lovers Cafe (⊙11am-6pm Tue-Sat) A kid-friendly place along the river with info, free internet, book swapping and light meals.

Shimoda Tourist Association (☎22-1531; ⊙10am-5pm) Pick up the useful *Shimoda Walking Map* and book accommodation. From the station, take a left, walk to the first intersection and you'll see it on the southeast corner. A branch near the Izu Cruise dock rents bicycles (¥500 per hour).

Shimoda International Club (sicshimoda@yahoo.co.jp) Offers guided tours (¥200 per person) on weekends and holidays.

ℹ Getting There & Away

Shimoda is as far as you can go by train on the Izu Peninsula. Limited-express Odoriko *tokkyū* trains run to Shimoda from Tokyo Station (¥6090, 2¾ hours) or Atami (¥3400, 80 minutes); regular Izukyūkō trains run from Atami (¥1890, 1½ hours) and Itō (¥1570, one hour). Try to catch Izukyū's Resort 21 train, with sideways-facing seats for full-on sea views.

Tōkai buses run to Dōgashima (¥1360, one hour) via Matsuzaki.

Tōkai Kisen (東海汽船; ☎22-2626) ferries serve the Izu Peninsula islands Kōzu-shima, Shikine-jima and Nii-jima (all ¥3890).

Car rental is available at **Toyota Rent-a-Car** (トヨタレンタカー; ☎27-0100) by the train station.

AROUND SHIMODA

RENDAI-JI & KANAYA ONSEN　　　蓮台寺・金谷温泉

The town of Rendai-ji is home to one of the best onsen on the peninsula, **Kanaya Onsen** (金谷温泉; admission ¥1000; ⊙9am-10pm). Its rangy, rambling building houses the biggest all-wood bath in the nation (mixed), called the *sennin-furo* (1000-person bath, a vast exaggeration). The women-only bath is nothing to sneeze at, and both sides have private outdoor baths as well. BYO towel, or buy one for ¥200.

The same building also houses the fabulously traditional **Kanaya Ryokan** (☎0558-22-0325; fax 23-6078; 114-2 Kouchi; r per person with/without 2 meals from ¥15,900/7480), which was built in 1929 and feels like it. Some of the tatami rooms are simple, while others are vast suites with private toilet. There are no restaurants nearby, so go for the inn's meals or pack your own.

From Izukyū Shimoda Station take the Izukyū line to Rendai-ji Station (¥160, five minutes), go straight across the river and main road to the T-junction and turn left; the onsen is 50m ahead on the right.

IRŌZAKI　　　　　　　　　　　　　石廊崎

The southernmost point of the peninsula is noted for its dramatic cliffs and lighthouse. From Shimoda, take bus 4 to Irōsaki-kōkō (¥860, 40 minutes) and head down the road on the left; the lighthouse is a 1km walk up from the harbour. Izu Cruise (p146), runs frequent 25-minute cruises around the rocky point (¥1200/600 per adult/child).

MATSUZAKI & DŌGASHIMA　　　松崎・堂ヶ島
☎0558

Things are much quieter on the west coast. The sleepy port of Matsuzaki is known for its streetscapes: some 200 traditional houses with *namako-kabe* walls. They're concentrated in the south of town, on the far side of the river. The **Tourist Information Center** (☎42-1190; ⊙8.45am-4.45pm) at the bus stop will hold your luggage for the day (¥100).

The **Izu Chōhachi Art Museum** (伊豆の長八美術館; 23 Matsuzaki; adult/child ¥500/free; ⊙9am-5pm) showcases the work of native son Irie Chōhachi (1815–99). His frescos and plaster works are unimaginably detailed – the staff supply magnifying glasses so you can get a better look. Each colour, no matter how intricate the design (be it a pine needle or a stitch on a kimono), gets its own layer of plaster. There are more Chōhachi works around town, in the **Chōhachi Memorial Hall** (長八記念館; 234-1 Matsuzaki; adult/child ¥400/300; ⊙9am-3.30pm Fri-Wed) and the former **Iwashina Elementary School** (岩科学校; 442 Iwashina-hokusoku; adult/child ¥300/free; ⊙9am-5pm), an attractive Meiji-era structure (1880) that combines Japanese and Western-style architecture. The latter is a 2km walk from the museum, past orchards and rice paddies.

Dōgashima, a short bus ride (¥260, five minutes) from Matsuzaki, is famous for its dramatic rock formations, which line the seashore. There is a **Tourist Information Center** (☎52-1268; ⊙8.30am-5pm Mon-Sat) in front of the bus stop that can help with onward bookings and transport info. **Cruises** (¥920/1880 for 20/50 minutes) from the nearby jetty take in the town's famous shoreline cave. The park just across the street from the bus stop has excellent views too; don't miss the **Tensōdō** (天窓洞), a natural window in the cave's roof.

🛏 Sleeping & Eating

Sanyo-sō Youth Hostel   HOSTEL $

(三余荘ユースホステル; ☑/fax 42-0408; www.jyh.or.jp; 73-1 Naka; dm member/nonmember ¥3360/3960) Amid rice fields 3km east of Matsuzaki, this is a delightfully antique lodging, a former landowner's home with fine (shared) tatami rooms. From Shimoda take a Dōgashima-bound bus and get off at the Yūsu-hosteru-mae bus stop (¥1160, 50 minutes); it's another ¥240 to Matsuzaki.

Mingei Sabō   SHOKUDO $$

(民芸茶房; 495-7 Matsuzaki; sets ¥1050-3150; ⏰7.30am-8.30pm) Here you'll find fishing paraphernalia on the walls and filling sets of fresh local seafood on the (picture) menu. It's near the port in Matsuzaki. From the art museum, walk straight across the river and keep going until the road comes around a curve; you'll see a painting of fish over the entrance.

ℹ Getting There & Away

Buses to Dōgashima (¥1360, one hour), via Matsuzaki, leave from platform 5 in front of Shimoda Station. From Matsuzaki, buses run via Dōgashima to Shuzen-ji (¥1970, 1½ hours), complete with fantastic views over Suruga-wan to Mt Fuji. When the air is clear and the mountain is blanketed with snow, you'll swear you're looking at a Hokusai print. The best views are between Ōkubo (大久保) and Tōi (土肥).

SHUZEN-JI ONSEN   修善寺温泉
☑0558

Inland Shuzen-ji Onsen is the Izu Peninsula's most charming town, a hot-spring village in a lush valley bisected by the rushing Katsura-gawa. The narrow lanes and criss-crossing bridges are perfect for strolling. Some of Japan's finest onsen ryokan are here as well. There's a **Tourist Information Office** (☑72-2501; ⏰9.30am-5pm) at Shuzen-ji Station. Shuzen-ji Onsen is a 10-minute bus ride from the station.

In the middle of Shuzen-ji Onsen is its namesake temple **Shuzen-ji** (964 Shuzen-ji; admission free; ⏰8.30am-4.30pm). It's said to have been founded over 1200 years ago by Kōbō Daishi, the Heian-period priest credited with spreading Buddhism throughout much of Japan.

History aside, the real reason to visit Shuzen-ji is to take a dip in one of its famous onsen. Right on the river is a foot bath called **Tokko-no-yu** (独鈷の湯; iron-club waters; admission free; ⏰24hr), rumoured to be Izu's oldest hot spring. Its name comes from a legend that its waters sprang from the rock when it was struck by Kōbō Daishi himself.

Inns around town offer day-use bathing, or try **Hako-yu** (筥湯; 925 Shuzen-ji; admission ¥350; ⏰noon-8.30pm), an elegant, contemporary facility identified by its wooden tower; bring your own soap.

🛏 Sleeping & Eating

🏆 TOP CHOICE Arai Ryokan   RYOKAN $$$

(新井旅館; ☑72-2007; www.arairyokan.net; fax 72-5119; 970 Shuzen-ji; r per person with 2 meals from ¥24,300; 🛜🖥) Long beloved by Japanese artists and writers, this gem of an inn was founded in 1872 and has kept its traditional, wood-crafted heritage. The bath hall, designed by artist Yasuda Yukihiko, is grand and the riverside rooms are magnificent in autumn, when the maples are ablaze.

Goyōkan   MINSHUKU $$

(五葉間; ☑72-2066; www.goyokan.co.jp; fax 72-8212; 765-2 Shuzen-ji; r per person with/without breakfast ¥7500/6450) Simple tatami rooms in the centre of everything, with river views. There are no private facilities, but the shared (indoor) baths are made of stone and *hinoki* cypress. Some English is spoken.

Zendera Soba   NOODLES $$

(禅寺そば; 761-1-3 Shuzen-ji; meals ¥630-1890; ⏰lunch Fri-Wed; 📖) This local institution serves its speciality namesake Zendera *soba* (¥1260) with a stalk of fresh wasabi root to grate yourself. It's steps from the bus station on the river side of the street, and has white and black banners.

ℹ Getting There & Away

From Tokyo, take the Tōkaidō line to Mishima (Kodama *shinkansen* ¥4400, one hour) then transfer to the Izu-Hakone Tetsudō for Shuzen-ji (¥500, 35 minutes). Buses connect Shuzen-ji Station to Shuzen-ji Onsen (¥210, 10 minutes), Itō (¥1100, one hour) and Dōgashima (¥2140, 1½ hours).

SOUTH OF TOKYO

Tokyo's cultural presence looms large in the Kantō area, but the area just to the south stands on its own. Spend a day (and definitely an evening) in Yokohama, Japan's second-largest city, and you'll discover an entirely different urban spirit. Further south, the fascinating old capital of Kamakura brims with temples, shrines and surprisingly hip restaurants.

Yokohama 横浜

♪045 / POP 3,680,000

Yokohama prides itself on its cosmopolitan roots. Though just 20 minutes south of central Tokyo, the city has a flavour and history all its own. While locals are likely to cite the uncrowded streets or neighbourhood atmosphere as the main draw, for visitors it's the breezy bay front, a popular date spot day and night.

Yokohama is a city of distinct districts, including Chinatown, historic Motomachi and Yamate, and the recent seaside development of Minato Mirai 21. Most of the sights are within 1km of the water, near stations on the JR Negishi line and the Minato Mirai line.

History

For most of its history, Yokohama was an unnoticed fishing village. Its fate changed abruptly in 1853–54 when the American fleet under Commodore Matthew Perry arrived off the coast to persuade Japan to open to foreign trade; in 1858 this little village was designated an international port.

Westerners were first relegated to an area within a moat in a district called Kannai (meaning 'inside the barrier') but later began to own property up the mountainside (Yamate). A Chinese community burgeoned as well, and the city expanded on reclaimed land.

Throughout the late 19th and early 20th centuries, Yokohama served as a gateway for foreign influence and ideas. Among the city's firsts-in-Japan: a daily newspaper, gas lamps and a train terminus (connected to Shimbashi in Tokyo).

The Great Kantō Earthquake of 1923 destroyed much of the city, with the rubble used to reclaim more land, including Yamashita-kōen. The city was devastated yet again in WWII air raids; occupation forces were initially based here but later moved down the coast to Yokosuka.

Yokohama continues to evolve. In recent decades the city has undertaken dramatic redevelopments of the harbour area and skyline.

⊙ Sights & Activities

MINATO MIRAI 21 みなとみらい21

This district of artificial islands used to be shipping docks, but the last three decades have transformed them into a planned city of tomorrow ('Minato Mirai' means 'port future'). Certain areas, namely the concrete sprawl and commercial complexes created in the early-'90s boom years, appear dated in retrospect. Recent additions, however, are of a more pedestrian sort, including the waterfront **Zō-no-hana Park** and a series of **promenades** connecting the area's main attractions.

Landmark Tower   NOTABLE BUILDING

(ランドマークタワ; 2-2-1-1 Minato Mirai; adult/child ¥1000/500; ◷10am-9pm; 飛Minato Mirai) Japan's tallest building (70 storeys and 296m high) has one of the world's fastest lifts (45km/h). The Landmark Tower Sky Garden observatory is on the 69th floor; on clear days there are views to Tokyo and Mt Fuji.

Yokohama Museum of Art   MUSEUM

(横浜美術館; www.yaf.or.jp/yma; 3-4-1 Minato Mirai; adult/child ¥500/free; ◷10am-6pm Fri-Wed; 飛Minato Mirai) Behind Landmark Tower, this modern-art museum hosts exhibitions that swing between safe-bet shows with European headliners and more daring ones with contemporary Japanese artists. It's noted for its building, designed by Pritzker Prize winner Tange Kenzō (1989).

Yokohama Port Museum   MUSEUM

(横浜みなと博物館; 2-1-1 Minato Mirai; museum & ship adult/child ¥600/300; ◷10am-5pm Tue-Sun; 飛Minato Mirai) On the harbour in front of Landmark Tower, this fan-shaped museum is largely dedicated to the **Nippon Maru sailing ship** (日本丸) docked adjacent. The four-masted barque (built in 1930) retains many original fittings.

Akarenga Sōkō   HISTORICAL BUILDING

(横浜赤レンガ倉庫; 1-1-2 Shinkō; ◷11am-8pm, some restaurants later; 飛Bashamichi) Akarenga Sōkō means 'red-brick warehouse', and these century-old structures have been refurbished into boutiques, restaurants, cafes and event spaces.

Cosmo World   AMUSEMENT PARK

(横浜コスモワールド; 2-8-1 Shinkō; rides ¥300-700; ◷11am-9pm; 飛Minato Mirai) The park is home to one of the world's tallest Ferris wheels, the 112.5m Cosmo Clock 21 (admission ¥700). There are kiddie rides here, too.

YAMASHITA-KŌEN AREA 山下公園周辺

This seaside, landscaped **park** (飛Motomachi-Chūkagai) is perfect for strolling and ship watching.

MT FUJI & AROUND TOKYO SOUTH OF TOKYO

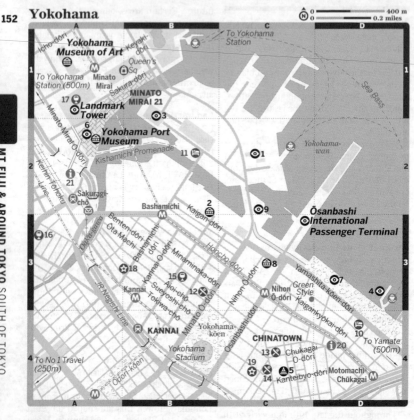

TOP CHOICE **Ōsanbashi International Passenger Terminal** NOTABLE BUILDING
(大さん橋国際客船ターミナル; 1-1-4 Kaigan-dōri; admission free; ⏰24hr; ℝNihon-ō-dōri) Just to the west of the park, this sleek, award-winning pier was designed by Farshid Moussavi and Alejandro Zaera Polo and completed in 2002. It has an attractive **roof deck**.

Yokohama Archives of History MUSEUM
(横浜開港資料館; 3 Nihon Ō-dōri; adult/child ¥200/100; ⏰9.30am-5pm Tue-Sun; ℝNihon-ō-dōri) Displays in English chronicle the city's history, from the opening of Japan through to the mid-20th century. It's inside the former British Consulate, on the main road across from Ōsanbashi pier.

Hikawa Maru MUSEUM
(氷川丸; Yamashita-kōen; adult/child & senior ¥200/100; ⏰10am-4.30pm Tue-Sun; ℝMotomachi-Chūkagai) Moored at the eastern end of the park, this restored 1930s passen-ger liner has art-deco fixings and stories to tell. Inside, you can wander from the 1st-class cabins (one of the staterooms was used by Charlie Chaplin) to the engine room.

BankART Studio NYK ART GALLERY
(www.bankart1929.com; 3-9 Kaigan-dōri; ⏰cafe 11.30am-11pm, gallery admission & hours vary; ℝBashamichi) This gallery and theatre in a former warehouse is a fixture on the local arts scene. You can sift through flyers for local events over drinks in the 1st-floor **cafe**.

YAMATE & MOTOMACHI 山手・元町
Southeast of Yamashita-kōen, the area of **Yamate** (ℝMotomachi-Chūkagai, Ishikawa-chō) offers a glimpse of Yokohama's cosmopolitan past, with early-20th-century Western-style architecture and fantastic views from the brick sidewalks of Yamate-hon-dōri (Bluff St). Private homes and churches here are still in use. Attractions include Harbour View Park and the **Foreigners' Cemetery**

Yokohama

(◷10am-5pm Tue-Sun), final resting place of 4000 foreign residents and visitors – the headstones carry some fascinating inscriptions. The shopping street in neighbouring **Motomachi** has some venerable old shops, though nearly all of the buildings are recent constructions.

CHINATOWN   中華街
Yokohama's **Chinatown** (Chūkagai; ▧Motomachi-Chūkagai, Ishikawa-chō) packs speciality shops and some 300 restaurants within a space of several blocks, marked by 10 elaborately painted gates. At its heart is the Chinese temple **Kantei-byō** (関帝廟; 140 Yamashita-chō; admission free; ◷9am-7pm), dedicated to Kanwu, the god of business.

SANKEI-EN   三渓園
Opened to the public in 1906, the landscaped gardens of **Sankei-en** (58-1 Honmoku-sannotani; adult/child ¥500/200; ◷9am-4.30pm) feature walking paths among ponds and medieval structures. From Yokohama or Sakuragi-chō Station, take bus 8 to Honmoku Sankei-en-mae (30 minutes).

🛏 Sleeping

Most domestic hotel brands have outposts in Yokohama. Both **Toyoko Inn** (www.toyoko-inn.com/eng) and **Washington Hotel** (www.wh-rsv.com/english) chains offer several affordable options around the city.

Hotel New Grand   HOTEL $$$
(ホテルニューグランド; ☎681-1841; www.hotel-newgrand.co.jp; fax 681-1895; 10 Yamashita-kōen-dōri; s/tw from ¥13,860/28,000; ⊜@; ▧Motomachi-Chūkagai) This old-line (1927) hotel has a prime waterfront location and was once a favourite of visiting foreign dignitaries (check out the timeless original lobby). Now it's a classy, upmarket option with some old-world charm, despite the addition of a tower in 1992.

Porto Yokohama   HOSTEL $
(ポルトヨコハマ; ☎263-6981; portoyokohama.jp; 3-10-3 Matsukage-chō; dm/d from ¥2500/4500; ⊜@☎; ▧Ishikawa-chō) Clean sheets and a fresh coat of paint transform two floors of a tenement house into a surprisingly attractive budget accommodation. It's run by a local community activist in one of the city's less, uh, touristy neighbourhoods. Rates include breakfast. Check the website for a map.

Navios Yokohama   HOTEL $$
(ナビオス横浜; ☎633-6000; www.navios-yokohama.com; fax 633-6001; 2-1-1 Shinkō; s/d from ¥8400/14,700; ▧Bashamichi; ⊜@☎) In convenient Minato Mirai, this is Yokohama's best midrange deal. Rooms are spotless and central, with city or sea views.

🍴 Eating

Chinatown offers the most interesting food options, though beware overpriced tourist traps. Yokohama is known for *yōshoku*, classic Western dishes (think hamburger

DON'T MISS

SHIN-YOKOHAMA RĀMEN MUSEUM

Noodle lovers, take note: the **Shin-Yokohama Rāmen Museum** (新横浜ラーメン博物館; www.raumen.co.jp/ramen; 2-14-21 Shin-Yokohama; adult/child ¥300/100, dishes around ¥900; ⊙11am-10pm; ℝShin-Yokohama) is devoted solely to *rāmen*, the Chinese-style noodles that (it's fair to say) Japan is bonkers about. Nine *rāmen* restaurants from around the country were handpicked to sell their wares in this replica of a 1958 *shitamachi* (downtown district). Order smaller, 'tasting' bowls to take advantage of the variety of miso, *shōyu* (soy sauce) and *tonkatsu* (pork) soups. When this clever 'food theme park' opened in 1994, it set off a wave of copycat establishments around the country enshrining other cult foods like *gyōza* (dumplings) and curry, though none have experienced the lasting popularity of the original. Getting there is a little complicated, so check the website for directions before heading out.

and stew) reinterpreted for local tastes. For an eclectic mix of cuisines, visit Akarenga Sōkō and the restaurant floors of Landmark Tower and Queen's Sq.

Manchinrō Honten   CHINESE **$$$**
(萬珍樓本店; ☑681-4004; english.manchinro .com; 153 Yamashita-chō; lunch/dinner courses from ¥2750/6600; ⊙11am-10pm; ⊖ⓓ; ℝMotomachi-Chūkagai) This elegant Cantonese restaurant is one of Chinatown's oldest (1892) and most respected, with chefs from Hong Kong. Look for the stone lions out the front. The newer annexe around the corner, Manchinrō Tenshinpo, specialises in yum cha (dim sum; dishes/courses from ¥725/3300).

Baikōtei   INTERNATIONAL **$**
(梅香亭; 1-1 Aioicho; mains ¥850-1550; ⊙lunch & dinner Tue-Sat; ⓓ; ℝKannai, Nihon Ō-dōri) This weathered classic with red-velour seating is famed for its *hayashi* rice (hashed beef in demi-glace sauce), and a mean *katsu-don* (pork cutlet). Look for the window that announces Baikō Emmies.

Ryūsen   CHINESE **$$**
(馬さんの店龍仙; 218-5 Yamashita-chō; mains from ¥1050; ⊙7am-3am; ⓓ; ℝIshikawa-chō) You can't miss friendly old Mr Ma sitting outside his small Shanghai-style eatery with a red awning, as he has done for years. The walls outside and inside are literally wallpapered with photos of tasty-looking dishes.

Chano-ma   ASIAN FUSION **$$**
(チャノマ; 3rd fl, Akarenga Sōkō Bldg 2; mains from ¥800; ⊙11am-11pm, to 5am Fri & Sat; ⓓ; ℝBashamichi) Dine on sushi rolls, salads and croquettes under tall ceilings, while serious club beats play. The most coveted seats are on mattresses, arranged around the open kitchen.

Bills   INTERNATIONAL **$$**
(ビルズ; Akarenga Sōkō Bldg 2; mains ¥1000-2000; ⊙9am-11pm; ⓓ; ℝBashamichi) This popular new outpost from Australian celebrity chef Bill Granger proves that Yokohama still has an appetite for foreign flavours. There's a glass terrace and a long line for Sunday brunch.

🍷 Drinking & Entertainment

Yokohama is a live-music city. The narrow streets of Noge-chō, just south of Sakuragi-chō Station, have a high concentration of small, intimate bars.

TOP CHOICE Kamome   LIVE MUSIC
(カモメ; www.yokohama-kamome.com; 6-76 Sumiyoshi-cho; live-music covers ¥3000-4000, drinks from ¥600; ⊙6-11pm; ℝBashamichi) This is the best place in town to catch some serious live music, with a line-up that includes veteran and up-and-coming talents playing jazz, funk, fusion and bossa nova. The interior is stark and sophisticated, the crowd stylish and multigenerational. Exit 3 of Bashamichi station points towards a side road; to get here, follow it for several blocks until you see the small neon sign on your right.

Craft Beer Bar   BAR
(クラフトビアバー; 2-31-3 Ōta-chō; drinks from ¥700; ⊙4-11.30pm Tue-Sun; ⊖; ℝBashamichi) This small counter bar has a revolving selection of 10 domestic craft brews on tap. There's no English menu, but you can just tell the barman what you want (ale, stout etc) and how you want it (pint or glass), and he'll happily oblige. Look for a plain wooden door in the alleyway, with English on the awning.

Downbeat   BAR

(ダウンビート; www.yokohama-downbeat.com, in Japanese; 1-43 Hanasaki-chō Bldg 2; drinks from ¥650; ⊙4-11.30pm Mon-Sat; ▣; ®Sakuragi-chō) *Jazz kissa,* which fall somewhere between cafes and bars, boast extensive jazz-record collections. This is one of the oldest (1956) in Yokohama, with over 3000 albums and some serious speakers. Occasional live music means an occasional cover charge. Look for the 2nd-floor red awning.

Windjammer   LIVE MUSIC

(ウィンドジャマー; 215 Yamashita-chō; live-music covers ¥400-600, drinks from ¥650; ⊙5pm-midnight; ▣; ®Motomachi-Chūkagai) The setting feels like the inside of a yacht – all the better to listen to live jazz nightly, from 8pm; look for the English sign.

Motion Blue   LIVE MUSIC

(モーション・ブルー・ヨコハマ; ☑226-1919; www.motionblue.co.jp; 3rd fl, Akarenga Sōkō Bldg 2; tickets ¥2100-8400; ⊙5-11.30pm Mon-Fri, 4-9.30pm Sat & Sun; ®Bashamichi) Upscale venue with a solid line-up of jazz, fusion, world music, J-pop and more.

Sirius   BAR

(シリウス; ☑221-1111; 2-2-1-3 Minato Mirai; cover charge after 5/7pm ¥1050/2100, cocktails from ¥1260; ⊙7am-1am; ®Sakuragi-chō) Cocktails with a view from the 70th floor of the Yokohama Royal Park Hotel.

❶ Information

Information about Yokohama is available on the web at www.welcome.city.yokohama.jp/eng/tourism.

Animi (アニミ; ⊙11am-9pm) Wi-fi, computers for rent (¥300) and curry (from ¥600), 15 minutes northwest of Minato Mirai Station.

Chinatown 80 Information Center (横浜中華街インフォメーションセンター; ☑662-1252; ⊙10am-9pm) A few blocks from Motomachi-Chūgakai Station.

Citibank (みなとみらい21総合案内所; ⊙24hr) International ATM outside the western exit of Yokohama Station, on the 2nd floor of a covered passageway attached to the Yokohama Bay Sheraton.

Minato Mirai 21 Information Center (☑211-0111; ⊙9am-6pm) English speakers and plenty of English-language maps and brochures, outside the northern exit of Sakuragi-chō Station.

No 1 Travel (☑231-0721; ⊙10am-6.30pm Mon-Fri, to 4.30pm Sat) For discount international travel; about 10 blocks southwest of Kannai Station, though the Isezaki shopping arcade.

Post office A block east of Sakuragi-chō Station, with foreign ATM service.

Yokohama Station Tourist Information Center (☑441-7300; ⊙9am-7pm) In the east–west corridor; English spoken.

❶ Getting There & Away

JR Tōkaidō, Yokosuka and Keihin Tōhoku lines run from Tokyo Station (¥450, 30 minutes) via Shinagawa (¥280, 20 minutes) to Yokohama Station. Some Keihin Tōhoku line trains continue along the Negishi line to Sakuragi-chō, Kannai and Ishikawa-chō. From Shinjuku, take the Shōnan-Shinjuku line (¥540, 35 minutes).

The private Tōkyū Tōyoko line runs from Shibuya to Yokohama (¥260, 25 minutes), after which it becomes the Minato Mirai subway line to Minato Mirai (¥440, 28 minutes) and Motomachi-Chūkagai (¥460, 30 minutes).

The Tōkaidō *shinkansen* stops at Shin-Yokohama Station, northwest of town, connected to the city centre by the Yokohama line.

To/From the Airport

The Narita Express (N'EX; ¥4180, 1½ hours) runs every 30 minutes to Yokohama. Frequent limousine buses run to/from the Yokohama City Air Terminal (YCAT, Sky Building; east of Yokohama Station, next to Sogō department store; www.ycat.co.jp) for Narita Airport (¥3500, two hours) or Haneda Airport (¥560, 30 minutes).

❶ Getting Around

BICYCLE Green Style (グリーンスタイル; 24-8 Yamashita-chō; per 3hr/day ¥1000/1800; ⊙11am-8pm Fri-Tue) rents bicycles on a back street near Yamashita-kōen.

BOAT Sea Bass ferries connect Yokohama Station with Minato Mirai 21 (¥400, 15 minutes) and Yamashita-kōen (¥700, express/local 20/50 minutes) from approximately 10am to 7pm. From Yokohama Station, take the east exit and pass through Sogō department store to reach the dock.

BUS Although trains are more convenient, Yokohama has an extensive bus network (adult/child ¥210/110 per ride). A special Akai-kutsu ('red shoe') bus loops every 20 minutes from 10am to 7pm through the tourist areas for ¥100 per ride.

SUBWAY The Yokohama City blue line (*shiei chikatetsu*) connects Yokohama with Shin-Yokohama (¥230, 11 minutes), Sakuragi-chō (¥200, three minutes) and Kannai (¥200, five minutes).

The '**Minato Burari**' day pass covers municipal subway and bus rides (including the Akai-kutsu bus, but not the Minato Mirai line) around Minato Mirai and Yamashita-kōen (adult/child ¥500/250); purchase at any subway station.

Kamakura 鎌倉

☎ 0467 / POP 174,000

Between 1185 and 1333, Kamakura was Japan's first feudal capital. Its glory days coincided with the spread of populist Buddhism in Japan, a legacy reflected in the area's high concentration of stunning temples and statuary. Contemporary residents have added a laid-back, earthy vibe complete with organic restaurants and summer beach shacks – which can be added to sunrise meditation and hillside hikes as reasons to visit. Just an hour from Tokyo, Kamakura does tend to get packed on weekends and in holiday periods, so make sure you plan accordingly.

History

The end of the Heian period was marked by a legendary feud between two great warrior families, the Minamoto (Genji) and the Taira (Heike). After the Taira routed the Minamoto, the third son of the Minamoto clan, called Yoritomo, was sent to live at a temple in Izu Peninsula. When the boy grew old enough, he began to gather support for a counterattack on his clan's old rivals. In 1180 Yoritomo set up his base at Kamakura, far away from the debilitating influences of Kyoto court life, close to other clans loyal to the Minamoto and, having the sea on one side and densely wooded hills on the others, easy to defend.

After victories over the Taira, Minamoto Yoritomo was appointed shōgun in 1192 and governed Japan from Kamakura. When he died without an heir, power passed to the Hōjō, the family of Yoritomo's wife.

The Hōjō clan ruled Japan from Kamakura for more than a century until, in 1333, weakened by the cost of maintaining defences against threats of attack from Kublai Khan in China, the Hōjō clan was defeated by Emperor Go-Daigo. Kyoto once again became the capital.

By the Edo period, Kamakura was practically a village again. With the opening of a rail line at the turn of the last century, the seaside town was reborn as a summer resort. Summer homes of wealthy Tokyoites still line the Shōnan coast.

⊙ Sights & Activities

The main attractions are located along the road from Kita-Kamakura Station (one stop before Kamakura) to Kamakura Station and also in Hase to the west. For shopping, head to narrow Komachi-dōri, to the left of Kamakura Station's east exit. The broad boulevard Wakayama-ōji runs from Tsurugaoka Hachiman-gū shrine to Yuiga-hama, a sandy beach with a smattering of eateries.

Kamakura

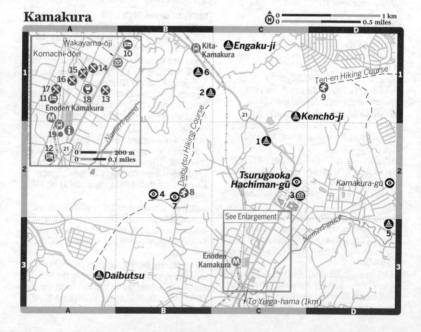

Kenchō-ji
TEMPLE

(建長寺; 8 Yamanouchi; adult/child ¥300/100; ⊙8.30am-4.30pm) Established in 1253, Kencho-ji is Japan's oldest Zen monastery and is still active today. It once comprised seven buildings and 49 subtemples, most of which were destroyed in the fires of the 14th and 15th centuries. However, the 17th and 18th centuries saw its restoration, and you can still get a sense of its splendour. The central Butsuden (Buddha hall) was brought piece by piece from Tokyo in 1647. Its Jizō Bosatsu statue, unusual for a Zen temple, reflects the valley's ancient function as an execution ground – Jizō consoles lost souls. Other highlights include a bell cast in 1253 and the juniper grove, believed to have sprouted from seeds brought from China by Kenchō-ji's founder some seven centuries ago.

Engaku-ji
TEMPLE

(円覚寺; 409 Yamanouchi; adult/child ¥300/100; ⊙8am-4.30pm Apr-Oct, to 3.30pm Nov-Mar) Engaku-ji, one of the five major Rinzai Zen temples in Kamakura, is on the left as you exit Kita-Kamakura Station. It was founded in 1282, allegedly as a place where Zen monks might pray for soldiers who lost their lives defending Japan against Kublai Khan. Engaku-ji remains an important temple, and a number of notable priests have trained here. All of the temple structures have been rebuilt over the centuries; the Shariden, a Song-style reliquary, is the oldest structure, last rebuilt in the 16th century. At the top of the long flight of stairs is the Engaku-ji bell, the largest bell in Kamakura, cast in 1301.

Tsurugaoka Hachiman-gū
SHRINE

(鶴岡八幡宮; 2-1-31 Yukinoshita; treasure hall adult/child ¥200/100; ⊙9am-4pm) Kamakura's most important shrine is, naturally, dedicated to Hachiman, the god of war. Minamoto Yoritomo himself ordered its construction in 1191 and designed the pine-flanked central promenade that leads to the coast. The sprawling grounds are ripe with historical symbolism: the Gempei Pond, bisected by bridges, is said to depict the rift between the Minamoto (Genji) and Taira (Heike) clans. Behind the pond is the **Kamakura Museum** (鎌倉国宝館; adult/child ¥300/100; ⊙9am-4pm), housing remarkable Buddhist sculptures from the 12th to 16th centuries.

Daibutsu
MONUMENT

(大仏; Great Buddha; 4-2-28 Hase; adult/child ¥200/150; ⊙7am-5.30pm) Kamakura's most iconic sight, an 11.4m bronze statue of Amida Buddha (*amitābha* in Sanskrit), is in Kōtoku-in, a Jōdo sect temple. Completed in 1252, it's said to have been inspired by Yoritomo's visit to Nara (where Japan's biggest Daibutsu holds court) after the Minamoto clan's victory over the Taira clan. Once housed in a huge hall, today the statue sits in the open, the hall having been washed away by a tsunami in 1495. For an extra ¥20, you can duck inside to see how the sculptors pieced the 850-tonne statue together.

Buses from stops 1 and 6 in front of Kamakura Station run to the Daibutsu-mae stop. Alternatively, take the Enoden Enoshima line to Hase Station and walk north for about five minutes. Better yet, take the Daibutsu Hiking Course (see p158).

GET ZEN

Too many temples and before you know it you're feeling anything but 'Zen'. *Zazen* (sitting meditation) can help you discover what you're missing – after all, temples were originally designed for this purpose (and not sightseeing). Both **Engaku-ji** (free; ⊘5.30-6.30am Apr-Oct, 6-7am Nov-Mar) and **Kenchō-ji** (temple admission ¥300; ⊘5-6pm Fri & Sat, enter before 4.30pm) hold beginner-friendly, public *zazen* sessions. Instruction is in Japanese, but you can easily manage by watching everyone else; arrive at least 15 minutes early.

Hase-dera
TEMPLE

(長谷寺; Hase Kannon; 3-11-2 Hase; adult/child ¥300/100; ⊘8am-4.30pm) About 10 minutes' walk from the Daibutsu, Hase-dera (Jōdo sect) is one of the most popular temples in the Kantō region. The focal point of the temple's main hall is a 9m-high carved wooden *jūichimen* (11-faced) Kannon statue. Kannon (*avalokiteshvara* in Sanskrit) is the bodhisattva of infinite compassion and, along with Jizō, is one of Japan's most popular Buddhist deities. According to legend, the temple dates back to AD 736, when the statue is said to have washed up on the shore near Kamakura.

Ennō-ji
TEMPLE

(円応寺; 1543 Yamanouchi; admission ¥200; ⊘9am-3.30pm) Across the road from Kenchō-ji is Ennō-ji, which is distinguished primarily by its collection of statues depicting the judges of hell. Presiding over them is a statue of Emma (Sanskrit name Yama; an Important Cultural Property), an ancient Hindu deity and ruler of hell's 10 kings. The statue is noted for its fierce gaze meant for the wicked (hopefully you won't have anything to worry about).

Tōkei-ji
TEMPLE

(東慶寺; 1367 Yamanouchi; admission ¥100; ⊘8.30am-4.30pm) Across the railway tracks from Engaku-ji, Tōkei-ji is famed as having served as a women's refuge. A woman could be officially recognised as divorced after three years as a nun in the temple precincts. Today, there are no nuns; the grave of the last abbess can be found in the cemetery, shrouded by cypress trees.

Daibutsu Hiking Course
HIKING

This 3km wooded trail connects Kita-Kamakura with the Daibutsu in Hase (allow about 1½ hours). The path begins at the steps just up the lane from pretty **Jōchi-ji** (浄智寺;1402 Yamanouchi; adult/child ¥200/100; ⊘9am-4.30pm), a few minutes from Tōkei-ji.

Along the course you'll pass **Zeniarai-benten** (銭洗弁天; admission free; ⊘8am-5pm), one of Kamakura's most alluring Shintō shrines. A cave-like entrance leads to a clearing where visitors come to bathe their money in natural springs, with the hope of bringing financial success. From here, continue down the paved road, turning right at the first intersection, walking along a path lined with cryptomeria and ascending through a succession of torii to **Sasuke-inari-jinja** (佐助稲荷神社; admission free; ⊘24hr) before meeting up with the Daibutsu path once again. To hike in the opposite direction, follow the road beyond Daibutsu and the trail entrance is on the right, just before a tunnel.

Sugimoto-dera
TEMPLE

(杉本寺; 903 Nikaidō; adult/child ¥200/100; ⊘8am-4.30pm) This small temple, founded in AD 734, is reputed to be the oldest in Kamakura. The ferocious-looking guardian deities and statues of Kannon are its main draw. Take a bus from stop 5 at Kamakura Station to the Sugimoto Kannon bus stop (¥190, 10 minutes).

Hōkoku-ji
TEMPLE

(報国寺; 2-7-4 Jōmyōji; bamboo garden admission ¥200; ⊘9am-4pm) Down the road from Sugimoto-dera, on the right-hand side, is this Rinzai Zen temple with quiet, landscaped gardens where you can relax under a red parasol with a cup of Japanese tea.

Zuisen-ji
TEMPLE

(瑞泉寺; 710 Nikaidō; adult/child ¥200/100; ⊘9am-4.30pm) The grounds of this secluded Zen temple make for a pleasant stroll and include gardens laid out by Musō Soseki, the temple's esteemed founder. To get here, take the bus from stop 4 at Kamakura Station and get off at Ōtōnomiya (¥190, 10 minutes); turn right where the bus turns left in front of Kamakura-gū, take the next left and keep following the road for 10 or 15 minutes.

Ten-en Hiking Course HIKING

(天園ハイキングコース) From Zuisen-ji you can access this trail, which winds through the hills for two hours before coming out at Kenchō-ji. From Kenchō-ji, walk around the Hojo (Main Hall) and up the steps to the trail.

✯ Festivals & Events

Kamakura Matsuri HISTORICAL

A week of celebrations held from the second Sunday to the third Sunday in April. It includes a wide range of activities, most of which are centred on Tsurugaoka Hachiman-gū.

Bonbori Matsuri LANTERNS

From 7 to 9 August, hundreds of lanterns are strung up around Tsurugaoka Hachiman-gū.

Reitai Matsuri MIKOSHI

Festivities between 14 and 16 September include a procession of *mikoshi* as well as, on the last day, a display of horseback archery.

🛏 Sleeping

Hotel New Kamakura HOTEL $$

(ホテルニューカマクラ; ☎22-2230; www.new kamakura.com; fax 22-0233; 13-2 Onarimachi; s/d from ¥4200/11,000; @) Charming, slightly shabby and a steal, this hotel built in 1924 has both Western- and Japanese-style rooms. There's a red carpet and a vintage vibe, though the economy rooms are rather plain. Rooms in the Original Wing have shared facilities. Exit west from Kamakura Station, take a sharp right down the alley and look for the art-deco sign.

Kamakura Hase Youth Hostel HOSTEL $

(鎌倉はせユースホステル; ☎/fax 24-3390; www1.kamakuranet.ne.jp/hase_yh/; 5-11 Sakanoshita; dm member/nonmember ¥3000/4000; ◉⌂) Three minutes from both Hase-dera and the beach, this tidy, modern hostel has an excellent location. It also has firm rules and even firmer bunks. From Kamakura Station take an Enoden Enoshima train to Hase Station.

Classical Hotel Ajisai HOTEL $$

(クラシカルホテルあじさい; ☎22-3492; www.hotel-ajisai.com; 1-12-4 Yukinoshita; s/tw from ¥6830/11,650; @) Across from Tsurugaoka Hachiman-gū, the 10-room Ajisai is a businesslike, affordable option with small, basic Western-style rooms. Fourth-floor rooms have shrine views.

Kamakura Park Hotel HOTEL $$$

(鎌倉パークホテル; ☎25-5121; www.kamak uraparkhotel.co.jp; fax 25-3778; 33-6 Sakanoshita; s/tw from ¥17,325/25,410; ◉⌂) A bit 1980s plush, with ocean views and marble baths. It's a 12-minute walk along the coast from Hase Station.

Lady's Inn White Hotel GUESTHOUSE $

(レディースインホワイトホテル; ☎22-4407; www014.upp.so-net.ne.jp/whitehotel, in Japanese; 2-20 Onarimachi; s/tw from ¥4500/9000) Just for ladies and decked out like a doll's house. Little English spoken; ask the tourist centre to call ahead.

🍴 Eating & Drinking

Vegetarians can eat well in Kamakura; pick up the free, bilingual **Vegetarian Culture Map** at the Tourist Information Center. *Shirasu* (tiny whitebait) are a local speciality, fished from nearby waters.

Snackers will love Komachi-dōri.

TOP CHOICE Matsubara-an NOODLES $$

(松原庵; 4-10-3 Yuiga-hama; lunch sets ¥2800, mains from ¥900; ⏰lunch & dinner) This upscale *soba* restaurant in a former residence captures the feel of early-20th-century Kamakura, when the area was a fashionable summertime retreat. There's no English menu, but you can't go wrong with the tempura *seiro soba* (al dente noodles served cold) or the set lunch (*ranchi kōsu*). From Yuiga-hama Station (on the Enoden line) head towards the beach and then take the first right. Look for the blue sign; the entrance is just to the left, with white door curtains.

Magokoro FUSION $$

(麻心; 2nd fl, 2-8-11 Hase; meals from ¥1000; ⏰lunch & dinner Tue-Sun; ✏◉) With eclectic fare like hemp-seed curry and additive-free sake, this organic joint is a favourite with the local green crowd. From Hase Station, walk to the beach and turn left onto the coastal road; you'll see the 2nd-floor picture windows on your left.

Bowls Donburi Café SUSHI $

(鎌倉どんぶりカフェbowls; 2-14-7 Komachi; meals ¥780-1250; ⏰11am-midnight; ◉@✏◉) The humble *donburi* (rice bowl) gets a hip, healthy remake here, with toppings such as seared tuna and avocado. You get a discount if you discover the word *atari* at the bottom of the bowl. There's an English sign over the doors.

Sông Bé Cafe
ASIAN FUSION $

(ソンベカフェ; 13-32 Onarimachi; dishes from ¥800; ⊘lunch & dinner Thu-Tue; 🖉🍴) This mellow day-to-evening joint near the Hotel New Kamakura serves up dishes like *pho* and green curry, with vegies sourced from the local farmers market. Look for the terrace out the front and flyers for local events inside.

Milk Hall
CAFE $

(ミルクホール; 2-3-8 Komachi; most dishes ¥600-1050; ⊘11am-10.30pm; 🍴) This local cafe-scene landmark is also an antiques shop and, by evening, a moody bar. Live jazz plays some nights. Head two blocks down Komachi-dōri, take a left and then another left down the first alley; the door has an English sign.

Bar Ram
BAR

(バー・ラム; 2-11-11 Komachi; drinks from ¥500; ⊘5pm-late) Kamakura has pockets of nightlife, including this hole in the wall in the lanes off Komachi-dōri. It's a *tachinomiya* (drink-while-standing bar) with plenty of old Rolling Stones vinyls and friendly banter. Look for the English sign.

Kamakura Ichibanya
RICE CRACKERS $

(鎌倉壱番屋; ⊘9am-6.30pm) Specialises in *senbei* (rice crackers); watch staff grilling them in the window or buy some 50 packaged varieties, including curry, garlic, *mentaiko* (spicy cod roe) or *uni* (sea urchin); look for the baskets on the corner.

Imo-no-kichikan
ICE CREAM $

(いも吉館; ⊘10am-6pm) Famous for softserve sweet-potato ice cream (¥295). Look for the giant plastic cone with lavender-hued ice cream.

ℹ Information

For information about both living and sightseeing in Kamakura, see www.city.kamakura.kanagawa.jp/english.

Kamakura Welcome Guides (www1.kamakuranet.ne.jp/kwga) Offers half-day tours with volunteer guides in English for a nominal fee; five days' notice is required.

Post office With ATMs; a short walk from Kamakura Station's east exit.

Tourist Information Center (鎌倉市観光協会 観光総合案内所; ☎22-3350; ⊘9am-5.30pm Apr-Sep, to 5pm Oct-Mar) Just outside Kamakura Station's east exit, this helpful tourist office distributes maps and brochures and can also make bookings for same-day accommodation.

ℹ Getting There & Away

JR Yokosuka-line trains run to Kamakura from Tokyo (¥890, 56 minutes) and Shinagawa (¥690, 46 minutes), via Yokohama (¥330, 27 minutes). Alternatively, the Shōnan Shinjuku line runs from the west side of Tokyo (Shibuya, Shinjuku and Ikebukuro, all ¥890) in about one hour, though some trains require a transfer at Ōfuna, one stop before Kita-Kamakura.

JR Kamakura-Enoshima Free Pass (from Tokyo/Yokohama ¥1970/1130) Valid for two days; covers the trip to and from Tokyo/Yokohama and unlimited use of JR trains around Kamakura, the Shōnan monorail between Ōfuna and Enoshima, and the Enoden Enoshima line.

Odakyū Enoshima/Kamakura Free Pass (from Shinjuku/Machida ¥1430/990) Valid for one day; includes transport to Fujisawa Station (where it meets the Enoden Enoshima line), plus use of the Enoden.

ℹ Getting Around

You can walk to most temples and shrines from Kamakura or Kita-Kamakura Stations. Sites in the west, like the Daibutsu, can be reached via the Enoden line from Kamakura Station to Hase (¥190) or by bus from Kamakura Station stops 1 and 6. Bus trips around the area cost either ¥170 or ¥190.

Rent-a-Cycle Kurarin (レンタサイクル; per hr/day ¥600/1600; ⊘8.30am-5pm) is outside the east exit of Kamakura Station, and right up the incline. Local rickshaw rides start at ¥2000 per person for 10 minutes.

EAST OF TOKYO

Chiba Prefecture, east and southeast of Tokyo, has few attractions for travellers, save the city of Narita. There are also decent surf beaches along the Kujūkuri-hama coastline, on the Pacific side of the Bōsō Peninsula.

Narita 成田

☑0476 / POP 127,000

Narita is chiefly known as the home of Japan's main international airport, but the older part of the city is a surprisingly pleasant stop. The centrepiece is the impressive temple **Narita-san Shinshōji** (成田山新勝寺; 1 Narita; admission free; ⊘24hr), surrounded by a pretty park, **Narita-san Kōen** (成田山公園), laced with walking paths, trees and ponds.

Pick up a map at the **Narita Tourist Information Center** (☎24-3198; ⊘8.30am-5.30pm) just outside the eastern exit of JR Narita Station, and head to **Omote-sandō**, the main drag. It winds like an eel towards the temple, past souvenir shops and restaurants.

Halfway down Omote-sandō, the **Tourist Pavilion** (☺9am-5pm Tue-Sun) has local-history exhibits. Across the street is the landmark eel house **Kawatoyo Honten** (川豊本店; 386 Naka-machi; meals ¥1260-1890; ☺10am-5pm Tue-Sun). The speciality here is *unajū* (¥1500), eel grilled, sauced and served over rice in a lacquer box. You can watch the chefs carving up the whip-like creatures right at the front table (perhaps not for the squeamish).

Most of the traditional shops shutter around 5pm, when Narita transforms into a hangout for the flight crews that descend nightly on the city. Evenings typically begin at the **Barge Inn** (ザ・ヴァージン; 538 Hanizaki-chō; meals around ¥1500, drinks from ¥400; ☺4pm-2am Mon-Fri, 11am-2am Sat & Sun), a sprawling British-style pub with indoor and outdoor seating owned by Virgin's Richard Branson.

Numerous chains operate hotels near the airport for those facing early flights, but none can compete with **Kirinoya Ryokan** (桐之屋旅館; ☎22-0724; www.naritakanko.jp/kirinoya; fax 22-1245; 58 Tamachi; s/d without bathroom ¥5250/9450; @) when it comes to history. The owner can trace his lineage back 50 generations, and his rambling old inn is filled with samurai armour and swords. Rooms are Japanese-style; call for pick-up (until 7pm) from either of Narita's train stations.

From Narita International Airport you can take the private Keisei line (¥250, 10 minutes) or JR (¥190/230 from Terminal 2/1, 10 minutes); Keisei-line trains are more frequent. From Tokyo, the easiest way to get to Narita is via the Keisei line from Keisei Ueno Station, taking the Cityliner limited express (¥1730, one hour), or the express (*kyūkō*; ¥810, 70 minutes). Note that most JR Narita Express trains do not stop at Narita.

IZU ARCHIPELAGO

The Izu Archipelago (伊豆諸島; Izu-shotō) comprises peaks of a submerged volcanic chain extending 300km into the Pacific. Although easily reached by ferry from Tokyo, the islands feel worlds away. Soaking in an onsen while gazing at the Pacific is the classic Izu-shotō activity. There is also excellent

If you have a long layover – including at least three hours to get out, away and back into the airport – consider making a quick detour into Narita city. There are international ATMs and luggage-storage facilities in both terminals; enquire at the English-speaking information counters.

hiking up the *mostly* dormant volcanoes and plenty of beach activities. Each island has its own character. We've listed our favourites; for more information on the whole chain, see www.tokyo-islands.com.

The islands can be crowded in the summer – it's often better to visit just outside this season, but typhoons can wreak havoc with your plans from late summer into early autumn and you'll need to plan for delays. Tourist information centres on each island have maps; you'll also need to register there for the (free) campsites.

ⓘ Getting There & Away

AIR ANA (全日空グループ　エアーニッポン; ☎0120-02-9222; www.ana.co.jp) has flights from Tokyo's Haneda Airport to Ō-shima (¥13,100, 30 minutes) and Hachijō-jima (¥19,800, 55 minutes).

  Shinchūō Kōkū (新中央航空; ☎0422-31-4191; www.central-air.co.jp, in Japanese) has flights between Chōfu Airport (on the Keiō line about 20 minutes from Shinjuku) and Ō-shima (¥9500, 25 minutes), Nii-jima (¥13,700, 40 minutes) and Kōzu-shima (¥14,900, 45 minutes).

  Tokyo Ai Land Shuttle (東京愛らんどシャトル; ☎0499-62-5222; www.tohoair.co.jp, in Japanese) flies helicopters between Miyake-jima and Ō-shima (¥11,340, 20 minutes).

BOAT Tōkai Kisen (東海汽船; ☎03-5472-9999, in Japanese; www.tokaikisen.co.jp) operates ferries between Tokyo and the Izu-shotō. Ferries sail to/from Tokyo's Takeshiba Pier, a 10-minute walk from the north exit of Hamamatsu-chō Station.

  High-speed hydrofoils service the inner islands (Ō-shima, To-shima, Nii-jima, Shikine-jima and Kōzu-shima), departing mornings from Tokyo (usually around 8am) and returning from the islands to Tokyo that same afternoon. The large passenger ferry *Camellia-maru* departs around 11pm for the inner islands, arriving early the next morning (stopping at all of the islands from north to south), before making its way back to Tokyo.

Second-class fares and travel times to/from Tokyo:

Ō-shima Hydrofoil ¥8170, 1¾ hours; ferry ¥5470, six hours.

Nii-jima Hydrofoil ¥10,580, three hours; ferry ¥7360, 8½ hours.

Shikine-jima Hydrofoil ¥10,580, 3¼ hours; ferry ¥7360, nine hours.

These islands are also serviced by ferries from the Izu Peninsula (see p149).

The outer islands (Miyake-jima, Mikura-jima and Hachijō-jima) are serviced by the large passenger ferry *Salvia-maru*, departing daily around 10.30pm and arriving at the islands the following morning, returning to Tokyo late the same evening. The journey between Tokyo and Hachijō-jima takes 11 hours and costs ¥10,330 in 2nd class.

Prices may change seasonally or to reflect fuel prices.

ⓘ Getting Around

Island hopping is easy on the daily ferries that run up and down the island chains. In addition, three ferries daily between Nii-jima and Shikine-jima (¥420, 10 minutes) make day trips possible.

Buses run on the larger islands, though they are infrequent. Hitching, while possible, is not that easy. Scooters (around ¥3000 per day) are ideal, though you'll need an international license to rent them. Bicycle rentals are widely available.

Ō-shima 大島

♫ 04992

The largest of the Izu islands and closest to Tokyo, Ō-shima is an easy overnight trip out of the city, but maintains a strong island vibe. It is dominated by 754m Mihara-san (三原山), a semidormant volcano that last erupted in 1986. The south coast has some good beaches, and you can round out your stay with a dip in one of the island's fine onsen. It's most beautiful when the camellia flowers are in bloom in late winter.

◉ Sights & Activities

If you've never peered into the maw of a recently erupted volcano, then we highly recommend a trip to the summit of **Mihara-san**. It's an awesome experience, and the concrete eruption shelters that line the path to the crater add a certain frisson to the approach. To get there, take a bus from Motomachi port to Miharasan-sancho-guchi (¥860, 25 minutes, five departures daily) and walk to the Kakō-tenbōdai observation point (about 45 minutes).

Ō-shima's southernmost point, **Toushiki-no-hana** (トウシキの鼻) is rocky and wave beaten, with good swimming in sheltered pools below Tōshiki Camp-jō. Don't even try to swim when the waves are high. To get there, take a Seminā-bound bus from Motomachi port to Minami-kōkō-mae (¥620, 30 minutes). About 5km east of this point is the island's best beach, Sa-no-hama (砂の浜), a fine stretch of black volcanic sand. Take a Seminaa-bound bus from Motomachi port to Sa-no-hama-iriguchi (¥420, 20 minutes).

Onsen are Ō-shima's other main attraction. **Motomachi Hama-no-yu** (元町浜の湯; admission ¥400; ⊙1-7pm), 10 minutes' walk north of the port, is a fine outdoor onsen with great ocean views. It's mixed bathing, so swimsuits are mandatory, and it can be crowded in summer. The more institutional, glitzy place next door is **Gojinka Onsen** (御神火温泉; admission ¥1000; ⊙9am-9pm), which has baths, a swimming pool and relaxation areas.

The southeastern end of the island has the charmingly nostalgic port of **Habu** (波浮), full of old buildings like the venerable **Ryokan Minato-ya** (旧港屋旅館; admission free; ⊙9am-4pm), now a museum with mannequins in period attire.

🛏 Sleeping & Eating

FREE **Tōshiki Camp-jō**   CAMPGROUND
(トウシキキャンプ場) Very close to the Minami-kōkō-mae stop, this well-maintained stretch of grass has a nice location right near the sea, as well as showers and a communal cooking area.

Akamon   HOTEL **$$**
(ホテル赤門; ☎2-1213; ooshima-akamon.com, in Japanese; fax 2-2860; 1-16-7 Motomachi; r per person from ¥6450) The tatami rooms here are nicer than the bland exterior suggests, and there's an onsen bath. An extra ¥1000 per person gets you a private cabin with twin beds; add ¥2000 for a room with a private *rotemburo*. It's just up the road from Motomachi port.

Hotel Shiraiwa   HOTEL **$$**
(ホテル白岩; ☎2-2571; www.h-shiraiwa.com, in Japanese; fax 2-1864; 3-3-3 Motomachi; r per person with 2 meals ¥8550-21,150; ⎙) This large hotel above Motomachi port seems stuck in the 1960s, but the Japanese- and Western-style rooms – some with harbour views – are still comfortable. Large common baths are a plus.

Otomodachi   SHOKUDŌ $$

(おともだち; 1-17-3 Motomachi; mains ¥800-2000; ⊘lunch & dinner) Simple set meals, like *jōsashimi teishoku* (special sashimi set; ¥1200), just 50m north of Motomachi pier. Look for the red shingles and large white signboard out the front.

ℹ️ Information

The **Ō-shima Tourist Association** (大島観光協会; ☎2-2177; ⊘8.30am-5.15pm) is located near the pier in Motomachi. Maps and sight descriptions can be found at www.town.oshima.tokyo.jp.

Nii-jima   新島

☎04992

Nii-jima competes with neighbouring Shi-kine-jima as the most appealing island in the Izu-shotō. It's got a ripping white-sand beach, two fine onsen and an easy laid-back vibe that'll make you think the islanders hauled a bit of Okinawa right to the doorstep of Tokyo. And there's a great camping ground within walking distance of the beach!

◎ Sights & Activities

The best beach anywhere near Tokyo is Nii-jima's fantastic **Habushi-ura** (羽伏浦), a blazing 6.5km stretch of white sand that runs over half the length of the island. Although it's really just a beach break, it attracts surfers from all over Kantō. Careful, though, because the waves and tide are very strong here. On the port side of the island, **Mae-hama** (前浜) stretches 4km and is a good alternative.

The island's other main attraction is one of Japan's most whimsical onsen, **Yuno-hama Onsen** (湯の浜温泉; admission free; ⊘24hr). It's a *rotemburo* with several tubs built into the rocks overlooking the Pacific, with a few Parthenon-inspired columns. It's a lot of fun and it's only five minutes' walk south of the Tourist Association. Bathing suits are required. About five minutes' walk south, **Mamashita Onsen** (まました温泉; regular/sand baths ¥300/700; ⊘10am-9.30pm Thu-Tue) has a good indoor bath and a sand bath – where you can experience the bizarre, body-warming (and slightly claustrophobic) sensation of being buried in hot sand.

Nii-jima's other attractions include the **Nii-jima Modern Glass Art Museum** (新島現代ガラスアートミュージアム; admission ¥300;

⊘9am-4.30pm Wed-Mon), 1km south of the port. There's some fine work made from naturally magnetic Koga stone (which is found only on Nii-jima and in Sicily). You can often see glass-blowers in action at the workshop next door.

🛏️ Sleeping & Eating

FREE **Habushi-ura Camp-jo**   CAMPGROUND
(羽伏浦キャンプ場) With a stunning mountain backdrop and spacious, grassy sites, this campground is a winner, and it's only about 10 minutes' walk to the beach. There are showers and plenty of barbecue pits to go around.

Saro   GUESTHOUSE $$
(サロー; ☎5-2703; saro-niijima.jp; 3-3-4 Honmura; r per person from ¥5500; ⊖🕾) Run by a young, artsy crowd, this new guesthouse (in a former *minshuku*) offers simple but stylish Western- and Japanese-style rooms, with shared bath. Downstairs it's a hip cafe, dishing up salads, pastas, and light Japanese fare; some English spoken.

Minshuku Hamashō   MINSHUKU $$
(民宿浜庄; ☎5-0524; fax 5-1318; 6-9-9 Honmura; r per person with 2 meals from ¥6800) Very close to Mae-hama beach, this rambling *minshuku* has friendly owners, good seafood and a great location. Mind the extremely 'playful' dog.

Sakaezushi   SUSHI $
(栄寿司; 5-2-9 Honmura; mains ¥650-2000; ⊘dinner) A few blocks from Mae-hama beach on the road to Habushi-ura, this popular local joint has sets like *shima-zushi* (island-style sushi; ¥1850). It's a white building with a blue door curtain.

ℹ️ Information

The **Nii-jima Tourist Association** (新島観光協会; ☎5-0001; ⊘8am-4pm) is about 200m south of the pier.

Shikine-jima   式根島

☎04992

About 6km south of Nii-jima, tiny Shikine-jima is a natural marvel: excellent seaside onsen and several sandy beaches all just 3.8 sq km. You can easily make your way around the island on foot, or on the *mama-chari* (granny bikes) that can be rented all over the island.

◉ Sights & Activities

Jinata Onsen (地鉈温泉; admission free; ⊙24hr) is one of the most dramatically located onsen we've seen: at the end of a narrow cleft in the rocky coastline, it's like the work of an angry axe-wielding giant. The waters, stained a rich orange from iron sulphide, are naturally 80°C; mixed with the cool ocean, they're just right. The tide affects the temperature, so bathing times change daily; check before making the steep descent. The access road is marked by a stone sign and a red arrow.

Near Ashizuki Port, **Matsugashita Miyabi-yu** (松が下雅湯; admission free; ⊙24hr) is near enough to the sea for stunning views but is not affected by the tides – the water is perfectly hot all the time. Look for the entrance near the boat ramp. A minute or so further down the coast is **Ashizuki Onsen** (足付温泉; admission free; ⊙24hr), another fine onsen built into the rocks at the water's edge. Like Jinata Onsen, the water temperature depends on the tide. All of the above are mixed bathing and require swimsuits.

Tomarikō-kaigan (泊港海岸) is a picturesque little beach in a sheltered cove with calm waters perfect for children. It's about 500m northwest of the ferry port, up and over the hill. **Naka-no-ura** (中の浦海岸) and **Ō-ura** (大浦海岸) beaches are an easy walk along the same coast.

🛏 Sleeping

FREE **Kamanoshita Camp-jo** CAMPGROUND (釜の下キャンプ場; ⊙Sep-Nov, Mar-Jun) Right near a fine beach and two free onsen, this little camping ground is great, especially in the quieter times of year, when you might have it to yourself. No showers here.

FREE **Ō-ura Camp-jo** CAMPGROUND (大浦キャンプ場; ⊙Jul & Aug) Right above a sandy cove, this camping ground is rather cramped and not well maintained, but the location is hard to beat. There are showers and barbecue pits.

La Mer B&B $$ (ラ・メール; ☎7-0240; www.shikine.com, in Japanese; fax 7-0036; r per person with 2 meals from ¥11,550; @) The island's most upscale lodging has spacious, if not plain, rooms set around a courtyard, and elaborate meals. It's uphill from the ferry port. Separate Early Bird bungalows (from ¥12,600 per cabin) are great for small groups. Rental bicycles available.

❶ Information

The **Shikine-jima Tourist Association** (式根島観光協会; ☎7-0170; ⊙8am-5pm) is at the pier.

Hachijō-jima 八丈島

☎04996

About 290km south of Tokyo, Hachijō-jima has a culture all its own, including a unique dialect and cuisine. With two volcanos and plenty of palms, it was once touted as a domestic Hawaii to honeymooners. These days the island has a laid-back, uncommercial vibe, attracting visitors for its hiking, diving and onsen.

◉ Sights & Activities

The island is dominated by two dormant volcanoes, 854m **Hachijō-Fuji** (八丈富士) and 701m **Mihara-yama** (三原山), covered with lush semitropical vegetation. The best hike is up Hachijō-Fuji; it's three hours from the Fuji-tōzan-michi-iriguchi bus stop or one hour from the trailhead. The one-hour walk around the crater rim is awesome, but watch for the large holes along the trail. On the Mihara-yama end of the island, try the hike to **Kara-taki** (唐滝), a lovely waterfall about an hour's hike inland and uphill from the settlement of Kashidate. **Nambara** (南原), on the west coast, is an impressive expanse of black rock formed by an eruption of Hachijō-Fuji.

TOP CHOICE **Urami-ga-taki Onsen** (裏見ケ滝温泉; admission free; ⊙10am-9pm) is not to be missed. Just below the road, it overlooks a waterfall – pure magic in the early evening. You'll need a swimsuit since it's mixed bathing. Take a Sueyoshi-bound bus from the port to Nakata-Shōten-mae and walk 20 minutes towards the ocean. Across the street there's a trail that leads to **Urami-ga-taki** (裏見ケ滝), a lovely waterfall only a few minutes away.

A 15-minute walk below Urami-ga-taki Onsen, towards the sea, is **Nakanogō-Onsen Yasuragi-no-yu** (中之郷温泉　やすらぎの湯; 1442 Nakanogō; admission ¥300; ⊙10am-9pm Fri-Wed), a quaint local onsen with a fine view over the Pacific from its inside baths.

Project WAVE (☎2-5407; www3.ocn.ne.jp/~p-wave/english.html) offers a variety of ecotourism options, including hiking, birdwatching, sea kayaking and scuba diving. Its owner, Iwasaki-san, speaks English.

Miyake-jima, 180km south of Tokyo, is one of the spookiest places in all of Japan. Lava flows in 1983 left some spectacular apocalyptic scenery and in 2000 its volcano **O-ya-ma** (御山) erupted again, forcing temporary evacuation of the island's residents. Tourist facilities reopened in 2005 but remain limited; check with the **Miyake-jima Tourism Association** (☏0499-45-1144) for volcanic-gas warnings. Underwater arches and coral beds make this island particularly attractive to divers. **Santomo** (サントモ; ☏0499-45-0532; santomo15.com, in Japanese; fax 0499-45-0527; r per person with 2 meals from ¥7900; 🛜), a cheery pension, restaurant and dive shop, offers **dive tours** from ¥6000.

In contrast, tiny **Mikura-jima**, just 20km further south, is covered in dense, raw forest. The island has only one village, of 300 people; the rest of the local mammalian population – 130 or so bottlenose dolphins – prefers the sea below. From April to October, locally run **snorkel tours** (about ¥6500 for two hours) offer a rare chance to swim up close with the playful cetaceans.

The number of tours, as well as visitors, to Mikura-jima is highly regulated and guests must book in advance. Scuba diving is not permitted and hikers must be accompanied by a guide; all of the rules are in the name of preservation. Very little English is spoken on the island; the **Mikura-jima Tourism Association** (☏0499-48-2022; fax 0499-48-7070) offers some rough **bungalows** (r per person ¥2000) and can assist in making arrangements.

Camping is not permitted on either island.

Miyake-jima (¥8230, seven hours) and Mikura-jima (¥9250, eight hours) are serviced by the *Salvia-maru* (see p161).

🛏 Sleeping & Eating

TOP CHOICE **Garden-sō** MINSHUKU **$$**
(ガーデン荘; ☏7-0014; www.h2.dion.ne.jp/~gardenso/; 3376 Nakanogō; r per person with 2 meals & without bathroom from ¥6800; 🐾@) This word-of-mouth favourite has heaps of personality, courtesy of its gregarious proprietress. The main building is a wonderfully traditional wooden house surrounded by palms, though the guest rooms (with shared bath) are comparatively ordinary. Within walking distance of Urami-ga-taki Onsen; pick-up service available.

TOP CHOICE **Ryōzanpaku** IZAKAYA **$$**
(梁山泊; 1672 Mitsune; mains from ¥1500; ☺dinner Mon-Sat; 🍴) Hachijō-jima has a number of local specialities like *ashitaba,* a local herb often served tempura style, and *shima-zushi*. This lively joint is the place to try them. It's on the main road between the airport and the ferry port. Look for the white vertical sign and sliding wooden doors.

FREE **Sokodo Camp-jō** CAMPGROUND
(底土キャンプ場; 4188 Mitsune) An excellent camping ground 500m north of Sokodo pier and near a beach, with toilets, cold showers and cooking facilities.

Mantenbō B&B **$$**
(満天望; ☏2-7250; www.mantenbo.jp; fax 2-7251; 930-2 Ōkago; r per person with 2 meals from ¥9450; ☺🛜) A family-run inn with spotless Western-style rooms and lots of natural light. The garden attracts birds (and birdwatchers); English spoken.

Sokodo-sō MINSHUKU **$$**
(そこど荘; ☏2-0092; www.sokodo-so.com, in Japanese; 1307 Mitsune; r per person with/without 2 meals from ¥7875/5250; ☺@) A popular choice up the road from Sokodo pier, with basic local-style rooms and bike rentals.

ℹ Information

In the centre of the island, **Hachijōjima Tourism Association** (八丈島観光協会; ☏2-1377; ☺8.15am-5.15pm) is next to the town hall on the main road.

OGASAWARA ARCHIPELAGO

You won't believe you're still in Japan, much less Tokyo! About 1000km south of downtown in the middle of the Pacific Ocean, this far-flung outpost of Tokyo Prefecture has pristine beaches and star-studded night skies. The Ogasawara Archipelago (小笠原諸島;

ONLY IN OGASAWARA

When scientists photographed the fabled giant squid *Architeuthis* for the first time ever in 2004, no wonder it was just off the Ogasawaras. The chain is home to dozens of rare and endangered species, such as the Bonin flying fox. From January to April humpback whales come within 500m of shore. While you're most likely to run into feral goats and hermit crabs, jungle hiking, snorkelling, diving, sea kayaking or taking a dolphin cruise virtually guarantees an exciting wildlife experience. And keep looking up! On a clear night, from the top deck of the *Ogasawara-maru* ferry, you'll see the Milky Way stretching from horizon to horizon through a breathtaking field of stars.

Ogasawara-shotō) is a nature-lover's paradise surrounded by tropical waters and coral reefs. Snorkelling, whale-watching, swimming with dolphins, and hiking are all on the bill.

The only way to get here is by a 25½-hour ferry ride from Tokyo. The ferry docks at Chichi-jima (父島; Father Island), the main island of the group. A smaller ferry connects this island to Haha-jima (母島), the other inhabited island.

The islands' earliest inhabitants were Westerners who set up provisioning stations for whaling ships working the Japan whaling grounds. You still see the occasional Western family name and face. You'll also see disused gun emplacements at the ends of most of the islands' beaches, built by the Japanese in hopes of repelling an anticipated Allied invasion in WWII (the big battles were fought further south on Iwo-jima).

Given the islands' nature, history and location, a trip here is one of Japan's great little adventures.

ℹ Getting There & Away

The *Ogasawara-maru* sails once a week between Tokyo's Takeshiba Pier (10 minutes from Hamamatsu-chō Station) and Chichi-jima (2nd class from ¥25,000 in July and August, from ¥22,000 September to June, 25½ hours). The *Hahajima-maru* sails five times a week between Chichi-jima and Haha-jima (¥3780, two hours). Contact **Ogasawara Kaiun** (小笠原海運; ☎03-3451-5171; www.ogasawarakaiun.co.jp); prices may change as per fuel charges. Other operators run day cruises from Chichi-jima to Haha-jima.

Chichi-jima   父島
☎04998
Beautifully preserved, gorgeous Chichi-jima has plenty of accommodation, restaurants, even a bit of tame nightlife. But the real attractions are the excellent beaches and outdoor activities.

◉ Sights & Activities

The two best beaches for snorkelling are on the north side of the island, a short walk over the hill from the village. **Miya-no-hama** (宮之浜) has decent coral and is sheltered, making it suitable for beginners. About 500m along the coast (more easily accessed from town) is **Tsuri-hama** (釣浜), a rocky beach that has better coral but is more exposed.

Good swimming beaches line the west side of the island, getting better the further south you go. The neighbouring coves of **Copepe** (コペペ海岸) and **Kominato-kaigan** (小港海岸), connected by an 800m trail, are particularly attractive. From Kominato-kaigan, you can continue over the hill and along the coast to the beguiling white sand of **John Beach** (ジョンビーチ), but note that it's a two-hour walk in each direction and there is no drinking water – bring at least 3L per person. The path to nearby Jinny beach is currently off-limits; the strong current makes it unsafe to swim to there, though sea kayaking is possible.

Many operators offer dolphin swimming and whale-watching, as well as trips to Minami-jima, an uninhabited island with a magical secret beach called **Ōgi-ike** (扇池). Stanley Minami, the English-speaking skipper of the **Pink Dolphin** (☎2-2096; www15.ocn.ne.jp/~pdolphin) runs half-/full-day tours (¥5000/8000) to Minami-jima and Haha-jima that include snorkelling and dolphin watching.

At Ōgiura Beach, **Rao Adventure Tours** (☎2-2081; web.me.com/boninrao/RAO/English_Page.html) organises jungle tours (¥4200 per half-day) and surf camps (¥15,000 per day).

Rental scooter is the best way to get around the island (available from ¥3000 per day).

🛏 Sleeping & Eating

Camping is not permitted on the island.

TOP CHOICE **Tetsuya** — BOUTIQUE HOTEL $$
(てつ家; ☎2-7725; www.tetuyabonin.com, in Japanese; fax 2-7726; r per person with 2 meals from ¥9800; ❄@🌐) This new hotel is the talk of the island for its multicourse meals that make innovative use of local ingredients. The thoughtfully designed rooms and open-air baths are even better. It's a five-minute walk from Kominato-kaigan.

Banana Inn — GUESTHOUSE $$
(バナナ荘; ☎2-2051; pinkdolphin.p1.bindsite.jp/banana.html; s/tw ¥5000/9000) Steps from the ferry pier, this humble inn has very basic Japanese- and Western-style rooms but lots of hospitality from owner John Washington, an Ernest Hemingway type who enjoys discussing local history. Note that the guesthouse may be closed September to December.

Marujō — SHOKUDŌ $$
(丸丈; mains from ¥1000; ☺lunch & dinner) This local favourite serves up fresh island seafood. Try the *sashimi moriawase* (mixed sashimi; ¥1575) or the *akaba karaage* (deep-fried rockfish; ¥1050). It's in town, on the street behind the main road; look for the white door curtains.

Rockwells — GUESTHOUSE $
(ロックウェルズ; ☎2-3838; rockwells.co.jp/ogasawara, in Japanese; dm ¥3000; r per person with 2 meals from ¥6900; 🌐) The closest thing you'll find to a beach shack on the island – simple accommodation and a bar three seconds from Ōgiura beach.

Ogasawara Youth Hostel — HOSTEL $
(小笠原ユースホステル; ☎2-2692; www.oyh.jp, in Japanese; fax 2-2692; dm members/nonmembers with 2 meals ¥5150/5750; P@) Clean, well-run hostel about 400m southwest of the pier; book early during summer.

🍷 Drinking

Yankee Town — BAR
(ヤンキータウン; drinks ¥700-1200; ☺8pm-2am Thu-Tue; 📶) A 15-minute walk east of the main pier, this driftwood bar is the perfect spot to chill with a pina colada. Follow the main coastal road towards Okumura and you'll see it on the left with the coloured lights.

ℹ Information

Chichi-jima Tourism Association (父島観光協会; ☎2-2587; ☺8am-12pm & 1.30-5pm) In the B-Ship building, about 250m west of the pier, near the post office. Ask for the helpful *Guide Map of Chichi-jima*; English spoken.

Ogasawara Visitor Center (小笠原ビジターセンター; ☺8.30am-5pm) Right on the beach past the village office, it has displays in English about the local ecosystem and history.

Haha-jima 母島

☎04998

Haha-jima is less developed than Chichi-jima and, with limited lodgings, sees far fewer visitors. Outside the summer season, you may even find yourself staring out over cerulean waters or spotting rare birds all by your lonesome.

👁 Sights & Activities

A road runs south from the village to the start of the **Minami-zaki Yūhodō** (南崎遊歩道), a hiking course that continues all the way to the **Minami-zaki** (南崎; literally 'southern point'). Along the way you'll find **Hōraine-kaigan** (蓬萊根海岸), a narrow

---

ECO VILLAGE, CHICHI-JIMA

Pelan Village (☎2-3386; www.pelan.jp; r per person from ¥4500; 🌐), the life's work of shaggy-haired Ryō Shimizu (and the occasional volunteer), is a Never-Never Land of rough wooden cabins, walkways and ladders perched on a leafy mountainside. On an island that sources most of its food from Tokyo, Pelan stands out for growing a fair amount of its own (enquire about WWOOFing opportunities; see p752). It is not, however, for dilettantes – conventional soaps and detergents are banned because water run-off goes directly to the crops.

Ryō-san also runs the **Pelan Sea Kayak Club**, which offers tours to some of the island's more enchanting spots (half-/full day ¥5000/10,000). Fees include equipment rental and meals cooked Pelan-style, on a wood-burning camp stove. Catching and grilling your own fish is optional.

beach with a decent offshore coral garden, and **Wai Beach** (ワイビーチ), with a drop-off that sometimes attracts eagle rays. Minami-zaki itself has a rocky, coral-strewn beach with ripping views of smaller islands to the south. Though tempting, the waters beyond the cove can whisk swimmers away.

Above Minami-zaki you'll find **Kofuji** (小富士), an 86m-high peak with fantastic views in all directions. Back in town, a four-hour hike loops through rare indigenous flora to **Mt Chibusa** (乳房山; 463m), the highest peak on the island.

Dive shop **Club Noah** (クラブノア母島; ☑3-2442; http://noah88.web.fc2.com, in Japanese; ⊙cafe 1-6pm) runs jungle-hiking and marine-life ecotours. It's in a white building on the far side of the fishing port; inside there's a **cafe** serving light meals (from ¥500).

Scooter (from ¥3000 per day) is the best way to get around the island. Many lodgings rent them, including the two listed here.

🛏 Sleeping & Eating

Note that camping is not permitted on the island.

Anna Beach Haha-jima Youth Hostel
HOTEL $

(アンナビーチ母島ユースホステル; ☑3-24 68; www.k4.dion.ne.jp/~annayh, in Japanese; fax 3-2371; dm members/nonmembers with 2 meals ¥5320/5920; ⊖⊙) A young family runs this tidy, cheery youth hostel in a bright yellow Western-style house overlooking the fishing port.

Island Resort Nanpū
HOTEL $$

(民宿　ナンプー; ☑3-2462; www.hahajima-nanpu.com/english; fax 3-2458; r per person with 2 meals ¥13,500; ⊖@⊙) This cosy new lodging has glossy wood-panelled rooms, friendly owners and good food. The rooms in the slightly older Minshuku Nanpū next door have big beds and shared bathroom for ¥10,000 per person.

ℹ Information

Haha-jima Tourist Association (母島観光協会; ☑3-2300; ⊙8am-5pm) is in the passenger waiting room at the pier.

The Japan Alps & Central Honshū

Best Places to Eat

» Atsuta Hōraiken (p178)
» Yabaton (p178)
» Kyōya (p192)
» Hotaruya (p232)

Best Places to Stay

» Yumoto Chōza (p203)
» Kōemon (p197)
» Beniya Mukayū (p238)
» Nakabusa Onsen (p220)
» Sumiyoshi Ryokan (p191)

Why Go?

Japan's heartland in both geography and attitude, Central Honshū (本州中部, 'Honshū Chūbu' in Japanese) stretches between the two great megalopolises in Kantō (home to Greater Tokyo) and Kansai (Osaka, Kyoto and Kōbe). This region is filled with modern commercial centres and traditional towns, the majestic Japan Alps (日本アルプス) and the rugged northern coastline.

In the region's central prefectures, hiking takes you through alpine uplands and onsen (hot spring) villages that offer welcome recovery for skiers. The Sea of Japan region (Hokuriku) boasts clifftop vistas, remarkable temples and incredible seafood.

Nagoya is the nation's industrial heart, with a can-do spirit and unique foods, while Hokuriku's hub is Kanazawa, a historic city that once housed samurai and geisha. Lovely Takayama is admired for its traditional riverside houses, wood crafts and verdant countryside. Matsumoto is popular for its striking 16th-century castle and many galleries.

When to Go
Nagoya

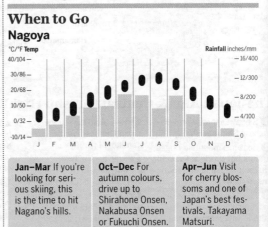

Jan–Mar If you're looking for serious skiing, this is the time to hit Nagano's hills.

Oct–Dec For autumn colours, drive up to Shirahone Onsen, Nakabusa Onsen or Fukuchi Onsen.

Apr–Jun Visit for cherry blossoms and one of Japan's best festivals, Takayama Matsuri.

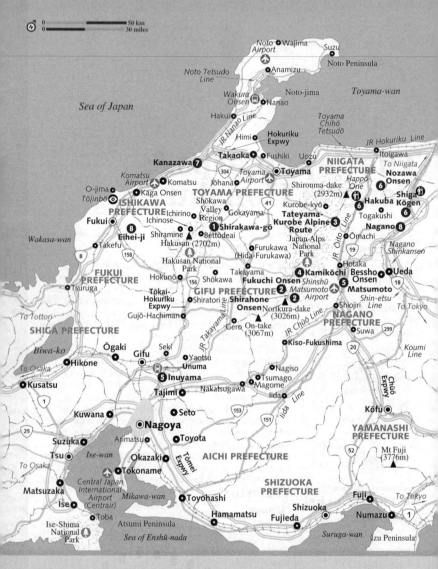

The Japan Alps & Central Honshū Highlights

1 Sleep in a thatch-roofed house in **Shirakawa-gō** (p197)

2 Soak in a mountain-ringed outdoor hot spring at **Fukuchi Onsen** (p203) and **Shirahone Onsen** (p202)

3 Ride trains, trolley buses and funiculars along the high-altitude **Tateyama-Kurobe Alpine Route** (p224)

4 Hike amid the stunning Japan Alps scenery of **Kamikōchi** (p199)

5 Step back in time at the **Inuyama-jō** (p183) and **Matsumoto-jō** (p216) castles

6 Ski, ski, ski at the Olympic resorts of **Shiga Kōgen** (p211), **Nozawa Onsen** (p212) and **Hakuba** (p213)

7 Take in arts in Kanazawa, from the ancient garden of **Kenroku-en** (p228) to the daring **21st Century Museum of Contemporary Art** (p227)

8 Train with Zen Buddhist monks in the 13th-century **Eihei-ji** (p239) or be awed by Nagano's **Zenkō-ji** (p204)

Climate

Central Honshū's climate varies with its landscape. In the lowlands the best times to visit are April and May or late September to early November; temperatures are mild and clear sunny skies are the norm. Expect heavy rains in the *tsuyu* (monsoon) season (typically a few weeks beginning in mid-June), followed by sticky summers (through mid-September) capped with a typhoon season. In the Japan Alps, November to March are cold and snowy. Many roads are impassable then, and the highest peaks might remain snow-covered until June. July and August tend to be most agreeable for mountain hikers; snows are generally melted and temperatures warmest.

❶ Getting There & Away

Central Japan International Airport (NGO), near Nagoya, provides easy access from abroad, and there are limited international flights into Komatsu (near Kanazawa; see p234) and Toyama (p223). Nagoya is a hub for rail travel nationwide, and a *shinkansen* (bullet train) line links Tokyo with Nagano.

❶ Getting Around

Nagoya is Chūbu's transport hub. The mountainous inland is best served by the JR Takayama and Chūō lines, which run north to south with hubs in Takayama (Takayama line) and Matsumoto and Nagano (Chūō line), respectively. The JR Hokuriku line follows the coast along the Sea of Japan, linking Fukui, Kanazawa and Toyama, and connecting to Kyoto and Osaka.

Chūbu's mountainous middle is served by bus, but plan carefully, as services can be inconvenient or stop entirely in bad weather. For some destinations, particularly Noto Peninsula, hiring a car makes sense.

NAGOYA

🎵 052 / POP 2.25 MILLION

If Kyoto is a gracious geisha and Tokyo is a preening teen forever seeking the newest and coolest, then Nagoya (名古屋) is their stalwart brother. He may not be the flashiest in the family, but through smarts, perseverance and duty, he provides the fortune that enables the others to live the lives they choose.

Japan's fourth-largest city, Nagoya is an industrial powerhouse; if measured on its own, its region would rank among the top 20 economies worldwide. It started long ago, with a heritage called *monozukuri* – making things. It's an article of faith that residents of this hard-working city can continue to earn a living even when everyone else is going broke. Toyota is only the most famous of the many manufacturers based here. It's even the birthplace of pachinko (Japanese pinball).

None of this marks Nagoya as a top-rank tourist destination, but since you're likely to pass through (Nagoya's a major transit hub), it's worth a detour for its impressive castle, important shrine and temples, unique and accessible cuisine, attractive port, and urban amusement on a far more relaxed scale than Tokyo or Osaka. Locals and expats alike take pride in the hometown character of this friendly city.

Nagoya also makes a useful base for day trips. From factory visits to ceramic villages to cormorant fishing, there's plenty in the region to keep you – need we say it? – busy.

On the western edge of the city centre, JR Nagoya Station (known locally as Meieki) is a city in itself, with department stores, boutiques, restaurants, hotels and observation decks on skyscrapers. Several train lines converge here, including *shinkansen* and the private regional lines Meitetsu and Kintetsu, and there are also subway and bus stations. Nagoya Station is quite large and confusing, so don't plan on a quick transfer.

From the east exit, Sakura-dōri runs towards the massive Eiffel Towerish TV tower, in the centre of the narrow Hisaya-ōdōri-kōen (Central Park). South and west of the TV tower are the Sakae and Nishiki districts, more atmospheric than Meieki and booming with shopping, dining and nightlife; the atmospheric Kakuōzan district is a few subway stops east of Sakae. The castle, Nagoya-jō, is just north of the city centre, while the Ōsu Kannon and, much further, Nagoya Port areas are to the south.

English-language signage and a convenient subway system make navigating Nagoya relatively easy.

History

Nagoya did not become a unified city until 1889, but it had a strong influence for centuries before. It is the ancestral home of Japan's 'three heroes': Oda Nobunaga, the first unifier of Japan, followed by the shōgun Toyotomi Hideyoshi and Tokugawa Ieyasu, whose dictatorial reign from Edo also ushered in an era of peace, prosperity and the arts. Ieyasu ordered the construction of Nagoya-jō, which became an important outpost for 16 generations of the Tokugawa family in this region, known as the Owari clan.

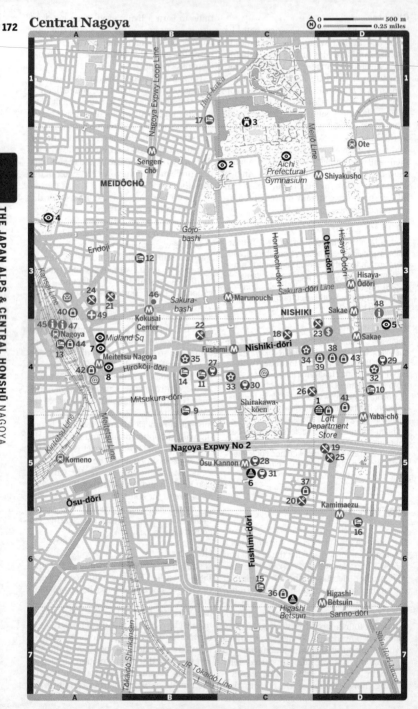

N 0 ____ 500 m
0 ____ 0.25 miles

17

3

2

Ote

Sengen-
chō

MEIDŌCHŌ

Aichi
Prefectural
Gymnasium

Shiyakusho

4

Endoji

Gojo-
bashi

Honmachi-dōri

Ōtsu-dōri

Hisaya-Ōdōri

Hisaya-
Ōdōri

12

Sakura-dōri Line

46

24

21

49

40

45

47

13

Nagoya

44

Midland Sq

7

42

8

Meitetsu Nagoya

Kokusai
Center

Sakura-
bashi

Marunouchi

NISHIKI

Sakae

48

5

Sakae

22

18

23

$

34

39

38

43

29

Hirokōji-dōri

35

27

Fushimi

Nishiki-dōri

Mitsukura-dōri

14

11

33

30

26

1

41

32

10

9

Shirakawa-
kōen

Loft
Department
Store

Yaba-chō

Komeno

Nagoya Expwy No 2

19

25

Ōsu Kannon

28

6

31

37

20

Kamimaezu

16

Ōsu-dōri

Fushimi-dōri

15

36

Higashi
Betsuin

Higashi-
Betsuin

Sanno-dōri

Nagoya grew into a centre of commerce, finance, industry, transport and shipping; during WWII some 10,000 Zero fighter planes were produced here. Manufacturing prominence led to massive Allied bombing – citizens were evacuated and roughly one quarter of the city was obliterated. The resulting blank slate allowed officials to plan the city you see today: wide avenues, subways, gleaming skyscrapers and green space.

Today, Nagoya continues as a worldwide leader in automobiles, machinery, electronics and ceramics. One look at Nagoya's many department stores shows the city's thriving commercial sector, though it's a mark of the severity of the current economic downturn in Japan that even Nagoyans are tightening their belts.

⊙ Sights

NAGOYA STATION AREA

Midland Square LANDMARK

(ミッドランドスクエア) Home to Toyota Motor Corporation, this skyscraper (247m) is Nagoya's tallest and the fifth-tallest in Japan. There is a chichi shopping centre on the lower floors, offices occupy the middle floors, and the top floors comprise the **Sky Promenade**

(⌨527-8877; www.noritake-elec.com/garden; 4-7-1 Meieki; garden adult/child/senior ¥700/300/500; ◷9.30am-11pm; ℞Nagoya), home of Japan's tallest outdoor observation deck (closed in bad weather), reached via passageways with some adventurously designed light murals.

Architecture fans should check out the exterior of the new **Spiral Towers**, a couple of blocks south.

Noritake Garden   GARDEN
(ノリタケの森; ⌨561-7290; www.noritake-elec.com/garden; 3-1-36 Noritake-shinmachi; garden admission free; ℞Kamejima) Take a stroll around Noritake Garden, the tree-planted grounds of the original 1904 factory of one of Japan's best-known porcelain makers. The **craft centre** (⌨561-7114; adult/child & senior ¥500/free; ◷10am-5pm) offers a peek at the production process and a museum of old Noritake pieces, plus a chance to glaze your own dish (¥1500). The **Noritake Gallery** (⌨562-9811; ◷10am-6pm Tue-Sun) has changing exhibitions of paintings, sculpture and ceramic works. Signage is in English throughout, and look for an early kiln and some atmospheric old chimneys, the remains of a 1933 tunnel kiln.

Naturally there are shopping opportunities, including the Box outlet store (open 10am to 6pm), with 30% to 40% discounts on discontinued items.

Toyota Commemorative Museum of Industry & Technology   MUSEUM
(トヨタテクノミュージアム産業技術記念館; ⌨551-6115; www.tcmit.org; 4-1-35 Noritake-shinmachi; adult/child ¥500/300; ◷9.30am-5pm Tue-Sat; ℞Sako, Meitetsu Nagoya line) Toyota, the world's largest automobile maker, started in another very Japanese industry: weaving. About 10 minutes' walk northwest of Noritake Garden, this excellent museum is on the site of the company's original Nagoya weaving plant (1911). It's filled with displays and demonstrations of metal processing and textile machinery, and hands-on experiences with principles of force, electronics and such, but the rubber meets the road in the 7900-sq-metre automotive pavilion; look out for humanoid robots, too. There's English signage, and an English-language audio guide for ¥200. See the box, p181, for information on factory tours.

NAGOYA CASTLE AREA
Nagoya-jō   CASTLE
(名古屋城; Nagoya Castle; 1-1 Honmaru; adult/child under 15 ¥500/100; ◷9am-4.30pm; ℞Shiyakusho, exit 7) Currently celebrating its 400th anniversary, Nagoya-jō was built by Tokugawa Ieyasu for his ninth son from 1610 to 1614. Although it was destroyed in WWII and replaced in 1959 with a concrete replica, it's worth a visit for the fine museum inside featuring armour, treasures and histories of the Oda, Toyotomi and Tokugawa families. A lift will save you climbing stairs. Note the 3m-long replicas of *shachihoko* (gilded dolphin-like sea creatures) at either end of the roof (and in every souvenir shop).

Within the castle grounds, the garden, Ninomaru-en (二の丸園), has a teahouse in an attractive setting. It's a sight during the cherry-blossom season (around early April), and on Fridays **ceremonial tea** (¥525; ◷9.30am-4pm Fri) is served here from a golden urn.

Nearby is the stately **Nagoya Noh Theatre** (名古屋能楽堂; ⌨231-0088; 1-1-1 San-no-maru; admission free; ◷9am-5pm), which has a small museum containing kimonos, masks, fans and art related to nō, the world's oldest continuously performed art.

Tokugawa Art Museum   MUSEUM
(徳川美術館; www.tokugawa-art-museum.jp; 1017 Tokugawa-chō; adult/child under 7 ¥1200/free; ◷10am-5pm Tue-Sun) A must for anyone with even a passing interest in Japanese culture and history, this museum has a 10,000-plus piece collection that includes National Treasures and Important Cultural Properties that once belonged to the shōgunal family: furnishings, arms and armour, tea-ceremony implements, calligraphy, painted scrolls, lacquerware, and masks and costumes from nō theatre. A priceless 12th-century scroll depicting *The Tale of Genji* (see p718) is locked away except for a short stint in late November; the rest of the year, visitors must remain content with a video.

The museum is three minutes' walk from the Tokugawaen-Shindeki bus stop, east of Nagoya-jō.

SAKAE & EAST
While Sakae doesn't have big-name attractions, it is ground zero for shopping and people-watching. The wide central park in the middle of Hisaya-ōdōri is busy all day, and Sakae's side streets are packed with revellers well into the night. For more classic sights, take a trip a few subway stops east of Sakae to Kakuōzan, a historic temple town.

International Design Centre Nagoya

GALLERY

(国際デザインセンター; 4th fl, 3-18-1 Sakae; adult/child under 16 ¥300/free; ⊙11am-8pm Wed-Mon; ⓡYaba-chō, exit 5 or 6) Just a short walk from Sakae, the futuristic, swooping Nadya Park skyscraper houses the International Design Centre Nagoya. It's a secular shrine to the deities of conceptualisation, form and function, from art deco to the present, from Electrolux to Isamu Noguchi, and from Arne Jacobsen to the Mini Cooper. Signage is in English.

Also in Nadya Park is the Loft department store (ロフト), which design-shoppers will find equally alluring. Nadya Park is about five minutes' walk from Yaba-chō Station.

Oasis 21

LANDMARK

(オアシス２１) Yes, it's a bus terminal, but if all the world's bus terminals were as interesting as OASIS 21, a recipient of good-design awards, everyone would take public transport. The 'galaxy platform', a fantastical glass disk, seems to hover three storeys above the ground, and you can climb it via stairs and go for a walk, particularly at night when it's adventurously lit.

SOUTH OF THE CITY CENTRE

Ōsu Kannon area

TEMPLE

(大須観音周辺) The much-visited Ōsu Kannon temple (大須観音; ⊙5.30am-7pm; ⓡŌsu Kannon, exit 2) traces its roots back to 1333 and was considered so auspicious that Tokugawa Ieyasu ordered it moved here around 1610. Although the current buildings are 20th-century reconstructions, it still retains a traditional atmosphere. Chanting is often piped throughout the temple grounds.

Ōsu is equally famous for the vibrant shopping district just east, which draws bargain hunters. See p180 for more on shopping.

Atsuta-jingū

SHRINE

(熱田神宮; www.atsutajingu.or.jp; 1-1-1 Jingū; admission free; ⊙24hr; ⓡJingū-mae, Meitetsu Nagoya line or Jingū-nishi, exit 2) Hidden among 1000-year-old cypress trees, the 1900-year-old Atsuta-jingū is one of the most sacred shrines in all of Shintō. It houses the *kusanagi-no-tsurugi* (sacred sword; literally the 'grass-cutting sword'), one of the *sanshu no jingi* (three regalia) that were, according to legend, handed down to the imperial family by the sun goddess Amaterasu-Ōmikami. (The other two are the curved jewels at the Imperial Palace in Tokyo, and the sacred mirror housed at Ise-jingū.) You won't be able to view the regalia, but don't feel left out; no one but the emperor and a few selected Shintō priests ever get to see them.

There is a small **Treasure Hall** (Hōmotsu-kan; adult/child ¥300/150; ⊙9am-4.30pm, closed last Wed & Thu of each month), housing a changing collection of Tokugawa-era swords, masks and paintings, including some Important Cultural Properties.

The shrine is about three minutes' walk west from Jingū-mae Station on the Meitetsu Nagoya line, or five minutes' walk east from Jingū-nishi Station on the Meijō subway line.

Nagoya/Boston Museum of Fine Arts

MUSEUM

(名古屋ボストン美術館; www.nagoya-boston .or.jp; 1-1-1 Kanayama-chō; special & long-term exhibitions adult/child ¥1400/free; ⊙10am-7pm Tue-Fri, to 5pm Sat & Sun; ⓡKanayama via JR, Meitetsu or Meijō subway lines) This excellent museum is a collaborative effort between Japanese backers and the Museum of Fine Arts, Boston. Rotating exhibitions showcase both Japanese and non-Japanese masterpieces, and have good English signage.

The museum is to the right of the south exit of Kanayama Station.

✴✍ Festivals & Events

Atsuta Matsuri

MARTIAL ARTS

Displays of martial arts, sumō and fireworks on 5 June at Atsuta-jingū (p175).

Dekimachi Tennō-sai

PARADE

On the first Saturday and Sunday of June there's a parade of floats with large *karakuri* (mechanical puppets) around the shrine, Susano-o-jinja, near the Tokugawa Art Museum.

Nagoya Bashō Sumō Tournament

SUMŌ

(愛知県体育館; ☏962-9300; 1-1 Honmaru; tickets from ¥1500) One of six annual championship tournaments, held over two weeks in July, at Aichi Prefectural Gymnasium. Arrive early in the afternoon to watch the lower-ranked wrestlers up close.

Minato Matsuri

PARADE

Street parade in Nagoya Port, around the third Sunday in July. There's a traditional parade, street dancers, fireworks and a water-logging contest that dates back to the Edo period.

SPORT

Sumō

A fascinating, highly ritualised activity steeped in Shintō beliefs, sumō is the only traditional Japanese sport that pulls big crowds and dominates primetime TV. The 2000-year-old sport, which is based on an ancient combat form called *sumai* (to struggle), attracts huge crowds on weekends. Tournaments take place over the span of 15 days, so unless you're aiming for a big match on a weekend, you should be able to secure a ticket. Sumō tournaments *(bashō)* take place in January, May and September at Ryōgoku Kokugikan in Tokyo (p107); in March at the Furitsu Taiiku-kan Gymnasium in Osaka; in July at the Aichi Prefectural Gymnasium in Nagoya (p175); and in November at the Fukuoka Kokusai Centre in Fukuoka (p571). Most popular are matches where one of the combatants is a *yokozuna* (grand champion). At the moment, sumō is dominated by foreign-born *rikishi* (sumō wrestlers), including Mongolian Asashōryū and Bulgarian Kotoōshū.

Soccer

Japan was already soccer-crazy when the World Cup came to Saitama and Yokohama in 2002. Now it's a chronic madness, and five minutes of conversation with any 10-year-old about why they like David Beckham should clear up any doubts you might have to the contrary. Japan's national league, also known as **J-League** (www.j-league.or.jp/eng), is in season from March to November and can be seen at stadiums around the country.

Baseball

Baseball was introduced to Japan in 1873 and became a fixture in 1934 when the Yomiuri started its own team after Babe Ruth and Lou Gehrig had swung through town. During WWII the game continued unabated, though players were required to wear unnumbered khaki uniforms and to salute each other on the field.

Today, baseball is still widely publicised and very popular, though many fans have begun to worry about the future of the sport in Japan, as some of the most talented national players, such as Matsui Hideki, Suzuki Ichirō and Matsuzaka Daisuke, migrate to major league teams in the USA. If you're visiting Japan between April and October and are interested in catching a game, two exciting places to do so are the historic Koshien Stadium, which is located just outside Osaka and was built in 1924 as Japan's first stadium, and Tokyo Dome (p107), affectionately known as the 'Big Egg' and home to Japan's most popular team, the Yomiuri Giants.

Nagoya Matsuri   PARADE

Nagoya's big annual event takes place in mid-October at Hisaya-ōdōri-kōen. It includes costume parades, processions of floats with *karakuri* puppets, folk dancing, music and a parade of flower-decorated cars.

Kiku-no-hana Taikai   FLOWERS

Chrysanthemum exhibition at Nagoya-jō in late October to late November. A *ningyō* (doll) pavilion incorporates flowers into scenes from Japanese history and legend.

🛏 Sleeping

Accommodation in Nagoya is clustered around Nagoya Station and Sakae. Ryokan listed here do not have en-suite toilet or bathroom, except where noted. All Western-style hotels listed provide LAN cables for in-room internet access.

TOP CHOICE / Nagoya Marriott Associa Hotel   HOTEL $$$

(名古屋マリオットアソシアホテル; ☎584-1111; www.associa.com/english/nma; 1-1-4 Meieki; s/d from ¥24,000/32,000; @@; ⒭Nagoya) The Marriott literally tops other hotels in town. The palmy lobby (accessed via an elevator from Nagoya Station) is on the 15th floor, and 774 spacious rooms, with big comfy beds and bathtub views of the city, start from the 20th, fitted with deluxe, well, everything. The 18th-storey gym also has views across the city.

Kimiya Ryokan
RYOKAN **$**

(きみ家旅館; ☎551-0498; hott@hotmail.com; 2-20-16 Nagono; r per person ¥4500, with breakfast/dinner ¥5000/6000; ®Kokusai Centre, exit 1) This friendly, 14-room, family-run ryokan is good value for its tatami rooms. The best ones overlook the garden. Not much English is spoken, but the owners dispense a helpful map and prepare Japanese meals. From the subway, walk north about five minutes. It's on the left, with English signage, before Endōji shopping arcade.

B Nagoya
HOTEL **$$**

(ザ・ビー 名古屋; ☎241-1500; www.ishinhotels.com; 4-15-23 Sakae; s/d from ¥5000/7500; ⊜@; ®Sakae, exit 13) A business hotel in Sakae that's as stylish as it is functional. Rooms make up for in panache (think PJs with piping and embroidered logos) what they lack in space. Look online for rates including breakfast.

Hilton Nagoya
HOTEL **$$$**

(ヒルトン名古屋; ☎212-1111, toll-free 0120-489-852; www.hilton.com; 1-3-3 Sakae; r from ¥17,500; ⊜@≋; ®Fushimi, exit 7) A soaring lobby with a piano player and manicured shrubs is your entree to Western-style rooms with Japanese touches such as *shōji* (rice-paper screens) and blackout panels on the windows. There's a well-equipped fitness centre and great views from upper rooms.

Petit Ryokan Ichifuji
RYOKAN **$$**

(☎914-2867; www.jin.ne.jp/ichifuji; 1-7 Saikōbashi-dōri, kita-ku; s/d with breakfast from ¥6400/9600; @; ®Heian-dōri, exit 2 via elevator) Well worth the 20-minute subway ride from Nagoya Station. It's dramatically lit, clean and comfortable, with designer basins and a communal cypress-wood bath. Japanese-Western fusion dinner (from ¥2480) is available with advance notice; after dinner the dining room turns into a little bar. From the station, walk south for three minutes. The ryokan is signposted in English, down a gravel alley across from the Pola store.

Westin Nagoya Castle
HOTEL **$$$**

(ウェスティンナゴヤキャッスル; ☎521-2121; www.castle.co.jp; 3-19 Hinokuchi-chō; s/d from ¥16,000/34,000; ⊜@☎≋; ®Sengen-chō) You can't get closer to Nagoya-jō than this, located across the moat. The castle is popular for its 'heavenly beds', spacious bathrooms, fitness facilities and restaurants. However, most singles are small and look to-

ward town, not the castle. Look for website-only specials. There's a shuttle bus to/from Nagoya Station.

Ryokan Meiryū
RYOKAN **$$**

(旅館名龍; ☎331-8686; www.japan-net.ne.jp/~meiryu; 2-4-21 Kamimaezu; s/d/tr ¥5250/8400/11,025; @☎; ®Kamimaezu, exit 3) This 22-room ryokan doesn't look like much from the outside, but inside it's quite professional, with some English-speaking staff, coin laundry, women's communal bath and a sauna in the men's. Home-style Japanese meals are available by reservation. From the station, walk along the street and take the first left. It's 1½ blocks down, on the left.

Ryokan Marutame
RYOKAN **$$**

(旅館丸為; ☎321-7130; www.jin.ne.jp/marutame; 2-6-17 Tachibana; s/tw ¥5250/8450; ®Higashi-Betsuin, exit 4) Narrow staircases testify to this ryokan's 50-year-plus history, yet it's modern with clean but basic Japanese rooms, English-speaking staff, coin-operated laundry and simple Japanese meals (breakfast/dinner ¥500/1200). Try for the lovely private *hanare* (apart) room in the back garden. From the station, cross the street, walk past the Nagoya Terebi building and Higashi Betsuin temple and turn right. It's on the left.

Richmond Hotel Nagoya Nayabashi
HOTEL **$$**

(リッチモンドホテル名古屋納屋橋; ☎212-1055; www.richmondhotel.jp; 1-2-7 Sakae; s/d/tw from ¥7500/10,800/15,500; ⊜@; ®Fushimi, exit 7) This business hotel offers relatively large, spick-and-span rooms in a minimalist shell, with dark-wood furniture, hi-tech desk lamps and English-language news on flat-panel TVs. Rates quoted here are 'member' rates; if you're not already a member, become one on registration (¥500).

Aichi-ken Seinen-kaikan Youth Hostel
HOSTEL **$**

(愛知県青年会館ユースホステル; ☎221-6001; www.jyh.or.jp; 1-18-8 Sakae; dm from ¥3360, HI member ¥2992; @; ®Fushimi, exit 7) This central, 50-bed hostel feels institutional, but it's usually the first budget place to fill up. Most options are Japanese-style dorms; there are also Western-style rooms with private toilet. From the station, walk west and take a left after the Hilton, from where it's two blocks further south. There is an 11pm curfew for dormitory guests.

Eating

Nagoya is famous for bold-flavoured local specialities, which, unlike in many other places in Japan, are also instantly palatable to non-Japanese tastes. *Kishimen* are flat, handmade wheat noodles, similar to *udon* (thick white noodles) and nicely chewy; *miso-nikomi udon* are noodles in hearty miso broth; and *miso-katsu* is breaded, fried pork cutlet with miso sauce. *Kōchin* (free-range chicken) is another local speciality, as are *tebasaki* (chicken wings). *Hitsumabushi* (charcoal-grilled eel sets) are also popular.

TOP CHOICE Yabaton TONKATSU $
(矢場とん; ☎252-8810; 3-6-18 Ōsu; dishes ¥735-1575; ⏰lunch & dinner Tue-Sun; ⓔ; 🚇Yaba-chō, exit 4) Throw caution to the wind at this spotless, workmanlike institution for *miso-katsu* that has been around since 1947. *Waraji-tonkatsu* is a cutlet flattened to as big as your head, or try *kani-korokke* (crab croquettes). *Yabaton-salada* (boiled pork with miso sesame sauce over vegetables) is kinda, sorta good for you. If all else fails, there's the delish *teppan-tonkatsu* (¥1350), which is a miso pork cutlet on a sizzling plate of cabbage. Look for the pig-in-an-apron logo.

TOP CHOICE Atsuta Hōraiken EEL $$
Honten (☎671-8686; 503 Kōbe-chō, Honten; mains ¥1890-3780; ⏰lunch & dinner, closed Mon; 🚇Temma-chō); Atsuta-jingū (☎682-5598; 2-10-26 Jingū, Atsuta-ku; ⏰lunch, dinner, closed Tues; 🚇Jingū-minami) This *hitsumabushi* shop, in business since 1873, is revered with good reason. Expect long queues during the summer peak season for *hitsumabushi,* basted in a secret *tare* (sauce) and served atop rice in a covered lacquered bowl (¥2730); add green onion, wasabi and *dashi* (fish broth) to your taste. Other *teishoku* (set menus) include tempura and steak. There's another branch a few blocks away, near Atsuta-jingū. The main branch has more atmosphere but also more smokers; avoid on Saturdays.

Tori Tori Tei IZAKAYA $
(とりとり亭; ☎566-3344; 2F, M-san Dining Bldg, 3-15-11 Meieki-Mae; small plates ¥360-1000; ⏰5pm-1am; 🚇Nagoya) This chain of *izakaya* centred on Nagoya chicken is a great introduction to local cuisine, with boisterous, smoky atmosphere and lots of beer going around. The standard is *tebasaki* (fried chicken wings; ¥150 each); other plates include *chikin namban furai* (Namban-style fried chicken; ¥680), and daikon salad. Look for the sign with black lettering behind the Royal Park Inn Nagoya.

Tiger Café CAFE $
(タイガーカフェ; ☎220-0031; 1-8-26 Nishiki; mains ¥600-2000, specials from ¥850; ⏰11am-3am Mon-Sat, to 11pm Sun; 🚇Fushimi) Fashionistas grace the windows of this faithful recreation of an old-style Parisian bistro, with tiled floors, white-shirted staff, sidewalk seating, art deco details and people smoking (even though you can't smoke in Paris bistros anymore). The smoked-salmon sandwich and *croque-monsieur* (toasted ham and cheese sandwich) are favourites, as are the good-value lunch specials.

Tarafuku IZAKAYA $
(たら福; ☎566-5600; 3-17-26 Meieki; dishes ¥400-800; ⏰dinner; ⓔ; 🚇Nagoya) Ambitious, young gourmets have turned the *izakaya* (pub-eatery) concept on its head, installing a stainless-steel kitchen in what looks from the outside like a falling-down house. East-West fusion dishes might include airy potato croquettes in a fried tofu crust; tomato and eggplant au gratin; house-cured ham, or beef, in wine sauce; plus wine and cocktail lists. Tarafuku is located diagonally across from both Tōyoko Inns.

Misen CHINESE $
(味仙; ☎238-7357; 3-6-3 Ōsu; dishes ¥580-1680; ⏰lunch & dinner, until 2am Fri & Sat; 🚇Yaba-chō, exit 4) Around the corner from Yabaton, Misen has little atmosphere and no English menu, but the *Taiwan rāmen* (egg noodles; ¥580) induces rapture – it's a spicy concoction of ground meat, chilli, garlic and green onion, served over noodles in a hearty clear broth. Other faves include *gomoku yakisoba* (stir-fried noodles; ¥630) and *mabōdōfu* (tofu in spicy meat sauce; ¥580).

Ebisuya NOODLES $
(えびすや; ☎961-3412; 3-20-7 Sakae; dishes from ¥700; ⏰lunch & dinner Mon-Sat; 🚇Sakae) One of the city's best-known *kishimen* chains, Ebisuya has a laid-back atmosphere and tasty, inexpensive bowls of noodles, which you can often catch being made by the chefs. There's a picture menu available.

Torigin Honten CHICKEN $
(鳥銀本店; ☎973-3000; 3-14-22 Nishiki; dishes ¥750-1950; ⏰dinner; ⓔ; 🚇Sakae) For top *kōchin,* Torigin has been going strong for decades. Chicken is served in many forms, including

kushiyaki (skewered), *kara-age* (deep-fried pieces), *zōsui* (mild rice hotpot) and sashimi (what you think it is). Individual dishes are a bit dainty for the price, but *teishoku* (set menus; from ¥3000) are more substantial. It's next door to BJ American Dining Bar.

Yamamotoya Sōhonke   NOODLES **$**
(山本屋総本家; ☎241-5617; 3-12-19 Sakae; dishes ¥976-1554; ☺lunch & dinner; ⓡSakae, Yaba-chō) This *miso-nikomi udon* shop has been in business since 1925, thanks to a lot of repeat customers. The basic dish costs ¥976. It's not really close to any subway station; it's a couple of blocks east of Shirakawa-kōen.

For cheap, informal, international eats, head to the Ōsu district. Expect to hear Portuguese at **Osso Brasil** (オッソ・ブラジル; ☎238-5151; 3-41-13 Ōsu; mains ¥700-1500; ☺10.30am-9pm Tue-Sun; ⓡKamimaezu, exit 8), a storefront serving Brazilian grills at lunchtime (all-you-can-eat on weekends, ¥1600) and snacks, while **Lee's Taiwan Kitchen** (李さんの台湾名物屋台; ☎251-8992; 3-35-10 Ōsu; mains around ¥450; ☺noon-8pm, closed Wed; ⓡKamimaezu, exit 8) does a big trade in take-out bubble tea and crackly *kara-age*. Other stands run from kebabs to crêpes to *okonomiyaki* (savoury pancakes).

🍷 Drinking

Smash Head   PUB
(スマッシュヘッド; ☎201-2790; 2-21-90 Ōsu; ☺noon-midnight Wed-Mon; ⓡŌsu Kannon, exit 2) Just north of Ōsu Kannon temple, this low-key spot in a faded brick building is both a pub and a motorcycle repair shop (no, really), where Guinness is the beverage of choice and teriyaki burgers are ¥850. But don't drink and ride or you may end up a...you know...

Eric Life   CAFE
(エリックライフ; ☎222-1555; 2-11-18 Ōsu; ☺noon-midnight Thu-Tue; ⓡŌsu Kannon, exit 2) Minimalist, kitsch-free and a teeny bit artsy, this cafe behind Ōsu Kannon temple is perfect for chilling over a coffee, cocktail or snack (lasagne ¥1100; *goma-negi udon* ¥750) Being in the Ōsu district, it draws a youngish crowd.

Shooters   BAR
(シューターズ; ☎202-7077; www.shooters-nagoya.com; 2-9-26 Sakae; ☺5pm-1am Mon-Thu, 11.30am-3am Fri-Sun; ⓡFushimi, exit 5) This US-style sports bar with over a dozen screens attracts a mostly *gaijin* (foreign), mostly raucous crowd. Japanese and foreign staff pour daily drink specials, and the menu includes burgers, pasta and Tex-Mex. It's on the 2nd floor of the Pola Building, diagonally across from Misono-za.

Elephant's Nest   BAR
(エレファントネスト; ☎232-4360; 1-4-3 Sakae; ☺5.30pm-1am Sun-Thu, to 2am Fri & Sat; ⓡFushimi, exit 7) Near the Hilton, Elephant's Nest is a favourite expat haunt, with a welcoming vibe, darts and traditional fare like Irish stew (¥1000). It's on the 2nd floor.

Red Rock Bar & Grill   PUB
(レッドロックバーアンドグリル; ☎262-7893; www.theredrock.jp; 4-14-6 Sakae; ☺5.30pm-late Tue-Sun; ⓡSakae, exit 13) On a Sakae side street, the Aussie-owned Red Rock has a warm ambience and plenty of pub food. Look for happy hours and specials such as 'Hump Night' on Wednesdays.

☆ Entertainment

Nagoya's nightlife might not match Tokyo's or Osaka's in scale but it makes up for it in ebullience. Check English-language listings magazines for dates and times.

Nagoya Blue Note   LIVE MUSIC
(名古屋ブルーノート; ☎961-6311; www.nagoya-bluenote.com, in Japanese; B2F 3-22-20 Nishiki; ⓡSakae) Foreign artists such as the Platters, McCoy Tyner Trio and Bill Frisell have recently graced this jazz and pop live stage, while Japanese performers have included the likes of Keiko Lee and the great Sadao Watanabe.

Misono-za   THEATRE
(御園座; ☎222-1481; www.misonoza.co.jp, in Japanese; 1-6-14 Sakae; ⓡFushimi, exit 6) This is the city's venue for kabuki theatre in February and October, although it does not have the translation facilities of theatres in other cities.

Nagoya Dome   SPORTS
(☎719-2121; ⓡNagoya Dome-mae Yada) Baseball fans will want to visit this 45,000-seat stadium, home of the Chunichi Dragons baseball team. It's also a venue for large concerts.

Electric Lady Land   NIGHTCLUB
(エレクトリックレディランド; ☎201-5004; www.ell.co.jp, in Japanese; 2-10-43 Ōsu; ⓡŌsu Kannon, exit 2) An intimate concert venue purveying the underground music scene in a cool, postindustrial setting. Nationally known bands perform in the 1st-floor hall, while the 3rd floor sees more up-and-coming acts.

Club JB's
NIGHTCLUB

(クラブジェービーズ; ☎241-2234; www.club-jbs
.jp; B1F Marumikonkō Bldg, 4-3-15 Sakae; 📮Sakae,
exit 13) Club kids (aged 20 and over) come for
an excellent sound system and famous DJs.

Shu
BAR

(シュー; ☎223-3788; 2F Manshin Bldg, 1-10-15
Nishiki; ⊙Wed-Mon; 📮Fushimi, exit 7) Nagoya
doesn't have a whole lot of options for gay
visitors from overseas (most operate as private clubs), but this tiny, chatty bar for gay
men welcomes all ages and nationalities.

🛍 Shopping

Both Meieki and Sakae boast gargantuan
malls and department stores, good for clothing, crafts and foods. Look for the department
stores **Maruei** (丸栄) and **Mitsukoshi** (三越)
in Sakae; **Takashimaya** (高島屋), **Meitetsu**
and **Kintetsu** (名鉄百貨店、近鉄百貨店)
near Nagoya Station; and **Matsuzakaya** (松
坂屋) in Sakae and near Nagoya Station. Regional crafts include *Arimatsu-narumi shi-
bori* (elegant tie-dying), cloisonné, ceramics
and Seki blades (swords, knives, scissors etc).

A youthful energy fills vintage clothing
shops, electronics and music shops, cafes
and a hodge-podge of old and new in the
Ōsu district, east of the temple around Ōsu
Kannon-dōri and its continuation, Banshō-
ji-dōri. **Komehyō** (コメ兵; 2-20-25 Ōsu, Naka-
ku; 📮Ōsu Kannon) is a multistorey discounter
that's recently taken over much of the real
estate, selling electronics, fashion, jewellery, house wares, used kimonos etc. Inside,
the ingenious **yen=g** (☎218-2122) sells used
clothing by weight. **Momijiya** (もみじや;
☎251-1313; 3-37-46 Ōsu) creates clothing and
accessories patterned after antique kimono
fabric, though look closely for its own cute,
contemporary twists.

Just east of Ōsu, Ōtsu-dōri is called the Akihabara of Nagoya for its proliferation of manga shops. Ōsu Kannon temple itself hosts a colourful antique market on the 18th and 28th
of each month, while Higashi Betsuin has a
flea market (☎321-9201; ⊙9am-2pm; 📮Higashi-
Betsuin, exit 4) on the 12th of each month.

Kinokuniya Books
BOOKSHOP

(紀伊國屋; ⊙10am-8pm; 📮Nagoya) In the
Meitetsu Men's-kan building, south of Nagoya Station. Has English-language titles.

Maruzen
BOOKSHOP

(丸善; ☎261-2251; 3-2-7 Sakae; 📮Sakae) On
busy Hirokōji-dōri. Has English-language
titles.

ℹ Information

Emergency
Ambulance & fire (☎119)
Nagoya International Centre (名古屋国際セン
ター; ☎581-0100; 1-47-1 Nagono; ⊙9am-7pm
Tue-Sun; 📮Kokusai Centre) Provides informa-
tion in English, including referrals.
Police (☎110)

Internet Access
Chikōraku (知・好・楽; 1-25-2 Meieki; 1st hr
¥490; ⊙24hr; 📮Nagoya) In the basement of
the Meitetsu Lejac building.
FedEx Kinko's (フェデックスキンコーズ; 2-3-31
Sakae; 1st 10min ¥250, 1st hr ¥1250; ⊙24hr;
📮Fushimi)
Nagoya International Centre (1-47-1 Nagono;
per 15min ¥100; ⊙9am-7pm Tue-Sun; 📮Koku-
sai Centre)

Internet Resources
Nagoya Convention and Visitors Bureau
(www.ncvb.or.jp) Good general website for
visitors.
Nagoya International Centre (www.nic
-nagoya.or.jp) Up-to-date event listings, plus
practical info for residents.

Medical Services
Nagoya's prefecture, **Aichi-ken** (☎249-9799;
www.qq.pref.aichi.jp), has a list of medical in-
stitutions with English-speaking staff, including
specialities and hours of operation.
Tachino Clinic (たちのクリニック; ☎541-9130;
Dai-Nagoya Bldg, 3-28-12 Meieki; 📮Nagoya)
Opposite the east exit of Nagoya Station; with
English-speaking staff.

Money & Post
Citibank (シティバンク) has 24-hour Cirrus ATMs
on the 1st floor of the Sugi building (📮Sakae,
exit 7) and in the arrival lobby at Central Japan
International Airport.
Eki-mae post office (タワーズ内郵便局; 📮Na-
goya) North of the station's east exit.
Nagoya Station post office (名古屋中央郵便
局名古屋駅前分室) Off the main concourse.

Tourist Information
English-language street and subway maps are
widely available at information centres and
hotels – the Convention & Visitors Bureau's free
Live Map Nagoya covers the basics. English-
language listings publications include *Japanzine*,
Avenues and *Nagoya Calendar*.

For information on onward transportation,
there is English-speaking staff at JR Nagoya
Station's ticket windows.
KNT Tourist (KNTツーリスト; ☎541-8686; 1-2-2
Meieki; ⊙10am-8pm Mon-Fri, to 6pm Sat & Sun;
📮Nagoya) For info on onward transportation.

Nagoya International Centre (☎581-0100; 1-47-1 Nagono; ⊗9am-7pm Tue-Sun; ⒭Kokusai Centre) This place has helpful English-speaking staff and information on both Nagoya and regional destinations. There's a library, overseas-TV newscasts and a bulletin board for postings.

Nagoya Tourist Information (名古屋市名 古屋駅観光案内所) Nagoya Station (☎541-4301; ⊗9am-7pm; ⒭Nagoya, in the central concourse); Kanayama Station (☎323-0161; ⊗9am-8pm; ⒭Kanayama); Sakae (☎963-5252; Oasis 21 Bldg; ⊗10am-8pm; ⒭Sakae) All locations have plenty of info and at least one English speaker on hand.

❶ Getting There & Away

Air

Many Nagoyans go to **Central Japan International Airport** (Centrair; NGO; www.centrair .jp/en), opened in 2005 on a manmade island in Ise-wan (Ise Bay) 35km south of the city, for an afternoon out. On the 4th floor are dozens of Japanese and Western shopping and dining options (at out-of-airport prices), plane-spotting from the observation deck, and **Fū-no-yu** (風の 湯; adult/child with towel ¥1000/600; ⊗8am-10pm), hot-spring baths, which are admittedly a little institutional.

Some 30 airlines connect Centrair with around 30 international cities (in Europe, North America, and especially Asia) and 20 Japanese cities, though you will find some are reached faster by train.

Boat

Taiheiyo ferry runs between Nagoya and Toma-komai (Hokkaido, from ¥10,500, 40 hours) via Sendai (from ¥7000, 21 hours 40 minutes) every second evening at 7pm. Take the Meikō subway line to Nagoya-kō Station and go to Nagoya Port.

Bus

JR and **Meitetsu Highway buses** operate services between Nagoya and Kyoto (¥2500, 2½ hours, hourly), Osaka (¥2900, three hours, hourly), Kobe (¥3300, 3½ hours), Kanazawa (¥4060, four hours, 10 daily), Nagano (¥4500, 4½ hours), and Tokyo (¥5100, six hours, 14 daily). Overnight buses run to Hiroshima (¥8400, nine hours).

Train

Nagoya is a major *shinkansen* hub, connecting with Tokyo (¥10,580, 1¾ hours), Shin-Osaka (¥6180, 50 minutes), Kyoto (¥5440, 35 minutes) and Hiroshima (¥13,630, 2½ hours). The private Meitetsu line is your best bet within the region.

To the Japan Alps, you can take the JR Chūō line to Nagano (Shinano *tokkyū* – limited express – ¥7330, 2¾ hours) via Matsumoto (¥5670, two hours). A separate line serves Takayama (Hida *tokkyū*, ¥5670, 2¼ hours).

❶ Getting Around

To/From the Airport

Central Japan International Airport is accessible from Nagoya Station via the Meitetsu Kūkō (Airport) line (*tokkyū*, ¥850, 28 minutes). A taxi from central Nagoya costs upwards of ¥13,000.

DON'T MISS

FAMOUS FACTORIES FOR FREE

Nagoya is the hub of a major industrial centre and visitors have a unique opportunity to visit some of the world's leading manufacturers. Bookings are required.

Two-hour tours of Toyota Motor Corporation's main plant in Toyota city depart from the **Toyota Kaikan Exhibition Hall** (☎0565-29-3355; www.toyota.co.jp/en/about_toyota/ facility/toyota_kaikan/museum; 1 Toyota-chō; ⊗11am Mon-Fri). Book online up to three months in advance. Allow at least one hour to get to Toyota city from central Nagoya; check the website for directions. See also the Toyota Commemorative Museum of Industry & Technology (p174).

Denso (☎0566-61-7215; www.globaldenso.com/en/aboutdenso/hall/gallery; Kariya City; ⊗9.30am-5pm Mon-Fri) is a company whose products you've probably used even if you don't know its name: its backbone is automotive components, but there are also industrial robots. Short visits (up to one hour) take place in the Denso Gallery, or you can visit the plant on a 2½-hour tour. It's a seven-minute walk from Kariya Station on the JR Tōkaidō line.

The Nagoya brewery of **Asahi Beer** (☎052-792-8966; www.asahibeer.co.jp/factory/brew ery/nagoya, in Japanese; 318 Nishi-kawahara, Moriyama-ku; ⊗9.30am-3pm, closed irregularly) welcomes visitors for 1¼-hour tours. Sample the wares for the tour's final 20 minutes – woo-hoo! Request about one month in advance for English-language guides. Take the JR Chūō line to Shin-Moriyama Station; it's a 15-minute walk.

If none of that starts your motor, visit www.sangyokanko.jp for more ideas.

Bus

The **Me~guru bus** (www.ncvb.or.jp/routebus/en/index.html; day pass adult/child ¥500/250) makes a convenient loop (close) to attractions in the Meieki, Sakae and castle areas, and offers discounted admission. It runs 9.30am to 5pm, hourly Tuesday to Friday and twice hourly on weekends.

Subway

Nagoya has an excellent subway system with six lines, clearly signposted in English and Japanese. Fares cost ¥200 to ¥320 depending on distance. One-day passes (¥740, ¥850 including city buses), available at ticket machines, include subway transport and discounted admission to many attractions. On Saturday and Sunday the *donichi eco-kippu* (Saturday-Sunday eco-ticket) gives the same benefits for ¥600 per day.

AROUND NAGOYA

This region, consisting of outlying Aichi-ken and southern Gifu-ken, offers plenty of easy day trips. The commuter towns of Tokoname and Arimatsu are historic centres for ceramics and tie-dyeing. Or for some 21st-century *monozukuri*, check out the factories making household-name brands. Easygoing Inuyama boasts National Treasures – its castle and teahouse. Both Inuyama and Gifu city are famed for *ukai* (cormorant fishing with trained birds).

Tokoname 常滑

0569 / POP 54,800

Clay beneath the ground of this bayside community has made Tokoname a hub for ceramic-making for centuries – during its height some 400 chimneys rose above its centre. Today, Tokoname still produces some ¥60 trillion in ceramics annually. Most of that is for plumbing and tiles, but teapots and *maneki-neko* (welcoming cat figurines at the entrance to shops and restaurants) are also signature designs. It all makes Tokoname's historic centre a visually interesting day trip from Nagoya or a quick detour from Central Japan International Airport. Pick up a map in English at **Tokoname Tourist Information** (常滑市観光案内所; ☑34-8888; ☺9am-5.30pm), inside Tokoname Station.

Yakimono Sanpo Michi (やきもの散歩道; Pottery Footpath) is a handsome 1.8km paved trail looping up and down hills around the town's historic centre. Lining the path are locally produced ceramics from historic pipes to roofing tiles and plaques decorated by school kids. Numbered plaques corresponding to the tourist office map indicate the stops along the way, and you'll pass kilns and chimneys, cafes and galleries selling the works of some 100 local ceramic artists, some at bargain prices.

The pipe-and-jug-lined lane **Dokanzaka** (土管坂; stop 9) is particularly photogenic, and go around the back at **Noborigama-hiroba** (登窯広場; Climbing Kiln Sq; stop 13) for a peek at the 10 square chimneys that served the gigantic, 1887 kiln. The restored **Takita-ke** (滝田家; Takita residence; admission ¥300; ☺9am-4.30pm Tue-Sun), c 1850, at stop 8 was the home of a shipping magnate family and exhibits a replica of the local trading ships called *bishu-kaisen,* and displays of ceramics, lacquer, furniture and oil lamps. Look for the *suikinkutsu,* a ceramic jar buried in the ground so that it rings like a *koto* (13-stringed instrument derived from a Chinese zither that is played flat on the floor) when water drips into it. A video is available with English translation.

With a little more time, visit **Inax Live Museum** (イナックスライブミュージアム; www.inax.co.jp/ilm; 1-130 Okueichō, Tokoname-shi; adult/child¥600/200; ☺10am-5pm, closed 3rd Wed of month), a cluster of buildings about a five-minute detour from the Pottery Footpath. Inax is one of Japan's top plumbing-equipment manufacturers. On the 2nd floor of Inax Kiln Plaza are some 150 Meiji- and Taisho-era toilets that are elaborately decorated. There are also small exhibits of tiles from around the world, and a workshop where you can try your own hand at tile-making (at an extra charge).

You won't have trouble finding cafes along the Pottery Footpath. **Koyōan** (古窯庵; ☑35-8350; mains ¥880-1800; ☺11.30am-5pm Tue-Sun, dinner by reservation) serves homemade *soba* (buckwheat noodles) on handsome ceramic-ware dishes, surrounded by wood-beamed ceilings and inlaid tiles. Specialities include *teuchi soba* (handmade *soba;* ¥880) and tempura *soba* (¥1780); set menus are available from ¥2100.

🛈 Getting There & Around

The private Meitetsu line connects Tokoname with Meitetsu Nagoya (*kyūkō*, ¥650, 40 minutes; *tokkyū* ¥1000, 30 minutes) and Central Japan International Airport (¥300, five minutes). Once in town, the Pottery Footpath is a few hundred metres from the train station.

Inuyama 犬山

♪0568 / POP 75,700

Dubbed the 'Japanese Rhine' since the 19th century, Inuyama's Kiso-gawa sets a pretty scene beneath its castle, a National Treasure. By day, the castle, quaint streets, manicured Uraku-en and 17th-century Jo-an Teahouse make for a pleasant ramble, while at night the scene becomes cinematic as fishermen practise *ukai* in season. Nearby attractions include architecture at Museum Meiji-mura and some rather racy shrines.

◉ Sights & Activities

Inuyama-jō　　　　　　　HISTORICAL BUILDING
(犬山城; 65-2 Kitakoken; adult/child ¥500/100; ◎9am-4.30pm) A National Treasure, Japan's oldest standing castle is said to have originated as a fort in 1440; the current *donjon* (main keep) dates from 1537 and has withstood war, earthquake and restoration to remain an excellent example of Momoyama-period architecture. Stone walls reach 5m high, and inside are narrow, steep staircases and military displays. There's a fine view of mountains and plains from the top storey.

Just south are the shrines **Haritsuna Jinja** (針綱神社) and **Sankō-Inari Jinja** (三光稲荷神社), the latter with interesting statues of *komainu* (protective dogs).

Marionette (Karakuri) Exhibition Room & Inuyama Castle Historical Museum　　　　　　　MUSEUM
Included in your admission ticket to Inuyama-jō are the following two collections.

One block south of Haritsuna Jinja and Sankō-Inari Jinja, the **Marionette (Karakuri) Exhibition Room** (からくり展示館; 8 Aza Kitakoken, Ōaza; admission purchased separately ¥100; ◎9am-5pm) contains a small display of Edo- and Meiji-era puppets. On Saturday and Sunday you can see the wooden characters in action (at 10.30am and 2pm).

To see the puppets as they were meant to be used, visit during **Inuyama Matsuri** (Inuyama Festival, on the first Saturday and Sunday in April; a scaled-down version is on the fourth Saturday in October), designated an Intangible Cultural Asset by the Japanese government. Dating back to 1635, the festival features a parade of 13 three-tiered floats decked out with lanterns and *karakuri*, which perform to music.

Nearby, the **Inuyama Castle Historical Museum** (犬山市文化資料館; admission purchased separately ¥100; ◎9am-5pm) has two of the festival floats on display. Four other floats are on exhibit at **Dondenkan** (どんでん館; adult/child ¥200/100; ◎9am-5pm), a few blocks south, accessed via a street of wood-built buildings.

Uraku-en & Jo-an Teahouse　　　　GARDEN
(有楽園・茶室如安; 1 Gomonsaki; admission adult/child ¥1000/600; ◎9am-5pm Mar-Nov, to

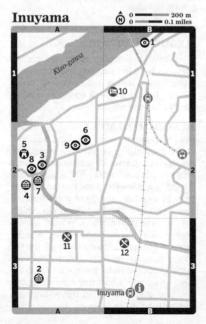

Inuyama

4pm Dec-Feb) The garden Uraku-en is 300m east of Inuyama-jō, in a corner of the grounds of the Meitetsu Inuyama Hotel. One of the finest teahouses in Japan and a National Treasure, Jo-an was built in 1618 in Kyoto by Oda Urakusai, a younger brother of Oda Nobunaga, and was relocated here in 1972. You can enjoy tea on the grounds for ¥500.

Cormorant Fishing FISHING

Ukai (鵜飼い) takes place close to Inuyama-yūen Station, by Twin Bridge Inuyama-bashi. Book your ticket at the tourist information office or **Kisogawa Kankō** (☑61-0057; www.kisogawa-kankou.com; adult/child Jul & Aug from ¥2800/1400, May-Jun & Sep-Oct from ¥2500/1250), near the cormorant-fishing pier.

Boats depart nightly at 7pm from June to August. In September and October boats depart at 6.30pm.

✨ Festivals & Events

In addition to **Inuyama Matsuri**, the city also hosts the summer **Nihon Rhine Matsuri**, every 10 August on the banks of the river, culminating in fireworks.

🛏 Sleeping & Eating

Rinkō-kan RYOKAN $$

(臨江館; ☑61-0977; fax 61-2505; www.rinkokan.jp; 8-1 Nishidaimon; r per person with/without 2 meals from ¥12,750/6450; @) Overlooking the river, this cheery, 20-room hot-spring ryokan makes the most of its 1960s building, featuring handsome Japanese-style accommodation with in-room bath, and stone common baths including *rotemburo* (outdoor baths). Dinner is served in your room.

Inuyama International Youth Hostel HOSTEL $

(犬山国際ユースホステル; ☑61-1111; fax 61-2770; www.inuyama-iyh.com; 161 Himuro, Tsugao; s/d/tr ¥3300/6200/8700; @) Also known as the Riverside Inuyama, this remote and modern and well-kept hostel offers large, comfortable, Japanese- and Western-style rooms, friendly staff and a stone common bath (BYOT). Reservations for meals (breakfast/dinner ¥840/1580) are recommended, as there are no restaurants nearby. It's 25 minutes' walk northeast of Inuyama-yūen Station – access it from along the river; from Inuyama Station, it's about a ¥1200 taxi ride.

Narita FRENCH $$

(なり多; ☑65-2447; 395 Higashikoken; 5-course meal from ¥3900; ⊙lunch & dinner) This is a chichi French restaurant in a 170-year-old building with attractive garden, specialising in five-course set meals. It's a block west of the Inuyama Miyako Hotel.

Fū CAFE $

(ふう; ☑61-6515; a-fuusan@md.ccnw.ne.jp; 558 Higashikoken; lunch ¥600; ⊙8am-6pm Thu-Tue) This friendly, low-key, family-run coffeeshop makes a different simple lunch daily and serves it until supplies run out. Phone (in Japanese) or email to enquire or reserve, and do not flake (bad karma). Or just enjoy coffee and cake. There's occasional live music.

ℹ Information

Inuyama's **tourist information office** (犬山観光案内所; ☑61-6000; ⊙9am-5pm) is in Inuyama Station. It dispenses useful English-language pamphlets and maps and can book accommodation and make referrals to river activities such as rafting. The castle and *ukai* area are closer to Inuyama-yūen Station, one stop north or about 15 minutes on foot. On the web, visit www.city.inuyama.aichi.jp/english/index.html.

ℹ Getting There & Away

Inuyama is connected with Nagoya (¥540, 30 minutes) and Meitetsu-Gifu Station in Gifu city (¥440, 35 minutes) via the Meitetsu Inuyama line. JR travellers can connect via Gifu to Unuma (¥320, 20 minutes) and walk across the Kisogawa to Inuyama.

Around Inuyama   犬山近辺

If you have the time, the region surrounding Inuyama has a few unusual and worthwhile attractions, as well as some decent farmland scenery. Be sure to check transport connections before you set out.

MUSEUM MEIJI-MURA 明治村

Few Meiji-period buildings have survived war, earthquake or rabid development, but this open-air **museum** (www.meijimura.com; 1 Uchiyama; adult/child ¥1600/600; ⊙9.30am-5pm Mar-Oct, to 4pm Nov-Feb, closed Mon Dec-Feb) has brought together over 60 of them from all over Japan to a lakeside 'village'. On exhibit are one-time public offices, private homes, banks and a sake brewery, as well as some forms of transport. Among them are the entryway designed by Frank Lloyd Wright for Tokyo's Imperial Hotel, the home of novelist Sōseki Natsume (who wrote *I am a Cat* and *Botchan*), and early Kyoto trams. Note the coming-together of Western and Japanese architectural styles, which is indicative of this era. Allow at least half a day to enjoy it at an easy pace.

A bus to Meiji-mura (¥410, 20 minutes) departs every 30 minutes from Inuyama Station's east exit.

ŌAGATA-JINJA   大縣神社

This 2000-year-old **shrine** (3 Aza Miyayama) is dedicated to the female Shintō deity Izanami and draws women devotees seeking marriage or fertility. The precincts of the shrine contain rocks (*hime-ishi*) and other items resembling female genitals.

The popular **Hime-no-Miya Matsuri** takes place here on the Sunday before 15 March (or on 15 March if it's a Sunday). Locals pray for good harvests and prosperity by parading through the streets bearing a *mikoshi* (portable shrine) with replicas of female genitals.

Ōgata-jinja is a 25-minute walk southeast of Gakuden Station on the Meitetsu Komaki line (¥220 from Inuyama, seven minutes).

TAGATA-JINJA   田県神社

Izanagi, the male counterpart of Izanami, is commemorated at this **shrine** (152 Tagatachō). The main hall has a side building containing images of phalluses, left as offerings by grateful worshippers.

The **Tagata Hōnen-sai Matsuri** takes place on 15 March at Tagata-jinja, when the highly photogenic, 2m-long, 60kg 'sacred object' is paraded, amid much mirth, around the neighbourhood. Arrive well before the procession starts at 2pm.

Tagata-jinja is five minutes' walk west of Tagata-jinja-mae Station on the Meitetsu Komaki line (¥290 from Inuyama, nine minutes).

Gifu   岐阜

♪ 058 / POP 420,000

Historically, Gifu has a strong association with Oda Nobunaga (p684), *daimyō* (domain lord) of the castle and bestower of the city's name in 1567. It was later visited by famed haiku poet Matsuō Bashō, who witnessed *ukai* here in 1688; Charlie Chaplin did the same in his day.

Contemporary Gifu shows little evidence of those historic times, due to a colossal earthquake in 1891 and a thorough drubbing in WWII. Still, the Nagara-gawa remains a popular destination for *ukai,* there's a re-

construction of the castle Gifu-jō atop the riverside mountain, Kinka-zan (329m), and a spiffed-up business district. Gifu is also known for handicrafts.

⊙ Sights & Activities

Cormorant Fishing   FISHING

(鵜飼い) During Gifu's cormorant fishing season (11 May to 15 October), boats depart nightly (except after flooding or on the night of a full moon) from the bridge, Nagarabashi. Or you can view the action from a distance by walking along the river east of the bridge.

Bookings are strongly advised. Tickets are sold at hotels or, if any tickets remain after 6pm, at the **booking office** (🖉262-0104 for advance reservations; www.ukai-gifucity.jp/ukai; adult/child ¥3300/2900; ⊙departures 6.15pm, 6.45pm & 7.15pm) just below Nagarabashi. Food and drink are not provided on the boats. On Monday to Friday, fares for the two later departures are ¥3000/2600 per adult/child. Take the bus to the Nagarabashi stop.

Gifu-kōen   GARDEN

(岐阜公園) At the foot of Kinka-zan, this is one of the loveliest city parks in Japan, with plenty of water and trees set into the hillside. Take the bus to the Gifu-kōen Rekishi Hakubutsukan-mae stop.

Gifu City History Museum

(岐阜市歴史博物館; 2-18-1 Ōmiya-chō; adult/child ¥300/150; ⊙9am-4.30pm Tue-Sun) Inside Gifu-kōen is the site of Oda Nobunaga's home.

Kinka-zan Ropeway

(金華山ロープウエー; 257 Senjōjiki-shita; return adult/child ¥1050/520; ⊙9am-5pm mid-Oct–mid-Mar, to 10.30pm late Jul-Aug, to 6pm mid-Mar–late Jul & Sep–mid-Oct) Also inside Gifu-kōen is a cable car to the summit.

Gifu-jō

(岐阜城; 18 Tenshukaku, Kinka-zan; adult/child ¥200/100; ⊙9.30am-30min before ropeway closure) From the summit you can check out Gifu-jō, a small but scenic modern reconstruction of the original castle. Those who'd rather huff it can hike to the castle (one hour).

Shōhō-ji   TEMPLE

(正法寺; 8 Daibutsu-chō; admission ¥150; ⊙9am-5pm) The main attraction of this orange-and-white temple is the papier-mâché *daibutsu* (Great Buddha; 1832), which is nearly

14m tall and is said to have been fashioned over 38 years using about a tonne of paper Sutras. The temple is a short walk southwest of Gifu-kōen. Get off at the Daibutsu-mae bus stop (from Gifu-kōen only).

🛏 Sleeping & Eating

The narrow streets between Nagarabashi-dōri and Kinka-zan-dōri (between the train stations) provide happy hunting for cafes, restaurants and *izakaya*.

Comfort Hotel Gifu   HOTEL **$$**
(コンフォートホテル岐阜; ☑267-1311; fax 267-1312; www.choice-hotels.jp/cfgifu, in Japanese; 6-6 Yoshino-machi; s/tw with breakfast ¥6500/11,550; ➔@🛜) Across from JR Gifu Station, this unpretentious, 219-room business hotel offers LCD TVs with wireless internet access from rooms and a coin laundry. Breakfast is a simple but plentiful Japanese/continental buffet.

Daiwa Roynet Hotel Gifu   HOTEL **$$**
(ダイワロイネットホテル岐阜; ☑212-0055; www.daiwaroynet.jp/gifu; fax 212-0056; 8-5 Kanda-machi; s/d from ¥7500/12,000; ➔@) A posher choice, with a minimalist design, nice linens and rooms outfitted with LAN cables for your computer. It's steps from Meitetsu-Gifu Station.

TOP CHOICE Utsuboya   CAFE **$**
(空穂屋; ☑215-7077; www.utsuboya.info, in Japanese; 38 Utsuboya-chō; ⏰10am-6pm Fri-Wed) A charming, atmospheric cafe and antiques gallery nestled in a wonderfully traditional house. The specialty here is homemade fried doughnuts (from ¥200). From the Hon-machi 3-chōme bus stop (en route to the Kinka-zan Ropeway), walk east along Nagarabashi-dōri and then turn right on the second street; you'll see it on the right in an old, tile-roofed shophouse.

Bier Hall   BAR
(ビアホール; ☑266-8868; 2-8 Tamamiya-chō; ⏰5.30pm-1am, Mon-Sat) For a nightcap, join expats and locals at the *wabi-sabi*-cool Bier Hall, which specialises in Guinness, pizzas, fried snacks and beef stew. It's a few doors behind the clothing shop 'Bad'.

🛍 Shopping

Gifu's craft tradition includes *wagasa* (oiled paper parasols/umbrellas) and *chōchin* (paper lanterns) elegantly painted with landscapes etc) though the number of arti-

sans is a mere fraction of their golden age in the Edo period (600 umbrella-makers then compared to a handful now). Souvenir shops sell mass-produced versions, or the tourist information office has a map of high-quality makers and/or sellers. Expect to pay ¥10,000-plus for a quality *wagasa* or *chōchin*. Shops keep irregular hours, so it's worth phoning ahead to make sure they're open.

Sakaida Eikichi Honten   WAGASA
(坂井田永吉本店; 27 Kanōnakahiroe-chō; ⏰9.30am-5.30pm Mon-Sat) This place makes and sells *wagasa* (from ¥10,000). It's a 10-minute walk from JR Gifu Station. Turn left from the south exit, and turn right at the second stoplight. Sakaida is at the next corner.

Ozeki Chōchin   CHŌCHIN
(オゼキ; 1-18 Oguma-chō; ⏰9am-5pm Mon-Fri) For Gifu *chōchin*, try Ozeki Chōchin. From Ken-Sōgōchōsha-mae bus stop, walk east. It's by the temple Higashi Betsuin.

ℹ Information

Tourist information office (☑262-4415; ⏰9am-7pm Mar-Dec, to 6pm Jan-Feb) On the 2nd floor of JR Gifu Station.

ℹ Getting There & Around

From Nagoya, take the JR Tōkaidō line (*tokkyū*, ¥1180, 20 minutes; *futsū*, ¥450, 30 minutes) to Gifu or the Meitetsu line to Meitetsu-Gifu (¥540, 35 minutes). Meitetsu trains also serve Inuyama (¥440, 35 minutes).

JR Gifu Station and Meitetsu-Gifu Station are a few minutes' walk apart in the southern city centre. Most of the sights are about 4km north, near Nagara-gawa and Kinka-zan, easily reachable by bus.

Buses to sights (¥200) depart from stops 11 and 12 of the bus terminal by JR Gifu Station's Nagara exit, stopping at Meitetsu-Gifu en route. However, ask before boarding, as not all buses make all stops.

Gujō-Hachiman   郡上八幡
☑0575 / POP 16,000

Nestled in the mountains at the confluence of several rivers, Gujō-Hachiman is a small, pleasant town famed for its **Gujō Odori**, Japan's third-largest folk dance festival, and for being the place where all of those plastic food models you see in restaurant windows come from.

The **tourist office** (観光協会; ☑67-0002; ☉8.30am-5pm) is by Shin-bashi in the centre of town, about five minutes' walk from the Jōka-machi Plaza bus terminal. For guided tours of Gujō-Hachiman in English, contact Gujoinus (pupi@zd.wakwak.com).

The festival first: following a tradition dating to the 1590s, townsfolk engage in frenzied dancing on 32 nights between mid-July and early September. Visitor participation is encouraged, especially during *tetsuya odori*, the four main days of the festival (13 to 16 August), when the dancing goes all night.

At other times of the year the town's sparkling rivers, narrow lanes and stone bridges make for a relaxing stopover.

Those incredibly realistic food models are one of life's great mysteries, and here's your chance to suss them out. In an old *machi-ya* (merchant house), **Shokuhin Sample Kōbō Sōsakukan** (食品サンプル工房創作館; admission free; ☉9am-5pm) lets you view the goodies and try creating them yourself (reservation required). Tempura (¥1000 for three pieces) and lettuce (free) make memorable souvenirs. It's about five minutes' walk from Jōka-machi Plaza.

Gujō-Hachiman's other attractions include the tiny hilltop castle **Gujō Hachiman-jō** (郡上八幡城; adult/child ¥300/150; ☉9am-5pm), which had been a humble fortress dating back to about 1600; the current, grander building dates from only 1933. It contains weapons, armour and the like, and offers fine views. From the bus terminal it's about 20 minutes' walk.

The town is also known for its waterways. A famous spring, **Sōgi-sui**, near the centre of town, is something of a pilgrimage site, named for a Momoyama-era poet. People who rank such things place Sōgi-sui at the top of the list for clarity.

Bizenya Ryokan (備前屋旅館; ☑65-2068; fax 67-0007; 264 Yanagi-machi; r per person with 2 meals from ¥11,550; Ⓟ) boasts large rooms, some with private facilities, around a handsome garden. This 12-room ryokan provides a relaxing, quietly upscale experience. It's located between the bus terminal and tourist office.

Nakashimaya Ryokan (中嶋屋旅館; ☑65-2191; fax 65-2192; www.nakashimaya.net; 940 Shinmachi; r from ¥5800; Ⓟ) is a delightfully well kept, comfortable inn between the station and the tourist office.

The most convenient access to Gujō-Hachiman is via bus from Gifu (¥1480, one hour). The private Nagaragawa Tetsudō line serves Gujō-Hachiman from Mino-Ōta (¥1320, 80 minutes, hourly), with connections via the JR Takayama line to Nagoya (¥1110, one hour) and Takayama (*tokkyū*, ¥4180, 1¾ hours; *futsū*, ¥1890, three hours). Buses also journey from Nagoya (¥3500, three hours) and Takayama (¥1600). Central Gujō-Hachiman is easily walkable, or bicycles are available for rent from the tourist office (¥300/1500 per hour/day).

HIDA DISTRICT

The centrepiece of this ancient, mountainous region (飛騨地域) is the handsome town of Takayama, known for merchant houses, temples and a strong craft tradition. Hida's signature architectural style is the thatch-roofed *gasshō-zukuri* (see the box, p190), while its culinary fame rests in Hida-*gyū* (local beef), *hoba-miso* (sweet miso paste grilled at the table on a magnolia leaf) and *soba*.

Takayama 高山
☑0577 / POP 93,000

With its old inns, shops and sake breweries, Takayama is a rarity: a 21st-century city (admittedly a small one) that's also retained its traditional charm. Vibrant morning markets, hillside shrines and a laid-back populace add to the town's allure, and it should be a high priority on any visit to Central Honshū. Give yourself at least two days to enjoy the place; it's easily tackled on foot or bicycle.

Takayama was established in the late 16th century as the castle town of the Kanamori clan, but in 1692 it was placed under direct control of the *bakufu* (shōgunate) in Edo. The present layout dates from the Kanamori period, and its sights include more than a dozen museums, galleries and exhibitions that cover lacquer and lion masks, folk craft and architecture.

Takayama remains the region's administrative and transport hub, and it makes a good base for trips around Hida and the Northern Japan Alps.

All of the main sights except Hida-no-Sato (Hida Folk Village) are in the centre of town, within walking distance of the station. Northeast of the station, Kokubun-ji-dōri, the main street, heads east, across the Miya-gawa (about 10 minutes' walk),

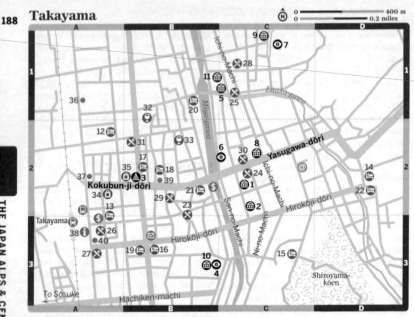

Takayama

⊙ Sights

1 Fujii Folkcraft Art Gallery	C2
2 Hida Folk Archaeological Museum	C2
3 Hida Kokubun-ji	B2
4 Jinya-mae Morning Market	B3
5 Kusakabe Mingeikan	C1
6 Miya-gawa Morning Market	C2
7 Sakurayama Hachiman-gū	C1
8 Takayama Shōwa-kan	C2
9 Takayama Yatai Kaikan (Festival Floats Exhibition Hall)	C1
10 Takayama-jinya	B3
11 Yoshijima-ke	B1

🛌 Sleeping

12 Asunaro Ryokan	A2
13 Best Western Hotel	A2
14 Hida Takayama Tenshō-ji Youth Hostel	D2
15 Hoshokaku	C3
16 J-Hoppers	B3
17 Minshuku Kuwataniya	B2
18 Rickshaw Inn	B2
19 Spa Hotel Alpina	B3
20 Sumiyoshi Ryokan	B1
21 Tanabe Ryokan	B2
22 Yamakyū	D2

⊗ Eating

23 Chapala	B2
24 Ebisu-honten	C2
25 Kyōya	C1
26 Myōgaya	A3
27 Orijin	A3
28 Rakuda	C1
29 Suzuya	B2
30 Takumi-ya	C2
31 Yamatake-Shōten	B2

🍸 Drinking

32 Red Hill Pub	B1
33 Rum Dance Hall	B2

🛍 Shopping

34 Mori no Kotoba	A2
35 Suzuki Chōkoku	B2

Information

36 International Affairs Office	A1
37 Kinki Nippon Tourist	A2
38 Tourist Information Office	A3

Transport

39 Hara Cycle	B2
40 Toyota Rent-a-Car	A3

THE JAPAN ALPS & CENTRAL HONSHŪ HIDA DISTRICT

where it becomes Yasugawa-dōri. South of Yasugawa-dōri is the historic, picturesque Sanmachi-suji (Sanmachi district) of immaculately preserved old homes. On signage, look for 古い町並み (*furui machinami*) or 'Old Private Homes' in English.

Hida-no-Sato is a 10-minute bus ride west of the station.

◎ Sights & Activities

Sanmachi-suji
NEIGHBOURHOOD

(三町筋) The centre of the old town, this district of three main streets (Ichi-no-Machi, Ni-no-Machi and San-no-Machi) is lined with traditional shops, restaurants and museums. Sake breweries are easily recognised by the spheres of cedar fronds: some open to the public in January and early February (the schedule is available at tourist offices); most of the year they just sell their wares. For beautiful nighttime shots, bring a tripod and set your camera's exposure to long.

Fujii Folkcraft Art Gallery

(藤井美術民芸館; Fujii Bijutsu Minzoku-kan; 69 San-no-Machi; adult/child ¥700/350; ⊙9am-5pm, often closed Tue-Fri early Dec-early Mar) A private collection in an old merchant's house, with folk craft and ceramics, particularly from the Muromachi and Edo periods.

Hida Folk Archaeological Museum

(飛騨民族考古館; Hida Minzoku Kōkō-kan; 82 San-no-Machi; adult/child ¥500/200; ⊙7am-5pm Mar-Nov, 9.30am-4pm Nov-Feb) A former samurai house boasting interesting secret passageways and an old well in the courtyard.

Takayama-jinya
HISTORICAL BUILDING

(高山陣屋; ☑32-0643; 1-5 Hachiken-machi; adult/child ¥420/free; ⊙8.45am-5pm Mar-Oct, to 4.30pm Nov-Feb) These sprawling grounds south of the Sanmachi district house the only remaining prefectural office building of the Tokugawa shōgunate. Takayama-jinya was originally built in 1615 as the administrative centre for the Kanamori clan but was later taken over by the *bakufu*. The main gate was once reserved for high officials. The present main building dates back to 1816 and it was used as the local government office until 1969.

As well as government offices, a rice granary and a garden, there's a torture chamber with explanatory detail. Free guided tours in English are available (reservations advised). Takayama-jinya is a 15-minute walk east of the train station.

Merchant Houses
HISTORICAL BUILDINGS

(吉島家・日下部民芸館) North of Sanmachi are two excellent examples of Edo-period merchants' homes, with the living quarters in one section and the commercial/warehouse areas in another.

Yoshijima-ke

(吉島家住宅; Yoshijima house; 1-51 Ōshinmachi; adult/child ¥500/300; ⊙9am-5pm Mar-Nov, to 4.30pm Wed-Sun Dec-Feb) Design buffs shouldn't miss Yoshijima-ke, which is well covered in architectural publications. Its lack of ornamentation allows you to focus on the spare lines, soaring roof and skylight. Admission includes a cup of delicious shiitake tea, which you can also purchase for ¥600 per can.

Kusakabe Mingeikan

(日下部民芸館; Kusakabe Folk Art Museum; 1-52 Ōshinmachi; adult/child ¥500/300; ⊙9am-4.30pm Mar-Nov, to 4pm Wed-Mon Dec-Feb) Down the block Kusakabe Mingeikan, built during the 1890s, showcases the striking craftsmanship of traditional Takayama carpenters. Inside is a collection of folk art.

Takayama Yatai Kaikan
MUSEUM

(高山屋台会館; Festival Floats Exhibition Hall; 178 Sakura-machi; adult/child ¥820/410; ⊙8.30am-5pm Mar-Nov, 9am-4.30pm Dec-Feb) A rotating selection of four of the 23 multitiered *yatai* (floats) used in the Takayama Matsuri can be seen at Takayama Yatai Kaikan. These spectacular creations, some dating from the 17th century, are prized for their flamboyant carvings, metalwork and lacquerwork. A famous feature of some floats is *karakuri,* mechanical puppets that perform amazing tricks and acrobatics courtesy of eight accomplished puppeteers using 36 strings. A video gives a sense of the festival.

The Yatai Kaikan is on the grounds of the stately hillside shrine **Sakurayama Hachiman-gū**; the shrine's main buildings are behind the Yatai Kaikan. Dedicated to the protection of Takayama, the shrine also oversees the festival.

Hida Kokubun-ji
TEMPLE

(飛騨国分寺; 1-83 Sōwa-chō; treasure hall adult/child ¥300/250; ⊙9am-4pm) Takayama's oldest temple, Hida Kokubun-ji was originally built in the 8th century and subsequently ravaged by fire; the oldest of the present buildings dates from the 16th century. The temple's treasure hall houses some Important Cultural Properties, and the courtyard boasts

Winter in the Hida region can be fierce, and inhabitants faced snow and cold long before the advent of propane heaters and 4WD vehicles. One of the most visible symbols of that adaptability is *gasshō-zukuri* architecture, seen in the steeply slanted straw-roofed homes that still dot the landscape around the region.

The sharply angled roofs were designed to prevent heavy snow accumulation, a serious concern in a region where nearly all mountain roads close from December to April. The name *gasshō* comes from the Japanese word for praying, because the shape of the roofs was thought to resemble two hands clasped in prayer. *Gasshō* buildings often featured pillars crafted from stout cedars to lend extra support. The attic areas were ideal for silk cultivation.

Larger *gasshō-zukuri* buildings were inhabited by wealthy families, with up to 30 people under one roof. Peasant families lived in huts so small that today they'd be considered fit only for toolsheds.

Development has made the *gasshō-zukuri* building an endangered species. Most examples have been gathered and preserved in folk villages, including Hida-no-Sato in Takayama and in Shirakawa-gō and Gokayama. So, two homes that are now neighbours may once have been separated by several days of travel on foot or sled. Local authorities have worked hard to re-create their natural surroundings, making it possible to imagine a bygone life in the Hida hills.

a three-storey pagoda and an impressively gnarled gingko tree, which is in remarkably good shape considering it's believed to be 1200 years old.

Takayama Shōwa-kan   MUSEUM
(高山昭和館; 6 Shimo-ichi-no-machi; adult/child ¥500/300; ⊙9am-6pm Apr-Oct, to 5pm Nov-Mar) Nostalgia for the mid-20th century is all the rage in Japan these days, and Takayama Shōwa-kan feels like a nostalgia bonanza from the era of Shōwa, the Japanese name for the previous emperor, known elsewhere as Hirohito. Though Shōwa ruled from 1926 to 1989, the museum concentrates on the period between 1955 and 1965, a time of great optimism between Japan's postwar malaise and pre-Titan boom. Lose yourself among the vehicles and movie posters, recreated storefronts, beauty salon and classroom.

Morning Markets   MARKET
(朝市) *Asa-ichi* (morning markets) take place every morning from 7am to noon, starting an hour earlier from April to October. The **Jinya-mae Morning Market** (陣屋前朝市) is in front of Takayama-jinya; the **Miya-gawa Morning Market** (宮川朝市) is larger, situated along the east bank of the Miya-gawa, between Kaji-bashi and Yayoi-bashi. The markets provide a pleasant way to start the day, with a stroll past rugged farm-folk at their vegetable stands and stalls selling crafts of wood or fabric, pickles, souvenirs and that all-important steaming cuppa joe (or beer or sake for the hearty).

Teramachi & Shiroyama-kōen   PARK
(寺町・城山公園) The hilly districts in the east of town are linked by a walking trail, which is particularly enjoyable in the early morning or late afternoon. Teramachi has over a dozen temples and shrines that you can wander around before taking in the greenery of Shiroyama-kōen. Various trails lead through the park and up the mountainside to the ruins of the castle, **Takayama-jō** (高山城跡).

Hida-no-Sato   HISTORICAL BUILDINGS
(飛騨の里; Hida Folk Village; 1-590 Okamoto-chō; adult/child ¥700/200; ⊙8.30am-5pm) The large, open-air Hida-no-Sato is highly recommended for its dozens of traditional houses, dismantled at their original sites throughout the region and rebuilt here. Allow at least three hours. During clear weather, there are good views across the town to the peaks of the Japan Alps.

Hida-no-Sato is in two sections. The western section features 12 old houses and a complex of traditional buildings. Displays are well presented and offer an excellent chance to see what rural life was like in previous centuries.

Hida-no-Sato is a 30-minute walk west from Takayama Station, but the route is not enjoyable. Either hire a bicycle, or catch a bus from Takayama bus station (高山濃飛バスセンター; ¥200, 10 minutes). The 'Hida-no-Sato setto ken' ticket combines return fare and admission to the park for ¥900. Be sure to check return times for the bus.

✥ Festivals & Events

From January to early February several of the sake breweries in Sanmachi-suji, many dating back to the Edo period, arrange tours and tastings.

Takayama Matsuri   PARADE
One of Japan's greatest festivals, the Takayama Matsuri is in two parts. On 14 and 15 April is the **Sannō Matsuri**; a dozen *yatai*, decorated with carvings, dolls, colourful curtains and blinds, are paraded through the town. In the evening the floats are decked out with lanterns and the procession is accompanied by sacred music. **Hachiman Matsuri**, on 9 and 10 October, is a slightly smaller version (see p189).

🛏 Sleeping

One of Takayama's pleasures is its variety of high-quality accommodation, both Japanese and Western, for all budgets. If visiting during festival times, book accommodation months in advance and expect to pay a 20% premium, or just commute in. The tourist information office can assist with lodging information.

TOP CHOICE Sumiyoshi Ryokan   RYOKAN $$
(寿美吉旅館; ☎32-0228; www.sumiyoshi-ryokan.com; 4-21 Hon-machi; r per person with/without meals from ¥11,550/7350; Ⓟ@) This delightfully traditional inn is set in an old merchant's house from the late Meiji period and is filled with antiques. Some rooms have river views through windows of antique glass, and the common baths are made of wood and slate tiles. One room has a private bath (¥13,650).

Tanabe Ryokan   RYOKAN $$$
(旅館田邊; ☎32-0529; fax 35-1955; www.tanabe-ryokan.jp; 58 Aioi-chō; r per person with 2 meals from ¥15,000; ◔@) Central, family-run inn with sweet, welcoming staff. There's art throughout, stone paths line the carpeted hallways, the 21 rooms are spacious, and dinner is *kaiseki*-style Hida cuisine. Rooms have en-suite bath, but the common baths with their beamed ceilings are worth a try. Some English is spoken.

Hōshōkaku   RYOKAN $$$
(宝生閣; ☎34-0700; www.hoshokaku.co.jp; fax 35-0717; 1-88 Baba-machi; r with meals from ¥18,000; Ⓟ) Surrounded by the lush greenery of Shiroyama-kōen park, this deliciously relaxing ryokan has outdoor hot springs with views over the city, and sumptuous *kaiseki* cuisine featuring Hida beef, freshwater fish and wild greens. It's a three-minute walk to the Jinya-mae morning market.

Rickshaw Inn   INN $$
(力車イン; ☎32-2890; www.rickshawinn.com; 54 Suehiro-chō; s without bathroom from ¥4900; tw with/without bathroom from ¥11,900/10,200; ◔@) Right off Kokubunji-dōri, this inn is excellent value and a travellers' favourite, offering pleasant Japanese- and Western-style rooms as well as a small kitchen, laundry facilities and a cosy lounge. Friendly English-speaking owners are founts of information about Takayama. Book well in advance.

Minshuku Kuwataniya   MINSHUKU $$
(民宿桑谷屋; ☎32-5021; www.kuwataniya.com; fax 36-3835; 1-50-30 Sowa-machi; r per person with/without bathroom ¥6450/4350; Ⓟ@) Takayama's longest-running *minshuku* (Japanese guesthouse; since the 1920s) has both Japanese- and Western-style rooms, high-def TVs (Japanese channels), simple onsen baths and free bicycle use. Dinner is available for ¥2310, and features Hida's famed beef (vegetarian options are available with advance notice), and breakfast is ¥840. It's half a block north of Hida Kokubun-ji.

Asunaro Ryokan   RYOKAN $$
(翌檜 ［あすなろ］; ☎33-5551, toll-free 0120-052-536; www.yado-asunaro.com; 2-96 Hatsuda-machi; r per person with/without meals from ¥11,550/6930; @) This excellent ryokan has handsome tatami rooms, a spacious onsen bath and decadent dinners and breakfasts. Several rooms have *irori* (hearth), and some have private bathrooms (all have toilets). The staff speaks some English.

Spa Hotel Alpina   HOTEL $$
(スパホテルアルピナ; ☎33-0033; www.spa-hotel-alpina.com, in Japanese; 5-41 Nada-cho; s/tw from ¥7200/13,000; Ⓟ◔@) This business hotel, which opened in 2008, is minimalist without being cold – crisp bedding, modular bathrooms and a variety of room types. The best part, though, is the onsen baths on the

top floor, including *rotemburo*, with views across the city. The breakfast buffet is ¥700. Some of the staff members speak English and can respond to email enquiries sent via the website.

Sōsuke
INN $

(惣助; ☎32-0818; www.irori-sosuke.com; fax 33-5570; 1-64 Okamoto-machi; r per person ¥5040; P@) West of the train station, Sōsuke has 13 pleasant tatami rooms, some with skylights and paper lanterns. English-speaking staff prepare excellent dinners (¥2100) and breakfasts (¥735), served at *hori-kotatsu* (low tables with a well beneath for your feet), including meals for vegetarians. The handsomely updated building dates from the 1800s and includes an *irori*. It's across a busy road from the hulking Takayama Green Hotel.

J-Hoppers
HOSTEL $

(ジェイホッパーズ飛騨高山ゲストハウス; ☎32-3278; http://takayama.j-hoppers.com; 5-52 Nada-machi; dm/r/tw per person from ¥2500/3200/2800; 🛜) Convenient location near the station, large dorm beds, Japanese-style private rooms and very outgoing, active staff (who can arrange tours to Mt Ontake and other out-of-the-way nature spots) make this hostel a compelling choice. For families, there are also quad private rooms with bunkbeds.

Best Western Hotel
HOTEL $$

(ベストウェスタンホテル高山; ☎37-2000; www.bestwestern.co.jp; 6-6 Hanasato-machi; s/d/tw from ¥9500/15,000/17,000; 🖨🛜) Very popular among overseas guests, this 78-room Western-style hotel offers crisp service and recently renovated, comfortably furnished rooms. There's a lounge and restaurant on-site, and wireless access from rooms. It's a block from the station.

Hida Takayama Tenshō-ji Youth Hostel
HOSTEL $

(ひだ高山天照寺ユースホステル; ☎32-6345; www.tenshoji.jp; fax 32-6392; 83 Tenshōji-machi; dm ¥3300, HI members ¥3000, add ¥1000 for private room; P🖨@) This peaceful hostel (with a rather early 10pm curfew) occupies an attractive hillside temple in Teramachi. Rooms are Japanese style, and you have a choice between shower near the rooms or small bath on the other side of the temple. The hostel is a 20-minute walk from the train station, or there's an infrequent bus service.

Yamakyū
INN $

(山久; ☎32-3756; www.takayama-yamakyu.com; 58 Tenshōji; r with/without meals ¥7980/5880; P@) This hillside inn, near the temples on the eastern side of town, is lined with antique-filled curio cabinets (glassware, tea bowls, the occasional bit of kitsch). Each of its 20 comfy tatami rooms has a sink and toilet, while bathing is in the signature water-wheel common baths. Some English is spoken. Yamakyū's about 20 minutes' walk from the station; staff can arrange for luggage pick-up with a couple of days' notice.

Hida Takayama Temple Inn Zenkō-ji
HOSTEL $

(飛騨高山善光寺宿坊; ☎32-8470; www.takayamahostelzenkoji.com; 4-3 Tenman-chō; dm/r per person ¥2500/3000; P🖨@🛜) At this temple (a branch of Nagano's famous Zenkō-ji, p204), private-room rooms are generously proportioned around a courtyard garden, and even the dorm-style rooms are handsome. There's a kitchen for guest use, no curfew and staff who speak excellent English.

🍴 Eating

Takayama's specialities include *soba, hoba-miso, sansai* (mountain vegetables) and Hida-*gyū*. You're likely to find many of these in meals at your inn. Street foods include *mitarashi-dango* (skewers of grilled riceballs seasoned with soy sauce), *shio-sembei* (salty rice crackers), and Hida-*gyū* served up on *kushiyaki* (skewers) and in *korokke* (croquettes) and *niku-man* (steamed buns).

TOP CHOICE Kyōya
IZAKAYA $$

(京や; ☎34-7660; 1-77 Ōshin-machi; mains ¥1200-5000; ⏰10am-10pm Wed-Mon; 🍴) This relaxing, atmospheric traditional eatery specialises in Hida regional dishes such as *hoba-miso* (Hida beef served on magnolia leaf, ¥1800). Seating is on tatami mats around long charcoal grills and under a cathedral ceiling supported by dark timbers. Look for the sacks of rice over the door; it's located by a picturesque canal near the Kusakabe Mingeikan.

Suzuya
SHOKUDŌ $$

(寿々や; ☎32-2484; 24 Hanakawa-chō; sets ¥1155-3100; ⏰11am-3pm & 5-8pm Wed-Mon; 🖊🍴) In the centre of town, Suzuya is one of Takayama's longstanding favourites, and it's highly recommended for local specialities like Hida beef, *hoba-miso* and various stews.

Orijin
IZAKAYA $

(おりじん; ☑36-4655; 4-108 Hanasato-chō; most dishes ¥315-819; ⊙dinner; 🅿) This wonderful local *izakaya* located a minute from the station has the usual *kushiyaki* and tofu steak, plus original dishes like sardines rolled in *yuba* (tofu skin), or big-as-a-beer-can grilled daikon in miso sauce. Or go for broke with Hida beef (¥1575). Look for the bamboo poles out the front.

Rakuda
CAFE $

(らくだ; ☑34-5574; 1-94 Ōshin-machi; mains ¥600-1000; ⊙10am-6pm Wed-Mon; 🅿) As laid-back as its namesake ('camel'), comfy Rakuda has curry lunches (¥850), open sandwiches topped with omelette and veggies (¥600), and goodies like chiffon cake (¥450). It's in a small square beside a mini parking lot.

Chapala
MEXICAN $

(チャパラ; ☑34-9800; 1 Hanakawa-chō; mains ¥600-980; ⊙dinner Mon-Sat, closed 1st Mon of each month; 🅿) Mexico is about as far from Japan as can be, but this little shop run by a Japanese enthusiast makes a fair stab at it. The taste and dainty portions of tacos, quesadillas and guac' and chips might not pass muster in California, Texas or Guadalajara, but the place is adorable and the owners earnest. Plus, you get to eat Mexican with chopsticks while swilling Coronas and margaritas.

Takumi-ya
BARBECUE $$

(匠家; ☑36-2989; 2 Shimo-Ni-no-Machi; mains downstairs ¥680-980, upstairs from ¥1280; ⊙lunch & dinner Thu-Tue) Hida beef on a burger budget. Adjacent to Takumi-ya's butcher shop is a casual restaurant (open 10am to 3pm) specialising in *rāmen* in Hida-beef broth and, for lunch, Hida *gyū-don* (beef and onion over rice; *gyū-don* and mini-*rāmen* combo for ¥1000). The upstairs restaurant serves *yakiniku* (Korean-style barbecue). It's next to the shop selling 'Total Fashion'. There's a photo menu.

Ebisu-Honten
NOODLES $

(恵比寿本店; ☑32-0209; 46 Kami-Ni-no-Machi; soba dishes ¥830-1530; ⊙10am-5pm Thu-Tue; 🍴) This Sanmachi shop has been making *teuchi* (handmade) *soba* since 1898. The menu explains the *soba*-making process. Go for *zaru* (cold) *soba* for the real flavour of the buckwheat, or try curry or *miso-nikomi* (in miso broth) style. It's on a side street and has a sign with a little roof on it.

Myōgaya
VEGETARIAN $$

(茗荷舎; ☑32-0426; 5-15 Hanasato-chō; mains around ¥1000; ⊙8am-3pm, 5-7pm Wed-Sun; ⊖🍴🅿) A good-for-you vibe pervades this tiny, organic restaurant and food shop, which is adorned with natural fibres, a block east of the train station. Look for tasty vegetarian curry with brown rice, samosas, fruit juices, dandelion tea and coffees. Reservations are requested on Saturdays.

Yamatake-Shōten
SHOKUDŌ $$

(山武商店; ☑32-0571; 1-70 Sōwa-chō; meals per person from around ¥3500; ⊙lunch & dinner Thu-Tue, closed 3rd Thu of month) This is a workmanlike butcher shop with a restaurant upstairs, and is an excellent place to sample Hida-*gyū*. Here's the drill: choose your own cut (pay by weight, from ¥1380 per 100g), which is plated and brought to the table for you to cook on an inset charcoal grill. Vegetables and simple desserts are included. Sides like kimchi and *gyū tataki* (marinated raw beef) are also for sale. There's a ¥420 seating charge.

🍷 Drinking

Asahi-machi, north of Kokubun-ji-dōri and west of the Miya-gawa, is Takayama's bar district, though don't go expecting a raucous time. The places listed here will point you in the right direction, or feel free to wander.

[TOP CHOICE] Red Hill Pub
PUB

(レッド・ヒル; ☑33-8139; 2-4 Sowa-chō; ⊙7pm-midnight, closed irregularly; 🛜) Locals and expats gather at this welcoming bar. There are snacks such as pita bread and *karai rāmen* (spicy *rāmen*, ¥700), an excellent selection of domestic and imported brews, cocktails like Sex on the Mountain, and an eclectic mix of tunes.

Rum Dance Hall
BAR

(☑36-1682; 29 Asahi-machi; ⊙7pm-late) This is a very chill bar with plenty of rum, *shōchū*, and delicious cocktails on offer, as well as laid-back, retro grooves spun by the English-speaking owner. Look for the large concrete building with a staircase and glass wall in the middle.

🔒 Shopping

Takayama is renowned for crafts. *Ichii itto-bori* (woodcarvings) are fashioned from yew and can be seen as intricate components of *yatai* or in shops around town.

THE JAPAN ALPS & CENTRAL HONSHŪ TAKAYAMA

Suzuki Chōkoku   CRAFTS
(鈴木彫刻; ☎32-1367; ⊙9am-7pm Wed-Mon)
Helmed by the one-time head of the
local *ittobori* association; sells figurines
and accessories priced from ¥750 to *how much?*

Mori no Kotoba   FURNITURE
(森のことば; Words from the Forest; ☎36-7005;
⊙9am-6pm Thu-Tue) Woodworking also
extends to furniture shops.

Takayama is also known for its *shunkei*
lacquerware. Many shops have outstanding
lacquerware and porcelain and, occasionally, good deals. Local pottery includes the
rustic *Yamada-yaki* and the decorative
Shibukusa-yaki styles.

Takayama's most ubiquitous souvenirs
are *saru-bobo* (monkey babies), dolls of
red cloth dressed in blue fabric, with pointy
limbs and featureless faces, recalling the
days when *obāsan* (grandmas) in this once-
impoverished town fashioned dolls for kids
out of readily available materials.

ℹ Information

Jūroku Bank (十六銀行) can change cash or
travellers cheques. For ATM users, the **main
post office** (高山郵便局; Hirokōji-dōri) is located a few blocks east of the station, and Ōgaki
Kyōritsu Bank, with foreign-card ATMs (大垣
共立銀行), is southeast of the station and also
near the Miya-gawa Morning Market.

City library (高山市図書館; ⊙9.30am-9.30pm)
Internet access, east of Sanmachi-suji.

International Affairs Office (国際情報セ
ンター; ☎32-3333, ext 2407; 2-18 Hanaoka)
To arrange a home visit, home stay or volunteer interpreter for non-Japanese languages
(including sign language). Located inside the
Takayama Municipal Office building; arrange
one month in advance.

Kinki Nippon Tourist (☎32-6901; 1-17 Hana-
oka-machi) For onward bus or train reservations within Japan.

Takayama Municipal Office (高山市役所;
2-18 Hanaoka; ⊙9am-5pm Mon-Fri), Internet
access; two computers.

Tourist information office (飛騨高山観光
案内所; ☎32-5328; ⊙8.30am-5pm Nov-Mar,
to 6.30pm Apr-Oct) Takayama's main tourist
office, directly in front of JR Takayama Station,
has knowledgeable English-speaking staff, as
well as English-language maps and information on sights (the *Hida Takayama* pamphlet is
a good start), accommodation, special local
events and regional transit. On the web, head to
www.hidatakayama.or.jp.

ℹ Getting There & Away

From Tokyo or Kansai, the most efficient way to
reach Takayama is to go via Nagoya on the JR
Takayama line (Hida *tokkyū*, ¥5670, 2¼ hours);
the mountainous train ride along the Hida-gawa
is *gorge*-ous. The same train then continues
on to Toyama (¥3480, 90 minutes), with connections to Kanazawa (additional ¥2050, 40
minutes).

Highway buses (☎32-1688; www.nouhibus
.co.jp/english) connect Takayama and Tokyo's
Shinjuku (¥6500, 5½ hours, several daily, reservations required). Takayama's bus station
(高山濃飛バスセンター) is adjacent to the train
station. Many roads in this region are closed
during winter, so bus schedules vary seasonally
and buses don't run at all during winter on some
routes. Check with the tourist office for cuurent
details.

For trips to Shirakawa-gō and the Northern
Japan Alps, see p199 and p199, respectively.

You'll find **Toyota Rent-a-Car** (トヨタレンタカ
ー; ☎36-6110) near the station.

ℹ Getting Around

Most sights in Takayama except Hida-no-Sato
can be covered easily on foot. You can amble
from the train station across to Teramachi in
about 20 minutes.

Takayama is bicycle-friendly. Some lodgings
lend cycles, or you can hire one (per hour/same
day about ¥300/1300) from **Hara Cycle** (ハラサ
イクル; ☎32-1657; Kokubun-ji-dōri).

Hida-Furukawa   飛騨古川

☎0577 / POP 26,000

Just 15 minutes by train from Takayama,
Hida-Furukawa is a relaxing riverside town
with photogenic streetscapes, peaceful temples and interesting museums, all framed
against mountains. It's also famous for Hadaka Matsuri (known as Naked Festival),
held each April.

◉ Sights

**Setokawa to
Shirakabe-dōzō**   HISTORIC DISTRICT
From the train station, walk right (north)
two blocks and turn left towards this historic canal district (瀬戸川と白壁土蔵
街, Seto River and White Wall Clay Storehouse Quarter), one of the region's prettiest
strolls. Its handsome streets boast white-
and dark-wood-walled shops, storehouses
and private homes. Carp-filled waterways
course through the district. You can buy fish
food for ¥50.

Hida Furukawa Matsuri Kaikan   MUSEUM

(飛騨古川まつり会館; Festival Exhibition Hall; 14-15 Ichinomachi; adult/child ¥800/400; ⊗9am-5pm Mar-Nov, to 4.30pm Dec-Feb) In the historic canal district, Hida Furukawa Matsuri Kaikan shows Furukawa's festival in all its glory. You can don 3-D glasses to watch a video of the festivities (with free English narration via iPod), see three of the *yatai* that are paraded through the streets, and watch a *karakuri* show. You can also try manipulating *karakuri* like those used on the *yatai*, and watch craftsmen demonstrating *kirie* (paper cut-outs) or *ittobori*. Drums used in the festival are on view in the barnlike structure diagonally to the left as you exit the exhibition hall.

Takumi-Bunkakan   MUSEUM

(匠文化館; Hida Craft Museum; 10-1 Ichinomachi; adult/child ¥300/100; ⊗9am-5pm, to 4.30pm winter, Fri-Wed) Across the square from Hida Furukawa Matsuri Kaikan, this museum is a must for woodworkers, craftspeople and design fans. In a hands-on room, you can try assembling blocks of wood cut into different joint patterns – not as easy as it sounds.

Follow the canal street westward for three blocks, then turn right to reach the riverside **Honkō-ji** (本光寺), an intricately carved temple that showcases Furukawa's fine craftsmanship. It is Hida's largest wooden temple. Though the temple was established in 1532, the current buildings are reconstructions from 1913 based on the original design, following a fire that destroyed 90% of the town.

From the temple, instead of retracing your steps, walk back along Ichi-no-Machi, a street sprinkled with shops selling woodworking and handcrafted toys, sake breweries (marked by the large balls of cedar fronds above the entrance) and traditional storehouses. Among them is **Mishima Wa-rosoku Ten** (三島和ろうそく店; Ichi-no-Machi; ⊗9am-4.30pm Thu-Tue), a shop that has made traditional candles for over two centuries.

✨ Festivals & Events

Furukawa Matsuri   PARADE

Furukawa Matsuri, as Hadaka Matsuri is formally known (it's also known as Naked Festival), takes place every 19 and 20 April with parades of *yatai*. The highlight is an event known as Okoshi Daiko in which, on the night of the 19th, squads of boisterous young men dressed in *fundoshi* (loincloths)

parade through town, competing to place small drums atop a stage bearing a giant drum. OK, it's not *naked*-naked, but we didn't make up the name.

Kitsune-bi Matsuri   PARADE

During the Fox Fire Festival, on the fourth Saturday in September, locals dress up as foxes, parade through the town by lantern light and enact a wedding at Okura Inari-jinja. The ceremony, deemed to bring good fortune, climaxes with a bonfire.

🛏 Sleeping & Eating

Hida Furukawa Youth Hostel   HOSTEL $

(飛騨古川ユースホステル; ☐/fax 75-2979; www.jyh.or.jp/english/toukai/hidafuru/index.html; 180 Nobuka; dm with meals ¥5800, HI members ¥4800; ⊗closed 30 Mar-10 Apr; ⊜@) A friendly and attractive 22-bed hostel, across from Shinrin-kōen. It's about 6km from the town centre, or 1.2km west of Hida-Hosoe Station (two stops north of Hida-Furukawa). In winter the hostel can help guests get set up for telemark skiing. Pick-up from the station is available after 6pm with advance notice. Both Japanese- and Western-style rooms are available.

Kitchen Kyabingu   SHOKUDŌ $

(キッチンきゃびんぐ; ☐73-4706; 6-8 Tonomachi; mains ¥850-2200; ⊗lunch & dinner Tue-Sun) This cosy lunch spot in the historic district serves Hida-*gyū*. Order the beef curry with rice (¥1050) or the *kyabingu teishoku* (¥2600), starring sizzling steak on a hot iron plate.

ℹ Information

Hida-Furukawa train and bus stations adjoin each other east of the town centre. Sights are within 10 minutes' walk. There's an **information office** (観光案内所; ☐73-3180; ⊗8.30am-5pm) at the bus station, dispensing the English *Hida Furukawa Stroll Map*, which is sufficient for most visitors. No English is spoken, though Takayama's tourist information office can help.

ℹ Getting There & Around

Some 20 daily trains run each way between Takayama and Furukawa. Hida-Furukawa train station is three stops north of Takayama (*futsū*, ¥230, 15 minutes), or you can bus it (¥360, 35 minutes). Central Furukawa is an easy stroll, or hire bikes at the taxi office **Miyagawa** (☐73-2321; per hr ¥200), near the station. Staff here can also store your luggage for ¥200 each day or a portion thereof.

Shirakawa-gō & Gokayama 白川郷・五箇山

These remote, dramatically mountainous districts between Takayama and Kanazawa are best known for farmhouses in the thatched, A-frame style called *gasshō-zukuri* (see the box, p190). They're rustic and lovely, particularly in clear weather or in the region's copious snows, and they hold a special place in the Japanese heart.

In the 12th century the region's remoteness is said to have attracted stragglers from the Taira (Heike) clan, virtually wiped out by the Minamoto (Genji) clan in a brutal battle in 1185. During feudal times Shirakawa-gō, like the rest of Hida, was under direct control of the Kanamori clan, connected to the Tokugawa shōgun, while Gokayama was a centre for the production of gunpowder for the Kaga region, under the ruling Maeda clan (see p225).

Fast-forward to the 1960s: when construction of the gigantic Miboro Dam over the river Shōkawa was about to submerge some local villages, many *gasshō* houses were moved out of harm's way to their current sites. Although much of what you'll find has been specially preserved for, and supported by, tourism, it still presents a view of rural life found in few other parts of Japan.

Most of Shirakawa-gō's sights are in the heavily visited community of Ogimachi; a new expressway from Takayama has made it even more crowded. In less-crowded Gokayama (technically not in Hida but in Toyama Prefecture), the community of Ainokura has the greatest concentration of attractions; other sights are spread throughout hamlets over many kilometres along Rte 156. Ogimachi and Ainokura are Unesco World Heritage Sites (as is the Gokayama settlement of Suganuma).

Even locals recognise that the community is becoming overrun with tour buses, traffic and souvenir-seekers, and there's passionate debate as to what to do about it. For you, the best advice is to avoid weekends, holidays, and cherry-blossom and autumn-foliage seasons.

Better, stay overnight in a *gasshō-zukuri* house that's been turned into an inn. Advance reservations are highly recommended; the Shirakawa-gō tourist information office by the parking area in Ogimachi can help with bookings (in Japanese), or via email in English at info@shirakawa-go.go.jp. Don't expect rooms with private facilities, though some inns have *irori* for guests to eat around.

SHIRAKAWA-GŌ 白川郷
☑ 05769

The region's central settlement, **Ogimachi**, has some 600 residents and over 110 *gasshō-zukuri* buildings, and is the most convenient place to orient yourself for tourist information and transport.

Ogimachi's **main tourist office** (Deai no Yakata; ☑ 6-1013; www.shirakawa-go.org; 2495-3 Ogimachi; ☺9am-5pm) is near the Shirakawa-gō bus stop. There's a free English map of Ogimachi. Limited English is spoken. There's a smaller tourist information office near the Ogimachi car park. Note that you cannot change money in Ogimachi and surrounding areas, and there are no post office ATMs here; credit cards are not accepted either, so bring enough cash.

⊙ Sights & Activities

On the site of the former castle, **Shiroyama Tenbōdai** (observation point) provides a lovely overview of the valley. It's a 15-minute walk via the road behind the east side of town. You can climb the path (five minutes) from near the intersection of Rtes 156 and 360, or there's a shuttle bus (¥200 one way) from the Shirakawa-gō bus stop.

Shirakawa-gō's big festival is held on 14 and 15 October at **Shirakawa Hachiman-jinja** (other festivals continue until the 19th), and features groups of dancing locals, taking part in the lion dance and *niwaka* (improvised buffoonery). The star is *doburoku,* a very potent unrefined sake. **Doburoku Matsuri Exhibition Hall** (adult/child ¥300/150; ☺9am-5pm Apr-Nov, closed during festivals) shows a video of the festival (in Japanese).

Gasshō-zukuri Minka-en　MUSEUM
(adult/child ¥500/300; ☺8.40am-5pm Apr-Nov, 9am-6pm Fri-Wed Dec-Mar) There are over two dozen relocated *gasshō-zukuri* buildings reconstructed in this open-air museum amid seasonal flowers. Several houses are used for demonstrating regional crafts such as woodwork, straw handicrafts and ceramics (in Japanese only, reservations required); many items are for sale.

You can wander away from the houses for a pleasant stroll through the trees further up the mountain. Feel free to take a picnic, but obey Shirakawa-gō custom and carry your rubbish out of town.

Wada-ke
HISTORIC BUILDING

(adult/child ¥300/150; ⊙9am-5pm) Shirakawa-gō's largest *gasshō* house, Wada-ke is a designated National Treasure. It once belonged to a wealthy silk-trading family and dates back to the mid-Edo period. Upstairs are silk-harvesting equipment and a valuable lacquerware collection.

Kanda-ke
HISTORIC BUILDING

(adult/child ¥300/150; ⊙9am-5pm) Of the other *gasshō* houses, Kanda-ke is the least cluttered with exhibits, which leaves you to appreciate the architectural details – enjoy a cup of herb tea in the 36-mat living room on the ground floor.

Nagase-ke
HISTORIC BUILDING

(adult/child ¥300/150; ⊙9am-5pm) This was the home of the doctors to the Maeda clan; look for displays of herbal medicine equipment. The *butsudan* (Buddhist altar) dates from the Muromachi period. In the attic, you can get an up-close look at the construction of the roof, which took 530 people to re-thatch.

Myōzen-ji Folk Museum
MUSEUM

(adult/child ¥300/150; ⊙8.30am-5pm Apr-Nov, 9am-4pm Dec-Mar) Next door to Ogimachi's small temple, Myōzen-ji Folk Museum displays the traditional paraphernalia of daily rural life.

Shirakawa-gō no Yu
ONSEN

(adult/child ¥700/300; ⊙10am-9.30pm) In central Ogimachi, Shirakawa-gō no Yu boasts a sauna, small *rotemburo* and large bath. Visitors staying at lodgings in town get a ¥200 discount.

Shiramizu no Yu
ONSEN

(しらみずの湯; 247-7 Hirase; adult/child ¥600/400; ⊙10am-9pm Thu-Tue) About 12km south of Ogimachi, off Rte 156 in Hirase Onsen, Shiramizu no Yu is a new onsen facility with views across the river valley, a treat during the autumn-foliage season; its waters are said to be beneficial for fertility.

Ōshirakawa Rotemburo
ONSEN

(大白川露天風呂; Ōshirakawa; admission ¥300; ⊙8.30am-5pm mid-Jun–Oct, to 6pm Jul & Aug) About another 40km up the Ōshirakawa river (via a mountain road with blind curves and no public transport), this onsen is much admired for its middle-of-nowhere setting and views of an emerald-green lake set amid the mountains. Getting there requires a private vehicle or taxi (60 to 90 minutes) from Ogimachi.

🛏️ Sleeping & Eating

Some Japanese is helpful in making reservations at one of Ogimachi's many *gasshō-zukuri* inns, originally private houses that now let out rooms. Rates include two meals. Expect a nightly heating surcharge (¥400 and up) during cold weather. Ogimachi has a few casual restaurants (look for *soba* or *hoba-miso*); most open only for lunch.

TOP CHOICE Kōemon
INN $$

(☑6-1446; fax 6-1748; 546 Ogimachi; r per person ¥8400; P) In the town centre, atmospheric Kōemon has five rooms with heated floors, dark-wood panelling and shared bathrooms. The fifth-generation owner speaks English and his love of Shirakawa-gō is infectious. Try to book the room facing the pond.

Shimizu
INN $$

(☑6-1914; www.shimizuinn.com; 2613 Ogimachi; r per person ¥8400; P) The location of this inn, a little removed from the town centre, means more quiet and a home-style feel. Its three rooms have six tatami each and are comfortably furnished, though the bath is tiny and guests often choose instead to go to the public onsen. Some English is spoken.

Magoemon
INN $$

(☑6-1167; fax 6-1851; 360 Ogimachi; r per person ¥10,500; P) Another friendly place, Magoemon has six slightly larger rooms, half with river views. Meals are served around the handsome *irori*.

Toyota Shirakawa-gō Eco-Institute
HOTEL $$

(トヨタ白川郷自然学校; ☑6-1187; www.toyota.eco-inst.jp; 223 Magari; d per person from ¥12,200; P) This eco-resort, a five-minute bus ride outside central Ogimachi, offers many activities: birdwatching, climbing Hakusan and more. Organic meals are served. Although it gets school and corporate groups, individual travellers are also welcome. Rates vary widely and include discounts for children.

Ochūdo
CAFE $

(落人; ☑090-5458-0418; 792 Ogimachi; cake sets ¥900; ⊙10.30am-5pm, closed irregularly; 🍴) Set around a large *irori* hearth in a 350-year-old *gasshō* house, this quaint cafe serves cake sets, *karē-raisu* (curry rice; ¥1000) teas and coffee. There's also an acoustic guitar if you feel like getting folksy. Look for the rocking chairs outside facing the rice paddy.

Irori SHOKUDŌ $
(☎6-1737; 374-1 Ogimachi; mains ¥700-1500; ⊙lunch) On the main road near Wada-ke, Irori serves regional specialities like *hoba-miso* and *yakidofu* (fried tofu), as well as *sansai* or *tempura soba* to patrons who gather around the warm hearths inside.

GOKAYAMA DISTRICT 五箇山
☎0763

North along the Shōkawa river and across the prefectural border in Toyama Prefecture, Gokayama is so isolated that road links and electricity didn't arrive until 1925.

Villages with varying numbers of *gasshō-zukuri* buildings are scattered over many kilometres along Rte 156. The following briefly describes some of the communities you'll come across as you travel north from Shirakawa-gō or the Gokayama exit from the Tōkai-Hokuriku Expressway; if your time is limited, head straight for Ainokura. There's a **tourist information office** (☎66-2468; 1235 Shimo-Nashi) in Nanto City.

⊙ Sights & Activities

Suganuma HISTORICAL BUILDINGS
(菅沼; www.gokayama.jp/english/index.html) This riverside World Heritage Site, 15km north of Ogimachi and down a steep hill, features an attractive if rather artificial-looking group of nine *gasshō-zukuri* houses.

Minzoku-kan
(民族館; Folklore Museum; ☎67-3652; adult/child ¥300/150; ⊙9am-4.30pm) This museum consists of two houses, with items from traditional life, and displays illustrating traditional gunpowder production.

Kuroba Onsen
(くろば温泉; 1098 Kamitaira-hosojima; adult/child ¥600/300; ⊙10am-9pm Wed-Mon) About 1km further up Rte 156, Kuroba Onsen is a complex of indoor-outdoor baths overlooking the river, with fine mountain views from its different storeys. Its low-alkaline waters are good for fatigue and sore muscles.

Kaminashi HISTORICAL BUILDINGS
(上梨) About 5km beyond Suganuma, the house museum **Murakami-ke** (村上家; adult/child ¥300/150; ⊙8.30am-5pm Apr-Nov, 9am-4pm Dec-Mar, closed 2nd & 4th Wed of each month) is one of the oldest in the region (dating from 1578). The proud owner shows visitors around and then sits them beside the *irori* and sings local folk songs. An English-language leaflet is available.

Also close by is the shrine **Hakusan-gū**. The main hall dates from 1502 and has been designated an Important Cultural Property. Its **Kokiriko Matsuri** (25 and 26 September) features costumed dancers performing with rattles that move like snakes. On the second day everyone joins in.

Ainokura HISTORICAL BUILDINGS
(相倉) This World Heritage Site is the most impressive of Gokayama's villages, with over 20 *gasshō* buildings in a valley amid splendid mountain views. It's less equipped for visitors than Ogimachi, which can be either a drawback or a plus. English pamphlets are at the booth by the central car park.

Ainokura Folklore Museum
(相倉民族館; admission ¥200; ⊙8.30am-5pm) Stroll through the village to this museum, with displays of local crafts and paper. It's divided into two buildings, the old Ozaki and Nakaya residences.

Gokayama Washi-no-Sato
(五箇山和紙の里; Gokayama Japanese Paper Village; adult/child ¥200/150; ⊙8.30am-5pm) Continue along Rte 156 for several kilometres until Gokayama Washi-no-Sato, where you will find displays of *washi* (Japanese handmade paper) art and a chance to make your own (from ¥500, reservations required, limited English spoken). It's inside the *michi-no-eki*, a sort of public rest station, with a helpful **tourist information office** (☎66-2223; ⊙8.30am-5pm).

🛏 Sleeping

Ainokura is a great place for a *gasshō-zukuri* farmhouse stay – depending on the time of year, it can be far less crowded than Ogimachi. Have a Japanese speaker contact the inns directly for reservations, or approach them yourself; note that rates may be higher in winter due to a heating charge.

Yomoshiro INN $$
(与茂四郎; ☎66-2377; fax 66-2387; per person with meals ¥8420) Try this welcoming four-room place, whose owner will demonstrate the *sasara*, a kind of noisemaker, upon request.

Goyomon INN $$
(五ヨ門; ☎66-2154; fax 66-2227; per person with meals ¥8000) Family-oriented.

Chōyomon INN $$
(長ヨ門民宿; ☎66-2755; fax 66-2765; per person with meals ¥8000) Try this 350-year-old place, with its atmospheric dark-wood sliding doors.

Camping ground CAMPGROUND $

(☎66-2123; per person ¥500; ⊙mid-Apr–late Oct) Ainokura also has a camping ground, about 1km from the centre of the village, that's closed if there's snow.

❶ Getting There & Away

Nōhi Bus Company (www.nouhibus.co.jp/english) operates seven buses daily linking Shirakawa-gō with Takayama (one way/return ¥2400/4300, 50 minutes). Some buses require a reservation. Two buses a day connect Kanazawa to Takayama (¥3300/5900, 2¼ hours), and to Shirakawa-go (¥1800/3200, 1¼ hours). Weather delays and cancellations are possible between December and March.

Just before Ainokura, buses divert from Rte 156 for Rte 304 towards Kanazawa. From the Ainokura-guchi bus stop it's about 400m uphill to Ainokura.

Kaetsuno Bus operates at least four buses a day between Takaoka on the JR Hokuriku line, Ainokura (¥1450, 90 minutes) and Ogimachi (¥2350, 2½ hours), stopping at all major sights. If you want to get off at unofficial stops (eg Kuroba Onsen), tell the driver.

By car, this region is about 50 minutes from Takayama, with interchanges at Gokayama and Shōkawa. From Hakusan, the scenic toll road Hakusan Super-Rindō ends near Ogimachi (cars ¥3150). In colder months, check conditions in advance with regional tourist offices.

NORTHERN JAPAN ALPS

Boasting some of Japan's most dramatic scenery, the Northern Japan Alps (北アルプス; also known as the Hida Mountains or Hida Sanmyaku; 飛騨山脈) contain stunning 3000m-plus peaks that even amateur hikers can climb. The chain is spread out over Gifu, Toyama and Nagano Prefectures. Large portions of the area are contained in the Chūbu-Sangaku National Park (中部山岳国立公園). Highlights include hiking the valleys and peaks of Kamikōchi and Shin-Hotaka Onsen, and soaking up the splendour of Shirahone Onsen or Hirayu Onsen. The northern part of the park extends to the Tateyama-Kurobe Alpine Route (p224).

❶ Information

Several maps and pamphlets are published in English by the Japan National Tourism Organization (JNTO) and local tourist authorities, with more detailed hiking maps in Japanese.

There are few banks in the area, and the only ATM in the communities listed in this section is at Hirayu Onsen's post office, which keeps shorter hours than most ATMs nationwide. Be sure you have enough cash on hand before setting out.

❶ Getting There & Around

The gateway cities to this area are Takayama and Matsumoto. Service from Takayama is by bus, while most travellers from Matsumoto catch the private Matsumoto Dentetsu train to Shin-Shimashima Station (¥680, 30 minutes) and transfer to buses – the ride in from either side is breathtaking. The main transit hubs are Hirayu Onsen and Kamikōchi. Bus schedules short-change visits to some areas and long-change others. Check schedules before setting out.

Hiring a car may save money, time and nerves. However, the road between Nakano-yu and Kamikōchi is open only to buses and taxis.

Kamikōchi   上高地

☎0260

The region's biggest drawcard, Kamikōchi offers some of Japan's most spectacular scenery along the rushing Azusa-gawa, and a variety of hiking trails from which to see it.

In the late 19th century, foreigners 'discovered' this mountainous region and coined the term 'Japan Alps'. A British missionary, Reverend Walter Weston, toiled from peak to peak and sparked Japanese interest in mountaineering as a sport. He is now honoured with a festival (on the first Sunday in June, the official opening of the hiking season), and Kamikōchi has become a base for strollers, hikers and climbers. It's a pleasure to meander along Kamikōchi's riverside paths lined with *sasa* (bamboo grass).

---

❶ HIKING THE JAPAN ALPS

Central Honshū is blessed, in the Shintō sense and every other way, with half of the nation's 100 famous mountains across many national parks, making it a key destination for hiking. This chapter presents some of the more popular destinations; enthusiastic hikers should pick up Lonely Planet's *Hiking in Japan* (2009) by David Joll, Craig McLachlan and Richard Ryall.

SAMPLE BUS ROUTES & DISCOUNTS: NORTHERN JAPAN ALPS

Within the Northern Alps, bus fares and schedules change seasonally and annually; the following are fares and travel times on common bus routes. If you are doing a lot of back-and-forth travel, consider the three-day 'Free Coupon' (¥6400) for unlimited bus transport within the Chūbu-Sangaku National Park and to Matsumoto and Takayama. From Takayama, Meitetsu's 'Marugoto Value Kippu' is a great deal: ¥5000 buys you two days' passage anywhere between Takayama and Shin-Hotaka, a ride on the Shin-Hotaka Ropeway and a soak in the *rotemburo* (outdoor bath) at Hirayu Onsen bus station. The Alps-wide Free Passport from Nōhi Bus, meanwhile, costs ¥10,000 and gives you four days' travel from Matsumoto to Kamikōchi, Shin-Hotaka, Takayama and even Shirakawa-gō. Find current fares and schedules at tourist offices in Matsumoto and Takayama, or at www.alpico.co.jp/access/route_k/honsen/info_e.html or www.nouhibus.co.jp.

Bus Fares

FROM	TO	FARE (¥; ONE WAY, OR ONE WAY/RETURN)	DURATION (MIN; ONE WAY)
Takayama	Hirayu Onsen	1530	55
	Kamikōchi	2660/4900	80
	Shin-Hotaka	2100	90
Matsumoto	Shin-Shimashima	680 (train)	30
	Kamikōchi	2400/4400	95
Shin-Shimashima	Naka-no-yu	1550	50
	Kamikōchi	1900/3300	70
	Shirahone Onsen	1400/2300	75
Kamikōchi	Naka-no-yu	600	15
	Hirayu Onsen	1130/2000	25
	Shirahone Onsen	1350	35
Hirayu Onsen	Naka-no-yu	540	10
	Shin-Hotaka	870	30

Kamikōchi is closed from 15 November to 22 April, and in peak times (late July to late August, and during the foliage season in October) can seem busier than Shinjuku Station. Arrive early in the day, especially during the foliage season. June to mid-July is the rainy season. It's perfectly feasible to visit Kamikōchi as a day trip, but you'll miss out on the pleasures of staying in the mountains and taking uncrowded early-morning or late-afternoon walks.

Visitors arrive in Kamikōchi at the bus station, which is surrounded by visitor facilities. A 10-minute walk from the bus station along the Azusa-gawa takes you to the bridge Kappabashi, named for a water sprite of Japanese legend, where most of the hiking trails start.

⊙ Sights & Activities

Onsen

Kamikōchi Onsen Hotel
ONSEN

(www.kamikouchi-onsen-spa.com; admission ¥800; ⊙7-9am & 12.30-3pm) On cold or drizzly days, the hot baths here are a refreshing respite.

Bokuden-no-yu
ONSEN

(admission ¥700; ⊙noon-5pm) The area's most unusual onsen – a tiny cave bath dripping with minerals. It's at the intersection at Naka-no-yu, just before the bus-only tunnel towards Kamikōchi proper. Enter the small shop next to the Naka-no-yu bus stop, pay and get the key to the little mountain hut housing the onsen. It is yours privately for up to 30 minutes.

Hiking & Climbing

The river valley offers mostly level, short-distance walks. A four-hour round trip starts east of Kappa-bashi along the right-hand side of the river past Myōjin-bashi (one hour) to Tokusawa (another hour) before returning. By Myōjin-bashi is the idyllic **Myōjin-ike** (admission ¥300), a pond whose clear waters mark the innermost shrine of **Hotaka-jinja**. There's also a track on the left-hand side of the river, though it's partly a service road.

West of Kappa-bashi, you can amble along the right-hand side of the river to **Weston Relief** (a monument to Kamikōchi's most famous hiker, Walter Weston; 15 minutes) or keep to the left-hand side of the river and walk to the pond **Taishō-ike** (40 minutes).

The visitor centre offers **guided walks** (in Japanese; per person ¥500) to destinations including Taishō-ike and Myōjin-ike. **Nature guides** (per hr approx ¥2000) and **climbing guides** (per day approx ¥30,000) may also be requested. It is always wise to request guides in advance, though English speakers cannot be guaranteed. Other popular hikes include the mountain hut at Dakesawa (2½ hours up) and Yakedake (four hours up, starting about 20 minutes west of the Weston Relief, at Hodaka-bashi). From the peaks, it's possible to see all the way to Mt Fuji in clear weather.

Dozens of long-distance options vary in duration from a couple of days to a week. Japanese-language maps of the area show routes and average hiking times between huts, major peaks and landmarks. Favourite hikes and climbs (which can mean human traffic jams during peak seasons) include Yariga-take (3180m) and Hotaka-dake (3190m) – also known as Oku-Hotaka-dake.

A steep but worthwhile hike connects Kamikōchi and Shin-Hotaka. The trail from Kappa-bashi crosses the ridge below Nishi Hotaka-dake (2909m) at Nishi Hotaka San-sō (Nishi Hotaka Mountain Cottage; three hours) and continues to Nishi Hotaka-guchi, which is the top station of the Shin-Hotaka Ropeway. The hike takes nearly four hours (because of a steep ascent). Or you could save an hour of sweat by hiking in the opposite direction. To reach the ropeway, take a bus from Takayama or Hirayu Onsen to Shin-Hotaka.

Other more distant hiking destinations include Nakabusa Onsen (allow three days) and Murodō (five days), on the Tateyama-Kurobe Alpine Route (p224). This allows you to indulge in a soak en route in Takama-ga-hara Onsen, one of the finest in Japan.

For long-distance hikes there are mountain huts available; enquire at the information centre for details. Hikers and climbers should be well prepared. Even during summer, temperatures can plummet, or the whole area can be covered in sleeting rain or blinding fog, and in thunderstorms there is no refuge on the peaks.

In winter, Kamikōchi is empty, but makes a beautiful spot for snowshoeing or cross-country skiing. You'll have to hike in from the entrance to the Kama Tunnel on Route 158.

🛏 Sleeping & Eating

Accommodation in Kamikōchi is pricey and advance reservations are essential. Except for camping, rates quoted here include two meals. Some lodgings shut down their electricity generators in the middle of the night (emergency lighting stays on).

Dotted along the trails and around the mountains are dozens of spartan *yama-goya* (mountain huts), which provide two meals and a futon from around ¥8000 per person; some also serve simple lunches. Enquire before setting out to make sure there's one on your intended route.

Kamikōchi Gosenjaku Lodge   INN $$
(☎95-2221; fax 95-2511; www.gosenjaku.co.jp; skier's bed per person ¥10,500, d/tr/q ¥17,850/16,800/15,750) This is a polished little place. Its 34 rooms are mostly Japanese-style plus some 'skier's beds', which are basically curtained-off bunk beds. Rooms all have sink and toilet, but baths are shared. Buffet-style meals are Japanese, Chinese and Western.

Kamikōchi Nishiitoya San-sō   INN $$
(☎95-2206; fax 95-2208; www.nishiitoya.com; dm from ¥8000, d per person ¥10,550;@) Recently refurbished, this friendly lodge with a cosy lounge dates from the early 20th century. Rooms are a mix of Japanese and Western styles, all with toilet and shared bath: a large onsen facing the Hotaka mountains. It's just west of Kappa-bashi.

Tokusawa-en   CAMPGROUND $
(☎95-2508; camp site/dm/r per person ¥500/9450/13,650) A marvellously secluded place, in a wooded dell about 3km northeast of Kappa-bashi. It's both a camping ground and a lodge, and has Japanese-style rooms (shared facilities) and hearty meals served in a busy dining hall.

Kamikōchi Konashidaira Kyampu-jō
CAMPGROUND $

(☎95-2321; www.nihonalpskankou.co.jp; camp site per person from ¥700, tents/bungalows from ¥2000/6000; ☺office 7am-7pm) About 200m past the visitor centre, this camping ground can get packed with tents. Rental tents (in July and August) and bungalows are available, and there's a small shop and restaurant (open from 7am to 2pm, and 4pm to 5.20pm).

Kamonji-goya
SHOKUDŌ $

(☎95-2418; dishes ¥600-2000; ☺8.30am-4pm; ▣) Kamikōchi's signature dish is *iwana* (river trout) grilled over an *irori*. Some trail huts serve it (along with the usual noodles and curry rice), but Kamonji-goya is worth seeking out. The *iwana* set is ¥1500, or there's *oden* (fish-cake stew), *soba* and *kotsu-sake* (dried *iwana* in sake) served in a lovely ceramic bowl. It's located near Myōjin-bashi, just outside the entrance to Myōjin-ike.

There's a shop at the bus station with cheap trail snacks or, at the other end of the spectrum, **Kamikōchi Gosenjaku Hotel** (☎95-2111) has pricey restaurants with French food and fancy cakes like Camembert torte with apples (¥630 per slice).

ℹ Information

Kamikōchi is entirely closed from 16 November to 22 April. Serious hikers and climbers might consider getting **insurance** (*hoken*; ¥1000 per person per day), available from window 3 at the Kamikōchi bus station. Weigh the benefits for yourself, but know that the out-of-pocket cost for a rescue 'copter starts at ¥800,000.

Kankō Ryokan Kumiai (Ryokan Association; ☎95-2405; ☺7am-5pm) At the Kamikōchi bus station; geared to booking accommodation, though non-Japanese speakers may want to book through the tourist information office in Matsumoto for Kamikōchi and Shirahone Onsen, as it has English-speaking staff.

Kamikōchi Information Centre (☎95-2433; ☺8am-5pm) A little bit further along from Kankō Ryokan Kumiai, and to the left, this centre provides hiking instructions and info on weather conditions, and also distributes the useful English *Kamikōchi Pocket Guide* with a map of the main walking tracks.

Kamikōchi Visitor Centre (☎95-2606; ☺8am-5pm) A 10-minute walk from the bus station along the main trail; the spiffy centre has displays on Kamikōchi's flora and fauna, and explanations of its geological history.

ℹ Getting Around

Private vehicles are prohibited between Naka-no-yu and Kamikōchi; access is only by bus or taxi, and then only as far as the Kamikōchi bus station. Those with private cars can use car parks en route to Naka-no-yu in the hamlet of Sawando for ¥500 per day; shuttle buses (¥1800 return) run a few times per hour.

Buses run via Naka-no-yu and Taishō-ike to the bus station. Hiking trails commence at Kappa-bashi, which is a short walk from the bus station.

Shirahone Onsen 白骨温泉
☎0263

Intimate, dramatic and straddling a deep gorge, this onsen resort town is one of the most beautiful in Japan. During the autumn-foliage season, and especially in the snow, it is just this side of heaven. All around the gorge are traditional inns (some more traditional than others) with open-air baths. Shirahone Onsen could also be a base for trips into Kamikōchi.

Shirahone means 'white bone', and it is said that bathing in the milky-blue hydrogen-sulphide waters here for three days ensures three years without a cold; the waters have a wonderful silky feel. The riverside **kōshū rotemburo** (公衆露天風呂; public outdoor bath; admission ¥500; ☺8.30am-5pm Apr-Oct), deep within the gorge, is separated by gender; the entrance is by the bus stop. Diagonally opposite, the **tourist information office** (観光案内所; ☎93-3251; ☺9am-5pm, irregular closures) maintains a list of inns that have opened their baths (admission from ¥600) to the public that day.

Budget travellers may wish to dip and move on; nightly rates start at ¥9000 with two meals. Advance reservations are highly recommended.

TOP CHOICE **Awanoyu Ryokan** (泡の湯旅館; ☎93-2101; www.awanoyu-ryokan.com; 4181 Shirahone Onsen; r per person incl 2 meals from ¥25,150; ▣) may be what you have in mind when you think onsen ryokan. Up the hill from most of Shirahone, it's been an inn since 1912 (the current building dates from 1940). It has private facilities in each room as well as single-sex common baths. There's also *kon-yoku* (mixed bathing), but not to worry: the waters are so milky that you can't see below the surface.

Tsuruya Ryokan (つるや旅館; ☎93-2331; fax 93-2029; www.tsuruya-ryokan.jp, in Japanese; 4202-6 Shirahone Onsen; r per person with 2 meals from ¥10,650; **P**) has both contemporary and traditional touches and great indoor and outdoor baths. Each of its 28 rooms has lovely views of the gorge; rooms with private toilet and sink are available for an extra charge.

Note: if you're driving to Shirahone, you'll have to take the road from Norikura-kōgen, as Route 300 from Sawando junction is under construction until 2013.

Hirayu Onsen 平湯温泉

♪0578

This onsen village is a hub for bus transport on the Takayama side of the park and makes a convenient base for excursions elsewhere. There's a pleasant, low-to-the-ground cluster of onsen lodgings, about half of which open for day-bathers; even the bus station has a rooftop **rotemburo** (admission ¥600; ⊘8.30am-5pm). The **information office** (☎89-3030; ⊘9.30am-5.30pm), opposite the bus station, has leaflets and maps and can book accommodation. No English is spoken.

Ryosō Tsuyukusa (旅荘つゆくさ; ☎89-2620; fax 89-3581; http://tuyukusa.okuhida-onsengo.com; 621 Hirayu; r per person with 2 meals ¥7500;**P**) is a recently redone eight-room mum 'n' dad *minshuku* with decent tatami rooms and a cosy mountain-view *rotemburo* of *hinoki* cypress. Go downhill from the bus station and left at the first narrow street. It's on the left before the road curves. No English is spoken here.

Practically in its own forest uphill from the bus station, the sprawling onsen ryokan **Hirayu-no-mori** (ひらゆの森; ☎89-3338; www.hirayunomori.co.jp; 763-1 Hirayu; r per person with 2 meals from ¥8000, bath day use ¥500; **P**) boasts 16 different *rotemburo* pools, plus indoor and private baths. After 9pm, they're exclusively for overnight guests. Rooms are Japanese-style, and meals are hearty and local.

The dignified **Hirayu-kan** (平湯館; ☎89-3111; www.hirayukan.com; 726 Hirayu; r per person with 2 meals from ¥13,800; **P**) has 60 rooms (Japanese, Western and combination style), plus a splendid garden and dreamy indoor and outdoor baths. All rooms have private facilities. It's a short walk past the turn-off for Tsuyukusa.

To reach the small **Hirayu Camping Ground** (平湯キャンプ場; ☎89-2610; fax 89-2130; www.hirayu-camp.com, in Japanese; 768-36 Hirayu; camp site per adult/child ¥600/400, bungalow from ¥5800, parking ¥1500; ⊘end Apr-end Oct), turn right out of the station and it's about 700m ahead on the left.

Fukuchi Onsen 福地温泉

♪0578

This relatively untouristed onsen town is one of the best in the Alps. It's a short ride north of Hirayu Onsen, and has rural charm, a morning market and two outstanding baths.

TOP CHOICE **Yumoto Chōza** (湯元長座; ☎89-2146; fax 89-2010; www.cyouza.com, in Japanese; Fukuchi Onsen; r per person with 2 meals from ¥23,000; **P**), one of Central Honshū's finest onsen ryokan, is reached by a long, rustic, covered walkway. Exquisite mountain cuisine is served at *irori* and you're surrounded by elegant traditional architecture and five indoor and two outdoor pools (visitors can bathe here between 2pm and 6pm for ¥750). Half of the 32 rooms have en-suite *irori*. Reservations are essential. By bus, get off at Fukuchi-Onsen-shimo.

A restaurant-cum-onsen, **Mukashi-banashi-no-sato** (昔ばなしの里; ☎89-2793; Fukuchi Onsen; bath ¥500; ⊘8am-5pm, closed irregularly; **P**) is set back from the street in a traditional farmhouse with fine indoor and outdoor baths, free on the 26th of each month. Out the front, there's an **asa-ichi** (morning market; ⊘6-10am daily Apr-Nov, Sat & Sun Dec-Mar) that's adorned with a wonderful collection of retro album covers. By bus, get off at Fukuchi-Onsen-kami bus stop.

Shin-Hotaka Onsen 新穂高温泉

♪0578

The reason to visit Shin-Hotaka Onsen, north of Fukuchi Onsen, is the **Shin-Hotaka Ropeway** (新穂高ロープウェイ; www.okuhi.jp/rop/frtop.html; Shin-Hotaka; 1 way/return ¥1500/2800; ⊘6am-4.30pm 1 Aug-last Sun in Aug, 8.30am-4.30pm late Aug-Jul). At 1308m, this two-stage cable car is Japan's – some say Asia's – longest, whisking you 2156m up Nishi Hotaka-dake (2909m). The entrance is a few minutes' walk uphill from Shin-Hotaka Onsen bus station. It's open additional hours at peak times.

Assuming clear weather, views from the top are spectacular, from observation decks and walking trails – in winter, snows can easily be shoulder deep. In season (only, please!), fit, properly equipped hikers with ample time can choose longer hiking options from the top cable-car station, Nishi Hotaka-guchi, including over to **Kamikōchi** (three hours), which is *much* easier than going the other way.

Just up the road above the bus terminal is the new **Okuhida no Yu onsen** (中崎山荘奥飛騨の湯; adult/child ¥800/400; ☺8am-8pm, closed irregularly; ❂) with large indoor baths and outdoor *rotenburo* commanding a spectacular vista of the mountains. There's a small dining room with offerings such as *hida-gyū* (Hida-style beef; ¥1800).

Information is available at **Oku-Hida Spa Tourist Information Centre** (奥飛騨温泉郷観光案内所; ☎89-2458; ☺10am-5pm) by the bus terminal. For transit information see the box, p200.

TOP CHOICE **Yarimikan** (槍見舘; ☎89-2803; fax 89-2309; www.yarimikan.com; Shin-Hotaka Onsen; r per person with meals from ¥15,900; ❂) is a deliciously traditional hot-springs ryokan on the Kamata-gawa river, with 10 indoor and riverside outdoor baths (some available for private hire; visitors can bathe between 11am and 2pm for ¥500) and only 16 rooms, keeping it intimate. The cuisine features local specialties such as Hida beef and grilled freshwater fish. It's just off Route 475, a few kilometres from the Shin-Hotaka Ropeway.

Closer to the ropeway and along a road that ascends from Route 475 is **Nonohana Sansō** (野の花山荘; ☎89-0030; http://nono87.jp, in Japanese; fax 89-2885; Shin-Hotaka Onsen; r per person with meals from ¥13,800; ❂), a newly opened hot-springs lodge. Though guestrooms are tatami-mat traditional, the lobby and fireplace lounge are refreshingly contemporary and there's an unusual open kitchen preparing local specialties. The large outdoor baths are also open to visitors (adult/child ¥800/500, open from 10am to 5pm).

NAGANO PREFECTURE

Known as Shinshū in earlier days, Nagano Prefecture (長野県; Nagano-ken) is one of Japan's most enjoyable visits, for the beauty of its mountainous terrain (it claims the title 'Roof of Japan'), traditional architecture, cultural offerings and unique foods.

Japan Alps National Park is the big draw, along with several quasi national parks that attract skiers, campers, hikers, mountaineers and onsen aficionados. Nagano, the prefectural capital, boasts a nationally important temple and makes a useful base for day trips, while Nagano-ken's second city, Matsumoto, mixes culture, outdoor pursuits and a National Treasure castle.

If you're travelling in Nagano-ken via the JR Chūō Line (which links Nagano with Nagoya via Matsumoto and the Kiso Valley), don't schedule too tight an onward connection, as the trains are frequently late (which is unusual for Japan).

Nagano   長野

◷026 / POP 387,800

The mountain-ringed prefectural capital, Nagano has been a place of pilgrimage since the Kamakura period. Back then it was a temple town centred on the magnificent Zenkō-ji. The temple still draws more than four million visitors every year.

Following Nagano's flirtation with international fame, hosting the Winter Olympic Games in 1998, the city has reverted to its friendly small-town self, if just a bit more worldly. While Zenkō-ji is the only real attraction in the city centre, Nagano is a great regional base for day trips.

Nagano is laid out on a grid, with Zenkō-ji occupying a prominent position overlooking the city centre from the north. Chūō-dōri leads south from the temple, doing a quick dogleg before hitting JR Nagano Station, 1.8km away; it is said that street-planners considered Zenkō-ji so auspicious that it should not be approached directly from the train. The private Nagano Dentetsu ('Nagaden') train line and most bus stops are just outside JR Nagano Station's Zenkō-ji exit.

◉ Sights

Zenkō-ji   TEMPLE

(善光寺; 491 Motoyoshi-chō; admission free; ☺4.30am-4.30pm summer, 6am-4pm winter, varied hours rest of year) This temple is believed to have been founded in the 7th century and is the home of the revered statue Ikkō-Sanzon, allegedly the first Buddhist image to arrive in Japan (in AD 552). Don't expect to see it, however; it is said that 37 generations of emperors have not seen the image, though millions of visitors flock here to view a copy every seven years during the Gokaichō Matsuri.

Zenkō-ji's immense popularity stems partly from its liberal welcoming of believers from all Buddhist sects, including women; its chief officiants are both a priest and a priestess. The current building dates from 1707 and is a National Treasure.

Visitors ascend to the temple via Nakamise-dōri and the impressive gates **Niō-mon** (仁王門) and **Sanmon** (山門 (三門)). In the *hondō* (main hall), the Ikkō-Sanzon image is in an ark left of the central altar, behind a dragon-embroidered curtain. To the right of the altar, visitors may descend a staircase to **Okaidan** (admission ¥500), a pitch-black tunnel that symbolises death and rebirth and provides the closest access to the hidden image (taller visitors watch your head!). As you navigate the twisting tunnel, dangle your arm along the right-hand wall until you feel something heavy, moveable and metallic – said to be the key to salvation, a bargain for the admission price.

Any bus from bus stop 1 in front of JR Nagano Station's Zenkō-ji exit will get you to the temple (¥100, about 10 minutes; alight at the Daimon bus stop).

✹✹ Festivals & Events

Gokaichō Matsuri RELIGIOUS
Five million pilgrims come to Zenkō-ji every seven years from early April to mid-May, to view a copy of Zenkō-ji's sacred Buddha image – the only time it can be seen. The next festival is in 2015.

Enka Taikai FIREWORKS
A fireworks festival with street food on 23 November.

🛏 Sleeping

Perhaps the most Nagano way to stay is in a *shukubō* (temple lodging) at one of Zenkō-ji's subtemples. Contact **Zenkō-ji** (☏186-026-234-3591) to book, at least one day in advance. Expect to pay ¥7000 to ¥10,000 per person with two meals.

Matsuya Ryokan RYOKAN $
(松屋旅館; ☏232-2811; fax 233-2047; www14 .ocn.ne.jp/~matuya, in Japanese; Zenkō-ji Kannai; r per person from ¥5250, with 2 meals from

---

ZENKŌ-JI LEGENDS

Few Japanese temples have the fascination of Zenkō-ji, thanks in part to the legends related to it. The following are just a few:

» **Ikkō-Sanzon** This image, containing three statues of the Amida Buddha, was brought to Japan from Korea in the 6th century and remains the temple's raison d'être. It's wrapped like a mummy and kept in an ark behind the main altar, and it's said that nobody has seen it for 1000 years. However, in 1702, to quell rumours that the ark was empty, the shōgunate ordered a priest to confirm its existence and take measurements. That priest remains the last confirmed person to have viewed it.

» **Following an Ox to Zenkō-ji** Long ago, an impious old woman was washing her kimono when an ox appeared, caught a piece of the cloth on his horn and ran away with it. The woman was as stingy as she was impious, and she gave chase for hours. Finally, the ox led her to Zenkō-ji, and she fell asleep under its eaves. The ox came to her in a dream, revealed himself to be the image of the Amida Buddha and disappeared. The woman saw this as a miracle and became a pious believer. Today, people in Kantō say, 'I followed an ox to Zenkō-ji', to mean that something good happened unexpectedly.

» **The Doves of Sanmon** Zenkō-ji's pigeon population is renowned, making the rattan *hatto-guruma* (wheeled pigeon) a favourite Nagano souvenir. Locals claim the birds forecast bad weather by roosting on the Sanmon gate. Visitors claim to see five white doves in the plaque above the central portal; the five short strokes in the characters for Zenkō-ji do look remarkably dove-like. See if you can spot them too. In the upper character (善, zen) they're the two uppermost strokes; in the middle character (光, kō) they're the strokes on either side of the top; and in the 'ji' (寺) it's the short stroke on the bottom left.

» **Binzuru** A follower of Buddha, Binzuru trained in healing. He was due to become a Bosatsu (bodhisattva, or enlightened one) and go to the land of the immortals, but the Buddha instructed him to remain on earth and continue to do good works. At most temples, images of Binzuru are outside the main hall, but at Zenkō-ji you'll find his statue just inside, worn down where visitors have touched it to help heal ailments of the corresponding parts of their own bodies; you can see the lines where the face was once replaced.

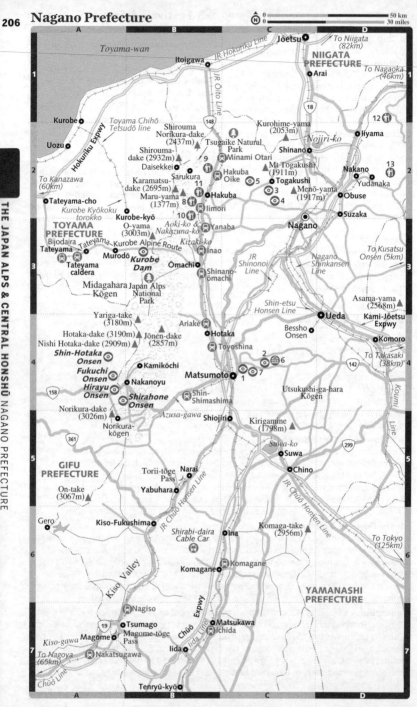

0 — 50 km
0 — 30 miles

Toyama-wan

Jōetsu

To Niigata
(82km)

NIIGATA
PREFECTURE

To Nagaoka
(46km)

Itoigawa

JR Hokuriku Line

JR Ōito Line

Arai

Kurobe

Toyama Chihō
Tetsudō line

Shirouma
Norikura-dake
(2437m)

Kurohime-yama
(2053m)

12

Iiyama

Uozu

Tsugaike Natural
Park

Nojiri-ko

Hokuriku Expwy

Shirouma-
dake (2932m)

Minami Otari

Shinano

Nakano

13

To Kanazawa
(60km)

Daisekkei

Sarukura

Hakuba
Oike

Mt Togakushi
(1911m)

Togakushi

Yudanaka

Tateyama-cho

Karamatsu-
dake (2695m)

Maru-yama
(1377m)

Hakuba

Menō-yama
(1917m)

Obuse

Kurobe Kyōkoku
torokko

Iimori

Suzaka

TOYAMA
PREFECTURE

Kurobe-kyō

O-yama
(3003m)

Aoki-ko &
Nakazuna-ko

Yanaba

Nagano

Bijodaira

Kurobe Alpine
Route

Kizaki-ko

To Kusatsu
Onsen (5km)

Tateyama

Murodō

Kurobe
Dam

Inao

JR
Shinonoi
Line

Nagano
Shinkansen
Line

Tateyama
caldera

Midagahara
Kōgen

Ōmachi

Shinano-
omachi

Japan Alps
National
Park

Asama-yama
(2568m)

Yariga-take
(3180m)

Shin-etsu
Honsen Line

Ueda

Kami-Jōetsu
Expwy

Hotaka-dake (3190m)
Nishi Hotaka-dake (2909m)

Jōnen-dake
(2857m)

Ariake

Hotaka

Bessho
Onsen

Komoro

Shin-Hotaka
Onsen

Toyoshina

To Takasaki
(38km)

Fukuchi
Onsen

Kamikōchi

Matsumoto

Utsukushi-ga-hara
Kōgen

Hirayu
Onsen

Nakanoyu

Shin-
Shimashima

Norikura-dake
(3026m)

Shirahone
Onsen

Norikura-
kōgen

Azusa-gawa

Shiojiri

Kirigamine
(1798m)

Suwa-ko

Suwa

GIFU
PREFECTURE

On-take
(3067m)

Torii-tōge
Pass

Narai

Chino

JR Chūō Honsen Line

Gero

Yabuhara

Kiso-Fukushima

JR Chūō Honsen Line

Shirabi-daira
Cable Car

Ina

Komaga-take
(2956m)

To Tokyo
(125km)

Kiso Valley

Komagane

Komagane

YAMANASHI
PREFECTURE

Nagiso

Tsumago

Magome-tōge
Pass

Chūō Expwy

Matsukawa

Ichida

Magome

Iida

Kiso-gawa

Nakatsugawa

To Nagoya
(65km)

Chūō Line

Tenryū-kyō

Iida Line

¥9450) Six generations of the Suzuki family have run this traditional inn just inside Zenkō-ji's Niō-mon. Even if the communal baths are a bit aged, the rest of the ryokan is exceedingly well maintained. Meals are seasonal *kaiseki* (Japanese haute cuisine). Add ¥1000 per person for rooms with private facilities. It's next to the statue of En-mei Jizō.

Shimizuya Ryokan   RYOKAN $
(清水屋旅館; ☎232-2580; fax 234-5911; 49 Daimon-chō; r per person from ¥4725) On Chūō-dōri, a few blocks south of Zenkō-ji, this friendly, family-run ryokan offers good value, with a smoky dark-wood interior, spotless tatami rooms (no private facilities), laundry machines and lots of ins, outs, ups, downs, nooks and crannies. It's been in the family for 130 years. No meals are served.

Hotel Metropolitan Nagano   HOTEL $$
(ホテルメトロポリタン長野; ☎291-7000; www.metro-n.co.jp; 1346 Minami-Ishido-chō; s from ¥9240, d & tw from ¥18,480; P@) An excellent choice by the station. The modern, elegant Metropolitan features airy, comfortable rooms, and there's a cafe, restaurant and top-floor lounge with broad views. Japan Rail Pass holders get a 20% discount. It's just outside the station's Zenkō-ji exit; sensitive sleepers should reserve a room facing away from the tracks.

1166 Backpackers   HOSTEL $
(1166 バックパッカーズ;☎217-2816; www.1166 bp.com; 1048 Nishi-machi; dm/r ¥2600/5600; @☎) This intimate, newly-opened hostel is set amid older buildings in the back streets near the road to Zenkō-ji. The friendly, informative owner can give you lots of tips about Nagano. Look for the beige building with a chalk signboard outside. No meals are served, but there's a kitchen and dining area for guests.

Holiday Inn Express Nagano   HOTEL $$
(ホリデイ・イン エクスプレス長野; ☎264-6000; www.ichotelsgroup.com; fax 264-5511; 2-17-1 Minami-Chitose; s/d/tw from ¥8800/16,000/17,000; ☺@) Built for the Olympics to cater to guests of overseas proportions, this professional 137-room hotel is a good deal for its large, Western-style rooms with LAN cable access. Breakfast is a Japanese-Western buffet (¥1100).

✖ Eating

Chō Bali Bali   ASIAN $
(チョーバリバリ; ☎229-5226; 1366-1 Ishidō-machi; mains from ¥600; ☺lunch, dinner Tue-Sun; ✍) This stylish space gathers lively crowds most nights and serves eclectic dishes from Indonesia, Thailand and Vietnam, with a touch of Italian for good measure; *yam-un-sen* is a spicy Thai salad with vermicelli. Highly recommended.

Gohonjin Fujiya   FUSION $
(藤屋御本陣; ☎232-1241; 80 Daimon-chō; mains ¥700-2700, courses from ¥2500; ☺lunch Mon-Fri, dinner nightly; 🍴) Until recently, this was Nagano's most venerable hotel (since 1648 – look for 'Hotel Fujiya' on signage), but it quit the hotel business and has transformed itself into the city's most venerable Western restaurant. Try sweet potato gnocchi with mascarpone sauce or *wa-gyū* (Japanese beef) sirloin. The imposing 1923 building mixes Japanese and art deco motifs.

India the Spice   CAFE $$
(インディア・ザ・すぱいす; ☎226-6136; 1418 Minami-ishido-chō; mains ¥1000-3000; ☺11.30am-11pm Mon-Thu & Sun, to midnight Fri & Sat) This eccentric cafe is festooned with every kind of wall clock imaginable, and specialises in variations on the theme of curry; lunch sets include *omu-karē* (rice wrapped in an omelette in keema curry sauce; ¥900). Going up Chūō-dōri, take a right when you see the food stall in a red bus beside the road, then take another right. Look for signboards and vine leaves around the entrance.

Asian Night Market
CAFE $

(アジアンナイトマーケット; http://asian
-night-market.net; 2-1 Higashi Go-chō; most dishes
under ¥1000; ☉noon-11pm; 🛜📖) Part cafe, part
humble-jumble Thai clothing and knickknack shop, this storefront is at once sweet
and hip. It has English-speaking staff, beer,
cocktails, soft drinks including Thai coffee,
Thai food, and nooks for browsing.

Sukitei
SUKIYAKI $$

(すき亭; ☎234-1123; 112-1 Tsumashina; lunch sets
¥1800-4450, sukiyaki from ¥2800; ☉lunch &
dinner Tue-Sun; 📖) Tops in town for succulent suki-
yaki. Meals include *udon, gyusashi* (beef
sashimi) and more. The price of the top-
grade beef is sky-high, but if you try it you
may never go back to the cheaper stuff. It's
set on the river, and is well worth the ¥1600
taxi ride from the station.

Marusei
SHOKUDŌ $

(丸清食堂; ☎232-5776; 486 Motoyoshi-chō; dish-
es ¥600-1800; ☉11am-6pm Thu-Tue) A stone's
throw from the temple on Nakamise-dōri,
tiny, unassuming Marusei serves *soba* and
a well-liked *tonkatsu* (deep-fried breaded
pork cutlet); the Marusei *bentō* (boxed meal;
¥1350) lets you try both.

Fujiki-an
NOODLES $

(藤木庵; ☎232-2531; 67 Daimon-chō; mains ¥800-
1500; ☉noon-2.30pm & 6pm-midnight Tue-Sun)
The clean, contemporary setting belies this
soba shop's history (since 1827) of making
fresh *soba* from the north of Nagano-ken.
There's a picture menu: *seiro-mori soba*
(cold *soba* on a bamboo mat; ¥900) lets the
flavour shine; other favourites are *sansai, ki-
noko* (mushroom) tempura (¥1400) or *nishin*
(herring; ¥1200).

Yayoi-za
SHIKUDŌ $$

(弥生座; ☎232-2311; 503 Daimon-chō; mains ¥945-
2650; ☉lunch & dinner, closed Tue & 2nd Wed each
month; 📖) A homey 150-year-old shop special-

Nagano

ising in *seiro-mushi* (ingredients steamed in a wood and bamboo box). The standard is *monzen seiro-mushi* (local beef and vegetables; ¥1680), while vegetarians can enjoy *on-yasai salada* (steamed vegetables in sesame sauce; ¥840). For dessert, try *kuri-an cream* (chestnut-paste mousse; ¥525).

🍷 Drinking

Bistro Liberty   BAR
(ビストロリバティー; ☺Wed-Sun;🖥) Nagano's most popular *gaijin* pub has Guinness on tap, decent pub food and a friendly crowd. From JR Nagano Station, take a right on busy Nagano-Ōdōri and another right (at the second stoplight) on Shōwa-dōri.

Groovy   LIVE MUSIC
(グルービー; http://kobe.cool.ne.jp/jazzgroovy/; cover ¥1000-3500) A music spot popular with jazz lovers for its live shows; check the website for schedule info. It's upstairs on Chūō-dōri, a six-minute walk from the train station.

ℹ Information

The website www.nagano-cvb.or.jp has information about sightseeing, transportation, accommodation and festivals.

There's a post office and international ATM in the West Plaza Nagano building opposite the station's Zenkō-ji exit. Other post offices include the Central Post Office (長野中央郵便局) on Chūō-dōri.

Internet Cafe Chari Chari (インターネットカフェ茶里茶里; 2F Daitō Bldg, Minami-ishido-chō; per hr ¥390; ☺24hr)

Nagano Tourist Information Centre (長野市観光情報センター; ☑226-5626; ☺9am-6pm) Inside JR Nagano Station, this friendly outfit has good English-language colour maps and guides to Nagano and the surrounding areas. Staff can book accommodation in the city centre.

ℹ Getting There & Away

Nagano *shinkansen* run twice hourly from Tokyo Station (Asama, ¥7460, 1¾ hours). The JR Shinonoi line connects Nagano with Matsumoto (Shinano *tokkyū*, ¥2970, 50 minutes) and Nagoya (Shinano *tokkyū*, ¥6620, 2¾ hours).

Togakushi   戸隠
♪026

This mountainous, forested region northwest of Nagano makes an excellent day trip. Hikers enjoy the refreshing alpine scenery from late spring to autumn, while winter belongs to the skiers. Togakushi has been famed for *soba* for centuries. Pick up English-language maps from the Nagano Tourist Information Centre.

Three sub-shrines – Togakushi-Hōkōsha (宝光社), Togakushi-Chūsha (中社) and Togakushi-Okusha (奥社) – each a few kilometres apart, together make up the **Togakushi Shrine**, which honours the 1911m-high Mt Togakushi. Intimate Chūsha is the most easily accessible; one tree here is said to be 700 years old. There's a little village by Chūsha with shops, restaurants and ryokan, and in winter there's the smallish, 10-lift **Togakushi Ski Park** (戸隠スキー場; day pass ¥4000), which has a local following.

Okusha, the innermost shrine, can be reached via bus or hiking trail. The direct path from Chūsha to Okusha bus stop takes about 25 minutes, or there's a longer route via **Kagami-ike** (鏡池; Mirror Pond) and the **Togakushi Botanic Garden** (森林植物園). From Okusha bus stop it's another 2km (40 minutes) to the shrine buildings, partially via a 500m-long, cedar-lined path (杉並木; *suginamiki*), planted in 1612.

From Okusha, avid alpinists can make the strenuous climb to the top of Mt Togakushi. In winter, Okusha is inaccessible except for hearty snowshoers, and attractions and businesses here are closed.

On the hill above the Okusha bus stop, the highlight of the **Togakushi Minzoku-kan** (戸隠民俗館; 3688-12 Togakushi; adult/child ¥500/350; ☺9am-5pm mid-Apr–mid-Nov) is the 'ninja house', cleverly concocted with trick doors, hidden staircases, a room that slopes upwards and others from which there is seemingly *no escape!* It pays tribute to the days when *yamabushi* (mountain monks) practised here, at what became the forerunner to *ninpo* (the art of stealth, as practised by ninja). Other buildings at Minzoku-kan contain museums of *ninpo* and local folklore.

In Chūsha, **Yokokura Ryokan** (横倉旅館; ☑254-2030; 3347 Chūsha; dm/with 2 meals ¥3045/5065, r per person with 2 meals from ¥7560;🅿) is in a thatch-roofed building from the early Meiji era, about 150m from the steps up to Chūsha. It's both a hostel and a ryokan, with tatami-room dorms (gender-separate) and private rooms. **Uzura Soba** (うずら家そば; ☑254-2219; dishes ¥800-1700; ☺lunch) serves handmade *soba* noodles until they run out. It's directly across from the steps to the shrine.

THE JAPAN ALPS & CENTRAL HONSHŪ NAGANO PREFECTURE

By Okusha bus stop, **Okusha no Chaya** (奥社の茶屋; ☑254-2222; mains ¥800-1680; ◷10am-4.30pm late Apr-late Nov) serves fresh *soba* (tempura *soba* set, ¥1450) in a minimalist, contemporary setting behind a glass wall that overlooks the forest; ice cream comes in seasonal flavours such as tomato, chestnut and wasabi.

Buses via the scenic routes from Nagano depart approximately hourly (7am to 7pm) and arrive at Chūsha-Miyamae bus stop by Chūsha shrine in about an hour (one way/return ¥1300/2400). To Okusha the one-way/return fare is ¥1280/2300. The Togakushi Kōgen Free Kippu pass (¥2500) gives unlimited rides on buses to and around Togakushi for three days. Buy tickets at **Kawanakajima Bus Co**, inside the Alpico Bus office by bus stop 7 in front of Nagano Station's Zenkō-ji exit.

Obuse 小布施

☑026 / POP 11,600

This little town northeast of Nagano occupies a big place in Japanese art history. The famed *ukiyo-e* (woodblock print) artist Hokusai (1760–1849) worked here during his last years. Obuse is also noted for its *kuri* (chestnuts), which you can sample steamed with rice or in ice cream or sweets.

The first stop should be **Hokusai-kan** (北斎館; 485 Ō-aza Obuse; adult/child ¥500/free; ◷9am-5.30pm Apr-Sep, to 4.30pm Oct-Mar), displaying some 30 of Hokusai's inspiring prints at any one time, as well as several colourful floats decorated with his imaginative ceiling panels. From the train station, cross the street and walk down the road perpendicular to the station; take the second right, then look for signs to the museum. It's a 10-minute walk from the station.

A block away, Hokusai's patron, Takai Kōzan, is commemorated in the **Takai Kōzan Kinenkan** (高井鴻山記念館; 805-1 Ō-aza Obuse; admission ¥300; ◷9am-6pm Apr-Sep, to 5pm Oct-Mar). This businessman was also an accomplished artist, albeit of more classical forms than Hokusai's; look for elegant Chinese-style landscapes.

Among Obuse's nine other museums, **Nihon no Akari Hakubutsukan** (日本のあかり博物館; Japanese Lamp & Lighting Museum; 973 Obuse-machi; adult/child ¥500/free; ◷9am-5pm late Mar-late Nov, 9.30am-4.30pm late Nov-late Mar, closed Wed except May, Aug, Oct, Nov) showcases lighting through Japanese history, including oil lamps and lanterns that will flip the switches of design fans. **Taikan Bonsai Museum** (盆栽美術館大観; 10-20 Obuse-machi; adult/child Apr-Nov ¥500/300, Dec-Mar ¥300/free; ◷9am-5pm) displays rare species and represents different Japanese landscapes.

Sample chestnut confections at **Chikufūdō** (竹風堂; 973 Obuse-machi; ◷8am-6pm), established in 1893. *Dorayakisan* (chestnut paste in pancake dumplings) are the standard.

Obuse is reached via the Nagano Dentetsu (Nagaden) line from Nagano (*tokkyū*, ¥750, 22 minutes; *futsū*, ¥650, 35 minutes). Obtain maps and information and hire bikes (¥400 per half-day) at **Obuse Guide Centre** (おぶせガイドセンター; ☑247-5050; ◷9am-5pm), en route to the museums from the station.

Yudanaka 湯田中

☑0269

This onsen village is known as the home of Japan's famous 'snow monkeys', a troop of some 200 Japanese macaques who live in and around the onsen baths. The monkeys and their mountain hot tub can be found at **Jigokudani Yaen-kōen** (地獄谷野猿公苑; Jigokudani Monkey Park; www.jigokudani-yaenkoen.co.jp; 6845 Ōaza-heian, Yamanouchi-machi; adult/child ¥500/250; ◷8.30am-5pm Apr-Oct, 9am-4pm Nov-Mar). The park has been operating since 1964, so the monkeys can no longer be described as truly wild, and they're often lured into the tub to gather food that's been placed there. Still, it's a unique chance to see them up close. It's a popular day trip from Nagano, and in winter it can be combined with a ski excursion to nearby Shiga Kōgen.

Across the river from Jigokudani, **Kōraku-kan** (後楽館; ☑33-4376; r per person with 2 meals from ¥10,545, onsen only adult/child ¥500/250; ◷noon-3pm) is a simple onsen hotel. Accommodation is basic, with small but clean-swept tatami rooms. Aside from the mountain vegetable tempura for overnight visitors, the highlight is the indoor and concrete riverside outdoor onsen. Bathe in the great outdoors, and some uninvited guests – of the decidedly hairy variety – may join you.

In peaceful central Yudanaka, **Uotoshi Ryokan** (魚歳旅館; ☑33-1215; www.avis.ne.jp/~miyasaka/; 2563 Sano, Yamanouchi-machi; s/d/tr/q from ¥4300/7980/11,970/15,960; @)

is basic but commendably hospitable. The English-speaking owner will demonstrate and let you try *kyūdō* (Japanese archery), pick you up at Yudanaka Station, or drop you off near the start of the Monkey Park trail on request. Dinner (from ¥2520) and breakfast (from ¥530) are available. From the station (seven minutes), walk left and follow the road over the river; when the road ends, turn right. It's 20m further on.

At Yudanaka station, there's the convenient hot springs of **Kaede no Yu** (楓の湯; 3227-1 Heian, Yamanouchi-machi; admission ¥300; ⊙10am-9pm, closed first Tue of every month) with footbaths, and indoor and outdoor bathing.

From Nagano, take the Nagano Dentetsu (Nagaden) line to Yudanaka terminus (*tokkyū*, ¥1230, 45 minutes; *futsū*, ¥1130, 1¼ hours); note that not all trains go all the way to Yudanaka. For Jigokudani Monkey Park, take the bus for Kanbayashi Onsen Guchi and get off at Kanbayashi Onsen (¥220, 15 minutes, eight daily), walk uphill along the road about 400m, and you'll see a sign reading 'Monkey Park' at the start of a tree-lined 1.6km walk.

Shiga Kōgen 志賀高原

☑0269

The site of several events in the 1998 Nagano Olympics and the 2005 Special Olympics World Winter Games, **Shiga Kōgen** (www .shigakogen.gr.jp/english; Hasuike, Shiga Kōgen; 1-day lift ticket ¥4800; ⊙8.30am-4.30pm Dec-Apr)

is Japan's largest ski resort and one of the largest in the world: 21 linked areas covering 80 runs. One lift ticket gives access to all areas as well as the shuttle bus between the various base lodges. There is a huge variety of terrain for all skill levels, as well as ski-only areas. In the Hasuike area, the **Shiga Kōgen Tourist Office** (志賀高原観光協会; ☑34-2323; ⊙9am-5pm) has English speakers who can help you navigate the slopes and can book accommodation. It's in front of the Shiga Kōgen ropeway station.

If you've got limited time, base yourself somewhere central like the Ichinose Family Ski Area, which has a central location and wide variety of accommodation and restaurants. The Nishitateyama area has good wide runs and generally ungroomed terrain. The Terakoya area is a little hard to get to but it is generally uncrowded and has good short runs and a pleasant atmosphere.

During the rest of the year, the mountains' lakes, ponds and overlooks make an excellent destination for hikers.

🛏 Sleeping & Eating

Hotels are scattered the length of Shiga Kōgen.

Hotel Shirakabasō HOTEL $$
(ホテル白樺荘; ☑34-3311; www.shirakaba.co.jp/ english/index.html; 7148 Hirao; r per person with 2 meals from ¥11,700; P🛆) Close to the cable-car base station and the Sun Valley ski area is this pleasant little hotel with a variety of rooms and its own indoor and outdoor onsen baths.

SHINSHŪ CUISINE: A ROGUE'S GALLERY

Nagano Prefecture is renowned for foods from the familiar to the, shall we say, challenging. You'll know a food is local if the name is preceded by Shinshū (信州), the region's ancient name. From the tamest, look for the following:

» *ringo* (りんご): apples, often as big as grapefruits. Ubiquitous in autumn.

» *kuri* (栗): chestnuts, especially in Obuse.

» *soba* (そば): buckwheat noodles, handmade from 100% buckwheat in speciality shops (ordinary *soba* contains as little as 50% buckwheat). These can be eaten either cold (*zaru-soba*; with wasabi and soy-based dipping sauce) or hot (*kake-soba*; in broth).

» *oyaki* (おやき): little wheat buns filled with vegetables, baked or steamed.

» wasabi (わさび): Japanese horseradish, grown in bogs particularly in Hotaka. You know grated wasabi from sushi and *soba*, and locals parboil the greens as drinking snacks. Some shops sell wasabi in cakes and ice cream.

» *basashi* (馬刺し): raw horse meat

» *hachinoko* (鉢の子): bee larvae

» *inago* (稲子): crickets

Hotel Heights Shiga Kōgen HOTEL $$
(ホテルハイツ志賀高原; ☎34-3030; www
.shigakogen.jp/heights/english/index.htm; Hotaru
Onsen; r per person with 2 meals from ¥6500; P)
Near the base of the Kumanoyu ski area, the
large Hotel Heights boasts clean Japanese-
and Western-style rooms and its own onsen.

Hotel Sunroute Shiga Kōgen HOTEL $$
(ホテルサンルート志賀高原; ☎34-2020;
www.shigakogen.com/hotel/sunroute, in Japanese;
Ichinose; r per person with 2 meals from ¥10,500;
P) Another place that caters to a Western
crowd. It's in the Ichinose village, a three-
minute walk from the Ichinose Diamond
ski lift, with great access to other ski areas.
The rooms are Western style with en-suite
baths; some have mountain views.

Villa Ichinose INN $$
(ヴィラ・一の瀬; ☎34-2704; www.villa101.biz/
english/index.htm; 7149 Hirao; r per person from
¥6000; P🛜) Popular with foreigners, and
its location in front of the Ichinose bus
stop can't be beat. There are Japanese-style
rooms (toilet only), and Western-style rooms
with a bathroom. It has wireless internet in
the lobby and a 24-hour public bath on the
2nd floor. It has English-speaking staff and
a friendly atmosphere.

Chalet Shiga INN $$
(シャレー志賀; ☎34-2235; www.shigakogen
.jp/chalet; Ichinose; r per person with 2 meals from
¥10,500; P) Also convenient to the slopes
is the Chalet Shiga, a nice place with clean
Western- and Japanese-style rooms and a
popular sports bar.

❶ Getting There & Away
Direct buses run between Nagano Station and
Shiga Kōgen, with frequent departures in ski
season (¥1600, 70 minutes). You can also take a
train from Nagano to Yudanaka and continue to
Shiga Kōgen by bus – take a Hase-ike-bound bus
and get off at the last stop (¥760, approximately
40 minutes).

Nozawa Onsen 野沢温泉
☎0269 / POP 3800
A compact town that is tucked into a corner
of the eastern Japan Alps, Nozawa Onsen is
a delightful onsen/ski resort. It feels like a
Swiss ski resort, and you may wonder where
you are – until you see a sign written entirely
in kanji. Although Nozawa is worth visiting
any time of year, skiing is the main attraction for foreign visitors.

On 15 January there is the **'Dosojin' Matsuri**, one of the three most famous fire festivals in Japan, to pray for good fortune and a
plentiful harvest in the coming year.

◎ Sights & Activities

Nozawa Onsen Ski Resort SKI AREA
(野沢温泉スキー場; www.nozawaski.com/winter/
en/; 1-day lift ticket ¥4600; ⏰Dec-Apr) The town is
dominated by the Nozawa Onsen Ski Resort,
which is one of Honshū's best. The ski area
here is more compact than, say, nearby Shiga
Kōgen, and it's relatively easy to navigate and
enjoy. The main base area is right around the
Higake gondola station. There is a good variety of terrain at all levels, and snowboarders should try the Karasawa terrain park or
the half-pipe at Uenotaira. Advanced skiers
will enjoy the steep and often mogulled Sch-
neider Course, while beginners and families
will enjoy the Higake Course.

Snowshoe tours are available from the
end of January, organised by the **Nozawa
Onsen ski school** (tours per person ¥4000,
snowshoe rental ¥1000; ⏰Tue, Thu & Sat 20 Jan-31
Mar), and there is a **snow-field sightseeing
tour** (雪原遊覧ツアー; ¥500; six times daily) in
a snowcat from early January to late March
from the rest house at Yunomine.

Onsen ONSEN
(⏰6am-11pm) After skiing or hiking, check
out the 13 free onsen dotted about the
town. Our favourite is **Ō-yu**, with its fine
wooden building, followed by the scalding-
hot **Shin-yu**, and the atmospheric old
Kuma-no-tearai (Bear's Bathroom). The
locals like to say about some of these that
they're so hot 'humans can't even enter'. If
you have silver jewellery, leave it in your
room unless you don't mind it turning
black for a day or so.

🛏 Sleeping & Eating
Nozawa Onsen Visitor Centre (野沢温泉
ビジターセンター; ☎85-3155; 9780-4 Toyosa-
to; ⏰8.30am-6pm), in the centre of town, can
help with accommodation, and has English-
speaking staff.

Pension Schnee INN $$
(ペンションシュネー; ☎85-2012; www.pen
sionschnee.com; 8276 Hikage-suki-jō; r per person
with 2 meals from ¥8400) On the slopes near the
Higake gondola base, this European-style hotel enjoys the best location in town. It's a ski-
in/ski-out place with comfortable pension-
style rooms and a woody dining room.

Lodge Nagano INN $

(ロッジながの; ☎090-8670-9597; www.lodgena gano.com; 6846-1 Ōaza Toyosato; r per person with breakfast from ¥4000, r in summer from ¥2500; 🛜) This is a popular foreign-run guesthouse that attracts a lot of Aussie skiers and, with Vegemite in the dining room, makes them feel right at home. It's a friendly, fun place with both bunk- and Japanese-style rooms, some with private bath. There's wi-fi and a house computer as well.

Lodge Matsuya INN $$

(ロッヂまつや; ☎85-2082; www.2u.biglobe.ne .jp/~onotaka, in Japanese; fax 85-3694; 9553 Nozawa Onsen; r per person with breakfast from ¥6000, with 2 meals from ¥8000) In the centre of town is this large, friendly, family-run place with both Western- and Japanese-style rooms.

Haus St Anton INN $$

(サンアントンの家; ☎85-3597; http://nozawa .com/stanton; 9515 Nozawa Onsen; r per person with 2 meals with/without bathroom from ¥14,000/11,550) In the centre of the village, this is a comfortable inn with an Austrian theme and very helpful, friendly staff. It has six attractive Western-style bedrooms in a variety of themes, and a dining area/bar with a woody, warm atmosphere. It is also very close to the supermarket and main shopping street.

🍷 Drinking

Main Street Bar Foot BAR

(マインストリトバーフット) For nightlife, try this place, right on the main drag. It's a casual place for an after-ski drink, with free internet and table soccer.

Stay BAR

(ステイ; www.seisenso.com) On the basement floor of the same building as Main Street Bar Foot, Stay is open late and run by a music-loving Japanese man who has lived abroad.

Minato Bar IZAKAYA

(みなと) The older crowd will prefer Minato. It's easy to find in the northern part of town, near the base of the gondola. It's a Japanese-style place that seats 50 and offers karaoke next door.

ℹ Getting There & Away

There are direct buses between Nagano Station's east exit and Nozawa Onsen (¥1400, 90 minutes, seven buses per day in winter, three buses per day in summer). Alternatively, take a JR Iiyama-line train between Nagano and Togari Nozawa Onsen Station (¥740, 55 minutes). Regular buses connect Togari Nozawa Onsen Station and Nozawa Onsen (¥300, 20 minutes, nine per day). The bus station/ticket office is about 200m from the main bus stop, which is directly in the middle of town. This can be a little confusing, but there are staff around to help get people where they need to be.

Hakuba 白馬

☎0261

At the base of one of the highest sections of the Northern Japan Alps, Hakuba is one of Japan's main skiing and hiking centres. In winter, skiers from all over Japan and increasingly from overseas flock to Hakuba's seven ski resorts. In summer, the region is crowded with hikers drawn by easy access to the high peaks. There are many onsen in and around Hakuba-mura, the main village, and a long soak after a day of action is the perfect way to ease your muscles.

For information, maps and lodging assistance, visit the **Hakuba Shukuhaku Jōhō Centre** (白馬宿泊情報センター; ☎72-6900; www.hakuba1.com, in Japanese; ⌚7am-6pm), to the right of the Hakuba train/bus station, or **Hakuba-mura Kankō Kyōkai Annai-jo** (白馬村観光案内所; ☎72-3232; ⌚8.30am-5.30pm), just outside the station to the right (look for the 'i' symbol). Online, visit www .vill.hakuba.nagano.jp/e/index.htm.

⊙ Activities

Happō-One Ski Resort SKI AREA

(八方尾根; www.hakuba-happo.or.jp, in Japanese; 1-day lift ticket ¥4600; ⌚Dec-Apr) Host of the downhill races at the 1998 Winter Olympics, Happō-One is one of Japan's best ski areas. The mountain views are superb, and beginner, intermediate and advanced runs cater to skiers and snowboarders.

Most runs go right down the face of the mountain, with several good burners descending from Usagidaira 109, the mountain's centre-point. Above this, two chairlifts run to the top, worth it for the views alone. On busy days, you can avoid lift-line bottlenecks by heading to areas like the Skyline 2.

The rest house at Usagidaira 109 is the largest eating establishment. The modern Virgin Café Hakuba has upscale ambience, while Café Kurobishi has excellent mountain views and cafeteria-style seating.

There are plenty of hire places in the streets around the base of the mountain, some with boots up to 31cm. All have roughly the same selection and prices (¥2500 to ¥3000 per day for skis/board and boots).

From Hakuba Station, a five-minute bus ride (¥260) takes you into the middle of Hakuba-mura; from there it's a 10-minute walk to the base of Happō-One and the main 'Adam' gondola base station. In winter, a shuttle bus makes the rounds of the village, lodges and ski base.

Hakuba 47 Winter Sports Park & Hakuba Goryū Ski Resort
SKI AREA

The interlinked areas of **Hakuba 47 Winter Sports Park** (Hakuba47ウィンタースポーツパーク; www.hakuba47.co.jp) and **Hakuba Goryū Ski Resort** (白馬五竜スキー場; www.hakubagoryu.com/e/index.html) form the second major ski resort (one-day lift ticket ¥4800, open December to April) in the Hakuba area. There's a good variety of terrain at both areas, but you'll have to be at least an intermediate skier to ski the runs linking the two. Like Happō-One, this area boasts fantastic mountain views; the restaurant Alps 360 is the place to enjoy them. The Genki Go shuttle bus from Hakuba-mura and Hakuba-eki provides the easiest access.

Hakuba Cortina Kokusai
SKI AREA

(白馬コルチナ国際; http://hakubacortina.jp/ski/index.html, in Japanese; 1-day lift ticket ¥3300; ☺Dec-Apr) This smaller ski area at the north end of the Hakuba valley is popular both with those wanting a break from the main ski areas, and with the richer crowd from Tokyo who want the resort experience. It also caters to more advanced skiers, but can be icy when there isn't new snow. Its main building is a massive European gothic structure with hotel, restaurants, ski rental and deluxe onsen. You can also get a combined ticket with neighbouring Norikura resort for more skiing terrain.

Onsen
ONSEN

There are many onsen in and around Hakuba-mura, but **Mimizuku-no-yu** (みみずくの湯; 5480 Ō-aza Hokujō; adult/child ¥500/250; ☺10am-9.30pm, enter by 9pm), near the Hotel Hakuba, has some of the best mountain views from the tub.

Hiking

In summer, take the gondola and the two upper chairlifts, and then hike along a trail for an hour or so to the pond Happō-ike on a ridge below Karamatsu-dake. From here, follow a trail for an hour up to Maru-yama, continue for 1½ hours to the Karamatsu-dake San-sō (mountain hut) and then climb

to the peak of **Karamatsu-dake** (唐松岳; 2695m) in about 30 minutes. The return fare is ¥2340 if purchased at the Hakuba tourist office, ¥2600 otherwise.

Evergreen Outdoor Centre
OUTDOOR ADVENTURES

(www.evergreen-hakuba.com) This place offers an array of half-day adventures with English-speaking guides from about ¥5000 year-round, including canyoning and mountain biking, as well as snowshoeing and backcountry treks in the winter.

🛏 Sleeping & Eating

The village of Hakuba-mura has a huge selection of accommodation. The Hakuba Shukuhaku Jōhō Centre can help arrange accommodation if you arrive without reservations.

Hakuba Tokyu Hotel
HOTEL $$

(白馬東急ホテル; ☎72-3001; www.tokyuhotelsjapan.com/en/TR/TR_HAKUB/index.html; Happō-wadanomori; r per person with breakfast from ¥13,700;🅿🤖) This is a deluxe hotel with all the amenities. The rooms are formal, with great views. The Grand Spa boasts the highest alkaline content in the area, and the hotel also has a gift shop, bar and restaurant with French and Japanese cuisine.

Hakuba Panorama Hotel
INN $$

(白馬パノラマホテル; ☎85-4031; www.hakuba-panorama.com; 3322-1 Hokujō; r per person with breakfast from ¥11,000;🅿🤖) About 300m from one of the lifts at Happō-One, this newly opened inn is run by a friendly Australian who also rents out separate chalets. The Panorama has barrier-free accessibility, large common baths (at extra cost) and 15 Western-style rooms with ensuite bathrooms.

Snowbeds Backpackers
INN $

(スノーベッズバックパッカーズ; ☎72-5242; www.snowbedsjapan.com; r per person from ¥3510;🅿@) One of Hakuba's cheapest, this place has fairly cramped bunk rooms and a nice communal area with a wood stove. It's foreign-run, so communication is no problem, and it's close to some good nightlife options.

Hakuba Highland Hotel
HOTEL $$

(白馬ハイランドホテル; ☎72-3450; fax 72-3067; www.hakuba-highland.net, in Japanese; 1582 Hokujō; r per person with 2 meals from ¥8400; 🅿) Located at the base of the Hakuba Highland ski area, this family-friendly hotel boasts a sensational view over the Hakuba range, clean and fairly spacious rooms and a great indoor-outdoor onsen.

Uncle Steven's Mexican Food   MEXICAN $$
(アンクルスティーブンス; ☑72-7569; www .unclestevenshakuba.com; Happō Gondola Rd; dinner meals ¥1000-4500; ☺11am-midnight) This is one of the most popular restaurants in Hakuba. The burrito, chimichanga and enchiladas are all quite authentic and the portions are big, though you may find it a little on the expensive side.

Bamboo Coffee Bar   CAFE $
(☑090-7017-5331; ☺8am-6pm; 📶) On the left as you exit Hakuba Staion, this recently opened Aussie-run cafe has great specialty coffees and panini sandwiches.

🍷 Drinking & Entertainment

Tracks Bar   BAR
(www.tracksbar.com) Located between Kamishiro Station and the base of Hakuba 47 Winter Sports Park and Hakuba Goryū Ski Resort area, this is one of the favourite night spots for the younger, foreign crowd, with live music, sports on a huge screen and regular events. There is also budget accommodation in the area.

The Pub   PUB
(Mominoki Hotel; www.mominokihotel.com) For a few drinks after a day on the slopes, try this British-style pub in the Mominoki Hotel. It offers pub food, live music and events and is just five minutes from the base of the hill in Hakuba village.

Hakuba Bike Bar   BAR
(www.bikebar-hakuba.com) This cavernous, disco-lit bar run by Australians is in the basement of a house in Hakuba Goryū, about 10 minutes' walk from the Sky 4 gondola. It has billiards, early evening film nights for families, and karaoke. The walls are decorated with an assortment of vehicles.

ℹ️ Getting There & Away

Hakuba is connected with Matsumoto by the JR Ōito line (tokkyū, ¥2570, 61 minutes; futsū, ¥1110, 99 minutes). Continuing north, change trains at Minami Otari to meet the JR Hokuriku line at Itoigawa, with connections to Niigata, Toyama and Kanazawa.

From Nagano, buses leave from Nagano Station (¥1500, approximately 70 minutes). There are also buses between Shinjuku Nishi-guchi, in Tokyo, and Hakuba (¥4700, 4½ hours).

Bessho Onsen   別所温泉

☑0268
This intimate, mountain-ringed onsen town, bisected by a gentle stream, is known as 'Little Kamakura' for its dramatic temples and the fact that it served as an administrative centre during the Kamakura period (1185–1333). It was also mentioned in *The Pillow Book* by the Heian-era poetess Sei Shōnagon and was later a retreat for writers, including Kawabata Yasunari.

Bessho's excellent waters, reputed to cure diabetes and constipation while beautifying your complexion, bring in tourists aplenty, but overall it feels undervisited. Web information is available at www.bessho-spa.jp/j_en glish/english_fls.htm.

The **Bessho Onsen Ryokan Association** (別所温泉旅館組合; ☑38-2020; ☺9am-5pm) is the local tourist office – at the train station. English speakers will be marginally better off enquiring at the **tourist office** (☑26-5001; ☺9am-6pm) in Ueda Station en route to Bessho; staff can book same-day accommodation in Bessho.

The National Treasure temple **Anraku-ji** (安楽時; ☑38-2062; adult/child ¥300/100; ☺8am-5pm Mar-Oct, to 4pm Nov-Feb), from AD 824–34 and renowned for its octagonal pagoda, is 10 minutes on foot from Bessho Onsen Station. The Tendai temple **Kitamuki Kannon** (北向観音; ☑38-2023; admission free; ☺24hr) is a few minutes' walk away, with some very old trees, sweeping valley views and a pavilion on stilts that's like a tiny version of Kyoto's Kiyomizu-dera. Its name comes from the fact that this Kannon image faces north, a counterpart to the south-facing image at Zenkō-ji in Nagano. About a 5km hike away are the temples **Chūzen-ji** (☑38-4538; adult/child ¥200/50; ☺9am-4pm) and **Zenzan-ji** (☑38-2855; adult/child ¥200/100; ☺9am-4pm, occasional winter closures), which feel like a real escape.

There are three central **public baths** (admission ¥150; ☺6am-10pm): Ō-yu (大湯) has a small *rotemburo;* Ishi-yu (石湯) is famed for its stone bath; and Daishi-yu (大師湯), most frequented by the locals, is usually cool.

TOP CHOICE **Ryokan Hanaya** (旅館花屋; ☑38-3131; http://hanaya.naganoken.jp, in Japanese; fax 38-7923; 169 Bessho Onsen; r per person for groups of 2 or more, with meals from ¥15,750) is a traditional gem set among lovely, manicured gardens. Spacious tatami rooms open onto the scenery; 14 rooms have their own baths supplied directly by hot springs. Some rooms have private onsen baths attached; guests without enjoy pleasant indoor and outdoor baths. Book far in advance.

Uematsu-ya (上松屋; ☑38-2300; fax 38-8501; www.uematsuya.com, in Japanese; r per person with 2 meals from ¥12,600) is neither historical nor traditional but kindly, well kept and good value. Its 32 rooms (both Japanese and Western style) are up nine storeys. There's an all-you-can-drink plan (females/males ¥2100/2625), plus indoor and outdoor baths. Some English is spoken.

The 13-bed **Mahoroba Youth Hostel** (上田まほろばユースホステル; ☑38-5229; fax 38-1714; www14.ueda.ne.jp/~mahoroba42731/; 40-1 Bessho Onsen; dm ¥3800, HI members ¥3200, meals ¥1200) is comfortable, secluded and surrounded by lush scenery, but doesn't have an onsen. It's an eight-minute walk south from the train station.

Access to Bessho Onsen is via Ueda, on the JR Nagano *shinkansen* (from Tokyo ¥6290, 1½ hours; from Nagano ¥2670, 12 minutes) or the private Shinano Tetsudō line from Nagano (¥740, about 35 minutes). At Ueda, change to the private Ueda Dentetsu line to Bessho Onsen (¥570, 30 minutes, approximately hourly).

Matsumoto　松本

☑0263 / POP 243,000

A traveller's favourite, Matsumoto has a superb castle, some pretty streets and an atmosphere that's both laid-back and surprisingly cosmopolitan.

Nagano-ken's second-largest city has been around since at least the 8th century. Formerly known as Fukashi, it was the castle town of the Ogasawara clan during the 14th and 15th centuries, and it continued to prosper through the Edo period. Today, Matsumoto's street aesthetic combines the black and white of its castle with *namakokabe* (lattice-pattern-walled) *kura* and Edo-period streetscapes in the Nakamachi district, and some smart 21st-century Japanese architecture. Plus, views of the Japan Alps are never much further than around the corner. The areas by the Metoba-gawa and Nakamachi boast galleries, comfortable cafes and reasonably priced, high-quality accommodation.

Utsukushi-ga-hara and Asama Onsens and the Utsukushi-ga-hara plateau are day trips, while Hotaka can be either a day trip or the start of a hiking route. Matsumoto is also a transit hub for Japan Alps National Park and the Kiso Valley.

◉ Sights & Activities

Matsumoto-jō　　　　HISTORICAL BUILDING
(松本城; 4-1 Marunōchi; adult/child ¥600/300; ⊙8.30am-5pm early-Sep–mid-Jul, to 6pm mid-Jul–Aug) Even if you spend only a couple of hours in Matsumoto, be sure to visit Matsumoto-jō, Japan's oldest wooden castle and one of four castles designated National Treasures – the others are Hikone, Himeji and Inuyama.

The magnificent three-turreted *donjon* was built c 1595, in contrasting black and white, leading to the nickname Karasu-jō (Crow Castle). Steep steps lead up six storeys, with impressive views from each level. Lower floors display guns, bombs and gadgets with which to storm castles, and a delightful *tsukimi yagura* (moon-viewing pavilion). It has a tranquil moat full of carp, with the occasional swan gliding beneath the red bridges. The basics are explained over loudspeakers in English and Japanese. You can also ask at the entrance about a free tour in English (subject to availability), or call the **Goodwill Guide Group** (☑32-7140), which gives free one-hour tours by reservation.

Matsumoto City Museum/Japan Folklore Museum
(松本市立博物館; 4-1 Marunōchi; ⊙8.30am-4.30pm) The castle grounds (and your admission ticket) also include the Matsumoto City Museum/Japan Folklore Museum, with small displays relating to the region's history and folklore.

Nakamachi　　　　NEIGHBOURHOOD
(中町) The narrow streets of this former merchant district make a fine setting for a stroll, as most of its storehouses have been transformed into cafes, galleries and craft shops specialising in wood, glass, fabric, ceramics and antiques. **Nakamachi Kura-Chic-Kan** (中町・蔵シック館; 'Classic-kan'; 2-9-15 Chūō; ⊙9am-10pm) is just one option, showcasing locally produced arts and crafts, with a relaxing coffee house next door.

Matsumoto Timepiece Museum　　MUSEUM
(松本市時計博物館; 4-21-15 Chūō; adult/student ¥300/150; ⊙9am-5pm Tue-Sun) Home to Japan's largest pendulum clock (on the building's exterior) and over 300 other timepieces, incuding fascinating medieval

Japanese creations, this museum shows Japan's love of *monozukuri,* the art of creating things.

Matsumoto City Museum of Art   MUSEUM

(松本市美術館; 4-2-22 Chūō; adult/child ¥400/free; ⏰9am-5pm Tue-Sun) This sleek museum has a good collection of Japanese artists, many of whom hail from Matsumoto or depict scenes of the surrounding countryside. Highlights include the striking avant-garde works of Kusama Yayoi (look for the 'Infinity Mirrored Room').

Japan Ukiyo-e Museum   MUSEUM

(日本浮世絵美術館; 2206-1 Koshiba, Shimadachi; adult/child ¥1050/530; ⏰10am-5pm Tue-Sun) Housing more than 100,000 wood-block prints, paintings, screens and old books, this renowned museum exhibits a minuscule fraction of its collection. There's an explanatory leaflet in English.

The museum is approximately 3km from Matsumoto Station, 15 minutes' walk from Ōniwa Station on the Matsumoto Dentetsu line (¥170, six minutes), or about ¥2000 by taxi.

Utsukushi-ga-hara & Asama Onsen   ONSEN

(美ヶ原温泉・浅間温泉) Northeast of town, Utsukushi-ga-hara Onsen (not to be confused with Utsukushi-ga-hara Kōgen) is the more beautiful of these two bathing areas, with a quaint main street and views across the valley. Asama Onsen's history is said to date back to the 10th century and includes writers and poets, though it looks quite generic now. **Hot Plaza Asama** (ホットプラザ浅間; adult/child ¥630/350; ⏰10am-11pm Wed-Mon) feels like a neighbourhood *sentō* but boasts many pools and sauna.

Both towns are easily reached by bus from Matsumoto's bus terminal (Utsukushi-ga-hara Onsen: ¥330, 18 minutes, twice hourly; Asama Onsen: ¥350, 23 minutes, hourly).

Utsukushi-ga-hara Kōgen   MOUNTAIN

(美ヶ原高原) Not to be confused with Utsukushi-ga-hara Onsen, this alpine plateau (2000m) is a popular warm-weather excursion from Matsumoto, reached via an ooh-and-ahh drive on twisty mountain roads called Azalea Line and Venus Line.

Utsukushi-ga-hara Bijutsukan   MUSEUM
(美ヶ原美術館; Utsukushi-ga-hara Open-Air Museum; adult/child/student ¥1000/700/800; ⊙9am-5pm late-Apr–mid-Nov) In the same vein (with the same owner) as the Hakone Open-Air Museum (p139), it's a large sculpture garden with some 350 pieces, mostly by Japanese sculptors. The surrounding mountains provide an inspiring backdrop in clear weather.

Nearby are pleasant walks and the opportunity to see cows in pasture (a constant source of fascination in Japan). **Furusatokan** (ふる里館), the shop at the hilltop farm, sells ice cream made from local *kokemomo* (lingonberries).

Buses (¥1300, 80 minutes) run several times daily in midsummer, with spotty-to-nonexistent service the rest of the season; check before you go. Taxis are expensive, so renting a car may make sense.

✴ Festivals & Events

Matsumoto-jō Sakura Matsuri   SPRING
Cherry-blossom time (late April) coincides with mood lighting at the castle.

Tenjin Matsuri   PARADE
The festival at Fukashi-jinja on 23 and 24 July features elaborately decorated *yatai*.

Takigi Nō Matsuri   THEATRE
This atmospheric festival during August features nō performances by torchlight, outdoors on a stage in the park below the castle.

Saitō Kinen Matsuri   MUSIC
About a dozen classical music concerts in memory of revered Japanese conductor and music educator Saitō Hideo (1902–72) held from mid-August to mid-September. Ozawa Seiji, conductor emeritus of the Boston Symphony Orchestra, is festival director.

Dōsojin Matsuri   CULTURAL
On the fourth Saturday in September, phallic merriment is to be had at the festival held in honour of *dōsojin* (roadside guardians) at Utsukushi-ga-hara Onsen.

Yohashira Jinja Matsuri   CULTURAL
This festival (aka Shintōsai) occurs around the beginning of October, featuring fireworks and large dolls.

Taimatsu Matsuri   PARADE
Around the start of October, Asama Onsen celebrates the spectacular fire festival with torch-lit parades that are accompanied by drumming.

Oshiro Matsuri   CULTURAL
The Castle Festival, from mid-October to 3 November, is a cultural jamboree that includes costume parades, puppet displays and flower shows.

🛏 Sleeping

Get away from the station (mostly cramped and charmless business hotels) for the many worthwhile lodgings within 10 minutes' walk, especially in Nakamachi.

TOP CHOICE Marumo   RYOKAN $
(まるも; ☑32-0115; fax 35-2251; 3-3-10 Chūō; r per person ¥5250, with breakfast ¥6300) Between Nakamachi and the rushing Metoba-gawa, this beautiful wooden ryokan dates from 1868 and has lots of traditional charm, including a bamboo garden and coffee shop. Although rooms aren't huge and don't have private facilities, it's quite popular, so book ahead.

Nunoya   INN $
(ぬのや旅館; ☑/fax 32-0545; 3-5-7 Chūō; r per person from ¥4500) Few inns have more heart than this pleasantly traditional charmer, with shiny wood floors and quality tatami rooms with shared bathrooms. No meals are served, but the cafes (and shops and galleries) of Nakamachi are just outside.

Seifūsō   RYOKAN $
(静風荘; ☑46-0639; http://homepage1.nifty.com/seihuso; fax 46-3266; 634-5 Minami-asama; r per person from ¥4725; Ⓟ@) This riverside inn outside the city centre has very helpful and welcoming staff, Japanese-style rooms and shared baths. Take bus 2 from Matsumoto Station to Minami-asama bus stop, or call ahead for a pickup.

Richmond Hotel   HOTEL $$
(リッチモンドホテル松本; ☑37-5000; www.richmondhotel.jp/e/matsumoto; 1-10-7 Chūō; s/d from ¥6000/8500; ◐@) Central and crisp, this 204-room business hotel offers decent-sized rooms, a minimum of fuss and LAN cable access. Rates are for *kai-in* (members); to become one, fill out a form and pay a one-time ¥500 charge at check-in. Even cheaper rates are often available online.

Hotel Buena Vista   HOTEL $$$
(ホテルブエナビスタ; ☑37-0111; www.buena-vista.co.jp; 1-2-1 Honjo; s/tw from ¥9240/19,645; ◐@) Long Matsumoto's sharpest Western hotel, the Buena Vista has been given a chic Barcelona-style makeover in its public

spaces: dark woods, stone, mood lighting and world beats in the lobby. The Sorpresa lounge on the 14th floor has the city's best views.

Sugimoto
RYOKAN $$

(旅館すぎもと; ☑32-3379; 451-7 Satoyamabe, Utsukushi-ga-hara Onsen; r per person from ¥15,000) You might want two nights in this fabulous ryokan on Utsukushi-ga-hara's main street: one to get acquainted with the facilities – onsen baths, jacuzzi, *mingei* (folk art) collection, tea room, underground passage, bar stocked with single malts etc – and the second to enjoy them. Rooms range in size and decor (Japanese, Western and mixed), but all are ineffably stylish. Dinner (¥6000, by reservation) includes bath admission.

✖ Eating & Drinking
For a quick coffee and cake, cafes line the banks of the Metoba-gawa and Nawate-dōri.

Kura
SHOKUDŌ $

(蔵; ☑33-6444; 1-10-22 Chūō; dishes from ¥300, teishoku ¥945-2100; ☑lunch & dinner Thu-Tue) Located near Nakamachi, Kura serves meticulously prepared sushi and tempura for lunch and dinner in a stylish former warehouse. For the daring: *basashi* (raw horse meat).

Shizuka
IZAKAYA $

(しづか; ☑32-0547; 4-10-8 Ōte; dishes ¥525-1365; ☑lunch & dinner Mon-Sat;🍴) Friendly, traditional *izakaya* serving favourites like *oden* and *yakitori* (skewers of grilled chicken). Some more challenging local specialities are on the English menu.

Vamonos
MEXICAN $

(バモノス; ☑36-4878; 1-4-13 Chūō; mains ¥750-900; ☑lunch & dinner) This sweet little Mexican cantina serves enchiladas, burritos, nachos, large salads and dainty but potent margaritas. Look for the sign on the 2nd floor.

Robata Shōya
YAKITORI $

(炉ばた庄屋; ☑37-1000; 11-1 Chūō; dishes ¥150-900; ☑dinner) On a corner in the town centre is this classic, lively *yakitori-ya* (restaurant specialising in *yakitori*), with a large selection of grills, seasonal specials and a (sort of) English menu.

Old Rock
PUB $

(オールドロック; ☑38-0069; 2-30-20 Chūō; mains from ¥750; ☑lunch & dinner;🍴) A block south of the river and across the street from Nakamachi, this popular *gaijin* pub attracts a lively crowd on weekend nights. Good lunch specials and a wide selection of beers are available.

Nomugi
NOODLES $$

(野麦; ☑36-3753; 2-9-11 Chūō; soba ¥1100; ☑lunch Thu-Mon) In Nakamachi, this is one of central Japan's finest *soba* shops. Its owner used to run a French restaurant in Tokyo before returning to his home town. There's one dish: *zaru-soba* in a wicker basket; plus *kake-soba* (¥1300), which is served during the colder months.

[TOP CHOICE] Coat
BAR

(メインバーコート; ☑34-7133; 2-3-24 Chūō; ☑6pm-12.30am Tue-Sun) Directly behind Old Rock, this sophisticated little bar is home to Matsumoto's most famous bartender. Hayashi-san's inventive *otomenadeshiko* cocktail won first prize at the Japan Bartenders Association competition early this decade.

🔒 Shopping
Matsumoto is synonymous with *temari* (embroidered balls) and doll-making (Takasago street, one block south of Nakamachi, has several doll shops). In addition to Nakamachi's galleries, Nawate-dōri north of the river is a colourful place for souvenirs and cafes. **Parco department store** (パルコ) has pride of place in the city centre.

Berami
TEMARI/DOLLS

(ベラミ; Belle Amie; ☑9am-7pm Mon, Tue, Thu, Fri & Sat, 10am-6pm Sun) *Temari* and dolls are found here. Doll styles include *tanabata* and *oshie-bina* (dressed in fine cloth).

ℹ Information
Although small streets radiate somewhat confusingly from the train station, soon you're on a grid. Any place on the Matsumoto map in this book is within 20 minutes' walk of the train station.

The main post office is located on Honmachi-dōri. For web information, visit www.city.matsumoto.nagano.jp.

JTB (☑35-3311; 1-2-11 Fukashi) For train and bus reservations.

Tourist information office Matsumoto Station (松本市観光案内所; ☑32-2814; 1-1-1 Fukashi; ☑9.30am-5.45pm); near castle gates (☑38-7176;☑9am-5.45pm;@) The branch inside Matsumoto Station, has English-language pamphlets and maps, and can book accommodation.

THE JAPAN ALPS & CENTRAL HONSHŪ MATSUMOTO

ⓘ Getting There & Away

Air

Shinshū Matsumoto airport has flights to Fukuoka, Osaka and Sapporo.

Bus

Alpico runs buses between Matsumoto and Shinjuku in Tokyo (¥3400, 3¼ hours, 18 daily), Osaka (¥5710, 5¼ hours, two daily), Nagoya (¥3460, 3½ hours, six daily) and Takayama (¥3100, 2½ hours, four daily). Reservations are advised. Matsumoto's bus station is in the basement of the Espa building across from the train station.

Car & Motorcycle

Hiring a car is often the best way to do side trips, and there are several agencies around the train station. Rates start at about ¥5250 for a half-day.

Train

Matsumoto is connected with Tokyo's Shinjuku Station (*tokkyū*, ¥6200, 2¾ hours, hourly), Nagoya (*tokkyū*, ¥5670, two hours) and Nagano (Shinano *tokkyū*, ¥2970, 50 minutes; *futsū*, ¥1110, 70 minutes).

ⓘ Getting Around

The castle and the city centre are easily covered on foot, or free bicycles are available for loan; enquire at the tourist information office. Three 'town sneaker' bus routes loop through the centre between 9am and 6pm from April to November (to 5.30pm December to March) for ¥100/300 per ride/day; the blue and orange routes cover the castle and Nakamachi.

An airport shuttle bus connects Shinshū Matsumoto airport with the city centre (¥540, 25 minutes). Buses are timed to flights. A taxi costs around ¥4500.

Hotaka 穂高
📞 0263

Not to be confused with Shin-Hotaka in Japan Alps National Park, Hotaka is home to Japan's largest wasabi (Japanese horseradish) farm. It is an easy day trip from Matsumoto and a popular starting point for mountain hikes.

The **tourist office** (観光案内所; 📞82-9363; ⊙9am-5pm Apr-Nov, 10am-4pm Dec-Mar) and **bicycle hire** (per hr from ¥200), the recommended way to get around, are outside the Hotaka Station exit. Both have basic maps, and the tourist office has some English-speaking staff and can make lodging reservations.

◉ Sights & Activities

Dai-ō Wasabi-Nōjo   WASABI FARM

(大王わさび農場; admission free; ⊙8.30am-5.30pm Jul & Aug, shorter hours rest of year) Fancy some wasabi beer? This farm is de rigueur for wasabi lovers, and even wasabi haters may have fun. An English map guides you among wasabi plants (130 tons of wasabi are grown in flooded fields here annually), restaurants, shops and workspaces, all set amid rolling hills.

The farm is about a 15-minute bike ride from Hotaka Station. There are also some calmer municipal wasabi fields.

Rokuzan Bijutsukan   MUSEUM

(碌山美術館; adult/child ¥700/150; ⊙9am-5.10pm Mar-Oct, to 4.10pm Nov-Feb, closed Mon Nov-Apr) Ten minutes' walk from the station, Rokuzan Bijutsukan showcases the work of Meiji-era sculptor Rokuzan Ogiwara (whom the Japanese have labelled the 'Rodin of the Orient') and his Japanese contemporaries. Strolling through the four buildings and garden, you may be struck by how much cross-cultural flow there was between East and West.

Jōnen-dake   HIKING

(常念岳) From Hotaka Station, it takes about 30 minutes by taxi (about ¥4800) to reach Ichi-no-sawa, from where experienced hikers can climb Jōnen-dake (2857m); the ascent takes about 5½ hours. There are many options for mountain hikes extending over several days in the region, but you must be properly prepared. Hiking maps and information are available at regional tourist information offices, although the more detailed maps are in Japanese. Get the taxi's *meishi* (business card) to phone for your return trip.

🛏 Sleeping

TOP CHOICE Nakabusa Onsen   INN $$

(中房温泉; 📞77-1488; www.nakabusa.com, in Japanese; 7226 Nakabusa; r per person with 2 meals from ¥9390; ⊙late Apr-late Nov) This rambling old place is a bather's delight – about a dozen indoor, outdoor and sand baths, some mixed and some very hot, can be enjoyed here at the end of a very windy mountain road. The older *honkan* wing has extremely basic rooms, so if you want to be more comfortable, stay in the newer *bekkan* wing. The best time to visit is late fall, when stunningly colourful foliage is topped by the snow-capped peaks.

Ariake-so
INN $$

(有明荘; ☑090-2321-9991; www.enzanso.co.jp/ariake; Nakabusa; dm/r per person with meals from ¥8800; ⊙late Apr-late Nov) Nestled up near Nakabusa Onsen, this is a seasonal 95-person lodge with basic rooms and a nourishing onsen (day use ¥600).

Azumino Pastoral Youth Hostel
HOSTEL $

(安曇野パストラルユースホステル; ☑83-6170; http://park2.wakwak.com/~pastoralyh, in Japanese; 8508 Ariake; dm ¥3960, HI members ¥3360, with 2 meals from ¥5900, HI members ¥5300) Amid farmland, 4km west of Hotaka Station (a one-hour walk), this pleasant hostel has plenty of rustic charm and rooms that sleep three to five people. It occasionally closes during the off season (typically in winter).

❶ Getting There & Away

Hotaka is about 30 minutes (¥320) from Matsumoto on the JR Ōito line.

Kiso Valley Region   木曽

☑0264
Thickly forested and alpine, southwest Nagano-ken is traversed by the twisting, craggy former post road, the Nakasendō. Like the more famous Tōkaidō, the Nakasendō connected Edo (present-day Tokyo) with Kyoto, enriching the towns along the way. Today, several small towns feature carefully preserved architecture of those days, making this a highly recommended visit.

TSUMAGO & MAGOME   妻籠・馬篭

These are two of the most attractive Nakasendō towns. Both close their main streets to vehicular traffic and they're connected by an agreeable hike.

Tsumago feels like an open-air museum, about 15 minutes' walk from end to end. It was designated by the government as a protected area for the preservation of traditional buildings, so no modern developments such as telephone poles are allowed to mar the scene. The dark-wood glory of its lattice-fronted houses and gently sloping tile roofs is particularly beautiful in early morning mist. Many films and TV shows have been shot on its main street.

Tsumago's **tourist information office** (観光案内館; ☑57-3123; fax 57-4036; ⊙8.30am-5pm) is in the centre of town, by the antique phone booth. Some English is spoken and there's English-language literature.

Down the street and across, **Waki-honjin** (脇本陣; adult/child ¥600/300; ⊙9am-5pm) is a former rest stop for retainers of *daimyō* on the Nakasendō. Reconstructed in 1877 under special dispensation from the emperor Meiji, it contains a lovely moss garden and a special toilet built in case Meiji happened to show up (apparently he never did). If some elements remind you of Japanese castles, that's because Waki-honjin was built by a former castle builder, out of work due to Meiji's antifeudal policies. The **Shiryōkan** (資料館; local history museum) here houses elegant exhibitions about Kiso and the Nakasendō, with some English signage.

Across from Shiryōkan, **Tsumago Honjin** (妻籠本陣; adult/child ¥300/150; ⊙9am-5pm) is where the *daimyō* themselves spent the night, though this building is more noteworthy for its architecture than its exhibits. A combined ticket (¥700/350) gives you admission to Waki-honjin and Shiryōkan as well.

Kisoji-kan (木曽路館; baths ¥700; ⊙10am-8pm), a few hilly kilometres above Tsumago, is a tourist facility with a raging souvenir shop. The real reason to visit is the *rotemburo* with panoramic mountain vistas. Some Tsumago lodgings offer discount tickets, and there's a free shuttle bus to/from Tsumago's car park No 1 (10 minutes, approximately hourly) and Nagiso (p222).

On 23 November, the **Fuzoku Emaki Parade** is held along the Nakasendō in Tsumago, featuring townsfolk in Edo-period costume.

In Gifu-ken, **Magome**, the next post town south, is more modern, with houses, restaurants, inns (and souvenir shops) lining a steep, cobblestone pedestrian road. Even if only some structures are Edo-style, Magome and its mountain views are undeniably pretty. At the **tourist information office** (観光案内館; ☑59-2336; fax 59-2653; ⊙8.30am-5pm mid-Mar–mid-Dec, 9am-5pm mid-Dec–mid-Mar), about halfway up the hill on the right, you can pick up maps, and staff will book accommodation.

Magome was the birthplace of the author Shimazaki Tōson (1872–1943). His masterpiece, *Ie* (The Family), records the decline of two provincial Kiso families. A **museum** (藤村記念館; admission ¥500; ⊙8.30am-4.45pm Apr-Oct, to 4.15pm Nov-Mar, closed 2nd Tue, Wed & Thu Dec) is devoted to his life and times, though it's pretty impenetrable for non-Japanese speakers.

Good gifts from both towns include toys, crafts and household implements made from Kiso *hinoki*.

The 7.8km hike connecting Tsumago and Magome reaches its peak at the top of the steep pass, Magome-tōge (elevation 801m). From here, the trail to/from Tsumago passes waterfalls, forest and farmland, while the Magome approach is largely along paved road. Free tea is on offer at the teahouse Tatebajaya (立場茶屋) along the way. It takes around 2½ hours to hike between the towns. The route is easier from Magome (elevation 600m) to Tsumago (elevation 420m) than the other way. English signage marks the route. The Magome-Tsumago bus (¥600, 30 minutes, at least three daily in each direction, except Monday to Friday from December to February) also stops at the pass.

If you're hiking between Magome and Tsumago, the towns offer a handy **baggage-forwarding service** (per bag ¥500; ⊘ daily late Jul-Aug, Sat, Sun & holidays late Mar-late Nov) from either tourist office to the other. Deposit your bags between 8.30am and 11.30am for delivery by 1pm.

🛏 Sleeping & Eating

It's worth a stay in these special towns, particularly Tsumago, to have them to yourself once the day trippers clear out. Both tourist information offices can help book accommodation at numerous ryokan. For street foods, look for *gohei-mochi,* skewered rice dumplings coated with sesame-walnut sauce, and in autumn you can't miss *kuri-kinton* (chestnut dumplings).

TOP CHOICE **Fujioto** RYOKAN $$
(藤乙; ⊅57-3009; Tsumago; www.takenet.or.jp/~fujioto; r per person ¥11,550) Another much-photographed, excellent ryokan, this place has impressive old-style rooms and a graceful garden, which you can enjoy over lunch such as Kiso Valley trout (*teishoku* ¥1350). It's a few doors down from the Waki-honjin in Tsumago.

Minshuku Daikichi MINSHUKU $$
(大吉旅館; ⊅57-2595; fax 57-2203; Tsumago; r per person with meals ¥10,000) Popular with foreign visitors, this place feels very traditional – with handsome tatami rooms and fine wood features – despite its 1970s construction. All rooms have a view. It's at the edge of Tsumago (take the right-hand fork uphill from the centre).

Matsushiro-ya RYOKAN $$
(松代屋旅館; ⊅57-3022; fax 57-3386; Tsumago; r per person ¥10,500; ⊘ Thu-Tue) One of Tsumago's most historic lodgings (parts date from 1804), Matsushiro-ya sits on the village's most picturesque street and offers large tatami rooms.

Magome-Chaya MINSHUKU $$
(馬籠茶屋; ⊅59-2038; www.magomechaya.com; Magome; s/d ¥5250/8190) This friendly, well-kept restaurant and *minshuku* is in the centre of Magome, near the water wheel.

Stalls throughout Tsumago sell street foods, and you can find a few little *shokudō* (all-round restaurants) near the path to the car park. **Yoshimura-ya** (吉村屋; ⊅57-3265; dishes ¥700-1500; ⊘ lunch, closed Thu; 🔊) is typical of these places and has an English menu; its speciality is handmade *soba* – try it with tempura.

ⓘ Getting There & Away
Nakatsugawa and Nagiso Stations on the JR Chūō line serve Magome and Tsumago, respectively, though both are still at some distance. Nakatsugawa is connected with Nagoya (*tokkyū*, ¥2740, 47 minutes) and Matsumoto (*tokkyū*, ¥3980, 1¼ hours). A few *tokkyū* daily stop in Nagiso (from Nagoya ¥3080, one hour); otherwise change at Nakatsugawa (*futsū* ¥320, 20 minutes).

Buses leave hourly from Nakatsugawa Station for Magome (¥540, 30 minutes). There's also an infrequent bus service between Magome and Tsumago (¥600, 25 minutes), via Magome-tōge.

Buses run between Tsumago and Nagiso Station (¥270, 10 minutes, eight per day), or it's an hour's walk.

Highway buses operate between Magome and Nagoya's Meitetsu Bus Centre (名鉄バスセンター; ¥1810, 1½ hours), as well as Tokyo's Shinjuku Station (¥4500, 4½ hours). These stop at the nearby interchange (Magome Intah; 馬籠インター), from where it's about 1.3km on foot uphill, unless it's timed with the bus from Nakatsugawa.

KISO-FUKUSHIMA 木曽福島
North of Tsumago and Magome and considerably more developed, Kiso-Fukushima's historical significance makes it a worthy few-hour side trip en route to these towns or from Matsumoto. It was an important checkpoint on the Nakasendō, and the town centre boasts a picturesque district of old residences.

From the station, cross the street and pick up an English map at the simple **tourist office** (木曽町観光協会; Kisomachi Kankō Kyōkai; ☎22-4000; 2012-10 Kiso-machi Fukushima; ⏰9am-4.45pm), and head down the hill towards the town centre. Sights are well signposted. To your right, between the Kiso-gawa and the train tracks, is **Ue-no-dan** (上の段), the old historic district full of atmospheric houses, many of which now serve as shops, cafes and galleries.

Another several minutes' walk leads you to the **Fukushima Sekisho-ato** (福島関所跡; Fukushima Checkpoint Site; adult/child ¥300/150; ⏰8am-5pm Apr-Oct, 8.30am-4pm Nov-Mar), a reconstruction of one of the most significant checkpoints on the Edo-period trunk roads. From its perch above the river valley, it's easy to see the barrier's strategic importance. Displays inside show the implements used to maintain order, including weaponry and *tegata* (wooden travel passes), as well as the special treatment women travellers received.

Tsutaya (おん宿蔦屋; ☎22-2010; fax 22-3166; www.kiso-tutaya.com, in Japanese; 5162 Kiso-machi Fukushima; r per person from ¥15,800) is a spiffy, newly opened hot-springs hotel located right in the centre of town. Splash out in traditional Japanese-style rooms with private barrel-shaped baths, or kick back in the common tubs partly open to the outdoors. The *kaiseki* cuisine here is especially delicious and includes lotus-root tempura and Shinshū steak cooked to perfection.

Kurumaya Honten (くるまや本店; ☎22-2200; 5367-2 Kiso-machi Fukushima; mains ¥630-1575; ⏰10am-5pm Thu-Tue; 📷) is one of Japan's most renowned *soba* shops. The classic presentation is cold *mori* (plain) or *zaru* (with strips of nori seaweed) on lacquer trays with a sweetish dipping sauce, or try it with *daikon orishi* (grated daikon radish) or hot with *jidori* (free-range chicken). It's just before the first bridge at the bottom of the hill on the right as you exit the station – look for the gears above the doorway.

In Ue-no-dan, **Bistro Matsushima-tei** (ビストロ松島体; ☎23-3625; 5250-1 Ue-no-dan; mains ¥1155-1900, lunch sets ¥1200-1800; ⏰lunch & dinner daily Jul-Oct, closed Wed Nov-Jun) serves a changing selection of handmade pizzas and pastas in a chichi-atmospheric setting befitting the building's history – a nice date spot. Or stop in for coffee and cake.

Kiso-Fukushima is a stop on the JR Chūō line (Shinano *tokkyū*), easily reached from Matsumoto (¥2610, 35 minutes), Nakatsugawa (¥2610, 35 minutes) and Nagoya (¥4500, 1½ hours).

Two daily buses travel each way (¥4500, 4¼ hours) between Kiso-Fukushima and Tokyo's Shinjuku Station (west exit).

TOYAMA PREFECTURE

Toyama Prefecture (富山県) is big in pharmaceuticals, zipper manufacturing and mountains. Visitors come for the latter, the Tateyama range, to the city's east and south, as well as the traditional thatched-roof houses of the Gokayama district (p198).

Toyama 富山

☑076 / POP 417,000

As a transit hub on the Hokuriku coast, Toyama City is known for its seafood (including *hotaruika,* firefly squid) and as a starting point for the Tateyama-Kurobe Alpine Route (p224).

The helpful **information office** (観光案内所; ☎432-9751; ⏰8.30am-8pm), inside Toyama Station, stocks maps and pamphlets on the city and Tateyama-Kurobe Alpine Route. Some English is spoken. Most lodgings and restaurants are outside the station's south exit, and sights are easily reachable by tram or bus.

Toyama Municipal Folkcraft Village (富山市民俗民芸村; 1118-1 Anyōbō; adult/child ¥500/250; ⏰9am-5pm) exhibits folk art, ceramics, tea ceremony implements, *sumi-e* (ink brush) paintings and more, in a variety of buildings snaking up a hillside. Atop the hill, the temple **Chōkei-ji** (長慶寺; ⏰24hr) offers awesome mountain views and 500-plus statues of *rakan* (Buddha's disciples) draped in colourful sashes. Toyama's free Museum Bus takes you to the Folkcraft Village (10 minutes, hourly from 10.30am to 4.30pm), from in front of the Toyama Excel Hotel Tōkyū.

North of the city centre is the bayside **Iwase** (岩瀬) neighbourhood, the well-preserved main street of the former shipping business district. Now it's filled with shops and private homes; even the banks look interesting. Take the Portram light rail line from Toyama Station's north exit to the terminus, Iwase-hama (¥200, 25 minutes), make a sharp left to cross the canal via Iwase-bashi (岩瀬橋) and you'll see signs in English. Rather than backtrack, you can return via Higashi-Iwase Station on the Portram.

There are many lodgings within a few minutes' walk of the train station's south exit. **Toyama Excel Hotel Tōkyū** (富山エクセルホテル東急; ☑441-0109; www.toyama-e.tokyuhotels.co.jp; CIC Bldg, 1-2-3 Shintomichō; s/d from ¥10,900/18,400; ☺@☎), located above the landmark CIC shopping centre, has large-ish singles, small twin rooms and LAN internet access. **Comfort Hotel Toyama Eki-mae** (コンフォートホテル富山駅前; ☑433-6811; www.choice-hotels.jp; 1-3-2 Takara-machi; s/d with breakfast from ¥5800/8500; @☎) is another business hotel. Neutral-palette rooms feature good beds, and buffet breakfast is decent for the price. It's across the street and to the right as you exit the station.

Shiroebi (white shrimp about 6cm long) is a regional speciality. **Shiroebi-tei** (白えび亭; ☑432-7575; mains ¥730-2200; ☺10am-8pm) and its *shiroebi ten-don* (*shiroebi tempura* over rice; ¥730), on the 3rd floor of Toyama Station, may be workmanlike, but locals swear by it.

Daily flights operate between Toyama and major Japanese cities, with less-frequent flights to Seoul and Shanghai.

The JR Takayama line runs south to Takayama (*tokkyū*, ¥3080, 90 minutes; *futsū*, ¥1620, two hours) and Nagoya (*tokkyū*, ¥8080, four hours). JR's Hokuriku line runs west to Kanazawa (*tokkyū*, ¥2410, 35 minutes; *futsū*, ¥950, 60 minutes), Kyoto (*tokkyū*, ¥7560, three hours) and Osaka (¥8290, 3½ hours); and northeast to Naoetsu (¥3980, 1¼ hours) and Niigata (¥6930, three hours).

Tateyama-Kurobe Alpine Route
立山黒部アルペンルート

This popular seasonal 90km route connects Toyama with Shinano-ōmachi in Nagano-ken via a sacred mountain, a deep gorge, a boiling-hot spring and glory-hallelujah mountain scenery. It is divided into nine sections with different modes of transport: train, ropeway, cable car, bus, trolley bus and your own two feet. Travel is possible in either direction; instructions here are from Toyama. The website www.alpen-route.com/ english/index.html has details. Avoid heavy luggage because there are many steps en route; it's best to courier your bags to your hotel on the other end.

The fare for the entire route is ¥10,560/17,730 one way/return; individual tickets are available. The route can be completed in under six hours one way, although you'll probably want to stop en route; some visitors find that a trip as far as Murodō, the route's highest point, is sufficient (¥6530 return). The route is open from mid-April to mid-November. During peak season (August to October), transport and accommodation reservations are strongly advised.

From Toyama Station take the chug-a-lug regional Chitetsu line (¥1170, one hour) through rural scenery to **Tateyama** (立山; 475m). There are plenty of ryokan in Tateyama if you make an early start or late finish.

From Tateyama, take the cable car (¥700, seven minutes) to **Bijodaira** (美女平) and then the bus (¥1660, 50 minutes) via the spectacular alpine plateau of Midagahara Kōgen to **Murodō** (室堂; 2450m). You can break the trip at Midagahara and do the 15-minute walk to see **Tateyama caldera** (立山カルデラ), the largest nonactive crater in Japan. The upper part of the plateau is often covered with deep snow until late into the summer; the road is kept clear by piling up the snow to form a virtual tunnel (great fun to drive through; for bus tours see the website earlier).

Murodō's beauty has been somewhat spoilt by a monstrous bus station, but short hikes take you back to nature. Just 10 minutes' walk north is the pond **Mikuri-ga-ike** (みくりが池), home to an inn of the same name that houses a small restaurant and Japan's highest **onsen** (adult/child ¥600/400; ☺9am-4pm). Twenty minutes further on is **Jigokudani Onsen** (Hell Valley Hot Springs): no bathing here, the waters are boiling! To the east, you can hike for about two hours – including a very steep final section – to the peak of **O-yama** (推山; 3003m) for an astounding panorama. Keen long-distance hikers with several days or a week to spare can continue south to Kamikōchi (p199).

Continuing on the route from Murodō, there's a bus ride (¥2100, 10 minutes) via a tunnel dug through Tateyama to **Daikanbō** (大観峰), where you can pause to admire the view before taking the cable car (¥1260, seven minutes) to Kurobe-daira, where another cable car whisks you down (¥840, five minutes) to Kurobeko beside the vast **Kurobe Dam** (黒部ダム).

There's a 15-minute walk from Kurobeko to the dam, where you can descend to the water for a cruise, or climb up to a lookout point, before taking the trolley bus to **Ogizawa** (扇沢; ¥1260, 16 minutes). From here, a bus ride (¥1330, 40 minutes) takes you down to Shinano-ōmachi Station (712m). From here there are frequent trains to Matsumoto (one hour), from where you can connect with trains for Tokyo, Nagoya and Nagano.

ISHIKAWA PREFECTURE

Ishikawa Prefecture (石川県; Ishikawa-ken), made up of the former Kaga and Noto fiefs, offers a blend of cultural and historical sights and natural beauty. Kanazawa, the Kaga capital and power base of the feudal Maeda clan, boasts traditional architecture and one of Japan's most famous gardens. To the north, the peninsula, Noto-hantō, has sweeping seascapes and quiet fishing villages. Hakusan National Park, near the southern tip of the prefecture, offers great hiking.

You can find good overviews at www.hot-ishikawa.jp.

Kanazawa 金沢

📞076 / POP 459,000

Kanazawa's wealth of cultural attractions makes it a highlight for visitors to Hokuriku. It is most famed for Kenroku-en, the fine former castle garden that dates from the 17th century. The experience is rounded out by handsome streetscapes of the former geisha and samurai districts, attractive temples and a great number of museums for a city of its size.

The city's main sights can be seen in a leisurely two days, and side trips to Noto-hantō are recommended.

History

Kanazawa means 'golden marsh', which is appropriate given its history. During the 15th century, Kanazawa was under the control of an autonomous Buddhist government, which was ousted in 1583 by Maeda Toshiie, head of the powerful Maeda clan of retainers to the shōgun.

Three centuries of bountiful rice production made the Kaga region Japan's wealthiest; it was known as Kaga-Hyaku-Man-Goku for the million *koku* (about five million bushels) of rice produced annually. Wealth allowed the Maeda to patronise cultural and artistic pursuits (see the box, p230), and today Kanazawa is one of Japan's key cultural centres. During WWII, the absence of military targets spared Kanazawa from destruction, preserving its historical and cultural sites, although it is an undeniably modern city with its share of functional (and some fanciful) contemporary architecture.

Sights & Activities

The site of the former Kanazawa-jō (Kanazawa Castle) and its gardens, including Kenroku-en, occupy the centre of town. The Katamachi district is a commercial and business hub. The Nagamachi samurai district is a short walk west, and the picturesque Higashi Chaya-gai (east geisha district) is northeast of the castle.

Kanazawa's labyrinthine layout befits its castle-town past, but bus service makes it easy to get from the train station to the main sightseeing districts, which can then be covered on foot.

The following information is arranged in geographical order, and can be used as a walking tour. If time is limited, must-sees are Kenroku-en, the 21st Century Museum of Contemporary Art, the Nagamachi and Higashi Chaya-gai districts and Ōmichō Market.

Nagamachi District   NEIGHBOURHOOD

(長町) Once inhabited by samurai, this attractive, well-preserved district (Nagamachi Buke Yashiki) framed by two canals features winding streets lined with tile-roofed mud walls. **Nomura Samurai House** (武家屋敷跡 野村家; 1-3-32 Nagamachi; adult/child/student ¥500/250/400; ☉8.30am-5.30pm Apr-Sep, to 4.30pm Oct-Mar), though partly transplanted from outside Kanazawa, is worth a visit for its decorative garden.

Towards Sai-gawa, **Shinise Kinenkan** (金沢市老舗記念館; 2-2-45 Nagamachi; adult/child ¥100/free; ☉9.30am-5pm) offers a peek at a former pharmacy and, upstairs, a moderate assortment of local traditional products. If the flowering tree made entirely of candy gives you a sweet tooth, slake it at *wagashi* (Japanese sweet) shops. **Tarō** (たろう; 📞223-2838; 1-3-32 Nagamachi; ☉8.30am-5.30pm), near the Nomura Samurai House, makes unusual flavours of *yōkan* (bean-paste gelatin) – our

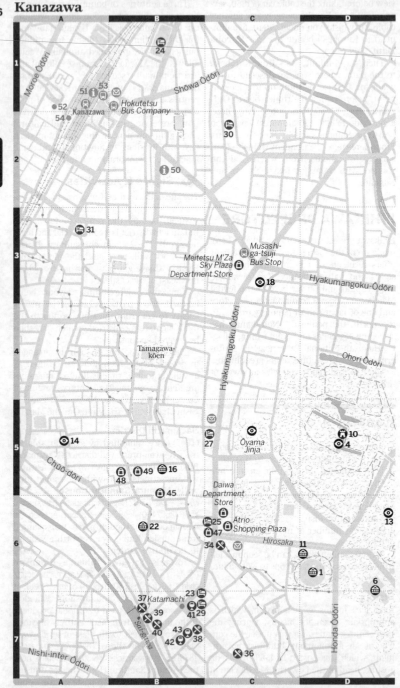

Moroe Ōdōri

1

24

Shōwa Ōdōri

51 53
52 Kanazawa
54
Hokutetsu Bus Company

30

2

50

31

3

Meitetsu M'Za Sky Plaza Department Store

Musashi-ga-tsuji Bus Stop

Hyakumangoku-Ōdōri

18

Tamagawa-kōen

4

Hyakumangoku Ōdōri

Ōhori Ōdōri

5

14

Chūō-dōri

27

Ōyama Jinja

10
4

48 49 16

45

Daiwa Department Store

22

13

25 Atrio Shopping Plaza
47

34

Hirosaka

11

6

1

6

Katamachi
37
39
40
43
42 38
23
41 29

Saigawa

36

7

Nishi-inter Ōdōri

Honda Ōdōri

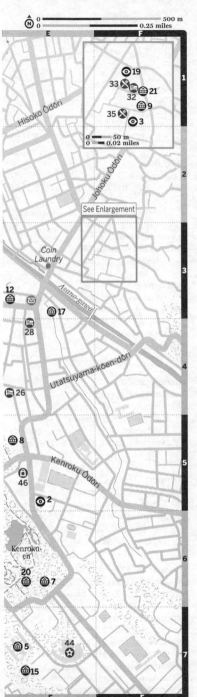

favourite is choco. **Murakami** (村上; ☎264-4223; 2-3-32 Nagamachi; ☺8.30am-5pm), across the canal, makes *fukusamochi* (red-bean paste and pounded rice in a crêpe) and *kakiho* (*kinako,* ie soybean flour, rolled in *kurogoma,* which are black sesame seeds).

In a nonhistoric building just outside Nagamachi (about 250m from the Nomura Samurai House), **Nagamachi Yūzen-kan** (長町友禅館; 2-6-16 Nagamachi; admission ¥350; ☺9am-noon & 1-4.30pm Fri-Wed) displays some splendid examples of *Kaga yūzen* kimono-dyeing and demonstrates the process. Enquire ahead about trying the silk-dyeing process yourself (¥4000).

21st Century Museum of Contemporary Art
MUSEUM

(金沢21世紀美術館; www.kanazawa21.jp; 1-2-1 Hirosaka; permanent collection adult/child ¥350/free; ☺10am-6pm Tue-Thu & Sun, to 8pm Fri & Sat) Designed by the acclaimed Tokyo architecture firm SANAA, this ultramodern museum opened in late 2004 and instantly became an 'it' building. A low-slung glass cylinder, 113m in diameter, forms the perimeter, and inside galleries and auditoria are arranged like boxes on a tray. Nongallery portions of the building are open daily from 9am to 10pm.

Oh yes, there's art too: temporary exhibits by leading contemporary artists from Japan and abroad, plus occasional music and dance performances. Check the website for events; admission charges may increase up to ¥1000 during special exhibitions.

Kanazawa Noh Museum
MUSEUM

(金沢能楽美術館; 1-2-25 Hirosaka; adult/child ¥300/free; ☺10am-6pm Tue-Sun) This modern museum gives a basic introduction to the mysterious art form of nō, the world's oldest continually performed art, with special emphasis on Kaga-style performance. Changing exhibits (costumes, masks etc) complement the ground floor, which is marked with an outline of a nō stage. Enthusiasts should also visit the Ishikawa Prefectural Nō Theatre (p233).

Kanazawa Castle Park
HISTORICAL BUILDING

(金沢城公園; 1-1 Marunouchi; grounds/Bldg free/¥300; ☺grounds 5am-6pm Mar-15 Oct, 6am-4.30pm 16 Oct-Feb, castle 9am-4.30pm) Originally built in 1580, Kanazawa-jō housed the Maeda clan for 14 generations; this massive structure was called the castle of 1000 tatami. That castle was destroyed by fire, but some reconstruction has taken place inside

Kanazawa

its moated walls, now rechristened Kanazawa Castle Park (Kanazawa-jō Kōen). The elegant gate **Ishikawa-mon** (石川門), rebuilt in 1788, provides a dramatic entry from Kenroku-en; holes in its turret were designed for *ishi-otoshi* (hurling rocks at invaders). Two additional buildings, the **Hishi-yagura** (菱櫓; diamond-shaped turret) and **Gojikken-Nagaya** (五十間長屋; armoury), were reconstructed in 2001, offering a glimpse of the castle's unique wood-frame construction.

Kenroku-en GARDEN
(兼六園; 1-1 Marunouchi; adult/child ¥300/100; ⊙7am-6pm Mar-15 Oct, 8am-4.30pm 16 Oct-Feb) The star attraction of Kanazawa, Kenroku-en is ranked as one of the great gardens of the Edo period and one of the top three gardens in Japan (the other two are Kairaku-en in Mito, and Kōraku-en in Okayama).

The name (*kenroku* means 'combined six') refers to a renowned garden from

Sung-dynasty China that required six attributes for perfection: seclusion, spaciousness, artificiality, antiquity, abundant water and broad views (on clear days you can see to the Sea of Japan). In 1676 Kenroku-en started as the garden of an outer villa of Kanazawa-jō, but later it was enlarged to serve the castle itself, reaching completion in the early 19th century; the garden opened to the public in 1871. In winter the branches of Kenroku-en's trees are famously suspended with ropes via a post at each tree's centre, forming elegant conical shapes that protect the trees from breaking under Kanazawa's heavy snows. In spring, irises turn Kenroku-en's waterways into rivers of purple.

Kenroku-en is certainly attractive, but enormous crowds can diminish its intimacy. Visit at opening time and you'll have the place to yourself.

Seison-kaku

(成巽閣; ☎221-0580; 2-1 Dewa-machi; adult/student ¥700/300; ☺9am-5pm Thu-Tue) Inside the park, Seison-kaku is a retirement villa built by a Maeda lord for his mother in 1863. Elegant chambers named for trees and animals are filled with furniture, clothing and furnishings. A detailed English-language pamphlet is available.

Ishikawa Prefectural Museum of Traditional Products & Crafts   MUSEUM

(石川県立伝統産業工芸館; 2-1 Kenroku-machi; adult/child ¥250/100; ☺9am-5pm, closed 3rd Thu of month Apr-Nov, closed Thu Dec-Mar) Behind Seison-kaku, this museum is not flashy but offers fine displays of over 20 regional crafts. Pick up the free English-language headphone guide.

Kanazawa Phonograph Museum   MUSEUM

(金沢蓄音器館; 2-11-21 Owari-chō; admission ¥300; ☺10am-5pm) Audio buffs will dig this museum of old-time phonographs (aka gramophones) and SP records. There are daily phonograph demonstrations at 11am, 2pm and 4pm.

Ishikawa Prefectural Art Museum   MUSEUM

(石川県立美術館; 2-1 Dewa-machi; adult/child ¥350/free; ☺9.30am-5pm) This museum specialises in antique exhibitions of traditional arts, with special emphasis on colourful Kutani porcelain, Japanese painting and *Kaga yūzen* (silk-dyed) fabrics and costumes. Admission prices are higher during special exhibitions.

Nakamura Memorial Museum   MUSEUM

(中村記念美術館; 3-2-29 Honda-machi; adult/child ¥300/free; ☺9.30am-5pm) Rotating exhibitions from the 600-piece collection of this museum usually include *chanoyu* (tea ceremony) utensils, calligraphy and traditional crafts from the collection of a wealthy sake brewer, Nakamura Eishun. You can enjoy a bowl of powdered tea for ¥100. Reached via a narrow flight of steps below the Ishikawa Prefectural Art Museum.

Honda Museum   MUSEUM

(本多蔵品館; 3-1 Dewa-machi; admission ¥500; ☺9am-5pm daily Mar-Oct, Fri-Wed Nov-Feb) The Honda family were chief retainers to the Maeda clan, and this museum exhibits the family collection of armour, household utensils and works of art. The bulletproof coat and the family vase are particularly interesting, and there's a detailed catalogue in English.

Gyokusen-en   GARDEN

(玉泉園; 1-1 Marunouchi; adult/child ¥500/350; ☺9am-4pm Mar–mid-Nov) For more intimacy and fewer crowds than Kenroku-en, this Edo-period garden rises up a steep slope. Enjoy a cup of tea here for an additional ¥700, while contemplating the tranquil setting.

Ōhi Pottery Museum   MUSEUM

(大樋美術館; Hashiba-chō; adult/child ¥700/500; ☺9am-5pm) This museum was established by the Chōzaemon family, now in its 10th generation. The first Chōzaemon developed this style in nearby Ōhi village, using a special slow-fired amber glaze, specifically for use in *chanoyu*.

Higashi chaya-gai   NEIGHBOURHOOD

(東茶屋街) North of the Ōhi Pottery Museum and across Asano-gawa, Higashi chaya-gai (Higashi Geisha District) is an enclave of narrow streets that was established early in the 19th century as a centre for geisha to entertain wealthy patrons. The slatted wooden facades of the geisha houses are romantically preserved.

One famous, traditional former geisha house is **Shima** (志摩; 1-13-21 Higashiyama; adult/child ¥400/300; ☺9am-6pm), dating from 1820. Note the case of elaborate combs and *shamisen* (three-stringed traditional instrument) picks. Across the street, **Kaikarō** (懐華樓; 1-14-8 Higashiyama; admission ¥700; ☺9am-5pm) is an early-19th-century geisha house refinished with contemporary fittings and art, including a red lacquered staircase.

GET LACQUERED, GO TO POT, DYE & BE GILDED

Much as the Medici family was the patron of some of the great artists of the Italian Renaissance, during the Edo period Kanazawa's ruling Maeda family fuelled the growth of important crafts. Many of these crafts are still practised today.

Kanazawa & Wajima Lacquerware

This luminous black lacquerware starts with hard, durable wood, such as *keyaki* (zelkova), or Japanese chestnut, finely carved with any defects removed or filled. Many layers of undercoating and middle coating are applied, each rubbed down with *washi* (Japanese paper) before the next application. Before the final topcoat, decoration is applied through *maki-e* (painting) or gilding. With the last coat of lacquer, artists must take great care that dust does not settle on the final product.

Ōhi Pottery

An aesthetic central to the tea ceremony is *wabi-sabi:* introspective, humble and understated, yet profound and prepared with great thought. The deliberately simple, almost primitive designs, rough surfaces, irregular shapes and monochromatic glazes of Ōhi pottery have long been favoured by tea practitioners. The same family, with the professional name Chōzaemon, has been keeper of the Ōhi tradition since the early Edo period.

Kutani Porcelain

Known for elegant shapes, graceful designs and bold hues of red, blue, yellow, purple and green, this underglaze ware could hardly be more different from Ōhi pottery. It is said to date back to the early Edo period, and shares design characteristics with Chinese porcelain and Japanese Imari ware. Typical motifs include birds, flowers, trees and landscapes.

Kaga Yūzen Silk Dyeing

This kimono-dyeing technique is characterised by sharp colours (red, ochre, green, indigo and purple) and realistic depictions of nature, such as flower petals that have begun to brown around the edges. It's highly specialised, labour-intensive work. A pattern is drawn on the fabric with grey-blue ink from spiderwort flowers and the lines are traced over with rice paste using a cone like a fine pastry tube; this keeps the dyes from running as they are painted onto the silk. The colours are filled in and coated with more rice paste and then the entire sheet of silk is dyed with the kimono's background colour. Only then is the fabric rinsed clean (traditionally in a river) and steamed to fix the colours. White lines between the elements, where the initial spiderwort ink has washed away, are a characteristic of *Kaga yūzen*. To dye the fabric for one kimono takes about three months.

Gold Leaf

It starts with a lump of pure gold the size of a ¥10 coin, which is rolled to the size of a tatami mat, as little as 0.0001mm thick. The gold leaf is cut into squares of 10.9cm – the size used for mounting on walls, murals or paintings – or then cut again for gilding on lacquerware or pottery. Tiny particles find their way into tea, sweets and hand lotion. Kanazawa makes over 98% of Japan's gold leaf.

The **Sakuda Gold Leaf Company** (金銀箔工芸さくだ; 1-3-27 Higashiyama; admission free; ◷9am-6pm) is a good place to observe the *kinpaku* (gold leaf) process and pick up some gilded souvenirs (including pottery, lacquerware and, er, golf balls). The tea served here contains flecks of gold leaf, meant to be good for rheumatism. Even the walls of the loos are lined with gold and platinum.

On most nights you can visit the local *sentō*, **Higashi-yu** (東湯; 1-13-2 Higashiyama; admission ¥370; ◷2pm-12.30am Mon & Wed-Sat, 1pm-12.30am Sun).

Teramachi District   NEIGHBOURHOOD

(寺町) This hilly neighbourhood across Sai-gawa, southwest of the centre, was established as a first line of defence and contains dozens of temples. **Myōryū-ji** (妙立寺; Ninja-dera; ☑241-0888; 1-2-12 Nomachi; admission ¥800; ⊙9am-4.30pm Mar-Nov, to 4pm Dec-Feb, reservations required) is a five-minute walk from the river. Completed in 1643, it was designed as a hideout in case of attack, and contains hidden stairways, escape routes, secret chambers, concealed tunnels and trick doors. The popular name refers to the temple's connection with ninja. Admission is by tour only – it's in Japanese but visual enough. Take Minami Ō-dōri across the river, take a left at the first major intersection, then the first right.

Nearby, **Kutani Kosen Gama Kiln** (九谷光仙窯; 5-3-3 Nomachi; admission free; ⊙9am-5pm) is a must for pottery lovers. Short tours give a glimpse of the process and the history of this fine craft. Try decorating porcelain yourself from ¥1050.

Ōmichō Market   MARKET

(近江町市場; 35 Ōmichō; ⊙9am-5pm) A warren of several hundred shops and restaurants, many of which specialise in seafood, this market bustles all day and is a great place for a break from sightseeing and to watch everyday people in action. Ōmichō functions like the outer market of Tokyo's Tsukiji Fish Market, but thanks to a recent makeover it's a lot more orderly and polished. It's between Katamachi district and Kanazawa Station. The nearest bus stop is Musashi-ga-tsuji.

🎎 Festivals & Events

Kagatobi Dezomeshiki   CULTURAL

In early January, scantily clad firemen brave the cold, imbibe sake and demonstrate ancient fire-fighting skills on ladders.

Asano-gawa Enyūkai   MUSIC

Performances of traditional Japanese dance and music are held on the banks of the Asano-gawa during the second weekend of April.

Hyakumangoku Matsuri   PARADE

In early June, Kanazawa's main annual festival commemorates the first time the region's rice production hit one million *koku* (around 150,000 tonnes). There's a parade of townsfolk in 16th-century costumes, *takigi nō* (torch-lit performances of nō drama), *tōrō nagashi* (lanterns floated down the river at dusk) and a special *chanoyu;* at Kenroku-en.

🏆 Pongyi   GUESTHOUSE $

(ポンギー; ☑225-7369; www.pongyi.com; 2-22 Rokumai-machi; dm, r per person from ¥2600; @) Run by a friendly Japanese man who did a stint in Southeast Asia as a monk, Pongyi is a charmingly renovated old shop along a mini canal. Cosy dorm beds are located in the attached vintage *kura* warehouse. The owner loves to involve guests in local festivals and traditions. It's five minutes from Kanazawa Station.

Yōgetsu   MINSHUKU $

(陽月; ☑252-0497; 1-13-22 Higashiyama; r per person with/without breakfast ¥5000/4500) This beautifully renovated 200-year-old geisha teahouse has only three rooms and features a circular *goemonburo* bath. It's located right in the picturesque Higashi-chaya district. No English is spoken.

Namaste   GUESTHOUSE $

(ナマステ; ☑255-1057; www.guesthouse-namaste.com; 6-14 Kasaichi-machi; dm/tw/tr ¥2500/5200/8500; @) A veteran traveler is host in this tranquil, renovated home near Kanazawa Station. Rooms are clean and simple, and there's a living room off the common kitchen.

Kanazawa Excel Hotel Tokyū   HOTEL $$$

(金沢エクセルホテル東急; ☑231-2411; www.tokyuhotels.co.jp; 2-1-1 Kōrinbo; s/d/tw from ¥14,500/24,200/22,500; ❄@) At 15 storeys (try for a room with views across the city to Hakusan National Park), Kanazawa city's most stylish hotel has sleek rooms, a slightly '80s retro design and plenty of amenities (including CNN on TV). It's also a winner for its central location in the heart of Katamachi.

Murataya Ryokan   RYOKAN $

(村田屋; ☑263-0455; http://murataya-ryokan.com; fax 263-0456; 1-5-2 Katamachi; s/tw ¥4700/9000; ❄@) Eleven well-kept rooms with friendly hosts await at this rather retro travellers' favourite in Katamachi, convenient to restaurants and nightlife; there's an English-language map of local establishments.

Matsumoto   RYOKAN $$$

(☑221-0302; fax 221-0303; 1-7-2 Owari-chō; r per person with 2 meals ¥25,000) This upscale inn bills itself as a *ryōri* (cuisine) ryokan; expect local dishes such as *nabe* (hot-pot). Huge rooms have private bathrooms. It's near the intersection of Hyakumangoku-ōdōri and Jūhoku-dōri, down a narrow street across from the post office. No English is spoken.

APA Hotel Kanazawa Chūō
HOTEL $$

(アパホテル金沢中央; ☎235-2111; www .apahotel.com; 1-5-24 Katamachi; s/d/tw from ¥8000/11,000/15,000; 🖨@) Towering above Katamachi, this 500-plus-room business hotel offers nicely appointed if cramped rooms. Guests have use of indoor and outdoor onsen baths on the 14th floor. Pick up an origami crane.

Hotel Dormy Inn Kanazawa
HOTEL $$

(ドーミーイン金沢; ☎263-9888; fax 263-9312; www.hotespa.net/hotels/kanazawa; 2-25 Horikawa-shinmachi; s/d/tw ¥8500/12,000/15,000; 🖨@) This brand-new hotel steps from the station is filled with futuristic art. Most of its 304 rooms are singles and have an inner door to keep out extraneous noise. It has a naturium- and calcium-rich onsen *rotemburo* on the top floor, and a coin laundry.

Kanazawa New Grand Hotel Annex
HOTEL $$

(金沢ニューグランドホテルアネックス; ☎233-7000; fax 265-6655; www.new-grand.co.jp, in Japanese; 1-50 Takaoka-machi; s/d & tw from ¥9817/18,480; 🖨@) Near both Nagamachi and Katamachi, this business hotel has nice-sized, up-to-date rooms. It's next door to the New Grand main building; you can reserve at either, but the Annex is newer and more polished.

Kanazawa Hakuchōrō Hotel
HOTEL $$$

(金沢白鳥路ホテル; ☎222-1212; www.hakucho ro.com; 6-3 Marunouchi; s/tw with breakfast from ¥12,000/20,000; 🖨📶) East meets West with room design (and dimensions) that could be from France or Germany and only-in-Japan touches like sashes across the beds and display cases of local crafts. Its out-of-the-way location means lots of quiet. Common onsen baths are available.

✗ Eating

Seafood is the staple of Kanazawa's *Kaga ryōri* (Kaga cuisine); even the most humble train-station *bentō* usually features some type of fish. *Oshi-zushi*, a thin layer of fish pressed atop vinegared rice, is said to be the precursor to modern sushi. Another favourite is *jibuni*, which is flour-coated duck or chicken stewed with shiitake and green vegetables. The Katamachi district and Ōmichō market are both great for browsing, packed with locals and visitors alike. Many restaurants have English menus available.

TOP CHOICE Hotaruya
KAISEKI $$

(蛍屋; ☎251-8585; 1-13-24 Higashiyama; lunch/ dinner courses from ¥3675/6300) To splurge on *Kaga ryōri* and step back in time, visit this shop in Higashi Chaya-gai; it's on the corner in a little square. You'll be rewarded with wood-beam and tatami room surroundings, and understated, standard-setting course meals. For lunch, try the *hanamachi kaiseki* set, ¥6300.

Jiyūken
SHOKUDŌ $

(自由軒; ☎252-1996; 1-6-6 Higashiyama; most mains ¥785-2990; ⊙closed Tue & 3rd Wed of month;📖) By Higashi Chaya-gai, this simple but welcoming spot has been serving *yō-shoku* (Japanese takes on Western cuisine; eg beef stew, grilled chicken, omelettes) since 1909. The *teishoku* is a steal at ¥920. There are plastic models in the window. Look for the stone front.

Legian
ASIAN $

(レギャン; ☎262-6510; 2-31-30 Katamachi; most dishes ¥600-1000; ⊙dinner; 🖉📖) For popular, authentic Indonesian cuisine head to this tiny spot by the river. Staff make annual trips to Indonesia to bone up on technique, and are happy to make vegetarian versions.

Oden Miyuki Honten
ODEN $

(三幸本店; ☎222-6117; 1-10-3 Katamachi; oden ¥100-400, most other dishes ¥400-600; ⊙dinner Mon-Sat) For fish in another form (ground and pressed into cakes and served in broth), *oden* is very satisfying, especially on chilly nights. Some of the staff are English-speaking.

Osteria del Campagne
ITALIAN $

(オステリアデルカンパーニュ; ☎261-2156; 2-31-33 Katamachi; mains ¥650-1950, set menus from ¥2500; ⊙dinner Mon-Sat) This cosy, quietly fashionable Italian bistro serves lovely set menus, including house-made focaccia, salads, pastas and desserts, plus hors d'oeuvres you can eat with chopsticks. It has an English menu and friendly, professional staff.

Kōtatsu
OKONOMIYAKI $

(やきやき香立; ☎261-6310; 32-1 Daiku-machi; mains ¥700-900; ⊙dinner Mon-Sat; 📖) More sophisticated than your everyday *okonomiyaki* place, Kōtatsu has a dark atmosphere and an assortment of sake and *shōchū*, and will cook your *okonomiyaki* for you. Salads are also available. It's beneath Arroz Spanish restaurant; there's a bubble motif on the brown wall outside.

Janome-sushi Honten   SUSHI $$
(蛇之目寿司本店; ☎231-0093; 1-1-12 Kōrinbō; mains ¥1200-3400, Kaga ryōri sets from ¥4000; ◷Thu-Tue) Highly regarded for sashimi and Kaga cuisine. One of our Japanese friends says that when he eats here, he knows he's really in Kanazawa. It's across a little stream from Siena clothing store.

Tamazushi   SUSHI $$
(玉寿司; ☎221-2644; 2-14-9 Katamachi; mains ¥1300-3300; ◷dinner Mon-Sat) Down near Sai-gawa in Katamachi, this classic sushi counter, backed by a painting of a nō stage, is one of Kanazawa's best. No English is spoken, but there's a picture menu. It's a brown-white building on your right as you enter from the main street.

☕ Drinking

Most of Kanazawa's bars and clubs are holes-in-the-wall, jam-packed into high-rises in Katamachi. Some are straightforward bars, others are barely disguised girlie clubs. Here are some of the former. Weekdays can be slow, but weekends tend to hop. For a quieter scene, peek into the lovely little bars of Higashi Chaya-gai.

Polé Polé   BAR
(ポレポレ; 2-31-30 Katamachi) In the same building (and sharing the same owners) as Legian restaurant, this dark, grungy and friendly bar has been an institution for decades for *gaijin* and locals – look for the signatures of foreign exchange students. The narrow floor is littered with peanut shells (proceeds from peanut sales go to charity), and the reggae music is loud.

Pilsen   PUB
(ぴるぜん; 1-9-20 Katamachi; ◷Mon-Sat; ▣) Munich by the Katamachi Scramble, this German-style place serves lots of beers and a menu including sausages, pasta and omelettes.

Baby Rick   BAR
(ベイビーリック; 1-5-20 Katamachi) This classy little shot bar has a billiard table, jazz and whisky (the good kind), and you can get dishes like spaghetti carbonara and homemade pizzas. It's in the basement level beneath Shidax karaoke. There's a ¥500 cover after 10pm.

I no Ichiban   IZAKAYA
(いの一番; 1-9-20 Katamachi) This slender *izakaya* serves plenty of cocktails and has ambience in spades – so much so that it's almost unrecognisable from the street. Look for the wood-panel screen and tiny stand of bamboo.

☆ Entertainment

Nō theatre is alive and well in Kanazawa, and performances are held weekly during summer at **Ishikawa Prefectural Nō Theatre** (石川県立能楽堂; ☎264-2598; 3-1 Dewamachi; admission free, performance tickets extra; ◷9am-4.30pm Tue-Sun).

🛍 Shopping

The Hirosaka shopping street, between Kōrinbō 109 (香林坊 109) department store and Kenroku-en, has some upmarket craft shops on its south side; department stores carry crafts too. At the Sakuda Gold Leaf Company (p230) you can find mirrors, chopstick rests and Buddhist prayer bells among many objects covered in gold leaf.

Kankō Bussankan   CRAFTS
(石川県観光物産館; Ishikawa Local Products Shop) For a quick view of Kanazawa crafts, you can visit Kankō Bussankan.

Kanazawa Kutani Museum   CERAMIC WARE
(金沢九谷ミュウジアム) On a corner in the Nagamachi samurai district in a wonderful old house with a garden, this is a lovely place if a bit of a misnomer; it's really a shop selling mostly high-end ceramic ware with a small museum of historic Kutani ware in the old storehouse and a cafe.

Libro Books   BOOKSHOP
(リブロ) Located downstairs from Ishikawa Prefectural International Exchange Centre (石川県国際交流センター), Libro sells English-language books and magazines.

ⓘ Information

There are post offices in Katamachi and in Kanazawa Station, and several coin-operated laundries, including in Higashi Chaya-gai and Katamachi. For information on the city, visit www.city.kanazawa.ishikawa.jp.

Ishikawa Foundation for International Exchange (☎262-5931; www.ifie.or.jp; 1-5-3 Honmachi; ◷9am-8pm Mon-Fri, to 5pm Sat & Sun) Offers information, a library, satellite-TV news and free internet access. It's on the 3rd floor of the Rifare building, a few minutes' walk southeast of the train station.

Kanazawa Goodwill Guide Network (KGGN; ☎232-3933; ◷10am-6pm) Inside the tourist information office at Kanazawa Station, it provides helpful English-language information and can help book hotels. Two weeks' notice is requested for free guiding in English.

Kanazawa tourist information office (石川県金沢観光情報センター; ☑232-6200; 1 Hiro-oka-machi; ☉9am-7pm) Friendly office inside Kanazawa Station. Pick up the bilingual map *Kanazawa Japan* (with details of sights, crafts and local specialities) and the English-language *Eye on Kanazawa*, which focuses on restaurants.

ⓘ Getting There & Away

Air

Nearby **Komatsu airport** (KMQ; www.komatsuairport.jp) has air connections with major Japanese cities, as well as Seoul, Shanghai and Taipei.

Bus

JR Highway Bus (☑234-0111; ☉reservations 9am-7pm) operates express buses from in front of Kanazawa Station's east exit, to Tokyo (¥7840, Ikebukuro seven hours, Shinjuku 7½ hours) and Kyoto (¥4060, 4¼ hours). **Hokutetsu Bus** (北陸鉄道予約センター; ☑234-0123; ☉reservations 8am-7pm) serves Nagoya (¥4060, four hours).

Train

The JR Hokuriku line links Kanazawa with Fukui (*tokkyū*, ¥2940, 50 minutes; *futsū*, ¥1280, 1½ hours), Kyoto (*tokkyū*, ¥6710, 2¼ hours), Osaka (*tokkyū*, ¥7440, 2¾ hours) and Toyama (*tokkyū*, ¥2810, 35 minutes), with connections to Takayama (total ¥5840, additional 90 minutes). From Tokyo take the Jōetsu *shinkansen* and change at Echigo-Yuzawa in Northern Honshū (¥12,710, four hours).

ⓘ Getting Around

Airport buses (¥1100, 40 minutes) are timed to aeroplane departures and arrivals, leaving from stop 6 in front of Kanazawa Station's east exit. Some buses also stop at Katamachi and Kōrinbō 109 department store but take one hour to reach the airport.

Hire bikes from **JR Kanazawa Station Rent-a-Cycle** (駅レンタサイクル; ☑261-1721; per hr/day ¥200/1200; ☉8am-8.30pm) – take an immediate left from Kanazawa Station's west exit – and **Hokutetsu Bicycle Rental** (北鉄レンタルサイクル; ☑263-0919; per 4hr/day ¥630/1050; ☉8am-5.30pm), by stop 4 out the west exit.

Any bus from station stop 7, 8 or 9 will take you to the city centre (¥200, day pass ¥900). The Kanazawa Loop Bus (single ride/day pass ¥200/500, every 15 minutes from 8.30am to 6pm) circles the major tourist attractions in 45 minutes. On Saturday, Sunday and holidays, the Machi-bus goes to Kōrinbō for ¥100.

Cars can be hired at rental agencies around the station.

Noto Peninsula   能登半島

With rugged seascapes, traditional rural life, fresh seafood and a light diet of cultural sights, Noto peninsula (Noto-hantō) atop Ishikawa-ken is a good escape from the Hokuriku region's urban sprawl. The lacquer-making town of Wajima is the hub of the rugged north, known as Oku-Noto, and the best place to stay overnight. Famous products include *Wajima-nuri* lacquerware, renowned for its durability and rich colours, Suzu-style pottery and locally harvested sea salt and *iwanori* seaweed. Check Kanazawa's **tourist information office** (☑076-232-6200) for the latest Noto-Hantō maps.

ⓘ Getting There & Around

In the centre of Oku-Noto, **Noto airport** connects the peninsula with Tokyo. **Furusato Taxi** (☑0768-22-7411) is a van service to locations around the peninsula. Fares start at ¥700 to nearby communities including Wajima (about 30 minutes).

Although there are trains, most sights can be reached by road only. For the west Noto coast, get off the JR Nanao Line at Hakui (*tokkyū*, ¥1370; *futsū*, ¥740), and connect to buses. For Oku-Noto, trains continue to Wakura Onsen, connecting to less frequent buses. **Hokutetsu** (☑076-234-0123) runs buses between Kanazawa and Wajima (¥2200, two hours, 10 daily).

Driving is the best way to see the peninsula. The 83km Noto Yūryo (能登有料; Noto Toll Rd) speeds you as far as Anamizu (toll ¥1180). Noto's mostly flat west coast also appeals to cyclists. However, cycling is not recommended on the Noto-kongō coast and east because of steep, blind curves.

WEST NOTO COAST
☑0767

During the Edo period, the Kita family administered over 200 villages from **Kita-ke** (喜多家; ☑28-2546; adult/child ¥500/200; ☉8.30am-5pm Apr-Oct, to 4pm Nov-Mar), at the pivotal crossroads of the Kaga, Etchū and Noto fiefs. Inside this splendid, sprawling home and adjacent museum, still in the hands of the same family (after about 400 years), are displays of weapons, ceramics, farming tools, fine and folk art, and documents. The garden has been called the Moss Temple of Noto.

Kita-ke is about 1km from the Komedashi exit on the Noto Toll Rd. By train, take the JR Nanao line to Menden Station; it's about 20 minutes' walk.

At times the 8km **Chirihama Nagisa Driveway** (千里浜なぎさドライブウエイ) in the Chirihama district of Hakui City (羽咋), resembles an early Daytona, as buses, motorcycles and cars roar past the breakers. Hakui is Noto's western transit hub, with frequent train connections to Kanazawa and less frequent bus connections along Noto's west coast.

Founded in 1294 by Nichizō, a disciple of Nichiren, the imposing **Myōjō-ji** (妙成寺; ☑27-1226; admission ¥500; ☉8am-5pm Apr-Oct, to 4.30pm Nov-Mar) remains an important temple for the sect. The grounds comprise many buildings, including 10 Important Cultural Properties, notably the strikingly elegant **Gojū-no-tō** (Five-Storeyed Pagoda). Pick up an English-language pamphlet.

The Togi-bound bus from Hakui Station can drop you at Myōjō-ji-guchi bus stop (¥420, 18 minutes); from here, it's under 10 minutes' walk.

NOTO-KONGŌ COAST AREA 能登金剛
☑0768

This rocky, cliff-lined shoreline extends for about 16km between Fukuura and Sekinohana, and is adorned with dramatic rock formations.

The manicured little town of Monzen, about 25km northeast of Ganmon, is home to majestic **Sōji-ji** (総持寺; ☑42-0005; fax 42-1002; adult/child ¥400/150; ☉8am-5pm), the temple established in 1321 as the head of the Sōtō school of Zen. After a fire damaged the buildings in 1898 the temple was restored, but it now functions as a branch temple; the main temple is in Yokohama. Sōji-ji welcomes visitors to experience one hour of *zazen* (seated meditation; ¥300, 9am to 3pm) and serves *shōjin-ryōri* (Buddhist vegetarian cuisine; ¥2500 to ¥3500). The temple also has accommodation for visitors (with two meals ¥6500; single women are prohibited). Reserve at least two days in advance.

Monzen is a bus hub with service to Kanazawa (¥2200, 2½ hours), Hakui (¥1510, 1½ hours) and Wajima (¥740, 35 minutes). For the temple, tell the driver 'Sōji-ji-mae'.

WAJIMA 輪島
☑0768 / POP 31,500

About 20km from Monzen, this fishing port on the north coast is the largest town in Oku-Noto and a historic centre for the production of *Wajima-nuri* (Wajima lacquerware) and, now, tourism. There's a prettily refurbished town centre and a lively morning market.

The **tourist information office** (☑22-1503; ☉8am-7pm) at the former Wajima train station (now called Michi-no-eki; 道の駅; still the bus station) provides English leaflets and maps, and staff can book accommodation. Limited English is spoken.

◉ Sights & Activities

Ishikawa Wajima Urushi Art Museum MUSEUM
(石川輪島漆芸美術館; ☑22-9788; adult/student ¥600/300; ☉9am-4.30pm) In the southwest corner of the town centre, this stately contemporary museum has a large, rotating collection of lacquerware in galleries on two floors; works are both Japanese and foreign, ancient and contemporary. It's about a 15-minute walk west of the train station. Phone ahead, as this museum closes between exhibitions.

Kiriko Kaikan MUSEUM
(キリコ会館; ☑22-7100; adult/child ¥600/350; ☉8am-5pm) A selection of the impressive illuminated lacquered floats used in the Wajima Taisai and other regional festivals is on display in this hall. Some of the floats are up to 15m tall. From Wajima Station, you can get there in 20 minutes on foot, or you can take the bus to Tsukada bus stop (¥150, six minutes).

✳ Festivals & Events

Gojinjō Daikō Nabune Matsuri DRUMMING
This festival culminating on 31 July features wild drumming by performers wearing demon masks and seaweed headgear.

Wajima Taisai PARADE
See Wajima's famous, towering, illuminated *kiriko* festival floats (late August).

🛏 Sleeping & Eating

Wajima has dozens of *minshuku* known for seafood meals worth staying in for. There are also some lovely restaurants by the harbour, though some close by early evening.

Tanaka RYOKAN **$$**
(たなか; ☑/fax 22-5155; www.oyado-tanaka.jp; 22-38 Kawai-machi; per person with meals from ¥8550; 🅿) This spotless 10-room inn has tatami-bed hybrid rooms, hot-spring baths (including a private-use *rotenburo*, extra charge), woodwork, and paper lanterns illuminating the wooden hallways. The *kaiseki* meals here feature local seafood and laquerware.

Fukasan MINSHUKU **$$**

(深三; ☎22-9933; fukasan@crux.ocn.ne.jp; r per person with meals ¥7950; ℗) By the harbour, this contemporary *minshuku* offers mood-lit rustic elegance, dark beams, high ceilings and an onsen.

Sodegahama Camping Ground CAMPGROUND **$**

(袖が浜キャンプ場; ☎23-1146; fax 23-1855; camp sites per person ¥1000) This camping ground is about 10 minutes west of town by bus. Take the local *noranke* bus (umi course, ¥100) or Nishiho bus (direction Zōza 雑座) to Sodegahama or hike for 20 minutes.

Madara-yakata SEAFOOD **$**

(まだら館; ☎22-3453; mains ¥800-2100; ☺lunch & dinner, closed irregularly) This restaurant serves local specialities, including *zosui* (rice hotpot), *yaki-zakana* (grilled fish) and seasonal seafood, surrounded by folk crafts. It's near the morning market street.

Shinpuku SEAFOOD **$$**

(伸幅; ☎22-8133; sushi per piece from ¥150, sets ¥1000-2500; ☺lunch & dinner, closed irregularly, mostly Wed) This tiny, assiduously local sushi shop serves fabulously fresh fish and seafood, and *iwanori* seaweed in the miso soup. Meals such as the *nigiri* set (¥1200)

Noto Peninsula

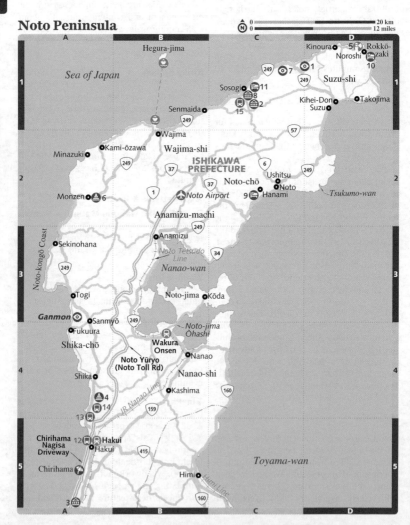

are a sure bet, while *asa-ichi-don* (¥2500) is a selection from the morning market over rice. It's on the main street, one block east of the Cosmo petrol station. There's a picture menu.

🛍 Shopping

Asa-ichi MARKET
(morning market; ☉8am–noon, closed 10th & 25th of month) This market is highly entertaining, though undeniably touristy. Some 200 fishwives ply their wares – seafood, crafts etc – with sass and humour that cuts across the language barrier. To find the market, walk north along the river from the Wajima Shikki Shiryōkan and turn right just before Iroha-bashi.

ℹ Getting There & Away

See p234 for information on Hokutetsu buses (☎22-2314) to Wajima. Buses to Monzen (¥740, 35 minutes) leave every one to two hours.

SUZU & NOTO-CHŌ 珠洲・能登町
☎0768
Heading east from central Wajima towards the end of the peninsula, you'll pass the famous slivered *dandan-batake* (rice terraces) at **Senmaida** (千枚田) before arriving in the coastal village of **Sosogi** (曽々木). After the Taira were defeated in 1185 (see p679), one of the few survivors, Taira Tokitada, was exiled to this region. The Tokikuni family, which claims descent from Tokitada, eventually divided into two clans and established separate family residences here, both now

Noto Peninsula

◉ Sights

😴 Sleeping

Transport

Important Cultural Properties. From Wajima, buses bound for Ushitsu stop in Sosogi (¥740, 40 minutes).

The first residence, **Tokikuni-ke** (時国家; Tokikuni Residence; adult/child ¥600/300; ☉8.30am–5pm), was built in 1590 in the style of the Kamakura period and has a *meishō tei-en* (famous garden). A few minutes' walk away, **Kami Tokikuni-ke** (上時国家; Upper Tokikuni Residence; adult/child ¥500/400; ☉8.30am–5pm), with its impressive thatched roof and elegant interior, was constructed early in the 19th century. Entry to either home includes a leaflet in English.

Several hiking trails are close by, and the rock formation **mado-iwa** (窓岩; window rock) is about 1km up the coast, just offshore. In winter, look for *nami-no-hana* (flowers of the waves), masses of foam that form when waves gnash Sosogi's rocky shore. Across from Mado-iwa Pocket Park, the well-kept, seven-room *minshuku* **Yokoiwaya** (横岩屋; ☎32-0603; fax 32-0663; Machinomachisosogi; r per person with meals from ¥8350;[P]) has welcomed guests for 150 years with comfortable rooms, onsen baths and outstanding seafood dinners; in most Japanese cities the dinner alone would easily cost this much. Look for the paper lantern, or request pick-up from Sosogi-guchi bus stop (曽々木口バス停).

The road northeast from Sosogi village leads past the **sea salt farms** (珠洲製塩) and **Gojira-iwa** (ゴジラ岩; Godzilla rock, for its shape) into the town of Suzu and the remote cape Rokō-zaki, the peninsula's furthest point. At the cape, you can amble up to the lighthouse in the village of **Noroshi** (狼煙); a signpost marks the distances to faraway cities (302km to Tokyo, 1598km to Shanghai). A coastal **hiking trail** runs west along the cape. It is rustic scenery, especially on weekdays when tourist buses run less frequently and Noroshi reverts to its sleepy fishing-village self.

As you head south, the road circles around the tip of the peninsula towards less dramatic scenery on the eastern coast, and, reluctantly, back towards Kanazawa.

Lamp no Yado (ランプの宿; ☎86-8000; www.lampnoyado.co.jp; 10-11 Jike, Misaki-machi; r per person with 2 meals from ¥19,000; [P][♨]), in remote Suzu, is a place that sparkles. This 13-room wood-built waterside village, far from the main drag, has been an inn since the 1970s, but the building goes back four centuries, to when people would escape to its curative waters for weeks at a time. Rooms (some two-storey) have private bathrooms and their own *rotemburo*. The pool is almost superfluous.

An Australian-Japanese couple runs the seaside inn-restaurant-bakery **Flatt's by the Sea** (民宿ふらっと; Minshuku Flatto; ☑62-1900; www.flatts.jp; r per person with meals from ¥13,500; ⊙Thu-Tue; ☎). It has just a few tables, and serves local seafood cuisine seasoned in part with *isshiri* squid sauce. The three 10-mat *minshuku* rooms have bang-on water views from across the street. For nonguests, meals are by reservation only, or just visit Flatt's bakery and cafe (closed Wednesday and Thursday) for basics or adventurous creations like chorizo rolls. It's near the inner elbow of Noto, in the town of Hanami.

Kaga Onsen   加賀温泉

☑0761

A centre for porcelain, lacquerware and hot springs, Kaga Onsen in southern Ishikawa-ken is perfect for art and nature lovers. This is a large area, centred on Kaga Onsen and Daishōji stations along the JR Hokuriku line, and is divided into three hot-springs areas: Katayamazu Onsen, Yamashiro Onsen, and Yamanaka Onsen; the last is the most scenic and worthwhile. Some of the region's finest ryokan can be found here as well.

◉ Sights & Activities

Kutaniyaki Art Museum   MUSEUM
(石川県九谷焼美術館; 1-10-13 Jikata-machi, Daishoji; admission ¥500; ⊙9am-5pm, closed Mon) Stunning examples of the local porcelain, which tends to be bright and colourful, are on display at this museum, an eight-minute walk from Daishōji Station.

Zenshō-ji   TEMPLE
(全昌寺; 1 Daishōji Shinmei-chō; admission ¥500; ⊙9am-5pm) The Daishoji neighbourhood is crammed with temples including Zenshō-ji, which houses over 500 amusingly carved Buddhist arhat sculptures.

Yamanaka Onsen   ONSEN
In quaint Yamanaka Onsen, the 17th-century haiku poet Basho rhapsodized on the chrysanthemum fragrance of the local mineral springs. It's still an ideal spot for chilling at the bathhouse **Kiku no Yu** (菊の湯; admission ¥420; ⊙6.45am-10.30pm), and for river walks

by the Kokusenkei gorge, spanned by the elegant **Korogi-bashi** (Cricket Bridge) and the whimsical, modern-art **Ayatori-hashi** (Cat's Cradle Bridge). Yamanaka Onsen is accessible by bus (¥410, 30 minutes) from Kaga Onsen station.

Yamashiro Onsen   ONSEN
A few kilometres closer to Kaga Onsen Station, Yamashiro Onsen is a sleepy town centred on a magnificent wooden bathhouse that was recently rebuilt. The **Kosōyu** (古総湯; admission ¥500, Sōyu combined ticket ¥700; ⊙6am-10pm) has beautiful stained-glass windows and a rest area on the top floor; neighbouring **Sōyu** (総湯) is a larger, more modern bathhouse. Two blocks to the northeast is **Kutaniyaki Kamamoto** (九谷焼窯元), a venerable porcelain kiln and shop.

🛏 Sleeping

These two ryokan, in Yamashiro and Yamanaka onsens, are perhaps the best part about visiting the area. The **Yamanaka Onsen Tourism Association** (☑78-0330; Yamanaka Onsen Bunka Kaikan, 5-1 Yamanaka Onsen) can also help with accommodation.

TOP CHOICE **Beniya Mukayū**   RYOKAN $$$
(べにや無何有; ☑77-1340; www.mukayu.com; fax 76-1340; 55-1-3 Yamashiro Onsen; per person with meals from ¥47,400; P@) Gorgeously minimalist, this deluxe inn designed by Kiyoshi Sey Takayama has a quiet, zen-like philosophy that pervades every aspect of the guest experience, from soaking in a private outdoor tub to clearing one's mind in the meditation hall (there are free morning yoga classes). Rooms are traditional Japanese-style, or a beautiful hybrid of Western beds and Japanese sitting rooms with bamboo flooring. The cuisine is equally eye-pleasing, and features dishes such as pike conger *shabu-shabu* (hot pot) and grilled *nodoguro* (blackthroat sea perch).

Kayōtei   RYOKAN $$$
(かよう亭; ☑78-1410; fax 78-1121; www.kayotei .jp; 1-20 Higashi-machi, Yamanaka Onsen; per person with meals from ¥39,000; P@) This delightful, opulent ryokan along the scenic Kokusenkei gorge has only 10 rooms, giving it an intimate feel. Some rooms have private outdoor baths facing the inn's private mountain. The staff is supremely hospitable, and can arrange a meal at a local trattoria if you're tired of *kaiseki*, as well as a Western-style breakfast.

ⓘ Getting There & Away

The JR Hokuriku line links Kaga Onsen with Kanazawa (*tokkyū*, ¥1780, 26 minutes; *futsū*, ¥740, 44 minutes) and Fukui (*tokkyū*, ¥1610, 20 minutes; *futsū*, ¥570, 48 minutes). A bus (¥700, 45 minutes, one daily April to November) links Yamanaka Onsen with Fukui-ken's famous Eihei-ji temple (p239).

Hakusan National Park
白山国立公園

For travellers with a thirst for exercise and time on their hands, this national park straddles four prefectures: Ishikawa, Fukui, Toyama and Gifu. The park has several peaks above 2500m; the tallest is Hakusan (2702m), a sacred mountain that, along with Mt Fuji, has been worshipped since ancient times. In summer, hiking and scrambling uphill to catch mountain sunrises are the main activities, while in winter skiing and onsen bathing take over.

For information, call **Hakusan Murodō Reservation Centre** (白山室堂予約センター; ☑076-273-1001) or **Shiramine Town Hall** (白山市白峰支所; ☑076-259-2011) in Japanese.

The alpine section of the park is crisscrossed with trails, offering treks of up to 25km. For hikers who are well equipped and in no hurry, there is a 26km trek to Ogimachi in Shōkawa Valley.

Those looking to hike on and around the peaks are required to stay overnight, mostly in giant dorms at either **Murodō Centre** (dm with 2 meals ¥7700; ⊙1 May-15 Oct) or **Nanryū Sansō** (南竜; Nanryū Mountain Lodge; ☑076-259-2022; dm with 2 meals ¥7600, camp sites ¥300, tent rental ¥2200, 5-person cabins ¥12,000; ⊙Jul-Sep). Getting to either of these requires a hike of 3½ to five hours, and when the lodges are full, each person gets about one tatami mat's worth of sleeping space. Camping is prohibited in the park except at Nanryū Sansō camping ground; there are several camping grounds outside the park. That doesn't stop the park from swarming with visitors, however. Reservations are recommended at least one week in advance.

The closest access point is Bettōdeai. From here it's 6km to Murodō (about 4½ hours' walk) and 5km to Nanryū (3½ hours). Ichirino, Chūgū Onsen, Shiramine and Ichinose have *minshuku*, ryokan and camping. Rates per person start from around ¥300 for camp sites, or around ¥7500 for rooms in inns with two meals.

ⓘ Getting There & Away

This is not easily done, even during the peak summer period. The main mode of transport is the **Hokutetsu Kankō** (☑076-237-5115) bus from Kanazawa Station to Bettōdeai. From late June to mid-October, up to three buses operate daily (¥2000, two hours). Return fares include a coupon for a stay at Murodō Centre (¥10,600).

If you're driving from the Shōkawa Valley, you can take the scenic toll road, Hakusan Super-Rindō (cars ¥3150).

FUKUI PREFECTURE

Fukui-ken (福井県) is quite off the beaten path for most travellers in Japan, but it has an excellent temple and coastal rock formations. Among Japanese, it's also known for its eyeglasses and a high number of nuclear powerplants.

Fukui 福井

☑0776 / POP 268.000

Thanks to a drubbing in WWII and an earthquake in 1948, Fukui, the prefectural capital, doesn't bubble over with big-name attractions like other Hokuriku towns, yet this friendly, down-to-earth city makes a useful sightseeing base.

Fukui Tourist Information Centre (☑20-5348; ⊙8.30am-7pm) dispenses English information and maps from beside the ticket gate at Fukui Station. If you are planning to visit both Eihei-ji and Tōjinbō, enquire here about a Free Pass (¥2000), offering unlimited bus transport to these destinations for two days.

JR trains connect Fukui with Kanazawa (*tokkyū*, ¥2940, 50 minutes; *futsū*, ¥1280, 1½ hours), Tsuruga (*tokkyū*, ¥2610, 35 minutes; *futsū*, ¥950, 55 minutes), Kyoto (¥4810, 1½ hours) and Osaka (¥5870, 1¾ hours).

Eihei-ji 永平寺

☑0776

In 1244 the great Zen master Dōgen (1200–53), founder of the Sōtō sect of Zen Buddhism, established Eihei-ji in a forest near Fukui. Today it's one of Sōtō's two head temples, one of the world's most influential Zen centres and a palpably spiritual place amid mountains, mosses and ancient cedars. Serious students of Zen should consider a retreat here – there are commonly some 150 priests and disciples in residence – but all are welcome to visit.

The **temple** (63-3102; adult/child ¥500/200; 9am-5pm) receives huge numbers of visitors as sightseers or for rigorous Zen training. Among the approximately 70 buildings, the standard circuit concentrates on seven major ones: San-mon (main gate), Butsuden (Buddha Hall), Hattō (Dharma Hall), Sō-dō (Priests' Hall), plus the *daikuin* (kitchen), *yokushitsu* (bath) and, yes, *tōsu* (lavatory). You walk among the buildings on wooden walkways in your stockinged feet (pretty chilly in cold weather). The Shōbōkaku exhibits many Eihei-ji treasures.

The temple is often closed for periods varying from a week to 10 days for religious observance. Before setting out, be sure to check www.sotozen-net.or.jp/kokusai/list/eiheiji.htm or with tourist offices.

You can attend the temple's four-day, three-night **sanrō experience program** (religious trainee program; 63-3640; fax 63-3631; www.sotozen-net.or.jp/kokusai/list/eiheiji.htm; fee ¥11,000), which follows the monks' training schedule, complete with 3.50am prayers, cleaning, *zazen* and ritual meals in which not a grain of rice may be left behind. Knowledge of Japanese is not necessary, but it helps to be able to sit in the half-lotus position. Everyone we've spoken to who has completed this course agrees it is a remarkable experience. Book at least two weeks in advance.

To get to Eihei-ji from Fukui, take the Keifuku bus (¥720, 35 minutes, at least three daily); buses depart from the east exit of Fukui Station.

Tōjinbō 東尋坊

On the coast about 25km northwest of Fukui are these towering **rock columns** and **cliffs**, a too-popular tourist destination that's also a place of legend: one says that Tōjinbō was an evil Buddhist priest who was cast off the cliff by angry villagers in 1182; the sea surged for 49 days thereafter, a demonstration of the priest's fury from beyond his watery grave.

Visitors can take a boat trip (¥1010, 30 minutes) to view the rock formations or travel further up the coast to **O-jima**, a small island with a shrine that is joined to the mainland by a bridge.

The most convenient connection to Tōjinbō is by bus via Awara Onsen Station (from Fukui: *tokkyū*, ¥1560, 10 minutes). *Futsū* trains are less expensive (¥320, 16 minutes), but less frequent. Buses to Tōjinbō depart Awara Onsen Station at 40 minutes past the hour and 10 minutes past the hour on weekends and holidays (¥730, 40 minutes).

Tsuruga 敦賀

Tsuruga, south of Fukui and north of Biwako, is a thriving port and train junction. **Shin Nihonkai ferry company** (0770-23-2222; www.snf.jp, in Japanese) has nine sailings a week to Tomakomai, Hokkaidō (2nd class from ¥9000, 19½ hours nonstop, 30½ hours with stops). Several of these stop en route at Niigata (¥5000, 12½ hours) and Akita (¥6500, 20 hours). Buses timed to ferry departures serve Tsuruga-kō port from Tsuruga Station (¥340, 20 minutes).

Japan in Pictures

Temples & Shrines »
Cuisine »
Onsen »
Hiking »
Festivals »

Glorious colour in the main worship hall of Itsukushima-jinja (p375), Miyajima

Temples & Shrines

Japan's two main religions, Shintō and Buddhism, are responsible for some of the most stunning architecture in the country. Buddhist temples range from quiet sanctuaries to bustling mercantile affairs. Likewise, Shintō shrines run the gamut from tiny mountaintop sanctuaries to sprawling downtown complexes.

Tōshō-gū (Nikkō)

1 In a country where the favoured colour for religious structures is bare wood, this shrine at Nikkō (p122) stands out like a peacock among pigeons.

Endless Shrine Gates at Fushimi-Inari Taisha (Kyoto)

2 There is something hypnotic about walking through the thousands of vermillion Shintō shrine gates (torii) at Kyoto's Fushimi-Inari Taisha (p274).

The Daibutsu at Tōdai-ji (Nara)

3 The 'cosmic Buddha' at Nara's Tōdai-ji (p334) is Japan's most powerful religious statue – spend a few moments basking in its strangely calming gaze.

Sensō-ji (Tokyo)

4 Sensō-ji (p80) is the religious heart of Tokyo, a kind of spiritual casbah where Buddhists and non-Buddhists alike come to buy amulets and plant incense sticks.

Kinkaku-ji (Kyoto)

5 The gold-covered main hall at this Kyoto temple (p270) is a shimmering apparition – even when you see it, you might not believe it.

Clockwise from top left
1. Tōshō-gū, Nikkō **2.** Shrine gates at Fushimi-Inari Taisha, Kyoto **3.** Daibutsu at Tōdai-ji, Nara **4.** Sensō-ji, Tokyo.

Cuisine

In a country famed for exquisite presentation and the ability to refine things to perfection, it's hardly surprising that local cuisine is among the best in the world. There are few more enjoyable pastimes than eating your way from one end of the archipelago to the other. For more on Japanese cuisine and drinks see p699.

Sweets

1 The sheer variety of *wagashi* (Japanese traditional sweets) is a testament to the Japanese imagination. Tour a department-store food floor to see all the creativity that goes into their production.

Sushi & Sashimi

2 Japan's greatest gift to the culinary world is always so much better on its home turf. The Japanese simply know how to handle fish better than anyone else – and rice, well, it's in their blood.

Tea & the Tea Ceremony

3 Japan is a tea lover's paradise: you'll find that there are almost as many types of tea as there are shades of green. And in the tea ceremony, the cup of tea becomes a secular sacrament.

Izakaya

4 If you want to really get inside Japan, you have to step into an *izakaya* (Japanese pub-style eatery). This is where the Japanese let their hair down.

Rāmen

5 Officially, *rāmen* (egg noodles) is a Chinese invention, but the Japanese have turned it into their own folk religion. You could spend years just sampling the different varieties.

Clockwise from top left
1. Japanese sweets 2. Sashimi 3. Traditional tea ceremony 4. Spread at an *izakaya* (pub-eatery).

Onsen

Hot water bubbles out of the ground throughout the Japanese archipelago, and the Japanese have built a whole culture around soaking in it. Ask any Japanophile what they like about Japan and, odds are, the word 'onsen' (hot springs) will be the first thing you hear.

Takaragawa Onsen (Gunma-ken)

1 These hot-spring baths (p129), within day-trip distance of Tokyo, are the classic riverside onsen.

Hōshi Onsen Chōjūkan (Gunma-ken)

2 Hōshi Onsen (p130) is one of our favourite onsen ryokan. What could be more relaxing than spending the night at a bathhouse inn?

Tsubo-yu Onsen (Kansai)

3 We can never get enough of this little onsen in a shack in the middle of a river way down in Wakayama-ken (p356).

Urami-ga-taki Onsen (Hachijō-jima)

4 This semitropical onsen (p164) is wrapped in greenery and looks more like Bali than Japan.

Dōgo Onsen (Ehime-ken)

5 On the island of Shikoku, Dōgo Onsen (see the box, p551) has a bathhouse straight out of Hayao Miyazaki's *Spirited Away*.

Right
1. *Rotemburo* (outdoor baths) at Takaragawa Onsen
2. Men's bathhouse at Hoshi Onsen

Hiking

Japan is one of the hiking world's best-kept secrets. You can go hut-to-hut in the Japan Alps, traverse the 'Big Snow Mountain' of Hokkaidō, climb volcanoes in Kyūshū, or saunter the hills around Kyoto. Wherever you go, you probably won't be alone: the Japanese are very keen hikers.

Daisetsuzan National Park (Hokkaidō)

1 The name means 'Big Snow Mountain' and for much of the year, this mountain massif (p505) in Hokkaidō lives up to its name. When the snow melts, the hiking is brilliant.

Kamikōchi (Nagano-ken)

2 An alpine sanctuary in the heart of the Japan Alps, Kamikōchi (p199) has some of Japan's most beautiful scenery.

Fuji-san (Shizuoka-ken)

3 What serious climber would come to Japan and not bag Japan's highest peak? If you're here in July or August, an ascent of Mt Fuji (p132) is a must.

Yakushima (Kagoshima-ken)

4 This island (p637) south of Kyūshū is home to the ancient Jōmon Sugi tree and some wonderfully mountainous hiking.

Aso-san (Kumamoto-ken)

5 This semi-active volcano (p601) in Kyūshū offers some excellent hiking and incredible views. The ever-present threat of eruption adds a certain thrill to the hiking.

Left
1. Steam rising from vents in Asahi-dake, Daisetsuzan National Park **2.** Nishi Hotaka-dake, Kamikochi

Festivals

Festivals, known as *matsuri* in Japan, are where the Japanese really let loose. Many *matsuri* are Shintō in origin, and when the sake starts flowing, the fires start burning and the people start dancing, you can really feel the ancient shamanic origins of the religion – the gods seem very near indeed.

Awa-odori Matsuri (Tokushima)

1 One of the biggest and most entertaining festivals in Japan is this rollicking dance party (see the box, p530) taking place in Tokushima in August.

Gion Matsuri (Kyoto)

2 Perhaps Japan's most important festival, the Gion Matsuri (p280) comes in two parts: several nights of revelry followed by a stately daytime procession of festival floats in July.

Yuki Matsuri (Sapporo)

3 This snow festival (p471), which takes place in Sapporo in February, gives new meaning to the words 'winter wonderland'.

Kurama-no-hi Matsuri (Kyoto)

4 For a true taste of primeval Shintō, the Kurama Fire Festival (p281) held in October in the tiny village of Kurama, just north of Kyoto, is highly recommended.

Sanja Matsuri (Tokyo)

5 With a parade of hundreds *mikoshi* (portable shrines), this is one of Tokyo's biggest festivals (p85). It's held in the old quarter of Asakusa in May.

Right
1. Dancers during Awa-odori Matsuri 2. Gion Matsuri float

Kyoto

♪075 / POP 1.47 MILLION

Best Places to Eat

» Yoshikawa (p286)

» Ōzawa (p289)

» Omen (p290)

» Ganko Zushi (p286)

» Ippūdō (p286)

Best Places to Stay

» Tawaraya (p283)

» Hyatt Regency Kyoto (p284)

» Tour Club (p282)

» Westin Miyako, Kyoto (p285)

» Hiiragiya (p283)

Why Go?

For much of its history, Kyoto (京都) *was* Japan. Even today, Kyoto is *the* place to go to see what Japan is all about. Here is where you'll find all those things you associate with the Land of the Rising Sun: ancient temples, colourful shrines and sublime gardens. Indeed, Kyoto is the storehouse of Japan's traditional culture, and it's the place where even the Japanese go to learn about their own culture.

With 17 Unesco World Heritage Sites (see the box, p279), more than 1600 Buddhist temples and over 400 Shintō shrines, Kyoto is one of the world's most culturally rich cities. It is fair to say that Kyoto ranks with Paris, London and Rome as one of those cities that everyone should see at least once in their lives. And, needless to say, it should rank at the top of any Japan itinerary.

When to Go
Kyoto

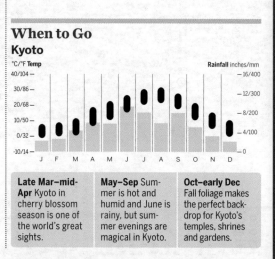

| Late Mar–mid-Apr Kyoto in cherry blossom season is one of the world's great sights. | May–Sep Summer is hot and humid and June is rainy, but summer evenings are magical in Kyoto. | Oct–early Dec Fall foliage makes the perfect backdrop for Kyoto's temples, shrines and gardens. |

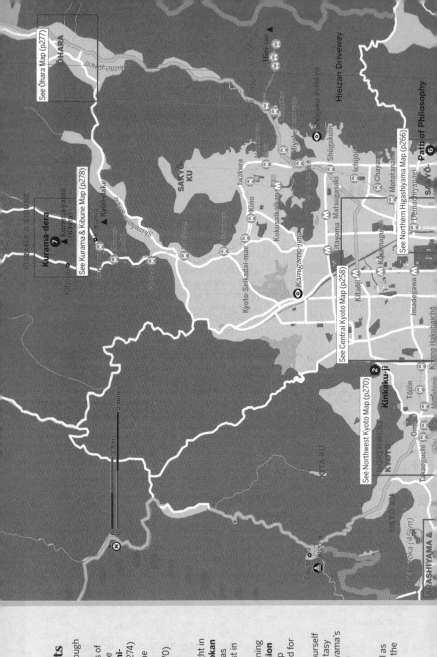

Kyoto Highlights

❶ Wander through the seemingly endless arcades of vermillion shrine gates at **Fushimi-Inari Taisha** (p274)

❷ Marvel at the golden hall of **Kinkaku-ji** (p270), floating over its tranquil pond

❸ Spend a night in a traditional **ryokan** (p281); Kyoto has some of the best in the country

❹ Take an evening stroll through **Gion** (p264) and keep your eyes peeled for geisha

❺ Immerse yourself in the green fantasy world of Arashiyama's **Bamboo Grove** (p271)

❻ Ponder the meaning of it all as you stroll along the

Path of Philosophy (p265)

7 Climb to the mountain temple of **Kurama-dera** (p277), then descend to the waiting hot spring below

8 Allow yourself to be dazzled by one of Kyoto's spring or fall **Geisha dances** (p293)

History

The Kyoto basin was first settled in the 7th century, and by 794 it had become Heian-kyō, the capital of Japan. Like Nara, a previous capital, the city was laid out in a grid pattern modelled on the Chinese Tang-dynasty capital, Chang'an (contemporary Xi'an). Although the city was to serve as capital of Japan and home to the Japanese imperial family from 794 to 1868 (when the Meiji Restoration took the imperial family to the new capital, Tokyo), the city was not always the focus of Japanese political power. During the Kamakura period (1185-1333), Kamakura served as the national capital, and during the Edo period (1600-1867), the Tokugawa shōgunate ruled Japan from Edo (now Tokyo).

Climate

The best and most popular times to visit Kyoto are the climatically stable and temperate seasons of spring (March to May) and autumn (late September to November).

Be warned that Kyoto receives close to 50 million domestic and international tourists a year. The popular sights are packed during the cherry-blossom and autumn-foliage seasons. Accommodation is hard to find during these times, so book well in advance. However, even during the busiest seasons in Kyoto, you can always find uncrowded spots if you know where to look (often just a few minutes' walk from the popular places).

◉ Sights

Like Manhattan, Kyoto is laid out in a grid pattern and is extremely easy to navigate. Kyoto Station, the city's main station, is located at the southern end of the city, and the JR and Kintetsu lines operate from here. The real centre of Kyoto is located around Shijō-dōri, about 2km north of Kyoto Station via Karasuma-dōri. The commercial and nightlife centres are between Shijō-dōri to the south and Sanjō-dōri to the north, and between Kawaramachi-dōri to the east and Karasuma-dōri to the west.

Although some of Kyoto's major sights are in the city centre, Kyoto's best sightseeing is on the outskirts of the city, along the base of the eastern and western mountains (known as Higashiyama and Arashiyama, respectively). Sights on the east side are best reached by bus, bicycle or the Tōzai subway line. Sights on the west side (Arashiyama etc) are best reached by bus or train (or by bicycle if you're very keen). Outside the city

itself, the mountain villages of Ōhara, Kurama and Takao make wonderful day trips and are easily accessible by public transport.

The Kyoto TIC (Tourist Information Centre) stocks the following maps: the *Kyoto City Map,* a useful map with decent insets of the main tourist districts; the oddly named *Kyoto Map for Tourist,* which is fairly detailed; the *Bus Navi: Kyoto City Bus Travel map,* the most useful guide to city buses; and the leaflet *Kyoto Walks,* which has detailed walking maps for major sightseeing areas in and around Kyoto (Higashiyama, Arashiyama, northwestern Kyoto and Ōhara).

KYOTO STATION AREA

Although most of Kyoto's attractions are further north, there are a few attractions within walking distance of the station (Map p253). The most impressive sight in this area is the vast Higashi Hongan-ji, but don't forget the station building itself – it's an attraction in its own right.

Kyoto Station   NOTABLE BUILDING

(京都駅; Map p253; Higashishiokō-ji-chō, Shiokōji sagaru, Karasuma-dōri, Shimogyō-ku) Kyoto's station building is a striking steel-and-glass structure – a futuristic cathedral for the transport age. Take some time to explore the many levels of the station, all the way up to the 15th-floor observation level. If you don't suffer from fear of heights, try riding the escalator from the 7th floor on the eastern side of the building up to the 11th-floor aerial skywalk, high over the main concourse.

In the station building you'll find several food courts (see p286), the Kyoto Prefectural International Centre (京都府国際センター), a performance space and an Isetan department store.

Kyoto Tower   NOTABLE BUILDING

(京都タワー; Map p253; Shichijō sagaru, Karasuma, Shimogyō-ku; admission ¥770; ⏰9am-9pm, last entry 8.40pm) If you want to orient yourself and get an idea of the layout of Kyoto as soon as you arrive in town, Kyoto Tower is the place to do it. Located right outside the Karasuma (north) gate of the station, this retro tower looks like a rocket perched atop the Kyoto Tower Hotel. The tower provides excellent views in all directions and you can really see why Kyotoites describe their city as a *bonchi* (a flat tray with raised edges). There are free mounted binoculars to use, and these allow ripping views over to Kiyomizu-dera (p262) and as far south as Osaka.

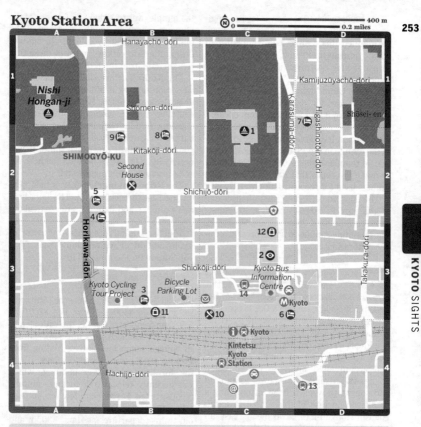

Kyoto Station Area

◎ Top Sights
Nishi Hongan-ji A1

◎ Sights
1 Higashi Hongan-ji C2
2 Kyoto Tower C3

🛏 Sleeping
3 APA Hotel Kyoto Ekimae.....................B3
4 Budget Inn..A2
5 Capsule Ryokan Kyoto A2
6 Hotel Granvia Kyoto C3
7 Matsubaya Ryokan...............................D1
8 Ryokan Shimizu....................................B2

9 Tour Club B2

✖ Eating
10 Cube C3
Eat Paradise...................................(see 10)

🛍 Shopping
11 Bic Camera..B3
Isetan Department Store.............(see 10)
12 Yodobashi Camera..............................C3

Transport
13 Airport Limousine Bus Stop................D4
14 Kyoto Station Bus Terminal C3

FREE **Higashi Hongan-ji** TEMPLE
(東本願寺; Map p253; Shichijō agaru, Karasuma-dōri, Shimogyō-ku; ⊙5.50am-5.30pm Mar-Oct, 6.20am-4.30pm Nov-Feb) A short walk north of Kyoto Station, this temple is the last word in all things grand and gaudy. Considering the proximity to the station, the free admission, the awesome structures and the dazzling interiors, this temple is an obvious spot to visit if you find yourself near the station.

In 1602, when Tokugawa Ieyasu engineered the rift in the Jōdo Shin-shū school, he founded this temple as a competitor to Nishi Hongan-ji. Rebuilt in 1895 after a series of fires destroyed all of the original structures, the temple is now the headquarters of the Ōtani branch of Jōdo Shin-shū.

In the corridor between the two main buildings you'll find a curious item encased in glass: a tremendous coil of rope made from human hair. Following the destruction of the temple in the 1880s, an eager group of female temple devotees donated their locks to make the ropes that hauled the massive timbers used for reconstruction.

The enormous Goei-dō (main hall) is one of the world's largest wooden structures, standing 38m high, 76m long and 58m wide. The adjoining Amida-dō hall is presently under restoration.

FREE Nishi Hongan-ji TEMPLE

(西本願寺; Map p253; Hanaya-chō sagaru, Horikawa-dōri, Shimogyō-ku; ⊙6am-5pm Nov-Feb, 5.30am-5.30pm Mar, Apr, Sep & Oct, to 6pm May-Aug) In 1591 Toyotomi Hideyoshi built this temple, known as Hongan-ji, as the new headquarters for the Jōdo Shin-shū (True Pure Land) school of Buddhism, which had accumulated immense power. Later, Tokugawa Ieyasu saw this power as a threat and sought to weaken it by encouraging a breakaway faction of this school to found Higashi Hongan-ji (higashi means 'east') in 1602. The original Hongan-ji then became known as Nishi Hongan-ji (nishi means 'west'). It now functions as the headquarters of the Hongan-ji branch of the Jōdo Shinshū school, with over 10,000 temples and 12 million followers worldwide.

The temple contains five buildings, featuring some of the finest examples of architecture and artistic achievement from the Azuchi-Momoyama period (1568–1600). The Goei-dō is a marvellous sight and the Daisho-in Hall has sumptuous paintings, carvings and metal ornamentation. A small garden and two nō (stylised Japanese dance-drama) stages are connected with the hall. The dazzling Kara-mon has intricate ornamental carvings.

Tō-ji TEMPLE

(東寺; 1 Kujō-chō, Minami-ku; admission to grounds free, Kondō & Treasure Hall ¥500; ⊙8.30am-5.30pm, to 4.30pm 20 Sep-19 Mar) This temple was established in 794 by imperial decree to protect the city. In 818 the emperor handed the temple over to Kūkai, the founder of the Shingon school of Buddhism. Many of the buildings were destroyed by fire or fighting during the 15th century; most of those that remain date from the 17th century.

The Kōdō (Lecture Hall) contains 21 images representing a Mikkyō (Esoteric Buddhism) mandala. The Kondō (Main Hall) contains statues depicting the Yakushi (Healing Buddha) trinity. In the southern part of the garden stands the five-storey pagoda, which burnt down five times. It was rebuilt in 1643 and is now the highest pagoda in Japan, standing 57m tall.

The Kōbō-san market-fair is held here on the 21st of each month. The fairs held in December and January are particularly lively.

Tō-ji is a 15-minute walk southwest of Kyoto Station or a five-minute walk from Tōji Station on the Kintetsu line.

Umekōji Steam Locomotive Museum MUSEUM

(梅小路蒸気機関車館; Kankiji-chō, Shimogyō-ku; adult/child ¥400/100, train ride ¥200/100; ⊙9.30am-5pm, closed Mon) A hit with steam-train buffs and kids, this museum features 18 vintage steam locomotives (dating from 1914 to 1948) and related displays. It's in the former Nijō Station building, which was recently relocated here and carefully reconstructed. For an extra few yen, you can take a 10-minute ride on one of the fabulous old trains (departures at 11am, 1.30pm and 3.30pm).

From Kyoto Station, take bus 33, 205 or 208 to the Umekō-ji Kōen-mae stop (make sure you take a westbound bus).

DOWNTOWN KYOTO

Downtown Kyoto (Map p256) looks much like any other Japanese city, but there are some excellent attractions to be found here, including Nishiki Market, the Museum of Kyoto, the Kyoto International Manga Museum and Ponto-chō. If you'd like a break from temples and shrines, then downtown Kyoto can be a welcome change. It's also good on a rainy day, because of the number of covered arcades and indoor attractions.

Nishiki Market MARKET

(錦市場; Map p256; Nishikikōji-dōri btwn Teramachi & Takakura; ⊙9am-5pm, varies for individual stalls, some shops closed on Wed) If you are interested in seeing all the really weird and wonderful foods that go into Kyoto cuisine, wander through Nishiki Market. It's in the centre of town, one block north of (and parallel to) Shijō-dōri, running west off Teramachi Shopping arcade and ending shortly before Daimaru department store. This market is a great place to visit on a rainy day or if you need a break from temple-hopping. The variety of foods on display is staggering, and the frequent cries of *Irasshaimase!* (Welcome!) are heart-warming.

Museum of Kyoto
MUSEUM

(京都文化博物館; Map p256; Takakura-dōri, Sanjō agaru, Nakagyō-ku; admission ¥500, extra for special exhibitions; ◎10am-7.30pm, special exhibitions to 6pm, to 7.30pm on Fri, closed Mon) This museum is worth visiting if a special exhibition is on. The regular exhibits, which include models of ancient Kyoto, audiovisual presentations and a small gallery dedicated to Kyoto's film industry, are not worth a special visit. On the 1st floor, the Roji Tempō is a reconstructed Edo-period merchant area showing 10 types of exterior latticework (this section can be entered free; some of the shops sell souvenirs and serve local dishes). The museum has English-speaking volunteer tour guides. The museum is a three-minute walk southeast of the Karasuma-Oike stop on the Karasuma and Tōzai subway lines.

Kyoto International Manga Museum
MUSEUM

(京都国際マンガミュージアム; Map p256; www.kyotomm.com/english; Oike agaru, Karasuma-dōri, Nakagyō-ku; adult/child ¥500/100; ◎10am-6pm, closed Wed) This fine museum has a collection of some 300,000 manga (Japanese comic books). Located in an old elementary school building, the museum is the perfect introduction to the art of manga. While most of the manga and displays are in Japanese, the collection of translated works is growing.

In addition to the galleries that show both the historical development of manga and original artwork done in manga style, there are beginners' workshops and portrait drawings on weekends. Visitors with children will appreciate the children's library and the occasional performances of *kami-shibai* (humorous traditional Japanese sliding-picture shows), not to mention the Astroturf lawn where the kids can run free. The museum hosts six month-long special exhibits yearly: check the website for details.

It's a short walk from the Karasuma-Oike Station on the Karuma line subway or the Tōzai line subway.

Ponto-chō
NEIGHBOURHOOD

(先斗町; Map p256) A traditional nightlife district and one of Kyoto's five geisha districts, Ponto-chō is a narrow alley running between Sanjō-dōri and Shijō-dōri just west of Kamo-gawa. It's best visited in the evening, when the traditional wooden buildings and hanging lanterns create a wonderful atmosphere of old Japan, perhaps combined with a walk in nearby Gion.

CENTRAL KYOTO

The area we refer to as Central Kyoto (Map p258) includes the Kyoto Imperial Palace Park, Nijō-jō Castle, a couple of important shrines and the Nishijin weaving district, among other things. It's flat and easy to explore by bicycle or on foot.

Kyoto Imperial Palace (Kyoto Gosho)
HISTORICAL BUILDING

(京都御所; Map p258) The original imperial palace was built in 794 and was replaced numerous times after destruction by fire. The present building, on a different site and smaller than the original, was constructed in 1855. Enthronement of a new emperor and other state ceremonies are still held here.

The Gosho does not rate highly in comparison with other attractions in Kyoto and you must apply for permission to visit. However, you shouldn't miss the park surrounding the Gosho (p256).

To get there, take the Karasuma line subway to Imadegawa or a bus to the Karasuma-Imadegawa stop and walk 600m southeast.

Imperial Household Agency

(宮内庁京都事務所; Map p258; ☎211-1215; ◎8.45am-noon & 1-5pm Mon-Fri) Permission to visit the Gosho is granted by the Kunaichō, the Imperial Household Agency, which is inside the walled park surrounding the palace, a short walk from Imadegawa Station on the Karasuma line. You have to fill out an application form and show your passport. Children can visit if accompanied by adults over 20 years of age (but are forbidden entry to the other three imperial properties of Katsura Rikyū, Sentō Gosho and Shūgaku-in Rikyū). Permission to tour the palace is usually granted the same day (try to arrive at the office at least 30 minutes before the start of the tour you'd like to join). Guided tours, sometimes in English, are given at 10am and 2pm from Monday to Friday. The tour lasts about 50 minutes.

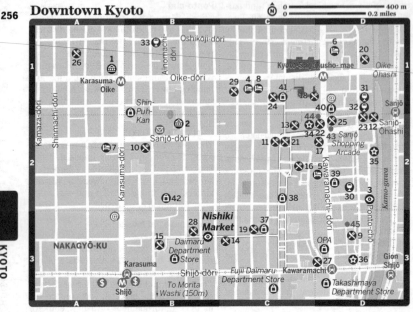

The Gosho can be visited without reservation during two periods each year, once in spring and once in autumn. The dates vary each year, but as a general guide, the spring opening is around the last week of April and the autumn opening is in the middle of November. Check with the TIC for exact dates.

The Imperial Household Agency is also the place to make advance reservations to see the Sentō Gosho, Katsura Rikyū and Shūgaku-in Rikyū.

Sentō Gosho Palace   HISTORICAL BUILDING

(仙洞御所; Map p258; ☎211-1215; Kamigyō-ku Kyoto gyoen) This palace is a few hundred metres southeast of the main Kyoto Gosho. It was originally built in 1630 during the reign of Emperor Go-Mizunō as a residence for retired emperors. The palace was repeatedly destroyed by fire and reconstructed but served its purpose until a final blaze in 1854 (it was never rebuilt).

The gardens, which were laid out in 1630 by Kobori Enshū, are superb. The route takes you past lovely ponds and pathways, and in many ways, a visit here is more enjoyable than a visit to the Gosho, especially if you are a fan of Japanese gardens. Visitors must obtain advance permission from the Imperial Household Agency and be over 20 years old. Tours (in Japanese) start at 11am and 1.30pm.

Kyoto Imperial Palace Park   PARK

(京都御苑; Map p258; Kamigyō-ku Kyoto gyoen; admission free; ☉dawn-dusk) The Kyoto Gosho and Sentō Gosho are surrounded by the spacious Kyoto Imperial Palace Park, which is planted with a huge variety of flowering trees and open fields. It's perfect for picnics, strolls and just about any sport you can think of. Take some time to visit the pond at the park's southern end, which contains gorgeous carp. The park is most beautiful in the plum- and cherry-blossom seasons (late February and late March, respectively). The plum arbour is located about midway along the park on the west side. There are several large *shidareze-zakura* ('weeping' cherry trees) at the north end of the park, making it a great cherry-blossom destination. The park is between Teramachi-dōri and Karasuma-dōri (to the east and west) and Imadegawa-dōri and Marutamachi-dōri (to the north and south).

TOP CHOICE Daitoku-ji   TEMPLES

(大徳寺; Map p258; 53 Daitokuji-chō, Murasakino, Kita-ku; admission free; ☉dawn-dusk) Daitoku-ji is a separate world within Kyoto – a collection of Zen temples, raked gravel gardens and wandering lanes. It is one of the most rewarding destinations in this part of the

KYOTO SIGHTS

city, particularly for those with an interest in Japanese gardens. The name Daitoku-ji confusingly refers to both the main temple here and the entire complex, which contains a total of 24 temples and subtemples. We discuss three of them here, but another five are open to the public.

The eponymous Daitoku-ji is on the eastern side of the grounds. It was founded in 1319, burnt down in the next century and rebuilt in the 16th century. The **San-mon** contains an image of the famous tea master, Sen-no-Rikyū, on the 2nd storey. If you enter via the main gate on the east side of the complex, Daitoku-ji will be on your right, a short walk north.

Just north of Daitoku-ji, **Daisen-in** (大仙院; Map p258; 54-1 Daitokuji-chō, Murasakino, Kita-ku; admission ¥400; ◔9am-5pm Mar-Nov,

to 4.30pm Dec-Feb) is famous for its two small gardens. At the western edge of the complex, **Kōtō-in** (高桐院; Map p258; 73-1 Daitokuji-chō, Murasakino, Kita-ku; admission ¥400; ◔9am-4.30pm) is famous for its stunning bamboo-lined approach and the maple trees in its main garden (try to visit in the foliage season).

The temple bus stop is Daitoku-ji-mae and convenient buses from Kyoto Station are buses 205 and 206. Daitoku-ji is also a short walk west of Kitaō-ji subway station on the Karasuma line.

Nijō-jō
CASTLE

(二条城; Map p258; 541 Nijōjō-chō, Horikawa Nishi iru, Nijō-dōri, Nakagyō-ku; admission ¥600; ◔8.45am-5pm, closed Tue in Dec, Jan, Jul & Aug; ◳Tōzai line to Nijō-jō-mae) This castle was

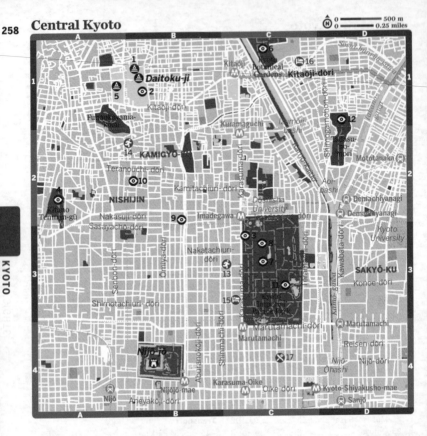

built in 1603 as the official Kyoto residence of the first Tokugawa shōgun, Ieyasu. The ostentatious style of its construction was intended as a demonstration of Ieyasu's prestige and also to signal the demise of the emperor's power. As a safeguard against treachery, Ieyasu had the interior fitted with 'nightingale' floors, as well as concealed chambers where bodyguards could keep watch.

After passing through the grand **Karamon** gate, you enter **Ninomaru Palace**, which is divided into five buildings with numerous chambers. The Ohiroma Yon-no-Ma (Fourth Chamber) has spectacular screen paintings. Don't miss the excellent **Ninomaru Palace Garden**, which was designed by the tea master and landscape architect Kobori Enshū.

To reach the castle, take the subway, or bus 9 from Kyoto Station to the Nijō-jō-mae stop.

Nishijin   NEIGHBOURHOOD
(西陣; Map p258) The Nishijin district is the home of Kyoto's textile industry, the source of the fantastically ornate kimonos and *obi* (ornamental kimono belts) for which the city is famous. It's one of Kyoto's more traditional districts, and there are still lots of good old *machiya* (traditional town houses) scattered about. To reach Nishijin, take bus 9 from Kyoto Station to the Horikawa Imadegawa stop.

Nishijin Textile Center
(西陣織会館; Map p258; Imadegawa Minami iru, Horikawa-dōri, Kamigyō-ku; admission free; ⏰9am-5pm) In the heart of the Nishijin textile district, this is worth a peek before starting a walk around the area. There are also displays of completed fabrics and kimonos, as well as weaving demonstrations and occasional kimono fashion shows. Unfortunately, these days, it's often overrun with large bus tours. It's on the southwest corner of the Horikawa-dōri and Imadegawa-dōri intersection.

Central Kyoto

Orinasu-kan

(織成館; Map p258; 693 Daikoku-chō, Kamigyō-ku; adult/child ¥500/350; ☺10am-4pm, closed Mon) This museum, housed in a Nishijin weaving factory, has impressive exhibits of Nishijin textiles. It's more atmospheric and usually quieter than the Nishijin Textile Center. The Susamei-sha building across the street is also open to the public and worth a look. It's a short walk north of the Nishijin Textile Center.

FREE **Shimogamo-jinja**   SHRINE

(下鴨神社; Map p258; 59 Izumigawa-chō, Shimogamo, Sakyō-ku; ☺6.30am-5pm; ⓡ Keihan line to Demachiyanagi) This shrine, dating from the 8th century, is a Unesco World Heritage Site. It is nestled in the fork of the Kamo-gawa and Takano-gawa rivers, and is approached along a shady path through the lovely Tadasu-no-mori. This wooded area is said to be a place where lies cannot be concealed and is considered a prime location to sort out disputes. The trees here are mostly broadleaf (a rarity in Kyoto) and they are gorgeous in the springtime.

The shrine is dedicated to the god of harvest. Traditionally, pure water was drawn from the nearby rivers for purification and agricultural ceremonies. The *hondō* (main hall) dates from 1863 and, like the Haiden hall at its sister shrine, Kamigamo-jinja, is an excellent example of *nagare*-style shrine architecture. The annual *yabusame* (horseback archery) event here is spectacular. It happens on 3 May from 1pm to 3.30pm in Tadasu-no-mori.

The shrine is only a one-minute walk from Shimogamo-jinja-mae bus stop; take bus 205 from Kyoto Station.

Kyoto Botanical Gardens   PARK

(京都府立植物園; Map p258; Shimogamohangichō, Sakyō-ku; gardens adult ¥200, child ¥80-150; ☺9am-5pm, greenhouse 9am-4pm) The Kyoto Botanical Gardens, opened in 1914, occupy 240,000 sq metres and feature 12,000 plants, flowers and trees. It is pleasant to stroll through the rose, cherry and herb gardens or see the rows of camphor trees and the large tropical greenhouse (adult ¥200, child ¥80 to ¥150). This is a good spot for a picnic or a bit of frisbee throwing. It's also a great spot for a *hanami* (cherry-blossom viewing) party and the blossoms here tend to hold on a little longer than those elsewhere in the city. The gardens are a five-minute walk west of Kitayama subway station (Karasuma line).

FREE **Kamigamo-jinja**   SHRINE

(上賀茂神社; Map p253; 339 Motoyama, Kamigamo, Kita-ku; ☺8am-5pm) This shrine is one of Japan's oldest and predates the founding of Kyoto. Established in 679, it is dedicated to Raijin, the god of thunder, and is one of Kyoto's 17 Unesco World Heritage Sites. The present buildings (over 40 in all), including the impressive Haiden hall, are exact reproductions of the originals, dating from the 17th to 19th centuries. The shrine is entered from a long approach through two torii (shrine gates). The two large conical white-sand mounds in front of Hosodono hall are said to represent mountains sculpted for gods to descend upon.

The shrine is a five-minute walk from Kamigamo-misonobashi bus stop; take bus 9 from Kyoto Station.

SOUTHERN HIGASHIYAMA

The Higashiyama district, which runs along the base of the Higashiyama mountains (Eastern Mountains), is the main sightseeing district in Kyoto and it should be at the top of your Kyoto itinerary. It is thick with impressive sights: fine temples, shrines,

KYOTO SIGHTS

Southern Higashiyama

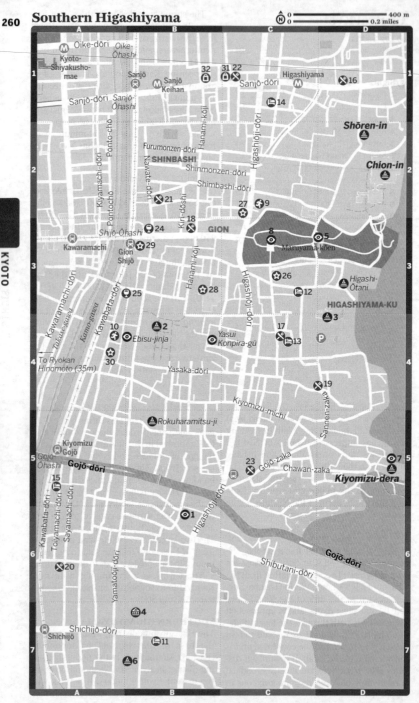

N 0 ———— 400 m
0 ———— 0.2 miles

Kyoto-Shiyakusho-mae
Oike-dōri
Oike-Ōhashi
Sanjō
Sanjō Keihan
Sanjō-dōri
Sanjō-dōri
Sanjō-Ōhashi
Higashiyama
32
31 22
14
16
Shōren-in
Chion-in
Furumonzen-dōri
SHINBASHI
Shinmonzen-dōri
Shimbashi-dōri
27 9
21
8 5
Maruyama-kōen
18
GION
24
29
Shijō-Ōhashi
Kawaramachi
Gion Shijō
26
Higashi-Ōtani
12
HIGASHIYAMA-KU
25
28
3
10
2
Ebisu-jinja
Yasui Konpira-gū
17 13
30
Yasaka-dōri
19
Sannen-zaka
Kiyomizu-michi
Rokuharamitsu-ji
Kiyomizu Gojō
23
Gojō-zaka
7
Gojō-Ōhashi
Gojō-dōri
Chawan-zaka
Kiyomizu-dera
15
1
Gojō-dōri
20
Shibutani-dōri
4
Shichijō-dōri
11
Shichijō
6

To Ryokan Hinomoto (35m)

Pontochō
Kiyamachi-dōri
Nawate-dōri
Hanami-kōji
Higashiōji-dōri
Kawaramachi-dōri
Kawabata-dōri
Kamo-gawa
Takase-gawa
Hanami-kōji
Kiri-dōshi
Higashiōji-dōri
Higashiōji-dōri
Kawabata-dōri
Toiyamachi-dōri
Sayamachi-dōri
Yamatoōji-dōri

KYOTO

Southern Higashiyama

KYOTO SIGHTS

gardens, museums, traditional neighbourhoods and parks. In this guide, we divide the Higashiyama district into two sections: Southern Higashiyama and Northern Higashiyama (p264).

This section starts at the southern end, around Shichijō-dōri, and works north to Sanjō-dōri. You could cover these in the order presented in a fairly long day.

Sanjūsangen-dō
TEMPLE
(三十三間堂; Map p260; 657 Sanjūsangendōmawari-chō, Higashiyama-ku; admission ¥600; ⊙8am-4.30pm, 9am-3.30pm 16 Nov-31 Mar; ⊠Keihan Shichijō) The original Sanjūsangen-dō was built in 1164 at the request of the retired emperor Go-shirakawa. The temple's name refers to the 33 (sanjūsan) bays between the pillars of this long, narrow building, which houses 1001 statues of the 1000-armed Kannon (the Buddhist goddess of mercy). The largest Kannon is flanked on either side by 500 smaller Kannon images, neatly lined up in rows.

There are an awful lot of arms, but if you're picky and think the 1000-armed statues don't have the required number of limbs, then you should remember to calculate according to the nifty Buddhist mathematical formula that holds that 40 arms are the equivalent of 1000 arms, because each saves 25 worlds.

At the back of the hall are 28 guardian statues in a great variety of expressive poses. The gallery on the western side of the hall is famous for the annual **Tōshi-ya Matsuri**, held on 15 January, during which archers shoot arrows the length of the hall.

The temple is a 1.5km walk east of Kyoto Station; alternatively, take bus 206 or 208 and get off at the Sanjūsangen-dō-mae stop.

Kyoto National Museum
MUSEUM
(京都国立博物館; Map p260; www.kyohaku.go.jp/eng/index_top.html; 527 Chaya-machi, Higashiyama-ku; adult/student ¥500/250; ⊙9.30am-6pm, to 8pm Fri, closed Mon) The Kyoto National Museum is housed in two buildings opposite Sanjūsangen-dō temple. It was founded in 1895 as an imperial repository for art and treasures from local temples and shrines. There are 17 rooms with displays of over a thousand artworks, historical artefacts and handicrafts. The permanent collection is

KYOTO IN...

Two Days

Even two days are enough to get a taste for the magic of Kyoto. On the morning of the first day, head to **Southern Higashiyama** and – if the energy level permits – spend the afternoon exploring **Northern Higashiyama**. You could just about make it from Kiyomizu-dera to Ginkaku-ji in one long day. The following day, head west to the **Arashiyama and Sagano Area** to visit the famed Bamboo Grove and Ōkōchi Sansō.

Four Days

Four days is about the perfect amount of time to allot Kyoto on a typical 10-day Japan trip. It gives you enough time to see quite a few of the big-name spots and add in a few *anaba* (secret spots). On the first two days, basically do the above two-day itinerary, but consider visiting **Southern Higashiyama** and **Northern Higashiyama** on separate days. After hitting these areas and the **Arashiyama and Sagano Area**, you've probably got one more day to play with. Maybe take a break from temple-hopping and hit some museums, or wander downtown and head up into the mountains to check out **Kibune and Kurama**.

One Week

If you're blessed with a full week in the old capital, our first advice is this: *slow down*. You'll want to do everything we mention in the above four-day itinerary, but at a slower pace, and you should consider 'stepping off the map' – ie just wandering into some temples or shrines and shops that aren't mentioned in this guide or hiking in the hills. Find your own perfect little garden and spend some time in meditation, thinking or napping. You'll also want to make a day trip to **Nara** and maybe even another one down to **Ise**.

---

excellent but somewhat poorly displayed; unless you have a particular interest in Japanese traditional arts, we recommend visiting this museum only when a special exhibition is on. Note that the museum is presently undergoing a partial reconstruction; you can still enter the museum but construction will be going on until late 2013.

Kawai Kanjirō Memorial Hall   MUSEUM
(河井寛治郎記念館; Map p260; 569 Kaneichō, Gojō-zaka, Higashiyama-ku; admission ¥900; ⊙10am-5pm, closed Mon & around 10-20 Aug & 24 Dec-7 Jan, dates vary each year) This museum is one of Kyoto's overlooked little gems, especially for those with an interest in Japanese crafts like pottery and furniture. The hall was the home and workshop of one of Japan's most famous potters, Kawai Kanjirō (1890–1966). The 1937 house is built in rural style and contains examples of Kanjirō's work, his collection of folk art and ceramics, and his workshop and a fascinating *noborigama* (a stepped kiln).

The hall is a 10-minute walk north of the Kyoto National Museum. Alternatively, take bus 206 or 207 from Kyoto Station and get off at the Umamachi stop.

Kiyomizu-dera   TEMPLE
(清水寺; Map p260; 1-294 Kiyomizu, Higashiyama-ku; admission ¥300; ⊙6am-6pm) This ancient temple was first built in 798, but the present buildings are reconstructions dating from 1633. As an affiliate of the Hossō school of Buddhism, which originated in Nara, it has successfully survived the many intrigues of local Kyoto schools of Buddhism through the centuries and is now one of the most famous landmarks of the city (for which reason it can get very crowded during spring and autumn).

The main hall has a huge veranda that is supported by pillars and juts out over the hillside. Just below this hall is the waterfall **Otowa-no-taki**, where visitors drink sacred waters believed to bestow health and longevity. Dotted around the precincts are other halls and shrines. At Jishu-jinja, the shrine up the steps above the main hall, visitors try to ensure success in love by closing their eyes and walking about 18m between a pair of stones – if you miss the stone, your desire for love won't be fulfilled! Note that you can ask someone to guide you, but if you do, you'll need someone's assistance to find your true love.

Before you enter the actual temple precincts, check out the **Tainai-meguri** (胎内めぐり; admission ¥100; ⊙9am-4pm), the entrance to which is just to the left (north) of the pagoda that is located in front of the main entrance to the temple (there is no English sign). We won't tell you too much about it as it will ruin the experience. Suffice to say that by entering the Tainai-meguri, you are symbolically entering the womb of a female bodhisattva. When you get to the rock in the darkness, spin it in either direction to make a wish.

The steep approach to the temple is known as Chawan-zaka (Teapot Lane) and is lined with shops selling Kyoto handicrafts, local snacks and souvenirs.

Check at the TIC for the scheduling of special night-time illuminations of the temple held in the spring and fall.

To get there from Kyoto Station take bus 206 and get off at either the Kiyōmizu-michi or Gojō-zaka stop and plod up the hill for 10 minutes.

Ninen-zaka & Sannei-zaka/Sannen-zaka
NEIGHBOURHOOD

(二年坂・三年坂) Just below and slightly to the north of Kiyomizu-dera, you will find one of Kyoto's loveliest restored neighbourhoods, the Ninen-zaka-Sannen-zaka area. The name refers to the two main streets of the area: Ninen-zaka and Sannen-zaka, literally 'Two-Year Hill' and 'Three-Year Hill' (the years referring to the ancient imperial years when they were first laid out). These two charming streets are lined with old wooden houses, traditional shops and restaurants. If you fancy a break, there are many teahouses and cafes along these lanes.

Kōdai-ji
TEMPLE

(高台寺; Map p260; 526 Shimokawara-chō, Kōdai-ji, Higashiyama-ku; admission ¥600; ⊙9am-5pm) This temple was founded in 1605 by Kita-no-Mandokoro in memory of her late husband, Toyotomi Hideyoshi. The extensive grounds include gardens that were designed by the famed landscape architect Kobori Enshū, and teahouses designed by the renowned master of the tea ceremony, Sen-no-Rikyū.

The temple is a 10-minute walk north of Kiyomizu-dera. Check at the TIC for the scheduling of special night-time illuminations of the temple (when the gardens are lit by multicoloured spotlights).

Maruyama-kōen
PARK

(円山公園; Map p260; Maruyama-chō, Higashiyama-ku) This park is a great place to escape the bustle of the city centre and amble around gardens, ponds, souvenir shops and restaurants. Peaceful paths meander through the trees and carp glide through the waters of a small pond in the centre of the park.

For two weeks in late March/early April, when the park's many cherry trees come into bloom, the calm atmosphere of the park is shattered by hordes of revellers enjoying *hanami* (blossom-viewing). For those who don't mind crowds, this is a good place to observe the Japanese at their most uninhibited. It is best to arrive early and claim a good spot high on the eastern side of the park, from which point you can safely peer down on the mayhem below.

The park is a five-minute walk east of the Shijō-Higashiōji intersection. To get there from Kyoto Station, take bus 206 and get off at the Gion stop. Alternatively, take the Tōzai subway line to the Higashiyama stop and walk south for about 10 minutes.

FREE Yasaka-jinja
SHRINE

(八坂神社; Map p260; 625 Gion-machi Kitagawa, Higashiyama-ku; ⊙24hr) This colourful shrine is just down the hill from Maruyama-kōen. It's considered to be the guardian shrine of neighbouring Gion and is sometimes endearingly referred to as 'Gion-san'. This shrine is particularly popular as a spot for *hatsu-mōde* (the first shrine visit of the new year). If you don't mind a stampede, come here around midnight on New Year's Eve or over the next few days. Surviving the crush is proof that you're blessed by the gods! Yasaka-jinja also sponsors Kyoto's biggest festival, Gion Matsuri.

Chion-in
TEMPLE

(知恩院; Map p260; 400 Rinka-chō, Higashiyama-ku; admission to grounds/inner buildings & garden free/¥400; ⊙9am-4.30pm) Chion-in was established in 1234 on the site where Hōnen, one of the most famous figures in Japanes Buddhism, taught his brand of Buddhism (Jōdo, or Pure Land, Buddhism) and eventually fasted to death. Today, the temple serves as the headquarters of the Jōdo sect, the most popular sect of Buddhism in Japan. It's the most popular pilgrimage temple in Kyoto and it's always a hive of activity. For visitors with a taste for the grand, this temple is sure to satisfy.

The oldest of the present buildings date back to the 17th century. The two-storey **San-mon**, a Buddhist temple gate at the main entrance, is the largest temple gate in Japan and prepares you for the massive scale of the temple. The immense main hall contains an image of Hōnen. It's connected to another hall, the Dai Hōjō, by a 'nightingale' floor (that sings and squeaks at every move, making it difficult for intruders to move about quietly).

Up a flight of steps southeast of the main hall is the temple's giant **bell**, which was cast in 1633 and weighs 70 tonnes. It is the largest bell in Japan. The bell is rung by the temple's monks 108 times on New Year's Eve each year.

The temple is close to the northeastern corner of Maruyama-kōen. From Kyoto Station take bus 206 and get off at the Chion-in-mae stop, or walk up (east) from Gion Shijō Station on the Keihan line.

TOP CHOICE **Shōren-in** TEMPLE
(青蓮院; Map p260; 69-1 Sanjōbō-chō, Awataguchi, Higashiyama-ku; admission ¥500; ⏰9am-5pm) This temple is hard to miss, with the giant camphor trees growing just outside its walls. Shōren-in was originally the residence of the chief abbot of the Tendai school of Buddhism. The present building dates from 1895, but the main hall has sliding screens with paintings from the 16th and 17th centuries. Often overlooked by the crowds that descend on other Higashiyama temples, this is a pleasant place to sit and think while gazing out over the beautiful gardens.

The temple is a five-minute walk north of Chion-in.

Gion NEIGHBOURHOOD
(祇園周辺; 🚃 Keihan line to Gion Shijō) Gion is Kyoto's famous entertainment and geisha district on the eastern bank of the Kamo-gawa. Modern architecture, congested traffic and contemporary nightlife establishments rob the area of some of its historical beauty, but there are still some lovely places left for a stroll and the district looks very attractive in the evening. Gion falls roughly between Sanjō-dōri and Gojō-dōri (north and south, respectively) and Higashiōji-dōri and Kawabata-dōri (east and west, respectively). In case you're wondering, Gion rhymes with 'key on'.

Hanami-kōji is the main north-south avenue of Gion, and the section south of Shijō-dōri is lined with 17th-century restaurants and teahouses, many of which are exclusive establishments for geisha entertainment.

Another must-see spot in Gion is **Shimbashi** (sometimes called Shirakawa Minami-dōri), which is one of Kyoto's most beautiful streets, and, arguably, among the most beautiful streets in all of Asia, especially in the evening and during cherry-blossom season. To get there, start at the intersection of Shijō-dōri and Hanami-kōji and walk north, then take the third left.

Kenin-ji TEMPLE
(建仁寺; Map p260; Komatsu-chō, Shijo sagaru, Yamatoōji-dōri, Higashiyama-ku; admission ¥500; ⏰10am-4.30pm) Founded in 1202 by the monk Eisai, Kenin-ji is the oldest Zen temple in Kyoto. It's an island of peace and calm on the border of the boisterous Gion nightlife district and it makes a fine counterpoint to the worldly pleasures of that area. The highlight here is the fine and expansive *kare-sansui* (dry landscape) garden. The painting of the twin dragons on the roof of the Hōdō hall is also fantastic; access to this hall is via two gates with rather puzzling English operating instructions (you'll see what we mean). It's at the southern end of Hanami-kōji street.

NORTHERN HIGASHIYAMA
The northern Higashiyama area (Map p266) at the base of the Higashiyama mountains is one of the city's richest areas for sightseeing. It includes such first-rate attractions as Nanzen-ji, Ginkaku-ji, Hōnen-in and Shūgaku-in Rikyū. You can spend a wonderful day walking from Keage Station on the Tōzai subway line all the way north to Ginkaku-ji via the Tetsugaku-no-Michi (the Path of Philosophy), stopping in the countless temples and shrines en route.

TOP CHOICE **Nanzen-ji** TEMPLE
(南禅寺; Map p266; Fukuchi-chō, Nanzen-ji, Sakyō-ku; admission grounds/Hōjō garden free/¥500, San-mon gate ¥300-400; ⏰8.40am-5pm Mar-Nov, to 4.30pm Dec-Feb) This is one of our favourite temples in Kyoto, with its expansive grounds and numerous subtemples. It began as a retirement villa for Emperor Kameyama but was dedicated as a Zen temple on his death in 1291. Civil war in the 15th century destroyed most of the temple; the present buildings date from the 17th century. It operates now as headquarters for the Rinzai school of Zen.

At its entrance stands the massive **San-mon**. Steps lead up to the 2nd storey, which has a fine view over the city. Beyond the gate is the main hall of the temple, above which you will find the **Hōjō**, where the **Leaping Tiger Garden** is a classic Zen garden well worth a look. (Try to ignore the annoying taped explanation of the garden.) While you're in the Hōjō, you can enjoy a cup of tea while gazing at a small waterfall (¥500, ask at the reception desk of the Hōjō).

Dotted around the grounds of Nanzen-ji are several subtemples that are often skipped by the crowds.

To get to Nanzen-ji from JR Kyoto or Keihan Sanjō Station, take bus 5 and get off at the Nanzen-ji Eikan-dō-michi stop. You can also take the Tōzai subway line from the city centre to Keage and walk for five minutes downhill. Turn right (east, towards the mountains) opposite the police box and walk slightly uphill (toward the mountains) and you will arrive at the main gate of the temple.

Nanzen-ji Oku-no-in

(南禅寺奥の院; Map p266; admission free; ☉dawn-dusk) Perhaps the best part of Nanzen-ji is overlooked by most visitors: Oku-no-in, a small shrine-temple hidden in a forested hollow behind the main precinct. To get there, walk up to the red-brick aqueduct in front of the subtemple of **Nanzen-in**. Follow the road/path that runs parallel to the aqueduct up into the hills, until you reach a waterfall in a beautiful mountain glen. Keep in mind that this is a sacred spot and worshippers come here to pray in peace. Please try to maintain a respectful silence.

Tenju-an

(天授庵; Map p266; 86-8 Fukuchi-chō, Nanzen-ji, Sakyō-ku; admission ¥400; ☉9am-5pm Mar-mid-Nov, to 4.30pm mid-Nov–Feb) This temple stands at the side of the San-mon. Built in 1337, the temple has a splendid garden and a great collection of carp in its pond.

Konchi-in

(金地院; Map p266; 86-12 Fukuchi-chō, Nanzen-ji, Sakyō-ku; admission ¥400; ☉8.30am-5pm Mar-Nov, to 4.30pm Dec-Feb) Just west of the main gate to Nanzen-ji (up some steps and down a side street), you will find Konchi-in, which has a dry garden designed by the master landscape designer Kobori Enshū. This garden is a good example of *shakkei*, or borrowed scenery; note how the mountains behind are drawn into the design.

Eikan-dō
TEMPLE

(永観堂; Map p266; 48 Eikandō-chō, Sakyō-ku; admission ¥600; ☉9am-5pm) Eikan-dō is a large temple famed for its varied architecture, gardens and works of art. It was founded in 855 by the priest Shinshō, but the name was changed to Eikan-dō in the 11th century to honour the philanthropic priest Eikan.

In the Amida-dō Hall, at the southern end of the complex, is the statue of Mikaeri Amida (Buddha Glancing Backwards). From the Amida-dō Hall, head north to the end of the covered walkway. Change into the sandals provided, then climb the steep steps up the mountainside to the **Tahō-tō** (Tahō Pagoda), where there's a fine view across the city.

Note that this temple is one of the city's most popular fall foliage spots; while it *is* stunning in November when the maples turn crimson, it also gets completely packed.

The temple is a 10-minute walk north of Nanzen-ji.

Tetsugaku-no-Michi (Path of Philosophy)
NEIGHBOURHOOD

(哲学の道; Map p266; Sakyō-ku Ginkaku-ji) The Tetsugaku-no-Michi is a pedestrian path that runs along a canal near the base of the Higashiyama. It's lined with cherry trees and a host of other blooming trees and flowers. It takes its name from one of its most famous strollers: 20th-century philosopher Nishida Kitarō, who is said to have meandered along the path lost in thought. It only takes 30 minutes to complete the walk, which starts just north of Eikan-dō and ends at Ginkaku-ji.

TOP CHOICE Hōnen-in
TEMPLE

(法然院; Map p266; 30 Goshonodan-chō, Shishigatani, Sakyō-ku; admission free; ☉6am-4pm) This fine temple was established in 1680 to honour Hōnen, the charismatic founder of the Jōdo school. It's a lovely, secluded temple with carefully raked gardens set back in the woods. Be sure to visit in November for the maple leaves. Normally, you cannot enter the main hall, but two special openings happen yearly (admission ¥500/800 fall/spring; 1-17 April and 1-7 November).

The temple is a 10-minute walk from Ginkaku-ji, on a side street that is accessible from the Tetsugaku-no-Michi; heading south on the path, look for the English sign on your left, then cross the bridge over the canal and follow the road uphill.

KYOTO

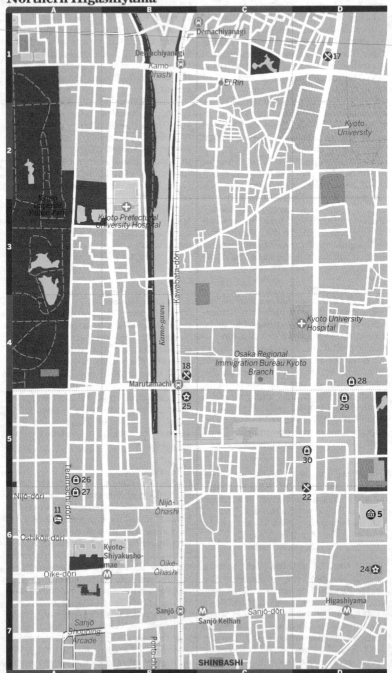

- Demachiyanagi
- Demachiyanagi
- Kamo-Ōhashi
- Ei Rin
- Kyoto University
- 17
- Kyoto Imperial Palace Park
- Kyoto Prefectural University Hospital
- Kawabata-dōri
- Kamo-gawa
- Kyoto University Hospital
- Osaka Regional Immigration Bureau Kyoto Branch
- 18
- Marutamachi
- 25
- 28
- 29
- Teramachi-dōri
- 26
- 27
- 30
- Nijō-dōri
- 11
- Nijō-dōri
- 22
- Oshikōji-dōri
- Nijō-Ōhashi
- 5
- Kyoto-Shiyakusho-mae
- Oike-dōri
- Oike-Ōhashi
- 24
- Sanjō
- Higashiyama
- Sanjō
- Sanjō Keihan
- Sanjō-dōri
- Sanjō Shopping Arcade
- Ponto-chō
- **SHINBASHI**

KYOTO

N 0 ————————— 400 m
0 ————————— 0.2 miles

Imadegawa-dōri

20 ✕ ✕ 19

23 ✕

Ginkaku-ji ⛩

10 ⊙   Hōnen-in ⛩

Yoshida-jinja ⊙

Takenaka
Inari-sha ⊙

Kaguraoka-dōri

Shirakawa-dōri

Munetada-jinja ⊙

Shinnyo-dō ⛩

Reikan-ji ⛩

Kurodani
Temple ⛩

Tetsugaku-no-Michi
(Path of Philosophy)

Kurodani
Pagoda ⛩

📇 15

Marutamachi-dōri

Okazaki-jinja ⊙

✕ 21

⊙ 2

Shira-kawa

1 ⛩

📇 14

Okazaki-kōen

🏛 4

🏛 8

Kyoto Municipal
📇 5

Biwako Sosui Canal

📇 12

Lake Biwa
Aqueduct
Museum ⊙

@

📇 13

9 ⛩

Nanzen-ji ⛩

3 ⛩

6 ⛩

7 ⛩

📇 16

Keage Ⓜ

HIGASHIYAMA-KU

Northern Higashiyama

KYOTO

Ginkaku-ji   TEMPLE
(銀閣寺; Map p266; 2 Ginkaku-ji-chō, Sakyō-ku;
admission ¥500; ⊙8.30am-5pm Mar-Nov, 9am-
4.30pm Dec-Feb) Ginkaku-ji is one of Kyoto's
premier sights. In 1482 Shōgun Ashikaga
Yoshimasa constructed a villa here as a genteel retreat from the turmoil of civil war. The
villa's name translates as 'Silver Pavilion', but
the shōgun's ambition to cover the building
with silver was never realised. After Yoshimasa's death, the villa was converted into a
temple.

Walkways lead through the gardens,
which include meticulously raked cones of
white sand (said to be symbolic of a mountain and a lake), tall pines and a pond in
front of the temple. A path also leads up the
mountainside through the trees.

Note that Ginkaku-ji is one of the city's
most popular sites, and it is almost always
crowded, especially during the spring and
autumn. We strongly recommend visiting
right after it opens or just before it closes.

From JR Kyoto or Keihan Sanjō Station,
take bus 5 and get off at the Ginkaku-ji-
michi stop. From Demachiyanagi Station or
Shijō Station, take bus 203 to the same stop.

Okazaki-kōen Area   NEIGHBOURHOOD
(岡崎公園) Right in the heart of the northern Higashiyama area, you'll find Okazaki-
kōen, which is Kyoto's museum district, and
the home of one of Kyoto's most popular
shrines, Heian-jingū.

Take bus 5 from Kyoto Station or Keihan
Sanjō Station and get off at the Kyoto Kaikan Bijutsu-kan-mae stop and walk north, or
walk up from Keihan Sanjō Station (15 minutes). All the sights listed here are within five
minutes' walk of this stop. Alternatively, take
the Tōzai subway line to Higashiyama Station and walk roughly north for five minutes.

Kyoto Municipal Museum of Art
(京都市美術館; Map p266; 124 Enshōji-chō,
Okazaki, Sakyō-ku; admission varies; ⊙9am-5pm,
closed Mon) The Kyoto Municipal Museum
of Art organises several major exhibitions
a year, including the excellent Kyoten exhibition, which showcases Japan's best living
artists. It's held from late May until early
June most years (check with the TIC for exact dates). Kyoto-related works form a significant portion of the permanent collection.

National Museum of Modern Art
(京都国立近代美術館; Map p266; www.mo
mak.go.jp/English; Enshōji-chō, Okazaki, Sakyō-
ku; admission ¥420; ⊙9.30am-5pm, closed Mon)
This museum is renowned for its compact
collection of contemporary Japanese ceramics and paintings.

Miyako Messe & Fureai-Kan
Kyoto Museum of Traditional Crafts
(みやこめっせ・京都伝統産業ふれあい館; Map p266; 9-1 Seishōji-chō, Okazaki, Sakyō-ku; admission free; 9am-5pm, closed Dec 29-Jan 3) The museum has exhibits covering things like wood-block prints, lacquerware, bamboo goods and gold-leaf work. It's in the basement of the Miyako Messe (Kyoto International Exhibition Hall).

Heian-jingū
(平安神宮; Map p266; Nishitennō-chō, Okazaki, Sakyō-ku; admission to shrine precincts/garden free/¥600; 6am-5pm Nov-Feb, 6am-6pm Mar-Oct) This impressive shrine complex was built in 1895 to commemorate the 1100th anniversary of the founding of Kyoto. The buildings are colourful replicas, reduced to two-thirds of the size of the Kyoto Gosho of the Heian period.

The spacious garden, with its large pond and Chinese-inspired bridge, is also meant to represent the kind of garden that was popular in the Heian period. About 500m in front of the shrine there is a massive orange *torii* (Shintō shrine gate). Although it appears to be entirely separate from the shrine, this is actually considered the main entrance to the shrine itself.

Two major events are held at the shrine: Jidai Matsuri (Festival of the Ages; p280), on 22 October, and *takigi nō*, from 1 to 2 June.

Shūgaku-in Rikyū HISTORICAL BUILDING
(修学院離宮; Map p250; Yabusoe, Shūgakuin, Sakyō-ku; admission free) This imperial villa was begun in the 1650s by the abdicated emperor Go-Mizunoo, and work was continued after his death in 1680 by his daughter Akenomiya.

Designed as an imperial retreat, the villa grounds are divided into three large garden areas on a hillside: lower, middle and upper. The gardens' reputation rests on their ponds, pathways and impressive use of 'borrowed scenery' in the form of the surrounding hills; the view from the Rinun-tei Teahouse in the upper garden is particularly impressive.

Tours, in Japanese, start at 9am, 10am, 11am, 1.30pm and 3pm (50 minutes). You must make advance reservations through the Imperial Household Agency (see p255 for details). An audio guide is available for non-Japanese speakers.

From Kyoto Station, take bus 5 and get off at the Shūgaku-in Rikyū-michi stop. The trip takes about an hour. From the bus stop it's a 15-minute walk (about 1km) to the villa. You can also take the Eiden Eizan line from Demachiyanagi Station to the Shūgaku-in stop and walk east about 25 minutes (about 1.5km) towards the mountains.

Hiei-zan & Enryaku-ji TEMPLE
(延暦寺; off Map p250; 4220 Honmachi, Sakamoto, Ōtsu city, Shiga; admission ¥550; 8.30am-4.30pm, 9am-4pm in winter) A visit to 848m-high Hiei-zan and the vast Enryaku-ji complex is a good way to spend half a day hiking, poking around temples and enjoying the atmosphere of a key site in Japanese history.

Enryaku-ji was founded in 788 by Saichō, also known as Dengyō-daishi, the priest who established the Tendai school. The complex is divided into three sections – Tōtō, Saitō and Yokawa. The **Tōtō** (eastern pagoda section) contains the Kompon Chū-dō (primary central hall), which is the most important building in the complex. The flames on the three Dharma (the law, in Sanskrit) lamps in front of the altar have been kept lit for over 1200 years. The Daikō-dō (great lecture hall) displays life-sized wooden statues of the founders of various Buddhist schools.

The **Saitō** (western pagoda section) contains the Shaka-dō, which dates from 1595 and houses a rare Buddha sculpture of the Shaka Nyorai (Historical Buddha). The Saitō, with its stone paths winding through forests of tall trees, temples shrouded in mist and the sound of distant gongs, is the most atmospheric part of the temple. Hold onto your ticket from the Tōtō section, as you may need to show it here.

The **Yokawa** is of minimal interest and a 4km bus ride away from the Saitō area.

You can reach Hiei-zan and Enryaku-ji by either train or bus. The most interesting way is the train-cable car-ropeway route.

By train, take the Keihan line north to the last stop, Demachiyanagi, and change to the Yase-Hieizanguchi-bound Eizan Dentetsu Eizan-line train (be careful not to board the Kurama-bound train that sometimes leaves from the same platform). At the last stop, Yase-Hieizanguchi (¥260), board the cable car (¥530, nine minutes) and then the ropeway (¥310, three minutes) to the peak, then walk down to the temples.

Alternatively, if you want to save money (by avoiding the cable car and ropeway), there are direct Kyoto buses from Kyoto and Keihan Sanjō Stations to Enryaku-ji, which take about 70 and 50 minutes, respectively (both cost ¥800).

KYOTO SIGHTS

NORTHWEST KYOTO

Northwest Kyoto has many excellent sights spread over a large area. Highlights include Kinkaku-ji (the famed Golden Pavilion) and Ryōan-ji, with its mysterious stone garden. Note that three of the area's main sites – Kinkaku-ji, Ryōan-ji and Ninna-ji – can easily be linked together to form a great half-day tour out of the city centre.

Kitano Tenman-gū   SHRINE

(北野天満宮; Map p258; Bakuro-chō, Kamigyō-ku; admission free; ⏴5am-6pm Apr-Oct, 5.30am-5.30pm Nov-Mar) This is a fine, spacious shrine on Imadegawa-dōri. If you're in town on the 25th of any month, be sure to catch the **Tenjin-san market-fair** here. It's one of Kyoto's two biggest markets and is a great place to pick up some interesting souvenirs.

From Kyoto Station, take bus 50 and get off at the Kitano-Tenmangū-mae stop. From Keihan Sanjō Station, take bus 10 to the same stop.

Kinkaku-ji   TEMPLE

(金閣寺; Map p270; 1 Kinkaku-ji-chō, Kita-ku; admission ¥400; ⏴9am-5pm) Kyoto's famed 'Golden Pavilion', Kinkaku-ji is one of Japan's best-known sights. The original building was built in 1397 as a retirement villa for Shōgun Ashikaga Yoshimitsu. His son converted it into a temple.

In 1950 a young monk consummated his obsession with the temple by burning it to the ground. The monk's story was fictionalised in Mishima Yukio's *The Golden Pavilion*. In 1955 a full reconstruction was completed that exactly followed the original design, but the gold-foil covering was extended to the lower floors.

Note that this temple can be packed almost any day of the year. We recommend going early in the day or just before closing.

To get to the temple from Kyoto Station, take bus 205 and get off at the Kinkaku-ji-michi stop. From Keihan Sanjō, take bus 59 and get off at the Kinkaku-ji-mae stop.

Northwest Kyoto

Ryōan-ji
TEMPLE

(龍安寺; Map p270; 13 Goryōnoshitamachi, Ryōan-ji, Ukyō-ku; admission ¥500; ⏲8am-5.30pm Mar-Nov, 8.30am-5pm Dec-Feb) This temple belongs to the Rinzai school of Zen and was founded in 1450. The main attraction is the garden arranged in the *kare-sansui* style. An austere collection of 15 rocks, apparently adrift in a sea of sand, is enclosed by an earthen wall. The designer, who remains unknown, provided no explanation.

The viewing platform for the garden can be packed solid but the other parts of the temple grounds are also interesting and less crowded. Among these, **Kyoyo-chi pond** is perhaps the most beautiful, particularly in autumn. If you want to enjoy the *kare-sansui* garden without the crowds, try to come right at opening time.

From Keihan Sanjō Station, take bus 59 to the Ryōan-ji-mae stop. Alternatively, you can walk to Ryōan-ji from Kinkaku-ji in about half an hour.

Ninna-ji
TEMPLE

(仁和寺; Map p270; 33 Omuroōuchi, Ukyō-ku; admission to grounds/Kondō Hall & Treasure Hall free/¥500; ⏲9am-5pm Mar-Nov, 9am-4.30pm Dec-Feb) This temple was built in 842 and is the head temple of the Omura branch of the Shingon school of Buddhism. The present temple buildings, including a five-storey pagoda, are from the 17th century. The extensive grounds are full of cherry trees that bloom in early April.

Admission to most of the grounds is free, but separate admission fees are charged for some of the temple's buildings, many of which are closed most of the year. To get there, take bus 59 from Keihan Sanjō Station and get off at the Omuro Ninna-ji stop. From Kyoto Station take bus 26.

Myōshin-ji
TEMPLE

(妙心寺; Map p270; 64 Myoshin-ji-chō, Hanazono, Ukyō-ku; admission to main temple/other areas of the complex ¥500/free; ⏲9.10-11.50am, 1pm-3.40pm, closed irregularly) The vast temple complex Myōshin-ji is a separate world within Kyoto, a walled-off complex of temples and subtemples that invites lazy strolling. Myōshin-ji dates back to 1342, and belongs to the Rinzai school. There are 47 subtemples, but only a few are open to the public.

From the north gate, follow the broad stone avenue flanked by rows of temples to the southern part of the complex. The eponymous Myōshin-ji is roughly in the middle of the complex. Your entry fee here entitles you to a tour of several of the buildings of the temple. The ceiling of the *hattō* (lecture hall) here features Tanyū Kanō's unnerving painting *Unryūzu* (meaning 'dragon glaring in eight directions'). Your guide will invite you to stand directly beneath the dragon; doing so makes it appear that it's spiralling up or down.

Another highlight of the complex is the wonderful garden of **Taizō-in** (退蔵院; admission ¥500; ⏲9am-5pm), a subtemple in the southwestern corner of the grounds.

The northern gate of Myōshin-ji is an easy 10-minute walk south of Ninna-ji; or take bus 10 from Keihan Sanjō Station to the Myōshin-ji Kita-mon-mae stop.

ARASHIYAMA & SAGANO AREA

Arashiyama and Sagano (Map p272), at the base of Kyoto's western mountains (known as the Arashiyama), is Kyoto's second-most important sightseeing district after Higashiyama. On first sight, you may wonder what all the fuss is about: the main street and the area around the famous Tōgetsu-kyō bridge have all the makings of a classic Japanese tourist trap. But once you head up the hills to the temples hidden among the greenery, you will understand the appeal.

Arashiyama's most stunning sight is the famous **bamboo grove**, which begins just outside the north gate of Tenryū-ji. Walking through this expanse of swaying bamboo is like entering another world and it ranks high on the list of experiences to be had in Japan.

Bus 28 links Kyoto Station with Arashiyama. Bus 11 connects Keihan Sanjō Station with Arashiyama. The most convenient rail connection is the ride from Shijō-Ōmiya Station on the Keifuku-Arashiyama line to Arashiyama Station (take the Hankyū train from downtown to get to Shijō-Ōmiya). You can also take the JR San-in line from Kyoto

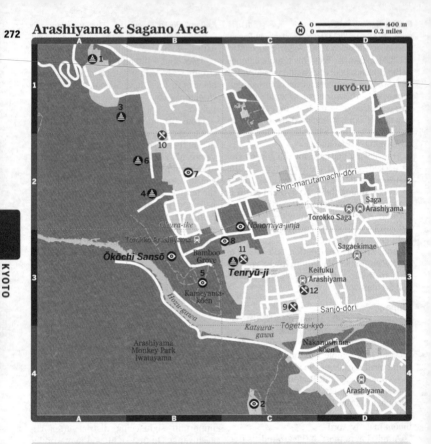

Arashiyama & Sagano Area

Station or Nijō Station and get off at Saga Arashiyama Station (be careful to take only the local train, as the express does not stop in Arashiyama).

The sites in this section are all within walking distance of Arashiyama Station. We suggest walking from this station to Tenryū-ji, exiting the north gate, checking out the bamboo grove, visiting Ōkōchi Sansō, then walking north to Giō-ji or Adashino Nembutsu-ji. If you have time for only one temple in the area, we recommend Tenryū-ji. If you have time for two, we suggest adding Giō-ji.

Kameyama-kōen
PARK

(亀山公園; Map p272) Southwest of Tenryū-ji, this park is a nice place to escape the crowds of Arashiyama. It's laced with trails, the best of which leads to a lookout over Katsura-gawa and up into the Arashiyama mountains. Keep an eye out for the monkeys, and keep children well away from the occasionally nasty critters. If you turn left when you reach the top of the bamboo grove, you'll find yourself in the park.

Tenryū-ji
TEMPLE

(天龍寺; Map p272; 68 Susukinobaba-chō, Saga Tenryū-ji, Ukyō-ku; admission ¥600; ☉8.30am-5.30pm, to 5pm 21 Oct-20 Mar) One of the major temples of the Rinzai school of Zen, Tenryū-ji was built in 1339 on the former site of Emperor Go-Daigo's villa after a priest had dreamt of a dragon rising from the nearby river. The dream was interpreted as a sign that the emperor's spirit was uneasy and the temple was constructed as appeasement – hence the name *tenryū* (heavenly dragon). The present buildings date from 1900, but the main attraction is the 14th-century Zen garden.

Arashiyama's famous **bamboo grove** lies just outside the north gate of the temple.

TOP CHOICE Ōkōchi Sansō
HISTORICAL BUILDING

(大河内山荘; Map p272; 8 Tabuchiyama-chō, Ogurayama, Saga, Ukyō-ku; admission ¥1000; ☉9am-5pm) This villa is the home of Ōkōchi Denjiro, an actor in samurai films. The superb gardens allow fine views over the city and are open to visitors. The gardens are particularly lovely during the autumn foliage season. The admission fee is hefty but includes tea and a cake (save the tea/cake ticket that comes with your admission). The villa is a 10-minute walk through the bamboo grove north of Tenryū-ji. When you get to the top of the bamboo grove, the entrance will be diagonally in front of you to the right.

The following sites are all located north of Ōkōchi Sansō. Strolling from Ōkōchi-Sansō all the way to Adashino Nembutsu-ji is a nice way to spend a few hours in Arashiyama/Sagano.

Jōjakkō-ji
TEMPLE

(常寂光寺; Map p272; 3 Ogura-chō, Ogurayama, Saga, Ukyō-ku; admission ¥400; ☉9am-5pm) If you continue north of Ōkōchi Sansō, the narrow road soon passes stone steps on your left that lead up to the pleasant grounds of Jōjakkō-ji. The temple is famous for its maple leaves and the Tahōtō pagoda. The

upper area of the temple precinct affords good views east over Kyoto. The temple is a 10-minute walk north of Ōkōchi Sansō.

Rakushisha
HISTORICAL BUILDING

(落柿舎; Map p272; 20 Himyōjin-chō, Ogurayama, Saga, Ukyō-ku; admission ¥200; ☉9am-5pm Mar-Dec, 10am-4pm Jan & Feb) This hut belonged to Mukai Kyorai, the best-known disciple of illustrious haiku (17-syllable poem) poet Bashō. Literally meaning 'House of the Fallen Persimmons', legend holds that Kyorai dubbed the house Rakushisha after waking one morning after a storm to find the persimmons he had planned to sell from the garden's trees scattered on the ground. The hut is a short walk downhill and to the north of Jōjakkō-ji.

Nison-in
TEMPLE

(二尊院; Map p272; 27 Monzenchōjin-chō, Nison-in, Saga, Ukyō-ku; admission ¥500; ☉9am-4.30pm) Nison-in is in an attractive setting on a wooded hillside. The long approach to the temple, which is lined with lovely maple trees, is the biggest drawcard. The temple is located a short walk north of Jōjakkō-ji.

Giō-ji
TEMPLE

(祇王寺; Map p272; 32 Kozaka, Saga Toriimoto, Ukyō-ku; admission ¥300; ☉9am-4.30pm, with seasonal variations) This quiet temple was named for a Heian-era *shirabyōshi* (traditional dancer) named Giō. Aged 21, Giō committed herself here as a nun after her romance with Taira-no-Kiyomori, the commander of the Heike clan. The temple is famous for its lovely expanse of moss, which lies in front of the thatch-roof main hall. It's about 10 minutes' walk north of Nison-in.

Adashino Nembutsu-ji
TEMPLE

(化野念仏寺; Map p272; 17 Adashino-chō, Saga Toriimoto, Ukyō-ku; admission ¥500; ☉9am-4.30pm, with seasonal variations) This rather unusual temple is where the abandoned bones of paupers and destitutes without next of kin were gathered. Thousands of stone images are crammed into the temple grounds, and these abandoned souls are remembered each year with candles here in the **Sentō Kuyō ceremony** held on the evenings of 23 and 24 August. The temple is about 15 minutes' walk north of Giō-ji.

Arashiyama Monkey Park Iwatayama
PARK

(嵐山モンキーパークいわたやま; Map p272; 8 Genrokuzan-chō, Arashiyama, Nishikyō-ku; adult/

child ¥550/250; ☺9am-5pm 15 Mar-15 Nov, to 4pm winter) Home to some 200 Japanese monkeys of all sizes and ages, this park is fun for kids and animal lovers of all ages.

Though it is common to spot wild monkeys in the nearby mountains, here you can see them close up. It makes for an excellent photo opportunity, not only for the monkeys but for the panoramic view over Kyoto. Refreshingly, it is the animals who are free to roam while the humans who feed them are caged in a box!

Just be warned: it's a steep climb up the hill to get to the monkeys. If it's a hot day, you're going to be drenched by the time you get to the spot where they gather.

The entrance to the park is up a flight of steps just upstream of the Tōgetsu-kyō bridge (near the orange torii of Ichitani-jinja). Buy your tickets from the machine to the left of the shrine at the top of the steps.

SOUTHEAST KYOTO
Southeast Kyoto (Map p250) contains some of Kyoto's most impressive sights, including Tōfuku-ji, with its lovely garden, and Fushi-Inari-Taisha, with its hypnotically beautiful arcades of Shintō shrine gates.

Tōfuku-ji   TEMPLE
(東福寺; Map p250; 15-778 Honmahi, Higashi-yama-ku; admission to garden/grounds ¥400/free; ☺9am-4pm Dec-Oct, 8.30am-4.30pm Nov) Founded in 1236 by the priest Enni, Tōfuku-ji belongs to the Rinzai sect of Zen Buddhism. As this temple was intended to compare with Tōdai-ji and Kōfuku-ji in Nara, it was given a name combining characters from the names of each of these temples.

The present temple complex includes 24 subtemples; at one time there were 53. The huge **San-mon** is the oldest Zen main gate in Japan. The **Hōjō** (abbot's hall) was reconstructed in 1890. The gardens, laid out in 1938, are well worth a visit. The northern garden has stones and moss neatly arranged in a chequerboard pattern. From a viewing platform at the back of the gardens, you can observe the Tsūten-kyō (Bridge to Heaven), which spans a valley filled with maples.

Note that Tōfuku-ji is one of Kyoto's most famous autumn-foliage spots, and it is invariably packed during the peak of colours in November. Otherwise, it's often very quiet.

Tōfuku-ji is a 20-minute walk (2km) southeast of Kyoto Station. You can also take a local train on the JR Nara line and get off at JR Tōfukuji Station, from which it's a 10-minute walk southeast. Alternatively, you can take the Keihan line to Keihan Tōfukuji Station, from which it's also a 10-minute walk.

Fushimi-Inari Taisha   SHRINE
(伏見稲荷大社; Map p250; 68 Yabunouchi-chō, Fukakusa, Fushimi-ku; admission free; ☺dawn-dusk) This stunning shrine complex was dedicated to the gods of rice and sake by the Hata family in the 8th century. As the role of agriculture diminished, deities were enrolled to ensure prosperity in business. Nowadays, the shrine is one of Japan's most popular, and is the head shrine for some 30,000 Inari shrines scattered the length and breadth of Japan.

The entire complex sprawls across the wooded slopes of Inari-yama. A pathway wanders 4km up the mountain and is lined with thousands of red torii. There are also dozens of stone foxes. The fox is considered the messenger of Inari, the god of the rice harvest (and, later on, business). The Japanese traditionally see the fox as a sacred, somewhat mysterious figure capable of 'possessing' humans. The key often seen in the fox's mouth is for the rice granary.

The walk around the upper precincts of the shrine is a pleasant day hike. It also makes for a very eerie stroll in the late afternoon and early evening, when the various graveyards and miniature shrines along the path take on a mysterious air.

To get to the shrine from Kyoto Station, take a JR Nara line train to Inari Station. From Keihan Sanjō Station take the Keihan line to Fushimi-Inari Station. The shrine is just east of both of these stations.

Daigo-ji   TEMPLE
(醍醐寺; Map p250; 22 Higashiōji-chō, Daigo, Fushimi-ku; admission to grounds most of year/cherry-blossom & autumn-foliage seasons free/¥600, to Sampō-in ¥600; ☺9am-5pm Mar-Nov, to 4pm Dec-Feb) Daigo-ji was founded in 874 by the priest Shobo, who gave it the name of Daigo. This refers to the five periods of Buddha's teaching, which were often compared to the five forms of milk prepared in India, the highest form of which is called *daigo* (ultimate essence of milk).

The temple was expanded into a vast complex of buildings on two levels: Shimo Daigo (Lower Daigo) and Kami Daigo (Upper Daigo). During the 15th century, the lower-level buildings were destroyed, with the sole exception of the five-storey pagoda.

Built in 951, this pagoda still stands and is lovingly noted as the oldest of its kind in Japan and the oldest existing building in Kyoto.

The subtemple **Sampō-in** is a fine example of the amazing opulence of that period. The Kanō paintings and the garden are special features.

To get to Daigo-ji, take the Tōzai subway line from central Kyoto to the last stop, Daigo, and walk east (towards the mountains) for about 10 minutes. Make sure that the train you board is bound for Daigo, as some head to Hama-Ōtsu instead.

Uji
NEIGHBOURHOOD

(宇治) Uji is a small city to the south of Kyoto. Its main claims to fame are Byōdō-in and tea cultivation. Uji's stone bridge – the oldest of its kind in Japan – has been the scene of many bitter clashes in previous centuries.

Uji is also home to **Ujigami-jinja**, a Unesco World Heritage Site. Despite this status, it's not one of the Kyoto area's more interesting sights. Those who wish to see it can find it by crossing the river (using the bridge near Byōdō-in) and walking about 10 minutes uphill (there are signs).

Uji can be reached by rail in about 40 minutes from Kyoto on the Keihan Uji line or JR Nara line.

When arriving in Uji by Keihan train, leave the station, cross the river via the first bridge on the right, and then turn left to find Byōdō-in. When coming by JR, the temple is about 10 minutes' walk east (towards the river) of Uji Station.

Byōdō-in

(平等院; 116 Uji renge, Uji-shi; admission ¥600; ⏰8.30am-5.30pm) This Buddhist temple was converted from a Fujiwara villa in 1052. The Hōō-dō (Phoenix Hall), more properly known as the Amida-dō, was built in 1053 and is the only original remaining building. The phoenix was a popular mythical bird in China and was revered by the Japanese as a protector of Buddha. The architecture of the building resembles the shape of the bird, and there are two bronze phoenixes perched opposite each other on the roof.

The building was originally intended to represent Amida's heavenly palace in the Pure Land. This building is one of the few extant examples of Heian-period architecture, and its graceful lines make one wish that far more of its type had survived to the present day. For a preview, take a look at the ¥10 coin.

Inside the hall is the famous statue of Amida and 52 Bosatsu (bodhisattvas) dating from the 11th century and attributed to the priest-sculptor Jōchō.

SOUTHWEST KYOTO

Southwest Kyoto (Map p250) is home to two notable sights, including the famous 'Moss Temple' (Saihō-ji) and Katsura-Rikyū.

Saihō-ji
TEMPLE

(西芳寺; Map p250; 56 Jingatani-chō, Matsuo, Nishikyō-ku; admission ¥3000) The main attraction at this temple is the heart-shaped garden designed in 1339 by Musō Kokushi. The garden is famous for its luxuriant moss, hence the temple's other name, Koke-dera (Moss Temple). While the reservation procedure is troublesome and the entry fee rather steep, a visit to the temple is highly recommended – the lush, shady garden is among the best in Kyoto.

Before you visit the garden, you will be asked to copy a Sutra using a Japanese ink brush. It's not as hard as it sounds, as you can trace the faint letters on the page – and don't worry about finishing. Once in the garden, you're free to move about as you wish.

Take bus 28 from Kyoto Station to the Matsuo-taisha-mae stop and walk 15 minutes southwest. From Keihan Sanjō Station, take Kyoto bus 63 to Koke-dera, the last stop, and walk for two minutes.

VISITING SAIHŌ-JI

Entry to Saihō-ji is part of a tour only, and advance reservation is required. To visit, send a postcard at least one week before the date you wish to come and include your name, number of visitors, address in Japan, occupation, age (you must be over 18) and desired date (choice of alternative dates preferred). Enclose a stamped, self-addressed postcard for a reply to your Japanese address – eg buy an Ōfuku-hagaki (send-and-return postcard set) at a Japanese post office. The address:

Saihō-ji
56 Kamigaya-chō
Matsuo, Nishikyō-ku
Kyoto-shi 615-8286
JAPAN

Katsura Rikyū   HISTORICAL BUILDING

(桂離宮; Katsura Detached Palace; Katsura Misono, Nishikyō-ku; admission free) This palace is considered to be one of the finest examples of Japanese traditional architecture. It was built in 1624 for the emperor's brother, Prince Toshihito. Every conceivable detail of the villa, the teahouses, the large pond with islets and the surrounding garden has been given meticulous attention.

Tours (around 40 minutes), in Japanese, commence at 10am, 11am, 2pm and 3pm. You should be there 20 minutes beforehand. An explanatory video is shown in the waiting room and a leaflet is provided in English. You must make advance reservations with the Imperial Household Agency (see p255 for details). Visitors must be over 20 years of age.

To get to the villa from Kyoto Station, take bus 33 and get off at the Katsura Rikyū-mae stop, which is a five-minute walk from the villa. The easiest access from the city centre is to take a Hankyū line train from Hankyū Kawaramachi Station to Hankyū Katsura Station, which is a 15-minute walk from the villa. A taxi from Hankyū Katsura Station to the villa will cost about ¥700. Note that some *tokkyū* (express) trains don't stop in Katsura.

KITAYAMA AREA

Starting on the north side of Kyoto city and stretching almost all the way to the Sea of Japan, the Kitayama (Northern Mountains) are a natural escape prized by Kyoto city dwellers. Attractions here include the village of Ōhara, with its pastoral beauty, the fine mountain temple at Kurama, the river dining platforms at Kibune, and the trio of mountain temples in Takao.

Ōhara   NEIGHBOURHOOD

(大原; Map p277) Since ancient times Ōhara, a quiet farming town about 10km north of Kyoto, has been regarded as a holy site by followers of the Jōdo school of Buddhism. The region provides a charming glimpse of rural Japan, along with the picturesque Sanzen-in, Jakkō-in and several other fine temples. It's most popular in autumn, when the maple leaves change colour and the mountain views are spectacular. During the peak foliage season of November, this area can get very crowded, especially on weekends.

Sanzen-in

(三千院; Map p277; 540 Raigōin-chō, Ōhara, Sakyō-ku; admission ¥700; ◎8.30am-5pm Mar-Nov, to 4.30pm Dec-Feb) Founded in 784 by the priest Saichō, Sanzen-in elongs to the Tendai sect of Buddhism. The temple's Yusei-en is one of the most photographed gardens in Japan, and rightly so. Take some time to sit and enjoy the garden.

After seeing Yusei-en, head off to the Ojo-gokuraku Hall (Temple of Rebirth in Paradise) to see the impressive Amitabha trinity, a large Amida image flanked by attendants Kannon, goddess of mercy, and Seishi, god of wisdom. After this, walk up to the hydrangea garden at the back of the temple, where in late spring and summer you can walk among hectares of blooming hydrangeas.

To get to Sanzen-in, follow the signs from Ōhara's main bus stop up the hill past a long arcade of souvenir stalls. The entrance is on your left as you crest the hill.

Jakkō-in

(寂光院; Map p277; 676 Kusao-chō, Ōhara, Sakyō-ku; admission ¥600; ◎9am-5pm Mar-Nov, to 4.30pm Dec-Feb) The history of Jakkō-in is exceedingly tragic. The actual founding date of the temple is subject to some debate (somewhere between the 6th and 11th centuries), but it gained fame as the temple that harboured Kenrei Mon-in, a lady of the Taira clan. In 1185 the Taira were soundly defeated in a sea battle with the Minamoto clan at Dan-no-ura. With the entire Taira clan slaughtered or drowned, Kenrei Mon-in threw herself into the waves with her grandson Antoku, the infant emperor; she was fished out – the only member of the clan to survive.

Unfortunately the main building of the temple burned down in May 2000 and the newly reconstructed main hall is lacking some of the charm of the original. Nonetheless, it's a nice spot and the walk there is pleasant.

Jakkō-in lies to the west of Ōhara. Walk out of the bus station up the road to the traffic lights, then follow the small road to the left. It's easy to get lost on the way, but any villager will be happy to point you in the right direction.

Kurama & Kibune   NEIGHBOURHOOD

(鞍馬・貴船; Map p278) Only 30 minutes north of Kyoto on the Eiden Eizan main line, Kurama and Kibune are a pair of tranquil valleys long favoured by Kyotoites as places to escape the crowds and stresses of the city below. Kurama's main attractions are its mountain temple and its onsen (hot springs). Kibune, over the ridge, is a cluster

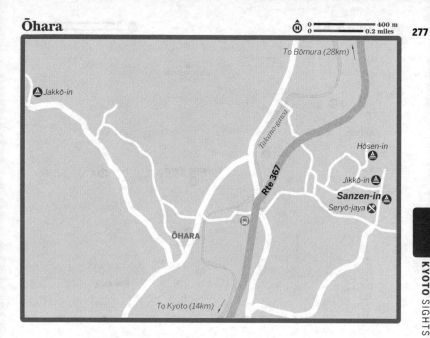

N 0 ────────── 400 m
0 ────────── 0.2 miles

To Bōmura (28km)

⛩ Jakkō-in

Takano-gawa

Rte 367

Hōsen-in ⛩

Jikkō-in ⛩

Sanzen-in ⛩
Seryō-jaya ✕

ŌHARA

To Kyoto (14km)

of ryokan overlooking a mountain stream. It is best enjoyed in the summer, when the ryokan serve dinner on platforms built over the rushing waters of the Kibune-gawa, providing welcome relief from the summer heat.

The two valleys lend themselves to being explored together. In the winter one can start from Kibune, walk for an hour or so over the ridge, visit Kurama-dera and then soak in the onsen before heading back to Kyoto. In the summer the reverse is best; start from Kurama, walk up to the temple, then down the other side to Kibune to enjoy a meal suspended above the cool river (unfortunately, restaurants in Kibune are known to refuse solo diners).

If you happen to be in Kyoto on the night of 22 October, be sure not to miss the **Kurama-no-hi Matsuri** (Kurama Fire Festival; p280), one of the most exciting festivals in the Kyoto area.

To get to Kurama and Kibune, take the Eiden Eizan line from Kyoto's Demachiyanagi Station. For Kibune, get off at the second-to-last stop, Kibune Guchi, take a right out of the station and walk about 20 minutes up the hill. For Kurama, go to the last stop, Kurama, and walk straight out of the station. Both destinations are ¥410 and take about 30 minutes to reach.

Kurama-dera
(鞍馬寺; Map p278; 1074 Kurama Honmachi, Sakyō-ku; admission ¥200; ◷9am-4.30pm) This temple was established in 770 by the monk Gantei from Nara's Tōshōdai-ji. After seeing a vision of the deity Bishamon-ten, guardian of the northern quarter of the Buddhist heaven, Gantei established Kurama-dera just below the peak of Kurama-yama. Originally under the Tendai sect, Kurama has been independent since 1949, describing its own brand of Buddhism as Kurama Kyō.

The entrance to the temple is just up the hill from the Eiden Eizan main line's Kurama Station. A tram goes to the top for ¥100; alternatively, hike up by following the main path past the tram station. The trail is worth taking if it's not too hot, as it winds through a forest of towering old-growth *sugi* (cryptomeria) trees. At the top there is a courtyard dominated by the *honden* (main hall). Behind the *honden,* a trail leads off to the mountain's peak.

At the top, you can take a brief detour across the ridge to Ōsugi-gongen, a quiet shrine in a grove of trees. Those who want to continue to Kibune can take the trail down the other side. It's a 1.2km, 30-minute hike from the *honden* to the valley floor of

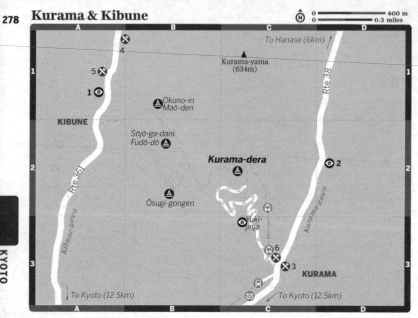

Kurama & Kibune

◎ **Top Sights**

◎ **Sights**

✖ **Eating**

Kibune. On the way down are two pleasant mountain shrines, Sōjō-ga-dani Fudō-dō and Okuno-in Maō-den.

Kurama Onsen

(鞍馬温泉; Map p278; 520 Kurama Honma-chi, Sakyō-ku; admission to outdoor/indoor bath ¥1100/2500; ◷10am-9pm) One of the few onsen within easy reach of Kyoto, Kurama Onsen is a great place to relax after a hike. The outdoor bath has a fine view of Kurama-yama; the indoor bath includes use of sauna and relaxation areas. Buy tickets from the machine outside the door of the main building (instructions are in Japanese and English).

To get to Kurama Onsen, walk straight out of Kurama Station, turn left up the main road and follow it for about 10 minutes. You'll see the baths down on your right. There's also a free shuttle bus that runs between the station and the onsen, leaving approximately every 30 minutes.

Kibune-jinja

(貴船神社; Map p278; 180 Kibune-chō, Kurama, Sakyō-ku; admission free; ◷6am-8pm Apr-Nov, 6am-6pm Dec-Mar) This shrine, halfway up the valley-town of Kibune, is worth a quick look, particularly if you can ignore the unfortunate plastic horse statue at its entrance. From Kibune you can hike over the mountain to Kurama-dera, along a trail that starts halfway up the village on the eastern side (or vice versa; see p277).

Takao   NEIGHBOURHOOD

(高雄; Map p250) Takao is a secluded mountain village tucked far away in the northwestern part of Kyoto. It is famed for autumn foliage and the temples of Jingo-ji, Saimyō-ji and Kōzan-ji.

There are two options for buses to Takao: an hourly JR bus that leaves from Kyoto Station, which takes about an hour to reach the Takao stop (get off at the Yamashiro-Takao stop); and Kyoto city bus 8 from

Shijō-Karasuma (get off at the Takao stop). To get to Jingo-ji from these bus stops, walk down to the river, then look for the steps on the other side.

Jingo-ji

(神護寺; Map p250; 5 Takao-chō, Umegahata, Ukyō-ku; admission ¥500; ◷9am-4pm) This is the best of the three temples in the Takao area. This mountain temple sits at the top of a long flight of stairs that stretch up from Kiyotaki-gawa to the temple's main gate. The Kondō (Gold Hall) is the most impressive of the temple's structures; it's roughly in the middle of the grounds, at the top of another flight of stairs.

After visiting the Kondō, head in the opposite direction along a wooded path to an open area overlooking the valley. Don't be surprised if you see people tossing small discs over the railing into the chasm below. These are *kawarakenage* – light clay discs that people throw to rid themselves of their bad karma. Be careful: it's addictive, and at ¥100 for two, it can become expensive. You can buy the discs at a nearby stall. The trick is to flick the discs very gently, convex side up, like a Frisbee. When you get it right, they sail all the way down the valley, taking all that bad karma away with them.

The other two temples are within easy walking distance of Jingo-ji.

Saimyō-ji

(西明寺; Map p250; 2 Makino-chō, Umegahata, Ukyō-ku; admission ¥500; ◷9am-5pm) This is the better of the two other temples. It's about five minutes' walk north of the base of the steps that lead up to Jingo-ji (follow the river upstream).

Kōzan-ji

(高山寺; Map p250; 8 Toganoo-chō, Umegahata, Ukyō-ku; admission ¥600; ◷8am-5pm) To get to Kōzan-ji you must walk back up to the main road and follow it north for about 10 minutes.

🏃 Activities

Funaoka Onsen
SENTO

(船岡温泉; Map p258; 82-1 Minami-Funaoka-chō-Murasakino Kita-ku; admission ¥410; ◷3pm-1am Mon-Sat, 8am-1am Sun & holidays) This old bath on Kuramaguchi-dōri is Kyoto's best. It boasts an outdoor bath, a sauna, a cypress-wood tub, an electric bath, a herbal bath and a few more for good measure. Be sure to check out the *ranma* (carved wooden pan-els) in the changing room. Carved during Japan's invasion of Manchuria, the panels offer insight into the prevailing mindset of that era. (Note the panels do contain some violent imagery, which may disturb some visitors.)

To find the bath, head west about 400m on Kuramaguchi-dōri from the Kuramaguchi-Horiikawa intersection. It's on the left, not far past Lawson convenience store. Look for the large rocks out the front.

Maika
GEISHA COSTUME

(舞香; Map p260; 📞551-1661; www.maica.tv/e/; Higashiyama-ku, Miyagawa suji 4-chōme 297; maiko/geisha from ¥6500/8000) If you ever wondered how you might look as a geisha,

> **DON'T MISS**

KYOTO UNESCO WORLD HERITAGE SITES

In 1994, 13 of Kyoto's Buddhist temples, three Shintō shrines and one castle met the criteria to be designated World Heritage Sites by the United Nations. Each of the 17 sites has buildings or gardens of immeasurable historical value and all are open for public viewing.

Castles

» Nijō-jō (p257)

Shrines

» Kamigamo-jinja (p259)
» Shimogamo-jinja (p259)
» Ujigami-jinja in Uji (p275)

Temples

» Byōdō-in (p275)
» Daigo-ji (p274)
» Enryaku-ji (p269)
» Ginkaku-ji (p268)
» Kinkaku-ji (p270)
» Kiyomizu-dera (p262)
» Kōzan-ji (p279)
» Ninna-ji (p271)
» Nishi Hongan-ji (p254)
» Ryōan-ji (p271)
» Saihō-ji (p275)
» Tenryū-ji (p273)
» Tō-ji (p254)

Kyoto has several shops that offer *maiko-henshin* (geisha transformation). Maika is a popular *maiko-henshin* shop in Gion. If you don't mind spending a bit extra, it's possible to head out in costume for a stroll through Gion (and be stared at like never before!). The process takes about an hour. Call to reserve at least one day in advance.

Club Ōkitsu Kyoto JAPANESE CULTURE
(京都桜橘倶楽部「桜橘庵」; Map p258; ☑411-8585; www.okitsu-kyoto.com; in the Kōdōkan, 524-1 Mototsuchimikado-chō, Shinmachi, Kamigyō-ku) Kyoto is a fine place to get a taste of traditional Japanese culture. Club Ōkitsu Kyoto offers an upscale introduction to various aspects of Japanese culture including tea ceremony and the incense ceremony. It also offers kimono dressing upon request (note that kimono dressing is not offered alone: it must be part of a package including tea ceremony and/or incense ceremony). The introduction is performed in an exquisite Japanese villa near the Kyoto Gosho and participants get a real sense of the elegance and refinement of traditional Japanese culture.

En TEA CEREMONY
(えん; Map p260; ☑080-3782-2706; 272 Matsubara-chō, Higashiyama-ku; tea ceremony per person ¥2000; ⊙3-6pm, closed Wed) A small teahouse near Gion where you can experience the Japanese tea ceremony with a minimum of fuss or expense. English explanations are provided and tea ceremonies are held at 3pm, 4pm, 5pm or 6pm (check the website for the latest times, as these may change). Reservations are recommended in high season. It's a little tricky to find: it's located down a little alley off Higashiōji-dōri – look for the sign just south of Tenkaippin Rāmen.

🍲 Courses

Uzuki COOKING
(www.kyotouzuki.com; 3hr class per person ¥4000) If you want to learn how to cook some of the delightful foods you've tried in Kyoto, we highly recommend Uzuki, a small cooking class conducted in a Japanese home for groups of two to four people. You will learn how to cook a variety of dishes and then sit down and enjoy the fruits of your labour. You can consult beforehand if you have particular dishes you'd like to cook. The fee includes all ingredients. Reserve via website.

☞ Tours

The following companies offer private tours of Japan:

Johnnie's Kyoto Walking WALKING
(http://web.kyoto-inet.or.jp/people/h-s-love) Hirooka Hajime, aka Johnnie Hillwalker, offers an interesting guided walking tour of the area around Kyoto station and the Higashiyama area.

Naoki Doi TAXI
(☑090-9596-5546; www3.ocn.ne.jp/~doitaxi) This English-speaking taxi driver offers private taxi tours of Kyoto.

🎎 Festivals & Events

There are hundreds of festivals happening in Kyoto throughout the year. Listings of these can be found in the *Kyoto Visitor's Guide* or *Kansai Scene*. The following are some of the major and most spectacular festivals. These attract hordes of spectators from out of town, so you will need to book accommodation well in advance.

Setsubun Matsuri at Yoshida-jinja FIRE
This festival is held on the day of *setsubun* (2, 3 or 4 February; check with the TIC), which marks the last day of winter in the Japanese lunar calendar. In this festival, people climb up to Yoshida-jinja in the northern Higashiyama area to watch a huge bonfire (in which old good luck charms are burned). It's one of Kyoto's more dramatic festivals. The action starts at dusk.

Aoi Matsuri PARADE
The Hollyhock Festival dates back to the 6th century and commemorates the successful prayers of the people for the gods to stop calamitous weather. These days the procession involves imperial messengers carried in ox carts and a retinue of 600 people dressed in traditional costume. The procession leaves at around 10am on 15 May from the Kyoto Gosho (p256) and heads for Shimogamo-jinja (p259).

Gion Matsuri PARADE
Perhaps the most renowned of all Japanese festivals, Gion Matsuri reaches a climax on 17 July with a parade of over 30 floats depicting ancient themes and decked out in incredible finery. On the three evenings preceding the main festival day, people gather on Shijō-dōri, many of them dressed in beautiful *yukata* (light summer kimonos), to look at

Common sense varies from place to place. In Kyoto, even if you dispense with common sense, you don't run the risk of serious trouble, but there are a few things to keep in mind to make everything easier and perhaps a little safer:

» **Look both ways** when exiting a shop or hotel onto a sidewalk, especially if you have young ones in tow – there is almost always someone on a bicycle tearing in your direction.

» **Bring a pair of slip-on shoes** to save you from tying and untying your shoes each time you visit a temple.

» **Don't take a taxi** in the main Higashiyama sightseeing district during cherry-blossom season – the streets will be so crowded that it will be faster to walk or cycle.

» **Get lost** once in a while. Grab a business card from your hotel and head out. You can't go too far wrong: the city is easy to navigate and the locals *will* help you find your way back.

» **Don't worry** about committing some dreadful faux pas. No one expects you to know all the rules. Just do what feels right and what would be polite in your own country.

the floats and carouse from one street stall to the next.

Daimon-ji Gozan Okuribi   FIRE

This festival, commonly known as Daimon-ji Yaki, is performed on 16 August as a means of bidding farewell to the souls of ancestors. Enormous fires are lit on five mountains in the form of Chinese characters or other shapes. The largest fire is always burned on Daimon-ji-yama, just above Ginkaku-ji (p268), in northern Higashiyama. The fires start at 8pm and the best position to watch from is the banks of the Kamo-gawa or, alternatively, pay for a rooftop view from a hotel.

Jidai Matsuri   PARADE

The Festival of the Ages is of comparatively recent origin, only dating back to 1895. More than 2000 people, dressed in costumes ranging from the 8th century to the 19th century, parade from Kyoto Gosho (p256) to Heian-jingū (p269) on 22 October.

Kurama-no-hi Matsuri   FIRE

In perhaps Kyoto's most dramatic festival, the Kurama Fire Festival, huge flaming torches are carried through the streets of Kurama (p276) by men in loincloths on 22 October (the same day as the Jidai Matsuri). Note that trains to and from Kurama will be completely packed with passengers on the evening of the festival (we suggest going early and returning late).

🛏 Sleeping

The most convenient areas in which to be based, in terms of easy access to shopping, dining and sightseeing attractions, are downtown Kyoto and the Higashiyama area. The Kyoto Station area is also a good place to be based, with excellent access to transport and plenty of shops and restaurants about. Transport information in the following listings is from Kyoto Station unless otherwise noted.

Welcome Inn Center (☎343-4887; ⏱10am-6pm, closed 2nd & 4th Tue of each month & New Year holidays) is a free booking service that can help you in English with accommodation at member hotels, ryokan and guesthouses in Kyoto and other parts of Japan. It's on the 9th floor of the Kyoto Station building. To get there from the main concourse of the station, take the west escalator to the 2nd floor, enter Isetan department store and take an immediate left, then look for the elevator on your left and take it to the 9th floor. It's right outside the elevator. Note that there was some uncertainty about its status at the time of writing – consider calling before going all the way up there, or ask at the Kyoto Tourist Information Center (p297).

For long-term rentals try **furnished apartments** (ザファーニッシュドアパートメント; ☎090-6660-7645; www.kyotojp.com/furnished-apt.html; 34 Hinoshitachō, Matsubara-sagaru, Takakura-dōri, Shimogyō-ku; apt per month 1/2 person from ¥98,000/140,000; 🚇Karasuma subway line to Gojō), which are located in the middle of Kyoto, and have everything you need for a longer stay, including simple kitchens, bathrooms and basic furniture. They are within walking distance of the shops and restaurants of downtown.

KYOTO STATION AREA

Hotel Granvia Kyoto   HOTEL $$$

(ホテルグランヴィア京都; Map p253; ☎344-8888; www.granvia-kyoto.co.jp/e/index.html; Shiokōji sagaru, Karasuma-dōri; s/ tw from ¥25,410/28,875; ☺@☎; ☒Kyoto Station, Karasuma central gate) Imagine stepping straight out of bed and into the *shinkansen* (bullet train). This is almost possible when you stay at the Granvia, an excellent hotel located directly above Kyoto Station. Rooms are clean, spacious and well appointed, with deep bathtubs. This is a very professional operation with some good on-site restaurants, some of which have views over the city.

Tour Club   GUESTHOUSE $

(旅倶楽部; Map p253; ☎353-6968; www.kyotojp.com; 362 Momiji-chō, Higashinakasuji, Shōmen-sagaru, Shimogyō-ku; dm ¥2450, d per person ¥3490, tw per person ¥3490-3885, tr per person ¥2960-3240; ☺@☎; ☒Kyoto Station, Karasuma central gate) Run by a charming and informative young couple, this clean, well-maintained guesthouse is a favourite of many foreign visitors. Facilities include wi-fi, bicycle rentals, laundry and free tea and coffee. The private rooms, which were recently refurbished, have en suite bathrooms. It's a 10-minute walk from Kyoto Station; turn north off Shichijō-dōri at the Second House coffee shop (looks like a bank) and keep an eye out for the English sign.

Budget Inn   GUESTHOUSE $$

(バジェットイン; Map p253; ☎344-1510; www.budgetinnjp.com; 295 Aburanokōji-chō, Shichijō sagaru, Shimogyō-ku; tr/q/5-person r per person ¥3660/3245/2960; ☺@☎♠; ☒Kyoto Station, Karasuma central gate) This well-run guesthouse is an excellent choice. It's got eight Japanese-style private rooms, all of which are clean and well maintained. All rooms have their own bathroom and can accommodate up to five people, making this a good spot for families. The staff here is very helpful and friendly, and laundry and bicycle rental are available. All in all, this is a great choice in this price range. It's a seven-minute walk from Kyoto Station; from the station, walk west on Shiokōji-dōri, turn north one street before Horikawa and look for the English-language sign out front.

Matsubaya Ryokan   RYOKAN $

(松葉家旅館; Map p253; ☎351-3727; www.matsubayainn.com; Nishi-iru Higashinotōin, Kamijuzūyachō-dōri, Shimogyō-ku; r per person from ¥4200; @; ☒Kyoto Station, Karasuma central gate) A short walk from Kyoto Station, this newly renovated ryokan has clean, well-kept rooms and a management that is used to foreign guests. Some rooms on the 1st floor look out on small gardens. Average room rates here run about ¥6510 per person. Matsubaya also has several serviced apartments in its adjoining Bamboo House section – these would be great for anyone planning a longer stay in the city. Breakfast is available from ¥500 to ¥800 (Western) or ¥1000 (Japanese).

Ryokan Shimizu   RYOKAN $

(京の宿しみず; Map p253; ☎371-5538; www.kyoto-shimizu.net; 644 Kagiya-chō, Shichijō-dōri, Wakamiya agaru, Shimogyō-ku; r per person from ¥5250; ☺@; ☒Kyoto Station, Karasuma central gate) A short walk north of Kyoto Station, this travellers' ryokan is quickly building a loyal following of foreign guests, and for good reason: it's clean, well run and friendly. Rooms are standard ryokan style with one difference: all have bathrooms. Bicycle rental is available. Saturdays and nights before holidays is extra ¥1050.

K's House Kyoto   GUESTHOUSE $

(ケイズハウス京都; ☎342-2444; http://kshouse.jp/kyoto-e/index.html; 418 Naya-chō, Shichijō agaru, Dotemachi-dōri, Shimogyō-ku; dm from ¥2300, s/d/tw per person from ¥3500/2900/2900; ☺@☎; ☒Kyoto Station, Karasuma central gate, Keihan Shichijō Station) K's House is a large Western-style backpackers' guesthouse with both private and dorm rooms. The rooms are simple but adequate and there are spacious common areas. There's also an on-site restaurant that serves cheap cafe drinks, alcohol and snacks, making this a great place to meet and hang out with other travellers. The staff can help arrange inexpensive onward travel around Japan. It's about a 10-minute walk from Kyoto Station.

APA Hotel Kyoto Ekimae   HOTEL $$

(アパホテル京都駅前; Map p253; ☎365-4111; Shiokōji sagaru, Nishinotōin-dōri, Shimogyō-ku; s/tw per person from ¥9500/9000; ☺@☎; ☒Kyoto Station, Karasuma central gate) Only five minutes on foot from Kyoto Station, this efficient business hotel is a good choice for those who want the convenience of a nearly stationside location. Rooms are adequate, with firm, clean beds and unit bathrooms. The staff is professional and is used to dealing with foreign guests.

Capsule Ryokan Kyoto
GUESTHOUSE **$**

(カプセル旅館京都; Map p253; ☎344-1510; www.capsule-ryokan-kyoto.com; 204 Tsuchihashicho, Shimogyo-ku; capsule bed ¥3500, tw per person ¥3990; ❀@☎; ☒Kyoto Station, Karasuma central gate) This unique new accommodation offers ryokan-style capsules (meaning tatami mats inside the capsules etc), as well as comfortable, cleverly designed private rooms. Each capsule also has its own TV and cable internet access point, while the private rooms have en suite bathrooms and all the amenities you might need. Free internet, wi-fi and other amenities are available in the comfortable lounge. It's located a seven-minute walk from Kyoto Station, near the southeast corner of the Horikawa-Shichijō intersection.

DOWNTOWN KYOTO

TOP CHOICE Tawaraya
RYOKAN **$$$**

(俵屋; Map p256; ☎211-5566; fax 221-2204; Fuyachō-Oike sagaru, Nakagyō-ku; r per person with 2 meals ¥42,263-84,525; ❀@; ☒Tōzai & Karasuma subway lines to Karasuma-Oike Station, exit 3) Tawaraya has been operating for over three centuries and is one of the finest places to stay in Japan. Entering this ryokan is like entering another world and you just might not want to leave. The ryokan has an intimate, private feeling and all rooms have bathrooms. The gardens are sublime and the cosy study is the perfect place to linger with a book. A night here is sure to be memorable and is *highly* recommended.

Hiiragiya
RYOKAN **$$$**

(柊屋; Map p256; ☎221-1136; fax 221-139; www.hiiragiya.co.jp/en; Anekōji-agaru, Fuya-chō, Nakagyō-ku; r per person with 2 meals ¥36,750-81,900; ❀@; ☒Tōzai & Karasuma subway lines to Karasuma-Oike Station, exit 3) This classic ryokan has hosted celebrities and dignitaries from around the world. From the decorations to the service to the food, everything at the Hiiragiya is first class. Rooms in the old wing have great old Japan style, while those in the new wing are pristine and comfortable. It's centrally located downtown within easy walk of two subway stations and lots of good restaurants.

Yoshikawa
RYOKAN **$$$**

(吉川; Map p256; ☎221-5544; www.kyoto-yoshikawa.co.jp; fax 221-6805; Tominokōji, Oike-sagaru,Nakagyō-ku; r per person with 2 meals from

¥30,000; @; ☒Tōzai & Karasuma subway lines to Karasuma-Oike Station or Kyoto Shiyakusho-mae Station) Located downtown, within easy walking distance of two subway stations and the entire dining and nightlife district, this superb traditional ryokan has beautiful rooms and a stunning garden. The ryokan is famous for its tempura and meals are of a high standard. Add an extra ¥5000 for peak season.

Hotel Unizo
HOTEL **$$**

(ホテルユニゾ京都; Map p256; ☎241-3351; Kawaramachi-dōri-Sanjō sagaru, Nakagyō-ku; s/d/tw from ¥8505/13,650/12,810; ❀; ☒bus 5 to Kawaramachi-Sanjō stop) They don't get more central than this downtown business hotel: it's smack-dab in the middle of Kyoto's nightlife, shopping and dining district and you can walk to hundreds of restaurants and shops within five minutes. It's a standard-issue business hotel, with small but adequate rooms and unit bathrooms. Considering the location and the condition of the rooms, it's great value.

Kyoto Hotel Ōkura
HOTEL **$$$**

(京都ホテルオークラ; Map p256; ☎211-5111; fax 254-2529; Kawaramachi-dōri, Oike, Nakagyō-ku; s/d/tw from ¥21,945/31,185/31,185; ❀@; ☒Tōzai subway line to Kyoto Shiyakusho-mae Station, exit 3) Located right in the midst of downtown, this is a well-run, comfortable hotel that claims the most convenient location of any luxury hotel in Kyoto. Rooms here are clean, spacious and comfortable and those on the upper floors have great views. There are several excellent on-site restaurants and bars, along with hundreds within easy walking distance of the hotel. If you exhaust the possibilities in and around the hotel, you can walk downstairs and hop right onto the subway.

Hiiragiya Bekkan (Annex)
RYOKAN **$$$**

(柊屋別館; Map p266; ☎231-0151; www.hiiragiya.com/index-e.html; fax 231-0153; Gokōmachi-dōri, Nijō sagaru, Nakagyō-ku; r per person with 2 meals from ¥21,000; ❀@; ☒Tōzai subway line to Shiyakusho-mae Station, exit North-10) Not far from the Hiiragiya main building, the Hiiragiya Bekkan Annex offers the traditional ryokan experience at slightly more affordable rates. The *kaiseki* (Japanese haute cuisine) served here is delicious, and the gardens are lovely. Rooms have en-suite bathrooms, but bathtubs are shared (there are four lovely bathtubs). As with many ryokan, some rooms can be a bit noisy.

WANT MORE?

For in-depth information, reviews and recommendations at your fingertips, head to the Apple App Store to purchase Lonely Planet's *Kyoto City Guide* iPhone app.

Alternatively, head to **Lonely Planet** (www.lonelyplanet.com/japan/kansai/kyoto) for planning advice, author recommendations, traveller reviews and insider tips.

Mitsui Garden Hotel Kyoto Sanjō HOTEL $$
(Map p256; ☎256-3331; www.gardenhotels.co.jp/eng/sanjo; fax 256-2351; 80 Mikura-chō, Nishiiru, Karasuma, Sanjō St, Nakagyō-ku; s/d/tw from ¥10,500/17,600/18,800; @; ⚑Tōzai & Karasuma subway lines to Karasuma-Oike Station, exit 6) Just west of the downtown dining and shopping district, this is a clean and efficient hotel that offers good value for the price and reasonably comfortable rooms. It's just a minute or two to the nearest subway station.

CENTRAL KYOTO

Palace Side Hotel HOTEL $
(ザ・パレスサイドホテル; Map p258; ☎415-8887; www.palacesidehotel.co.jp/english/fr-top-en.html; fax 415-8889; Kamigyō-ku, Karasuma-dōri, Shimotachiuri agaru; s/tw/d from ¥6000/9000/9800; @; ⚑Karasuma line to Marutamachi Station) Overlooking the Kyoto Imperial Palace Park, this excellent value budget hotel has a lot going for it, starting with a friendly English-speaking staff, great service, washing machines, an on-site restaurant, well-maintained rooms and free internet terminals. The rooms are small but serviceable. It's a three-minute walk from the subway.

Ryokan Rakuchō RYOKAN $
(洛頂旅館; Map p258; ☎721-2174; fax 791-7202; 67 Higashi-hangi chō, Shimogamo, Sakyō-ku; s/tw/tr ¥5300/9240/12,600; @; ⚑Karasuma subway line to Kitaōji Station; ⚑bus 205, Furitsu-daigaku-mae stop) There is a lot to like about this fine little foreigner-friendly ryokan in the northern part of town: it's entirely non-smoking, there is a nice little garden and the rooms are clean and simple. Meals aren't served, but the owners can supply a good map of local eateries.

Ryokan Hinomoto RYOKAN $
(旅館ひのもと; off Map p260; ☎351-4563; www.ryokan-hinomoto.jp/eng_info; fax 351-3932; 375 Kotake-chō, Matsubara agaru-Kawaramachi-dōri; 1/2 person from ¥4200/8400; @; ⚑bus 17 or 205 to Kawaramachi-Matsubara stop) This cute little ryokan is very conveniently located for shopping and dining in downtown Kyoto, as well as sightseeing on the east side of town. It's got a nice wooden bathtub and simple rooms. It's a nice, cosy place to stay and there is LAN cable internet access.

SOUTHERN HIGASHIYAMA

Hyatt Regency Kyoto HOTEL $$$
(ハイアットリージェンシー京都; Map p260; ☎541-1234; www.kyoto.regency.hyatt.com; fax 541-2203; 644-2 Sanjūsangendō-mawari, Higashiyama-ku; r ¥19,000-46,000; @; ⚑Keihan Shichijō Station) The Hyatt Regency is an excellent, stylish, foreigner-friendly hotel at the southern end of Kyoto's southern Higashiyama sightseeing district. Many travellers consider this the best hotel in Kyoto. The staff here is extremely efficient and helpful (there are even foreign staff members – something of a rarity in Japan). The on-site restaurants and bar are excellent. The stylish rooms and bathrooms have lots of neat touches. The concierges are knowledgeable about the city and they'll even lend you a laptop to check your email if you don't have your own. It's a five-minute walk from the station.

Ryokan Uemura RYOKAN $$
(旅館うえむら; Map p260; ☎/fax 561-0377; Ishibe-kōji, Shimogawara, Higashiyama-ku; r with breakfast per person ¥9000; @; ⚑bus 206 to Higashiyama-Yasui stop) This beautiful little ryokan is at ease with foreign guests. It's on a quaint cobblestone alley, just down the hill from Kōdai-ji. Rates include breakfast, and there is a 10pm curfew. Book well in advance, as there are only three rooms. Note that the manager prefers bookings by fax and asks that cancellations also be made by fax (with so few rooms, it can be costly when bookings are broken without notice).

Sakara Kyoto INN $$$
(桜香楽; Map p260; sakarakyoto@gmail.com; 541-2 Furukawa-cho Higashiyama-ku; r from ¥10,000 to ¥25,000; @; ⚑Tōzai subway line to Higashiyama Station) This modern Japanese-style inn is conveniently located in a covered pedestrian shopping arcade just south of Sanjō-dōri, about 50 metres from Higashiyama Subway Station. It's great for couples and families, and rooms can accommodate up to five people. Each room has bath/shower, kitchenette and laundry facilities. Reservation is by email only.

Gion Hatanaka
RYOKAN $$$

(祇園畑中; Map p260; ☎541-5315; www.the
hatanaka.co.jp/english/index.html; fax 551-0553;
Yasaka-jinja Minami-mon mae, Higashiyama-ku; r
per person with 2 meals from about ¥30,000; ☺☍;
🚈Keihan Shijō Station or Hankyū Kawaramachi Station) Climb a flight of beautiful, stone stairs
to reach the entrance to Gion Hatanaka, a
fine ryokan right in the heart of the Southern Higashiyama sightseeing district (less
than a minute's walk from Yasaka-jinja). Despite being fairly large, this ryokan manages
to retain an intimate and private feeling. In
addition to bathtubs in each room, there is
a huge wooden communal bath. The rooms
are clean, well designed and relaxing. This
ryokan offers regularly scheduled geisha entertainment that non-guests are welcome to
join. Wi-fi is in the lobby only.

Seikōrō Ryokan
RYOKAN $$$

(Map p260; ☎561-0771; http://ryokan.asia/seikoro;
fax 541-5481; 467 Nishi Tachibana-chō, 3 chō-me,
Gojō sagaru, Tonyamachi-dōri, Higashiyama-ku;
r per person with 2 meals from ¥24,150; ☺@☍;
🚈bus 17 or 205 to Kawaramachi-Gojō stop) The
Seikōrō is a classic ryokan with fine rooms
and a grandly decorated lobby. It's fairly spacious, with excellent, comfortable rooms,
attentive service and a fairly convenient
midtown location. Several rooms look over
gardens and all have private baths.

Ryokan Motonago
RYOKAN $$$

(旅館元奈古; Map p260; ☎561-2087; www.moton
ago.com; fax 561-2655; 511 Washio-chō, Kōdaiji-michi,
Higashiyama-ku; r per person with 2 meals from
¥17,850; ☺@; 🚈bus 206 to Gion stop) This ryokan
may have the best location of any ryokan in
the city: right on Nene-no-Michi in the heart
of the Higashiyama sightseeing district. It's
got traditional decor, friendly service, nice
bathtubs and a few small Japanese gardens.

NORTHERN HIGASHIYAMA

TOP CHOICE Westin Miyako, Kyoto
HOTEL $$$

(ウェスティン都ホテル京都; Map p266;
☎771-7111; www.westinmiyako-kyoto.com; fax
751-2490; Keage, Sanjō-dōri, Higashiyama-ku; d &
tw from ¥33,500, Japanese-style r from ¥41,500;
☺@☍☍; 🚈Tōzai subway line to Keage Station, exit
2) This grande dame of Kyoto hotels occupies a commanding position overlooking the
Higashiyama sightseeing district (making
it one of the best locations for sightseeing
in Kyoto). Rooms are clean and well maintained, and the staff is at home with foreign
guests. Rooms on the north side have great

views over the city to the Kitayama mountains. There is a fitness centre, as well as a
private garden and walking trail. The hotel
even has its own ryokan section for those
who want to try staying in a ryokan without
giving up the convenience of a hotel.

Three Sisters Inn Main Building
RYOKAN $$

(スリーシスターズイン洛東荘本
館; Map p266; ☎761-6336; fax 761-6338; 18
Higashifukunokawa-chō, Okazaki, Sakyō-ku;
s/d/tr from ¥9345/13,650/20,475; ☺; 🚈bus 5,
Dōbutsuen-mae stop) This is a good foreigner-friendly ryokan with a loyal following of foreign guests. It's well situated in Okazaki for
exploring the northern Higashiyama area.

Three Sisters Inn Annex
RYOKAN $$

(スリーシスターズイン洛東荘別館; Map
p266; ☎761-6333; fax 761-6338; 89 Irie-chō, Okazaki, Sakyō-ku; s/d from ¥10,810/18,170/23,805, s/d
without bathroom ¥5635/11,270; ☺@☍; 🚈bus
100, Okazakimichi stop or bus 5, Dōbutsuen-mae
stop) In the same neighbourhood as the preceding, this is also a good choice for those
in search of a moderately-priced ryokan.
The features are similar to the main building, but it's somewhat more intimate and the
garden walkway adds to the atmosphere.

Kyoto Garden Ryokan Yachiyo
RYOKAN $$$

(旅館八千代; Map p266; ☎771-4148; www
.ryokan-yachiyo.com/top/englishtop.html; fax 771-4140; 34 Fukuchi-chō, Nanzen-ji, Sakyō-ku; r per
person with 2 meals ¥15,000-60,000; ☺☍; 🚈Tōzai
subway line to Keage Station, exit 2) Located just
down the street from Nanzen-ji temple, this
large ryokan is at home with foreign guests.
Rooms are spacious and clean, and some
look out over private gardens. There is an
excellent on-site restaurant with a choice of
tatami (woven floor matting) and table seating. For convenient evening strolling, this is
a good bet. The price varies depending on
dates and meals.

Koto Inn
GUESTHOUSE $$$

(古都音; Map p266; ☎751-2753; koto.inn@gmail
.com; 373 Hori-ike-chō, Higashiyama-ku; d from
¥15,000; ☺☍@; 🚈Tōzai subway line to Higashiyama station) Conveniently located near the
Higashiyama sightseeing district and two-minutes' walk from the Tōzai subway line,
this vacation rental is good for families,
couples and groups who want a bit of privacy. It's got everything you need and is decorated with lovely Japanese antiques. While
the building is traditionally Japanese, all
the facilities are fully modernised.

✗ Eating

Kyoto is a great place to make a full exploration of Japanese cuisine and you'll find good restaurants in every budget bracket. If you tire of Japanese food, there are plenty of excellent international restaurants to choose from. You'll find the thickest concentration of eateries in downtown Kyoto, but also plenty of choice in Southern Higashiyama/Gion and in and around Kyoto Station.

Because Kyoto gets a lot of foreign travellers, you'll find a surprising number of English menus, and most places are quite comfortable with foreign guests – it's rare to see waiters running for the exits at the first sign of a foreign face.

KYOTO STATION AREA

The new Kyoto Station building is chock-a-block with restaurants, and if you find yourself anywhere near the station around mealtime, this is probably your best bet in terms of variety and price.

There are several food courts scattered about the station building. The best of these can be found on the 11th floor on the west side of the building: the **Cube** food court and Isetan department store's **Eat Paradise** food court. In Eat Paradise, we like Tonkatsu Wako for *tonkatsu* (deep-fried breaded pork cutlet), Tenichi for sublime tempura, and Wakuden for approachable *kaiseki* fare. To get to these food courts, take the west escalators from the main concourse all the way up to the 11th floor and look for the Cube on your left and Eat Paradise straight in front of you.

Other options in the station include Kyoto Rāmen Koji, a collection of seven *rāmen* (egg noodle) restaurants on the 10th floor (underneath the Cube). Buy tickets from the machines, which don't have English but have pictures on the buttons. In addition to *rāmen,* you can get green-tea ice cream and other Japanese desserts at Chasen, and *tako-yaki* (battered octopus pieces) at Miyako.

About five minutes' walk north of the station, Yodobashi Camera has a wide selection of restaurants on the 6th floor, and an international supermarket with lots of take-away items on the B2 floor.

DOWNTOWN KYOTO

Downtown Kyoto has the best variety of approachable Japanese and international restaurants.

TOP CHOICE Yoshikawa   TEMPURA $$$
(Map p256; ☑221-5544; Oike sagaru, Tominokōji, Nakagyō-ku; lunch ¥3000-25,000, dinner ¥6000-25,000; ⏰11am-2pm & 5-8.30pm; 📶) This is the place to go for delectable tempura. It offers table seating, but it's much more interesting to sit and eat around the small counter and observe the chefs at work. It's near Oike-dōri in a fine traditional Japanese-style building. Reservation required for tatami room; counter and table seating unavailable on Sunday.

Kane-yo   JAPANESE UNAGI $$
(かねよ; Map p256; ☑221-0669; Rokkaku, Shin-kyōgoku, Nakagyō-ku; unagi over rice from ¥950; ⏰11.30am-8.30pm; 📶) This is a good place to try *unagi* (eel). You can sit downstairs with a nice view of the waterfall or upstairs on the tatami. The *kane-yo donburi* set (¥950) is great value; it's served until 2pm. Look for the barrels of live eels outside and the wooden facade.

Café Bibliotec HELLO!   CAFE $
(カフェビブリオティックハロー！; Map p258; ☑231-8625; 650 Seimei-chō, Yanaginobanba higashi iru, Nijō, Nakagyō-ku; food from ¥850, coffee ¥450; ⏰11.30am-midnight, closed irregularly; 📶) Like its name suggests, books line the walls of this cool cafe located in a converted *machiya.* You can get the usual range of coffee and tea drinks here, as well as light cafe lunches. Overall, this may be our favourite cafe in Kyoto, and it's worth the walk from the centre of town. Look for the plants out front.

TOP CHOICE Ippūdō   RĀMEN $
(一風堂; Map p256; ☑213-8800; 653-1 Bantōya-chō, Nishikikōji higashiiru, Higashinotōin, Nakagyō-ku; rāmen around ¥750-950; ⏰11am-2am; 📶) There's a reason that there's usually a line outside this rāmen joint at lunchtime: the *rāmen* is awesome and the bite-sized *gyōza* (Chinese dumplings) are to die for. We recommend the *gyōza* set meal, which costs ¥750 or ¥850, depending on your choice of *rāmen*. It's on Nishiki-dōri, next to a post office and diagonally across from a Starbucks. There's a big English sign.

Ganko Zushi   SUSHI $$
(がんこ寿司; Map p256; ☑255-1128; 101 Nakajima-chō, Kawaramachi Higashi iru, Sanjō-dōri, Nakagyō-ku; lunch/dinner ¥1000-2000/3000; ⏰11am-11pm; 📶) Near Sanjō-ōhashi bridge, this is a good place for sushi or just about anything else. There are plenty of sets to

Yes, we know: the idea of dining in a department store sounds as appetizing as dining in a gas station. However, Japanese department stores, especially those in large cities like Tokyo and Kyoto, are loaded with good dining options. And, unlike many street-level shops, they're usually fairly comfortable with foreign diners (if there's any communication trouble, they can always call down to the bilingual ladies at the information counter).

On their basement floors, you'll find *depachika* (from the English word 'department' and the Japanese word *chika*, which means 'underground'). A good *depachika* is like an Aladdin's cave of gustatory delights that rivals the best gourmet shops in any Western city. Meanwhile, on their upper floors, you'll usually find a *resutoran-gai* ('restaurant city') that includes restaurants serving all the Japanese standards – sushi, noodles, tonkatsu, tempura – along with a few international restaurants, usually French, Italian and Chinese.

If you find yourself feeling peckish in downtown Kyoto, here are some good department dining options:

» **Takashimaya** At the corner of Shijō and Kawaramachi streets, this elegant department store has an incredible food floor (on the B1 level) and the best department store *resutoran-gai* in the city (on the 7th floor).

» **Daimaru** On the north side of Shijō, between Kawaramachi and Karasuma streets, Daimaru has a food floor that rivals the one at Takashimaya (note the awesome Japanese sweet section) and a solid *resutoran-gai* on the 8th floor.

» **Fuji Daimaru** On the south side of the Shijō-Teramachi intersection, the Tavelt food floor on the B1 level of this department store is the cheapest of the three in this section. It usually has a great selection of take-away sushi/sashimi and fruit.

choose from, but we recommend ordering sushi à la carte. There's a full English menu, the kitchen is fast and they are used to foreigners. Look for the large display of plastic food models in the window.

Merry Island Café INTERNATIONAL $$
(メリーアイランド　カフェ; Map p256; ☎213-0214; Oike agaru, Kiyamachi-dōri, Nakagyō-ku; lunch from ¥1050; ⊙11.30am-11pm; 🗐) This popular lunch/dinner restaurant strives to create the atmosphere of a tropical resort. The menu is *mukokuseki* (without nationality) and most of what is on offer is pretty tasty. It does a good risotto and occasionally has a nice piece of Japanese steak. In warm weather the front doors are opened and the place takes on the air of a sidewalk cafe.

Kerala INDIAN $
(ケララ; Map p256; ☎251-0141; 2F KUS Bldg, Sanjō agaru, Kawaramachi, Nakagyō-ku; lunch/dinner from ¥850/2600; ⊙11.30am-2pm & 5-9pm, closed irregularly; 🖋🗐) This is where we go for reliable Indian lunch sets – great *thalis* that include two curries, good naan bread, some rice, a small salad etc. Dinners are à la carte. It's on the 2nd floor; look for the display of food in the glass case at street level.

Biotei VEGETARIAN $
(びお亭; Map p256; ☎255-0086; 2F M&I Bldg, 28 Umetada-chō, Higashinotōin Nishi iru, Sanjō-dōri, Nakagyō-ku; lunch from ¥840; ⊙lunch & dinner, closed Sun, Mon & holidays, dinner Thu & lunch Sat; 🖋🗐) Located diagonally across from the Nakagyō post office, this is a favourite of Kyoto vegetarians. Best for lunch, it serves a daily set of Japanese vegetarian food (the occasional bit of meat is offered as an option, but you'll be asked your preference). It's up the metal spiral steps.

🖋 Shizenha Restaurant
Obanzai VEGETARIAN $
(自然派レストランおばんざい; Map p256; ☎223-6623; 199 Shimomyōkaku-ji-chō, Oike agaru, Koromonotana-dōri, Nakagyō-ku; lunch/dinner ¥840/2100; ⊙11am-2pm & 5-9pm, closed dinner Wed; 🖋) A little out of the way but good value, Obanzai serves a good buffet-style lunch/dinner of mostly organic vegetarian food. It's northwest of the Karasuma-Oike crossing, set back from the street a bit. Lunch on weekends is ¥1050.

Park Café CAFE $
(パークカフェ; Map p256; ☎211-8954; 1F Gion Bldg, 340-1 Aneyakō-ji kado, Gokomachi-dōri, Nakagyō-ku; drinks from ¥450; ⊙noon-11pm) This

hip little cafe always reminds us of a Melbourne coffeeshop. It's on the edge of the downtown shopping district and a convenient place to take a break.

Café Independants
CAFE $

(カフェ　アンデパンダン; Map p256; ☎255-4312; B1F 1928 Bldg, Sanjō Gokomachi kado, Nakagyō-ku; salads/sandwiches from ¥400/800; ⏰11.30am-midnight) Located beneath a gallery, this cool subterranean cafe offers a range of light meals and good cafe drinks in a bohemian atmosphere. A lot of the food offerings are laid out on display for you to choose from – with the emphasis on healthy sandwiches and salads. Take the stairs on your left before the gallery.

Ootoya
SHOKUDŌ $

(大戸屋; Map p256; ☎255-4811; 2F Goshoame Bldg, Sanjō-dōri, Kawaramachi higashi iru, Nakagyō-ku; meals from ¥600; ⏰11am-11pm) Ootoya is a clean, modern Japanese restaurant that serves a range of standard Japanese dishes at bargain-basement prices. It's popular with Kyoto students and young office workers. The large picture menu makes ordering a breeze. Look for the English sign just west of Ganko Sushi.

Karafuneya Coffee Honten
CAFE $

(からふねや珈琲本店; Map p256; ☎254-8774; Kawaramachi Sanjō sagaru, Nakagyō-ku; simple meals ¥800-900; ⏰9am-1am; 🖬) Japan is famous for its plastic food models, but this place takes food to a whole new level – it's like some futuristic dessert museum. We like the centrepiece of the display: the mother of all sundaes that goes for ¥10,000-18,000 and requires advance reservation to order. Lesser mortals can try the tasty *matcha* parfait for ¥780 or any of the cafe drinks and light meals on offer.

Honke Tagoto
NOODLES $

(本家田毎; Map p256; ☎221-3030; 12 Ishibashi-chō, Kawaramachi Nishi iru, Sanjō-dōri, Nakagyō-ku; noodle dishes from ¥840; ⏰11am-9pm; 🖬) One of Kyoto's oldest *soba* restaurants makes a good break for those who have overdosed on *rāmen*. It's in the Sanjō covered arcade and you can see inside to the tables.

Mishima-tei
JAPANESE SUKIYAKI $$

(三嶋亭; Map p256; ☎221-0003; 405 Sakurano-chō, Sanjō sagaru, Teramachi-dōri, Nakagyō-ku; sukiyaki lunch/dinner from ¥8700/12,700; ⏰11.30am-10pm, closed Wed; 🖬) In the Sanjō covered arcade, this is a good place to sample sukiyaki: there is even a discount for foreign travellers! Special lunch ¥4505 until 3pm.

A-Bar
IZAKAYA $

(居酒屋A（あ）; Map p256; ☎213-2129; Nishikiyamachi-dōri; dishes ¥160-680; ⏰6pm-1am) This student *izakaya* (pub-eatery) with a log-cabin interior is popular with expats and Japanese students for a raucous night out. The food is fairly typical *izakaya* fare, with plenty of fried items and some decent salads. It's a little tough to find – look for the small black-and-white sign at the top of a flight of steps.

Musashi Sushi
SUSHI $

(寿しのむさし; Map p256; ☎222-0634; Kawaramachi-dōri, Sanjō agaru, Nakagyō-ku; all plates ¥137; ⏰11am-10pm) This is the place to go to try *kaiten-zushi* (conveyor-belt sushi). Sure, it's not the best sushi in the world, but it's cheap, easy and fun. Look for the mini sushi conveyor belt in the window. It's just outside the entrance to the Sanjō covered arcade.

Tagoto Honten
KAISEKI $$

(田ごと本店; Map p256; ☎221-1811; 34 Otabi-chō, Shijō dōri Kawaramachi Nishiiru, Shimogyō-ku; lunch/dinner from ¥1600/3700; ⏰lunch 11am-3pm, dinner 4.30-9pm; 🖬) Across the street from Takashimaya department store, this longstanding Kyoto restaurant serves approachable *kaiseki* fare in a variety of rooms, both private and common. The kiku set (¥1600) includes some sashimi, a bit of tempura and a variety of other nibblies. *Kaiseki* dinner courses start at ¥6300 and you must reserve in advance. This is a good spot for those who want a civilised meal downtown in relaxing surroundings. At present, there's no English sign: look for pictures of the food and the stone and wooden front; the entrance is down the narrow alley.

Warai
OKONOMIYAKI $

(わらい; Map p256; ☎257-5966; 1F Mizukōto Bldg, 597 Nishiuoya-chō, Takakura Nishiiru, Nishikikōji-dōri, Nakagyō-ku; okonomiyaki from ¥600; ⏰11.30am-1am; 🖬) This Nishiki-dōri restaurant is a great place to try *okonomiyaki* (savoury pancakes) in casual surroundings. It can get a little smoky, but it's a fun spot to eat. It's got sets from as little as ¥650 at lunch. It's about 20m west of the west end of Nishiki Market; look for the English sign in the window.

Rāmen Kairikiya
RĀMEN $

(ラーメン魁力屋; Map p256; ☑251-0303; 1F Hijikata Bldg, 435-2 Ebisu-chō, Sanjō agaru, Kawaramachi-dōri, Nakagyō-ku; rāmen from ¥600; ☺11am-3am; ☝) Not far from the Sanjō-Kawaramachi intersection, this popular rāmen specialist welcomes foreigners with friendly staff. It's got several types of rāmen to choose from and tasty sets that include things like fried rice, fried chicken or gyōza, all for about ¥800. It's pretty easy to spot: look for the red and white sign and the words 'There is an English menu.'

Kyō Kurabu
VEGETARIAN $

(京倶楽部; Map p256; ☑222-1831; 215 Kajiyachō, Nishikikōji-dōri; meals from around ¥1000; ☺11am-7pm or 8pm, closed Tue; ☝) This restaurant in Nishiki Market is a great spot to take a break from exploring the market. The menu is pan-Asian and meals can be had for about ¥1000. You can also just have a drink. It's up the stairs two doors down (west) from Aritsugu knife shop; look for the signs that read 'Café Dining' and 'kyo club'.

Ike Tsuru
JUICE BAR $

(池鶴; Map p256; ☑221-3368; Nishikikōji-dōri, Yanaginobanba-Higashi-iru, Nakagyō-ku; juice around ¥450; ☺9am-6.30pm, closed Wed) We love this fruit juice specialist in Nishiki Market. In addition to all the usual favourites, it sometimes has durian on hand and can whip up a very unusual durian juice. Look for the fruit on display – it's on the south side of the market, a little east of Yanaginobanba-dōri.

SOUTHERN HIGASHIYAMA

Kasagi-ya
JAPANESE TEAHOUSE $

(かさぎ屋; Map p260; ☑561-9562; 349 Masuya chō, Kōdai-ji, Higashiyama-ku; ☺11am-6pm, closed Tue; ☝) At Kasagi-ya, on the Ninen-zaka slope near Kiyomizu-dera, this funky old wooden shop has atmosphere to boot and friendly staff. It's a great place for a cup of green tea and a Japanese sweet to power you through a day of sightseeing in Higashiyama. *Matcha* tea with a sweet costs ¥700. It's hard to spot; you may have to ask someone in the area to point it out.

TOP CHOICE Ōzawa
TEMPURA $$

(おおざわ; Map p260; ☑561-2052; Minami gawa, Gion Shirakawa Nawate Higashi iru, Higashiyama-ku; meals from ¥3990; ☺5-10pm, closed Thu; ☝) On the most beautiful street in Gion, this restaurant offers good tempura in traditional Japanese surroundings. Unless you choose a private tatami room, you'll sit at the counter and watch as the chef prepares each piece of tempura. Lunch available on advance request.

Kagizen Yoshifusa
JAPANESE TEAHOUSE $

(鍵善良房; Map p260; ☑561-1818; 264 Gion machi Kita gawa, Higashiyama-ku; kuzukiri ¥900; ☺9.30am-6pm, closed Mon; ☝) One of Kyoto's oldest and best-known *okashi-ya* (sweet shops) sells a variety of traditional sweets and has a peaceful tearoom in back where you can sample cold *kuzukiri* (transparent arrowroot noodles), served with a *kuro-mitsu* (sweet black sugar) dipping sauce. It's in a traditional *machiya* up a flight of stone steps.

Machapuchare
VEGETARIAN $$

(マチャプチャレ; Map p260; ☑525-1330; 290 Kamihorizume-chō, Sayamachi-dōri Shōmen sagaru, Higashiyama-ku; obanzai lunch set ¥1050; ☺11.30am-2pm, closed Tue; ☝) This organic vegetarian restaurant serves a sublime vegetarian *obanzai* set (Kyoto home-style cooking). The problem is, the restaurant keeps somewhat irregular hours and the *obanzai* is not always available. Get a Japanese speaker to call and check before trekking here.

Asuka
SHOKUDŌ $

(明日香; Map p260; ☑751-9809; 144 Nishi-machi, Jingū-michi Nishi iru, Sanjō-dōri, Higashiyama-ku; meals from ¥850; ☺11am-10pm, closed Mon; ☝) With an English menu, and a staff of old Kyoto *mama-sans* at home with foreign customers, this is a great place for a cheap lunch or dinner while sightseeing in the Higashiyama area. The tempura *moriawase* (assorted tempura set) is a big pile of tempura for only ¥1000. Look for the red lantern and the pictures of the set meals.

Hisago
NOODLES $

(ひさご; Map p260; ☑561-2109; 484 Shimokawara-chō, Higashiyama-ku; meals from ¥900; ☺11.30am-7.30pm, closed Mon; ☝) If you need a quick meal while in the main southern Higashiyama sightseeing district, this simple noodle and rice restaurant is a good bet. It's within easy walking distance of Kiyomizu-dera and Maruyama-kōen. *Oya-ko-donburi* (chicken and egg over rice; ¥980) is the speciality of the house. There is no English sign; look for the traditional front and the small collection of food models on display. In the busy seasons, there's almost always a queue outside.

Shibazaki NOODLES $$

(柴崎; Map p260; ☎525-3600; 4-190-3 Kiyomizu, Higashiyama-ku; soba from ¥1000; ☺11am-6pm, closed Tue except national holidays; 📶) For excellent *soba* noodles and well-presented tempura sets (among other things) in the area of Kiyomizu-dera, try this comfortable and spacious restaurant. After your meal, head upstairs to check out the sublime collection of Japanese lacquerware – it's the best we've seen anywhere. Look for the low stone wall and the *noren* curtains hanging in the entryway.

Ryūmon CHINESE $$

(龍門; Map p260; ☎752-8181; Kita gawa, Higashiōji Nishi iru, Sanjō-dōri, Higashiyama-ku; dinner set from ¥3000; ☺5pm-5am) The place looks like a total dive, but the food is reliable and authentic, as the crowds of Chinese residents will attest. There's no English menu, but there is a picture menu and some of the waiters can speak English. Decor is strictly Chinese kitsch, with the exception of the deer head over the cash register – we're still trying to figure that one out.

NORTHERN HIGASHIYAMA

TOP CHOICE Omen NOODLES $$

(おめん; Map p266; ☎771-8994; 74 Jōdo-ji Ishibashi-cho, Sakyō-ku; noodles from ¥1100; ☺11am-9pm, closed one day a month irregularly, usually Thu; 📶) This noodle shop is named after the thick, white noodles served in a hot broth with a selection of seven fresh vegetables. Just say *'omen'* and you'll be given your choice of hot or cold noodles, a bowl of soup to dip them in and a plate of vegetables (you put these into the soup bowl with some sesame seeds). It's a great bowl of noodles but don't stop there: the à la carte menu is also fantastic – ranging from excellent tempura to healthy vegetable dishes. It's about five minutes' walk from Ginkaku-ji in a traditional Japanese house with a lantern outside. Note that there's often a line during tourist high season.

Goya JAPANESE (OKINAWAN) $

(ゴヤ; Map p266; ☎752-1158; 114-6 Nishida-chō, Jōdo-ji, Sakyō-ku; ☺noon-4.30pm & 5.30pm-midnight, closed Wed; 📶) We love this Okinawan-style restaurant for its tasty food, stylish interior and comfortable upstairs seating. It's the perfect place for lunch while exploring northern Higashiyama and it's just a short walk from Ginkaku-ji. At lunch it serves simple things like taco rice (¥880) and *gōya*

champurū (bitter melon stir-fry; ¥680), while dinners are more à la carte affairs with a wide range of *izakaya* fare, much of it with an Okinawan twist.

Hinode Udon NOODLES $

(日の出うどん; Map p266; ☎751-9251; 36 Kitanobō-chō, Nanzenji, Sakyō-ku; noodle dishes from ¥450; ☺11am-5pm, closed Sun; 📶) Filling noodle and rice dishes are served at this pleasant little shop. Plain *udon* (thick white noodles) here is only ¥450, but we recommend you spring for the *nabeyaki udon* (pot-baked *udon* in broth) for between ¥850 and ¥1000. This is a good spot for lunch when temple-hopping near Ginkaku-ji or Nanzen-ji.

Karako RĀMEN $

(唐子; Map p266; ☎752-8234; 12-3 Tokusei-chō, Okazaki, Sakyō-ku; rāmen from ¥630; ☺11.30am-2pm & 4.30pm-midnight, closed Tue) This is our favourite *rāmen* restaurant in Kyoto. While it's not much on atmosphere, Karako has excellent *rāmen* – the soup is thick and rich and the *chāshū* (pork slices) melt in your mouth. We recommend the *kotteri* (thick soup) *rāmen*. Look for the red lantern outside.

🍃 Earth Kitchen Company JAPANESE (BENTŌ) $

(アースキッチンカンパニー; Map p266; ☎771-1897; 9-7 Higashi Maruta-chō, Kawabata, Marutamachi, Sakyō-ku; lunch ¥735; ☺10.30am-6.30pm Mon-Fri, closed Sat & Sun) Located on Marutamachi-dōri near the Kamo-gawa, this is a tiny spot that seats just two people but does a bustling business serving tasty takeaway lunch *bentō*. If you fancy a picnic lunch for your temple-hopping, this is the place.

🍃 Cafe Proverbs 15:17 VEGETARIAN $

(カフェプロバーブズ15:17; Map p266; ☎707-6856; Domus Hyakumanben 3F, 28-20 Tanakamonzen-chō, Sakyō-ku; drinks/food from ¥300/750; ☺11.45am-10pm, from noon Sun, to 6pm Wed, closed Mon; 📶📶) This is a pleasant spot for a cuppa or a light vegetarian meal. Lunch sets include green curry, sandwiches and Japanese fare. It's on the 3rd floor but there's a small sign on street level.

Grotto KAISEKI $$

(ぐろっと; Map p266; ☎771-0606; 114 Jōdo-ji Nishida-chō, Sakyō-ku; dinner course ¥4750; ☺6pm-midnight, closed Sun; 📶) This stylish little place along Imadegawa-dōri serves a tasty dinner set menu that will take you through the major tastes in Japanese gastronomy. The fare is simple counter *kaiseki* or *kappō* (a series of little dishes). It's a great way to spend two or three hours with someone special. Reservations are recommended. The master speaks English.

ARASHIYAMA & SAGANO AREA

Arashiyama Yoshimura   NOODLES $$

(Map p272; ☎863-5700; Togetsu-kyō kita, Ukyō-ku; soba dishes from ¥1050, set meals from ¥1575; ⏰11am-5pm; 🍴) For a tasty bowl of *soba* noodles and a million-dollar view over the Arashiyama mountains and the Togetsu-kyō bridge, head to this extremely popular eatery just north of the famous bridge, overlooking the Katsura-gawa. There's an English menu but no English sign; look for the big glass windows and the stone wall.

Komichi   CAFE $

(こみち; Map p272; ☎872-5313; 23 Ōjōin-chō, Nison-in Monzen, Saga, Ukyō-ku; matcha ¥650; ⏰10am-5pm, closed Wed) This friendly little teahouse is perfectly located along the Arashiyama tourist trail. In addition to hot and cold tea/coffee drinks, it serves *uji kintoki* (sweet *matcha* over shaved ice, sweetened milk and sweet beans – sort of a Japanese Italian ice) in summer and a variety of light noodle dishes year-round. The picture menu helps with ordering. The sign is green and black on a white background.

Yoshida-ya   SHOKUDŌ $

(よしだや; Map p272; ☎861-0213; 20-24 Tsukurimichi-chō, Saga Tenryū-ji, Ukyō-ku; lunch from ¥750; ⏰10.30am-4pm, closed Wed) This quaint and friendly little *teishoku-ya* (set-meal restaurant) is the perfect place to grab a simple lunch while in Arashiyama. All the standard *teishoku* favourites are on offer, including things like *oyako-donburi* for ¥850. You can also cool off here with a refreshing *uji kintoki* (¥650). It's the first place south of the station and it's got a rustic front.

Shigetsu   JAPANESE (TŌFU) $$

(篩月; Map p272; ☎882-9725; 68 Susukinobaba-machi, Saga Tenryū-ji, Ukyō-ku; lunch sets ¥3500, ¥5500 & ¥7500; ⏰11am-2pm) To sample *shōjin-ryōri* (Buddhist vegetarian cuisine) try Shigetsu in the precinct of Tenryū-ji. It has beautiful garden views.

ŌHARA

Seryō-jaya   SHOKUDŌ $$

(Map p277; ☎744-2301; Ōhara Sanzenin hotori, Sakyō-ku; lunch sets from ¥2000; ⏰11am-5pm)

Just by the entry gate to Sanzen-in, Seryō-jaya serves tasty *soba* noodles and other fare. There is outdoor seating in the warmer months. Look for the food models.

KURAMA

🏆 Yōshūji   VEGETARIAN $$

(Map p278; ☎741-2848; 1074 Honmachi, Kurama, Sakyō-ku; meals from ¥1050; ⏰10am-6pm, closed Tue; 🍴) Yōshūji serves superb *shōjin-ryōri* in a delightful old Japanese farmhouse with an *irori* (open hearth). The house special, a sumptuous selection of vegetarian dishes served in red lacquered bowls, is called *kurama-yama shōjin zen* (¥2600). Or if you just feel like a quick bite, try the *uzu-soba* (*soba* topped with mountain vegetables; ¥1050). You'll find it halfway up the steps leading to the main gate of Kurama-dera; look for the orange lanterns out the front.

Aburaya-shokudō   SHOKUDŌ $

(Map p278; ☎741-2009; 252 Honmachi, Kurama, Sakyō-ku; udon & soba from ¥600; ⏰9.30am-4.30pm, closed irregularly) Just down the steps from the main gate of Kurama-dera, this classic old-style *shokudō* (all-round restaurant) reminds us of what Japan was like before it got rich. The *sansai teishoku* (¥1750) is a delightful selection of vegetables, rice and *soba* topped with grated yam.

KIBUNE

Visitors to Kibune from June to September should not miss the chance to cool down by dining at one of the picturesque restaurants beside the Kibune-gawa. Meals are served here on platforms (known as *kawa-doko*) suspended over the river, as cool water flows just underneath. Most of the restaurants offer some kind of lunch special for around ¥3000. For a full *kaiseki* dinner spread (¥5000 to ¥10,000) have a Japanese speaker call to reserve in advance. Be warned that restaurants in Kibune have been known to turn away solo diners.

Kibune Club   CAFE $

(Map p278; ☎741-3039; 76 Kibune-chō, Kurama, Sakyō-ku; coffee from ¥500; ⏰11.30am-6pm summer, 11.30am-5pm winter) The exposed wooden beams and open, airy feel of this rustic cafe make it a great spot to stop for a cuppa while exploring Kibune. In the winter, it sometimes cranks up the wood stove, which makes the place rather cosy. It's easy to spot.

Hirobun
JAPANESE $$

(Map p278; ☎741-2147; 87 Kibune-chō, Kurama, Sakyō-ku; noodles served until 4pm from ¥600, kaiseki courses from ¥8400; ⏰11.30am-9pm) This is a good place to sample riverside or 'above-river' dining in Kibune. There's a friendly crew of ladies here who run the show and the food is quite good. Note that it does not accept solo diners for *kaiseki* courses (but you can have noodles). Look for the black-and-white sign and the lantern. Reserve for dinner.

🍷 Drinking

Kyoto has a great variety of bars, clubs and *izakayas,* all of which are good places to meet Japanese folks. And if you happen to be in Kyoto in the summer, many hotels and department stores operate rooftop beer gardens with all-you-can-eat-and-drink deals and good views of the city.

In addition to the places listed here, the *izakaya* A-Bar (p288) is a fun place to drink. Also, all the top-end hotels listed in the Sleeping section have at least one good bar on their premises. We particularly like the Tōzan bar at the Hyatt.

There are two good sources of information on bars and entertainment in Kyoto:

Kansai Scene This magazine has listings of foreigner-friendly bars as well as detailed event listings.

Deep Kyoto (www.deepkyoto.com) This website has listings on little-known Kyoto bars, cafes and restaurants, as well as some event information.

McLoughlin's Irish Bar & Restaurant
BAR

(マクラクランズ・アイリッシュバー＆レストラン; Map p256; ☎212-6339; 8F The Empire Bldg, Kiyamachi, Sanjō-agaru, Nakagyō-ku; ⏰6pm-1am, closed Tue; @📶) With a fine view over the city, free wi-fi and good food, this bar is a nice place to spend an evening in Kyoto. There's a great selection of local and international craft beers. It's also a good place to meet local expats and Japanese. It hosts music events as well.

Gael Irish Pub
BAR

(ザガエルアイリッシュパブ; Map p260; ☎525-0680; 2F Ōtō Bldg, Nijūikken-chō, Yamatoōji-dōri agaru, Shijō, Higashiyama-ku; drinks from ¥500; ⏰5pm-1am, later Thu-Sun) A cosy little Irish bar on the doorstep of Gion. It offers good food, excellent beer and friendly staff, as well as occasional live music. It's a great place to meet local expats and see what's going on in town. It's up a flight of steps.

Sama Sama
BAR

(サマサマ; Map p256; ☎241-4100; 532 Kamiōsaka-chō, Sanjō agaru, Kiyamachi, Nakagyō-ku; drinks from ¥600-700; ⏰6pm-2am, 6pm-4am Fri & Sat, closed Tue) This place seems like a very comfortable cave somewhere near the Mediterranean. Scoot up to the counter or make yourself at home on the cushions on the floor and enjoy a wide variety of drinks, some of them Indonesian (where the owner hails from). It's down an alley just north of Sanjō; the alley has a sign for Sukiyaki Komai Tei.

Kisui
IZAKAYA

(器粋; Map p260; ☎585-6639; 1F 2-239 Miyagawa-suji, Higashiyama-ku; drinks from ¥600; ⏰6pm-midnight, closed Sun; 📷) This little one-counter *izakaya* at the north end of the Miyagawa geisha district is a good place to knock a few back. The cheerful owner is sure to make you welcome and you can order food from the upstairs restaurant to eat. It's on the 1st floor, opposite a park, on the corner. There is no English sign.

TOP CHOICE Yoramu
BAR

(ヨラム; Map p256; ☎213-1512; 2F Ōtō Bldg, Nijō-dōri, Nakagyō-ku; sake tasting sets from ¥1200; ⏰6pm-midnight, closed Sun, Mon & Tue) Named for Yoramu, the Israeli sake expert who runs the place, this is highly recommended for anyone who wants an education in sake. It's very small and can only accommodate a handful of people. By day, it's a *soba* restaurant.

Ing
BAR

(イング; Map p256; ☎255-5087; Nishikiyamachi-dōri, Takoyakushi agaru, Nakagyō-ku; snacks ¥250-700, drinks from ¥500; ⏰6pm-2am Mon-Thu, to 5am Fri-Sun) This little joint is the place for cheap bar snacks, drinks and good music. It's on the 2nd floor of the Royal building.

☆ Entertainment

Most of Kyoto's cultural entertainment is of an occasional nature, and you'll need to check with the TIC or *Kansai Scene* to find out whether anything interesting coincides with your visit.

Clubs

World
NIGHTCLUB

(ワールド; Map p256; ☎213-4119; 97 Shinmachi Shijō-agaru, Nishi-Kiyamachi, Shimogyō-ku; admission ¥2500-3000; ⏰10pm-5am, closed Mon, Tue bar only) World is Kyoto's biggest club and it naturally hosts some of the biggest events. It has two floors, a dance floor and lockers where you can leave your stuff while you dance the night away. Events include everything from deep soul to reggae to techno to salsa. Drinks from ¥500.

Metro

NIGHTCLUB

(メトロ; Map p266; ☑752-4765; BF Ebisu Bldg, Marutamachi sagaru, Kawabata, Sakyō-ku; admission ¥500-3000; ☺10pm-3am) This is one of the most popular and vibrant clubs in town. It holds a variety of themed events and occasional live bands or international DJ events. It's inside exit 2 of the Keihan Marutamachi Station.

Geisha Dances

In the spring and autumn, Kyoto's geisha (or, properly speaking, *geiko* and *maiko*) perform fantastic dances, usually on seasonal themes. For a small additional fee, you can participate in a brief tea ceremony before the show. We *highly* recommend seeing one of these dances if you are in town when they are being held. Ask at the tourist information centre or at your lodgings for help with ticket purchase. Tour companies can also help with tickets.

TOP CHOICE Gion Odori

DANCE

(祇園をどり; ☑561-0224; Higashiyama-ku-Gion; admission/with tea ¥3500/4000; ☺shows 1.30pm & 4pm) Held at Gion Kaikan Theatre (祇園会館; Map p260) near Yasaka-jinja; 1 to 10 November.

Kamogawa Odori

DANCE

(鴨川をどり; ☑221-2025; Ponto-chō-Sanjō sagaru; normal/special seat/special seat with tea ¥2000/4000/4500; ☺shows 12.30pm, 2.20pm & 4.10pm) Held at Ponto-chō Kaburen-jō Theatre (Map p256), Ponto-chō; 1 to 24 May.

Kitano Odori

DANCE

(北野をどり; ☑461-0148; Imadegawa-dōri-Nishihonmatsu nishi iru; admission/with tea ¥4000/4500; ☺shows 1.30pm & 4pm) At Kamishichiken Kaburen-jō Theatre (上七軒歌舞練場), east of Kitano-Tenman-gū; 15 to 25 April.

Kyō Odori

DANCE

(京をどり; ☑561-1151; Kawabata-dōri-Shijō sagaru; non-reserved/reserved seat ¥2000/4000, plus ¥500 with tea; ☺shows 12.30pm, 2.30pm & 4.30pm) Held at Miyagawa-chō Kaburen-jō Theatre (宮川町歌舞練場; Map p260), east of the Kamo-gawa between Shijō-dōri and Gojō-dōri; from the first to the third Sunday in April.

Miyako Odori

DANCE

(都をどり; ☑561-1115; Higashiyama-ku-Gion-chō South; seat reserved/nonreserved/reserved with tea ¥4000/2000/4500; ☺shows 12.30pm, 2pm, 3.30pm & 4.50pm) At Gion Kōbu Kaburen-jō Theatre (祇園甲部歌舞練場; Map p260), near Gion Corner; throughout April.

Geisha Entertainment

If you want to see geisha perform and actually speak with them, one of the best ways is at **Gion Hatanaka** (祇園畑中; Map p260), a Gion ryokan that offers the **Kyoto Cuisine & Maiko Evening** (☑541-5315; www.kyoto-maiko .jp; Yasaka Jinja Minamimon-mae, 505 Minamigawa, Gion-machi, Higashiyama-ku; per person ¥18,000; ☺6-8pm, every Mon, Wed, Fri, Sat & selected dates). Here, you can enjoy elegant Kyoto *kaiseki* food while being entertained by real Kyoto *geiko* and *maiko*.

Kabuki

Minami-za Theatre

THEATRE

(南座; Map p260; ☑561-0160; Shijō-Ōhashi; performances ¥4200-12,600; ☺irregular) This grand theatre in Gion is the oldest kabuki venue in Japan and it's a great place to get acquainted with this most beguiling of Japanese theatrical arts. The major event of the year is the Kao-mise Festival (1 to 26 December), which features Japan's finest kabuki actors. Other performances take place on an irregular basis. Ask at the tourist information centre or at your lodgings for help with ticket purchase. Tour companies can also help with tickets.

Karaoke

Jumbo Karaoke Hiroba Kawaramachi Branch

KARAOKE

(ジャンボカラオケ広場; Map p256; ☑231-6777; 29-1 Ishibashi-chō, Sanjō dōri, Kawaramachi Nishi iru, Nakagyō-ku; per person per 30min before/after 7pm from ¥100/300; ☺11am-5am) If you feel like giving the vocal chords a workout with the Japanese national pastime (karaoke), then head to this popular 'karaoke box' in the Sanjō shopping arcade. It has enough English songs to keep foreign guests entertained.

Musical Performances

Musical performances featuring the koto, *shamisen* and *shakuhachi* are held in Kyoto on an irregular basis. Traditional performances of *bugaku* (court music and dance) are often held at Kyoto shrines during festival periods. Occasionally contemporary butoh dance is also performed in Kyoto. Check with the tourist information centre to see if any performances are scheduled to be held while you are visiting the city.

Nō

Kanze Kaikan Nō Theatre
THEATRE

(観世会館; Map p266; ☎771-6114; 44 Okazaki Enshoji-chō, Sakyō-ku; admission ¥3000-4000; ☺10.30am-5pm Tue-Sun) This is the main theatre for performances of nō. *Takigi nō* is a picturesque form of nō performed in the light of blazing fires. In Kyoto this takes place on the evenings of 2 and 3 June at Heian-jingū – tickets cost ¥3000 if you pay in advance (ask at the tourist information office for the location of ticket agencies) or you can pay ¥4000 at the entrance gate.

Traditional Dance, Theatre & Music

Gion Corner
THEATRE

(ギオンコーナー; Map p260; ☎561-1119; Yasaka Hall, 570-2 Gionmachi Minamigawa, Higashiyama-ku; admission ¥3150; ☺performances nightly at 7.40pm & 8.40pm 1 Mar-30 Nov, closed 16 Aug, Fri, Sat & Sun from 7pm Dec-Feb) The shows presented here are a sort of crash course in Japanese traditional arts. You get a chance to see snippets of the tea ceremony, koto music, ikebana, *gagaku* (court music), *kyōgen* (ancient comic plays), *Kyōmai* (Kyoto-style dance) and *bunraku* (puppet plays).

🔒 Shopping

The heart of Kyoto's shopping district is around the intersection of Shijō-dōri and Kawaramachi-dōri. The blocks to the north and west of here are packed with stores selling both traditional and modern goods. Kyoto's largest department stores (Hankyū, Takashimaya, Daimaru and Fujii Daimaru) can be found in this area.

Some of the best shopping and people-watching can be had along Kyoto's three downtown shopping arcades: Shinkyōgoku shopping arcade, Teramachi shopping arcade and Nishiki Market. Teramachi and Shinkyōgoku run parallel to each other in the heart of downtown. The former has a mix of tasteful and tacky shops; the latter specialises in tacky stuff for the hoards of schoolkids who visit Kyoto every year. Nishiki branches off Shinkyōgoku to the west, about 100m north of Shijō-dōri.

The place to look for antiques in Kyoto is Shinmonzen-dōri, in Gion (Map p260). The street is lined with great old shops, many of them specialising in one thing or another (furniture, pottery, scrolls, prints etc). You can easily spend an afternoon strolling from shop to shop, but be warned: if something strikes your fancy you're going to have to break out the credit card – prices here are steep!

Teramachi-dōri (Map p258), between Oike-dōri and Marutamachi-dōri, has a number of classic old Kyoto arts, crafts, antiques and tea shops. This is probably the best place for shopping if you're after 'old Kyoto' items.

Kōjitsu Sansō
OUTDOOR GEAR

(Map p256; ☎708-5178; 5F Kyoto Yodobashi, 590-2 Higashi shiokōji-chō, Karasuma dōri Shichijō sagaru, Shimogyōku; ☺9.30am-10pm) If you plan to do some hiking or camping while in Japan, you can stock up on equipment at this excellent little shop. It's down a flight of steps, the entrance to which is to the right of a convenience store.

Art Factory
CLOTHING

(Map p256; ☎213-3131; 498 Higashigawa-chō, Teramachi, Takoyakushi agaru, Nakagyō-ku; ☺11am-8pm) A T-shirt with your name written in kanji, katakana or hiragana across the chest is a great souvenir, and this place can make them in just a few minutes. If you don't fancy your own name on the shirt, you can also get the name of your country or choose from a variety of Japanese words and slogans. Look

---

MARKETS

If you're in town when one of the following markets is on, by all means go! Markets are the best places to find antiques and bric-a-brac at reasonable prices and are the only places in Japan where you can actually bargain for a better price.

On the 21st of each month, **Kōbō-san Market** (弘法さん（東寺露天市）) is held at Tō-ji (p254) to commemorate the death of Kōbō Daishi (Kūkai), who in 823 was appointed abbot of the temple.

Another major market, **Tenjin-san Market** (天神さん（北野天満宮露天市）), is held on the 25th of each month at Kitano Tenman-gū (p270), marking the day of the birth (and, coincidentally, the death) of the Heian-era statesman Sugawara Michizane (845-903).

for the T-shirts displayed outside (strangely, there is no sign in English or Japanese, but they call themselves 'Art Factory').

Bic Camera
ELECTRONICS

(ビックカメラ; Map p253; ☎353-1111; Kyoto Station Bldg, 927 Higashi Shiokōji-chō, Shimogyō-ku; ⏰10am-9pm) This vast new electronics/camera shop is directly connected to Kyoto Station via the Nishinotōin gate; otherwise, it's accessed by leaving the north (Karasuma) gate and walking west. You will be amazed by the sheer amount of goods it has on display. Just be sure that an English operating manual is available. For computer parts, keep in mind that not all items on offer will work with English operating systems.

Yodobashi Camera
ELECTRONICS

(ヨドバシカメラ; Map p253; ☎351-1010; 590-2 Higashi Shiokōji-chō, Shimogyō-ku; ⏰9.30am-10pm) A major new rival for the above, this mammoth shop sells a similar range of electronic goods, camera and computer products and also has a restaurant floor, supermarket, bookshop, cafe and, well, the list goes on. It's a few minutes' walk north of Kyoto Station.

TOP CHOICE Aritsugu
KNIVES

(有次; Map p256; ☎221-1091; 219 Kajiya-chō, Gokomachi nishi iru, Nishikikōji-dōri, Nakagyō-ku; ⏰9am-5.30pm) Located in Nishiki Market, this is one of the finest knife shops in Japan. There's usually someone on hand who can help you in English. If you purchase a knife, staff put a final edge on it with a giant stone sharpening wheel before packaging it.

TOP CHOICE Morita Washi
JAPANESE CRAFTS

(森田和紙; off Map p256; ☎341-1419; 1F Kajioha Bldg, 298 Ōgisakaya-chō, Bukkō-ji agaru, Higashinotōin-dōri, Shimogyō-ku; ⏰9.30am-5.30pm, to 4.30pm Sat, closed Sun & holidays) Not far from Shijo-Karasuma, this wonderful shop sells a fabulous variety of handmade washi (Japanese paper) for reasonable prices. It could be our favourite shop in Kyoto.

Kamiji Kakimoto
JAPANESE CRAFTS

(紙司柿本; Map p266; ☎211-3481; 54 Tokiwagi-chō, Nijō agaru, Teramachi, Nakagyō-ku; ⏰9am-6pm, closed irregularly) This place sells a good selection of washi (Japanese paper). It even stocks washi computer paper.

Rakushikan
JAPANESE CRAFTS

(楽紙館; Map p256; ☎221-1070; Takoyakushi-dōri Takakura nishi iru, Nakagyō-ku; ⏰10.30am-6pm,

closed Mon, first/last week of the year) This downtown Kyoto paper specialist carries an incredible variety of washi and other paper products in its spacious store. You can also try your hand at making your own washi here (ask at the counter for details).

TOP CHOICE Zōhiko
JAPANESE CRAFTS

(象彦; Map p266; ☎752-7777; 10 Okazaki Saishōji-chō, Sakyō-ku; ⏰9.30am-6pm, closed Wed) This is our favourite lacquerware shop in Kyoto. While the outside is nondescript, the inside is a treasure trove of beautiful lacquerware and there's a fine gallery upstairs. It's very near Heian-jingū.

Kyūkyo-dō
JAPANESE CRAFTS

(鳩居堂; Map p256; ☎231-0510; 520 Shimo-honnōjimae-chō, Aneyakōji agaru, Teramachi, Nakagyō-ku; ⏰10am-6pm Mon-Sat, closed Sun & 1-3 Jan) This old shop in the Teramachi covered arcade sells a selection of incense, shodō (calligraphy) goods, tea-ceremony supplies and washi. Prices are on the high side but the quality is good.

Kyoto Handicraft Center
JAPANESE CRAFTS, SOUVENIRS

(京都ハンディクラフトセンター; Map p266; ☎761-5080; 21 Entomi-chō, Shōgoin, Sakyō-ku; ⏰10am-7pm, closed 1-3 Jan) Just north of the Heian-jingū, this is a huge cooperative that sells, demonstrates and exhibits crafts (wood-block prints and yukata are a good buy here). It's the best spot in town for buying Japanese souvenirs and is highly recommended.

Kagoshin
JAPANESE CRAFTS

(籠新; Map p260; ☎771-0209; 4 chō-me, Sanjō-dōri, Sanjō-Ōhashi higashi, Higashiyama-ku; ⏰9am-6pm, closed Mon) This small shop sells a wide variety of inexpensive bamboo products like flower holders and baskets.

Kyoto Sanjō Takematsu
JAPANESE CRAFTS

(Map p260; ☎751-2444; 3-39 Sanjō-dōri, Higashiyama-ku; ⏰10am-7pm) Just a few doors from Kagoshin, it's almost a carbon copy.

Tōzandō
SWORDS

(東山堂; Map p266; ☎762-1341; 24 Shōgoin Entomi-chō, Sakyō-ku; ⏰10am-7pm) If you're a fan of Japanese swords and armour, you have to visit this wonderful shop on Marutamachi (diagonally opposite the Kyoto Handicraft Center). It's got authentic swords, newly made Japanese armour, martial arts goods etc and there's usually someone on hand who can speak English.

Ippōdō   TEA
(Map p266; ☎211-3421; Teramachi-dōri, Nijō, Nakagyō-ku; ⏱9am-7pm Mon-Sat, to 6pm Sun & holidays, cafe 11am-5pm) This is an old-fashioned tea shop selling all sorts of Japanese tea. You can ask to sample the tea before buying. There's an excellent adjoining cafe that sells a variety of green tea drinks and Japanese sweets – it's a highly recommended spot to relax while shopping on Teramachi.

Junkudō   BOOKSHOP
(ジュンク堂書店; Map p256; ☎253-6460; Kyoto BAL Bldg, 2-251 Yamazaki-chō, Sanjō sagaru, Kawaramachi-dōri, Nakagyō-ku; ⏱11am-8pm) In the BAL Building, this shop has a great selection of English-language books on the 5th and 8th floors. This is Kyoto's best bookshop now that the old Maruzen and Random Walk bookshops have closed (you may remember these shops if you visited in the past). There is an excellent cafe on the top floor, which has a great view over Kyoto to the Higashiyama mountains. You can get light meals here as well as drinks.

ⓘ Information

Immigration Office
Osaka Regional Immigration Bureau Kyoto Branch (大阪入国管理局京都出張所; Map p266; ☎752-5997; 4F Kyoto Second Local Joint Government Bldg, 34-12 Marutamachi Kawabata Higashi iru, Higashi Marutamachi, Sakyō-ku; ⏱9am-noon & 1-4pm Mon-Fri)

Internet Access
Kinko's (キンコーズ; Map p256; ☎213-6802; 651-1 Tearaimizu-chō, Takoyakushi sagaru, Karasuma-dōri, Nakagyō-ku; first 10min ¥262, then every 10min ¥210; ⏱24hr Mon-Fri, 8am-10pm Sat, Sun, holidays)
Kyoto International Community House (京都市国際交流会館;KICH; Map p266; ☎752-3010; 2-1 Torii-chō, Awataguchi, Sakyō-ku; per 30min ¥200; ⏱9am-9pm Tue-Sun) The machines here have Japanese keyboards and allow access to only a limited number of sites. There's also wi-fi here (you have to register, but it's free – ask at the main information desk). Closed Tuesday when Monday is a holiday.
Media Café Popeye (ポパイ; Map p256; ☎253-5300; www.mediacafe.jp/branch/sanjokawaramachi/index.html, in Japanese; B1, 42-6 Ebisu-cho, Sanjō agaru, Kawaramachi, Nakagyō-ku; per hr ¥420; ⏱24hr) This is convenient when you're downtown.
Tops Café (トップスカフェ; Map p253; ☎681-9270; www.topsnet.co.jp, in Japanese; Kyoto-eki, Hachijō-guchi; per 15min ¥120, plus ¥200 registration fee; ⏱24hr) This is an all-night

manga/internet cafe where you can actually spend the night in the booths if you want. It's just outside the south (Hachijō) exit of Kyoto Station.

Internet Resources
Kyoto Temple Admission Fees (www.templefees.com)
Kyoto Visitor's Guide (www.kyotoguide.com)

Media
The free *Kyoto Visitor's Guide* is the best source of information on upcoming events. It has restaurant reviews, day walks, detailed maps, useful information sections and feature articles about various aspects of the city. Pick up a copy as soon as you arrive in Kyoto. It's available at the TIC, Kyoto International Community House and most major hotels.

Another excellent source of information about Kyoto and the rest of the Kansai area is *Kansai Scene*, a monthly English-language listings magazine. Apart from lively articles, it has a large section of ads for employment, travel agencies, meetings etc. It's available at Junkudō bookshop, and a variety of other foreigner-friendly shops and accommodations in Kyoto.

Medical Services
Kyoto University Hospital (京都大学医学部附属病院; Map p266; ☎751-3111; 54 Shōgoinkawara-chō, Sakyō-ku; ⏱reception 8.30-11am, medical examination starts at 9am) Best hospital in Kyoto. There is an information counter near the entrance that can point you in the right direction.

Money
Most of the major banks are near the Shijō-Karasuma intersection, two stops north of Kyoto Station on the Karasuma line subway.

International transactions (like wire transfers) can be made at **Bank of Tokyo-Mitsubishi UFJ** (三菱東京UFJ銀行; Map p256; ☎221-7161; ⏱9am-3pm Mon-Fri, 10am-5pm Sat, closed Sun, ATM 24hr), which is at the southeast corner of this intersection. There is another branch one block southwest of the intersection. Other international transactions can be made at **Citibank** (シティバンク; Map p256; ☎212-5387; ⏱office 9am-3pm Mon-Fri, ATM 24hr), just west of this intersection.

Finally, you can change travellers cheques at most post offices around town, including the Kyoto Central Post Office, next to Kyoto Station. Post offices also have ATMs that accept most foreign-issued cards. If your card doesn't work at postal ATMs, try the ATMs in 7-Eleven convenience stores. Failing that, try **Citibank**, which has a 24-hour ATM that accepts most foreign-issued cards.

Post

Kyoto Central Post Office (京都中央郵便局; Map p253; ☎365-2471; 843-12 Higashishiokōji-chō, Shimogyō-ku; ◷9am-9pm Mon-Fri, to 7pm Sat, Sun & holidays, ATMs 12.05am-11.55pm Mon-Sat, to 8pm Sun & holidays) Conveniently located next to Kyoto Station (take the Kara-suma exit; the post office is on the northwest-ern side of the station). There's an after-hours service counter on the southern side of the post office, open 24 hours a day, 365 days a year. The ATMs here are open *almost* 24 hours a day.

Tourist Information

Kyoto Tourist Information Center (TIC; 京都総合観光案内所; Map p253; ☎343-0548; 2F Kyoto Station Bldg; ◷8.30am-7pm) Located in the main concourse on the 2nd floor of the Kyoto Station building that runs between the *shinkansen* station and the front of the station (near Isetan department store), this is the main tourist information centre in Kyoto. English speakers are always on hand and occasionally, speakers of other European and Asian languages are available. It stocks useful maps of the city, as well as bus maps, and can answer most of your questions. Note that it's called 'Kyo Navi' in Japanese (in case you have to ask someone).

Kyoto City Tourist Information (京都市観光案内所; Map p253; ☎343-6655; ◷8.30am-7pm) Inside the new Kyoto Station building, on the 2nd floor. Though it's geared towards Japanese visitors, an English-speaking staff member is usually on hand.

Travel Agencies

IACE TRAVEL (IACEトラベル; Map p256; ☎212-8944; 4F Dai15 Hase Bldg, 688 Takanna-chō, Shijo agaru, Karasuma dōri, Nakagyō-ku; ◷office 10am-7pm Mon-Fri, to 11am-6pm Sat)

KNT (近畿日本ツーリスト; Map p256; ☎255-0489; 437 Ebisu-chō, Sanjo agaru, Kawarama-chi dōri, Nakagyō-ku; ◷office 10.30am-7pm Mon-Fri, to 6.30pm Sat, Sun & holidays)

Useful Organisations

Kyoto International Community House (KICH; Map p266; ☎752-3010; 2-1 Torii-chō, Awatagu-chi, Sakyō-ku; ◷9am-9pm) An essential stop for those planning a long-term stay in Kyoto, but it can also be quite useful for short-term visi-tors. Here you can send and receive faxes, and use the internet (there are terminals and wi-fi). It has a library with maps, books, newspapers and magazines from around the world, and a no-tice board displaying messages regarding work, accommodation, rummage sales etc. KICH is in eastern Kyoto. It's closed Monday, except when Monday is a national holiday, then it's closed Tuesday. Take the Tōzai line subway from central Kyoto and get off at Keage Station, from which it's a 350m (five-minute) walk downhill.

✪ Getting There & Away

Travel between Kyoto and other parts of Japan is a breeze. Kansai is served by the Tōkaidō and San-yō *shinkansen* (bullet train) lines, several JR main lines and a few private rail lines. It is also possible to travel to/from Kyoto and other parts of Honshū, Shikoku and Kyūshū by long-distance highway buses. Finally, Kyoto is served by two airports. Kyoto is also relatively close to Nagoya, in case you can only get a flight to Centrair airport.

Air

Kyoto is served by Osaka Itami Airport (ITM), which principally handles domestic traffic, and the Kansai International Airport (KIX), which principally handles international flights. There are frequent flights between Tokyo and Itami (around ¥24,600, 80 minutes), but unless you're very lucky with airport connections you'll prob-ably find it as quick and more convenient to take the *shinkansen*. There are ample connections to/from both airports, though the trip to/from Kansai International Airport takes longer and costs more.

Bus

Overnight JR buses run between Tokyo Sta-tion (Nihonbashi-guchi/arrival, Yaesu-guchi/departure long-distance bus stop) and Kyoto Station Bus Terminal (京都駅前バスターミナル; Map p253).

The trip takes about eight hours and there are usually departures nightly in either direction, at 10.10pm, 10.30pm, 11pm (daily from Tokyo to Kyoto) and 11pm (daily from Kyoto to Tokyo). The fare is ¥6700 to ¥8100 one way. You should be able to grab some sleep in the reclining seats. There is a similar service to/from Shinjuku Sta-tion's Shin-minami-guchi in Tokyo.

Other JR bus transport possibilities include Kanazawa (one way ¥3800 to ¥4060) and Hiro-shima (one way ¥4300 to ¥5500).

Train

SHINKANSEN (TOKYO, OSAKA, NAGOYA & HAKATA) Kyoto is on the Tōkaidō-San-yō *shinkansen* line, which runs between Tokyo and northern Kyūshū, with stops at places like Nagoya, Osaka, Kōbe, Himeji and Hiroshima en route. The *shinkansen* operates to/from Kyoto Station (Kyoto's main train station). On the Tokyo end, it operates from Kyoto, Shinagawa and Shin-Yokohama stations. Fares and times for Hikari (the second-fastest type of *shinkansen*) between Kyoto and the following cities are as follows.

Tokyo ¥13,220; two hours, 43 minutes
Nagoya ¥5440; 40 minutes
Shin-Osaka ¥2730; 15 minutes
Hiroshima ¥10,790; two hours
Hakata ¥15,210; three hours, 22 minutes

NARA The private Kintetsu line (sometimes written in English as the Kinki Nippon railway) links Kyoto (Kintetsu Kyoto Station, south side of the main Kyoto Station building) and Nara (Kintetsu Nara Station). There are fast direct *tokkyū* (¥1110, 33 minutes) and ordinary express trains (¥610, 40 minutes), which may require a change at Saidai-ji.

The JR Nara line also connects Kyoto Station with JR Nara Station (express, ¥690, 41 minutes), and this is a great option for Japan Rail Pass holders.

OSAKA The fastest train other than the *shinkansen* between Kyoto Station and Osaka is the JR *shinkaisoku* (special rapid train), which takes 29 minutes (¥540). In Osaka, the train stops at both Shin-Osaka and Osaka Stations.

There is also the cheaper private Hankyū line, which runs between Hankyū Kawaramachi, Karasuma and Ōmiya Stations in Kyoto and Hankyū Umeda Station in Osaka (*tokkyū* or limited express Umeda-Kawaramachi, ¥390, 40 minutes). These trains are usually more comfortable than the JR trains, and if you board at Kawaramachi or Umeda, you can usually get a seat.

Alternatively, you can take the Keihan main line between Demachiyanagi, Sanjō, Shijō or Shichijō Stations in Kyoto and Keihan Yodoyabashi Station in Osaka (*tokkyū* to/from Sanjō ¥400, 51 minutes). Yodoyabashi is on the Midōsuji subway line. Again, these are more comfortable than JR trains and you can usually get a seat if you board in Demachiyanagi or Yodoyabashi.

TOKYO The *shinkansen* line has the fastest and most frequent rail links. The journey can also be undertaken by a series of regular JR express trains, but keep in mind that it takes around eight hours and involves at least two (often three or four) changes along the way. The fare is ¥7980. Get the staff at the ticket counter to write down the exact details of each transfer for you when you buy your ticket.

ⓘ Getting Around

To/From the Airport

OSAKA ITAMI AIRPORT　大阪伊丹空港

There are frequent limousine buses between Osaka Itami airport and Kyoto Station (the Kyoto Station airport bus stop is opposite the south side of the station, in front of Avanti department store). Buses also run between the airport and various hotels around town, but on a less regular basis (check with your hotel). The journey should take around 55 minutes and the cost is ¥1280. Be sure to allow extra time in case of traffic.

At Itami, the stand for these buses is outside the arrivals hall; buy your tickets from the machines and ask one of the attendants which stand is for Kyoto (hint: you've got a better chance of getting a seat if you board at the South Terminal).

MK Taxi Sky Gate Shuttle limousine van service (☑778-5489) offers limousine van service to/from the airport for ¥2300. Call at least two days in advance to reserve, or ask at the information counter in the arrivals hall on arrival in Osaka.

KANSAI INTERNATIONAL AIRPORT (KIX)　関西国際空港

The fastest, most convenient way to travel between KIX and Kyoto is on the special Haruka airport express, which makes the trip in about 78 minutes. Most seats are reserved (¥3290, ¥3490, ¥3690 depending on season) but there are usually two cars on each train with unreserved seats (¥2980). Open seats are almost always available, so you don't have to purchase tickets in advance. First and last departures from Kyoto to KIX are 5.46am and 8.15pm; first and last departures from KIX to Kyoto are 6.33am Mon-Fri, 6.42am Sat, Sun and holidays and 10.16pm. Note that the Haruka is one of the few trains in Japan that is frequently late (although not usually by more than a few minutes). We suggest leaving a little extra time when heading from Kyoto to the airport to catch a flight.

If you have time to spare, you can save some money by taking the *kankū kaisoku* (Kansai airport express) between the airport and Osaka Station and taking a regular *shinkaisoku* to/from Kyoto. The total journey by this method takes about 92 minutes with good connections and costs ¥1830, making it the cheapest option.

It's also possible to travel by limousine bus between Kyoto and KIX (¥2500, about 90 minutes). In Kyoto, the bus departs from the same place as the Itami-bound bus.

A final option is the **MK Taxi Sky Gate Shuttle limousine van service** (☑778-5489), which will pick you up anywhere in Kyoto city and deliver you to KIX for ¥3500. Call at least two days in advance to reserve. The advantage of this method is that you are delivered from door to door and you don't have to lug your baggage through the train station. MK has a counter in the arrivals hall of KIX, and if there's room they'll put you on the next van to Kyoto. A similar service is offered by **Yasaka Taxi** (☑803-4800).

Bicycle

Kyoto is a great city to explore on a bicycle; with the exception of outlying areas it's mostly flat and there is a bike path running the length of the Kamo-gawa.

Unfortunately, Kyoto must rank near the top in having the world's worst public facilities for bike parking, and the city regularly impounds bikes parked outside regulation bike-parking areas. If your bike does disappear, check for a poster in the vicinity (in both Japanese and English) indicating the time of seizure and the inconvenient place you'll have to go to pay a ¥2000 fine and retrieve your bike.

There are two bicycle-parking lots in town that are convenient for tourists: one in front of Kyoto Station (Map p256) and another off Kiyamachi-dōri, between Sanjō-dōri and Shijō-dōri . It costs ¥150 per day to park your bicycle here. Be sure to hang onto the ticket you pick up as you enter.

BICYCLE PURCHASE

If you plan on spending more than a week or so exploring Kyoto by bicycle, it might make sense to purchase a used bicycle. A simple *mama chari* (shopping bike) can be had for as little as ¥3000. Try the used-cycle shop **Ei Rin** (栄輪; Map p266; ☑752-0292; 28-4 Sekiden-chō, Tanaka, Sakyō-ku; ☺9.30am-7.30pm, closed year-end/year-beginning holidays) on Imadegawa-dōri, near Kyoto University. Otherwise, you'll find a good selection of used bikes advertised for sale on the message board of the Kyoto International Community House (see p297).

BICYCLE RENTAL

☑**Kyoto Cycling Tour Project** (KCTP; 京都サイクリングツアープロジェクト; Map p253; ☑354-3636; www.kctp.net/en/index.html; ☺9am-7pm) A great place to rent a bike. These folk rent bikes (¥1000 per day) that are perfect for getting around the city. KCTP also conducts a variety of excellent bicycle tours of Kyoto with English-speaking guides. These are a great way to see the city (check the website for details).

Public Transport

BUS Kyoto has an extensive network of bus routes providing an efficient way of getting around at moderate cost. Many of the routes used by visitors have announcements in English. The core timetable for buses is between 7am and 9pm, though a few run earlier or later.

The main bus terminals are Kyoto Station on the JR and Kintetsu lines, Sanjō Station on the Keihan line/Tōzai subway line, Karasuma-Shijō Station on the Hankyū line/Karasuma subway line, and Kitaōji Station on the Karasuma subway line. The bus terminal at Kyoto Station is on the north side and has three main departure bays (departure points are indicated by the letter of the bay and number of the stop within that bay).

The TIC (p297) stocks the *Bus Navi: Kyoto City Bus Sightseeing Map*, which is a good map of the city's main bus lines. This map is not exhaustive. If you can read a little Japanese, pick up a copy of the regular (and more detailed) Japanese bus map available at major bus terminals throughout the city.

Bus stops usually display a map of destinations from that stop on the top section. On the bottom section there's a timetable for the buses serving that stop. Unfortunately, all of this information is in Japanese, and nonspeakers will simply have to ask locals for help.

Entry to the bus is usually through the back door and exit is via the front door. Inner-city buses charge a flat fare (¥220), which you drop into the clear plastic receptacle on top of the machine next to the driver on your way out. A separate machine gives change for ¥100 and ¥500 coins or ¥1000 notes.

On buses serving the outer areas, you take a numbered ticket (*seiri-ken*) when entering. When you leave, an electronic board above the driver displays the fare corresponding to your ticket number (drop the *seiri-ken* into the ticket box with your fare).

The main bus information centre (京都バス案内書; Map p253) is located in front of Kyoto Station. Here you can pick up bus maps, purchase bus tickets and passes (on all lines, including highway buses), and get additional information. Nearby, there's a convenient English/Japanese bus-information computer terminal; just enter your intended destination and it will tell you the correct bus and bus stop.

Three-digit numbers written against a red background denote loop lines: bus 204 runs around the northern part of the city and buses 205 and 206 circle the city via Kyoto Station. Buses with route numbers on a blue background take other routes.

When heading for locations outside the city centre, be careful which bus you board. Kyoto city buses are green, Kyoto buses are tan and Keihan buses are red and white.

SUBWAY Kyoto has two efficient subway lines, which operate from 5.30am to 11.30pm. The minimum fare is ¥210 (children ¥110).

The quickest way to travel between the north and south of the city is the Karasuma subway line. The line has 15 stops and runs from Takeda in the far south, via Kyoto Station, to the Kyoto International Conference Hall (Kokusaikaikan Station) in the north.

The east-west Tōzai subway line crosses Kyoto from Uzumasa-Tenjingawa in the west, meeting the Karasuma line at Karasuma-Oike Station, and continuing east to Sanjō Keihan, Yamashina and Rokujizō, in the east and southeast.

Taxi

Kyoto taxi fares start at ¥640 for the first 2km. The exception is **MK Taxis** (☑778-4141), whose fares start at ¥580.

MK Taxis also provides tours of the city with English-speaking drivers. For a group of up to four, prices start at ¥21,800 for a three-hour tour. Another company offering a similar service is **Kyōren Taxi Service** (☑672-5111).

Most Kyoto taxis are equipped with satellite navigation systems. If you are going somewhere unusual, it will help the driver if you have the address or phone number of your destination, as both of these can be programmed into the system.

Kansai

Why Go?

Kansai (関西) is the heart of Japan. Nowhere else in the country can you find so much of historical and cultural interest in such a compact area. Indeed, if you had to choose only one region to explore, Kansai would be the easy choice. Kyoto, covered in the preceding chapter, is hands down the most rewarding destination in Japan for the traveller, and it makes a good base for exploring the region.

Nara, Japan's first permanent capital, is a dense collection of traditional sights and is home to Japan's most impressive Buddhist temple: Tōdai-ji. Osaka is a great place to sample Japanese city life in all its mind-boggling intensity, while Kōbe is one of Japan's most attractive cities. In Mie-ken you'll find Ise-jingū, Japan's most sacred Shintō shrine, and in Wakayama-ken there are great onsen (hot springs), a rugged coastline and the temple complex of Kōya-san, Japan's most important Buddhist centre.

Best Places to Eat

» Café Absinthe (p314)
» Misono (p322)
» Tempura Asuka (p338)
» Imai Honten (p314)
» Fukutei (p327)

Best Places to Stay

» Guesthouse Sakuraya (p337)
» Arietta Hotel (p311)
» Blue Sky Guesthouse (p355)

When to Go
Osaka

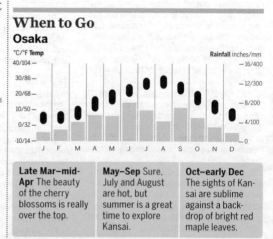

Late Mar–mid-Apr The beauty of the cherry blossoms is really over the top.	**May–Sep** Sure, July and August are hot, but summer is a great time to explore Kansai.	**Oct–early Dec** The sights of Kansai are sublime against a backdrop of bright red maple leaves.

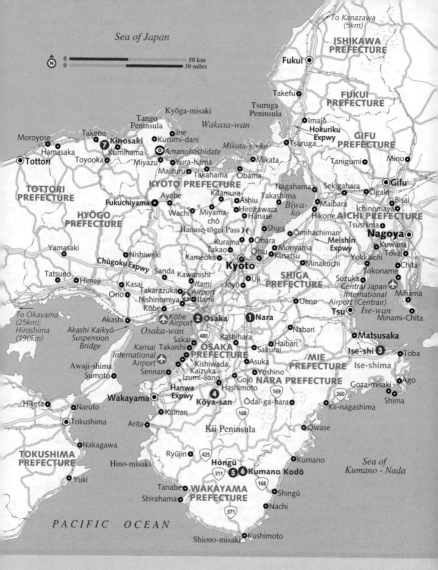

Kansai Highlights

1 Gaze in awe at the **Great Buddha** (Daibutsu) at Nara's Tōdai-ji (p334)

2 Feast your eyes on the colourful human parade of Osaka's **Dōtombori** area (p305)

3 Feel the power radiating from the main hall of **Ise-jingū**

(p358), Japan's most sacred Shintō shrine

4 Wander the mystical forest of Kōya-san's **Oku-no-in** (p348)

5 Soak in the restorative waters of the three onsen of **Hongū** (p355)

6 Walk the ancient pilgrimage trails of Wakayama's **Kumano Kodō** (p352)

7 Put on your *yukata* (light cotton kimono) and stroll from onsen to onsen in the quaint town of **Kinosaki** (p360)

OSAKA

♪ 06 / POP 2.66 MILLION

Osaka (大阪) is the working heart of Kansai. Famous for its down-to-earth citizens and the colourful *Kansai-ben* (Kansai dialect) they speak, it's a good counterpart to the refined atmosphere of Kyoto. First and foremost, Osaka is famous for good eating: the phrase *kuidaore* (eat 'til you drop) was coined to describe Osakans' love for good food. Osaka is also a good place to experience a modern Japanese city: it's only surpassed by Tokyo as a showcase of the Japanese urban phenomenon.

This isn't to say that Osaka is an attractive city; almost bombed flat in WWII, it is an endless expanse of concrete boxes, pachinko (pinball) parlours and elevated highways. But the city somehow manages to rise above this and exert a peculiar charm. At night, Osaka really comes into its own; this is when all those drab streets come alive with flashing neon, beckoning residents and travellers alike with promises of tasty food and good times.

Osaka's highlights include Osaka-jō and its surrounding park, Osaka Aquarium with its enormous whale sharks and manta rays, the *Blade Runner* nightscapes of the Dōtombori area, and the wonderful Open-Air Museum of Old Japanese Farmhouses. But Osaka has more to offer than its specific sights; like Tokyo, it is a city to be experienced in its totality, and casual strolls are likely to be just as rewarding as structured sightseeing tours.

History

Osaka has been a major port and mercantile centre from the beginning of Japan's recorded history. During its early days, Osaka was Japan's centre for trade with Korea and China. In the late 16th century, Osaka rose to prominence when Toyotomi Hideyoshi, having unified all of Japan, chose Osaka as the site for his castle. Merchants set up around the castle and the city grew into a busy economic centre. This development was further encouraged by the Tokugawa shōgunate, which adopted a hands-off approach to the city, allowing merchants to prosper unhindered by government interference.

In the modern period, Tokyo has usurped Osaka's position as the economic centre of Japan, and most of the companies formerly headquartered in Osaka have moved east.

Osaka is still an economic powerhouse, however, and the city is ringed by factories churning out the latest in electronics and hi-tech products.

⊙ Sights & Activities

Osaka is usually divided into two areas: Kita and Minami. Kita (Japanese for 'north') is the city's main business and administrative centre, and contains two of its biggest train stations: JR Osaka and Hankyū Umeda.

Minami (Japanese for 'south') is Osaka's entertainment district, and contains the bustling shopping and nightlife zones of Namba and Shinsaibashi. It's also home to two major train stations, JR Namba and Nankai Namba stations.

The dividing line between Kita and Minami is formed by two rivers, the Dōjima-gawa and the Tosabori-gawa, between which you'll find Nakano-shima, a relatively peaceful island that is home to the Museum of Oriental Ceramics. About 1km southeast of Nakano-shima is Osaka-jō and its surrounding park, Osaka-jō-kōen.

To the south of the Minami area there's another group of sights clustered around Tennō-ji Station. These include Shitennō-ji, Tennō-ji-kōen, Den-den Town (the electronics neighbourhood) and the retro entertainment district of Shin-Sekai.

The bay area, to the west of the city centre, is home to another set of attractions including the excellent Osaka Aquarium and Universal Studios Japan theme park.

Keep in mind that while JR Osaka Station is centrally located in the Kita area, if you're coming from Tokyo by *shinkansen* (bullet train) you will arrive at Shin-Osaka Station, which is three stops (about five minutes) north of Osaka Station on the Midō-suji subway line.

At the visitor information offices, pick up a free copy of the first-rate *Osaka City Map,* which has insets of the city's most important areas and a map of the excellent subway/tram/train system. These offices also stock the *Osaka Japan Tourist Guide,* a more detailed booklet with maps, descriptions of sites and plenty of other useful information.

KITA AREA キタ

By day, Osaka's centre of gravity is the Kita area (Map p304). While Kita doesn't have any great attractions to detain the traveller, it does have a few good department stores, lots of places to eat and the eye-catching Umeda Sky building. Note that the JR Osaka

The **Kansai Thru Pass** is an excellent way to get around Kansai on the cheap. This pass – available at the travel counter in the arrivals hall of Kansai International Airport and at the main bus information centre in front of Kyoto station – allows unlimited travel on most bus and train lines in Kansai except the Japan Railways (JR) line. (The pass covers travel on the Nankai line, which serves Kansai International Airport.) It also qualifies you for discounts at several attractions around Kansai. The pass does not cover the Ise-shima region.

When you buy the pass, be sure to pick up the handy companion English guide-map, which shows all the bus and train lines available.

Two-/three-day passes cost ¥3800/5000. It's possible to purchase multiple passes for longer explorations of Kansai. Like the Japan Rail Pass, however, these passes are only available to travellers on temporary visitor visas (you'll have to show your passport). For more on the pass, visit **Kansai Thru Pass** (www.surutto.com/conts/ticket/3dayeng).

Station and much of the surrounding area is presently being rebuilt; we've tried to anticipate the changes, but keep in mind that some information was unavailable as this book went to press.

Umeda Sky Building   NOTABLE BUILDING
(梅田スカイビル) Just northwest of Osaka Station, the Umeda Sky building is Osaka's most dramatic piece of modern architecture. The twin-tower complex looks like a space-age version of Paris' Arc de Triomphe. The view from the top is impressive, particularly after sunset, when the lights of the Osaka–Kōbe conurbation spread out like a magic carpet in all directions.

There are two observation galleries: one outdoors on the roof and one indoors on the floor below. Getting to the top is half the fun, as you take a glassed-in escalator for the final five storeys (definitely not for vertigo sufferers). Tickets for the **observation decks** (1-1-88 Ōyodonaka, Kita-ku; admission ¥700; ☉10am-10.30pm; ☒JR line to Osaka) include the escalator ride and can be purchased on the 3rd floor of the east tower. Last entry 10pm.

Below the towers, you'll find **Takimi-kōji Alley** (滝見小路), a re-creation of an early Shōwa-era market street crammed with restaurants and *izakaya* (pub-eateries).

The building is reached via an underground passage that starts just north of both Osaka and Umeda stations (Map p304).

Osaka Museum of Housing & Living   MUSEUM
(大阪くらしの今昔館; Map p306; 6-4-20 Tenjinbashi, Kita-ku; admission ¥600; ☉10am-5pm Wed-Mon, closed day after national holiday, 3rd Mon & 27 Dec-3 Jan; ☒Tanimachi line to Tenjinbash-isuji Rokuchōme, exit 3) Two subway stops from Umeda is the Osaka Museum of Housing & Living, which contains a life-sized reproduction of an entire 1830s Edo-period Osaka neighbourhood. You can enter and inspect shophouses, meeting halls, drug stores and even an old-style *sentō* (public bath). The rooms and houses are dimly lit in order to re-create the ambience of pre-electric Osaka. The museum also contains a room filled with dioramas of post-Meiji Osaka neighbourhoods, including an interesting community of buses that were converted into homes following WWII.

To get there, from the station's exit 3, go through the glass doors to the left of the escalator and take the elevator to the 8th floor. There's no English sign.

CENTRAL OSAKA
Osaka Museum of History   MUSEUM
(大阪歴史博物館; Osaka Rekishi Hakubutsukan; Map p306; 4-1-32 Ōtemae, Chūō-ku; admission ¥600; ☉9.30am-5pm, to 8pm Fri, closed Tue & year-end/new-year holidays, closed Wed if preceding Tue is a national holiday; ☒Tanimachi line to Tanimachi-yonchōme) Just southwest of Osaka-jō, the Osaka Museum of History is housed in a fantastic new sail-shaped building adjoining the Osaka NHK Broadcast Center. The display floors of the museum occupy the 7th to the 10th floors.

The displays are broken into four sections by floor; you start at the top and work your way down, passing in time from the past to the present. The displays are very well done and there are plenty of English explanations; taped tours are available.

The museum is a two-minute walk northeast of Tanimachi-yonchōme Station.

OSAKA SIGHTS & ACTIVITIES

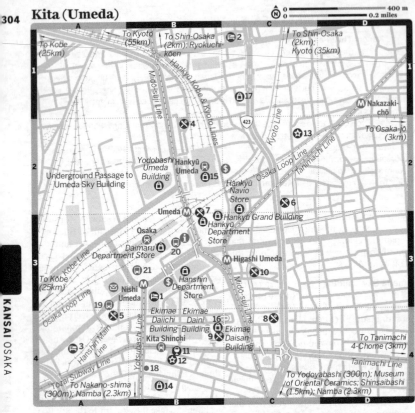

Osaka-jō   CASTLE

(大阪城; Map p306; 1-1 Osaka-jō, Chūō-ku; admission grounds/castle keep free/¥600; ⊙9am-5pm, to 7pm Aug; ⓇJR Osaka Loop line to Osaka-jō-kōen) This castle was built as a display of power by Toyotomi Hideyoshi after he achieved his goal of unifying Japan. One hundred thousand workers toiled for three years to construct an 'impregnable' granite castle, finishing the job in 1583. However, it was destroyed just 32 years later, in 1615, by the armies of Tokugawa Ieyasu.

Within 10 years the castle had been rebuilt by the Tokugawa forces, but it was to suffer a further calamity when another generation of the Tokugawa clan razed it rather than let it fall to the forces of the Meiji Restoration in 1868.

The present structure is a 1931 concrete reconstruction of the original, which was refurbished in 1997. The interior of the castle houses an excellent collection of displays relating to the castle, Toyotomi Hideyoshi and the city of Osaka. On the 8th floor there is an observation deck offering 360-degree views of Osaka and surrounding areas.

The castle and park are at their best in the spring-cherry-blossom and autumn-foliage seasons. Last entry is 30 minutes before closing.

The Ōte-mon gate, which serves as the main entrance to the park, is a 10-minute walk northeast of Tanimachi-yonchōme Station (sometimes written as Tanimachi 4-chome) on the Chūō and Tanimachi subway lines. You can also take the JR Osaka Loop line, get off at Osaka-jō-kōen Station and enter through the back of the castle.

Modern Transportation Museum   MUSEUM

(交通科学博物館; off Map p306; 3 Namiyoke, Minato-ku; adult/child ¥400/100; ⊙10am-5.30pm Tue-Sun, closed year-end/new-year holidays, closed Tue if preceding Mon is a national holiday; ⓇJR Osaka Loop line to Bentenchō, south exit) If you've

Kita (Umeda)

got kids in tow or just love those trains, then you'll want to check out the small but interesting Modern Transportation Museum, on the west side of town and easily accessed by the JR Osaka Loop line. The displays focus mostly on trains, but there are also some great models of ships and aircraft, several decent interactive displays, as well as life-sized *shinkansen* that you can climb inside to check out what things look like from the engineer's seat. Outside, there are several real steam and electric engines and passenger cars that you can climb inside (one is a working restaurant car). Finally, don't miss the great model-train layout at the far end of the building.

To get there from the station, take a hard left out of the turnstiles and it's across the street.

NAKANO-SHIMA 中之島

Sandwiched between Dōjima-gawa and Tosabori-gawa, this island is a pleasant oasis of trees and riverside walkways in the midst of Osaka's unrelenting grey. It's also home to **Osaka City Hall** (大阪市役所; Map p306) and **Nakano-shima-kōen** (中之島公園; Map p306) on the eastern end of the island, a good place for an afternoon stroll or picnic lunch. If you're coming from Kyoto, Nakano-shima is just north of Yodoyabashi Station, the terminus of the Keihan line. If you're coming by JR, it's about 15 minutes' walk south of JR Osaka Station.

Museum of Oriental Ceramics MUSEUM
(大阪市立東洋陶磁美術館; Map p306; 1-1-26 Nakanoshima, Kita-ku; admission ¥500; ⏰9.30am-5pm Tue-Sun, closed Tue if preceding Mon is a national holiday; 🚇Midō-suji line to Yodoyabashi) With more than 2700 pieces in its permanent exhibits, this museum has one of the finest collections of Chinese and Korean ceramics anywhere in the world. At any one time, approximately 300 of the gorgeous pieces from the permanent collection are on display, and there are often special exhibits (which cost extra). Last entry 4.30pm.

To get to the museum, go to Yodoyabashi Station on either the Midō-suji line or the Keihan line (different stations). Walk north to the river and cross to Nakano-shima. Turn right, pass the city hall on your left, bear left with the road, and look for the squat brown brick building.

MINAMI AREA ミナミ

A few stops south of Osaka Station on the Midō-suji subway line (get off at either Shinsaibashi or Namba Station), the Minami area (Map p308) is *the* place to spend the evening in Osaka. Its highlights include the Dōtombori Arcade, the National Bunraku Theatre, Dōguya-suji Arcade and Amerika-Mura.

Dōtombori NEIGHBOURHOOD
(道頓堀) Dōtombori is Osaka's liveliest nightlife area. It's centred on Dōtombori-gawa and **Dōtombori Arcade** (道頓堀; Map p308), a strip of restaurants and theatres where a peculiar type of Darwinism is the rule for both people and shops: survival of the flashiest. In the evening, head to **Ebisu-bashi** bridge to sample the glittering

OSAKA SIGHTS & ACTIVITIES

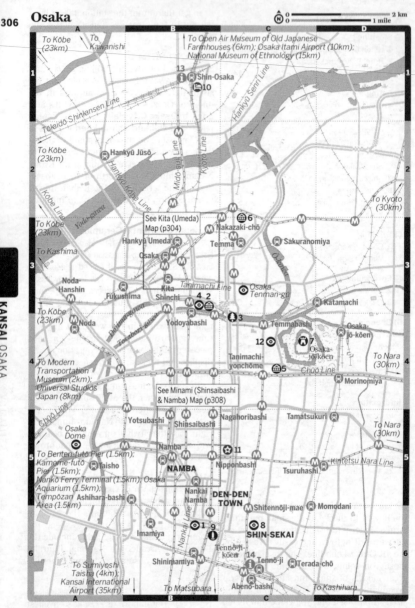

nightscape, which brings to mind a scene from the science-fiction movie *Blade Runner*. Nearby, the banks of the **Dōtombori-gawa** have recently been turned into attractive pedestrian walkways and this is the best vantage point for the neon madness above.

Only a short walk south of Dōtombori Arcade you'll find **Hōzen-ji** (法善寺; Map p308), a tiny temple hidden down a narrow alley. The temple is built around a moss-covered **Fudō-myōō statue**. This statue is a favourite of people employed in *mizu*

Osaka

shōbai (water trade), who pause before work to throw some water on the statue. Nearby, **Hōzen-ji Yokochō** is a tiny alley filled with traditional restaurants and bars.

To the south of Dōtombori, in the direction of Nankai Namba Station, is a maze of colourful arcades with more restaurants, pachinko parlours, strip clubs, cinemas and who knows what else. To the north of Dōtombori, between Midō-suji and Sakai-suji, the narrow streets are crowded with hostess bars, discos and pubs. This district, along with Amerika-Mura, is the place to do your bar hopping.

Dōguya-suji Arcade   MARKET

(道具屋筋; Map p308) If you desperately need a *tako-yaki* (octopus ball) fryer, a red lantern to hang outside your shop or plastic food models to lure the customers in, this shopping arcade is the place to go. You'll also find endless knives, pots, pans and just about anything else that's even remotely related to the preparation and consumption of food.

Amerika-Mura   NEIGHBOURHOOD

(アメリカ村; Map p308) Amerika-Mura (America Village, also known as Ame-Mura) is a compact enclave of trendy shops and restaurants, with a few discreet love hotels thrown in for good measure. The best rea-

son to come is to check out the hordes of colourful Japanese teens living out the myth of America. These days, the look is hip-hop for guys and and tiny shorts for the girls. The peculiar name, by the way, comes from the presence of several shops that sprang up here after the war and sold various bits of Americana, like Zippo lighters and American T-shirts.

In the middle of it all is **Amerika-Mura Triangle Park** (アメリカ村三角公園; Map p308), an all-concrete park with benches where you can sit and watch the parade of fashion victims. Ame-Mura is one or two blocks west of Midō-suji, bounded on the north by Suomachi-suji and on the south by Dōtombori-gawa.

If you're on a tight budget, this is the best place to eat and drink in Osaka, as the place is chock-a-block with cheap *izakaya* and restaurants.

TENNŌ-JI & AROUND   天王寺公園

Shin-Sekai   NEIGHBOURHOOD

(新世界) For something completely different, take a walk through this retro entertainment district just west of Tennō-ji-kōen. At the heart of it all you'll find crusty old **Tsūten-kaku** (Map p306), a 103m-high structure that dates back to 1912 (the present tower was rebuilt in 1969). When the tower first went up, it symbolised everything new and exciting about this once-happening neighbourhood (*shin-sekai* is Japanese for 'new world'). Now, Shin-Sekai is a world that time forgot, home to ancient pachinko parlours, rundown theatres, dirt-cheap restaurants and all manner of raffish and suspicious characters.

Shitennō-ji   TEMPLE

(四天王寺; Map p306; 1-11-18 Shitennō-ji, Tennōji-ku; admission garan/garden ¥300/300; ⊘garan 8.30am-4.30pm Apr-Sep, to 4pm Oct-Mar, garden 10am-4pm; ☒Tanimachi line to Shitennōji-mae, southern exit) Founded in 593, Shitennō-ji has the distinction of being one of the oldest Buddhist temples in Japan, although none of the present buildings are originals. Unfortunately, most are the usual concrete reproductions, with the exception of the big stone torii (shrine gate) that dates back to 1294, making it the oldest of its kind in Japan. Apart from the torii, there is little of real historical significance, and the absence of greenery in the raked-gravel grounds makes for a rather desolate atmosphere. The adjoining **museum** (admission ¥200) is of limited interest.

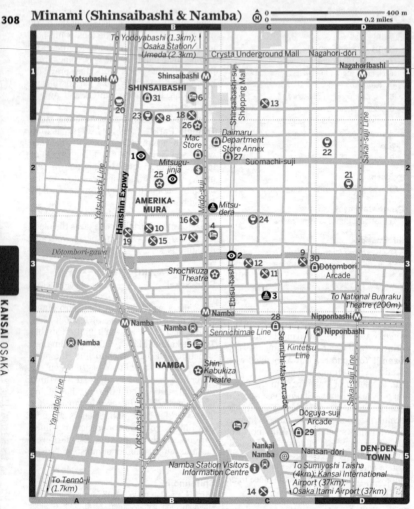

Take the southern exit from the station, cross to the left side of the road and take the small road that goes off at an angle away from the subway station. The entrance to the temple is on the left.

FREE Sumiyoshi Taisha SHRINE
(住吉大社; off Map p306; 2-9-89 Sumiyoshi, Sumiyoshi-ku; ⊙dawn-dusk; ℝNankai main line to Sumiyoshi-taisha) This shrine is dedicated to Shintō deities associated with the sea and sea travel, in commemoration of a safe passage to Korea by a 3rd-century empress. Having survived the bombing

in WWII, Sumiyoshi Taisha actually has a couple of buildings that date back to 1810. The shrine was founded in the early 3rd century and the buildings that can be seen today are faithful replicas of the ancient originals. They offer visitors a rare opportunity to see a Shintō shrine that predates the influence of Chinese Buddhist architectural styles.

The shrine is next to both Sumiyoshi-taisha Station on the Nankai main line and Sumiyoshi-tori-mae Station on the Hankai line (the tram line that leaves from Tennō-ji Station).

Minami (Shinsaibashi & Namba)

TEMPŌZAN AREA 天保山エリア

Trudging through the streets of Kita or Minami, you could easily forget that Osaka is actually a port city. A good remedy for this is a trip down to Tempōzan (off Map p306), the best of Osaka's burgeoning seaside developments. On an island amid the busy container ports of Osaka Bay, Tempōzan has several attractions to lure travellers, especially those with children in tow. To reach Tempōzan, take the Chūō subway line west from downtown Osaka and get off at Osakakō Station. Take exit 1 out of the station, go straight at the bottom of the stairs and walk for 300m to reach the following attractions.

Before hitting the main attractions, you might want to get some perspective on it all by taking a whirl on the **giant Ferris wheel** (大観覧車; Daikanransha; 1-1-10 Kaigan-dōri, Minato-ku; admission ¥700; ⊗10am-10pm, last ticket 9.30pm). Said to be the largest Ferris wheel in the world, the 112m-high wheel offers unbeatable views of Osaka, Osaka Bay and Kōbe. Give it a whirl in the evening to enjoy the vast carpet of lights formed by the Osaka–Kōbe conurbation.

Next to the Ferris wheel, **Tempōzan Marketplace** (天保山マーケットプレース; 1-1-10 Kaigan-dōri, Minato-ku; admission free; ⊗shops 11am-8pm, restaurants to 9pm) is a shopping and dining arcade that includes the **Naniwa Kuishinbō Yokochō** (なにわ食いしんぼ横丁; 1-1-10 Kaigan-dōri, Minato-ku; admission free; ⊗11am-8pm), a faux Edo-period food court where you can sample all of Osaka's culinary specialities.

TOP CHOICE Osaka Aquarium AQUARIUM
(海遊館; off Map p306; www.kaiyukan.com; 1-1-10 Kaigan-dōri, Minato-ku; adult/child ¥2000/900; ⊗10am-8pm) Osaka Aquarium is easily one of the best aquariums in the world and it's well worth a visit, particularly if you've got kids or if you love sharks. The aquarium is built around a vast central tank, which houses the star attractions: one whale shark and one manta. But these are only the beginning: you'll also find a huge variety of other sharks, including leopard sharks, zebra sharks and hammerhead sharks. There are also countless other species of rays and fish.

A walkway winds its way around the main tank and past displays of life found on eight different ocean levels. The giant spider crabs in the Japan Ocean Deeps section look like alien invaders from another

OSAKA SIGHTS & ACTIVITIES

planet. Presentations have both Japanese and English captions and an environmentally friendly slant to them.

The aquarium is at the west end of the Tempōzan complex, just past Tempōzan Marketplace.

OTHER AREAS

Open-Air Museum of Old Japanese Farmhouses
PARK

(日本民家集落博物館; off Map p306; ☑6862-3137; 1-2 Hattori Ryokuchi, Toyonaka-shi; admission ¥500; ⊙9.30am-5pm Tue-Sun, closed year-end/new-year holidays, closed Tue if preceding Mon is a national holiday; ⊠Midō-suji line to Ryokuchi-kōen, west exit) In Ryokuchi-kōen, this fine open-air museum features 11 traditional Japanese country houses and other structures brought here from all over Japan. All have been painstakingly reconstructed and filled with period-era tools and other displays. Most impressive is the giant *gasshō-zukuri* (thatch-roofed) farmhouse from Gifu-ken.

The parklike setting, with plenty of trees and bamboo, gives the museum a pleasantly rustic air – and the whole place comes alive with fiery red maple leaves during the November foliage season. For anyone even remotely interested in traditional Japanese architecture, we highly recommend this excellent attraction. An English-language pamphlet is available. Last entry by 4.30pm.

To get there, walk northwest from the station into the park.

Universal Studios Japan
AMUSEMENT PARK

(ユニバーサルスタジオジャパン; Universal City; adult/child ¥6100/4100; ⊙10am-5pm Mon-Fri, to 6pm Sat, Sun & holidays; ⊠JR Osaka Loop line to Universal City) Universal Studios Japan is Osaka's answer to Tokyo Disneyland. Closely based on its two sister parks in the USA, the park features a wide variety of rides, shows, restaurants and other attractions; hours vary seasonally.

To get there, take the JR Loop line to Nishi-kujō Station, switch to one of the distinctively painted Universal Studio shuttle trains and get off at Universal City Station. From Osaka Station the trip costs ¥170 and takes about 15 minutes. There are also some direct trains from Osaka Station (ask at the tourist office for times; the price is the same).

National Museum of Ethnology
MUSEUM

(国立民族学博物館; off Map p306; ☑6876-2151; 10-1 Senri Expo Park, Suita; admission ¥420; ⊙10am-5pm Thu-Tue, closed year-end/new-year holidays & Thu if preceding Wed is a national holiday; ⊠Midō-suji line to Senri-chūō, then east on Osaka Monorail to Banpaku-kinen-kōen) Located in Osaka Banpaku-kōen (World Expo Park), this museum is arguably Osaka's best. It's well worth the trip from downtown Osaka or Kyoto, especially if there's a good special exhibit on (check *Kansai Scene* or the tourist information offices for upcoming exhibits).

The museum provides a whirlwind tour through the cultural artefacts of many of the world's cultures. Exhibits range from Bollywood movie posters to Thai *túk-túk* (motorised transport), with Ainu textiles, Bhutanese mandalas and Japanese festival floats in between. There is little English signage, but most of the materials are self-explanatory. You can borrow a sheet of English explanations from the reception desk.

From the station, go left, cross the bridge over the highway, buy a ticket from the machines, go through the turnstile and walk towards the huge Tower of the Sun statue. Once past the statue, you will see the museum about 250m in front of you to the northwest (it's got several towers on its roof that resemble cooling towers). From Kyoto, you can take the Hankyū line to Minami Ibaraki Station and change there to the Osaka Monorail.

Festivals & Events

Tōka Ebisu
TRADITIONAL

From 9 to 11 January, huge crowds of more than a million people flock to the Imamiya Ebisu-jinja (今宮戎神社; Map p306) to receive bamboo branches hung with auspicious tokens. The shrine is near Imamiya Ebisu Station on the Nankai line.

Tenjin Matsuri
TRADITIONAL

Held on 24 and 25 July, this is one of Japan's three biggest festivals. Try to make the second day, when processions of *mikoshi* (portable shrines) and people in traditional attire start at Osaka Temman-gū and end up in O-kawa (in boats). As night falls, the festival is marked with a huge fireworks display.

Kishiwada Danjiri Matsuri
TRADITIONAL

Osaka's wildest festival on 14 and 15 September, a kind of running of the bulls except with *danjiri* (festival floats), many weighing over 3000kg. The *danjiri* are hauled through the streets by hundreds of people using ropes, and in all the excitement there have been a couple of deaths – take care and stand back. Most of the action takes place on the second day. The best place to see it is west of Kishiwada Station on the Nankai *honsen* line (main rail line, from Nankai Station).

🛏 Sleeping

There are plenty of places to stay in and around the two centres of Kita and Minami. You can also explore Osaka from a base in Kyoto, and you'll find more budget accommodation in the old capital, which is only about 40 minutes away by train. Keep in mind, however, that the trains stop running a little before midnight (party-goers take note).

KITA AREA

Minami has a bigger selection of restaurants and shops, but the Kita area is convenient if you want fast access to transport, with plenty of hotels around the stations.

Hilton Osaka
HOTEL $$$

(ヒルトン大阪; Map p304; ☎6347-7111; fax 6347-7001; 1-8-8 Umeda, Kita-ku; s ¥18,000-47,000, d & tw ¥21,000-51,000; @🛜🏊; 🚇JR line to Osaka) Just south of JR Osaka Station, this is an excellent hotel at home with foreign guests. The rooms are clean and light, with a Japanese touch, and there's a 15m pool in the fitness centre. The views from the 35th-floor Windows on the World bar are awesome, and there are two floors of great restaurants below the hotel.

Hotel Sunroute Umeda
HOTEL $$

(ホテルサンルート梅田; Map p304; ☎6373-1111; fax 6374-0523; www.sunroute.jp/HotelInfoSVE; 3-9-1 Toyosaki, Kita-ku; s/d/tw from ¥8820/12,600/15,750; @; 🚇Midō-suji line to Nakatsu) The Sunroute is a good business hotel about 15 minutes' walk north of JR Osaka Station. The rooms are small but clean and some have good views over Osaka. It's just north of Hankyū Umeda.

Ritz-Carlton Osaka
HOTEL $$$

(ザ・リッツ・カールトン大阪; Map p304; ☎6343-7000; fax 6343-7001; www.ritzcarlton.com/en/Properties/Osaka/Default.htm; 2-5-25 Umeda, Kita-ku; d/tw from ¥58,138; @🛜🏊; 🚇Hanshin line to Umeda, west exit, or JR line to Osaka, Sakurabashi exit) A short walk from JR Osaka and Hankyū Umeda stations in Kita, the Ritz-Carlton is an elegant oasis in the heart of the city. Rooms are well appointed, comfortable and spacious, and the staff is polite and efficient. There is a pool, fitness centre and 24-hour business centre, as well as four on-site restaurants, one on-site bar and an on-site lounge.

MINAMI AREA

TOP CHOICE Arietta Hotel
HOTEL $$

(アリエッタホテル; ☎6267-2787; fax 6267-2789; www.thehotel.co.jp/en/arietta_osaka; 3-2-6 Azuchi-machi, Chūō-ku; s/tw from ¥7500/15,000; @; 🚇Midō-suji line to Honmachi) Located in Honmachi, which is about 10 minutes' walk north of the hopping Minami district (and served by the convenient Midō-suji subway line), the new Arietta has a lot going for it: clean minimalist rooms with everything you need at very competitive prices. It's a nice place to come home to after a day of exploring.

Cross Hotel Osaka
HOTEL $$

(クロスホテル大阪; Map p308; ☎6213-8281; fax 6213-8640; www.crosshotel.com/eng_osaka/index.html; 2-5-15 Shinsaibashisuji, Chūō-ku; s/d/tw from ¥19,635/24,255/27,720; @; 🚇Midō-suji line to Namba) Stylish rooms, excellent service and an awesome location make the Cross a fine choice at the upper end of the midrange bracket. It's right smack in the middle of Minami – you'd have to sleep under Ebisu-bashi bridge to achieve a more central location.

Swissotel Nankai Osaka
HOTEL $$$

(スイスホテル南海大阪; Map p308; ☎6646-1111; http://osaka.swissotel.com; 5-1-60 Namba, Chūō-ku; d/tw from ¥34,650/48,510; @; 🚇Midō-suji line to Namba) This is Minami's most elegant hotel, with stunning views and direct connections to KIX airport via Nankai-line trains that depart from Namba Station below the hotel. Rooms are clean and well appointed. There is a gym and excellent dining options on-site and nearby.

Hotel Nikkō Osaka
HOTEL $$$

(ホテル日航大阪; Map p308; ☎6244-1281; fax 6245-2432; www.jalhotels.com/domestic/kansai/osaka/index.html; 1-3-3 Nishi-Shinsaibashi, Chūō-ku; s ¥11,000-24,000, d ¥13,000-30,000, tw ¥13,000-35,000; @; 🚇Midō-suji line to Shinsaibashi) The Nikkō is a good base for shopping in Minami. It's an efficient hotel with decent rooms and views from the upper floors. There is direct access to Shinsaibashi subway station.

First Cabin
HOTEL $

(ファーストキャビン; Map p308; ☎6631-8090; info@first-cabin.jp; http://first-cabin.jp/en/store_midosuji-namba/index.php; 4th fl, Midōsuji-Namba Bldg, 4-2-1 Namba, Chūō-ku; per person ¥4800; @; 🚇Midō-suji line to Namba, exit 13) First Cabin is a good example of a new wave of Japanese capsule hotels: instead of coffin-like capsules, you get a tiny private room, sort of like a suite on an Airbus 380 (hence the name). Rooms are segregated by gender, as are the large common baths and showers. This is a good place to stay if you want to be close to the Minami action at an affordable price, but don't expect it to be quiet.

OTHER AREAS

Shin-Osaka Youth Hostel
HOSTEL $

(新大阪ユースホステル; Map p306; ☎6370-5427; fax 6370-5428; www.osaka-yha.com/shin-osaka; 1-13-13 Higashinakajima, Higashiyodoga-wa-ku; dm/tw ¥3300/4500; @☎; ☒JR line to Shin-Osaka, east exit) Five minutes' walk from Shin-Osaka Station, this is the closest hostel to the centre of town. The rooms are clean and well maintained, and there are great views across the city. A variety of private rooms are available, including one barrier-free room. The east exit out of Shin-Osaka Station is only marked from the upper floors of the station; cross the road and go left, passing a small convenience store and a sushi restaurant; turn right just past the sushi restaurant and walk 200m and you will see the large building on your left. Elevators are at the back.

Hotel Nikkō Kansai Airport
HOTEL $$$

(☎072-455-1111; www.nikkokix.com/e/top.html; fax 072-455-1155; 1 Senshū Kūkō kita, Izumisano-shi; s/d/tw ¥21,945/32,340/32,340; @☎☒; ☒JR Kansai Kūkō line to Kansai Kūkō) This is the only hotel at KIX and it charges accordingly. But if you can live with that, it's a decent place to spend the night. The rooms are fairly spacious with some good views. Note that check-in can be slow when a lot of flights are arriving at once.

✖ Eating
KITA
Japanese
Yukari
OKONOMIYAKI $$

(ゆかり; Map p304; ☎6311-0214; Ohatsutenjin-dōri, Sonezaki; pancakes ¥1000-2000; ☺11am-1am; ☒☒; ☒JR line to Osaka) A short walk from JR Osaka Station, this popular restaurant in the Ohatsutenji-dōri shopping arcade is a good place to try that great Osaka favourite: okonomiyaki (savoury Japanese 'pancakes' with a variety of fillings). They're cooked on a griddle right in front of you and there's even a vegetarian menu. There's a small English sign.

Ganko Umeda Honten
SUSHI $$

(がんこ梅田本店; Map p304; ☎6376-2001; 1-5-11 Shibata; lunch from ¥780; ☺11.30am-4am; ☒; ☒JR line to Osaka) Big is the operative word at this giant but approachable dining hall alongside Hankyū Umeda Station that serves a wide variety of Japanese dishes starting with sushi (if you want just sushi, you can sit at the counter and order à la carte). Look for the picture of the guy with the headband; it's just south of the DD House complex.

Umeda Hagakure
NOODLES $

(梅田はがくれ; Map p304; ☎6341-1409; B2 fl, Osaka Ekimae Daisan Bldg, 1-1 Umeda; noodles ¥500-600; ☺11am-2.45pm & 5-7.45pm Mon-Fri, 11am-2.30pm Sat & Sun; ☒JR line to Osaka) Locals line up outside this place for the fantastic udon noodles. Take the central escalator to the B2 floor, take a right, walk 25m and take another right; it is on the left with a small English sign. There are pictures outside to help with ordering. Our pick here is tenzaru (udon served on a plate with tempura; ¥1100). Whatever you do, don't go on a weekday between noon and 1pm (this is when the local office workers line up for lunch).

Dōjima Hana
TONKATSU $

(堂島花; ☎6345-0141; 2-1-31 Dōjima, Kita-ku; lunch ¥1000-1500, dinner ¥3000; ☺11am-11pm Mon-Sat, lunch Sun; ☒JR line to Osaka) If you crave something a little kotteri (rich and fatty), we recommend the tasty tonkatsu (pork cutlets) at this restaurant a stone's throw from the excellent Junkudō bookshop. We recommend the rōsukatsu teishoku (pork cutlet roast teishoku; small/medium ¥700/800). There is a limited picture menu and an English sign.

Food Courts

Of course, a lot of the dining action in Kita can be found in the seemingly endless shopping arcades, department store restaurant floors and entertainment/dining complexes. If you want to rub shoulders with the local salarymen, check out the **Shin-Umeda Shokudō-Gai** (新梅田食道街; Map p304), which is located down the escalators and to the right of the main exit of Hankyū Umeda Station (just past the McDonald's). There are heaps of good cheap restaurants in this area that compete for the lunch/dinner custom with cheap set meals, many of which are displayed outside, making ordering easy.

Okonomiyaki Sakura

OKONOMIYAKI $

(お好み焼きさくら; Map p304; ☑6364-7521; 9-10 Kakuda-chō; ⊙10.30am-11pm; 📵; 🚇Hankyū line to Umeda) A foreigner-friendly *okonomiyaki* specialist with an English menu. There is a map in the middle of the food court, and Okonomiyaki Sakura is Nos 10 and 16 on the map. Look for the glass sliding doors and the counter.

Gourmet Traveler

FOOD COURT $

(Map p304; B2 fl, Herbis Plaza complex) Gourmet Traveler at the Herbis Plaza complex (ハービスプラザ) is located a five-minute walk west of JR Osaka Station between the Hilton and the Ritz Carlton hotels. Here, you will find everything from Belgian beer restaurants to Indian curry houses, as well as a smattering of Japanese places for good measure.

Shinkiraku

TEMPURA $$

(新善楽; Map p304; ☑6345-3461; 1-8-16 Umeda, Kita-ku; lunch/dinner ¥800/4000; ⊙11am-2.30pm & 5-11pm Mon-Fri, 11am-2.30pm & 4-10pm Sat, Sun & holidays; 📵; 🚇JR line to Osaka) Another top food court is Hilton Plaza (ヒルトンプラザ), on the B2 floor beneath the Hilton Osaka, where you will find this excellent tempura specialist that packs 'em in at lunchtime. At lunch try the *ebishio-tendon* (shrimp tempura over rice; ¥880) and at dinner try the *tempura course* (¥5250). Take the escalator to the B2 floor, go right and look for the small English sign.

International

Org Life

CAFE $

(オルグオーガニックライフ; Map p304; ☑6312-0529; 7-7 Dōyama-chō, Kita-ku; drinks from ¥360, lunch ¥900-3000, dinner ¥3000; ⊙lunch & dinner; 🚇JR line to Osaka) At this open-plan, casual cafe you can grab a light meal or quick pick-me-up while exploring Kita. Order a pasta or risotto lunch for ¥900, and finish it off with cake and coffee. It's easy to spot, with an English sign. There's no English menu, but there is a picture menu and 'pasta lunch' or 'risotto lunch' will get your point across.

Tucusi Tapas & Charcoal Grill

SPANISH $$

(ツクシタパスアンドチャコールグリル; Map p304; ☑6362-2948; 2-5-30 Sonezaki; dinner ¥3000; ⊙5pm-3am; 📵; 🚇Midō-suji line to Yodoyabashi) Spanish food is all the rage in Japan and Tucsi has the good stuff. It's a slick, modern spot oddly located in a sort of netherworld east of Kita-Shinchi. Eat at the bar

or grab a table. Like most tapas spots, this place is as much about drinking as eating. There is an English sign.

MINAMI

Japanese

You will find lots of good Japanese choices in Minami, including a huge variety of dirt-cheap *izakaya* in Ame-Mura.

🏆 TOP CHOICE Shinsaibashi Madras 5

CURRY $

(マドラス心斎橋店; Map p308; ☑6213-0858; 2-7-22 Nishi-Shinsaibashi, Chūō-ku; meals ¥1000-2000; ⊙11am-1am; 🚇Midō-suji, Yotsubashi or Nagahori Tsurumiryokuchi line to Shinsaibashi, Namba or Yotsubashi) If you've never tried Japanese-style curry rice, this new Ame-Mura restaurant is a good place to get acquainted with it. The clean, well-lit space has friendly staff, and you can choose from tomato-, beef- or chicken-based curries and a variety of toppings. You can even get *genmai* (brown rice) if you wish. The *mikusu furai* (mixed fry; ¥1080) curry is a good choice.

Ume no Hana

JAPANESE $$

(梅の花; Map p308; ☑6258-3766; 11th fl, OPA Bldg, 1-4-3 Nishi-Shinsaibashi, Chūō-ku; average lunch/dinner ¥2000/5000; ⊙11am-3pm & 5-9pm; 📵; 🚇Midō-suji line to Shinsaibashi) This is part of an upscale chain that serves a variety of tofu-based dishes. The elevator is on the southeast side of the building (entry from the street – look for the sign reading 'OPA Restaurant & Cafe').

Nishiya

NOODLES $$

(にし家; Map p308; ☑6241-9221; 1-18-18 Higashi Shinsaibashi, Chūō-ku; noodle dishes from ¥630, dinner ¥3000-4000; ⊙11am-11pm Mon-Sat, to 9.30pm Sun; 📵; 🚇Midō-suji, Yotsubashi or Nagahori Tsurumiryokuchi line to Shinsaibashi) An Osaka landmark that serves *udon* noodles and a variety of hearty *nabe* (cast-iron pot) dishes for reasonable prices, including a tempura *udon* (¥1155). Look for the semirustic facade and the food models.

DŌTOMBORI ARCADE

Minami is all about *shōtengai* (shopping arcades). **Dōtombori Arcade** (道頓堀; Map p308; Dōtombori, Chūō-ku; 🚇Midō-suji line to Namba) is the heart of Minami, and it's crammed with eateries. This is not the place to go for refined dining, but if you want heaping portions of tasty food in a very casual atmosphere, it can be a lot of fun. And because it sees a lot of tourists, most of the big restaurants here have English menus.

OSAKA EATING

TOP CHOICE Imai Honten   NOODLES $$

(今井本店; Map p308; ☎6211-0319; 1-7-22 Dōtombori, Chūō-ku; noodles from ¥578; ⊙11am-10pm Thu-Tue; ▣) One of the area's oldest and most revered *udon* specialists and our favourite place on the strip. Try the *tendon* (tempura over rice; ¥1575). An oasis of calm amid the chaos (the no-mobile-phone policy ensures quiet), it's sandwiched between two pachinko parlours. There's no English sign, but the traditional front stands out among the glitter.

Chibō   OKONOMIYAKI $$

(千房; Map p308; ☎6212-2211; 1-5-5 Dōtombori, Chūō-ku; okonomiyaki from ¥850; ⊙11am-1am Mon-Sat, to midnight Sun; ▣) A great *okonomiyaki* specialist. There's an English sign in addition to the English menu. Try the house special *Dōtombori yaki*, a toothsome treat with pork, beef, squid, shrimp and cheese for ¥1550. Some tables look out over the canal. Last orders an hour before closing.

AMERIKA-MURA

If you want to combine your dining with drinking and want to rub shoulders with Osaka's hip young things, head to Ame-Mura, which is home to some of Japan's cheapest *izakaya*. No one would accuse these places of serving refined food, but if you are happy with the Japanese equivalent of pub grub, it's hard to think of a more enjoyable place to eat. Note that these places tend to come and go, so if you can't find one of the following, it's probably closed: head to the next one on the list.

Tori Kizoku   IZAKAYA $

(鳥貴族; Map p308; ☎6251-7114; 2nd fl, 1-8-15 Nishi-Shinsaibashi, Chūō-ku; dishes/drinks ¥294; ⊙6pm-5am, last order 4.30am; ▣; ⊠Midō-suji line to Shinsaibashi) The name means 'chicken nobility', but the prices at this casual *yakitori* (chicken cooked on skewers) are decidedly common. Look for the gaudy yellow and red sign and the number 280 (indicating that all skewers cost just ¥280).

Umiya Goofy   IZAKAYA $

(ウミヤ グーフィー; Map p308; ☎6213-0538; B1, 2nd fl, 2-8-19 Nishi-Shinsaibashi, Chūō-ku; dishes ¥2000; ⊙5pm-5am, last order 4.30am; ⊠Midō-suji line to Shinsaibashi) Cram into this popular student *izakaya* to enjoy some good greasy food, all of which goes very well with the ¥380 draft beers. There's an English sign. Note: we're not entirely sure why they call the place 'Goofy'. Maybe it's because the prices are so low it's just silly.

Yume-hachi   IZAKAYA $

(ゆめ八; Map p308; ☎6212-7078; 1st fl, 2-16-9 Nishi-Shinsaibashi, Chūō-ku; dishes ¥330; ⊙5pm-5am; ⊠Midō-suji line to Shinsaibashi) Not to be outdone, everything on the menu at this *izakaya* is ¥330. Some of the dishes are surprisingly good, especially considering the price. There's an English sign.

NAMBA PARKS

If you want a huge variety of places to choose from all under one roof, head to the new Namba Parks complex, just south of Namba Station. Here, you'll find eight floors of restaurants, with most of the usual Japanese and international choices represented. Best of all, there's a rooftop garden area with potted trees and benches – a nice break from the surrounding concrete and neon.

Sai-ji-ki   VEGETARIAN $$

(菜蒔季; Map p308; ☎6636-8123; 6th fl, Namba Parks, 2-10-70 Namba naka, Naniwa-ku; lunch/dinner from ¥1600/2100; ⊙11am-11pm, enter by 9pm; ✏; ⊠Midō-suji, Sennichimae, Yotsubashi line to Namba) This vegetarian restaurant serves an all-you-can eat buffet of mostly Japanese food for ¥1799. If you go at lunchtime, be prepared to sit in line.

International

TOP CHOICE Café Absinthe   MEDITERRANEAN $$

(カフェアブサン; ☎6534-6635; 1st fl, South Yotsubashi Bldg, 1-2-27 Kitahorie, Nishi-ku; lunch ¥1000-2000, dinner ¥2000-3000; ⊙3pm-1am, closed Tue; ▣; ⊠Midō-suji line to Shinsaibashi) For fantastic alcoholic and non-alcoholic drinks and juices and an incredibly diverse menu of Mediterranean food (something of a rarity in Kansai), this friendly restaurant on the western edge of Ame-Mura is a must. The drinks and food here cost a little more, but they're worth it when you factor in the quality of the ingredients and the atmosphere. And, yes, it does serve the eponymous absinthe. Needless to say, this place can easily double as a nightspot.

Slices Bar & Cafe   CAFE $

(スライセズバーアンドカフェ; Map p308; ☎6211-2231; 1st fl, Yoshimoto Bldg, 2-3-21 Nishi-Shinsaibashi, Chūō-ku; pizza slices/whole from ¥400/2600; ⊙noon-midnight Sun-Fri, to 2am Sat; ▣; ⊠Midō-suji line to Namba or Shinsaibashi) If you need a break from Japanese food and want something casual, stop into this foreigner-friendly pizza joint for a slice or two. In addition to pizza, it serves wraps, bagels, salads and fries. There's a big English sign.

Banco
CAFE $

(バンコ; Map p308; ☑080-6113-2504; 1-9-26 Nishi-Shinsaibashi, Chūō-ku; drinks ¥400; ⊙noon-2am; ⓘ; ℝMidō-suji line to Shinsaibashi) This cafe could have been airlifted straight from Greenwich Village. It's an intimate spot to fill up on caffeine to start a day of shopping or an evening of bar hopping.

Krungtep
THAI $$

(クンテープ; Map p308; ☑4708-0088; 1-6-14 Dōtombori, Chūō-ku; lunch buffet ¥1200, dinner dishes from ¥1000; ⊙11.30am-11pm, closed 3-5pm weekdays; ⓘ; ℝMidō-suji line to Namba) Dōtombori's most popular Thai place serves fairly authentic versions of the standard favourites like green curry and fried noodles. Look for the small English sign – it's on the B1 floor.

🍷 Drinking

Osaka is a hard-working city, but when quitting time rolls around, Osakans know how to party. Take a stroll through Minami on a Friday night and you'd be excused for thinking there's one bar for every resident of the city. Whatever your taste, you're sure to find something to your liking among this vast array of bars and clubs. For up-to-date info on upcoming bar/club/music events in Osaka, check **iflyer** (http://iflyer.tv/).

KITA

Minami might be Osaka's real nightlife district, but there are plenty of bars, clubs and *izakaya* in the neighbourhoods to the south and east of Osaka Station.

Captain Kangaroo
BAR

(Map p304; 1-5-20 Sonezakishinchi, Kita-ku; drinks from ¥500; ⊙6pm-5am Mon-Sat, to midnight Sun; ⓘ; ℝJR line to Osaka) This popular bar in the Kita-Shinchi district, a short walk from JR Osaka Station, draws a good crowd of expats and Japanese. It's a friendly place to start an evening in Kita.

Windows on the World
BAR

(ウィンドーズオンザワールド; Map p304; 1-8-8 Umeda, Kita-ku; ⊙5.30pm-12.30am Mon-Thu & Sun, to 1am Fri & Sat; ⓘ; ℝJR line to Osaka) An unbeatable spot for drinks with a view – it's on the 35th floor of the Hilton Osaka. Be warned that there's a ¥1750 per person table charge and drinks average ¥2000.

MINAMI

This is the place for a wild night out in Osaka. You simply won't believe the number of bars, clubs and restaurants that are packed into the narrow streets and alleys of Dōtombori, Shinsaibashi, Namba and Ame-Mura. See also the Minami eating section for some *izakaya* and cafes that serve as watering holes.

Zerro
BAR

(ゼロ; Map p308; 2-3-2 Shinsaibashi-suji, Chūō-ku; drinks from ¥500; ⊙7pm-5am; ⓘ; ℝMidō-suji line to Namba or Shinsaibashi) Zerro is the perfect place to start off your evening, with a wide assortment of food and drink, as well as some of the most energetic bartenders around. Live DJs every weekend will have you grooving and shaking until the wee hours of the morning. Check the tasty Friday Night Roast with freshly oven-roasted meat and vegetables every Friday evening.

Cinquecento
BAR

(チンクエチェント; Map p308; 2-1-10 Higashi-Shinsaibashi, Chūō-ku; drinks ¥500; ⊙7.30pm-5am Mon-Sat, 8pm-3am Sun; ⓘ; ℝMidō-suji line to Namba or Shinsaibashi) This cosy, appropriately named bar is the perfect place to go to meet local expats and make new friends. Everything on the menu is ¥500, with a hearty selection of food and the most extensive martini selection in the city. Knock back a few before heading off to the nearby clubs.

Rock Rock
BAR

(ロックロック; Map p308; 1-8-1 Nishi-Shinsaibashi, Chūō-ku; drink/food from ¥500/600; ⊙7pm-5am; ⓘ; ℝMidō-suji line to Namba or Shinsaibashi) Ever dreamed of running into a famous rock star in a small, intimate setting? Well, you now have your chance, as Rock Rock is the home to official after-parties for just about every international act imaginable. Nightly events with a modest cover charge showcase some of Osaka's finest rock DJs. In case you're curious, past visitors to the bar include James Hatfield, Rob Halford, Keanu Reeves, Lady Gaga and a host of others.

Murphy's
BAR

(マーフィーズ; Map p308; 1-6-3 Higashi-Shinsaibashi, Chūō-ku; drinks ¥400-3000; ⊙5pm-1am Sun-Thu, to 4am Fri & Sat; ⓘ; ℝSakai-suji line to Nagahoribashi) This is one of the oldest Irish-style pubs in Japan, and a good place to rub shoulders with local expats and Japanese. It's on the 6th floor of the Reed Plaza Shinsaibashi building, a futuristic building with what looks like a rocket moulded on the front.

Tavola 36 BAR

(タボラ36; Map p308; 5-1-60 Namba, Chūō-ku; ⏰6pm-11.30pm; ⓘ; ⒭Midō-suji line to Namba) If you want drinks, a killer view and upscale surroundings, this is the place to be in Minami. It's an Italian restaurant-bar on the 36th floor of the Swissotel Nankai Osaka. There's a ¥1260 per person table charge after 6pm and drinks start at ¥1200.

☆ Entertainment

For up-to-date listings of forthcoming club events, check *Kansai Scene*.

Clubs

Karma NIGHTCLUB

(カーマ; Map p304; ☎6344-6181; 1-5-18 Sone-zakishinchi, Kita-ku; ⒭JR line to Osaka) A long-standing club in Kita that is popular with Japanese and foreigners alike. On weekends it usually hosts techno events with cover charges averaging ¥2500.

Grand Café NIGHTCLUB

(グランドカフェ; Map p308; ☎6213-8637; 2-10-21 Nishi-Shinsaibashi, Chūō-ku; ⒭Midō-suji or Yotsubashi line to Shinsaibashi) This hip underground club hosts a variety of electronica-DJ events. There's a comfy seating area and several dance floors. Look for the blue sign at street level.

TOP CHOICE Onzieme (11) NIGHTCLUB

(オンジェム; Map p308; ☎6243-0089; 1-4-5 Nishi-Shinsaibashi, Chūō-ku; ⒭JR line to Osaka) Those eager for a taste of Osaka nightlife at its craziest should head to the city's largest and most lively club. An assortment of local and internationally acclaimed house, hip-hop and techno DJs showcase their talents nightly, with the posh interior reminiscent of some of the more famous London establishments. Don't miss the monthly Hollywood parties with DJ Bento and friends.

Traditional Japanese Entertainment

Osaka has plenty of traditional cultural shows. Unfortunately, not much of it is regularly scheduled. For information on upcoming shows, check with the tourist information offices or *Kansai Scene*.

National Bunraku Theatre THEATRE

(国立文楽劇場; Map p306; 1-12-10 Nipponbashi, Chūō-ku; ⒭Sennichimae or Sakai-suji line to Nipponbashi) Although *bunraku*, or puppet theatre, did not originate in Osaka, the art form was popularised at this theatre. The most famous *bunraku* playwright was Chikametsu

Monzaemon (1653–1724), who wrote plays set in Osaka concerning the classes that traditionally had no place in Japanese art: merchants and the denizens of the pleasure quarters. Not surprisingly, *bunraku* found a wide audience among these people, and a theatre was established to put on the plays of Chikametsu in Dōtombori. Today's theatre is an attempt to revive the fortunes of *bunraku*.

Performances are only held at certain times of the year: check with the tourist info offices. Tickets normally start at around ¥2300 or ¥5800; earphones and program guides in English are available. This is probably the best place in Japan to see *bunraku*. Just be warned that performances sell out quickly.

Osaka Nōgaku Hall THEATRE

(大阪能楽会館; Map p304; 2-3-17 Nakasakinishi, Kita-ku; ⒭JR line to Osaka) A five-minute walk east of Osaka Station, this hall holds nō (stylised dance-drama) shows about twice a month, most of which cost ¥5000 to ¥6000.

🔒 Shopping

Osaka has almost as many shops as it has restaurants. The major department stores are clustered around JR Osaka and Hankyū Umeda stations in Kita. High-end fashion shops and international luxury brands have their outlets along Midō-suji, the main street of Minami, between Shinsaibashi and Namba subway stations.

Osaka's speciality is electronics, and **Den Den Town** is Osaka's version of Tokyo's Akihabara. Taking its name from the Japanese word for electricity, *denki,* Den Den Town is an area of shops almost exclusively devoted to electronic goods. To avoid sales tax, check if the store has a 'Tax Free' sign outside and bring your passport. Most stores are closed on Wednesday. Take the Sakai-suji subway line to Ebisu-chō Station and take exit 1 or exit 2. Alternatively, it's a 15-minute walk south of Nankai Namba Station.

For anything related to cooking and eating, head to the **Dōguya-suji Arcade** (道具屋筋) in Minami.

Kōjitsu Sansō OUTDOOR GEAR

(好日山荘; Map p304; Osaka Ekimae Daisan Bldg, 1-3 Umeda, Kita-ku; ⏰10.30am-8pm; ⒭JR line to Osaka) If you need a new backpack or any other kind of outdoor gear, head to this excellent shop on the ground floor at the northwest corner of the Ekimae Daisan building.

Bic Camera
ELECTRONICS

(ビックカメラ; Map p308; 2-10-1 Sennichimae, Chūō-ku; ⊙10am-9pm; ®Midō-suji line to Namba) Bic Camera is a one-stop shop for everything related to cameras, electronics and computers (but note that many computer-related items are designed for operation with a Japanese system). You are likely to find some of the best prices in the city at this vast shop.

Tokyu Hands
DEPARTMENT STORE

(東急ハンズ; 3-4-12 Minamisenba, Chūō-ku; ⊙10.30am-8.30pm; ®Midō-suji line to Shinsaibashi) If you love gadgets, don't miss Tokyu Hands. From tools for jobs you didn't know existed to curios to please people with everything, this place is stocked to the rafters with things that you probably don't need but may very well want. Even if you don't buy anything, it's fun to browse.

Village Vanguard
BOOKSHOP

(ヴィレッジヴァンガード; Map p308; 1-10-28 Nishi-Shinsaibashi, Chūō-ku; ⊙11am-11pm; ®Midō-suji line to Shinsaibashi) Officially, this place is a bookshop, but books are only half the story: between the cluttered racks of books and magazines are all sorts of odd curios – probably the stuff that Tokyu Hands deemed too arcane for its shelves. Some of these novelty items would make great 'only available in Japan' gifts for the folks back home.

Namba Parks
MALL

(なんばパークス; Map p308; 2-10-70 Nambanaka, Naniwa-ku; ⊙11am-9pm; ®Midō-suji, Sennichimae, Yotsubashi line to Namba) They call it 'Namba Parks' because of all the trees in flower pots around the upper levels of this new shopping complex in Namba. It consists of floor after floor of shops, interspersed with a wide variety of restaurants, both international and Japanese. It's a good place to go for a break from the Minami mayhem.

Junkudō
BOOKSHOP

(ジュンク堂書店; Map p304; ⊙10am-9pm; ®JR line to Osaka) This giant bookshop has the best selection of foreign and Japanese-language books in Osaka. It's inside the Dōjima Avanza Building in Kita, about 10 minutes' walk from Osaka Station. Most English-language books are on the 3rd floor along with a cafe. English travel guides, including a good selection of Lonely Planet guides, are on the 2nd floor.

Athens
BOOKSHOP

(アテネ書店; Map p308; ⊙10am-10pm; ®Midō-suji line to Shinsaibashi) This Minami bookshop has a good selection of English books and magazines on its 4th floor.

Maruzen & Junkudō Shoten Umeda Branch
BOOKSHOP

(MARUZEN&ジュンク堂書店梅田店; Map p304; ⊙10am-10pm; ®JR line to Osaka) While this place wasn't open when we were researching this guide, it should be open by the time you read this. It is slated to be the largest bookshop in the city.

Kinokuniya
BOOKSHOP

(紀伊國屋書; Map p304; ⊙10am-10pm; ®Hankyū line to Umeda) Inside Hankyū Umeda Station, this shop has a decent selection of foreign books and magazines.

ℹ Information

Immigration Offices

Osaka Immigration Office (大阪入国管理局; Map p306; www.immi-moj.go.jp/english/soshiki/kikou/osaka.html; ⊙9am-4pm Mon-Fri; ®Tanimachi line to Temmabashi) The main office for the Kansai region is a three-minute walk from exit 3 of Temmabashi Station on the Keihan main line.

Internet Access

Aprecio (アプレシオ; Map p308; Minami; per 30min from ¥150; ⊙24hr; ®Midō-suji line to Namba)

Money

Citibank (シティバンク) Osaka Ekimae (Map p304; www.citibank.co.jp/en/bankingservice/branch_atm/kansai/br_osakaekimae.html; ⊙9am-3pm Mon-Fri, ATM 24hr; ®Hankyū line to Umeda or JR line to Osaka); Shinsaibashi (Map p308; www.citibank.co.jp/en/bankingservice/branch_atm/kansai/br_shinsaibashi.html; ⊙9am-3pm Mon-Fri, ATM 24hr; ®Midō-suji line to Shinsaibashi); Umeda (Map p304; www.citibank.co.jp/en/bankingservice/branch_atm/kansai/br_umeda.html; ⊙9am-3pm Mon-Fri, ATM 8am-10pm; ®Hankyū line to Umeda or JR line to Osaka)

Post

Osaka Central Post Office (大阪中央郵便局; Map p304; ®JR line to Osaka) Next to JR Osaka Station. Has a 24-hour service window.

Tourist Information

All the offices listed here can help book accommodation if you visit in person. For information on upcoming events, pick up a copy of *Kansai Scene* magazine at any of the bookshops listed under Shopping.

Umeda Visitors Information Office (大阪市ビジターズインフォメーションセンター・梅田; Map p304; ☎6345-2189; Kita; ☺8am-8pm, closed 31 Dec-3 Jan) is the main tourist information office in Osaka. It's a little tricky to find: from JR Osaka Station, exit the Midō-suji ticket gate/exit, turn right, and walk about 50m. The office is just outside the station, beneath a pedestrian overpass. From the subway, go out exit 9, and look for it outside the station, beside the bus terminal. Note that the station was under construction at the time of research and there was word that this office might move again.

Similar offices with the same opening hours:

Namba Station Visitors Information Office (難波駅観光案内; Map p308; ☎6631-9100)

Shin-Osaka Station Visitors Information Office (大阪市ビジターズインフォメーションセンター・新大阪; Map p306; ☎6305-3311) On the 3rd floor between the central *shinkansen* gate and the regular lines' east gate.

Tennō-ji Station Visitors Information Office (大阪市ビジターズインフォメーションセンター・天王寺; Map p306; ☎6774-3077)

Osaka Itami and Kansai International airports also have information counters:

Kansai International Airport Information Center (☎072-455-2500; 2nd fl North & Central, 1st fl North & South, 4th fl North, South & Central zones; ☺24hr)

Osaka Itami Airport Information Center (☎6856-6781; 1st fl, Terminal Arrival Lobby, North & South zones; ☺North zone 8am-9.15pm, South zone 6.30am-9.15pm)

Travel Agencies

No 1 Travel Osaka (大阪No1トラベル; Map p304; www.no1-travel.com/kix/no1air/index .htm; 3rd fl, Kyo-Tomi Bldg, 1-3-16 Sonezaki-shinchi, Kita-ku; ☺10am-6.30pm Mon-Fri, 11am-5pm Sat; ☐JR line to Osaka) Located in Umeda, this helpful travel agency has English speakers and competitive prices. The sign on street level here presently reads 'H.I.S. Travel'.

❶ Getting There & Away

Air

Osaka is served by two airports: Osaka Itami Airport (ITM), which handles only domestic traffic, and the newer Kansai International Airport (KIX), which handles all international and some domestic flights. Itami is conveniently located right in Osaka itself; KIX is on an artificial island in Wakayama-ken.

Boat

The **Japan China International Ferry Company** (www.shinganjin.com/index_e.php) connects Shanghai and Osaka/Kōbe (one way 2nd class ¥20,000/Y1300, around 48 hours). A similar service at similar prices is provided by the **Shanghai Ferry Company** (www.shanghai -ferry.co.jp/english/). These ferries operate from the Osaka Nankō international ferry terminal, which can be reached by taking the New Tram service from Suminoe-kōen Station to Nankogu-chi Station.

Domestic ferries operate from Nankō ferry terminal and Kamome-futō and Benten-futō piers for various destinations around Honshū, Kyūshū and Shikoku. Destinations (2nd-class fares) include Beppu (from ¥9000, 11½ hours), Miyazaki (from ¥10,000, 12¾ hours), Shibushi (from ¥11,900, 14¾ hours) and Shinmoji (from ¥6000, 12 hours) in Kyūshū; and Shōdo-shima (from ¥3900, 4½ hours) and Niihama (from ¥5500, 9¼ hours) in Shikoku.

For details about sailing schedules and bookings contact the tourist information offices.

Bus

There is a long-distance highway bus service between Osaka and cities all across Honshū, Shikoku and some cities in Kyūshū. Destinations include Tokyo (from ¥3500, eight hours), Nagasaki (¥11,000, 10 hours) and Kagoshima (¥12,000, 12 hours). Most buses depart from JR Osaka Station; check with the tourist information offices for more details.

Train

Osaka is on the Tōkaidō–San-yō *shinkansen* line that runs between Tokyo and Hakata (Kyūshū): Hikari *shinkansen* run to/from Tokyo (¥13,750, three hours) and to/from Hakata (¥14,590, three hours). Other cities on this line include Hiroshima, Kyoto, Kōbe and Okayama.

KYOTO The *shinkansen* is the fastest way to travel between Kyoto and Osaka (¥2730, 14 minutes). The second-fastest way is a JR *shinkai-soku* (special rapid train) between JR Kyoto Station and JR Osaka Station (¥540, 28 minutes).

Another choice is the cheaper and more comfortable private Hankyū line that runs between Hankyū Umeda Station in Osaka and Hankyū Kawaramachi, Karasuma and Ōmiya stations in Kyoto (*tokkyū* limited express train to Kawaramachi ¥390, 44 minutes).

Alternatively, you can take the private Keihan main line between Sanjō, Shijō or Shichijō stations in Kyoto and Keihan Yodoyabashi Station in Osaka (*tokkyū* to Sanjō ¥400, 51 minutes). Yodoyabashi is on the Midō-suji subway line.

KŌBE The *shinkansen* is the fastest way to travel between Kōbe and Osaka (¥2810, 13 minutes, from Shin-Kōbe Station to Shin-Osaka Station). The second-fastest way between Kōbe and Osaka is a JR *shinkaisoku* train between JR Osaka Station and Kōbe's Sannomiya and Kōbe stations (¥390, 24 minutes).

There is also the private Hankyū line, which takes a little more time but is cheaper and usually less crowded/more comfortable. It runs from Osaka's Hankyū Umeda Station to Kōbe's Sannomiya Station (*tokkyū*, ¥310, 29 minutes).

NARA The JR Kansai line links Osaka (Namba and Tennō-ji stations) and Nara (JR Nara Station) via Hōryū-ji (*yamatoji kaisoku*, ¥780, 42 minutes).

The private Kintetsu Nara line also connects Osaka (Kintetsu Namba Station) with Nara (Kintetsu Nara Station). *Kyūkō* (express) and *futsū* services take about 36 minutes and cost ¥540. *Tokkyū* trains do the journey in five minutes less time but at almost double the cost, making them a poor option.

ⓘ Getting Around

To/From the Airport

OSAKA ITAMI AIRPORT There are frequent **limousine buses** (Osaka Airport Transport Co; www.okkbus.co.jp/eng/index.html) running between the airport and various parts of Osaka. Buses run to/from Shin-Osaka Station every 20 minutes from about 8am to 9pm (¥490, 25 minutes). Buses run at about the same frequency to/from Osaka and Namba stations (¥620, 25 minutes). At Itami, buy your tickets from the machine outside the arrivals hall. (Hint: you've got a better chance of getting a seat if you board at the South Terminal.) In Kita, these buses operate from a boarding point a short walk west of JR Osaka Station. In Minami, the stop is in Namba, near the Midō-suji subway line's Namba Station, near exit 7.

KANSAI INTERNATIONAL AIRPORT (KIX) The fastest way between KIX and Osaka is the private Nankai Express Rapit, which runs to/from Nankai Namba Station on the Midō-suji subway line (¥1390, 35 minutes). The JR Haruka limited airport express runs between KIX and Tennō-ji Station (¥2270, 29 minutes) and Shin-Osaka Station (¥2980, 45 minutes).

Regular JR express trains called *kankū kaisoku* also run between KIX and Osaka (¥1160, 63 minutes), Kyōbashi (¥1160, 70 minutes), Tennō-ji (¥1030, 49 minutes) and JR Namba (¥1030, 56 minutes) stations.

The Osaka City Air Terminal (OCAT), in JR Namba Station, allows passengers on Japanese and some other airlines to check in and deposit baggage before boarding trains to the airport. Check with your airline for details.

There are a variety of bus routes between KIX and Osaka. **Limousine buses** (Kansai Airport Transportation Enterprise; www.kate .co.jp/pc/index_e.html) travel to/from Osaka Umeda, OCAT Namba, Uehonmachi and Nankō (Cosmo Sq) stations. The fare is ¥1500 (¥1000 OCAT) for most routes and the journeys take an average of 50 minutes, depending on traffic conditions.

Bus

Osaka has an extensive bus system, but it is nowhere near as easy to use as the train/subway network. Japanese-language bus maps are available from the tourist offices.

Train

Osaka has a good subway network and, like Tokyo, a JR loop line (known as the JR Kanjō-sen) that circles the city area. In fact, there should be no need to use any other form of transport while you are in Osaka unless you stay out late and miss the last train.

There are eight subway lines, but the one that most short-term visitors are likely to find most useful is the Midō-suji line, which runs north to south, stopping at Shin-Osaka, Umeda (next to Osaka Station), Shinsaibashi, Namba and Tennō-ji stations. Most rides cost between ¥200 and ¥300.

If you plan on taking a lot of subway rides, consider buying a 'one-day free ticket'. For ¥850 (or ¥600 on Fridays and the 20th of every month) you get unlimited travel on any subway, the New Tram line and all city buses (but not the JR line). These tickets can be purchased from some of the ticket machines in most subway stations; push the button for 'one-day free ticket' (*kyōtsū ichinichi jōsha ken*) then press the illuminated button reading '¥850'.

KŌBE

♪ 078 / POP 1.53 MILLION

Perched on a hillside overlooking the sea, Kōbe (神戸) is one of Japan's most attractive cities. It's also one of the country's most cosmopolitan places, having served as a maritime gateway to Kansai from the earliest days of trade with China. One of Kōbe's best features is its relatively small size – most of the sights can be reached on foot from the main train stations. And this is the main appeal of Kōbe: rather than a collection of sights, Kōbe is a city that is best enjoyed by casual wandering, enjoying the neighbourhoods and stopping in the many good restaurants and cafes as the whim strikes you. The most pleasant neighbourhoods to explore are Kitano, Chinatown and, after dark, the bustling area around Sannomiya Station.

⊙ Sights

Kōbe's two main entry points are Sannomiya and Shin-Kōbe stations. Shin-Kōbe Station, in the northeast of town, is where the *shinkansen* stops. A subway (¥200, two

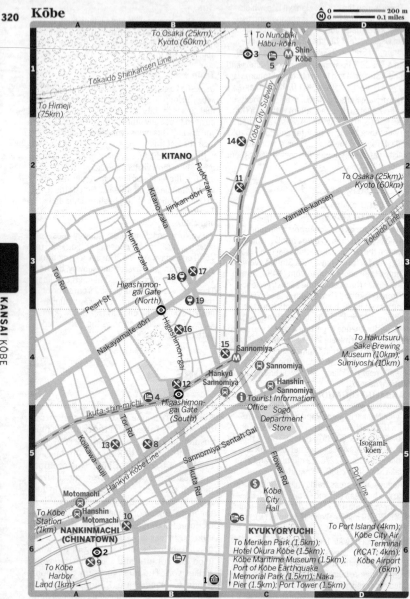

KANSAI KŌBE

minutes) runs from here to the downtown Sannomiya Station, which has frequent rail connections with Osaka and Kyoto. It's possible to walk between the two stations in around 20 minutes. Sannomiya Station marks the city centre, although a spate of development in Kōbe Harbor Land is starting to swing the city's centre of gravity towards the southwest. Before starting your exploration of Kōbe, pick up a copy of the *Kōbe City Map* at one of the two information offices.

Kōbe

Kitano
NEIGHBOURHOOD

(北野) Twenty minutes' walk north of San-nomiya is the pleasant hillside neighbour-hood of Kitano, where local tourists come to enjoy the feeling of foreign travel without leaving Japanese soil. A European–American atmosphere is created by the winding streets and *ijinkan* (literally 'foreigners' houses'), which housed some of Kōbe's early Western residents. Admission to some houses is free, for others it costs ¥300 to ¥700, and most are open from 9am to 5pm daily. Although these brick and weatherboard dwellings may not hold the same fascination for Western travel-lers that they hold for local tourists, the area itself is pleasant to stroll around and is dot-ted with good cafes and restaurants.

Nunobiki Hābu-kōen
GARDEN

(布引ハーブ公園; Nunobiki Herb Garden; admis-sion ¥200; ◷10am-5pm) The **Shin-Kōbe cable car** (新神戸ロープウェイ; Shin-Kōbe Rope-way; 1 way/return ¥750/1200; ◷9.30am-5.30pm; ◉Seishin-Yamate line or JR San-yō shinkansen to Shin-Kōbe) leaves from behind the Crowne Plaza Kōbe hotel near Shin-Kōbe Station and ascends to a mountain ridge 400m above the city. The views from the top over Kōbe and

the bay are particularly pretty after sunset. The complex of gardens, restaurants and shops below the top station is known as the Nunobiki Hābu-kōen. Note that you can eas-ily walk down to the bottom station from the Herb Garden in about 30 minutes.

Kōbe City Museum
MUSEUM

(神戸市立博物館; Kōbe Shiritsu Hakubutsukan; 24 Kyō-machi, Chūō-ku; admission ¥200; ◷10am-5pm, closed Mon & New Year holidays; ◉JR Kōbe line to Sannomiya) This museum has a collec-tion of so-called *namban* (literally 'southern barbarian') art and occasional special exhib-its. *Namban* art is a school of painting that developed under the influence of early Jesuit missionaries in Japan, who taught Western painting techniques to Japanese students. The entrance is on the building's east side.

Nankinmachi (Chinatown)
NEIGHBOURHOOD

(南京町) Nankinmachi, Kōbe's Chinatown, is a gaudy, bustling, unabashedly touristy collection of Chinese restaurants and stores that should be familiar to anyone who's vis-ited Chinatowns elsewhere in the world. The restaurants here tend to be overpriced and may disappoint sophisticated palates, but the place is fun for a stroll, particularly in the eve-ning when the lights of the area illuminate the gaudily painted facades of the shops.

Kōbe Harbor Land & Meriken Park
NEIGHBOURHOOD

(神戸ハーバーランド) Five minutes' walk southeast of Kōbe Station, Kōbe Harbor Land is awash with megamall shopping and dining developments. This may not appeal to foreign travellers the way it does to the lo-cal youth, but it's still a nice place for a stroll in the afternoon.

A five-minute walk to the east of Harbor Land you'll find Meriken Park, on a spit of reclaimed land jutting out into the bay. The main attraction here is the **Kōbe Maritime Museum** (Kōbe Kaiyō Hakubutsukan; 2-2 Hatoba-chō, Chūō-ku; admission ¥500; ◷10am-5pm, closed Mon & 29 Dec-3 Jan; ◉JR Kōbe line to Mo-tomachi). The museum has a small collection of ship models and displays, with some Eng-lish explanations.

FREE Hakutsuru Sake Brewery Museum
MUSEUM

(白鶴記念造酒資料館; 4-5-5 Sumiyoshi Minami-machi, Higashinada-ku; ◷9.30am-4.30pm, closed Mon, New Year holiday & O-Bon; ◉Hanshin main line to Sumiyoshi) The Nada-ku area of Kōbe is one of Japan's major sake-brewing centres and the dominant brewer here is the famous Hakutsuru company. The Hakutsuru Sake Brewery Museum provides a fascinating look into traditional sake-making methods. There is not much in the way of English explanations, but the free English pamphlet should get you started. Free sake tasting is possible after you tour the facilities (ask at the counter).

Take the Hanshin line eight stops east from Sannomiya (¥180, seven minutes if you switch train at Mikage, 15 minutes if you take the Hanshin *honsen* train; express trains do not stop) and get off at Hanshin Sumiyoshi Station. Exit the station, walk south to the elevated highway and cross the pedestrian overpass; take a right at the bottom of the steps; take your first left, then a right and look for it on the right (there is no English sign). You have to sign in at the gate. Use the blue-and-white crane logo atop the modern wing of the factory as your guide.

✨ Festivals & Events

Luminarie, Kōbe's biggest yearly event, is held every evening from around 2 to 13 December to celebrate the city's miraculous recovery from a 1995 earthquake that killed over 6000 people (check with the Kōbe tourist information office as the exact dates change slightly every year). The streets southwest of Kōbe City Hall are decorated with countless illuminated metal archways, which when viewed from within look like the interior of some otherworldly cathedral.

🛌 Sleeping

Hotel Trusty   BOUTIQUE HOTEL **$$$**
(ホテルトラスティ神戸; ☑330-9111; fax 330-9112; 63 Naniwamachi, Chūō-ku; s/d/tw from ¥9800/15,400/18,900; @; ℝJR Kōbe line, Hankyū to Sannnomiya) The name of the place screams 'standard-issue business hotel', but this intimate little hotel in Kōbe's Kyūkyoryūchi district is actually a super-stylish boutique hotel. The rooms are on the small side, but they are very clean and have all the amenities that you might need. It's within relatively easy walking distance of the stations.

B Kōbe   HOTEL **$$$**
(ザ・ビー神戸;☑333-4880;www.ishinhotels.com/theb-kobe/en/index.html; fax 333-4876; s/d/tw from ¥9450/16,800/18,900; @;ℝSeishin-Yamate line to Sannomiya) The centrally located B Kōbe is a good utilitarian choice if you've got business in Kōbe or just want a clean place to lay

your head in the evening. Some of the rooms are quite small, but if you're only there at night this shouldn't matter too much.

Crowne Plaza Hotel Kōbe   HOTEL **$$$**
(クラウンプラザ神戸; ☑291-1121; www.ichotels group.com/h/d/cp/1/en/hotel/osakb; fax 291-1151; s ¥8800-12,000, d& tw ¥14,000-25,000; @⦿;ℝSeishin-Yamate line or JR San-yō shinkansen to Shin-Kōbe) You'll feel on top of the world as you survey the bright lights of Kōbe from this perch atop the city. Conveniently located near JR Shin-Kōbe Station, this first-class hotel offers clean and fairly spacious rooms and has an English-speaking staff. Downstairs in the Oriental Avenue shopping centre (アベニュー), you'll find several good restaurants to choose from.

Oriental Hotel   HOTEL **$$$**
(☑326-1500; fax 326-1669; www.orientalhotel.jp/index_eng.html; d/tw from ¥30,030/33,495;@;ℝJR Kōbe line, Hanshin or Hankyū to Sannnomiya or Motomachi) Not to be confused with the two other Oriental hotels in Kōbe, this refurbished hotel in the Kyūkyōryūchi district is very well designed, with smart rooms, competent staff and a convenient location next to the Kōbe City Museum.

🍴 Eating

Japanese

Misono   STEAKHOUSE **$$**
(みその; ☑331-2890; 7th & 8th fl, Misono Bldg, 1-1-2 Shimoyamate dōri, Chūō-ku; lunch/dinner ¥2500/12,000; ⊘lunch & dinner; ⓘ; ℝHanshin Kōbe line or Kōbe line to Sannomiya Station, West exit) If you're a carnivore, you probably want to sample some of Kōbe's famous beef. One of the more approachable spots to try these heavenly steaks is at Misono, which occupies two of the upper floors of a building not far from Sannomiya Station. The restaurant isn't particularly luxurious, but the steaks are good and you can enjoy a bit of a view as you dine. There's an English sign at street level.

Wakkoqu   STEAKHOUSE **$$**
(和黒; ☑262-2838; 3rd fl, Shin Kōbe Oriental Avenue shopping mall, 1-1 Kitano-chō, Chūō-ku; lunch/dinner from ¥3234/8250; ⊘11.45am-10.30pm, last order 9.30pm, ⓘ; ℝSeishin-Yamate line or JR San-yō shinkansen to Shin-Kōbe) A more elegant spot to try Kōbe beef, on the 3rd floor of the Oriental Avenue shopping centre (アベニュー) at the base of the Crowne Plaza Kōbe hotel, just outside the elevator bank on the south side. The name 'Wakkoqu' is written

in English on the menu displayed outside (and the menu is partially translated into English).

Mikami

SHOKUDŌ **$**

(味加味; ☎242-5200; 2-5-9 Kanō-chō, Chūō-ku; meals from ¥500; ☺11am-3pm & 5-10pm, closed Wed; ⓘ; ⓡJR Kōbe line to Sannomiya) This is a friendly spot for good-value lunch and dinner sets of standard Japanese fare. Noodle dishes are available from ¥500 and *teishoku* (set meal) from ¥1000. Look for the large doghouse outside and a small English sign.

Ganko Sushi

SUSHI **$$**

(がんこ寿司; ☎331-6868; 2-5-1 Kitanagasa-dōri, Chūō-ku; lunch/dinner from ¥714/2000; ☺11.30am-11pm; ⓘ; ⓡJR Kōbe line to Sannomiya or Motomachi) For good sushi and just about any other Japanese dish you crave, this casual, easy-to-enter restaurant near Motomachi Station is a good call. We particularly recommend ordering sushi à la carte here. The staff are used to foreigners; look for the small sign that says 'Japanese food restaurant'.

Toritetsu

YAKITORI **$$**

(とり鉄; ☎327-5529; 1-16-12 Nakayamate-dōri, Chūō-ku; dinner from ¥3000; ☺5pm-midnight; ⓡJR Kōbe line to Sannomiya) Almost opposite the Hotel Area One Kōbe on Higashimongai, this bustling *yakitori* restaurant is a good place to eat, drink and watch the chefs labour over their grills. The sign says '*yakitori*' in English and there is some English on the menu.

Kintoki

SHOKUDŌ **$**

(金時; ☎331-1037; 1-7-2 Motomachi-dōri, Chūō-ku; set menu around ¥600-700; ☺10.30am-9pm, to 8pm Sat, to 7pm Sun, closed holidays; ⓡJR Kōbe line to Motomachi) This atmospheric old *shokudō* serves the cheapest food in the city. You can order standard noodle and rice dishes from the menu (plain *soba* or *udon* noodles are ¥250) or choose from a variety of dishes laid out on the counter. Look for the blue-and-white awning about 20m north of the shopping street arcade.

International

TOP CHOICE R Valentino

ITALIAN **$$**

(アール ヴァレンティーノ; ☎332-1268; 3rd fl, 4-5-13 Kanō-chō, Chūō-ku; pasta from ¥1500, lunch/dinner main from ¥1400/3800; ☺11.30am-2pm & 5.30-9pm; ⓘ; ⓡJR, Hanshin or Hankyū line to Sannomiya Station) Pizzas cooked in a brick oven are the draw at this Sannomiya Italian restaurant. It's very casual and comfortable and

there's an English/Italian menu. The Italian owner can explain the specials and make recommendations.

Ganso Gyōza-en

CHINESE **$**

(元祖ぎょうざ苑; ☎331-4096; 2-8-11 Sakae machi-dōri, Chūō-ku; 6 gyōza ¥420; ☺11.45am-3pm & 5-8.30pm, closed Mon; ⓘ; ⓡJR Kōbe line to Motomach) This is the best spot in Nankinmachi for *gyōza* dumplings, either fried (*yaki gyōza*) or steamed (*sui gyōza*). Use the vinegar, soy sauce and miso on the table to make a dipping sauce. It's next to a small parking lot – look for the red-and-white awning and English sign.

Modernark Pharm

INTERNATIONAL **$**

(モダナーク ファーム; ☎391-3060; 3-11-15 Kitanagasa-dōri, Chūō-ku; lunch & dinner from ¥850; ☺11.30am-10.30pm, to 10pm Sun; ⓓⓘ; ⓡJR Kōbe line to Motomachi) This interesting little restaurant serves tasty sets of Japanese and Western dishes, including burritos and rice dishes. There are some veggie choices here. Look for the plants.

Vieni

ITALIAN **$**

(ヴィエニ; ☎252-1323; 1-22-26 Nakayamate-dōri, Chūō-ku; espresso from ¥400, pasta from ¥1400; ☺11am-midnight, closed Mon; ⓘ; ⓡJR, Hanshin or Hankyū line to Sannomiya Station) This Italian cafe serves excellent expresso as well as various alcoholic drinks. The Italian fare on offer here is quite good and the owners speak some English. A nice spot for a break in the Kitano area, it also hosts occasional music events.

Nailey's Café

INTERNATIONAL **$**

(ネイリーズ カフェ; ☎231-2008; 2-8-12 Kanō-chō, Chūō-ku; coffee from ¥450, lunch from ¥1050, dinner main from ¥800; ☺lunch & dinner; ⓘ; ⓡSeishin-Yamate line or JR San-yō shinkansen to Shin-Kōbe) This hip little cafe serves espresso, light lunches and dinners. The menu here is Europe-influenced and includes such things as pizza, pasta and salads. This is a good spot for an evening drink.

🍷 Drinking

Kōbe has a large foreign community and a number of bars that see mixed Japanese and foreign crowds. For Japanese-style drinking establishments, try the *izakaya* in the neighbourhood between the JR tracks and Ikuta-jinja. Also bear in mind that a lot of Kōbe's nightlife is centred around the city's many cafes, most of which transform into bars come evening.

KŌBE DRINKING

Jazz Live & Restaurant Sone
LIVE MUSIC

(ジャズライブ・レストランソネ; ☏221-2055; 1-24-10 Nakayamate-dōri, Chūō-ku; drink/food from ¥750/850; ⏰5-11.30pm Mon-Sat, to 11pm Sun; 🅿; 🚉JR, Hanshin or Hankyū line to Sannomiya Station) Said to be the birthplace of Japanese jazz, this famous Kitano club is still one of the best places in the city to see live music. Check with the tourist information offices about upcoming events.

Sonic
BAR

(ソニック; 1-13-7, Nakayamate-dōri, Chūō-ku; drink/food from ¥750/850; ⏰5-11.30pm Mon-Sat, to 11pm Sun; 🅿; 🚉JR, Hanshin or Hankyū line to Sannomiya Station) This friendly international sports bar is a good place to meet local Japanese and expats.

ℹ Information

Tourist Information

Citibank (シティバンク; ⏰9am-3pm Mon-Fri, ATM 24hr; 🚉JR Kōbe line to Sannomiya) Next to Kōbe City Hall; the ATM accepts international cards.

Tourist information office (神戸市総合インフォメーションセンター; ☏322-0220; ⏰9am-7pm) The city's main tourist information office is on the ground floor on the south side of JR Sannomiya Station's west gate (follow the signs for Santica, the underground shopping mall). There's a smaller information counter on the 2nd floor of Shin-Kōbe Station, right outside the main *shinkansen* gate. Both information centres carry the free *Kōbe City Map*.

ℹ Getting There & Away

Air

Skymark Airlines (www.skymark.jp/en) operates out of Kōbe Airport, with destinations including Tokyo (Haneda; ¥12,800, 70 minutes), Sapporo (Shin-Chitose; ¥19,800, one hour and 55 minutes) and Okinawa (Naha; ¥17,800, two hours and 15 minutes).

Boat

China Express Line (www.celkobe.co.jp/CCP017.html) operates a ferry (2nd class from ¥22,000, around 48 hours) between Kōbe and Tientsin. It departs Kōbe every Thursday at midnight.

There are regular ferries between Kōbe and Shikoku (Niihama) and Kyūshū (Shinmoji and Ōita). Most ferries depart from Rokkō Island and are operated by **Ferry Sunflower** (www.ferry-sunflower.co.jp, in Japanese). Destinations include Shinmoji (Hankyū Ferry; www.han9f.co.jp/en/index.html; ¥6000) Niihama (Orange Ferry; www.orange-ferry.co.jp, in Japanese; ¥5500) and Ōita (¥9000).

Bus

Buses run between Kōbe (Sannomiya Bus Terminal) and Tokyo (Shinjuku highway bus terminal and JR highway bus terminal – JR 高速バスターミナル) at Tokyo Station. The journey costs from ¥6000 and takes around 9½ hours. Buses depart in the evening and arrive early the following day.

Train

Kōbe's JR Sannomiya Station is on the JR Tōkaidō line. A JR *shinkaisoku* train on this line is the fastest way between Kōbe and Osaka Station (¥390, 24 minutes) or Kyoto (¥1050, 54 minutes).

Two private lines, the Hankyū and Hanshin lines, also connect Kōbe and Osaka. The Hankyū line is the more convenient of the two, running between Kōbe's Hankyū Sannomiya Station and Osaka's Hankyū Umeda Station (*tokkyū*, ¥310, 29 minutes). The Hankyū line also has connections between Kyoto and Osaka, so you can travel between Kyoto and Kōbe (*tokkyū*, ¥600, 65 minutes, change at Jūsō or Umeda).

Shin-Kōbe Station is on the Tōkaidō/San-yō *shinkansen* line. The Hikari *shinkansen* goes to/from Fukuoka (¥14,270, two hours and 52 minutes) and to/from Tokyo (¥14,270, three hours and 10 minutes). Other stations on this line include Osaka, Kyoto, Nagoya and Hiroshima.

ℹ Getting Around

To/From the Airport

ITAMI OSAKA AIRPORT There are direct limousine buses to/from Osaka's Itami airport (¥1020, 40 minutes). In Kōbe, the buses stop on the southwestern side of Sannomiya Station.

KŌBE AIRPORT The easiest way to get to/from Kōbe's spanking-new airport is with the Portliner, which makes the trip between Sannomiya (downtown Kōbe) and the airport in 18 minutes and costs ¥320. A taxi costs between ¥2500 and ¥3000, and takes 15 to 20 minutes.

KANSAI INTERNATIONAL AIRPORT (KIX) There are a number of routes between Kōbe and KIX. By train, the fastest way is the JR *shinkaisoku* to/from Osaka Station, and the JR *kanku kaisoku* between Osaka Station and the airport (total cost ¥1660, total time 87 minutes with good connections). There is also a direct limousine bus to/from the airport (¥1900, 1¼ hours), which is more convenient if you have a lot of luggage. The Kōbe airport bus stop is on the southwestern side of Sannomiya Station.

Public Transport

Kōbe is small enough to travel around on foot. The JR, Hankyū and Hanshin railway lines run east to west across Kōbe, providing access to most of Kōbe's more distant sights. A subway line also connects Shin-Kōbe Station with Sannomiya Station (¥200, two minutes). There is also a city-loop bus service that makes a grand-circle tour of most of the city's sightseeing spots (per ride/all-day pass ¥200/600). The bus stops at both Sannomiya and Shin-Kōbe stations; look for the retro-style green buses.

HIMEJI

📞 079 / POP 536,367

Himeji-jō, the finest castle in all of Japan, towers over the small city of Himeji (姫路), a quiet city on the *shinkansen* route between Osaka and Okayama/Hiroshima. In addition to the castle, the city is home to the Hyōgo Prefectural Museum of History and Kōko-en, a small garden alongside the castle. If you're a fan of castles, a visit to Himeji is a must. You can visit it as a day trip from Kyoto, Nara or Osaka, or as a stopover en route to Hiroshima.

◉ Sights

Himeji-jō
CASTLE

(姫路城; 68 Honmachi; adult/child ¥400/100; ⊙9am-5pm Sep-May, to 6pm Jun-Aug) The most magnificent castle in Japan, Himeji-jō is also one of only a handful of original castles in the country (most others are modern concrete reconstructions). In Japanese it is sometimes called *shirasagi*, or 'white heron', a title that derives from the castle's stately white form.

Although there have been fortifications in Himeji since 1333, today's castle was built in 1580 by Toyotomi Hideyoshi and enlarged some 30 years later by Ikeda Terumasa. Ikeda was awarded the castle by Tokugawa Ieyasu when the latter's forces defeated the Toyotomi armies. In the following centuries it was home to 48 successive lords.

The castle has a five-storey main keep (*tenshū*) and three smaller keeps, and the entire structure is surrounded by moats and defensive walls punctuated with rectangular, circular and triangular openings for firing guns and shooting arrows. The walls of the main keep also feature *ishiotoshi* – openings that allowed defenders to pour boiling water or oil onto anyone who made it past the defensive slits and was thinking of scaling the walls. All things considered, visitors are recommended to pay the admission charge and enter the castle by legitimate means.

It takes around 1½ hours to follow the arrow-marked route around the castle. Last entry is an hour before closing.

Kōko-en
GARDEN

(好古園; 68 Honmachi; admission ¥300; ⊙29 Apr-31 Aug 9am-6pm, 1 Sep-28 Apr to 5pm, closed 29 & 30 Dec) Just across the moat on the western side of Himeji-jō is Kōko-en, a reconstruction of the former samurai quarters of the castle. There are nine separate Edo-style gardens, two ponds, a stream, a tea arbour (¥500 for *matcha* powdered green tea and a Japanese sweet) and the restaurant Kassui-ken, where you can enjoy a *bentō* (boxed meal; ¥1575) of *anago* (conger eel, a local speciality) while gazing over the gardens. While the garden doesn't have the subtle beauty of some of Japan's older gardens, it is well done and especially lovely in the autumn-foliage season.

Note that a joint ticket to both the Kōko-en and Himeji-jō costs only ¥560, a saving of ¥140. These can be purchased at both the entrance to Kōko-en and Himeji-jō. Enter by 30 minutes before closing.

Hyōgo Prefectural Museum of History
MUSEUM

(兵庫県立歴史博物館; Hyōgo Kenritsu Rekishi Hakubutsukan; 68 Honmachi; admission ¥200; ⊙10am-5pm, closed Mon & the day after national holidays) This museum has good displays on Himeji-jō and other castles around Japan. In addition, the museum covers the main periods of Japanese history, with some English explanations. At 10.30am, 1.30pm and 3.30pm, one lucky person can even try on a suit of samurai armour or a kimono (ask at the front desk to be included in the lottery).

The museum is a five-minute walk north of the castle. Enter by 30 minutes before closing.

ℹ️ HIMEJI-JŌ RENOVATION

Himeji-jō is undergoing a massive renovation, from late 2009 until early 2014. During most of this period, the main keep (*tenshū*) of the castle will be covered by a scaffoldlike structure that will obscure it from view. The rest of the castle will not be covered by any structure. It will be possible to enter the castle during the reconstruction period, although some areas (most notably, the castle keep) may be closed to the public from time to time. Call Himeji tourist information office if you have any questions.

Himeji

✿ Festivals & Events

The **Nada-no-Kenka Matsuri**, held on 14 and 15 October, involves a battle between three *mikoshi*, which are battered against each other until one smashes. Try to go on the second day, when the festival reaches its peak (around noon). It is held five minutes' walk from Shirahamanomiya Station (10 minutes from Himeji Station on the San-yō-Dentetsu line); follow the crowds. The train company lays on extra trains on the day of the *matsuri*.

🛏 Sleeping

Himeji is best visited as a day trip from other parts of Kansai. If you'd like to stay, however, there are plenty of choices.

Tōyoko Inn   HOTEL $
(東横イン; ☎284-1045; 97 Minamiekimae-chō; s/d/tw ¥5480/7980/7980;@🛜) This efficient business hotel is a good choice if you want to be close to the station. The rooms are serviceable, well maintained and, as usual in a business hotel, fairly small. As with other Tōyoko Inns, just about everything you need is supplied, including free breakfast.

APA Hotel Himejieki-kita   HOTEL $$
(☎284-4111; 98 Higashiekimae-chō; s/d from ¥7500/13,000; @) This centrally located business hotel is pretty much everything a good hotel should be: well run and clean with reasonable-sized rooms (for a business hotel, that is). It's within easy walking distance of the castle and lots of restaurants.

Himeji

Hotel Nikkō Himeji
HOTEL $$$

(ホテル日航姫路; ☎222-2231; 100 Minamie-kimae-chō; s/d/tw ¥10,925/20,700/20,700; @) A stone's throw from the south side of the station, this hotel offers stylish and fairly spacious rooms and is the best choice for those who are looking for something nicer than a business hotel. The rooms here are larger and the bathtubs have almost enough room to stretch out in. Some of the upper rooms on the north side have views of the top of the castle.

✗ Eating

Most of the restaurants in Himeji are located in the shopping arcades north of the station (on the way to the castle).

TOP CHOICE Fukutei
KAISEKI $$

(ふく亭; ☎222-8150; 75 Kamei-chō; lunch/dinner from ¥1500/3000; ⊙11.30am-2.30pm & 5-10pm Mon-Fri, 11.30am-2.30pm & 5-9pm Sat & Sun; 🉑) This stylish, approachable restaurant is a great lunch choice if you want something a little civilised. The fare here is casual *kaiseki*: a little sashimi, some tempura and the usual nibbles on the side. At lunch try the excellent *omakese-zen* (tasting set; ¥1500). There's a small English sign.

Me-n-me
NOODLES $

(めんめ; ☎225-0118; 68 Honmachi; noodles from ¥550; ⊙11.30am-6pm, closed Wed; 🉑) They make their own noodles at this homey little noodle joint a few minutes' walk from the castle. It's not fancy, but if you want an honest, tasty bowl of *udon* to power you through the day, this is the spot. There's usually an English sign on the street.

Rāmen-no-Hōryū
RĀMEN $

(ラーメンの寶龍; ☎288-1230; 316 Eki-mae-chō; chāshūmen ¥880; ⊙11.30am-midnight Mon-Sat, to 11pm Sun) For good *gyōza* and hearty bowls of *rāmen* we recommend this friendly *rāmen* joint near the station. Buy your tickets from the machine (staff usually rush around to help you do this, since the buttons are labelled in Japanese). It's roughly opposite Starbucks – look for the faux wooden facade painted with large white swirls.

ⓘ Information

In Himeji Station, you'll find the **Himeji Tourist Information Office** (姫路市観光案内所[姫路観光なびポート]; ☎287-0003; ⊙9am-7pm, closed 29 & 30 Dec) on the ground floor of

ⓘ AKASHI KAIKYŌ BRIDGE

On the way to Himeji by train from Kyoto, Osaka or Kōbe, take a look out the train window at the newly constructed Akashi Kaikyō Suspension Bridge. Its 3910m span links the island of Honshū with Awaji-shima, making it the longest suspension bridge in the world. It comes into view on the southern side of the train, approximately 10km west of Kōbe.

Himeji Station, not far from the central gate (clearly marked with signs as you exit the turnstiles). While you're there, pick up a copy of the useful *Places of Interest Downtown Himeji* map or *Himeji Tourist Guide & Map*. The castle is a 15-minute walk (1200m) straight up the main road from the north exit of the station. If you don't feel like walking, free rental cycles are available from an underground parking area halfway between the station and the castle; enquire at the information office.

ⓘ Getting There & Away

If you've got a Japan Rail Pass or are in a hurry, a *shinkansen* is the best way to reach Himeji to/from Kyoto (Hikari, ¥5130, 55 minutes), Hiroshima (Nozomi, ¥8270, 58 minutes) and Shin-Osaka (Hikari, ¥3640, 39 minutes). If you don't have a pass, a *shinkaisoku* on the JR Tōkaidō line is the best way to reach Himeji from Kyoto (¥2210, 91 minutes), Osaka (¥1450, 61 minutes) and Kōbe (¥950, 37 minutes). From Okayama, to the west, a *tokkyū* JR train on the San-yō line takes approximately two hours including transit time and costs ¥1450.

SHIGA PREFECTURE

Just across the Higashiyama mountains from Kyoto is Shiga Prefecture (滋賀県; Shiga-ken), dominated by Biwa-ko, Japan's largest lake. The small prefecture has a variety of attractions that are easily visited as day trips from Kyoto. The major attractions here are the towns of Nagahama, with its Kurokabe Square neighbourhood of glass artisans, and Hikone, with its fine original castle. Other worthwhile destinations include temples like Mii-dera and Ishiyama-dera, and the Miho Museum, which is worth a trip just to see the building and the compound in which it is located.

Ōtsu 大津

📞077 / POP 333,909

Ōtsu has developed from a 7th-century imperial residence (the city was capital of Japan for just five years) into a lake port and major post station on the Tōkaidō highway between eastern and western Japan. It is now the capital of Shiga-ken.

The **information office** (📞522-3830; ⏰8.40am-5.25pm) is at JR Ōtsu Station.

◉ Sights

Mii-dera   TEMPLE
(三井寺; 246 Onjōji-chō; admission ¥500; ⏰8am-5pm) Mii-dera is a short walk northwest from Keihan Hama-Ōtsu Station. The temple, founded in the late 7th century, is the head branch of the Jimon branch of Tendai Buddhism. It started its days as a branch of Enryaku-ji (延暦寺) on Hiei-zan, but later the two fell into conflict, and Mii-dera was repeatedly razed by Enryaku-ji's warrior monks. The Niō-mon gate here is unusual for its roof, made of layers of tree bark rather than tiles. It looks particularly fine when framed by the cherry trees in early April.

✨ Festivals & Events

Ōtsu Dai Hanabi Taikai   FIREWORKS
If you're in town on 8 August, be sure to catch the Ōtsu Grand Fireworks Festival. Starting at dusk, the best spots to watch are along the waterfront near Keihan Hama-Ōtsu Station. Be warned that trains to and from Kyoto are packed for hours before and after the event.

Ōtsu Matsuri   TRADITIONAL
Takes place in early to mid-October at Tenson-jinja, close to JR Ōtsu Station. Ornate floats are displayed on the first day and paraded around the town on the second day.

ℹ Getting There & Away
From Kyoto, take the JR Tōkaidō line from JR Kyoto Station to JR Ōtsu Station (¥190, nine minutes), or travel on the Kyoto Tōzai subway line to Hama-Ōtsu Station (¥410, 21 minutes from Sanjō Keihan Station).

Ishiyama-dera 石山寺

This Shingon-sect **temple** (1-1-1 Ishiyama-dera; admission ¥500; ⏰8am-4.30pm) was founded in the 8th century. The room beside the *hondō*

(main hall) is famed as the place where Lady Murasaki wrote *The Tale of Genji*. The temple precincts are in a lovely forest with lots of good trails to explore, including the one that leads up to Tsukimitei hall, from which there are great views over Biwa-ko.

The temple is a 10-minute walk from Keihan Ishiyama-dera Station (continue along the road in the direction that the train was travelling). Take the Kyoto Tōzai-line subway from Sanjō Keihan Station in Kyoto to Keihan Hama-Ōtsu and change there to a Keihan-line Ishiyama-dera-bound *futsū* (¥640, 50 minutes including transit time). Alternatively, take the JR Tōkaidō line from JR Kyoto Station to JR Ishiyama-dera Station (*kaisoku* or *futsū* trains only, ¥230, 13 minutes) and switch to the Keihan line for the short journey to Keihan Ishiyama-dera Station (¥160).

Miho Museum

This **museum** (ミホミュージアム; 📞0748-82-3411; www.miho.or.jp; 300, Momodani, Shigaraki; adult/child ¥1000/300; ⏰10am-5pm, closed Mon early Jun-early Jul, mid-end Aug, mid-end Dec) is visually stunning, located in the countryside of Shiga-ken near the village of Shigaraki. The IM Pei–designed museum houses the Shumei Family art collection, which includes examples of Japanese, Middle Eastern, Chinese and south Asian art.

A visit to the museum is something like a visit to the secret hideout of an archvillain in a James Bond film, and there is no doubt that the facility is at least as impressive as the collection. Since a trip to the museum from Kyoto or Osaka can take the better part of a day, we highly recommend calling the museum to check what's on before making the trip.

To get there, take the JR Tōkaidō line from Kyoto or Osaka to Ishiyama Station, and change to a **Teisan Bus** (Teisan Konan Kōtsu; www.teisan-konan-kotsu.co.jp, in Japanese) bound for the museum (¥800, approximately 50 minutes).

Hikone 彦根

📞0749 / POP 111,800

Hikone is the second-largest city in the prefecture and of special interest to visitors for its lovely castle, which dominates the town. The adjoining garden is also a classic and is a must-see after your visit to the castle.

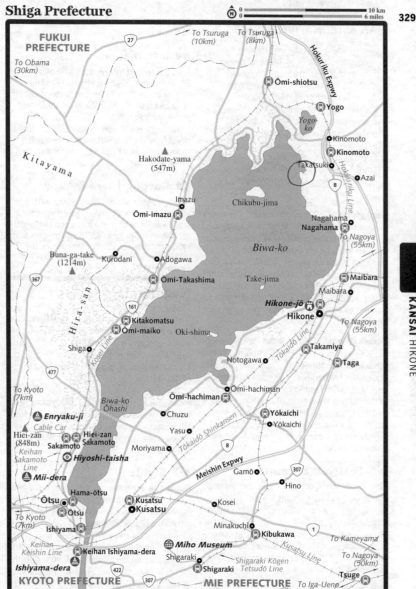

⊙ Sights

Hikone-jō CASTLE

(彦根城; 1-1 Konki-chō; admission ¥600; ◉8.30am-5pm) This castle was completed in 1622 by the Ii family, who ruled as *daimyō* (domain lords) over Hikone. It is rightly considered one of the finest castles in Japan. Much of it is original, and you can get a great view across the lake from the upper storeys. Surrounded by more than 1000 cherry trees, the castle is a very popular spot for springtime *hanami* (blossom-viewing) activities.

WORTH A TRIP

AN ALTERNATIVE CASTLE

Since Himeji-jō will be undergoing renovations until 2014, those who wish to see an original (rather than rebuilt) castle in Kansai should consider a trip out to Hikone to see Hikone-jō. While it's nowhere near as big or impressive as Himeji-jō, it's quite lovely in its own right and is a good example of Japanese castle architecture. If you've got a Japan Rail Pass and can take the *shinkansen* as far as Maibara, you can do this as a half-day trip from Kyoto.

Genkyū-en
GARDEN

(admission incl in castle ticket; ⊘8.30am-5pm) After visiting the castle, don't miss nearby Genkyū-en, a lovely Chinese-influenced garden that was completed in 1677. Ask someone at the castle to point you in the right direction. There's a teahouse in the garden where ¥500 gets you a cup of *matcha* and a sweet to enjoy as you relax and gaze over the scenery.

Yumekyō-bashi Castle Road
NEIGHBOURHOOD

(夢京橋キャッスルロード) About 400m southwest of the castle (marked on the *Street Map & Guide to Hikone* map and accessible via the Omote-mon or Ōte-mon gate of the castle), this street of traditional shops and restaurants is the ideal spot for lunch after exploring the castle, and a browse in the shops is a nice way to round out your visit to Hikone.

★ Festivals & Events

The **Birdman Contest**, held in summer (dates differ every year) at Matsubara Beach in Hikone, is a fantastic celebration of the human desire to fly – ideally without the use of fossil fuels. Here you will find contestants launching themselves over Biwa-ko in all manner of flimsy human-powered flying machines.

✕ Eating

Monzen-ya
NOODLES **$**

(もんぜんや; ☎24-2297; soba ¥780; ⊘11am-7pm, closed Tue) Our favourite spot for a bite in Yumekyō-bashi Castle Rd is Monzen-ya, a great little *soba* place that serves such things as *nishin-soba* (*soba* noodles with herring; ¥880). Starting from the castle end of the

street, it's about 100m on the left – look for the white *noren* curtain with black lettering in the doorway.

ℹ Information

The good **tourist information office** (☎22-2954; ⊘9am-5.30pm) is on your left at the bottom of the steps as you exit the west exit of Hikone Station. It stocks the excellent *Street Map & Guide to Hikone*.

The castle is a 10-minute walk straight up the street from the station (take a left before the shrine, then a quick right, or walk through the shrine grounds).

ℹ Getting There & Away

Hikone is about an hour (*shinkaisoku*, ¥1110) from Kyoto on the JR Tōkaidō line. If you have a Japan Rail Pass or are in a hurry, you can take the *shinkansen* to Maibara (¥3300, 20 minutes from Kyoto) and then backtrack from there on the JR Tōkaidō line to Hikone (¥180, five minutes).

Nagahama 長浜

☎0749 / POP 125,738

Nagahama is a surprisingly appealing little town on the northeast shore of Biwa-ko, which can easily be teamed up with a trip to Hikone. The main attraction here is the Kurokabe Square neighbourhood northeast of the station.

If you're in the area from 14 to 16 April, check out the **Nagahama Hikiyama Matsuri**, in which costumed children perform Hikiyama *kyōgen* (comic drama) on top of a dozen festival floats decked out with elaborate ornamentation.

⊙ Sights

Kurokabe Square
NEIGHBOURHOOD

(黒壁スクエア) Many of the old *machiya* (townhouses) and *kura* (storehouses) in this attractive old neighbourhood (it's not really a square) have been converted into shops and galleries highlighting the town's traditional (and modern) glass industry. Exit the east side of Nagahama Station, cross the bus boarding area towards Heiwado supermarket, walk around the supermarket to the left, then go right on the main street and take the first left after Shiga Bank; after about 100m on your right (at the corner), you will find the **Kurokabe Information Centre** (黒壁インフォメーションセンター; ☎65-8055; ⊘10am-6pm, to 5pm Nov-Mar), which has maps of the area.

Kurokabe Museum of Glass Art MUSEUM
(黒壁美術館; admission ¥600; ⊙10am-5pm) We like the small collection of glass *objets* at this museum. While you're here, ask them to demonstrate the *suikinkutsu*, a strange 'musical instrument' formed from an overturned urn into which water is dripped. It's about 50m north of the information centre, on the opposite side of the street. Last entry 4.30pm.

FREE Giant Kaleidoscope LANDMARK
(巨大万華鏡; kyodaimangekyō; ⊙dawn-dusk) Our hands-down favourite attraction in Kurokabe Square is the Giant Kaleidoscope, which is located off a shopping arcade north of the Kurokabe Museum of Glass Art. From the museum, walk north to the next street and take a right. About 30m after entering the arcade, you will see a sign reading 'Antique Gallery London'. It's in an open area behind this shop.

Daisū-ji TEMPLE
(大通寺; admission to garden/grounds ¥500/free; ⊙9am-4.30pm, closed year-end/new-year holidays) Not far from the Giant Kaleidoscope, Daitsū-ji, is a Jodo-Shin-sect temple that's worth a quick look (we don't recommend paying to enter the garden, though).

✕ Eating

Torikita NOODLES $
(翼果楼; ☑63-3663; dishes from ¥840; ⊙from 11am until noodles are sold out, closed Mon) For a tasty lunch while exploring Nagahama, drop into this atmospheric restaurant, which positively oozes 'old Japan' charm. The signature dish here is *yakisaba-sōmen* (thin noodles with cooked mackerel; ¥840) – it's a toothsome dish indeed. There is no English menu, but there are pictures on the Japanese menu. It's about 15m before the information office when approaching from the station, on the same side of the street – the name is written in English on the sign.

❶ Getting There & Away

Nagahama is on the JR Tōkaidō line (*shinkai-soku*, ¥1280, 66 minutes from Kyoto). Be aware that not all *shinkaisoku* from Kyoto go all the way to Nagahama; you may have to change in Maibara, which is a 10-minute ride south of Nagahama by *shinkaisoku* (¥190). If you've got a Japan Rail Pass, you can take the *shinkansen* to Maibara (¥3300, 20 minutes from Kyoto) and then switch to a local JR train for the short trip to Nagahama.

☑0742 / POP 369,000

The first permanent capital of Japan, Nara (奈良) is one of the most rewarding destinations in the country. Indeed, with eight Unesco World Heritage Sites, Nara is second only to Kyoto as a repository of Japan's cultural legacy. The centrepiece is, of course, the Diabutsu, or Great Buddha, which rivals Mt Fuji and Kyoto's Golden Pavilion (Kinkaku-ji) as Japan's single most impressive sight. The Great Buddha is housed in Tōdai-ji, a soaring temple that presides over Nara-kōen, a park filled with other fascinating sights that lends itself to relaxed strolling amid the greenery and tame deer.

Nara's best feature is its small size: it's quite possible to pack the most worthwhile sights into one full day. Many people visit Nara as a side trip from Kyoto, and comfortable express trains link the cities in about half an hour. Of course, it's preferable to spend two days here if you can. If your schedule allows for two days in Nara, you might spend one in Nara-kōen and the other seeing the sights to the west and southwest of Nara city (areas known as Nishinokyō and Ikaruga, respectively).

History
Nara is at the northern end of the Yamato Plain, where members of the Yamato clan rose to power as the original emperors of Japan. Until the 7th century, however, Japan had no permanent capital, as Shintō taboos concerning death stipulated that the capital be moved with the passing of each emperor. This practice died out under the influence of Buddhism and with the Taika reforms of 646, when the entire country came under imperial control.

At this time it was decreed that a permanent capital be built. Two locations were tried before a permanent capital was finally established at Nara (which was then known as Heijōkyō) in 710. Permanent status, however, lasted a mere 75 years. When a priest by the name of Dōkyō managed to seduce an empress and nearly usurp the throne, it was decided to move the court to a new location, out of reach of Nara's increasingly powerful clergy. This led to the new capital being established at Kyoto, about 35km to the north.

Although brief, the Nara period was extraordinarily vigorous in its absorption of

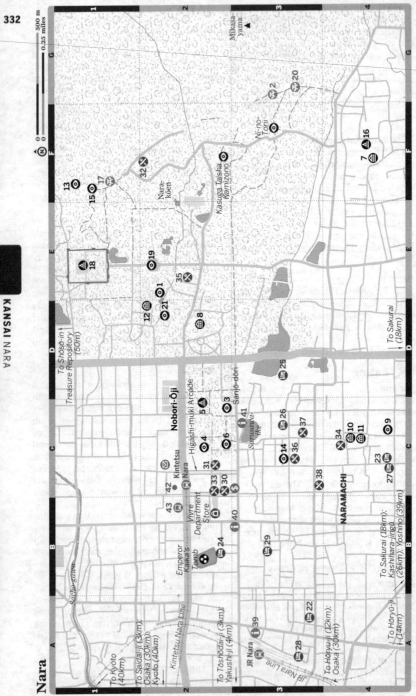

Nara

500 m
0.25 miles

To Kyoto
(40km)

To Saidai-ji (3km);
Osaka (30km);
Kyoto (40km)

To Shōsō-in
Treasure Repository
(50m)

Mikasa-
yama

Ni-no-
Torii

Kasuga Taisha
Kamizono

Nara-kōen

Emperor
Kaika's
Tomb

Nobori-Ōji

Higashi-muki Arcade

Sanjō-dōri

Kintetsu
Nara

Vivre
Department
Store

Shimsawa-
ike

NARAMACHI

To Tōshōdai-ji (3km);
Yakushi-ji (4km)

JR Nara

To Sakurai (18km);
Kashihara-jingū
(26km); Yoshino (39km)

To Hōryū-ji (12km);
Osaka (30km)

To Hōryū-ji
(14km)

To Sakurai
(18km)

Nara

◎ Sights

influences from China, a process that laid the foundations of Japanese culture and civilisation. And with the exception of an assault on the area by the Taira clan in the 12th century, Nara was subsequently spared the periodic bouts of destruction wreaked upon Kyoto, and a number of magnificent buildings have survived.

◉ Sights

Nara retains the grid pattern of streets laid out in Chinese style during the 8th century. There are two main train stations: JR Nara and Kintetsu Nara. JR Nara Station is a little west of the city centre (but still within walking distance of the sights), while Kintetsu Nara is right in the centre of town. Nara-kōen, which contains most of the important sights, is on the eastern side, against the bare flank of Wakakusa-yama. Most of the other sights are west or southwest of the city and are best reached by bus or train. It's easy to cover the city centre and the major attractions in nearby Nara-kōen on foot, although buses do ply the city.

Nara tourist information offices stock the useful *Nara Sight Seeing Map*. If you want something more detailed, ask if they have any copies of the excellent *Nara City Sightseeing Map*. If you read a bit of Japanese and want to explore Nara Prefecture, ask for a copy of *Nara-Yamatoji Kankō Mappu*.

NARA-KŌEN AREA   奈良公園
Many of Nara's most important sites are located in Nara-kōen, a fine park that occupies much of the east side of the city. The park is home to about 1200 deer, which in pre-Buddhist times were considered messengers of the gods and today enjoy the status of National Treasures. They roam the park and surrounding areas in search of handouts from tourists, often descending on petrified children who have the misfortune to be carrying food. You can buy *shika-sembei* (deer biscuits) from vendors for ¥150 to feed to the deer.

Our Nara-kōen walking tour is the best way to take in all the major sights in a day.

Nara National Museum
MUSEUM

(奈良国立博物館; Nara Kokuritsu Hakubutsu-kan; ☑050-5542-8600; 50 Noboriōji-chō; admission ¥500; ⊙9.30am-5pm) The Nara National Museum is devoted to Buddhist art and is divided into two sections, housed in different buildings. Built in 1894, the **Nara Buddhist Sculpture Hall & Ritual Bronzes Gallery**, contains a fine collection of *butsuzō* (statues of Buddhas and Bodhisattvas). The Buddhist images here are divided into categories, each with an excellent English explanation, making this an excellent introduction to Mahayana Buddhist iconography. The newer East and West wings, a short walk away, contain the permanent collections (sculptures, paintings and calligraphy) and are used for special exhibitions.

A special exhibition featuring the treasures of the **Shōsō-in Hall**, which holds the treasures of Tōdai-ji, is held in the newer wings in May, as well as from 21 October to 8 November (call the Nara City Tourist Information Centre to check, as these dates vary slightly each year). The exhibits include priceless items from the cultures along the Silk Road. If you are in Nara during these periods and are a fan of Japanese antiquities, you should make a point of visiting the museum, but be prepared for crowds. Enter by 4.30pm.

Kōfuku-ji
TEMPLE

(興福寺) This temple was transferred here from Kyoto in 710 as the main temple for the Fujiwara family. Although the original temple complex had 175 buildings, fires and destruction as a result of power struggles have left only a dozen standing. There are two **pagodas** – three storeys and five storeys – dating from 1143 and 1426, respectively. The taller of the two is the second-tallest in Japan, outclassed by the one at Kyoto's Tō-ji by a few centimetres. Note that a new hall is being built in the centre of the temple grounds and construction isn't expected to be completed until 2018.

The **Kōfuku-ji National Treasure Hall** (興福寺国宝館; 48 Noborioji-chō, Kokuhō-kan; admission ¥600; ⊙9am-5pm) contains a variety of statues and art objects salvaged from previous structures. Enter by 4.45pm.

TOP CHOICE Isui-en & Neiraku Art Museum
GARDEN

(依水園・寧楽美術館; 74 Suimon-chō; admission museum & garden ¥650; ⊙9.30am-4.30pm, closed Tue & New Year holidays) This garden, dating from the Meiji era, is beautifully laid out and features abundant greenery and a pond with ornamental carp. It's without a doubt the best garden in the city and well worth a visit. For ¥500 you can enjoy a cup of tea on tatami mats overlooking the garden.

The adjoining art museum, Neiraku Bijutsukan, displays Chinese and Korean ceramics and bronzes (admission is included in garden entry). Enter by 4pm.

FREE Yoshiki-en
GARDEN

(吉城園; 68 Noborioji-chō; ⊙9.30am-5pm Mar–27 Dec) This garden, located next door to Isui-en (to the right when you're facing the entrance of Isui-en), is a stunner. Originally a residence of the high priest of Tōdai-ji, it fell into private hands. The present garden was laid out in 1918 and contains a lovely thatch-roof cottage, a pond and several walking paths. It's particularly lovely in November and early December, when the maples turn a blazing crimson. Best of all, at the time of writing, entry was free for foreign tourists! Enter by 4.30pm.

TOP CHOICE Tōdai-ji
TEMPLE

(東大寺) Nara's famous Daibutsu (Great Buddha) is housed in the Daibutsu-den Hall of this grand temple. It's Nara's star attraction and can often be packed with tour groups and schoolchildren from across the country, but it's big enough to absorb huge crowds and it belongs at the top of any Nara itinerary.

Before you enter the temple be sure to check out the **Nandai-mon** (東大寺南大門), an enormous gate containing two fierce-looking **Niō guardians**. These recently restored wooden images, carved in the 13th century by the sculptor Unkei, are some of the finest wooden statues in all of Japan, if not the world. They are truly dramatic works of art and seem ready to spring to life at any moment. The gate is about 200m south of the temple enclosure.

Note that most of Tōdai-ji's grounds can be visited free of charge, with the exception of the main hall, the Daibutsu-den Hall.

Daibutsu-den Hall

(大仏殿; Hall of the Great Buddha; 406-1 Zōshi-chō; admission ¥500; ⊙8am-4.30pm Nov-Feb, to 5pm Mar, 7.30am-5.30pm Apr-Sep, to 5pm Oct) Tōdai-ji's Daibutsu-den is the largest wooden building in the world. Unbelievably, the present structure, rebuilt in 1709, is a mere two-thirds of the size of the original! The

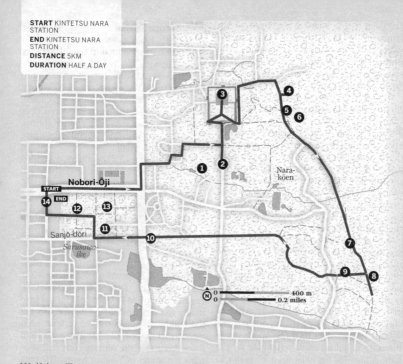

START KINTETSU NARA STATION
END KINTETSU NARA STATION
DISTANCE 5KM
DURATION HALF A DAY

Walking Tour
Nara-kōen

❯ Start at Kintetsu Nara Station and walk straight up Nobori-Ōji, passing Kōfuku-ji on your right. Go left and visit ❶ **Isui-en**, one of Nara's finest gardens. Walk north from the garden entrance, take the next major right after about 100m and walk east to come out in front of Tōdai-ji. Go right to inspect the massive ❷ **Nandai-mon**, the main gate. Admire the Niō guardians and then continue to ❸ **Tōdai-ji**.

Take the southeast exit, then a hard left and walk along the temple enclosure. Just past the pond, take a right up the hill following the stone-paved path. This leads to an incredibly atmospheric stretch that takes you up to an open plaza in front of ❹ **Nigatsu-dō** and ❺ **Sangatsu-dō** halls. Climb the steps to Nigatsu-dō to enjoy the view from the verandah, which takes in the graceful curves of the Daibutsu-den and most of the Nara plain.

Return to the plaza and exit heading south, passing between a log-cabinlike structure and gaudy ❻ **Tamukeyama-hachimangū** (手向山八幡宮). Follow the broad path through the woods, descend two staircases and follow the 'Kasuga Shrine' signs. You'll come to a road leading uphill to the left; follow it, passing under the slopes of Wakakusa-yama. At Musashino Ryokan (look for the small English sign), walk straight down the steps, cross a bridge, jog left, and at the T-intersection take a left up to ❼ **Kasuga Taisha** (you'll have to work around the side to find the main entrance).

Leave the shrine via the main entrance and bear left up the path to ❽ **Wakamiya-jinja** (若宮神社), passing several small shrines on the way. After seeing the shrine, retrace your steps towards Kasuga Taisha and take a left down the steps which lead back towards the centre of town. You'll pass first through ❾ **Ni-no-Torii** and then continue down the broad wooded arcade to ❿ **Ichi-no-Torii**. Cross the street and you'll soon see the ⓫ **Kōfuku-ji pagoda**. Walk through the Kōfuku-ji grounds, passing between the ⓬ **Nanen-dō** and ⓭ **Hokuen-dō** halls, and take the narrow lane that leads down to Higashi-muki Arcade. A quick right here will bring you back to where you started: ⓮ **Kintetsu Nara Station**.

Daibutsu (Great Buddha) contained within is one of the largest bronze figures in the world and was originally cast in 746. The present statue, recast in the Edo period, stands just over 16m high and consists of 437 tonnes of bronze and 130kg of gold.

The Daibutsu is an image of Dainichi Buddha (also known as Vairocana Buddha), the cosmic Buddha believed to give rise to all worlds and their respective Buddhas. Historians believe that Emperor Shōmu ordered the building of the Buddha as a charm against smallpox, which ravaged Japan in preceding years. Over the centuries the statue took quite a beating from earthquakes and fires, losing its head a couple of times (note the slight difference in colour between the head and the body).

As you circle the statue towards the back, you'll see a wooden column with a hole through its base. Popular belief maintains that those who can squeeze through the hole, which is exactly the same size as one of the Great Buddha's nostrils, are ensured of enlightenment. There's usually a line of children waiting to give it a try and parents waiting to snap their pictures. Adults sometimes try it, but it's really something for the kids. A hint for big kids: it's a lot easier to go through with both arms held above your head – and someone on either end to push and pull helps, too.

Nigatsu-dō & Sangatsu-dō

The Nigatsu-dō and Sangatsu-dō halls are almost sub-temples of Tōdai-ji. They are an easy walk east (uphill from the Daibutsu-den). You can walk straight east up the hill, but we recommend taking a hard left out of the Daibutsu-den exit, following the enclosure past the pond and turning up the hill. This pathway is among the most scenic walks in all of Nara. For details, see the Nara-kōen walking tour, p335.

As you reach the plaza at the top of the hill, the **Nigatsu-dō** (二月堂; admission free) is the temple hall with the verandah overlooking the plaza. This is where Nara's Omizutori Matsuri is held. The verandah affords a great view over Nara, especially at dusk. Opening hours here are the same as those of the Daibutsu-den.

A short walk south of Nigatsu-dō is **Sangatsu-dō** (三月堂; admission ¥500), which is the oldest building in the Tōdai-ji complex. This hall contains a small collection of fine statues from the Nara period. It's open the same hours as the Daibutsu-den.

FREE Kasuga Taisha SHRINE

(春日大社; 160 Kasugano-chō; ⊙dawn-dusk) This shrine was founded in the 8th century by the Fujiwara family and was completely rebuilt every 20 years, according to Shintō tradition, until the end of the 19th century. It lies at the foot of the hill in a pleasant, wooded setting with herds of sacred deer awaiting handouts. As with similar shrines in Japan, you will find several subshrines around the main hall.

The approaches to the shrine are lined with hundreds of lanterns, and there are many hundreds more in the shrine itself. The lantern festivals held twice a year at the shrine are a major attraction.

While you're in the area, it's worth walking a few minutes south to the nearby shrine of **Wakamiya-jinja**.

Shin-Yakushi-ji SHRINE

(新薬師寺; 1352 Takabatake-chō; admission ¥600; ⊙9am-5pm) This temple was founded by Empress Kōmyō in 747 in thanks for her husband's recovery from an eye disease. Most of the buildings were destroyed or have been reconstructed, but the present main hall dates from the 8th century. The hall contains sculptures of Yakushi Nyorai (Healing Buddha) and a set of 12 divine generals.

It's about 15 minutes' walk from Wakamiya-jinja; follow the trail south through the woods. When you come to the main street, look for the small signs in English leading up (south) into a suburban neighbourhood.

Nara City Museum of Photography MUSEUM

(奈良市写真美術館; Nara-shi Shashin Bijutsu-kan; ☏22-9811; 600-1 Takabatake-chō; admission ¥500; ⊙9.30am-5pm, closed Mon) Around the corner from Shin-Yakushi-ji, this small museum is worth a visit if you are in the area or interested in a particular exhibit (there is no permanent collection). Ask at any of the tourist offices before making the trek. Enter by 4.30pm.

NARAMACHI 奈良町

South of Sanjō-dōri and Sarusawa-ike pond you will find Naramachi, a traditional neighbourhood with many well-preserved machiya and kura. It's a nice place for a stroll before or after hitting the big sights of Nara-kōen, and there are several good restaurants in the area to entice the hungry traveller. There is a lot of creative energy here and residents are eager to share their culture with travellers.

FREE Naramachi Shiryō-kan Museum
MUSEUM

(奈良町資料館; 14 Nishishinya-chō; ⊘10am-4pm Sat & Sun) Has a decent collection of bric-a-brac from the area, including a display of old Japanese coins and bills.

FREE Naramachi Koushi-no-Ie
NOTABLE BUILDING

(ならまち資料館; 44 Gangōji-chō; ⊘9am-5pm, closed Mon) A traditional Japanese house that you can enter and explore.

FREE Naramachi Monogatari-kan
GALLERY

(奈良町物語館; 2-1 Nakanoshinya-chō; ⊘10am-5pm) An interesting little gallery that holds some worthwhile exhibitions.

FREE Saka-gura Sasaya
SAKE

(☑27-3383; ⊘10am-7pm, closed Tue) If all this sightseeing has made you thirsty, drop in for a tasting (prices range from ¥100 to ¥500 per sample) of the various types of sake produced in Nara Prefecture (all sake is also available for purchase). There is a useful English explanation sheet. Look for the sake barrels and a sign in the window reading 'sake'.

Tours

Nara Kōtsū (☑22-5263) runs daily bus tours on a variety of routes, two of which include Nara city sights only and two of which include more distant sights including Hōryū-ji and the burial mounds around Asuka. Prices for the all-day trips range from ¥3000 to ¥7000 for adults (including all temple fees and an English audio guide). Nara Kōtsū has offices opposite JR Nara Station and across the street from Kintetsu Nara Station.

For something more intimate, try one of the private tours operated by one of the Kyoto-based private tour operators (see p280) or one of Nara's volunteer guide organisations (see p339).

Festivals & Events

The dates for some of these festivals vary, so it's best to check with the Nara or Kyoto tourist information offices.

Yamayaki
TRADITIONAL

In early January (the day before Seijin-no-hi or Coming-of-Age Day), the Grass Burning Festival commemorates a feud many centuries ago between the monks of Tōdai-ji and Kōfuku-ji: Wakakusa-yama is set alight at 6pm, with an accompanying display of fireworks.

Mantōrō
LANTERNS

Held in early February at Kasuga Taisha at 6pm, the Lantern Festival involves the lighting of 3000 stone and bronze lanterns around Kasuga Taisha – it's impossibly atmospheric, as you can imagine. A *bugaku* dance takes place in the Apple Garden on the last day. This festival is also held around 14 August in the O-Bon (Festival of the Dead) holiday period.

Omizutori
TRADITIONAL

On the evening of 12 March, the monks of Tōdai-ji parade huge flaming torches around the balcony of Nigatsu-dō and rain down embers on the spectators to purify them. The water-drawing ceremony is performed after midnight.

Takigi Onō
NŌ

Open-air performances of nō are held after dark by the light of blazing torches at Kōfuku-ji and Kasuga Taisha, on 11 and 12 May.

Shika-no-Tsunokiri
DEER-ANTLER CUTTING

Those deer in Nara-kōen are pursued in a type of elegant rodeo into the Roku-en (deer enclosure) close to Kasuga Taisha on Sundays and holidays in October. They are then wrestled to the ground and their antlers sawn off. Tourist brochures hint that this is to avoid personal harm, though it's not clear whether they are referring to the deer fighting each other or the deer mugging the tourists.

Sleeping

Although Nara can be visited as a day trip from Kyoto, it is pleasant to spend the night here, allowing for a more relaxing pace.

TOP CHOICE Guesthouse Sakuraya
GUESTHOUSE $$

(桜舍; ☑/fax 24-1490; www.guesthouse-sakuraya.com; 1 Narukawa-chō; per person incl breakfast ¥6000; ☎) This brand-new three-room guesthouse is a charming place to stay. It's described as a guesthouse, but it feels more like a ryokan – the rooms are traditional and the building is an atmospheric stunner. There's a lovely little central garden and a comfortable common room. The owner offers a Discovery of Japanese Culture course for ¥3000. Keep in mind that it's a traditional and relatively small place, so partiers should look elsewhere.

Ryokan Matsumae
RYOKAN $

(旅館松前; ☎22-3686; fax 26-3927; www.mat
sumae.co.jp/english/index_e.html; 28-1 Higashitera
hayashi-chō; per person without bathroom from
¥5250; ⊚) This friendly little ryokan lays
claim to an incredibly convenient location in
Naramachi, a short walk from all the sights.
The rooms are typical of a ryokan: tatami
mats, low tables, TVs and futons. Some of
the rooms are a little dark, but the feeling
here is warm and relaxing.

Guesthouse Nara Komachi
GUESTHOUSE $

(ゲストハウス奈良小町; ☎87-0556; guest-
house@wave.plala.or.jp; 41-2 Surugamachi; dm from
¥2500, r per person from ¥3800; ⊚) One of the
best accommodation bargains in Nara is
this excellent new guesthouse. Choose from
dorm rooms or Western- or Japanese-style
private rooms with en suite bathrooms/
showers. There's a self-catering kitchen and
cheap bicycle rentals.

Super Hotel Lohas JR Nara-eki
HOTEL $$

(スーパーホテルLohas・JR奈良駅; ☎27-
9000; www.superhoteljapan.com/en/s-hotels/nara
-lohas.html; fax 27-9008; 1-2 Sanjōhonmachi; s/tw
¥6980/12,800; ⊚) Connected to JR Nara Sta-
tion by an elevated walkway, this new Super
Hotel has a lot going for it: clean compact
rooms with en suite bathrooms, efficient
service and a large communal 'onsen' bath.
Room rates include breakfast.

Nara Hotel
HOTEL $$$

(奈良ホテル; ☎26-3300; www.narahotel.co.jp/
english/index.html; fax 23-5252; 1096 Takabatake-
chō; s/tw from ¥18,480/33,495; ⊚) This grande
dame of Nara hotels is a classic, with high
ceilings and the smell of polished wood all
around. All the rooms are spacious and
comfortable with big beds. Unfortunately,
some of the bathrooms have cramped unit
baths. The rooms in the Shinkan (new
wing) are nice, but we recommend the
Honkan (main building) for its great retro
atmosphere.

Ryokan Seikansō
RYOKAN $

(☎/fax 22-2670; 29 Higashikitsuji-chō; per person
without bathroom from ¥4200; ⊚) This traditional ryokan has reasonable rates and a
good Naramachi location. The rooms are
clean and spacious with shared bathrooms
and a large communal bathtub. The management is used to foreign guests and there
is a nice Japanese garden. It's a little long in
the tooth, but the friendly reception makes
up for it.

Ugaya Guesthouse
GUESTHOUSE $

(ウガヤゲストハウス; ☎95-7739; www.ugaya
.net/en/index.html; 4-1 Okukomori-chō; dm from
¥2500, r per person without bathroom from ¥3000;
⊚) This casual backpackers' guesthouse offers a tight warren of rooms and dorms and
convivial communal areas a short walk from
the sights of Naramachi. This is a sociable
place and a good place to meet other travellers. Grab a copy of the excellent map when
you check in.

Hotel Fujita Nara
HOTEL $$

(ホテルフジタ奈良; ☎23-8111; fax 22-0255;
www.fujita-nara.com/e/index.html; 47-1 Shimosanjō-
chō; s/d/tw from ¥8000/11,000/13,600; ⊚)
Right smack in downtown Nara and close
to both main train stations, this efficient
midrange hotel hits all the right notes: clean
rooms, reasonable prices and some English-
speaking staff. It's a good choice for those
who want a conveniently located hotel.

✖ Eating

Nara is chock-a-block with good restaurants,
most of which are near the train stations
and in Naramachi. There aren't many good
choices in Nara-kōen, but we list one spot
halfway between Tōdai-ji and Kasuga Taisha
for those exploring that area.

Mellow Café
CAFE $

(メロー　カフェ; ☎27-9099; 1-8 Konishi-chō;
lunch from ¥980; ⊙11am-11.30pm; ⊡) Located
down a narrow alley (look for the palm tree)
not far from Kintetsu Nara Station, this
open-plan cafe is a pleasant spot to fuel up
for a day of sightseeing. The menu centres
on pasta and pizza (there's a brick oven).
There's an English sign and menu.

Falafel Garden
FELAFEL $

(ファラフェルガーデン; ☎24-2722; 13-2 Hi-
gashimuki Minamimachi; lunch from ¥950; ⊙11am-
9pm; ⊡) About midway along the Konishi
shopping arcade, this felafel specialist is a
great place for vegetarians and anyone in
need of a break from noodles and rice.

Tempura Asuka
TEMPURA $$

(天ぷら飛鳥; ☎26-4308; 11 Shōnami-chō; meals
¥1500-5000; ⊙11.30am-2.30pm & 5-9.30pm,
closed Mon; ⊡) This reliable restaurant
serves attractive tempura and sashimi sets
in a relatively casual atmosphere. At lunchtime try its nicely presented *yumei-dono
bentō* (a box filled with a variety of tasty
Japanese foods) for ¥1600. There is an English sign.

Nonohana Ohka
CAFE $

(野の花黄花; ☎22-1139; 13 Nakashinyamachi; coffee & tea ¥500-600; ⊙11am-5pm, closed Mon; 🖬) With indoor and outdoor garden seating, this cafe is one of our favourite places for a pick-me-up when in Naramachi. The cakes are usually very good here and they go down a treat with the excellent tea. Look for the glass front and the sign reading 'cafe'.

Tachibana
CAFE $

(たちばな; ☎31-6439; 18-1 Nishiterabayashi-chō; coffee from ¥400; ⊙11am-6pm; closed Wed; 🖬) This friendly little cafe/gallery in Naramachi is a great place to sample a cup of green tea. Once you're done enjoying your tea, head upstairs to check out the wonderful collection of ceramics from Kyoto and Nara artists. There's no English sign at present, but the English/Japanese menu is displayed outside.

Silk Road
SHOKUDŌ $$

(シルクロードの終着駅; ☎25-0231; 16 Kasugano-chō; meals ¥1000; ⊙10am-7pm; 🖬) If you've got kids in tow, head into the Yumekaze Hiroba dining/shopping complex across from the Nara National Museum to find this wonderful 'train-centric' restaurant. There are two huge model train layouts, which kids can actually control while eating bowls of standard Japanese curry rice and similar favourites.

Kura
JAPANESE $$

(蔵; ☎22-8771; 16 Kōmyōin-chō; oden ¥80-150; ⊙5pm-10pm, closed Thu; 🖬) This rustic Naramachi restaurant specialises in *oden*, a stew of various foods like eggs, Japanese radishes and tofu simmered in a rich broth (it's better than that might sound). For a taste of old Japan, try this friendly spot.

Ten Ten Café
CAFE $

(テンテンカフェ; ☎26-6770; 19 Wakido-chō; meals from ¥750; ⊙11.30am-6pm; 🖬) Operated by a singer-songwriter, and a venue for lots of live music, this airy cafe is a fine spot for a drink or light meal in the Naramachi area. It serves a daily lunch special for ¥750. Look for the English sign and plants out front.

Kasugano
SHOKUDŌ $

(春日野; meals from ¥600; ⊙9am-5pm; 🖉🖬) If you're exploring Nara-kōen, lunchtime often finds you somewhere between Tōdai-ji and Kasuga Taisha. A good choice in this area is Kasugano, a restaurant/souvenir shop at the base of Wakakusa-yama. Take a seat in the woodsy annexe cafe section here rather than the main tables in the shop area (the menu is the same). Dishes include things like tempura *soba* (¥800). It's the third shop house from the northern end of this strip. Note that most of the souvenir shops in this same strip also have on-site restaurants that serve similar fare and most have English menus.

Doutor
CAFE $

(ドトール) If you just need a quick cuppa or an eat-in or takeaway sandwich, there is a branch of the coffee shop chain in the Konishi Arcade (a five-minute walk from Kintetsu Nara).

❶ Information

The main **JR Nara Station information centre** (☎22-9821; ⊙9am-5pm), in the old Nara Station building just outside the east exit of JR Nara Station, is the city's main tourist information centre and English speakers are usually on hand. If you start from Kintetsu Nara Station, try the helpful **Kintetsu Nara Station information office** (☎24-4858; ⊙9am-9pm), which is near the top of the stairs above exit 3 from the station.

There are several other information offices in Nara, including the **Nara City Tourist Information Centre** (奈良市観光センター; ☎22-3900; ⊙9am-9pm) and the **Sarusawa Tourist Information Office** (猿沢観光案内所; ☎26-1991; ⊙9am-5pm).

The information centres can put you in touch with volunteer guides who speak English and other foreign languages, but you must book at least one day in advance. Two of these services are the **YMCA Goodwill Guides** (☎45-5920; www4.kcn.ne.jp/~eggymca/egghomepage.html) and **Nara Student Guides** (☎26-4753; www.narastudentguide.org).

❶ Getting There & Away

Bus

There is an overnight bus service between Tokyo's Shinjuku (Shinjuku highway bus terminal) and Nara (one way/return ¥8400/15,120). In Nara, call **Nara Kōtsū Bus** (☎22-5110; www.narakotsu.co.jp/kousoku/index.html, in Japanese) or check with the Nara City Tourist Information Centre for more details. In Nara, overnight buses leave from stop 8 in front of JR Nara Station and from stop 20 outside Kintetsu Nara Station. In Tokyo, call **Kantō Bus** (☎03-3371-1225; www.kanto-bus.co.jp, in Japanese) or visit the Shinjuku highway bus terminal in person.

Airport limousines (¥2000, 90 minutes to Kansai International Airport; ¥1440, 60 minutes to Itami Airport) leave from stop 9 in front of JR Nara Station and stop 20 (Kansai International Airport) and 12 (Itami Airport) outside Kintetsu Nara Station.

Buses to sights west (Yakushi-ji and Tōshōdai-ji) and southwest (Hōryū-ji) leave from stop 10, diagonally across from JR Nara Station, and stop 8 outside Kinetsu Nara Station.

Train

KYOTO The Kintetsu line, which runs between Kintetsu Kyoto Station (in Kyoto Station) and Kintetsu Nara Station, is the fastest and most convenient way to travel between Nara and Kyoto. There are *tokkyū* (¥1110, 33 minutes) and *kyūkō* (¥610, 40 minutes). The *tokkyū* trains run directly and are very comfortable; the *kyūkō* usually require a change at Saidai-ji.

The JR Nara line also connects JR Kyoto Station with JR Nara Station (*JR miyakoji kaisoku*, ¥690, 41 minutes) and there are several departures an hour during the day.

OSAKA The Kintetsu Nara line connects Osaka (Kintetsu Osaka Namba Station) with Nara (Kintetsu Nara Station). *Kaisoku* and *futsū* services take about 36 minutes and cost ¥540. *Tokkyū* services do the journey in five minutes but cost almost double, making them a poor option.

The JR Kansai line links Osaka (Namba and Tennō-ji stations) and Nara (JR Nara Station). A *kaisoku* connects Namba and JR Nara Station (¥540, 45 minutes) and Tennō-ji and JR Nara Station (¥450, 30 minutes).

ⓘ Getting Around

To/From the Airport

Nara is served by Kansai International Airport (KIX). There is a **limousine bus service** (Nara Kōtsū; www.narakotsu.co.jp/kousoku/limousine/nara_kanku.html, in Japanese) between Nara and the airport with departures roughly every hour in both directions (¥2000, 90 minutes). At Kansai International Airport, ask at the information counter in the arrivals hall, and in Nara visit the ticket office in the building across from Kintetsu Nara Station. Reservations are a good idea.

For domestic flights, there are **limousine buses** (Nara Kōtsū; www.narakotsu.co.jp/kousoku/limousine/nara_itami.html, in Japanese) to/from Osaka's Itami airport (¥1440, 60 minutes).

Bus

Most of the area around Nara-kōen is covered by two circular bus routes: bus 1 runs anticlockwise and bus 2 runs clockwise. There's a ¥200 flat fare. You can easily see the main sights in the park on foot and use the bus as an option if you are pushed for time or get tired of walking. If you plan to ride a lot, the one-day Free Pass costs ¥500.

Buses to Ikaruga and Nishinokyō (for Yakushi-ji, Tōshōdai-ji and Hōryū-ji) leave from stop 10 diagonally across from JR Nara Station and from stop 8 outside Kinetsu Nara Station.

AROUND NARA

In the area around Nara, southern Nara-ken was the birthplace of imperial rule and is rich in historical sites that are easily accessible as day trips from Osaka, Kyoto or Nara, provided that you make an early start. Of particular historical interest are the *kofun* (burial mounds) that mark the graves of Japan's first emperors; these are concentrated around Asuka. There are also several isolated temples where you can escape the crowds that plague Nara's city centre. Further afield, the mountaintop town of Yoshino is one of Japan's cherry-blossom meccas.

Easily reached by rail, Yamato-Yagi and Sakurai serve as useful transport hubs for the region. Keep in mind that the Kintetsu line is more convenient than JR for most of the destinations in this section.

Temples Southwest of Nara

While Nara city has some impressive ancient temples and Buddhist statues, if you want to go right back to the roots of Japanese Buddhism it's necessary to head to three temples southwest of Nara: Hōryū-ji, Yakushi-ji and Tōshōdai-ji.

Hōryū-ji is one of the most important temples in all of Japan, largely for historical reasons. However, its appeal is more academic than aesthetic, and it's quite a slog through drab suburbs to get there. Thus, for most people we recommend a half-day trip to Yakushi-ji and Tōshōdai-ji, which are easy to get to from Nara and very pleasant for strolling.

If you want to visit all three temples, head to Hōryū-ji first (it's the most distant from the centre of Nara) and then continue by bus 97 or 98 (¥560, 39 minutes) up to Yakushi-ji and Tōshōdai-ji, which are a 10-minute walk apart. Obviously, this can also be done in reverse. Of all the buses that ply the southwest temple route, bus 97 is the most convenient, with English announcements and route maps (it also pulls off the main road and enters the Yakushi-ji parking lot).

HŌRYŪ-JI 法隆寺

Hōryū-ji (admission ¥1000; ⊙8am-5pm 22 Feb-3 Nov, to 4.30pm 4 Nov-21 Feb) was founded in 607 by Prince Shōtoku, considered by many to be the patron saint of Japanese Buddhism. Legend has it that moments after his birth, Shōtoku stood up and started praying. Hōryū-ji is renowned not only as the oldest temple in Japan but also as a repository for some of the country's rarest treasures. Several of the temple's wooden buildings have survived earthquakes and fires to become the oldest of their kind in the world.

The temple is divided into two parts, **Sai-in** (West Temple) and **Tō-in** (East Temple). The entrance ticket allows admission to Sai-in, Tō-in and the Great Treasure Hall. A detailed map is provided and a guidebook is available in English and several other languages.

The main approach to the temple proceeds from the south along a tree-lined avenue and continues through the Nandai-mon and Chū-mon gates before entering the Sai-in precinct. As you enter, you'll see the **Kondō** (Main Hall) on your right and a pagoda on your left.

The Kondō houses several treasures, including the triad of the **Buddha Sakyamuni**, with two attendant Bodhisattvas. Though it is one of Japan's great Buddhist treasures, it's dimly lit and barely visible – you will need a torch (flashlight) to see it. Likewise, the pagoda contains clay images depicting scenes from the life of Buddha, which are barely visible without a torch.

On the eastern side of Sai-in are the two concrete buildings of the **Daihōzō-in** (Great Treasure Hall), containing numerous treasures from Hōryū-ji's long history.

Given the cost of admission and the time it takes to get here from central Nara, we recommend that you give careful thought to committing at least half a day to visiting this temple.

ⓘ Getting There & Away

To get to Hōryū-ji, take the JR Kansai line from JR Nara Station to Hōryū-ji Station (¥210, 11 minutes). From there, bus 72 shuttles the short distance between the station and the bus stop Hōryū-ji Monmae (¥180, eight minutes). Alternatively, take bus 52 or 97 from either JR Nara Station or Kintetsu Nara Station and get off at the Hōryū-ji-mae stop (¥760, 60 minutes). Leave the bus stop and walk west for about 50m, cross the road and you will see the tree-lined approach to the temple.

YAKUSHI-JI   薬師寺

This **temple** (admission ¥500; ⓧ8.30am-5pm) houses some of the most beautiful Buddhist statues in all Japan. It was established by Emperor Temmu in 680. With the exception of the **East Pagoda**, which dates to 730, the present buildings either date from the 13th century or are very recent reconstructions.

Entering from the south, turn to the right before going through the gate with guardian figures and walk to the **Tōin-dō** (East Hall). The hall houses a famous Shō-Kannon image, built in the 7th century and showing obvious influences of Indian sculptural styles. Exit the Tōin-dō and walk west to the **Kondō** (Main Hall).

The Kondō was rebuilt in 1976 and houses several images, including the famous **Yakushi Triad** (the Buddha Yakushi flanked by the Bodhisattvas of the sun and moon), dating from the 8th century. They were originally gold, but a fire in the 16th century turned the images an appealingly mellow black.

Behind (north of) the Kondō is the **Kō-dō** (Lecture Hall), which houses yet another fine Buddhist trinity, this time Miroku Buddha with two Bodhisattva attendants. You can exit to the north behind this hall and make your way to Tōshōdai-ji.

ⓘ Getting There & Away

To get to Yakushi-ji, take bus 97 from JR Nara Station or Kintetsu Nara Station and get off at the Yakushi-ji Parking Lot stop (*Yakushijo Chūshajō*; ¥240, 22 minutes). The temple is a short walk north of the parking lot. You can also take bus 52, 63, 70, 72, 88 or 97 from these stations and get off at the Yakushi-ji Higashi-guchi stop (¥250, 15 minutes). From this stop, walk 100m south (same direction the bus was travelling) to a Mobil station, cross the road to the west, and walk west across a canal. From the main road it's 250m to the temple's south entrance.

You can also take a *futsū* on the Kintetsu Kashihara line (which runs between Kyoto and Kashihara-jingū-mae) and get off at Nishinokyō Station, which is about a 200m walk northwest of Yakushi-ji (and 600m walk south of Tōshōdai-ji). If you're coming from Nara, you will have to change trains at Yamato-Saidaiji (¥200, five minutes; *kyūkō* and *tokkyū* do not stop at Nishinokyō). If you're coming from Kyoto, take a *kyūkō* as far as Yamato Saidaiji and then change to the *futsū* (¥610, 40 minutes).

TŌSHŌDAI-JI   唐招提寺

This **temple** (admission ¥600; ⓧ8.30am-5pm, last entry by 4.30pm) was established in 759 by the Chinese priest Ganjin (Jian Zhen), who had been recruited by Emperor Shōmu to reform Buddhism in Japan. The temple grounds are pleasantly wooded and make a good contrast to nearby Yakushi-ji, which is largely devoid of greenery.

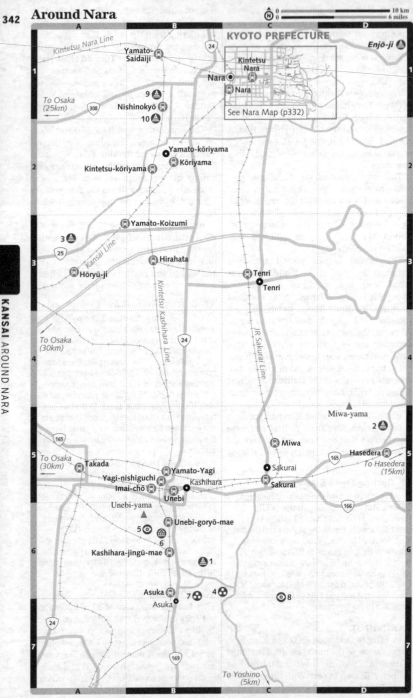

N 0 ━━━━━━━━━━ 10 km
0 ━━━━━━━━━━ 6 miles

KYOTO PREFECTURE

Kintetsu Nara Line

Enjō-ji

Yamato-Saidaiji

Kintetsu Nara

Nara

Nara

See Nara Map (p332)

To Osaka (25km)

9

Nishinokyō

10

Yamato-kōriyama

Kōriyama

Kintetsu-kōriyama

Yamato-Koizumi

3

Kansai Line

Hirahata

Tenri

Tenri

Hōryū-ji

Kintetsu Kashihara Line

To Osaka (30km)

JR Sakurai Line

Miwa-yama

2

Miwa

Hasedera

To Osaka (30km)

Takada

Yamato-Yagi

Sakurai

To Hasedera (15km)

Yagi-nishiguchi

Kashihara

Sakurai

Imai-chō

Unebi

Unebi-yama

Unebi-goryō-mae

5

6

Kashihara-jingū-mae

1

Asuka

7   4

8

Asuka

To Yoshino (5km)

Around Nara

◎ Sights

The **Kondō** (Golden Hall), roughly in the middle of the grounds, contains a stunning Senjū (thousand-armed) Kannon image. Behind this, the **Kōdō** (Lecture Hall), contains a beautiful image of Miroku Buddha.

Tōshōdai-ji is a 500m walk north of Yakushi-ji's northern gate.

Around Yamato-Yagi 大和八木周辺

Easily reached on the Kintetsu line from Osaka, Kyoto or Nara, Yamato-Yagi is the most convenient transport hub for sights in southern Nara-ken. From Kyoto take the Kintetsu Nara/Kashihara line direct (*kyūkō*, ¥860, 57 minutes). From Nara take the Kintetsu Nara line to Saidaiji and change to the Kintetsu Kashihara line (*kyūkō*, ¥430, 27 minutes). From Osaka's Uehonmachi Station, take the Kintetsu Osaka line direct (*kyūkō*, ¥540, 34 minutes). If you've got a Japan Rail Pass, you can reach the Kashihara area from Nara by taking the JR Nara/Sakurai lines and getting off at Unebi (¥480, 39 minutes).

KASHIHARA 橿原

Three stops south of Yamato-Yagi, on the Kintetsu Kashihara line, is Kashihara-jingū-mae Station (¥200 from Yamato-Yagi, five minutes; all trains stop). As noted above, you can also take the JR Nara/Sakurai line from Nara. There are a couple of interesting sights within easy walking distance of this station.

◎ Sights

FREE **Kashihara-jingū** SHRINE
(橿原神宮) This shrine, at the foot of Unebi-yama, dates back to 1889, when many of the buildings were moved here from Kyoto Gosho (Kyoto Imperial Palace). The shrine buildings are built in the same style as those of Ise-jingū's Grand Shrine and are a good example of classical Shintō architecture. The shrine is dedicated to Japan's mythical first emperor, Jimmu, and an annual festival is held here on 11 February, the legendary date of Jimmu's enthronement. The vast, parklike grounds are pleasant to stroll around.

The shrine is five minutes' walk from Kashihara-jingū-mae Station; take the central exit out of the station and follow the main street in the direction of the mountain.

Nara Prefecture Kashihara Archaeological Museum MUSEUM
(奈良県橿原考古学研究所付属博物館; Nara Ken-ritsu Kashihara Kōkogaku Kenkyūjo Fuzoku Hakubutsukan; ☑0744-24-1185; admission ¥400, foreign passport holders free; ◎9am-5pm, closed Mon) This museum is highly recommended for those with an interest in the history of the Japanese people. The objects on display come from various archaeological sites in the area, including several *kofun*. Although most of the explanations are in Japanese, there's enough English to give you an idea of what's going on. However, if you want to get the most out of the museum, bring a Japanese friend to explain things. Foreigners can enter free, but you'll need your passport to take advantage of this great deal.

To get there from Kashihara-jingū, walk out the northern gate of the shrine (to your left when you stand with your back to the main hall), follow the wooded avenue for five minutes, cross the main road and continue on in the same direction for 100m before turning left at the first intersection. It's on the left soon after this turn. Note that it's not well marked in English (look for a sign reading 'The Museum, Archeological Institute of Kashihara, Nara Prefecture').

Asuka 飛鳥

☑0744 / POP 6141
The Yamato Plain in central Nara-ken is where the forerunners of Japan's ruling Yamato dynasty cemented their grip on power. In these pre-Buddhist days, huge earthen burial mounds were used to entomb deceased emperors. Some of the best examples of these burial mounds, or *kofun*, can be found around the town of Asuka, an hour or so south of Nara on the Kintetsu line.

There's a **tourist information office** (☎54-3624; ⊙8.30am-5pm, closed New Year holidays) outside Asuka Station, but it didn't stock any useful maps the last time we were there. The best way to explore the area is by bicycle. **Manyō Rent-a-Cycle** (レンタサイクル万葉) rents bikes for ¥300 an hour or ¥900 a day. Manyō is across the street from the station, and also stocks a useful English map of the area.

Two tombs worth seeing are **Takamatsuzuka-kofun** (高松塚古墳) and **Ishibutai-kofun** (石舞台古墳; admission ¥250; ⊙8.30am-5pm). Takamatsuzuka-kofun, which looks like a grassy mound, is located in a pleasant wooded park that you can explore on foot or by bicycle. Ishibutai-kofun, which is composed of vast rocks in an open area, is said to have housed the remains of Soga no Umako but is now completely empty.

If you have time, take a look at **Asuka-dera** (飛鳥寺; admission ¥350; ⊙9am-5.15pm Apr-Sep, to 4.45pm Oct-Mar), which dates from 596 and is considered the first true temple in all of Japan. Housed within is the oldest remaining image of Buddha in Japan – it looks pretty good considering it's been around for more than 1300 years.

If you'd like a bite to eat while in Asuka, try **Café Rest Ashibi** (あしびの郷; ☎0742-26-6662; meals from ¥1000; ⊙10am-6pm). The *yaki curry* (baked curry; ¥1000) is a tasty dish (vegetarians should note that it contains meat). To get there, exit the station and follow the canal to the right for about 150m.

Asuka is five stops south of Yamato-Yagi (change at Kashihara-jingū-mae) and two south of Kashihara-jingū-mae on the Kintetsu Yoshino line (¥220 from Yamato-Yagi, 10 minutes; *tokkyū* trains stop at Asuka).

Around Sakurai 桜井周辺

There are a few interesting places to visit close to the town of Sakurai, which can be reached directly from Nara on the JR Nara/Sakurai line (*futsū*, ¥320, 30 minutes). To reach Sakurai via Yamato-Yagi (when coming from Kyoto or Osaka), take the Kintetsu Osaka line from Yamato-Yagi (*junkyū*, ¥200, seven minutes).

⊙ Sights

Tanzan-jinja SHRINE
(談山神社; admission ¥500; ⊙8.30am-4.30pm) South of Sakurai, this shrine can be reached by Sakurai City Community Bus from stand 1 outside the southern exit of Sakurai Station (¥480, 25 minutes). Enshrined here is Nakatomi no Kamatari, patriarch of the Fujiwara line, which effectively ruled Japan for nearly 500 years. Legend has it that Nakatomi met here secretly with Prince Naka no Ōe over games of kickball to discuss the overthrow of the ruling Soga clan. This event is commemorated on the second Sunday in November by priests playing a game of kickball.

The central structure of the shrine is an attractive 13-storey pagoda, best viewed against a backdrop of maple trees ablaze with autumn colours (November and early December).

Hase-dera TEMPLE
(長谷寺; admission ¥500; ⊙8.30am-5pm Apr-Sep, 9am-4.30pm Oct-Mar) Two stops east of Sakurai on the Kintetsu Osaka line is Hasedera Station (¥200, six minutes). From the station, it's a 20-minute walk to lovely Hase-dera. After a long climb up seemingly endless steps, you enter the main hall and are rewarded with a splendid view from the gallery, which juts out on stilts over the mountainside. Inside the top hall, the huge Kannon image is well worth a look. The best times to visit this temple are in the spring, when the way is lined with blooming peonies, and in autumn, when the temple's maple trees turn a vivid red. From the station, walk down through the archway, cross the river and turn right onto the main street that leads to the temple.

Murō-ji TEMPLE
(室生寺; admission ¥600; ⊙8.30am-4.30pm, to 4pm Dec-Feb) Founded in the 9th century, this temple has strong connections with Esoteric Buddhism (the Shingon sect). Women were never excluded from Murō-ji as they were from other Shingon temples, and it is for this reason that it came to be known as 'the Woman's Koya'. Unfortunately, the temple's lovely five-storey pagoda, which dates from the 8th or 9th century, was severely damaged in a typhoon in the summer of 1999. The newly rebuilt pagoda lacks some of the rustic charm of the old one. Nonetheless, Murō-ji is a secluded place in thick forest and is well worth a visit.

After visiting the main hall, walk up to the pagoda and then continue on behind the pagoda in the direction of **Oku-no-in**, a temple hall located at the top of a very steep flight of steps. If you don't feel like making the climb, at least go about 100m past the pagoda to see the mammoth cedar tree growing over a huge rock here.

To get there from Sakurai, take the Kintetsu Osaka line from Sakurai to Murōguchi-ōno Station (*kyūkō*, ¥340, 16 minutes). Then switch to a bus to Murō-ji (bus 43, ¥420, 15 minutes). In spring, there is a direct bus between Hase-dera and Murō-ji (¥830, end of April to early May, one or two buses per hour between 11am and 3pm).

Yoshino 吉野

☑ 0746 / POP 9053

Yoshino is Japan's top cherry-blossom destination. For a few weeks in early to mid-April, the blossoms of thousands of cherry trees form a floral carpet gradually ascending the mountainsides. It's definitely a sight worth seeing, but the narrow streets of the village become jammed tight with thousands of visitors at this time, and you'll have to be content with a day trip unless you've booked accommodation long in advance. Once the cherry-blossom petals fall, the crowds depart and Yoshino reverts to a sleepy village with a handful of shrines and a couple of temples to entertain day trippers.

◉ Sights

Kimpusen-ji TEMPLE
(金峯山寺; admission ¥400; ⊙8.30am-4.30pm, enter by 4pm) Walk about 400m uphill from the cable-car station and you will come to the stone steps leading to the Niō-mon gate of the temple. Check out the fearsome **Kongō Rikishi** (guardian figure statues) in the gate and then continue on to the massive **Zaō-dō Hall** of the temple. Said to be the second-largest wooden building in Japan, the hall is most interesting for its unfinished wooden columns. For many centuries Kimpusen-ji has been one of the major centres for Shugendō, and pilgrims have often stopped here to pray for good fortune on the journey to Ōmine-san.

Yoshimizu-jinja SHRINE
(吉水神社) Continuing another 300m up the street brings you to a side road to the left (the first turn past the post office) that leads to this small shrine that has a good view back to Kimpusen-ji and the *hito-me-sen-bon* (1000 trees in a glance) viewpoint.

The shrine has played host to several important historical figures. Minamoto Yoshitsune, a legendary swordsman and

general, fled here after incurring the wrath of his brother, the first Kamakura shōgun. Emperor Go-Daigo set up a rival southern court in Yoshino after a dispute for succession broke out in Kyoto, and stayed here while his palace was being built. The shrine displays a collection of scrolls, armour and painted murals from the emperor's stay (admission ¥400). It also entertained Toyotomi Hideyoshi and his 5000-person *hanami* party in 1594.

Nyoirin-ji TEMPLE
(如意輪時; admission ¥400;⊙9am-4pm) Take the left fork on the road just above Yoshimizu-jinja and the dilapidated **Katte-jinja** (勝手神社) shrine to reach Nyoirin-ji, a temple that preserves both the relics of Emperor Go-Daigo's unlucky court and his tomb itself.

The right fork leads uphill, where you will soon pass the two recommended accommodation options here, **Kizō-in** (喜蔵院) on your left and then **Chikurin-in** (竹林院) on the right, which has a wonderful garden.

A few minutes' walk further on there is another fork, where you'll find a wooden torii and some steps leading up to a shrine. Take the left fork and the next right up the hill for the 3km hike to **Kimpu-jinja** (金峯神社), a small shrine in a pleasantly wooded mountain setting.

⌑ Sleeping

Yoshino-yama Kizō-in SHUKUBŌ $
(吉野山喜蔵院; ☑ 32-3014; per person with 2 meals ¥10,000; ⊙Mar-Dec) Kizō-in temple doubles as the local youth hostel and is the cheapest option in town. It's a pleasant place to stay, and several of the hostel's rooms look out across the valley.

Chikurin-in Gumpōen RYOKAN $$$
(竹林院群芳園; ☑ 32-8081; www.chikurin.co.jp /e/home.htm; r per person with 2 meals ¥13,650-31,500, without bathroom ¥12,600-21,000;@) Not far past Kizō-in, on the opposite side of the street, this is an exquisite temple that now operates primarily as a ryokan. Both present and previous emperors have stayed here, and a look at the view afforded by some of the rooms explains why. Reservations are essential for the cherry-blossom season, and a good idea at all other times. Even if you don't plan to stay at the temple, you should at least visit its splendid garden (admission ¥300).

✕ Eating

Hōkon-an
CAFE **$**

(芳魂庵; ☎32-8207; ⊙9am-5.30pm) This is an atmospheric little teahouse, where you can sip your tea while enjoying a lovely view over the valley. The *matcha* (¥650) comes with a homemade Japanese sweet. Look for the rustic wooden facade and large ceramic urn on the left, just past the post office. Hours are irregular but it's open daily in April.

Nakai Shunpūdō
SHOKUDŌ **$**

(中井春風堂; ☎32-3043; ⊙9am-5pm) With a limited picture menu, this restaurant serves a *kamameshi teishoku* (rice cooked in an iron pot; ¥1500) and other typical lunch favourites; the view from the windows is great. It's about 5m past the information office, on the opposite side – look for the ceramic *tanuki* (Japanese raccoon dog) figure out front.

Nishizawaya
SHOKUDŌ **$**

(西澤屋; ☎32-8600; ⊙9am-5pm; 🅿) Run by a bunch of friendly ladies, this homey restaurant serves a *shizuka gozen* set, which includes a broiled *ayu* (sweetfish) and a small hotpot filled with vegetables and tofu (¥1500). It's directly across the street from Katte-jinja; look for the plastic food on display.

❶ Information

Yoshinoyama Visitor Centre (☎32-3081/8014; ⊙9am-5pm Tue-Sun, closed Jan, Feb & day following national holidays) is about 500m up the main street from the top cable-car station, on your right just after Kimpusen-ji (look for the large tan-and-white building). It can help with *minshuku* (guesthouse) bookings if necessary.

❶ Getting There & Away

Visitors to Yoshino first arrive at Yoshino Station, and then make their way up to the village proper by cable car or on foot. The cable car costs ¥350/600 one way/return. The walk takes about 15 minutes; follow the path that leaves from beside the cable-car station. Note that the cable car stops running at 5pm – plan your day accordingly or you'll have to walk down.

To get to Yoshino Station from Kyoto or Nara, take the Kintetsu Nara Kashihara line to Kashihara-jingū-mae (*kyūkō* from Kyoto, ¥860, 66 minutes; *kyūkō* from Nara, ¥480, 36 minutes) and change to the Kintetsu Yoshino line (*kyūkō*, ¥460, 52 minutes; *tokkyū* ¥960, 39 minutes).

You can take a direct train on the Kintetsu Minami Osaka–Yoshino line from Osaka (Abenobashi Station, close to Tennō-ji Station) to Yoshino (*kyūkō* ¥950, 89 minutes; *tokkyū* ¥1450, 75 minutes).

The closest JR station to Yoshino is Yoshino-guchi, which has connections with Nara, Osaka and Wakayama. From there, you'll have to take the private Kintetsu line (*kyūkō* ¥370, 35 minutes; *tokkyū* ¥870, 26 minutes).

KII PENINSULA

The remote and mountainous Kii Peninsula (紀伊半島; Kii-hantō) is a far cry from central Kansai's bustling urban sprawl. Most of the attractions are found in Wakayama-ken, including the mountaintop temple complex of Kōya-san, one of Japan's most important Buddhist centres. To the south, the ancient pilgrimage trails of the Kumano Kodō converge on the town of Hongū, which is also home to several fine onsen.

Other Wakayama-ken attractions include the beachside onsen resort of Shirahama, on the west coast of the peninsula, and the rugged coastline of Shiono-misaki and Kii-Ōshima, at the southern tip of the peninsula.

The JR Kii main line (Kinokuni line) runs around the coast of the Kii-hantō, linking Shin-Osaka and Nagoya stations (some trains originate/terminate at Kyoto Station). Special Kuroshio and Nankii *tokkyū* trains can get you around the peninsula fairly quickly, but once you step off these express trains you're at the mercy of slow local trains and buses, so plan accordingly. For this reason, renting a car is a good option for exploring this area.

Kōya-san
高野山

☎0736 / POP 3840

Kōya-san is a raised tableland in northern Wakayama-ken covered with thick forests and surrounded by eight peaks. The major attraction here is the Kōya-san monastic complex, which is the headquarters of the Shingon school of Esoteric Buddhism. Though not quite the Shangri-la it's occasionally described as, Kōya-san is one of the most rewarding places to visit in Kansai, not just for the natural setting of the area but also as an opportunity to stay in temples and get a glimpse of long-held traditions of Japanese religious life.

Although it is just possible to visit Kōya-san as a day trip from Nara, Kyoto or Osaka, it's *much* better to reduce the travel stress and stay overnight in one of the town's excellent *shukubō* (temple lodgings). Keep in mind that Kōya-san tends to be around 5°C

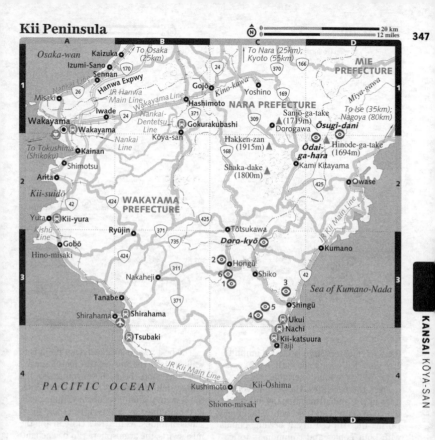

colder than down on the plains, so bring warm clothes if you're visiting in winter, spring or autumn.

Whenever you go, you'll find that getting there is half the fun – near the end of its journey, the train winds through a series of tight valleys with mountains soaring on all sides, and the final vertiginous cable-car leg is not for the faint of heart.

History

The founder of the Shingon school of Esoteric Buddhism, Kūkai (known after his death as Kōbō Daishi), established a religious community here in 816. Kōbō Daishi travelled as a young priest to China and returned after two years to found the school. He is one of Japan's most famous religious figures and is revered as a Bodhisattva, calligrapher, scholar and inventor of the Japanese *kana* syllabary.

Followers of Shingon believe that Kōbō Daishi is not dead, but rather that he is meditating in his tomb in Kōya-san's Oku-

Kii Peninsula

◎ **Sights**

no-in Cemetery, awaiting the arrival of Miroku (Maitreya, the future Buddha). Food is ritually offered in front of the tomb daily to sustain him during this meditation. When Miroku returns, it is thought that only Kōbō Daishi will be able to interpret his heavenly message for humanity. Thus,

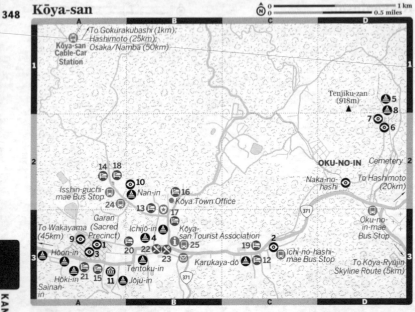

the vast cemetery here is like an amphitheatre crowded with souls gathered in expectation of this heavenly sermon.

Over the centuries, the temple complex grew in size and attracted many followers of the Jōdo (Pure Land) school of Buddhism. During the 11th century, it became popular with both nobles and commoners to leave hair or ashes from deceased relatives close to Kōbō Daishi's tomb.

Kōya-san is now a thriving centre for Japanese Buddhism, with more than 110 temples remaining and a large population. It is the headquarters of the Shingon school, which numbers 10 million members and presides over nearly 4000 temples all over Japan.

◉ Sights

The precincts of Kōya-san are divided into two main areas: the Garan (Sacred Precinct) in the west, where you will find interesting temples and pagodas, and the Oku-no-in, with its vast cemetery, in the east.

TOP CHOICE Oku-no-in   TEMPLE

(奥の院) Any Buddhist worth their salt in Japan has had their remains, or just a lock or two of hair, interred in this cemetery/temple complex to ensure pole position when Miroku Buddha comes to earth.

The best way to approach Oku-no-in is to walk or take the bus east to Ichi-no-hashi-mae bus stop. From here you cross the bridge, **Ichi-no-hashi** (一の橋), and enter the cemetery grounds along a winding, cobbled path lined by tall cedar trees and thousands of tombs. As the trees close in and the mist swirls, the atmosphere can be enchanting, especially as night falls.

At the northern end of the graveyard, you will find the **Tōrō-dō** (燈籠堂; Lantern Hall), which is the main building of the complex. It houses hundreds of lamps, including two believed to have been burning for more than 900 years. Behind the hall you can see the closed doors of the **Kūkai mausoleum** (空海の墓).

On the way to the Lantern Hall is the bridge **Mimyo-no-hashi** (御廟橋). Worshippers ladle water from the river and pour it over the nearby Jizō statues as an offering for the dead. The inscribed wooden plaques in the river are in memory of aborted babies and those who died by drowning.

Between the bridge and the Tōrō-dō is a small wooden building the size of a large phone booth, which contains the **Miroku-ishi** (みろく石). Pilgrims reach through the holes in the wall to try to lift a large, smooth boulder onto a shelf. The weight of the stone

Kōya-san

is supposed to change according to your weight of sin. We can only report that the thing was damn heavy!

Buses return to the centre of town from the Oku-no-mae bus stop, or you can walk back in about 30 minutes.

Kongōbu-ji
TEMPLE

(金剛峯寺; admission ¥500; ⊘8.30am-5pm) This is the headquarters of the Shingon school and the residence of Kōya-san's abbot. The present structure dates from the 19th century and is definitely worth a visit.

The main hall's **Ohiro-ma room** has ornate screens painted by Kanō Tanyu in the 16th century. The **rock garden** is interesting for the sheer number of rocks used in its composition, giving the effect of a throng of petrified worshippers eagerly listening to a monk's sermon.

Admission includes tea and rice cakes served beside the stone garden.

Garan
TEMPLE

(伽藍; admission to each bldg ¥200; ⊘8.30am-5pm) In this temple complex of several halls and pagodas, the most important buildings are the **Dai-tō** (大塔; Great Pagoda) and **Kondō** (金堂; Main Hall). The Dai-tō, rebuilt in 1934 after a fire, is said to be the centre of the lotus-flower mandala formed by the eight mountains around Kōya-san. It's well worth entering the Dai-tō to see the **Dainichi-nyōrai** (Cosmic Buddha) and his four attendant Buddhas. It's been repainted recently and is an awesome sight. The nearby **Sai-tō** (西塔; Western Pagoda) was most recently rebuilt in 1834 and is more subdued.

Treasure Museum
MUSEUM

(霊宝館; Reihōkan; admission ¥600; ⊘8.30am-5.30pm May-Oct, to 5pm Nov-Apr) The Treasure Museum has a compact display of Buddhist works of art, all collected in Kōya-san. There are some very fine statues, painted scrolls and mandalas. Enter 30 minutes before closing.

Tokugawa Mausoleum
MONUMENT

(徳川家霊台; Tokugawa-ke Reidai; admission without joint ticket ¥200; ⊘8.30am-5pm) Built in 1643, the Tokugawa Mausoleum consists of two adjoining structures that serve as the mausoleums of Tokugawa Ieyasu (on the right) and Tokugawa Hidetada (on the left), the first and second Tokugawa shōguns, respectively. They are ornately decorated, as with most structures associated with the Tokugawa shōguns. The mausoleum is not far from the Namikiri-fudō-mae bus stop (波切不動前バス亭).

🎎 Festivals & Events

Aoba Matsuri
TRADITIONAL

Held on 15 June to celebrate the birth of Kōbō Daishi. Various traditional ceremonies are performed at the temples around town.

Rōsoku Matsuri
CANDLES

This more interesting festival is held on 13 August in remembrance of departed souls. Thousands of mourners light candles along the approaches to Oku-no-in.

🛌 Sleeping

More than 50 temples in Kōya-san offer temple lodgings (shukubō). A stay at a shukubō is a good way to try shōjin-ryōri (Buddhist vegetarian cuisine – no meat, fish, onions or garlic). Most shukubō also hold morning prayer sessions, which guests are welcome to join.

Most lodgings *start* at ¥9500 per person including two meals. There is a lot of variation in prices, not just between temples but also within them, depending upon room, meals and season (needless to say, the more you pay, the better will be the room and the meals). Most places ask that you check in by 5pm.

While we list phone numbers for the *shukubō* in this section, most places prefer that you reserve at least a week in advance by fax through the **Kōya-san Tourist Association** (56-2616; fax 56-2889; www.shukubo.jp/eng); the homepage has a form to be used for fax reservations. Even if you contact the temples directly, you will usually be asked to go to the Tourist Association to pick up a reservation slip-voucher. If you prefer to reserve by email, you can call the Tourist Association and request their email address.

Fukuchi-in SHUKUBŌ $$
(福智院; 56-2021; fax 56-4736; r per person with 2 meals from ¥12,600, single travellers ¥15,750; @) This fine temple has outdoor baths with onsen water and a lovely garden designed by the famous designer Shigemori Mirei.

Sōji-in SHUKUBŌ $$
(総持院; 56-2111; fax 56-4311; r per person with 2 meals from ¥15,750, single travellers ¥18,900) At home with foreign guests, this temple has a lovely garden and some rooms with en suite baths. There is one barrier-free room with Western-style beds. The top rooms here are among the best in Kōya-san.

Rengejō-in SHUKUBŌ $$
(蓮華定院; 56-2233; fax 56-4743; r per person with 2 meals from ¥9500, single travellers ¥12,500) This lovely temple has superb rooms, many with garden views, fine painted *fusuma* (sliding doors) and interesting art on display. English is spoken here; sometimes explanation of Buddhist practices and meditation is available.

Ekō-in SHUKUBŌ $$
(恵光院; 56-2514; fax 56-2891; ekoin@mbox .co.jp; r per person with 2 meals from ¥10,000; @) One of the nicer temples in town, Ekō-in is run by a friendly bunch of young monks and the rooms look onto beautiful gardens. This is also one of the two temples in town (the other is Kongōbu-ji) where you can study *zazen* (seated meditation); call ahead to make arrangements for this.

Kōya-san Youth Hostel HOSTEL $
(高野山ユースホステル; 56-3889; fax 56-3889; dm ¥3960; @) This hostel is a friendly and comfortable budget choice if the prices at the temples are out of your range. It's closed for parts of December and January. Call ahead for reservations.

Henjōson-in SHUKUBŌ $$
(遍照尊院; 56-2434; fax 56-3641; r per person with 2 meals from ¥15,750, without bathroom ¥12,600) Nice rooms and communal baths make this a good choice.

Yōchi-in SHUKUBŌ $$
(桜池院; 56-2003; fax 56-3628; r per person with 2 meals from ¥11,000) A simple, friendly and well-located temple.

Haryō-in SHUKUBŌ $$
(巴陵院; 56-2702; fax 56-2936; r per person with 2 meals from ¥6825) This temple is one of the cheaper *shukubō* and functions as a *kokumin-shukusha* (people's lodge).

Muryōkō-in SHUKUBŌ $$
(無量光院; 56-2104; fax 56-4555; r per person with 2 meals ¥9500;) A fine place with an interesting morning Buddhist ceremony.

Shōjōshin-in SHUKUBŌ $$
(清浄心院; 56-2006; fax 56-4770; r per person with 2 meals from ¥9,600 or ¥11,100;) Friendly spot.

Eating

The culinary speciality of Kōya-san is *shōjin-ryōri,* which you can sample at your temple lodgings. If you're just in town for the day, you can try *shōjin-ryōri* at any of the temples that offer *shukubō*. Ask at the Kōya-san Tourist Association office and staff will call ahead to make reservations. Prices are fixed at ¥2700, ¥3700 and ¥5300, depending on how many courses you have. In addition, there are a few *shokudō* around town (but note that most close late in the afternoon).

Maruman SHOKUDŌ $
(丸万; 56-2049; noodle dishes from ¥450; 9am-5pm) This simple *shokudō* is a good spot for lunch (opening hours are irregular, though it's usually closed on Wednesday). All the standard lunch items are represented by plastic food models in the window; *katsudon* (fried pork cutlet over rice) is ¥820. It's just west of the tourist office on the main street – look for the food models in the window. If this is full or doesn't suit, Nankai Shokudō next door is similar.

ℹ Information

A joint ticket (*shodōkyōtsu-naihaiken;* ¥1500) that covers entry to Kongōbu-ji, the Kondō, Daitō, Treasure Museum and Tokugawa Mausoleum can be purchased at the Tourist Association office.

Kōya-san Tourist Association (高野山観光協会; ☑56-2616; fax 56-2889; ⊙Jan & Feb 8.30am-4.30pm, Mar-Jun & Sep-Dec to 5pm, Jul & Aug to 5.45pm) In the centre of town in front of the Senjūin-bashi bus stop (千手院橋バス停), this tourist information centre stocks maps and brochures, and English speakers are usually on hand.

Kōyasan Interpreter Guide Club (☑090-1486-2588/090-3263-5184; www.geocities.jp/koyasan_i_g_c) This club offers four-hour private tours of Kōya-san for ¥5000 per group for groups of up to five people. It also offers regularly scheduled tours on Wednesday from April to September for ¥1000 per person. The morning tour meets at Ichi-no-hashi at 8.30am, lasts three hours and covers Oku-no-in, Garan and Kongōbu-ji. The afternoon tour meets at Kongōbu-ji at 1pm, takes three hours, and covers Kongōbu-ji, Garan and Oku-no-in.

ℹ Getting There & Away

Unless you have a rental car, the best way to reach Kōya-san is by train on the Nankai-Dentetsu line from Osaka's Namba Station. The trains terminate at Gokurakubashi, at the base of the mountain, where you board a funicular railway (five minutes, price included in train tickets) up to Kōya-san itself. From the cable-car station, you take a bus into the centre of town (walking is prohibited on the connecting road).

From Osaka (Namba Station) you can travel directly on a Nankai-Dentetsu line *kyūkō* to Kōya-san (¥1230, one hour and 40 minutes). For the slightly faster *tokkyū* service with reserved seats you need to pay a supplement (¥760). Nankai-Dentetsu offers the Kōya-san World Heritage ticket for ¥3310; this ticket covers entry to the main sites and round-trip *tokkyū* fare from Osaka's Nankai Namba Station.

From Kyoto go via Namba in Osaka (taking the Nankai-Dentetsu line from Namba). Or, if you've got a Japan Rail Pass, take the JR line to Hashimoto, changing at Nara, Sakurai and Takada en route. From Hashimoto, you have no choice but to take the private Nankai-Dentetsu line to Kōya-san (¥1890, 2½ hours).

If you plan to continue on from Kōya-san to Hongū in Wakayama, return to Hashimoto and take the JR line to Gōjō (¥200, 15 minutes), then continue by bus to Hongū (¥3200, four hours).

ℹ Getting Around

Buses run on three routes from the top cable-car station via the centre of town to Ichi-no-hashi and Oku-no-in. The fare to the tourist office in the centre of town at Senjūin-bashi is ¥280. The fare to the final stop, Oku-no-in, is ¥400. An all-day bus pass (*ichi-nichi furee kippu;* ¥800) is available from the bus office outside the top cable-car station, but once you get into the centre of town you can reach most destinations quite easily on foot (including Oku-no-in, which takes about 30 minutes). Note that buses run infrequently, so you should make a note of the schedule before setting out to see the sights.

If you don't feel like walking, bicycles can be rented (per hour/day ¥400/1200) at the Kōyasan Tourist Association office.

Tanabe 田辺

☑0739 / POP 81,522

Tanabe, a small city on the west coast of Wakayama, serves as the main gateway to the Kumano Kodō. It's a friendly place with a very enlightened local government that has made huge efforts to welcome foreign tourists.

Just outside the train station, there's a useful **tourist information office** (☑25-4919) that stocks useful maps of the area as well as a 'gourmet map' that lists local restaurants with English menus.

Miyoshiya Ryokan (美吉屋旅館; ☑0739-22-3448; www.miyoshiya-ryokan.com/english.html; r per person from ¥3200; @) is a simple travellers' ryokan. It is located three minutes' walk from the Kii-Tanabe station. Once you exit the station, turn left at the first traffic signal. Follow this road about 300m and it will be on your right. There is a small English sign near the door

The JR Kii main line connects Shingū with JR Shin-Osaka Station (*tokkyū,* ¥7010, four hours; change at Tennōji) and Shin-Osaka Station (direct *tokkyū,* ¥7010, four hours).

Buses running between Tanabe and Hongū (¥2000, two hours) make a loop of the three surrounding onsen (Watarase, Yunomine and Kawa-yu). These buses also stop at several places, which serve as trailheads for the Kumano Kodō.

Shirahama 白浜

☑0739 / POP 23,506

Shirahama, on the southwest coast of the Kii-hantō, is Kansai's leading beach resort and has all the trappings of a major Japanese tourist attraction – huge resort

KANSAI TANABE

KUMANO KODŌ: JAPAN'S ANCIENT PILGRIMAGE ROUTE

From the earliest times, the Japanese believed the wilds of the Kii Peninsula to be inhabited by *kami*, Shintō deities. When Buddhism swept Japan in the 6th century, these *kami* became *gongen* – manifestations of the Buddha or a Bodhisattva – in a syncretic faith known as *ryōbu*, or 'dual Shintō'.

Japan's early emperors made pilgrimages into the area. The route they followed from Kyoto, via Osaka, Tanabe and over the inner mountains of Wakayama, is known today as the Kumano Kodō: the Kumano Old Road. Over time, the popularity of this pilgrimage spread from nobles to common folk and *yamabushi* priests (wandering mountain ascetics).

In 2004 Unesco declared the Sacred Sites and Pilgrimage Routes in the Kii Mountain Range to be World Heritage sites. Many sections of the route have been restored and there is good accommodation en route, making it possible to perform your own 'pilgrimage' through the mountains of Wakayama.

Most of the routes converge on the town of Hongū, which is home to Hongū Taisha, the most important of the three sacred shrines of the pilgrimage; the other two are Hayatama Taisha in Shingū and Nachi Taisha in Nachi Katsuura. Typical routes involve taking a bus from the town of Tanabe, on the west coast of Wakayama, and walking for two days to Hongū, but many variations and longer/shorter trips are possible.

The **Tanabe City Kumano Tourism Bureau** (www.tb-kumano.jp/en/index.html), one of the most progressive tourism outfits in all Japan, has detailed information and maps on the routes. You can access its English-language accommodation booking site via the homepage, making trip planning a snap.

hotels, aquariums, amusement parks etc. However, it also has several good onsen, a great white-sand beach and rugged coastal scenery.

Because the Japanese like to do things according to the rules – and the rules say the only time you can swim in the ocean is from late July to the end of August – the place is almost deserted outside the peak season. Thus, this is a great place to visit in June or September, and we've swum in the sea here as late as mid-October.

There's a **tourist information office** (☑42-2900; ☺9.30am-6pm) in the station, where you can pick up a map to the main sights and accommodation. Since the station is a fair distance from the main sights, you'll need to take a bus (one way/all-day pass ¥330/1000, 15 minutes to the beach) or rent a bicycle if you arrive by rail. The JR office at the station rents bicycles (¥500 per day); unfortunately, no one would describe these as performance vehicles.

🔘 Sights & Activities

Shirara-hama   BEACH
(白良浜) Shirara-hama, the town's main beach, is famous for its white sand. If it reminds you of Australia, don't be surprised – the town had to import sand from Down Under after the original stuff washed away. This place is packed during July and August,

but in the low season it can actually be quite pleasant. The beach is hard to miss, as it dominates the western side of town.

Onsen
In addition to its great beach, Shirahama has some of Japan's oldest developed onsen (they're even mentioned in the *Nihon Shoki*, one of Japan's earliest literary texts).

Shirasuna-yu   ONSEN
(しらすな湯; 864 Shirahama-chō, Nishimuro-gun; admission May-Sep ¥100, Oct-Apr free; ☺10am-3pm, to 7pm Jul-15 Sep) An open-air onsen off the boardwalk in the middle of Shirara-hama. You can soak here and then dash into the ocean to cool off – not a bad way to spend an afternoon.

Sakino-yu Onsen   ONSEN
(崎の湯温泉; 1688 Shirahama-chō, Nishimuro-gun; admission ¥300; ☺8am-5pm, enter by 4.30pm, closed Wed) A fantastic bath built on a rocky point with great views of the Pacific Ocean (and you can climb down the rocks to cool off if the waves aren't too big). Come early in the day to beat the crowds. It's 1km south of the main beach; walk along the seafront road and look for the point below the big Hotel Seymor.

Shirara-yu   ONSEN
(白良湯; 3313-1 Shirahama-chō, Nishimuro-gun; admission ¥300; ☺7am-11pm Wed-Mon, noon-

11pm Tue, enter by 10.30pm) A pleasant bath right on the north end of Shirara-hama (the main beach).

Murono-yu ONSEN
(牟婁の湯; 1665 Shirahama-chō, Nishimuro-gun; admission ¥300; ⊘noon-11pm Thu, 7am-11pm Fri-Wed) A simple onsen in front of Shirahama post office, on the way to the Sakino-yu Onsen.

Coastal Scenery
Just around the point south of the Sakino-yu Onsen are two of Shirahama's natural wonders. **Senjō-jiki** (千畳敷; Thousand Tatami Mat Point) is a wildly eroded point with stratified layers that actually resemble the thousand tatami mats it is named for.

More impressive is the 50m cliff face of **Sandan-heki** (三段壁; Three-Step Cliff), which drops away vertiginously into the sea. While you can pay ¥1200 to take a lift down to a cave at the base of the cliff, it's better simply to clamber along the rocks to the north of the cliff – it's stunning, particularly when the big rollers are pounding in from the Pacific.

If you'd like to enjoy more rugged coastal scenery, walk south along the coast another 1km from Sandan-heki to **Isogi-kōen** (いそぎ公園), where the crowds are likely to be thinner and the scenery just as impressive.

These natural attractions can be reached on foot or bicycle from the main beach in around 30 minutes, or you can take a bus from the station (¥430, 20 minutes to Senjō-jiki, bus stop 'Senjō-guchi'), from which you can walk to the others.

🛏 Sleeping

Minshuku Katsuya MINSHUKU $
(民宿かつ屋; ☑42-3814; fax 42-3817; 3118-5 Shirahama-chō, Nishimuro-gun; r per person without meals ¥3500) Katsuya is the best-value *minshuku* in town and it's very central, only two minutes' walk from the main beach. It's built around a small Japanese garden and has its own natural onsen bath. There is red-and-white Japanese writing on the building and faint English on a small sign.

Kokumin-shukusha Hotel
Shirahama GUESTHOUSE $
(国民宿舎ホテルシラハマ; ☑42-3039; fax 42-4643; 813 Shirahama-chō, Nishimuro-gun; r per person with 2 meals ¥6900) This is a good bet if Katsuya is full, and offers similar rates. It's a little dark and showing its age, but the rooms are spacious and there is an onsen

bath. It's just off Miyuki-dōri, 100m past the post office towards the beach (look for a parking lot and the black, blue, red and white sign). The tourist information office at the station has maps.

Hotel Ginsui HOTEL $$
(ホテル銀翠; ☑42-3316; fax 43-1301; Hama dōri, Shirahama-chō, Nishimuro-gun; s/d/tw from ¥6300/9450/11,550; @🕾) If you'd prefer a hotel, this is a very reasonable choice within easy walking distance of the beach. It's got everything you need and the staff are efficient. Considering the location, it's a good deal.

🍴 Eating
There are many restaurants in the streets just in from the beach. If you'd like to self-cater, Sakae Supermarket is five minutes' walk from the main beach.

Kiraku SHOKUDŌ $
(喜楽; ☑42-3916; 890-48 Shirahama-chō, Nishimuro-gun; ⊘11am-2pm & 4-9pm, closed Tue) There is nothing fancy about this friendly little *shokudō* that serves standard *teishoku* for around ¥1200. There is a limited picture menu to help with ordering. It's about 5m in from Miyuki-dōri, on the beach side, close to a coin laundry (look for the plants out the front).

ℹ Getting There & Away
Shirahama is on the JR Kii main line. There are *tokkyū* trains from Shin-Osaka Station (¥5450, two hours and 12 minutes). There also *futsū* trains on the same line (¥3260, 5½ hours). The same line also connects Shirahama to other cities on Kii-hantō such as Kushimoto, Nachi, Shingū and Wakayama city. A cheaper alternative is offered by **Meikō Bus** (www13.ocn .ne.jp/~meikobus, in Japanese; ⊘9am-6pm), which runs buses between JR Osaka Station and Shirahama (one way/return ¥2700/5000, about 3½ to four hours).

Kushimoto, Shiono-misaki & Kii-Ōshima
串本・潮岬・紀伊大島

☑0735

The southern tip of Kii Peninsula has some stunning coastal scenery. Shiono-misaki, connected to the mainland by a narrow isthmus, has some fine rocky vistas, but the real action is over on Kii-Ōshima, a rocky island accessible by bridge.

The main attraction on Kii-Ōshima is the coastal cliffs at the eastern end of the island, which can be viewed from the park around **Kashino-zaki Lighthouse** (樫野崎灯台). Just before the park, you'll find the **Toruko-Kinenkan Museum** (トルコ記念館; 1025-25 Kashino, Kushimoto-chō, Higashimuro-gun; admission ¥250; ☉9am-5pm), which commemorates the sinking of the Turkish ship *Ertugrul* in 1890.

Backtracking about 1km towards the bridge, there are small English signs to the **Japan–US Memorial Museum** (日米修交記念館; 1033 Kashino, Kushimoto-chō, Nishimuro-gun; admission ¥250; ☉9am-5pm), which commemorates the visit of the US ship *Lady Washington* in 1791, a full 62 years before Commodore Perry's much more famous landing in Yokohama in 1853. There is a lookout just beyond the museum from which you can see the magnificent **Umi-kongō** (海金剛) formations along the eastern point of the island.

If you're without your own transport, the best way to explore Kii-Ōshima is by renting a bicycle at Kushimoto Station (per four hours/full day ¥600/1000), but be warned that there are a few big hills en route and these bikes are better suited to shopping than cruising. Otherwise, there are buses from the station, but take note of schedules, as departures are few and far between.

Misaki Lodge Youth Hostel (みさきロッジジュースホステル; ☎62-1474; fax 62-0529; 2864-1 Shionomisaki, Kushimoto-chō; per person dm without meals/minshuku with 2 meals from ¥4500/7350) is the best place to stay in the area. It's on the southern side of the cape overlooking the Pacific. Take a Shionomisaki-bound bus from Kushimoto Station (20 minutes) and get off at Koroshio-mae.

Kushimoto is one hour from Shirahama by JR *tokkyū*, and 3½ hours (¥6280) from Shin-Osaka. *Futsū* services are significantly cheaper but take almost twice as long.

Nachi & Kii-Katsuura 那智・紀伊勝浦

The Nachi and Kii-Katsuura area has several sights grouped around the sacred **Nachi-no-taki** (那智の滝), Japan's highest waterfall (133m). **Nachi Taisha** (那智大社), near the waterfall, was built in homage to the waterfall's *kami* (Shintō spirit god). It is one of the three great shrines of Kii-hantō, and worth the climb up the steep steps to get there. Next to the shrine, **Sanseiganto-ji** (山青岸渡寺) is a fine old temple.

The most atmospheric approach to the falls and the shrine is the fantastic tree-lined arcade of **Daimon-zaka**. To get to Daimon-zaka, take a bus from Nachi or Kii-Katsuura Station and get off at the Daimon-zaka stop (ask the bus driver to drop you at Daimon-zaka and he'll point you in the right direction from the stop). The way isn't marked in English, but it's roughly straight uphill just in from the road. From the bus stop to the shrine is roughly 800m, most of it uphill. It's fine in winter, but in summer you'll get soaked, so consider doing it in reverse (check bus schedules carefully before setting out).

Daimon-zaka takes you up to the steps at the base of the shrine. After visiting the shrine, walk down to the falls. At the base of the falls is **Nachiyama-oku-no-in** (那智山奥の院), where you can pay ¥200 to hike up to a lookout with a better view of the falls.

The **Nachi-no-Hi Matsuri** (Fire Festival) takes place at the falls on 14 July. During this lively event, *mikoshi* are brought down from the mountain and met by groups bearing flaming torches.

Buses to the waterfall and shrine leave from Nachi Station (¥470, 17 minutes) and from Kii-Katsuura Station (¥600, 25 minutes). Buses to the Daimon-zaka stop leave from Nachi Station (¥330, 11 minutes) and from Kii-Katsuura Station (¥410, 19 minutes).

ⓘ Getting There & Away

Nachi and Kii-Katsuura (the stations are only two stops apart) can be reached by JR Kii main-line trains from Shin-Osaka Station (*tokkyū*, ¥6700, three hours and 45 minutes; *futsū*, ¥4310, six hours excluding transit times) and from Nagoya Station (*tokkyū*, ¥7510, three hours and 40 minutes; *futsū*, ¥3920, 5½ hours excluding transit times). *Futsū* are significantly cheaper but take almost twice as long.

Shingū 新宮

☎0735 / POP 32,479

The small city of Shingū, on the east coast of Wakayama, functions as a useful transport hub for access to the Kumano Kodō pilgrimage route and the onsen village of Hongū. There's a helpful **information office** (☎22-2840; ☉9am-5.30pm) at the station.

A two-minute walk north of the station, **Hase Ryokan** (長谷旅館; ☎22-2185; fax 21-6677; r per person with 2 meals from ¥6300; @) is a comfortable and reasonable choice. Call from the station and someone will collect you, or ask at the information office for a map.

The JR Kii main line connects Shingū with Nagoya Station (*tokkyū*, ¥7190, three to 3½ hours) and Shin-Osaka Station (*tokkyū*, ¥7010, four hours).

There are buses between Shingū and Hongū, about half of which make a loop of the three surrounding onsen (Watarase, Yunomine and Kawa-yu).

Hongū 本宮

Hongū is a good starting point for the onsen nearby. The **Kumano Hongu Heritage Centre** (◷9am-5pm) has detailed information in English about the sacred Kumano region. Hongū is also home to **Kumano Hongū Taisha** (熊野本宮大社), one of the three famous shrines of the Kumano Sanzan. The shrine is close to the Hongū Taishamae bus stop (the buses listed in this section stop there).

Blue Sky Guesthouse (蒼空げすとはうす; ☑42-0800; www.kumano-guesthouse.com/eng.html; 1526 Hongū, Hongū-chō; r per person from ¥6000 incl breakfast; ☎) is an excellent new guesthouse with clean, comfortable rooms a short walk from the Hongū information centre. Follow the main highway 10 minutes to the south end of town and there are signs in English pointing the way.

Buses leave for Hongū from JR Gojō Station and Kintetsu Yamato-Yagi Station in the south (¥4000, five hours), Kii-Tanabe in the west (¥2000, two hours) and Shingū in the

KANSAI HONGŪ

LOCAL KNOWLEDGE

BRAD TOWLE ON THE KUMANO KODŌ

'A pilgrimage to Kumano is like copulating with the universe,' or so says my boss. For people looking for an off-the-beaten-path destination in a natural environment – a place to slow down, relax and experience the spiritual countryside of Japan – the enigmatic Kumano region might be for you. And don't forget the great isolated onsen, delicious authentic cuisine and friendly locals!

I first came to this isolated sacred region in 1999 to teach English in the small village of Hongū. I couldn't speak Japanese and knew nothing of the rich spiritual history around me, but I could feel something special...and over 10 years later, I am still here! I am now responsible for grassroots tourism development in Tanabe City, a challenging and rewarding job, and I'm still trying to decipher all of the complexities and symbolism of this sacred place.

The Kumano faith is based on prehistoric forms of nature worship – I guess that's where the cosmic sex comes in! – and over the centuries has mixed with other religions, such as Buddhism. The focal points of worship are the Hongū Taisha, Hayatama Taisha and Nachi Taisha 'grand shrines', which are connected via the Kumano Kodo pilgrimage routes. I like the fact that the Kumano faith is not defined or standardised, and is open to reinterpretation by those who visit; it's a universal sacred site.

The best way to visit Kumano would probably be to follow the general flow of pilgrims from the 9th century – how could over 1000 years of pilgrimage tradition be wrong? Find your way down the west coast of the Kii-hantō peninsula from Kyoto or Osaka to Tanabe (or travel through Kōya-san). Tanabe has some great *izakaya* pubs. From here, head into the mountainous Hongū area. Following the pilgrimage route from Hosshinmon-oji to Kumano Hongū Taisha is a great half-day walk. There are some excellent onsen in Hongū, including Yunomine and Kawa-yu, and many visitors spend a few nights here.

You can then travel along the Kumano-gawa to Shingū and Hayatama Taisha (there is also a lovely boat trip offered part-way), and then onto Nachi Taisha to see Japan's highest waterfall, the awe-inspiring Nachi Falls. Don't miss the Daimon-zaka Slope staircase! You can complete your visit by soaking in another onsen bath in Katsuura to contemplate your experiences.

A couple of words of advice: travel responsibly, respect the locals' faith, take your time, and open your mind. One last thing: be careful, the universe might try to make some moves on you!

Brad Towle is the International Tourism Promotion & Development Director for the Tanabe City Kumano Tourism Bureau

southeast (¥1500, 60 to 80 minutes), which has the most departures of these three access points. Most Hongū buses also stop at Kawa-yu, Watarase and Yunomine onsen (in that order), but be sure to ask before boarding. Keep in mind that departures are few in any direction.

Needless to say, since bus departures are limited, exploring the area by rental car is a good idea. Renting a car at Tanabe, Shirahama or Wakayama City and heading inland is the normal route, but you can also start further north and go via Kōya-san.

Yunomine, Watarase & Kawa-yu Onsen

These three onsen are among the best in all of Kansai. Because each has its own distinct character, it's worth doing a circuit of all three. There are several ryokan and *minshuku* in the area, but if you are on a tight budget it's possible to camp on the riverbanks above and below Kumano Hongū Taisha. See Hongū for transport details.

Note that you can walk between the three onsen in this section relatively easily. The tunnel at the west end of the village at Kawa-yu connects to Watarase Onsen (the total journey is a little less than 1km). From Watarase Onsen, it's about 3km west along Rte 311 to reach Yunomine.

YUNOMINE ONSEN   湯峰温泉

The town of Yunomine is nestled around a narrow river in a wooded valley. Most of the town's onsen are contained inside ryokan or *minshuku* but charming little **Tsubo-yu Onsen** (つぼ湯温泉; admission ¥750; ☺6am-9.30pm, enter by 9pm) is open to all. It's right in the middle of town, inside a tiny wooden shack built on an island in the river. Buy a ticket at the *sentō* next to **Tōkō-ji** (東光寺), the temple in the middle of town. The *sentō* itself is open the same hours as the onsen and entry is ¥250; of the two baths at the *sentō*, we suggest the *kusuri-yu* (medicine water; ¥380), which is 100% pure hot-spring water.

🛏 Sleeping

Yunomine has plenty of *minshuku* and ryokan for you to choose from.

Minshuku Yunotanisō   MINSHUKU $$
(民宿湯の谷荘; ☎0735-42-1620; r per person with 2 meals ¥8000) At the upper end of the

village, this *minshuku* is exactly what a *minshuku* should be: simple, clean and welcoming. The food is very good and there's an excellent onsen bath on the premises.

Ryokan Yoshino-ya   RYOKAN $$
(旅館よしの や; ☎0735-42-0101; r per person with 2 meals from ¥8970) Located very close to Tsubo-yu, this is a slightly more upscale place with a lovely *rotemburo* (outdoor bath). It's fairly new and the location can't be beat. Like Yunotanisō, it's a friendly and well-run spot.

KAWA-YU ONSEN   川湯温泉

Kawa-yu Onsen is a natural wonder, where geothermally heated water percolates up through the gravel banks of the river that runs through the middle of the town. You can make your own private bath here by digging out some of the stones and letting the hole fill with hot water; you can then spend the rest of the day jumping back and forth between the bath and the cool waters of the river. Admission is free and the best spots along the river are in front of Fujiya ryokan. We suggest bringing a bathing suit unless you fancy putting on a 'naked *gaijin*' show for the whole town.

In the winter, from November to 28 February, bulldozers are used to turn the river into a giant *rotemburo*. Known as the **Sen-nin Buro** (仙人風呂; admission free; ☺6.30am-10pm), the name is a play on the word for 'thousand', a reference to the fact that you could just about squeeze 1000 bathers into this open-air tub.

🛏 Sleeping

Pension Ashita-no-Mori   HOTEL $$
(ペンションあしたの森; ☎0735-42-1525; ashitanomori-kawayu@za.ztv.ne.jp; fax 0735-42-1333; r per person with 2 meals from ¥10,650) This hotel is in a pleasant wooden building with a good riverside location. Rooms are adequate in size and well maintained. It has its own private onsen bath, and inside baths are onsen as well.

TOP CHOICE Fujiya   RYOKAN $$
(富士屋; ☎0735-42-0007; www.fuziya.co.jp/english/index.html; fax 0735-42-1115; r per person with 2 meals from ¥15,900; 🖥) Next door, this is a more upmarket ryokan with tasteful rooms: spacious, clean and tastefully decorated. For a very civilised place to stay after a day in the river baths, this is the spot. Needless to say, it's got its own private onsen bath as well.

WATARASE ONSEN わたらせ温泉

This **onsen** (admission ¥700; ⏰6am-10pm, entry by 9.30pm) is built around a bend in the river directly between Yunomine Onsen and Kawa-yu Onsen. It's not as interesting as its neighbours, but does boast a nice collection of *rotemburo*. Baths get progressively cooler as you work your way out from the inside bath.

ISE

♪0596 / POP 133,788

The Ise (伊勢) region, on Mie Prefecture's Shima Peninsula, is famous for Ise-jingū, Japan's most sacred Shintō shrine. The shrine is in Ise-shi, the main city of the region. Although Ise-shi is rather drab, it's worth making the trip to visit the spectacular shrine, arguably Japan's most impressive. Its only rival is Nikkō's Tōshō-gū, which is as gaudy as Ise-jingū is austere. Ise is also home to a lovely traditional street, Kawasaki Kaiwai.

Ise is easily reached from Nagoya, Kyoto or Osaka and makes a good two-day trip from any of these cities (you can even do it as a day trip from these cities if you take Kintetsu express trains). If you're wondering about how to pronounce Ise, it sounds like 'ee-say'.

⊙ Sights & Activities

If you have some time to kill in town before or after visiting the shrines, take a stroll down atmospheric **Kawasaki Kaiwai** (河崎界隈), a street lined with traditional Japanese houses and shops. It's a little tricky to find: start at the Ise Pearl Pier Hotel, cross the street, go down the side street that runs next to and behind Eddy's Supermarket (yes, that's the name), and take a left down the street 50m before the canal; Kawasaki Kaiwai parallels this canal, on its west side (but it's not the street that runs right along its banks – it's the one before that). The atmospheric old buildings begin about 200m north of where you turn left.

Ise-shima

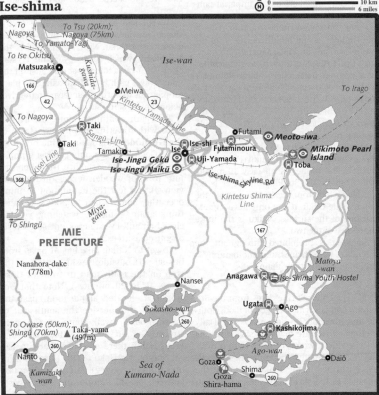

FREE Ise-jingū

SHRINE

(伊勢神宮; ☉sunrise-sunset) Dating back to the 3rd century, Ise-jingū is the most venerated Shintō shrine in Japan. Shintō tradition has dictated for centuries that the shrine buildings be replaced every 20 years, with exact imitations built on adjacent sites according to ancient techniques – no nails, only wooden dowels and interlocking joints.

Upon completion of the new buildings, the god of the shrine is ritually transferred to its new home in the Sengū No Gi ceremony, first witnessed by Western eyes in 1953. The wood from the old shrine is then used to reconstruct the torii at the shrine's entrance or is sent to shrines around Japan for use in rebuilding their structures. The present buildings were rebuilt in 1993 (for the 61st time) at a cost exceeding ¥5 billion. They'll next be rebuilt in 2013.

You may be surprised to discover that the main shrine buildings are almost completely hidden from view behind wooden fences. Only members of the imperial family and certain shrine priests are allowed to enter the sacred inner sanctum. This is unfortunate, as the buildings are stunning examples of pre-Buddhist Japanese architecture. Don't despair, though, as determined neck craning over fences allows glimpses of the upper parts of buildings (at least if you're tall). You can get a good idea of the shrine's architecture by looking at any of the lesser shrines nearby, which are exact replicas built on a smaller scale.

There are two parts to the shrine, Gekū (外宮; Outer Shrine) and Naikū (内宮; Inner Shrine). The former is an easy 10-minute walk from Ise-shi Station; the latter is accessible by bus from the station or from the stop outside Gekū. If you only have time to visit one of the shrines, Naikū is the more impressive of the two.

Smoking is prohibited throughout the grounds of both shrines, and photography is forbidden around their main halls.

Gekū

(外宮) The Outer Shrine dates from the 5th century and enshrines the god of food, clothing and housing, Toyouke-no-Ōkami. Daily offerings of rice are made by shrine priests to the goddess, who is charged with providing food to Amaterasu-Ōmikami, the goddess enshrined in the Naikū. A stall at the entrance to the shrine provides a leaflet in English with a map.

The main shrine building here is the **Goshōden**, which is about 10 minutes' walk from the entrance to the shrine. Across the river from the Goshōden, you'll find three smaller shrines that are worth a look (and are usually less crowded).

From Ise-shi Station or Uji-Yamada Station it's a 10-minute walk down the main street to the shrine entrance; the shrine is southwest of both stations. Note that it's slightly easier to find if you start from Ise-shi Station (be sure to exit the south side of the station).

Naikū

(内宮) The Inner Shrine is thought to date from the 3rd century and enshrines the sun goddess, Amaterasu-Ōmikami, who is considered the ancestral goddess of the imperial family and the guardian deity of the Japanese nation. Naikū is held in even higher reverence than Gekū because it houses the sacred mirror of the emperor, one of the three imperial regalia (the other two are the sacred beads and the sacred sword).

A stall just before the entrance to the shrine provides the same English leaflet given out at Gekū. Next to this stall is the **Uji-bashi**, which leads over the crystal-clear Isuzu-gawa into the shrine. Just off the main gravel path is a **Mitarashi**, the place for pilgrims to purify themselves in the river before entering the shrine.

The path continues along an avenue lined with towering cryptomeria trees to the **Goshōden**, the main shrine building. As at Gekū, you can only catch a glimpse of the top of the structure from here, as four rows of wooden fences obstruct the view. If you feel the temptation to jump over the fence when nobody's around, think again – they're watching you on closed-circuit TV cameras not so cleverly disguised as trees!

To get to Naikū, take bus 51 or 55 from bus stop 11 outside Ise-shi Station or the stop on the main road in front of Gekū (¥410, 15 to 20 minutes). Note that bus stop 11 is located about 100m past the main bus stop outside the south exit of Ise-shi Station (walk south on the main street). Get off at the Naikū-mae stop. From Naikū there are buses back to Ise-shi Station via Gekū (¥410, 15 to 20 minutes from bus stop 2). Alternatively, a taxi between Ise-shi Station and Naikū costs about ¥2000.

✨ Festivals & Events

Ise-jingū is Japan's most sacred shrine and it's not surprising that it's a favourite destination for *hatsu-mōde* (first shrine visit of the new year). Most of the action takes place in the first three days of the year, when millions of worshippers pack the area and accommodation is booked out for months in advance.

The **Kagura-sai**, celebrated in early April and mid-September, is a good chance to see performances of *kagura* (sacred dance), *bugaku* dance, nō and Shintō music.

🛏 Sleeping

Hoshide-kan RYOKAN $
(星出館; ☎28-2377; fax 27-2830; 2-15-2 Kawasaki; r per person with/without 2 meals ¥7900/5200; ☻) In Ise-shi, this is a quaint wooden ryokan with some nice traditional touches. Go straight past Ise City Hotel, and it's on the right (there is a small English sign). It's at the second light (400m) past the train tracks. Look for the large traditional building with cedars poking out of tiny gardens.

Asakichi Ryokan RYOKAN $$
(麻吉旅館; ☎22-4101; fax 22-4102; 109 Nakano chō; r per person with 2 meals ¥12,600) Located a short bus or taxi ride outside the city centre, this charming ryokan is a nice place to stay if you want a real Japanese experience. The ryokan is built on a hillside, with rooms at various levels. There's a nice common bath and three rooms have en suite baths. A taxi from the station will cost about ¥1000, or take bus 1 or 2 from stop 2 outside Uji-Yamada Station to Asakichi Ryokan.

Ise Pearl Pier Hotel HOTEL $$
(パールピアホテル; ☎26-1111; www.pearlpier .com; 2-26-22 Miyajiri; s ¥7875-8400, d ¥12,600, tw ¥16,800/18,900; ☻🖵) The Pearl Pier is a good business hotel a short walk from Ise-shi Station. The 'deluxe' rooms may be worth the cash if you've been feeling cramped in business hotels. To get there from Ise-shi Station, take a left (east) outside the station, walk past a JTB travel agency, take a left at the first traffic light, and cross the tracks. You'll see it on the left.

Ise-Shima Youth Hostel HOSTEL $
(伊勢志摩ユースホステル; ☎0599-55-0226; ise@jyh.gr.jp; 1219-82 Anagawa, Isobe-chō, Shima-shi; r per person with breakfast from ¥4620; 🖵) Built on a hill overlooking an attractive bay, this is a great place to stay for budget travel-

lers. It's close to Anagawa Station on the Kintetsu line south of Ise-shi (only *futsū* trains stop). Walk east out of the station along the waterfront road; it's uphill on the right.

🍴 Eating & Drinking

Daiki SHOKUDŌ $$
(大善; ☎28-0281; meals from ¥1500; ⏱11am-9pm; 🖹) Our favourite place to eat in Ise-shi bills itself as 'Japan's most famous restaurant'. It's a great place to sample seafood, including *ise-ebi* (Japanese lobsters), served as set meals for ¥5000; ask for the *ise-ebi teishoku* and specify *yaki* (grilled), *niita* (boiled) or *sashimi* (raw). Simpler meals include tempura *teishoku* (¥1500). It's outside and to the right of Uji-Yamada Station (walk past the Toyota Rentacar lot); there's a small English sign reading 'Kappo Daiki' and 'Royal Family Endorsed'.

Nikōdōshiten JAPANESE $
(二光堂支店; ☎24-4409; 19 Ujiimazaike-chō; ⏱11am-4pm, closed Wed & Thu; 🖹) At Naikū there are plenty of good restaurants in the Okage-yokochō Arcade, just outside the shrine (to find this place, look to your left as you cross Uji-bashi bridge to enter the shrine). In the arcade, Nikōdōshiten is a good place to try some of the local dishes in a rough, roadhouse atmosphere. *Ise-udon* (thick noodles in a dark broth; small/large bowl ¥450/600) is the speciality. For a bigger meal, try the *ume-chiri gohan setto* (*ise-udon* with rice and side dishes; ¥800). The restaurant is 100m up from the southern (shrine) end of the arcade, on the right. There is no English sign; Ichishina, the shop just before it, has an English sign.

Tamaya BAR $
(珠家; ☎24-0105; 2-17-23 Kawasaki; drink/food from ¥600/1000; ⏱7pm-midnight, closed Sun; 🖹) In the Kawasaki Kaiwai district, this excellent bar-restaurant in an old *kura* is a friendly spot for a drink or a light meal. It's just down a narrow street off Kawasaki Kaiwai on the left as you walk north (look for a white-and-red sign on a utility pole that reads 'Tamaya The Lounge').

ℹ Information

Across the street from Naiku (about 10 minutes' walk from Ise-shi Station), **Ise Tourist Information Centre** (伊勢市観光協会; ☎28-3705; ⏱8.30am-5pm) has the useful *Map of Ise* and can answer your questions and help you find accommodation.

ℹ️ Getting There & Away

There are rail connections between Ise-shi and Nagoya, Osaka and Kyoto on both the JR and the Kintetsu lines. If you've got a Japan Rail Pass, the easiest way to get there (even if coming from Kyoto/Osaka) is to take a *shinkansen* to JR Nagoya Station, then switch to a JR *kaisoku* Mie train to Ise-shi Station (¥1940, 90 minutes).

For those travelling without a Japan Rail Pass, the Kintetsu line is by far the most convenient way to go and the *tokkyū* are comfortable and fast. Kintetsu fares and travel times to/from Ise-shi include Nagoya (*tokkyū*, ¥2690, one hour and 20 minutes), Osaka (Uehonmachi or Namba stations, *tokkyū*, ¥3030, one hour and 46 minutes) and Kyoto (*tokkyū*, ¥3520, two hours).

Note that there are two stations in Ise: Ise-shi Station and Uji-Yamada Station, which are only a few hundred metres apart (most trains stop at both). Get off at Ise-shi Station for destinations and accommodation described in this section.

NORTHERN KANSAI

The spectacular coastline of northern Kansai (関西北部) is known for its sandy beaches, rugged headlands, rocky islets and laid-back atmosphere. The JR San-in line runs the length of the area, but it spends a fair bit of time inland and in tunnels. The best way to see the coastline is on wheels, whether it be a rental car, a motorbike, a bicycle or by thumb.

Without a doubt, the best place to base yourself for an exploration of this area is the onsen town of Kinosaki, which is just over two hours from Kyoto by comfortable JR express trains.

Moroyose 諸寄

Moroyose, in Hyōgo-ken, near the border with Tottori-ken, is a pleasant little seaside town with a decent sand beach. **Youth Hostel Moroyose-sō** (諸寄荘ユースホステル; ☏0796-82-3614; 461 Moroyose; r without meals per person ¥3435, in winter ¥3645) is a good spot to stay for backpackers, with fairly large rooms for a YH and breakfast/dinner for ¥600/1000. It's a 10-minute climb uphill from the eastern end of the beach. Moroyose is on the JR San-in line; the station is in the centre of town, very close to the beach.

Takeno 竹野

Takeno is a pleasant little fishing village and summer resort with two good sandy beaches: **Benten-hama** (弁天浜) to the west and **Takeno-hama** (竹野浜) to the east. To get to Benten-hama, exit Takeno Station and turn left at the first light and walk straight for about 15 minutes (you will cross one big street en route). To get to Takeno-hama, go straight out of the station and walk for around 20 minutes. There is an **information office** (☏0796-47-1080; ⏰8.30am-5pm) on the beachfront at Takeno-hama in an orange brick building. This office can help with accommodation in local *minshuku* and ryokan.

Bentenhama camping area (弁天浜キャンプ場; ☏0796-47-0888; campsites per adult/child ¥1000/500; ⏰Jul & Aug) is on the seafront at Benten-hama. It's a decent, if crowded, spot to pitch a tent. **Kitamaekan** (北前館; ☏0796-47-2020; onsen adult/child ¥500/300; ⏰10am-10pm Mon-Sat, from 7am Sun) is an onsen complex where the baths are on the 2nd floor with a great view of the beach and sea. It's at Takeno-hama, in a large grey building about 150m west of the information office.

Takeno Station is on the JR San-in line, an easy trip from Kinosaki (¥190, nine minutes). The train trip is a good chance to enjoy some of the coastal scenery.

Kinosaki 城崎

☏0796 / POP 4134

Kinosaki is one of the best places in Japan to sample the classic Japanese onsen experience. A willow-lined canal runs through the centre of this town, and many of the houses, shops and restaurants retain something of their traditional charm. Add to this the delights of crab fresh from the Sea of Japan in winter, and you'll understand why this is one of our favourite overnight trips from the cities of Kansai.

👁️ Sights & Activities

Kinosaki's biggest attraction is its seven onsen. Guests staying in town stroll the canal from bath to bath wearing a *yukata* (light cotton kimono) and *geta* (wooden sandals). Most of the ryokan and hotels in town have their own *uchi-yu* (private baths), but also provide their guests with free tickets to the ones outside (*soto-yu*).

The following is the full list of Kinosaki's onsen, in order of preference (you can get a map from the information office or your lodgings):

TOP CHOICE **Gosho-no-yu**   ONSEN
(御所の湯; admission ¥800; ⊙7am-11pm, enter by 10.30pm, closed 1st & 3rd Thu) Lovely log construction, a nice two-level *rotemburo* and fine maple colours in autumn. The entry area is decorated like the Kyoto Gosho (Imperial Palace).

Sato-no-yu   ONSEN
(さとの湯; admission ¥800; ⊙1-9pm, enter by 8.40pm, closed Mon) Fantastic variety of baths, including Arab-themed saunas, rooftop *rotemburo* and a 'Penguin Sauna' (basically a walk-in freezer – the only one we've seen anywhere – good after a hot bath). Women's and men's baths shift floors daily, so you'll have to go two days in a row to sample all of the offerings.

Kou-no-yu   ONSEN
(鴻の湯; admission ¥600; ⊙7am-11pm, enter by 10.30pm, closed Tue) Nothing fancy, but a good *rotemburo* and pleasant inside baths.

Ichi-no-yu   ONSEN
(一の湯; admission ¥600; ⊙7am-11pm, enter by 10.30pm, closed Wed) Wonderful 'cave' bath.

Yanagi-yu   ONSEN
(柳湯; admission ¥600; ⊙3-11pm, enter by 10.40pm, closed Thu) Worth a quick soak as you make your way around town. Nice wooden construction.

Mandara-yu   ONSEN
(まんだら湯; admission ¥600; ⊙3-11pm, enter by 10.40pm, closed Wed) Small wooden *rotemburo*.

Jizo-yu   ONSEN
(地蔵湯; admission ¥600; ⊙7am-11pm, enter by 10.40pm, closed Fri) Spacious main inside tub but no *rotemburo*. Good if others are crowded.

In addition to the town's great onsen, visitors might want to have a peek at the **Kinosaki Mugiwarazaikudenshokan** (城崎麦わら細工伝承館; admission ¥300; ⊙9am-5pm, enter by 4.30pm, closed last Wed of every month), which has displays on one of the local handicrafts known as *mugiwarazaiku*, a decorative technique that employs barley straw cut into tiny pieces and applied to wood to form incredibly beautiful patterns. It's located off the canal, a short walk from Ichi-no-yu onsen.

🛏 Sleeping

TOP CHOICE **Nishimuraya Honkan**   RYOKAN $$$
(西村屋本館; ☑32-2211; www.nishimuraya.ne.jp/honkan/english/index.html; fax 32-4456; r per person with 2 meals from ¥37,950; 🛜) This classic is the ultimate inn here. If you would like to try the high-class ryokan experience, this is a good place. The two onsen baths are exquisite and most of the rooms look out over private gardens. The excellent food is the final touch.

Suishōen   RYOKAN $$
(水翔苑; ☑32-4571; www.suisyou.com/en; fax 32-4575; r per person with 2 meals ¥14,000-20,000, r per person without meals ¥6300-9000; 🛜) This excellent modern ryokan is a short drive from the town centre, but they'll whisk you straight to the onsen of your choice in their own London taxi and pick you up when you're done. It's a strangely pleasant feeling to ride in the back wearing nothing but a *yukata*! The rooms are clean and well kept, and the private onsen is great, with indoor and outdoor baths. Wi-fi is in the lobby only.

Mikuniya   RYOKAN $$
(三国屋; ☑32-2414; www.kinosaki3928.com/english/index.htm; fax 32-2679; r per person with 2 meals from ¥18,900; 🛜) About 150m on the right on the street heading into town from the station, this ryokan is a good choice. The rooms are clean, with nice Japanese decorations, and the onsen bath is soothing. There is an English sign.

Tsuruya   RYOKAN $$
(つるや; ☑32-2924; info@kinosaki-tsuruya.com; fax 32-3704; r per person with 2 meals from ¥10,330, without meals from ¥5590) A few metres before Kou-no-yu onsen (as you approach from the station), this simple ryokan is comfortable with foreign guests. The rooms are plain but sufficient and the manager is helpful and speaks some English.

🍴 Eating

Crab from the Sea of Japan is a speciality in Kinosaki during the winter months. It's called *kani* and the way to enjoy it is in *kani-suki*, cooked right at your table in a broth with vegetables. Note that most restaurants in Kinosaki shut down very early. This is because most people opt for the two-meal option at their accommodation. You should consider doing the same, at least during *kani* season.

Daikō Shōten

SHOKUDŌ $$

(大幸商店; ☑32-3684; ⊙10am-9pm, to 11pm in summer) This seafood shop/*izakaya* is a great place to try freshly caught local seafood in a casual atmosphere. From November until mid-April (the busy tourist season for Kinosaki), the restaurant section is upstairs, while the downstairs is given over to selling vast quantities of crabs and other delights. For the rest of the year, the restaurant is on the ground floor. *Teishoku* are available from ¥1480, but you'll never go wrong by just asking for the master's *osusume* (recommendations). It's diagonally across from Mikuniya, about 50m back toward the station.

Orizuru

SUSHI $$

(をり鶴; ☑32-2203; meal ¥3000; ⊙lunch & dinner, closed Tue; 📖) For decent sushi and crab dishes, try this popular local sushi restaurant on the main street. You can get a *jō-nigiri* (superior sushi set; ¥3700) or try the crab dishes in winter. It's between Ichi-no-yu and Gosho-no-yu, on the opposite side of the street. There is a small English sign.

Koyume

IZAKAYA $$

(こ夢; ☑32-2695; ⊙5-11.30pm) This tiny *izakaya* serves a variety of food and sake, and is a good place to rub shoulders with the locals. There are a few counter seats and some tatami mat seating. It's on the small street behind Jizo-yu and Yanagi-yu. There is no English sign, so find it by looking for the script listed here.

ℹ Information

Opposite the station is an **accommodation information office** (お宿案内所; ☑32-4141; ⊙9am-6pm), where the staff will gladly help you find a place to stay and make bookings, as well as provide maps of the town. The same office has rental bicycles available for ¥400/800 per two hours/day (return by 5pm).

ℹ Getting There & Away

Kinosaki is on the JR San-in line and there are a few daily *tokkyū* from Kyoto (¥4710, two hours and 22 minutes) and Osaka (¥5450, two hours and 42 minutes).

Tango Peninsula 丹後半島

Tango-hantō is a peninsula that juts up into the Sea of Japan on the north coast of Kansai. The inside of the peninsula is covered with thick forest, idyllic mountain villages and babbling streams, while the serrated coast alternates between good sandy beaches and rocky points.

The private Kita-kinki Tango Tetsudō rail line runs between Toyooka and Nishi-Maizuru, cutting across the southern base of the peninsula and stopping en route at Amanohashidate. Thus, if you want to check out the rest of the peninsula you'll have to go by road. A large car park and restaurant mark the start of the 40-minute round-trip walk (about 3km) to the **Kyōga-misaki Lighthouse** (経ヶ岬灯台).

The village of **Ine** (伊根), on a perfect little bay on the eastern side of the Tango-hantō, is particularly interesting. There are *funaya* houses that are built right out over the water, under which boats are drawn in, as if in a carport. The best way to check it out is by boat, and **Ine-wan Meguri** (☑0772-42-0321) tour boats putter around the bay (¥660, 30 minutes) from March to December. Buses (¥910) reach Ine in half an hour from Amanohashidate.

There are several fine *minshuku* in the small village of Ine, including **Yoza-sō** (与謝荘; ☑0772-32-0278; 507 Hirata; per person with 2 meals from ¥11,550).

Amanohashidate 天橋立

☑0772 / POP 21,000

Amanohashidate (the Bridge to Heaven) is rated as one of Japan's 'three great views'. The 'bridge' is really a long, narrow, tree-covered (8000 pine trees!) sand spit, 3.5km in length. There is good swimming, as well as beach showers, toilet facilities and covered rest areas, the length of the spit. It's a good example of a Japanese tourist circus, but it is pleasant enough and there are some decent attractions like the village of Ine in the vicinity.

The town of Amanohashidate consists of two separate parts, one at each end of the spit. At the southern end there are a number of hotels, ryokan and restaurants, a popular temple and Amanohashidate Station. There's an **information counter** (☑22-8030; ⊙10am-6pm) at the station. To get to the bridge from the station, take a right out of the station and walk along the main road for 200m to the first light and take a sharp left.

At the southern end of the bridge, **Amanohashidate View Land** (天橋立ビューランド; chairlift/monorail round trip ¥850; ⊙9.10am-5pm 21 Aug-20 Jul, 8.40am-6pm 21 Jul-20 Aug) is serviced by chairlift and monorail.

From here, you are supposed to view Amanohashidate by turning your back to it, bending over and observing it framed between your legs! (It supposedly makes Amanohashidate look like it is 'floating'.)

At the northern end, **Kasamatsu-kōen** (傘松公園; funicular/chairlift round trip ¥640; ◎8am-4.30pm) offers similar views and another chance to view the world from between your legs.

🛏 Sleeping & Eating

Amanohashidate Youth Hostel   HOSTEL **$**
(天橋立ユースホステル; ☎27-0121; per person with/without 2 meals ¥4500/2950; @) This fine hostel has good views down towards Amanohashidate, friendly owners, well-kept rooms and an excellent hillside location. Internet is available in the lobby only. To get there, take a bus (¥510, 20 minutes) from JR Amanohashidate Station and get off at the Jinja-mae bus stop. From the stop, walk to the main hall of the shrine, take a right and leave the shrine precinct then turn left up the hill and walk 50m, take a right and follow the sign for Manai Shrine. Turn at the stone torii, walk 200m uphill and it's on the right.

Amanohashidate Hotel   HOTEL **$$**
(天橋立ホテル; ☎22-4111; per person with 2 meals from ¥20,000; ◉) This hotel about 100m west of the station commands the best views of Amanohashidate. Rooms are mixed Japanese/Western style and there are several good communal baths that afford views of Amanohashidate and the bay. The hotel serves special crab cuisine in winter.

Resutoran Monju   NOODLES **$$**
(れすとらん文珠; ☎22-2805; meals from ¥1000; ◎9.30am-4pm, closed Thu) There are several decent but slightly overpriced *shokudō* at the southern end of Amanohashidate, including Resutoran Monju, which has *asari udon* (*udon* noodles with clams), a local speciality, for ¥1000. Look for the red-and-white sign as you approach Chion-ji (the temple at the southern end of Amanohashidate).

❶ Getting There & Away

The Kita-kinki Tango Tetsudō line runs between JR stations at Toyooka to the west and Nishi-Maizuru to the east. Amanohashidate Station is on this line, 1¼ hours from Toyooka (*futsū*, ¥1160) and 40 minutes from Nishi-Maizuru (*futsū*, ¥620). There are several direct trains from Kyoto daily, but JR pass holders will have to fork out for the Kita-kinki Tango Tetsudō part of the route (from Kyoto ¥4380, two hours; from Osaka ¥5240, 2¼ hours).

❶ Getting Around

You can cross Amanohashidate on foot, by bicycle or on a motorcycle of less than 125cc capacity. Bicycles can be hired at a number of places for ¥400/1600 for two hours/a day.

Maizuru   舞鶴

There's nothing overly appealing about the two ports of Nishi-Maizuru and Higashi-Maizuru, but they play an important part in the area's transport networks. If you've come from the west on the Kita-kinki Tango Tetsudō trains, Nishi-Maizuru is the end of the line and where the JR Obama line comes out to meet the coast. If you're on your way to Amanohashidate, this is where you'll have to change to the private line.

There are regular ferry services between Higashi-Maizuru and Otaru in Hokkaidō (2nd class ¥9000, 20 hours). Call **Shin-Nihonkai Ferry** (☎06-6345-2921; www.snf.jp, in Japanese) for details.

Hiroshima & Western Honshū

Best Places to Eat

» Okonomi-mura (p372)
» Tōshō (p372)
» Yabure-Kabure (p408)
» Yakigaki-no-hayashi (p376)

Best Places to Stay

» Hattōji International Villa (p389)
» Benesse House (p397)
» Tsutsuji-sō (p397)
» Hana Hostel (p370)
» Santora (p399)
» Yoshidaya (p420)

Why Go?

Travelling in Western Honshū (本州西部) reveals a tale of two coastlines. San-yō (literally 'sunny side of the mountains'), looking out over the Inland Sea, boasts the bigger cities, the charming narrow-laned portside and hillside towns, ceramic history and the fast train. This is the coast that holds the region's big name – indelibly scarred, thriving, come-have-a-drink-with-us Hiroshima.

On the other side of the dividing Chūgoku mountain range, San-in (literally 'in the shade of the mountains') gazes out across the expanse of the Japan Sea. Up here, it's all about an unhurried pace, onsen villages that see few foreigners, historic sites, wind-battered, rugged coastal views, and warm welcomes.

Turn away from both coasts and take an inland route for hikes along gorges and through caves. Or leap (by ferry or cycle) off the mainland altogether to the Inland Sea and its galaxy of islands.

When to Go

Hiroshima

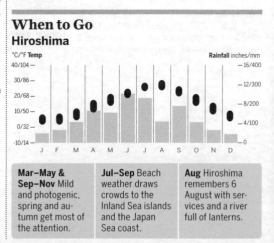

Mar–May & Sep–Nov Mild and photogenic, spring and autumn get most of the attention.

Jul–Sep Beach weather draws crowds to the Inland Sea islands and the Japan Sea coast.

Aug Hiroshima remembers 6 August with services and a river full of lanterns.

Getting Around

The *shinkansen* (bullet train), linking Okayama with major cities along the San-yō coast to Shimonoseki, is the fastest way to get around. On the San-in coast along the Sea of Japan, the *shinkansen* is not an option. Train services are generally infrequent and it's hard to completely avoid the slow local services. If you're in a hurry up here, it's worth hiring a car. The major rail link between the two coasts runs between Okayama and Yonago.

HIROSHIMA & AROUND

Hiroshima 広島

📞 082 / POP 1,174,200

To most people, Hiroshima means just one thing. The city's name will forever evoke thoughts of 6 August 1945, when Hiroshima became the target of the world's first atomic-bomb attack. Hiroshima's Peace Memorial Park is a constant reminder of that day, and it attracts visitors from all over the world. But leafy Hiroshima, with its wide boulevards and laid-back friendliness, is a far from depressing place. Present-day Hiroshima is home to a thriving and internationally minded community, and it's worth spending a couple of nights here to experience the city at its vibrant best.

⊙ Sights

Most sights can be reached either on foot or with a short tram ride. To catch a tram to the Atomic Bomb Dome and Peace Memorial Park area, hop on tram 2 or 6 at the terminal in front of the station (south exit) and get off at the Genbaku-dōmu-mae stop.

Atomic Bomb Dome   HISTORIC RUINS

Perhaps the starkest reminder of the destruction visited upon Hiroshima is the Atomic Bomb Dome (原爆ドーム; Genbaku Dōmu), across the river from the Peace Memorial Park. Built by a Czech architect in 1915, the building served as the Industrial Promotion Hall until the bomb exploded almost directly above it. Everyone inside was killed, but the building itself was one of very few left standing anywhere near the epicentre. Despite local misgivings, a decision was taken after the war to preserve the shell of the building as a memorial. Declared a Unesco World Heritage Site in December 1996, the propped-up ruins are floodlit at night, and have become a grim symbol of the city's tragic past.

Peace Memorial Park   PARK

From the Atomic Bomb Dome, cross over into Peace Memorial Park (平和記念公園; Heiwa-kōen), which is dotted with memorials, including the **cenotaph** (原爆死没者慰霊碑), which contains the names of all the known victims of the bomb. The cenotaph frames the **Flame of Peace** (平和の灯), which will only be extinguished once the last nuclear weapon on earth has been destroyed, and the Atomic Bomb Dome across the river.

Just north of the road through the park is the **Children's Peace Monument** (原爆の子の像), inspired by Sadako Sasaki. When Sadako developed leukaemia at 11 years of age in 1955, she decided to fold 1000 paper cranes. In Japan, the crane is the symbol of longevity and happiness, and she was convinced that if she achieved that target she would recover. She died before reaching her goal, but her classmates folded the rest. The story inspired a nationwide spate of paper-crane folding that continues to this day.

Nearby is the **Korean Atomic Bomb Memorial** (韓国人原爆犠牲者慰霊碑). Many Koreans were shipped over to work as slave labourers during WWII, and Koreans accounted for more than one in 10 of those killed by the atomic bomb.

Peace Memorial Museum   MUSEUM

(平和記念資料館; www.pcf.city.hiroshima.jp; 1-2 Nakajima-chō, Naka-ku; admission ¥50; ⊙8.30am-5pm, to 6pm Mar-Nov, to 7pm Aug) The lower floor of Hiroshima's peace museum presents the history of the city and, interestingly, explains the living conditions and sentiment during the war years leading up to the dropping of the bomb. Upstairs, along with a depressing display showing the development of even more destructive weapons in the years since, are rooms filled with items salvaged from the aftermath of the explosion. The displays here are harrowing – ragged clothes, glasses, a child's melted lunch box – and there are some gruesome photographs of victims. It can be overwhelming, and you might not want to bring young children through here, but it's a must see in Hiroshima. In the corridor on the way out, it's well worth taking time to watch the video testimonials of survivors.

TOP CHOICE Hiroshima National Peace Memorial Hall for the Atomic Bomb Victims   MEMORIAL

(国立広島原爆死没者追悼平和祈念館; 1-6 Nakajima-chō, Naka-ku; ⊙8.30am-6pm Mar-Nov, to 5pm Dec-Feb, to 7pm Aug) A walkway circles

Hiroshima & Western Honshū Highlights

1 Eating and drinking well in cosmopolitan **Hiroshima** (p365)

2 Gaining a new perspective at the art installations of **Naoshima** (p396)

3 Hiring a bike and going island hopping via the **Shimanami Kaidō** (p383) to Shikoku

4 Slowing down and listening to the waves on

Manabe-shima (p399) in the Inland Sea

5 Seeing the floating shrine of Itsukushima-jinja and staying at a ryokan on **Miyajima** (p374)

6 Seeing where the gods go on holiday at **Izumo Taisha** (p417)

7 Spending a night in a restored farmhouse in the hills at **Hattōji** (p389)

8 Strolling around the moated castle before a gorgeous Shinji-ko (Lake Shinji) sunset in **Matsue** (p413)

9 Exploring the World Heritage **Iwami Ginzan silver mine district** (p418)

Hiroshima

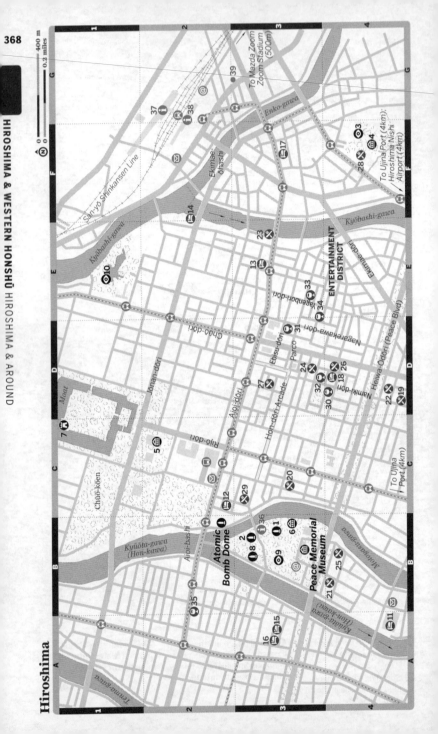

N

0   400 m
0   0.2 miles

To Mazda Zoom
Zoom Stadium
(500m)

San-yo Shinkansen Line

Ekimae-
ōhashi

Enko-gawa

Kyōbashi-gawa

ENTERTAINMENT
DISTRICT

Kyōbashi-gawa

To Ujina Port (4km);
Hiroshima Nishi
Airport (4km)

Kyōbachi-gawa

Nagarekawa-dōri

Yagenbori-dōri

Chūō-dōri

Jōnan-dōri

Ebisu-dōri

Parco

Namiki-dōri

Heiwa-Ōdōri (Peace Blvd)

Aioi-dōri

Rijō-dōri

Hondōri Arcade

To Ujina
Port (4km)

Chūō-kōen

Moat

Aioi-bashi

Kyōbashi-gawa
(Hon-kawa)

Atomic
Bomb Dome

Peace Memorial
Museum

Motoyasu-gawa

Kyōbashi-gawa
(Hon-kawa)

Tenma-gawa

Hiroshima

down to a contemplative underground hall of remembrance, and a room where the names and photographs of atomic-bomb victims are kept, along with testimonies from survivors, in several languages. It was built by architect Tange Kenzō, who also designed the museum, cenotaph and eternal flame. The testimonies, which can be viewed on video, vividly evoke the chaos of the time.

Shukkei-en   GARDEN
(縮景園; 2-11 Kami-nobori-chō; admission ¥250, combined ticket with museum ¥600; ⊙9am-6pm Apr-Sep, to 5pm Oct-Mar) Modelled after Xi Hu (West Lake) in Hangzhou, China, Shukkei-en was built in 1620 for *daimyō* (domain lord) Asano Nagaakira. The garden's name means 'contracted view', and it attempts to re-create grand vistas in miniature. The garden was totally destroyed by the bomb, though many of the trees and plants survived to blossom again the fol-

lowing year, and the park and its buildings have long since been restored to their original splendour.

Hiroshima-jō   CASTLE
(広島城; Hiroshima Castle; 21-1 Moto-machi, Naka-ku; admission ¥360; ⊙9am-6pm Mar-Nov, to 5pm Dec-Feb) Also known as Carp Castle (Rijō; 鯉城), Hiroshima-jō was originally constructed in 1589, but much of it was dismantled following the Meiji Restoration. The remainder was totally destroyed by the bomb and rebuilt in 1958. There's not a lot to see inside, but there's a moat, and the surrounding park is a pleasant place for a stroll.

Hiroshima Museum of Art   ART GALLERY
(ひろしま美術館; www.hiroshima-museum.jp; 3-2 Moto-machi, Naka-ku; admission ¥1000; ⊙9am-5pm) In an interesting 1970s building, this museum has a decent collection of minor works by well-known painters, including Picasso, Gauguin, Monet and Van Gogh.

VOLUNTEER GUIDES: PEACE MEMORIAL MUSEUM

Yasuko Yamaoka, a retired junior high-school teacher, and Keiko Hasegawa, a mother and housewife, have volunteered as guides at the Peace Memorial Museum for eight and 10 years respectively. Yasuko became a volunteer after years of interest in peace education during her teaching career. Keiko applied for the six-month volunteer training after bringing her then elementary-school-aged sons to the museum. 'Even though I was born and raised in Hiroshima, and my father was one of the bomb survivors, I realised I couldn't explain much to my sons', she says. 'I later saw an ad calling for guides to help convey the history to the next generation, and I felt, this is *my* job.'

Both are passionate about helping visitors, especially young people, get a deeper understanding of what took place here. 'We can look at the science and numbers of what happened,' Yasuko says, 'but what happened to the people, the living things, that is the most important. This is what I want people and leaders to come and see – what happened to *each* person. If we say 200,000 people died, that means there are 200,000 individual stories of agony'.

Among the museum's many displays, both guides nominate the personal items as the most profound. 'I usually encourage people to look at the lunch box, or the remains of the child's uniform', Keiko says. Yasuko adds that, for her, the display of burnt, blistered roof tiles is also important. 'Roof tiles are made in extreme heat over many hours in a kiln, and still these tiles became burnt and glassy', she emphasises. 'Many people just feel them quickly and walk past. But we should take time to look at them and really understand.' These salvaged objects all have a story to tell, they say. 'The people died, but these items are here. They survived, and are telling us what happened.'

Hijiyama-kōen `PARK`

Hijiyama-kōen is noted for its cherry blossoms in spring, It's a 20-minute walk south of JR Hiroshima Station.

Hiroshima City Museum of Contemporary Art `ART GALLERY`

(広島市現代美術館; www.hcmca.cf.city.hiroshima.jp; 1-1 Hijiyama-kōen, Minami-ku; admission ¥360, additional fee for temporary exhibits; ⊙10am-5pm, closed Mon) In Hijiyama-kōen, this gallery has frequently changing exhibits by modern Japanese and international artists.

`FREE` **Mazda Museum** `MUSEUM`

(マツダミュージアム; www.mazda.com/mazdaspirit/museum; ☎252-5050) Popular for the chance to see the 7km assembly line – the longest in the world. See the website for tour times; reservations are required. The museum is a short walk from JR Mukainada (向洋) Station, two stops from Hiroshima on the San-yō line.

🏃 Activities

A love of **baseball** is not a prerequisite for having a great time at a Hiroshima Carp game (www.carp.co.jp, in Japanese). It's just as much fun watching the rowdy, organised enthusiasm of the crowd, especially when the despised Tokyo Giants come to town. Games

are played in the Mazda Zoom-Zoom Stadium, a short walk southeast of the station. For schedule information in English, see www.japanball.com, or ask at the tourist office.

🎎 Festivals & Events

Peace Memorial Ceremony `MEMORIAL SERVICE`

On 6 August, the anniversary of the atomic bombing, a memorial service is held in Peace Memorial Park and thousands of paper lanterns for the souls of the dead are floated down the Kyūōta-gawa from in front of the Atomic Bomb Dome.

🛏 Sleeping

Hiroshima has numerous accommodation options in every price bracket. In particular, budget travellers can rejoice – Hiroshima's hostels and guesthouses offer good-quality rooms with personalised service that you don't get at some of the bigger hotels. Even if you're not carrying a backpack, you'll likely be quite comfortable at most hostels here.

`TOP CHOICE` **Hana Hostel** `HOSTEL $`

(広島花宿; ☎263-2980; http://hiroshimahostel.jp; 1-15 Kojin-machi, Minami-ku; dm/s/tw ¥2500/3900/6800; ⊛@☎) Hana is more guesthouse than backpacker joint, with a choice of Japanese- or Western-style private rooms, some with (small) en suite. Cosy lamp lighting and traditional decoration make the tatami rooms the top pick here. The only downside for light sleepers is occasional street noise. From the station go immediately left along the train tracks, continue past the railway crossing (not over it) and turn right. It's opposite the temple.

K's House Hiroshima
HOSTEL $

(ケイズハウス広島; ☎568-7244; www.ks house.jp/hiroshima-e; 1-8-9 Matoba-chō; dm/s/tw from ¥2500/4500/7000; ⊜@🛜) K's House has a great location not too far from the station. There are small dorms and comfortable tatami rooms with shared shower rooms, or pay a little more for a room with bed and en suite. The kitchen is modern and not too cramped, there's a rooftop terrace, and the staff are helpful. Note that the entrance is at the back of the block – turn left off Aioi-dōri.

J-Hoppers Hiroshima
HOSTEL $

(ジェイホッパーズ広島ゲストハウス; ☎233-1360; http://hiroshima.j-hoppers.com; 5-16 Dobashi-chō, Naka-ku; dm/tw per person with shared bathroom ¥2300/2800; ⊜@🛜) This popular old favourite feels more like someone's house than a standard hostel. The rooms are small and getting scuffed here and there, but it's a cosy place and the friendly crew are in the process of redecorating. There are both dorm beds and private tatami rooms. Bikes can be rented (¥500 per day).

Sera Bekkan
RYOKAN $$

(世羅別館; ☎248-2251; fax 248-2768; www.yado .to, in Japanese; 4-20 Mikawa-chō Naka-ku; per person with/without meals from ¥12,600/8400; ⊜) Off Namiki-dōri in this traditional ryokan with good-sized tatami rooms, large baths, a peaceful garden and great hospitality. Look for the dark-red-brick building on a corner across from a small car park.

Hiroshima Inn Aioi
RYOKAN $$$

(広島の宿相生; ☎247-9331; fax 247-9335; www .galilei.ne.jp/aioi, in Japanese; 1-3-14 Ōtemachi Naka-ku; per person with meals from ¥19,900) Kick back in your *tabi* (split-toe socks) and enjoy city and park views from your room, or from the large bath on the 7th floor. The meals are an elaborate traditional spread of dishes, and you can opt for breakfast or dinner only. It's just near the Atomic Bomb Dome.

Hotel Active!
HOTEL $$

(ホテルアクティブ！広島; ☎212-0001; www .hotel-active.com/hiroshima, in Japanese; 15-3 Nobori-chō Naka-ku; s/d incl breakfast from ¥5980/7875; ⊜@) This very chic hotel has designer couches, satiny coverlets and extra-comfy desk chairs. It's right in the heart of things – within stumbling distance of bars and restaurants – and the bejewelled staff are pleasant. A buffet-style breakfast is included in the rates.

Ikawa Ryokan
RYOKAN $

(いかわ旅館; ☎231-5058; fax 231-5995; www .ikawaryokan.net; 5-11 Dobashi-chō Naka-ku; s/tw from ¥4725/9450; @) On a quiet side street (near J-Hoppers), this is a large family-run hotel-style ryokan with three connected wings, one recently renovated. There are Japanese- and Western-style rooms, all very clean, and most have private bathrooms (though there's also a large public bath). Some English is spoken.

Hotel Flex
HOTEL $$

(ホテルフレックス; ☎223-1000; www.hotel -flex.co.jp; 7-1 Kaminobori-chō Naka-ku; s/d from ¥6300/9000; ⊜@) Curves, concrete and light are the features at this designer hotel set right on the river. Rooms are bright – even the smallest have large windows – though some rooms could do with a new coat of paint. Naturally, rooms on the river side of the building have the views, and you can choose the option of a more deluxe terrace room, or a stylish split-level maisonette.

Aster Plaza International Youth House
HOTEL $

(広島市国際青年会館; ☎247-8700; hiyh.pr .arena.ne.jp; 4-17 Kako-machi Naka-ku; s/tw ¥3620/6260; @) With good views from the top floors of a huge municipal building, this city-run hotel represents excellent value for foreign travellers, who get roomy well-equipped modern accommodation at budget prices. There's a 1am curfew. You can also book via email: kokusei@hiyh. pr.arena.jp.

✗ Eating

Hiroshima is famous for oysters and *okonomiyaki* (savoury pancakes; batter and cabbage, with vegetables and seafood or meat cooked on a griddle), served Hiroshima-style with noodles. You'll come across plenty of places serving both.

Sandan Gorge (三段峡; Sandan-kyō) is an 11km ravine about 50km northwest of Hiroshima. A mostly paved trail follows the Shiki-gawa through the gorge, providing visitors with access to fresh air, waterfalls and forests. The hike is very popular in autumn, when the leaves change colour. Ask at the tourist office in Hiroshima, or pick up a copy of Lonely Planet's *Hiking in Japan* for full details.

A dozen buses a day run from the Hiroshima bus centre to Sandan-kyō Station (¥1200 to ¥1400, 1½ hours), at the southern end of the gorge. The gorge is also accessible by car from Shimane-ken along Rte 191.

TOP CHOICE Okonomi-mura
OKONOMIYAKI $

(お好み村; 5-13 Shintenchi Naka-ku; dishes ¥700-1000; ⊙11am-2am) Twenty-five stalls spread over three floors, all of them serving the same thing – this Hiroshima institution is a good place to get acquainted with the local speciality of *okonomiyaki*, and chat with the cooks over a hot griddle. It's close to the Parco department store; look for the sign jutting out into the street.

Tōshō
TOFU $$

(豆匠; ☎506-1028; www.toufu-tosho.jp, in Japanese; 6-24 Hijiyama-chō Minami-ku; lunch/dinner courses from ¥1890/5000; ⊙lunch & dinner) A traditional wooden building in a beautiful garden setting, Tōshō specialises in home-made tofu (the menu has some pictures), served in a surprising variety of tasty forms. It's a short walk from Danbara 1 chōme (段原一丁目) tram stop, left uphill after the Hijiyama shrine.

Hassei
OKONOMIYAKI $

(八誠; 4-17 Fujimi-chō Naka-ku; dishes ¥450-1200; ⊙lunch & dinner Tue-Sat, dinner Sun; 📷) The walls of this popular *okonomiyaki* joint are covered with the signatures of celebrity visitors. Unless you're a sumō wrestler, you'll probably find a half-order more than enough to be getting on with at lunchtime. Look for the wooden sign next to the doorway.

Kaki-tei
OYSTERS $$

(牡蠣亭; ☎221-8990; www.kakitei.jp, in Japanese; 11 Hashimoto-chō Naka-ku; ⊙lunch & dinner, closed Tue) This intimate bistro on the riverbank specialises in oysters prepared in a variety of mouth-watering ways. Grilled options include *champagne cream yaki* (¥850 for two). The daily oyster lunch is ¥1200. There's no English menu, but the friendly staff will help you figure things out. Look for the green *noren* (cloth curtain hung in the entrance) and the words 'Oyster Conclave'.

Cha Cha Ni Moon
JAPANESE $$$

(茶茶貳ムーン; ☎241-7444; 2-6-26 Ōtemachi Naka-ku; courses from ¥3500; ⊙5pm-midnight; 📷) Sophisticated minimalist chic prevails in this softly lit old house. There's a bar downstairs and two floors of intimate semiprivate dining rooms upstairs. The beautifully presented dishes here are based on traditional Kyoto cuisine. Look for the small orange sign out the front.

Chari
CAFE $

(茶里; 2-5 Nakajima-chō Naka-ku; ⊙lunch & dinner; 😊) This low-ceilinged narrow cafe-restaurant near the Peace Memorial Museum is a good place for a coffee or lunch stop. There are a few wooden tables and a solo-diner-friendly long bench. Lunch sets, from ¥750, include a *teishoku* (set meal) of *udon* (thick white noodles), and there are curries and cakes on the menu.

Shanti Vegan Cafe
VEGETARIAN & VEGAN $

(ヴィーガンカフェ; www.shanti-yoga.net/cafe.html, in Japanese; 2nd fl, Mondano Bldg 2-20 Mikawa-chō; lunch/dinner sets ¥850/1500; ⊙11.30am-8.30pm; 😊🍽) Eat hearty vegan and vegetarian meals at this simple cafe beneath a yoga studio. There's no English menu, but you can't really go wrong since there's a choice of two set meals up on the chalkboard. Sets feature pasta, brown rice and tasty specialities like *renkon* (lotus root) burger.

Bakudanya
NOODLES $

(ばくだん屋; www.bakudanya.net; 6-13 Fujimi-chō Naka-ku; ⊙11.30am-midnight, to 1am Fri & Sat) Come to this simple street-corner stall to try another famous Hiroshima dish: *tsukemen*, a cold *rāmen*-like dish in which noodles and soup come separately. This is the original outlet; the chain has now spread across the country. A *nami* (medium-sized) serving of *tsukemen* is ¥750. Look for the green awning.

Spicy Bar Lal's
INDIAN $

(スパイシーバーラルズ; ☎504-6328; 5-12 Tatemachi Naka-ku; curries ¥930-1000; ☺lunch & dinner; ✍📶) This colourful Indian and Nepalese restaurant serves filling lunch specials and plain naan the size of a small African country. A range of imported beers and veg options make this a nice change, if you ever get tired of *okonomiyaki*.

Ristorante Mario
ITALIAN $$

(リストランテマリオ; ☎248-4956; www.san mario.com, in Japanese; 4-11 Nakajima-chō Naka-ku; dishes ¥1000-2500; ☺lunch & dinner Mon-Fri, 11.30am-10pm Sat & Sun; 📶) A cosy ivy-clad place serving honest Italian food with good service, and a romantic atmosphere in the evenings. Weekday lunch courses start at ¥1180. Try to reserve on weekends.

Zucchini
TAPAS $$

(ズッキーニ; ☎546-0777; 1-5-18 Otemachi Naka-ku; meals ¥400-2800; ☺5.30pm-1am; 📶) Very lively Spanish-style tapas restaurant serving all the usual ham, cheese and fish goodies and paellas from ¥1400. It's a two-storey glass-fronted affair on the corner – you can't miss it.

🍷 Drinking

The city's thrumming main entertainment district is made up of hundreds of bars, restaurants and karaoke joints crowding the lanes between Aioi-dōri and Heiwa-Ōdōri in the city centre.

Organza
BAR, CAFE

(ヲルガン座; ☎295-1553; www.organ-za.com, in Japanese; 2nd fl, Morimoto Bldg Tōkaichi-machi; ☺5.30pm-2am Tue-Fri, 11.30am-2am Sat, 11.30am-midnight Sun, closed Mon) Bookshelves, floral wallpaper, old-fashioned furniture and a piano add to the busy retro surrounds at this dimly lit lounge bar. Organza hosts an eclectic schedule of live events (from acoustic guitar to cabaret), some with a cover charge, and it gets busy. Lunch is served on weekends.

Nawanai
IZAKAYA

(なわない; Fujimi Bldg, 12-10 Kanayama-chō Naka-ku; ☺6pm-midnight) This basement *izakaya* is an atmospheric place to mingle with locals over fresh fish and a range of local sakes. Try *ko-iwashi* (baby sardines), available either as sashimi or tempura (¥600). There is no English menu, but the owners will make sure you don't go home hungry – or thirsty. Take the fourth left off Yagenbori-dōri and look up and left for the illuminated sign in Japanese. Nawanai's in the basement.

Ninjō Ganko Yatai
IZAKAYA

(人情がんこ屋台; ☺6.30pm-7am) Six small *izakaya* squeezed into one large room make up this convivial spot, where beer and sake come with the usual *izakaya* fare, as well as some local-style *okonomiyaki*. Take the sixth right off Yagenbori-dōri, and look for the lanterns and rope curtain over the sliding-door entrance.

Kuro-sawa
BAR

(黒澤; 5th fl, Tenmaya Ebisu Bldg, 3-20 Horikawa-chō Naka-ku; ☺6pm-2.30am Mon-Thu, to 3.30am Fri & Sat, to 12.30am Sun; 📶) This is a trendy 'Japanese-style public house', hewn from concrete, with seating at the bar or on velvet chairs in a raised red-carpet area. It's worth coming for a drink just for the bizarre toilet experience. Food also served. It's in Ebisu-dōri arcade, on the 5th floor of a building opposite the Italian Tomato Café.

Koba
BAR

(コバ; 3rd fl, Rego Bldg, 1-4 Naka-machi; dishes ¥700-1200; ☺6pm-2am, closed Wed) Cross the pool of water and go up the narrow stairs to this laid-back place, where the welcoming rock-music-loving guys behind the bar serve drinks and cook up small meals. It's in a concrete building, just behind Stussy.

Lotus
BAR

(ロータス; 5th fl, Namiki Curl Bldg, 3-12 Mikawa-chō; drinks from ¥650; ☺6pm-3am; 📶) Take off your shoes and relax on the raised floor amid cushions, or sip cocktails at the bar. It's on a side street just off Namiki-dōri.

ℹ Information

INTERNET ACCESS There is free wi-fi in the Peace Park and along Heiwa-Ōdōri from 8.30am to 7pm (to 6pm in winter, to 8pm August). When you first connect, you'll need to register before you start using.

Futaba@Cafe (フタバ@アットカフェ; 2-22 Matsubara-chō; membership fee ¥105, 1st hr ¥400; ☺24hr) On the 6th floor of a book and CD store, with a yellow sign to the left as you exit the station.

International Exchange Lounge (国際交流ラウンジ; Peace Memorial Park; ☺9am-7pm Apr-Sep, to 6pm Oct-Mar) Has free internet access (30-minute limit) and some basic tourist information.

HIROSHIMA & WESTERN HONSHŪ HIROSHIMA & AROUND

MONEY Higashi Post Office has ATMs that accept international cards, as do 7-Elevens. Hiroshima Rest House tourist information centre has a list of banks and post offices that change money and travellers cheques.

POST Higashi (広島東郵便局; 2-62 Matsubara-chō Minami-ku; ◷9am-7pm Mon-Fri, to 5pm Sat, to 12.30pm Sun) The post office most convenient to the station, outside the south exit.

TOURIST INFORMATION Hiroshima Rest House (広島市平和記念公園レストハウス; ☑247-6738; 1-1 Nakajima-machi Naka-ku; ◷8.30am-5pm) In the Peace Memorial Park, next to Motoyasu-bashi. Has comprehensive information about the city and the island of Miyajima.

Tourist information office (広島市観光案内所; ◷9am-5.30pm) JR Hiroshima Station South (☑261-1877) JR Hiroshima Station North (☑263-6822) There's also another branch downstairs.

WEBSITES The following are useful:

Hiroshima Navigator (www.hcvb.city.hiroshima.jp) Tourist and practical information, downloadable audio guides to the sights and more.

Get Hiroshima (www.gethiroshima.com) A good resource, particularly if you're staying in Hiroshima more than a few days.

ⓘ Getting There & Away

AIR Hiroshima Airport (www.hij.airport.jp) Hiroshima's main airport, 40km east of the city, with bus connections to/from Hiroshima Station (¥1300, 48 minutes).

Hiroshima Nishi airport (www.hij.air port.jp/nishi/, in Japanese) Four kilometres southwest of the city centre on the coast. There are regular buses to/from Hiroshima Station (¥240, 20 minutes).

BUS Long-distance buses connect Hiroshima with all the major cities. Buses depart from the **Hiroshima Bus Centre** (広島バスセンター; www.h-buscenter.com, in Japanese), located on the 3rd floor between the Sogo and AQ'A shopping centres by the Kamiya-cho Nishi tram stop.

FERRY There are connections to Matsuyama in Shikoku across the Inland Sea, with **Setonaikai Kisen Ferry** (☑253-1212; www.setonaikaikisen.co.jp), via standard car ferry (¥3500, 2¾ hours, 10 daily) or high-speed service (¥6900, one hour and 15 minutes, 14 daily). The port (広島港) is the last stop on trams 1, 3 and 5 bound for Ujina (宇品). Tram 5 runs from Hiroshima Station.

TRAIN Hiroshima is on the JR San-yō line, which passes through and westwards to Shimonoseki. It's also a major stop on the Tokyo–Osaka–Hakata *shinkansen* line. From Hiroshima:

Hakata ¥8190, 1¼ hours

Osaka ¥9440, 1½ hours

Tokyo ¥17,540, four hours

ⓘ Getting Around

BICYCLE Many hostels and hotels have bikes for hire.

Nippon Rent-a-car (ニッポンレンタカー; ☑264-0919; 3-14 Kojin-machi; bike rental per 2hr/day ¥263/735; ◷24hr), a few blocks southeast of the station, has a limited number of bikes for rent.

TRAM Hiroshima has an extensive tram service that will get you almost anywhere you want to go for a flat fare of ¥150. If you have to change trams to get to your destination, you should ask for a *norikae-ken* (transfer ticket). Pay when you get off.

Miyajima 宮島

☑0829 / POP 1970

The small island of Miyajima is a Unesco World Heritage Site and one of Japan's biggest tourist attractions, and is easily reached from Hiroshima. Its star attraction is the oft-photographed vermilion torii (shrine gate) of Itsukushima-jinja, which seems to float on the waves at high tide – a scene that has traditionally been ranked as one of the three best views in Japan. Besides this feted view, Miyajima has some good hikes, temples, and cheeky deer that rove the streets and will snatch anything out of the hands of unsuspecting tourists.

ⓞ Sights & Activities

Turn right as you emerge from the ferry terminal and follow the waterfront for 10 minutes to get to the shrine. The shopping street, packed with souvenir outlets and restaurants, as well as the world's largest *shakushi* (rice scoop), is a block back from the waterfront.

ⓘ **TRAM PASSES**

If you'll be taking at least four tram trips in a day, get a **one-day trip card** (¥600). A day pass that covers your tram trips plus return ferry to Miyajima is ¥800. The **two-day trip card** (¥2000) is a great deal, covering tram trips, ferry, and ticket for the ropeway on Miyajima. Buy passes from the conductors on board, from the station or at various hotels and hostels.

Itsukushima-jinja
SHRINE

(厳島神社; 1-1 Miyajima-chō; admission ¥300; ⏱6.30am-6pm Mar–mid-Oct, to 5.30pm mid-Oct–Nov, Jan & Feb, to 5pm Dec) Going back as far as the late 6th century, Itsukushima-jinja gives the island its real name. The shrine's present form dates·from 1168, when it was rebuilt under the patronage of Taira no Kiyomori, head of the doomed Heike clan. Its pier-like construction is a result of the island's holy status: commoners were not allowed to set foot on the island and had to approach the shrine by boat through the **floating torii** (大鳥居) out in the bay. Much of the time, however, the shrine and torii are surrounded by mud: to get the classic view of the torii that adorns the brochures, you'll need to come at high tide.

On one side of the floating shrine is a **floating nō stage** (能舞台) built by local lord Asano Tsunanaga in 1680 and still used for nō (stylised dance-drama) performances every year from 16 to 18 April.

Senjō-kaku
PAVILION

(千畳閣; 1-1 Miyajima-chō; admission ¥100; ⏱8.30am-4.30pm) Dominating the hill immediately to the north of Itsukushima-jinja is this huge pavilion built in 1587 by Toyotomi Hideyoshi. The atmospheric hall is constructed with massive pillars and beams, and the ceiling is hung with paintings. It looks out onto a colourful five-storey **pagoda** (五重塔) dating from 1407.

Daigan-ji
TEMPLE

(大願寺; 3 Miyajima-chō; ⏱9am-5pm) Miyajima has several important Buddhist temples, including the 1201 Daigan-ji, just south of the shrine, which dates back to the Heian period and is dedicated to Benzaiten, the Japanese name for Saraswati (the Hindu goddess of good fortune). The seated image of Yakushi Nyorai here is said to have been carved by Kōbō Daishi.

Daishō-in
TEMPLE

(大聖院; 210 Miyajima-chō; ⏱8am-5pm) Just south of town at the foot of Mt Misen, Daishō-in is a worthwhile stopping point on the way up or down the mountain. This hingon temple is crowded with interesting things to look at: from Buddhist images and prayer wheels to sharp-beaked *tengu* (bird-like demons) and a cave containing images from each of the 88 Shikoku pilgrimage temples.

Tahō-tō
PAGODA

(多宝塔) South of Itsukushima-jinja, stone steps (before the History & Folklore Museum) lead up from the road to this picturesque pagoda. There's a pleasant, short path looping around from here and back down to the road.

Miyajima History & Folklore Museum
MUSEUM

(歴史民俗資料館; 57 Miyajima-chō; admission ¥300; ⏱8.30am-5pm, closed Mon) Set in a fine garden, this museum combines a 19th-century merchant house with exhibitions on trade in the Edo period, as well as displays connected with the island.

Misen
WALK

The ascent of Misen (弥山; 530m) is the island's finest walk. You can avoid most of the uphill part of the climb by taking the two-stage **ropeway** (1 way/return ¥1000/1800; ⏱9am-5pm), which leaves you with a 20-minute walk to the top. There are monkeys and deer around the cable-car station, and some fantastic views – on clear days you can see across to the mountain ranges of Shikoku. Close to the summit is a **temple** where Kōbō Daishi meditated for 100 days following his return from China in the 9th century. Next to the main temple hall close to the summit is a flame that's been burning continually since Kōbō Daishi lit it 1200 years ago. From the temple, a path leads down the hillside to Daishō-in and Itsukushima-jinja. The descent takes a little over an hour. A four-hour hike of Misen is detailed in Lonely Planet's *Hiking in Japan*.

Miyajima Public Aquarium
AQUARIUM

(宮島水族館; www.sunameri.jp/eng/index.html) Miyajima's newly renovated aquarium reopened in August 2011, complete with all the usual sealife suspects and interactive displays.

🎎 Festivals & Events

Kangen-sai
MUSIC, BOATS

Shintō ritual held in summer, on the 17th of the sixth lunar-calendar month.

Hiwatarishiki
FIRE-WALKING

The island's monks walk across fire on 3 November. You can join in, if you're keen.

🛏 Sleeping

It's well worth staying on the island – you'll be able to enjoy the evening quiet after the day trippers have left. The Miyajima Hotel Directory (www4.ocn.ne.jp/~miyayado) has a list of the island's accommodation.

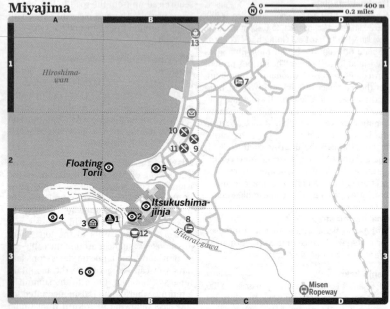

Guest House Kikugawa
RYOKAN $$

(ゲストハウス菊がわ; ☎44-0039; fax 44-2773; www.kikugawa.ne.jp; 796 Miyajima-chō; s/tw from ¥7140/12,600; ❸@🛜) This charming inn is built in traditional style and has lovely wooden interiors. There are Western- and Japanese-style rooms, all with attached bathrooms. The tatami rooms are slightly larger and one has a loft-like bedroom. Meals are available. Heading inland from the ferry terminal, turn right as you walk out of the tunnel and you'll see it on the left across the road from the small Zonkō-ji (存光寺) temple.

Iwasō Ryokan
RYOKAN $$$

(岩惣; ☎44-2233; www.iwaso.com; Momiji-dani Miyajima-chō; per person with 2 meals from ¥19,950) The Iwasō, open since 1854, offers the grand ryokan experience in exquisite gardens, a few minutes' walk from the throng. It's especially stunning in autumn when Momiji-dani (Maple Valley) explodes with colour. There are three wings (a stay in the Hanare costing the most), with a relaxing onsen in the main building.

Backpackers Miyajima
HOSTEL $

(バックパッカーズ宮島;☎56-3650;www.backpackers-miyajima.com/index_e.html; dm ¥2500-3000; ❸@🛜) Not actually on the island,

but a short walk from the mainland ferry terminal in Miyajima-guchi.

🍴 Eating & Drinking

There are plenty of eateries along and around the main strip, where you can try the local oysters, as well as eel in various guises (on rice, or perhaps in a steamed bun). Most restaurants shut down after the crowds go home.

TOP CHOICE Yakigaki-no-hayashi
OYSTERS $$

(焼がきのはやし; ☎44-0335; www.yakigaki-no-hayashi.co.jp; 505-1 Miyajima-chō; dishes ¥700-1400; ⏰10.30am-5pm, closed Wed; 📷) The oysters in the tank and on the barbecue outside are what everyone is eating here. Try a plate of *nama-gaki* (raw oysters) or *kaki-furai* (crumbed, fried oysters) for ¥1300. It's not all about the slimy shell-dwellers – there are other meals, such as *udon* sets (¥850), on offer too.

Mame-tanuki
RESTAURANT, IZAKAYA $$

(まめたぬき; ☎44-2131; 1113 Miyajima-chō; ⏰lunch & 5-11pm, closed dinner Tue; 📷) At this friendly place on the main shopping street there's a floor-level wooden counter, with a space to dangle your legs underneath. By day there are lunch sets, such as *anago*

Miyajima

meshi (steamed conger eel with rice; ¥1575) and fried oysters, and at night Mame-tanuki is one of the few places that's open late, serving drinks and *izakaya*-style small dishes. There's no smoking in the evening. Look for the large blue sign with white writing.

Kaki-ya   OYSTERS $$
(牡蠣屋; ☎ 44-2747; www.kaki-ya.jp; in Japanese; 539 Miyajima-chō; plate of 4 oysters ¥1000; ⏰ 10am-6pm; 📶) Kaki-ya is a sophisticated oyster bar on the main street. It serves delicious local oysters freshly grilled on the barbecue by the entrance, along with beers and wines by the glass.

Coffee Souko   CAFE $
(珈琲創庫; 280 Miyajima-chō; coffees ¥250-450; ⏰ 11am-5pm, irregular in low season) Across the river behind the shrine is this little cafe, where coffees go for less than in the main street. Get your latte to go or grab one of the few tables. Look for the red van inside.

ℹ Information

Tourist information counter (宮島観光案内所; ☎ 44-2011; www.miyajima.or.jp; 1162-18 Miyajima-chō; ⏰ 9am-5pm) In the ferry terminal.

ℹ Getting There & Away

The mainland **ferry terminal** is a short walk from Miyajima-guchi Station on the JR San-yō line, halfway between Hiroshima (¥400, 27 minutes) and Iwakuni. The ferry terminal can also be reached by tram 2 from Hiroshima (¥270, 70 minutes), which runs from the station and goes past Genbaku Dome.

FERRY Regular ferries shuttle across from Miyajima-guchi (¥170, 10 minutes). JR Pass holders should use the one operated by JR. High-speed ferries (¥1800, 30 minutes, six to eight daily) operate direct to Miyajima from Hiroshima's Ujina port. Another ferry (¥1900, 45 minutes, eight to 12 daily) runs between Miyajima and the Peace Memorial Park in Hiroshima.

ℹ Getting Around

Everywhere on the island is within easy walking distance. **Bicycles** can be hired from the JR office in the ferry terminal at a cost of ¥320 for two hours.

Iwakuni   岩国

☎ 0827 / POP 143,800

About an hour away from Hiroshima by train or bus, Iwakuni makes for a worthwhile half-day trip, or a stop-off en-route between Yamaguchi and Hiroshima. The main reason to come here is to see the five-arched Kintai-kyō bridge and take a walk around the Kikkō-kōen area to which it leads.

◎ Sights

Kintai-kyō   BRIDGE
(錦帯橋; Brocade Sash Bridge; admission ¥300, combination incl cable car & castle ¥930; ⏰ 24hr) Iwakuni's chief claim to fame is the graceful Kintai-kyō, built in 1673 during the rule of feudal lord Kikkawa Hiroyoshi. It has been restored several times since then, most recently in 2003–04, but remains an impressive sight, with Iwakuni-jō just peeping out from atop the green hills behind. In the feudal era only members of the ruling class were allowed to use the bridge, which linked the samurai quarters on the west bank of Nishiki-gawa with the rest of the town. Today, anyone can cross over for a small fee.

SAIJŌ

A short train ride east of Hiroshima is the town of **Saijō** (西条; http://saijosake.com), home to 10 sake breweries, eight of which are clustered within easy walking distance of the station. The brewers here know their stuff – Saijō has been producing sake for around 300 years – and most open up their doors to curious and thirsty visitors.

Heading down the road leading straight out from the station, you'll find the **tourist office** (◎10am-4pm, closed Mon) on the left, where you can pick up an English map of the breweries. West from here is well-known **Kamotsuru** (www.kamotsuru.jp, in Japanese), with a large tasting room screening a DVD about the district. Nearby is one of Saijō's oldest breweries, **Hakubotan** (www.hakubotan.co.jp, in Japanese), with a lovely broad-beamed display and tasting room with Munakata woodblock prints on the wall. In the area east of the station you'll find **Kamoki**, the smallest brewery here. Try the chiffon cake (¥400) in the attached **Sakagura Cafe** (◎10.30am-5pm, closed Mon). When you're done tasting, you can pay your respects to the god of sake at Matsuo-jinja, a short walk away behind the station.

A great time to come to Saijō is during the Sake Matsuri (http://sakematsuri.com, in Japanese), held the second weekend in October.

Saijō is 35 minutes by train from Hiroshima (¥570).

Kikkō-kōen
PARK

What remains of the old samurai quarter now forms pleasant Kikkō-kōen (吉香公園) on the west bank of the river, across the bridge. Within it are old residences and a couple of museums. Worth a look is the **Mekata Family Residence** (旧目加田家住宅; admission free; ◎9.30am-4.30pm, closed Mon), the former home of a middle-ranking samurai family from the mid-Edo period. Reptile enthusiasts and kids might want to pop next door to the small **White Snake Viewing Facility** (白蛇観覧所; admission ¥100; ◎9am-5pm), where several of the bizarre albino snakes unique to Iwakuni are on display.

Iwakuni-jō
CASTLE

(岩国城; admission ¥260; ◎9am-4.45pm, closed mid-end Dec) The original Iwakuni-jō was built by Hiroie, the first of the Kikkawa lords, between 1603 and 1608. Just seven years later, the Tokugawa shogunate passed a law limiting the number of castles *daimyō* were allowed to build, and the castle at Iwakuni was demolished. It was rebuilt not far from its original setting in 1960. There is nothing much of interest inside, but there are good views from the hilltop setting.

You can get to the castle by **cable car** (1 way/return ¥320/540; ◎every 20min 9am-5pm) or on foot via the pleasant path beside the youth hostel.

Ukai
CORMORANT FISHING

(☎28-2877; boat rides per person ¥3500; ◎6.30pm Jun-Aug) Watch from the riverbank (for free) at Kintai-kyō as fishermen and their feathered workers hunt by torchlight, or take a boat ride. Daily in summer, except when rain makes the water muddy, or on nights with a full moon.

🛏 Sleeping

If you're keen to stay in Iwakuni, you can find a couple of good options in the bridge and park area.

Hangetsu-an
RYOKAN **$$**

(半月庵; ☎41-0021; www.gambo-ad.com/hotel; fax 43-0121; 1-17-27 Iwakuni; per person with/without meals from ¥12,000/¥6000) Built as a teahouse in the early Meiji period, this traditional place has well-maintained tatami rooms and serves local food. The 'deluxe' suite (¥16,000) has garden views. *Sudomari* (stay without meals) is only available on weekdays. From the bus centre near Kintai-kyō, walk towards the bridge and take the left opposite the bridge entrance. It's on the left.

Iwakuni Youth Hostel
HOSTEL **$**

(岩国ユースホステル; ☎43-1092; fax 43-0123; www.geocities.jp/iwakuniyouth/englishtop.html; dm members/nonmembers ¥2835/3835) The large hostel has a friendly caretaker and a tranquil location behind the park on the west bank of the river. Meals are available.

🍴 Eating

There are small eateries in the park and stalls along the riverside. Local specialities include *iwakuni-zushi*, a sushi made in large square molds, and *renkon* (lotus root) cooked in *korokke* (croquette) form.

Midori-no-sato
SUSHI, NOODLES $

(緑の里; 1-4-10 Iwakuni; meals ¥580-1050; ◷10am-6pm; ⊜) This pleasant restaurant has set menus including an *iwakuni-zushi* set (¥1050) that comes with *renkon* noodles, and *udon* dishes from ¥580. From the bus centre near Kintai-kyō, walk towards the bridge and take the left opposite the bridge entrance. It's on the right.

ⓘ Information

Tourist information (☑41-1477; www.iwakuni -kanko.com, in Japanese) JR station (☑21-6050; ◷10am-5pm, closed Mon); *shinkansen* station (◷10.30am-3.30pm, closed Wed)

ⓘ Getting There & Away

BUS The bridge and park are a 20-minute bus ride (¥240) from Iwakuni Station. There are also buses (¥280, 20 minutes) from Shin-Iwakuni. Buses leave regularly. If coming from Hiroshima, it works out cheaper to get the Iwakuni bus from Hiroshima bus centre, which also handily drops you at Kintai-kyō (¥800, 50 minutes to an hour, hourly).

TRAIN The main Iwakuni Station is on the San-yō line, west of Hiroshima (¥740, 50 minutes). Shin-Iwakuni *shinkansen* station is half an hour by bus from the main town.

Tomo-no-ura 鞆の浦

☑084 / POP 5000

Perfectly situated in the middle of the Inland Sea coast, Tomo-no-ura flourished for centuries as a stopping-off point for boats travelling between western Japan and the capital, until the arrival of steam put an end to the town's glory days. Not a lot has happened here since. The town is not completely unspoilt, but the old harbour and the narrow streets that surround it retain much of the flavour of the Edo-period heyday.

Brochures and maps are available at JR Fukuyama Station and at various hotels in Tomo-no-ura itself. It's easy to get around the town on foot, but bikes can be hired (¥300 for two hours) from a booth next to the ferry terminal.

◉ Sights

Tomo-no-Ura Historical Museum MUSEUM
(鞆の浦歴史民俗資料館; www.tomo-rekimin .org, in Japanese; admission ¥150; ◷9am-5pm, closed Mon) This museum sits at the top of the hill behind the ferry pier. Nearby is the site of the **old castle**, of which nothing remains but a few foundation stones. Stone steps lead down from here to a network of nar-

row streets lined with old houses and shops, which then leads towards the harbour.

Fukuzenji TEMPLE
(福禅寺) Close to the ferry pier, this temple dates back to the 10th century. Adjoining it is **Taichōrō** (対潮楼; admission ¥200; ◷8am-5pm), built in the 1690s. This is where you go for a classic view out across a narrow channel to the uninhabited island of Benten-jima, and its shrine.

Jōyatō LANTERN
(常夜燈) The road along the shoreline from Taichōrō leads to the main harbour area, dominated by the stone lantern that used to serve as a lighthouse.

Ōta Residence HISTORICAL BUILDING
(太田家住宅; admission ¥400; ◷10am-5pm, closed Tue) Close to the lantern in the harbour area, the former Ōta residence is a fine collection of restored buildings from the mid-18th century. Guided tours take you through the impressive family home and workplace. There is an English pamphlet.

Amo Chinmi Processed Seafoods Company FACTORY
(阿藻珍味; www.amochinmi.com, in Japanese; 1567-1 Ushiroji Tomo-chō) Amo Chinmi has its factory and shop at the far western end of the harbour. In the factory premises, **Uonosato** (うをの里; admission free, ◷9am-5pm, closed Mon) processes much of the locally caught fish. You can watch the workers making prawn *sembei* (rice crackers) and *chikuwa* (processed fish sausages). Tomo-no-ura is also famous for *homei-shu* (保命酒), a medicinal liquor made from rice, *shōchū* (a distilled spirit made from potato and barley) and 16 types of herbs. Among the houses a few blocks back from the waterfront, you can find stalls offering samples.

Iō-ji TEMPLE
(医王寺) Around the harbour and inland slightly from the Ōta Residence are a dozen or so temples. Up a steep hill to the west of the harbour, Iō-ji was reputedly founded by Kōbō Daishi in the 900s. A path leads from the temple to the top of a bluff, from where there are more great views.

Sensui-jima ISLAND
Sensui-jima is just five minutes across the water by regular ferry (¥240 return). On the island there's a campground, a couple of hotels and good views, especially at sunset.

🛏 Sleeping

The town is small enough to be seen in half a day. If you are interested in spending the night here, it's worth staying on nearby Sensui-jima.

Kokuminshukusha Sensui-jima RYOKAN **$$**
(国民宿舎仙酔島; ☎970-5050; www.tomonoura .co.jp/sen/02shukusha.html, in Japanese; 3373-2 Ushiroji Tomo-chō; per person with meals from ¥9800; 🍴) This is a reasonably priced option on Sensui-jima, right on the beach, with Japanese- and Western-style rooms and wonderful baths.

Keishōkan Sazanami-tei RYOKAN **$$$**
(景勝館漣亭; ☎982-2121; www.keishokan.com; 421 Tomo Tomo-chō; per person with 2 meals from ¥18,000) Inside the modern exterior are traditional rooms, some with their own *rotemburo* (outdoor bath), and an impressive array of baths. Meals include fresh fish from the Inland Sea.

Tomo Seaside Hotel HOTEL **$$**
(鞆シーサイドホテル; ☎983-5111; www.tomo noura.co.jp/tomo, in Japanese; per person with 2 meals from ¥8800) This is slightly rundown and caters mainly to families and tour groups, but it's close to the sights and comfortable enough, with tatami rooms and an onsen.

🍴 Eating

@Cafe CAFE **$**
(Jōyatōmae Tomo-chō; meals ¥600-1200; ⏰11am-8pm, closed Wed) This modern cafe is a good place to stop for a break and a bite in town. It is situated in a 150-year-old building beside the stone lighthouse in the harbour. There's a small menu consisting of pasta dishes and other meals for around ¥1000.

Tabuchiya CAFE, JAPANESE **$**
(田渕屋; www.geocities.jp/tabuchiya, in Japanese; Tomo Tomo-chō; ⏰10.30am-6.30pm, closed Wed) Coffee and light meals, including *hayashi raisu* (beef in sauce on rice; ¥1000). Walk past the Ōta Residence away from the harbour and look for the green *noren* on your left.

ℹ Getting There & Away

Buses run every 15 minutes from outside JR Fukuyama Station (¥510, 30 minutes), which is a main hub on the San-yō line east of Onomichi and west of Kurashiki.

Onomichi 尾道

☎0848 / POP 145,200

Onomichi is a gritty, old-timey seaport town whose hills are full of temples and literary sites. Film director Ōbayashi Nobuhiko was born in Onomichi, and the town has featured in a number of Japanese movies, notably Ozu's *Tokyo Story*. It's also known for its *rāmen*, and you'll find plenty of places dishing it up. But for many travellers, Onomichi is the base from which to cycle the Shimanami Kaidō, the system of road bridges that allows people to island-hop their way across the Inland Sea to Shikoku.

⊙ Sights

The modern town stretches east from the station along a thin corridor between the railway tracks and the sea. Most of the places of interest are on the other side of the tracks, in the series of steep flagstoned streets that ladder the hillside. There are also some interesting sights on the islands accessible by ferry and/or bike from Onomichi; nearby Ikuchi-jima (p383) is a popular half-day trip.

Historical Temple Walk TRAIL, TEMPLES
(古寺めぐり) This well-signed trail, taking in 25 old temples, starts just east of the station: take the inland road from the station and cross the railway tracks by the statue of local author Hayashi Fumiko. About a third of the way along the route is a **cable car** (1 way/return ¥280/440; ⏰every 15min 9am-5.15pm) that whisks you up to the hilltop **Senkō-ji** (千光寺), the best known and most impressive of Onomichi's temples, and its pleasant park.

Onomichi Literature Museum MUSEUM
(文学記念室; 13-28 Tsuchidō; admission with Shiga Naoya residence ¥300; ⏰9am-5pm Nov-Mar, to 6pm Apr-Oct, closed Tue Dec-Feb) Close to the fourth temple along the temple walk, Hōdo-ji, this museum features displays on the lives and works of Hayashi Fumiko and other writers connected with Onomichi. It's all in Japanese, but the proprietor speaks English and will delight in taking you through it all at length.

Shiga Naoya Residence NOTABLE BUILDING
(志賀直哉旧居; 8-28 Tsuchi-dō; admission with Onomichi Literature Museum ¥300; ⏰9am-5pm Nov-Mar, to 6pm Apr-Oct, closed Tue Dec-Feb) Around the corner from the literature museum is the house where Shiga Naoya, another of Japan's major 20th-century writers, lived from 1912 to 1913.

🛏 Sleeping

Miyako Ryokan   RYOKAN $

(都旅館; ☎22-3853; www.miyako-ryokan.jp, in Japanese; 13-4 Nishi Gosho-machi; per person with/without breakfast ¥5500/4750) This is a charming little place with the odd 'nostalgic' touch, like a stained-glass porthole window and Tiffany-style lamps. The neat tatami rooms and one (small) Western-style room share the bathroom. It's a five-minute walk from the station – go immediately right as you exit, then left at the third traffic lights. Look for the yellow exterior.

Uonobu Ryokan   RYOKAN $$$

(魚信旅館; ☎37-4175; fax 37-3849; www.uonobu .jp, in Japanese; 2-27-6 Kubo; per person with meals from ¥16,800) Right on the waterfront, this elegantly old-fashioned place is renowned for its seafood. Nonguests can eat here too, but you'll need to reserve by 5pm the previous day. It's a good 20-minute walk from the station. Look for the imposing traditional building on the right just after the city hall (市役所). There are paper lanterns outside.

Green Hill Hotel Onomichi   HOTEL $$

(グリーンヒルホテル尾道; ☎24-0100; http:// gho.hotwire.jp/index_e.html; 9-1 Higashi Gosho-ma-chi; s/tw from ¥7875/15,750; ⊟@) Directly above the ferry port and a minute's walk from the station, this comfortable, well-appointed hotel could hardly be better located. Pay a little more for a room on the sea-view side.

🍴 Eating

Go left out of the station to find eateries along the waterfront and in the arcade one block inland.

Yamaneko   CAFE, RESTAURANT $

(やまねこ; 2-9-33 Tsuchidō; dishes ¥700-950; ⏰11.30am-10pm, to midnight Sat & Sun, closed Mon) Retro furnishings, battered-looking walls decorated with local artwork, and a mellow playlist add up to a relaxed spot for a drink or light meal (pasta carbonara is ¥930). Find it on a corner along the waterfront road, a 15-minute walk from the station, just before Royal Hotel. Look for the cats.

Onomichi Rāmen Ichibankan   RĀMEN $

(尾道ラーメン壱番館; www.f-ichibankan.com, in Japanese; 2-9-26 Tsuchidō; dishes ¥530-890; ⏰11am-7.30pm, closed Fri) Opposite the Sumi-yoshi shrine on the waterfront, a 15-minute walk from the station, this popular noodle shop is a good place to try Onomichi *rāmen*, characterised by thick slabs of juicy pork. Its best seller is the *kaku-ni rāmen* (角煮ラーメン; noodles with eggs and tender cuts of fatty pork) for ¥890.

Yasuhiro Sushi   SUSHI & SASHIMI $$

(保広寿司; yasuhiro.co4.jp, in Japanese; 1-10-12 Tsuchidō; ⏰lunch & dinner, closed Mon) Enjoy excellent local seafood in this cosy, traditional black-and-white building on the seafront, five to 10 minutes' walk from the station. Try the *sashimi teishoku* (¥1600) at lunchtime. Prices start from around ¥8000 in the evening.

ℹ Information

Onomichi City website (www.city.onomichi .hiroshima.jp) A good source of information on sights, accommodation and transport links.

Tourist information office (☎20-0005; ⏰9am-6pm) Supplies maps and can help with booking accommodation. Inside Onomichi Station.

ℹ Getting There & Away

BICYCLE Onomichi Port Rent-a-Cycle (☎22-5332; per day ¥500, deposit ¥1000; ⏰7am-6pm) is in the car park next to the ferry terminal. Bikes with gears and electric-assist bikes available.

BUS Regular buses run to Imabari (¥2200), in Shikoku, from Onomichi Station (some originating in Shin-Onomichi Station), with a transfer at Inno-shima. It takes up to two hours, depending on the connection.

FERRY Ferries run to Imabara from Habu port on Inno-shima and Miyaura port on Ōmi-shima. There are no ferries linking Onomichi with Ōmi-shima.

Ferries from Onomichi run to the following destinations:

Ikuchi-jima (Setoda) ¥800, 40 minutes, nine daily

Inno-shima (Habu) ¥850, 45 minutes, six daily

Inno-shima (Shigei) ¥400, 20 minutes, nine daily

Mukai-shima ¥100, five minutes, every 10 minutes

TRAIN Onomichi is on the main JR San-yō line. The Shin-Onomichi *shinkansen* station is 3km north. Regular buses (¥180, 15 minutes) connect the two. On the San-yō line:

Fukuyama ¥410, 20 minutes

Hiroshima ¥1450, 1½ hours

OKAYAMA & AROUND

Okayama Prefecture (岡山県; Okayama-ken) is known for its rural character, and the villa at Hattōji offers one of Japan's

CYCLING THE SHIMANAMI KAIDŌ

The Setouchi Shimanami Kaidō (瀬戸内しまなみ海道; Shimanami Sea Route) is a chain of bridges linking Onomichi in Hiroshima Prefecture with Imabari in Ehime Prefecture on Shikoku, via six Inland Sea islands. Besides being remarkable feats of engineering (the monster Kurushima-kaikyō trio at the Imabari end are among the longest suspension bridges in the world), the bridges make it possible to cycle the whole way across. Breezing along, 50m or more above the island-dotted sea, is an amazing experience and a highlight of a trip to this part of Japan.

The Route

The route begins on Mukai-shima (a quick boat ride from Onomichi) and crosses Inno-shima, Ikuchi-jima, Ōmi-shima, Hakata-jima and Ōshima, before the final bridge to reach Imabari. The 'recommended' route is well marked and signed with information boards and maps, but there's nothing stopping you from taking detours and plotting your own course from bridge to bridge. Much of the 'recommended' route is fairly flat, with the odd minor hill, but there are thigh-burning inclines leading up to each bridge entrance.

Distance & Time

The total 'recommended' route from Onomichi to Imabari is roughly 70km, and could be done in eight or so hours, depending on your fitness and propensity to stop and take pictures. You could take the ferry part of the way, such as to Ikuchi-jima, and bike the rest. Or, a good day trip from Onomichi is to cycle to Ikuchi-jima (about 30km) and return to Onomichi on the ferry in the afternoon.

Sights

The ride itself – passing by citrus groves, beaches and glittering views of the sea – is satisfying enough, but there are plenty of reasons to stop and get off your bike.

INNO-SHIMA

On Inno-shima (因島), once the base of one of the three Murakami pirate clans, there's a modern-replica **pirate castle** (因島水軍城; admission ¥310; ◎9.30am-5pm, closed Thu). Or cycle up to **Shirataki-yama** (白滝山) to see a collection of sculptures of the 500 Rakan disciples of the Buddha.

IKUCHI-JIMA

There's very little doing in Setoda, the main town of Ikuchi-jima (生口島), but it does have the remarkable temple complex of **Kōsan-ji** (耕三寺; admission ¥1200; ◎9am-5pm). Shortly after the death of his beloved mother in 1934, local steel-tube magnate and arms manufacturer Kanemoto Kōzō became a Buddhist priest and sank his fortune into a series of garishly coloured temple buildings. The result is a chaos of over-the-top Buddhist kitsch, consisting of some 2000 exhibits. Don't miss the 1000 Buddhas Cave and its series of

great countryside getaways. The area is also home to Kurashiki and its well-preserved merchant quarter, the Kibiji district cycling route, and a coastline that provides jumping-off points for some of the most popular islands in the Inland Sea.

Okayama 岡山

☑086 / POP 709,600

The most many travellers see of Okayama is the blur of colour as they fly through on the *shinkansen* to Hiroshima. But it's worth stepping off the train, if only to spend a few hours strolling around Kōraku-en, one of Japan's top three gardens, which is overlooked by the city's crow-black castle. If you have a few days up your sleeve, make Okayama your base for day trips to other attractions in the region.

The city itself is pleasant and laid-back, and is proud of its connection to Momotarō, the demon-quelling boy hero of one of Japan's best-known folk tales. You will spot his face beaming out at you all over town.

graphically illustrated hells. Just past Kōsan-ji is the **Ikuo Hirayama Museum of Art** (平山郁夫美術館; www.hirayama-museum.or.jp, in Japanese; admission ¥700; ⏱9am-5pm), dedicated to the life and work of the well-travelled, famous Setoda-born artist. The collection here includes several striking works inspired by Ikuo's journeys in India and along the Silk Road.

ŌMI-SHIMA

The mountainous island of Ōmi-shima (大三島) is home to one of the oldest Shintō shrines in western Japan, **Ōyamazumi-jinja** (大山祇神社; admission Treasure Hall & Kaiji Museum ¥1000; ⏱8.30am-5pm), near Miyaura port. The deity enshrined here is the brother of Amaterasu, the sun goddess. The present structure dates from 1378, but in the courtyard is a 2600-year-old camphor tree, and the treasure hall contains the most important collection of ancient weapons found anywhere in Japan. Heading past the shrine, cycle your way back to the present with a look at the modern sculpture in the **Tokoro Museum** (ところミュージアム大三島; www.city.imabari.ehime.jp/bunka/tokoro; admission ¥300; ⏱9am-5pm, closed Mon), from where there are also fabulous views.

Sleeping

Ikuchi-jima is a good place to stay overnight. The friendly **Setoda Shimanami Guesthouse** (瀬戸田しまなみゲストハウス; ☎27-3137; www7.enjoy.ne.jp/~kymy-y/eshimanami.html; 58-1 Tarumi Setoda-chō; per person with/without meals ¥4600/3000), also called Hostel Setoda Tarumi Onsen, is right on Sunset Beach and has its own onsen. Accommodation is in individual tatami rooms and payment is by cash only. If you're not arriving on two wheels, a pick-up can be arranged from Setoda ferry port. Tourist offices have lists of accommodation on other islands and can help with reservations.

Information

The tourist office in Onomichi, and those on each of the islands, can help with all the information you need, including an excellent map (in English) showing the routes, distances and locations of bike terminals along the way. The Japanese version is downloadable from www.go-shimanami.jp, and there are basic maps, plus bus and ferry schedules, at www.city.onomichi.hiroshima.jp/english/kanko/shimanami/shimanami.html.

If you need to get heavy luggage across, contact **Kuroneko Yamato** (www.kuronekoyamato.co.jp), whose *takkyūbin* service will deliver it for you by the next business day (around ¥1900 depending on size).

Bikes & Costs

Bike hire is ¥500 per day, plus ¥1000 deposit. You don't get the deposit back if you return the bike to a different rental place along the route. There are bike-hire terminals in Onomichi and in Imabari, and on each island in between. Bridge tolls for cyclists are between ¥50 and ¥200 per bridge, and it costs up to ¥150 to take your bike on a ferry.

⦿ Sights

Kōraku-en
GARDEN

(後楽園; www.okayama-korakuen.jp; 1-5 Kōraku-en; admission ¥400; ⏱7.30am-6pm Apr-Sep, 8am-5pm Oct-Mar) Kōraku-en draws the crowds with its reputation as one of the three most beautiful gardens in Japan. Built on the orders of *daimyō* Ikeda Tsunemasa, it was completed in 1700 and, despite suffering major damage during floods in the 1930s and air raids in the 1940s, remains much as it was in feudal times. It was opened to the public in 1884.

Unusually for a Japanese garden, it is mostly expansive lawns (though, as usual, you can't walk on them). The garden is broken up by ponds, teahouses and other Edo-period buildings, including a stage for nō, and even has a small tea plantation and rice fields. The highlights change with the seasons – in spring the groves of plum and cherry blossoms are stunning, white lotuses unfurl in summer, and in autumn the maple trees are a delight for photographers. There are also seasonal events (fancy some harvest-moon viewing?) – check the website.

Okayama

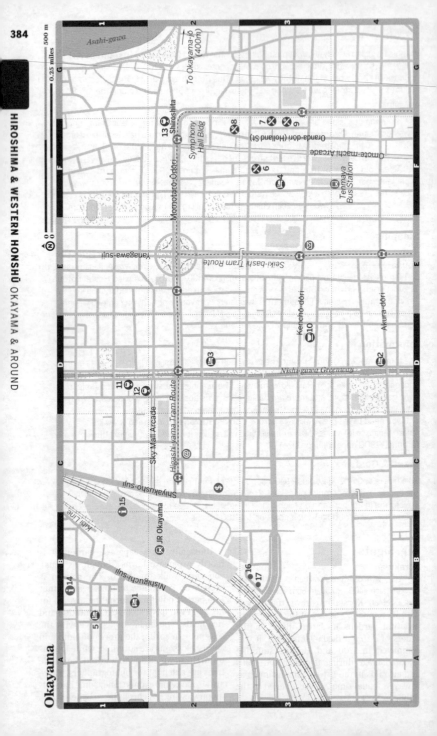

0 500 m
0 0.25 miles

Asahi-gawa

To Okayama-jō (400m)

Shiroshita

Symphony Hall Bldg

Oranda-dōri (Holland St)

Omote-machi Arcade

Tennaya Bus Station

Momotaro-Odori

Yanagawa-suji

Seiki-bashi Tram Route

Kenchō-dōri

Akura-dōri

Nishi-gawa Greenway

Sky Mall Arcade

Higashi-yama Tram Route

Shiyakusho-suji

Kibi Line

JR Okayama

Nishiguchi-suji

Okayama

The park is a 20-minute walk up Momotarō-Ōdōri from the station. Alternatively, take the Higashi-yama tram to the Shiroshita stop (¥100) then follow the signs.

Okayama-jō CASTLE
(岡山城; 2-3-1 Marunouchi; admission ¥300, additional charge for special exhibitions; ⏱9am-5pm) Nicknamed U-jō (烏城; Crow Castle) because of its colour, the striking black Okayama Castle was built by *daimyō* Ukita Hideie and completed in 1597. Much of the castle was dismantled after the Meiji Restoration and most of what remained burnt down during WWII air raids. The castle was rebuilt in 1966.

The imposing exterior – its gilded fish-gargoyles flipping their tails in the air – is the castle's most impressive aspect, and you can enjoy it for nix by walking around the grounds, or looking from across the river. Inside the *donjon* (main keep) museum, modern finishes and an elevator mar the 16th-century feel, but there are a few interesting displays, and views from the top floor.

Yumeji Art Museum ART GALLERY, MUSEUM
(夢二郷土美術館; www.yumeji-art-museum.com; 2-1-32 Hama; admission ¥700; ⏱9am-5pm, closed Mon) Prominent Taishō-era artist and poet Takehisa Yumeji (1884–1934) is particularly known for his *bijin-ga* (images of beautiful women), and various wistfully posed ladies feature among the paintings, prints and screens on display at this small museum. It's just across the river on the northeast side of Kōraku-en, about a 15-minute walk from the Shiroshita tram stop.

Okayama Prefectural Museum MUSEUM
(岡山県立博物館; www.pref.okayama.jp/kyoiku/kenhaku/hakubu.htm; 1-5 Kōraku-en; admission ¥250; ⏱9am-6pm, closed Mon) A range of historical artefacts from the region, including documents, tools, armoury and Bizen pottery. The museum is near the entrance to Kōraku-en.

Hayashibara Museum of Art MUSEUM
(林原美術館; www.hayashibara-museumofart.jp, in Japanese; 2-7-15 Marunouchi; admission ¥300; ⏱9am-5pm, closed Mon) Small museum with exhibits of scrolls, armour and paintings that were once the property of the Ikeda clan (who ruled Okayama for much of the Edo period). Find Hayashibara near the back entrance of the castle.

🏃 Tours

Okayama has a small army of **volunteer guides**, some English-speaking, who are keen to share their knowledge free of charge. Make arrangements at least a couple of days in advance by contacting friendly Okayama aficionado **Masako Sugiyama** (☎222-2121), at Central Hotel Okayama (regardless of whether you're staying there).

🛏 Sleeping

Modern midrange and budget hotels (mostly chains) dominate the scene in Okayama. For a more traditional ryokan experience, consider staying in nearby Kurashiki.

TOP CHOICE Kōraku Hotel HOTEL $$
(後楽ホテル; ☎221-7111; www.hotel.kooraku.co.jp; 5-1 Heiwa-chō; s/tw from ¥7500/15,000; ❄@) Kōraku has classy touches like local museum pieces displayed on each floor, and stylish rooms with plenty of breathing space. Corner rooms (from ¥20,000), with large curved windows, are especially luxurious. Staff members speak English, as does the enthusiastic manager, who you'll likely come across mingling with guests in the lobby. Throw in a convenience store, a restaurant and a handy location and it's hard to beat.

Central Hotel Okayama
HOTEL **$$**

(セントラルホテル岡山; ☎222-2121; www
.c-hotelokayama.co.jp, in Japanese; 1-10-28 Tama-
chi; s/tw from ¥5600/9200; ❄@) There are a
couple of pleasant surprises behind the rath-
er pedestrian name – the first is the thought-
fully designed wood-hued rooms, with
neatly hidden amenities; for the second, ask
to see the room at the top. Some English is
spoken – if you can't navigate the Japanese
website, call or email (info@c-hotelokaya
ma.co.jp).

Saiwai-sō
HOTEL **$**

(ビジネスホテル幸荘; ☎254-0020; http://
w150.j.fiw-web.net, in Japanese; fax 254-9438;
24-8 Ekimoto-chō; s/tw ¥4200/7600; ☎❄) This
'happy house' declares itself Okayama's
first business hotel but it's not typical of
that genre, having mostly tatami rooms
(go for one of these) spread throughout a
warren-like building. Some rooms have
shared bathrooms. Groups and families are
welcomed (up to eight people from ¥3600
per person). And where else will you find
an old-school video-game table in the hotel
lounge? The affable owners speak a little
English.

Okayama View Hotel
HOTEL **$$**

(岡山ビューホテル; ☎224-2000; www.oka
view.jp; 1-11-17 Naka Sange; s/tw from ¥6300/
10,500; ❄@☎) Blonde-wood fittings and
beds on the floor in the 'concept' rooms
here make this an attractive modern Japanese option. Rooms are small but the hotel
is in a good spot between the station and
the garden.

ANA Hotel Okayama
HOTEL **$$$**

(岡山全日空ホテル; ☎898-1111; www.anahotel
-okayama.com, in Japanese; 15-1 Ekimoto-chō; s/
tw from ¥13,860/24,255; ❄@) This top-end
chain hotel has gorgeous rooms, several
restaurants and great views from its Sky
Bar. There are numerous 'plans' and
significant savings to be had if you book
online.

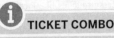

TICKET COMBO

Save a few yen with a combination
ticket (¥560) covering entry to both
Kōraku-en and Okayama-jō. Passes
including other local museums are also
available. Buy combination tickets at
whichever site you visit first.

✗ Eating

Tori-soba Ōta
NOODLES **$**

(とりそば太田; www.torisoba.com, in Japanese;
1-7-24 Omote-chō; dishes ¥650-990; ☺11am-8pm,
closed Mon; ❄📵) The name of this little
countertop restaurant is also its trademark
dish: *tori-soba* (steaming bowls of noodles
packed with chicken and served in a tasty
broth). Other options are variations on the
chicken, noodle and spring onion theme
and even the small serve is a decent feed.
Look for the big blue sign opposite Chūgoku
Bank.

Okabe
TOFU **$**

(おかべ; 1-10-1 Omote-chō; dishes ¥800-850;
☺11.30am-2.30pm, closed Sun) This street-
corner tofu restaurant is recognisable by the
big illustration of a heavily laden tofu seller
in a straw hat. Squeeze in at the counter and
watch the team of women chopping and fry-
ing as you wait. There are only two things on
the menu: an *okabe teishoku* (set meal with
several types of tofu; ¥800) and a *namayu-
uba-don teishoku* (dried 'tofu skin' on rice,
with soup; ¥850).

Shiromi Chaya
NOODLES, TEA **$**

(城見茶屋; 272-2920; 1-7 Kōraku-en; dishes ¥550-
750; ☺8am-5pm, closed Mon; 📵) Relax under-
cover on a tatami platform overlooking the
river and take in great views of the castle
at this perfectly placed eatery outside the
south gate of Kōraku-en. As well as standard
tasty *udon* and *soba* offerings, there are rice-
based dishes, *chirashi-zushi* (sushi rice with
egg and fish toppings) and teas, plus menus
in various languages. It can get busy in
garden-viewing high season.

Padang Padang
ITALIAN, FRENCH **$$**

(パダンパダン; www.padangpadang.jp, in
Japanese; ☎223-6665; 1-7-10 Omote-chō; dishes
¥1000-2000; ☺6pm-midnight, closed Tue; 📵)
Despite its name, this mellow restaurant
focuses on French and Italian pasta, meat
and risotto dishes, served to a North African
soundtrack. There is occasional live music
and it's a good spot for a glass of wine after
a day of sightseeing.

Quiet Village Curry Shop
CURRY **$**

(クワイエットビレッジカレーショップ;
1-6-43 Omote-chō; dishes ¥780-880; ☺11.30am-
7.30pm, closed Mon; ✒) This cosy curry restaurant consists of one long table, where
the menu is disguised as a notebook. Some
English is spoken and there are vegetarian
and vegan options.

DON'T MISS

NAKED FESTIVAL

If you're in the area on the third Saturday in February, head to Saidai-ji for the **Saidai-ji Eyō**, also known as the Hadaka Matsuri (Naked Festival). It takes place at the Kannon-in temple, where a chaotic crowd of around 10,000 men in loincloths and *tabi* (split-toe socks) fight over two sacred *shingi* (wooden batons) while freezing water is poured over them. The fun kicks off at 10pm, though there's also a version for elementary-school boys earlier in the evening. Regular trains run to Saidai-ji from Okayama (¥230, 17 minutes).

🍷 Drinking

Izayoi no Tsuki   IZAKAYA
(いざ酔いの月; 1-10-2 Ekimae-chō; ⊙5pm-midnight) A convivial atmosphere, walls decorated with sake labels, and an enormous drink menu – just what you want from a local *izakaya*. There are numerous sakes from Okayama Prefecture (around ¥500) and beers from local microbreweries – try the Doppo pilsner or a Kibi Doteshita Bakushu ale. Izoyoi is just back from the corner off the Sky Mall arcade. The bar's name is written in large characters across a yellow moon.

Saudade na Yoru   BAR, CAFE
(サウダーヂな夜; www.saudade-ent.com/saudade, in Japanese; 2nd fl, Shiroshita bldg, 10-16 Tenjin-chō; ⊙6pm-3am) This 2nd-floor lounge bar overlooking the Symphony Hall building makes all the right retro-chic moves, including a rough concrete floor, mismatched furniture and ornate-glass lighting. It has a good drinks list (most priced around ¥700), coffees and a limited food and snacks menu. A ¥300 cover charge applies after 9pm.

5 Deli   JUICE BAR
(1-1-11 Tamachi; juices ¥400; ⊙9am-11pm Mon-Fri, 10am-11pm Sat, 10am-9pm Sun) Funky little bar with a good range of juices and coffee.

Aussie Bar   PUB
(オージーバー; 1-10-21 Ekimae-chō; ⊙7pm-3am) An expat-run watering hole that's popular with the city's English-speaking population.

ℹ Information

ATMs at 7-Eleven stores accept international cards.

Bank of Tokyo-Mitsubishi UFJ (三菱東京UFJ銀行; ☑223-9211; 6-36 Honmachi; ⊙9am-3pm Mon-Fri) Cashes travellers cheques.

Comic Buster (コミックバスター; www.comicbuster.jp/kameiten/33_okayama; per 10min/3hr ¥80/980; ⊙24hr) Internet access.

Momotarō Tourist Information Centre (ももたろう観光センター; www.okayama-japan.jp/en; ☑222-2912; ⊙9am-8pm) Maps and information on Okayama and the region. Some English spoken. In the basement complex below the station – take the east exit and the stairs down on the right.

Okayama Central Post Office (岡山中央郵便局; 2-1-1 Naka Sange; ⊙9am-7pm Mon-Fri, to 5pm Sat, to 12.30pm Sun) International ATM.

Okayama International Centre (岡山国際交流センター; ☑256-2914; www.opief.or.jp/english; 2-2-1 Hōkan-chō; ⊙9am-5pm, closed Sun) Has information in English on sights throughout the region and resources for foreign residents. Free internet access (30 minutes).

Tourist information counter (観光案内所; ⊙9am-6pm) In the station, by the entrance to the *shinkansen* tracks.

ℹ Getting There & Away

AIR Okayama airport (www.okayama-airport.org/en) is 20km northwest of the city centre. Regular buses (¥740, 30 minutes) run between the airport and the station.

BUS Buses to Shin-Okayama port (¥480, 40 minutes, one or two per hour) leave from Okayama Station, also stopping at Tenmaya bus station in the city centre.

FERRY See the Shōdo-shima and Naoshima sections for information on accessing these islands.

TRAIN Major destinations on the San-yō *shinkansen* line:

Hakata ¥11,550, one hour 50 minutes

Hiroshima ¥5350, 35 minutes

Kyoto ¥6820, one hour

Osaka ¥5350, 45 minutes

Tokyo ¥15,850, 3½ hours

Other destinations:

Takamatsu (Shikoku) ¥1470, one hour, two to three times per hour

Yonago (Tottori Prefecture) ¥4620, two hours, hourly

Okayama Prefecture and Kagawa Prefecture, on the island of Shikoku, are linked by the legend of Momotarō, the Peach Boy, who emerged from the stone of a peach and, backed up by a monkey, a pheasant and a dog, defeated a three-eyed, three-toed people-eating demon. The island of Megi-jima, off Takamatsu in Shikoku, is said to be the site of the clash with the demon. Momotarō may actually have been a Yamato prince who was deified as Kibitsuhiko. His shrine, Kibitsu-jinja, lies along the route of the Kibiji bicycle ride.

There are statues of Momotarō at JR Okayama Station; he and his sidekicks feature on manhole covers; and the city's biggest street is named after him. One of the most popular souvenir treats from Okayama is also Momotarō's favoured sweet, *kibi-dango*, a soft *mochi*-like dumpling made with millet flour.

ⓘ Getting Around

Okayama can be seen on foot or with a couple of short tram rides.

BICYCLE JR Eki-Rinkun Rent-a-cycle (レンタサイクル駅リンくん; ☑223-7081; per day ¥300; ☺7am-11pm)

CAR Eki Rent-a-Car (駅レンタカー; ☑224-1363; per day from ¥5770; ☺8am-8pm)

TRAM Trams run from in front of the station. The Higashi-yama line takes you to the main attractions, going all the way up Momotarō-Ōdōri, then turning right. The Seiki-bashi line turns right earlier, passing the Central Post Office. Travel within the central city area costs ¥100.

Bizen　　　　　　　　　　　備前

☑0869 / POP 37,800

The Bizen region has been renowned for its ceramics since the Kamakura period (1185–1333). The pottery produced here tends to be earthy and subdued, and has been prized by dedicated tea-ceremony aficionados for centuries. Travellers with an interest in pottery may find the gritty Bizen town of **Imbe** (伊部) and its kilns a worthwhile side trip from Okayama.

Most places of ceramic interest are within easy walking distance of Imbe Station. The **information counter** (☑64-1100; www.touyuukai.jp; ☺9am-6pm, closed Tue), inside the souvenir shop on the left as you exit the platform, has a handy *Inbe Walk* map, in English, showing the locations of kilns, shops and other sites.

On the 2nd floor of the station building is a gallery run by the **Friends of Bizen-yaki Ceramics Society** (岡山県備前焼陶友会; www.touyuukai.jp; admission free; ☺9.30am-5.30pm, closed Tue), selling a wide range of ceramics by contemporary potters.

The sombre-looking concrete building to the right as you exit the station is the

Okayama Prefectural Bizen Ceramics Art Museum (岡山県備前陶芸美術館; admission ¥700; ☺9.30am-5pm, closed Mon), with pieces from the Muromachi (1333–1568) and Momoyama (1568–1600) periods, plus work by several modern artists who have been designated 'Living National Treasures'.

The station area is pretty uninspiring, but walking up the road leading north you begin to spot the smoking chimneys and the bamboo groves of the hills behind the town. There are several galleries and shops on this road and many more along the road that forms a T-intersection at the end. Lanes running uphill from here are dotted with potters' workshops, some selling their wares directly to the public.

Go right at the T-intersection then left up a lane to glimpse the kiln ruins of **Tempogama** (天保窯), dating from c 1832, now fenced off for protection. Look for the red iron roof. Back on the road, further along from the turn for the ruins, is **Amatsu-jinja** (天津神社), decorated with Bizen-yaki figures of the animals of the Chinese zodiac. From here there is also a pretty walk up to **Imbe-jinja** (忌部神社).

You can drop in at some of the kilns to watch the professionals at work, and several kilns in the area offer the chance to try your hand at making your own masterpiece. Try **Bishūgama** (備州窯; ☑64-1160; www.gift.or.jp/bisyu; bisyu@gift.or.jp; 302-2 Imbe Bizen-shi; ☺9am-3pm), where making a piece will set you back ¥2625 or ¥3675, depending on the type of firing you choose. Reservations are required. Go right at the T-intersection, pass the Amatsu-jinja entrance, and you'll find the rear of Bishūgama near the end of the road.

There is one direct train an hour to Imbe from Okayama (¥570, 40 minutes) on the Akō line (赤穂線), bound for Banshū-Akō (播州赤穂) and Aioi (相生).

Kibiji 吉備路

The largely rural Kibiji district around Okayama is best explored on two wheels, following a popular **cycling route** across the Kibi plain. It takes in several interesting temples and shrines, an ancient burial mound and an old sake brewery, passing through rice fields along the way.

To get to the starting point, take a local JR Kibi line train from Okayama to Bizen Ichinomiya (備前一宮; ¥200, 11 minutes, about every half-hour). From here, the mostly flat cycling route runs west for roughly 15km to the station at Sōja (総社), where you can drop off your bike and take a train back to Okayama. It can take as little as a couple of hours if you're just peddling on through, but allow three or four if you want to wander around the sights or take a few detours (ie get lost) here and there.

Uedo Rent-a-Cycle (ウエドレンタサイクル; ☎086-284-2311; ☉9am-6pm) is on the right at the front of Bizen Ichinomiya Station. It occasionally closes in bad weather. If no one is around, try asking the guard at the nearby bike parking lot, who may be able to call and get it opened up for you. Bike rental is ¥1000 if you're returning the bike at Sōja.

From here, follow the route map (in Japanese) you receive with the bike, and the blue 'Kibiji District' road signs along the course. Despite this guidance, it's easy to take a wrong turn at the start, and even easier at the end near Sōja. Most locals will be able to set you straight – just ask them for the Kibiji *jitensha dōro* (Kibiji bike path).

The first shrine you'll pass is the **Kibitsuhiko-jinja** (吉備津彦神社), fronted by a pond near the start of the bicycle path. Not far from here is the **Kibitsu-jinja** (吉備津神社). This major shrine is dedicated to an ancient warrior who subdued a local bandit/demon called Ura and brought the area under central control. Many people believe that these exploits were the ultimate source of the Momotarō legend (see the box, p388). You'll see Momotarō's peachy features looking out at you from the votive tablets in front of the shrine.

WORTH A TRIP

HATTŌJI

As you head up through the hills past the farms and thatched-roof houses to Hattōji (八塔寺), the crowds and vending machine–packed streets of big-city Japan begin to feel delightfully out of reach.

The chief reason to journey out here is to stay at the **Hattōji International Villa** (八塔寺国際交流ヴィラ; Kagami Yoshinaga-chō Bizen-shi; ☉🏠), a restored farmhouse that is one of two remaining places established by the prefectural government in the late 1980s as accommodation for foreigners. This is an excellent option for those weary of the fast lane, and a great opportunity to get a sense of Japan outside the well-touristed urban centres.

The house itself has four large tatami rooms separated by sliding doors, a shared bathroom and kitchen, and bicycles that are free to use. There's an open hearth in the common area, where you can burn charcoal for the full olden-days effect, and near the villa you'll find hiking tracks, shrines and temples (where it's possible to join morning meditation). There are a couple of eateries in the area but hours are irregular – stock up on groceries in Okayama or Yoshinaga before you come to Hattōji.

For reservations, contact the **International Villa Group** (☎086-256-2535; www.hare net.ne.jp/villa; fax 086-256-2576; ☉phone reservations 9am-noon & 1-5pm Mon-Fri) in Okayama. Rates are ¥3500 per person. You can also pay ¥25,000 (for up to eight people) to have exclusive use of the house.

Buses (¥200, 30 minutes, five to six daily Monday to Saturday) run to Hattōji from Yoshinaga Station (吉永駅) on the JR San-yō line, accessible by train (¥570, 33 minutes, roughly every hour) from Okayama. The bus drops you near the villa entrance. See the International Villa Group website for the latest schedule.

While you're near Yoshinaga Station, it's worth visiting the historic Edo-period **Shizutani Gakko** (閑谷学校; Shizutani School; admission ¥300; ☉9am-5pm), the first public school in Japan, its wood interiors and Bizen-yaki roof tiles now beautifully preserved. The school is about 3km from the station – 10 minutes by taxi, or about 40 minutes on foot. Ask at the station for directions.

Pedalling on, you'll pass the **Koikui-jinja** (鯉喰神社), located slightly off the main route by the river, and the 5th-century **Tsukuriyama-kofun** (造山古墳). The fourth-biggest *kofun* tomb in Japan, this is thought to mark the final resting place of a local king who ruled the Kibi region when this area was a rival power to the Yamato court (which eventually came to rule all of Japan).

The next major stop on the route is the **Bitchū Kokobun-ji** (備中国分寺), a temple with a picturesque five-storey pagoda. The oldest buildings here date from the Edo period, but the first temple on this site was built in the 8th century. Across the main road from the temple is the **Miyake Sake Brewery Museum** (三宅酒造資料館; ☏0866-92-0075; admission ¥400; ☻10am-4pm, Tue-Fri & 1st & 3rd Sat of month). Look for the large white building. The brewery has been in the same family for over 100 years, and there is a small museum of old brewing paraphernalia, as well as opportunities to taste and buy.

From here, it's a few kilometres to Sōja, where you can return your bicycle at **Araki Rent-a-Cycle** (荒木レンタサイクル; ☏0866-92-0233; ☻9am-6pm), at the side of the bus area in front of the station.

Kurashiki 倉敷

☏086 / POP 475,400

Kurashiki's main attraction is its Bikan quarter (美観地区), an area of historic buildings by an old willow-edged canal, where a picturesque group of black-and-white warehouses has been converted into museums.

In the feudal era the warehouses were used to store rice brought by boat from the surrounding countryside. Later, the town became an important textile centre, under the Kurabō Textile Company. Owner Ōhara Magosaburō built up a collection of European art, and opened the Ōhara Museum of Art in 1930.

◉ Sights

Ōhashi House HISTORICAL BUILDING
(大橋家住宅; Ōhashi-ke Jūtaku; 3-21-31 Achi; admission ¥500; ☻9am-5pm, closed Mon) Between the station and the canal area is the beautifully restored Ōhashi House, built in 1793. The house belonged to one of Kurashiki's richest families and was built at a time when prosperous merchants were beginning to claim privileges that had previously been the preserve of the samurai.

Ōhara Museum of Art ART GALLERY
(大原美術館; www.ohara.or.jp; 1-1-15 Chuō; admission ¥1300; ☻9am-5pm late Jul, Aug, Oct & Nov, closed Mon rest of yr) This is Kurashiki's premier museum, housing the predominantly Western art collection amassed by local textile magnate Ōhara Magosaburō (1880–1943), with the help of artist Kojima Torajirō (1881–1929). The varied assemblage of paintings, prints and sculpture features works by Picasso, Cézanne, El Greco and Matisse, and one of Monet's water-lilies paintings (said to have been bought from the man himself by Torajirō while visiting Monet's home in 1920). While no rival to the major galleries of Europe, it's an interesting collection and one of the town's biggest attractions for Japanese tourists.

The valid-all-day ticket gets you into the museum's **Craft and Asiatic Art Gallery**, the **contemporary Japanese collection** housed in an annexe behind the main building, plus the **Kojima Torajirō Memorial Museum** (児島虎次郎記念館).

Japan Rural Toy Museum MUSEUM
(日本郷土玩具館; 1-4-16 Chuō; admission ¥400; ☻9am-5pm) Four rooms are crammed with displays of wooden toys, masks, dolls and spinning tops (including a world record breaker), and a colourful array of kites just beckoning to be put on a breeze. You can purchase a new toy of your own in the attached shop.

Kojima Torajirō Memorial Hall MUSEUM
(www.ivysquare.co.jp/cultural/torajiro.htm, in Japanese; 7-2 Honmachi; admission ¥500; ☻9am-5pm, closed Mon) Kojima Torajirō was the European-style painter who went above and beyond in helping Ōhara build up his art collection; head to this museum to immerse yourself in his life.

Ivy Square SQUARE, MUSEUM
(アイビースクエア) Present-day Ivy Square was once the site of Ōhara's Kurabō textile factories. The company moved into more modern premises a long time ago, and the red-brick factory buildings (dating from 1889) now house a hotel, restaurants, shops and yet more museums, including the **Kurabō Memorial Hall** (7-1 Honmachi; admission ¥350; ☻9am-5pm), where you can learn all about the history of the Japanese textile industry.

Kurashiki Museum of Folk-craft   MUSEUM
(倉敷民芸館; 1-4-11 Chūō; admission ¥700; ⊙9am-5pm Mar-Nov, to 4.15pm Dec-Feb, closed Mon) Housed in an attractive complex of rice warehouses dating from the late 18th century, with interesting exhibits of ceramics, glassware, textiles and furniture.

Achi-jinja   SHRINE
(阿智神社; 12-1 Honmachi) A short walk from the canal area are the steep stone steps that lead up to this shrine in the **Tsurugata-yama-kōen**, a park that overlooks the old area of town.

🛏 Sleeping

Kurashiki is a good place to spend a night in a ryokan, soaking up the olde-worlde atmosphere. There are also plenty of Western-style business hotels around the station and along Chūō-dōri, but if you're considering one of these you might be better off staying in Okayama, where you'll get nicer digs for less money. The Kurashiki tourist office has a list of accommodation and can help with bookings.

Ryokan Kurashiki   RYOKAN $$$
(旅館くらしき; ☑422-0730; www.ryokan-kurashiki.jp; fax 422-0990; 4-1 Honmachi; per person with 2 meals from ¥32,200) By the canal in the heart of the historic district and incorporating several beautifully restored Edo-period buildings, this is probably the best ryokan in town. The spacious suites all have tatami lounge areas with attached twin-bed rooms and bathrooms. Dinner is a multicourse *kaiseki* (Japanese haute cuisine) affair featuring delicacies from the Inland Sea. Some English is spoken.

Ryokan Tsurugata   RYOKAN $$
(鶴形; ☑424-1635; www.turugata.jp, in Japanese; fax 424-1650; per person with 2 meals ¥13,800-33,600) This welcoming ryokan in a converted building right in the historic area has tatami rooms overlooking a garden, and meals featuring local seafood. Prices vary according to room size and most have shared bathrooms. A little English is spoken.

Dormy Inn Kurashiki   HOTEL $$
(ドーミーイン倉敷; ☑426-5489; www.hotespa.net/hotels/kurashiki; s/tw from ¥5000/8000; ⊜@) The pick of the Western-style chains, this relatively new hotel is not far from the historic district and has a little something extra to tip the scales in its favour – an onsen on the top floor.

Kurashiki Youth Hostel   HOSTEL $
(倉敷ユースホステル; ☑422-7355; www.jyh.or.jp/english/chugoku/kurasiki/index.html; 1537-1 Mukōyama; dm members/nonmembers ¥2940/3540; ⊜) An OK option if your need to save money outweighs your need for a convenient location – it's up the hill southeast of Ivy Square. From the station, take bus 6 and get off at Shimin-kaikan-mae (市民会館前), then walk up through the cemetery.

🍴 Eating

Within the historic area you'll pay a little more for the atmosphere that goes with your food. You'll find cheaper, quick-eats options along Chūō-dōri and in the arcades running from the station. Or just grab a sandwich and find a spot to sit on the edge of the canal.

Kana Izumi   NOODLES $
(かな泉; ☑421-7254; www.kanaizumi.co.jp, in Japanese; 8-33 Honmachi; ⊙11am-8pm, closed Mon) Slurp back freshly made *sanuki-udon* (a type of wheat noodle) dishes, such as *sansai udon* (*udon* with mountain vegetables; ¥650), at this speciality restaurant back from the canal. Full set meals include a *tempura teishoku* for ¥1600. You can also buy noodles in the attached shop to take home and cook for yourself. Look for the purple flag on the corner with the name in white.

Mamakari-tei   SEAFOOD $$
(ままかり亭; ☑427-7112; 3-12 Honmachi; ⊙11am-2pm & 5-10pm, closed Mon) This traditional eatery, in a 200-year-old warehouse with chunky beams and long wooden tables, is famed for the sardine-like local speciality. This tasty fish is supposed to induce bouts of uncontrollable feasting, so that people are obliged to *kari* (borrow) more *mama* (rice) from their neighbours in order to carry on with their binge. *Mamakari-zushi* is ¥800; lunchtime-only set meals include a *mamakari teishoku* for ¥2625.

Kamoi   SUSHI & SASHIMI $$
(カモ井; ☑422-0606; 1-3-17 Chūō; dishes ¥1050-2625; ⊙10am-6pm, closed Mon; ⊜🄟) A large, pleasant canal-side restaurant opposite the Ōhara Museum, serving sashimi set meals, seafood-and-rice dishes, and some desserts (from ¥525). You can get the local sardine-like speciality here in *mamakari-zushi* form for ¥1050.

HIROSHIMA & WESTERN HONSHŪ OKAYAMA & AROUND

Bukkake Udon
NOODLES $

(ぶっかけうどん; 2-3-23 Achi; dishes ¥440-840;
⊗7am-9pm) In the less-than-atmospheric
Bios Arcade across from the station, this local chain serves up the tasty Kurashiki *udon*
speciality – called *bukkake udon* (from
bukkakeru, meaning to pour or splash)
because you tip the sauce over the noodles
yourself. *Tempura bukkake* is ¥590. Or try
a *niku* (meat) *kimuchi bukkake* for ¥680.
Look for the sign with a ぶ in a yellow oval.

🍷 Drinking

Coffee-Kan
CAFE

(倉敷珈琲館; www.kurashiki-coffeekan.com; in
Japanese; 4-1 Honmachi; coffees ¥500-850; ⊗10am-
5pm; 📷) The low-ceilinged, wood-and-brick
interior of this caffeine-lovers' paradise is
thick with the aroma of freshly roasted beans.
The menu features coffee and coffee only,
though you can choose hot or cold. It's on the
canal next to Ryokan Kurashiki.

SWLABR
BAR

(2-18-2 Achi; ⊗6pm-3am) After the Bikan area
closes down, relax with the good music and
friendly staff at SWLABR. It's the green
weatherboard house on the corner, a couple
of blocks southeast of the station. Cocktails
cost ¥600.

🛍 Shopping

Wander down the lanes off the main canal-
side strip to find lots of small shops selling
souvenirs, crafts and food.

Komachi
CRAFTS, ACCESSORIES

(小町; 6-17 Honmachi; ⊗10am-6pm, closed Tue &
Wed) Handmade on site at this small shop
are souvenir craft items, such as dolls,
trinkets and accessories, using material
from old kimonos. Look for the sign with
the words 'I make an accessory with an
old kimono'.

ℹ Information

Tourist Information Office (倉敷駅前観光案
内所; ☑424-1220; 2nd fl, Kurashiki City Plaza,
1-7-2 Achi; ⊗9am-7pm) Just out of the station on the second level and to the right. Free
internet access (15 minutes) for sightseeing
information only.

Kurashikikan Tourist Information (倉敷館観
光案内所; ☑422-0542; 1-4-8 Chūō; ⊗9am-
6pm) Larger centre near the Naka-bashi bridge
at the bend in the canal. Also has a rest area.

ℹ Getting There & Away

Kurashiki is on the JR San-yō main line. Shin-
Kurashiki, on the *shinkansen* line, is two stops
further west. Regular trains from Kurashiki
serve the following destinations:

Kurashiki

◎ Top Sights

◎ Sights

🛏 Sleeping

✖ Eating

☕ ◯ Drinking

🛍 Shopping

Information

Fukuyama ¥740, 40 minutes
Okayama ¥320, 14 minutes
Shin-Kurashiki ¥190, seven minutes

Shōdo-shima   小豆島

📞 0879 / POP 31,200

Famed for its olive groves and as the setting of the classic film *Nijūshi-no-hitomi* (Twenty-Four Eyes; it tells the story of a village school teacher and her young charges), Shōdo-shima makes an enjoyable day trip or overnight escape from big-city Japan. It has a smattering of sights but is mainly appealing for its mountainous landscape, scenic coastal roads and Inland Sea vistas. The island is popular during summer and when the autumn leaves are at their peak in October and November. Come out of season and you'll find a sleepy isle with very few fellow travellers.

◎ Sights & Activities

AROUND THE COAST

FREE **Shōdo-shima Olive Park**   PARK, ONSEN
(小豆島オリーブ公園; www.olive-pk.jp, in Japanese; Nishimura-misaki 1941-1; ⊘8.30am-5pm) This park is where the island's olive-growing activities are celebrated with several whitewashed buildings, some fake Grecian ruins, a museum, and opportunities to buy olive-themed souvenirs. It's worth tolerating the kitsch for the **Sun Olive Onsen** (サン・オリーブ温泉; admission ¥700; ⊘noon-9pm), where you can enjoy fabulous views of the Japanese Aegean from a variety of herbal baths.

Marukin Soy Sauce Historical
Museum   MUSEUM
(マルキン醤油記念館; www.marukin-chuyu.com/kodawari/shoyu/kinenkan.html, in Japanese; Nouma; admission ¥210; ⊘9am-4pm) Shōdo-shima's first olives were planted in 1908, but the island was famous for its soy beans long before that, and several old soy-sauce companies are still in business here (as frequent whiffs around the island will remind you). Marukin is situated in an old black-and-white building on the main road between Kusakabe and Sakate. There are good English explanations, and souvenirs available include soy sauce–flavoured ice cream.

Twenty-Four Eyes Movie Village   MOVIE SET
(二十四の瞳映画村; www.24hitomi.or.jp, in Japanese; Tanoura; admission ¥700, combined ticket with the old school ¥790; ⊘9am-5pm) Just north of Sakate is the turn-off to the picturesque fishing village of **Tanoura** (田ノ浦), site of the village school that featured in the film *Twenty-Four Eyes*. The film was based on a novel by local writer Tsuboi Sakae and was a huge hit in postwar Japan. The set used in the 1980s remake of the original 1954 B&W film is now open to the public as this movie village, where busloads of tourists gather to wallow in nostalgia.

Misaki Branch School   HISTORIC SCHOOL
(岬の分教場; www.24hitomi.or.jp, in Japanese; admission ¥200, combined ticket with the movie village ¥790; ⊘9am-5pm) Also worth seeing in Tanoura is this perfectly preserved 1902 school, setting for the *Twenty-Four Eyes* story and the 1954 film. It's a short walk from the movie village on the road back to Sakate.

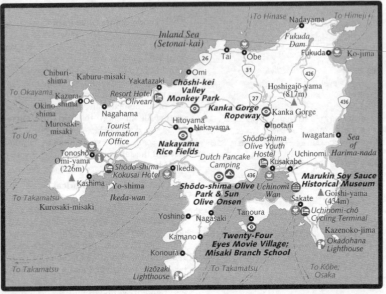

CENTRAL MOUNTAINS
Kanka Gorge Ropeway   CABLE CAR, GORGE
(寒霞渓ロープウエイ; www.kankakei.co.jp, in Japanese; 1 way/return ¥700/1250; ☉8.30am-5pm, to 4.30pm late Dec-late Mar) The cable car is the main attraction in the central mountains, making a spectacular trip through Kanka-kei, particularly when the gorge is ablaze with autumn colours (though be warned that many others have the same idea). Of course, you could just take in the breathtaking views of the Inland Sea from the area around the upper cable-car station without taking the ride. An alternative for keen walkers is to climb between the lower and upper cable-car stations via the **Omote 12 Views** (表12景; 2.3km) and **Ura Eight Views** (裏8景; 1.8km) tracks. There are other scenic walks from the upper station, including a hike to the eastern peak of **Hoshigajō-yama** (星ヶ城東峰; 817m).

On weekends, and on weekdays during peak periods, there are four buses a day from Kusakabe port to the lower cable-car station (紅雲亭; Kōuntei). There are no buses during winter.

Nakayama Rice Fields   RICE TERRACES
(中山千枚田; Nakayama Senmaida) About 4km inland from the Ikeda ferry terminal are Nakayama's 'thousand rice fields'. The terraces are pretty in any season but are especially picturesque after rice planting in late April or early May, when the water-filled fields become a hillside of mirrors.

Chōshi-kei Valley Monkey Park   MONKEY PARK
(銚子渓お猿の国; Nouma; admission ¥370; ☉8.20am-5pm) Large troupes of monkeys will come right up to you here as they squabble for food. For a less intense monkey encounter, look out for them on the way up to the park area, where they're sometimes found lazing on the road.

🎎 Festivals & Events
Nōson Kabuki   KABUKI
Shōdo-shima was famous during the Edo period for its tradition of rural kabuki (stylised Japanese theatre), and two 17th-century thatched theatres survive in the mountain villages east of Tonoshō. Performances are held on 3 May at the Rikyū Hachiman Shrine in Hitoyama (肥土山) and on the second Sunday in October at the Kasuga Shrine in Nakayama (中山).

🛏 Sleeping & Eating
Tonoshō offers a variety of hotels and simple places to eat, particularly along the road running straight back from the

waterfront. For the youth hostel and Dutch Pancake Camping, the nearest port is at Kusakabe.

Dutch Pancake Camping
CAMPGROUND, PANCAKES **$**

(ダッチ・パンケーキ・キャンピング; ☑82-4616; ww8.tiki.ne.jp/~dpc; 1765-7 Nishimura Otsu, Shōdoshima-chō; per person/camp site ¥800/1000) Run by a Dutchman and his Japanese wife, this friendly spot is in an idyllic setting, with views out to sea. Full price details are on the website. The **Dutch Café Cupid & Cotton** (pancakes from ¥600; ⊙11am-5pm, closed Wed & Thu; ⊠), in a cosy knick-knack-filled windmill just behind the campsite, serves savoury and sweet 'real Dutch' pancakes, as well as coffee. Lunch sets are ¥850. Turn right at the top of the Olive Park complex and look for the small sign pointing up a narrow, partly unpaved road on the left.

Minshuku Maruse
MINSHUKU **$**

(民宿マルセ; ☑62-2385; http://new-port.biz/maruse/1.htm, in Japanese; Tonoshō-kō; s/tw without bathroom ¥3650/7000; ☎) This welcoming, neatly kept place next to Tonoshō's post office, a short walk from the ferry terminal, has Japanese-style rooms. Meals are available and the filling dinner features local seafood.

Resort Hotel Olivean
RESORT **$$$**

(リゾートホテルオリビアン; ☑65-2311; www.olivean.com; Yū-higaoka; s/tw incl breakfast from ¥13,650/23,100; ⊝@☎☒☺) This grand complex has it all: tennis courts, onsen, swimming pool, restaurants and sunset views from spacious Western- and Japanese-style accommodation. Even furry friends are well catered for in designated pet-friendly rooms. There are courtesy buses to the resort from Tonoshō.

Shōdo-shima Olive Youth Hostel
HOSTEL **$**

(小豆島オリーブユースホステル; ☑82-6161; www.jyh.gr.jp/shoudo; 1072 Nishimura, Uchinomi-chō; dm members/nonmembers ¥3255/3885; ⊝☎) This pleasant hostel has bunk-bed dorms and tatami rooms. Meals and bike rental are available. Buses stop in front of the hostel (at the Orību-Yūsu-mae stop), or it's about a 20-minute walk from Kusakabe port.

Business Hotel New Port
HOTEL **$$**

(ビジネスホテル・ニューポート; ☑62-6310; www.new-port.biz, in Japanese; s/tw from ¥4200/7800; @) Run by the same friendly management as at Minshuku Maruse, this small

business hotel is handy if you want to stay near the Tonoshō port. Head right out of the ferry terminal – it's on the right about a minute's walk away.

ⓘ Information

Tonoshō, at the western end of the island, is the biggest town and the usual point of arrival from Takamatsu or Okayama.

Tourist information booth (☑62-5300; ⊙8.30am-5.15pm) Inside the Tonoshō ferry terminal.

www.town.shodoshima.lg.jp Tourist information, maps and links to ferry schedules.

ⓘ Getting There & Away

See the boxed text, p396, for the main ferry routes to and from Shōdo-shima's ports. There is also a service from Osaka (from ¥4100 per person, 3½ hours), operating daily during Golden Week, two weekends in July, and daily in August. Contact **Ferry Sunflower** (☑06-6614-1013; www.ferry-sunflower.co.jp, in Japanese) for the latest details.

ⓘ Getting Around

The most convenient way to see the island is by car – it's worth hiring one for the day to take in all the scenic routes. (Note you can bring a car on some ferries but it will cost about as much as hiring one on the island.) Cycling can also be enjoyable if you have plenty of time, but you'd want to be keen – there are some serious climbs heading inland. If you're taking the buses, it's advisable to check the timetables and plan your itinerary in advance.

BICYCLE Bikes can also be rented at the youth hostel near Kusakabe and at the Cycling Terminal Inn (Elies-sō) in Sakate port.

Asahiya Rent-a-Cycle (旭屋レンタサイクル; ☑62-0162; www.asahiya.org, in Japanese; gearless bikes per hr ¥300; ⊙8.30am-5pm) Inside the Asahiya hotel, opposite the post office in Tonoshō, a short walk from the ferry terminal.

ⓘ BUS & FERRY COMBO

If you're going to Shōdo-shima from Okayama, pick up a *Kamome bus kippu* (one way ¥1200), a discounted combination ticket covering the bus from Okayama Station to Shin-Okayama port plus the ferry to Shōdo-shima. They're sold at the booth in the bus terminal of Okayama Station, and in the Tonoshō ferry terminal.

ORIGIN	DESTINATION	FARE (¥)	DURATION	FREQUENCY (PER DAY)
Himeji	Fukuda	1480	1hr 40min	7
Shin-Okayama	Tonoshō	1000	70min	13
Takamatsu	Tonoshō (regular)	670	1hr	15
Takamatsu	Tonoshō (high speed)	1140	30min	16
Takamatsu	Ikeda	670	1hr	8
Takamatsu	Kusakabe (regular)	670	1hr	5
Takamatsu	Kusakabe (high speed)	1140	45min	5
Uno	Tonoshō	1200	1½hr	7

Ishii Rent-a-Cycle (石井レンタサイクル; ☑62-1866; www7.ocn.ne.jp/~ishii-c/rental. htm, in Japanese; Olive-dōri; gearless bikes per day ¥1000, mountain & electric bikes ¥2000; ☺8.30am-5pm) It's worth the walk here to get a bicycle with gears. It's about 2km from Tonoshō port – ask at the ferry terminal for directions.

BUS Shōdo-shima Olive Bus (小豆島オリーブ バス; ☑62-0171; www.shodoshima-olive-bus. com, in Japanese; 1-/2-day pass ¥2000/2500) operates services around the island. The most frequent, at one or two per hour, runs between Tonoshō and Kusakabe ports, passing Ikeda and Olive Park. Some continue on to Sakate port, passing the Marukin Soy Sauce Historical Museum; some head north to Fukuda port. There are infrequent services along the north coast, inland to Nakayama, and to Tanoura. There are no services to the Monkey Park.

CAR Japaren (ジャパレン; ☑62-4669; car.orix. co.jp, in Japanese; 6hr from ¥5145; ☺8.30am-6pm) has an English guide and basic touring map in English. Walk about two minutes along the road heading right out of the Tonoshō ferry terminal.

Naoshima 直島

☑087 / POP 3300

The arty isle of Naoshima has certainly come up in the world. Until not too long ago, this small island was no different from many others in the Inland Sea: home to a dwindling population subsisting on the joint proceeds of a dying fishing industry and the old-age pension. Today, as the location of the Benesse Art Site Naoshima, Naoshima is one of the area's biggest tourist attractions, offering a unique opportunity to see some of Japan's best contemporary art in gorgeous natural settings.

The project started in the early '90s, when the Benesse Corporation chose Naoshima as the setting for its growing collection of modern art. Naoshima is now home to a number of world-class art galleries and installations, and there are smaller galleries worth seeking out.

In addition to the main sites, numerous works of outdoor art are situated around the coast, including the pumpkin sculpture by Kusama Yayoi that has become a symbol of the island.

◉ Sights & Activities

Art House Project ART INSTALLATIONS
(家プロジェクト; combined ticket ¥1000; ☺10am-4.30pm, closed Mon) In the old fishing village of Honmura (本村), half a dozen traditional buildings have been restored and turned over to contemporary artists to use as the setting for creative installations. Some of them are more exciting than others. Highlights include Ōtake Shinrō's shacklike **Haisha** house, its Statue of Liberty sculpture rising up through the levels; James Turrell's experiment with light in **Minami-dera**, where you enter in total darkness...and wait; and Sugimoto Hiroshi's play on the traditional **Go'o Shrine**, with a glass staircase, and underground 'Stone Chamber' (those who are claustrophobic or wide of hip will want to give this a miss).

The sites are within walking distance of each other. Take the Naoshima bus to the Nōkyō-mae stop, where you can buy your Art House Project ticket (includes a map of the sites) from the tobacco shop and start exploring. Or buy a ticket at the first site you visit.

Benesse House Museum   ART GALLERY

(ベネッセハウス; www.benesse-artsite.jp/en/ benessehouse-museum; admission ¥1000; ⊙8am-9pm) Award-winning architect Andō Tadao designed this stunning museum and hotel on the south coast of the island. Among the works here are pieces by Andy Warhol, David Hockney, Jasper Johns, and Japanese artists such as Ōtake Shinrō.

Chichū Art Museum   ART GALLERY

(地中美術館; www.benesse-artsite.jp/en/chichu; admission ¥2000; ⊙10am-6pm, to 5pm Oct-Feb, closed Mon) A short walk from Benesse House is another Andō creation. A work of art itself, the museum consists of a series of cool concrete-walled spaces sitting snugly underground, lit by natural light. It provides a remarkable setting for several Monet water-lilies paintings, some monumental sculptures by Walter de Maria and installations by James Turrell. Outside is the Chichū garden, created in the spirit of Monet's garden in Giverny.

Lee Ufan Museum   ART GALLERY

(李禹煥美術館; www.benesse-artsite.jp/en/ lee-ufan; admission ¥1000; ⊙10am-6pm, to 5pm Oct-Feb, closed Mon) The latest in Benesse's suite of museums is yet another design from the irrepressible Andō. It houses works by the renowned Korean-born artist (and philosopher) Lee Ufan, who was a leading figure in the Mono-ha movement of the 1960s and 1970s.

Naoshima Bath – I Heart Yū   PUBLIC BATH

(直島銭湯; www.naoshimasento.jp; admission ¥500; ⊙2-9pm Tue-Fri, 10am-9pm Sat & Sun, closed Mon) Take a soak at this colourful fusion of Japanese bathing tradition and contemporary art, designed by Ōtake Shinrō, where the elephant in the room is, actually, an elephant in the room. It's a couple of minutes' walk inland from Miyanoura port.

🛏 Sleeping

The accommodation scene is dominated by *minshuku* (Japanese guesthouses), which is good news if you've stayed in one too many bland business hotels on your travels. The Tourist Information Centre in Miyanoura has a complete list of lodgings.

TOP CHOICE Tsutsuji-sō   CAMPGROUND $

(つつじ荘; ☎892-2838; http://tsutsujiso.no-blog. jp/blog/english; fax 892-3871; per person from ¥3675; ⊛) Perfectly placed on the beachfront not far from the Benesse Art Site area is this encampment of Mongolian-style *pao* tents. The cosy tents sleep up to four, have a small fridge and heater (but no air-con), and shared bathroom facilities. The tent-averse can opt instead for one of the caravans or cottages. See the downloadable leaflet on the website for full details. Meals are available if reserved in advance. Cash only.

Benesse House   BOUTIQUE HOTEL $$$

(☎892-3223; www.benesse-artsite.jp/en/benesse-house; tw/ste from ¥31,185/48,510; ⊛) A stay at this unique Andō-designed hotel-museum is a fabulous experience for art and architecture enthusiasts. Take the monorail to the hilltop 'Oval' wing, where rooms are arranged around a pool of water open to the sky, stay by the sea at a 'Beach' suite, or stick close to the art in the 'Museum' lodgings. Rooms have a clean, modern design and feature artworks from the Benesse collection. Best of all, you can roam around the Benesse House museum whenever the mood takes you.

Minshuku Oyaji-no-umi   MINSHUKU $

(民宿おやじの海; ☎892-2269; http://yopopo .moo.jp, in Japanese; per person incl breakfast ¥4200; @🛜) This is a good option for friendly, family-style lodgings, with tatami rooms (separated by sliding doors) and shared bathroom, in an old house close to the Art House Project in Honmura.

Gallery Inn Kuraya   GUESTHOUSE $

(ギャラリーインくらや; ☎892-2253; kuraya -naoshima.net, in Japanese; per person incl breakfast ¥5000; ⊛) Kuraya Gallery offers accommodation to the public when it's not occupied by

---

MARK YOUR DIARIES

After a successful maiden running in 2010, the fantastic **Setouchi International Art Festival** (瀬戸内国際芸術祭; setouchi-artfest.jp) is scheduled to come around again in 2013. This new festival of art, music, drama and dance has a calendar of events occurring on seven Inland Sea islands, many on Naoshima. It all happens between late July and October, during which time additional ferries link the islands. Check the website closer to the time for the low-down on event and ferry passes, and book your accommodation well in advance.

GALLERY OWNER TALKS ART

Tell us about your gallery. Gallery Kuraya is mainly for artists who are not established yet, but going to be. It is my pleasure to see them have the chance to show their work to many people who visit Naoshima. **Why Naoshima?** I am originally from the Tokyo area, and I like the slow and relaxing lifestyle on this island. **There are many art sites on Naoshima. Do you have a favourite?** I personally like Benesse House Museum as it has a variety of work by many artists, in a nice building. Also, I recommend walking on the Benesse beach area, looking at the outdoor artworks here and there. If you stay at the hotel, the night view from the window is the best.

visiting artists – a Japanese-style room in the old house, or a room within the wood-floored gallery. English is spoken. It's near Honmura port, on the left as you head towards the Art House Project's 'Ishibashi'.

Cin.na.mon   GUESTHOUSE $
(シナモン; ☎840-8133; www.cin-na-mon.jp; per person without bathroom incl breakfast ¥4000) Above this cafe-bar near the port in Miyanoura are three comfortable tatami rooms.

Dormitory in Kūron   HOSTEL $
(ドミトリーin九龍; ☎892-2424; http://kawloon.gozaru.jp, in Japanese; dm ¥2800; @ 🛜) Basic dormitory accommodation just back from the ferry port in Miyanoura. Note that you'll pay ¥3500 if you show up without a reservation. Some English is spoken.

🍴 Eating & Drinking

There are a few cafes in the Art House Project area and eateries near the port at Miyanoura. Most can be found on the tourist office map.

Genmai-Shinshoku Aisunao   CAFE $
(玄米心食あいすなお; http://aisunao.jp, in Japanese; meals ¥600-900; ⊙11am-5pm; 😔 🍴) A tranquil rest stop within the Art House Project area, Aisunao has seating on raised tatami flooring, and a decidedly health-conscious menu – try the tasty Aisunao lunch set (¥800), with local brown rice, soup and vegies. Desserts (such as soy-milk ice cream), juices and fair-trade coffees are also on offer. It's around the corner from 'Gokaisho'.

Museum Restaurant Issen   KAISEKI $$$
(日本料理一扇; ☎892-3223; www.benesse-artsite.jp/en/benessehouse/restaurant_cafe.html; dinner courses ¥6000-12,000; ⊙breakfast, lunch & dinner; 😔 🍴) The artfully displayed *kaiseki* dinners at this Benesse House basement restaurant are almost too pretty to eat. Courses feature seafood, but there is a veg-dominated option (request a couple of days ahead), and the menu changes with the seasons. Breakfast and lunch are also served. Reservations are recommended.

Cin.na.mon   CURRY, BAR $
(シナモン; www.cin-na-mon.jp; curries ¥700-1000; ⊙11am-3pm & 5-10pm; 🍴) The laid-back brothers here serve curries, cakes and smoothies by day, and open up the bar (with numerous cocktails and a food menu) at night. It's a short walk from the Miyanoura port.

Café Maruya   CAFE $
(カフェまるや; http://cafe-maruya.jp, in Japanese; lunch special ¥800; ⊙11am-6pm, closed Mon) In Honmura, Maruya serves coffee and does a good *higawari ranchi* (daily lunch special; ¥800), sometimes with seasonal local seafood.

ℹ️ Information

Tourist Information Centre (☎892-2299; www.naoshima.net; ⊙8.30am-6pm) In the Marine Station at the Miyanoura ferry port. Has a full list of accommodation options (some also on the website) and a useful bilingual map of the island (downloadable from the website).

ℹ️ Getting There & Away

Travelling via Naoshima is a good way to get from Honshū to Shikoku, or vice versa. See www1.biz.biglobe.ne.jp/~shikoku (in Japanese) for ferry-timetable details. Ferries run to the main port of Miyanoura from the following destinations:

Takamatsu ¥510, one hour, six to eight daily
Uno ¥280, 15 to 20 minutes, 15 daily

There are also five ferries a day from Uno to the port of Honmura (¥280, 20 minutes). Uno is at the end of the JR Uno line, about an hour from Okayama (¥570). There may be a quick change of trains at Chayamachi (茶屋町).

Getting Around

It's possible to get around the main sights on foot (for example, it's just over 2km from Miyanoura port to Honmura).

BICYCLE Cafe Ōgiya Rent-a-Cycle (☎892-3642; per day ¥500; ☺9am-7pm) is inside the Marine Station at the Miyanoura ferry port. A few electric bikes are also available (per day ¥2000).

BUS Minibuses run between Miyanoura, Honmura and Tsutsuji-sō (per trip ¥100) once or twice an hour. From Tsutsuji-sō, there's a free Benesse shuttle, stopping at all the Benesse Art Site museums.

Kasaoka Islands 笠岡諸島

Located between Kurashiki and Fukuyama, the port of Kasaoka is the jumping-off point for six small islands connected to the mainland only by boat. In particular, the islands of Shiraishi-jima and Manabe-shima are worth visiting to enjoy the slower pace of life as it used to be lived all over the Inland Sea.

Kasaoka is 40 minutes west of Okayama and 25 minutes west of Kurashiki on the JR San-yō line. From the station, it's a five-minute stroll down to the port and the ferry terminal, from where eight **Sanyō Kisen** (三洋汽船; ☎0865-62-2866) boats a day run to Shiraishi-jima (¥650 or ¥1130, 35 minutes or 22 minutes) and on to Manabe-shima (¥990 or ¥1710, one hour and 10 minutes or 44 minutes). Five of these are express services, which cost almost double but don't save that much time. See www.city.kasaoka.okayama.jp/002g/000a.html (in Japanese) for the schedule.

SHIRAISHI-JIMA 白石島
☎0865 / POP 750

Sleepy Shiraishi-jima is popular in the summer for its beaches and there are some good walking paths. Go-everywhere Buddhist saint Kōbō Daishi stopped off here on his way back from China in 806; the temple associated with him, **Kairyū-ji** (開龍寺), incorporates a trail of small shrines leading to a huge boulder on top of the hill.

Visitors can stay at the great-value **International Villa** (per person ¥3500), where communal accommodation is available on a hillside overlooking the beach. For reservations, contact **International Villa Group** (☎086-256-2535; www.harenet.ne.jp/villa; fax 086-256-2576; ☺phone reservations 9am-noon & 1-5pm Mon-Fri) in Okayama.

Alternatively, there are several *minshuku* on the beach, including **San-chan** (民宿さんちゃん; ☎68-3169; fhp.jp/sanchan,

in Japanese; per person with/without 2 meals ¥6000/3000), with no-frills Japanese-style rooms with shared bathrooms. Resident expat Amy Chavez runs the **Mooo! Bar** (☺summer) on the beach and can arrange sailing trips to other islands.

MANABE-SHIMA 真鍋島
☎0865 / POP 300

Nearby Manabe-shima is home to more cats than people, and its one small town is an atmospheric maze of old wooden houses, a solitary village shop that has been in business since the Meiji period, and an old-fashioned school with fewer than 10 pupils at last count. As with everywhere in this part of Japan, Kōbō Daishi got here first – the great man spent time at the **Enpukuji** (円福寺) temple.

More recently, the island has seen an increase in French visitors since the publication of Florent Chavouet's wonderful illustrated book *Manabé Shima*. The locals are sure to show you a copy (and point themselves out in it).

A good reason to venture out here is to stay at the waterfront ryokan **Santora** (島宿三虎; ☎68-3515; www.kcv.ne.jp/~santora, in Japanese; fax 68-3516; per person with 2 meals ¥10,500; ❷❋) so you can laze about in its outdoor saltwater bath while watching boats sail by. The rooms are spacious, the shared indoor bathroom has sea views, and the meals feature local seafood and vegies grown by the friendly owners. Those on a tighter budget should ask for the 'easy plan' (¥7000 per person), which gets you a pared-down supper and light breakfast. Or upgrade and go for one of the *hanare* (separate) cabins (from ¥12,600 per person with meals), which have private bathrooms and huge balconies looking out to sea.

There are few places to eat out on the island (most with irregular hours) – the helpful staff at the ferry-terminal office can give you some tips.

YAMAGUCHI & AROUND

Yamaguchi 山口
☎083 / POP 196,600

During the 100 years of civil war that bedevilled Japan until the country was reunited under the Tokugawa in the early 17th century, Yamaguchi prospered as an alternative capital to chaotic Kyoto. In 1550 Jesuit

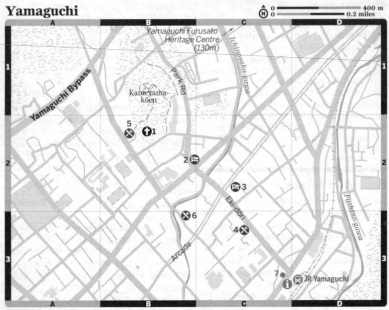

missionary Francis Xavier paused for two months here on his way to the imperial capital, and quickly returned when he was unable even to find the emperor in Kyoto. Yamaguchi today is a surprisingly small prefectural capital with a handful of sights.

⊙ Sights & Activities

St Francis Xavier Memorial Church CHURCH
(ザビエル記念聖堂; www.xavier.jp; donation ¥100; ⊙visiting hours 9am-5.30pm) Yamaguchi was a major centre of Christian missionary activity before the religion was outlawed in 1589. The church has the look of a large tent, and sits above the town in Kameyama-kōen. Built in 1952 in honour of St Francis Xavier, it burned down in 1991 and was rebuilt in 1998. The ground-floor **Christian museum** (admission ¥300; ⊙9am-5.30pm, closed Wed) contains exhibits on the life of Xavier and the early history of Christianity in Japan, most of it in Japanese only. Steps opposite the church lead up the hill to views of Yamaguchi.

Yamaguchi Furusato Heritage Centre HISTORIC BUILDING
(山口ふるさと伝承総合センター; ☎928-3333; www.c-able.ne.jp/~denshou; 12 Shimotatekōji; ⊙9am-5pm) The ground floor of the 1886 sake merchant building (the Manabi-kan; まなび館) has a small display of local crafts, including some Ōuchi dolls, but the building itself is interesting. Go upstairs to get a closer look at the large dark-wood beams, and don't miss the delightful tea-ceremony room made from old sake-brewing barrels – it's in the garden. The modern learning centre is behind the old building, where you can see lacquer ware being made, or make your own lacquer-ware chopsticks (¥840) – reservation required.

Kōzan-kōen PARK, TEMPLES
North of the town centre is Kōzan Park (香山公園), where the five-storey pagoda of **Rurikō-ji** (瑠璃光寺), a National Treasure dating from 1404, is picturesquely situated beside a small lake. The park is also the site of the **Tōshun-ji** (洞春寺) and the graves of the Mōri lords.

Jōei-ji TEMPLE, GARDEN
(常栄寺; 2001 Miyano-shimo; garden admission ¥300; ⊙garden 8am-5pm) About 4km northeast of the JR station, Jōei-ji is notable for its Zen garden, **Sesshutei**, designed by the painter Sesshū. From the garden, a trail leads uphill through the woods to several more shrines.

Yamaguchi

Yuda Onsen   ONSEN

Just west of the city is the 800-year-old
Yuda Onsen. The area is covered in a rash of
hotels and bathing facilities, mostly along a
busy main road; it's not a place for totter-
ing between baths in your *yukata*. Still, if
you've got a bit of time to kill in Yamaguchi,
a soak here isn't a bad way to spend a few
hours.

You can use the baths at the large **Hotel
Kamefuku** (ホテルかめ福; 4-5 Yuda Onsen;
admission ¥800; ☺11.30am-10pm), the less-
crowded **Kokuminshukusha Koteru** (国民
宿舎小てる; 4-3-15 Yuda Onsen; admission ¥400;
☺8am-noon & 3-10pm) and, for a taste of luxury, the traditional ryokan **Umenoya** (梅乃
屋; 4-3-19 Yuda Onsen; admission ¥800; ☺1.30pm-
midnight).

There's a **tourist information office**
(☑901-0150; 2-1-23 Yuda Onsen; ☺9am-7pm) on
the main road, where you can pick up a map
and guide to all the baths.

Buses run regularly to Yuda Onsen bus
stop from Yamaguchi Station (¥190, 10 minutes). They drop you on the main strip, Yuda
Onsen-dōri, a short walk from the tourist
office (just keep walking in the direction of
the bus). Yuda Onsen Station is one stop on
the local train line (¥140). From the station,
follow the red road for about 1km to get to
the busy main T-intersection. Turn right for
the tourist office.

✿✿ Festivals & Events

Gion Matsuri   DANCE
On 20, 24 and 27 July, during the Gion
Matsuri, the *Sagi-mai* (Egret Dance) is
held at Yasaka-jinja.

Tanabata Chōchin Matsuri   LANTERNS
From 6 to 7 August, thousands of decorated lanterns illuminate the city.

🛏 Sleeping

There's not much choice in central Yamaguchi. There are Western-style chains clustered
around Shin-Yamaguchi station, and while
it's not an inspiring area, nearby Yuda Onsen
does have a few good Japanese-style options.

Matsudaya Hotel   RYOKAN $$$
(ホテル松田屋; ☑922-0125; www.matsudaya
hotel.co.jp, in Japanese; fax 925-6111; 3-6-7 Yuda
Onsen; s & tw with 2 meals from ¥22,000; @🛜) At
this centuries-old, now modernised, ryokan,
you can bathe in history – right in the tub
where once dipped the plotters of the Meiji
Restoration. The ryokan's garden setting
and excellent service will likely ease any
present-day rebellious thoughts. Matsudaya
is on the main drag in Yuda Onsen.

Taiyō-dō Ryokan   RYOKAN $
(太陽堂旅館; ☑922-0897; fax 922-1152; 2-3
Komeya-chō; per person from ¥3500) The Taiyō-
dō could do with a spruce up, but it does
have a massage chair in the lobby. The tatami rooms are comfortable and bathrooms
are shared. It helps to be able to speak a little Japanese. The ryokan is in the shopping
arcade just off Eki-dōri, beside a bakery.

Sunroute Kokusai Hotel
Yamaguchi   HOTEL $$
(サンルート国際ホテル山口; ☑923-3610;
www.sunroute.jp; 1-1 Nakagawara-chō; s/tw from
¥6825/12,180; ⊜@) This modern hotel has
stylish, neutral-toned rooms, and is in a
good location in the centre of town.

Kokuminshukusha Koteru   GUESTHOUSE $$
(国民宿舎小てる; ☑922-3240; fax 928-6177;
www.c-able.ne.jp/~koteru, in Japanese; 4-3-15
Yuda Onsen; per person with/without meals
¥7500/5400) Two blocks north of the main
street in Yuda Onsen, this is a good-value
family-run place with Japanese-style
rooms and cheery staff.

🍴 Eating & Drinking

Sabō Kō   CAFE $
(茶房幸; 1-2-39 Dōjōmonzen; dishes ¥600-900;
☺11.30am-6pm, closed Tue; ⊜) A cosy atmosphere prevails in this crowded little eatery, where customers perch on wooden
stools sipping coffee. The speciality on the
Japanese-only menu is *wafū omuraisu*
(Japanese-style rice omelette; ¥800) but it

also serves curries and *soba*. Look for the small wood-covered place with ceramic pots sticking out of the exterior plasterwork.

Hub
RESTAURANT, BAR $$

(ハブ; 2nd fl, 2-4-19 Dōjōmonzen; meals ¥880-1200; ⊗noon-3am, closed Tue) Overlooking the main shopping street, this stylish cafe-restaurant serves Asian-style rice dishes, and pastas (such as an Italian tomato spaghetti lunch set, ¥980), and is a relaxing space for a late-night drink. Look for the grey sign next to the entrance, just around the corner off Eki-dōri.

La Francesca
ITALIAN $$$

(ラフランチェスカ; ☏934-1888; http://xavier-cam.co.jp/lafrancescajp; 7-1 Kameyama; ⊗lunch & dinner; ✿🅿) Excellent Italian food is the main attraction at this elegant Tuscan villa, on the left as you head up the hill to the St Francis Xavier Memorial Church. Set-course options include the *Pranzo* (¥1890) at lunchtime and *Verde* (¥5250) in the evenings. The menu changes seasonally.

ℹ Information

Tourist Information Office (山口観光案内所; http://yamaguchi-city.jp) JR station (☏933-0090; ⊗9am-6pm) On the right, inside the station; *shinkansen* station (⊗9am-6.30pm) On the 2nd floor, *shinkansen* exit side.

ℹ Getting There & Away

See p405 for details on the *SL Yamaguchi-gō* steam train.

BUS Chūgoku JR Bus (www.chugoku-jrbus.co.jp, in Japanese) runs nine to 11 buses daily to Hagi (Higashi-Hagi Station; ¥1680, one hour and 10 minutes) from Yamaguchi Station (some originating at Shin-Yamaguchi). **Bōchō Bus** (www.bochobus.co.jp, in Japanese) runs buses to Higashi-Hagi Station (¥1970, 1½ hours, at least hourly) from Shin-Yamaguchi.

TRAIN Yamaguchi Station is on the JR Yamaguchi line. Shin-Yamaguchi station is 10km southwest in Ogōri on the San-yō *shinkansen* line. The Yamaguchi local service connects the two (¥230, 25 minutes).

Destinations on the *shinkansen* line:

Hiroshima ¥4620, 30 minutes to one hour
Shimonoseki ¥1110 to ¥2050, 56 minutes to 25 minutes

ℹ Getting Around

It's possible to walk to the central sights from Yamaguchi Station, but Jōei-ji is about 4km away. It's possible to catch a bus part of the way – ask at the station for details. A taxi might be an easier option if you don't want to walk or cycle.

BICYCLE Fukutake (福武老舗; ☏922-0915; Eki-dōri 1-4-6; hire 1st 2hr ¥300, per additional hr ¥100; ⊗8am-7pm) is located across from the station.

Akiyoshi-dai
秋吉台

The rolling Akiyoshi-dai tablelands are dotted with curious rock spires, beneath which are hundreds of limestone caverns. One of these is **Akiyoshi-dō** (www.karusuto.com; admission ¥1200; ⊗8.30am-4.30pm), the largest limestone cave in Japan.

It is size that makes the cave impressive. It extends about 10km, at some points 100m wide (though public access is limited to a 1km section), and a river flows through it. The watery reflection of the towering cave walls at times gives the dizzying impression you're walking over a deep ravine. But you can leave the spelunking gear at home – there's a paved route, regular pushbutton information points that belt out explanations in various languages, and an elevator in the middle that takes you up to a lookout.

Despite the development, Akiyoshi-dō is a good side trip from Yamaguchi or Hagi, if you have time, or a stop en route between the two.

ℹ Getting There & Away

Buses go to the cave from the following stations:
Yamaguchi ¥1130, 55 minutes, 10 daily
Shin-Yamaguchi ¥1140, 45 minutes, nine daily
Higashi-Hagi ¥1760, one hour and 10 minutes, 10.50am and 1.45pm
Mine ¥600, 20 minutes, nine daily

Buses leaving from Yamaguchi Station also stop at Yuda Onsen. Buses to Higashi-Hagi from the cave leave at 1pm and 3.40pm.

Tsuwano
津和野

☏0856 / POP 8400

A highlight of this region, Tsuwano is a relaxing, 700-year-old mountain town with an important shrine, a ruined castle, and an evocative samurai quarter. It also has a wonderful collection of carp swimming in the roadside water channels – in fact, there are far more carp here than people.

◉ Sights & Activities

TONOMACHI DISTRICT

Only the walls and some fine old gates from the former samurai quarter of Tonomachi (殿町) remain, but it's an attractive area for strolling. The water channels that run alongside the picturesque Tonomachi road are home to numerous carp, bred to provide food in the case of emergency. As you're walking, look out for *sugidama* (cedar balls) hanging outside a few old sake breweries.

Catholic Church   CHURCH
(津和野カトリック教会; Tonomachi; ⊙8am-5.30pm Apr-Nov, to 5pm Dec-Mar) The church here is a reminder of the town's Christian history. Hidden Christians from Nagasaki were exiled here in the early Meiji period. It's interesting to peep inside to see tatami mats instead of pews.

Katsushika Hokusai Museum   MUSEUM
(葛飾北斎美術館; 254 Ushiroda-guchi; admission ¥500; ⊙9.30am-5pm, closed Dec & Jan) Near the post office, this museum features a small collection by the Edo-period artist and his disciples, and shows the woodblock process plate by plate.

AROUND TOWN

Taikodani-Inari-jinja   SHRINE
(太鼓谷稲成神社; ⊙8am-4.30pm) Just above the castle chairlift station, thriving Taikodani-Inari-jinja, built in 1773 by the seventh lord Kamei Norisada, is one of the five major Inari shrines in Japan. Walk up the hillside to it through a tunnel created by hundreds of torii (lit up beautifully at night). There are great views of the valley and mountains from the top.

TOP CHOICE Morijuku Museum   MUSEUM
(杜塾美術館; 542 Morimura; admission ¥300; ⊙9.30am-5pm) This is something of mixed bag. The lovely preserved building itself once served as the home of a *shōya* (village headman). Downstairs is a collection of soft-edged scenes painted by local-born artist Nakao Shō, a roomful of bullfight sketches by Goya, and a framed set of beautifully embroidered Taishō-era kimono collars. The caretaker will gladly point out the features of the building, including the pinhole camera hidden away upstairs.

Chapel of St Maria   CHAPEL
The tiny Maria-dō (マリア聖堂; Mary Chapel) dates from 1951. More than 150 'hidden Christians' were imprisoned in a Buddhist temple on this site in the early years of the Meiji Restoration; 36 died before a law allowing freedom of religion was passed in 1873. A procession is held here on 3 May.

Tsuwano-jō   CASTLE
(津和野城; chairlift ¥450; ⊙chairlift 10am-5pm, irregular hr winter) The broken walls of Tsuwano-jō brood over the valley. A chairlift takes you up the hillside, and there's a further 15-minute walk to the castle ruins. There's nothing here but the walls, but there are good views over the town and the valleys.

SOUTH OF TOWN

FREE Nishi Amane Former
Residence   HISTORICAL BUILDING
(西周旧居; Ushiroda; ⊙9am-5pm) Worth taking a walk along the river to see is the thatched-roof former residence of Nishi Amane (1829–97), a philosopher and political scientist prominent in the Meiji government.

Mori Ōgai Former
Residence   HISTORICAL BUILDING
(森鴎外旧宅; www.town.tsuwano.lg.jp/shisetsu/ougai.html, in Japanese; Machida; admission ¥100; ⊙9am-5pm, closed Mon Dec-early Mar) Across the river from the Nishi Amane house is the old residence of Mori Ōgai (1862–1922), a highly regarded novelist who served as a physician in the Imperial Japanese Army. It's next to the Mori Ōgai Memorial Museum.

Nagomi-no-sato   ONSEN
(なごみの里; www.nagomi-nosato.com, in Japanese; 256 Washibara; admission ¥600; ⊙10am-9pm, closed Thu) An onsen complex a 15-minute walk along the main road south of the Mori museum.

✦✦ Festivals & Events

Yabusame   ARCHERY
At Washibara Hachiman-gū (鷲原八幡宮), south of town about 4km from the station, archery contests on horseback are held on the second Sunday in April.

Sagi Mai Matsuri   DANCE
The Heron Dance Festival sees processions of dancers dressed as herons, on 20 and 27 July.

🛏 Sleeping

You could see Tsuwano in a day trip from Yamaguchi, but staying the night gives you

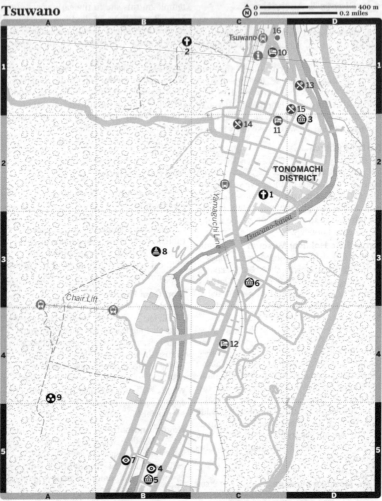

the chance to enjoy one of the town's *min-shuku* or ryokan, and a walk through the quiet lamp-lit streets in the evening.

Hoshi Ryokan MINSHUKU $
(星旅館; ☏72-0136; fax 72-0241; 53-6 Ushiroda; per person with/without meals ¥7000/5000) You'll get a warm, family welcome at this big, slightly creaky *minshuku* located a minute from the station. The tatami rooms are spacious and there's a shared family-style bathroom.

Noren Yado Meigetsu RYOKAN $$
(のれん宿明月; ☏72-0685; www.gambo-ad .com/area.php?ar=12, in Japanese; fax 72-0637;

665 Ushiroda-guchi; per person with 2 meals from ¥10,500) This is a traditional ryokan on a narrow lane off Tonomachi. *Fusuma* (sliding screen doors) slide open in the rooms to reveal a garden, and there are soothing, wood-panelled shared bathrooms. Some rooms have private bathrooms. Look for the old-fashioned gate with a red-tiled roof.

Wakasagi-no-yado Minshuku MINSHUKU $
(民宿わかさぎの宿; ☏/fax 72-1146; www .gambo-ad.com/area.php?ar=12, in Japanese; 98-6 Morimura-guchi; per person with/without 2 meals ¥7500/4700) This well-kept *minshuku* is on the main road between Tonomachi and the

Tsuwano

Mori Ōgai house. Bathrooms are shared. Walking from the station, look for the building with a checked-tile design on the facade and a curtain with a picture of a heron.

✖ Eating & Drinking

There are a few cafes and eateries on the main Tonomachi street, and more along the (less picturesque) street that runs to the right from the station. There's not a lot open at night, as many people eat at their accommodation.

Tsurube NOODLES $
(つるべ; 384-1 Ushoroda-guchi; dishes ¥550-900; ⊙11am-4pm, closed Fri) The speciality here is fresh wheat noodles handmade on the premises, like *sansai zaru udon* (noodles with wild vegetables; ¥840) and *umeboshi udon* (noodles with dried plum; ¥630). It's next to the graveyard.

Yūki FISH $$
(遊亀; 271-4 Ushiroda; meals ¥1300-3000; ⊙10.30am-7pm, closed Thu) The *tsuwano teishoku* (a carp-themed sampler of local dishes; ¥2800) is recommended at this elegantly rustic restaurant, which has wooden tables and the sound of running water. There are *koi* (carp) in a pool in the floor here, and more on the menu. Look for the old-fashioned building with a brown *noren* and small pine tree outside.

Pommes Soufflées ITALIAN $$
(ポンム・スフレ; ☑72-2778; www.tsuwano .ne.jp/pomme; 284 Ushiroda; dishes ¥840-1470; ⊙lunch & dinner, closed Thu; ⊙) The menu at this modern cafe-restaurant includes pastas and pizzas, plus there's a range of sweet bready items you can have with your coffee. Course menus are priced from ¥1575 to ¥4200. Reservations are recommended for dinner.

ℹ Information

Tourist Information Office (津和野町観光協会; ☑72-1771; Ekimae; ⊙9am-5pm) Immediately to the right as you exit the station.

ℹ Getting There & Away

BUS There is a service to Hagi (¥2130, one hour and 45 minutes, five daily).

TRAIN Tsuwano is on the JR Yamaguchi line. There are a few limited-express services direct from Shin-Yamaguchi (¥1150). Otherwise there's a change at Yamaguchi.

Yamaguchi ¥950, one hour and 10 minutes, 10 daily

Masuda ¥570, 40 minutes, nine daily

STEAM TRAIN The **SL Yamaguchi** (SL Yamaguchi-gō; www.c571.jp, in Japanese) runs from Shin-Yamaguchi to Tsuwano from mid-March to late November on weekends and holidays. It costs ¥1620 and takes two hours. Check the latest schedules and book well ahead at JR and tourist information offices.

ℹ Getting Around

Most attractions are within walking distance of the station. There are no local buses, so taxis are the only four-wheeled option.

Kamai-shōten (かまい商店; ☑72-0342; bike hire per 2hr/day ¥500/800; ⊙8am-sunset) Bicycle hire in front of the station.

Shimonoseki 下関

☑083 / POP 280,900

At the extreme western tip of Honshū, Shimonoseki is separated from Kyūshū by a narrow strait, famous for a decisive 12th-century clash between rival samurai clans. The expressway crosses the Kanmon Straits (Kanmon-kaikyō) on the Kanmon-bashi, while another road, the *shinkansen* railway line and the JR railway line all tunnel underneath. You can even walk to Kyūshū through a tunnel under the water. Shimonoseki is also an important connecting point

Shimonoseki

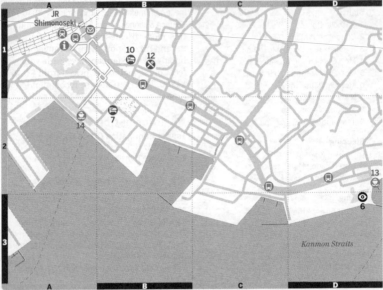

to South Korea. The town is famous for its seafood, particularly *fugu*, the potentially lethal pufferfish.

◉ Sights & Activities

Karato Ichiba   MARKET

(唐戸市場; www.karatoichiba.com, in Japanese; 5-50 Karato; ⊙5am-1pm Mon-Sat, 8am-3pm Sun) A highlight of a trip to Shimonoseki is an early-morning visit to the Karato fish market. It's a great opportunity to try sashimi for breakfast or lunch, and the fish doesn't get any fresher – a fair bit of it will still be moving. Note that the market is occasionally closed on Wednesday.

Buses to Karato (¥190) leave from outside the station, the earliest at 6.27am, and take about seven minutes.

Shimonoseki Kaikyō-kan   AQUARIUM

(海響館; www.kaikyokan.com; 6-1 Arukapōto; adult/child ¥2000/900; ⊙9.30am-5.30pm) In Karato, a short walk from the market, Shimonoseki's aquarium has penguins, dolphins, and sea-lion shows, plus a blue-whale skeleton and tanks of *fugu*.

Akama-jingū   SHRINE

(赤間神宮; 4-1 Amidaiji-chō; ⊙24hr) Bright vermilion, Akama-jingū is a shrine dedicated to the seven-year-old emperor Antoku, who

died in 1185 in the battle of Dan-no-ura. At the left side of the shrine is a statue of Miminashi Hōichi (Earless Hōichi), the blind bard whose musical talents get him into trouble with ghosts in a story made famous by Lafcadio Hearn (see the box, p417).

The shrine is between Karato and Hinoyama, about a five-minute walk from the Karato market area. From the station, get off the bus (¥230, 10 minutes) at the Akamajingū-mae bus stop.

Hino-yama Park   MOUNTAIN, ROPEWAY

(火の山公園; ropeway 1-way/return ¥300/500; ⊙10am-5pm Mar-Nov, closed Tue & Wed) About 5km northeast of JR Shimonoseki Station, there are superb views over the Kanmon Straits from the top of 268m-high Hinoyama. To get to the ropeway (火の山ロープウェイ), get off the bus at Mimosusōgawa (御裳川; ¥230). From here it's a steep 10-minute walk to the ropeway entrance. There are buses that drop you at the entrance (Hino-yama ropeway stop), but they only run once an hour from the station.

Dan-no-ura Memorial   MEMORIAL

Across the road from the Mimosusōgawa bus stop is a memorial (壇ノ浦銅像) marking the spot where the decisive clash between the Minamoto and Taira clans took

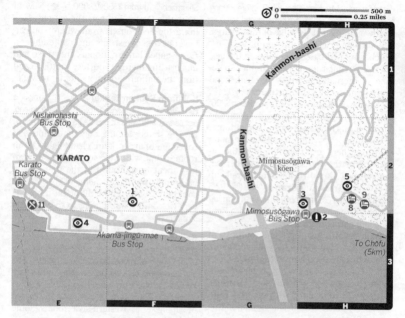

place in 1185. This is where Taira no Tokiko plunged into the sea with the young emperor Antoku in her arms, rather than surrender to the enemy. The statues depict Yoshitsune (the victorious Minamoto general) and Taira no Tomomori, who tied an anchor to his feet and leapt into the sea at Dan-no-ura when it became clear that his side had lost. Local legend holds that the Heike crabs that live in these waters and have strange face-like patternings on their shells are the reincarnations of angry Taira warriors.

FREE Kanmon Tunnel   TUNNEL
(関門トンネル人道; bike admission ¥20; ☉6am-10pm) This is where you come to get that picture of yourself with one foot in Honshū and the other in Kyūshū. For the 780m submarine walk to Kyūshū, head down to the tunnel via the lifts by the Mimosusōgawa bus stop.

CHŌFU   長府
Chōfu – east of Shimonoseki Station along the coastal road – is home to the old castle town area. While little remains of the castle itself, there are earth walls and samurai gates, several temples and shrines, and inviting narrow streets, making it an atmospheric spot for a wander.

Shimonoseki

◎ Sights

1 Akama-jingū F2
2 Dan-no-ura Memorial H3
3 Kanmon Tunnel Pedestrian
    Entrance H2
4 Karato Ichiba E3
5 Ropeway to Hino-yama Lookout H2
6 Shimonoseki Kaikyō-kan D3

🛏 Sleeping

7 Dormy Inn Shimonoseki B2
8 Hinoyama Youth Hostel H2
9 Kaikyō View Shimonoseki H2
10 Kokumin Ryokan Tenkai B1

🍴 Eating

Kaiten Karato Ichiba Sushi .... (see 4)
11 Kamon Wharf E2
12 Yabure-Kabure B1

Transport

13 Ferry to Kyūshū D2
14 Shimonoseki International
    Ferry Terminal A2

The **Shimonoseki City Art Museum** (下関市立美術館; www.city.shimonoseki.yama guchi.jp/bijutsu, in Japanese; Chōfu Kuromon

Higashi-machi 1-1; admission ¥200, more during special exhibitions; ⊙9.30am-5pm, closed Mon) is on the main road at the edge of the old area. It houses an eclectic collection of local art, which is rotated based on changing themes. There are regular temporary exhibits, sometimes of international artists. Across the road from the museum is **Chōfu-teien** (長府庭園; Chōfu Kuromon Higashi-machi 8-11; admission ¥200; ⊙9am-5pm), a garden set around a pond and famous for its flowers in spring and autumn.

Continue a few minutes along the main road from here and turn inland at the canal. Follow the signs and the small river, Dangu-gawa (壇具川), for a nice walk up to National Treasure **Kōzan-ji** (功山時; 1-2-3 Chōfu Kawabata; ⊙9am-5pm), the family burial temple of the local Mōri lords, with a Zen-style hall dating from 1327.

Walk the area just south and southeast of the temple to see some old walls and gates. Also in this area you'll find **Nogi-jinja** (乃木神社), one of several shrines in Japan dedicated to renowned general Nogi Maresuke (1849–1912), who, along with his wife, committed *seppuku* (ritual suicide) upon the death of Emperor Meiji.

Regular buses go along the main coastal road from Shimonoseki Station heading to Chōfu (¥350, 20 minutes). For the art museum and garden, get off at Bijustukan-mae.

🎎 Festivals & Events

Sentei Festival   HISTORICAL

Held at Akama-jingū 2 to 4 May to remember the Heike women who worked as prostitutes to pay for rites for their fallen relatives. On 3 May women dressed as Heian-era courtesans form a colourful procession at the shrine.

🛏 Sleeping

🏆 CHOICE Hinoyama Youth Hostel   HOSTEL $

(火の山ユースホステル; ☎222-3753; www.e-yh.net/shimonoseki; 3-47 Mimosusogawa-chō; dm ¥3200; ⊜@🔊) Amazing views of the straits and welcoming service make this one of the best youth hostels in Western Honshū. You can take a bus from the station to Hinoyama (¥230, 25 minutes, hourly), from where it's a short walk. Note that the caretakers sometimes need to pop out – let them know if you're coming to drop off your bags.

Dormy Inn Shimonoseki   HOTEL $$

(ドーミーイン下関; ☎223-5489; www.hotespa.net/hotels/shimonoseki, in Japanese; 3-40 Shinmachi; s/d from ¥5500/8000; ⊜@) New in 2010, this Dormy Inn gets the vote for having a top-floor onsen from where you can look out over the straits and bathe under a *fugu*-shaped lantern. Rooms are stylish and modern and there's a courtesy shuttle to and from the station (though it's not far to walk).

Kokumin Ryokan Tenkai   RYOKAN $

(国民旅館天海; ☎222-3676; 1-16-8 Takezaki-chō; per person with/without private bath ¥5500/4300) Up the stairs past the dog statue and odd collection of artwork are clean, light tatami rooms (some with wide-screen TVs). You can just about turn around in the tiny private bathrooms, but there's plenty of space in the communal ones. The lady of the house is very welcoming, but it helps to speak a little Japanese.

Kaikyō View Shimonoseki   HOTEL $$

(海峡ビューしものせき; ☎229-0117; fax 229-0114; www.kv-shimonoseki.com, in Japanese; 3-58 Mimosusogawa-chō; per person with 2 meals from ¥9975) Perched up on Hino-yama, Kaikyō View has professional service and the choice of Japanese- or Western-style rooms. Some of the Japanese-style rooms don't have private bathrooms. The hotel has a fabulous onsen with sea views – nonguests can also use it from 11am to 3pm (entry ¥700), except on Wednesday.

🍴 Eating

Close to the fish market is the Kamon Wharf (カモンワーフ) area with eateries and shops specialising in the local goodies – seekers of only-in-Japan culinary experiences can look out for the *uni*-flavoured ice cream (うにソフトクリーム; sea urchin) and *fugu* burgers (ふぐバーガー). Note that whale meat *(kujira)* is on the menu at many seafood places in Shimonoseki. Check for くじら or クジラ if you'd rather avoid it.

🏆 CHOICE Yabure-Kabure   FUGU $$$

(やぶれかぶれ; ☎234-3711; http://820.jp, in Japanese; 2-2-5 Buzenda-chō; lunch/dinner set menu from ¥3150/5250; ⊙lunch & dinner) There's only one thing on the menu in this boisterous spot: pick from a range of *fugu* set menus, such as the Ebisu course (¥5250), which features the cute little puffer in raw, seared, fried and drowned-in-sake incarnations. A lunchtime *tetsuyaki setto* (set meal with grilled *fugu*) is ¥3150. You can also order individual dishes. Look for the blue-and-white puffer fish outside.

FERRIES TO KOREA & CHINA

The **Shimonoseki International Ferry Terminal** (下関港国際ターミナル; www.shi monoseki-port.com) is the boarding point for ferries to Busan, Korea, and Qīngdǎo, China. Check with the ferry companies for the latest schedules. The port website also has information. There are currently no passenger ferry services to Shànghǎi.

Kampu Ferry (関釜フェリー; ☎224-3000; www.kampuferry.co.jp, in Japanese) Operates the Shimonoseki–Busan ferry. There are daily departures at 7pm from Shimonoseki, arriving in Busan at 8.30am the following morning. One-way fares start at ¥9000 for 2nd class.

Orient Ferry Ltd (オリエントフェリー; ☎232-6615; www.orientferry.co.jp, in Japanese) Ferries between Shimonoseki and Qīngdǎo. One-way/return tickets start from ¥15,000/27,000 from Shimonoseki, leaving noon Wednesday and Saturday, arriving at 4pm the following day.

Kaiten Karato Ichiba Sushi SUSHI & SASHIMI $ (海転からと市場寿司; www.kaitenkaratoich ibazusi.com, in Japanese; 2nd fl, 5-50 Karato; per plate ¥105-525; ☺lunch & dinner; 🅿) This revolving sushi restaurant on the 2nd floor, right above the fish market, is a great place to get your hands on the freshest fish without needing to know what they're all called. It's closed when the market closes on some Wednesdays.

ℹ Information

Shimonoseki Post Office (下関郵便局; 2-12-12 Takezaki-chō; ☺9am-4pm) Money exchange and ATMs.

Tourist Information Office (下関駅観光案内所; www.city.shimonoseki.yamaguchi.jp; ☺9am-7pm) JR station (☎232-8383); shinkansen station (☎256-3422)

ℹ Getting There & Away

FERRY Kanmon Kisen (☎222-1488; www.kanmon-kisen.co.jp, in Japanese) ferries run two or three times hourly from the Karato area of Shimonoseki to Moji in Kyūshū (¥390, five minutes). Regular **Kanmon Kaikyō** (☎266-6371; www.kkferry.co.jp, in Japanese) ferries run between Karato and Kokura in Kyūshū (¥200, 13 minutes).

TRAIN *Shinkansen* trains stop at Shin-Shimonoseki station, two stops from JR Shimonoseki (¥190, 10 minutes).

Tawarayama Onsen
俵山温泉

☎0837

Nestled in the mountains, Tawarayama Onsen is a small village that has a reputation as a favoured hidden spa for *tōji* (curative bathing). The story goes that an injured monkey once healed itself in the waters here. The only monkeys you'll see these days are the ones painted on the street and peering at you from the tasty *manjū* sold around town.

There is a narrow main strip lined with a mix of old and newer ryokan, none of which has its own bath. Instead, guests go out to bathe in the two public baths: **Machi-no-yu** (町の湯; admission ¥390; ☺6am-10.30pm) and the newer **Hakuen-no-yu** (白猿の湯; admission ¥700, early morning & late evening ¥500; ☺7am-9pm). If you're looking for a place to stay, try popular **Izumiya** (泉屋; ☎29-0231; fax 29-0232; http://member.hot-cha.tv/~htc02178, in Japanese; per person with meals from ¥8925; 🅿), a well-maintained old inn with wooden floors and a garden. The friendly managers can pick up guests at Nagato-Yumoto Station. See www.tawarayama-onsen.com (in Japanese) for more.

Tawarayama is not especially convenient to anywhere, which for some is part of its appeal. There's a direct bus from Shimonoseki (¥1610, one hour and 50 minutes, seven daily). Or get to Nagato-Yumoto Station (on the JR Mine line), from where there is one bus an hour to Tawarayama Onsen (¥510, 25 minutes).

Hagi
萩

☎0838 / POP 53,700

The quiet town of Hagi is known for producing some of the finest ceramics in Japan, and has a well-preserved old samurai quarter. During the feudal period, Hagi was the castle town of the Chōshū domain, which, together with Satsuma (corresponding to modern Kagoshima in southern Kyūshū), was instrumental in defeating the Tokugawa government and ushering in a new age after the Meiji Restoration.

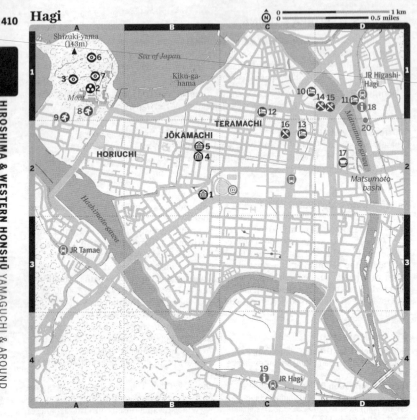

◎ Sights

The main area of interest is the old samurai residential district of *jōkamachi* (城下町), and surrounds, where there are many streets lined with whitewashed walls, enclosing old houses. Nearby is a nice beach (when it's clean) and bay views. There are also a few sights further afield on the edges of town.

Kikuya House   HISTORICAL BUILDING
(菊屋家住宅; 1-1 Gofuku-machi; admission ¥500; ⊙9am-5.30pm) The Kikuya family were merchants rather than samurai. As official merchants to the *daimyō* their wealth and connections allowed them to build a house well above their station. This house dates from 1604 and has a fine gate and attractive gardens, as well as numerous construction details and materials that would normally have been forbidden to the merchant class.

Kubota House   HISTORICAL BUILDING
(旧久保田家住宅; 1-3 Gofuku-machi; admission ¥100; ⊙9am-5pm) Across the street from Kikuya House is Kubota House, a renovated residence from the late Edo period that served as a clothing store and sake brewery.

Shizuki-kōen   PARK, RUINS
(指月公園; castle admission with Asa Mōri House ¥210; ⊙8am-6.30pm Apr-Oct, to 4.30pm Nov-Feb, to 6pm March) There's not much of the old **Hagi-jō** to see, apart from the typically imposing outer walls and the surrounding moat. The castle was built in 1604 and dismantled in 1874 following the Meiji Restoration. But the grounds are a pleasant park, with the **Shizukiyama-jinja** (志都岐山神社), the **Hanano-e Tea House** (花江茶亭) from the mid-19th century, and other buildings. From the castle ruins you can climb the hillside to the 143m peak of Shizuki-yama.

Hagi

Hagi Uragami Museum
MUSEUM

(山口県立萩美術館・浦上記念館; 586-1 Hiyako; admission ¥1000; ⊙9am-4.30pm, closed Mon) Here you'll find a superb collection of ceramics and wood-block prints. There are fine works by Katsushika Hokusai and Utamaro Kitagawa.

Shōin-jinja
SHRINE

(松陰神社; admission treasure house ¥500) This shrine, with a garden and small complex, was founded in 1890 and is dedicated to Meiji Restoration movement leader Yoshida Shōin. His old house and the school where he agitated against the shogunate in the years leading up to the revolution are also here, as well as a treasure house (宝物館). The shrine is located southeast of Higashi-Hagi Station, about 500m from the east end of Matsumoto bridge, over the train tracks. The circle bus drops you out the front.

Itō Hirobumi House
NOTABLE BUILDING

(伊藤博文旧宅; admission ¥100; ⊙9am-5pm) About 200m from Shōin-jinja is the thatched early home of the four-term prime minister, who was a follower of Yoshida Shōin, and who later drafted the Meiji Constitution. It's interesting to see the contrast between this humble place and the impressive mansion he lived in during his years in Tokyo, which is next door, having been moved to Hagi after his death.

Tōkō-ji
TEMPLE

(東光寺; admission ¥300; 1647 Chintō; ⊙8.30am-5pm) East of the river, near Shōin-jinja, stands pretty Zen Tōkō-ji, built in 1691 and home to the tombs of five Mōri lords. The stone walkways on the hillside behind the temple are flanked by almost 500 stone lanterns, which were erected by the lords' servants.

Kasa-yama
MOUNTAIN AREA

About 5km east of the town is the 112m dormant volcano Kasa-yama (笠山). The pond at the mountain's base, **Myōjin-ike** (明神池), is connected to the sea, and shelters a variety of saltwater fish.

Further up the mountain from the pond is **Hagi Glass Associates** (萩ガラス工房; ☑26-2555; www.hagi-glass.jp, in Japanese; Myōjin-ike Koshigahama; admission free; ⊙9am-6pm, demonstrations 9am-noon & 1-4.30pm), where quartz basalt from the volcano is used to make extremely tough Hagi glassware. There is a showroom and a shop, and visitors can make their own piece of glassware (glass-blowing classes ¥3150). Next door is Hagi's own beer and citrus-juice factory, **Yuzuya Honten** (柚子屋本店; www.e-yuzuya .com, in Japanese; Myojin-ike Koshigahama; admission free; ⊙9am-5pm).

The road continues to the top of Kasa-yama, from where there are fine views along the coast and a tiny 30m-deep crater, and there is a walking track around the coast. From late February to late March a beautiful grove of camellias here is in bloom.

Kasa-yama is close enough to make a good bicycle ride from Hagi. A bus from Higashi-Hagi Station drops you about eight-minutes' walk from Hagi Glass Associates.

🏃 Activities

Hagi-yaki is noted for its fine glazes and delicate pastel colours, and connoisseurs of Japanese ceramics rank it as some of the best. At a number of shops and kilns you can

POTTED HISTORY

During his Korean peninsula campaigns in 1592 and 1598, Toyotomi Hideyoshi abducted whole families of potters as growing interest in the tea ceremony generated desire for the finest Korean ceramics. The firing techniques brought over all those centuries ago live on in Japanese ceramics today.

see *hagi-yaki* being made, and browse the finished products. The tourist office has a complete list.

Jōzan   POTTERY MAKING
(城山; ☎25-1666; 31-15 Horiuchi Nishi-no-hama; lessons ¥1680; ◷8am-4pm) You can try your hand at making the pottery in this large workshop; once fired, items can be shipped anywhere in Japan.

Hagi-jō Kiln   KILN, POTTERY
(萩城窯; 2-5 Horiuchi; ◷8am-5pm) In Horiuchi (within the walls of the old castle ruins); has some fine pieces.

🛏 Sleeping

Hagi no Yado Tomoe   RYOKAN $$$
(萩の宿常茂恵; ☎22-0150; fax 25-0152; www .tomoehagi.jp; 608-53 Kōbō-ji Hijiwara; per person from ¥17,000) The finest inn in Hagi, the historic Tomoe has gorgeous Japanese rooms with garden views, beautifully prepared cuisine and luxurious baths. Prices vary according to season, and there are often discounted plans on the website.

Nakamura Ryokan   RYOKAN $
(中村旅館; ☎22-0303; http://nakamura-r.ftw.jp , in Japanese; fax 26-0303; 56 Furuhagi-machi; s/ tw ¥5250/8400) The ivy-covered Nakamura is a friendly place divided into modern and older buildings. It has large tatami rooms and there's a big pine by the entrance.

Hagi Royal Intelligent Hotel   HOTEL $$
(萩ロイヤルインテリジェントホテル; ☎21-4589; http://hrih.jp, in Japanese; 3000-5 Chintō; s/ tw incl breakfast ¥5900/7400; ◒@) Walk out of Higashi-Hagi Station and straight into this modern hotel. The large rooms have some quirky features – the magnetic dartboard and puzzles will keep you entertained – plus spacious showers that spray you at all angles. There's an onsen downstairs, and some staff members speak English.

Minshuku Abugawa   MINSHUKU $
(民宿阿武川; ☎22-2739; www.gambo-ad.com/ area.php?ar=11, in Japanese; per person from ¥4200) The tatami rooms are basic but clean, and there's a nice shared onsen and friendly older owners. You'll need to break out a bit of Japanese here.

🍴 Eating & Drinking

Hagi Shinkai   SEAFOOD $$
(萩心海; ☎26-1221; 370-71 Hijiwara; set meals ¥4000-6000; ◷lunch & dinner) This is a popular seafood joint, a few minutes' walk from Higashi-Hagi Station. Seating is arranged around a large open tank in the floor, so you can peer at the doomed fish as you eat. There's a *sashimi teishoku* (¥2415), or ask for the manager-recommended *Shinkai teishoku* (¥1050/1890 at lunch/dinner), which includes sashimi, tempura and *cha-wanmushi* (steamed savoury egg custard). Look for the white building with the lighthouse.

Cafe Tikal   CAFE $
(長屋門珈琲・カフェティカル; http://hagi -nagayamoncoffee.jimdo.com, in Japanese; 298-1 Hijiwara; coffee from ¥250; ◷9.30am-8pm, to 6pm Sun, closed Mon) Through the old gate of the Kogawa family residence is this small cafe with large windows looking on to a pleasingly unkempt garden. Sit among the knick-knacks and books at one of the few wooden tables and choose from a range of coffees, including a mountainous cappuccino. Cakes are also served.

Don Don Udonya   NOODLES $
(どんどん; 377 San-ku Hijiwara; dishes ¥390-700; ◷9am-9pm; 📶) A popular spot serving tasty *udon*, with plastic models in the window. *Udon teishoku* (*udon* set) goes for ¥580 and there are *donburi* standards like *oyako-don* (¥500). There's a cheaper morning selection. It's in a big black-and-white building on the right as you head away from the station.

Maru   IZAKAYA $$
(まる; 78 Yoshida-chō; meals ¥700-1200; ◷5-11pm, closed Sun) A relaxed and modern young people's *izakaya*, Maru features the local beef, *kenran-gyū* (見蘭牛), available as sashimi (¥850), sushi (¥1000) or garlic steak (¥650). It also serves all the usual *izakaya* favourites. Try the *Hagi no kuramoto ude-dameshi setto* (¥1000) for a tasting set from six local sake breweries. Look for the large wooden door marked with a circle.

ℹ️ Information

Get off at JR Higashi-Hagi for the main sights. Western and central Hagi are effectively an island created by the two rivers Hashimoto-gawa and Matsumoto-gawa; eastern Hagi (with the major JR station Higashi-Hagi) lies on the eastern bank of the Matsumoto-gawa.

Hagi City Library (萩市立萩図書館; 2nd fl, 552-26 Emukai; ⏱9.30am-5.30pm, to 7pm Wed & Sat, closed Mon) Free internet access on 2nd floor. You may need to show ID.

Tourist Information Office (萩市観光案内所; ☎25-3145; ⏱9am-5pm) Located inside Higashi-Hagi Station. Has a good English cycling-walking map. There's another tourist office near Hagi Station.

ℹ️ Getting There & Away

BUS Long-distance bus connections (from Higashi-Hagi Station via Hagi Bus Centre):

Shin-Yamaguchi ¥1970, 1½ hours, at least hourly

Tsuwano ¥2130, one hour and 45 minutes, five daily

Yamaguchi ¥1680, one hour and 10 minutes, nine to 11 daily

TRAIN Hagi is on the JR San-in line, which runs along the north coast from Tottori and Matsue. Local services between Shimonoseki and Higashi-Hagi (¥1890) take up to three hours, depending on transfers. If you're going to Tsuwano and have a JR Pass, you'll want to go by train up the coast to Masuda (¥1110, one hour and 15 minutes), then change to the JR Yamaguchi line for Tsuwano.

ℹ️ Getting Around

Some sights are on the edges of town and Hagi is a good place to explore by bicycle if you're not keen on walking. There are plenty of hire places.

BICYCLE Hagi Rainbow Cycles (萩レインボーサイクル; ☎25-0067; 2960-19 Chintō; hire per hr/day ¥150/1000; ⏱8am-5pm) is to the left outside Higashi-Hagi Station.

BUS The handy *māru basu* (まぁ—るバス; circle bus) takes in Hagi's main attractions. There are east- (東回り) and west-bound (西回り) loops, with two services per hour at each stop. One trip costs ¥100, and one-/two-day passes cost ¥500/700. Both routes stop at Higashi-Hagi Station.

MATSUE & AROUND

Along the northern San-in coastline on the Sea of Japan is Shimane Prefecture (島根県; Shimane-ken), of which Matsue is the capital. It may be off the beaten track, but there is no shortage of reasons to visit. Cities are few and far between, the pace of life is decidedly slower than on the San-yō coast and the people are particularly friendly towards visitors.

Matsue   松江

☑0852 / POP 193,300

With its fine castle and spectacular sunsets over Shinji-ko (Lake Shinji), Matsue is an appealing city with some interesting historical attractions. The city straddles the Ōhashi-gawa, which connects Shinji-ko with Nakanoumi, a saline lake. Most of the main attractions are in a compact area in the north, where you'll find the castle – a rare original. Matsue is also a good base for sojourns to other places of interest in Shimane Prefecture and you could easily spend a few lazy days here.

👁 Sights

Matsue-jō CASTLE

(松江城; Matsue Castle; www.matsue-tourism.or.jp/m_castle, in Japanese; 1-5 Tonomachi; admission ¥550, foreigners with ID ¥280; ⏱8.30am-6.30pm Apr-Sep, to 5pm Oct-Mar) Dating from 1611, picturesque Matsue-jō has a wooden interior showcasing treasures belonging to the Matsudaira clan. Known as Plover Castle for the graceful shape of its gable ornaments, Matsue-jō is one of only 12 original keeps left in Japan, making it worth having a look inside. There are dioramas of the city, as well as fine displays of armoury, including a collection of interesting helmets. The design of each helmet is said to reflect the personality of its wearer – look for the one with the big ears. From the top of the castle there are great unobstructed views.

It's pleasant to walk around the castle grounds (free entry) and along the surrounding moat, with its charming bridges and pines reaching out across the water. A good way to see the castle area is a trip on a **Horikawa Sightseeing Boat** (¥1200, foreigners with ID ¥800; ⏱every 15-20min 9am-5pm). The characterful boatmen circumnavigate the castle moat and then zip around the city's canals and beneath a series of bridges.

**Koizumi Yakumo (Lafcadio Hearn)
Memorial Museum** MUSEUM

(小泉八雲記念館; www.matsue-tourism.or.jp/yakumo, in Japanese; 322 Okudani-chō; admission

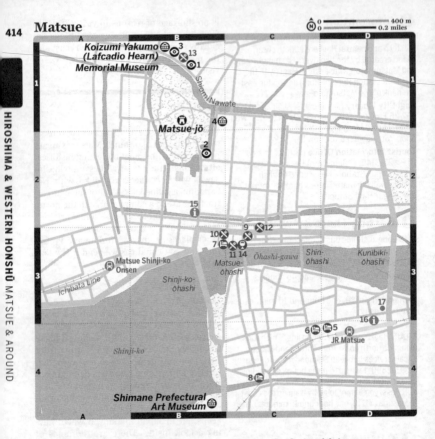

¥300, foreigners with ID ¥150; ⊘8.30am-6.30pm Apr-Sep, to 5pm Oct-Mar) This memorial museum has displays on the life and work of the well-travelled Lafcadio Hearn, as well as some of the man's personal effects – including his dumb-bells, his spectacles, and a stack of Japanese newspapers on which he wrote words and phrases to teach English to his son. Hearn enthusiasts should pop round next door to have a look at his **old residence** (小泉八雲旧居; admission ¥350; ⊘9am-4.30pm), where he lived for 15 months.

Buke Yashiki Samurai
Residence   HISTORICAL BUILDING
(武家屋敷; www.matsue-tourism.or.jp/buke, in Japanese; 305 Kitahori-chō; admission ¥300, foreigners with ID ¥150; ⊘8.30am-6.30pm Apr-Sep, to 5pm Oct-Mar) Built for a middle-ranking samurai family during the early 18th century, Buke Yashiki is an immaculately preserved house and garden.

Shimane Prefectural Art
Museum   ART GALLERY
(島根県立博物館; www1.pref.shimane.lg.jp/contents/sam; 1-5 Sodeshi-chō; admission ¥300; ⊘10am-6.30pm, to 30min after sunset Mar-Sep, closed Tue) With its white undulating roof and huge glass windows facing the lake, the Shimane Prefectural Art Museum building itself is an impressive sight. Inside, it displays rotating exhibits from its collection of wood-block prints (there are some Hokusai among them), as well as European paintings and contemporary art. The sunset views from the museum's 2nd-floor platform or outside by the water also draw crowds here – see the website for a sunset schedule. The museum is a 15-minute walk west of the station.

Matsue History Museum   MUSEUM
(松江歴史館; www.matsu-reki.jp, in Japanese; 279 Tono-machi; admission ¥500; ⊘8.30am-6.30pm, to 5pm Oct-Mar, closed 3rd Thu of month) Matsue's

Matsue

new museum, which was opened in March 2011, has various displays and articles relating to the clan history of Matsue and its castle.

🛏 Sleeping

Terazuya   RYOKAN **$**

(旅館寺津屋;   ☎21-3480; www.mable.ne
.jp/~terazuya; fax 21-3422; 60-3 Tenjin-machi; per
person with/without 2 meals ¥7350/4200; @🛜)
You'll find a warm welcome and clean,
simple tatami rooms at this family-run
ryokan, opposite Matsue Tenmangū shrine.
Some English is spoken, and the owners can
pick you up from the station. While a canal
runs behind the ryokan, so does the JR line
bridge – fortunately there's very little traffic

at night in these parts. It has a shared bathroom and an 11pm curfew, and there's free coffee and toast. Cash only.

Minamikan   RYOKAN **$$$**

(皆美館;   ☎21-5131; www.minami-g.co.jp/min
amikan, in Japanese; fax 26-0351; 14 Suetsugu
Honmachi; per person with breakfast/2 meals from
¥14,010/23,250) A refined inn on the edge of
the lake, Minamikan has a choice of 'modern', 'retro' and 'classic' rooms, all with broad
views across the water. The top-end 'modern'
(from ¥30,180 with two meals) has a tatami
room with attached twin beds and private
cypress-wood onsen. The cheaper 'classic'
has seen the likes of literary great Kawabata
Yasunari pass through. The ryokan entrance
is set back from the road.

Matsuekan   RYOKAN **$**

(松江館;   ☎21-4679; http://matsuekan.com, in
Japanese; fax 25-3513; 494-5 Asahimachi; per per-
son with/without 2 meals from ¥8500/4800; @🛜)
Matsuekan has Japanese-style accommodation and it's located a short walk from the
station. Most of the rooms have private toilets and wash basins, and there are shared
bathrooms – the newest of these is a larger,
communal one. Note that some rooms have
station-area views.

Green Rich Hotel Matsue   HOTEL **$$**

(グリーンリッチホテル松江駅前;   ☎27-
3000; www.gr-matsue.com, in Japanese; 493-1
Asahimachi; s/tw from ¥5950/9900; ⊜@🛜) A
modern chain hotel going for a designer
look with dark-toned furnishings and backlit headboards. Most inviting is the large,
sunken public bath on the 1st floor.

🍴 Eating & Drinking

Yakumo-an   NOODLES **$**

(八雲庵; 308 Kita Horiuchi; dishes ¥700-1150;
🕙10am-3.30pm; 🐾) Next door to the samurai
house, this *soba* (buckwheat noodle) restaurant and its beautiful grounds are an excellent place to sample the local *warigo soba*.
Try the tasty *soba kamo nanban* (noodles
with slices of duck in broth). Look for the
large gate topped by a lantern.

Naniwa   JAPANESE **$$**

(なにわ;   ☎21-2835; 21 Suetsugu Honmachi;
🕙lunch & dinner) Next to Matsue-ōhashi
bridge, this bright, wood-themed restaurant
is a tranquil spot for *unameshi* (eel and rice;
¥2625). Courses featuring the local specialities start at ¥4200 for a Shinji-ko course (see
the box, p416).

Kawa-kyō
IZAKAYA $

(川京; 65 Suetsugu Honmachi; meals ¥800-1575; ⏱6-10.30pm, closed Sun; ➥🈲) You can count on a friendly welcome at this *izakaya*-style restaurant, which specialises in the 'seven delicacies' from Shinji-ko. Look for the white sign with black lettering and the bamboo-roofed menu display outside.

Nakria
JAPANESE, INTERNATIONAL $$

(菜厨; 33-7702; http://hwsa8.gyao.ne.jp/nakria, in Japanese; 2nd fl Matsuya Bldg, 13 Suetsugu Honmachi; ⏱lunch & dinner, closed Mon; 🈲🈲) Stylish Nakria serves set lunches of pasta, curry or steamed pork, plus meals and snacks in the evening to go with your wine. There are vegetarian set options – let them know what you don't eat and they'll do their best. It's in the building opposite the Pasta Factory.

Cafe Bar EAD
BAR, CAFE

(カフェバーEAD; 36 Suetsugu Honmachi; drinks from ¥525; ⏱8.30pm-midnight, to 1am Fri & Sat, closed Tue & Wed) There are great river views from the terrace of this relaxed bar-cafe, found as you head away from the bridge. Snacks include homemade pizzas (from ¥735). The entrance is on the left as you come off the bridge. Take the stairs to the 3rd floor.

Tsurumaru
SEAFOOD $

(鶴丸; 1-79 Higashi Honmachi; dishes ¥600-1050; ⏱5.30-10.30pm, closed Sun; 🈲) The smell of fish grilling over coals permeates this restaurant, which specialises in the cuisine of the Oki Islands. The menu features things like *eri-yaki konabe* (hot spicy soup cooked over a flame at your table; ¥630) and sashimi. You'll know it by the *noren* with the crane on it, and the rustic folk-singing that drifts into the street.

LAKE DELICACIES

Matsue's *kyodo ryōri* (regional cuisine) includes the 'seven delicacies' from Shinji-ko.

» *suzuki* or *hōsho yaki* – steam-baked and paper-wrapped bass

» *shirauo* – whitebait tempura or sashimi

» *amasagi* – sweet tempura or teriyaki

» *shijimi* – freshwater clams in miso soup

» *moroge ebi* – steamed shrimp

» *koi* – baked carp

» *unagi* – grilled freshwater eel

ℹ️ Information

Shimane International Centre (しまね国際センター; 31-5056; 3rd fl, Town Plaza Shimane, 8-3 Tonomachi; ⏱8.30am-7pm Mon-Fri, to 5pm Sun, closed Sat) Information, a small library (with a number of antique Lonely Planet guides) and internet access. Good resources for long-term foreign residents.

Tourist Information Office (松江国際観光案内所; 21-4034; www.kankou-matsue.jp; 665 Asahimachi; ⏱9am-6pm) Friendly assistance directly in front of JR Matsue Station. Internet access available.

ℹ️ Getting There & Away

Matsue is on the JR San-in line, which runs along the San-in coast. You can get to Okayama via Yonago on the JR Hakubi line. It's ¥480 to Yonago (35 minutes), then ¥4620 to Okayama by *tokkyū* (two hours and 15 minutes). Highway buses operate to Japan's major cities.

ℹ️ Getting Around

BICYCLE Matsue is a good place to explore by bicycle; these can be rented close to Matsue station at **Mazda Rent-a-Car** (マツダレンタカー; 26-8787; 466-1 Asahimachi; per day ¥300; ⏱8.30am-6pm).

BUS The red streetcar-like Lake Line buses follow a set route around the city's attractions every 20 minutes. One ride costs ¥200; a day pass is available for ¥500.

Oki Islands
隠岐諸島

📞 08512 / POP 21,700

North of Matsue are the Oki-shotō, with spectacular scenery and steep cliffs. Strictly for those who want to get away from it all, they were once used to exile prisoners (as well as two emperors) who came out on the losing side of political squabbles. The group consists of several islands, including the three Dōzen islands and the larger Dōgo. The 7km-long cliffs of the Oki Kuniga coast of **Nishi-no-shima**, at times falling 250 sheer metres into the sea, are particularly noteworthy. **Kokubun-ji** on Dōgo dates from the 8th century. **Bullfights** are an attraction on Dōgo during the summer months – not man versus bull, but bull versus bull.

The islands make a great getaway. If you're keen to go, allow at least a couple of days and keep in mind that ferry services are subject to change or halt without notice due to bad weather. Your first stop should be the very helpful information office at Mat-

Born to a Greek mother and an Anglo-Irish army surgeon on the island of Lefkada in the Ionian Sea, Patrick Lafcadio Hearn (1850–1904) grew up in Dublin and studied in England before being packed off at 19 with a one-way ticket to America. He eventually found work as a journalist in Cincinnati – until he scandalised acquaintances by marrying a black woman and found himself cast out from polite society. Hearn fled to New Orleans, where he wrote about voodoo and began to develop the taste for the exotic that would characterise his writing on Japan. After two years in the French West Indies, Hearn accepted an assignment from *Harper's* magazine to travel to Japan.

Hearn soon became famous for the articles and books in which he introduced the wonders of this faraway land to the English-speaking world. Eager to stay on after his contract with *Harper's* ran out, Hearn did what many others have done since, and took a job teaching English. For 15 idyllic months he lived in the provincial castle town of Matsue, where he married Koizumi Setsu, the daughter of a local samurai family. After a stint in Kumamoto and a period as a journalist in Kobe, he finally settled in Tokyo – 'the most horrible place in Japan' – where he was appointed professor of English Literature at Tokyo Imperial University. He became a naturalised citizen in 1895 and died less than 10 years later, at the age of 54.

Although Japan has changed almost beyond recognition since Hearn lived here, his best pieces are still well worth reading today. His first Japan-themed collection, *Glimpses of Unfamiliar Japan* (1894), contains his famous essay on Matsue – 'Chief City of the Province of the Gods', as well as an account of his trip to Izumo, where he was the first European allowed inside the gates of the ancient shrine. *Kwaidan*, a collection of ghost stories, was made into a successful film by Kobayashi Masaki in 1964.

sue Station to pick up maps and brochures. There's also the Japanese-only website www.e-oki.net. The islands have some *minshuku* and other forms of accommodation, and places to camp.

Ferry services to the Oki Islands from Shichirui and Sakai-minato, which are northeast of Matsue, are operated by **Oki Kisen** (📞0851-22-1122; www.oki-kisen.co.jp, in Japanese). Check the website or ask at the Matsue Station tourist office for the latest schedule details.

Izumo 出雲

📞0853 / POP 143,800

Just west of Matsue, Izumo has one major attraction – the great Izumo Taisha shrine, which ranks with Ise-jingū as one of the most important shrines in Japan. The shrine and surrounding area can be visited as a day trip from Matsue.

◎ Sights

Izumo Taisha   SHRINE
(出雲大社; 195 Kizuki Higashi Taisha-chō; ◎6am-8pm) Perhaps the oldest Shintō shrine of all, Izumo is second in importance only to Ise-jingū, the home of the sun goddess

Amaterasu. The shrine is as old as Japanese history – there are references to Izumo in the *Kojiki*, Japan's oldest book – and its origins stretch back into the age of the gods. Impressive as the structure is today, it was once even bigger. Records dating from AD 970 describe the shrine as the tallest building in the country; there is evidence that the shrine towered as high as 48m above the ground during the Heian period. It may well have been too high for its own good – the structure collapsed five times between 1061 and 1225, and the roofs today are a more modest 24m.

The current appearance of the main shrine dates from 1744. The main hall is currently undergoing one of its periodic rebuildings, and until May 2013 the deity will take up residence in a temporary shrine in front of the main hall.

The shrine is dedicated to Ōkuninushi, who, according to tradition, ceded control over Izumo to the sun goddess' line – he did this on the condition that a huge temple would be built in his honour, one that would reach as high as the heavens. Long revered as a bringer of good fortune, Ōkuninushi is worshipped as the god of marriage, and visitors to the shrine summon the deity by clapping four times rather than the usual two.

DON'T MISS

ADACHI MUSEUM OF ART

East of Matsue in Yasugi is this excellent **museum** (足立美術館; www.adachi-museum .or.jp; 320 Furukawa-chō, Yasugi-shi; admission ¥2200, foreigners with ID ¥1100; ⊙9am-5.30pm, to 5pm Oct-Mar), founded by local businessman and art collector Adachi Zenkō. The collection includes more than 100 paintings by Yokoyama Taikan (1868–1958) and a good selection of works by other major Japanese painters of the 20th century. There's also a delightful 'pictures for children' gallery. But for many the real attraction is the stunning **gardens**, regularly voted among the best in Japan. Sit and contemplate the perfectly clipped mounds of the Dry Landscape Garden – in the distance, mountains rise up as though part of the garden itself. Take the JR line to Yasugi (安来; ¥400, 25 minutes), where there's a free shuttle bus to the museum (10 daily from 9.05am to 4.15pm).

Huge *shimenawa* (twisted straw ropes) hang over the entry to the main buildings. Those who can toss and lodge a coin in them are said to be blessed with good fortune. Visitors are not allowed inside the main shrine precinct, most of which is hidden behind huge wooden fences. Ranged along the sides of the compound are the *jūku-sha,* which are long shelters where Japan's myriad deities stay when they come for their annual conference.

Shimane Museum of Ancient Izumo
MUSEUM
(島根県立古代出雲歴史博物館; 99-4 Kizuki Higashi Taisha-chō; admission ¥600, foreigners with ID ¥300; ⊙9am-6pm, to 5pm Nov-Feb, closed 3rd Tue of month) Just to the right of the shrine's front gate, this museum contains exhibits on local history. These include reconstructions of the shrine in its pomp, and recordings of the annual ceremonies held to welcome the gods to Izumo. There is also a superb collection of bronze from the ancient Yayoi period.

FREE Kodai Izumo Ōyashiro Mokei Tenjikan
SHRINE MODEL
(古代出雲大社模型展示館; Ancient Izumo Shrine Model Hall; ⊙8.30am-4.30pm) To get an idea of the original size of Izumo Taisha, check out the scale model of the shrine as it was about 800 years ago, housed in a small hall on the corner opposite the main shrine gate entrance.

✹ Festivals & Events

Kamiari-sai
SHINTŌ
The 10th month of the lunar calendar is known throughout Japan as Kan-na-zuki (Month without Gods). In Izumo, however, it is known as Kami-ari-zuki (Month with Gods), for this is the month when all the Shintō gods congregate at Izumo Taisha.

The Kamiari-sai is a series of events to mark the arrival of the gods in Izumo. It runs from the 11th to the 17th of the 10th month according to the old calendar; exact dates vary from year to year.

ℹ Information

Izumo Taisha is 8km northwest of central Izumo. The shrine area is basically one sleepy street that leads up to the shrine gates. The Ichibata-line Taisha Ekimae Station is at the foot of the street close to the shrine.

Tourist information office (☎53-2298; 1346-9 Kizuki Minami Shinmondōri Taisha-chō; ⊙9am-5.30pm) In the station building; has pamphlets and maps, though these may only be in Japanese. Check at Matsue Station tourist office for information in English.

ℹ Getting There & Away

The private, old-fashioned **Ichibata line** starts from Matsue Shinjiko-onsen Station in Matsue and rattles along the northern side of Shinji-ko to Taisha Ekimae Station (one way/return ¥790/1500, one hour, with a transfer at Kawato, 川跡).

The **JR line** runs from JR Matsue Station to JR Izumo-shi Station (¥570, 42 minutes), where you can transfer to an Ichibata train to Izumo Taisha (¥480), or to a bus to the shrine (¥490, 25 minutes).

Iwami Ginzan 石見銀山

About 6km inland from Nima Station on the San-in coast west of Izumo is the old Iwami Ginzan silver mine, a Unesco World Heritage Site since 2007. In the early 17th century, the mine produced as much as 38 tonnes of silver annually, making it the most important mine in the country at a time when Japan was producing around a third of the world's silver every year. The Tokugawa shogunate had direct control over the 500 or so mines in the area.

Ōmori is a small town within the silvermine site, with carefully restored houses lining the main street. At one end of the street is the Daikansho Ato bus stop, across the road from the **Ōmori Daikansho Ato** (大森代官所跡; Former Magistrate's Office; admission ¥500; ⊗9am-5pm, to 4pm Dec-Feb). Inside this is the **Iwami Ginzan Museum** (石見銀山資料館; admission ¥500; ⊗9am-5pm, to 4pm Dec-Feb), containing various documents, tools and silver-related items. Not far up the old road on the left is the lovingly restored **Kumagai Residence** (熊谷家住宅; admission ¥500; ⊗9.30am-5pm, closed Mon), rebuilt in 1801 after an earthquake destroyed most of the town the previous year. The house belonged to a merchant family who made their fortune as officials in the silver trade. The road continues past more old residences and a few temples. Further along on a road to the left off the main road is an interesting temple, **Rakan-ji** (羅漢寺; 804 Ōmori-chō; admission ¥500; ⊗8am-5pm). Opposite the temple is the wonderful **Gohyakurakan** (五百羅漢) where, crowded into two small caves, there are 500 diminutive stone statues of the Buddha's disciples, each showing a different expression – some smiling, some turning their head to chat to their neighbour. The collection was completed in 1766, after 25 years of work.

A little over 2km further up the main street is the **Ryūgenji Mabu Shaft** (龍源寺間歩; admission ¥400; ⊗9am-5pm, to 4pm 24 Nov-19 Mar), which has been widened substantially from its original size. One glance at the original tunnel that stretches beyond the fence at the end of the accessible area should be enough to make most people glad they weren't born as 17th-century miners. Past the Ryūgenji mine shaft, a hiking trail leads 12km to Yunotsu on the coast, following the old route along which silver was hauled to port.

South of Rakan-ji, the **Iwami Ginzan World Heritage Centre** (石見銀山世界遺産センター; 1597-3 Ōmori-chō; admission ¥300; ⊗9am-5pm) has exhibits on the history of the mines and the surrounding area. Tours leave from here to the larger **Ōkubo mine shaft** (大久保間歩; ☏84-0750; tours ¥3800; ⊗9.30am, 10am, 1.30pm & 2pm Fri-Sun & holidays Mar-Nov).

The **tourist information office** (☏89-0333; ⊗9am-5pm May-Sep, to 4pm Oct-Apr) is by the car park close to Rakan-ji. Buses run to the Ōmori Daikansho-ato from Ōda (¥610, 25 minutes, 18 per day) and Nima (¥390, 15 minutes, five per day) Stations; some buses continue on to the World Heritage Centre (¥730). Within the mine area, shuttle buses connect the Ōmori Daikansho-ato and the World Heritage Centre every 15 minutes (¥200).

Iwami Ginzan could be visited on a (very long) day trip from Matsue. Alternatively, it's good to combine a trip here with a stay at a ryokan in nearby Yunotsu. Another good option for accommodation in the area is near Nima Station, at the **Jōfuku-ji Youth House** (城福寺ユースハウス; ☏88-2233; www.14.plala.or.jp/joufukuji; 1114 Nima-machi Nima-chō; r per person ¥3000; @). Accommodation is in comfortable tatami rooms in a Buddhist temple. Meals are available, and the owners can collect you from the station.

Yunotsu 温泉津

☏0855

Three stations south of Nima is the coastal onsen town of Yunotsu (www2.crosstalk.or.jp/yunotsu, in Japanese), one of the ports from where silver from the Iwami Ginzan mines was shipped to the capital and beyond. Now a protected historic area, it consists of a couple of narrow streets of well-preserved wooden buildings and two atmospheric public baths where you can soak up the mineral-rich waters with the locals.

On the main street of the town, recognisable by the statue outside and the large blue sign, **Motoyu Onsen** (元湯温泉; admission ¥300; ⊗5.30am-9pm) traces its history back 1300 years, to when an itinerant priest came across a *tanuki* (racoon) nursing its wounded paw in the waters here. There are no fancy shower heads and racks of shampoo in the wash area here – just grab a wooden bucket, run the tap and give yourself a good splash down. A short walk away on the other side of the street is the relatively modern **Yakushinoyu Onsen** (薬師湯温泉; admission ¥300; ⊗5am-9pm), discovered when hot water bubbled up from the ground after an earthquake in 1872.

There are a number of places to stay, including the 100-year-old **Ryokan Masuya** (☑65-2515; fax 65-2516; www.ryokan-masuya.com; per person with 2 meals from ¥10,600), down the street towards the sea from the two public baths. Some English is spoken, and accommodation is in tatami rooms (a Western-style room is available, but go for the Japanese-style ones).

🖉 **Yoshidaya** (吉田屋; ☑65-2014; www.lets .gr.jp/yoshidaya; fax 65-2412; per person with/without 2 meals from ¥8550/4500; 🛜) is a creaky 80-year-old building with spacious tatami rooms. The staff here do various works in the community, including with local elderly women farmers, who sell *mottainai* vegetables (imperfect-looking vegies that wouldn't normally sell in a store) to use in the meals here. It's not always possible to stay here on weekdays – call ahead to check. Payment is by cash only. Yoshidaya is a few doors down from Motoyu Onsen, heading towards the sea.

Yunotsu is on the San-in line, west down the coast from Matsue (¥1450, 1½ hours to two hours). Coming out of Yunotsu Station, go left, then follow the road around to the right along the waterfront until you reach the main street of ryokan. It's a 10- to 15-minute walk.

Sanbe-san 三瓶山

About 20km inland from Ōda is Sanbe-san, an old volcano with grassy slopes that reaches 1126m. It takes about an hour to climb from **Sanbe Onsen** and five hours to walk around the caldera. You can have a dip in the onsen on your return. Day-trippers can try the outdoor baths at **Kokuminshukusha Sanbesō** (国民宿舎さんべ荘; ☑0854-83-2011; www.sanbesou.jp, in Japanese; Shigaku Sanbe-chō Ōda-shi; baths ¥500, r per person from ¥7400; ⊙10.30am-9pm), where accommodation is available. The area is a popular ski centre in winter. Buses run between Ōda Station and Sanbe Onsen (¥830, 40 minutes).

TOTTORI & AROUND

Although Tottori Prefecture (鳥取県; Tottori-ken) is the least populous of Japan's 47 prefectures, it has a wealth of coastal scenery, sand dunes, onsen and volcanoes. The snag is it takes time and a bit of planning to get to some areas – this is a good place to hire a car. Summer is the best time to visit.

Tottori 鳥取

☑0857 / POP 197.300

Tottori is a medium-sized city that attracts crowds of Japanese tourists coming to take pictures of each other next to camels on the famous sand dunes. There's not a lot to keep you here once you've made the obligatory trip to the sand, but it's a decent base for exploring the nearby coastal areas.

◉ Sights & Activities

Tottori-sakyū (The Dunes)   SAND DUNES

Used as the location for Teshigahara Hiroshi's classic 1964 film *Woman in the Dunes,* the Tottori sand dunes (鳥取砂丘) are on the coast about 5km from the city. There's a viewing point on a hillside overlooking the dunes, along with a car park and the usual array of tourist schlock. The dunes stretch for over 10km along the coast and, at some points, can be about 2km wide. You can even get a 'Lawrence of Arabia' photo of yourself accompanied by a camel. There are maps and pamphlets at the **Sand Pal Tottori Information Centre** (サンドパルとっとり; 2083-17 Yūyama, Fukube-chō; ⊙9am-6pm).

Loop buses (p421) run to the dunes area. Regular buses sail out to the dunes from Tottori Station (¥360, 20 minutes). The closest stop to the dunes is Sakyū-Sentā (砂丘センター; Dunes Centre). There is a **cable car** (¥300; ☑8.30am-4.30pm) from here down.

Tottori-jō & Jinpū-kaku Villa   CASTLE, MUSEUM

(鳥取城跡・仁風閣; 2-121 Higashi-machi; villa admission ¥150; ⊙9am-5pm, closed Mon) Tottori's castle once overlooked the town, but now only the foundations remain. Below is the elegant Jinpū-kaku Villa, built as accommodation for the Taishō emperor when he visited as Crown Prince in 1907, and now used as a museum.

Hinomaru Onsen   PUBLIC BATH

(日乃丸温泉; 401 Suehiro Onsen-chō; admission ¥350; ⊙6am-midnight, closed 2nd Mon of month except Jan & Aug) There are a number of inner-city onsen within a short walk of the station. If you can brave the scorching hot waters, try soaking with the locals at this *sentō* in the heart of the entertainment district.

🛏 Sleeping

Matsuya-sō   GUESTHOUSE $

(松屋荘; ☑22-4891; 3-814 Yoshikata Onsen; s/tw ¥3675/6300) About a 15-minute walk from

Tottori

Tottori

◉ Sights
1 Hinomaru Onsen B1

🛏 Sleeping
2 Green Hotel Morris A1
3 Matsuya-sō B2

🍴 Eating
4 Jujuan B2
5 Tottori-ya B2

🍸 Drinking
6 Chocolate A1

Transport
7 Cal Rent-a-Car A3
8 Rent-a-Cycle A2

alities in this airy restaurant. There are set courses, such as the *kaisen gozen* (grilled seafood and vegetables with sides; ¥4800), and a seasonal menu that may include crab and other locally sourced goodies. It has a brown awning with what looks like a smiley face on it.

Chocolate   CAFE, BAR
(チョコレート; 611 Sakae-machi; drinks from ¥550; ⊙10am-midnight, to 2am Fri & Sat, closed Tue) A long, narrow cafe-bar selling beer, cocktails and coffee (but not chocolate). Food is also served (pastas around ¥800).

ⓘ Information

Tourist Information Office (鳥取市観光案内所; ☎22-3318; www.torican.jp; ⊙9.30am-6.30pm) To the right at the front of the station, with English-language pamphlets and maps.

Internet & Comic Cafe Hills (www.hills.cjb.net, in Japanese; per 30min ¥180; ⊙24hr) Internet access; on the 3rd floor of the building.

ⓘ Getting There & Away

Tottori is on the coastal JR San-in line. Major destinations:

Matsue ¥2210, 2¼ hours; express service ¥3470, 1½ hours

Okayama express via Yonago ¥4270, two hours

Toyooka local service ¥1450, 2½ hours

ⓘ Getting Around

BUS A loop bus (¥300/600 per ride/day pass) operates on weekends, holidays and between 20 July and 31 August. It connects the station with the dunes. Red- and blue-roofed minibuses

the station and behind a high-rise apartment building, this *minshuku*-style lodging has simple Japanese rooms and shared bathrooms. From the station, go straight and turn right onto Eiraku-dōri (永楽通り). Look for the yellowish sign on the left.

Green Hotel Morris   HOTEL $$
(グリーンホテルモーリス; ☎22-2331; www.hotel-morris.co.jp/tottori, in Japanese; 2-107 Imamachi; s/tw from ¥5250/11,550; ➚@) Stylish, neutral-toned rooms, large spa baths and a sauna on site make Morris a great Western-style option. It's close to the station, and there's a buffet breakfast for ¥500.

🍴 Eating & Drinking

Tottori-ya   YAKITORI $
(とっ鳥屋; 585-1 Yamane; ⊙5pm-midnight) This bustling *yakitori* (skewers of grilled chicken) place has *yakikushi moriawase* (grilled chicken assortments) at ¥609 for six sticks, or ¥1207 for 12. The veg five-stick option is ¥504, or select from a large menu of individual sticks and rice dishes. Look for the rope curtain hanging over the door.

Jujuan   SEAFOOD, GRILL $$
(ジュジュアン; 751 Suehiro Onsen-chō; ⊙lunch & dinner) Fresh seafood and local beef *sumibiyaki* (charcoal grilled) are the speci-

There are several onsen areas dotted across Tottori Prefecture. If you have time, consider taking a soak at one of these.

Hawai Onsen (はわい温泉; www.hawai-togo.jp, in Japanese) West of Tottori city and just north of Kurayoshi (倉吉) Station is Tōgō-ike, with Hawai Onsen on its western side. Among the many hotels with baths here, you'll find friendly local *sentō* **Hawai Yūtown** (ハワイゆーたうん; www.supersentou.com/4_chugoku/05_hawai.htm, in Japanese; admission ¥350; ☉9am-9pm, closed Thu). Pick up a map of the other baths in the area from the information centre. Buses to Hawai Onsen run from Kurayoshi Station.

Hamamura Onsen (浜村温泉) You can also take a dip in the delightful indoor and outdoor baths at Hamamura, further east along the train line from Kurayoshi. From Hamamura Station, head straight and take the first major turning on the right. **Hamamura Onsen Kan** (浜村温泉館; admission ¥420; ☉10am-10pm, closed 1st Wed of month) is on the left, a seven-minute walk from the station.

Iwai Onsen (www.iwaiya.jp) East of Tottori city is Iwai Onsen, said to be the oldest onsen in the region and known for its curative waters. This small collection of ryokan is about eight minutes by bus from Iwami Station along Rte 9. Day trippers can relax at modern *sentō* **Iwai Yukamuri Onsen** (岩井ゆかむり温泉; http://yukamuri.net, in Japanese; admission ¥300; ☉6am-10pm). It's right by the bus stop and has an old-fashioned, white-and-blue exterior.

(¥100 per ride) ply smaller, inner-city loops from the station every 20 minutes. Regular city buses depart from the station and travel to the dunes area (¥360, 20 minutes). There are maps and timetables available at the information office.

BICYCLE Rent-a-Cycle (per day ¥500; ☉8am-6.30pm) is outside the station.

CAR Take the main road leading straight out from the south side of the station, then take a left turn at the first major intersection. **Cal Rent-a-Car** (☎24-0452; 1-88 Tomiyasu; 24hr from ¥3800; ☉8am-8pm) is in a petrol station on the right.

Daisen 大山
☎0859

Although it's not one of Japan's highest mountains, at 1729m Daisen looks impressive because it rises straight from sea level – its summit is only about 10km from the coast.

The popular climb up the volcano is a five- to six-hour return trip from **Daisen-ji** (大山寺) temple. Up a stone path is **Ōgamiyama-jinja** (大神山神社) shrine, the oldest building in western Tottori-ken. From the summit, there are fine views over the coast and, in perfect conditions, all the way to the Oki Islands. Pick up a copy of Lonely Planet's *Hiking in Japan* for detailed information on hiking Daisen.

Buses run to the temple from Yonago (¥800, 50 minutes, five daily from 7.20am to 6.10pm) with **Nihon Kōtsu** (www.nihonkotsu.co.jp, in Japanese). At the temple is the **Daisen-ji Tourist Information Centre** (☎52-2502; ☉8.30am-5pm Mon-Fri, to 6.30pm Sat & Sun), with brochures, maps and hiking information. Staff can arrange bookings at the local ryokan.

The mountain catches the northwest monsoon winds in the winter, bringing lots of snow to western Japan's top skiing area. **Daisen Kokusai Ski Resort** (大山国際スキー場; ☎52-2321; www.daisen.net) is one of four linked ski hills on the lower slopes.

San-in Coast National Park 山陰海岸国立公園

The coastline east from the Tottori dunes stretching all the way to the Tango-hantō in Kyoto-fu is known as the San-in Kaigan Kokuritsu Kōen – the San-in Coast National Park. There are sandy beaches, rugged headlands and pines jutting into the blue sky. To get the most out of your travels here, having a car is the best option. However, it is possible to get to some sites via train and bus.

Near the edge of Hyōgo Prefecture is **Uradome Kaigan** (浦富海岸), a scenic stretch of coastline. Forty-minute **cruises** (☎0857-73-

1212; cruises ¥1200; ⊘every 20min 9.10am-4.10pm Mar-Nov) leave from the fishing port of Ajiro (網代), 35 minutes east of Tottori by bus from JR Tottori Station. The bus goes via the dunes, so it's possible to visit the dunes and do the cruise as a day trip from Tottori. Take a bus bound for Iwami and Iwai Onsen and get off at Kutsui-Ōhashi (杏井大橋). Boat is the only way to see the islets and craggy cliffs, with pines clinging precariously to their sides.

Uradome (浦富) and **Makidani** (牧谷), two popular beaches, are a few kilometres east. The closest station is Iwami on the JR San-in line, 2km from the coast, where there's a **tourist information office** (☎0857-72-3481; ⊘9am-6pm, closed Mon). You can rent bicycles at the office and arrange accommodation in the area.

Along this stretch of coast are walking tracks that are part of the **Chūgoku Shizen Hodō** (中国自然歩道; Chūgoku Nature Walking Path), linking to tracks in neighbouring prefectures. The **Tottori Prefecture website** (www.pref.tottori.lg.jp, in Japanese) has guides and information.

Northern Honshū (Tōhoku)

POP 9.8 MILLION

Best Places to Eat

» Shinzaemon-no-Yu (p450)

» Restaurant Yamazaki (p432)

» Aomori-ichiba (p428)

» Jintako (p428)

» Akita Kakunodate Nishi-nomiyage (p439)

Best Places to Stay

» Tsuru-no-yu Onsen (p437)

» Aoni Onsen Ryokan (p443)

» Sukayu Onsen Ryokan (p429)

» Takamiya (p450)

» Towada Hotel (p434)

Why Go?

> The rough sea, stretching out towards Sado, the Milky Way.
>
> *Matsuo Bashō,* The Narrow Road to the Deep North *(1689)*

On 11 March 2011, the Great East Japan Earthquake struck off the eastern coast of Tōhoku (東北). The resulting tsunami reached heights of nearly 40m and travelled inland as far as 10km. It left behind a path of near-absolute destruction, claimed tens of thousands of lives and instigated a Level 7 (major) nuclear disaster. At press time, the aftermath of these events was still being widely felt in the region and emotionally across all of Japan. Although Iwate, Miyagi and Fukushima Prefectures will need time to rebuild, transport infrastructure was largely unaffected elsewhere. Tōhoku remains a recommended destination for outdoor enthusiasts in search of hiking, onsen and skiing. Physical beauty aside, a trip to Tōhoku also encourages tourism to recommence where its economic effects are needed most.

When to Go
Aomori

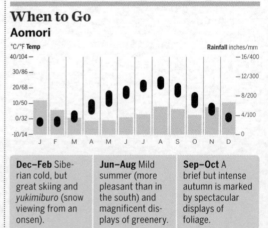

Dec–Feb Siberian cold, but great skiing and *yukimiburo* (snow viewing from an onsen).

Jun–Aug Mild summer (more pleasant than in the south) and magnificent displays of greenery.

Sep–Oct A brief but intense autumn is marked by spectacular displays of foliage.

Northern Honshū (Tōhoku) Highlights

1 Getting away from the mainland crush on **Sado-ga-shima** (p453), a former island of exile

2 Soaking your worries away in Nyūtō Onsen on the shores of **Tazawa-ko** (p435)

3 Traipsing around the verdent shores of **Towada-ko** (p433), the largest crater lake on Honshū

4 Hiking through the sacred trio of peaks that comprise **Dewa Sanzan** (p444), and seeking out tutelage from the famed *yamabushi* (mountain priests)

5 Strolling alongside immaculately preserved samurai mansions in **Kakunodate** (p438), Tōhoku's 'Little Kyoto'

6 Dodging ice-covered trees known as 'snow monsters' at **Zaō Onsen** (p449)

7 Tracing the steps of Bashō with a deeply spiritual pilgrimage to the mountaintop temples at **Yamadera** (p448)

History

Tōhoku was settled during the 7th to 9th centuries by the Ezo people, who are believed to have been related to the Ainu of Hokkaidō. Originating in central Honshū, they spread northward over the generations in search of new arable land.

In the 11th century the Northern Fujiwara clan ruled from Hiraizumi, a settlement reputed to have rivalled Kyoto in its majesty and opulence.

Date Masamune represents the cornerstone of Tōhoku's feudal history. In 1601, construction commenced on Date's castle at the former fishing village of Sendai. The clan would go on to rule for close to 300 years, a reign that ushered in Tōhoku's lofty golden age.

Unfortunately, Tōhoku faded into obscurity when the Meiji Restoration wiped out clan rule. It suffered almost a century of neglect, a trend that was reversed only after WWII and the subsequent drive for development based on industrial growth.

ⓘ Getting There & Around

CAR & MOTORCYCLE

Exploration of the more remote parts of Tōhoku is generally possible with local train and minor bus connections, but car rental is preferable. Be advised, however, that roads in this region can be severely affected by winter weather, which can change very quickly.

TRAIN

The JR Tōhoku *shinkansen* (bullet train) line travels as far as Aomori. From there, limited-express and local trains run further north to Hokkaidō.

Local transport revolves around three major JR railway lines. Two of these run down the east and west coasts, while the third line snakes down between them in the centre.

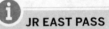

JR EAST PASS

Those without JR Passes should consider investing in the **JR East Pass** (p764), which provides unlimited travel by JR rail in the Tōhoku region for four flexible days, or five or 10 consecutive days. As with the Japan Rail Pass, this can only be purchased outside Japan.

AOMORI PREFECTURE

Aomori-ken (青森県), at the curious northern tip of Honshū, is split in the middle by Mutsu-wan, Noheji-wan and Aomori-wan, the bays cradled in the arm of the axe-shaped Shimokita Peninsula. Somewhat lacking in public transport, this is a prefecture where having a rental car will really open up some of Japan's most remote and wildly exotic areas. The ethereal volcanic landscapes around Osore-zan are where Aomori's people come to commune with the dead. The verdant nature clinging to the shores of Towada-ko is definitely more rooted in this world.

Aomori　　　青森

📮 017 / POP 311,000

Aomori functions as a stop-over point for travellers breaking up the journey between Tokyo and Hokkaidō, and as a transport hub for destinations around the prefecture. Aside from a couple of museums that might appeal to the artistically minded, there is little here in the way of tourist sights. However, the atmosphere of the city completely changes during the Nebuta festival in the first week of August, when illuminated floats parade down the streets, followed by throngs of raucous merrymakers dancing to the tune of drums and woodwinds.

◉ Sights

Aomori-ken Ritsu-bijyutsukan　　MUSEUM
(青森県立美術館; www.aomori-museum.jp/en/index.html; 185 Yasuta-Aza Chikano; admission ¥500; ⊙9am-6pm Jun-Sep, 9.30am-5pm Oct-May, closed 2nd & 4th Mon of month) Located approximately 1km west of the station, the Aomori Prefectural Museum of Art has a decent variety of works on display, including a large outdoor exhibition of Jōmon-era (10,000–400 BC) replica artefacts. There are clear English signs marking the path.

Munakata Shikō Kinenkan　　MUSEUM
(棟方志功記念館; http://munakatashiko-museum.jp/schedule_e.html; 2-1-2 Matsubara; admission ¥500; ⊙9.30am-5pm Tue-Sun) Situated 5km east of the station is this museum, which houses a collection of prints, paintings and calligraphy by Munakata Shikō (1903–1975), an Aomori native who won international fame in his lifetime. Buses bound for Nakatsutui leave from stop 2 outside the train station for the Munakata Shikō Kinenkan-dōri stop (¥190, 15 minutes).

Aomori Prefecture

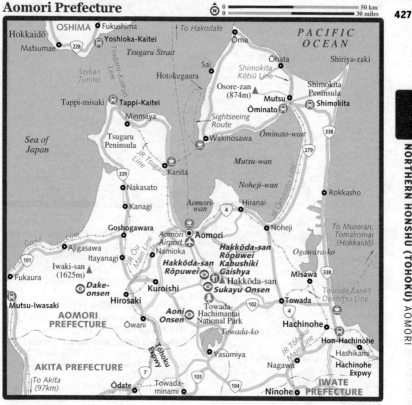

★ Festivals & Events

Nebuta Matsuri
PARADES

Held from 2 to 7 August, the Nebuta Matsuri (www.nebuta.or.jp/english/index_e.htm) has parades of colossal illuminated floats accompanied by thousands of rowdy, chanting dancers. The parades start at sunset and last for hours; on the final day the action starts around noon. As this is one of Japan's most famous festivals, you will need to book in advance if you harbour any hopes of actually scoring a hotel room for a night or two.

🛏 Sleeping

Hotel JAL City Aomori
HOTEL $$

(ホテルJALシティ青森; ☎732-2580; http://jalhotels.com; fax 735-2584; 2-4-12 Yasukata; s/tw ¥9200/14,000; @ ☎) If it is good enough for the Japan Airlines flight attendants, it is certainly good enough for us. Recent renovations have spruced up the place from floor to ceiling with fresh carpeting, bold paints and edgy furniture. From street level, it's an easy building to spot with the JAL logo emblazoned proudly on the exterior.

Aomori Grand Hotel
HOTEL $$

(青森グランドホテル; ☎723-1011; www.agh.co.jp, in Japanese; 1-1-23 Shin-machi; s/d from ¥6500/10,000; @ ☎ 🚻) Across from the Ai Plaza (アイ・プラザ), this is by far the best value in town. Cookie-cutter rooms are mostly lacklustre, but the pick of the litter do have sea views. The central location is also conducive to moving around the city on foot.

Aomori Moya Kogen Youth Hostel
HOSTEL $

(青森雲谷高原ユースホステル; ☎764-2888; 9-5 Yamabuki, Moya; dm from ¥3360; @) An alternative to the urban scene, this homey hostel lies 12km south of the city out in the 'burbs. Buses departing from stop 9 outside the train station can drop you off in front of the hostel (¥590, 40 minutes, last bus 8.20pm).

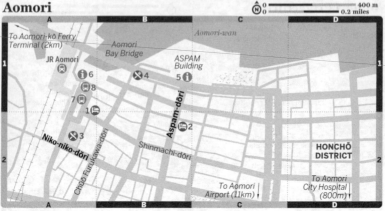

Aomori

🛏 Sleeping
1 Aomori Grand Hotel A1
2 Hotel JAL City Aomori B2

🍴 Eating
3 Aomori Ichiba A2
4 Jintako B1

Information
5 Prefectural Tourist Information
   Counter B1
6 Tourist Information Office A1

Transport
7 Aomori City Buses A1
8 JR Highway Bus Stop JR A1

🍴 Eating

Aomori-ichiba MARKET **$**
(⊙5am-6.30pm; 1-11-1 Furokawa; snacks from ¥300; 🅿) The best place in Aomori to grab a snack is at this fish and produce market near the station. Aomori is famous for a number of local and regional speciality items including scallops, codfish, apples, pickled vegetables and many, many others. You can easily spend an hour perusing all of the food stalls, stopping here and there to sample the bounty from sea and land.

Jintako SEAFOOD **$$$**
(甚太古; 🕿722-7727; 1-6-16 Yasukata; set meals without drinks ¥6000; ⊙dinner, closed 1st & 3rd Sun) Housed in an unassuming beige building (look for the wooden sign) on the waterfront, this restaurant serves formal seafood

dinners set to the tune of the *tsugaru jamis-en,* a version of the traditional three-stringed *shamisen* (guitar). Reservations are necessary – if you don't speak Japanese, ask the staff at tourist information to call for you.

ⓘ Information

Aomori City Hospital (青森市民病院; 🕿734-2171; 1-14-20 Katsuda)
Prefectural tourist information counter (青森県観光総合案内所; 🕿734-2500; 2nd fl, ASPAM Bldg, 1-1-40 Yasukata; ⊙9am-6pm) English-speaking staff and free internet.
Tourist information office (青森市観光交流情報センター; 🕿723-4670; ⊙8.30am-5.30pm) Provides English-language pamphlets and a city map.

ⓘ Getting There & Away

Air
From Aomori Airport, 11km south of the city centre, flights head to/from Tokyo, Osaka, Nagoya and many other destinations. Airport buses are timed for flights and depart from Aomori Station (¥560, 40 minutes).

Boat
Seaikan (🕿42-5561) operates eight daily ferries (year-round) between Aomori and Hakodate (from ¥4000, four hours). Ferries depart from Aomori-kō on the western side of the city – it's a 10-minute taxi ride from Aomori Station (around ¥1300).

Bus
Highway buses depart from the bus terminal across from the train station, and connect Aomori to major cities throughout Honshū. There are also regional buses to the Shimokita Peninsula, Hakkōda and Towada-ko – see each section for more information.

Train

Frequent *tokkyū* (limited-express) trains on the JR Tsugaru Kaikyō line run between Aomori and Hakodate on Hokkaidō (¥5140, two hours), via the Seikan Tunnel (see the box, p477).

There are several daily departures on the *Kamoshika* limited-express train that runs on the JR Ōu main line between Aomori and Akita (¥5250, 2¾ hours). *Futsū* (local) trains on this line connect Aomori to Hirosaki (¥650, 45 minutes).

Hakkōda-san   八甲田山

♪ 017

Hakkōda-san, which translates to 'many peaks and marshlands', is a region of intense natural beauty with a dark history. In 1902, a regiment of 210 Japanese soldiers training in the winter weather were caught in a sudden and severe snow storm. All but 11 men perished, carving out a place for Hakkōda-san in the collective Japanese psyche.

Today, most hikers tackle Honshū's northernmost volcanic range between May and October. Yet the blistery winter months are a great time for skiing and snowboarding. Even if you do catch a chill, take comfort in the fact that Hakkōda-san is home to one of Tōhoku's best onsen, Sukayu.

⊙ Sights

Hakkōda-san Rōpuwei   ROPEWAY
(八甲田山ロープウエイ; www.hakkoda-ropeway.jp, in Japanese; 1 way/return ¥1150/1800; ⊙9am-4.20pm) For anyone who wants a taste of the alpine without having to brave the steep ascent, this scenic ropeway quickly whisks you up to the summit of Tamoyachidake (田茂萢岳; 1324m). From there you can follow an elaborate network of hiking trails, though purists prefer the magnificent one-day loop that starts and finishes in Sukayu Onsen Ryokan.

✦ Activities

Hakkōda-san   HIKING
(八甲田山) Hakkōda-san's quintessential hike spans 12km in distance, and can be completed in a gruelling but highly rewarding day. The trailhead is right around the corner from Sukayu Onsen Ryokan. Things start out relatively flat as you wind through marshlands, but eventually the pitch starts to increase in the shadow of Ōdake (大岳; 1584m). The ridge trail continues to Idodake (井戸岳; 1550m) and Akakura-dake (赤倉岳; 1548m) before connecting to Tamoyachi-dake (田茂萢岳; 1326m).

After stopping in the ropeway terminal for a quick pick-me-up, follow the descending trail through wildflower-filled marshes and rolling pasturelands. Arriving back at Sukayu Onsen Ryokan before nightfall, it's time to indulge in a post-hike beer and the obligatory muscle-relaxing soak.

Hakkōda-san Rōpuwei Kabushiki Gaisha   SKIING & SNOWBOARDING
(八甲田ロープウェー株式会社; www.hakkoda-ropeway.jp, in Japanese; 5-time pass ¥4900; ⊙9am-4.20pm) Compared with other ski mountains across Tōhoku and Hokkaidō, Tamoyachi-dake is fairly modest in scope. The plus side is that you can expect frozen fir trees, piles of wet snow and scant to no crowds. There are five runs in total, varying from short beginner hills to long and winding intermediate trails. The highlight is the 'Forest Course', which cuts through the tree line, and has a few steep and speedy pitches. There are limited goods and services at the ropeway building aside from equipment rental (¥3500 per day).

🛏 Sleeping

TOP CHOICE **Sukayu Onsen Ryokan**   RYOKAN $$
(酸ヶ湯温泉; ☎738-6400; www.sukayu.jp, in Japanese; r per person with/without 2 meals from ¥10,650/6975, bath-only admission ¥600; ⊙7am-5.30pm) Plucked right out of an *ukiyo-e* wood-block painting, Sukayu is a delight for all five senses. Look at the dark wood, milky water and steam; listen to the gurgle of the water; feel its penetrating heat or knead tired shoulders with its *utase-yu* (massaging stream of water); smell the sulphur; and, if you dare, taste the water itself – it's lemony, almost like *ponzu* (citrusy sauce). On a cold day, relaxing here is hard to beat, and one of the baths is rumoured to hold up to 1000 people (though you'll rarely see more than 25 at any one time).

Sukayu Camping Ground   CAMPGROUND $
(酸ヶ湯キャンプ場; ☎738-6566; www.sukayu.jp/camp; camp sites from ¥500) A good spot to pitch a tent with clean facilities and rental supplies. If you have a car, it's located at the end of a small access road immediately south of Sukayu Onsen Ryokan.

❶ Getting There & Away

Two daily buses leave from stop 8 outside Aomori Station, pass by the Hakkōda Ropeway-eki stop (¥1070, 50 minutes), and terminate at the next stop, Sukayu Onsen (¥1300, one hour).

Shimokita Peninsula
下北半島

♪ 0175 / POP 120,000

Remote, axe-shaped Shimokita-hantō is centred on Osore-zan (恐山; 874m), a barren volcano that is regarded as one of the most sacred places in all of Japan. Osore, which means fear or dread, is an appropriate name given that the peak is the stage for Buddhist purgatory. With flocks of jet-black ravens swarming about, and sulphur-infused tributaries streaming by, it's not too hard to make the metaphysical leap.

⊙ Sights & Activities

Osorezan-bodaiji   SHRINE
(恐山菩提寺; admission ¥500; ⊙6am-6pm May-Oct) This holy shrine at the top of Osore-zan is a somewhat terrifying, strangely atmospheric place that's popular with pilgrims seeking to commune with the dead. Several stone statues of the child-guardian deity, Jizō, overlook hills of craggy, sulphur-strewn rocks and hissing vapour. According to ritual, visitors are encouraged to help lost souls with their underworld penance by adding stones to the cairns. You can even bathe on hell's doorstep at the free onsen to the side as you approach the main hall.

Hotokegaura   SCENIC COASTLINE
(仏ヶ浦) The western edge of the peninsula is a spectacular stretch of coastline dotted with 100m-tall wind-carved cliffs, which are said to resemble Buddhas. Between April and October, round-trip sightseeing boats for Hotokegaura depart from Wakinosawa at 10.45am and 2.45pm (¥3800, two hours). Services are often suspended in poor weather.

✿ Festivals & Events

Osore-zan Taisai   SPIRITUAL
These two annual festivals (held from 20 to 24 July and from 9 to 11 October) attract huge crowds who come to consult *itako* (mediums) and try to contact dead family members.

⌷ Sleeping

TOP CHOICE Wakinosawa Youth Hostel   HOSTEL $
(脇野沢ユースホステル; ☎44-2341; www.wakinosawa.com; 41 Wakinosawasenokaware, Mutsu; dm with 2 meals from ¥6000) This stand-out hostel is charmingly perched on a hillside at

ℹ BRING YOUR RIDE

With a sparsely inhabited coastline and a largely abandoned interior, Shimokita might as well be off the grid. While public transport does run (however infrequent it might be), this is one destination where having your own rental car will make all the difference. You should also stock up on necessary supplies before heading to the peninsula as facilities are extremely limited.

Wakinosawa village, about 15 minutes west of the ferry pier – call ahead for a pick-up if you don't have a car. Both Western- and Japanese-style dormitory rooms are available, all of which are adorned with rich hardwoods and country furnishings. While it helps to speak a bit of Japanese, the owners are extremely accommodating and can drive you to a local onsen before dinner. They're also dedicated naturalists who unofficially catalogue the movements of the local Japanese macaques. With the right bit of luck, they can help you track down a few furry little snow monkeys.

Plaza Hotel Mutsu   HOTEL $$
(プラザホテルむつ; ☎23-7111; www.0175.co.jp/plaza, in Japanese; 2-46 Shimokita-chō, Mutsu; r from ¥5000; @☎) This is an average-issue business hotel with institutional furniture. However, the price is right, especially if you book online and lock in the offered discount rate. In addition, it's conveniently located just a two-minute walk northwest of the station.

ℹ Getting There & Away

Bus
There are a few daily direct buses between JR Aomori Station and the bus terminal in Mutsu (¥2520, 2½ hours). Infrequent local services also connect Mutsu to Wakinosawa (¥1790, 1½ hours), Osore-zan (¥750, 40 minutes) and Ōma (¥1880, two hours).

Boat
There are several daily *kaisoku* (rapid) trains on the JR Tsugaru line between Aomori and Kanita (¥1290, 25 minutes). From Kanita, **Mutsuwan** (☎422-3020) runs two to three daily ferries to Wakinosawa (¥1420, one hour).

Higashi Nihon (☎0120-756-564) runs two to three daily ferries between Hakodate on Hokkaidō and Ōma (¥1370, 1¾ hours).

Hirosaki 弘前

☑ 0172 / POP 183,000

Established in the feudal era by the Tsugaru clan, the historic town of Hirosaki remains one of Tōhoku's principal cultural centres. Although it faded in prominence after political power shifted to Aomori, Hirosaki remains elegant and graceful. The town is centred on castle grounds, complete with extant keeps and towers, and highlighted by its beautiful canopies of majestic cherry trees. Hirosaki also serves as a convenient jumping-off point for the spiritual trek up to Iwaki-san.

◉ Sights

Hirosaki-kōen   PARK

(弘前公園) This expansive public park has been shaped over the centuries by three castle moats, and landscaped by overhanging cherry trees (there are more than 5000 in total). You can either burn a bit of shoe leather hiking out here, or take any local bus from stop 2 to Shiyaku-sho-mae (¥100, 20 minutes), which is located right across from the park.

Hirosaki-jō

(弘前城; admission ¥300; ☺9am-5pm Apr-Nov) At the heart of the park lie the ancient remains of this castle, which was originally constructed in 1611. Rather tragically, only 16 years later the castle was burnt to the ground after being struck by lightning. Two centuries on, one of the corner towers was rebuilt, and it presently contains a small museum housing samurai weaponry.

Chōshō-ji   TEMPLE

(長勝寺; admission ¥500; ☺8am-5pm Apr-Oct, 9am-4pm Nov–mid-Dec) A 10-minute walk southwest of the castle ruins brings you to an atmospheric temple district redolent of feudal times. The focus here is on Chōshō-ji, the largest temple, which harbours rows of mausoleums built for the rulers of the Tsugaru clan.

✸✸ ☀ Festivals & Events

Neputa Matsuri   PARADES

From 1 to 7 August, Hirosaki celebrates its Neputa Matsuri, famous for the illuminated floats parading every evening to the accompaniment of flutes and drums. The festival is generally said to signify ceremonial preparation for battle, expressing sentiments of bravery for what lies ahead and of heartache for what lies behind.

🛏 Sleeping

Best Western Hotel New City Hirosaki   HOTEL $$$

(ベストウェスタンホテルニューシティ弘前; ☑37-0700; fax 37-1229; 1-1-2 Ohmachi; s/d from ¥9000/18,000; @🛜🐾) More of a low-key boutique hotel than an anonymous business hotel, the Best Western is a thoroughly modern and surprisingly intimate instalment of this international chain. The property is attached to JR Hirosaki Station and shopping complex, and equipped with an excellent health and fitness centre.

Hirosaki Grand Hotel   HOTEL $$

(弘前グランドホテル; ☑32-1515; http://breezbay-group.com/hirosaki-gh; fax 32-1810;

DON'T MISS

IWAKI-SAN

Soaring above Hirosaki is the sacred volcano of **Iwaki-san** (岩木山; 1625m), a popular peak for Shintō pilgrims. Tradition dictates that summit-bound travellers should first make an offering to the guardian god at **Iwaki-san Jinja** (岩木山神社), and then walk through the torii into sacred space. The trail to the top offers stunning views of the **Shirakami-sanchi** (白神山地), a Unesco-protected mountain range with virgin forests of Japanese beech trees. After peaking at the summit, the pilgrimage trail winds gradually down past the smaller peak of **Tori-no-umi-san** (鳥ノ海山), and eventually terminates in the village of **Dake-onsen** (岳温泉).

From early April to late October there are up to eight buses daily from the **Hirosaki bus terminal** (弘前バスターミナル) to Iwaki-san Jinja (¥880, 50 minutes). From Dake-onsen, there are up to eight buses daily back to the Hirosaki bus terminal (¥900, one hour). The entire 9km hike should take you around 6½ hours, which means that you can easily summit Iwaki-san on a day trip from Hirosaki if you get an early enough start.

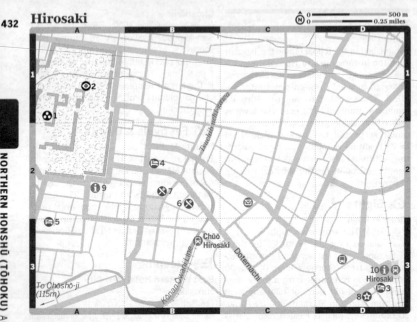

Hirosaki

1 Ichiban-chō; s/d from ¥5000/6980; @) A very affordable business hotel with good service, decent restaurants and moderate-sized rooms, the Hirosaki Grand is within easy walking distance of the castle. It's a fairly nondescript grey building – look for the large 'G' sign.

Hirosaki Youth Hostel HOSTEL **$**
(ひろさきユースホステル; ☑33-7066; www .jyh.or.jp/english/touhoku/hirosaki/index.html; 11 Mori-machi; dm from ¥3045; @) Tucked away on a side street two blocks south of the outer moat, this hostel is identifiable by the large 'YH' sign on the exterior. Although it lacks the personality of the region's other guesthouses, the price is right, and you're smack in the middle of the town's main sights.

✖ Eating & Drinking

TOP CHOICE Restaurant Yamazaki FRENCH **$$**
(☑38-5515; 41 Oyakata-chō; courses from ¥3675; ⊙11.30am-2pm & 5.30-8.30pm, closed Sun; 🍴) Given its rich history and well-developed culture, Hirosaki gravitates towards the refined, especially on the dinner menu. At Restaurant Yamazaki, classic French cuisine with a subtle Japanese twist is served in a variety of tasting courses that change with the seasons. Don't let the location near the bowling alley fool you – the humble entrance (look for the green banners) opens up to a formal continental dining room set with bone china and crystal stemware.

Manchan CAFE **$**
(万茶ン; ☑35-4663; 36-6 Dotemachi; sweets around ¥750; ⊙9.30am-8pm, closed 1st & 3rd Thu)

A lovely little cafe that is reportedly one of the oldest in the region, Manchan is the perfect spot for an afternoon tea and a flaky pastry (there's no English menu, but you can easily choose what you want from the display case). The cafe is across the street from the Nakasan department store – look for the bifurcated cello standing guard.

☆ Entertainment

Live House Yamauta   LIVE MUSIC
(ライブハウス山唄; 1-2-7 Ōmachi; dinner & show per person from ¥3000; ⊙5-11pm, closed alternate Mon) Just a few steps down the road from the station (look for the English sign), this popular venue offers nightly performances of traditional Japanese folk music alongside locally influenced *izakaya* dishes. Call ahead for reservations – the staff caters well for foreign guests.

ℹ Information

Hirosaki Sightseeing Information Centre (弘前市立観光館; ☑37-5501; ⊙9am-6pm) Inside the Kankōkan (tourism building).
Main post office (弘前郵便局; 18-1 Kita Kawarake-chō) Has an international ATM.
Tourist information office (弘前市観光案内所; ☑26-3600; ⊙8.45am-6pm) Offers free internet access.

ℹ Getting There & Away

Hourly *tokkyū* on the JR Ōu main line run between Aomori and Hirosaki (¥1460, 35 minutes), and Hirosaki and Akita (¥2520, three hours).

Aoni Onsen   青荷温泉

A seriously atmospheric, but seriously isolated hot-springs town, Aoni Onsen exists in a time warp. Here, oil lamps replace electricity, open hearths replace kitchen appliances and bathing is elevated to a fine art. For an authentic look at the inner workings of an Edo-period ryokan, Aoni Onsen is a must.

TOP CHOICE **Aoni Onsen Ryokan** (青荷温泉旅館; ☑0172-54-8588; www.yo.rim.or.jp/~aoni/index.htm, in Japanese; fax 54-2655; r per person with 2 meals from ¥9600, baths ¥500) is known as a *lampu-no-yado*, or quite literally a 'lamp mansion'. The proprietors here work hard to suspend your reality and transport you back to a simpler age. There is no electricity, it can get a bit drafty here in the winter months and food is basic. But the tranquil experience of shuffling down dimly lit wooden corridors while the snow gently falls outside will inspire you to craft haiku. And then there are the wood- and rock-framed baths themselves, which occupy both indoor and outdoor space, and incorporate the surrounding nature into their design. The babbling brook, swaying forest and rolling hills all play a role in elevating your bathing experience to the transcendental.

Aoni Onsen is located alongside Rte 102 between Hirosaki and Towada-ko. If you don't have a car, you're going to have to work to get out here. Consider the journey a means of filtering out all except the true onsen buffs. By public transport, take the private Kōnan Tetsudō line from Hirosaki to Kuroishi (¥420, 30 minutes, six daily); Kōnan buses connect with arriving passengers for Niji-no-ko (¥750, 10 minutes), from where shuttle buses run to Aoni (free, 30 minutes, six daily).

Note that reservations are mandatory – if you don't speak Japanese, consult with English staff at any regional tourist information centre. Also be sure to enquire about local weather, as heavy snowfall can quickly alter your travel plans.

Towada-ko   十和田湖

☑0176 / POP 6000
Along with Tazawa-ko in Akita Prefecture, Towada-ko is the focal point of the 855-sq-km **Towada-Hachimantai National Park** (十和田八幡平国立公園). A vast wilderness area of beech forests, volcanic ranges, molar-shaped peaks, crater lakes and alpine plateaus, Towada-Hachimantai attracts outdoor enthusiasts year-round. It's also a great place for a scenic drive or a quiet riverside amble.

Towada-ko is the largest crater lake in Honshū (52km in circumference), and boasts famously transparent waters and impressive scenery. In the past, it was much more difficult to access than nearby Tazawa-ko, and resultantly much less developed for mass tourism. Of course, this is all set to change following the construction of the sparkling new Shichinohe-Towada *shinkansen* station, which puts the lake within easy striking distance of regional transport hubs.

🏃 Activities

Oirase-gawa   HIKING
(奥入瀬川) This winding river, which drains Towada-ko into the Pacific Ocean, is marked by cascading waterfalls, carved-out gorges

Towada-ko ⊙

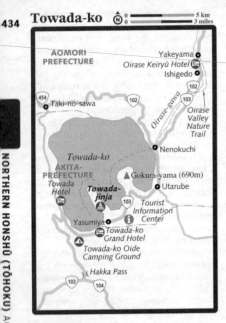

AOMORI PREFECTURE

Yakeyama
Oirase Keiryū Hotel
Ishigedo
102
454
Taki-no-sawa
102
103
Oirase-gawa
Oirase Valley Nature Trail
Towada-ko
Nenokuchi
AKITA PREFECTURE
Towada Hotel
Gokura-yama (690m)
Utarube
Towada-jinja
103
Tourist Information Center
Yasumiya
Towada-ko Grand Hotel
Towada-ko Oide Camping Ground
Hakka Pass
103
104

and plenty of gurgling rapids. Casual hikers can follow the river for a 14km stretch connecting Nenokuchi, a small tourist outpost on the eastern shore of the lake, to Yakeyama, from where relatively frequent buses return to either Nenokuchi (¥660, 30 minutes) or the main tourist hub of Yasumiya (¥1100, one hour). The entire hike should only take you about three hours. Set out in the early morning or late afternoon to avoid the slow-moving coach parties.

Towada-ko   SCENIC CRUISES

(十和田湖) To get a sense of the lake's enormous scale, you really need to leave the shoreline. Formed by a series of violent volcanic eruptions eons ago, Towada-ko is a roughly circular caldera lake hemmed in by rocky coastlines and dense forests. In the autumn months, the dying leaves erupt in a fiery display that stretches to the horizon.

From the docks in Yasumiya, you have a couple of options for scenic cruises, the best of which is the one-hour circuit between Yasumiya and Nenokuchi (one way ¥1400). Boats leave roughly every hour from April to early November between 8am and 4pm. There is also a year-round 40-minute loop-circuit (¥1100), which is preferable if it's too cold to hike for extended periods along the Oirase-gawa.

🛏 Sleeping

Towada Hotel   HOTEL $$$

(☎75-1122; www.towada-hotel.com, in Japanese; Namariyama, Towadako, Kosaka-machi, Kazuno-gun; r per person with 2 meals from ¥14,700; @🤶) The Towada Hotel is a pre-WWII construction defined by its dramatic lobby of hulking timbers that rise to a chandelier-lit cathedral ceiling. Japanese-style rooms are equally historic, but the newer Western-style rooms in the annexe are comparatively lacking in character. All guests have access to the lakefront onsen, which offers total seclusion – all alone on the southwestern shores, you certainly won't see too many people milling about. With that said, consider having access to your own car as something of a prerequisite for staying out here.

Oirase Keiryū Hotel   HOTEL $$

(☎74-2121; www.oirase-keiryuu.jp, in Japanese; 231 Tochikubo Oirase, Towada; r per person with 2 meals from ¥14,000; @🤶🍴) A very large hotel that caters to the package crowds, the Oirase Keiryū lies near the trailhead for the Oirase-gawa hike. There is a standard mix of Japanese-style tatami and Western rooms on offer, in addition to a string of hot springs along the river. The standout feature of the property is its cavernous dining hall, with picture windows edging the forest and sloping eaves of panelled hardwood.

Towada-ko Grand Hotel   HOTEL $

(十和田湖グランドホテル; ☎75-1111; Yasumiya-sanbashi-mae, Towada-kohan, Towada-chō, Kamikita-gun; r per person with 2 meals from ¥5800; @🤶) South of the ferry pier in Yasumiya is this pleasant cross between a European chalet and a Japanese inn. It's another favourite of the package-holiday set, who queue up for the all-inclusive price and central location, so you will need to brave the crowds if you end up staying here.

Towada-ko Oide Camping Ground   CAMPGROUND $

(十和田湖生出キャンプ場; ☎75-2368; www.bes.or.jp/towada/camp.html; camp sites ¥300; ⊙25 Apr-5 Nov) About 4km west of Yasumiya.

ⓘ Information

Tourist information centre (十和田湖総合案内所; ☎75-2425; ⊙8am-5pm) Has English-language pamphlets.

Getting There & Away

BUS From April to November, JR buses run several times per day between Aomori and Yasumiya (¥3000, three hours). A limited network of local buses run around the lakeside. Infrequent connections are reason enough to bring your own wheels.

TRAIN Frequent trains on the JR Tohoku *shinkansen* line run between Shichinohe-Towada and Shin-Aomori (¥2920, 15 minutes).

AKITA PREFECTURE

Japan's sixth-largest prefecture, Akita-ken (秋田県) is shaped by the Oū-sanmyaku and Dewa mountain ranges. Between the soaring peaks lies a series of high alpine trails, which provide access to some of the region's holiest shrines. At lower altitudes, towns and cities have sprung up in the fertile valleys, including the prefectural capital of Akita, and the feudal city of Kakunodate, a storehouse of samurai culture. And then there is Tazawa-ko and its partner destination of Nyūtō Onsen, an immensely popular summer-holiday retreat for Tokyoites fleeing to cooler northern altitudes.

Tazawa-ko 田沢湖

☎0187 / POP 13,000

At 423m, Tazawa-ko is Japan's deepest lake, complete with sandy beaches, wooded shores and vacationing families either paddling rowboats across still waters or skiing down snow-covered slopes. The area is also home to the atmospheric Nyūtō Onsen, which is tucked up at the top of a winding mountain road, and is famous for its mineral-enriched milky-white water. As if all of this isn't enough of a selling point, consider the fact that Tazawa-ko also has its own dedicated *shinkansen* station, which makes it an easy-to-access rural getaway.

Sights

Tazawa-ko LAKE

(田沢湖) Public beaches surround the lake itself, yet swimming is a frigid proposition outside the balmy summer months. If you're not a member of the polar-bear club, you can rent all manner of boats in the town of Tazawa Kohan during the spring, summer and autumn months. A stroll by the lake at sunset is a treat at any time of year, and is

---

THE GREAT EAST JAPAN EARTHQUAKE

Officially known as the Higashi-nihon Dai-shinsai (東日本大震災), the Great East Japan Earthquake was a 9.0-magnitude 'megathrust' event that occurred at 2.46pm (JST) on 11 March 2011. Estimates suggest that the epicentre was located 72km east of Tōhoku's Oshika Peninsula, at the junction of the Pacific and North American Plates. Since modern record-keeping began in the early 20th century, it was the most powerful earthquake to hit Japan, and among the five strongest ever recorded.

Just minutes after the quake struck, a massive tsunami surged over the coastline of northeast Honshū. Some residents had time to flee to higher ground or take refuge in designated shelters, but many did not. The tsunami was far larger and more powerful than anyone could have imagined. Protective seawalls were overwhelmed by waves that crested at nearly 40m in height. The surge flooded over 500 sq km of land and reached up to 10km inland. At press time, the Japanese National Police Agency had confirmed 14,728 dead, over 10,808 missing and presumed dead, and more than 126,000 living in evacuation shelters.

In regard to infrastructure, more than 190,000 buildings were either heavily damaged or destroyed. Roads and railways were washed away, Fujinuma Dam burst and Sendai airport was submerged up to the second level of the passenger terminal. But by far the most widely publicised and serious damage to infrastructure occurred at the Fukushima One nuclear powerplant. For details on this, see the box on p736.

In response to the Great East Japan Earthquake, we have removed coverage of the affected areas from this guidebook. However, we believe that travel in other parts of Tōhoku remains safe, with the caveat that you continue to stay informed on the latest developments (see p748 for resources). Relief efforts were under way at the time this book went to press, and while volunteer opportunities are limited to those with professional training and expertise, donations are being widely accepted by various charities and NGOs. To find out more, see the box on p752.

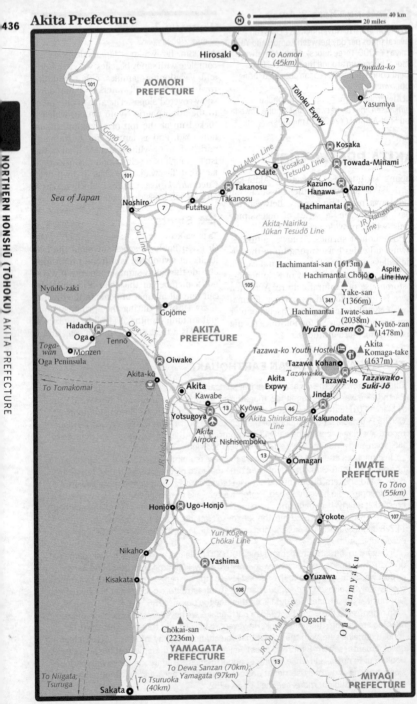

NORTHERN HONSHŪ (TŌHOKU) AKITA PREFECTURE

0 | 40 km
0 | 20 miles

Hirosaki

To Aomori (45km)

Towada-ko

AOMORI PREFECTURE

101

Tōhoku Expwy

Yasumiya

7

Gonō Line

Kosaka

Towada-Minami

JR Ōu Main Line

Kosaka Tetsudō Line

Ōdate

Kazuno-Hanawa

Kazuno

101

Takanosu

Takanosu

Noshiro

Sea of Japan

Futatsui

7

Hachimantai

JR Hanawa Line

Ōu Line

Akita-Nairiku Jūkan Tesudō Line

105

Hachimantai-san (1613m)

Aspite Line Hwy

Hachimantai Chōjō

Yake-san (1366m)

341

Iwate-san (2038m)

Hachimantai

Nyūtō-zan (1478m)

Nyūdō-zaki

Gojōme

AKITA PREFECTURE

Nyūtō Onsen

Tazawa-ko Youth Hostel

Akita Komaga-take (1637m)

Hadachi

Oga

Tennō

Ōga Line

Oiwake

Tazawa Kohan

Tazawa-ko

Tazawa-ko

Tazawako-Suki-Jō

Toga-wan

Monzen

Oga Peninsula

Akita-kō

Akita

Akita Expwy

Jindai

To Tomakomai

Kawabe

13

Kyōwa

46

Kakunodate

Akita Shinkansen Line

Yotsugoya

Akita Airport

Nishisemboku

JR Uetsu Main Line

13

Omagari

IWATE PREFECTURE

To Tōno (55km)

7

Honjō

Ugo-Honjō

Yokote

107

Yuri Kōgen Chōkai Line

Nikaho

Yashima

108

Kisakata

Yuzawa

Ō - s a n - m y a k u

Chōkai-san (2236m)

YAMAGATA PREFECTURE

Ogachi

JR Ōu Main Line

To Dewa Sanzan (70km); Yamagata (97km)

7

To Niigata; Tsuruga

To Tsuruoka (40km)

13

MIYAGI PREFECTURE

Sakata

the preferred activity for romance-seeking Japanese couples and bonding families. There is also a 20km perimeter road, which is perfect for a slow drive or a vigorous bike ride – rentals are available in Tazawa Kohan (¥400 per hour).

Nyūtō Onsen
ONSEN

(乳頭温泉) Nyūtō is one of Japan's choicest hot springs, and a must-visit for any aspiring onsen aficionado. The area is home to no fewer than eight rustic ryokan, each with a different character and different baths. All offer healing waters that are great for an away-from-it-all soak. Many also feature *konyoku* or mixed-sex baths (when it comes to bathing, the Japanese certainly aren't shy!) The two most famous bathhouses are Tsuru-no-yu and Kuroyu – see Sleeping for more information.

🏃 Activities

Akita Komaga-take
MOUNTAIN CLIMBING

(秋田駒ヶ岳) Straddling the border with Iwate Prefecture, this mountainous area is admired for its summer wildflowers, fall foliage and rare prevalence of both dry and wet plant species. If you have two days to spare, you can pursue a 17km-long course that takes in three peaks, overnights in a picturesque mountain hut and finishes up with a rewarding soak in the healing waters of Nyūtō Onsen.

You can access the trailhead at Komaga-take Hachigōme (eighth station) by taking one of seven daily buses (all depart before 1.30pm) from Tazawa-ko station (¥1000, one hour). From eighth station, it should take you about two to three hours to reach the summit of Oname-dake (男女岳; 1637m).

From here, you should press on to the eastern edge of the oval-shaped pond below, and claim your space at the Amida-ike Hi-nan Goya (阿弥陀池避難小屋) unmanned mountain; it's recommended that you leave a small tip (¥1000). If it's still light outside, you can double back for 20 minutes or so and scale O-dake (男岳; 1623m).

On the second day, it will take you about seven hours to descend to Nyūtō Onsen, though not without first summiting Yoko-dake (横岳; 1583m). The descending trail follows the ridgeline most of the way, and eventually winds through expansive marsh-lands that harbour all manner of avian life. The circuit ends at the bus stop for Nyūtō Onsen, which signals that your hot bath is just ahead.

Tazawako-Sukī-Jō
SKIING & SNOWBOARDING

(たざわ湖スキー場; www.snowjapan.com/e/spotlight/tazawa.html; 1-day lift tickets ¥3800; ☉Dec-Apr) With Tokyo little more than a three-hour *shinkansen* ride away, this winter-sports destination sees a good amount of foot traffic once the snow starts to fall. The powder accumulates over 13 runs that wind down Akita Komaga-take and overlook the nearby shores of Tazawa-ko.

Trails are evenly divided between beginner, intermediate and advanced levels. However, they tend to be a bit on the shorter side with the exception of the 1.6km-long Kokutai and Shirakaba runs. Six lifts do a reasonable job of keeping the queues to a relative minimum, but it can get very busy here on peak weekends.

You'll find English-language signs on the mountains and in the restaurants. There are three large cafeteria-style eateries serving the usual fast-food-leaning staples in addition to local specialities such as ginger *rāmen* (egg noodles) and Tazawako micro-brews if you're in the mood for a gourmet *après-ski*. Full equipment rental is available for ¥3500 per day. Tazawako-Sukī-Jō is located on the road to Nyūtō Onsen, and can be accessed by local bus or car in the winter months.

🛌 Sleeping

The ryokan listed below are found within the precincts of Nyūtō Onsen.

TOP CHOICE Tsuru-no-yu Onsen
RYOKAN $$

(鶴の湯温泉; ☏46-2139; www.tsurunoyu.com/english.html; fax 46-2100; 50 Kokuyurin, Sendat-suzawa; r per person with 2 meals ¥8500-15,900, baths ¥500; @🛜) The most storied onsen in Nyūtō, Tsuru-no-yu has been in the business for almost four centuries. The reason for its enduring fame is the mineral-rich spring containing sulphur, sodium, calcium chloride and carbonic acid, which combine to form a distinctive milky-white colour. According to local lore, a hunter once saw a *tsuru* or crane healing its wounds in the spring, and reported the fortuitous discovery to his lord. The hot spring was soon designated the official bathhouse of the Akita clan's ruling elite. Today it's fortunately open to commoners and nobles alike. The mixed *rotemburo* (outdoor bath) is positively jubilant, though shyer folks can take refuge in the indoor sex-segregated baths. Accommodation is extremely varied, ranging from tiny six-mat tatami rooms that share bathrooms to compartmentalised suites that open up to the forest. Regardless of where you bed down, the evening hours are a nostalgic affair distinguished by hearty meals cooked over the *irori* (sunken hearth) and guests in *yukata* (light cotton kimono) dining and socialising by lantern light.

Taenoyu
RYOKAN $$$

(妙乃湯; ☑46-2740; www.taenoyu.com, in Japanese; fax 46-2207; 2-1 Komagatake, Obonai; r per person with 2 meals from ¥12,855, baths ¥700; ⊚) What Taenoyu lacks in history, it more than makes up for in style. Capitalising on the fact that it's been in existence for decades instead of centuries, this boutique ryokan specialises in sophisticated refinement. Sleeping quarters are framed by rich hardwoods and elaborate furnishings, and locavore meals are built around wild plants foraged on the grounds. Bathing options are comprehensive, including private family onsen, reclining cypress tubs, mixed *rotemburo* (open-air bath), rock-lined springs and indoor relaxation pools.

Kuroyu Onsen
RYOKAN $$

(黒湯温泉; ☑46-2214; www.kuroyu.com, in Japanese; fax 46-2280; 2-1 Aza-kuroyuzawa, Obonai; r per person with 2 meals from ¥11,700, baths ¥500) At the streamside Kuroyu, you'll easily feel like you've stepped into a Japanese woodblock print. With a bathing tradition dating back more than 300 years (albeit not as ancient as Tsuru-no-yu), Kuroyu is famous for its hydrogen-sulphide spring that is said to ease high blood pressure, diabetes and arteriosclerosis. Check out the waterfall jets, which erupt from the wall and channel cascades of water onto your shoulders and back. Japanese-style rooms are fairly standard, though the forest setting is the stage for a relaxing retreat.

Tazawa-ko Youth Hostel
HOSTEL $

(田沢湖ユースホステル; ☑43-1281; www.jyh .or.jp/yhguide/touhoku/tazawako/index.html, in Japanese; fax 43-0842; 33-8 Kami-Ishigami, Obonai; r from ¥3090; ⊚) Rooms at the YH are clean and functional, and you can expect good Japanese home cooking.

ℹ️ Information

Folake (☑43-2111; ⊚8.30am-6.30pm) Inside the train station; tourist information and free internet.

ℹ️ Getting There & Away

Bus

Buses connect the train station to Tazawa Kohan, a small transport hub on the eastern shores of the lake. From here, it takes about 40 minutes travelling northwest by bus or car to reach Nyūtō Onsen and the ski slopes.

Frequent local buses run between JR Tazawa-ko Station and Tazawa Kohan (¥350, 10 minutes), and between Tazawa Kohan and Nyūtō Onsen (¥650, 40 minutes). Note that these services terminate after sunset.

Car & Motorcycle

If you're driving, a well-maintained network of local roads branches off the Akita Expressway (秋田自動車道) running east from Akita.

Train

JR Tazawa-ko Station is located a few kilometres southeast of the lake, and serves as the area's main access point.

Several hourly trains on the Akita *shinkansen* line run between Tazawa-ko and Tokyo (¥15,240, three hours), and between Tazawa-ko and Akita (¥3280, 55 minutes) via Kakunodate (¥1560, 15 minutes).

Kakunodate 角館

☑0187 / POP 13,000

Established in 1620 by Ashina Yoshikatsu, the lord of the Satake clan, Kakunodate is known as 'Little Kyoto', and presents a thoughtful, immersive experience for anyone interested in catching a glimpse of the samurai era. While the castle that once guarded the feudal town is no more, the *bukeyashiki* – or samurai district – is splendidly preserved. A veritable living museum of Japanese culture and history, the *bukeyashiki* consists of orderly mansions surrounded by cherry trees and lush garden expanses. It only takes an hour or so to stroll through the district, but staying overnight allows you to soak up the historic atmosphere sans tourist masses.

👁 Sights

Kakunodate Rekishimura Aoyagi-ke
MUSEUM

(角館歴史村青柳家; www.samuraiworld.com/ english/index.html; 3 Omotemachi, Shimochō; admission ¥500; ⊚9am-5pm Apr-Oct, to 4pm Nov-Mar) Each of the samurai mansions that make up this museum complex is impressive in its own right, but the highlight of the *bukeyashiki* is this agglomeration of mini-exhibits. Here you'll find everything from

Aoyagi family heirlooms and folk art to valuable antiques including old-time cameras, gramophones and classic jazz records. There is also an impressive amount of samurai weaponry.

Bukeyashiki Ishiguro-ke NOTABLE BUILDING
(武家屋敷石黒家; Omotemachi; admission ¥300; ⏲9am-5pm) Built in 1809, this was the residence of the Isihiguro family, advisers to the Satake clan, and it's one of the oldest buildings in the district. A descendant of the family still lives here, but some rooms are open to the public. In addition to samurai gear, don't miss the weathered maps and the precision scales for doling out rice.

Kakunodate Kabazaiku Denshōkan MUSEUM
(角館樺細工伝承館; 10-1 Omotemachi Shimochō; admission ¥300; ⏲9am-5pm Apr-Oct, to 4.30pm Nov-Mar) Inside you'll find exhibits and demonstrations on *kabazaiku,* which is the craft of covering household or decorative items in fine strips of cherry bark. This pursuit was first taken up by lower-ranking and masterless samurai in times of hardship.

Festivals & Events

Cherry-blossom tunnel CHERRY BLOSSOM
On the river embankment, a 2km tunnel of cheery blossom comes alive in April or May. Some of the *shidarezakura* (drooping cherry) trees in the *bukeyashiki* are up to 300 years old, and were originally brought from Kyōtō.

Hikiyama Matsuri TRADITIONAL
From 7 to 9 September, Kakunodate celebrates the Hikiyama Matsuri, in which participants haul around enormous seven-tonne *yama* (wooden carts) to pray for peaceful times, accompanied by folk music and dancing.

Sleeping

TOP CHOICE Tamachi Bukeyashiki Hotel BOUTIQUE HOTEL $$
(田町武家屋敷ホテル; ☎52-2030; www.bukeyashiki.jp, in Japanese; fax 52-1701; 52 Tamachi; r with 2/1 meals from ¥15,750/11,125) A Western-style hotel of mind-blowing opulence that preserves the original character and structure of the samurai mansion. While it's only been in the business for a few decades, you can easily imagine travel-worn samurai crashing here for the night, albeit on tatami mats and not on plush sleeper beds. But that is precisely why this stand-alone boutique gets our top marks: it's a masterful blend of historic ambience and tasteful luxury with a heaving dose of urbane style.

Ishikawa Ryokan RYOKAN $$
(石川旅館; ☎54-2030; 32 Iwasemachi; r with 2 meals from ¥9000) This Edo-period ryokan continues to operate just as it did in the time of travelling samurai. The present building dates from the early 20th century, with a few antiques strewn about for good measure. The amiable owners do a good job of making guests feel welcome, and the home-cooked meals are heart-healthy spreads.

Folkloro Kakunodate HOTEL $$
(フォルクローロ角館; ☎53-2070; Nakasugazawa 14; s/tw/q ¥7350/12,600/21,000) Located next to Kakunodate Station; prices decrease for multiple-day stays.

Eating

Akita Kakunodate Nishinomiyage SHOKUDŌ $$
(あきた角館西宮家; ☎52-2438; bento from ¥1500; ⏲10am-8pm; 📄) Although it's generally packed with tourists, there's lots of room to spare at this massive warehouse, built by the Nishinomiya family almost a century ago. The food is average, best described as Japanese comfort (tempura, noodles), but dining at long tables under hulking wooden beams, surrounded by authentic period pieces is part of the experience.

Kosendō NOODLES $
(古泉洞; ☎53-2902; noodles from ¥750; ⏲lunch & dinner; 🖉) The town's most historically significant lunch spot is this wooden schoolhouse. The speciality is the *inaniwa-udon* (udon noodles in a mushroom soup; ¥850).

Information

Tourist information office (角館町観光協会; ☎54-2700; ⏲9am-6pm mid-Apr–Sep, to 5.30pm Oct–mid-Apr) Outside the station in a small building shaped like a *kura* (traditional Japanese storehouse).

Getting There & Away

Several hourly trains on the Akita *shinkansen* line run between Kakunodate and Tazawa-ko (¥1560, 15 minutes), and between Kakunodate and Akita (¥2940, 45 minutes).

Infrequent local trains also run on the JR Tazawako line between Kakunodate and Tazawa-ko and (¥320, 20 minutes), and between Kakunodate and Akita (¥1280, 1¾ hours), with a change at Ōmagari to the JR Ōu main line.

Akita 秋田

♪ 018 / POP 336,000

The northern terminus of the aptly dubbed Akita *shinkansen,* this sprawling commercial city and prefectural capital is one of the region's principal transport hubs, and you'll probably pass through once or twice on your northern travels. For the Japanese, the city is more famous for its '*Akita-bijin*' (a beautiful woman from Akita), who is rumoured to have the fairest complexion in the country. This is somewhat ironic given how ugly the city itself can be. Fret not, however, as there are a couple of local delicacies on the menu worth seeking out.

◉ Sights

Akita's few sights cluster in the city centre near the train station, so you can easily get around without fear of getting too lost.

Senshū-kōen   PARK

(千秋公園) Originally constructed in 1604, Akita's castle was destroyed with other feudal relics during the Meiji 'enlightenment'. However, the hallowed ruins still frame this leafy park just 10 minutes due west of the station. The park protects a few odd walls, turrets and guardhouses, and an observation platform that delivers appealing views of the city.

At the heart of the park lies the **Hirano Masakichi Bijutsukan** (http://hirabi.m78.com; 3-7 Senshū Meitoku-chō; admission ¥610; ⊙10am-5.30pm Tue-Sun May-Sep, to 5pm Tue-Sun Oct-Apr), a famous art museum renowned for its enormous painting, *Events of Akita*. Reputed to be the world's largest canvas painting, it measures 3.65m by 20.5m and depicts traditional Akita life throughout the seasons.

Akarenga Kyōdokan   MUSEUM

(www.city.akita.akita.jp/city/ed/ak, in Japanese; 3-3-21 Ōmachi; admission ¥200; ⊙9.30am-4.30pm) This Meiji-era, Renaissance-style, red-brick building now operates as a folk museum. Inside, you'll find wood-block prints of traditional Akita life by self-taught artist Katsuhira Tokushi. Head west from the park and continue south past the Akita New City department store to find the museum.

✸ Festivals & Events

Akita Kantō Matsuri   LANTERNS

From 3 to 6 August, Akita celebrates the visually stunning Pole Lantern Festival (www.kantou.gr.jp/english/index.htm). When evening falls on the city centre, more than 160 men skilfully balance giant poles, weighing 60kg and hung with illuminated lanterns, on their heads, chins, hips and shoulders, to the beat of *taiko* drumming groups.

🛏 Sleeping

Richmond Hotel Akita Ekimae   HOTEL $$

(♪884-0055; www.richmondhotel.jp/en/akita/index.php?lang=en; 2-2-26 Naka-dōri; r from ¥8700; @✿☃) Opened to the public in 2009, this sparkling new property is conveniently located just a few blocks in front of the train station. Bucking the trend of dated quarters that characterises far too many business hotels in Japan, rooms at the Richmond are sleek and shiny. Note that prices vary considerably based on size, view and amenities, so shop around before swiping your credit card.

Naniwa Hotel   HOTEL $

(ホテルなにわ; ♪832-4570; www.hotel-naniwa.jp, in Japanese; 6-18-27 Nakadōri; r per person with/without 2 meals ¥6000/3150; @) This family-run hotel consists of cutesy and cosy tatami rooms as well as appealing extras including free massage chairs, a beautiful 24-hour *hinoki* (Japanese cypress) bath and meals made with the owners' own home-grown rice. From the station, turn left at the Topico plaza, and head south until you hit the major throughway – it's the red building with a wooden entrance.

Akita Castle Hotel   HOTEL $$

(秋田キャッスルホテル; ♪834-1141; www.castle-hotel.co.jp, in Japanese; 1-3-5 Nakadōri; s/d from ¥6500/7000; @) The Akita Castle Hotel has a great location – you can survey the castle moat from the south as you indulge in a fine French meal. Despite the somewhat Stalinistic concrete exterior, Western- and Japanese-style rooms have been recently updated to reflect a more capitalist world.

🍴 Eating & Drinking

You can't leave Akita without sampling *kiritanpo* (kneaded rice wrapped around bamboo spits and then barbecued over a charcoal fire). The rice is then cooked in a soy-flavoured chicken broth with noodles, onions, Japanese parsley and field mushrooms to make a hotpot called *kiritanpo-nabe*. Another Akita speciality is salted and fermented *hatahata* (a local fish).

Otafuku   HOTPOT $$

(お多福; ♪862-0802; 4-2-25 Ōmachi; kiritanpo from ¥2520; ⊙lunch & dinner; ♪) Specialising

Akita

Akita

⊙ Sights
1	Akarenga Kyōdokan	A2
2	Hirano Masakichi Bijutsukan	B2
3	Senshū-kōen	B1

⊜ Sleeping
4	Akita Castle Hotel	A2
5	Naniwa Hotel	B3
6	Richmond Hotel Akita Ekimae	B2

⊗ Eating
7	Daiichi-kaikan Kawabataten	A3
8	Otafuku	A2

⊜ Drinking
9	Green Pocket	A2

in *kiritanpo-nabe,* this restaurant is in a traditional black and beige wooden building on the western banks of the Kawabata-gawa.

Daiichi-kaikan Kawabataten   HOTPOT $$
(☎823-4141; 5-1-17 Ōmachi 3F; shottsuru from ¥1050; ⊗5-10.30pm) Complementing Otafuku is this unassuming spot tucked away on the 3rd floor of a nondescript white building just a few blocks south. The house speciality is *shottsuru-nabe* (¥2520), a hotpot made with *hatahata,* green onions and fresh tofu.

Green Pocket   BAR
(グリーンポケット; 5-1-7 Ōmachi; ⊗7pm-midnight Mon-Sat) One place that definitely bucks the neon trend of the Kawabata-dōri entertainment district is this little gem at the street's southern end. Decked out in authentic period panelling, it has an old-time piano in the corner, Vivien Leigh prints on the walls and a fabulously decadent selection of whiskies and fine wines. Classy.

❶ Information

Akita Red Cross Hospital (秋田赤十字病院; 222-1 Naeshirosawa Aza Kamikitatesaruta)

Tourist information office (秋田市観光案内所; ☎832-7941; www.akitafan.com/language/en/index.html; ⊗9am-7pm) Opposite the *shinkansen* tracks on the 2nd floor of Akita Station.

❶ Getting There & Away

Air

From Akita Airport, 21km south of the city centre, flights head to/from Tokyo, Osaka, Nagoya, Hiroshima, Sapporo and many other destinations.

Frequent buses run between JR Akita Station and the airport (¥890, 40 minutes).

Boat

From the port of Akita-kō, **Shin Nihonkai** (☎880-2600) runs ferries to Tomakomai on Hokkaidō (from ¥4200, 10 hours) leaving at 7am on Tuesday, Wednesday, Friday, Saturday and Sunday.

One bus runs at 6.05am from JR Akita Station to Akita-kō (¥390, 30 minutes), 8km northwest of the city.

Bus

Highway buses depart from the **bus station** (バス乗り場), in front of the east exit of the train station, and connect Akita to major cities throughout Honshū.

Car & Motorcycle

If you're driving, the **Akita Expressway** (秋田自動車道) runs east from Akita.

Train

Several hourly trains on the JR Akita *shinkansen* run between the northern terminus of Akita and the southern terminus of Tokyo (¥16,470, four hours) via Tazawako (¥3080, one hour) and Kakunodate (¥2940, 45 minutes).

Infrequent local trains also run on the JR Ōu main line between Akita and Kakunodate (¥1280, 1¾ hours), with a change at Ōmagari to the JR Tazawako line. Finally, there are a few *tokkyū* each day on the JR Uetsu line connecting Akita with Niigata (¥7020, 3¾ hours).

YAMAGATA PREFECTURE

While it's not as famous as its neighbouring prefectures, Yamagata-ken (山形県) is nevertheless home to several of Tōhoku's top attractions. At the top of the list is tiny but tranquil Zaō Onsen, famous for its enormous *rotemburo* and challenging ski slopes. A close second is the sacred trio of peaks at Dewa Sanzan, which are revered by *yamabushi* and hikers alike. A humble contender, Yamadera offers temple buffs and Bashō fans some spectacular photo opportunities, while the towns of Yonezawa and Tendō have a quiet charm of their own, namely *wagyū* (beef) and chess.

Tsuruoka   鶴岡

☎0235 / POP 139,000

Tsuruoka is a pleasant enough place to spend the night and get some rest. This is a good thing as you're going to need plenty of shut-eye if you plan on tackling nearby Dewa Sanzan. Indeed, Tsuruoka serves as the take-off point for Tōhoku's most famous trio of mountains, But don't dash off too quickly, as this former castle town in the middle of the Shōnai plain was once an important city in its own right. Established by the Sakai clan, one of feudal Yamagata's most important families, Tsuruoka continues to hold onto a few noteworthy relics of its proud past.

◉ Sights & Activities

Chidō Hakubutsukan   MUSEUM
(致道博物館; 10-18 Kachū-shinmachi; admission ¥700; ◷9am-4.30pm) Founded in 1950 by the former Lord Shōnai in order to develop and preserve local culture, this museum features Sakai-family artefacts, a family residence, two Meiji-era buildings, a traditional storehouse and a *kabuto-zukuri* (a farmhouse with a thatched roof shaped like a samurai helmet).

The museum is on the southwest corner of Tsuruoka-kōen, the site of the former Sakai castle. You can either walk for about 15 minutes southwest from JR Tsuruoka Station, or take a bus from stop 1 – frequent buses bound for Yunohama Onsen pass by the Chidō Hakubutsukan-mae stop (¥200, 10 minutes).

Zenpō-ji   TEMPLE
(善寶寺) Seven kilometres west of Tsuruoka is this Zen-Buddhist temple, complete with five-tier pagoda and large gateway. It dates from the 10th century, when it was dedicated to the Dragon King, guardian of the seas. Near the temple is a more contemporary attraction, the famous *jinmen-gyo* (human-faced carp). When viewed from above, these curious fish actually do appear to have human faces. From the station, take a bus bound for Yunohama Onsen to the Zenpō-ji stop (¥580, 30 minutes).

✷✷ Festivals & Events

Tenjin Matsuri   MASKS
At this festival, which takes place on 25 May, people stroll around in masks and costume for three days on end, serving sake and keeping an eye out for friends and acquaintances. The object is to make it through the festival without anyone recognising you, whereupon local lore states you'll have good luck for the rest of your life.

⊨ Sleeping

Tsuruoka Washington Hotel   HOTEL $$
(鶴岡ワシントンホテル; ☎25-0111; www .tsuruoka-wh.com, in Japanese; fax 25-0110; 5-20 Suehiro-machi; s/d from ¥6930/10,972; @☎) Directly outside the station's south exit, Tsuruoka's instalment of the Washington Hotel is true to the brand name, offering affordable, well-maintained rooms and a convenient location.

Tokyo Daiichi Hotel Tsuruoka   HOTEL $$
(東京第一ホテル鶴岡; ☎24-7662; www .tdh-tsuruoka.co.jp, in Japanese; fax 24-7610; 2-10 Nishiki Machi; s/d from ¥8662/12,705; @☎) A huge yellow-brick building just one minute southwest of the station next to bus station, this upmarket business hotel has standard rooms and an above-average *rotemburo* and sauna.

Narakan   HOTEL $$
(奈良館; ☎22-1202; 2-35 Hiyoshimachi; r per person with 2 meals from ¥6300) Head five minutes south along the main street leading out from the station to reach this Western-style inn distinguished by its tall chimney. Rooms are a bit on the small side, but you'll eat well – and you need the calories before hitting Dewa Sanzan.

ⓘ Information

Tourist information office (☎25-7678; ◷10am-5pm Nov-Feb, 9.30am-5.30pm Mar-Oct) To the right as you exit JR Tsuruoka Station; can book accommodation and has information about Dewa Sanzan.

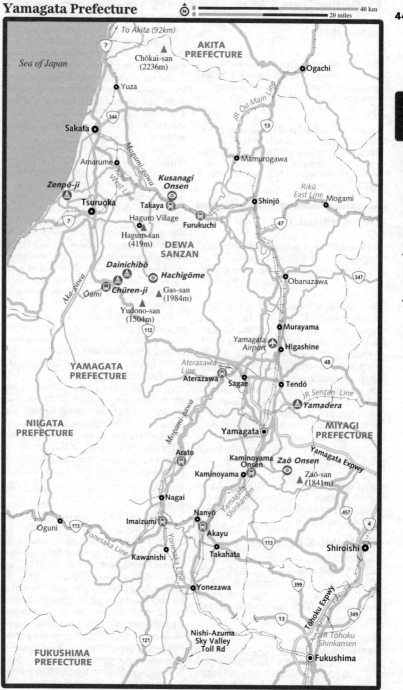

Getting There & Away

For detailed information on accessing Dewa Sanzan, see p447.

Bus

There are a few buses each day between Tsuruoka and Yamagata (¥2400, 1¾ hours), though services are often cut back during the winter months due to snowdrifts.

Train

A few daily *tokkyū* on the JR Uetsu main line run between Tsuruoka and Akita (¥3820, 1¾ hours), and between Tsuruoka and Niigata (¥4330, 1¾ hours). There are also a few daily *futsū* running on the same line between Tsuruoka and Akita (¥2210, 2¾ hours).

Dewa Sanzan 出羽三山

♪ 0235

> How cool it is, a pale crescent shining, above the dark hollow of Haguro-san.
> *Matsuo Bashō,* The Narrow Road to the Deep North *(1689)*

Dewa Sanzan is the collective title for three sacred peaks – Haguro-san, Gas-san and Yudono-san – which are believed to represent birth, death and rebirth respectively. Together they have been worshipped for centuries by *yamabushi* and followers of the Shugendō sect. During the annual pilgrimage seasons, you can see white-clad pilgrims equipped with wooden staff, sandals and straw hat, and fleece-clad hikers equipped with poles, waterproof boots and bandana.

Of course, it is the *yamabushi,* with their unmistakable conch shells, chequered jackets and voluminous white pantaloons, that keep the tradition alive. Whether stomping along precipitous trails or sitting under icy waterfalls, these devoted mountain men embrace severe ascetic exercises to discipline both body and spirit.

Sights & Activities

Tradition dictates that you start at Haguro-san and finish at Yudono-san, which is why we're presenting the pilgrimage in this order. However, feel free to follow the circuit in the opposite direction, which is certainly one way of going against the crowd.

Haguro-san   SACRED MOUNTAIN

Because it has the easiest access, Haguro-san (羽黒山; 419m) attracts a steady flow of tourists. At the base of the mountain in Haguro village is the **Ideha Bunka Kinenkan** (いで

は文化記念館; admission ¥400; ⊙9am-4.30pm Wed-Mon Apr-Nov, 9.30am-4pm Wed-Mon Dec-Mar), a small history museum featuring films of *yamabushi* rites and festivals. Although the exhibits are in Japanese, they provide excellent context for the climb to follow.

The orthodox approach to the shrine on the summit requires pilgrims to climb 2446 steps, but buses run straight to the top. The climb can be done in a leisurely hour, though you might be lapped by gaggles of sprightly senior citizens.

From the bus stop, walk straight ahead through the torii and continue across the bridge. En route you'll pass **Gojū-no-tō** (五重塔), a weather-beaten, five-storey pagoda dating from the 14th century. Then comes a very long slog up the hundreds of stone steps arranged in steep sections. Pause halfway at an ancient teahouse known as **Ni-no-sakachaya** (二の坂茶屋; admission incl tea ¥700; ⊙8.30am-5pm Apr-Nov) for refreshment and breathtaking views. If you detour to the right, you'll come upon the temple ruins of **Betsu-in** (別院), visited by Bashō during his pilgrimage here.

The scene at the summit can be a bit anticlimactic if the crowds are thick. However, you can still have a contemplative moment in front of the **San-shin Gōsaiden** (三神合祭殿), a vivid red hall that enshrines the deities of all three mountains.

At the top of Haguro-san you have a couple of options to consider. In the summer, regular morning buses travel directly from the summit to the eighth station of Gas-san. Alternatively, purists can follow the 20km ridge hike to the peak of Gas-san. If you miss the bus, or you want to rest up for the ridge hike, accommodation is available at Saikan.

Gas-san   SACRED MOUNTAIN

Accessible from July to September, Gas-san (月山; 1984m) is the highest of the three sacred mountains. Coming from Haguro-san, the peak is usually accessed from the trailhead at **Hachigōme** (八合目; eighth station). This route then passes through an alpine plateau to **Kyūgōme** (九合目; ninth station) in 1¾ hours, and then grinds uphill for another 1¼ hours. At the summit, pilgrims flock to **Gassan-jinja** (月山神社; admission incl ritual purification ¥500; ⊙6am-5pm), though not without first being purified: bow your head to receive a priest's benediction before rubbing your head and shoulders with sacred paper, which is then placed in the fountain.

Another year is gone, a traveller's shade on my head, straw sandals at my feet.
Matsuo Bashō, Account of Exposure to the Fields *(1685)*

Regarded as Japan's master of haiku, Matsuo Bashō (1644–94) is credited with elevating its status from comic relief to Zen-infused enlightenment.

Bashō was born into a samurai family, and served the feudal lord Yoshitada into his late teenage years. Moving first to Kyoto, and then to Edo, Bashō found success as a published poet, but ultimately found the acclaim to be spiritually unsettling. He eventually turned to Zen, and the philosophy had a deep impact on his work. In fact, comparisons have been made between his haiku and Zen *kōan* (short riddles), intended to bring about a sudden flash of insight in the listener.

Bashō was also influenced by the natural philosophy of the Chinese Taoist sage Chuangzi, and began to examine nature uncritically. Later he developed his own poetic principle by drawing on the concept of *sabi,* a kind of spare, lonely beauty.

When he reached his 40s, Bashō decided to give his career away in favour of travelling throughout Japan, seeking to build friendships and commune with nature as he went. He published evocative accounts of his travels, including *The Records of a Weather-Beaten Skeleton* and *The Records of a Travel-Worn Satchel,* but his collection *The Narrow Road to the Deep North,* detailing his journey throughout Tōhoku in 1689, is probably the most famous.

From the summit, you could head down to eighth station and stay at Gas-san Sanrōsho, which may be something of a necessity if you walked the entire ridgeline. However, the flow of pilgrims will be pressing on with the steep descent to Yudono-san. This takes another three hours or so, and you'll have to carefully descend rusty ladders chained to the cliff sides, and pick your way down through a slippery stream bed at the end of the trail.

Yudono-san SACRED MOUNTAIN
Accessible from May to October, Yudono-san (湯殿山; 1504m) is the spiritual culmination of the Dewa Sanzan trek. Coming from Gas-san, it's just a short walk from the stream bed at the end of the down climb to **Yudono-san-jinja** (湯殿山神社; admission ¥500; ☺6am-5pm, closed Nov-Apr). This sacred shrine is not a building, but rather a large orange rock continuously lapped by water from a hot spring. It has the strictest rituals of the three, with pilgrims required to perform a barefoot circuit of the rock, paddling through the cascading water.

To finish the pilgrimage, it's a mere 10-minute hike further down the mountain to the trailhead at **Yudono-san Sanrōsho** (湯殿山参籠所), which is marked by a torii and is adjacent to the to **Sennin-zawa** (仙人沢) bus stop.

From here, you have a number of options: spend the night at Yudono-san Sanrōjo, catch a direct bus back to Tsuruoka, catch the bus or walk along the 3km toll road to the Yudono-san Hotel, or take a detour to Dainichibō and Chūren-ji.

Dainichibō & Chūren-ji TEMPLES
Off Rte 112, halfway between Yudono-san and Tsuruoka in the village of Ōami, these two seemingly ordinary country temples house the mummies of priests who have become 'living Buddhas'. The ascetic practice of self-mummification, outlawed since the 19th century, involved coming as close to death as possible through starvation, before being buried alive while meditating.

Both temples are located close to the Ōami bus stop, and there are colourful signs to follow. The mummy at **Dainichibō** (大日坊; admission ¥500; ☺8am-5pm) is dressed in bright reddish-orange robes, and is looking rather ghoulish with his leathery skin. From the bus stop, head into the village, make a left at the post office, and continue walking for about 10 minutes.

The **Chūren-ji** (注連寺; admission ¥500; ☺8.30am-5pm) mummy, which is no less freakish looking, is allegedly a reformed murderer who became a powerful Buddhist priest. From the bus stop, head north along the road, carefully following signs at all of the junctions. Appropriately enough, the temple is after the graveyard.

Buses are spaced about two hours apart, which leaves time to look around, and still make your connection back to Tsuruoka.

✱✱ Festivals & Events

The peak of Haguro-san is the site of several major festivals.

Hassaku Matsuri   HARVEST
Yamabushi perform ancient fire rites on 31 August and 1 September to pray for a bountiful harvest.

Shōrei-sai   RELIGIOUS
On New Year's Eve, *yamabushi* perform similar rituals to those at the Hassaku Matsuri in competition with each other after completing 100-day-long austerities.

🥾 Courses

If you haven't yet found your calling, consider becoming a *yamabushi*.

Dewa Sanzan-jinja   RELIGIOUS
(☑62-2355) This temple at the top of Haguro-san is where you should enquire about becoming a 'real' *yamabushi*. Note that these courses are extremely intense, not for the faint of heart and only really a viable option if you have an excellent command of Japanese – and a good bit of time and money to burn.

Ideha Bunka Kinenkan   CULTURAL
(☑62-4727) For those who are happy being just a *yamabushi* apprentice, this museum in Haguro village runs minicourses that include fasting, mountain sprints and morning wake-up calls. Here too you need to have a command of Japanese – phone ahead to enquire about dates. A three-day course starts at ¥34,600.

🛏 Sleeping

Sleeping options are listed in order from start to finish of the Haguro-san–Yudono-san pilgrimage route.

🏯 Saikan   SHUKUBŌ $$
(斎館; ☑62-2357; r per person with 2 meals ¥7350) Located at the top of Haguro-san, this is the most famous *shukubō* (temple lodging) at Dewa Sanzan. The approach skirts past towering trees and through an imposing gate before arriving at a secluded temple. The grounds overlook the grand sweep of valleys below, while the building itself has been weathered by the ages and is imbued with an air of stoic grandeur. In keeping with the traditions of the *yamabushi*, meals are wholly vegetarian. Come with an open mind as one bite of the foraged mushrooms and mountain vegetables will ensure that you won't be dreaming about steak any time soon.

Gas-san Sanrōsho   HUT $$
(月山参籠所; ☑090-3022-1191; r per person with 2 meals ¥7000; ☺closed Oct-Jun) Located at eighth station on Gas-san, this mountain hut sees much less tourist traffic than Saikan. But if you follow the ridge trail to Gas-san – and thus extend the hike to three days – this is where you will inevitably spend the night. Facilities and food are basic, but the close quarters are conducive to meeting new friends.

Yudono-san Sanrōsho   LODGE $$
(湯殿山参籠所; ☑54-6131; r per person with 2 meals from ¥7000; ☺closed Nov-Apr) At the end of your second day, consider staying here rather than pressing on in search of creature comforts. In marked contrast to the serenity and sanctity of Saikan, this airy mountain lodge is full of jovial pilgrims celebrating the completion of their multiday circuit. Meat and fish is on offer in case you've been missing it, as is plenty of beer and sake to help get the conversation flowing.

Yudono-san Hotel   HOTEL $$
(湯殿山ほてる; ☑54-6231; www7.plala.or.jp/yudono/index.html; r per person from ¥9600) If you prefer some privacy at the end of the trek, bypass Yudono-san Sanrōsho and catch the bus or hike down the road to this onsen hotel. Rooms are run-of-the-mill, and meals are served in a glorified cafeteria, but there's something to be said for a fluffy bed and a hot bath after days on the trail.

ℹ Information

Theoretically, if you hiked at a military pace and timed the buses perfectly, you might be able to cover all three peaks in one day. However, this would leave you no time to enjoy the scenery, and the chances of missing a key bus connection are very high. If you want to tackle all three mountains, it's best to devote two or three days, especially if you eschew buses in favour of foot leather.

Before setting out, it's recommended that you book accommodation, and stock up on maps, at the tourist information office in Tsuruoka. Also note that transport can grind to a halt once the snow starts to pile up – it's best to time your visit between July and September when all three mountains are open to hikers.

ⓘ Getting There & Around

Directions are given in the same sequence as the trek.

Hourly buses run from Tsuruoka to Haguro village (¥700, 35 minutes), several of which then continue on to Haguro-sanchō (Haguro summit; ¥1050, 50 minutes).

From early July to late August, and then on weekends and holidays until late September, there are up to four daily buses from Haguro-sanchō to Gas-san as far as Hachigōme (¥1370, one hour).

Between June and early November, there are up to four daily buses from the Yudono-san Sanrōsho trailhead at Yudono-san to Tsuruoka (¥1550, 1½ hours), which also pass by the Yudono-san Hotel (¥100, five minutes) and Ōami (¥1020, 45 minutes).

Yamagata 山形

📞 023 / POP 255,000

Yamagata is a thriving industrial centre with a sizeable student population, making for a more youthful vibe than in comparable *inaka* (rural) cities. While it's a bit short on sights, Yamagata is an excellent base for day trips to Yamadera, Tendō and Yonezawa, and also serves as a transit point for Zaō Onsen.

◉ Sights & Activities

Hirashimizu Pottery District POTTERY DISTRICT
(平清水陶器地域) The fiery kilns lining the Hazukashi-kawa (Embarrassed River) turn out beautiful bluish-grey spotted-glaze pieces. Known as *nashi-seiji* (pear skin), these stunning pieces are displayed for sale in attached workshops. To get here, buses bound for Nishi-Zaō or Geikō-dai run hourly or half-hourly from stop 5 outside Yamagata Station to the Hirashimizu stop (¥200, 15 minutes).

Shichiemon-gama POTTERY STUDIO
(七右エ門窯; 153 Hirashimizu; ⊗8.30am-5.30pm, pottery making 9am-3pm) This renowned studio offers formal instruction (in Japanese) in pottery making.

✦✦ Festivals & Events

Hanagasa Matsuri TRADITIONAL
In early August; features large crowds of dancers wearing *hanagasa* (flower-laden straw hats) and singing folk songs.

Yamagata International Documentary Film Festival FILM
This biennial event (www.yidff.jp) takes place over one week in October, and screens films from over 70 countries, along with retrospectives, symposiums and a Japanese panorama.

🛏 Sleeping & Eating

Guesthouse Mintaro Hut GUESTHOUSE $
(ゲストハウスミンタロハット; 📞2797-1687; www.mintarohut.com, in Japanese; 5-13 Ōtemachi; s/d ¥3500/6000; @🛜) This brand-new guesthouse is run by the very hospitable English-speaking Sato-san, who works hard to ensure a warm and familial atmosphere. The main common area is built around a radiant stove, creating a relaxed, ski-chalet atmosphere that is conducive to chatting with fellow travellers. Wood-framed rooms with clean lines share communal facilities, and inexpensive but tasty cooked-to-order meals are available around the clock. Mintaro Hut is located just off the northeast corner of the central park.

Tōyoko Inn Yamagata Eki Nishiguchi HOTEL $$
(東横イン山形駅西口; 📞644-1045; www.toyoko-inn.com/hotel/00097, in Japanese; 1-18-13 Jōnan-machi; s/d ¥3980/7770; @🛜) Business hotels cluster around JR Yamagata Station, but this is the best value for your money. Just a minute's walk from the station's west exit, this reliable chain offers the standard-issue Japanese business-hotel room.

Sakaeya Honten NOODLES $
(栄屋本店; 📞623-0766; 2-3-21 Honchō; hiyashi rāmen ¥700; ⊗11.30am-7.30pm Thu-Tue) A tasty Yamagata speciality is *hiyashi rāmen* (chilled soup noodles), and it is served up in huge doses here. Facing east from the AZ store, take the first side street to your right.

ⓘ Information

Tourist information office (山形市観光案内センター; 📞647-2266; ⊗8.30am-8pm) On the 2nd floor of Yamagata Station, in a small glass booth.

ⓘ Getting There & Away

Bus

There are a few buses each day between Yamagata and Zaō Onsen (¥860, 40 minutes).

Train

There are several hourly trains on the JR Yamagata and Tōhoku *shinkansen* lines between Tokyo and Yamagata (¥11,030, three hours).

There are also frequent *kaisoku* on the JR Senzan line between Yamagata and Yamadera (¥230, 20 minutes).

TENDŌ & YONEZAWA

On this worthwhile day trip from Yamagata, you can learn about *shōgi* (将棋; general's chess or Japanese chess), dine on delightfully marbled beef, and be back at your hotel with plenty of time to spare.

Tendō

Tendō (天童) produces around 90% of the country's *shōgi* pieces annually. This exquisite art was started during the Edo period by samurai who had fallen upon hard times after their salaries were cut by the Tendō lord.

The **Tendō Shōgi Museum** (天童市将棋資料館; 1-1-1 Hon-chō; admission ¥300; ⊗9am-6pm Thu-Tue), which is part of JR Tendō Station, displays chess sets from Japan and abroad. You can also see *shōgi* pieces being made at **Eishundō** (栄春堂; 1-3-28 Kamatahonchō; admission free; ⊗8am-6pm Wed-Mon), a 15-minute walk straight out from the station, just past the Tendō Park Hotel.

If you're here on the last weekend in April, head to the central park for the theatrical **Ningen Shōgi** (人間将棋) when outdoor chess matches are played using real people as pieces.

There are regular *futsū* on the JR Ōu main line between Yamagata and Tendō (¥230, 20 minutes).

Yonezawa

Carnivores should head here to chow down on Yonezawa beef, famous for its tenderness and flavour, and arguably rivalling Kobe's own. Yonezawa (米沢) is also home to the ruined 17th-century castle of the Uegugi clan.

The foundations of the castle now form the boundaries of **Matsugasaki-kōen** (松ヶ崎公園). Inside the park is the **Uesugi Museum** (米沢市上杉博物館; admission ¥400; ⊗9am-4.30pm, closed every 4th Wed, closed Mon Dec-Mar), which displays Uesugi-clan artefacts including samurai armour and precious handicrafts.

Yonezawa beef is on the menu everywhere, but **Tokiwagyū-nikuten** (登起波牛肉店; ☎24-5400; www.yonezawabeef.co.jp/info/eng.html; 2-3 Chūō; meals from ¥4200; ⊗11am-9pm, closed Tue; 🅿) dates from the Edo period, and specialises in *shabu-shabu* (pieces of thinly sliced beef or pork cooked quickly with vegetables in boiling water and then dipped in sauce; ¥4500) and sukiyaki (sliced meat simmered with vegetables and sauce; ¥4200). Ask the staff at the tourist information centre in JR Yonezawa Station to mark the location on a map – it's a bit out of the way in the northern Chūō district.

Regular *futsū* run on the JR Ōu main line between Yonezawa and Yamagata (¥820, 45 minutes).

Yamadera   山寺

☎023 / POP 1500

Stillness, seeps into the stones, the cry of cicadas.

Matsuo Bashō, The Narrow Road to the Deep North *(1689)*

A favourite destination of the itinerant haiku master, Yamadera is an atmospheric cluster of temples and shrines that is perched precariously on lush and wooded slopes. The town was founded in AD 860 by priests who carried with them the sacred flame from Enryaku-ji near Kyoto, and supposedly the same flame is still alight today. It is believed that Yamadera's rock faces are the boundaries between this world and the next.

⊙ Sights

Risshaku-ji   TEMPLE COMPLEX
(立石寺; ⊗8am-5pm; admission ¥300) The 'Temple of Standing Stones', more commonly known as Yamadera, lies at the top of a rock-hewn staircase that has been weathered over the centuries by unrelenting elements. With more than 1000 steps and occasional gusts of wind to contend with – not to mention the heaving tourist throngs, and the swarms of noisy cicadas in the warmer

months – the spiritual climb belies the cliché that the journey is more important than the destination.

Once you've passed through the San-mon (山門) gate and entered the Oku-no-in (奥の院; Inner Sanctuary), you might find yourself at a loss for words. The views of the surrounding mountains and bucolic countryside below are spectacular, especially on a clear summer day. The inspiration for Bashō's haiku can be all-encompassing.

If you're not in a rush to climb down, a network of trails branch off the main prayer hall, and lead to various smaller shrines and lookout points. These side trails are also typically devoid of tourists, so you can easily find a reflective spot to pen a few of your own original haiku. For a better shot at a measure of the meditative bliss that so inspired Bashō, visit on a day trip from Yamagata early in the morning or late in the afternoon, or spend the night in relative peace and quiet.

Bashō Kinenkan   MUSEUM
(山寺芭蕉記念館; admission ¥400; ⊘9am-4.30pm, closed Mon Dec-Feb) Back down in the village near the train station, this biographical museum exhibits scrolls and calligraphy related to Bashō's famous northern journey.

🛏 Sleeping

Pension Yamadera   PENSION $$
(山寺ペンション; ☑695-2134; 4273-1 Yamadera; r per person with 1/2 meals 7000/9640; @) Located next to JR Yamadera Station, this modest pension is good for a quick stay if you want to slow things down and take in the sights and sounds of Yamadera by night. Slanting ceilings and exposed beams instil a sense of country comfort, and *soba* dinners bring out the best in the local buckwheat crop.

❶ Getting There & Away

There are frequent *kaisoku* on the JR Senzan line between Yamadera and Yamagata (¥230, 20 minutes).

Zaō Onsen   蔵王温泉

☑023 / POP 14,000

Zaō Onsen is a small hot-springs town with some big skiing. Even bigger are its *juhyō* (ice monsters), which are conifers that have been frozen solid by harsh Siberian winds. Skiing or snowboarding through fields of

lurking ice monsters is a surreal experience unique to Zaō. Other times of the year, Zaō attracts visitors with great hiking opportunities, not to mention the chance to soak in the *dai-rotemburo,* a tub so big that it can literally hold hundreds of bathers.

🔾 Sights & Activities

Zaō Onsen   SKIING & SNOWBOARDING
(蔵王温泉; www.zao-spa.or.jp, in Japanese; 1-day lift tickets ¥4800; ⊘Dec-Apr) Zaō is arguably home to the best slopes in Northern Honshū. In comparison to heavyweight Hokkaidō, you shouldn't come here expecting spine-tingling chutes, but rather a huge breadth of beginner and intermediate runs. In fact, it's possible to ski all the way from the highest point of the mountain right down to the base without ever turning down a black diamond or getting stuck in a field of moguls.

But don't come expecting boring bunny slopes. On the contrary, Zaō is distinguished by its broad and winding courses, some of which reach nearly 10km in length! With 40 ropeways and ski lifts spanning 14 spidery courses with multiple off-shoots, it's almost impossible to swish down the exact same route twice. Of course, you might want to have a second go at the Juhyō Kōgen (樹氷高原; Ice Monster Plateau), which reaches its peak ferocity in frigid February. At this time, blizzards are particularly severe, so dress appropriately.

English signage is excellent, and full equipment rental is available at various locations throughout the village. Zaō Onsen also offers a full complement of bars, cafes, restaurants and onsen, making for a truly memorable *après-ski*. Trust us on this point. There is nothing quite like the sensation of stripping off your ski-wear, sliding into an onsen bath and uncorking a bottle of micro-brewed sake. Once you've worked up a sweat – and a hunger – simmering hot pot awaits you at any number of places just around the next corner.

Zaō Sky Cable   RIDING & HIKING
(蔵王スカイケーブル; 1 way/return ¥750/1200; ⊘8.30am-5pm May-Oct) In the warmer months, this cable car whisks you over the conifers and up **Zaō-san** (蔵王山) to within spitting distance of **Okama** (御釜), a volcanic crater of shimmering cobalt blue. Hiking around the lake is a joy, with Buddhist statues and monuments hidden among the greenery.

BEST SKIING

» Zaō Onsen (p449)

» Naeba (p459)

» GALA Yuzawa (p458)

» Tazawa-ko (p435)

» Myōkō Kōgen (p460)

Zaō Onsen Dai-rotenburo ONSEN
(蔵王温泉大露天風呂; admission ¥450; ⏱6am-7pm May-Oct) Hikers congregate en masse for a soak at this gigantic outdoor hot-spring pool, which can easily hold up to 200 people. The sulphur-stained rocks set the stage for the spectacle that is hundreds of complete strangers bathing naked together in joyful unison.

🛌 Sleeping & Eating

Accommodation abounds, but reservations are essential if you're visiting during the ski season or on weekends in summer. If you speak Japanese, it pays to call ahead – alternatively, have tourist information phone around for a vacancy.

TOP CHOICE Takamiya RYOKAN $$$
(高見屋; ☎694-9333; www.zao.co.jp/takamiya, in Japanese; fax 694-2166; 54 Zaō Onsen; r per person with 2 meals from ¥16,950; 📶📧) There is no shortage of upmarket ryokan in town, though Takamiya gets our pick for its emphasis on the classics. Meals are incredibly opulent *kaiseki ryōri* (traditional Japanese formal banquets served in multiple courses) that span a couple of hours, while intimate bathing takes place in one of several nostalgic onsen that are hundreds of years old. Rooms vary according to price, though each one is an artful blend of antique rustic fixtures with carefully placed modern amenities. If you're travelling with someone you love, some rooms even come complete with their own private *rotemburo,* allowing for intimate bathing by moonlight.

Ki-no-sato RYOKAN $$
(季の里; ☎694-2288; www.zao-kinosato.co.jp, in Japanese; 1271-1 Zaō Onsen; r per person with 2 meals from ¥13,800; 📶📧) Ki-no-sato may lack the history of Takamiya, but it remains a stately ryokan with sleek environs and exemplary service. Indoor onsen baths have floor-to-ceiling picture windows overlooking the frozen hinterlands, while steamy open-air baths are exposed to the elements. Japanese-style tatami rooms are comfortable if slightly understated, while well-portioned meals feature Yonezawa beef and the fruits of the sea.

Pension Boku-no-Uchi PENSION $$
(ペンションぼくのうち; ☎694-9542; www.bokunouchi.com; 904 Zaō Onsen; r per person with 2 meals from ¥7200) Next to the Lawson convenience store, this family-run place is the perfect compromise between Western- and Japanese-style accommodation. Guests can use the 24-hour sulphur bath, take meals in the ski-lodge-esque dining room and then turn in for the night in tatami rooms.

Lodge Chitoseya LODGE $
(ロッジちとせや; ☎694-9145; fax 694-9145; 954 Zaō Onsen; r per person with/without 2 meals from ¥6090/3675; 📧) Right near the bus station, this relaxed lodge is very budget-friendly, and attracts a youthful crowd of skiers and hikers. You'll also eat very well here, as the delightful couple in charge serve up original meals that are a mix of Japanese-inspired and fusion favourites.

TOP CHOICE Shinzaemon-no-Yu SHABU-SHABU $$
(新左衛門の湯; ☎693-1212; 905 Kawa-mae Zaō Onsen; meals from ¥1500; ⏱lunch & dinner, closed irregularly) Luxurious bath-cum-banqueting house – come here to soak those ski pains away (the onsen is open 10am to 9.30pm; baths are ¥600), and then feast on the winter warmer that is *shabu-shabu* (¥3600) in simple, natural-wood elegance. The restaurant occupies a traditional wooden building across from the ropeway.

ℹ Getting There & Away

Hourly buses run between the bus terminal in Zaō Onsen and JR Yamagata Station (¥860, 40 minutes).

During peak ski season, private companies run overnight shuttles between Tokyo and Zaō. Prices can be as low as ¥7000 return – enquire at tourist information centres in Tokyo for more information.

NIIGATA PREFECTURE

While not technically part of Tōhoku proper, Niigata-ken (新潟県) serves as a stepping stone to the northern lands. The onsen town of Echigo-Yuzawa was the setting for Kawabata's acclaimed novel *Snow Country,* while the slopes at GALA Yuzawa, Naeba and Myōkō Kōgen attract powder fiends. Of

course, the star in Niigata Prefecture's crown is undeniably the persimmon-peppered island of Sado-ga-shima, a former penal colony that is today one of the Honshū's top outdoors destinations.

Niigata 新潟

♪025 / POP 812,000

The prefectural capital of Niigata serves as a transport hub and a springboard for nearby Sado-ga-shima. Although there's little to keep you here for more than the time it takes to change trains or board a ferry, Ni-

igata is an attractive city that is bisected by the Shinano-gawa, which generates a great swath of blue sky wherever you look.

⊙ Sights

On the northwestern banks of the Shinano-gawa is **Hakusan-kōen** (白山公園; ⊙dawn-dusk), a small park containing a shrine, Hakusan-jinja (白山神社), to the local god of marriage. The grounds also preserve a fine lotus pond and the historic Meiji-era teahouse **Enkikan** (燕喜館; admission free, tea ¥300; ⊙9am-5pm), which was transplanted from Kyoto and reconstructed here.

✲ Festivals & Events

Sake-no-jin   SAKE

Sake aficionados won't want to miss this event, held on the third weekend each March. It's a mammoth bacchanal, highlighting more than 175 varieties of sake from all over Japan. *Kampai!*

Niigata Matsuri   PARADES

From the first or second weekend (varies yearly) in August, the streets are filled with afternoon parades of colourful floats and shrines. At night thousands of folk dancers parade across the span of the Bandai-bashi. A bumper fireworks display on the final night lights up the Shinano-gawa, as a passage of decorated boats carries the shrine of the local god of the sea.

🛏 Sleeping

Hotel Okura Niigata   HOTEL $$

(ホテルオークラ新潟; ☎244-6111; www.okura
-niigata.com/english/index.html; fax 224-7060; 53 Kawabata-cho; s/d from ¥8925/14,700; @🛜🅿) Arguably the finest hotel in Niigata, the Hotel Okura has a picturesque location next to the Bandai-bashi, and offers sweeping views of the Shinano-gawa, particularly from the formal French restaurant on the 15th floor. Accommodation is in carefully muted rooms that are stately without being too overbearing.

Dormy Inn Niigata   HOTEL $$

(ドーミーイン新潟; ☎247-7755; www.hotespa
.net/hotels/niigata, in Japanese; fax 247-7789; 1-7-14 Akashi; s/d from ¥4500/7350; @) Across the street from the NTT Building, the Dormy Inn is pioneering a great concept for budget business hotels. Prices are kept low by offering rooms that are tight, relatively featureless and lacking in bathrooms, though guests can take advantage of the on-site onsen and sauna, as well as the large and surprisingly sociable cafeteria.

Ueda Ryokan   RYOKAN $$

(植田旅館; ☎225-1111; www.uedaryokan.com, in Japanese; fax 225-1110; 2120 Yonnochō; r per person with/without meals from ¥7350/3780; @) This pleasant Japanese-style inn occupies a quiet spot just beyond the river's edge.

🍴 Eating & Drinking

Niigata is famous for the high standard of its rice, seafood and sake, so be sure to treat yourself before pushing on. You'll also find plenty of little hole-in-the-wall places here where you can dine and drink to your heart's content.

Honchō Ichiba   MARKET

(本町市場; ⊙10am-5pm, closed irregularly) If you want a feast for both the eyes and the stomach, check out this energetic produce and seafood market that occupies several pedestrian arcades.

ℹ Information

Niigata central post office (新潟中央郵便局; 2-6-26 Higashi Ōdori; ⊙7am-11pm Mon-Fri, 9am-7pm Sat, Sun & holidays) Offers postal and ATM cash services.

Niigata International Friendship Centre (新潟国際友好会館; ☎225-2777; Kurosuparu Niigata Bldg, 3-2086 Ishizuechōdōri; ⊙9am-9.30pm Mon-Sat, to 5pm Sun & holidays, closed every 4th Mon) Has a small library and helpful staff for general tourist information.

Niigata University Medical & Dental Hospital (新潟大学医歯学総合病院; 1-757 Asahimachi-dōri)

Tourist information centre (新潟駅万代口観光案内センター; ☎241-7914; ⊙9am-6pm) To the left of Niigata Station's Bandai exit.

ℹ Getting There & Away

Air

From Niigata Airport, 13km north of the city centre, flights head to/from Tokyo, Osaka, Nagoya, Hiroshima, Sapporo and many other destinations.

Buses run from stop 11 outside Niigata Station to the airport every half-hour from 6.40am to 6.40pm (¥370, 25 minutes); a taxi should cost around ¥2000.

Boat

From the port of Niigata-kō, **Shin-Nihonkai** (☎273-2171) ferries run at 10.30am daily, except Monday, to Otaru on Hokkaidō (¥6200, 18 hours). To get to Niigata-ko, take any bus bound for Rinko-nichōme from stop 3 at Niigata Station and get off at Suehiro-bashi (¥200, 20 minutes).

From the Sado Kisen terminal, there are frequent ferries and hydrofoils to Ryōtsu on Sado-ga-shima (see p454). Buses to the terminal (¥200, 15 minutes) leave from stop 6 at Niigata Station 45 minutes before sailing.

Alternatively, a taxi to either Niigata-kō or the Sado Kisen terminal should cost around ¥1200.

Bus

Highway buses depart from the **Bandai bus centre** (万代シティバスセンター), and connect Niigata to major cities throughout Honshū.

Car & Motorcycle

If you're driving, the **Hokuriku Expressway** (北陸自動車道) runs between Tokyo and the greater Niigata area.

Train

There are several hourly trains on the Jōetsu *shinkansen* between Niigata and Tokyo (¥10,270, 2¼ hours) via Echigo-Yuzawa Onsen (¥5240, 50 minutes).

There are a few *tokkyū* each day on the JR Uetsu line between Niigata and Tsuruoka (¥4330, 1¾ hours), and between Niigata and Akita (¥7020, 3¾ hours).

For accessing the port of Naoetsu-kō, where you can grab a ferry or hydrofoil to the town of Ogi on Sado-ga-Shima, there are a few *tokkyū* each day on the JR Shinetsu line between Niigata and Naoetsu (¥5020, 1¾ hours). From the station, it's a 10-minute bus ride (¥200) and then a 15-minute walk to the port.

Sado-ga-shima 佐渡島

☑ 0259 / POP 66,000

Despite being Japan's sixth-largest island, Sado-ga-shima is relatively undeveloped, and is characterised by rugged natural beauty and eccentric reminders of its rich and evocative past. Framed by mountainous backdrops, vast orchards of persimmon trees stretch across cultivated fields, while small fishing villages bustle with life along the rocky shores of the Sea of Japan. Travellers escape to this remote island throughout the warm summer months, but crowds peak during the third week in August for the Earth Celebration, headlined by the world-famous Kodo Drummers.

History

Sado has always been something of a far-flung destination, just not always a voluntary one. During the feudal era, the island was a notorious penal colony where out-of-favour intellectuals were forever banished. The illustrious list of former prisoners includes Emperor Juntoku, nō (stylised dance-drama) master Ze-Ami, and Nichiren, the founder of one of Japan's most influential Buddhist sects. When gold was discovered near the village of Aikawa in 1601, there was a sudden influx of miners, who were often vagrants press-ganged from the mainland and made to work like slaves.

LOCAL KNOWLEDGE

SADO'S 'OTHER' FESTIVALS

There is no denying the splendour of the Earth Celebration, but amid the crush of humanity that descends on Sado, sometimes you can lose sight of the island's bucolic charm. Thus it shouldn't come as a surprise that locals are quick to tout Sado's 'other' festivals, which in true Japanese fashion, typically involve a unique type of local food.

For a full list of all the weird and wonderful events on Sado, see www.visitsado.com.

Sado Hon-maguro Matsuri (佐渡本まぐろ祭り; Sado Tuna Festival; Ryōtsu; late June) Mid-summer is peak season for catching tuna in the Sea of Japan. Fresh fish is on the menu all over the island, and tuna-cutting exhibitions take place in Ryōtsu.

Wataru from Ryōtsu

Asari-sagashi Dai-kai (アサリさがし大会; Clam Search Convention; Jogahama; mid-July) My kids love this one! They get to splash around in the ocean while searching for clams. We bring them home, and cook them in a big pot with miso, *dashi* (fish stock) and leeks.

Eriko from Sawata

Sazae Matsuri (さざえ祭り; Turban Shell Festival; Ogi; late July) Have you ever eaten a turban shell? We look for them at night while holding flaming torches. Their insides are delicious when grilled with soy and sake, and you can keep the shell as a unique souvenir.

Akira from Ogi

Chinowa Matsuri (茅の輪まつり; Straw Circle Festival; Ogi; 30 June) We celebrate summer by passing through a straw circle and casting off six months of uncleanliness. Then we eat delicate dumpling made with steamed iris petals.

Akiko from Ogi

NORTHERN HONSHŪ (TŌHOKU) NIIGATA PREFECTURE

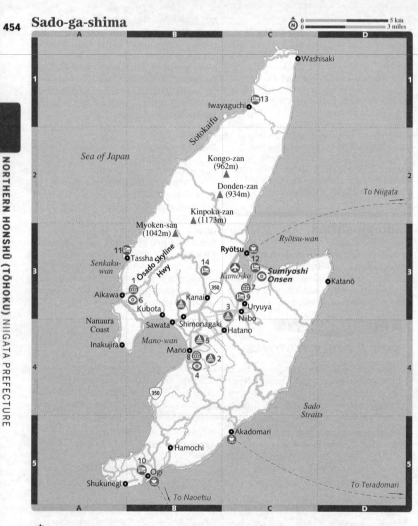

0   5 km
0   3 miles

Washisaki

Iwayaguchi · 13

Sotokaifu

Sea of Japan

Kongo-zan
(962m)

Donden-zan
(934m)

To Niigata

Kinpoku-zan
(1173m)

Myoken-san
(1042m)

Ryōtsu-wan

11 · Tassha Skyline
Senkaku-
wan   Ōsado Skyline Hwy

Ryōtsu · 12
14   Kamo-ko

Sumiyoshi
Onsen

Katanō

Aikawa
6
Kubota

Kanai   350   9
Uryuya
3
Nanaura
Coast   Sawata Shimonagaki   Niibo
Inakujira   Mano-wan   Hatano

5
Mano
8   2
4

350

Sado
Straits

Akadomari

Hamochi

10
Ogi
Shukunegi

To Naoetsu

To Teradomari

Festivals & Events

Earth Celebration   ARTS

One of Sado's biggest draws is this three-day music, dance and arts festival (www.kodo.or.jp) held during the third week in August. The event features *okesa* (folk dances), *on-idaiko* (demon drum dances) and *tsuburo-sashi* (a phallic dance with two goddesses). However, the focal point of the Earth Celebration is the performance of the Kodo Drummers, who live in a small village north of Ogi but spend much of the year on tour across the globe. Considered to be one of the most elite drumming groups on the planet,

its members are required to adhere to strict physical, mental and spiritual training regimens. If you're interested in attending, be advised that you will need to buy tickets and arrange accommodation well in advance.

ℹ️ Getting There & Away

Sado Kisen (☎03-5390-0550) runs car ferries and passenger-only hydrofoils between Niigata and Ryōtsu. There are up to five ferries (¥2440/17,500 one way per person/car, 2½ hours) and 14 jetfoils (¥6340, one hour) per day, though service is greatly reduced outside the summer months.

Sado-ga-shima

From Naoetsu-kō, about 90km southwest of Niigata, there are also up to three daily car-ferry services to Ogi (¥2650/19,500 one way per person/car, 2½ hours), which are particularly useful for visiting during the Earth Celebration.

ⓘ Getting Around

Bicycle

Cycling is an enjoyable way to move around the towns, but long-distance cruising is not recommended given the island's steep changes in elevation. Bicycle rental is available at various locations for around ¥400 to ¥1500 per day.

Bus

Local buses are fine on the main routes, though services to other parts of the island are restricted to two or three a day, and often halted in the winter.

If you plan to make extended use of local buses, there's an English-language timetable available from the ferry terminals and tourist information offices. The ¥2000 unlimited-ride bus pass, also in English, is a good-value option valid for two consecutive days on weekends only.

Car & Motorcycle

You really need a private vehicle to access the island's most scenic parts, and a good number of accommodation options are situated far from bus stops. Ferries from Honshū can accommodate cars for a substantial fee, though it's far cheaper to simply pick one up at the port in Ryōtsu. Be advised that distances between villages are long, and winding roads can be very slow going, so always make sure you fill up the tank whenever possible.

Sado's main hub, Ryōtsu is a low-key port town with little in the way of sights. Unless you're feeling seasick from the ferry and need some time to recuperate, it's recommended that you get your bearings, make any necessary travel arrangements and press on as quickly as possible.

A nice introduction to the island's ancient culture is the **Sado Nōgaku-no-sato** (佐渡能楽の里; admission ¥500; ⊙8.30am-5pm), a high-tech museum of nō drama situated approximately 3km south of town. Here you'll find displays of masks and costumes as well as nō performances enacted by a cast of animatronics actors.

About 4km further southwest is **Konpon-ji** (根本寺; admission ¥300; ⊙8am-4pm), a temple that occupies the location where Nichiren was first brought when exiled to Sado in 1271. Any bus on the Minami line between Ryōtsu and Sawata can drop you off at the Nōgaku-no-sato-mae and Konpon-ji-mae bus stops.

If you do need to stay the night, the **Sado Seaside Hotel** (佐渡シーサイドホテル; ☑27-7211; http://sadoseasidehotel.yuyado.net, in Japanese; fax 27-2713; 80 Sumiyoshi; r per person with 2 meals from ¥9450; @) is a Western-style drive-up motel with sea-view rooms and a decent onsen, located just 2km south of the ferry terminal. If you don't have your own wheels, it provides a free shuttle service to and from the port.

Small restaurants and cafes line Ryōtsu's main street, and feature seasonal specialities from the sea. Persimmons are also everywhere, and *hoshi-gaki* (dried winter persimmon) is a common food, even appearing in the traditional *yōkan* (bean jelly) sweets, some flecked with real gold.

The island's main **tourist information centre** (☑23-3300; ⊙8.30am-5pm, to 6.50pm Jun-Aug) is located in the street behind the coffee and souvenir shops across from the ferry terminal. You can ask the English-speaking staff here to help you arrange car rental. There are numerous companies in Ryōtsu, and you should expect to pay upwards of ¥10,000 per day.

For detailed transport information on accessing Ryōtsu and Sado-ga-shima by ferry, see p454.

SAWATA & AROUND 佐和田

Some 5km southwest of Ryōtsu, Sawata serves as Sado's main administrative and population centre. With Kyokushin Air's sudden cessation in 2008, Sawata itself is rather forlorn these days. But if you look beyond the drabness and the dearth of sights, and head out into the surrounding area, you'll find two noteworthy accommodation options that serve as excellent bases for exploring the island.

TOP CHOICE Green Village (グリーンヴィレッジ; ☎22-2719; www.e-sadonet.tv/~gvyh/eng/index.html; 750-4 Niibo Uryuya; dm/s ¥3600/4000, breakfast/dinner ¥700/1500; @) is one of our favourite accommodation spots is this adorable little cottage that looks as though it was scooped up from some far-flung European hamlet and plopped down in the middle of Sado. The wonderfully accommodating hosts can help you arrange all manner of activities, and stuff you full of home-baked apple pie before sending you on your way. Accommodation is in spotless six-person dormitories or a handful of private rooms with shared facilities. Your hosts speak basic English, and if you drop them a line in advance, they can arrange all of your meals, and make sure you know how to get here. From Ryōtsu, regular buses on the Minami line heading towards Sawata can drop you off at the Uryūya stop, from where you need to continue for 10 minutes and turn left at the first bend.

A great little *minshuku* is **Tōkaen** (桃華園; ☎63-2221; www.on.rim.or.jp/~toukaen, in Japanese; fax 63-1051; 1636-1 Otsu; s with/without 2 meals from ¥8400/4200), which has an attractive but isolated location in the middle of the central plains. It's a great escape, especially considering that the owners are avid outdoors folk who know every trail on the island, and will let you unwind in their *shiogama-buro* (rock-salt bath) at the end of a hard day. Any bus travelling on the Hon line between Ryōtsu and Aikawa via Kanai can drop you off at the Shinbo Undōkōen-mae stop, from where it's another 3km north on foot. If you tell the driver you're going to Tōkaen, they will drop you off a bit closer.

Regular buses run on the Minami line between Ryōtsu and Sawata (¥570, 40 minutes), and on the Hon line between Aikawa and Sawata (¥390, 20 minutes).

MANO & AROUND 真野

Although Mano was the provincial capital and cultural centre of the island from early times until the 14th century, it has since played younger sibling to more heavily pop-

BEST SCENIC DRIVES

» Sado-ga-shima (p453)
» Tazawa-ko (p435)
» Shimokita Peninsula (p430)
» Towada-ko (p433)

ulated Sawata. But unlike the fading administrative capital, Mano retains a vast wealth of historical attractions.

The entrance to a peaceful 7km-long nature trail is located just west of **Konponji** along the Minami bus route between Ryōtsu and Sawata, near the Danpū-jō bus stop. From the trailhead, it's a short walk to **Myōsen-ji** (妙宣寺; admission free; ☉9am-4pm), which was founded by one of Nichiren's disciples, and features a distinctive five-storey pagoda.

The trail then passes through rice fields and up old wooden steps set into the hillside to **Kokubun-ji** (国分寺; admission free; ☉8am-4pm), Sado-ga-shima's oldest temple, dating from AD 741. Another 3km takes you past marvellous lookout points to **Mano Go-ryō** (真野御陵), the tomb of Emperor Juntoku.

From there, it's a short walk down to **Sado Rekishi Densetsukan** (佐渡歴史伝説館; admission ¥700; ☉8am-5.30pm Apr-Nov, to 5pm Dec-Mar), where more tireless robots illustrate dioramas of Sado's history and festivals.

At the heart of the tiny and unpretentious village of Mano, you'll find the equally modest **Itōya Ryokan** (伊藤屋; ☎55-2019; www.visitsado.com/en/05plan/03accom/inn-find-id.php?id=a040012, in Japanese; fax 55-2677; 278 Mano-shinmachi; r with/without 2 meals ¥8400/5250; @), just 50m southwest of the Shinmachi traffic signal. This historic house is full of handicrafts from across the island, and evening dishes feature fish and shellfish from the deep sea. There is also an inviting *hinoki* bath here in case you catch a chill.

Mano's **tourist information office** (☎55-3589; ☉9am-5.30pm Apr-Oct), located at the junction of Rtes 350 and 65, can provide information on hikes and temples in the vicinity.

Regular buses run on the Minami line between Mano and Ryōtsu (¥630, 45 minutes), and between Mano and Sawata (¥260, 13 minutes). There are also regular buses between Mano and Ogi (¥810, 50 minutes).

OGI 小木

Although the area is home to the famed Kodo Drummers, Ogi is little more than a minor port that sees much less ferry traffic than Ryōtsu. During the Earth Celebration, Ogi does become something of a heaving metropolis, but for the rest of the year it's a drowsy village with some minor tourist attractions.

For Japanese visitors, Ogi is famous for its *taraibune,* boats made from huge barrels that are rowed by women in traditional fisher-folk costumes. In the olden days, they were used for collecting shellfish. Today they're mainly used for giving **rides** (¥450, 10 minutes, from 8.30am to 4.30pm) to tourists. Tickets are available at the marine terminal.

If you want to cover a bit more ground, you can take a **sightseeing boat** (¥1400, 45 minutes, from 8.30am to 4.30pm April to November) on a circle tour that runs from the marine terminal to the Sawa-zaki lighthouse and back.

For travellers who are more independent, the coastal areas in these parts are riddled with remote caves and coves, which can be accessed either by bike or rental car. There are a multitude of opportunities here for independent exploration, so put the guidebook down and see what you can discover.

If you're catching a ferry back to Honshū, the **Minshuku Sakaya** (さかや民宿; ☎86-2535; fax 86-2145; 1991 Ogi-chō; r per person with 2 meals ¥7350) is conveniently located just a few minutes' walk east of the Ogi ferry terminal. It's a fairly basic and unassuming spot, but the seafood is fresh and the staff is delightful.

While it's certainly a bit bleak from the exterior, the five-storey **Hotel New Kihachiya** (ホテル ニュー 喜八屋; ☎86-3131; www.kihachiya.com, in Japanese; 1935-21 Ogi-chō; r per person with meals from ¥10,000; @) in the centre of town is a surprisingly upmarket spot. Sprawling Japanese- and Western-style rooms – some with sea views – are complemented by a sparkling onsen and a large dining room hosting nightly formal feasts.

The **tourist office** (☎86-3200; ☉9am-5.30pm Apr-Oct) is a few minutes' walk west of the bus terminal. If Ogi is your entry point to the island, you can ask the English-speaking staff here to help you arrange car rental. There are a handful of companies in Ogi, and again, you should expect to pay upwards of ¥10,000 per day.

Regular buses run on the Ogi line between Ogi and Sawata (¥910, 1¼ hours) via Mano (¥810, 50 minutes).

For detailed transport information on accessing Ogi and Sado-ga-shima by ferry, see p454.

AIKAWA 相川

From a tiny hamlet, Aikawa grew almost overnight into a 100,000-person boom town when gold was discovered nearby in 1601. Mining amid some incredibly rough and rugged conditions continued until the end of the Edo period, a sufficient length of time to associate Sado with hardship and suffering. Today, the town is dwindling with each passing generation, but the scars of its mining past remain up in the hills.

From Aikawa bus terminal, it's a 40-minute walk (or a much shorter drive) up a steep mountain to the once bountiful **Sado Kinzan** (佐渡金山; ☎74-2389; www .sado-kinzan.com/en; 1305 Shimoaikawa; admission 1/2 courses ¥800/1200; ☉8am-5pm Apr-Oct, 8.30am-4.30pm Nov-Mar), the infamous 'Golden Mountain' that produced large quantities of gold and silver until its demise in 1989. The main tourist route descends into the chilly depths, where you'll encounter robots that dramatise the perilous existence of former miners. A second route brings you through century-old hauling tunnels, and leads a further 300m up the mountain to the original opencast mine where you can still see the remains of the workings.

It takes around 30 minutes to return on foot (of course, it's much less by car) down the mountain road to Aikawa. On the way you'll pass several temples and **Aikawa Kyōdo Hakubutsukan** (相川郷土博物館; ☎74-4312; Sakashita Machi; admission ¥300; ☉8.30am-5pm), a folk museum with more exhibits putting face and shape to the old mining town.

In the town centre, squeezed between the water and the main post office, is the affordably priced **Hotel Manchō** (ホテル万長; ☎74-3221; www.sado-royal.co.jp, in Japanese; 952-1575 Aikawa-orito; r per person with/without 2 meals from ¥5880/10,500; @☎). It's one of the oldest spots in town, and the Japanese-style rooms are a bit worn, but the location is convenient, and the restaurant is popular among locals.

Along the town's southern waterfront is the **Hotel Ōsado** (ホテル大佐渡; ☎74-3300; www.oosado.com, in Japanese; 288-2

Aikawakabuse; r per person with/without 2 meals from ¥13,275/7000; @🛜), where you can watch the sun set over the Sea of Japan while you sprawl in a *rotemburo*. Accommodation is in a mixed assortment of Western- and Japanese-style rooms, the best of which face the sea.

There's a small **tourist information centre** (📞74-2220; ⏰9am-5.30pm Apr-Oct) beside the bus terminal.

Regular buses run on the Nanaura Kaigan line between Aikawa and Ryōtsu (¥780, one hour) via Sawata (¥390, 20 minutes).

SOTOKAIFU   外海府

Sado's rugged northern coast is a dramatic landscape of sheer sea cliffs dropping off into deep blue waters. Roads are narrow and windy, which lead to harrowing but exhilarating coastal drives. Indeed, this is one area in Sado where having a rental car will make a big difference.

In order to truly appreciate the beauty of the region, you're going to have to head out into the bay. During the summer months, glass-bottom boats depart from the village of **Tassha** (達者), and embark on a 30-minute cruise of **Senkaku-wan** (尖閣湾, ¥850).

There are some wonderful youth hostels along this stretch of Sado's coast. In the fishing village of **Iwayaguchi** (岩谷口), just south of the bus stop, you'll find the **Sotokaifu Youth Hostel** (外海府ユースホステル; 📞78-2911; www.jyh.or.jp/yhguide/hokushinestu/sotokaif/index.html, in Japanese; fax 78-2931; 131 Iwayaguchi; dm from ¥3360, breakfast/dinner ¥760/1260), which is a traditional Sado-style house that has been converted by its loving owners into a very chilled-out accommodation spot. The property is centred on a traditional hearth cooking stove where hungry guests tend to congregate in the evening hours.

Another great option is the **Sado Belle Mer Youth Hostel** (佐渡ベルメールユースホステル; 📞75-2011; http://sado.bellemer.jp, in Japanese; 369-4 Himezu; dm from ¥3360, breakfast/dinner ¥760/1260), a more modern building that is scenically perched near the shore about five minutes on foot from the Minami-Himezu bus stop. This property is run by a knowledgeable Japanese family, who can give you some good outdoor tips for exploring Sado's wildest stretch of coastline.

A few daily buses run on the Kaifu line between Iwayaguchi and Aikawa (¥1010, 70 minutes).

Echigo-Yuzawa Onsen
越後湯沢温泉

📞025 / POP 8660

Echigo-Yuzawa Onsen was the setting for Nobel Prize–winning writer Kawabata Yasunari's *Snow Country,* a novel about decadent onsen geisha. Hedonistic hot springs and Kawabata memorabilia remain major tourist drawcards for Japanese literary buffs, though most tourists tend to focus on the town's close proximity to the snow-covered slopes at GALA Yuzawa.

⊙ Sights & Activities

GALA Yuzawa   SKIING & SNOWBOARDING
(ガーラ湯沢; www.galaresort.jp/winter/english; day lift tickets ¥4300; ⏰Dec-May) One of Tōhoku's most popular ski resorts, GALA Yuzawa is located just 200km north of Tokyo, and is easily accessed by *shinkansen*. You can quite literally wake up early in the morning in Tokyo, hit the slopes after breakfast, and be back home for dinner and a movie. With such incredible ease of access, GALA Yuzawa is predictably packed, especially on weekends and holidays, but you can't beat the convenience.

GALA Yuzawa is divided into a northern and a central area, which together offer 15 runs. There is also a southern area, though at the time of research it was closed for redevelopment. With the exception of a few runs at the bottom of the mountain, almost all trails are intermediate and beginner level. As a result, GALA Yuzawa is especially popular among families and novices. Courses from top to bottom are moderate in length, with the longest stretching for 2.4km. Three quad lifts alongside 12 triple and double lifts help to thin the crowds, but expect queues at peak times.

Given its popularity and proximity to Tokyo, GALA Yuzawa is a massive resort complete with its own onsen and fitness spa, as well as a multitude of bars, restaurants and accommodations. English is everywhere, and you'll see plenty of other foreigners here. Full equipment rental is available for a somewhat pricey ¥4800 per day. From JR Echigo-Yuzawa station, free shuttle buses run to the resort every 15 minutes from morning until early evening.

Yukiguni-kan   MUSEUM
(雪国館; admission ¥500; ⏰9am-4.30pm Thu-Tue) Sitting 500m north of the station, this wonderful little museum displays memora-

bilia from the life of Kawabata, in addition to interesting displays that bring his classic book to life.

🛏 Sleeping

Most visitors are day trippers from the capital, but you can spend the night if you'd like, and aim to be the first one on the slopes the following day.

🏷 Hakuginkaku Hana-no-yoi   RYOKAN $$
(白銀閣華の宵; ☎784-3311; www.hakugin.com/English.html; fax 784-4680; r per person with/without 2 meals from ¥13,650/10,500; @📶) Right outside the station's east exit is this foreigner-friendly ryokan and secluded refuge from the madding crowds. After a day on the slopes, you'll relish the opportunity to soak contemplatively in the brisk outdoor *hinoki* tub or in the indoor marble bath. Dinner is served in the room, so you can stretch your legs out on the tatami.

NASPA New Ōtani   HOTEL $$
(NASPAニューオータニ; ☎780-6111, 0120-227-021; www.naspa.co.jp/english; r per person with breakfast from ¥10,000; @🛜📶) Overlooking the town and the ski grounds, the New Otani has reasonably sized Western-style rooms and a whole range of resort facilities. It is also very conducive for travelling with little kids. A small *rotemburo* is a great way to soak the soreness away, and around-the-clock restaurants and buffet spreads help you keep up your energy levels. Free shuttles run between the station and the resort.

ℹ Getting There & Away

Bus
Echigo-Yuzawa Onsen is connected to Naeba by regular local buses (¥650, 40 minutes).

Train
There are several hourly trains on the Jōetsu *shinkansen* between Echigo-Yuzawa Onsen and Tokyo (¥6490, 1¼ hours), and between Echigo-Yuzawa Onsen and Niigata (¥5240, 50 minutes).

Naeba   苗場
☎025
Naeba is a little town with a lot going on. If you come in late July, the Fuji Rock Festival (see the box, p460) is three days of musical madness – like Woodstock, only with toilets and less mud – and up to 100,000 people show up to hang out, listen to great bands and enjoy the party atmosphere. In the win-

ter months, Naeba (and adjacent Kagura) is where you'll find some of the most challenging skiing and snowboarding in the whole of Tōhoku.

🏃 Activities

Naeba Sukī-Jō   SKIING & SNOWBOARDING
(苗場スキー場; www.princehotels.co.jp/ski/naeba; day lift ticket/combined Naeba & Kagura ¥4000/5000; ⊙Nov-May) Naeba is an impressive resort with 27 courses fairly evenly divided among the various skill levels. The longest run (4km) starts at the top of the mountain, and winds through birch forests and mogul fields prior to dropping a full kilometre in elevation. The snow tends to be dry and light, and there are plenty of ungroomed areas where you can carve up some serious powder.

Naeba offers a snow park and sledding hill where the little ones can roam free, as well as a freestyle snowboarding course complete with rails, half pipes and kickers. As at GALA Yuzawa, English is everywhere, and you definitely won't be the only foreigner on the slopes. At the bottom of the hill, you'll find the N-Plateau, which is a massive complex complete with a full food court, onsen, convenience store and ski shop. You can also rent equipment here for ¥4300 per day.

Six- and eight-person gondolas do a pretty decent job of keeping the crowds in check at peak times. But if you find the lines a little too long for your liking, you can always jump on the awesomely named Dragondola (トラゴンドラ). Spanning a distance of 5.5km, this is reportedly the longest gondola in the world, and whisks you away to Kagura in just 15 minutes.

Kagura Sukī-Jō   SKIING & SNOWBOARDING
(かぐらスキー場; www.princehotels.co.jp/ski/kagura; day lift ticket/combined Naeba & Kagura ¥4200/5000; ⊙Nov-May) Naeba is an even more attractive winter destination when you consider that it's contiguous with Kagura, an impressive mountain in its own right. Divided into the Tashiro, Kagura and Mitsumata areas, this resort offers up an additional 22 runs that are divided 45/35/20 among beginner, intermediate and advanced runs.

But don't let the numbers fool you – Kagura has a lax policy on back-country skiing, which means that experienced alpinists can really have an extreme adventure up here. For those who feel more comfortable sticking to the trails, fret not, as one of the courses here reaches an impressive 6km in

Music lovers head to Japan in late July for the **Fuji Rock Festival** (www.fujirockfestival.com). There's no better location than the ski resort in Naeba, Niigata Prefecture: mountains rise on both sides of a forested valley, littered with several stages. Here you'll find foreign and home-grown rock, hip-hop, experimental jazz, techno, punk and reggae, all just a two-hour train ride from Tokyo.

More than 100,000 people attend Fuji Rock, and most camp up on a mountain as accommodation tends to be booked out. What to bring? You won't need your skis so much as some sunscreen and, yes, sturdy boots. Most years see two days of blue skies and sun followed by rain. You may find yourself swimming in mud.

Held in late September, the two-day **Asagiri Jam** (www.asagirijams.org, in Japanese) festival is perhaps more deserving of the name 'Fuji Rock Festival' – it's located in the beautiful foothills that surround Mt Fuji. Asagiri Jam is low-key, and the line-up isn't announced beforehand. The emphasis is more on creating a good vibe rather than pulling in big names. Dub, techno, jazz and, of course, rock are featured. There are no hotels around here, so bring a tent or stay up all night.

The two-day **Summer Sonic** (www.summersonic.com/2010/english/) draws major international acts and is held during early August in Chiba, next to Tokyo, and Osaka. Chiba's line-up plays the next day in Osaka, and vice-versa.

Then there's the three-day **Rock in Japan** (www.rock-net.jp, in Japanese) festival, set in acres of green fields in Ibaraki Prefecture, a two-hour train ride from Tokyo. In many ways, this festival epitomises the Japanese music scene today – all performers are Japanese – and it spans everything from J-Pop stars to ageing crooners.

---

length. With the combined pass, you can also return to Naeba by the Dragondola at any time, or alternatively take one of the free shuttle buses that depart from the bottom of the Mitsumata area.

🛏 Sleeping

Naeba gets its fair share of day trippers. Bedding down here or in Echigo-Yuzawa Onsen helps you get the most out of your ski holiday.

Prince Hotel Naeba HOTEL $$
(プリンスホテル苗場; ☎789-2211; www.prince hotels.co.jp/naeba; fax 789-3140; San-goku; r per person from ¥8000; @ 🛜 🚃) All of the ski action in Naeba centres on this monolithic resort, which is in the business of catering to your every whim and fancy. On offer is a range of Western-style rooms and suites that vary considerably in size, amenities and price – check online for specials – in addition to a whole slew of bars, cafes, restaurants and health and fitness facilities.

❶ Getting There & Away

Echigo-Yuzawa Onsen is connected to Naeba by regular local buses (¥650, 40 minutes). Free shuttle buses to the Prince Hotel also run this route, though you need to be a registered guest to take advantage of this service.

During peak ski season, private companies run overnight shuttles between Tokyo and Naeba. Prices can be as low as ¥7000 return – enquire at tourist information centres in Tokyo for more information.

Myōkō Kōgen 妙高高原
☎0255

This up-and-coming skiing and snowboarding destination comprises a sprawling collection of powder-rich winter resorts that line the Myōko mountain range. On the whole, the region is much less developed for mass tourism than GALA Yuzawa (p458) and Naeba, for example, but this off-the-beaten-path appeal is precisely why you should visit.

Akakura Onsen Sukī-Jō (赤倉温泉スキー場; www.akakura-ski.com, in Japanese; day lift tickets ¥3900; ⊙Dec-Apr) is one of the more popular resorts, especially among travellers with small children. All but two of the 20 runs were laid out with the needs of novice skiers in mind, and even the black diamonds are little more than short chutes. But the high-quality powder and picturesque setting ensure a good time for everyone. Family restaurants, many drawing inspiration from European chalets, are scattered around the slopes. Full equipment rental for skiers/

snowboarders is available for ¥4000/4950 per day. English signage is generally available.

For off-piste excitement, check out the local telemark experts, **Myōkō Backcountry Ski School** (妙高バックカントリースキースクール; ☎87-2392; www.myokokogen.org/mbss/english.php), for guided tours in English through the backwoods terrain, as well as personalised one-on-one instruction. Prices are variable depending on the length and type of tour or course, so contact the ski school for more information.

The tranquil **Hotel Alp** (ホテルアルピ; ☎87-3388; www.alp-myoko.com/english/index.html; 585-90 Akakura Onsen, Myoko-shi; r per person with 2 meals from ¥13,000; @ 🛜 🦽) lies at the base of the slopes, and is extremely conducive to a ski-in, ski-out holiday. There are fewer than 20 rooms on the premises, allowing for a sense of intimacy not found at the resort hotels. Be sure to spend some quality time in the therapeutic sauna, perfect for thawing out your joints.

The Nagano *shinkansen* runs once or twice every hour between Tokyo and Nagano (¥7770, 1¾ hours). Nagano is connected to Myōkō Kōgen by the JR Shinetsu line; hourly *kaisoku* (¥960, 45 minutes) ply this route. From Myōkō Kōgen JR station, shuttle buses and taxis run to Akakura Onsen Sukī-Jō and other ski resorts.

Sapporo & Hokkaidō

Best Places to Eat

» Kani-honke (p473)

» Kita-no-aisukurīmu Yasan (p484)

» Takechan (p497)

» Kunen-kōbō Yamadori (p505)

» Marukibune (p515)

Best Places to Stay

» La Vista Hakodate Bay (p479)

» Ginrinsō (p482)

» Green Leaf (p487)

» Akan Yuku-no-sato Tsuruga (p516)

» Biei Potato-no-Oka (p504)

Why Go?

A frozen hinterland with a wild frontier spirit, Hokkaidō (北海道) is defined by everything that Japan's southern islands are not. Aside from a few major cities such as Sapporo (札幌), the untamed north country is a hauntingly beautiful wilderness, on par with the Canadian Rockies or New Zealand's South Island.

For the thrill-seeking traveller in search of sweeping vistas, amazing wildlife, wide open roads and overwhelming emptiness, Hokkaidō is a refreshing contrast to the crushing density of Honshū. In fact, the image of cruising across these hinterlands is associated with unfettered freedom in the minds of the Japanese.

From November to March, a Siberian cold descends on the island, providing some of the best skiing in Japan and the eastern hemisphere. When Hokkaidō thaws, and the bears awaken from their hibernation, the island lures hikers in search of rugged backcountry terrain and remote onsen.

When to Go
Sapporo

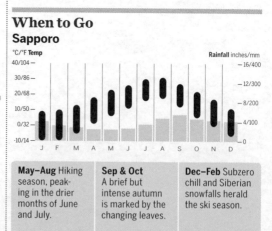

| **May–Aug** Hiking season, peaking in the drier months of June and July. | **Sep & Oct** A brief but intense autumn is marked by the changing leaves. | **Dec–Feb** Subzero chill and Siberian snowfalls herald the ski season. |

History

The Ainu, Hokkaidō's indigenous people, have shaped this island's history.

After the glaciers receded, the Ainu settled here and called the land Ainu Moshiri – Ainu meaning 'human' and Moshiri meaning 'world'. Until the Edo period (1600–1868), the Ainu and the Japanese, remarkably, had relatively little contact with each other. However, this changed when the Matsumae clan established a major foothold for themselves in southwestern Hokkaidō, and successfully bargained with the Ainu. They succeeded in creating a trade monopoly, which was lucrative for the clan, but would ultimately prove disastrous to the Ainu people.

By the end of the Edo period, trade and colonisation had begun in earnest, and by the time the Meiji Restoration began in 1868, the Ainu culture was under attack. Many Ainu customs were banned, women were forbidden to get tattoos, men were prohibited from wearing earrings and the Kaitakushi (Colonial Office) was created to encourage mainland Japanese people to migrate northward. When the Meiji period ended, the Ainu had become de facto second-class citizens, and by the start of the 20th century, the mainland Japanese population on the island topped one million.

With world attention focused on Hokkaidō when Sapporo hosted the 1972 Winter Olympics, Japan felt the need to ease restrictions on the Ainu. Sadly, however, it would take another 26 years before significant protections were written into law. Though marginalised for much of the past century, the Ainu have recently won recognition as an important part of Japanese cultural heritage, and are re-establishing themselves. Today, the Ainu are proudly continuing their traditions while still fighting for further recognition of their unique culture.

National Parks

Hokkaidō boasts some of Japan's oldest and most beautiful national parks. Daisetsuzan National Park, centrally located near Asahikawa city, is a must-see. This stunning expanse of mountain ranges, volcanoes, onsen (hot springs), lakes and hiking tracks is Japan's largest, covering 2309 sq km.

Akan National Park, near Kushiro, has onsen, volcanoes and hiking. In spring, thousands of cranes flock to Kushiro Shitsugen National Park, one of Japan's largest marshlands; deer, foxes, *shima-risu* (none other than the humble chipmunk!) and a host of birds are abundant. The northern islands of Rebun and Rishiri offer superb hiking and views of seaside cliffs, volcanic mountains and (in season) hillsides of flowers.

Shiretoko National Park, in the northeast, is as remote as it gets: two-thirds of it doesn't have roads. Ponds as glassy as reflecting pools, rivers with brown bears munching salmon, waterfalls more delicate than rice-paper paintings – the scenery is stunning, but tourists are told quite plainly that if they venture into restricted areas they will be fined, eaten by Higuma bears... or both.

❶ Getting There & Away

AIR

Sapporo is the main hub of all Hokkaidō traffic, though Hakodate and other smaller cities also offer direct flights to many of Japan's larger cities.

BOAT

For those without Japan Rail (JR) Passes, domestic ferries from Honshū are a low-cost alternative to train travel. Hokkaidō also serves as a jumping-off point for the maritime route to Russia (see p498).

TRAIN

If you are coming from Tokyo, consider taking either the *Hokutosei* sleeper train or the more luxurious *Cassiopeia* to save time. Note that the *shinkansen* (bullet train) does not offer a service direct to Hokkaidō, at least not until 2015 at the earliest. Take it as far north as Shin-Aomori, and then transfer to the *tokkyū* (limited express).

❶ Getting Around

AIR

Sapporo and Hakodate both have flights to all other major Hokkaidō cities.

BICYCLE

For fans of greener ways to get around, Hokkaidō is a good place to tour by bike. *Charida* (bicycle riders) are a common sight on major roads. Rider houses or cycling terminals (see p742) are also cheap, common and great places to meet other cyclists as well as bikers.

BUS

Within cities, buses are convenient and usually cheap. Ask about a *norihō dai* (all-day) pass if you're going to use them a lot – there's often a substantial discount.

Sapporo & Hokkaidō Highlights

❶ Drinking beer straight from the source in **Sapporo** (p466)

❷ Staring down a Hello Kitty snowwoman at the **Sapporo Yuki Matsuri** (Snow Festival; p471)

❸ Carving up the slopes at **Niseko** (p485) or **Furano** (p503)

❹ Charting a path through the wilderness in **Daisetsuzan National Park** (p505)

❺ Saying goodbye to stress as you steam at **Noboribetsu Onsen** (p489)

❻ Discovering enormous, ancient *marimo* (balls of algae) in **Akan National Park** (p513)

❼ Dining on fresh *uni* (sea-urchin roe) and *ikura* (salmon eggs) in **Otaru** (p482)

❽ Strolling through 19th-century streetscapes in historic **Hakodate** (p477)

❾ Heading to the 'end of the world' in the Unesco World Heritage site of **Shiretoko National Park** (p518)

❿ Taking a plane or ferry out to the remote islands of **Rishiri-Rebun-Sarobetsu National Park** (p498) to photograph the summer wildflowers

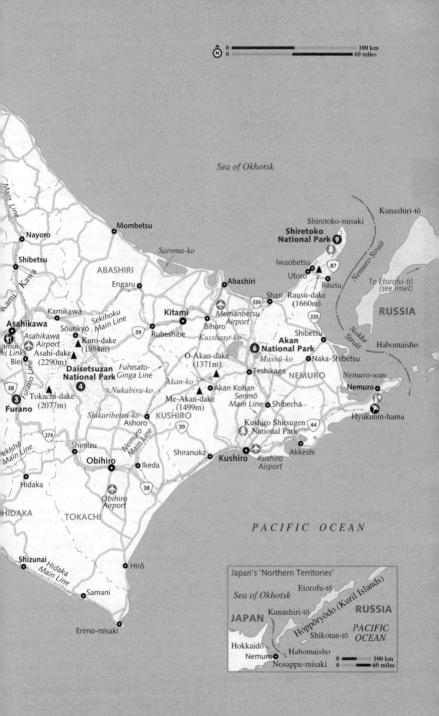

0   100 km
0   60 miles

Sea of Okhotsk

Kunashiri-tō

Shiretoko-misaki

Shiretoko National Park 9

Mombetsu

Saroma-ko

Nayoro

Shibetsu

ABASHIRI

Engaru

Abashiri

Iwaobetsu

Utoro

Rausu

Nemuro Strait

To *Etorofu-tō* (see inset)

RUSSIA

Kamikawa

Sekihoku Main Line

Shari

334

Rausu-dake (1660m)

87

335

Habomaisho

Nokke Strait

Asahikawa

Sōunkyō

Kitami

Bihoro

Memanbetsu Airport

39

Rubeshibe

Shibetsu

Asahikawa Airport

Kuro-dake (1984m)

Kussharo-ko

Akan National Park 6

Naka-Shibetsu

ki Links

Asahi-dake (2290m)

O-Akan-dake (1371m)

Mashū-ko

Bei

Daisetsuzan National Park 4

Furusato-Ginga Line

Akan-ko

Teshikaga

NEMURO

Nemuro-wan

Nemuro

38

Furano Line

Nukabira-ko

Me-Akan-dake (1499m)

Akan Kohan

Senmō Main Line

3

Tokachi-dake (2077m)

Furano

Shikaribetsu-ko

Ashoro

KUSHIRO

Shibecha

Hyakunin-hama

39

Nemuro Main Line

ekisho Main Line

Shimizu

Obihiro

Ikeda

Shiranuka

Kushiro Shitsugen National Park

44

Akkeshi

HIDAKA

Hidaka

Obihiro Airport

38

Kushiro

Kushiro Airport

274

TOKACHI

PACIFIC OCEAN

Shizunai

Hidaka Main Line

Hirō

Samani

Erimo-misaki

Japan's 'Northern Territories'

Sea of Okhotsk

Etorofu-tō

JAPAN

Kunashiri-tō

Hoppōryōdo (Kuril Islands)

RUSSIA

Shikotan-tō

PACIFIC OCEAN

Hokkaidō

Nemuro

Habomaisho

Nosappu-misaki

0   100 km
0   60 miles

ℹ️ ROAD TRIP

Shaped a bit like the squashed head of a squid, Hokkaidō is often divided into five subprefectures: *Dō-nan* (southern), *Dō-ō* (central), *Dō-hoku* (northern), *Dō-tō* (eastern) and Tokachi. Public transport leaves a lot to be desired, though Hokkaidō is fortunately conducive to travel by car – or better yet by motorcycle.

You'll need lots of time to tackle this largely undeveloped land mass, but you'll be rewarded with a road trip unlike any other in Japan. Quick tip: distances in Hokkaidō can be deceiving, so make a point of travelling early on in the day, especially in the winter months.

For a list of the best scenic drives, see the box, p481.

CAR & MOTORCYCLE

Private-vehicle rental is recommended as the island's beauty is in its landscapes. Car-rental rates vary, but if you walk in off the street expect to pay between ¥7000 and ¥10,000 per day, plus the cost of fuel (which can certainly add up!). You will need an International Driving Permit, which you must get from your home country prior to arrival in Japan.

TRAIN

Trains run frequently on the trunk lines, but reaching remote locations involves infrequent connections. In addition to the country-wide JR Rail Pass, there is also a Hokkaidō Rail Pass: a three-/flexible four-/five-day pass costs ¥15,000/19,500/19,500.

SAPPORO

📞 011 / POP 1.90 MILLION

Japan's fifth-largest city, and the prefectural capital of Hokkaidō, Sapporo (札幌) is a surprisingly dynamic and cosmopolitan urban centre that pulses with energy despite its extreme northerly latitude. Designed by European and American architects in the late 19th century, Sapporo is shaped by its wide grid of tree-lined streets and ample public-park space, which contribute to the city's surprising level of liveability. Even if you get cold easily, you can always get your energy back over a hot meal, a great proposition given Sapporo's wholly deserved gastronomic reputation.

As the island's main access point and transport hub, Sapporo serves as an excellent base for striking out into the wilds. But don't check out too quickly: Sapporo is a major tourist destination in itself, especially for those partial to the delicious liquid gold that is Sapporo beer. If you're planning long periods of time hiking in isolation, you might want to first indulge in a bit of the raucous nightlife of the Susukino district. And of course, if the calendar month happens to read February, don't miss out on the Sapporo Yuki Matsuri, a winter carnival highlighted by frozen sculptures of everything from brown bears and *tanuki* (racoon dogs) to Godzilla and Doraemon.

History

Sapporo is one of Japan's newest cities, and lacks the temples and castles found in its more southerly neighbours. However, it has a long history of occupation by the Ainu, who first named the area Sari-poro-betsu or 'a river which runs along a plain filled with reeds'.

The present-day metropolis was once nothing but a quiet hunting and fishing town in the Ishikari Plain of Hokkaidō. While the Ainu were left alone until 1821, everything changed when the Tokugawa *shōgunate* (military government) created an official trading post that would eventually become Sapporo. The city was declared the capital of Hokkaidō in 1868, and its growth was carefully planned.

In the 20th century, Sapporo emerged as a major producer of agricultural products. Sapporo Beer (see p470), the country's first brewery, was founded in 1876, and quickly became synonymous with the city itself. In 1972, Sapporo hosted the Winter Olympics, and the city's annual Sapporo Yuki Matsuri, begun in 1950, attracts more than two million visitors.

In recent years, Sapporo has experienced something of a cultural and spiritual renaissance, especially as more and more youths are choosing to flee their lives in the Tokyo and Osaka areas in search of a new start.

👁 Sights

We're not going to lie to you – Sapporo can be bitterly cold, especially when the Arctic winds are blowing and the snow is piling up. However, if you dress appropriately – and maybe get a beer or two into your system – Sapporo is actually a very walkable city. The gridded streets (a rarity in Japan) make for very simple navigation, and most of the major sights are clustered together in the city centre.

Of course, if your body starts to go numb, you can always take advantage of the city's subway, tram and bus lines.

Enquire at the various concession offices about the Sapporo Selection discount ticket, which retails for ¥1500. This allows you to enter three of the six cooperating tourist sights, including Sapporo Terebi-tō observatory, Sapporo Winter Sports Museum and the Moiwa-yama Ropeway.

Hours for attractions listed are for high season (generally April to September); most of them have reduced hours the rest of the year.

Hokudai Shokubutsuen   BOTANICAL GARDEN
(北大植物園; www.hokudai.ac.jp/fsc/bg; N3W8 Chūō-ku; combined ticket ¥400, winter greenhouse only ¥110; ⊙9am-4.30pm) One of Sapporo's must-sees, this beautiful outdoor garden is the botanical showpiece of Hokkaidō University. Here you'll find more than 4000 plant varietals, all attractively set on a meandering 14-hectare plot just 10 minutes on foot southwest of the station. Of particular note is the small section dedicated to Ainu wild foods and medicinal plants, though English-language signage is sadly in short supply.

Sapporo Terebi-tō   NOTABLE BUILDING
(さっぽろテレビ塔; www.tv-tower.co.jp/en/; Ōdōri-nishi 1-chōme Chūō-ku; admission ¥700; ⊙9am-10pm) There's no way you'll miss this Eiffel Tower–shaped affair at the east of Ōdōri-kōen, which stands alongside Tokyo Tower (p59) in the category of misplaced monuments. Still, the views from the top of the 90m-tall tower are very impressive, especially when the sun drops below the horizon and Sapporo lights up for the night. During Sapporo Yuki Matsuri, a trip up here is pretty much obligatory.

Sapporo Winter Sports Museum   MUSEUM
(札幌ウィンタースポーツミュージアム; www.sapporowintersportsmuseum.com, in Japanese; 1274 Miyano-mori Chūō-ku; admission ¥600; ⊙8.30am-6pm) Housed in the ski-jump stadium built for the Sapporo Olympics, this highly amusing museum includes a computerised ski-jump simulator that allows you to try your skills without potentially breaking every bone in your body. Even if you do land a few virtual jumps, a chairlift ride to the launch point of the actual ski jump used in the 1972 games should serve as a quick reality check. To reach the museum, take the Tozai line to Maruyama, and then take exit

2 for the Maruyama bus terminal. Next, take bus 14 to Okurayama-iriguchi (15 minutes, ¥200); from here, it's a 10-minute walk uphill to the stadium.

Moiwa-yama Ropeway   ROPEWAY
(藻岩ロープウェイ; www.sapporo-dc.co.jp/eng; tickets ¥600; ⊙10.30am-9.30pm) Panoramic views of Sapporo can be had from this scenic ropeway, which runs 1200m up the slopes of Moiwa-san. At the top is a large tourist complex where you can linger over a meal, shop for Hokkaidō-related paraphernalia or scan the cityscape with high-powered binoculars. You can easily access the ropeway by taking the tram to the Rōpuwei-iriguchi stop, and then walking west towards the hill for around 10 minutes.

Sapporo-shi Tokei-dai   CLOCK TOWER
(札幌市時計台; www15.ocn.ne.jp/~tokeidai/english.html; N1W2 Chūō-ku; admission ¥200; ⊙8.45am-5pm Tue-Sun) While it may not be at the top of your list, no Japanese tourist can leave Sapporo without snapping a photo of the city's signature landmark, the clock tower. Built in 1878, the clock has never missed tolling the hour for more than 130 years. Impressive – though the clock tower is also known as one of Japan's top three *gakkari* (disappointing) spots, mainly because the brochure photos often remove the urban metropolis that dwarfs the small building. The clock tower is just two minutes on foot from exit 7 of Ōdōri station.

NAVIGATING THE GRID

Sapporo, laid out in a Western-style grid pattern, is relatively easy to navigate. Blocks are labelled East, West, North and South in relation to a central point near Sapporo Terebi-tō (the TV Tower) in the city centre. For example, the famous landmark Tokei-dai (Clock Tower) is in the block of North 1, West 2 (Kita Ichi-jo, Nishi Ni-chōme) – N1W1. Ōdōri-kōen, a narrow grass-covered section ending at Sapporo Terebi-tō, is a major city feature, dividing the city east–west, into north–south halves. South of Ōdōri is the downtown shopping district with shops and arcades. Susukino, the club and entertainment district, is located mainly between the South 2 and South 6 blocks.

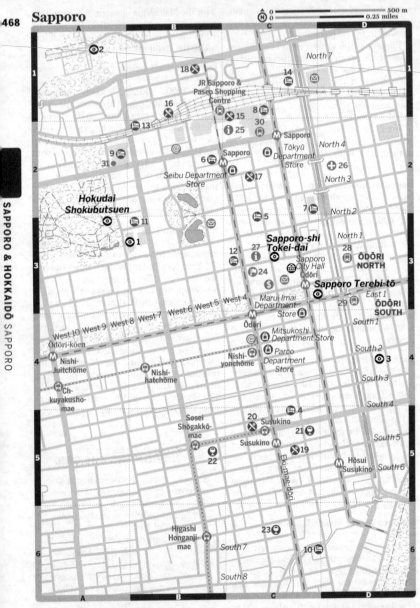

North 7

JR Sapporo &
Paseo Shopping
Centre

North 4

North 3

North 2

North 1

Sapporo
Tōkyū
Department
Store

*Hokudai
Shokubutsuen*

Seibu Department
Store

**Sapporo-shi
Tokei-dai**

Sapporo
City Hall
Ōdōri

ŌDŌRI
NORTH

Sapporo Terebi-tō

East 1

ŌDŌRI
SOUTH

South 1

*Marui Imai
Department
Store*

Ōdōri

*Mitsukoshi
Department Store*

*Parco
Department
Store*

South 2

South 3

South 4

West 10 West 9 West 8 West 7 West 6 West 5 West 4

Ōdōri-kōen

Nishi-
Juitchōme

Nishi-
hatchōme

Nishi-
yonchōme

Chi-
kuyakusho-
mae

Sosei
Shōgakkō-
mae

Susukino

South 5

Susukino

Hōsui
Susukino

South 6

Eki-mae-dōri

Higashi
Honganji-
mae

South 7

South 8

Hokkaidō University   UNIVERSITY
(北海道大学; Hokkaidō Daigaku; www.hokudai
.ac.jp/en/index.html; ☉dawn-dusk) Established
in 1876, this university is a scenic place,
with a number of unique buildings. The Furukawa Memorial Hall and the Seikatei are
noteworthy, and several campus museums
are open to the public. The bust of William
S Clark, the founding vice-president of the
university, is a famous landmark. Upon his
departure in 1877, Professor Clark famously
told his students: 'Boys, be ambitious!'

Hokkaidō Ritsubun-gakukan MUSEUM
(北海道立文学館; www.h-bungaku.or.jp, in Japanese; Nakashima-kōen 1-4 Chūō-ku; admission ¥250; ⊘Tue-Sun) This museum offers the opportunity to see the private side of many of Japan's famous novelists, primarily those with a Hokkaidō connection. Letters, memorabilia, books and short films all help viewers understand why these writers have earned a place in the canon of Japanese literature. The museum is scenically located in Nakajima park in the southern district.

Ni-jō Ichiba MARKET
(二条市場; S3E1&2 Chūō-ku; ⊘7am-noon) Buy a bowl of rice and select your own sashimi toppings, gawk at the fresh delicacies or sit down at a shop in Ni-jō, one of Hokkaidō's best fish markets. Sea urchin and crab are favourites; as is Hokkaidō's version of 'Mother and Child' (oyakodon), a bowl of rice topped with salmon and roe. Get there early for the freshest selections and the most variety; things close up by noon and individual restaurants have their own hours.

FREE Toyohira-gawasake Kagakukan MUSEUM
(豊平さけ科学館; www.sapporo-park.or.jp/sake/english/e_index.html; 2-1 Makomanai-kōen; ⊘9.15am-4.45pm Tue-Sun) This museum is a tribute to one of the world's most delicious fish. Check out more than 20 species of salmon in varying stages of development, as well as a few odd salamanders, turtles and frogs. Bring the kids! It's in Makomanai Park near the Olympic stadium. Take the subway to Makomanai Station, then board any bus to Kyogijo bus stop (15 minutes, ¥200). From here it's a five-minute walk.

FREE Hokkaidō Jingu TEMPLE
(北海道神宮; www.hokkaidojingu.or.jp/eng/index.html) This temple is nestled in a forest so dense that it's easy to forget that the city is just beyond the grounds. Attention has been paid to labelling the natural surroundings: a large plaque lists a number of local birds and the largest trees have identification signs. The temple lies a few blocks east of Maruyama-kōen station (exit 1).

SAPPORO BEER

Let's face it: 'Sapporo' means beer. After visiting Germany (and being favourably impressed), Kihachirō Ōkura returned and selected Sapporo as the lucky place to start what would become Japan's first beer brewery, founded in 1876.

Sapporo Beer-En (サッポロビール園; www.sapporo-bier-garten.jp/foreign/english .php; N7E9 Higashi-ku; admission free; ☉beer garden 11.30am-10pm, tours 9am-3.40pm), part museum, part beer garden, is located in the original Sapporo Beer brewery, almost due east of JR Sapporo Station. Visitors wanting to belly up to the trough should take the free one-hour tour (recorded English commentary provided), which includes a tasting (¥200 per beer) and most likely a slight buzz! The adjoining beer garden has four restaurants spanning a variety of cuisines – purists should note that pints of Sapporo were meant to be enjoyed with the local grilled-lamb speciality, *jingisukan* (Genghis Khan). There is also a great gift shop where you can snag a few reprints of nostalgic beer posters from the early 20th century.

To get here take the Tōhō subway to the Higashi-Kuyakusho-mae stop (exit 4). Head south along Higashi-Nana-Chōme-dōri to N8E8 (about 10 minutes) and look to the left. The large brick chimney with the distinct Sapporo trademark star is unmistakable. The building itself is at N7E9. By bus, take the Chūō Bus Higashi 63 and get off at the Kitahachi Higashinana (N8E7) stop. The building will be right in front of you. Note that while tour reservations aren't essential, they're not a bad idea – if you don't speak Japanese, ask tourist information or your hotel staff to phone ahead for you.

Hokkaidō Brewery (サッポロビール北海道工場; Toiso 542-1 Eniwa-shi; ☉tours 9am-3.30pm), the current brewing and bottling facility – and a must for diehard fans – is a 40-minute train ride from Sapporo. The mammoth production plant seems more like something out of a James Bond movie rather than a place where beer is made: technicians in white lab coats peer into test tubes; immaculate stainless-steel tanks are covered with computerised gauges and dials; and video cameras monitor the bottles as they whizz by. The 40-minute tour is self-guided and English is minimal, but you'll be rewarded with a refreshing 20 minutes to tipple at the end. Admission is free, but you need to make reservations a few weeks in advance.

Take the JR Chitose line towards the airport, and get off at the Sapporo Beer Teien Station. Head away from the tracks towards the giant white silos with the Sapporo logo; the entrance is a 10-minute walk away.

FREE Hokkaidō Ritsukindai-bijyutsukan MUSEUM
(海道立近代美術館; www.aurora-net.or.jp/art/dokinbi, in Japanese; N1W17 Chūō-ku; adult/student ¥450/220; ☉9.30am-5pm Tue-Sun)
A comprehensive collection of modern works by primarily Japanese artists. The museum is a few blocks north of Nishi-18-chōme station (exit 4) on the Tozai line.

FREE Hokkaidō Ainu Kyōkai CULTURAL CENTRE
(北海道アイヌ協会; www.ainu-assn.or.jp/english/eabout01.html; 7th fl, Kaderu 2.7 Community Centre, N2W7 Chūō-ku; ☉9am-5pm Mon-Sat)
Across the street from the botanical gardens, this cultural centre offers an interesting display room of robes, tools and historical information on the Ainu.

FREE Moerenuma-kōen SCULPTURE PARK
(モエレ沼公園; www.sapporo-park.or.jp/moere/english.php; 1-1 Moeru-kōen, Higashi-ku; ☉7am-10pm) Completed in 2005, this former waste-treatment plan is now a reclaimed green belt full of modern sculptures. To reach the park, take bus 79 from the Kanjo-dōri Higashi subway stop.

🏃 Activities

Sapporo Teine SKIING & SNOWBOARDING
(サッポロテイネ; www.sapporo-teine.com/snow, in Japanese; day passes ¥4800; ☉9am-4pm) With Niseko (p485) just around the corner, alpine enthusiasts aren't too keen on spending any more time in Sapporo than they have to. But you can't beat Teine for convenience, as the slopes lie quite literally on the edge of the city.

With only 15 runs and nine lifts, Teine caters primarily to families with children. The highlights include a 4km-long beginner trail that undulates from the highland zone down to the village, and then continues into a low-lying valley. There is also an exhilarating 700m black-diamond chute that was featured in the downhill rotation at the Sapporo Olympics.

Cafeteria-style restaurants are located at each of the various levels, and offer winter warmers such as udon, *rāmen* and curry rice. Full equipment rental for skiers/snowboarders is available for ¥4000/4950 per day. English signage is a bit limited, and foreigners are in short supply compared to Niseko.

Just 15 minutes from Sapporo by local train, Teine can get very crowded, particularly on weekends and school holidays. Frequent trains on the JR Hakodate line run between Sapporo and Teine (¥260). From JR Teine Station, shuttle buses conveniently whisk you back and forth to the slopes.

✹✷ Festivals & Events

Sapporo Yuki Matsuri   SNOW

Drawing more than two million visitors, the annual Sapporo Yuki Matsuri (www.snowfes.com/english) takes place from 7 to 13 February, and is arguably one of Japan's top festivals. Its humble origins back to 1950, when local high-school students built six snow statues in Ōdōri-kōen. Five years later, the Japan Self-Defence Force from the nearby Makomanai base upped the ante by building the city's first gigantic snow sculptures. By 1974, the event had grown into an international contest attracting teams from more than a dozen countries. Taking weeks and weeks to carve, past snow sculptures have included life-sized statues of Hideki Matsui, entire frozen stages for visiting musical acts, ice slides and mazes for the kiddies and – of course – a cutesy-cool Hello Kitty statue or two. You can view these icy behemoths in Ōdōri-kōen as well as in other locations around the city. The festival also highlights the best in regional food and drink from across the island, and you can expect all kinds of wild and drunken revelry, particularly once the sun sets (at these latitudes, it's quite early!). Finding reasonably priced accommodation can be extremely difficult, so book as far in advance as possible.

Ōdōri Nōryō Gāden   BEER

The summer beer festival is held in Ōdōri Kōen from mid-July to mid-August. Sapporo, Asahi and microbrewers set up outdoor beer gardens, offering a variety of beers and other beverages, as well as food and snacks.

Hokkai Bonodori   TRADITIONAL

Families welcome back the spirits of the dead in mid-August. The festival provides viewers with glimpses of traditional songs, dances and summer *yukata* (light, cotton kimonos).

🛏 Sleeping

Sapporo offers a diverse range of accommodation ranging from budget crash pads to lavish escapes. Advance reservations are necessary during Sapporo Yuki Matsuri, and potentially on weekends during peak winter snowfall and peak summer wildflowers.

If you're looking for a place to crash in an emergency, internet cafes across the city are open 24 hours, offer reclining chairs and hot showers, and are often cheaper than even the cheapest of hotels.

Love hotels in Susukino are another colourful if slightly promiscuous option, and are as clean as (or cleaner than!) budget hostels and hotels. Check in after 11pm for the lowest rates.

Nakamuraya Ryokan   RYOKAN $$

(中村屋旅館; ☎241-2111, 241-2118; www.naka mura-ya.com/english.html; N3W7-1 Chūō-ku; r per person high season from ¥7875, low season ¥7350;

QUIRKY HOKKAIDŌ EVENTS

Sapporo Yuki Matsuri might grab most of the headlines, but there are plenty of quirky Hokkaidō events worth seeking out. Here are a few of our favourites:

» **Marimo Matsuri** in Akan Kohan – return fuzzballs of algae to Akan-ko (p516)

» **Orochon-no-hi** (Fire Festival) in Abashiri – fire dancers gyrate in flames (p511)

» **Japan Cup Zenkoku Inu-zori Wakkanai Taikai** (Japan Cup Dogsled Race) in Wakkanai – watch as dogs dash and fur flies (p496)

» **Kyōkoku Hi Matsuri** (Fire Festival) at Sōunkyō Onsen – flaming arrows are shot into a gorge (p509)

» **Come Back Salmon Night** in Abashiri – grill seafood while watching salmon return to spawn (p511)

» **Heso Matsuri** (Navel Festival) in Furano – celebrate innies and outies in style (p504)

@🛜) Located on a small side street that right angles the entrance to the botanical gardens, this charming little Japanese-style inn is a wonderful introduction to the pleasures of the island. A variety of different plans are available, featuring tatami rooms of varying shapes and sizes, as well as lavish feasts incorporating the unique flavours of Hokkaidō. All guests can also relax in the on-site bath, and the owner-managers are well equipped to deal with the needs of foreigner travellers.

Cross Hotel Sapporo HOTEL $$

(☎272-0010; www.crosshotel.com/eng_sapporo; N3W2 Chūō-ku; s/d from ¥10,000/12,600; @🛜) This shimmering modernist tower is located about five minutes south of the JR Sapporo Station on foot. The interior is a veritable designer's showcase, with chic rooms categorised according to three thematic styles: urban, natural and hip. The hotel's signature restaurant is an organic Italian eatery with a companion lounge and cocktail bar. As an added bonus, there is a steel- and glass-enclosed onsen that allows you to stare out at the city while you soak in a steaming tub.

JR Tower Hotel Nikko Sapporo HOTEL $$$

(☎251-2222; fax 251-6370; www.jrhotelgroup .com/eng/hotel/eng101.htm; N5W2 Chūō-ku; s/d from ¥18,000/26,000; @🛜) You can't beat the location at this lofty hotel, which is firmly attached to the JR Sapporo Station. Taking advantage of such great heights, the Hotel Nikko Sapporo offers plush rooms priced by floor, a spa with a view on the 22nd floor, and both Western and Japanese restaurants perched on the 35th floor. The views from the top are some of the best in the city, so be sure to stop by for dinner (see Mikuni Sapporo in Eating), a drink (see Sky J in Drinking) or even a beauty treatment at the on-site holistic spa.

Ino's Place HOSTEL $

(イノーズプレイス; ☎832-1828; http://inos -place.com/e/; dm/s/d from ¥2900/4300/7600; @🛜) While youth hostels in Japan are often stale and sterilised affairs with strict rules and little to no English on hand, Ino's Place is a true backpackers' spot with all the fixings. Friendly and bilingual staff are on hand to make your stay warm and welcome, while clean rooms, private lockers, free internet, no curfew, a Japanese bath, laundry facilities, a kitchen and a communal lounge space sweeten the deal. To reach Ino's, take the Tōzai line to the Shiroishi stop (four past Ōdōri); take exit 1 and walk straight for a few minutes along the main street in the direction of the Eneos petrol station. Turn right at the Marue supermarket and you'll see a detached two-storey white building – you've arrived!

Hotel Gracery Sapporo HOTEL $$

(☎251-3211; www.gracery.com/en/sapporo/index .html; N4W4-1 Chūō-ku; s/d from ¥6000/10,000; @🛜) The former Sapporo Washington Hotel has been completely remodelled and subsequently relaunched as a stylish yet affordable boutique hotel. The design is minimalist meets industrial with a splash of colour. Rooms vary in price depending on the design and layout, and there are even specially designated executive and women's-only floors. The property is connected to the JR Sapporo Station by an underground shopping passage, which comes in handy when the mercury drops.

Hotel Monterey Edelhof Sapporo HOTEL $$$

(ホテルモントレエーデルホフ札幌; ☎242-7111; fax 232-1212; www.hotelmonterey .co.jp/eng/index.htm; N2W1 Chūō-ku; s/d from ¥15,500/17,000; @🛜) A few minutes south of the station, opposite the JR Sapporo Railway Hospital, this seemingly modern hotel lords it over the street like a concrete monolith, though the interior is fully decked out in a somewhat out-of-place but surprisingly amenable Austrian theme. While the opulent lobby and ornate rooms are Continental inspired, the various dining rooms and onsen are Japanese through and through.

Sapporo Grand Hotel HOTEL $$$

(札幌グランドホテル; ☎261-3311; fax 231-0388; www.grand1934.com/english/index.html; N1W4 Chūō-ku; r from ¥20,000; @🛜) Established in 1934 as the first European-style hotel in Sapporo, this grand old dame now occupies three adjacent buildings that lie at the southeast corner of the former Hokkaidō government building. Fairly subdued rooms vary considerably in price and style, though all guests are seemingly treated to VIP service from arrival to checkout.

Sapporo International Youth Hostel HOSTEL $

(札幌国際ユースホステル; ☎825-3120; www.youthhostel.or.jp/kokusai; 6-5-35 Toyohira-ku; dm/r per person from ¥3300/3800; @🛜)

Housed in a surprisingly modern and stylish building that could give most business hotels a run for their money, this well-conceived youth hostel has perfected the basics by offering simple but sparkling rooms to budget travellers. Both Western- and Japanese-style private rooms are available, as well as 'dorm rooms' featuring four full-sized beds. The closest subway stop is Gakuen-mae (exit 2) on the Toho line; the hostel is just two minutes from the station behind the Sapporo International Student Centre.

Marks Inn Sapporo
HOTEL $$

(マークスイン札幌; ☎512-5001; www.marks-inn.com/sapporo/english.html; S8W3 Chūō-ku; s/d from ¥4500/6000; @☎) If you want private accommodation, you really can't get cheaper than this business hotel on the edge of the Susukino entertainment district, right across from the canal. Rooms are a bit cramped, but the feathery beds are soft, and become even softer if you party too hard in Susukino and stumble back in the wee hours of the morning.

Capsule Inn Sapporo
HOTEL $

(カプセル・イン札幌; ☎251-5571; www.capsuleinn-s.com/english.html; S3W3-7 Chūō-ku; r per person ¥2800) If you're a man of simple needs who doesn't get scared easily by small spaces, this XY-chromosome-only capsule hotel offers your standard berth plus a sauna, large bathroom, coin laundry and even a 'book corner' with reclining chairs. It's located a stone's throw from the Susukino subway station on the Nanboku line. Take exit 1, go to the KFC and turn right on the side street – you should see the inn on the left, about halfway down. A 6am-to-6pm 'rest' is also an option (¥1200).

Keiō Plaza Hotel Sapporo
HOTEL $$$

(京王プラザホテル札幌; ☎271-0111; www.keioplaza-sapporo.co.jp/english/index2.html; N5W7 Chūō-ku; r from ¥20,000; ❄@☎✈) Lies at the northeast corner of the botanical gardens, and offers a suite of upmarket amenities.

Tōyoko Inn Sapporo-eki Kita-guchi
HOTEL $$

(東横イン札幌駅北口; ☎728-1045; fax 728-1046; www.toyoko-inn.com/e_hotel/00066; N6W1-4-3 Kita-ku; s/d Nov-May ¥5040/6800, Jun-Oct ¥6825/9240; @☎) A convenient clutch of Tōyoko Inns grace the JR station environs. Look for considerable discounts in the winter months.

Sapporo House Youth Hostel
HOSTEL $

(札幌ハウスユースホステル; ☎726-4235; www.youthhostel.or.jp/English/c_sapporohouse.htm; N6W6-3-1 Kita-ku; dm from ¥3750; @) A few minutes on foot west of JR Sapporo Station, located just beside the train tracks.

🍴 Eating

In addition to its namesake beer, Sapporo is famous for its miso-based *rāmen* (egg noodles), which makes use of Hokkaidō's delicious butter and fresh corn. The city also serves up some truly incredible seafood, winter-warming stews and *jingisukan*, an easy-to-love dish of roasted lamb that pays tribute to everybody's favourite Mongol warlord, Genghis Khan.

For a complete rundown of the island's unique cuisine, see the box, p484.

TOP CHOICE Kani-honke
SEAFOOD $$$

(札幌かに本家; ☎222-0018; N3W2 Chūō-ku; set courses from ¥4000; ⏰11.30am-10pm) The frigid seas surrounding Hokkaidō are extremely bountiful and yield some of the tastiest crustaceans on the planet. There is no better place to dine on all manner of exotic crab than at the famous Kani-honke, which serves up elaborate *kaiseki ryōri* (Japanese cuisine following strict rules of etiquette) centred on these juicy little critters. Seasonal set courses are priced according to the size and rarity of the crab, so simply choose depending on how much you want to spend. Don't miss the opportunity to sample the *tarabagani* (red king crab), which is considered to be the most expensive yet most delicious decapod known to humankind.

Yosora-no-Jingisukan
JINGISUKAN $$

(夜空のジンギスカン; ☎219-1529; www.yozojin.com/main-yozora.htm; 10th fl, S4W4 Chūō-ku; plates from ¥850; ⏰5pm-2.30am) Genghis Khan is on the menu everywhere, though at this speciality restaurant, located on the 10th floor of the My Plaza building, across from a 7-Eleven, you can grill up tender slices of locally raised lamb, as well as more exotic cuts from Australia and Iceland. There is no English, though the handy picture menu makes ordering a breeze.

Shōjin Restaurant Yō
VEGAN $$

(精進レストラン葉; ☎562-7020; S17W7-2-12 Chūō-ku; dishes from ¥1250; ⏰11.30am-4.30pm Mon & Tue, to 8pm Thu-Sun; ☎🅿) Macrobiotic, organic and vegan fare that's attractively presented and very tasty. The shop is beautifully

style bar and Zen-style flower arrangements. To get here, take the Nanboku line and get off at Horohirabashi. Go left out of the station and veer right at the first traffic signal. The road curves, passing a park (on the right). Go straight through the next signal and turn left when you hit the next one (at the tram line); the restaurant is a few doors down on the right.

Mikuni Sapporo
FRENCH $$$

(☎251-0392; 9th fl, Stellar Pl, N5W2 Chūō-ku; lunch/dinner courses from ¥3200/8000; ⊙lunch & dinner) Classical French with a subtle Japanese twist is *de rigueur* at this much-celebrated restaurant, located on the 9th floor of the JR Tower at Sapporo Station. Seasonality dictates the menu, with the culinary palette spanning from sun-ripened produce to winter hauls of snow crab. Although it's pricey to call forth a bottle, Mikuni has one of the largest and most extensive wine cellars in the city. There is French but no English on the menu – non-Francophones can select a course based on price. Stop by for lunch if you want a reasonable splurge.

Kushidori
YAKITORI $$

(串鳥; ☎758-2989; www.sapnet.ne.jp/kusidori, in Japanese; N7W4-8-3 Kita-ku; skewers from ¥150; ⊙4.30pm-12.30am) A famous Sapporo-only chain serving a variety of *yakitori* (skewers of grilled chicken) and grilled vegetables, Kushidori is usually packed with boisterous college kids and 20-somethings. While there is no English menu, you can simply point at what you want, and the chef will grill it for you – choose from either *tare* (sauce) or *shio* (salt). There are locations all around the city, including one just a few blocks north of JR Sapporo Station (look for the English sign).

Rāmen Yokochō
RĀMEN $

(元祖さっぽろラーメン横丁; ⊙11am-3am) This famous alleyway in the Susukino entertainment district is crammed with dozens of *rāmen* shops, and you'll most likely wind up here in a noble attempt to vanquish your hangover. Anyone with a yen for *rāmen* shouldn't miss it, but it can be difficult to find. Take the Nanboku line to Susukino and walk south to the first crossroad. Turn left (east); Rāmen Yokochō is halfway down on the right. If you can't find it just ask – it's one place people *will* know. Hours vary for different shops, though prices are consistently cheap, with a bowl of noodles setting you back no more than ¥1000.

Hirihiri-dō
JAPANESE SOUP CURRY $

(スープカレー工房ひりひり堂; ☎643-1710; N2-27-5W2 Nishu-ku; soups from ¥850; ⊙lunch & dinner Tue-Sun) A Sapporo staple, soup curry is an inventive way to warm the body and spice up your palette, especially on a blistery winter day. As its name implies, soup curry is quite simply a soupier version of Japanese curry – there is no English menu here, but it's easy enough to trust your nose and point to the best-smelling vat. The restaurant is located just outside JR Sapporo Station's west exit – look for the red building with the pepper on the window.

Ni-jō Ichiba
MARKET $$

(⊙5am-9am) The fish market is one of the best places in town for sushi and sashimi so fresh it's still twitching.

Esta
RESTAURANTS $$

(エスタ; ⊙7am-9pm) Fussy eaters who like to window shop should head straight to this giant restaurant floor that forms part of the Paseo Shopping Centre at JR Sapporo Station; one major path to the subway leads right through it. Listen for the singsong '*Ikagadeshou~~ka?*' (Take a look?) and you'll know you've arrived.

🍷 Drinking & Entertainment

Sapporo-ites are famous for their love of the drink, though you can hardly blame them as the beer here really does seem to taste better. (If you want to drink delicious Sapporo lager straight from the source, don't miss Sapporo Beer-En; see the box, p470.) While there are literally hundreds of bars and clubs scattered throughout the city, all of the action and nightlife revolves around Susukino, the largest entertainment district north of Tokyo.

The places listed are all within easy stumbling distance of the Susukino subway station, and are some of Sapporo's party landmarks, though you can always simply follow the crowds to whatever is new and trendy. Generally, some bars and most clubs have a cover charge of ¥1000 to ¥3000 on Friday and Saturday nights, which often includes one or two drinks.

Sky J
LOUNGE

(35th fl, JR Tower, N5W2 Chūō-ku; ⊙11.30am-2.30pm & 5.30pm-close) There is some truth to the observation that cocktails seem to taste better when consumed at great heights. Here on the 35th floor of the JR Tower, the views of the Sapporo skyline twinkle to the tune of live piano and jazz music, not to mention the muted whispers of sophisticated patrons dressed to the nines.

alife
CLUB

(エーライフ; www.alife.jp/pc, in Japanese; B1F Tailki Bldg, S4W6 Chūō-ku; ⊗8pm-close) This well-heeled club brings a bit of the Tokyo high life to the far north. Although the thermometer might be dropping outside, it's always hot and heavy in this cavernous joint, so dress to impress!

500 Bar
BAR

(ファイブハンドレッドバー; 1st fl, Hoshi Bldg, S4W2 Chūō-ku; ⊗6pm-5am Mon-Sat, to 2am Sun & holidays) Usually packed, even on weekdays, with a mix of foreign and local clientele, every drink on the menu here is ¥500, hence the name (pronounced *'gohyakubaa'*). This is one of the franchise's several locations in Sapporo, right across the street from the Susukino subway station's Nanboku line.

Booty
CLUB

(ブーティー; www.booty-disco.com; S7W4 Chūō-ku; ⊗8pm-close) There's always plenty of booty at this discotheque and lounge bar, which serves up Western-style fast food alongside urban beats. The rotating schedule incorporates the best in hip-hop, R&B and reggae, which attracts a young and clubby crowd.

❶ Information

Internet Access

Comic Land (コミックランド三越前店; http://i-comicland.com; 2nd fl, Hinode Bldg, S1W4 Chūō-ku; per 30min from ¥200; ⊗24hr) Has showers and reclining chairs; offers fixed fees as well as half-hourly rates.

i-café (アイ・カフェ; http://sapporocrh.i-cafe.ne.jp, in Japanese; N5W5 Gochōme 2-12 Chūō-ku; per 30min from ¥200; ⊗24hr) Provides free snacks in addition to the usual coffee/drinks.

Medical Services

Dial 119 for a medical emergency. JR Sapporo and Sapporo City hospitals require that non-emergency patients arrive before noon.

JR Sapporo Railway Hospital (JR札幌病院; 241-4971; N3E1 Chūō-ku) Close to JR Sapporo Station; no emergency room.

Medical Plaza Sapporo (メディカルプラザ札幌; 209-5410; N5W2 Chūō-ku) Conveniently located on the 7th and 8th floors of the JR Tower in JR Sapporo Station.

Sapporo City General Hospital (市立札幌病院; 726-2211; N11W13 1-1 Chūō-ku) Offers 24-hour emergency care.

Money

With the exception of 7-Eleven convenience stores, ATMs on the street do not accept non-Japanese-issued cards. However, you can always withdraw cash from the postal ATMs.

Post

Sapporo Chūō Post Office (札幌中央郵便局; N6E1-2-1 Higashi-ku)

Sapporo Ōdōri Post Office (札幌大通郵便局; 2-9 Ōdōri-nishi, Chūō-ku)

Tourist Information

Hokkaidō-Sapporo Food & Tourist Information Centre (北海道さっぽろ「食と観光」情報館; 213-5088; fax 213-5089; www.welcome.city.sapporo.jp/english/index.html; N5W3 Chūō-ku, JR Sapporo Station Nishi-dōri Kitaguchi; ⊗8.30am-8pm) Located on the 1st floor of Sapporo Stellar Pl, inside JR Sapporo Station. This is the island's mother lode of tourist information, so stock up on maps, timetables, brochures and pamphlets, and be sure to make use of the friendly and helpful bilingual staff.

Sapporo International Communication Plaza Foundation (札幌国際プラザ; 211-3670; www.plaza-sapporo.or.jp/english/index_e.html; 1st fl, MN Bldg, N1W3 Chūō-ku; ⊗9am-5.30pm) An extensive list of English resources, as well as free internet access.

Travel Agencies

IACE Travel (IACEトラベル; 219-2796; fax 219-2766; 9th fl, Kita San Jō Bldg, N3W3 Chūō-ku; ⊗10am-7pm Mon-Fri, to 4pm Sat, closed Sun) A popular Japanese travel agency that also caters to foreigners, and is useful for making international travel arrangements.

JTB Shop (JTBショップ; 241-6201; N3W3 Chūō-ku; ⊗10am-7pm) This popular Japanese travel agency is useful for making domestic travel arrangements, including plane and train bookings.

❶ Getting There & Away

Air

Sapporo's main airport is **New Chitose Airport** (新千歳空港; Shin-Chitose Kūkō), about 40km south of the city. Domestic destinations include Tokyo, Osaka, Nagoya, Hiroshima and many others. See p755 for details of international flights.

There's a smaller airport at **Okadama** (丘珠空港; Okadama Kūkō), about 10km north of the city, which has limited service to cities in Hokkaidō.

Bus

Highway buses connect Sapporo with the rest of Hokkaidō, and are generally cheaper than trains and even time-competitive on some routes. **Sapporo Eki-mae bus station** (札幌駅バスターミ

ナル) is the main terminal, just southeast of JR Sapporo Station, beneath Esta. The **Chūō bus station** (中央バス札幌ターミナル; southeast of JR Sapporo Station) and **Ōdōri bus centre** (北海道中央バス札幌ターミナル) are also departure spots. At all three departure points you will find ticket booths from where you can purchase tickets to major cities throughout Hokkaidō.

Some sample destinations, which have frequent daily departures from Sapporo Eki-mae:

Asahikawa ¥2000, two hours
Furano ¥2100, three hours
Niseko ¥2300, three hours
Noboribetsu Onsen ¥2100, two hours
Tōya-ko Onsen ¥2700, 2¾ hours
Wakkanai ¥6000, six hours

From Chūō bus station there are a few departures a day to Abashiri (¥6210, 6¼ hours) and Obihiro (¥3670, 4¼ hours).

Buses to Hakodate depart from both the Chūō and Ōdōri bus stations (¥4680, 5¼ hours).

Discounted round-trip tickets are available for most routes.

Car & Motorcycle

The best place in Hokkaidō to pick up a rental car is at the New Chitose Airport. While you might have to backtrack a bit if you're heading north, some people find this preferable to picking up a vehicle in Sapporo, and subsequently navigating through the busy city centre. There are just under a dozen different companies located in the arrivals area on the 1st floor, which makes it easy to shop around the various booths and quickly compare prices.

If you'd prefer to pick up your vehicle in Sapporo, it's recommended that you deal with **Toyota Rent a Car** (トヨタレンタカー; http://rent.toyota.co.jp/en/index.html; N5E2-1 Chūō-ku; ⏲8am-10pm). In addition to being conveniently located near JR Sapporo Station, the company is a bit better at dealing with foreigners than most rental-car dealers. There's no guarantee the staff will speak English – if you have problems, you can always try to make arrangements in advance through the tourist information centre.

Train

The **Hokutosei** (北斗星; www.jreast.co.jp/cassiopeia/hokutosei/index.html) is a *tokkyū* sleeper train that runs between Tokyo's JR Ueno Station and JR Sapporo Station. There is one departure in both directions every evening, and the total journey time is around 16½ hours, which puts you in your destination the following morning. Ticket prices vary depending on the distance travelled, as well as the type of accommodation you choose.

The base fare for a journey from Tokyo to Sapporo is ¥17,930, plus an extra ¥2940 limited-express train charge. On top of this, you need to pay a fee for accommodation – prices range from ¥6300 for a private sleeping berth to ¥17,180 for the 'royal room'. Note that this flat fee is charged regardless of starting or ending location. If you're travelling on a JR Pass, you do not have to pay the base fare and limited-express charge, but you have to pay the accommodation fare. Full-on French and formal Japanese meals are available on board with advance reservation, though meal service is not included in the ticket price.

A much more luxurious option is the **Cassiopeia** (カシオペア; www.jreast.co.jp/cassiopeia), a *tokkyū* sleeper train that runs three times a week between Tokyo and Sapporo. There are three evening departures in both directions every week, and the total journey time is also around 16½ hours. Base fares and limited-express train charges are equivalent to the *Hokutosei*, and are again waived if you have a JR Pass, though accommodation is more expensive, ranging from ¥13,350 for a twin room to ¥25,490 for a full-on suite. These prices are on par with an upmarket hotel, and sleeper cars on the *Cassiopeia* are something akin to a four-star resort on wheels. The night train also has sophisticated dining cars offering Michelin-star quality meals, which are not included in the ticket price, and must be booked in advance. Note that single travellers must pay for the full price of a room, so it's advised that you have a travel companion.

Reservations for both the *Hokutosei* and the *Cassiopeia* can be made at any JR ticket counter or travel agency. These trains are very popular and often booked solid, particularly in the summer months, so make a reservation as far in advance as possible.

Additionally, there are hourly trains on the JR Tōhoku *shinkansen* between Tokyo and Hachinohe (¥15,350, three hours). Hachinohe is connected to Sapporo by the JR Tsugaru Kaikyō line and Hakodate lines – hourly *tokkyū* trains run through the Seikan Tunnel (see the box, p477) between Hachinohe and Hakodate (¥7230, three hours), and between Hakodate and Sapporo (¥8590, 3½ hours).

There are hourly *kaisoku* (rapid) trains on the JR Hakodate line between Sapporo and Otaru (¥620, 40 minutes). Finally, Super Kamui *tokkyū* trains run twice an hour between Sapporo and Asahikawa (¥4480, 1½ hours).

ⓘ Getting Around

To/From the Airport

New Chitose Airport is accessible from Sapporo by *kaisoku* train (¥1340, 35 minutes) or bus (¥1000, 1¼ hours). There are also convenient bus services connecting the airport to various Hokkaidō destinations including Niseko.

A modern marvel of Japanese engineering, this railway tunnel travels beneath the Tsugaru Strait, connecting the islands of Honshū and Hokkaidō. With a total length of 53.85km, including a 240m-deep and 23.3km-long undersea portion, the Seikan Tunnel (青函トンネル) is the deepest and longest undersea tunnel in the world.

Prior to 2006, you could actually get off the train and take a subterranean tour of the tunnel's inner workings. However, since the Hokkaidō *shinkansen* is currently under construction, and scheduled for completion in 2015, tours will not recommence during the shelf life of this book. But once construction concludes, it is likely that passengers will be allowed to disembark and tour the station as in the past.

For Okadama airport, buses leave every 20 minutes or so from in front of the ANA ticket offices, opposite JR Sapporo Station (¥400, 30 minutes).

Bus & Tram

JR Sapporo Station is the main terminus for local buses. From late April to early November, tourist buses loop through major sights and attractions between 9am and 5.30pm; a one-day pass costs ¥750, single trips are ¥200 (basic fee).

There is a single tram line that heads west from Ōdōri, turns south, then loops back to Susukino (すすきの). The fare is a flat ¥170.

Taxi

Taxis are a quick and comfortable way to move around the city, but you'll pay substantially for the convenience factor. Flagfall is ¥650, which gives you 2km (1.5km after 11pm), after which the meter starts to clock an additional ¥90 for every 300m, or two minutes in traffic.

Subway

Sapporo's three subways are efficient. Fares start at ¥200 and one-day passes cost ¥800 (weekend-only passes are ¥500 per day). There are also ¥1000 day passes that include the tram and buses as well. The pay-in-advance With You card (various denominations available) can be used on subways, buses, trams, and Jōtetsu and Chūō buses; unlike the one-day passes, it does not expire at midnight.

SOUTHERN HOKKAIDŌ

Southern Hokkaidō (道南; Dō-nan) is often bypassed entirely by Sapporo-bound travellers, who use the capital's transportation network as a springboard for more remote destinations. However, this is unfortunate as it's certainly worth getting off the train in Hakodate, a prominent Meiji-era port that is one of the most atmospheric cities in Hokkaidō. Dō-nan is also home to a couple of small but historically significant towns, which bear striking architectural reminders of the Edo period.

Hakodate 函館

📞 0138 / POP 288,000

Built on a narrow strip of land between Hakodate Harbour to the west and the Tsugaru Strait to the east, hourglass-shaped Hakodate is the southern gateway to the island of Hokkaidō. Under the Kanagawa Treaty of 1854, the city was one of the first ports to open up to international trade, and as such hosted a small foreign community. Much of that influence can still be seen in the Motomachi district, a steep hillside that is sprinkled with wooden buildings and brick churches. You can also get a sense of history by riding nostalgic trams through the orderly streets, or by watching the squid boats, with their traditional lantern lights, bob gently in the bay.

⊙ Sights

Hours for attractions listed are for peak season (generally April to October); most have reduced hours the rest of the year.

Motomachi HISTORIC DISTRICT
(元町) On Mt Hakodate's lower slopes, this area is home to the lion's share of 19th-century sites, and commands stunning panoramic views of the bay. The places in the following listings are all located in close proximity to one another, and are easily reached on foot.

To get to Motomachi, take tram 5 from the station and get off at the Suehiro-chō stop, then walk uphill for 10 minutes. Alternatively, get off at the end of the line and walk along the waterfront first, visit the cemetery, then stop at the buildings as you walk uphill to Suehiro-chō.

Central Hakodate

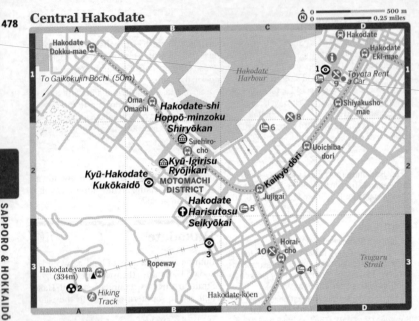

Central Hakodate

Kyū-Hakodate Kukōkaidō
(旧函館区公会堂; 11-13 Motomachi; admission ¥300; ⊙9am-7pm) The old Public Hall of Hakodate Ward is an ornate mansion awash in pale blues and yellows that reigns regally over the district. Inside are items of historical interest relating to the city, although the main appeal is the wonderful colonial-style architecture – and the opportunity for visitors to dress up! In true Japanese fashion, you can indulge in a bit of costume play by donning a Meiji-era high-collar dress, and prancing around the estate like a reigning monarch.

Kyū-Igirisu Ryōjikan
(旧イギリス領事館; 33-14 Motomachi; admission ¥300, afternoon tea from ¥550; ⊙9am-7pm) From 1913 to 1934, this whitewashed mansion served as the British consulate, though today it's primarily used as a tea salon for sightseers in need of some bergamot-scented afternoon respite.

Hakodate Harisutosu Seikyōkai
(函館ハリストス正教会; 3-13 Motomachi; admission ¥200; ⊙10am-5pm Mon-Fri, 10am-4pm Sat, 1-4pm Sun) Dating from 1916, this beautiful old Russian Orthodox church is adorned with distinctive copper domes and spires.

Gaikokujin Bochi
(外国人墓地; ⊙dawn-dusk) The Foreigners' Cemetery, an interesting slice of local history, has the graves of sailors, clergy and

others who unfortunately died far away from their homelands. Many of the graves are marked with English, Russian or French inscriptions.

Hakodate-shi Hoppō-minzoku Shiryōkan (函館市北方民族資料館; 21-7 Suehiro-chō; admission ¥300; ⊙9am-7pm) The Hakodate City Museum of Northern Peoples is a recommended place to learn about the Ainu and their material culture. English signs have been added to some exhibits.

Hakodate-yama   MOUNTAIN

(函館山) This small mountain (334m) offers a memorable view of Hakodate, especially at night when the twinkling city lights contrast the dark waters. A **ropeway** (ロープウェイ; www.334.co.jp/en/index.html; one way/return ¥640/1160; ⊙10am-10pm) whisks you to the top in a few minutes.

A 10-minute walk from the summit is a car park. At its far end there is an overgrown path that leads to moss-covered walls and buttresses, the ruins of an old fort, **Hakodateyama Yōsai** (函館山要塞; admission free). It's refreshingly deserted, and you can happily clamber around, Indiana Jones–style, among ferns with fronds the size of palm leaves.

Take tram 2 or 5 to the Jūjigai stop, and walk a few minutes uphill to the ropeway platform. Alternatively, a summit-bound bus (¥360, 30 minutes) leaves directly from the station, and stops at several viewing places as it winds to the top. Those wanting to rough it old style can take the **hiking track** (from May to late October).

FREE Hakodate Asa-ichi   MARKET

(函館朝市; ⊙5am-noon) Located just to the right of JR Hakodate Station, this market is a great place for hungry seafood lovers. Like tightly packed ammo, freshly caught squid glisten in ice-stuffed Styrofoam. Most of the live commerce is over by 8am, but you can still pick up snacks and souvenirs during the closing hours.

FREE Goryō-kaku   FORT

(五稜郭) Japan's first Western-style fort was built in 1864 in the shape of a five-pointed star (*goryō-kaku* means 'five-sided fort'), and was designed to trap attackers in deadly crossfire. Nothing remains of the actual fort structure, but the landscaped grounds and moat are picturesque, and the moss-covered walls are quite fun to scramble upon.

To reach the fort, take tram 2 or 5 to the Goryōkaku-kōen-mae stop. From there it's a 10-minute walk.

Yachigashira Onsen   ONSEN

(谷地頭温泉; 20-7 Yachigashira; admission ¥390; ⊙6am-9.30pm, closed every 2nd & 4th Tue) On the southern edge of Hakodate-yama is this enormous hot spring, one of Hokkaidō's oldest, with dark iron-laden water. To get here, take tram 2 to Yachigashira, the final stop. On foot, continue to the first intersection and then turn right – you'll see the public bathhouse complex on the left shortly after you turn.

★★ Festivals & Events

Hakodate Goryōkaku Matsuri   HISTORY

Held on the third weekend in May, this festival features a parade of townsfolk dressed in the uniforms of the soldiers who took part in the Meiji Restoration battle of 1868.

Hakodate Minato Matsuri   PORT

During the Hakodate Port Festival in early August, groups of seafood-fortified locals (reportedly 10,000 of them) move like waves doing an energetic squid dance.

☷ Sleeping

TOP CHOICE La Vista Hakodate Bay   HOTEL $$$

(ラビスタ函館ベイ; ☑23-6111; www.hotespa .net/hotels/lahakodate/english_room.html; 12-6 Toyokawacho; r from ¥13,300; @☎) This truly excellent upmarket hotel benefits from its location in Nishi-hatoba, a waterfront district with a variety of eateries in converted warehouses and English-style buildings. Rooms are very small, but the space constraints are forgivable given the art-deco interior design – indirect lighting, soothing hues, low-lying furniture, stained-wood accents and antique replicas. Check out the in-room coffee sets, which let you grind your own beans before setting up a slow-drip cup. There is also a rooftop onsen and spa complex, complete with soaking tubs overlooking the mountains and the bay, a *rotemburo* (outdoor bath) that lets you bathe outside in the midst of a snowfall, a sauna and steam room duo, an *akasuri* body-scrubbing station and a dedicated massage studio.

La Villa Concordia   HOTEL $$$

(ヴィラ・コンコルディア; ☑24-5300; http:// villa-concordia.com, in Japanese; 3-5 Suehiro; r from ¥42,000; @☎) Although it operates as

MATSUMAE & ESASHI

On this worthwhile day trip you can visit the only castle on Hokkaidō, explore the regal dwellings of the island's former fishing barons, and be back in Hakodate with enough time to watch the sunset from atop Hakodate-yama.

Matsumae

Prior to the start of the Meiji era, this town was the stronghold of the Matsumae clan and the centre of Japanese political power in Hokkaidō. As a result, Matsumae (松前) is home to the only castle on the island. **Matsumae-jō** (松前城; admission ¥270; ⏰9am-5pm mid-Apr–Dec) dates from the 19th century, and currently houses feudal relics and a small collection of Ainu items.

Frequent *tokkyū* on the JR Esashi line run between Hakodate and Kikonai (¥1620, 35 minutes). Regular buses run between JR Kikonai Station and Matsumae (¥1220, 1½ hours).

Esashi

If Matsumae was Hokkaidō's Edo-period political centre, then Esashi (江差) was its economic lifeblood. Prior to the depletion of fishing stocks in the early 20th century, a number of *nishingoten* (herring barons' homes) dominated the shoreline. Today several of these buildings remain – **Yokoyama-ke** (横山家; admission ¥300; ⏰9am-5pm) and **Kyū Nakamura-ke Jyūtaku** (旧中村家住宅; admission ¥300; ⏰9am-5pm) in particular are well preserved.

Frequent *tokkyū* on the JR Esashi line run between Hakodate and Kikonai (¥1620, 35 minutes). Kikonai is connected to Esashi by the JR Esahi line – a few daily *kaisoku* ply this route (¥900, one hour).

---

a full-service resort and spa, La Villa Concordia is packaged as a boutique hotel, which ensures that you'll have customised attention throughout your stay – even if Japanese isn't your first language. Rooms range in size from deluxe studios with kitchenettes to full-on suites overlooking the harbour. Round out your stay with a pampering beauty treatment and a proper meal of Italian-French fusion. The property is located one block from the Suehiro-chō 3 traffic light – look for the white neoclassical structure.

Hakodate Youth Guesthouse HOSTEL $
(函館ユースゲストハウス; ☎26-7892; www12.ocn.ne.jp/~hakodate, in Japanese; 17-6 Hōraimachi; dm Oct-Jun ¥3800, Jul & Sep ¥4200, Aug ¥4500; @🔒) Wholesome, family-friendly accommodation complete with 9am home-made ice-cream parties and 11pm curfews, the Hakodate Youth Guesthouse is a relaxed and affordable base for budget travellers. It's conveniently located near the Hōrai-chō tram stop – after getting off the tram, turn left at the first light, then go past two more lights and turn right. The guesthouse is across the street from a supermarket and car park.

Tōyoko Inn Hakodate Eki-mae Asaichi HOTEL $$
(東横イン函館駅前朝市; ☎23-1045; www.toyoko-inn.com/e_hotel/00063/index.html; 22-7 Ōtemachi; s/d Nov-May ¥4210/6825, Jun-Oct ¥5460/7980; @📶) While it's positively characterless in comparison to more upmarket offerings, this Tōyoko clone remains the most affordable choice for budget-conscious travellers in need of private space. It's located just steps away from the morning market, and only three minutes on foot from JR Hakodate Station.

🍴 Eating & Drinking

Hakodate Rāmen Kamome RĀMEN $
(函館らーめん かもめ; ☎22-1727; 8-2 Wakamatsuchō; rāmen from ¥580; ⏰6.30am-3.30pm) A famous noodle shop (just look for the blue awning) where you can put your culinary skills to the test – you can start with a basic bowl of miso *rāmen* (¥580), and add *kani* (crab), *ebi* (shrimp), *ika* (squid), *hotate* (scallops) and/or *uni* for a few hundred extra yen. The shop is located across the street from the fish market, so you can be reassured that everything here is fresh.

Hakodate Beer
PUB $$

(はこだてビール; ☎23-8000; 5-22 Ōtemachi; dishes from ¥650; ☺11am-10pm; 🅿) Next to the Hakodate Kokusai Hotel (函館国際ホテル), this expansive brick building has live music and boisterous crowds. Scan the English menu, and choose from a variety of microbrews – from cold ales and golden wheat beers to dark stouts – to complement homemade pizzas and various items from the grill including fresh-caught squid and locally made sausages.

Hishī
CAFE $

(ひし伊; ☎27-3300; 9-4 Hōraichō; snacks from ¥525; ☺10am-5pm) Hishi-sabō, part cafe, part antique shop, is an unmistakable ivy-covered *kura* (mud-walled storehouse) that is situated just one block west from the Hōrai-chō tram stop. Even if you are not in the market for a used kimono, you cannot go wrong with a cup of English tea and a tasty gourmet waffle (*waffuru-setto;* ¥890).

ℹ Information

Hakodate Tourist Information Centre (函館市観光案内所; ☎23-544; ☺9am-7pm Apr-Oct, to 5pm Nov-Mar) Inside JR Hakodate Station.

ℹ Getting There & Away
Air

From Hakodate Airport, just a few kilometres east of the city centre, there are international flights to Seoul, and domestic flights to various destinations including Sapporo, Tokyo, Kansai and others.

Frequent buses run direct between Hakodate Airport and JR Hakodate Station (¥300, 20 minutes), or you can simply take a taxi (¥2000).

Boat

From Hakodate Harbour, **Higashi Nihon** (☎0120-756-564) operates eight daily ferries (departing year-round) between Aomori and Hakodate (from ¥4000, four hours), and two to three daily ferries between Hakodate and Ōma (¥1370, 1¾ hours) on the Shimokita Peninsula. The ferry terminal, where you also buy your tickets, is on the northeast corner of Hakodate Harbour.

Regular shuttle buses (¥250, 15 minutes) as well as taxis (¥1500) run between the ferry terminal and the train station.

Bus

There are five to six daily buses between JR Hakodate Station and Sapporo's Chūō bus station and Ōdōri bus centre (¥4680, 5¼ hours).

Car & Motorcycle

If you've just arrived in Hokkaidō, Hakodate is a good place to pick up a rental car and start your road-tripping adventure across the island. The recommended **Toyota Rent a Car** (トヨタレンタカー函館駅前; ☎26-0100; www.rent.toyota.co.jp; 19-2 Ōtemachi; ☺8am-8pm) has a branch office a few blocks southwest of the station.

Train

Frequent *tokkyū* on the JR Tsugaru Kaikyō line run between Hakodate and Aomori (¥5340, two hours) via the Seikan Tunnel (see the box, p477). There are also frequent *tokkyū* on the JR Hakodate line between Hakodate and Sapporo (¥8590, 3½ hours). Finally, a combination of *tokkyū* and *kaisoku* trains run on the JR Hakodate line between Hakodate and Niseko via Oshamambe (¥5410, 3½ hours).

For information on trains between Hakodate and Tokyo, see p476.

ℹ Getting Around

Single-trip fares on trams and buses are generally between ¥200 and ¥250, and are determined by how long you ride. One-day (¥1000) and two-day (¥1700) passes offer unlimited rides on both trams and buses (¥600 for tram alone), and are available at the tourist information centre or from the drivers. These passes are also good for the bus to the peak of Hakodate-yama.

CENTRAL HOKKAIDŌ

Central Hokkaidō (道央; Dō-ō) is where Hokkaidō garners its deserved reputation for stunning national parks, world-class ski slopes and rustic onsen towns. Although the scenic port town of Otaru is the largest population centre, the focus is on Niseko, where legendary powder attracts skiers and snowboarders from across the globe. And, while the French might have invented *après-ski*, it is the Japanese who have elevated this concept to an art form. After a long day on the frozen slopes, retire to a steamy onsen while nursing a fine bottle of sake – bliss!

BEST SCENIC DRIVES

» Hakodate (p477) to Sapporo (p466)
» Shikotsu-tōya National Park (p489)
» Asahikawa (p492) to Wakkanai (p496)
» Furano (p503) to Biei (p504)
» Pretty much anywhere in Eastern Hokkaidō (p510)

Otaru 小樽

♪ 0134 / POP 138,000

Resist the temptation to beeline straight for Niseko, and escape to Otaru for a weekend, a day or even an afternoon. One of Hokkaidō's most popular tourist destinations for Japanese visitors, Otaru is a romantic port town steeped in a rich history that dates back to its glory days as a major herring centre. Otaru was the terminal station for Hokkaidō's first railroad, and today nostalgic warehouses still line the picturesque canal district. Whether you stroll through the snow while holding your sweetheart's hand, or pace off the perfect shot while steadying your Nikon, Otaru will be a memorable visit.

⊙ Sights

Otaru Canal
CANAL

(小樽運河; Otaru Unga) Walk beneath the old Victorian-style gas lamps lining this historic canal, and admire the charismatic warehouses dating from the late 19th and early 20th centuries.

Kyū-Nippon Yūsen Kabushiki Kaisha Otaru-shiten

(旧日本郵船株式会社小樽支店; admission ¥300; ◉9.30am-5pm Tue-Sun) Lying behind the park at the northern end of the canal is the old Nippon Yūsen Company Building. Before the collapse of the herring industry, much of Hokkaidō's shipping orders were processed here. The interior of the building has been restored to its former grandeur, and provides a revealing look at the opulence of the era.

Otaru-shi Sōgō Hakubutsukan

(小樽市総合博物館; admission ¥300; ◉9.30am-5pm Tue-Sun) This small but engaging museum is housed in a restored warehouse dating from 1893, and has displays on Hokkaidō's natural history, some Ainu relics, and various special exhibitions on herring, ceramics and literature.

Nichigin-dōri
STREET

(日銀通り) Once known as the 'Wall Street of the North', Nichigin-dōri is lined with elegant buildings that speak to Otaru's past life as a prominent financial centre.

FREE Nippon-ginkō KyūOtaru-shiten

(日本銀行旧小樽支店金融資料館; ◉9.30am-5pm Tue-Sun) Don't miss the old Bank of Japan (日本銀行), a classic brick building that was designed by the same architect responsible for Tokyo Station. The exterior is marked by owl keystones, which pay homage to the Ainu guardian deity, while an impressive 100m-high ceiling highlights the interior.

🏃 Activities

K's Blowing
GLASS-BLOWING

(ケーズブローイング; www.ks-blowing.jp; lessons ¥1800-2500; ◉9am-4.30pm) At this famous gallery and studio, you can take a short lesson in glass-blowing (in English). Prices are based on what you want to make – simple but elegant cups, bowls and vases are all within your capacity.

🛏 Sleeping

TOP CHOICE Ginrinsō
RYOKAN $$$

(銀鱗荘; ♪54-7010; www.ginrinsou.com; 1-1 Sakura, Otaru Chikko; s/d with meals from ¥68,295/105,3000; @) Part of the Luxury Ryokan Collection, this is one of Hokkaidō's most spectacular accommodations, and a worthwhile splurge if you want to experience a living piece of history. Ginrinsō was originally constructed in 1873 as a herring estate, though in 1938 it began a new life as a top-end ryokan. Perched high on a bluff in Otaru Chikko, Ginrinsō stands like a sentry guarding the rocky coastline. The interior is given form by hand-shaped cedar beams and adorned with priceless antiques. The outdoor *rotemburo* is carved out of the rock, and faces out towards the sunset over Ishikari-wan. Lavish meals of French-Japanese fusion are served in a Meiji-style dining hall illuminated by chandeliers and candelabras. The property is located south of Otaru proper in close proximity to Otaru Chikko Station, but the staff can arrange transport from either Sapporo or Otaru with advance notice.

Hotel Nord Otaru
HOTEL $$

(ホテルノルド小樽; ♪24-0500; www.hotel nord.co.jp/english/index.htm; 1-4-16 Ironai; s/d from ¥7350/12,600; @) The Hotel Nord is a European-style hotel that fronts the warehouses along Otaru Canal. Check-in takes place beneath a vaulted ceiling, while sunlight (however faint at these extreme latitudes) illuminates a series of stained-glass windows. Fairly standard-issue rooms are priced according to size and view – the larger, canal-facing rooms are by far the most atmospheric.

Otaru

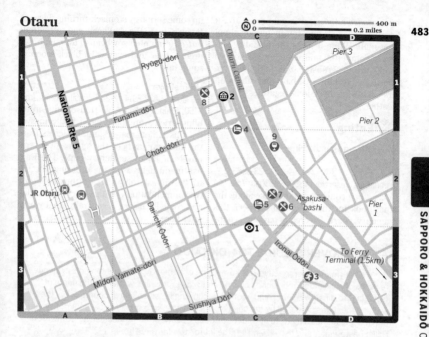

Hotel Vibrant Otaru
HOTEL $$

(ホテルヴィブラントオタル; ☑31-3939; www.vibrant-otaru.jp/en_index.html; 1-3-1 Ironai; s/d from ¥5500/6500, vault r from ¥10,500; @) A stylish renovation of a historic Otaru bank resulted in this justifiably 'vibrant hotel', which is located across the road from the main post office. The lobby is very attractive with period-piece furniture, including wrought-iron tables, though the somewhat disappointing rooms are of the business-hotel variety. For a memorable night's stay, shell out a bit of extra cash and bed down in the old bank vault!

Otarunai Backpackers' Hostel Morinoki
HOSTEL $

(おたるないバックパッカーズホステル杜の樹; ☑23-2175; http://backpackers-hostel.infotaru.net/en/; 4-15 Aioi-chō; dm ¥3200; @⊚) This is a great little backpacker spot that is worlds apart from your usual Japan YH offerings. Accommodation is in fairly simple male and female dormitories, though guests are treated to kitchen, laundry and internet facilities, as well as bilingual staff, communal lounges, and a laid-back and congenial vibe. The hostel is about a 20-minute walk from JR Otaru Station – exit, turn right and head straight through a series of traffic lights until you see the au-Mobile shop on the left-hand side.

Otaru

⊙ Sights
1 Nippon-ginkō KyūOtaru-shiten C3
2 Otaru-shi Sōgō Hakubutsukan C1

Activities, Courses & Tours
3 K's Blowing...D3

⊜ Sleeping
4 Hotel Nord Otaru C2
5 Hotel Vibrant Otaru C2

⊗ Eating
6 Denuki-kōji C2
7 Kita-no-aisukurīmu Yasan C2
8 Uminekoya B1

⊜ Drinking
9 Otaru Sōko No 1 ....C2

Turn left here, and continue straight until you see the big stone gate; make a right and you'll see the hostel on your left-hand side after about 100m.

Grand Park Hotel
HOTEL $$

(グランドパーク小樽; ☑21-3111; www.park hotelgroup.com/gpot; 11-3 Chikko, Otaru Chikko; r from ¥10,000, vault r from ¥10,500; @⊚) This business-friendly hotel is connected to JR Otaru Chikko Station by an indoor shopping mall. While it lacks the nostalgic setting of competing midrange hotels, modern rooms are generously sized, and the large offering of restaurants, bars and stores offers plenty of diversions regardless of the weather.

✕ Eating

TOP CHOICE Kita-no-aisukurīmu Yasan

ICE CREAM $

(北のアイスクリーム屋さん; ☎23-8983; 1-2-18 Ironai; ice cream from ¥350; ◷9.30am-7pm; ◨) Housed in a converted warehouse along the canal (look for the ice-cream banner), this legendary Otaru ice-cream parlour scoops up some seriously stomach-turning flavours. If you're up to the challenge, you can sample *nattō* (fermented soy beans), tofu, crab, sea urchin, beer and even a jet-black scoop of squid ink.

Uminekoya

SEAFOOD $$

(海猫屋; ☎32-2914; 2-2-14 Ironai; dishes from ¥750; ◷lunch & dinner; ◨) Housed in a crumbling brick warehouse laced with vines of ivy, this famous bar-restaurant across from the museum has been the setting for several novels of Japanese literary fame. The English menu helps with the ordering, though it's best to ask the waiter for their *osusume* (recommendation), as the catch of the day and some local sake is generally what you're after here.

A FOOD LOVER'S GUIDE TO HOKKAIDŌ

From a gourmand's perspective, it is something of a tragedy that little tangible evidence remains of Hokkaidō's indigenous cuisine. In 1878, a Yorkshire woman by the name of Isabella Bird dined with Ainu, and wrote the following lip-smacking account: 'Soon, the evening meal was prepared by the chief's principal wife, who tipped into a soot pot swinging over the flames a mixture of wild roots, beans, seaweed, shredded fish, dried venison, millet paste, water and fish oil, and left the lot to stew for three hours.'

Of course, the frontier spirit is still alive and well on the island, and Hokkaidō does remain a foodie's paradise. One Ainu dish that has survived the passage of time is **ruibe** (ルイベ), which is simply a salmon that has been left out in the Hokkaidō midwinter freeze, sliced up sashimi style, and then served with high-grade soy sauce and water peppers.

The Ainu tradition of hotpots is also being fostered by modern Japanese, and you'll find winter-warming **nabemono** (鍋物) all across the island. A particularly delicious variant of this dish is **ishikari-nabe** (石狩鍋), a rich stew of cubed salmon, miso, mirin, potatoes, cabbage, tofu, leek, kelp, wild mushrooms and sea salt. Sapporo-ites are also fond of their original **sūpu-karē** (スープカレー), which is quite literally a soupy variant of Japanese curry.

In addition to salmon, another cold-water speciality is **kani-ryōri** (かに料理; crab cuisine). The long-legged crabs of Wakkanai and Kushiro fetch the highest prices, though anything from Hokkaidō's icy waters will be packed with flavour. Crab appears in a variety of manifestations on the menu, though we're partial to boiled crustaceans served alongside a dish of melted butter.

Dairy cows flourish in the island's wide open expanses, which is reason enough to add a bit of lactose to your diet. **Hokkaidō milk** is used in everything from ice cream and cappuccinos to creamy soups and sauces, while Hokkaidō butter is best served atop a bowl of **rāmen** (ラーメン).

There are variants on everybody's favourite soup-noodle dish across the island, though the most famous is the miso-based **Sapporo rāmen**. If you want to be a purist, wash down your bowl with a pint of the legendary lager that is **Sapporo bīru** (札幌ビール).

And finally, no culinary account of Hokkaidō is complete without mention of Sapporo's beloved **jingisukan** (ジンギスカン), which was perhaps best summed up by British writer Alan Booth: 'I ordered the largest mug of draft beer on the menu and a dish of mutton and cabbage, which the Japanese find so outlandish that they have dubbed it *jingisukan* (Ghenghis Khan) after the grandfather of the greatest barbarian they ever jabbed at. The beer, as always, was about one-third froth, but a single portion of Ghenghis was so huge that it took an hour to eat – compensation for the loss of fluid ounces...'

Otaru Sushi-kō
SUSHI $$

(小樽すし耕; ☑21-5678; 2-2-6 Ironai; sushi set from ¥1470; ⊙noon-8.30pm; ☑) For Japanese travellers, eating Otaru is *all* about sushi – local specialities include *sake* (salmon), *ikura* (salmon roe), *uni* and *kani*. Inside this grey-brick warehouse (look for the English sign) about 500m east of the canal along Ironai Ōdōri, there are just six seats at the counter, ensuring personalised attention from the supremely skilled sushi chef.

If you're the type of person who enjoys scouting out good eateries before sitting down at the table, check out the **Denuki-kōji** (出抜小路; 1-1 Ironai; ⊙10am-8pm), located on the southern banks of Asakusa-bashi. This tourist-friendly complex contains a dozen or so restaurants spanning a variety of cuisines – most have plastic models out the front to help attract indecisive diners.

🍷 Drinking

Otaru Sōko No 1
BREW PUB $$

(小樽倉庫No. 1; 5-4 Minato-machi; dishes from ¥800; ⊙11am-10pm; ☑) Also housed in a converted warehouse, Sōku No 1 offers a nice selection of microbrewed drafts, plus German culinary fare to complement its Bavarian decor. Meat and potatoes are a big hit, but you're free to choose something a little more heart-healthy. There is live music here occasionally to provide some background accompaniment to your meal. An 'Otaru Beer' sign marks the brewery, which is along the banks of the canal.

❶ Getting There & Away

Boat

From Otaru Harbour, **Shin-Nihonkai** (☑22-6191) ferries run at 10.30am from Tuesday to Saturday, and at 7.30pm on Sunday, to Niigata (from ¥6200, 18 hours), returning every day but Monday.

To get to the ferry terminal, take the bus from stop 4 in front of JR Otaru Station (¥210, 30 minutes).

Car & Motorcycle

If you're driving, the **Sapporo Expressway** (札幌自動車道) runs between Otaru and the greater Sapporo area.

Train

There are hourly *kaisoku* on the JR Hakodate line between Otaru and Sapporo (¥620, 40 minutes) via Otaru Chikko (¥200, five minutes), and occasional *kaisoku* between Otaru and Niseko (¥1410, two hours).

Niseko
ニセコ

☑0136 / POP 4650

Hokkaidō is dotted with world-class ski resorts, but the reigning prince of powder is unquestionably Niseko. Despite its village status, Niseko boasts four interconnected resorts, which together contain more than 800 skiable hectares. Niseko also experiences northwest to southeast Siberian weather fronts, which produce a soft and light powdery snow that is perfect for carving. In fact, Niseko was named by *Forbes* magazine as the world's second-snowiest ski resort, with an annual average snowfall of more than 15m! (It was pipped at the post by the Mt Baker Ski Area in Washington State, USA.) Niseko is predictably popular with international jet-setting ski bums – many of whom own second homes here – resulting in a diverse dining and nightlife scene that is atypical of far-flung rural Japan.

🎿 Activities

Niseko United
SKIING & SNOWBOARDING

(ニセコユナイテッド; www.niseko.ne.jp/en; 8-hr/1-day pass ¥4900/5900; ⊙8.30am-9.30pm Nov-Apr) Niseko United is the umbrella name for four resorts, namely Niseko Annupuri, Niseko Village, Grand Hirafu and Hanazono. What makes Niseko United stand out from the competition is that you can ski or snowboard on all four slopes by purchasing a single all-mountain pass. This electronic tag gives you access to 18 lifts and gondolas, as well as free rides on the intermountain shuttle bus. If you're planning on skiing for several days, a week or even the season, you can also buy discounted multiday passes.

While it's difficult to generalise about such a massive area, Niseko United offers arguably some of the finest skiing in Japan and Asia – and the whole world for that matter. Niseko caters for skiers and snowboarders of all skill levels, and it's possible to spend several days here without repeating the same course. In total there are around 60 beginner, intermediate and advanced runs with a 2m to 3m snow base. And while the hype can be pretty overwhelming at times, the powder here is close to perfect, especially after a blizzard when the sky clears.

Swishing down the slopes, the first thing you'll be struck by is the perfect conical volcano Yōtei-zan (羊蹄山; 1898m), which looms ominously across the valley. Known in Japanese as *ezo-fuji* or the 'Fuji of the North',

Yōtei-zan provides a dramatic backdrop unlike any other. The second point worth highlighting is the variability of the terrain. Beginner courses tend to be wide and curvy with few natural obstacles to get in the way. Intermediate courses straighten out and increase dramatically in pitch. Advanced runs are mogul fields that either drop down from the peak or precariously hug the tree lines.

Rental equipment is of very high quality, and can be picked up virtually everywhere at fairly standard but affordable prices. In fact, a good number of rental shops will deliver (and pick up) equipment straight to your accommodation. As with the all-mountain pass, you can save a bit of money by renting equipment over a longer period. Rental shops also typically have a few Australian staff on hand to help English-speaking customers. Indeed, almost half of the tourists at Niseko are from Oz, which means that English is everywhere you look and listen.

Niseko United also benefits from well-developed facilities, both on the mountain and in the various towns at the base. At every point on the slopes, you're never more than a kilometre away from a hot drink and an energy-rich meal. Some of the mountain chalets like the Lookout Cafe on the Niseko Village course are fashionable affairs with crab pasta and herbal teas. Others like the 1000m Hut on the Hirafu course are modest dwellings with steamed buns and cups of hot cocoa.

At the base, most of the *après-ski* action is in Hirafu, though luxury seekers harbour in the Hilton, and locals tend to stick to Annupuri. But what unites travellers of all types is the love of onsen bathing after a long day of exposure to the elements. Trust us – there is nothing quite like the feeling of stepping out of your skis or snowboard, stripping off all of your clothing and jumping into an onsen. The scene is even more surreal during a blizzard when frozen flakes melt mid-air into steamy vapour clouds. Most hotels either have an onsen on the premises, or can point you in the direction of the nearest bathhouse.

Finally, be sure to check the *Local Rules Guide* (available from the information centre), as accidents do happen and avalanches are a possibility after heavy snows. Note that Australian and New Zealand walkie-talkies are banned in Niseko United as they interfere with local TV transmitters – you will be fined heavily if you are caught using one, so don't take the risk.

Goshiki Onsen   HIKING
(五色温泉) While the mild summer months may represent low season in Niseko, this is actually the best time of the year to tackle some of the area's challenging wilderness hikes. There is a 16km circuit that starts just west of the summit of Niseko Annupuri at Goshiki Onsen, and traverses several summits in the western Niseko range. This hike can be tackled in six to seven hours, and the trailhead is accessible by local bus lines. From Goshiki Onsen, you can also take a side trip by hiking east for two hours up the summit of Niseko Annupuri (ニセコアンヌプリ; 1308m). If it's a clear day, the panorama at the top will be of the Niseko United ski resort as well as of neighbouring Yōtei-zan.

Yōtei-zan   HIKING
Yōtei-zan is covered in alpine flowers during the summer, though you're going to face a 10-hour, 10km slog to the top to see them. The Ezo violet in particular is a rare endemic found above the 1600m threshold. From the peak, the Sea of Japan, the Pacific and Lake Toya are all visible. And in comparison to the real Fuji, Ezo Fuji sees few hikers, ensuring long bouts of silent contemplation. The trailhead for Yōtei-zan is at Yōtei-zan Tozan-guchi (羊蹄山登山口), which is south of Kutchan near JR Hirafu Station, and is accessible by local bus lines.

🛶 Courses
While skiing and snowboarding are Niseko's principal drawcards, you can also come here for ice climbing, snowshoeing and dog sledding, as well as canoeing, kayaking and river rafting in the summer. The **Niseko Outdoor Centre** (ニセコアウトドアセンター; ☑44-1133; www.noc-hokkaido.jp/e/index.html), near the Annupuri ski slope, and the **Niseko Adventure Centre** (ニセコアドベンチャーセンター; ☑23-2093; www.nac-web.com/e_index.htm), in the village of Hirafu, can organise activities in addition to short courses for novices and newbies.

🛏 Sleeping

Niseko proper is spread out along the base of the four slopes, with nothing close to the various train stations. The closer you get to the slopes themselves, the more options you'll have. Hirafu and Annupuri host the vast majority of accommodations, while Niseko Village is centred on the upmarket Hilton. Most places will provide pick-up and drop-off, or you can take buses and shuttles to move about. Spontaneous travellers can take their chances and show up without reservations, but it's strongly recommended that you book well in advance.

┌TOP┐
└CHOICE┘ Green Leaf   RESORT $$$

(ザ・グリーンリーフホテル; ☎44-3311, 44-3398; www.thegreenleafhotel.com/; Niseko Village; r from ¥33,000; @🛜♨🏊) A recent renovation of an ageing Niseko Village property has resulted in one of the most sophisticated joints on the mountain. The brainchild of a New York City interior-design firm and the late Soichiro Tomioka (1922–94), whose work appears in the MOMA, the Green Leaf is a walkable canvas of whimsical artwork. Contemporary rooms are distinguished by designer furniture and freeform lighting sources, and the on-site spa and onsen help to facilitate a deep and therapeutic sleep. The lobby appears to have been flown in straight from Aspen, as evidenced by the cowskin leather lounge chairs and polished stone surfaces. *Après-ski* cocktails of top-shelf liquor are served on the rooftop around a wood-burning firepit. Meals are buffet style, and incorporate a revolving assortment of local Hokkaidō specialities, Western standards and Japanese fusion creations. As a final lure to dedicated powder fiends, the close proximity to the Morino and Banzai chairlifts allows for easy ski-on, ski-off trips up and down the mountain.

Hilton Niseko Village   RESORT $$$

(ニセコヒルトンヴィレジ; ☎44-1111; fax 44-3224; www.hiltonworldresorts.com/Resorts/Niseko; Niseko Village; r from ¥20,000; @🛜♨🏊) There is no shortage of resort hotels in Niseko, though the Hilton enjoys the best location of all – it is quite literally attached to the Niseko Gondola. As you might expect from the luxury moniker, spacious Western-style rooms at the Hilton are complimented by a whole slew of amenities spread out across a self-contained village. Compared to stand-alone accommodation in the area,

you really can't beat the Hilton in regard to convenience. Equipment rental and valet service is available on site, and it's less than a five-minute walk from your room to the gondola. The trade-off is an almost total lack of Japanese character, and the abundance of large tour groups. Check the website before arriving as special deals are usually available, which combine discounted room rates with breakfast and dinner buffets.

Annupuri Village   CHALET $$$

(アンヌプリ・ヴィレジ; ☎59-2111; fax 59-2112; www.annupurivillage.com; Niseko Annupuri; chalets for 4-10 people from ¥74,000-110,000; @🛜) If you're travelling with a large group of friends, consider giving the resort hotels a pass and renting an immaculately designed ski chalet in Annupuri Village, located at the base of the Annupuri ski slopes. Natural hardwoods and picture windows are featured prominently from floor to ceiling, while rich stone fireplaces, spa-quality bathroom fixtures, professional kitchens and plasma TVs add a touch of modern class.

Jam Garden   PENSION $$

(ジャムガーデン; ☎22-6676; www.jamgarden.com, in Japanese; 37-89 Kabayama, Kucchan-chō; r per person with 2 meals ¥8000) Right near the ski lift at Hirafu, this deluxe farmhouse comes complete with its own Jacuzzi and sauna. Western-style rooms and country cooking are also on offer once you pry yourself away from the nearby slopes of Hirafu.

Niseko Kōgen Youth Hostel   HOSTEL $

(ニセコ高原ユースホステル; ☎/fax 44-1171; www13.ocn.ne.jp/~kogenyh/index2.html, in Japanese; 336 Aza Niseko; dm winter/summer ¥3200/3000, breakfast/dinner ¥500/1000; @) This *Winnie the Pooh*–themed hostel occupies a converted schoolhouse, and is famous among travellers for the owner's incredible accordion solos. It's 5km from Niseko Station and about 1km west of the slopes at Annupuri.

Niseko Annupuri Youth Hostel   HOSTEL $

(ニセコアンヌプリユースホステル; ☎58-2084; www.annupuri-yh.com, in Japanese; 470-4 Niseko; dm with 2 meals ¥5380) This mountain lodge constructed entirely from hardwood sits conveniently close to the Annupuri ski grounds. In between runs, guests congregate in front of the fire, swapping ski tips and tucking into delicious meals.

Niseko Tourist Home
GUESTHOUSE **$**

(ニセコツーリストホーム; ☎44-2517; http://niseko-th.com, in Japanese; dm Nov-Apr/Mar-Oct ¥3500/2500, with 2 meals ¥5000/4000; @) A clean and inexpensive A-frame about 4km from Niseko Station, the always-busy Tourist Home is a great budget base. Attracting a more Japanese crowd than the internationally minded youth hostels, the delightful owners have a lot of pride in their small ski town.

✖ Eating & Drinking

Many of the lodges and ryokan offer great meals cooked to order, and the slopes have plenty of snacks, pizza, *rāmen* and other goodies to stave off the munchies while you're in your gear. After hours, things are tricky because lodging is spread out and buses are inconvenient, but there are plenty of watering holes in Hirafu (usually packed with boisterous, fun-loving Aussies).

TOP CHOICE Barn
FRENCH **$$**

(ザ・バーン; ☎55-5553; 188-9 Aza-Yamada, Hirafu; lunch/dinner courses ¥1800/4300; ⏰11.30am-2pm & 6pm-11am, closed Mon summer; @) Housed in a modernist rendition of an old Hokkaidō barn, this self-described French Alpine Bistro sets the bar on the Hirafu dining scene. Signature dishes apply French reductions to locally procured meats, fish and vegetables, which are accompanied by hearth-baked bread and freshly made ice cream. As if this wasn't enough to make die-hard foodies rejoice, you can also order up a bottle of Boyer-Gontard, which comes from the owner's personal vineyard in Burgundy, France. The visually striking steel-and-glass barn is located two blocks south of the Seicomart in Hirafu.

Niseko Pizza
ITALIAN **$$**

(ニセコピザ; ☎55-5553; 188-9 Aza-Yamada; Hirafu; pizzas from ¥1300; ⏰4pm-late; @) This authentic family-run pizzeria headed by the affable Cezar is a popular late-night spot. Classic pies cater to big appetites, while gourmet variations and pastas suit more discerning palettes. Bonus: Niseko Pizza delivers, so no need to brave the cold if you suddenly develop a hankering for melted mozzarella! The pizzeria is in a brick building with English signage across from the Park Hotel in Hirafu.

Downtown Cafe
CAFE **$**

(ダウンタウンカフェ; ☎23-3354; Hirafu; breakfast sets ¥1000; ⏰7.30am-11pm winter, to 6pm summer; @) A local landmark that sits aside the main traffic light in downtown Hirafu, this New York City–inspired cafe has the obligatory cup of joe and toasted bagel with a smear of cream cheese. Sweet tooths can find comfort in all manners of danishes and pastries, not to mention pizza, sandwiches and tap beer for the lunch and dinner crowds.

Brick
PUB

(ザ・ブリック; Hirafu; ⏰5pm-late; @) A towering brick building smack in the middle of Hirafu proper, this character-laden spot is perfect for pub grub, a frosty pint or an expertly mixed cocktail. Early on in the evening, the Brick mostly caters to the burger and beer crowd, but things get much livelier later on when the DJ starts spinning and the hard alcohol starts to empty from the shelves.

ℹ Information

At the base of the ski slopes lie several towns and villages that compose Niseko's population centre. Most of the restaurants and bars are clustered together in **Hirafu** (ひらふ), while **Annupuri** (アンヌプリ), **Niseko Village** (ニセコビレッジ) and **Hanazono** (花園) are much quieter and less developed. Further east are **Kutchan** (倶知安) and **Niseko** (ニセコ) proper, which are more permanent population centres that remain decidedly Japanese.

There are very small **tourist information offices** (☎Niseko 44-2468, Kutchan 22-5151; www.niseko.gr.jp/eigo.html; ⏰10am-7pm) in JR Niseko and Kutchan Stations that can provide pamphlets, maps, bus timetables and help with bookings.

To meet the winter crush, the **Hirafu Welcome Centre** (ひらふウエルカムセンター; ☎22-0109; www.grand-hirafu.jp/winter/en/index.html; ⏰8.30am-9pm) – which is where direct buses to/from New Chitose Airport originate and terminate – also provides English-language information.

ℹ Getting There & Away

Bus

During the ski season, a couple of companies run regular highway buses from JR Sapporo Station and New Chitose Airport to Niseko. The trip takes around three hours depending on road conditions, costs ¥2300 (return ¥3850) and drops off at the welcome centre in Hirafu before continuing on to the Hilton and Annupuri. Reservations are necessary, and it's recommended that you book well ahead of your departure date. If you don't speak Japanese, ask the staff at the tourist information centres or your accommodation to make a reservation for you.

WORTH A TRIP

RUSUTSU

Compared to neighbouring Niseko, Rusutsu (ルスツ; population 2000) is something akin to the runt of the litter. It is much, much less developed, and vastly pales in size and scope. On the flip side, however, the slopes aren't nearly as crowded, and the lack of foreigners results in a decidedly more traditional ambience.

There is some serious powder waiting for you at the **Rusutsu Resort** (ルスツリゾート; ☑0136-46-3111; http://en.rusutsu.co.jp; lift tickets day/night ¥5100/2000; r from ¥9500; ☺day 9am-5pm, night 4-9pm Nov-Apr), which boasts well-groomed trails and fantastic tree runs – at times, you're often the first person passing through the powder! The resort caters equally to skiers and snowboarders, has trails of all difficulty levels, 18 lifts, more than two dozen runs, a 100m half pipe and numerous off-piste options. The lodge itself offers Western-style rooms in the Swiss-inspired north and south wings, while larger suites overlook the slopes in the modern tower. Book in advance as discounted packages including room, lift ticket and meal plan are often available.

During the ski season, several companies run highway buses from Sapporo and New Chitose Airport to Niseko via Rusutsu (¥1990, two hours). If you're driving, Rte 230 runs between Sapporo and Tōya-ko via Rusutsu.

Chūō Bus (☑011-231-0500; www.chuo-bus .co.jp, in Japanese)

Donan Bus (☑0123-46-5701; www.donanbus .co.jp, in Japanese)

Car & Motorcycle

Scenic Rte 5 winds from Sapporo to Otaru around the coast, and then cuts inland through the mountains down to Niseko. Having a car will also certainly make it easier to move between the various ski slopes, though drive with extreme caution as fatalities have tragically occurred here in the past. In the summer (low season), public transport drops off, which provides more incentive to pick up a car in Sapporo.

Train

While there is a JR Hirafu Station, it is far from the town itself, and is not well serviced by local buses. From JR Niseko and JR Kutchan Stations, you will need to switch to local buses to access the villages at the base of the ski slopes. For these reasons, it's recommended that you travel to Niseko via highway bus or car. If however the bus lines are fully booked, *futsū* trains run on the JR Hakodate line between Sapporo and Niseko (¥2400, two hours) via Kutchan (¥2090, 1¾ hours).

ⓘ Getting Around

There are twice-hourly local buses linking JR Kutchan and JR Niseko Stations to Hirafu, Niseko Village, Annupuri and Hanazono. Pick up a schedule from the tourist information centres so that you don't miss your connection. Also, if you've purchased an all-mountain pass, you can ride the free hourly shuttle bus between the villages.

Shikotsu-tōya National Park 支笏洞爺国立公園
☑0142

Shikotsu-tōya National Park (993 sq km) is largely mountainous wilderness that is criss-crossed by rugged hiking trails, marked by two picturesque caldera lakes, and home to Hokkaidō's premier hot-spring town, Noboribetsu Onsen.

NOBORIBETSU ONSEN 登別温泉
☑0143

Noboribetsu is the sum total of two dozen or so bathhouses clustered tightly together along a narrow, winding street. If you can overlook the mass commercialisation, then you're in for an onsen experience par excellence. The rejuvenating water here originates from a volcanic sulphurous 'hell' not far above.

⊙ Sights

Dai-ichi Takimoto-kan ONSEN
(第一滝本館; www.taki motokan.co.jp/english; onsen baths ¥2000; ☺9am-5pm). This massive and unmistakable compound has more than 15 kinds of baths, ranging from take-your-skin-off scalding to cryogenic freeze-inducing cold.

Noboribetsu Grand Hotel ONSEN
(登別グランドホテル; www.nobogura.co.jp/ english; onsen baths ¥1000; ☺12.30-5pm & 6.30-8pm) Half the price (and size), the star attraction is the domed ceiling, giving the impression of a spacious Roman-era bath.

Shikotsu-tōya National Park

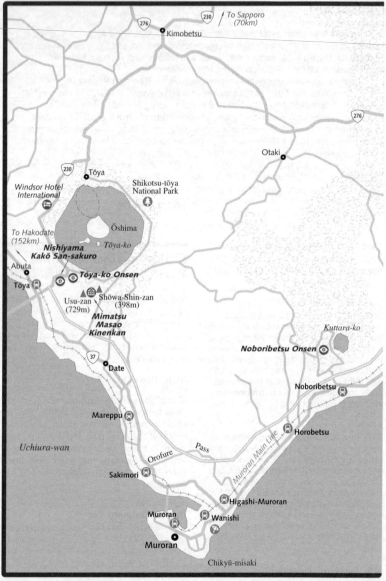

Jigokudani

HELL VALLEY

(地獄谷) A short walk uphill reveals what may await us in the afterlife: sulphurous gases, hissing vents and seemingly blood-stained rocks.

🛏 Sleeping

🏆 Ryotei Hanayura

RYOKAN $$$

(旅亭花ゆら; ☎84-2322; fax 84-2035; http:hanayura.com/en/index.html; 100 Noboribetsu Onsen; r per person with 2 meals from ¥23,625;

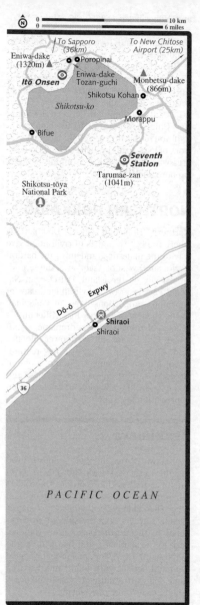

isn't too hard given that there are only two dozen rooms, some of which have private outdoor baths.

Dai-ichi Takimoto-kan   HOTEL $$

(第一滝本館; ☎84-3322; www.takimotokan .co.jp/english; 55 Noboribetsu Onsen; r per person with 2 meals from ¥9150; @ 🍴) The town's most famous hot spring also doubles as a resort hotel, offering both Western- and Japanese-style rooms spread out over several wings of varying quality. Meals are offered either buffet style in the crowded main dining room, or served in your room for an additional charge. You will also get complimentary access to the hot-springs complex, which definitely represents a substantial saving.

Noboribetsu Grand Hotel   HOTEL $$

(登別グランドホテル; ☎717-8899; fax 84-2543; www.nobogura.co.jp, in Japanese; 154 Noboribetsu Onsen; r per person with 2 meals from ¥8500 @ 🍴) The Grand Hotel was once a favourite of the imperial family, although today it principally caters to package travellers on the tour-bus circuit. Still, there are some decent Western- and Japanese-style rooms to be had, and having around-the-clock access to the beautiful baths is a treat in itself.

ℹ Getting There & Away

BUS

Highway buses run frequently between Noboribetsu and Sapporo (¥2100, two hours). From April to November, regular buses also run between Noboribetsu and Tōya (¥1530, 1¼ hours), and between Noboribetsu and New Chitose Airport (¥1330, 1¼ hours).

CAR & MOTORCYCLE

If you're driving, Noboribetsu is easily accessed by the **Dō-ō Expressway** (道央自動車道) running between Sapporo and Hakodate.

TRAIN

Frequent *tokkyū* run on the JR Muroran line between JR Noboribetsu Station and Hakodate (¥6700, 2½ hours), between Noboribetsu and Sapporo (¥4360, 1¼ hours), and between Noboribetsu and Tōya Station (¥2650, 35 minutes). Local buses run every 30 minutes between JR Noboribetsu Station and Noboribetsu Onsen (¥330, 15 minutes).

@ 🛜) If you find the other properties in town to be a bit over the top, fear not as Hanayura is the embodiment of what an intimate ryokan ought to be. Classically Japanese in style and service, the emphasis here is on personalised attention, which

TŌYA-KO ONSEN   洞爺湖温泉

As the closest onsen town to Sapporo and New Chitose Airport, Tōya-ko is a popular and convenient spot for scenic soaking.

The landscape is distinguished by two active volcanoes, namely **Shōwa-Shin-zan** (昭和新山; 398m) and **Usu-zan** (有珠山; 729m). The former regularly belches sulphurous fumes, while the latter has quieted somewhat since erupting in 2000.

There's a **ropeway** (有珠山ロープウェイ; http://wakasaresort.com/usuzan/en/index.html; return ¥1450; ⊙8am-5pm) that runs from the base of Usu-zan to a small viewing platform overlooking the steaming crater.

Nearby is the **Mimatsu Masao Kinenkan** (三松正夫記念館; admission ¥300; ⊙8am-5pm Apr-Oct, 9am-4pm Nov-Mar), a memorial hall to local postmaster Mimatsu Masao. In 1946, he purchased Shōwa-Shin-zan, and subsequently saved it from the mining companies.

FREE **Nishiyama Kakō San-sakuro** (西山火口散策路; ⊙closed 10 Nov-20 Apr) is a promenade that skirts hissing fissures and bubbling ponds. Note that the area is sometimes closed due to dangerous levels of toxic gas – if there is no one there when you arrive, you know why!

A cruise ship–shaped resort on the northwestern shores of the lake, the **Windsor Hotel International** (ザ・ウィンザーホテル洞爺; ☑0120-29-0500; www.windsor-hotels.co.jp/en/toya; Shimizu Abuta-chō; r from ¥33,600; @⊙⊠) offers luxury rooms and palatial suites, not to mention a dozen restaurants including a Michelin three-star bistro by French chef Michel Bras. There is a free shuttle bus between the hotel and JR Tōya Station.

Fronting the lake in the centre of town is the **Hotel Grand Tōya** (ホテルグランドトーヤ; ☑75-2288; fax 75-3434; www.grandtoya.com; 144 Tōyako Onsen, Tōyako-chō, Abuta-gun; r per person with 2 meals from ¥8500; @), a much more modest onsen hotel with a colourful open-air bath, and a tiny cafe with al fresco seating in the summer months.

Frequent *tokkyū* run on the JR Muroran line between JR Tōya Station and Hakodate (¥5340, 1¾ hours), between Tōya and Sapporo (¥5760, 1¾ hours), and between Tōya

and Noboribetsu (¥2650, 35 minutes). Local buses run every 30 minutes between JR Tōya Station and Tōya-ko Onsen (¥320, 25 minutes).

Highway buses run frequently between Tōya and Sapporo (¥2700, 2¾ hours). From April to November, regular buses also run between Tōya and Noboribetsu Onsen (¥1530, 1¼ hours), and between Tōya and New Chitose Airport (¥2140, 2½ hours).

If you're driving, a well-maintained network of local roads branches off the Dō-ō Expressway (道央自動車道) running between Sapporo and Hakodate.

NORTHERN HOKKAIDŌ

Northern Hokkaidō (道北; Dō-hoku) is where the last trappings of civilisation give way to the majestic grandeur of the natural world. Southwest of Asahikawa, the second-largest city on the island, Daisetsuzan National Park is a raw and virgin landscape of enormous proportions. West of Wakkanai, in the shadow of Siberia, Rishiri-Rebun-Sarobetsu National Park is a dramatic islandscape famous for its wildflower blooms. And, in case you still need a few reminders of human settlement, Furano is one of Hokkaidō's most famous ski resorts, and home to one of the world's only belly-button appreciation festivals!

Asahikawa 旭川

☑0166 / POP 355,000

Asahikawa carries the dual honour of having the most days with snowfall in all of Japan, as well as the record for the coldest temperature (-40°C). Less picturesque than other Hokkaidō cities, Asahikawa is mainly used by travellers as a transit point for Wakkanai to the north, Daisetsuzan National Park to the southeast, and Biei and Furano to the south. However, you'll probably spend the night here at some point, and there are some noteworthy museums, a zoo and breweries to visit before pressing on.

⊙ Sights

Kawamura Kaneto Ainu Kinenkan MUSEUM (川村カ子トアイヌ記念館; 11 Kitamonchō; admission ¥500; ⊙8am-6pm Jul & Aug, 9am-5pm Sep-Jun) Kaneto Kawamura, an Ainu chief, became a master surveyor and helped to lay the tracks for several of Hokkaidō's railways.

BEST ONSEN

» Tōya-ko Onsen (p491)
» Noboribetsu Onsen (p489)
» Asahidake Onsen (p507)
» Sōunkyō Onsen (p508)
» Kawayu Onsen (p513)

DON'T MISS

SHIKOTSU-KO

Completely surrounded by soaring volcanoes, Shikotsu-ko (支笏湖) is the second-largest caldera lake in Japan, and a conducive spot for independent exploration. If you're looking to get off the beaten path in Shikotsu-tōya, lace up your hiking boots, tie a bear bell to your rucksack and keep on reading...

Monbetsu-dake (紋別岳; 866m) is one of the easiest hikes in the area. The trail starts at the northern end of Shikotsu Kohan, and it should take you around 1½ hours to reach the summit.

A much more challenging ascent is **Eniwa-dake** (恵庭岳; 1320m), which lies on the northwestern side of the lake. A 3½-hour hike will bring you to the crater, though enquire locally as trail conditions near the top can be dangerous.

On the southern side of the lake is **Tarumae-zan** (樽前山; 1041m), an active volcano that is the area's most popular hike. Due to poisonous gases, the crater itself is usually closed, but you can reach the rim from the **seventh station** (only accessible by private car) in about 40 minutes.

When you're ready to take a break from all the hiking, **Itō Onsen** (いとう温泉; admission ¥700; ⊙10am-4pm) on the northern shores of the lake is a great place to quite literally soak up the atmosphere. This onsen is famous for its unobstructed views of the lake, so feel free to let it all hang out and embrace Mother Nature.

The area is served by the towns of Shikotsu Kohan (支笏湖畔) and Morappu (モラップ). Local bus connections are limited, which means that you will really need your own wheels to get the most out of the area.

In 1916, after eye problems forced him to retire, he used his accumulated wealth to create the first Ainu museum. Take bus 24 from bus stop 14 in front of the station to the Ainu Kinenkan-mae stop (¥170, 15 minutes).

FREE **Otokoyama Jyōzō** SAKE BREWERY
(男山酒造; www.otokoyama.com/english/index
.html; 2-7 Nagayama; ⊙9am-5pm) If you want a free tipple, take the 30-minute tour of this legendary brewery, which appears in old *ukiyo-e* (woodblock prints) and historic literature. Take bus 67, 68, 70, 71, 667 or 669 from bus stop 18 in front of the station, and get off at Nagayama 2-jō 6-chōme (¥200, 20 minutes); from there it's a two-minute walk (look for the large white cube that rests on the roof of the building).

FREE **Takasago Meiji Jyōzō** SAKE BREWERY
(高砂明治酒造; http://takasagoshuzo.com, in Japanese; 17 Miyashitadōri; ⊙9am-5.30pm Mon-Sat) If you want to turn the afternoon into a sake crawl, Takasago Meiji has a 30-minute free tour of its own. From January to March it also has an *aisudōmu*, a sake-filled ice dome where you can warm up with a drink. Take bus 1, 3 or 17 from bus stop 17 in front of the station to 1-jō 18-chōme (¥150, 10 minutes). It's a large whitewashed building with a cedar ball hanging outside the door.

Even if you don't speak Japanese, English pamphlets and friendly staff help make both tours worthwhile.

Asahiyama Dōbutsukan ZOO
(旭山動物園; www5.city.asahikawa.hokkaido.jp/
asahiyamazoo/zoo/English/top.html; Kuranuma; admission ¥800; ⊙9.30am-5.15pm May-Oct, 10.30am-3.30pm Nov-Apr) The country's northernmost zoo attracts even more visitors than Tokyo's Ueno Zoo. As you might imagine, the star attractions here are cold-weather animals, including the ever-popular polar bears, penguins and seals. As far as zoos go, Asahiyama gets good marks for its attempts to create naturally styled enclosures for the animals. Buses 41, 42 or 47 run between bus stop 5 in front of the station and the entrance to the zoo (¥400, 40 minutes).

Hokkaidō Folk Arts & Crafts Village MUSEUM
(北海道伝統美術工芸村; www.yukaraori.co.jp, in Japanese; 3-1-1 Minamigaoka; combined tickets ¥1200) Located 5km southwest of the train station, this collection of three museums provides an overview of the island's traditional folk arts. A free shuttle runs every hour or two between the village and the Kureyon Parking, next to the Asahikawa Washington Hotel.

✲✲ Festivals & Events

Yuki Matsuri   SNOW

Held in Asahikawa every February. While second to the one in Sapporo, this festival is still impressive, with ice sculptures, food and fun seasonal events.

Kotan Matsuri   TRADITIONAL

Takes place in late September on the banks of the Chubestu-gawa, south of the city. During the festival you can see traditional dances, music and *kamui-nomi* and *inau-shiki*, prayer ceremonies offered to the deities of fire, the river, *kotan* (the village) and the mountains.

🛏 Sleeping

Loisir Hotel Asahikawa   HOTEL $$$

(ロワジールホテル旭川; ☎25-8811; fax 25-8200; www.solarehotels.com/english/loisir/hotel-asahikawa/guestroom/detail.html; Nanajō-dōri; s/d from ¥17,400/19,700; @🛜) An easy-to-spot white tower block overlooking the city's park, the Loisir is Asahikawa's best hotel, equipped with minimalist rooms decked out in soft hues and natural shades. First-class amenities include a large gym and spa as well as four fine restaurants, one of which is a 15th-floor French bistro with a view.

Tokiya Ryokan   RYOKAN $

(時屋旅館; ☎23-2237; fax 26-3874; www.tokiya.net/english.html; 9-2 Nijō-dōri; r per person with shared/private bathroom ¥4500/5000; @🛜) North of the station, on the opposite side of the street from the Asahikawa bank, this traditional inn is very well priced, and is a much more atmospheric choice than the standard business hotels. Well-decorated Japanese-style rooms have either shared or private facilities, though all guests can scrub down in the small but refreshing *sento* (public bath).

Tōyoko Inn Asahikawa Ekimae   HOTEL $$

(東横イン旭川駅前; ☎27-1045; fax 27-1046; www.toyoko-inn.com/e_hotel/00069/index.html; 9-164-1 Ichijō-dōri; s/d from ¥5985/9240; @) This popular chain's clean and convenient Asahikawa clone.

Asahikawa Terminal Hotel   HOTEL $

(旭川ターミナルホテル; ☎24-0111; fax 21-2133; www.asahikawa-th.com/contents/intl/english/english.htm; 7 Miyashita; s/d from ¥4500/5000; @) A reliable spot, conveniently located inside the JR Asahikawa Station.

🍴 Eating

There is a *rāmen* shop on virtually every street in Asahikawa. This is welcome news given that the city's home-grown blend is a light but flavourful variation of the *shōyu* (soy sauce) variety.

Saroma-ko To Barō-mura   SEAFOOD $$

(サロマ湖とばろう村; ☎22-6426; 6-1 Sanjō-dōri; small plates from ¥500; ☺dinner) Come here for the freshest seafood prepared with care by a chef who's not afraid to close the restaurant if the shellfish doesn't meet his finicky standards. Try the *hotate-no-sashimi* (scallop sashimi; ¥900) or the *kaki-no-sakemushi* (oysters steamed in sake; ¥1100). Prices vary depending on the quality and the season. The restaurant is easily found by looking for the string of traditional Japanese lanterns.

Tenkin   IZAKAYA $$

(天金; ☎17-6400; 7 Yonjō-dōri; small plates from ¥500; ☺dinner; 🅿) One of the oldest *izakaya* in town, Tenkin is a box-shaped hall with wood trim that is marked by large golden characters. The menu is broad, but the recurring themes are winter warmers such as *nabe* (stew cooked in a cast-iron pot) as well as all manner of seafood – check out the tanks near the entrance to see what's fresh.

🍷 Drinking

Den   BAR

(ザ・デン; 5th fl, Yoshitake 2 Bldg, Nijō-dori; drinks from ¥500; ☺5.30pm-1am) This is a highly recommended Australian-run international bar where you can have some drinks, meet some peeps and party the night away. The owner is a long-time resident of Hokkaidō and can give you some tips about the island. The bar is on the 5th floor, but a large English sign on the street marks the entrance.

ℹ Information

JR Asahikawa Station is on the south side of the city. A large pedestrian avenue extends out for a few blocks, and most of the hotels and restaurants listed here are within easy walking distance. Museums and sights, on the other hand, are spread out across the city and will often require a bus ride.

Tourist information counter (☎22-6704; ☺8.30am-7pm Jul-Sep, 10am-5.30pm Oct-Jun) Inside Asahikawa Station – be sure to ask for the very useful bus-stop map.

Although Ainu culture was once declared 'dead' by the Japanese government, the past few decades have seen people of Ainu descent assert their ethnicity both politically and culturally.

In 1899 the Hokkaidō Former Natives Protection Act formalised decades of Meiji-era discrimination against the Ainu, denying them land ownership and giving the governor of Hokkaidō sole discretion over the management of communal Ainu funds. Thus, the Ainu became dependent on the welfare of the Japanese state.

Although this law had been amended over the years, many Ainu people objected to it, right down to its title, which used the word *kyūdo-jin* ('dirt' or 'earth' people) to describe them. It was once the standard among people of Ainu descent to hide their ethnicity out of fear of discrimination in housing, schools and employment; out of an estimated 100,000 Ainu, only 25,000 acknowledged it publicly.

In the 1980s various Ainu groups called for the law's repeal, and in 1998 the Japanese government replaced the law with one that allocated government funds for Ainu research and the promotion of Ainu language and culture, as well as better education about Ainu traditions in state schools.

If you're interested in learning more about the Ainu, we recommend the following:

Shiraoi's **Poroto Kotan** (ポロトコタン) is a lakeside village of reconstructed traditional Ainu buildings, anchored by the **Ainu Museum** (アイヌ民族博物館; Ainu Minzoku Hakubutsukan; www.ainu-museum.or.jp/english/english.html; admission ¥750; 8.45am-5pm). Museum exhibits are labelled in both Japanese and English, and in the village you might catch demonstrations of Ainu crafts and cultural performances. Frequent *tokkyū* and *kaisoku* on the JR Muroran line run between Shiraoi and Sapporo (¥3200, one hour) via Noboribetsu (¥350, 20 minutes).

In the village of Nibutani, which is located in the northern outskirts of Biratori village, **Nibutani Ainu Culture Museum** (二風谷アイヌ文化博物館; Nibutani Ainu Bunka Hakubutsukan; www.town.biratori.hokkaido.jp/biratori/nibutani, in Japanese; admission ¥400; 9am-5pm mid-Apr–mid-Nov, 9am-5pm Tue-Sun mid-Nov–mid-Apr, closed mid-Dec–mid-Jan) has arguably better collections and more attractive displays, although most information is in Japanese only. Visitors could easily spend half a day watching documentary videos about Ainu folk crafts, traditional dances, epic songs and traditional ceremonies. Other highlights include a loom for weaving traditional tree-bark cloth and some enormous canoes hewn from entire tree trunks.

Across Nibutani's main street, amid some traditional huts, the **Kayano Shigeru Ainu Memorial Museum** (萱野茂二風谷アイヌ資料館; Kayano Shigeru Nibutani Ainu Shiryōkan; admission ¥400; 9am-5pm Apr-Nov, by appointment Dec-Mar) houses the private collection of Kayano Shigeru, the first person of Ainu descent to be elected to the Japanese Diet.

A combined ticket for both Nibutani museums costs ¥700. Unfortunately, access to Nibutani is a trial on public transport, though it's a quick and easy trip by car: Rte 237 runs straight to the town.

Other useful sources of information include the **Foundation for the Research & Promotion of Ainu Culture** (アイヌ文化振興研究推進機構; Ainu Bunka Shinkō-kenkyū Suishinkikoū; 011-271-4171; www.frpac.or.jp/eng/index.html) in Sapporo, the **Ainu Culture Centre** (アイヌ文化交流センター; Ainu Bunka Kōryū Centā; 03-3245-9831) in Tokyo and the **Ainu Association of Hokkaidō** (北海道アイヌ協会; Hokkaidō Utari Kyōkai; 011-221-0462; www.ainu-assn.or.jp, in Japanese) in Sapporo.

ℹ️ Getting There & Around

Air

Asahikawa's small airport is located about 15km outside the city. From here, there are domestic flights to various destinations including Tokyo, Osaka, Nagoya and others. Buses between the airport and JR Asahikawa Station (¥570, 35 minutes) are timed to connect with arrivals and departures.

Bus

Some sample destinations, which have frequent daily departures from the bus stops in front of the JR Asahikawa Station, include Sapporo (¥2000, two hours), Wakkanai (¥4700, 4¾ hours), Furano (¥860, 1½ hours) and Biei (¥520, 50 minutes).

Car & Motorcycle

If you want to pick up a car before heading either north, south or east, the recommended **Toyota Rent a Car** (トヨタレンタカー; ☎23-0100; 9-396-2 Miyashitadōri; ☉8am-8pm Apr-Oct, to 7pm Nov-Mar) has a branch office right outside the station.

Train

Super Kamui *tokkyū* run twice an hour between Asahikawa and Sapporo (¥4480, 1½ hours). There are just a couple of *tokkyū* on the JR Sōya line each day between Asahikawa and Wakkanai (¥7870, 3¾ hours), and on the JR Sekihoku line between Asahikawa and Abashiri (¥7750, four hours). Finally, there are regular *kaisoku* on the JR Furano line between Asahikawa and Furano (¥1040, 1¼ hours) via Biei (¥530, 35 minutes).

Wakkanai 稚内

☎0162 / POP 41,000

Wakkanai, Japan's most northern mainland city, changes wildly with the seasons. From November to March, it's something akin to a remote Siberian outpost, home to hearty fishermen, kelp farmers and a harpseal colony. Outside the winter months, it's a pleasantly mild port city that serves as a departure point for ferries to Rishiri-tō and Rebun-tō, two dramatic wildflower-dotted islands that rank among Hokkaidō's highlights, and – assuming you have your visa in order – a trip across the border to the Russian city of Korsakov.

◉ Sights

Most attractions are outside town.

Wakkanai Shikai Hyaku-nen Kinen-tō   TOWER

(稚内開基百年記念塔; admission ¥400; ☉closed Nov-Apr) Atop a grassy hill a few blocks from the train station is the town's centennial memorial tower. On a clear day you can see Russia, just like former Alaskan governor Sarah Palin!

Noshappu-misaki   CAPE

This cape (ノシャプ岬; Map p500), the second most northern point in mainland Japan, is a nice place for a picture or a picnic, or just to watch the water for a while. If it's a clear day, look for the green flash as the sun slips below the horizon. The cape is a pleasant walk (35 minutes) or bike ride (15 minutes) away from town. Along the way, look out for the kelp-drying yards (they look like gravel-covered car parks if they're not covered with kelp) along the shoreline.

Sōya-misaki   CAPE

Thirty kilometres from Wakkanai, this cape (宗谷岬) is the real thing: mainland Japan's most northern point. Among the cape's various monuments is one dedicated to the victims of Korean Airlines flight 007, which was shot down in 1983 by a Soviet fighter jet. Birdwatchers will love seeing hawks sitting side by side with seagulls and terns on the wave-washed black sand. There are four return buses each day, departing from JR Wakkanai Station (¥2430, one hour each way).

Sarobetsu Genya   MARSHLANDS

While technically part of Rishiri-Rebun-Sarobetsu National Park, these marshlands (サロベツ原; Map p500) are best accessed from Wakkanai. Approximately 35km south of town, Sarobetsu Genya is full of colour every spring, with dramatic blooms of rhododendrons, irises, lilies and many other types of flowers. Frequent *futsū* on the JR Sōya line run between Wakkanai and Toyotomi (¥900, 45 minutes). Toyotomi is connected to the park entrance by regular local buses (¥430, 15 minutes).

🏃 Activities

FREE **Harp Seals**   WATCHING WILDLIFE

There is some wonderful wildlife-watching in Bakkai, where a few hundred harp seals (Map p500) arrive each year and stay from November to the end of March. A basic viewing hut (free) provides shelter, a toilet and some information about the seals. Frequent *futsū* run on the JR Sōya line between Wakkanai and Bakkai (¥260, 15 minutes). Dress warmly as the hut is a 30-minute walk from JR Bakkai Station, and temperatures can be well below freezing.

🎭 Festivals & Events

Japan Cup Zenkoku Inu-zori Wakkanai Taikai   DOGSLED RACE

In late February, Wakkanai hosts the biggest dogsled race in Japan. The track winds through some truly inhospitable frozen terrain, though everyone warms up back in the city where festivities carry on well into the night.

🛏 Sleeping

The youth hostels are occasionally closed in the winter, so it's best to phone ahead.

🌿 Wakkanai Youth Hostel
HOSTEL $

(稚内ユースホステル; Map p500; ☏23-7162; www7.plala.or.jp/komadori-house; 3-9-1 Komadori; dm/r from ¥3150/4200; @) The Wakkanai Youth Hostel is perched on top of a hill, and has a commanding view of the surrounding town and ocean. While still a youth hostel, it feels more homey, almost like a *minshuku* (Japanese guesthouse) rather than an institution, and it sources everything locally. It's a 15-minute walk from Minami-Wakkanai Station – follow the signs.

Saihate Ryokan
RYOKAN $

(さいはて旅館; Map p500; ☏23-3556; 2-11-16 Chūō; per person with/without 2 meals from ¥6500/3700) Right next to the bus and ferry terminals, this is a very convenient place to bed down before hopping on a ship out to Rishiri-Rebun-Sarobetsu National Park. Although it can get a bit noisy, simple Japanese- and Western-style rooms are well maintained, and meals usually feature the area's famous sea urchin and salmon roe.

ANA Hotel Wakkanai
HOTEL $$

(稚内全日空ホテル; Map p500; ☏23-8111; www.ana-hotel-wakkanai.co.jp, in Japanese; s/d from ¥5400/9300; @🛜) Tall, sleek and stylish, this place seems a bit out of place in downtown Wakkanai – walk to the waterfront and you can't miss it. Truth be told, this level of luxury is a bit incongruous with the local atmosphere, but the ANA does good business with travellers who like to indulge in creature comforts, even in extreme places.

Wakkanai Moshiripa Youth Hostel
HOSTEL $

(稚内モシリパユースホステル; Map p500; ☏24-0180; www.moshiripa.net, in Japanese; 2-9-5 Chūō; dm/r from ¥3960/4800) Located between JR Wakkanai Station and the ferry port (look for the dark-blue, three-storey building) – dormitories and private rooms are functional without much fuss. But the management is warm and friendly, even if the temperatures outside are cold and unforgiving.

✕ Eating

TOP CHOICE Takechan

SEAFOOD $$

(竹ちゃん; ☏22-7130; 2-8-7 Chūō; dishes from ¥1000; ⊘lunch & dinner) This is a famous Wakkanai restaurant where you can sample *tako-shabu* (¥1575), an octopus variant of traditional shabu-shabu. Steady your chopsticks, and then slowly dip slices of tentacle into steaming broth. For the squeamish, there is safety in *sōyakurōshi*, a strip steak carved from Japan's northernmost free-range cows. Exit JR Wakkanai Station, walk straight through the first light and then turn right at the next corner. Walk for two more blocks and you'll see a white wooden building with black trim on your left-hand side.

Narazushi
SUSHI $$

(なら鮨; ☏23-6131; 2-13 Chūō; sets from ¥1300; ⊘lunch & dinner) One block southwest of Takechan, you will find this sushi spot, which is easily identified by the giant shrimp stamped on the exterior curtain. From the picture menu, you can choose between a variety of house specialities, each featuring various combinations of cold-water fish, crustaceans and echinoderms (think: sea urchins) brought from Japan's northern seas.

ℹ Information

JR Wakkanai Station is right next to the bus terminal, and both are just 10 minutes on foot from the ferry port. If you're heading out to the islands (or across the border to Russia), it's wise to stock up on money – an international ATM is available at the **post office** (⊘8.45am-7pm Mon-Fri, 9am-5pm Sat & Sun), due west of the train station. You can pick up maps and get your bearings at the **tourist information counter** (☏22-1216; www.welcome.wakkanai.hokkaido.jp/en; ⊘10am-6pm) located inside the train station.

ℹ Getting There & Around

Air

From Wakkanai Airport, about 10km east of the city centre, there are a couple of flights a day to Sapporo and Tokyo. Regular buses run between JR Wakkanai Station and the airport (¥590, 35 minutes).

Bus

There are a couple of daily buses in either direction between JR Wakkanai Station and Sapporo (¥6000, six hours), as well as Asahikawa (¥4700, 4¾ hours).

Boat

For information on ferries to Rishiri-tō and Rebun-tō, see p499 and p502, respectively.

For details about a trip to Russia, see the box, p498.

FERRY TO/FROM RUSSIA

From mid-May to late October, an unusual excursion from Wakkanai is a ferry trip to the city of Korsakov on Sakhalin Island in Russia. Most Japanese tourists make this journey with a tour group, but with a little planning, it's fairly easy to go on your own.

In order to qualify for a Russian tourist visa, you will need to obtain an invitation letter from a hotel or tourist agency in the country. With a reservation, this letter can usually be emailed to you without any hassle.

You can then apply for the visa at the **Russian embassy** (Map p60; 03-3583-4445; www.rusconsul.jp; 2-1-1, Azabudai, Minato-ku, Tokyo; 9.30am-12.30pm Mon-Fri) in Tokyo or at the **Russian consulate** (在札幌ロシア連邦総領事館; 011-561-3171~2; www.rusconsul.jp; 2-5 12-chōme Nishi, Minami 14-jo, Chūō-ku; 9.30am-12.30pm Mon-Fri) in Sapporo. Note that fees vary considerably depending on your nationality, and waits of up to two weeks are not uncommon.

From Wakkanai Harbour, **Heartland Ferry** (ハートランドフェリー; 011-233-8010; www.heartlandferry.jp/english/index.html) operates four to nine monthly ferries (May to October) in both directions between Wakkanai and Karsakov (7½ hours). At the time of research, a 2nd-class one-way/return ticket cost ¥24,000/38,000. Note, however, that these prices are subject to change. If you're not returning to Japan, you may be asked to show an onward ticket at customs in Russia.

Car & Motorcycle

Long and lonely Rte 40 runs between Asahikawa and Wakkanai. If you're heading out to Rishiri-Rebun-Sarobetsu National Park, parking is available at the ferry terminal for ¥1000 per night.

Train

There are just a couple of *tokkyū* each day on the JR Sōya line between Asahikawa and Wakkanai (¥8070, 3¾ hours).

Rishiri-Rebun-Sarobetsu National Park
利尻礼文サロベツ国立公園

In case mainland Hokkaidō isn't remote enough for you, take a trip out to the islands of Rishiri-tō and Rebun-tō, which lie just off the coast of Wakkanai. While the islands are virtually abandoned in the winter months, from May through August, Rishiri-tō and Rebun-tō burst to life with wildflower blooms, drawing visitors by the boatload. This is also the best time to summit Rishiri-zan (1721m), a near-perfect cinder cone rising like a miniature Mt Fuji from the surrounding sea. The national park also includes the flower-filled marshlands of Sarobetsu Genya, best accessed from Wakkanai (see p496).

RISHIRI-TŌ
利尻島
0163 / POP 5000

While Rishiri-tō might not have the same concentration of wildflowers as its more popular sibling, the island is home to one of Japan's '100 Famous Mountains'. Rishiri-zan is certainly an arresting sight when viewed from Wakkanai or Rebun-tō, but the mountain takes on even more epic proportions when scaled on a demanding day hike.

Activities

The two most reliable hiking tracks to the summit of **Rishiri-zan** (利尻山) start about 3km from town (from the ferry port) at **Oshidomari** (鴛泊) and **Kutsugata** (沓形). The journey between both towns is 18km, and it should take you about eight to 10 hours depending on your pace. Limited bus service runs to the start of each track; otherwise you must walk, hitch, taxi or ask staff at your lodging if they can drop you off.

Just past the eighth station is **Rishiri-dake Yamagoya** (利尻岳山小屋), an unstaffed mountain hut that perches on the edge of a precipice, and provides the bare minimum for a roof over your head (no water). It is possible to spend the night here, but it is bloody cold, colder still with the wind-chill factor. However, it's impossibly beautiful, especially on a crystal-clear night when the Russian city of Korsakov is visible in the distance.

From the hut, it is a steep climb on loose scree past the ninth station to the peak, though there are some ropes to assist with tricky footing. There are actually two peaks, namely **Kita-mine** (北峰) and **Minami-mine**

(南峰), the latter just 2m higher. Also of interest is the appropriately named **Rōsoku-dake** (ローソク岳; Candle Rock), which lies on the descending trail to Kutsugata.

🛏 Sleeping

It's best to phone ahead in the winter months as the places listed here are closed irregularly. Note that meals are best taken at your accommodation since restaurants on the island are limited. Finally, you can usually arrange to be collected from the port or the airport if you call ahead to any of these accommodation listings.

Rishiri Fuji Kankō Hotel   HOTEL $$
(利尻富士観光ホテル; ☎82-1531; fax 82-1897; www15.plala.or.jp/fujikan, in Japanese; per person with 2 meals from ¥15,900; ⊘closed Dec-Feb; @🐾) Just two minutes on foot from the port, Oshidomari's ageing upmarket offering is a firm favourite for package holiday makers and large tour groups. Although the Fuji Kankō can be positively swamped during the crowded summer months, it offers low-key but comfortable rooms of varying shapes and styles as well as full resort amenities and sit-down dinners.

Island Inn Rishiri   HOTEL $$
(アイランドインリシリ; ☎84-3002; fax 84-3340; www.island-inn-rishiri.com, in Japanese; r per person with 2 meals ¥16,500; @) Just behind the ferry terminal in Kutsugata, the Island Inn sees a bit less package-tourism traffic than the Fuji Kankō. Above-average Western-style rooms come with either ocean or mountain views, and there is also a large banquet hall with buffet dinners and a wonderfully invigorating onsen-fed bath – the perfect indulgence after hiking Rishiri-zan.

Pension Misaki   PENSION $$
(ペンションみさ; ☎82-1659; fax 82-2176; www.misaki.burari.biz/sub01.htm, in Japanese; r per person with 2 meals ¥8925) An informal place with harbour-view, Japanese-style rooms and a Japanese bath, this whitewashed pension is just a few minutes on foot from Oshidomari port. While it's not the fanciest place on the island, it is a decent midrange option where you can expect good service and hearty seafood dinners.

Rishiri Green Hill Youth Hostel   HOSTEL $
(利尻グリーンヒルユースホステル; ☎82-2507; www.youthhostel.or.jp/English/n_rishiri.htm; dm from ¥3960; ⊘Mar-Sep) About 25 minutes' walk from Oshidomari port or a short bus ride to the Gurīn-Hiru-Yūsu-Hosuteru-mae stop, the island's youth hostel is a sociable spot for assembling an impromptu hiking party. But unfortunately the dormitories are less than spotless, and the building itself is completely lacking in personality.

Hokuroku Kyampu-jō   CAMPGROUND $
(利尻北麓野営場; ☎82-2394; campsites per person ¥300) Located right near the start of the Rishiri-zan track.

Kutsugata-Misaki Kyampu-jō   CAMPGROUND $
(杏形岬公園キャンプ場; ☎84-2394; campsites per person ¥300) Just south of the ferry terminal in Kutsugata.

ℹ Information

Information booths (Oshidomari ☎82-2201; ⊘8am-5.30pm 15 Apr-15 Oct; Kutsugata ☎84-3622; ⊘10am-4.30pm May-Sep) provide maps and details about transport, sights and hiking. Staff can also help you book accommodation.

ℹ Getting There & Around

AIR
From Rishiri-tō Airport, just a few kilometres west of Oshidomari, there are a couple of flights a day to Wakkanai, more in the summer tourist season. Local buses run infrequently by the airport, which means you're better off taking a taxi into town for around ¥1200.

BICYCLE
Bicycling is a great way to see the island – rent one from the youth hostels or shops near the Oshidomari ferry terminal – a leisurely circuit of the island (56km) takes anywhere from five to seven hours. There is also a 29km cycling path that runs through woods and coastal plains from Oshidomari past Kutsugata.

BOAT
From Wakkanai Harbour, **Heartland Ferry** (ハートランドフェリー; ☎011-233-8010) operates

QUICK TIPS

Prepare properly for a mountain hike and pay particular attention to the season and weather – late June through mid-September is best. Aim for an early start if you're not planning to spend the night atop the mountain. Excellent maps and hiking details (mainly in Japanese) are available at the information booths and the youth hostel.

Rishiri-Rebun-Sarobetsu National Park

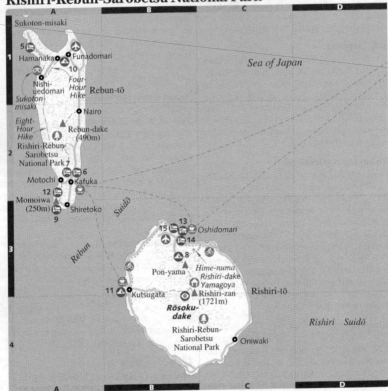

Rishiri-Rebun-Sarobetsu National Park

two to four daily ferries (year-round) between Wakkanai and Oshidomari (from ¥2080, 1¾ hours). Slightly less frequent ferries run in both direction from Oshidomari and Kutsugata Harbours to Kafuka (¥830, 45 minutes) on Rebun-tō. All ferry tickets are available for purchase at the various ports.

BUS

Regular local buses run in both directions around the island's perimeter, completing a circuit in about two hours (¥2200). The trip from Oshidomari to Kutsugata (¥730) takes 30 to 50 minutes, depending on whether the bus stops at the airport.

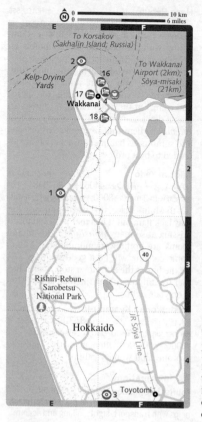

A relaxed 2½-hour hike runs from Su-koton-misaki along the coast to the scenic overlook at **Sukai-misaki** (澄海岬) before turning inland for another 1½ hours of hiking to reach the bus stop at **Hamanaka** (浜中). Alternatively, you can continue south from Sukai-misaki and hike the entire length of the island, arriving eight hours later in the village of **Motochi** (元地).

Another popular hike is from **Nairo** (内路), halfway down the east coast, to the top of **Rebun-dake** (礼文岳; 490m). The peak is subdued in comparison to the volcanic splendour of neighbouring Rishiri. But the hike is a pleasant four-hour return journey, and the view from the summit helps to give perspective on the shape of Rebun.

Near the port in **Kafuka** (香深) there is a wildflower loop leading across a backbone of spectacular highlands to **Momoiwa** (桃岩; Peach Rock). The trail then winds down through more flowers and bamboo to the lighthouse at **Shiretoko** (知床). It's a great two-hour taste of the island's beauty for those without a lot of time.

🛏 Sleeping

Once again, note that it's best to phone ahead in the winter months as the places listed here are closed irregularly. Note that meals are best taken at your accommodation since restaurants on the island are limited. Finally, you can usually arrange to be collected from the port or the airport if you call ahead to any of the following accommodation listings.

TOP CHOICE **Momoiwa-sō Youth Hostel** HOSTEL $
(桃岩荘ユースホステル; ☑86-1421; www .youthhostel.or.jp/n_momoiwaso.htm, in Japanese; dm ¥3645, breakfast/dinner ¥630/1050; ◎Jun-Sep) Famous for hard hikes by day and camp songs and craziness until lights out at 10pm, this eclectic youth hostel (located in an old herring house) has a devoted cult following. With an absolutely stunning location on Rebun's southwest side, it's just a few minutes' walk from several hiking tracks and has easy access to the rock-strewn sea. Beds are a combination of Japanese-style dorms (on tatami mats) and bunks. Staff can pick you up when the ferry docks: look for the flags and the enthusiastic guys yelling '*okae-rinasai!*' (welcome home!). If you're coming by yourself, you can take a Motochi-bound bus and get off at the Yūsu-mae station (15 minutes), from where it's another 15-minute walk.

REBUN-TŌ   礼文島
☑0163 / POP 3200

Shaped like an arrowhead (or a dried squid), Rebun is a naturalist's dream. In the glorious summertime, fields of over 300 species of wildflower explode into colour. The terrain is varied, and each walking track is unique. The beaches also harbour all sorts of cool finds, from interesting (and edible!) marine animals to semiprecious stones.

🏃 Activities

Most people come to Rebun-tō to hike, whether it is the eight-hour version or some of the tamer two- to four-hour options.

For starters, it's a good idea to take a bus to the northern tip of the island, **Sukoton-misaki** (スコトン岬). From here, you can hike your way back south, passing breathtaking cliff-side vistas, fields of flowers, dwarf-bamboo thickets, woody forests and tiny fishing villages tucked tightly into the island's many coves.

TRAIL SAFETY

Anyone injured while hiking on Rebun has to be rescued by boat, so heed our advice for maximising trail safety. As a general rule, group hiking is always encouraged – if you're travelling alone, consider meeting a few new friends in the hostels. You should also watch the weather carefully and plan ahead. Warm layers and rain gear are recommended.

Finally, do *not*, under any circumstances, drink unpurified water. After being introduced from Russia in the 1930s, foxes colonised the island and contaminated the streams with their faeces. This means that *Echinococcus multilocularis* is present, which can cause a deadly tapeworm infection.

Hanashin   HOTEL $$

(はな心; ☑86-1648; www16.plala.or.jp/hanasin, in Japanese; r per person with/without bathroom & 2 meals ¥10,800/8800; 🐾@) A great compromise between the larger hotels and the no-frills youth hostel, the Nature Inn is something of an ecolodge divided into two wings, offering the choice between functional tatami rooms with shared bathrooms and slightly larger rooms with private facilities. Guests divide by sex for a predinner soak in the on-site *sento*, and then congregate in the cafeteria for country-style meals prepared by an attentive family. The property is a 25-minute walk north from Kafuka-kō. By bus, head in the Shimadomari direction and get off at 'Youth Iriguchi'.

Field Inn Seikan-sō   HOSTEL $

(フィールドイン星観荘; ☑87-2818; http://homepage1.nifty.com/seikanso/main/p030000.htm, in Japanese; dm with 2 meals ¥6000; ⊙May-Oct) This dormitory-style accommodation is more peaceful than Momoiwa-sō, which may appeal to some hikers who can do without all the cheesiness. Nestled on a small ledge in the middle of a grassy field, Seikan-sō very much gives the impression of a rural field station, not to mention the fact that it's a convenient jumping-off point for a number of hikes. Take a bus to Sukoton-misaki (ask the driver to let you off at Seikan-sō). After getting off the bus, take the unpaved road to the west. Staff can pick you up at the ferry if you phone ahead.

Hana Rebun   HOTEL $$$

(花れぶん; ☑86-1177; www.hanarebun.com, in Japanese; r with 2 meals from ¥17,850; @🐾) Competing with the package-holiday hotels on neighbouring Rishiri, this upmarket spot packs in the crowds during the busy summer months. You might want to consider elsewhere if you're searching for peace and calm. On the other hand, if tourists en masse don't scare you, there is an excellent *rotemburo* here that overlooks Rishiri-zan, and sumptuous banquet dinners that are attended to by a professional staff.

Kāchan Yado   MINSHUKU $$

(かあちゃん宿; ☑86-1406; fax 86-2188; r per person with 2 meals ¥8000; ⊙Jun-Aug) Translating to Mum's Place, this warm and cosy inn may lack flair, but it has that personal touch missing at so many *minshuku*. Tiny tatami rooms are nothing memorable, but Mum's home cooking will be a good memory. Get off the bus at the Shiretoko stop, walk a further five minutes along the road and the inn is on your right.

Kushukohan Kyampu-jō   CAMPGROUND $

(久種湖畔キャンプ場; ☑87-3110; campsites per person/tent ¥600/500, 4-person cabins ¥2000; ⊙May-Oct) Offers attractive lakeside camping and woodsy cabins.

🛈 Information

Tourist information counter (☑86-2655; ⊙8am-5pm mid-Apr–Oct) At the ferry terminal; helps with transport, sights, hiking and accommodation.

🛈 Getting There & Around

AIR

From Rebun-tō Airport, at the very northern tip of the island, there are a couple of flights a day to Wakkanai, more in the summer tourist season. The closest bus stop to the airport is Kūkō-shita ('Below the Airport'), which means you'll still need to walk 15 minutes to the terminal.

BOAT

From Wakkanai Harbour, **Heartland Ferry** (ハートランドフェリー; ☑011-233-8010) operates two to five daily ferries (year-round) between Wakkanai and Kafuka (from ¥2300, two hours). Slightly less frequent ferries run in both directions from Kafuka to Oshidomari and Kutsugata Harbours (¥830, 45 minutes) on Rebun-tō. All ferry tickets are available for purchase at the various ports.

BUS

Up to five buses per day run along the island's main road from Kafuka in the south to Sukoton-misaki in the north (¥1180, 70 minutes). There are also bus routes from Kafuka to Shiretoko (¥280, 15 minutes) and Motochi (¥440, 20 minutes) – check the timetable at the Kafuka ferry terminal on arrival.

Furano 富良野

☎0167 / POP 25,230

One of Japan's most inland towns, Furano receives extreme amounts of powdery snow, and is ranked as one of the country's top skiing and snowboarding destinations. Rather surprisingly, a continental climate descends on the area outside the winter months, fostering a burgeoning wine industry, producing award-winning cheeses and enabling sprawling fields of lavender to spring to life. For Japanese tourists who can't manage the time and money to summer in the south of France, Furano is regarded as something of a close second.

⊙ Sights

The real appeal of Furano is simply exploring and getting lost in the beautiful nature surrounding the town. However, if you want to focus your sightseeing a bit more, there are a number of gourmet attractions worth checking out.

Having the luxury of your own wheels will enhance your visit, and allow you to (proverbially speaking) stop and smell the roses. But public transport is available – frequent shuttle buses leave from bus stop 4 across from JR Furano Station, stopping at the various sights listed here (¥150 per trip).

FREE Farm Tomita   LAVENDER FARM
(ファーム富田; Map p506; www.farm-tomita. co.jp/en; ⊙9am-4.30pm Oct-late Apr, 8.30am-6pm late Apr-Sep) You really have to see Farm Tomita to believe it, though try to imagine expansive fields of carefully delineated flowers blooming in succession. Given the French connection, the Japanese tend to go wildest over the lavender, but the seasonal fields are just as visually arresting and olfactorally intoxicating. The lavender theme continues at the cafe and gift shop, where lavender-infused products include soft creams, puddings, jellies, pastries and sodas. From roughly June to September, JR actually opens up a temporary station known as Lavender Batake (ラベンダー畑; Lavender Farm; Map p506) to accommodate the influx of tourists.

FREE Furano Wine Kōjō   WINERY
(ふらのワイン工場; Map p506; www.furanow ine.jp, in Japanese; ⊙9am-4.30pm, closed Sat & Sun Nov-Apr) If you're not going skiing or getting behind the wheel, the Furano Wine Factory (ふらのワイン工場), about 4km northwest of the station, gives tours explaining the wine-making process, and obliges visitors with a complimentary tipple.

FREE Furano Budō-kajū Kōjō   GRAPE-JUICE FACTORY
(ふらのぶどう果汁工場; Map p506; ⊙9am-4.30pm, closed weekends Sep-May) If you're going skiing or getting behind the wheel, Furano Budō-kajū Kōjō, about 1.5km away, gives tours explaining the grape juice–making process, and obliges visitors with a complimentary non-alcoholic tipple.

FREE Furano Chīzu Kōjō   CHEESE FACTORY
(富良野チーズ工場; Map p506; www.furano -cheese.jp; ⊙9am-5pm May-Oct, to 4pm Nov-Apr, closed 1st & 3rd Sat & Sun of month Nov-Apr) Foodies should continue on to the cheese factory – try the squid-ink brie.

FREE Furano Aisu-miruku Kōjō   ICE-MILK FACTORY
(富良野アイスミルク工房; Map p506; www .furano-cheese.jp; ⊙9am-5pm May-Oct, to 4pm Nov-Apr, closed 1st & 3rd Sat & Sun of month Nov-Apr) Adjacent is the ice-milk factory, which offers cool treats to beat the summer heat.

🏃 Activities

Furano Skī-Jō   SKIING & SNOWBOARDING
(富良野スキー場; Map p506; www.princehotels. co.jp/ski/furano_e/index.html; lift tickets full day/ night only ¥4200/1500; ⊙day 8.30am-5pm, night 5-9pm) Lying between two Prince hotels, this world-class winter-sports resort has hosted 10 FIS World Ski Cup events and two FIS World Snowboarding Cup events. Yet to the benefit of savvy foreign travellers, Furano remains relatively undiscovered, especially in comparison to its spotlight-hogging rival, Niseko. To make a fair comparison, Furano does not allow for off-piste skiing, but there is plenty here to catch your fancy.

The 23 slopes are predominantly beginner and intermediate. The handful of advanced runs are very steep, a bit short and are typically ungroomed with some seriously deep snow drifts. The more novice-friendly courses, all with perfect powder, can run up

DON'T MISS

BIEI

With the dramatic mountains of Daisetsuzan National Park in the background, Biei (美瑛; population 11,000) is an artist's and nature-lover's mecca. With the freedom of a rental car, you can cruise for hours along blissful country roads lined with fields of sunflowers, lavender and white birch.

Biei Potato-no-Oka (美瑛ポテトの丘; ☎0166-92-3255; www.potatovillage.com/eng/top. html; dm/r per person from ¥4960/6100, 4-person cottages ¥22,000, 3-/5-person log houses ¥13,650/21,000; @ 🛜) is an endearing youth hostel perched at the top of a field of potatoes. A variety of accommodation options are available in dormitories, rooms with private bathrooms, and positively adorable cottages and log houses. Guests congregate at night for hearty dinners (extra cost) featuring local produce, most notably potatoes!

Rte 237 runs between Asahikawa and Biei, but the real appeal of Biei is simply exploring the detours, getting lost and stopping to enjoy the rural flavour. If you don't have a car, there are *kaisoku* on the JR Furano line between Biei and Furano (¥620, 40 minutes).

to 3km in length. They also wind scenically through pristine birch forests, and open up in sections to tremendous views. Eleven lifts, including the fastest gondola in Japan, help to keep the crowds in check.

The two Prince hotels provide a wonderful *après-ski* atmosphere of fine dining, lively drinking and curative onsen soaking. Full equipment rental is available for ¥4500 per day. English signage is adequate.

🎎 Festivals & Events

Heso Matsuri   BELLY BUTTONS
Humorously known as Heso-no-machi (Belly-Button Town), Furano is in the centre of Hokkaidō: the middle. This geographic distinction has given rise to the town's famous navel festival on 28 and 29 July. If you've been pining for a place where you can strip off your shirt and have a traditional mask painted onto your torso before you go revelling, you've come to the right festival. *Tobiiri odori* ('jump right in') dancing is part of the fun; as with sumō, it helps to be a bit on the heavy side!

Furano Wine Festival   WINE
Coinciding with the grape harvest every September, this festival offers tastings and bacchanal merriment. A barbecue lets you buy local produce and then grill it for yourself, while costumed revellers stamp barefoot on grapes in a barrel.

🛏 Sleeping

New Furano Prince Hotel   HOTEL $$
(Map p506; ☎22-1111; www5.princehotels.co.jp/en/newfurano/; s/d with breakfast & lift tickets from ¥14,000/16,000; @ 🛜 ♨) Lying at opposite

ends of the ski slopes near the gondolas, both Prince hotels are snazzy places with a variety of restaurants, bars, and lounge areas. If we had to choose, however, the New Furano wins out for its modern sheen, though we confess that the 'new' moniker may be subliminally influencing. While the rooms themselves are nothing more than standard issue, the service here is impeccable, and the convenience factor helps to maximise your slope time. Note that the cheapest prices are available if you book online in advance.

Furano Prince Hotel   HOTEL $$
(富良野プリンスホテル; Map p506; ☎23-4111; www5.princehotels.co.jp/en/furano; s/d with breakfast & lift tickets from ¥12,500/15,000; @ 🛜 ♨) Somewhat akin to an oversized A-frame chalet, the Furano Prince Hotel is the older sibling that has aged gracefully, thanks to a number of interior makeovers. Once again, you're paying for convenience, amenities and service, though costs can be kept at a reasonable level if you book well in advance.

Furano Natulux Hotel   BOUTIQUE HOTEL $$$
(富良野ナチュラクスホテル; ☎22-1777; fax 23-1070; www.natulux.com/en/index.html; s/d from ¥12,600/18,900; @ 🛜) If you came to Furano to ski, then you really can't beat the location and the amenities of the two Prince properties. But when it comes to style, the Natulux wins out, hands down. Located directly across from JR Furano Station, this brand-new boutique hotel is reminiscent of a converted loft apartment with exposed sheetrock walls and modernist urban fur-

nishings. Rooms are very tiny and therefore not for the claustrophobic, but things open up a bit in the rock-lined *sento*. The cafe is also a great place to indulge in a wine and cheese fondue set – both locally sourced, of course!

Furano Youth Hostel
HOSTEL $

(富良野ユースホステル; ☑44-4441; www.4.ocn.ne.jp/~furanoyh/english.htm; 3-20 Okamati Naka-Furano-Cho; dm/s/d with breakfast & dinner ¥3360/5460/8820; @) Just west of JR Naka-Furano Station, the Furano Youth Hostel occupies a big farmhouse complete with an expansive deck overlooking the countryside. The best part of staying here is the free breakfast and dinner (except Sunday night – the chef takes a break!), which are simple but tasty self-service meals featuring local produce.

Alpine Backpackers
HOSTEL $

(アルパインバックパッカーズ; ☑22-1311; fax 23-4385; www.alpn.co.jp/english/index.html; dm per person ¥2500, tw/q ¥5000/10,000; @🛜) The perfect crash pad for anyone with plans to spend every waking moment on the slopes, Alpine Backpackers is conveniently located just a few minutes' walk from the Kitanomine lift near the Prince Hotel. True to its moniker, backpackers are well catered for with cooking facilities, laundry machines, and a boiling onsen that gets the aches and pains out after skiing.

🍴 Eating & Drinking

TOP CHOICE Kunen-kōbō

Yamadori
JAPANESE CURRY $

(くんえん工房 YAMADORI; ☑39-1810; 4-14 Asahi-machi; dishes from ¥1000; ⊙lunch & dinner; 🗾) Furano is famous for its curries, a potent winter warmer that heats from within. But rather than serving it simply over rice, Yamadori tops off the dish with a fresh omelette and a sliced sausage in a local concoction known as *omu-karē* (¥1000). You'll find this neat little treat in a cutesy-cool pink farm house with white trim, just around the northwest corner of the Natulux Hotel.

Chīzu Rāmen-no-mise Karin
CHEESE RĀMEN $

(チーズラーメンの店かりん; ☑22-1692; 9-12 Moto-machi; dishes from ¥1000; ⊙11am-8pm) As you've no doubt figured out by now, Furano is also famous for its cheese. While you can be a traditionalist and eat it by the slice, we prefer ours shredded over a bowl of *rāmen*. This excessively high-calorie indulgence can

be found in a fairly nondescript brown-and-white building (look for the red curtain) three blocks east and one block north of the public library. There is no English menu, but just say *'cheezu rāmen'* and you're golden.

Bars are everywhere in the town centre, and closer to the slopes in the vicinity of the Prince hotels. In the summer months the action tends to cluster along the main drag heading southwest from the station. Peak snow season shifts the focus to the two Prince properties.

❶ Information

Tourist information office (☑23-3388; www.furanotourism.com/english/home.htm; ⊙9am-6pm) Stock up on maps and pamphlets, get some last-minute help booking accommodation, rent bicycles and even check your internet for free.

❶ Getting There & Away

Bus

Frequent buses run between Furano and Sapporo (¥2100, three hours), as well as between Furano and Asahikawa (¥860, 1½ hours).

Car & Motorcycle

Rte 237 runs between Asahikawa and Furano, though be extremely careful in the winter months as this route can be icy and treacherous. As a word of caution, Furano's roads have the highest rate of traffic fatalities in the country. Also, be sure to pick up a good map from tourist information as it's very easy to get lost in the mountains.

Train

There are frequent *kaisoku* on the JR Furano line between Furano and Asahikawa (¥1040, 1¼ hours). For Sapporo (¥4030, 2½ hours), take a frequent *futsū* on the JR Nemuro line to Takikawa, and then change to the hourly Super Kamui *tokkyū*.

A *Lavender Express* special seasonal train also runs direct between Furano and Sapporo (from ¥4040, two hours) daily from early June to 31 August, and on weekends and holidays from September to the end of October.

Daisetsuzan National Park 大雪山国立公園

Known as 'Nutakukamushupe' in Ainu, Daisetsuzan or 'Big Snow Mountain' is Japan's largest national park, covering more than 2300 sq km. A vast wilderness area of soaring mountains, active volcanoes, remote

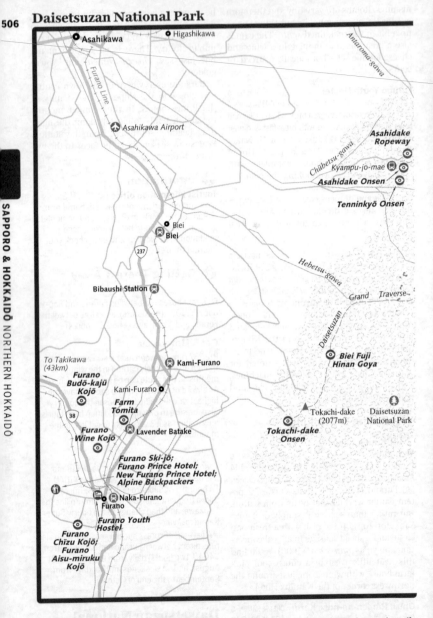

onsen, clear lakes and dense forests, Daisetsuzan is the kind of place that stressed-out workers in Tokyo and Osaka dream about on their daily commute.

Virtually untouched by human hands, the park has minimal tourism, with most visitors basing themselves in the hot-spring villages on the periphery. From the comfort of your onsen hotel, you can make small forays into the park's interior, summiting peaks and hiking through valleys on challenging day routes.

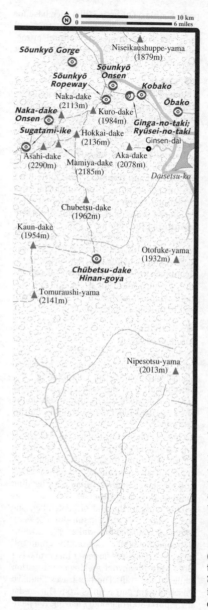

Sōunkyō Gorge

Niseikaushuppe-yama
(1879m)

Sōunkyō
Ropeway

Sōunkyō
Onsen

Kobako

Naka-dake
(2113m)

Ōbako

Naka-dake
Onsen

Kuro-dake
(1984m)

Ginga-no-taki;
Ryūsei-no-taki

Sugatami-ike

Hokkai-dake
(2136m)

Ginsen-dai

Asahi-dake
(2290m)

Mamiya-dake
(2185m)

Aka-dake
(2078m)

Daisetsu-ko

Chubetsu-dake
(1962m)

Kaun-dake
(1954m)

Otofuke-yama
(1932m)

Chūbetsu-dake
Hinan-goya

Tomuraushi-yama
(2141m)

Nipesotsu-yama
(2013m)

0   10 km
0   6 miles

However, if you have the right gear, and you've done a bit of planning, you can tackle Japan's most hardcore multiday hike, the Daisetsuzan Grand Traverse (see the box, p509), which shatters any notions you have of Japan being small and densely packed.

ASAHIDAKE ONSEN
旭岳温泉

☑0166

This forested hot-springs resort has a dozen or so small inns at the base of Asahi-dake. Serious hikers head here for the start of the Daisetsuzan Grand Traverse. There are plenty of other options, many of which wind through unique terrain offering a mix of volcanic activity, fields and foliage. Whether you're here for a full-on hike or just a few day trails, be good to your body by spending ample time in the area's healing onsen.

🏃 Activities

Asahidake Ropeway
ROPEWAY

(朝日岳 ロープウェイ; Map p506; one way/return Jul–mid-Oct ¥1500/2800, mid-Oct–Jun ¥1000/1800; ⏱6am-4.30pm Jul–mid-Oct, 9am-4pm mid-Oct–Jun) This ropeway runs to within in easy hiking distance of **Asahi-dake** (旭岳; 2290m), Hokkaido's tallest peak.

Before embarking on the final climb, don't miss **Sugatami-ike** (姿見池), a picture-postcard pond that reflects the contrasting images of snow in the foreground and steaming Asahi-dake in the background.

The climb up the south ridge and over the west flank is a constant incline, but it should only take you about two hours if you're in good shape. Once atop the peak, you'll have a 360-degree view of Daisetsuzan National Park to revel in.

You can follow the 1.7km loop track that leads for about 50 minutes around the area before returning to the ropeway's upper terminal, or embark on the Daisetsuzan Grand Traverse.

Back in town, most onsen, even at the higher-end hotels, are open for day use to the general public. Prices range from ¥500 up to ¥1500 – bringing your own wash cloth and towel can shave a few hundred yen off the price.

🛏 Sleeping & Eating

🏨 Hotel Beamonte
HOTEL $$$

(ホテルベアモンテ; ☎97-2321; www.bearmonte.jp, in Japanese; r per person with 2 meals from ¥10,650) Across from the visitors centre, this is Asahidake's most sophisticated accommodation. Modelled after an alpine chalet, the Beamonte combines elegant rooms (some with polished wooden floors) and a stunner of an onsen, offering a variety of indoor and outdoor rock tubs. Prices vary substantially depending on the season, and it can be quite full at times; calling ahead is a good plan. Visiting the bath only is possible for ¥1500.

SAPPORO & HOKKAIDŌ DAISETSUZAN NATIONAL PARK

Daisetsuzan Shirakaba-sō INN $

(大雪山白樺荘; ☎97-2246; fax 97-2247; http://
park19.wakwak.com/~shirakaba/english.html; dm
¥4870, dm/r per person with 2 meals ¥6890/7940;
@) Something of a cross between a youth
hostel and a ryokan, this mountain lodge
near the ropeway's lower terminal offers
comfortable Japanese- and Western-style
rooms and hot-spring baths. There is a large
kitchen available if you're self-catering, but
it's worth going for the meal plan as the
English-speaking staff specialises in heart-
healthy dishes. If you're looking to recruit
some fellow hikers for the grand traverse,
this is probably the best spot to do so.

Lodge Nutapukaushipe LODGE $$

(ロッジ・ヌタプカウシペ; ☎97-2150; r per
person with 2 meals from ¥7500, rāmen from ¥750)
Next door to Shirakaba-sō, this log cabin–
style accommodation is an intimate choice,
offering just a handful of private rooms. The
property is also highlighted by a wonder-
ful onsen built from rich woods, as well as
a *rāmen* shop that tops traditional noodle
blends with local mountain vegetables – ask
for the *sansai rāmen*.

ℹ Information

Hikers should pay a visit to the **Asahidake
Visitors Centre** (☎97-2153; www.town.higashi
kawa.hokkaido.jp/vc, in Japanese; ☉9am-5pm
daily Jun-Oct, to 4pm Tue-Sun Nov-May), which
has excellent maps that the staff will mark with
daily track conditions. An onsen map is also
available here, which lists the locations, prices
and hours of the various baths.

ℹ Getting There & Away

From 15 June to October, there are five buses
in both directions between bus stop 4 in front
of JR Asahikawa Station and Asahidake Onsen
(¥1320, 1½ hours). The first bus, which leaves
Asahikawa and Asahidake at 9.10am and 9.15am
respectively, is direct, while all others require a
quick transfer in Higashikawa. All other times of
the year, there are only one or two daily buses in
both directions.

If you're driving, follow Rtes 237, 213 and 160
from Asahikawa to Asahidake Onsen. Note that
these roads are very dangerous in the snowy
winter months, so drive with extreme caution.

SŌUNKYŌ ONSEN 層雲峡温泉
☎01658

Daisetsuzan's second major gateway is this
onsen town on the park's northeastern edge,
which provides secondary access to the
grand traverse (see the box, p509). Even if
you're not planning to hike the length of the

park, Sōunkyō Onsen is still a nice base for
shorter forays into the park's interior, and
there are some impressive natural attrac-
tions in the area that are worth seeking out
between dips in the hot springs.

⊙ Sights

Sōunkyō (層雲峡; Layer Cloud Gorge) is a
string of gorges that stretches for approxi-
mately 8km beyond Sōunkyō Onsen. Don't
miss the breathtaking waterfalls, namely
Ryūsei-no-taki (流星の滝; Shooting Stars
Falls) and **Ginga-no-taki** (銀河の滝; Milky
Way Falls). Also noteworthy are **Ōbako** (大
箱; Big Box) and **Kobako** (小箱; Little Box),
two unique sections of perpendicular rock
formations. If you don't have a rental car, a
number of shops along the main street rent
mountain bikes (¥2000 per day).

After a hard day of cycling, **Kurodake-
no-yu** (黒岳の湯; admission ¥600; ☉10am-9pm
Thu-Tue) offers handsome hot-spring baths
including a 3rd-floor *rotemburo* – it's on the
town's main pedestrian street. You can also
soothe your aching feet in the free foot bath
next to the Ginsenkaku Hotel.

🏃 Activities

Sōunkyō ropeway ROPEWAY

(大雪山層雲峡・黒岳ロープウェイ; www
.rinyu.co.jp/kurodake; ☉8am-7pm Jul-Aug, closed
intermittently in winter) This combination rope-
way-chairlift provides fast and easy access
to Kuro-dake. One-way/return tickets on the
ropeway cost ¥100/1850 and on the chairlift
¥400/600.

Once at the top, you have three options:
you can explore Kurodake for a few hours
before returning to Sōunkyō Onsen, head
to Asahidake on an all-day, no-return excur-
sion, or spend the next three days heading
south on the grand traverse.

From July to the end of September, one
bus a day goes to **Ginsen-dai** (銀泉台),
where the trailhead **Aka-dake** (赤岳; 2078m)
is located. Set a bit back from the grand tra-
verse, Aka-dake sees far fewer hikers and is a
nice escape for anyone seeking near isolation
while on the trail. The bus leaves Sōunkyō
Onsen at 6am and returns from Ginsen-dai
at 2.15pm (¥800, one hour), leaving you plen-
ty of time for your ascent and descent.

🎎 Festivals & Events

Hyōbaku Matsuri ICE

From the end of January to the end of
March, this festival features ice sculptures,
tunnels and domes, some lit up.

DAISETSUZAN GRAND TRAVERSE

Hokkaidō's ultimate outdoor experience, the Daisetsuzan Grand Traverse is a roughly five-day, 55km hike connecting two active volcanoes, **Asahi-dake** and **Tokachi-dake** (十勝岳; 2077m), which lie at the northern and southern areas of the park respectively.

The hiking season runs from early July to late October, and there are guaranteed sources of fresh water (sometimes snow!) throughout this time frame. A tent and camping gear are preferable to the extremely bare-bones huts, and you'll need to carry in your own food and cooking supplies. This is also bear country, so be smart and tie a bell to your rucksack.

You should also pick up a topographic map of the area – we recommend anything by the Japanese company **Yama-to-kogen-chizu** (山と高原地図) – and be sure to talk to the staff at the **Asahidake Visitors Centre** (see p508). One last thing: make sure you're in peak physical condition as the grand traverse is anything but a walk in the park.

The trail starts from atop the ropeway in the village of Asahidake Onsen, and leads up and over Asahi-dake on the first day. As if this wasn't enough of an initial shock, you'll still need to traverse **Mamiya-dake** (間宮岳; 2185m) and **Naka-dake** (中岳; 2113m) before reaching shelter at the crossroads beneath **Kuro-dake** (黒岳; 1984m). Over a seven- to eight-hour period, you'll ascend 1450m, descend 650m and cover no less than 15km of tough-going, mountainous terrain.

Your first night's lodging will be at **Kuro-dake Ishimuro** (黒岳石室; ☎0165-85-3031; campsites per person ¥200, huts ¥2000), which has a fresh-water supply and a state-of-the-art bio-toilet (instead of flushing, you're asked to pedal after doing your business!). If you're not completely knackered, it's about 30 minutes to the top of Kuro-dake for an unforgettable sunset.

On the second day, you can cut the hike short by taking a combination ropeway-chair-lift down to the village of **Sōunkyō Onsen**. Otherwise, it's seven to nine hours and 18km on the edge of an escarpment along the plateau of **Takane-ga-hara** (高根ガ原). Before the day is done, you'll need to scale **Chūbetsu-dake** (忠別岳; 1962m) before reaching the unmanned A-frame shelter **Chūbetsu-dake Hinan-goya** (忠別岳避難小屋). There is a basic toilet here, and the snow melt can be boiled.

The third day, a mere 5km, 10-hour walk, is a welcome respite. You will continue south through head-high brush pine and scale **Kaun-dake** (化雲岳; 1954m) before arriving at the base of **Tomuraushi-yama** (トムラウシ山; 2141m), one of Japan's famous '100 mountains' that is seemingly an enormous pile of boulders. After a good deal of boulder-hopping, you can bed down in the unmanned campsite of **Minami-numa Kyampu-jō** (南沼キャンプ場). There is plenty of melting water here, but no toilets to speak of.

Did you get plenty of rest? Good, because the fourth and most difficult day is a nine- to 10-hour, 17km slog to the seemingly abandoned shelter of **Biei Fuji Hinan Goya** (美瑛富士避難小屋). If the going gets tough, you can always break down this route into two days, but be advised that you will need to make sure your food and water supplies are adequate. The latter option also entails camping at **Futago-numa** (双子沼), a cramped and muddy clearing that sits in no-man's land between escape points on an exposed ridge.

Finally, on the last day, you will tackle the moonscape of Tokachi-dake before descending into the village of **Tokachi-dake Onsen**, where you can reward yourself with a much-needed bath in the hot springs. Happy trails!

Kyōkoku Hi Matsuri   FIRE

This celebration on the last Saturday in July is meant to purify the hot springs and appease the mountain and fire deities. Revellers perform traditional Ainu owl dances and drumming, climaxing with archers shooting flaming arrows into the gorge.

🛏 Sleeping

Ginsenkaku   RYOKAN $$

(銀泉閣; ☎5-3003; www.ginsenkaku.com, in Japanese; r per person with 2 meals high/low season from ¥15,900/10,500; ☎) A Japanese style-inn with European architectural flourishes, Ginsenkaku is a very professional operation located in the centre of the village. Traditionally minded tatami rooms are the scene of lavish nightly feasts, though not before you give yourself a good scrub down in the steamy common baths, including a *rotemburo* with a view.

Sōunkyō Youth Hostel

HOSTEL $

(層雲峡ユースホステル; ☑5-3418; www.youth hostel.or.jp/sounkyo; dm per person with/without 2 meals ¥4830/3150; ⊙ Jun-Oct; @) Dwarfed by the larger block-style resorts, this humble wooden hostel is about a 10-minute walk uphill from the bus station. Offering bunk-bed accommodation, as well as basic but filling meals, this is a great place to meet other hikers before tackling the trails in the park.

Taisetsu Hotel

HOTEL $$

(ホテル大雪; ☑5-3211; www.taisetsu-g.com/english/taisetsu1.htm; r per person with 2 meals from ¥10,000; @🛜♨) This sprawling resort up on the hill sees its fair share of the tour-group circuit, though the encompassing views and nature-wrapping bath complex offer plenty of respite from the crowds. The cheapest packages are run-of-the-mill tatami rooms paired with buffet dinners, but you can upgrade to in-room dining and onsen-equipped suites if you're in need of a splurge.

ⓘ Getting There & Away

There are up to seven buses a day in both directions between Sōunkyō Onsen and Asahikawa (¥1950, 1¾ hours) via Kamikawa. JR Rail Pass holders can travel for free between Asahikawa and Kamikawa, and then catch the bus between Kamikawa and Sōunkyō Onsen (¥800, 35 minutes). These buses also run between Sōunkyō Onsen and Akan Kohan (¥3260, 3½ hours) in Akan National Park.

There are also a couple of buses a day to Kushiro (¥4790, 5¼ hours) via Akan Kohan (¥3260, 3½ hours). Finally, there are two buses a day to Obihiro (¥2200, 80 minutes), which follow a scenic route via Nukabira-ko.

If you're driving, Rte 39 connects Sōunkyō Onsen to Asahikawa in the west and Abashiri in the east.

TOKACHI-DAKE ONSEN 十勝岳温泉

Northeast of Furano, this remote hot-spring village is the traditional end point for the grand traverse (see the box, p509). It is much less crowded than Asahidake and Sōunkyō Onsen, but still serves as a good base for hikes into Daisetsuzan National Park.

For instance, if you're not embarking on the entirety of the grand traverse, you can still climb the peak Tokachi-dake in a long day. This route undulates through a seemingly lifeless moonscape of sandy patches and rocky ledges.

With Furano so close by, most travellers choose to press on. However, a decent mid-range spot where you can unwind after hiking is the **Kamihoro-sō** (カミホロ荘; ☑0167-45-2970; http://tokachidake.com/kamihoro, in Japanese; s/d incl 2 meals from ¥15,700/25,400; @). Despite looking like an American motel from the front, inside you'll find pleasant Japanese-style rooms and hot-spring baths fronting the distant mountains. If coming by bus, get off at Kokumin-shukusha-mae, which is almost right in front of Kamihoro-sō.

Frequent *futsū* run on the JR Furano line between Furano and Kami-Furano (¥350, 20 minutes). Kami-Furano Station is connected to Tokachi-dake Onsen by regular buses (¥500, 20 minutes). If you're driving, just take it slow along windy Rte 291.

EASTERN HOKKAIDŌ

Eastern Hokkaidō (道東; Dōtō) is the Japanese equivalent of Canada's Yukon Territory, a harsh yet hauntingly beautiful landscape that has been shaped by vast temperature extremes. In the winter months, dramatic ice floes off the coast of Abashiri can be seen from the decks of icebreakers. But Akan Kohan, an Ainu cultural stronghold, and Shiretoko, a pristine national park, are best explored during the mild summers. Not so coincidentally, this is also when all of the bears that live here are most active!

Abashiri 網走

☑0152 / POP 40,000

To the Japanese, Abashiri is as synonymous with the word 'prison' as Alcatraz is to Westerners. Winters here are as harsh as they come, and the mere mention of the prison here (still in operation) sends chills through the spines of even the most hardened individuals. Abashiri is also famous for its frozen seas, which can be explored on icebreakers, and its coral-grass blooms, which burst into life every September. Throughout the warmer months, Abashiri serves as a jumping-off point for both Akan National Park and Shiretoko National Park.

◎ Sights

A ¥900 day pass gives all-day entry on a tourist-loop bus, which connects the bus and train stations to the various museums.

Abashiri Kangoku Hakubutsukan MUSEUM
(網走監獄博物館; www.kangoku.jp/world/index.htm; admission ¥1050; ⊙8am-6pm Apr-Oct, 9am-5pm Nov-Mar) Housed in the remains of the original Meiji-era structure, this dark and foreboding museum details the reasons that this historic prison was so feared. Inmates braved brutally cold winters with thin bedding and virtually no warmth: one lone pipe ran the entire length of the corridors, providing the bare minimum of heat for cell-bound prisoners.

FREE **Abashiri Keimusho** PRISON
(網走刑務所; ⊙9am-4pm) Across the river from the old prison is this modern construction, a very real and very secure working prison home to just under 800 inmates. Given the notoriety of its precursor, the modern prison has become something of a tourist attraction, complete with a tiny museum and gift shop where crafts made by inmates can be purchased. It's also possible to walk around outside the prison walls, though further entry and photographs are prohibited.

Okhotsk Ryūhyō-kan MUSEUM
(オホーツク流氷館; www.ryuhyokan.com, in Japanese; admission ¥520; ⊙8am-6pm Apr-Oct, 9am-4.30pm Nov-Mar) Next to the old prison is this ice-floe museum, which has an interesting display relating to the tiny *kurione* (sea angel), a funky relative of the sea slug that has become the de facto Abashiri mascot.

Hokkaido-ritsu Hoppō-minzoku Hakubutsukan MUSEUM
(北海道立北方民族博物館; www.hoppohm.org/english/index.htm; admission ¥450; ⊙9.30am-4.30pm Tue-Sun) A few minutes' walk downhill from the summit of Tento-zan is this museum of northern cultures, a state-of-the-art place with numerous exhibits of Ainu, Native American, Aleutian and other indigenous cultures.

🏃 Activities

Aurora ICEBREAKER CRUISING
(おーろら; http://ms-aurora.com/abashiri/en; cruises ¥3000; ⊙9am-6pm) From roughly late January to mid-March, the *Aurora* departs four to six times a day from Abashiri port for one-hour cruises into the frozen Sea of Okhotsk. Looking out at a snow-white plain of frozen floes from the deck of an icebreaker is a surreal experience, and the sound of bergs grinding together from the force of the sea's currents make a deep impression on all who hear it. As you might imagine, dressing warmly is essential if you want to enjoy this truly Siberian cruise.

Sango Sōgunraku CORAL-GRASS VIEWING
(サンゴ草群落) Known as salt pickle or glasswort in other parts of the world, the humble marsh plant of coral glass gets its 15 minutes of fame in mid-September, when it turns bright red. Busloads of tourists flock to a few boardwalk viewing spots. Nature lovers will enjoy the bird life, as the marshes attract not only seagulls but also curlews, terns, egrets, herons and more.

Ryūhyō Norokko-gō SIGHTSEEING TRAIN
(流氷ノロッコ号) Running concurrently with the *Aurora* is this sightseeing train, puttering along twice a day from Abashiri to Shiretoko-shari Station (¥810, 40 minutes) through a field of utterly white snow. Stare out at this frozen landscape while eating toasted *surume* (squid) and nursing a can of Sapporo lager.

In the fall, a cycling road runs for 25km from Abashiri proper to the coral-grass-viewing areas and beyond, providing some beautiful views of lakes, forests and pumpkin fields. In the summer, the northern coastal areas are perfect for beachcombing with lots of sand dollars and other small shells.

🎆 Festivals & Events

Come Back Salmon Night SALMON
A welcome to the lake's most famous (and delicious!) fish. Each year (mid-October to mid-December, depending on the fish's schedules) the salmon run upstream, greeted by bright spotlights that illuminate the fish as they pass into Abashiri-ko. Nearby grilling stations serve *sanma* (a dark, oily and delicious seasonal fish that's distantly related to mackerel, but smaller), scallops, squid and venison, often with free tastes. Salmon – the guest of honour – is *not* served...not *that* night anyway.

Orochon-no-hi FIRE
Held on the last Saturday in July, this festival derives from the shamanistic rites of the indigenous Gilyak people, who once lived in the Abashiri area.

🛏 Sleeping

Abashiri Central Hotel
HOTEL $$

(網走セントラルホテル; ☎44-5151; www
.abashirich.com, in Japanese; Minami-ni-jō-nishi,
San-chōme; s/tw from ¥6300/10,500; @) A few
minutes' walk east of the station in front of
Chūō bridge, the Abashiri Central is the best
hotel in town despite its fairly innocuous
price tag. Rooms are decked out in soft and
muted colours to provide for a relaxing stay,
while the recommended restaurant serves
up seasonal offerings from Abashiri's frozen
but nurturing seas.

🏖 Abashiri Gensei-kaen Youth Hostel
HOSTEL $

(網走原生花園ユースホステル; ☎46-2630;
http://sapporo.cool.ne.jp/genseikaen, in Japanese;
dm per person with 2 meals ¥5200; closed Nov-Jan;
@) This rural farmhouse turned youth hostel
is located in the middle of the **Wakka Gensei-
kaen** (ワッカ原生花園), a coastal wildflower
garden that is 20km long and 700m wide and
boasts more than 300 species. It's about a
15-minute drive east of Abashiri in the village
of Kitahama, or you can take a *futsū* on the JR
Senmō line from Abashiri to Kitahama (¥260,
20 minutes). The hostel is a 10-minute walk or
a quick drive southeast from the station.

Hotel Route Inn Abashiri Eki-mae
HOTEL $$

(ホテルルートイン網走駅前; ☎44-5511; fax
44-5512; www.route-inn.co.jp/search/hotel/index.
php?hotel_id=502, in Japanese; 1-2-13 Shin-chō;
s/d ¥6050/10,450; @🛜) Directly across from
JR Abashiri Station, this instalment of the
Route Inn chain offers the usual boring business rooms. However, a nice perk here aside
from the convenient location is the large
winter-warming onsen.

🍴 Eating & Drinking

Kandō Asa-ichi
SEAFOOD $

(感動朝市; ☎43-7670; 6.30-9.30am Mon-Fri, to
10.30am Sat & Sun mid-Jul–15 Oct) A great option for fresh-fish lovers: select your own
seafood and cook it on one of the open-air
grills. Shuttles leave from hotels to the market, located on the outskirts of the town; ask
your lodging for details.

Murakami
SUSHI $

(むらかみ; ☎43-1147; www.drive-net.com/mu
rakami, in Japanese; Minami-san-jō-nishi, Ni-chōme;
platters from ¥1400; lunch & dinner) Two blocks
east and one block south of the Central Hotel is this small sushi bar (look for the red-
and-blue sign), which is locally famous for

its high-quality fish. The owner changes the
menu daily based on what's fresh from the
boat, so it's best to just ask for his *osusume*.

Abashiri Bīru-kan
PUB $$

(網走ビール館; www.takahasi.co.jp/beer/yaki
niku/index.html, in Japanese; Minami-ni-jō-nishi,
Yon-chōme; meat plates from ¥780, beers from
¥500; lunch & dinner) A famous Hokkaidō
microbrewery with various flavours on tap,
the Abashiri Beer Hall offers refreshing tast-
er sets that are the perfect accompaniment
to *yaki-niku* (grilled meat) courses. There is
no English, but the mouth-watering picture
menu makes things easy.

ℹ Information

The **tourist information office** (☎44-5849;
9am-5pm) outside Abashiri Station has
English-language maps and a wide offering of
pamphlets on Eastern Hokkaidō.

ℹ Getting There & Away

Air

From Memanbetsu Airport, about 15km south
of the city centre, there are domestic flights to
various destinations including Sapporo, Tokyo
and Osaka. Airport buses (¥750, 30 minutes) are
approximately timed to flights and run from the
bus station via Abashiri Station to the airport.

Bus

There are a few highway buses each day in both
directions between the bus terminal in Abashiri
(1km east of the train station), and the Chūō bus
station in Sapporo (¥6210, 6¼ hours). Between
June and mid-October there are three daily buses
from Memanbetsu Airport via Abashiri bus termi-
nal to Utoro in Shiretoko National Park (¥3000,
2½ hours). Finally, there is one direct bus daily
linking Abashiri and Shari (¥1120, 1¼ hours).

Car & Motorcycle

Hiring a car is the best option for those who want
to get to the more remote sections of Shiretoko
and Akan National Parks. Various car-rental
agencies, including **JR Hokkaido Rent a Lease**
(ジェイアール北海道レンタリース; www.jrh-
rentacar.jp; 8am-6pm Jan-Apr & Nov-Dec, to
8pm May-Oct), are located in front of the station.

Train

Frequent *tokkyū* on the JR Sekihoku line run
between Abashiri and Asahikawa (¥7750, four
hours) via Bihoro (¥1440, 25 minutes), where
you can catch onward buses to Akan National
Park. There are just a couple of *futsū* each day
on the JR Senmō main line between Abashiri and
Kushiro (¥3570, 3½ hours) via Shiretoko-shari
(¥810, 40 minutes).

Akan National Park
阿寒国立公園

This expansive park (905 sq km) contains volcanic peaks, large caldera lakes, thick forests and rejuvenating onsen, though the six million or so visitors who come here each year are more interested in snapping photos of algae. Of course, we're not talking about any old clump of green slime, but rather *marimo (Cladophora aegagropila),* a surprisingly cute and increasingly rare spherical form of algae that has been declared a national treasure. Even if the appeal of *marimo* is lost on you, Akan is big enough that even at peak times, it's easy to get away from it all, particularly if you're looking to hike or meander around isolated forest and mountain tracks.

Kawayu Onsen bus station is 10 minutes by bus from JR Kawayu Onsen Station, one of the main access points for the national park. JR Mashū Station and the adjacent town of Teshikaga, a little further south, is an alternative access point.

KAWAYU ONSEN   川湯温泉
♪015

Kawayu is a quiet onsen town that is home to more than two dozen hot springs, but it's the surrounding area where Akan National Park really comes to life. From errant monster sightings in crater lakes to hard-boiled eggs in sulphurous pools, there is plenty here to keep you busy between bath times.

⊙ Sights

FREE **Wakoto Onsen**   HOT SPRING
(和琴温泉) Special not for what it has, but for what it doesn't, Wakoto is merely a scalding-hot pool in the middle of nowhere on the southern shore of a beautiful lake. Best reached by car or bicycle, the onsen has none of the razzle-dazzle of most spa resorts. There's no electricity, no soap, no buckets, not even any doors on the bathhouse: you just strip, dip and enjoy. Not for everyone, but true onsen buffs will appreciate it. It has a view of the western side of Kussharo-ko and, in season, snow geese fly overhead as the sun slips behind the mountains. Not for the shy either, as it's a *konyoku* (mixed-sex bath) and there's algae on the rocks, which makes getting in and out a slippery affair. If it's too hot when you stick a toe in, try moving further away (towards the lake, not the bathhouse) and you'll find it's a slightly cooler shade of scalding.

Iō-zan   MOUNTAIN SPRING
(硫黄山) This hellish mountain (512m) comes complete with steaming vents, sunshine-yellow sulphur and onsen-steamed eggs. You'll hear the sellers calling *Tamago! Tamago! Tamago! Tamago!* (Eggs!) even before you reach the car park. Although they don't taste much different from a regular kitchen-boiled egg, they're a sickly brownish-green. The 4km walk between JR Kawayu Onsen Station and Kawayu Onsen passes Iō-zan along the way.

Mashū-ko   LAKE
(摩周湖) Considered by many to be Japan's most beautiful lake, Mashū-ko once held the world record for water clarity (it was eventually topped by Oregon's Crater Lake), with visibility of 35m. The island in the middle, which is hauntingly beautiful, was known by the Ainu as the Isle of the Gods.

Kussharo-ko   LAKE
(屈斜路湖) The park's other major lake is famous for its swimming, boating and volcanically warmed sands. Naka-jima (中島) is the aptly named 'middle island' that's in the centre of the lake, which reportedly has its own version of the Loch Ness monster, Kusshi.

Kawayu Sumō Kinenkan   MUSEUM
(川湯相撲記念館; admission ¥310; ⊙9am-9pm Jun-Sep, to 5pm Oct-May) Sumō fans will enjoy this small museum dedicated to a hometown hero.

Kotan-ainu Minzoku-shiryōkan   MUSEUM
(コタンアイヌ民族資料館; admission ¥400; ⊙9am-5pm mid-Apr–Oct) In the village of Kussharo Kotan; displays traditional Ainu tools and crafts.

ⓘ ACCESSING AKAN NATIONAL PARK

The main access points for Akan are Bihoro and Abashiri to the north, and Kushiro to the south. Inside the park itself, you can base yourself in the towns of Kawayu Onsen and Akan Kohan, while Teshikaga (aka Mashū) serves as a useful transport hub. While it is possible to access the area by public transport, having your own car will make it much easier to get around and visit the various sights. A rental car is also something of a must if the next stop on you itinerary is Shiretoko National Park.

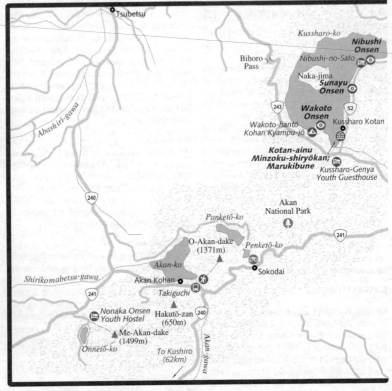

SAPPORO & HOKKAIDŌ EASTERN HOKKAIDŌ

🛏 Sleeping

TOP CHOICE **Kussharo-Genya Youth Guesthouse**

HOSTEL $

(屈斜路原野ユースゲストハウス; ☎484-2609; www.gogogenya.com/intro/e-intro.htm; dm/r per person from ¥4300/5200, breakfast/dinner ¥600/1300; @) Located just off of Rte 243 on the southern shores of Kussharo-ko, this wonderfully designed youth hostel is an architectural treat, both inside and out. Reminiscent of a large wooden church lording it over fields of vegetables, Kussharo-Genya charms guests with vaulted ceilings, lofty skylights and polished wooden floors; keeps them busy with a constantly changing list of activities; and sends them away stuffed to the brim with gourmet meals centred on Hokkaidō delicacies. If you don't have a car, the English-speaking staff will pick you up from JR Mashū Station provided you make an advance reservation.

Mashū-ko Youth Hostel

HOSTEL $

(摩周湖ユースホステル; ☎482-3098; www.masyuko.co.jp/english/yhe.htm; dm ¥3000-3500, s ¥4500-7400, d ¥5000-9000, breakfast/dinner ¥760/1260; @) A modern and comfortable base for exploring Akan National Park, this youth hostel is a 10-minute drive from downtown Teshikaga, and offers the usual Western-style accommodation with shared facilities. However, the personality of the property is raised significantly at the next-door Great Bear, a European-style mess hall where you can dine with fellow hostellers at the long table. Once again, if you don't have a car, the English-speaking staff will pick you up at JR Mashū Station with an advance reservation.

Nibushi-no-Sato

MINSHUKU $$

(☎483-2294; www1.ocn.ne.jp/~kussie; r per person with 2 meals ¥8550; @🛜🅿) This family-run *minshuku* sits on the northwestern shores of Kussharo-ko off Rte 52, and is very accom-

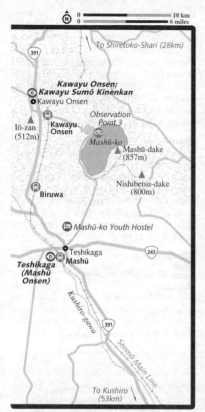

out canoe. Inside you'll find a variety of local specialities including *howaito-rāmen* (noodles in milk broth; ¥1000) and the sashimi of *parimono* (a local river fish; ¥1000). Ainu-music performances (¥3000) are given on certain Saturday nights; be sure to call for a reservation as seating is limited.

ℹ Information

Kawayu Eco-Museum Centre (川湯エコミュージアムセンター; ☑483-4100; www6.marimo .or.jp/k_emc, in Japanese; ⊙8am-5pm May-Oct, 9am-4pm Nov-Apr) The park visitors centre has handy hiking maps (in Japanese).

ℹ Getting There & Around

BUS

Depending on the season – services drop off in the winter – there are up to three buses a day between Kawayu Onsen bus station and Bihoro (¥1920, 2½ hours), which run via the scenic Bihoro Pass. Bihoro is accessed by train from Abashiri.

CAR & MOTORCYCLE

Kawayu Onsen is accessed by Rte 391, which runs north–south between Abashiri and Kushiro. Between Mashū Station and Akan Kohan on Rte 241 is a particularly scenic stretch with an outstanding lookout at Sokodai that overlooks Penketō-ko and Panketō-ko.

TRAIN

Frequent *tokkyū* on the JR Sekihoku line run between Abashiri and Bihoro (¥1440, 25 minutes).

Frequent *kaisoku* run north on the JR Senmō main line between Kawayu Onsen and Shiretoko-shari (¥900, 45 minutes), and south between Kawayu Onsen and Kushiro (¥1790, 1¾ hours) via Mashū (¥350, 20 minutes).

JR Kawayu Onsen Station is a 10-minute bus ride from the town centre (¥280); buses are timed to meet most of the trains.

AKAN KOHAN   阿寒湖畔
☑0154

The resort town of Akan Kohan has one of the largest Ainu *kotan* in Hokkaidō, and is recommended for anyone interested in this ancient culture. The town is also where you can catch a glimpse of *marimo*, the most famous algae ever to bob to the surface – then you can quickly leave behind the tourist throngs on a hike into the national park.

⊙ Sights

Ainu Kotan   VILLAGE

(アイヌコタン) It's definitely a tourist-orientated affair, yet the *kotan* on the western edge of the village is inhabited by one of

modating to foreign travellers. The property has a casual log-cabin feel complete with a small but sublime private onsen, and the owners can point out some great local walks, bike trails and birdwatching spots. Nibushino-Sato is a short drive from Kawayu Onsen bus station; alternatively you can call ahead for a pick-up.

Wakoto-hantō Kohan
Kyampu-jō   CAMPGROUND $

(和琴半島湖畔キャンプ場; ☑484-2350; camp sites ¥450, cabins ¥4500; ⊙mid-May–Oct) Along Rte 234 south of the Bihoro Pass, and accessible by private vehicle or bus from Mashū, Bihoro and Kawayu Onsen.

✕ Eating

 Marukibune   LOCAL SPECIALITIES $

(丸木舟; ☑484-2644; dishes from ¥650; ⊙11am-7.30pm) Next door to the museum of Ainu folklore in Kussharo Kotan, this popular restaurant is named after an Ainu-style dug-

the largest remaining Ainu communities in Hokkaidō. The Ainu are generally indistinguishable in appearance from the Japanese due to generations of intermarriage, but there are material signs of their rich culture. The most obvious of these are the woodcrafts, leatherwork and other handmade items, which are on sale at shops throughout the *kotan*.

Onnechise

(オンネチセ; admission ¥1000) At the top of the hill, there are Ainu dance performances here six times a day in the high season, and at least once a day the rest of the year.

Ainu Seikatsu Kinenkan

(アイヌ生活記念館; admission ¥300; ☺10am-10pm May-Oct) Next door to the Onnechise is this tiny museum celebrating Ainu lifestyles of yesteryear.

🏃 Activities

The highest mountain in the park, **Me-Akan-dake** (雌阿寒岳; Female Mountain; 1499m), is an active volcano that is usually closed due to emissions of poisonous gas. Ask at the tourist information office about current conditions.

O-Akan-dake
HIKING

(雄阿寒岳) About 6km east of Akan Kohan is O-Akan-dake (Male Mountain; 1371m). Buses to Kushiro pass the Takiguchi trail entrance five minutes out of Akan Kohan. The ascent takes a fairly arduous 3½ hours, and the descent takes about another 2½ hours. From the peak there are very fine views of Penketō-ko and Panketō-ko, and on clear days you can see as far as Daisetsuzan National Park.

Hakutō-zan
HIKING

(白湯山) The shorter climb to the observation platform on Hakutō-zan (650m) affords fine views of the lakes and the surrounding peaks. Starting 2km south of town, the ascent takes about an hour, winding through birch and fir forests and past several groups of bubbling sulphur hot springs (too hot to bathe in: don't try!).

🛏 Sleeping

TOP CHOICE **Akan Yuku-no-sato Tsuruga**
RYOKAN $$$

(あかん遊久の里鶴雅; ☎67-2531; www.tsuruga-g.com/english/01tsuruga/01tsuru-facility.html; 4-6-10, Akan Onsen; r per person with 2 meals from ¥23,000; @🛜) If you're looking for a worth-

---

MARIMO VIEWING

Akan-ko is famous for *marimo* (まりも; *Cladophora aegagropila*), spheres of algae that are both biologically interesting – it takes as long as 200 years for them to grow to the size of a baseball – and very, very *kawaii* (cute). Akan *marimo* grow only in a few places in the world, and they became endangered after being designated a national treasure: suddenly, everyone in Japan wanted to have one. The building of a powerplant (which actually lowered the lake level several inches) obviously did nothing to help the plight of these green benthic fuzzballs.

The Ainu finally came to the rescue by starting the **Marimo Matsuri** (まりも祭り), held in mid-October, which returns *marimo* to Akan-ko, one by one. Their numbers are growing, but they are sometimes affected by natural disasters – typhoons can push as much as 50% of them out of the lake. Luckily, locals quickly return them to the water as soon as the winds have subsided. On that note, please try to resist the urge to buy a bottled *marimo* on a keychain, even though they're widely available throughout Akan Kohan – and all of Hokkaidō, for that matter.

Akan Kohan Eco-Museum Centre (阿寒湖畔エコミュージアムセンター; http://business4.plala.or.jp/akan-eco; admission free; ☺9am-5pm Wed-Mon) on the eastern edge of town has well-maintained exhibits with lots of photographs, and a number of *marimo* in aquarium tanks. It also has hiking maps and displays about the local flora and fauna. The *bokke* (bubbling clay pools) walk starts from the museum, and makes a shaded, breezy loop out to the lake and back through some pine forest, with views of obliging tufted-eared squirrels, chipmunks and birds.

The best way to actually get up close and personal with *marimo* is to take a **sightseeing cruise** (☎67-2511; www.akankisen.com/_eng/index.html; trips ¥1850), which makes an 85-minute loop from the docks around the lake. Included in the trip is a brief 15-minute stop at a small observation centre where you can hopefully spot a few balls of algae photosynthesising on the surface of the water.

while splurge, this stunner of a ryokan offers refined elegance in the truest Japanese sense. A variety of tatami rooms are on offer, some of which feature private soaking tubs, rocking chairs in front of picture windows and silk cushions strategically strewn about hewn-wooden floors. Regal meals are built around never-ending courses of edible art, while two floors of onsen bliss run the gamut from ceramic tubs to open-air rock-garden baths.

Nonaka Onsen Youth Hostel
HOSTEL $

(野中温泉ユースホステル; ☎0156-29-7454; www.youthhostel.or.jp/English/e_nonaka.htm; Ashoro-chō Moashoro 159; dm from ¥3510, breakfast/dinner ¥760/1260; @🚲) Complete with its own onsen, this is a very popular spot that's often booked solid by hikers in the busy summer months. The remote hostel is snuggled between a forested hillside and the shores of Onneto-ko off Rte 241. It's preferable that you have your own car if you stay here, though buses bound for Meakan Onsen can drop you off if you ask the driver.

Hoteru Gosensui
HOTEL $$

(ホテル御前水;☎67-2031; www.akanko.co.jp/gozensui-top.html; 4-5-1 Akan Onsen; r per person with 2 meals from ¥8550; @🛜) While this white block of concrete in the town centre isn't nearly as atmospheric as other choices, it provides excellent value and proximity to the main tourist sights. Western-style rooms with low-lying beds are adequate, and the onsen is above average with wood-panelled walls and a large skylight. Seasonal menu items are a tasty affair, including lake fish served with its own salted eggs.

Akan Lakeside Kyampu-jō
CAMPGROUND $

(阿寒湖畔キャンプ場;☎67-3263; 5-1 Akan Onsen; campsites per person ¥630; ☺Jun-Sep) About a five-minute walk west of the village centre; has shady pitches, and even an *ashiyu* (foot bath) for cleaning off those muddy feet.

🍷 Drinking

Pan de Pan
CAFE $

(パンデパン; 1-6-6 Akan Onsen; ☺8.30am-6.30pm; 🏠) This monochromatic cafe in the town centre (look for the English sign) is nothing but wall-to-wall red-washed wooden furniture. Being surrounded by so much intense colour is certainly an upper! If you're still feeling down, you can drink a filter coffee and nosh on some fresh-baked sweet bread until your stomach fills and your mind eases.

ℹ Information

Buses arrive at the terminal on the eastern edge of the village. Here you'll find a **tourist information office** (☎67-3200; www.lake-akan.com/en/index.html; 2-1-15 Akan-ko Onsen; ☺9am-6pm) that stocks pamphlets and trail guides in English.

ℹ Getting There & Away

There are up to seven buses a day in both directions between Asahikawa and Akan Kohan (¥5210, 4½ hours) via Sōunkyō Onsen (¥3260, 3½ hours) in Daisetsuzan National Park. There are also a couple of buses a day between Akan Kohan and Kushiro (¥4790, 5¼ hours).

If you're driving, Akan Kohan runs along Rte 240, which (of course!) has been renamed **Marimo Kokudō** (まりも国道).

Kushiro
釧路

☎0154 / POP 189,000

A large and rather unsightly port city, Kushiro fails to captivate tourists. It does, however, serve as the southern gateway to Akan National Park, as well as the jumping-off point for 269-sq-km **Kushiro Shitsugen National Park** (釧路湿原国立公園), Japan's largest expanse of undeveloped wetland. Kushiro Shitsugen is nearly the size of Tokyo, and provides shelter for thousands of different species of wildlife.

To reach Kushiro Shitsugen, you can take trains from Kushiro to the **Hosooka Observatory** (細岡展望台; ☺9am-7pm summer, to 5pm winter) on the eastern side of the park, or a bus (¥660, 40 minutes) to the **Kushiro Observatory** (釧路湿原展望台; admission ¥400; ☺8.30am-6pm summer, 9am-5pm winter) on the west. The former is atop a lookout where you can easily appreciate the grand scale of this wetland preserve.

Most Japanese visitors to Kushiro Shitsugen are keen on spotting a *tanchō-zuru* (red-crested white crane), the traditional symbol of both longevity and Japan. The peak crane season is winter to early spring, but even in August a few stragglers may be around if you're lucky. Foxes dart around the undergrowth in search of prey, so keep your eyes peeled. Deer are also so common in this area that the trains have a special *shika-bue* (deer whistle) to scare them off.

Around the corner from JR Kushiro Shitsugen Station is the **Kushiro Shitsugen Tōro Youth Hostel** (釧路湿原とうろユースホステル; ☎87-2510; www.sip.or.jp/~tohro/sub1.htm, in Japanese; dm from ¥3360, breakfast/dinner ¥630/1050), which has bunk-style rooms that are big enough not to feel cramped, and a great viewing deck from which you can survey the national park.

Next to the train station in Kushiro is the **Kushiro Royal Inn** (釧路ロイヤルイン; ☑31-2121; www.royalinn.jp, in Japanese; s/d from ¥5300/7500; @), an efficient business hotel with space-saving micro-rooms and a modest dining room on the top floor.

Just to the right of Kushiro station on the corner after Lawson convenience store, the impressive **Washō Market** (和商市場; www .washoichiba.com; 25-13 Kurokane-chō; items from ¥200; ⊙8am-6pm Mon-Sat) features every possible seafood one can imagine, plus a food court with *bentō* and other prepared dishes.

ⓘ Getting There & Away

Air

Kushiro's small airport is located about 10km northwest of the city. From here, there are domestic flights to various destinations including Tokyo, Osaka, Nagoya and others. Buses between the airport and JR Kushiro Station (¥910, 45 minutes) are timed to connect with arrivals and departures.

Bus

There are a couple of buses a day between Sōunkyō Onsen and Kushiro (¥4790, 5¼ hours) via Akan Kohan (¥1530, 2¼ hours). There are also up to five daily buses between Rausu and Kushiro (¥4740, 3½ hours).

Car & Motorcycle

Rte 319 runs north–south between Abashiri and Kushiro.

Train

There are just a couple of *futsū* each day on the JR Senmō main line between Kushiro and Abashiri (¥3570, 3½ hours) via Shiretoko-shari (¥2730, 2½ hours), Kawayu Onsen (¥1790, 1½ hours) and Kushiro Shitsugen (¥350, 20 minutes).

SHARI 斜里
☑0152 / POP 13,000

The town of Shari is built up around JR Shiretoko-shari, the closest train station to Shiretoko. With that said, you're still about an hour by bus or car from the entrance to the national park.

FREE **Koshimizu Gensei Kaen** (小清水原生花園; ⊙closed Nov-Apr) is an 8km stretch of wildflowers along the coast, only 20 minutes from Shari. Visit in late June with your own wheels and catch it at its peak: over 40 species of flowers simultaneously blooming.

Unless you miss your onward bus connection, there is little reason to spend the night. If you do get stuck, however, there are a few convenient spots right near the station, including the **Shari Central Hotel** (斜里セントラルホテル; ☑23-2355; s/d from ¥4800/8000). Look for the English sign atop a concrete gate, as well as the European-styled octagon adjacent to your typical business hotel.

There are just a couple of *futsū* each day on the JR Senmō main line between Shiretoko-Shari and Abashiri (¥810, 50 minutes), and between Shiretoko-Shari and Kushiro (¥2730, 2½ hours) via Mashū (¥1230, 1¼ hours).

There is one direct bus daily linking Abashiri and Shari (¥1120, 1¼ hours). There are between five and nine buses daily between Shari and Utoro (¥1490, 1¼ hours), but only three in summer that continue on as far as Iwaobetsu (¥1770, 1¼ hours).

Surprisingly well-maintained Rte 334 runs up the coast from Abashiri to Shari, and continues to the village of Iwaobetsu.

Shiretoko National Park
知床国立公園

Shiretoko-hantō, the peninsula that makes up Shiretoko National Park, was known in Ainu as 'the end of the world.' As remote as it gets, this magnificent stretch of land has virtually no sealed roads within its boundaries. Hiking tracks are present, but they're poorly maintained, wind over slippery boulders

---

ⓘ WARNING: BEAR ACTIVITY

The peninsula of Shiretoko-hantō is home to around 600 brown bears, the highest density in Hokkaidō. Hikers are thus strongly advised not to go into the forest in the early morning or at dusk, and to avoid hoofing it alone. Tying a bell to your rucksack is also recommended as bears will flee if they hear loud noises. If you're camping, tie up your food and do not bury your rubbish. Bear activity picks up noticeably during early autumn when the creatures are actively foraging for food ahead of their winter hibernation. Be especially cautious at this time.

WHY DO YOU LOVE HOKKAIDŌ? *MATTHEW D FIRESTONE*

While updating the Hokkaidō chapter for this guidebook, I spent a good deal of time talking to random strangers. As you might imagine, gathering and fact-checking travel information takes a lot of time and energy, though it's a great way to pick the brains of all the locals you meet. In fact, I made a point to ask everybody I met the same simple question: 'Why do you love Hokkaidō?' Residents of the island provided me with some truly notable quotables, a few of which are listed here:

Hokkaidō isn't Japan. Seriously. I mean, have you ever walked to the bus stop in Tokyo, and wondered whether or not you would cross paths with a bear?

Tomo from Furano

Have you tasted our crab? It's the best in world. I've never been to Alaska, but I don't need to go. We catch it right here, and eat it right here, and that's why it's the best.

Daisuke from Wakkanai

Do you have *uni* (sea-urchin roe) in your country? I love to buy *uni* fresh from the market, and then mix it with cream and eat it with pasta. It's delicious!

Mariko from Otaru

We invented beer, right here in Sapporo! Well, I guess maybe it came from Germany first, but the Japanese were drinking sake before we came to the rescue!

Haruki from Sapporo

This island makes you tough. Tokyo-ites complain when the rain soaks their shoes. We complain when the snow buries our houses.

Ichiro from Kushiro

and disappear at times on cliff sides. If the weather turns frigid or you slip and break an ankle, you'll need to hope that a passing fishing boat spots you – before the bears do. However, the reward is obvious. Shiretoko, a Unesco World Heritage Site, is Japan's last true wilderness.

☉ Sights & Activities

Shiretoko Traverse   HIKING
The classic traverse is a two-day hike that stretches for 25km from **Iwaobetsu Onsen** (岩尾別温泉) to **Kamuiwakka-yu-no-taki** (カムイワッカ湯の滝). It winds up and down the spine of the peninsula, with views of violent seas on both sides, and takes in old-growth pine forests and several active volcanic peaks. While it probably goes without mention, you need to be properly equipped to tackle this route, and you shouldn't underestimate the difficulty of the terrain that awaits you.

The first day is an 8km hike to the campsite at **Mitsumine** (三ツ峰), which should take about five to six hours. Before setting out on the trail, you can soak (for free!) in the natural hot springs scattered about the village of Iwaobetsu Onsen. From here,

you'll head southeast along a rocky saddle before arriving in the shadow of **Rausu-dake** (羅臼岳; 1661m). A round-trip journey to the top and down again will give you a closer look at the hotly disputed Kurils (see p520). Back on the main circuit, you're just an hour or so away from your first night's rest.

The second day is a slightly more taxing 18km hike that can take up to eight hours to complete. The trails pass by fields of summer wildflowers and marshlands before turning into a rock scramble on the slopes of **Iō-zan** (硫黄山; 1563m). After coming down, you'll be reminded of the surrounding volcanic activity at the steaming vents of **Shinfunkaguchi** (新噴火口). Just before the trail-end and the adjacent bus stop lies Kamuiwakka-no-taki, a cascade of hot water running down a succession of natural *rotemburo*.

At the time of research, however, the Iō-zan descent leading to Kamuiwakka-no-taki was temporarily closed due to rock falls. While it is expected that the circuit will open in its entirety during the shelf life of this book, be sure to enquire with the park service (see Information) before setting out.

DON'T MISS

NEMURO

The main attraction of this tiny town (population 3100) is its view of several islands that are currently occupied by Russia, despite being the subject of heated debate. Nemuro (根室) is also the easternmost part of Japan, so travellers who like to collect '-mosts' should be sure to come here.

The bus between JR Nemuro Station and the easternmost tip, **Nosappu-misaki** (納沙布岬), passes a number of gravel car parks that serve as kelp-drying areas. When laid out in rows, the drying kelp looks like black strips of twisted leather.

At the tip, you will find the **Nosappu-misaki Heiwa-no-tō** (ノサップ岬平和の塔; admission ¥900; ☺8.30am-15min after sunset), a viewing tower that overlooks the disputed **Chisima Retto** (千島列島; Kuril Islands).

The Kurils are a volcanic archipelago that stretches for 1300km northeast to Kamchatka, Russia, and separate the Sea of Okhotsk from the Pacific Ocean. The original demarcation line between Japan and Russia dates back to the 1855 Treaty of Shimoda, which divided the chain into the Japanese-controlled South Kurils and the Russian-controlled North Kurils.

The subsequent 1875 Treaty of St Petersburg awarded Japan control of the entire chain. The Kurils were later seized by Russian military forces in the closing months of WWII. The ongoing dispute over control arose from ambiguities in the 1945 Yalta Treaty and the 1951 Treaty of San Francisco.

The Japanese contend that the San Francisco treaty renounced their control of the North Kurils but secured their right to the South Kurils. The former USSR, however, did not sign this treaty, in protest. The Russians contend that Yalta protects their WWII land acquisitions. The Japanese counter that this treaty did not specify territorial claims in the Kurils.

Although sparsely populated, the Kurils have valuable mineral deposits, possibly oil and gas reserves, and are surrounded by rich fishing grounds. In 2010, Russian President Dmitry Medvedev landed on the Kurils, and promised its residents development assistance. Japan in turn condemned the visit, and diplomatic tensions were high at the time of research.

There are a few *futsū* each day on the JR Nemuro line between Kushiro and Nemuru (¥2420, 2½ hours). Buses, which are timed with train arrivals, bring you from the train station out to Nosappu-misaki (one way/return ¥1040/1900, 50 minutes). Buses leave Nosappu-misaki about every two hours until 6.35pm.

If the trail remains closed, you can cut the traverse short by doubling back to Iwaobetsu Onsen. Alternatively, you can turn south from Rausu-dake and exit the park at **Rausu** (羅臼). Although this fishing village once grew wealthy on the herring industry, these days there isn't much here except for some enchanting coastal scenery.

Shiretoko-go-ko   SCENIC AREA

(知床五湖) A scenic region with mountain-backed lakes that is easily accessible from Iwaobetsu Onsen and suited for relaxed day-hiking.

Kamuiwakka Cruising   CRUISES

(カムイワッカクルーザーツアー; ☎24-3060; 1/3hr trips ¥3100/8000) Boats depart from the pier in Utoro, and take in the Shiretoko coastline including Kamui-wakka-no-taki.

🛏 Sleeping

🏆 Shiretoko Iwaobetsu Youth Hostel   HOSTEL $

(知床岩尾別ユースホステル; ☎24-2311; www4.ocn.ne.jp/~iwayh/english/e-top.html; dm from ¥3200, breakfast/dinner from ¥700/800; ☺Mar-Nov) In the small village of Iwaobetsu Onsen, just off Rte 334, this is a popular base for hikers, providing easy access to the Shiretoko traverse and the Shiretoko-go-ko region. As well as organising hiking parties, the hostel also provides numerous chances to spot wildlife. Bear, deer and fox are all regulars in the surrounding woods, and the knowledgeable staff can provide all sorts of helpful spotting tips.

Marumi   RYOKAN $$

(まるみ; ☎88-1313; www.shiretoko-rausu.com, in Japanese; r per person with 2 meals from ¥11,500;

@) If you find yourself exiting the park at Rausu, this well-regarded ryokan has both Western-style and tatami rooms overlooking the sea, not to mention lovely seafood meals, a *rotemburo* and a sauna. After the downward climb from Rausu-dake, this is a wonderful place to build up your energy before returning to civilisation.

Kinoshita-goya   MOUNTAIN HUT $
(木下小屋; ☎24-2824; dm from ¥1575; ☉Jun-Sep) Located right at the trailhead for the Shiretoko traverse and Rausu-dake, you can always overnight at this spartan log house in a pinch. Snacks and hot drinks are available, and there is tiny mixed *rotemburo* out back.

There are a number of undeveloped campgrounds along the Shiretoko traverse, including **Mitsumine Kyampu-jō** (三ツ峰キャンプ地). Here and elsewhere, you will need to be entirely self-sufficient. If you do come across running water, boil it before you bottle it – fox faeces carry *Echinococcus multilocularis* (see p502).

❶ Information

Hiking must be arranged in advance: there are steep fines for anyone caught hiking off-limits or after hours. Be sure to register at the **Shiretoko Nature Centre** (知床ネイチャーセンター; ☎24-2114; www.shiretoko.or.jp/snc_eng/en_about.htm; ☉8am-5.40pm mid-Apr–mid-Oct, 9am-4pm mid-Oct–mid-Apr), which provides valuable maps and park info.

❶ Getting There & Around
Bus

There are between five and nine buses daily between Shari and Utoro (¥1490, 50 minutes), but only three in summer that continue on as far as Iwaobetsu (¥1770, 1¼ hours).

From late April to October, buses run four times daily from Utoro (¥900, 50 minutes) along the northern side of the peninsula, passing the nature centre, the youth hostel, Shiretoko-go-ko and Kamuiwakka-no-taki before terminating at Shiretoko-ōhashi. During this time frame, there are also buses four times daily between Utoro and Rausu via the dramatic Shiretoko-Toge pass (¥1310, 55 minutes).

Finally, there are up to five daily buses between Rausu and Kushiro (¥4740, 3½ hours).

Car

While not essential, having a car will make it easier to access the park, as well as to move up and down the coastline. As a disclaimer, there are no sealed roads within the park's boundaries, except for a short northwest–southeast road that connects the town of Utoro (on the northwestern edge) with Rausu (on the southern side); in two-thirds of the park there are no roads at all.

TOKACHI

The name Tokachi (十勝) is as synonymous with wine in Japan as Beaujolais is for Westerners. While its name doesn't fit neatly in with the cardinal monikers of Hokkaidō's other subprefectures, Tokachi was a historic but short-lived province that was established in the late 19th century. Today, the region is largely agricultural and has few major tourist draws, though it does boast some lively wine-scented countryside that's worth exploring if you have some time at the end of your trip.

Obihiro   帯広
☎0155 / POP 171,000

A former Ainu stronghold, the modern city of Obihiro was founded in 1883 by the Banseisha, a group of colonial settlers from Shizuoka Prefecture in Central Honshū. Squeezed in between the Hidaka and Daisetsuzan mountain ranges, Obihiro is a friendly, laid-back city without much for tourists. However, you will need to pass through briefly en route to Ikeda and Erimo-misaki.

A great place to break for the night is the **Toipirka Kitaobihiro Youth Hostel** (トイピルカ北帯広ユースホステル; ☎30-4165; http://homepage1.nifty.com/TOIPIRKA/english/main_eng.htm; dm from ¥3200, breakfast/dinner ¥600/1000; @🖧), an attractive log house with Western-style beds and nightly tea time. It's near Tokachigawa Onsen, a cluster of resort-style onsens and hotels along the Tokachi-gawa. If you phone ahead, the staff can pick you up from the station in Obihiro.

❶ Getting There & Away
Air

Obihiro's tiny airport is located about 25km southwest of the city. From here, there are domestic flights to various destinations including Tokyo, Osaka, Nagoya and others. Buses between the airport and JR Obihiro Station (¥1000, 45 minutes) are timed to connect with arrivals and departures.

Bus

There are a few departures in both directions between the bus terminal adjacent to the station in Obihiro and the Chūō bus station in Sapporo (¥3670, 4¼ hours). There are also regular buses running between Obihiro and Sōunkyō Onsen (¥2200, 80 minutes).

Car & Motorcycle

Rte 274 runs between Sapporo and Obihiro, while Rte 38 connects Obihiro to Kushiro.

Train

Frequent *tokkyū* run on the JR Nemuro line between Obihiro and Sapporo (¥7220, 2½ hours), and between Obihiro and Kushiro (¥4880, 1½ hours).

Ikeda 池田

♪ 015 / POP 8500

Located amid the grape fields of the eastern Tokachi plain, Ikeda is a small farming town that became famous in the 1960s when the municipal government started experimented with winemaking. While conservative oenophiles might not consider Japanese wines in the same league as Old World classics and other New World upstarts, pull out a bottle of Ikeda and decide for yourself. Judging by the giant corkscrew sculpture in the station, the folks here hope you will.

In our humble opinion, some perfectly quaffable wines are made at **Wain-jō** (ワイン城; Wine Castle; www.tokachi-wine.com, in Japanese; 83 Kiyomi, Ikeda-chō; admission free; ⊙factory tours 9am-5pm), set on a hillside overlooking the town. A tour (in Japanese only) guides you through the production process and there's a tasting afterwards. To get here head south along the train track from the station; you'll see the hill on your left shortly afterwards (look for the ferris wheel).

What goes well with wine? Cheese, of course! The rather optimistically named **Happiness Dairy** (ハッピネスデーリィ; http://happiness-dairy.com, in Japanese; 104-2 Kiyomi, Ikeda-chō; admission free; ⊙9.30am-5.30pm Mon-Fri, to 6pm Sat, Sun & holidays summer, to 5pm Mon-Fri, to 5.30pm Sat, Sun & holidays winter) takes you through the entire process, from walking in the wheat fields with the milk cows to tasting the final product, be it fresh cheese or rum-raisin gelato. From Wain-jō head east on Rte 39 about 200m, then turn left at the T-junction, head 500m north and turn right at the cross section. Go 300m and the shop is on your right.

There is also a burgeoning artists' community in Ikeda that produces some lovely craft goods. The **Moon Face Gallery & Cafe** (画廊喫茶ムーンフェイス; 132 Kiyomi, Ikeda-chō; admission free; ⊙10am-6pm Wed-Mon) displays works by locals while serving up tasty cappuccinos and espressos. The **Spinner's Farm Tanaka** (スピナーズファーム・タナカ; www12.plala.or.jp/spinner, in Japanese; admission free; ⊙10am-6pm Apr-Oct, to 5.30pm Nov-Mar, closed 2nd Sat of each month) is a wool-weaving workshop.

Friendly management and delicious dinners including a complimentary glass of local wine make **Ikeda Kita-no-Kotan Youth Hostel** (池田北のコタンユースホステル; ♪572-3666; www11.plala.or.jp/kitanokotan, in Japanese; dm with 2 meals from ¥5600; @⊚) a real treat. The hostel is within easy walking distance of the Toshibetsu Station, one stop west of Ikeda (¥200, five minutes). From the station take the main road south, turn left at the first intersection and the hostel is where the road ends. Look for the Victorian-style white-panelled house with a blue roof.

Frequent *futsū* run on the JR Nemuro line between Obihiro and Ikeda (¥440, 30 minutes).

Erimo-misaki 襟裳岬

♪ 01466

This remote cape is far off the beaten path, but with its windswept cliffs and dramatic ocean vistas, and kelp strung up to dry like giant shoelaces, it's a good day trip for anyone with their own wheels and a lot of extra time.

The history of this unique place is something of an ecological miracle. Beginning in the Meiji era, the hills surrounding this kelp-farming community were gradually deforested, so by the 1950s it was nicknamed Erimo Desert. Sand blew into the ocean, destroying the kelp, and the community faced a stark choice: reforest or leave. Thanks to the locals' perseverance and a vast number of seedlings, the hills now boast a Japanese black pine forest.

Those same great offshore winds and Pacific swell make for spectacular surfing breaks for anyone daring enough to bring along a board and wetsuit, but check with locals about rips and safety before paddling out into the waves. Across from the deserted JR bus stop there's a small bluff that makes a good spot to take a snapshot of the fishing boats below.

Ten minutes' drive further, at the cape itself, is an entire museum dedicated to wind, namely **Kaze-no-Yakata** (風の館; www9.ocn. ne.jp/~kaze, in Japanese; 366-3 Tōyō, Erimo-chō; admission ¥300; ⏰8.30am-6pm May-Sep, 9am-5pm Oct-Apr, closed Dec-Feb). There are plenty of weather-related films and displays, but the undisputed highlight is being blasted by gale-force winds inside an artificial wind tunnel.

Kuril seals, which bask all year round on the rocks below, are called *zenigata-azarashi* (money-shaped) because the white spots on their black bodies are reminiscent of old Japanese coins. Here, you can also pick out your own crab or conch and have it grilled at the restaurant-shacks beside the car park. Bring a windbreaker: outside feels just as gusty as the wind tunnel does.

When things warm up a bit outside the winter months, the **Hyakunin-hama Ōtokyampu-jō** (百人浜オートキャンプ 場; ☎4-2168; campsites ¥510, bungalows ¥5090; ⏰20 Apr-20 Oct) is a popular campground among the surfing set. It's located on the beach at Hyakunin-hama, 8km northeast of the cape, right near the lighthouse. If you don't have your own gear, rental tents and gear are available, as are furnished bungalows.

At the tip of the cape, just around the corner from the wind museum, you will find the **Minshuku Misaki-sō** (民宿みさき荘; ☎3-1316; www.goodinns.com/misakiso, in Japanese; Erimo-misaki Tōdaimoto, Erimo-chō; r per person with 2 meals ¥9500; @), a surprisingly homey option at the seeming end of the world. The speciality of the house is crab, which should be obvious given the huge crab-adorned sign that greets travellers upon arrival.

Seemingly abandoned Rte 34 hugs the coastline, and provides an incredibly scenic drive for anyone who has no other pressing engagements elsewhere in the world.

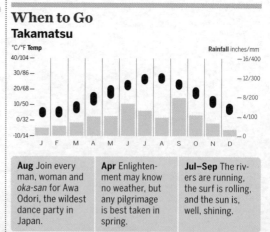

Shikoku

Best Places to Eat

» Goshiki Sōmen Morikawa (p554)

» Gosankeshi (p544)

» Bijin-tei (p561)

» Hirome Ichiba (p544)

Best Places to Stay

» Chiiori (p538)

» Kaiyu Inn (p547)

» Funaya (p554)

» Shimanto-gawa Youth Hostel (p545)

» Utoco Deep Sea Therapy Hotel (p540)

Why Go?

The birthplace of revered Buddhist ascetic, Kōbō Daishi (774–835), Shikoku (四国) is synonymous with natural beauty and the pursuit of spiritual perfection. The 88 Temple route is Japan's most famous pilgrimage, even if some *henro* (pilgrims) today make the trek in air-conditioned comfort.

Yet this is not merely a place for passive soul-searching. The stunning Iya Valley, a rugged and ancient Pacific Ocean coastline, gorgeous free-flowing rivers and mountain ranges all beckon to be explored firsthand. If the inner demons are restless, there are Takamatsu, Kōchi and Matsuyama, attractive and youthful cities with excellent regional cuisine and all the trappings of 'mainland' modernity.

Travellers are quietly heralding the virtues of the island where 12th-century Heike warriors disappeared into the mountains to escape their Genji pursuers. Easy to access from Honshu via two glorious feats of engineering, Shikoku offers an adventurous retreat from the outside world. Just like Kōbō Daishi would have wanted.

When to Go
Takamatsu

Aug Join every man, woman and *oka-san* for Awa Odori, the wildest dance party in Japan.

Apr Enlightenment may know no weather, but any pilgrimage is best taken in spring.

Jul–Sep The rivers are running, the surf is rolling, and the sun is, well, shining.

ⓘ Getting There & Around

This chapter follows the same clockwise loop that most visitors have used to travel around Shikoku over the past 1000 years. Most visitors arrive on the island by train from Okayama or by highway bus from Osaka, Kyoto and Tokyo. The Iya Valley and the two southern capes are probably best explored by car, as many towns there have tricky bus and train connections.

AIR

All Nippon Airways (www.ana.co.jp) and **Japan Airlines** (www.jal.co.jp) services connect Matsuyama, Kōchi, Takamatsu and Tokushima in Shikoku with Tokyo, Osaka and other major centres.

BOAT

Nankai Ferry (南海フェリー; ☑636-0750; www.nankai-ferry.co.jp) runs daily connections between Tokushima and Wakayama (¥2400, two hours, eight daily)

Ocean Tōkyū Ferry (オーシャン東九フェリー; ☑662-0489; www.otf.jp) departs once daily to/from Tokyo.

Setonaikai Kisen ferry (☑082-253-1212, Matsuyama booking office 089-953-1003; ☺9am-7pm) has regular hydrofoil connections between Matsuyama and Hiroshima (¥6300, 1¼ hours, 14 daily).

Matsuyama is also a stopping point for ferries run by **Diamond Ferry company** (☑951-0167; www.diamond-ferry.co.jp) between Osaka and Kōbe, and Ōita (Kyūshū). There is one sailing a day each way.

Jumbo Ferry (☑811-6688) runs between Takamatsu and Kōbe (¥1800, three hours and 40 minutes, five daily).

BUS

Three bridge systems link Shikoku with Honshū. In the east, the Akashi Kaikyō-ōhashi connects Tokushima with Kōbe in Hyōgo-ken via Awaji-shima (Awaji Island). The Shimanami Kaidō (p383) is an island-hopping series of nine bridges (with bike paths!) leading from Imabari in Ehime-ken to Onomichi near Hiroshima.

TRAIN

The Seto-ōhashi bridge runs from Okayama to Sakaide, west of Takamatsu. This is the only one of the bridges to carry trains. JR and private Kotoden trains run to all regions, except the tips of the two southern capes.

TOKUSHIMA PREFECTURE

The traditional starting point for generations of pilgrims, Tokushima Prefecture (徳島県) is home to the first 23 of Shi-

koku's 88 Temples. Notable attractions in this region include the lively Awa-odori Matsuri (Awa-odori Festival), which takes place in Tokushima in August; the mighty whirlpools of the Naruto Channel between Tokushima and Awaji-shima; the dramatic scenery of the Iya Valley; and the surf beaches of the southern coast.

Tokushima 徳島

☑088 / POP 270,000

With Mt Bizan looming in the west, and Shinmachi-gawa (Shinmachi River) cutting a gentle swathe through the middle, Tokushima is an appealing modern city and, with a number of nearby temples, makes a popular starting point for pilgrims.

Every August, the Awa-odori Matsuri, a traditional dance festival, attracts thousands of Japanese from across the country. At other times, the Naruto whirlpools have visitors in a spin.

⊙ Sights & Activities

Bizan SITE

(眉山) Bizan means 'eyebrow' and the site surrounding the 280m-high summit raises the interest of most visitors to Tokushima. As you arrive at the foot of Bizan, at the southwestern end of Shinmachibashi-dōri, you pass **Awa Odori Kaikan** (阿波おどり会館; ☑611-1611; 2-20 Shinmachibashi; admission ¥300; ☺9am-5pm, closed 2nd & 4th Wed), which features extensive exhibits relating to the Awa-odori Matsuri and dance. The dance is performed at 2pm, 3pm and 4pm daily (with an additional performance at 11am on weekends), with a nightly performance at 8pm (afternoon/evening performances ¥500/700). From the 5th floor, a **cable car** (☑652-3617; one way/return Nov-Mar ¥600/1000, return Apr-Oct ¥600; ☺9am-5.30pm Nov-Mar, to 9pm Apr-Oct & during cherry-blossom season) whizzes you to the top of Bizan for fine views over the city. A combined ticket covering the museum, cable car and dance show is ¥1500.

Awa Puppet Theatre THEATRE

(阿波十郎兵衛屋敷; ☑665-2202; 184 Honura; museum admission ¥400; ☺9.30am-5pm) For hundreds of years, puppet theatre thrived in the farming communities around Tokushima. The traditional dramas can still be seen at Awa Jūrobei Yashiki, in the former residence of Bandō Jūrobei, a samurai who allowed himself to be executed

Shikoku Highlights

1 Follow time-worn paths along the pilgrimage of the **88 Temples** (p534)

2 Find seclusion, if not enlightenment, like Kōbō Daishi did at **Muroto-misaki** (p540)

3 Surf world-class waves at **Ohkihama** (p547), one of Japan's best beaches, then paddle down the beautiful **Shimanto-gawa**

4 Hike up sacred **Ishizuchi-san** (p556), one of Japan's most gripping ascents

5 Get off the beaten path in the **Iya Valley** (p535), where you can swing across vine

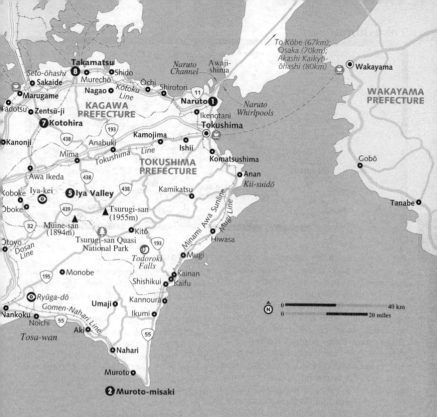

bridges and white-water raft down icy Yoshina-gawa

6 Take a soak in the historic **Dōgo Onsen** (p551) in the castle-town metropolis of Matsuyama

7 Trek up 1368 stone steps to pay homage to the god of seafarers at **Kompira-san** (p557) in the town of Kotohira

8 Walk off Japan's most famous noodles with a stroll

through Takamatsu's exquisite Edo-period garden, **Ritsurin-kōen** (p559)

Tokushima

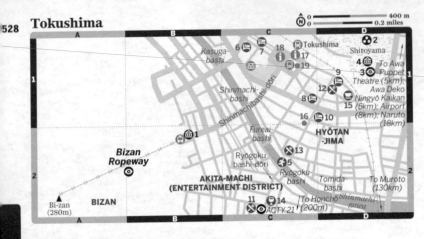

for a crime he didn't commit in order to preserve the good name of his master. The tale provided inspiration for the drama *Keisei Awa no Naruto*, first performed in 1768. Sections from the play are performed at 11am daily, and at 11am and 2pm on weekends. More puppets can be seen at nearby **Awa Deko Ningyō Kaikan** (阿波木偶人形会館; Awa Puppet Hall; ☎665-5600; 1-84 Honura; admission ¥400; ⏱9am-5pm, closed 1st & 3rd Wed of the month). To get to the museum, take a bus for Tomiyoshi Danchi (富吉団地) from Tokushima Station and get off at the Jūrobei Yashiki-mae stop (¥270, 20 minutes).

Chūō-kōen   PARK
(中央公園) Northeast of the train station, on the slopes of Shiroyama, is Chūō-kōen, where you'll find the scant ruins of Tokushima-jō (Tokushima Castle). Built in 1585 for Hachisuka Iemasa after he was granted the fiefdom of Awa by Toyotomi Hideyoshi, most of the castle was destroyed in 1875 following the Meiji Restoration. If you're having problems imagining the former grandeur of the site, **Tokushima Castle Museum** (徳島城博物館; 1-8 Jōnai; admission ¥300; ⏱9am-5pm, closed Mon) contains an impressive reconstruction of the castle town at its peak, as well as the *daimyō's* (domain lord's) boat, some displays of armour, and letters to the local lord from Hideyoshi and the first Tokugawa shogun, Ieyasu. The displays are all in Japanese. The beautiful **Senshūkaku-teien** (千秋閣庭園; admission ¥50, incl in museum ticket) is an intimate 16th-century garden featuring rock bridges and secluded ponds.

☞ Tours

Boats (ひょうたん島一周遊覧船) cruise around the 'gourd-shaped' Hyōtan-jima (Hyōtan Island) in central Tokushima. The tours cost ¥100 and leave from Ryōgoku-bashi (両国橋; Ryōgoku Bridge) on the Shinmachi-gawa every 20 minutes from 1pm to 3.40pm on Saturday and Sunday from mid-March to mid-October, and daily from 20 July to 31 August. In July and August there are additional departures every 40 minutes from 5pm to 7.40pm.

☆ Festivals & Events

Every August Tokushima is the location for one of the biggest parties in Japan, when the fabulous **Awa-odori Matsuri** (Awa-odori Festival) takes place to mark the O-bon holidays.

🛏 Sleeping

Sakura-sō   MINSHUKU $
(さくら荘; ☎652-9575; fax 652-2220; 1-25 Terashima-honchō-higashi; per person without bathroom ¥3000) The delightful older lady in charge readily welcomes lost foreigners to her charming *minshuku* (guesthouse), which has large, good-value tatami (woven floor matting) rooms. It's a few blocks east of the train station, past the NHK TV studio. Look for the sign on the right: さくら荘.

Agnes Hotel Tokushima   BOUTIQUE HOTEL $$
(アグネスホテル徳島; ☎626-2222; fax 626-3788; www.agneshotel.jp, in Japanese; 1-28 Terashima-honchō-nishi; s/d with small breakfast from ¥6300/12,600; ⊜@🛜) Hip little Agnes lies 200m west of the station and offers a

Tokushima

more sophisticated aesthetic than the usual business hotel. The rooms have stylish interiors, and the foyer pastry cafe is a destination in its own right. There's internet access in the lobby, and LAN access in all rooms.

Hotel Astoria
HOTEL $$

(☑653 6151; fax 653-6350; 2-26-1 Ichiban-cho; s/tw ¥6300/8400; ⊜@⊛) A less formal vibe pervades this neat family hotel tucked off the main drag. The narrow rooms are well appointed, with spacious bathrooms and firm beds. There is LAN internet access in rooms, and a popular cafe-restaurant in the lobby. It's across the road from the giant Tōyoko Inn signage.

Tōyoko Inn
HOTEL $$

(東横イン徳島駅前; ☑657-1045; fax 657-1046; www.toyoko-inn.com; 1-5 Ryōgoku Honchō; s/tw with small breakfast ¥6300/9000; ⊜@⊛) This popular chain hotel is a good option, with small but clean and comfortable rooms. There is LAN internet access in rooms, and there are computer consoles in the lobby.

Hotel Clement Tokushima
HOTEL $$$

(ホテルクレメント徳島; ☑656-3111; www.hotelclement.co.jp; 1-61 Terashima-honchō-nishi; s/d ¥10,200/19,700; ⊜@) Directly on top of the station building, luxurious Hotel Clement boasts 18 floors and 250 comfortable, spacious Western-style rooms. Although it's more expensive than other business hotels, the extra yen gets you a whole smattering of amenities including a spa and a range of restaurants and bars.

Four Season Hotel Tokushima
BOUTIQUE HOTEL $$

(☑622-2203; 1-54-1 Terashima-honchō-nishi; s/tw with small breakfast from ¥8400/13,600; ⊜@⊛) The newest hotel in Tokushima is not *quite* the famous chain, but the 23 rooms are stylish nonetheless, à la their sister hotel, the Agnes, just down the road.

✘ Eating & Drinking

Tokushima's main entertainment district is in Akita-machi across the river, along the streets around the landmark ACTY 21 building.

TOP CHOICE YRG Café
CAFE $

(☑656-7899; 1-33-4 Terashima Honchō Higashi; meals ¥600-1200; ⊠) This super cute coffee shop down by the train tracks is run by super talented, English-speaking Takao. 'Yellow, Red, Green' sells hip jewellery and postcards and mix CDs, not to mention whopping cups of chai latte (¥400) and nutritious, comforting meals that change weekly.

Masala
INDIAN $

(マサラ; ☑654-7122; Terashima-honchō-nishi; vegie curry ¥750 ⊙11am-9.30pm; ⊠) Sometimes all you need is a good, authentic curry. The Indian staff serve veggie curries and a range of enormous, piping hot naan breads. This branch of the small Shikoku-based chain is on the 5th floor of the Clement Plaza.

Tori-kō
YAKITORI $

(鳥甲; ☑657-0125; 2-19 Ryōgoku Honchō; ⊙4-10.30pm, closed Mon) This atmospheric spot is thick with the smell of delicious local

SHIKOKU TOKUSHIMA

DON'T MISS

AWA-ODORI MATSURI

The Awa-odori is the largest and most famous *bon* (Japanese Buddhist custom that honours one's ancestors) dance in Japan. Every night from 12 to 15 August, men, women and children don *yukata* (light cotton kimono) and straw hats and take to the streets to dance to the samba-like rhythm of the theme song 'Awa Yoshikono', accompanied by the sounds of *shamisen* (three-stringed guitars), *taiko* (drums) and *fue* (flutes). More than a million people descend on Tokushima for the festival every year, and accommodation is at a premium.

chicken grilling on coals. Orders like *tsukune* (chicken meat balls) and *tebasaki* (chicken wings) are ¥300 for two sticks; the *Awa-odori Sanmai* course (a selection of different cuts of the local gourmet chicken) is ¥3000. Look for the wooden menu boards covering the walls outside.

Saffron CAFE $
(☑656-0235; 2-10-2 Ichiban-cho; meals ¥800-1000; ☉10am-4pm) The huge Japanese omelettes (fried and folded egg filled with spiced rice and covered in sweet, brown sauce) at this very cosy lunch spot make delicious hangover food. Linger for a scoop of homemade ice cream and hang out with the friendly owner. It's around the corner from Sakura-sō guesthouse, with an English sign.

Kisuke SEAFOOD $$
(喜助; ☑652-1832; dishes ¥600-1500 ☉5pm-1am) Named after an *anime* character who always arrives in the nick of time, Kisuke has built a reputation for imaginative seafood dishes over the past 16 years. Turning left into a side street off the north end of Ryōgoku Honchō – it's on the first corner. The exterior is a striking, modern design of wood and steel.

Wine IZAKAYA $
(☑657-7477; 1st fl, 12-1 Konya-machi; dishes ¥500-1800; ☉5pm-1am) The pick of the all-you-can-drink joints in Tokushima is this three-floor number that offers the usual spread of well-presented Japanese staples in generous proportions. For ¥3500 you will get seven courses, including sashimi and delicious salads. Get there early on weekends.

Ingrid's International Lounge KARAOKE BAR
(☑626-0067; www.ingridsinternational.com; 2-19 Sakae-machi 2 Chome; ☉6pm-late; 🏠) Filipino Ingrid is Tokushima's go-to-girl for expatriate gossip and all-night karaoke. It's hard to find, tucked among the hostess clubs in

the southwest of Akita-machi, but there's nothing duplicitous about this Tokushima travellers' institution. Beware: Ingrid never forgets a face!

Leaf Bar BAR
(☑652-3547; Ryōgokubashi; cover charge ¥500; ☉5pm-3am) This small 6th-floor bar diagonally opposite the ACTY 21 building is a gamer's fantasy with manga posters, Tekken on the big screen, groups of dolled-up Japanese girls drinking cocktails and squealing over the top of mainstream American R&B. Food is available and a (very) small beer costs ¥350.

Ray Charles BAR
(レイチャールズ; ☑652-0878; Ryōgokubashi; ☉7pm-3am, to 4am Fri & Sat) A dimly lit bar where people drift in to shoot the breeze with the bow-tied bartenders and listen to American oldies. Draft Carlsberg is ¥700. It recently moved premises half a block south, but the old sign is still up.

ⓘ Information

There are coin lockers at the station, and the ATMs at the post office (郵便局) accept international cards.

Japan Travel Bureau (JTB; ☑623-3181; 1-29 Ryōgoku Honmachi; ☉10am-6pm, closed Wed)

Tokushima Prefecture International Exchange Association (徳島県国際交流協会; TOPIA; ☑656-3303; www.topia.ne.jp; ☉10am-6pm) On the 6th floor of the station building. English-speaking staff. Internet access is available (¥50 for 10 minutes).

Tourist information office (徳島総合観光案内所; ☑622-8556; ☉9am-8pm) In a booth outside the station.

ⓘ Getting There & Around

TO/FROM THE AIRPORT Tokushima's **airport** (☑699-2831; www.tokushima-airport.co.jp) is reached by bus (¥430, 25 minutes, buses timed to coincide with flights) from in front of the station.

BUS JR highway buses connect Tokushima with Tokyo (¥10,000, nine hours) and Nagoya (¥6600, 4½ hours); there are also buses to Takamatsu (¥1600, 1½ hours), Hiroshima (¥6000, 3¾ hours, two daily) and Kansai airport (¥4000, 2¾ hours).

Bike Rental bicycles (貸し自転車; per half/full day ¥300/500, deposit ¥3000; ⊙9am-5pm) are available from the underground bike park to the left as you leave the station.

TRAIN Tokushima is just over an hour by train from Takamatsu (¥2560 by *tokkyū* – limited express). For the Iya Valley and Kōchi, change trains at Awa Ikeda (阿波池田, ¥1580, 1½ hours).

Around Tokushima

NARUTO WHIRLPOOLS   鳴門のうず潮
At the change of tides, seawater whisks through the narrow channel between Shikoku and Awaji-shima at such speed that ferocious whirlpools are created. The Naruto-no-Uzushio are active twice a day. Check www.uzusio.com/shio4-6.html for a timetable or visit the tourist office.

For an up-close and personal view of the whirlpools, you can venture out into the Naruto Channel on one of the **tourist boats** that depart from the waterfront in Naruto. **Naruto Kankō Kisen** (鳴門観光汽船; ☑088-687-0101; per person ¥1530-2200) is one of several companies making regular trips out (every 20 minutes from 9am to 4.20pm) from the port, close to the Naruto Kankō-kō bus stop. For a bird's-eye view, you can walk out along **Uzu-no-michi** (渦の道; ☑088-683-6262; admission ¥500; ⊙9am-6pm, to 5pm Oct-Feb), a 500m-long walkway underneath the Naruto-ōhashi, which puts you directly above the action.

The best way to get to the whirlpools is to take a bus bound for Naruto-kōen (鳴門公園) from bus stop 1 in front of Tokushima Station (¥600, one hour, hourly from 9am) and get off at Naruto Kankō-kō (鳴門観光港).

If you want to stare into the abyss a bit longer, **Mizuno Ryokan** (旅館公園水野; ☑088-772-0013; s/d from ¥10,000/15,000) has beautiful, spacious Japanese-style rooms with fabulous sea views and efficient, foreigner-friendly service.

WALKING PILGRIMS

The *henro* (pilgrim on the 88 Temple walk) is one of the most distinctive sights of any trip to Shikoku. They're everywhere you go, striding along busy city highways, cresting hills in remote mountain valleys and tapping their colourful walking sticks – lonely figures in white, trudging purposefully through heat haze and monsoonal downpour alike on their way from temple to temple. Who are these people, and what drives them to leave the comforts of home for months at a time in order to make a journey of more than 1400km on foot?

Although the backgrounds and perhaps motives of the *henro* may differ widely, the pattern and routine of life on the road is very similar for everyone who undertakes the trail. The dress is uniform, too: *hakue* (white garments) to signify sincerity of purpose and purity of mind; the *sugegasa* (straw hat) that has protected pilgrims against sun and rain since time immemorial; and the *kongōzue* (colourful staff). Pilgrims believe that the *kongōzue* is an embodiment of the Daishi himself, who accompanies all pilgrims on their journey – hence the inscription on so many pilgrims' backpacks and other paraphernalia: 同行二人 *(dōgyō ninin)*, meaning 'two people on the same journey'. The routine at each temple is mostly the same, too: a bang on the bell and a chant of the Heart Sutra at the Daishi-dō (one of the two main buildings in each temple compound), before filing off to the *nōkyōsho* (desk), where the pilgrims' book is inscribed with beautiful characters detailing the name of the temple and the date of the pilgrimage.

If you're eager to become an *aruki henro* (walking pilgrim) yourself, you'll need to budget around 60 days (allowing for an average distance of 25km a day) to complete the circuit. Travellers who don't have the time or inclination for the whole thing can get a taste of what it's all about by following one of the *henro*-for-a-day minicircuits mentioned in the Around Tokushima and Uwajima (p548) sections. Other cities with concentrations of temples within easy reach of each other include Matsuyama (p550) in Ehime-ken and Zentsū-ji (p557) in Kagawa Prefecture.

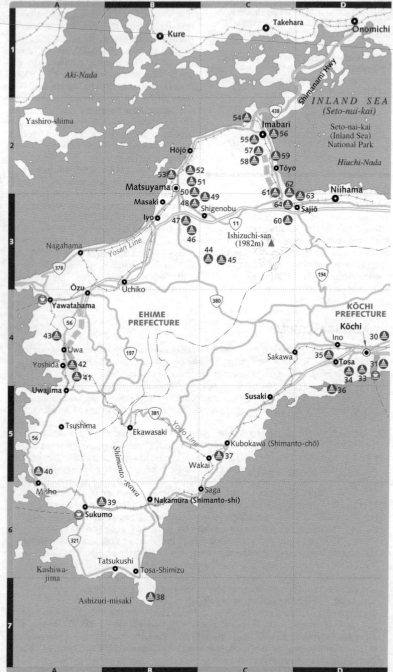

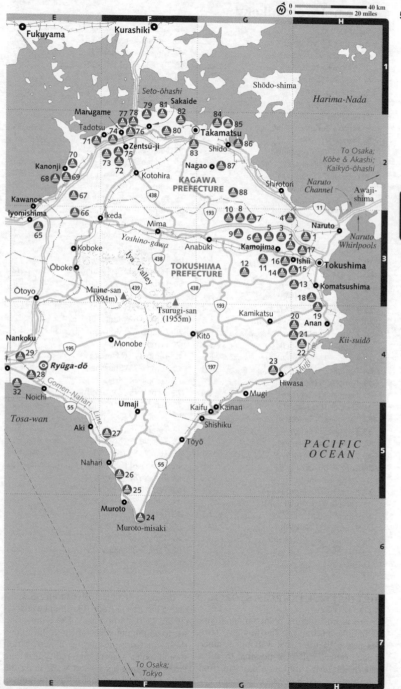

0 ⎯⎯⎯ 40 km
0 ⎯⎯⎯ 20 miles

Fukuyama
Kurashiki

Shōdo-shima

Harima-Nada

Seto-ōhashi

79 81 Sakaide
Marugame 77 78   82   84 85
Tadotsu 74   76   80 ● Takamatsu   86
71   75   83   Shido   *To Osaka;*
70   73 ● Zentsū-ji   Nagao 87   *Kōbe & Akashi;*
72   Kanonji   Kotohira   *Kaikyō-ōhashi*
68 69   **KAGAWA**   Shirotori
PREFECTURE   *Naruto*
67   (438)   88   *Channel*   Awaji-
Kawanoe   (193)   10 8   4   *shima*
Iyomishima   66   Ikeda   9   7   Naruto   (11)
65   Mima   5 3 2 1   *Naruto*
Yoshino-gawa   Anabuki   6   17   *Whirlpools*
Koboke   **TOKUSHIMA**   Kamojima   16 Ishii   ● Tokushima
Ōboke   **PREFECTURE**   12   11 14 15
Ōtoyo   Muine-san   (439)   13   Komatsushima
(1894m)   Tsurugi-san   (438)   18
(1955m)   (193)   Kamikatsu   19
Nankoku   (195) Monobe   Kitō   20 Anan
29   *Ryūga-dō*   21 *Kii-suidō*
28   (197)   22
32   *Gomen-Nahari*   23
Noichi   *Line*   Umaji   Kaifu Kainan
Tosa-wan   Aki   Shishiku   *PACIFIC*
27   Mugi   *OCEAN*
Nahari   Tōyō
26   (55)
25
Muroto
24
Muroto-misaki

To Osaka;
Tokyo

SHIKOKU AROUND TOKUSHIMA

88 Temples of Shikoku

◎ Sights

THE FIRST FIVE TEMPLES: RYŌZEN-JI TO JIZŌ-JI

Naruto is the starting point for Shikoku's 88 Temple pilgrimage. The first five temples are all within easy walking distance of each other, making it possible to get a taste of the *henro* trail on a day trip from Tokushima.

To get to Temple 1, **Ryōzen-ji** (霊山寺), take a local train from Tokushima to Bandō (板東; ¥260, 25 minutes). The temple is a 10- to 15-minute walk (about 700m) along the main road; the map at Bandō Station should point you in the right direction. From Ryōzen-ji it's a short walk along the main road from the first temple to the second, **Gokuraku-ji** (極楽寺), and another 2km from here to Temple 3, **Konsen-ji** (金泉寺). There are more-or-less regular signposts (in Japanese) pointing the way. Look for the signs by the roadside marked *henro-michi* (へんろ道 or 遍路道), often decorated with a red picture of a *henro* in silhouette. From here, it's about 5km along an increasingly rural path to **Dainichi-ji** (大日寺), and another 2km to **Jizō-ji** (地蔵寺), where there's an impressive **collection of statues** (admission ¥200) of the 500 Rakan disciples of the Buddha. From the Rakan (羅漢) bus stop on the main road in front of the temple you can catch a bus to Itano (板野) Station, where a train will take you back to Tokushima (¥350, 30 minutes).

Iya Valley   祖谷渓

The spectacular Iya Valley is a special place, its staggeringly steep gorges and thick mountain forests luring travellers to seek respite from the hectic 'mainland' lifestyle. Winding your way around narrow cliff-hanging roads as the icy blue water of the Yoshino-gawa shoots along the ancient valley floors is a blissful travel experience. The active soul can pick up some of the country's finest hiking trails around Tsurugi-san or try world-class whitewater rafting in the Ōboke and Koboke Gorges.

For the more sedentary, three top-notch onsen (hot springs) are well within reach, while evening entertainment is nothing more strenuous than sampling the local Iya *soba* (buckwheat noodles) and reliving your day's visual feast.

The earliest records of the valley describe a group of shamans fleeing from persecution in Nara in the 9th century. At the end of the 12th century, Iya famously became the last refuge for members of the vanquished Heike clan following their defeat at the hands of the Minamoto in the Gempei Wars. Their descendants are believed to live in the mountain villages to this day.

Access to the area is via Ōboke Station, reached by train from Takamatsu, Kōchi or Tokushima with a change at Awa Ikeda. Getting around the valley itself involves some planning, because Iya's sights are widespread, and public transport is sporadic at the best of times. Infrequent buses travel between Awa Ikeda, Ōboke and Iya, but the best way to explore the region is with your own wheels – rental cars are available in Shikoku's larger cities.

ŌBOKE & KOBOKE   大歩危・小歩危

Ōboke and Koboke are two scenic gorges on the Yoshino-gawa. South of Ikeda on Old Rte 32 between Koboke and Ōboke, whitewater rafting and kayaking trips run from April to late November. Sensational rafting trips run courtesy of **Happy Raft** (ハッピーラフト; ☑0887-75-0500; www.happyraft.com), close to JR Tosa Iwahara Station across the border in Kōchi Prefecture, which operates daily trips with English-speaking guides (half-day ¥5500 to ¥7500, full day ¥10,000 to ¥15,500).

River Station West-West (☑0887-84-1117; www.west-west.com, in Japanese) is a new, slightly generic tourist complex that offers rafting from the well-known Mont Bell group, and an excellent cafe and *soba* restaurant. Still, it lacks the thrill of Happy Raft.

A great place to warm up after a chilling plunge is **Iya Onsen** (祖谷温泉; ☑0883-75-2311; www.iyaonsen.co.jp, in Japanese; Matsuo Matsumoto 367-2; admission ¥1500; ☺7am-9pm, 7am-7pm Jan-Feb), on Old Rte 32, where a cable car descends a steep cliff-face to some sulphurous open-air baths overlooking the river. Accommodation (per person with meals

---

VINE BRIDGES

The wisteria vine bridges of the Iya Valley are glorious remnants of a remote and timeless Japan. Crossing the bridges has for centuries been notoriously difficult, which well suited the bandits and humbled warriors who took refuge in the secluded gorges. The bridges were feats of ancient engineering, undertaken roughly a thousand years ago, and were formed by tying together the wild vines that hung on either side of the 45m-wide valley. Only in recent years have the bridges been reinforced with side rails, planks and wire. But it's not only the acrophobic among us who will get the wobbles.

Only three *kazura-bashi* survive, one heavily touristed bridge at Nishi Iya and another pair of 'husband and wife' bridges at Higashi Iya, which is a further 30km east – the secluded, deep gorge setting is worth the extra effort.

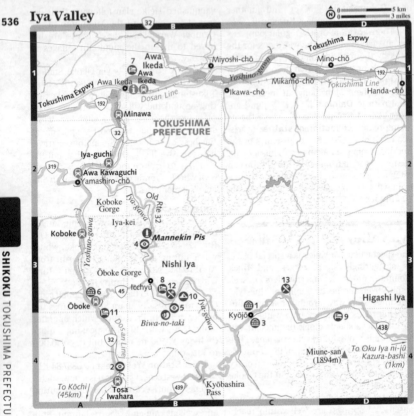

SHIKOKU TOKUSHIMA PREFECTURE

from ¥16,320) is available. Infrequent buses run from Awa Ikeda Station, bound for the Kazura-bashi.

Lapis Ōboke (ラピス大歩危; ☎0883-84-1489; admission ¥500; ☉9am-5pm), located just north of JR Ōboke Station, is a geology museum that doubles as a tourist information centre.

Ku-Nel-Asob (空音遊; ☎090-9778-7133; www.k-n-a.com; dm ¥2600; P) offers simple but attractive accommodation in communal tatami rooms. The friendly English-speaking owners can provide free pick-ups/drop-offs at JR Ōboke Station, 3km away. Since the house doesn't have a bath, a ride to nearby Iya Onsen is offered for ¥500, including entry to the onsen.

Run by a popular rafting company, **Happy Guest House** (☎0887-75-0500; per person ¥3000) is an ideal spot to rest your water-logged bones. The self-contained and fully restored farmhouse is a fine example of modern Japanese interiors. It overlooks the Yoshino Valley, and sleeps four in a spotless tatami room.

Another excellent option is **Midori no Tokeidai** (みどりの時計台; ☎0887-72-0202; ¥3500 per guest), a delightfully decorated former school building that houses many 'in-the-know' Japanese and foreign guests.

Awa Ikeda Youth Hostel (阿波池田ユースホステル; ☎0883-72-5277; dm with breakfast ¥3525), an isolated hostel with huge communal tatami rooms and a do-it-yourself vibe, is set aside the serene Mitsugon-ji mountain temple. Make sure you book ahead if you need to be picked up at JR Awa Ikeda Station, 5km away, and if you require meals.

There is spectacular scenery in the deep canyons along Old Rte 32 – infrequent public buses (¥880, 55 minutes, 7.15, 10.15am and 12.15pm) ply this narrow route between Awa Ikeda and the Iya Valley.

Iya Valley

NISHI IYA 西祖谷

Kazura-bashi (かずら橋; admission ¥500; ◎sunrise-sunset) is a remarkable vine bridge that's one of only three left in the valley (the other two are further east in Higashi Iya). Nearby, **Biwa-no-taki** is an impressive, 50m-high waterfall. The approach via the monstrous, concrete car park is a mild dampener.

Kazura-bashi Camping Village (かずら橋キャンプ村; ☑090-1571-5258; campsite ¥500, plus per person ¥200, 4-5-person bungalow from ¥5200; ◎Apr-Nov) is a camping ground 500m upriver from the vine bridge. The atmosphere is rustic, and the basic facilities are well cared for.

Hotel Kazura-bashi (ホテルかずら橋; ☑0883-87-2171; www.kazurabashi.co.jp; per person with meals from ¥15,900) is about a kilometre north of the bridge. The comfortable tatami rooms have terrific mountain views and there's a hilltop onsen.

For a taste of local Iya *soba*, try **Iya Bijin Keikoku-ten** (祖谷美人渓谷店; ☑0883-87-2009; 9-3 Zentoku; meals ¥600-1000; ◎8am-5pm), in an attractive black-and-white building with lanterns hanging out the front. A plate of *zaru soba* (cold noodles with seaweed strips) is ¥700.

HIGASHI IYA 東祖谷

Head 30km east to the spectacular **Oku Iya Ni-jū Kazura-bashi** (奥祖谷二重かずら橋; admission ¥500; ◎sunrise-sunset) in Higashi Iya, where two secluded vine bridges hang side by side high over the river. A self-propelled, three-seated wooden cable-cart is another fun way to cross the river; there's a small public camping area on the other side.

The **Higashi Iya Folk Museum** (東祖谷民族資料館; ☑0883-88-2286; admission ¥300; ◎9.30am-5pm) is in a large red building in Kyōjō, displaying historic artefacts and items relating to the Heike legend.

Several kilometres up a narrow, winding road near Kyōjō, **Buke Yashiki** (武家屋敷喜多家; ☑0883-88-2893; admission ¥300; ◎9am-5pm, closed Tue & Dec-Mar) is a thatched-roof samurai-house museum commanding spectacular views of the valley. Beside the house is a Shintō shrine that is home to a massive cedar tree dating back more than 800 years.

Iyashi no Onsen-kyō (いやしの温泉郷; ☑0883-88-2975; fax 0883-76-7080; www.sobanoyado.jp, in Japanese; per person with meals from ¥13,800, bungalow per person from ¥4350), off the main road between Kyōjō and the Higashi Iya vine bridges, is a hotel and hot-springs complex with six Japanese-style and six Western-style rooms, a bungalow and a restaurant. Nonguests can use the onsen (open 8.30am to 3.30pm October and November, to 4pm April to September, closed Wednesday) for ¥1500.

At **Soba Dōjō** (そば道場; ☑0883-88-2577; ◎11am-5pm Fri-Wed), also on Rte 438, you can sample a bowl of *zaru soba* (¥800) and even make your own (¥2500; reservation required). The restaurant has a reddish roof, and a yellow curtain hanging over the door.

TSURUGI-SAN 剣山

At 1955m, Tsurugi-san is the second-highest mountain in Shikoku and provides excellent and challenging hiking opportunities, as well as some fairly basic snowboarding from December to February. A **chairlift** (return/one way ¥1800/1000) goes most of the way up, after which it is a leisurely 30-minute walk to the summit. If you decide to climb all the way, you'll pass the Tsurugi-jinja (Tsurugi Shrine) en route, which is close to a natural spring of drinkable water.

Off the peak to the west at 1750m, the **Kame-ga-mori Hutte** (瓶ヶ森ヒュッテ; ☑0897-56-0537; per person own sleeping bag ¥700, with bedding ¥3800, with two meals ¥6500; ◎late Apr–mid-Oct) is the pick of the few sleeping options. For more detailed information on ascending Tsurugi-san and Miune-san, check out Lonely Planet's *Hiking in Japan*.

CHIIORI – A RURAL RETREAT

High on a mountainside in the remote Iya Valley, looking out over forested hillsides and plunging gorges, is one of Japan's most unusual places to stay.

Chiiori – 'The Cottage of the Flute' – is a once-abandoned 18th-century thatched-roof farmhouse that has been painstakingly restored towards its original brilliance. Unlike many such examples of cultural heritage in Japan, where concrete and plastic have wrecked the architectural aesthetic, here glistening red-pine floorboards surround open-floor hearths under soaring rafters. Set amid steep hillsides dotted by thatched houses and forests strewn with narrow mountain paths, Iya was for centuries an example of an untouched coexistence of man and nature, albeit one that offered residents little hope of wealth and comfort.

In recent decades, however, the locals' traditional lifestyle and the balance with the environment have been rapidly upset; employment moved from agriculture to government-subsidised and frequently pointless construction, the effects of which – eg paved riverbeds – can be seen from almost any roadside. Part of the project's mission has been working with residents to promote sustainable, community-based tourism and realise the financial potential of traditional life – which until recently many locals saw as backward and valueless. It is a work in progress – many thatched roofs in the area are still hidden by corrugated tin sheets – but by adding to the growing number of tourists visiting the area, largely because of the work of those involved in Chiiori, visiting here helps to encourage those conservation efforts.

The house was bought as a ruin by the author and aesthete Alex Kerr in the early 1970s, and he went on to romanticise the Iya Valley in his award-winning book *Lost Japan*. Chiiori remains a beautiful and authentic destination for sensitive travellers.

Public transport is available at the bottom of the mountainside from the nearest train station, JR Oboke – about 30km away – but buses are infrequent, and having your own vehicle is a better option. It costs ¥6500 per person so stay, which includes two delicious meals. Chiiori itself can sometimes arrange pick-ups.

To learn more about the project log onto www.chiiori.org.

Southern Tokushima Prefecture 徳島県南部

The slow-paced highway running south from Tokushima-*shi* (city) passes through prosperous little agricultural towns fronted by lazy surf beaches and marine industry machinery, and flanked by hidden temples and spectacular rocky bluffs.

The JR Mugi line runs down the coast as far as Kaifu, just short of the border. From Kaifu, the private Asa Kaigan railway runs two stops further to Kannoura, just across the border. From here, you can continue by bus to the cape at Muroto-misaki and on to Kōchi city. Coming the other way, trains run from Kōchi as far as Nahari – but you'll have to rely on buses to get you around the cape.

HIWASA 日和佐
☎0884

The major attraction in the small coastal town of Hiwasa is **Yakuō-ji** (薬王寺), Temple 23, and the last temple in Tokushima Prefecture. Yakuō-ji dates back to the year 726, and is famous as a *yakuyoke no tera* (a temple with special powers to ward off ill fortune during unlucky years). The unluckiest age for men is 42; for women, 33 is the one to watch out for. Kōbō Daishi is said to have visited in 815, the year of his own 42nd birthday. The long set of stone steps leading up to the main temple building comes in two stages: 33 steps for the women, followed by another 42 for the men. The tradition is for pilgrims to put a coin on each step – if you come when it's busy, you may find the steps practically overflowing with one-yen coins.

About 1.5km from the centre of town is Ōhama (大浜) beach, a long stretch of sand where sea turtles come to lay their eggs from May to August each year.

The best accommodation option is at Yakuō-ji's **shukubō** (☎77-1105; fax 77-1486; per person with meals ¥7300). The tatami rooms here are spacious and well kept, and filling meals are served. It's in a modern building across the road from the temple.

SOUTH TO MUROTO-MISAKI

A short train ride south from Hiwasa is the sleepy fishing town of **Mugi** (牟岐), where the winding streets of the old fishing port make an interesting stopover. A 45-minute (3km) walk along the coast past the fishing port is **Mollusc Mugi Shell Museum** (貝の資料館モラスコむぎ; ☑0884-72-2520; admission ¥400; ⊙9am-4.30pm, closed Mon), where there's an impressive collection of shells and tropical fish in an idyllic setting on a quiet beach. There is an old Hachiman shrine in the centre of the town, and boats run out to the island of Teba-jima (出羽島).

Glass-bottomed boats tour the waters around Takegashima island near Shishikui, run by **Blue Marine** (ブルーマリン; ☑0884-76-3100; cruises ¥1800; ⊙9am-4pm, closed Tue). **Sea kayaking** (マリンジャム; ☑0884-76-1401; per person ¥2500; ⊙10am & 2pm) is available at the same place, inside the Marine Jam Building.

🛏 Sleeping & Eating

There are plenty of places to stay along the coast at Kannoura, Shishikui and Ikumi.

TOP CHOICE Minshuku Ikumi   MINSHUKU $
(民宿いくみ; ☑0887-24-3838; www.ikumiten.com; Ikumi; per person with breakfast ¥4100) A charming family-run affair, and a popular surfer's choice, thanks to the well-presented rooms and the helpful, knowledgeable owner, Ten.

White Beach Hotel Ikumi   HOTEL $$
(ホワイトビーチホテル見見; ☑0887-29-3018; www.wbhotel.net/ikumi, in Japanese; Ikumi; per person ¥4000-5000) Close by Minshuku Michishio is this place, which has Japanese- and Western-style rooms and a beachfront restaurant called Oluolu (it offers meals from ¥800, and is open for lunch and dinner – a picture menu is available).

Minshuku Michishio   MINSHUKU $$
(民宿みちしお; ☑0887-29-3471; fax 0887-29-3470; Ikumi; per person with meals from ¥5775) Another good option on the beach, with Japanese- and Western-style rooms and a restaurant serving tasty *okonomiyaki* (savoury pancakes; butter and cabbage cooked with seafood or meat on a griddle).

Shirahama White Beach Hotel   HOTEL $
(白浜ホワイトビーチホテル; ☑0887-29-3344; www.wbhotel.net, in Japanese; Kannoura; per person from ¥6000) A slightly faded modern resort hotel that's directly on the beach at Kannoura. In the summer, camping is available on the beach next to the hotel.

Hotel Riviera   HOTEL $$
(ホテルリビエラししくい; ☑0884-76-3300; fax 0884-76-3910; www.hotel-riviera.co.jp, in Japanese; Shishikui; per person with meals from ¥12,000) In Shishikui, with upmarket Western- and Japanese-style rooms. Nonguests can use the sea-view onsen baths (¥600; from 11am to 10pm).

LOCAL KNOWLEDGE

TEN IN IKUMI

Where and when did you learn to surf? I grew up in Osaka and started surfing at Isonoura in Wakayama 30 years ago. I've been living (and surfing) in Ikumi for 10 years.

What are three things that a surfer needs to know about Tokushima? Like anywhere, you must communicate with the local surfers; if you do, they are very friendly. There are many options for surfing here: beach breaks, reefs and river mouths. If the waves are closing out, then somewhere else might be perfect.

Where are your favourite places to surf in Shikoku? Ikumi beach is my favourite surfing point. Tainohama, Tebajima and Kaifu are also good, especially if elsewhere is too big.

When is the best time to surf in Shikoku? July to October.

Do many foreigners surf here? Not so many, but some foreigner surfers living in this area and European surfers come to my accommodation every year.

Do you think the surfing scene in Shikoku is growing? According to the older surfers, the surfing story of Shikoku started about 40 years ago, and has steadily grown since then.

Where is your favourite place to surf outside Japan? Hawaii, and Noosa (Australia)!
Ten Taguchi, local surfer extraordinaire

SURFING TOKUSHIMA

Southern Tokushima is a surfer's paradise, with world-class river mouths, consistent barrels and relatively few surfers in the water. Despite the prevalence of concrete on the shoreline, this region has mostly gorgeous white-sand beaches and relaxed, friendly locals.

Surfing equipment is available for hire at numerous places in the one-street beach-bum town of **Ikumi** (生見), where you'll find most of the best places to stay. For money, there is a post office with an international ATM in Kaifu, and another in Kannoura.

Aunt Dinah　　　　　　　　　CURRY $
(☎0887-29-2080; Kannoura; meals ¥750-1500; ☺9.30am-9.30pm, closed Tue) Old-time country music and a range of curries available (seafood curry ¥890).

ⓘ Getting There & Away

Trains run as far south as Kannoura. There are also buses from Mugi to Kannoura (¥770, 45 minutes, 14 per day), stopping at Kaifu and Shishikui on the way. Seven buses a day run from Kannoura to Muroto-misaki, via Ikumi (¥1390, 40 minutes). Buses run as far as Aki (安芸; ¥2880, two hours), where you can transfer to a train to Kōchi. On the last 40km to the cape, the road hugs the coast, hemmed in by mountains and sea.

KŌCHI PREFECTURE

The largest of Shikoku's four prefectures, Kōchi Prefecture spans the entire Pacific coastline between the two capes of Muroto-misaki and Ashizuri-misaki. Cut off from the rest of Japan by the mountains and sea, the province once known as Tosa was traditionally regarded as one of the wildest and remotest places in the country.

Although the trip through Tosa makes up more than a third of the pilgrimage, only 16 of the 88 Temples are located in the province. In fact, it's 84km from the last temple in Tokushima Prefecture at Hiwasa before you get to the first temple in Kōchi Prefecture at Muroto-misaki. The longest distance between temples is also in Kōchi: a crippling

87km from Temple 37 (岩本寺; Iwamoto-ji) in Kubokawa to Temple 38 (金剛福寺; Kongōfuku-ji) at Ashizuri-misaki.

Kōchi Prefecture is a good place for outdoor types. Whale-watching, rafting, hiking and camping are all options here. Kōchi Prefecture brims with scenic spots, especially along the Shimanto-gawa, one of the last undammed rivers in Japan.

Tokushima to Kōchi

Continuing further south, you'll pass more pretty fishing villages tucked away along a painfully slow-paced oceanside highway. It's a beautiful, desolate coastal drive, and all the more remarkable for its proximity to the bright lights of Kōchi.

MUROTO-MISAKI　　　　　　　　室戸岬
☎0887
Kōbō Daishi found enlightenment on this gorgeous, wild cape, and it's easy to ponder why as you reach the 'doorway to the land of the dead'. Visitors can explore Kōbō Daishi's rather murky bathing hole among the rock pools, and the Shinmeikutsu cave (神明窟) where he once meditated.

A huge white statue of the saint stares out to sea just north of the cape. Temple 24, **Hotsumisaki-ji** (最御崎寺; also known as Higashi-dera) was founded by Kōbō Daishi in the early 9th century. It's at the top of a steep hill directly above the point. Next to the temple, accommodation is available at the peaceful **shukubō temple lodgings** (☎23-0024; per person with/without meals ¥5775/3885), a modern building with spotless tatami rooms.

For something different, **Utoco Deep Sea Therapy Hotel** (☎22-1811; r per person from ¥20,000) is a remarkable concept hotel that aims to harness the restorative powers of the ocean in a science fiction setting. The design is elegant, each room a spacious, silent retreat with electronic toilets and cloudlike beds. A whole menu of massage and saltwater spa therapy is available, plus a menu that scours the hidden depths of the sea. Utoco is located on the shoreline, 100m before Daishi's statue.

Seven buses a day run west from the cape to Nahari or Aki (安芸; ¥1300, 1½ hours), where you can change to the JR line for a train to Kōchi (one hour). Trains between Aki and Kōchi take anywhere between 45 minutes and 1½ hours, depending on connections at Gomen (tickets cost between

¥1150 and ¥1460). There are also buses up the east coast to Kannoura and Mugi in Tokushima Prefecture.

RYŪGA-DŌ 龍河洞
⏺0887

Accessible by bus from Tosa-Yamada Station on the Dosan line is the limestone cave **Ryūga-dō** (⏺53-2144; www.ryugadou.or.jp, in Japanese; admission ¥1000; ⏱8.30am-5pm, to 4.30pm Dec-Feb). The cave has some interesting stalactites and stalagmites, and traces of prehistoric habitation. The route gets quite steep in places. About 1km of the 4km cave is toured in the standard visit. Advance reservations and an additional ¥500 are required for the *bōken kōsu* (adventure course; 冒険コース), where you get to don helmet and overalls and follow a guide for a 90-minute exploration of the inner reaches of the cave.

There are five buses a day to Ryūga-dō from Tosa-Yamada Station (¥440, 20 minutes). Tosa-Yamada Station is 30 minutes from Kōchi by local train (¥350), or 15 minutes by *tokkyū* (limited express train; ¥600).

Kōchi 高知
⏺088 / POP 335,000

Kōchi is a smart, compact city with a deserved reputation for enjoying a good time. The castle here is largely undamaged, and remains a fine example of Japanese architecture. Excellent access to the Ashizuri-misaki, Iya Valley and southern Tokushima, and easy day trips to caves, beaches and mountains make Kōchi perhaps the perfect base for travels around the island. The town also boasts a samurai of great national significance. During the Meiji Restoration, Sakamoto Ryōma was instrumental in bringing down the feudal government.

⊙ Sights & Activities

Kōchi-jō CASTLE
(高知城; Kōchi Castle; 1-2-1 Marunouchi; admission ¥400; ⏱9am-5pm) Kōchi-jō is one of just a dozen castles in Japan to have survived with its original *tenshu-kaku* (keep) intact. The castle was originally built during the first decade of the 17th century by Yamanouchi Katsutoyo, who was appointed *daimyō* by Tokugawa Ieyasu after he fought on the victorious Tokugawa side in the Battle of Sekigahara in 1600. A major fire destroyed much of the original structure in 1727, and the castle was largely rebuilt between 1748 and 1753.

The castle was the product of an age of peace – it never came under attack, and for the remainder of the Tokugawa period it was more like a stately home than a military fortress.

Godaisan PARK
(五台山) Several kilometres east of the town centre is the mountain of Godaisan, where there are excellent views out over the city from a **lookout point** (展望台) in a park. A short walk away at the top of the hill is **Chikurin-ji** (竹林寺), Temple 31 of the 88, where the main hall was built by the second Tosa *daimyō*, Yamanouchi Tadayoshi, in 1644. The extensive grounds also feature a five-storey pagoda and thousands of statues of the Bodhisattva Jizō, guardian deity of children and travellers. The **Treasure House** (宝物館; admission ¥400; ⏱9am-5pm) hosts an impressive collection of Buddhist sculpture from the Heian and Kamakura periods; the same ticket gets you into the lovely late-Kamakura-period garden opposite. Descending the steps by the Treasure House brings you to the entrance gates of the **Kōchi Prefectural Makino Botanical Gardens** (高知県立牧野植物園; admission ¥500; ⏱9am-5pm), a beautiful network of gardens and parkland featuring more than 3000 different plant species. These gardens are named for Makino Tomitarō, the 'Father of Japanese Botany'.

The **My-Yū** circular bus stops at Godaisan on its way to Katsura-hama from Kōchi Station (all-day ticket ¥900, 25 minutes). The bus usually operates on weekends only, but runs daily during Golden Week (19 July to 31 August) and the New Year holidays.

Katsura-hama BEACH
(桂浜) Katsura-hama is a popular **beach** 13km south of central Kōchi at the point where Kōchi's harbour empties out into the bay. Unfortunately, strong currents prohibit swimming. Just before you get to the beach itself is **Sakamoto Ryōma Memorial Museum** (坂本龍馬記念館; 830 Jōsan; admission ¥400; ⏱9am-5pm), where the exhibits are dedicated to the life of a local hero who was instrumental in bringing about the Meiji Restoration in the 1860s. Born in Kōchi in 1835, Ryōma brought about the alliance between the Satsuma (modern Kagoshima) and Chōshū (Yamaguchi) domains that eventually brought down the Tokugawa shogunate. He was killed in Kyoto in 1867, aged 32.

SHIKOKU KŌCHI PREFECTURE

Kōchi

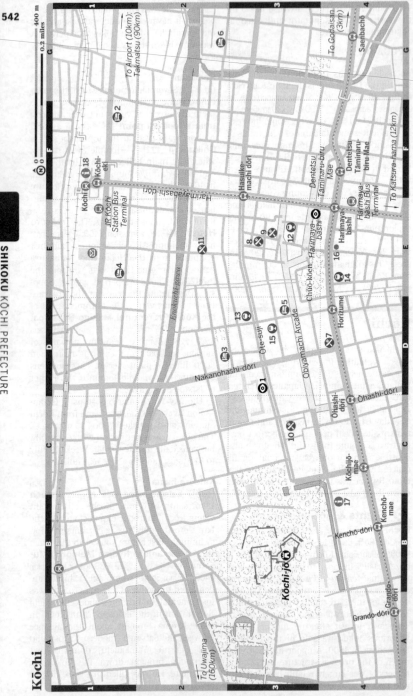

N

0   400 m
0   0.2 miles

To Godaisan
(3km)

Saenbachō

To Katsura-hama (12km)

To Airport (10km);
Takmatsu (90km)

Dentetsu
Tāmiharu-biru
Mae

Dentetsu
Tāmiharu-biru
Mae

Harimaya-
bashi Bus
Terminal

Harimaya-
bashi

Hasuike-
machi dōri

Harimayabashi-dōri

Kōchi-
eki

Kōchi

JR Kōchi
Station Bus
Terminal

Chūō-kōen

Harimaya-bashi

Horizume

Obiyamachi Arcade

Enokuchi-gawa

Nakanohashi-dōri

Ōte-suji

Ōhashi-
dōri

Ōhashi-dōri

Kōchijō-
mae

Kōchi-jō

Kenchō-
mae

Kenchō-dōri

Grando-
dōri

Grando-dōri

To Uwajima
(160km)

Kōchi

There is an **aquarium** (桂浜水族館; ☎841-2437; admission ¥1100; ⏰9am-5.30pm) on the beach, and a small shrine on the hillside. Buses run to Katsura-hama from Kōchi Station (¥610, 30 minutes, six daily) and Harimaya-bashi (¥560, 25 minutes, frequent).

The bloodthirsty traveller might enjoy the **Tosa Dog Fighting Centre** (土佐闘犬センター; admission ¥500, fighting tournaments ¥1500; ⏰9am-4pm), which runs regular tournaments and sells fluffy versions of the tough Tosa breed.

Sunday Market
MARKET

(日曜市; Ōte-suji; ⏰5am-6pm Sun Apr-Sep, 6am-5pm Sun Oct-Mar) Our favourite street market in Shikoku, 300 years old, takes place every Sunday along the main road leading to the castle. Colourful stalls sell fresh produce, tonics and tinctures, knives, flowers, garden stones and wooden antiques.

Tosa Washi Paper Museum
MUSEUM

(いの町紙の博物館) Make your own Japanese paper for ¥300. At Ino, about 10km west of Kōchi.

🎎 Festivals

Kōchi's lively **Yosakoi Matsuri** (Yosakoi Festival; よさこい祭り) on 10 and 11 August perfectly complements Tokushima's Awa-odori Matsuri (12 to 15 August). There's a night-before event on 9 August and night-after effort on 12 August, but 10 and 11 August are the big days. The short-lived **Havanero Matsuri** is promising to return in September 2011. Fingers crossed, as this outdoor hip-hop and reggae party is a sure-fire hit.

🛏 Sleeping

TOP CHOICE **Tosa Bekkan**
MINSHUKU $

(とさ別館; ☎883-5685; fax 884-9523; 1-11-34 Sakura-chō; per person ¥3800) One of the most relaxed and comfortable *minshuku* on the island is set in a quiet residential area 15 minutes' walk (900m) from the station. The spacious Japanese-style rooms are a bargain and meals are available with advance notice. To get here, follow the tramlines straight ahead from the station and turn left when you see Green Hotel on your right. Look out for signs on the telegraph posts with the name in Japanese.

Kochi Youth Hostel
HOSTEL $

(高知ユースホステル酒の国共和国; ☎823-0858; fax 823-0859; www.kyh-sakenokuni.com; 4-5 Fukuigashi-machi; dm/s with breakfast ¥2415/3150; @) This charming wood-panelled hostel behind the Engyoujiguchi Station doubles as a sake tasting house (sampling courses ¥500). The tatami rooms are simple and comfortable, and the food is excellent quality and value. The friendly host Tomio Kondo is very welcoming to foreign guests.

Comfort Inn
HOTEL $$

(コンフォートホテル高知駅前; ☎883-1441; fax 884-3692; 2-2-12 Kita-Honmachi; s/tw with breakfast ¥5400/7200; P❄@🌐) This large hotel has friendlier staff than at many business hotels, and the rooms are excellent for the price. There are consoles with internet in the lobby, a good complimentary breakfast and enough long, empty corridors for a horror film.

Hotel No 1 Kōchi HOTEL $$
(ホテルNO. 1高知; ☎873-3333; fax 875-9999; www.hotelno1.jp/kochi, in Japanese; 16-8 Nijūdai-machi; s/tw ¥5140/7870; P⊖@) This business hotel is in a quiet area between the station and the castle. Western-style rooms are on the small side, but the rooftop onsen is a nice touch. There is LAN access in all rooms, and there are internet consoles in the lobby.

Petit Hotel HOTEL $$
(☎826-8156; 1-8-13 Kitahon-machi; s/tw ¥6100/8340; ⊖@) This excellent business hotel near Kōchi Station is an astute alternative to the larger chains. Service is efficient and friendly, and the rooms are reasonably spacious, particularly the sparkling clean bathrooms.

Richmond Hotel HOTEL $$$
(リッチモンドホテル高知; ☎820-1122; www.richmondhotel.jp/e/kochi/index.htm; 9-4 Obiyamachi; s ¥11,000, d ¥16,000-20,000; P⊖@) Kōchi's classiest hotel has immaculate rooms and professional service, plus it's located just off the main shopping arcade in the heart of the city. There are public consoles with free internet access; rental laptops are also available and LAN access is in all rooms.

Sansuien HOTEL $$$
(三翠園; ☎822-0131; www.sansuien.co.jp, in Japanese; 1-3-35 Takajō-machi; per person with meals from ¥13,800; P) Three blocks south of the castle along Kenchō-mae Dōri is this classy multistorey hotel with luxurious onsen baths and a garden incorporating a series of buildings that once formed part of the *daimyō's* residence. The Japanese tatami rooms far outweigh their Western counterparts for both size and comfort. Nonguests can use the baths from 10am to 4pm (¥900).

Eating

Kōchi's main entertainment district is in the area around the Obiyamachi arcade and the Harimaya-bashi junction where the tramlines meet. Local specialities include *katsuo tataki* (lightly seared bonito fish). After a night of drinking, head to Green Rd, a small street lined till late with open-air noodle stalls.

TOP CHOICE **Gosankeshi** SEAFOOD $$
(dishes ¥600-2500; ⌚6pm-1am) Named after the auspicious carp, this is Kōchi's hottest spot for high quality, affordable seafood. Sweet, pan-fried *ebi* (shrimp) and delectable *tai* (snapper) dishes are whipped up on demand by young, affable chefs. It's in the heart of the party district and makes an ideal predrinking feast.

Hirome Ichiba ARCADE $
(ひろめ市場; ☎822-5287; 2-3-1 Obiyamachi; ⌚8am-11pm, from 7am Sun; ⓔ) Some hundred or so mini restaurants specialising in everything from *gomoku rāmen* (seafood noodles) to *tacoyaki* (octopus balls); this is the hub of Kōchi's cheap eats scene. On weekends, it positively heaves with young people drinking hard and happy. It's at the end of the main arcade, just before the castle.

Hakobe OKINOMIYAKI $
(はこべ; ☎823-0084; 1-2-5 Obiyamachi; dishes ¥600-1000; ⌚11am-midnight) This is one of the few remaining cook-it-yourself *okinomiyaki* joints in Kōchi (¥630) serving cheap and cheerful Japanese pancakes, with good English spoken by the waiters. The 'mix' of *ika* (squid) and *ebi* and *tori* (chicken) is heavenly. Other alternatives include *buta* (pork) and *yasai* (vegetables). It's slap bang in the heart of the arcade.

Uofuku IZAKAYA $$
(魚福; ☎824-1129; 2-13 Nijūdai-chō; dishes ¥600-1500; ⌚5-11pm, closed Sun) Uofuku is a fabulous curb-side *izakaya* (pub-eatery) on a quiet backstreet behind the arcade. Fish is the order of the day, handpicked from the tank by the door. The menu is a mess of kanji; try the *katsuo tataki* (around ¥1200) or ask for *osusume* (a recommendation). This is a good place for adventurous eaters to try *shutō* – the pickled and fermented innards of the bonito fish (¥450), which locals regard as a delicacy.

Café Panda SEAFOOD $$
(パンダ; ☎872-4698; Sakai-machi; ⌚lunch & dinner; ⓔ) Contemporary bar meals with an emphasis on healthy seafood dishes are on offer at this classy new establishment decked out in floorboards, white furniture and glass tables. The light electronic soundtrack kicks on until 2am.

Drinking & Entertainment

Famille Horse Shoe Bar BAR
(☎090-5711-9958; Hirome Ichiba; ⌚11am-11pm) Pull up one of five stools in the heart of the food market and watch the world go by as the young owner plies you with wisdom and whisky. Beers cost ¥600 and shots are two-for-one.

Love Jamaican
NIGHTCLUB

(☑872-0447; 3rd fl, 1-5-5 Obiyamachi; ⊙7pm-3am)
This fully legit reggae and hip-hop club is
a hive of after-hours mayhem thanks to a
classy sound system, generous drink deals
and a manicured young crowd.

Habotan
IZAKAYA

(葉牡丹; ☑872-1330; 2-21 Sakai-machi; ⊙11am-
11pm) Red lanterns mark out this locals' *izakaya*. The menu, plastered over the walls, is
in Japanese, but the food is under glass on
the counter, so you can always point. *Sashimi moriawase* (a selection of sashimi) is
¥1050. Local fare includes Tosa-tsuru sake
and Dabada Hiburi, a *shōchū* (distilled grain
liquor) made from chestnuts. It's opposite
Chūō Kōen, near several banks.

Also recommended:

Amontillado Pub
PUB

(アモンティラード; ☑875-0899; 1-1-17 Obiyamachi; ⊙5pm-1am) Irish bar serving pints
of Guinness for ¥900.

Boston Cafe Bar
BAR

(ボストンカフェ; ☑875-7730; 1-7-9 Ōte-
suji; ⊙5.30pm-2am, to after 2am Sat & Sun)
Friendly, American-themed neighbourhood
bar.

ⓘ Information

Coin lockers and a left-luggage office are in the
station, and international ATMs are available at
the post office next to the station.

JTB (☑823-2321; 1-21 Sakai-chō; ⊙10am-
6pm, closed Wed) Close to the Harimayabashi
intersection.

Kōchi International Association (高知県国
際交流協会; ☑875-0022; www.kōchi-kia.or.jp;
4-1-37 Honmachi; ⊙8.30am-5.30pm, closed
Sun) Free internet access, a library and English
newspapers.

Tourist information office (高知市観光案内
所; ☑826-3337; ⊙9am-5pm) Helpful office
inside JR Kōchi Station.

ⓘ Getting There & Around

TO/FROM THE AIRPORT Kōchi's Ryōma airport, about 10km east of the city, is accessible
by bus (¥700, 35 minutes) from the station.
There are daily flights to/from Tokyo, Nagoya,
Osaka and Fukuoka (¥23,700, 45 minutes, three
daily).

BUS The My-Yū circular bus runs to Godaisan
and Katsurahama from Kōchi Station.

TRAIN Kōchi is on the JR Dosan line, and is
connected to Takamatsu (*tokkyū* ¥4760, two
hours and 10 minutes) via Awa Ikeda (*tokkyū*
¥2730, one hour and nine minutes). Trains also

run west to Kubokawa (*tokkyū* ¥2560, one hour),
where you can change for Nakamura (for the
Shimanto-gawa).

TRAM Kōchi's colourful tram service (¥190 per
trip) has been running since 1904. There are
two lines: the north–south line from the station intersects with the east–west tram route
at the Harimaya-bashi (はりまや橋) junction.
Pay when you get off, and ask for a *norikae-ken*
(transfer ticket) if you have to change lines.

Kōchi to Ashizuri-misaki

The quiet stretch of coast between Kōchi
and Ashizuri-misaki offers a number of interesting diversions. Tosa-wan (Tosa Bay)
was once a major whaling centre; today,
whale-watching is increasingly popular
along the coast. There are kayaking opportunities along the Shimanto-gawa, one of
the last free-flowing rivers in Japan, and an
exquisite beach at Ohkihama. At the cape
itself, there's some rugged scenery and Temple 38 on the Shikoku pilgrim trail.

The train line from Kōchi parts at Wakai.
The JR Yodo line heads northwest through
the mountains to Uwajima in Ehime-ken,
while the private Tosa-Kuroshio line heads
around to Nakamura and ends at Sukumo.
There is also a bus service to Ashizuri-misaki from Nakamura Station (¥1930, one hour
and 40 minutes, nine daily).

In the town of Kuroshio-machi not far
from Nakamura, **Ōgata Whale Watching**
(☑0880-43-1058; fax 0880-43-1527; http://sunabi
.com/kujira, in Japanese; per person ¥5000) runs
three four-hour trips daily between late
April and October, leaving at 8am, 10am and
1pm. Tosa Irino and Tosa Kamikawaguchi
are the closest stations to Kuroshio-machi
on the Tosa-Kuroshio railway line.

TOP CHOICE **Shimanto-gawa Youth Hostel**
(四万十川ユースホステル; ☑0880-54-1352;
www16.plala.or.jp/shimanto-yh, in Japanese; nonmembers per person with 2 meals ¥5980; ❄) is a
charming place and reason enough to get
upstream. A friendly couple oversee excellent
accommodation in shared bedrooms and run
regular canoeing trips on the river (¥8400 for
a regular day's touring; cheaper introductory
courses are available for beginners). The hostel closes from mid-December to late January.

The hostel is 4.5km away from Kuchiya-
nai (口屋内), accessible by (infrequent) buses from Ekawasaki Station and Nakamura.
Given enough notice, the manager will pick
you up.

Little traffic and stunning scenery make Shikoku one of the best driving destinations in Japan. There's also a lack of regular public transport services in some areas, namely around the two southern capes and the Iya Valley, so your international license can at last come in handy. Our favourite drive is along the banks of the Shimanto-gawa on Rte 381. Here you vie with the odd truck for single-lane access to some of the narrowest, bendiest, prettiest roads in the country, boxed in by rocky cliffs on one side and the shimmering Shimanto-gawa on the other. It feels like you're in a rally driving video game where the animated cars just know how to avoid you.

Kawarakko (かわらっこ; ☎0880-31-8400; www.kawarakko.com, in Japanese; campsite ¥2100, autocamping ¥3150) is a riverside campground run by an adventure company. Canoes, mountain bikes and even tents are available to hire should you fancy a spontaneous night under the stars.

NAKAMURA 中村
☎0880 / POP 37,900

Nakamura, recently renamed Shimanto-shi, is a good place to organise trips on the beautiful **Shimanto-gawa** (四万十川). Staff at the **tourist information office** (☎35-4171; ☉8.30am-5pm), located on the right side of the highway as you enter town from the north, can provide information on kayaking and canoe trips, and camping and outdoor activities. A number of companies offer **river cruises** on traditional fishing boats called Yakata-bune (¥2000 for 50 minutes); the tourist information office has a full list. Bike rental is available here (per five hours/one day ¥600/1000) too, allowing you to scoot out to the river under your own steam.

In front of the station, decent Western-style rooms are available at the **Dai-ichi Hotel Nakamura** (中村第一ホテル; ☎0880-34-7211; fax 0880-34-7463; s/d ¥5000/10,500). A post office with international ATM is a short walk away.

Ashizuri-misaki 足摺岬
☎0880

Like Muroto-misaki, Ashizuri-misaki is a rugged, picturesque promontory that's famous for its other-worldly appearance and violent weather.

On the cape at Ashizuri-misaki there's an imposing statue of locally born hero John Manjirō. Born in 1836 as Nakahama Manjirō, the young fisherman was swept onto the desolate shores of Tori-shima, 600km from Tokyo Bay, in 1841. Five months later, he and his shipmates were rescued by a US whaler passing by, and granted safe passage to Hawaii. After moving to Massachusetts and learning English, 'John' finally returned to Japan and later played a leading role in diplomatic negotiations with the USA and other countries at the end of the Tokugawa period.

Ashizuri-misaki is also home to Temple 38, **Kongōfuku-ji** (金剛福寺), which has breathtaking views of the promontory and the Pacific Ocean. A short walk back towards civilisation is **Ashizuri Youth Hostel** (足摺ユースホステル; ☎88-0324; dm per person ¥3960), run by a cute older couple, who provide large, well-cared-for tatami rooms. With advance notice, meals are available. More upmarket is **Ashizuri Kokusai Hotel** (足摺国際ホテル; ☎0880-88-0201; fax 0880-88-1135; www.ashizuri.co.jp, in Japanese; r per person with meals from ¥13,650), which has onsen baths overlooking the sea. It's located 50m from the hostel.

EHIME PREFECTURE

Occupying the western region of Shikoku, Ehime Prefecture (愛媛県) has the largest number of pilgrimage temples – 27 of them, to be precise. Like Tosa, the southern part of the prefecture has always been considered wild and remote; by the time pilgrims arrive in Shikoku's largest city, Matsuyama, they know that the hard work has been done. There are large clusters of temples around Matsuyama and the Shimanami-kaidō bridge system, which links Shikoku with Honshū.

Prefectural highlights are the immaculately preserved feudal castle and historic Dōgo Onsen in Matsuyama, and the sacred peak of Ishizuchi-san (1982m), the tallest mountain in western Japan.

Uwajima 宇和島

☑0895 / POP 62,000

Uwajima is an unhurried rural town that draws a steady trickle of titillated travellers to its academically inclined sex museum and attached Shintō fertility shrine. The surrounding islands and coastline are keenly fish farmed, though day trips are still pretty and peaceful. Uwajima is also noteworthy as a centre for traditional bullfighting.

◉ Sights & Activities

Taga-jinja & Sex Museum   MUSEUM/SHRINE
(多賀神社; ☑22-3444; www3.ocn.ne.jp/~deko boko, in Japanese; admission ¥800; ☉8am-5pm) Once upon a time, many Shintō shrines had a connection to fertility rites. Of those that remain, Taga-jinja is one of the best known. The grounds of the shrine are strewn with tree-trunk phalluses and numerous statues and stone carvings. Inside, the museum is packed with anthropological erotica from all corners of the procreating world. The shrine is 500m northwest of town, over the Suka-gawa.

Uwajima-jō   CASTLE
(宇和島城; admission ¥200; ☉9am-4pm) Dating from 1601, Uwajima-jō is a small three-storey castle on an 80m-high hill in the centre of town. The present structure was rebuilt in 1666 by the *daimyō* Date Munetoshi. The *donjon* (main keep) is one of only 12 originals left in Japan; there is nothing much to see inside. The surrounding park, **Shiroyama-kōen** (城山公園), is open from sunrise to sunset, and is a pleasant place for a stroll.

Date Museum   MUSEUM
(伊達博物館; 9-14 Goten-machi; admission ¥500; ☉9am-5pm, closed Mon) The well-presented exhibits at the excellent Date Museum are dedicated to the Date family, who ruled Uwajima from the castle for 250 years during the Tokugawa period. The explanations are mostly in Japanese, but a lot of the stuff on display – swords, armour, palanquins and lacquerware – is pretty self-explanatory.

Municipal Bullfighting Ring   BULLFIGHTING RING
(宇和島市営闘牛場; admission ¥3000) *Tōgyū* (闘牛) can probably be called a sort of bovine sumō. Victory is achieved when one animal forces the other to its knees, or when one turns tail and flees from the ring. Fights are held on 2 January, the first Sunday of April, 24 July, 14 August and the fourth Sunday of October. Directions to the bullfighting ring are available at the tourist information office.

WORTH A TRIP

DETOUR: OHKIHAMA

About 40 minutes south of Nakamura, on the bus to Ashizuri-misaki, is **Ohkihama** (大岐浜), Shikoku's most magnificent sandy white beach. The only souls to frequent this unspoilt 2km stretch shielded by neat rows of pine trees are the pick of the region's surfers, some egg-laying turtles and the odd, grinning clam diver. Facing east means you can watch the sun and moon rise from your beach towel, and warm currents ensure swimming is possible year-round.

Most travellers shoot through en route to the cape, but a stay at **Kaiyu Inn** (☑0880-82-8500; www.kaiyu-inn.jp; s from ¥8500, extra person from ¥2500) is itself worth the visit to Shikoku. The accomplished owner, Mitsu, studied agriculture in the USA before serving a hotel apprenticeship in Bali. Here he has redesigned a white concrete 1960s conference centre into a sublime yet affordable contemporary retreat. Each room has been designed by a different emerging Japanese architect and, coupled with Mitsu's keen aesthetical eye and extensive designer furniture collection, has created spaces worthy of Conde Naste covers, each with Pacific Ocean views. The communal meals are inventive, super fresh and organic, and feature famed local clams, catch-of-the-day fish, and loads of fruit and vegetables.

The addition of a boiler-fired luxury **onsen** (¥1500/3000 for guests/nonguests) completes the holiday experience. This ecofriendly day spa is itself a day-trip destination, with tranquil views of Ohkihama from the stylish baths, featuring imported heat-conducive stone and adjustable temperature gauges. Never has the word 'wellness' felt so apt.

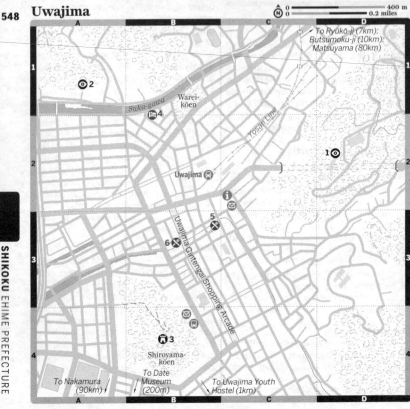

Uwajima

⊙ Sights
1 Municipal Bullfighting Ring D2
2 Taga-jinja & Sex Museum A1
3 Uwajima-jō B4

🛏 Sleeping
4 Tsukigase B1

🍴 Eating
5 Hozumi-tei B3
6 Wabisuke B3

Temples 41-42   TEMPLE
A great way to get a taste of the 88 Temple
pilgrimage without having to slog it out
along busy main roads is to take a bus from
Uwajima Station direct to Temple 42, **But-
sumoku-ji** (仏木寺; ¥510, 40 minutes). After
admiring the thatched bell-house and the
statues of the seven gods of good fortune,
follow the clearly marked *henro* trail back
through picturesque farming villages and
rice paddies to Temple 41, **Ryūkō-ji** (龍光
寺). Here, a steep stone staircase leads up
to a pleasant temple and shrine overlooking
the fields. It's a little over 5km in all. From
outside Ryūkō-ji there are signs to Muden
Station (務田駅), a 15-minute (800m) walk
away. From here, you can catch a train or
bus back to Uwajima.

🛏 Sleeping & Eating

Tsukigase   RYOKAN $$
(月ヶ瀬; ☎22-4788; fax 22-4787; 1-5-20 Miyu-
ki-machi; per person with/without meals from
¥10,000/6000; ℗) Between Warei-kōen and
the bridge to Taga-jinja is this family-run
ryokan, which features traditionally decorat-
ed tatami rooms. Guests can take advantage
of the stunning on-site onsen complete with
mountain views, as well as some excellent
food in the adjacent restaurant.

Uwajima Youth Hostel
HOSTEL $

(宇和島ユースホステル; ☎22-7177; fax 22-7176; www2.odn.ne.jp/~cfm91130; 166-11 Daichojioku Hinoe; dm foreign traveller special rate ¥2100; P ⊖ @) This out-of-the-way hostel is hidden 2.5km uphill from the station, though it's friendly and decidedly low-key. The dorm rooms and showers are spotless, and trips to surrounding islands can be arranged. Look for the directions to Uwatsuhiko-jinja (English sign) and the small white and green 'YH' sign. From here, a small path leads up the hill to the hostel.

Wabisuke
SEAFOOD $$

(和日輔; ☎24-0028; 1-2-6 Ebisu-machi; dishes ¥1000-1500; ⊙lunch & dinner) This restaurant, washed by the gentle sounds of running water, is an elegant spot to try the local *tai* (sea bream) specialities, available here as a *tai-meshi go-zen* (sea bream set course; ¥1880). There is a picture menu, and the young staff speak some English.

Hozumi-tei
IZAKAYA $$

(ほづみ亭; ☎22-0041; 2-3-8 Shinmachi; dishes ¥750-1500; ⊙lunch & dinner Mon-Sat) This formal *izakaya* has been serving up local food for over 70 years. The menu is all in Japanese, but if you say the words '*Kyōdo ryōri*' (郷土料理) – meaning 'local cuisine' – the friendly owner should unlock his secrets. A course of the local *tai-meishi* is ¥2100.

ℹ Information

There are coin lockers at the station and international ATMs at the post office that's next to the tourist information office.

Tourist information office (宇和島市観光協会; ☎22-3934; ⊙8.30am-5pm Mon-Fri, 9am-5pm Sat & Sun) Across the road from JR Uwajima Station; offers free internet access.

ℹ Getting There & Around

Uwajima is on the JR Yosan line, and can be reached from Matsuyama (*tokkyū* ¥2900, 1½ hours) via Uchiko (*tokkyū* ¥2210, one hour). You can hire bicycles (¥100 per hour) from the tourist information office.

Uwajima to Matsuyama

There are several worthwhile stops along the western coast between Uwajima and Matsuyama, including Ōzu, with its recently reconstructed castle, and Uchiko, a town that grew rich on wax in the 19th century

and is home to several elegant old buildings. From Uwajima, the JR Yodo line runs to Kubokawa and Kōchi; the JR Yosan line heads north to Matsuyama.

YAWATAHAMA
八幡浜

☎0894 / POP 41,200

Throughout the centuries, pilgrims from Kyūshū traditionally arrived in Yawatahama by ferry, and then started and ended their pilgrimage at nearby Temple 43 – **Meiseki-ji** (明石寺).

Nankai Ferry (☎0120-732-156) runs from Yawatahama to Beppu (¥3120, three hours, six daily) and Saganoseki (¥2320, 2¼ hours, six to seven daily) on Kyūshū. Yawatahama-kō port is a five-minute bus ride (¥150) or 20-minute (1.5km) walk from Yawatahama Station. To walk there, turn left out of the station and head straight until you hit the sea.

Harbor Plaza Hotel (☎22-0022; www.harbor.or.jp, in Japanese; 1 Nakano-machi; s/tw ¥7140/11,550), just off the main north–south thoroughfare, is the best choice for a sleepover.

ŌZU
大洲

☎0893 / POP 50,000

On the Yosan line northeast of Yawatahama is Ōzu, where traditional **ukai** (鵜飼; cormorant river fishing) takes place on the Hijikawa from 1 June to 20 September. **Sightseeing boats** (☎24-2029; cruises per person ¥3000; ⊙depart 6.30pm, return 9pm) follow the fishing boats down the river as the cormorants catch fish. Reservations are required. Less strenuous **cruises** (¥100; ⊙10am-4pm) run across the river during April and May.

Ōzu-jō (大洲城; ☎24-1146; joint ticket with Garyūsansō ¥800; ⊙9am-5pm) is one of Japan's most authentically reconstructed castles. Other buildings in the grounds are original survivals from the Edo period. The castle is an impressive sight above the river, especially at night.

Garyūsansō (臥龍山荘; admission ¥500, or joint ticket with Ōzu-jō ¥800; ⊙9am-5pm), across town from the castle, is an elegant Meiji-period teahouse and garden in an idyllic spot overlooking the river.

Ōzu Kyōdokan Youth Hostel (大洲郷土館ユースホステル; ☎24-2258; http://homepage3.nifty.com/ozuyh; San-no-maru; dm per person ¥3200) is a delightful place to stay at the foot of the castle. The tatami rooms are fit for an army, and the hostel doubles as a museum, featuring interesting curios from the town's boom years as a Tokugawa-period castle town.

UCHIKO 内子

Uchiko is undergoing a mini-renaissance, with a growing number of domestic travellers taking interest in this handsome town with its prosperous past. During the late Edo and early Meiji periods, Uchiko boomed as a major producer of wax, resulting in a number of exquisite houses along a street called Yōkaichi that still stand today.

◉ Sights

Uchiko-za
THEATRE

(内子座; admission ¥300; ☺9am-4.30pm) About halfway between the station and Yōkaichi is Uchiko-za, a magnificent traditional kabuki theatre. Originally constructed in 1916, the theatre was completely restored in 1985, complete with a revolving stage. Performances are still held at the theatre; call ahead for a schedule.

Museum of Commerce & Domestic Life
MUSEUM

(商いと暮らし博物館; admission ¥200; ☺9am-4.30pm) A few minutes' walk further north along the main road from Uchiko-za is the Museum of Commerce & Domestic Life, which exhibits historical materials and wax figures portraying a typical merchant scene of the early 20th century.

Yōkaichi
HISTORIC DISTRICT

(八日市) Uchiko's picturesque main street has a number of interesting buildings, many now serving as museums, souvenir stalls, craft shops and charming teahouses. The old buildings typically have cream-coloured plaster walls and 'wings' under the eaves that serve to prevent fire spreading from house to house.

On the left as you walk up the street, look for **Ōmori Rōsoku** (☺9am-5pm, closed Mon & Fri), Uchiko's last remaining candle manufacturer. The candles are still made by hand here, according to traditional methods, and you can watch the candle-makers at work.

As the road makes a slight bend, several well-preserved Edo-era buildings come into view, including **Ōmura-tei** and **Hon-Haga-tei**, the latter of which is a fine example of a rich merchant's home. The Hon-Haga family established the production of fine wax in Uchiko, winning awards at World Expositions in Chicago (1893) and Paris (1900).

Further on, the exquisite **Kami-Haga-tei** is a wax merchant's house within a large complex of buildings related to the wax-making process. The adjacent **Wax Exhibition Room** (admission ¥400; ☺9am-4.30pm) has good English explanations on the wax-making process and the town's prosperous past.

🛏 Sleeping & Eating

At least one luxury hotel had its sights set on Uchiko at the time of research.

Matsunoya Ryokan
RYOKAN $$$

(☎44-5000; www.dokidoki.ne.jp/home2/matunoya, in Japanese; 1913 Uchiko; r per person with/without 2 meals ¥12,600/7500; @) Still the best place to stay in town, this smart, central ryokan has neatly kept tatami rooms and an attractive, spacious reception area. The attached Poco a Poco restaurant serves delicious pasta. Set meals (including crème brulee!) start at ¥1000.

Mother Restaurant
CAFE $

(☎44-5463; lunch ¥800-1000) Near the turn-off to Yōkaichi St is this friendly Japanese diner that prepares a tasty two-choice lunch menu and good, strong coffee.

❶ Information

There are coin lockers at the station.

Tourist information booth (☎43-1450; ☺9.30am-5pm Thu-Tue) You can pick up an English map at this booth, located on your right as you leave JR Uchiko Station.

❶ Getting There & Around

Uchiko is 25 minutes from Matsuyama by *tokkyū* (¥1250, hourly) and by *futsu* (local train; ¥740, one hour). Yōkaichi is 1km north of Uchiko Station, and is well signposted in English.

Matsuyama 松山

Located in a lush river basin, Shikoku's largest city is handsome and refined, with a hint of 'mainland' hustle. Matsuyama is famed across Japan for Dōgo Onsen Honkan, a luxurious 19th-century public bathhouse built over ancient hot springs. The finest castle on the island towers above the stylish trams criss-crossing the city streets, the harbour glistening in the distance. Matsuyama is also home to seven of the 88 Temples, including Ishite-ji, one of the most famous stops on the pilgrimage.

◉ Sights

Matsuyama-jō
CASTLE

(松山城; admission ¥500; ☺9am-5pm, to 5.30pm Aug, to 4.30pm Dec & Jan) Perched on top of Mt Katsuyama in the centre of town, the castle

According to legend, Dōgo Onsen (道後温泉) was discovered during the age of the gods when a white heron was found healing itself in the spring. Since then, Dōgo has featured prominently in a number of literary classics, and won itself a reputation for the curative powers of its waters. The mono-alkaline spring contains sulphur, and is believed to be particularly effective at treating rheumatism, neuralgia and hysteria.

Dōgo Onsen Honkan (道後温泉本館; ☎089-921-5141; 5-6 Dōgo-yunomachi; ☺6am-11pm), the main building, was constructed in 1894, and designated as an important cultural site in 1994. The three-storey, castle-style building incorporates traditional design elements, and is crowned by a statue of a white heron to commemorate its legendary origins. Although countless famous people have passed through its doors, Dōgo Onsen Honkan is perhaps best known for its inclusion in the famous 1906 novel *Botchan* by Natsume Sōseki, the greatest literary figure of Japan's modern age, who based his novel on his time as a schoolteacher in Matsuyama in the early 20th century.

Even if you're well versed in onsen (hot springs) culture, Dōgo can be a bit confusing as there are two separate baths (and four pricing options) from which to choose. The larger and more popular of the two baths is *kami-no-yu* (神の湯; water of the gods), which is separated by gender and adorned with heron mosaics. A basic bath costs ¥400, while a bath followed by tea and *senbei* (rice crackers) in the 2nd-floor tatami room costs ¥800, and includes a rental *yukata* (light cotton kimono). A rental towel and soap will set you back a further ¥50. The smaller and more private of the two baths is the *tama-no-yu* (魂の湯; water of the spirit), which is also separated by gender and adorned with simple tiles. A bath followed by tea and *dango* (sweet dumplings) in the 2nd-floor tatami room costs ¥1200, while the top price of ¥1500 allows you to enjoy your snack in a private tatami room on the 3rd floor.

Although there are English-language pamphlets on hand to clarify the correct sequence of steps, Dōgo Onsen can be a bit intimidating if you don't speak Japanese. After paying your money outside, you should enter the building and leave your shoes in a locker. If you've paid ¥400, go to the *kami-no-yu* changing room (signposted in English), where you can use the free lockers for your clothing. If you've paid ¥800 or ¥1200, first go upstairs to receive your *yukata,* and then return to either the *kami-no-yu* or *tama-no-yu* (also signposted in English) changing room. After your bath, you should don your *yukata* and retire to the 2nd-floor tatami room to sip your tea and gaze down on the bath-hoppers clip-clopping by in *geta* (traditional wooden sandals). If you've paid top whack, head directly to the 3rd floor, where you will be escorted to your private tatami room. Here, you can change into your *yukata* before heading to the *tama-no-yu* changing room, and also return after your bath to sip tea in complete isolation.

Regardless of which option you choose, you are allowed to explore the building after taking your bath. On the 2nd floor, there is a small **exhibition room** displaying artefacts relating to the bathhouse, including traditional wooden admission tickets. If you've taken one of the pricier upstairs options, you can also take a guided tour (in Japanese) of the private **imperial baths**, last used by the royal family in 1950. On the 3rd floor, the corner tatami room (which was the favourite of Natsume Sōseki) has a small **display** (in Japanese) on the life of the writer.

Dōgo can get quite crowded, especially on weekends and holidays, although at dinner time it's usually empty, because most Japanese tourists will be dining at their inns. If you want to escape the crowds, one minute on foot from the Honkan (through the shopping arcade) is **Tsubaki-no-yu** (椿の湯; admission ¥360; ☺6am-11pm), Dōgo Onsen's hot-spring annexe, frequented primarily by locals. If you don't want a full bath, there are also nine free **ashi-yu** (足湯; foot baths) scattered around Dōgo Onsen where you can take off your shoes and socks and warm your feet. The most famous one is located just opposite the station at the start of the arcade. Here, you can also check out **Botchan Karakuri Clock** (坊ちゃんからくり時計), which was erected as part of Dōgo Onsen Honkan's centennial in 1994. It features figures based on the main characters from *Botchan*, who emerge to take a turn on the hour from 8am to 10pm.

Matsuyama

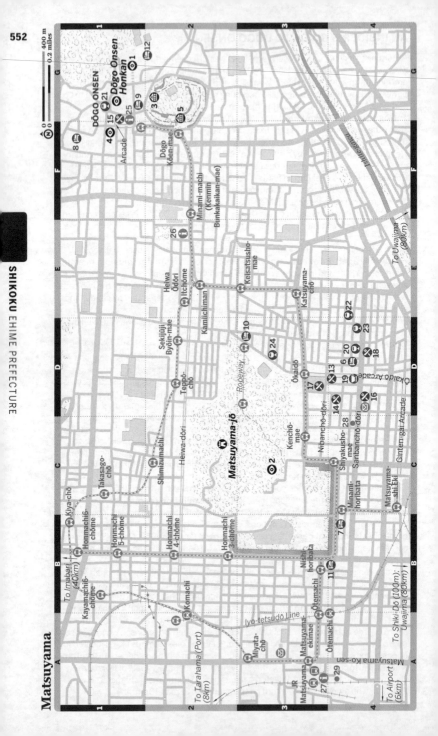

DŌGO ONSEN

DŌGO ONSEN
Dōgo Onsen
Honkan

Matsuyama-jō

To Imabari (40km)
To Tarahama (Port) (8km)
To Airport (6km)
To Shiki-Dō (100m); Uwajima (80km)
To Uwajima (80km)

Iyo-tetsudō Line
Matsuyama Ko-sen

Okaidō Arcade
Ginten-gai Arcade

0   400 m
0   0.2 miles

dominates the city, as it has for centuries. Matsuyama-jō is one of Japan's finest surviving castles, and one of the very few with anything interesting to look at inside: there are excellent English-language displays.

A ropeway (one way/return ¥260/500) is on hand to whisk you up the hill, though there is a pleasant pathway if you prefer to walk. It's worth walking down via the back slopes of the castle and stopping off at **Ninomaru Shiseki Tei-en** (二之丸史跡庭園; admission ¥100; ⏰9am-5pm, to 5.30pm Aug, to 4.30pm Dec & Jan) in the outer citadel of the fort, consisting of old gardens and modern water features.

Ishite-ji
TEMPLE

East of Dōgo Onsen is **Ishite-ji** (石手寺), 51st of the 88 Temples, and one of the largest and most impressive in the circuit. *Ishite* means 'stone hand' and comes from a legend associated with Kōbō Daishi. A statue of Kōbō Daishi overlooks the temple from the hillside.

Shiki Memorial Museum
MUSEUM

(子規堂; 16-3 Suehiro-chō; admission ¥50; ⏰8.30am-5pm) Just south of Matsuyama-shi Station, in the temple grounds of Shōjūzen-ji. Part of the house where famous haiku poet Shiki Masaoka (1867–1902) spent the first 17 years of his life.

Dōgo-kōen
PARK

(道後公園) A small park containing the site of Yuzuki-jō, the former residence of the Kōno clan that ruled Iyo province in feudal times. Articles unearthed during recent excavations are on display in **Yuzuki-jō Museum** (湯築城資料館; admission free; ⏰9am-5pm, closed Mon), near the west entrance of the park.

Isaniwa-jinja
SHRINE

Designated a National Treasure, this shrine (伊佐爾波神社) was modelled on Kyoto's Iwashimizu-Hachimangū and was built in 1667. It's located a short walk east of Dōgo Onsen.

🛏 Sleeping

Matsuyama Youth Hostel
HOSTEL $

(松山ユースホステル; ☎933-6366; www.matsuyama-yh.com/english/index.html; 22-3 Dōgo-himezuka; dm ¥2625, r per person ¥3360; P🛜@) This excellent hilltop hostel is famous for its immaculate dorms, stellar service and friendly, communal atmosphere. It's also a great base for multiple visits to Dōgo Onsen, since it's a 10-minute walk up the hill east of the complex. It's a good idea to reserve in advance here. Meals are available.

Dōgo Kan
HOTEL $$

(道後舘; ☎941-7777; www.dogokan.co.jp, in Japanese; 7-26 Dōgo Takōchō; per person with meals Mon-Fri from ¥15,000, Sat & Sun from ¥21,000) The Kishi Kurokawa–designed Dōgo Kan is a naturally sympathetic structure with a hint of divine decadence. On a slope behind the Tsubaki-no-yu public baths, you'll find grand tatami rooms and an elaborate series of private baths. The Western rooms are appreciably cheaper, but lack any real 'Dōgo-ness'.

Funaya
RYOKAN $$$

(ふなや; ☎947-0278; fax 943-2139; www.dogo-funaya.co.jp, in Japanese; 1-33 Dōgo Yunomachi; per person with meals from ¥22,050) Natsume Sōseki took refuge here from his writer's block and aching limbs, and so should you if you can afford it. The beauty lies on the inside, from the central garden and private onsen to the exquisite surrounding tatami rooms fit (and fitted) for Japanese royalty. It's a short walk from the Dōgo Onsen tram station along the road that leads up to Isaniwa-jinja.

Hotel JAL City
HOTEL $$

(☎913-2580; 1-10-10 Otemachi; s/tw ¥6800/10,900) The No 5 tram runs right past the door of the best business hotel in Matsuyama. The new JAL hotel is a tasteful offering with near five-star service and exemplary dining. The rooms are a bit bland, but very spacious and comfortable. The castle is a short walk away.

Guest House Matsuyama
HOSTEL $

(ゲストハウスまつやま; ☎934-5296; fax 934-5296; www.sophia-club.net/guesthouse; 8-3-3 Okaido-chō; s/tw from ¥2500/4000; @) Tamanoi-san is Matsuyama's jovial resident expert who welcomes guests to his neat budget guesthouse in a cool strip by the ropeway. There's a choice between Japanese and Western rooms; ask to see a few. There's complimentary internet and bicycle hire.

Check Inn Matsuyama
HOTEL $$

(チェックイン松山; ☎998-7000; fax 998-7801; www.checkin.co.jp/matsuyama, in Japanese; 2-7-3 Sanban-chō; s/tw from ¥4380/7700; P☺@) This swish hotel is excellent value for money, with well-equipped modern rooms, chandeliers in the lobby and an onsen on the roof. A short walk from the Ōkaidō arcade (大街道), the hotel is convenient to the city's nightlife and restaurants. LAN internet is in all rooms and there are consoles in the lobby.

Dai Ichi Hotel Matsuyama
HOTEL $$

(☎943-1011; fax 921-4111; 2-5-5 Honmachi; s/tw ¥6800/10,900) Spacious and comfortable rooms, along with satellite TV and a dim-sum restaurant, make this hotel near the castle moat a good option. It's directly opposite the Honmachi 3-chōme (本町三丁目) tram stop.

🍴 Eating

The area around the Ginten-gai and Ōkaidō shopping arcades in central Matsuyama is full of places to eat and drink.

Café Bleu
CAFE $

(☎907 0402; 2-2-8 Okaido 402; meals ¥600-900; ⊙11am-11pm) This lovely little music cafe on the edge of the Ōkaidō arcade serves tasty, simple lunches to a bookish clientele. The decor includes groovy album covers, music photography and vintage typewriters. Beer and generous cocktails are also available.

Ohana Cafe
FAST FOOD $

(オハナカフェ; ☎993 3668; 2-2-8 Okaido; burgers from ¥600; ⊙11am-11pm) This Hawaiian burger joint in the heart of Matsuyama is a happening little business. The four-seater lunch counter and one comfy booth are permanently packed during happy lunch hours, and the tiny, many varied burgers are sweet and delicious. The fruity enchiladas are pretty good too. It's off Okaido Arcade, past Café Bleu and on the right.

Café Jumelle
VEGETARIAN $$

(☎947-6370; 3-4-14 Niban-chō; meals ¥700-1500; ⊙10am-10pm) Matsuyama has a revelatory organic food store and cafe that serves up heartening soy-based meals with clean flavours and crisp presentation. It's a godsend for vegans and for anyone who loves a lightly sugared dessert.

Goshiki Sōmen Morikawa
JAPANESE $$

(五色そうめん森川; ☎933-3838; 3-5-4 Sanban-chō; meals ¥700-1500; ⊙11am-8.30pm; 🖃) Next to the central post office is this elegant Matsuyama institution, which specialises in goshiki sōmen (thin noodles in five different colours). You'll recognise it by the piles of colourful noodles in the window waiting to be snapped up and taken home as souvenirs. Set meals are around ¥1500; there is a picture menu.

Tengu no Kakurega
IZAKAYA $

(てんぐの隠れ家; ☎931-1009; 2-5-17 Sanban-chō; dishes ¥400-1200; ⊙5pm-midnight, to 1am Fri & Sat) A chic young people's izakaya serving *yakitori* and other dishes in a pleasant setting; paper screens give onto a little garden at the back. It's tucked away and a little hard to find – heading away from the post office, look for the small sign on the right in the second block after the Ōkaidō arcade.

Also recommended:

Futaba JAPANESE $
(ふたば; ☑945-9508; 13-22 Yuno-machi Dogo; dishes ¥800-2000; ☺lunch & dinner) Excellent noodles and *nabe* (Japanese hotpot) for your post-onsen replenishment.

🍷 Drinking

The bulk of drinking establishments are concentrated in Ichiban-chō and Niban-chō amid the network of neon-lit streets either side of the Ōkaidō arcade.

Sala Sol BAR
(3rd fl, Ciel Bld 2-3-5 Sanbanchō; drinks from ¥600; ☺8.30pm-3am, closed Mon) The town's most popular foreigner bar is surprisingly cool, with excellent music and generous drink specials. It's also one for the few places in town where people dance...all night long.

Dōgo Biiru-kan BREWERY
(道後麦酒館; 20-13 Dōgo Yunomachi; ☺11am-9pm) Right by Dōgo Onsen Honkan, this place brews its own beer, and is a good spot for a drink and a bite to eat after a relaxing soak. The names of the beers (¥840) are allusions to novelist Natsume Sōseki and his famous novel, *Botchan*. There's also a decent range of food available from a picture menu (such as *iwashi no karaage* – fried sardines – for ¥550).

Peggy Sue Saloon BAR
(ペギー・スー; 2nd fl, 1-2-9 Nibanchō; drinks from ¥700; ☺8.30pm-3am, closed Mon) Run by a music nut with a fondness for country music, this friendly bar is a treasure trove of cowboy-themed Americana. There's a Wurlitzer jukebox, and several guitars and mandolins on the walls that are just waiting for someone to take them down and start picking. The 2nd-floor sign is visible from street level. It's in a cluster of bars just east of Okaido Arcade.

Underground Cafe BAR
(2nd fl, Okazaki-Sangyo Bldg; ☺noon-4am) A local and expat secret bar hang-out that feels more Honshu than Shikoku and serves Mexican food on the side. It's off the street leading to the ropeway; look for the Union Jack flag, so coolly out of context.

Chocobar BAR
(2-2-6 Sanbanchō; drinks from ¥700; ☺5pm-late) This tiny shot bar located on a busy road has a regular hip-hop soundtrack and colourful decor. It's one of the few places in Matsuyama where passers-by can watch you get drunk.

Also recommended:

Cafe BC CAFE
The best coffee in Matsuyama. The lady of the house also makes killer sandwiches (¥500).

ℹ Information

ATMs accepting international cards can be found at the central post office and at the post office that's a couple of minutes' walk north of JR Matsuyama Station.

Ehime Prefectural International Centre (愛媛県国際交流協会; EPIC; ☑943-6688; www .epic.or.jp; 1-1 Dōgo Ichiman; ☺8.30am-5pm, closed Sun) Provides advice, internet access and bike rental. EPIC is near the Minami-machi or Kenmin Bunkakaikan-mae (南町) tram stop. Look for the red question mark.

JTB (☑931-2281; 4-12-10 Sanbanchō; ☺10am-6pm, closed Sun) In the centre of town.

Tourist information office JR Matsuyama Station (☑931-3914; ☺8.30am-8.30pm); Dōgo Onsen-mae (道後観光案内所; ☑921-3708; ☺8am-4.45pm) The main office is located inside JR Matsuyama Station, while a branch office is near the tram terminus for Dōgo Onsen.

ℹ Getting There & Away

BOAT The superjet hydrofoil, run by the **Setonaikai Kisen ferry** (☑082-253-1212, Matsuyama booking office 089-953-1003; ☺9am-7pm), has regular hydrofoil connections between Matsuyama and Hiroshima (¥6300, 1¼ hours, 14 daily). The Hiroshima–Matsuyama ferry (¥2900, 2¾ hours, 10 daily) is also a popular way of getting to/from Shikoku.

Matsuyama is a stopping point for ferries run by **Diamond Ferry company** (☑951-0167; www .diamond-ferry.co.jp) between Osaka and Kōbe, and Ōita (Kyūshū). There is one sailing a day each way.

BUS There are JR Highway buses that run to/from Osaka (¥6700, 5½ hours, five daily) and Tokyo (¥12,200, 12 hours, one daily), and there are frequent buses to major cities in Shikoku.

TRAIN The JR Yosan line connects Matsuyama with Takamatsu (*tokkyū* ¥5500, 2½ hours), and there are also services across the Seto-ōhashi to Okayama (*tokkyū* ¥6120, 2¾ hours) on Honshū.

ℹ Getting Around

TO/FROM THE AIRPORT Matsuyama's airport, 6km west of the city, is easily reached by bus (¥330, 20 minutes, hourly) from the front of the JR Matsuyama Station.

BICYCLE RENTAL (per day ¥300; ☉9am-6pm Mon-Sat) Available at the large bicycle park to the right as you exit JR Matsuyama Station.

TRAM Tickets cost a flat ¥150 for each trip (pay when you get off). A day pass costs ¥300. Lines 1 and 2 are loop lines, running clockwise and anti-clockwise around Katsuyama (the castle mountain). Line 3 runs from Matsuyama-shi station to Dōgo Onsen, line 5 goes from JR Matsuyama station to Dōgo Onsen, and line 6 from Kiya-chō (木屋町) to Dōgo Onsen. If you're lucky with timing you can ride the Botchan Ressha (坊ちゃん列車), small trains that were imported from Germany in 1887. Named for Natsume Sōseki's famous novel, they ran up and down Matsuyama's streets for 67 years, and they're back in occasional use.

Around Matsuyama

ISHIZUCHI-SAN   石鎚山

At 1982m, Ishizuchi-san is the highest peak in western Japan, and was traditionally considered to be a holy mountain. Ishizuchi attracts pilgrims and climbers alike, particularly during the July and August climbing season. During the winter (late December to late March) skiing is possible.

To get to the Nishi-no-kawa cable-car station (on the northern side of the mountain), take the direct bus (¥990, 55 minutes, four daily) from Iyo-Saijo Station.

You can climb up one way and down the other or make a complete circuit from Nishi-no-kawa to the summit, down to Tsuchigoya and then back to Nishi-no-kawa. Allow all day and an early start for the circuit. For detailed information on hiking Ishizuchi-san, see Lonely Planet's *Hiking in Japan*.

Ishizuchi Fureai-no-Sato   HOTEL $
(石鎚ふれあいの里; ☎0897-59-0203; 1-25-1 Nakaoka, Saijo-shi; cabins from ¥1170/2920) The cabins are cosy and the complex is completely self-contained – with a small onsite restaurant, *ofuro* (public bath) and outdoor cooking area.

KAGAWA PREFECTURE

Formerly known as Sanuki, Kagawa Prefecture (香川県) is the smallest of Shikoku's four regions, and the second smallest of the country's 47 prefectures. It has plenty to offer though, including the site of a celebrated shrine of Kompira-san at Kotohira, reached via a stirring stair climb, and the handsome port city of Takamatsu with its world-renowned Japanese garden.

The region's hospitable weather and welcoming people have always been a comfort to pilgrims as they come to the end of their journey. Today, it's an important point of arrival, too, since the only rail link with Honshū is via the Seto-ōhashi bridge to Okayama. Equally importantly, it's a short ferry ride to the remarkable Inland Sea island of Naoshima.

Matsuyama to Takamatsu

The JR Yosan line runs around the coast between Takamatsu and Matsuyama. At Tadotsu, the JR Dosan line splits off and runs south to Zentsū-ji and Kotohira, through the Iya Valley and eventually to Kōchi.

KANONJI   観音寺
♪0875 / POP 65,000

Coming east from Ehime-ken, the first town of consequence in Kagawa Prefecture is Kanonji, notable as the only spot on the pilgrimage trail to have two of the 88 Temples on the same grounds: Temple 68, **Jinne-in** (神恵院), and Temple 69, **Kanon-ji** (観音寺). It's also known for the odd **Zenigata** (銭形), a 350m-circumference coin-shaped sculpture in the sand dating from 1633. The coin and its inscription are formed by huge trenches dug in the sand, and are said to have been dug overnight by the local population as a welcome present to their feudal lord. For the best views of the sculpture, you'll need to climb the hill in Kotohiki-kōen, 1.9km northwest of Kanonji Station (not far from the two temples). A small **tourist information office** (☎25-3839), over the bridge from the station, has maps. Kanonji is considerably closer to Takamatsu (*tokkyū* ¥2210, 48 minutes) than Matsuyama (*tokkyū* ¥4130, one hour and 38 minutes).

MARUGAME   丸亀
♪0877 / POP 110,700

An interesting detour from the 88 Temple circuit is in Marugame, home to **Marugame-jō** (丸亀城; admission ¥200; ☉9am-4.30pm). The castle dates from 1597, and is one of only 12 castles in Japan to have its original wooden *donjon* intact.

At **Uchiwa-no-Minato Museum** (うちわ
の港ミュージアム; admission free; ◎9.30am-
5pm, closed Mon) there are displays and craft
demonstrations showing how *uchiwa* (traditional paper fans) are made. The museum
is in the harbour, a few minutes' walk from
the station.

Bike hire (☎25-1127; per day ¥200, deposit
¥500) is available from the bicycle park
across from the station. By bike, it is less
than an hour from Marugame to Zentsū-ji.
Marugame is easily covered as a day trip
from Takamatsu (*tokkyū* ¥1050, 25 minutes).

ZENTSŪ-JI 善通寺
☎0877 / POP 34,000

If you only have time for one temple, then
make it **Zentsū-ji** (善通寺), number 75 of the
88 Temples and the place where Kōbō Daishi was born. It is also the largest temple –
most of the other 88 could fit comfortably
into the car park here. The temple boasts a
truly magnificent five-storey pagoda and giant camphor trees that are said to date back
as far as Daishi's childhood. Visitors can
venture into the basement of the **Mie-dō**
(御影堂; admission ¥500) building and traverse a 100m-long passageway (戒壇めぐり)
in pitch darkness: by moving carefully along
with your hand pressed to the wall (painted
with mandalas, angels and lotus flowers),
you are said to be safely following Buddha's
way. If you're on a bike, there are several other pilgrimage temples within easy reach of
this one, including Temple 73, **Shusshaka-ji**
(出釈迦寺).

The temple is about 1km from the JR
Zentsuji Station, straight ahead as you exit.
On the right you'll find a number of well-
priced, casual restaurants and an incongruously large hip-hop music store. There's
some faux-period street lighting as you
reach the temple.

KOTOHIRA 琴平
☎0877 / POP 10,900

The small mountain village of Kotohira is
home to one of Shikoku's most famous tourist attractions, Kompira-san, a Shintō shrine
dedicated to the god of seafarers. The 1368
steep stone steps are a rite of passage for
many Japanese, with plenty of interesting
en-route distractions.

◎ Sights

Kompira-san TEMPLE
(金刀比羅宮) Kompira-san or, more formally, Kotohira-gū, was originally a Buddhist and Shintō temple dedicated to the

guardian of mariners. It became exclusively
a Shintō shrine after the Meiji Restoration.

A lot of fuss is made about how strenuous
the climb (1368 steps) to the top is, but if
you've made it this far in Japan, you've probably completed a few long ascents to shrines
already.

The first notable landmark on the long
climb is **Ō-mon** (大門), a stone gateway
that leads to **Hōmotsu-kan** (宝物館; Treasure
House; admission ¥500; ◎8.30am-5pm), where
the collection of treasures is pretty under-
whelming for such a major shrine. Nearby
you will find five traditional-sweets vendors
at tables shaded by large white parasols. A
symbol of ancient times, the vendors (the
Gonin Byakushō – Five Farmers) are descendants of the original families that were
permitted to trade within the grounds of the
shrine. Further uphill is **Shoin** (書院; Reception Hall; admission ¥500; ◎8.30am-4.30pm),
a designated National Treasure that dates
from 1659 and has some interesting screen
paintings and a small garden.

Continuing the ascent, you eventually
reach large **Asahino Yashiro** (旭社; Shrine
of the Rising Sun). Built in 1837, this large
hall is dedicated to the sun goddess Amaterasu, and is noted for its ornate wood-carv-
ing. From here, the short final ascent, which
is the most beautiful leg of the walk, brings
you to **Gohonsha** (御本社; Gohon Hall) and
Ema-dō (絵馬堂; Ema Pavilion). The latter
is filled with maritime offerings ranging
from pictures of ships and models to modern ship engines. From this level, there are
spectacular views that extend right down to
the coast and over the Inland Sea.

Incurable climbers can continue for another 500 or so steps up to **Oku-sha** (Inner
Shrine), which features stone carvings of
tengu (long-nosed mountain demons) on
the cliff.

Kanamaru-za THEATRE
(金丸座; ☎73-3846; admission ¥500; ◎9am-
5pm) Japan's oldest kabuki playhouse,
though it had a lengthy stint as a cinema
before falling out of use. The restorations
are superb; wander backstage and see the
revolving-stage mechanism, basement trap
doors and a tunnel out to the front of the
theatre. The playhouse is 200m east of the
main approach to Kompira-san.

Kinryō-no-Sato MUSEUM
(金陵の郷; admission ¥310; ◎9am-5pm) This
sake museum, located along the main

SHIKOKU MATSUYAMA TO TAKAMATSU

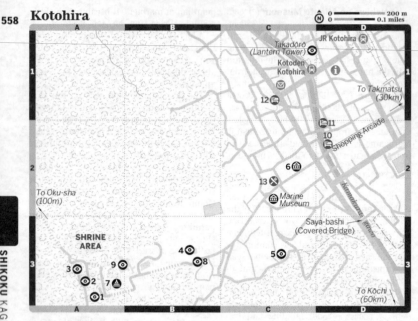

Kotohira

approach to the shrine, is in the old premises of a brewery that has owned the building since 1789. At the end of the tour you can try three different Kinryō sakes for ¥100 a glass.

🛏 Sleeping & Eating

Kotobuki Ryokan
RYOKAN $$

(ことぶき旅館; ☑73-3872; 245-5 Kotohira-cho; per person with 2 meals ¥6800; P) This welcom-ing ryokan with comfortable tatami rooms and warm hospitality is conveniently situ-ated by the riverside. Umbrellas, internet ac-cess and spotless shared bathrooms are all available. Turn left for the arcade and some small restaurants; turn right for the shrine.

Kotohira Riverside Hotel
HOTEL $$

(☑75-1880; 246-1 Kotohira-cho; d with breakfast ¥9000) This well-run business hotel has a very good upstairs restaurant overlooking the river and excellent Western rooms.

Kotosankaku
RYOKAN $$$

(琴参閣; ☑75-1000; fax 75-0600; www.koto sankaku.jp/index_en.html; 685-11 Kotohira-cho; per person Mon-Fri from ¥9600, Sat & Sun from ¥17,850; P 🏊) One of the biggest ryokans in Shikoku, this well-designed grand dame has superla-tive Japanese- and Western-style rooms and a summer-time pool. The onsen complex is open to nonguests (¥1200, from 10.30am to 3pm). Hotel prices are halved during the week.

Kompira Udon
NOODLES $

(こんぴらうどん; ☑73-5785; meals ¥500-950; ⊘8am-5pm) Just short of the first set of steps leading up Kompira-san, this is one of doz-ens of *Sanuki udon* joints in Kotohira. Look for the giant udon bowl outside.

Information

There are coin lockers at the station, and the ATMs at the post office accept international cards.

Tourist information centre (琴平観光会館内 観光案内所; ☎75-3500; ⊙9.30am-8pm) Found along the main road, to the left as you exit the JR Kotohira Station. Has local maps, and bikes available for hire (¥100/500 per hour/day).

Getting There & Away

You can travel to Kotohira on the JR Dosan line from Kōchi (*tokkyū* ¥3810, one hour and 38 minutes) and Ōboke. For Takamatsu and other places on the north coast, change trains at Tadotsu. The private Kotoden line has regular direct trains from Takamatsu (¥610, one hour).

Takamatsu 高松
☑087 / POP 425,000

Takamatsu is a sparkling port city with a spectacular garden, solid nightlife and efficient transport links with the mainland by rail, road and sea. There's an air of prefectural capital among the well-heeled locals and wide boulevards, which all lead to wonderful Ritsurin-kōen. The city also serves as a base for a number of unique day trips, notably to the olive groves of Shōdo-shima and the island of Naoshima in the Inland Sea.

◉ Sights

Ritsurin-kōen PARK
(栗林公園; 1-20-16 Ritsurinchō; admission ¥400; ⊙sunrise-sunset) One of the most beautiful gardens in the country, Ritsurin-kōen dates from the mid-1600s and took more than a century to complete. Designed as a walking garden for the *daimyō's* enjoyment, the park winds around a series of ponds, tearooms, bridges and islands. To the west, Shiun-zan (Mt Shiun) forms an impressive backdrop to the garden. The classic view of Engetsu-kyō bridge with the mountain in the background is one of the finest in Japan.

Enclosed by the garden are a number of interesting sights, including **Sanuki Folkcraft Museum** (讃岐民芸館; admission free; ⊙8.45am-4.30pm), which displays local crafts dating back to the Tokugawa dynasty. If you're a fan of *matcha* (powdered green tea) and traditional sweets, there are a number of teahouses in the park, including 17th-century **Kikugetsu-tei**, where you can have *matcha* for ¥710, and the lovely thatched-roof **Higurashi-tei**, which dates from 1898.

The easiest way to reach Ritsurin-kōen is by taking the frequent direct bus (¥230, 15 minutes) from JR Takamatsu Station.

Takamatsu-jō CASTLE
(高松城; 2-1 Tamamo-chō; admission ¥200; ⊙sunrise-sunset) The site of Takamatsu's castle now forms delightful Tamamo-kōen, a park where the walls and moat (filled with sea water) survive, along with several of the original turrets. Each spring a swimming race is held in the cool seawater moat to honour an age-old chivalrous tradition. The original castle was built in 1588 for Itoma Chikamasa, and was the home of the region's military rulers until the Meiji Restoration, which happened nearly 300 years later. In 2008 work began on a reconstruction of the main keep – however, it was still far from finished at the time this book went to print.

Takamatsu City Museum of Art ART GALLERY
(10-4 Konya-machi; admission ¥200; ⊙9.30am-5pm) This impressive inner-city gallery is testament to Takamatsu's quality art scene. The light and spacious refitting of a former Bank of Japan building is a stroke of curatorial genius, well served by interesting exhibitions on rotation from across Japan and the world.

🛏 Sleeping

Castle Hotel Takamatsu HOTEL $
(キャッスルホテル高松; ☎851-0606; fax 851-0607; 4-8 Tsuruya-machi; s/d ¥3500/5250; P@) This musty bargain slightly north of the Kataharamachi Station is run by a fabulous English-speaking owner who loves to accommodate indie travellers. The hotel is a fairly nondescript concrete number – and easy to miss if you don't read hiragana – but the tatami rooms are enormous for the price, with deep-seated baths and comfortable futons. There's LAN internet access in all rooms.

Area One Hotel HOTEL $$
(☎823 7801; 2-23 Nishi-no-marucho; s/tw from ¥5000/7600) Opposite the JR station is this no-fuss business hotel from a reliable, designed-focused chain. Rooms are spacious and stylish, all representing excellent value. Useful extras such as desk lamps, laptops and humidifiers are available for rent in the lobby. The restaurant next door serves a delicious, cheap breakfast (¥500) for hotel guests.

Hotel No 1 Takamatsu　　　　HOTEL $$
(ホテルNo.1高松; ☎812-2222; fax 812-0002; www.hotelno1.jp/takamatsu, in Japanese; 2-4-1 Kankō-dōri; s/d ¥5140/7870; P◉♨@) Three blocks east and three blocks south of Koto-den Kawaramachi Station, this is a sparkling business hotel with standard rooms and a rooftop men-only *rotemburo* (outdoor bath) with sweeping views of the city (the women's baths are on the 2nd floor). There is internet access in the lobby, and there are LAN connections in all rooms.

Dormy Inn Takamatsu　　　　HOTEL $$
(さぬきの湯ドーミーイン高松; ☎832-5489; fax 835-5657; www.hotespa.net/hotels/takamatsu, in Japanese; 1-10-10 Kawaramachi; s/d ¥6600/9000; ♨@) The Dormy is a little bit different from the usual big hotel fare, with its keen eye for design and a location at the heart of the entertainment district. The rooms are sleek and spacious, while the service is top notch for the price. The onsen and *rotemburo* on the top floor are welcome additions. There's LAN access in all rooms.

ANA Hotel Clement Takamatsu　　HOTEL $$$
(全日空ホテルクレメント高松; ☎811-1111; fax 811-1100; ww.anaclement.com; 1-1 Hamano-chō; s/d ¥12,474/23,100; P♨@) This eye-catching ultramodern hotel is one of the first buildings you see as you exit JR Takamatsu Station. The rooms are spacious, and there's a good selection of bars and restaurants with sweeping views of the Inland Sea.

✕ Eating

Restaurants and bars are clustered in the covered arcades and entertainment district to the west side of the tracks between Koto-den Kataharamachi and Kawaramachi stations. People in Takamatsu are serious about their udon (delicious, thick white noodles made from wheat), and no trip here would be complete without at least one bowl of the famous speciality, *Sanuki udon*. Look for the words *te-uchi udon* （手打ちうどん), meaning 'handmade noodles'.

Kanaizumi　　　　NOODLES $
(かな泉; ☎822-0123; 9-3 Konyamachi; medium serving of noodles with 2 toppings ¥500; ◷9.30am-5pm) A self-service, self-explanatory noodle joint that is ideal for famished victims of culture shock. You can choose between *shō* (small), *chū* (medium) or *dai* (large) helpings of *kake udon* (udon in broth) or *zaru udon* (cold udon, with a dipping sauce), and then

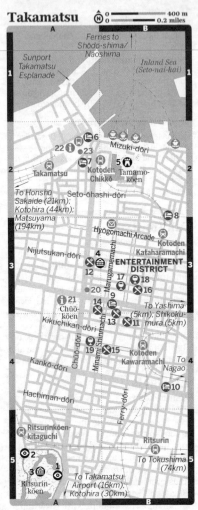

help yourself to a wide variety of toppings. It's located by the Takamatsu City Museum of Art.

Tsurumaru　　　　NOODLES $
(鶴丸; ☎821-3780; 9-34 Furubaba-chō; curry udon ¥700; ◷8pm-3am, closed Sun) Sit at the counter and watch the noodles being pounded by hand in this popular spot, which is busy with the bar-hopping crowd until late into the night. The delicious *karē udon* (curry udon) is the most popular choice here. Look for the curtain over the door with a picture of a crane on it.

Bijin-tei　　　　　　　　　　SEAFOOD **$$**
(美人亭; ☎861-0275; 2-2-10 Kawara-machi; dishes ¥700-1500; ☺5-10pm, closed Sun) Smiling *mama-san* sees all at this discrete, seafood *izakaya*. Point to the menu items already plated – the pickled *taco* (octopus) is a mouthful – or ask for an *o-susume* (recommendation). It's on the ground floor of a building containing several snack bars and karaoke joints. Look for the sign with the shop's name on it in kanji: 美人亭.

King's Yawd　　　　　　　　JAMAICAN **$**
(☎837 2660; 1-2-2 Tokishin-machi; dishes ¥800-900; ☺noon-late, closed Sun; 🚃) Dreadlocked Kalli and his laid-back staff serve up genuine Caribbean flavour in the heart of Takamatsu. Think platters of jerk chicken (¥800), fiery fish curries (¥900) and tropical fruit desserts. The generous cocktails blend perfectly with the Rastafarian vibes emanating from the sound system and the red, yellow and green decor. The legendary weekend parties are popular with both locals and expats.

Ofukuro　　　　　　　　　VEGETARIAN **$**
(おふくろ; ☎861-0275; 2-2-10 Kawara-machi; dishes ¥500-1500; ☺5-10pm, closed Sun; 🚃) This fabulous *washofu* (local eating house) in the heart of the entertainment district offers a well-priced and hearty dining experience. A number of delicious, preprepared vegetarian and fish dishes sit on the counter. The complimentary salad and miso soup make minimeals. It's next door to a popular *yakitori* restaurant, east of Minami-shinmachi.

Tokiwa Saryō　　　　　　　SEAFOOD **$$$**
(ときわ茶寮; ☎861-5577; 1-8-2 Tokiwa-chō; dishes ¥1200-3600; ☺lunch & dinner) An old Japanese inn with a pond and excellent sashimi sets. It's off the Tokiwa arcade from Ferry Dōri, take the second left; it's the building on the right with the big white lantern.

🍷 Drinking

Anbar　　　　　　　　　　　　BAR
(アンバー; 1st fl, Dai-ichi Bldg, 8-15 Furubaba-chō; ☺8pm-midnight, closed Thu) The company of surreal feline imagery is an interesting companion to a fine, pensive whisky. There's an English sign outside, and plenty of hip weirdos inside.

Grandfather's　　　　　　　　BAR
(Tamachi-cho; ☺7pm-late) The scene here is so smooth you'll fall off your seat as the bookish owner spins vintage '60s and '70s funk and soul records from his enormous collection. Meanwhile, otherworldly waitresses hover through smoke to present your free-poured, icy cool beverages.

Cancun　　　　　　　　　　　BAR
(カンクン; 6-23 Furubaba-chō; ☺6pm-3am, closed Sun) A hodge-podge of bric-a-brac and bad lighting, Cancun is about as far from Mexico as you can get without leaving Kagawa. There's a wide range of drinks (most ¥700 to ¥800), and the friendly young bar staff speak some English and know the party scene well.

Information

The free Kagawa Welcome Card is available at Kagawa International Exchange or the tourist information office (you'll need to show your passport), or you can print one out online from www.21kagawa.com/visitor/kanko/index.htm. The card provides minor discounts around the prefecture. There are coin lockers and a left-luggage office at JR Takamatsu Station, and international ATMs at the central post office (located near the northern exit of Marugamemachi Arcade).

JTB (851-2117; 7-6 Kajiyamachi; 10am-6pm, closed Sun)

Kagawa International Exchange (アイパル香川香川国際交流会館; I-PAL Kagawa; 837-5901; www.i-pal.or.jp, in Japanese; 1-11-63 Banchō; 9am-6pm Tue-Sun) In the northwest corner of Chūō-kōen, with a small library, satellite TV and internet access.

Tourist information office (高松市観光案内所; 851-2009; 9am-6pm) In the plaza outside the station.

Getting There & Around

BICYCLE Takamatsu is flat, and excellent for biking. The city offers a great deal on its 'blue bicycles' (¥200 per day; photo ID is required), which can be picked up at **Takamatsu-shi Rental Cycles** (高松駅前広場地下レンタサイクルポート; 821-0400; 7am-10pm) in the underground bicycle park outside JR Takamatsu Station.

BUS There are bus services to/from Tokyo (¥10,000, 9½ hours, one daily), Nagoya (¥6800, 5½ hours), Kyoto (¥4800, three hours and 40 minutes) and most other major cities.

TRAIN Takamatsu is the only city in Shikoku with regular rail links to Honshū. There are frequent trains to Okayama (¥1470, 55 minutes, every half-hour), where you can connect to *shinkansen* (bullet train) services that will whizz you to any of the major cities in just a few hours.

From Takamatsu, *tokkyū* trains on the JR Kōtoku line run southeast to Tokushima (¥2560, one hour and seven minutes, hourly); the JR Yosan line runs west to Matsuyama (¥5500, 2½ hours, hourly); and the JR Dosan line runs to Kōchi (¥4760, 2½ hours, hourly). The private Kotoden line also runs direct to Kotohira (¥610, one hour, frequent).

Around Takamatsu

In addition to places listed here, Takamatsu is a great stepping-off point for the olive groves of Shōdo-shima (p393) and the wonderful art of Naoshima (p396) in the Inland Sea, both less than an hour by boat from the ferry port close to Takamatsu Station.

YASHIMA 屋島

About 5km east of Takamatsu is the 292m-high tabletop plateau of Yashima, where you'll find **Yashima-ji** (屋島寺), number 84 of the 88 Temples. This was the site of a decisive battle between the Genji and Heike clans in the late 12th century, and the temple's **Treasure House** (admission ¥500; 9am-5pm) exhibits artefacts relating to the battle. Just behind the Treasure House is the **Pond of Blood**, where victorious Genji warriors washed the blood from their swords.

At the bottom of Yashima, about 500m north of the station, is **Shikoku-mura** (四国村; 9-1 Shimanaka; admission ¥800; 8.30am-6pm, to 5.30pm Nov-Mar), an excellent village museum that houses old buildings transported here from all over Shikoku and neighbouring islands. The village's fine kabuki stage came from Shōdo-shima (p394), which is famous for its traditional farmers' kabuki performances. There is also an excellent **restaurant** serving, you guessed it, *Sanuki udon* (from ¥450) in an old farmhouse building down a stone staircase to the right.

Yashima is six stops from Kawaramachi on the private Kotoden line (¥240). Shuttle buses run from the station to the top of the mountain (¥100) every half an hour from 9.30am to 4.30pm, but the short uphill walk is gentle enough.

ISAMU NOGUCHI GARDEN MUSEUM イサムノグチ庭園美術館

It's worth considering an excursion to the town of Murechō, east of Takamatsu, to witness the fascinating legacy of noted sculptor Isamu Noguchi (1904–88). Born in Los Angeles to a Japanese poet and an American writer, Noguchi set up a studio and residence here in 1970. Today the **complex** (www.isamunoguchi.or.jp; 3-5-19 Murechō; tours ¥2100; 1hr tours 10am, 1pm & 3pm Tue, Thu & Sat, by appointment) is filled with hundreds of Noguchi's works, and holds its own as an impressive art installation. Inspiring sculptures are on display in the beautifully restored Japanese buildings and in the surrounding landscape.

Visitors should fax or email ahead for reservations, preferably two weeks or more in advance (see the website for reservations and access details).

Kyūshū

Best Places to Eat

» Hamakatsu (p590)

» Ippudō (p573)

» Kawashima Tōfu (p579)

» Toyotsune (p629)

» Ajimori (p611)

Best Places to Stay

» Hakusuikan (p616)

» Yoyōkaku (p579)

» With the Style (p571)

» Yamada Bessou (p628)

» Wasuki (p598)

Why Go?

Japan's southern- and westernmost main island is its warmest, friendliest and (we're partial) most beautiful, with active volcanic peaks, rocky, lush and palmy coastlines, and onsen virtually everywhere. Much Japanese history was made in Kyūshū (九州) – Jōmon ruins, Shintō's sun goddess, wealthy trading ports, cloistered foreigners, samurai rebels and one of the earth's greatest wartime tragedies all loom large.

Today, burgeoning Fukuoka is a multicultural metropolis. In picturesque Nagasaki, tragedy contrasts deftly with a colourful trading history, Kumamoto's castle is one of Japan's finest, and the volcanic Aso caldera is the world's largest. Coastal towns such as Karatsu and Arita are legendary pottery centres. Steam pours from the very earth in Beppu, while the relatively lightly populated prefectures of Kagoshima and Miyazaki have wide open vistas outside their laidback capitals. Peppered throughout are relaxing hot-spring towns and hiking opportunities.

When to Go
Fukuoka

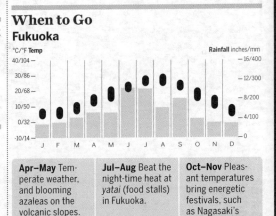

Apr–May Temperate weather, and blooming azaleas on the volcanic slopes.

Jul–Aug Beat the night-time heat at *yatai* (food stalls) in Fukuoka.

Oct–Nov Pleasant temperatures bring energetic festivals, such as Nagasaki's Kunchi Matsuri.

Kyūshū Highlights

① Join the night owls for beer and *yakitori* skewers at a **Fukuoka** (p572) *yatai* food stall

② Be moved – and charmed – by **Nagasaki** (p581)

③ Soak in a **Beppu** (p625) *onsen au naturel*

④ See where the last samurai made their last stand at **Kumamoto-jō** (p597)

⑤ Marvel at Japan's unique ceramics traditions in **Arita, Imari** and **Karatsu** (p578)

⑥ Commune with Shintō's sun goddess in **Takachiho** (p623)

⑦ Recharge in a riverside *rotemburo* (outdoor baths) in tranquil **Kurokawa Onsen** (p604)

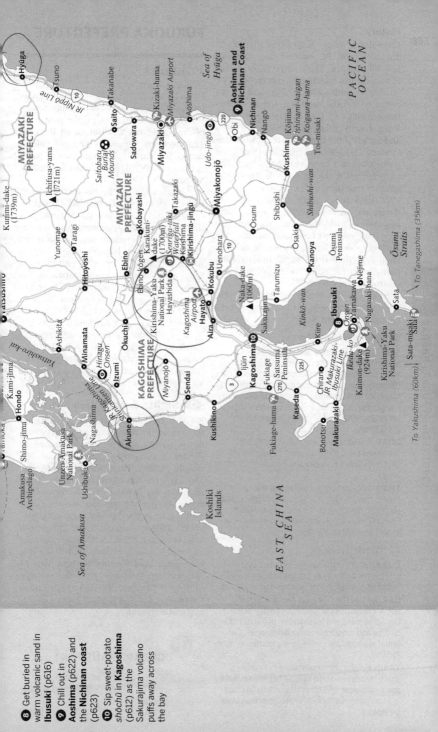

8 Get buried in warm volcanic sand in **Ibusuki** (p616)

9 Chill out in **Aoshima** (p622) and the **Nichinan coast** (p623)

10 Sip sweet-potato *shōchū* in **Kagoshima** (p612) as the Sakurajima volcano puffs away across the bay

Excavations near Kagoshima dating to around 10,000 BC indicate that southern Kyūshū was the likely entry point of the Jōmon culture, which gradually crept north.

Japan's trade with China and Korea began in Kyūshū, and the arrival of Portuguese ships in 1543 initiated Japan's at-times thorny relationship with the West and heralded the beginning of its 'Christian Century' (1549–1650). With Christianity, the Portuguese also brought gunpowder weaponry, heralding the ultimate decline of the samurai tradition.

In 1868 rebels from Kyūshū were instrumental in carrying through the Meiji Restoration, which ended the military shōgunate's policy of isolation, marking the birth of modern Japan. During the ensuing Meiji era (1868–1912), rapid industrialisation caused profound social, political and environmental change.

Sadly, this historically rich region is best known for one event – the 9 August 1945 atomic bombing of Nagasaki.

ⓘ Getting There & Away

AIR Fukuoka Airport is Japan's third largest, servicing destinations in Asia and Japan. In addition to frequent domestic connections, Ōita (Beppu), Kagoshima, Kumamoto, Miyazaki and Nagasaki airports all have flights to Seoul, and Kagoshima, Nagasaki and Kitakyūshū airports serve Shanghai, and Miyazaki Taipei, but not always daily.

BOAT There are sea connections to Kyūshū from Osaka and Okinawa. High-speed ferries shuttle between Fukuoka and Busan, in South Korea.

TRAIN The opening of the Kyūshū *shinkansen* (bullet train) in March 2011 brought high-speed rail travel directly from Shin-Osaka to Hakata Station (Fukuoka), Kumamoto and Kagoshima, as well as some smaller towns.

ⓘ Getting Around

BUS Kyūshū's extensive highway bus system is often the best way to get around. See www.rakubus.jp/english for routes and reservations.

CAR Outside the cities, car rental is a good option. Without a car, you'll miss many of the best-preserved and least-known of the island's diverse and most impressive landscapes. Car-rental agencies are conveniently located all over Kyūshū.

TRAIN Kyūshū *shinkansen* lines run north–south through western Kyūshū between Hakata and Kagoshima, and other major Kyūshū cities are connected by *tokkyū* (limited express) train services.

FUKUOKA PREFECTURE

Fukuoka 福岡

♪ 092 / POP 1,462,000

Fukuoka is Kyūshū's largest city and growing fast. It's made up of two former towns, the Fukuoka castle town on the west bank of the Naka-gawa and Hakata on the east. The two towns merged in 1889 as Fukuoka, though the name Hakata still remains widely in use; eg it's Fukuoka Airport but Hakata Station.

Whatever you call it, this youthful, user-friendly metropolis in Fukuoka Prefecture (福岡県) has a cosmopolitan charm, particularly after dark, peppered with the flavours of its Asian neighbours. Hakata traces its trading history back some 2000 years, which continues today with visitors from Seoul and Shanghai. Among Japanese, the city is famed for its 'Hakata *bijin*' (beautiful women), SoftBank Hawks baseball team and hearty Hakata *rāmen* (egg noodles).

If Fukuoka doesn't burst with sights like Tokyo or Kyoto, its friendly atmosphere, warm weather and contemporary attractions – art, architecture, shopping and cuisine – make up for it, and it's a good base for regional excursions.

⊙ Sights & Activities

For visitors, Fukuoka can be divided into three main districts. Hakata, the old *shita-machi* (downtown), is now dominated by Fukuoka's *shinkansen* stop, the busy JR Hakata Station. Three subway stops away and across the Naka-gawa is Fukuoka's beating heart, the Tenjin district, featuring boutiques, eateries and nightlife. Above ground, Tenjin centres around Watanabe-dōri, paralleled underground by Tenjin Chikagai, a long shopping arcade with mood lighting and cast-ironwork ceilings that make it a cool refuge from the summer heat. West of Tenjin is trendy Daimyō, Fukuoka's homage to Tokyo's Omote-sandō-dōri (p70) minus the crowds, heading towards Fukuoka's former castle grounds.

ⓘ CHEAP TRANSPORT

See p765 and p759 for information on discounted all-you-can-ride passes on JR Kyūshū and Kyūshū buses.

The coastal neighbourhoods, best reached by bus or taxi, have many attractive sights, restaurants and hotels.

HAKATA AREA

Fukuoka Asian Art Museum   ART GALLERY
(福岡アジア美術館; http://faam.city.fukuoka.lg .jp/eng/home.html; 7th & 8th fl, Riverain Centre Bldg, 3-1 Shimokawabata-machi; admission ¥200; 🕙10am-8pm, closed Wed; 🚇Nakasu-Kawabata) On the upper floors of the large Hakata Riverain Centre (博多リバレイン), the Fukuoka Asian Art Museum houses the world-renowned **Asia Gallery** and additional galleries for special exhibits (note that the admission fee varies) and artists in residence. Changing exhibits cover contemporary works from 23 countries, from East Asia to Pakistan.

Hakata Machiya Furusato-kan   MUSEUM
(博多町家ふるさと館; www.hakatamachiya.com, in Japanese; 6-10 Reisen-machi; admission ¥200; 🕙10am-6pm; 🚇Gion) Spread over three *machiya* (traditional town houses), this newly renovated folk museum re-creates a Hakata *nagare* (neighbourhood unit) from the late Meiji era. The replica buildings house historical photos and displays of traditional Hakata culture, festivals, crafts and performing arts, as well as recordings of impenetrable Hakata-ben (dialect). Artisans are frequently on hand offering demonstrations.

Shrines & Temples   SHRINES
The intimate **Kushida-jinja** (櫛田神社), municipal Shintō shrine of Hakata, traces its history to AD 757 and sponsors the Hakata Gion Yamakasa Matsuri (p570). It has float displays and a local history **museum** (1-41 Kami-kawabata; admission ¥300; 🕙10am-5pm; 🚇Gion or Nakasu-Kawabata) chiefly featuring the festival.

Sumiyoshi-jinja (住吉神社; 2-10-7 Sumiyoshi) is said to be Japan's original Sumiyoshi *taisha* (shrine). On its north side is **Rakusuien** (楽水園; admission/tea ¥100/300; 🕙9am-5pm, closed Tue), a pretty garden and teahouse built by a Meiji-era merchant, serving an outdoor tea ceremony.

Tōchō-ji (東長寺; 2-4 Gokushō-machi; 🚇Gion) has Japan's largest wooden Buddha (created 1992) and some impressively carved Kannon (goddess of mercy) statues. It is said to date from AD 806 and to have been founded by Kūkai, the founder of the Shingon school of Buddhism.

Shōfuku-ji (聖福寺; 6-1 Gokushō-machi; 🚇Gion) is a Zen temple founded in 1195 by

Eisai, who introduced Zen and tea to Japan; the nation's first tea plants are said to have been planted here.

Canal City   NOTABLE BUILDING
(キャナルシティ; www.canalcity.co.jp/eg; 1-2 Sumiyoshi, Hakata-ku) Once-futuristic Canal City may be showing its age (it opened in 1996), but it still attracts crowds with its artificial canal with illuminated fountain symphony, hotels, multiplex cinema, playhouse, and about 250 boutiques, bars and bistros.

TENJIN AREA

Fukuoka-jō & Ōhori-kōen   HISTORIC PARK
(福岡城・大濠公園) Only the walls remain of what was once Fukuoka-jō, but the castle's hilltop site (Maizuru-kōen) provides good views of the city.

Ōhori-kōen, adjacent to the castle grounds, has the traditionally styled **Nihonteien** (Japanese Garden; 1-7 Ōhori-kōen; admission ¥240; 🕙9am-5pm Sep-May, to 6pm Jun-Aug, closed Mon; 🚇Ōhori-kōen). It's a more recent construction (1984) around a pond with stone gardens and a teahouse.

Nearby, the **Fukuoka Art Museum** (www .fukuoka-art-museum.jp/english; 1-6 Ōhori-kōen; admission ¥200; 🕙9.30am-5pm Tue-Sun Sep-May, to 7pm Tue-Sat, to 5pm Sun Jul & Aug; 🚇Ōhori-kōen) has ancient pottery and Buddhist guardians on one floor; works by Basquiat, Brancusi, Rothko and Warhol upstairs; and galleries pairing Western artists with Japanese contemporaries. Most exhibits change every few months.

Chūō-kōen   PARK
(中央公園) Some attractive historic Western architecture populates this park by City Hall, most notably the French Renaissance-styled **Former Prefectural Hall & Official Guest House** (旧福岡県公会堂貴賓館; 6-29 Nishi-nakasu; admission ¥240; 🕙9am-5pm Tue-Sun, closed 29 Dec-3 Jan; 🚇Nakasu-Kawabata or Tenjin), dating from 1910 and with a fantastic French cafe where you can watch the scene. A couple of blocks north, the copper-turreted **Akarenga Bunka-kan** (福岡市赤煉瓦文化館; Red Brick Cultural Centre; admission free; 🕙9am-9pm Tue-Sun, closed 28 Dec-3 Jan) was built in 1909 by the same architect who designed Tokyo Station and now hosts simple historical exhibits.

COASTAL FUKUOKA
Fukuoka's coast is easiest reached by bus from Tenjin or Hakata. Fukuoka Tower and Yahoo! Japan Dome are west of the city centre.

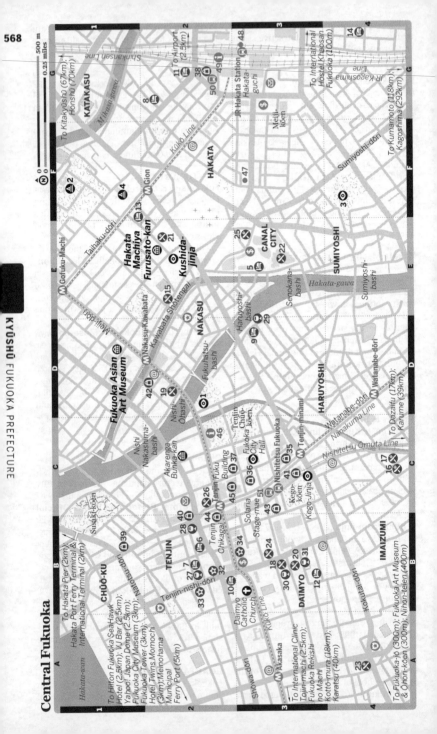

Central Fukuoka

500 m
0.25 miles

Hakata-wan

To Hilton Fukuoka SeaHawk
Hotel (2.5km); VJ Bar (2.5km);
Yahoo! Japan Dome (2.5km);
Fukuoka City Museum (3km);
Fukuoka Tower (3km);
Hotel Twins Momochi
(3km);Meinohama
Municipal
Ferry Port (5km)

To Hakata Pier (2km);
Hakata Port Ferry Terminal &
International Terminal (2km)

CHŪO-KU

TENJIN

DAIMYO

IMAIZUMI

To International Clinic
Tojin-machi(2.5km);
Fukuoka Rekishi
no Machi

To Fukuoka-jo (300m); Fukuoka Art Museum
& Ohori-koen (300m); Nihon-teien (400m)

To Dazaifu (17km);
Karume (39km)

HARUYOSHI

SUMIYOSHI

CANAL
CITY

HAKATA

KATAKASU

To Kitakyūshū (67km);
Honshū (70km)

Mikasa-gawa

To Airport
(2.5km)

JR Hakata Station

Hakata-
guchi

Meiji-
koen

To International
Hostel Khaosan
Fukuoka (100m)

To Kumamoto (118km);
Kagoshima (292km)

Shinkansen Line

Kūkō Line

Fukuoka Asian
Art Museum

Hakata
Machiya
Furusato-kan

Kushida-
Jinja

NAKASU

Hakata-gawa

Nishi
Nakashima-
bashi

Akarenga
Bunka-kan

Tenjin Fuku
Building

Fukuoka
City
Hall

Tenjin
Chūō-
koen

Nishitetsu Fukuoka

Solaria
Stage-mae

Kego-
koen

Kego-Jinja

Daimyo
Catholic
Church

Tenjin
Chikagai

Gion

Susaki-koen

Nishi-
Ohashi

Fukuhatsu-
bashi

Haruyoshi-
bashi

Senokawa-
bashi

Sumiyoshi-
bashi

JR Kagoshima
Line

Sumiyoshi-dōri

Watanabe-dōri

Nishitetsu Omuta Line

Nanakuma Line

Kokutai-dōri

Showa-dōri

Kūkō Line

Tenjin-nishi-dōri

Natsu-dōri

Taihaku-dōri

Meiji-dōri

Gofuku-Machi

Nakasu-Kawabata

Kawabata Shotengai

Fukuoka Tower LANDMARK

(福岡タワー; www.fukuokatower.co.jp/english/index.html; 2-3-26 Momochi-hama; admission ¥800; ◉9.30am-10pm Apr-Sep, to 9pm Oct-Mar) Standing above the Momochi district, a modern mix of corporate headquarters, hotels, large shopping and entertainment venues and apartment blocks, is the 234m-tall Fukuoka Tower, a symbol of the city and mostly hollow (its main purpose is as a broadcast tower). At 120m, the classy **Sky Lounge Refuge** cafe is a great place to soak up the views, especially at dusk. While you're here, drop into the Robosquare (see p574) nearby.

Fukuoka City Museum MUSEUM

(http://museum.city.fukuoka.jp/english/index_e.html; 3-1-1 Momochi-hama; admission ¥200; ◉9.30am-5.30pm Tue-Sun Sep-Jun, to 7.30pm Tue-Sat, to 7pm Sun Jul & Aug) The Fukuoka City Museum displays artefacts from local history and culture, the pride of the museum being an ancient 2.3 sq cm, 109g golden seal with an inscription proving Japan's historic ties to China.

Yahoo! Japan Dome STADIUM

(ヤフードーム; www.hawkstown.com) This monolithic, retractable-roof stadium is the

MOJIKŌ & YAHATA

Most visitors don't get to the industrial city of Kitakyūshū at the island's far north, but two enclaves there can be combined for a worthwhile day trip from Fukuoka.

Mojikō (門司港), Kyūshū's closest point to Honshū, has been a port since 1889, and its harbourside 'Retro Town' is a trove of Meiji- and Taishō-period architecture, handsome brick buildings that once housed shipping companies and customs houses, and a drawbridge for pedestrians. A bit further on, you can walk under the Gempei Strait via the tunnel to Shimonoseki on Honshū. A row of shops along the waterside serves Mojikō's signature dish, *yaki-curry* (curry rice broiled with melted cheese on top; see p573).

Yahata (八幡) is a one-time industrial town that has cleaned up its act with inspirational results. **Kitakyūshū Kankyō Museum** (北九州市環境ミュージアム; Kitakyūshū Environment Museum; 2-2-6 Higashida Yahata; admission ¥100; ⊙9am-5pm, closed Mon) tells of the environmental degredation of Kyūshū in the early industrial period (including the notorious Minamata disease that struck near Kumamoto in the 1950s) via 'radioramas' with sound available in English. Interactive exhibits illustrate the effects of pollution. Steps away, the futuristic **Kitakyūshū Innovation Gallery & Studio** (北九州イノベーションギャラリー; www.kigs.jp; 2-2-11 Higashida Yahata; ⊙9am-7pm Tue-Fri, to 5pm Sat & Sun) offers changing special exhibits (¥500) and an excellent chronology of technological innovation. Across the road is a towering **steel foundry** from 1901, now cleaned up and a great place for a *bentō* (boxed meal) lunch.

From Hakata, transfer at Kokura (*shinkansen* ¥3300, 15 minutes; *tokkyū* limited express ¥2050, 45 minutes) for the 15-minute ride (¥270) to either Mojikō or Space World Station (for Yahata).

home field of Fukuoka's much-loved Soft-Bank Hawks baseball team. Tours (in Japanese) are offered and there's a museum of the life of **Oh Sadaharu**, the world's all-time home-run king, although if you're less than a die-hard fan it may be hard to catch.

A small city has grown up around the stadium, including the impressive César Pelli–designed **Hilton Fukuoka Sea Hawk** hotel. Yahoo! Japan Dome is about 1km northwest of Tōjin-machi Station. Frequent direct buses go to Yahoo! Dome from Tenjin bus centre (about 15 minutes).

Nearby Islands   ISLANDS

A quick ferry ride from Fukuoka, pretty **Nokonoshima** (能古島) mixes natural and man-made parks. The latter, called **Island Park** (www.nokonoshima.com; adult/child ¥1000/500), gets the most visitors, with a swimming beach, fields of seasonal wildflowers, huts selling crafts, and sweeping ocean views. Bicycle rental (per hour/day ¥300/1000) and English maps are available at Noko Market, by the ferry dock. Buses 300 and 301 depart frequently from Nishitetsu Tenjin bus terminal (¥360, 20 minutes) for Meinohama Municipal Ferry Port.

Ferries to delightfully rural **Shikanoshima** (志賀島), where fresh seafood restaurants line the harbourside streets, depart hourly (¥650, 33 minutes) from Bayside Place, along with seasonal sightseeing cruises around Hakata Bay. Shikanoshima also has a **fishing shrine** (志賀海神社), decorated with deer antlers, and a popular **beach** about 5km east of the shrine.

FREE Fukuoka Rekishi no Machi

Kottō-mura   CRAFT VILLAGE

(福岡歴史の町骨董村; ☎806-0505; 439-120 Tokunaga, Nishi-ku; ⊙10am-6pm, closed Thu; ®JR Chikuhi line from Meinohama to Kyūdai-gakken-toshi) Around 15 working potters, weavers and paper-makers exhibit and sell their wares at this rustic historical village and antiques cooperative. It's out of the way, but a nice diversion with bargains to be found. It's about ¥1000 by taxi from Kyūdai-gakken-toshi Station, or you may be able to arrange station pick-up if you phone.

Festivals & Events

Hakozaki-gū Tamatorisai
(Tamaseseri)   TRADITIONAL

On 3 January, two groups of young men clad in loincloths raucously chase a wooden ball in the name of good fortune, at Hakozaki-gū shrine.

Hakata Dontaku Matsuri TRADITIONAL

On 3 and 4 May, Fukuoka's Meiji-dōri vibrates to the percussive shock of *shamoji* (wooden serving spoons) being banged together like castanets, with *shamisen* (three-stringed instrument) accompaniment.

Hakata Gion Yamakasa Matsuri TRADITIONAL

The city's main festival is held from 1 to 15 July, climaxing at 4.59am on the 15th, when seven groups of men converge at Kushida-jinja to race along a 5km-long course carrying huge *mikoshi* (portable shrines). According to legend, the festival originated after a 13th-century Buddhist priest was carried aloft, sprinkling holy water over victims of a plague.

Kyūshū Bashō Sumō Tournament SUMŌ

Held over two weeks at the Fukuoka Kokusai Centre during mid-November. Spectators start lining up at dawn for limited same-day tickets (*tōjitsu-ken;* ¥3400 to ¥15,000).

🛏 Sleeping

Fukuoka is popular for business and pleasure, with plenty of quality accommodation at all budgets. Stay near JR Hakata Station for convenience if railing around, but Tenjin is a better bet if you plan to spend a few days shopping and playing.

HAKATA AREA

TOP CHOICE **With the Style** HOTEL $$$

(ウィズザスタイル福岡; ☑433-3900; www .withthestyle.com; 1-9-18 Hakataeki-minami; r with breakfast, minibar & welcome drinks from ¥39,270; ⊖@; ᵣHakata) We don't know what the name means, but 'style' is indeed the byword at this sleek, designer hotel. You could easily imagine yourself poolside in Hollywood around the fountain courtyard, each of the 16 rooms exudes rock-star cool, and guests can reserve complimentary private use of the rooftop spa or penthouse bar. With a sushi bar and steakhouse on-site, it's an inner-city retreat to savour.

Ryokan Kashima Honkan RYOKAN $$

(和風旅館 鹿島本館; ☑291-0746; fax 271-7995; 3-11 Reisen-machi; r per person without bathroom from ¥6300; @; ᵣGion) This charmingly creaky, unpretentious ryokan is pleasantly faded and focused around a Meiji-era garden. Oozing atmosphere, it's a great place to sample traditional Japan. The friendly owners communicate well in English.

Grand Hyatt Fukuoka HOTEL $$$

(グランドハイアット福岡; ☑282-1234; http:// fukuoka.grand.hyatt.com; 1-2-82 Sumiyoshi; s/d from ¥28,000/34,000; P⊖@☱) Ensconced amid the fountains of Canal City, this massive yet sumptuous property's warm, light-filled rooms synthesise traditional Japanese aesthetics (*shoji* screen room dividers) with contemporary comforts. Suites are magnificent and decadent.

Nishitetsu Inn Hakata HOTEL $$

(西鉄イン博多; ☑413-5454; fax 413-5466; 1-17-6 Hakata-ekimae; s/d from ¥6900/13,300; ⊖@; ᵣHakata) This shiny, spotless 500-room transit hotel has decent-sized rooms but really scores additional points for its common sauna and onsen baths. Visit them in a spiffy waffle-pattern *yukata* (light cotton kimono).

International Hostel Khaosan Fukuoka HOSTEL $

(☑404-6035; www.khaosan-fukuoka.com; 11-34 Hiemachi; dm/s/tw from ¥2400/3500/5200; ⊖@⟨中⟩; ᵣHakata) This 19-room hostel offers bare-bones accommodation and a communal TV, plus roof deck for meeting other travellers. From Hakata Station, head down Chikushi-dōri and turn left at Hotto Motto *bentō* (boxed meal) shop.

Hotel New Simple HOTEL $

(ホテルニューシンプル; ☑411-4311; www .hotel-newsimple.jp; 1-23-11 Hakata-ekimae; dm/s/ tw ¥3000/4200/7140; ᵣGion) This boxy, no-frills, inexpensive lodging lives up to its name.

TENJIN AREA

Il Palazzo HOTEL $$$

(☑716-3333; www.ilpalazzo.jp; 3-13-1 Haruyoshi; s/d from ¥22,050/25,200; ⊖@; ᵣNakasu-Kawa-bata) Don't be put off by the windowless, colonnaded facade of burnt orange and obsidian. The lobby is as glossy as black lipstick, the 62 rooms are slick and soothing, staff couldn't be sweeter, and you're just steps from Nakasu-gawa and Tenjin hot spots (yet hidden on a quiet street).

Plaza Hotel Premier HOTEL $$

(プラザホテルプルミエ; ☑734-7600; www .plaza-hotel.net; 1-14-13 Daimyō; s/tw from ¥8200/14,000; P⊖@; ᵣTenjin or Akasaka) Located in trendy Daimyō, the Premier is a smooth operator rivalling far pricier hotels. The night vibe on the street outside is ubercool and its Trattoria Bal Musette could be straight out of Paris.

La Soeur Hotel Monterey
HOTEL $$

(ホテルモントレ ラ・スール福岡; ☏726-7111; https://www.hotelmonterey.co.jp/eng/index.html; 2-8-27 Daimyō; s/d from ¥13,860/23,100; ☻@; ⓡTenjin) A popular wedding spot, this 182-room property has a prime location and well-appointed rooms with contemporary French touches and parquet floors. Check the website for online, pay-in-advance bargains.

Hotel Ascent
HOTEL $$

(ホテルアセント福岡; ☏711-1300; fax 711-1717; 3-3-14 Tenjin; s/d from ¥7245/13,650; ☻@; ⓡTenjin) This hotel has 263 spiffy rooms in the heart of Tenjin, with a chic Italian restaurant in the lobby.

Hotel Etwas Tenjin
HOTEL $$

(ホテルエトワス天神; ☏737-3233; fax 737-3266; 3-5-18 Tenjin; s/d incl light breakfast ¥5800/7800; ☻@; ⓡTenjin) Recently refurbished and good value. Lively Oyafuko-dōri is around the corner.

COASTAL FUKUOKA AREA

Hilton Fukuoka Sea Hawk
HOTEL $$$

(☏844-8111; www.hilton.com; 2-2-3 Jigyohama; s/d from ¥12,600/23,100; P☻@⊠) If you want to make an impression, you can hardly do better anywhere in Japan. The lobby restaurant of this César Pelli–designed hotel soars like its namesake, and at 1052 rooms it's Asia's largest Hilton. With the right room and weather, on game days you can watch the SoftBank Hawks without leaving the hotel.

Hotel Twins Momochi
HOTEL $

(☏852-4800; www.twinsmomochi.jp, in Japanese; 1-7-4 Momochi-hama, Sawara-ku; s/d from ¥5800/7800; P☻@) Room types vary at this great-value couple- and family-friendly hotel; they're perhaps inspired by IKEA, but all have refreshingly personal touches. There's a coin laundry and shared kitchenettes.

✘ Eating

To most Japanese, Hakata means *tonkotsu rāmen* – noodles in a distinctive broth made from pork bones. Other specialities include *yakitori* (grilled chicken on skewers), *yakiniku* (Korean-style grilled beef) and fresh seafood.

The Fukuoka way to eat is at *yatai* (屋台), mobile hawker-style food stalls with simple counters and seats; Fukuoka claims more *yatai* than in the rest of Japan combined! Let the aromas and chatty conversation lead you to the best cooking and the best companions. For a more local experience, try around Tenjin or Nagahama. *Yatai* open at dusk and most seats are soon taken.

Tenjin Nobunaga
YAKITORI $$

(☏721-6940; 2-6-21 Tenjin; skewers from ¥263; ☻dinner; ⓡTenjin) Nobunaga is raucous and rowdy, and that's just the chefs. There's no English menu but it's easy to choose from the skewers behind the counter. Another house speciality is *potato-mochiage* (¥420), a fried dumpling of mashed potato, cheese and *mochi* (pounded rice). Look for the red lanterns just to the right of Big Echo karaoke hall.

Murata
NOODLES $

(信州そばむらた; ☏291-0894; 2-9-1 Reisen-machi; soba from ¥850; ☻11.30am-9pm, closed 2nd Sun of month; ✐; ⓡGion) Down the street from the Hakata Machiya Furusato-kan, this lovely eatery makes homemade *soba* (buckwheat noodles) in the style of the Shinshū area of central Japan (around Nagano), prepared in a variety of ways. Try *oroshi-soba* (cold noodles topped with grated daikon) for ¥950.

Sushikō Minatomachi Honten
SUSHI $$

(☏761-1659; 2-11-18 Minatomachi; meals from ¥1050; ☻10am-10pm) Sushi here can be two completely different experiences: elegant and dignified on the 2nd floor, or served together with other dishes in a rollicking upstairs beer garden that's open year-round for inclement weather (all you can eat and drink for women/men from ¥2500/3150). Its sister conveyor-belt sushi shop, fresh and friendly **Kintarō** (☏737-8750; sushi ¥100-500; ☻lunch & dinner), is on the ground floor.

Fish Man
IZAKAYA $$

(Sakana Otoko; ☏717-3571; 1-4-23 Imaizumi; teishoku ¥680-1280; ☻lunch & dinner; ◧; ⓡTenjin-minami) Fish Man's decor is all post-industrial minimalism with lacquered plywood and big windows, the better to show off the deft, unconventional presentations of seafood fresh from the Nagahama market across town: *kaidan-zushi* (sushi served on a wooden spiral staircase), *tsubotai no misoyaki* (miso-grilled snapper) or a *maguro* hamburger served on a steel plate.

Afterwards, stop for dessert at Fish Man's adorable affiliated cake shop **Henry & Cowell** (☏741-7888; 1-3-11 Imaizumi; ☻10am-9pm), just down the street.

Not unlike Pavlov's dogs, Fukuokans salivate at the mention of Hakata *rāmen* (egg noodles). The distinctive local style is called *tonkotsu rāmen*, noodles in a hearty broth made from pork bones. You can find it all over town, but two chains have national reputations.

Ippudō (🕿781-0303; 1-12-61 Daimyō; rāmen ¥700-800; ⏱11am-2am Sun-Thu, 10.30am-4am Fri & Sat; 📷; 🚇Tenjin) has workmanlike and always bustling branches in Tenjin, serving the best-selling Akamaru Modern (with black sesame oil and a fragrant *umami-dama*, or flavour ball), Shiromaru Classic (with thin noodles) and Karaka (spicy *rāmen*).

Ichiran (🕿713-6631; 2-1-57 Daimyō; rāmen from ¥690; ⏱10am-7am; 📷; 🚇Tenjin) is an entirely different experience, with multiple branches around town. Purchase tickets from a vending machine at the entrance, sit at one of the individual booths and fill out a form (available in English) detailing your order: doneness of noodles, level of spice, thickness of broth etc. Then enjoy in peace (or dislocation, depending on your perspective).

And if for some reason Hakata-style *rāmen* doesn't satisfy, in Canal City there's **Rāmen Stadium** (ラーメンスタジアム; 🕿282-2525; 5th fl, Canal City; rāmen from ¥550; ⏱11am-10.30pm), an entire floor of eight *rāmen* vendors imported from the length and breadth of Japan.

Taigen Shokudō
KOREAN $

(🕿752-5589; 1-1-5 Akasaka; dishes from ¥780; ⏱lunch & dinner; 🚇Akasaka) Locally popular place for Korean BBQ grilled behind the counter and served on sizzling *teppan* (steel plates). A great bargain at lunchtime. There's no English menu, but order the *yakiniku teishoku* (set meal with salad, soup and rice; ¥880) or *Taigen teishoku* (*yakiniku* set meal plus hamburger, beef cutlet and sausage; ¥1200). It's next to Core 21 Akasaka.

Curry Honpo
CURRY $

(伽哩本舗; 🕿262-0010; www.curry-honpo.com; 6-135 Kami-kawabata; curry from ¥670; ⏱lunch & dinner; 🖉📷; 🚇Nakasu-Kawabata) Can't make it to Mojikō (see p570)? Try the Kawabata Shōtengai location of the famous shop for some *yaki-curry* (broiled curry rice with cheese), which the English menu disturbingly refers to as 'combustion curry'. The standard is pork combustion curry (¥870). It's the fake-wood-panelled storefront in the arcade.

No No Budo
BUFFET $$

(野の葡萄; 🕿714-1441; IMS Bldg, 1-7-11 Tenjin; lunch/dinner ¥1680/2200; ⏱lunch & dinner; 🖉; 🚇Tenjin) The IMS building (天神イムズ) has prime skyline views from its 12th- and 13th-floor restaurants, including No No Budo. The busy self-serve gourmet buffet has good-for-you Japanese and Western fish and meat dishes, noodles, salads, soups and nice pastries. An extra ¥1300 buys all-you-can-drink beer, wine and cocktails.

Jacques Monod
FRENCH $$

(🕿724-8800; 6-29 Nishi-Nakasu; set menus ¥980-2700; ⏱11am-midnight; 🚇Nakasu-Kawabata or Tenjin) Quietly chic indoor-outdoor cafe at the Former Prefectural Hall, serving full and light meals.

West
NOODLES $

(🕿273-1591; 9-3 Gionmachi; ⏱11am-11pm) Popular, inexpensive chain for *udon* (thick white wheat noodles), tempura (often served with *udon;* ¥280 to ¥680) and *yakiniku* (all-you-can-eat ¥1980 to ¥3380). Multiple locations.

🍷 Drinking

The weekend starts on Thursday in multicultural, party-friendly Fukuoka. Tenjin and Daimyō's streets are safe, easy to explore and great for people-watching. The main drag, Oyafuko-dōri, roughly translates to 'street of unruly children' because of the cram schools that once lined it. In a way, the cap still fits. Nakasu Island, while one of Japan's busiest entertainment districts, is often sleazy.

For the latest on Fukuoka's cloistered gay scene, consult *Fukuoka Now* magazine (www.fukuoka-now.com) or, if you can read Japanese, www.k-toom.com.

International Bar
BAR

(インターナショナルバー; 4th fl, Urashima Bldg, 3-1-13 Tenjin; 🚇Tenjin) There's free karaoke on Tuesdays at this tiny bar. Like the name implies, it's one of the original places in Fukuoka for locals and *gaijin* (foreigners) to connect, in a time warp of red velvet seating with hip-hop beats.

KYŪSHŪ FUKUOKA

Mitsubachi
BAR

(ミツバチ; 5th Hotel East, 3-4-65 Haruyoshi; 圓Nakasu-Kawabata) Enjoy views of Hakata and Canal City across the Naka-gawa through giant windows in this pretty dining bar. Inside it's like a contemporary log cabin.

Craic & Porter Beer Bar
PUB

(http://craic.mine.nu; 3-5-16 Tenjin; 圓Tenjin) A tiny taste of Ireland with open windows and about 10 premium import beers on tap. Owner Mike is a friendly character, with plenty of experience in Japan. It's above ABC flower shop on Oyafuko-dōri.

Morris
PUB

(7th fl, Stage 1 Nishidōri Bldg, 2-1-4 Daimyō; ⊙from 5pm; @; 圓Tenjin) One of the better pubs in Japan, attracting a nice mix of Japanese and *gaijin*. Begin your evening with happy-hour cocktails (¥250; 5pm to 7pm) on the awesome patio perched high above trendy Daimyō. There's a good beer selection and tasty pub food.

Small Spaces
BAR

(1-13-12 Daimyō; 圓Tenjin or Tenjin-Minami) While this corner bar may be a little tricky if you can't speak Japanese, it's worth a look. Small Spaces is all about young Japanese doing their own thing. The cool glow spills out onto the street through the open door and white-shuttered windows of this little wooden shack. Peace, man.

VJ Bar
BAR

(34th fl, Fukoka Hilton Sea Hawk, 2-2-3 Jigyohama; ⊙6pm-1am) Bar with expensive views, 123m above the ground.

☆ Entertainment

Juke Joint
BAR

(ジュークジョイント; ☑762-5596; http://juke-records.net/jukejoint, in Japanese; 2nd fl, 1-9-23 Maizuru; 圓Tenjin) Funsters can select the tunes at this Fukuoka original DJ lounge. The eclectic music collection is the work of record-shop owner 'Kinky' Ko Matsumoto. Drinks start at ¥500, plus there's spicy seafood gumbo (that's right) and no cover charge.

Dark Room
BAR

(ザ・ダークルーム; ☑725-2989; www.thedarkroom.biz; 8th fl, Tenjin Bacchus-kan, 3-4-15 Tenjin; ⊙6pm-2am; 圓Tenjin) Dark, rocky and loud, this is a cool urban rock oasis with a killer sound system, pool table, foosball, friendly dudes behind the bar and a spiral staircase leading to a fun, summer-only rooftop patio.

Sam & Dave
NIGHTCLUB

(サムアンドデイブ; ☑713-2223; www.samanddave.jp; 3rd fl, West Side Bldg, Tenjin Nishi-dōri; 圓Tenjin) Like its sister bars around Japan, Sam & Dave's vacillates between being somewhere fun to shake your ass, and just another boozy big-beat meat-market nightclub. Hope for a good crowd and you could be lucky, whatever you fancy. It's best Fridays and Saturdays.

🛍 Shopping

For contemporary fashion, low-rise boutiques in the Daimyō district show off local designers.

Shōgetsudō
TRADITIONAL DOLLS

(☑291-4141, 5-1-22 Nakasu; ⊙9am-7pm; 圓Nakasu-Kawabata) White-faced clay Hakata *ningyō* (Hakata dolls) depicting women, children, samurai and geisha are a popular Fukuoka craft. This place sells them and offers painting workshops (¥1575 to ¥2100).

Hakata Ichijū
KIMONO

(3rd fl, 5-1-22 Nakasu; ⊙noon-7.30pm; 圓Nakasu-Kawabata) An understated store offering obis, kimonos and accessories in the distinctive Hakata-ori weaving style (also at Tenjin's department stores).

Mandarake
MANGA

(5-7-7 Tenjin; ⊙noon-8pm; 圓Tenjin) The Fukuoka branch of Mandarake is Kyūshū's largest manga store with several storeys of games, comic books and DVDs.

Robosquare
ELECTRONICS

(2nd fl, TNC Bldg, 2-3-2 Momochihama; ⊙closed 2nd Tue) Near Fukuoka Tower, Robosquare sells robotics and salutes all things cyborg with demonstrations, robot performances and small exhibits of current technology.

Department Stores
DEPARTMENT STORES

Fukuoka's department stores occupy a three-block gauntlet of Watanabe-dōri in Tenjin. **Tenjin Core** (天神コア), **Mitsukoshi** (三越), **Daimaru** (大丸), **Solaria Plaza** (ソラリアプラザ), the **IMS Building** (天神イムズ) and **mina tenjin** are all favourites, as is the subterranean **Tenjin Chikagai** (天神地下街).

Bookshops
BOOKSHOPS

If you're looking for reading material, **Junkudō Fukuoka** (ジュンク堂書店; 1st-4th fl, Media Mall, Tenjin; ⊙10am-8.30pm; sells foreign paperbacks, while **Kinokuniya** (紀伊國屋; 6th fl, Fukuoka Kōtsū Centre Bldg,

Hakata-eki; ⊘10am-9pm; ℝHakata) has a huge selection of Japanese- and English-language books, magazines and DVDs.

❶ Information

Internet Access

Cybac Café (サイバックカフェ; www.cybac.com, in Japanese; 2nd fl, 3-2-22 Tenjin; registration fee ¥300, per 1st 30min/subsequent 15min ¥300/100; ⊘24hr; ℝTenjin)

Kinko's Akasaka (キンコーズ赤坂店; 2-12-12 Daimyō; ⊘24hr; ℝAkasaka); Chikushiguchi (キンコーズ筑紫口店; 2-5-28 Hakata-eki higashi; ⊘24hr); Hakata-ekimae (キンコーズ博多駅前店; 2-19-24 Hakata-ekimae; ⊘8am-10pm; ℝHakata) Ten minutes' access for ¥210.

Media Café Popeye (www.media-cafe.net, in Japanese) Hakata-ekimae (メディアカフェポパイ博多; 8th fl, Fukuoka Kōtsū Centre Bldg; ⊘24hr; ℝHakata); Nakasu (メディアカフェポパイ中州店; 8th fl, Spoon Bldg, 5-1-7 Nakasu; ⊘24hr; ℝNakasu-kawabata); Tenjin (メディアカフェポパイ天神店; 2nd fl, Nishitetsu Imaizumi Bldg, 1-12-23 Imaizumi; ⊘24hr; ℝTenjin-minami) Each has a free soft-drink bar, massage chairs and couples' booths. Offers ¥510 for the first 60 minutes, then ¥80 per subsequent 10 minutes.

Media

Fukuoka Now (www.fukuoka-now.com) Indispensable monthly English-language street mag with detailed city maps. It should be the first thing you source to find out what's on.

Yokonavi.com (www.yokonavi.com/eg) A comprehensive Fukuoka/Hakata tourist information site.

Medical Services

International Clinic Tojin-machi (☎717-1000; http://internationalclinic.org; 1-4-6 Jigyo, Chūō-ku; ℝTōjin-machi, exit 1) Contact this fluent multilingual clinic for general medical services and emergencies. From the station, walk upstairs and continue two blocks.

Money

In addition to post office and Seven Bank ATMs, banks and ATMs offer currency exchange at Fukuoka Airport, there's a 24-hour Citibank ATM (シティバンク ATM) in Tenjin, and most banks around JR Hakata Station and Tenjin handle foreign-exchange services.

Post

The central post office (福岡中央郵便局) is one block northeast of Tenjin subway station, and Hakata post office (博多郵便局) is just outside JR Hakata Station's Hakata-guchi.

Tourist Information

ACROS Fukuoka (アクロス福岡; ☎725-9100; www.acros.or.jp/r_facilities/information.html, in Japanese; Cultural Information Centre, 2nd fl, ACROS Bldg, 1-1-1 Tenjin; ⊘10am-6pm, closed 29 Dec-3 Jan; ℝNakasu-Kawabata or Tenjin) Has plenty of English-language information on the prefecture. If you're into architecture, the building itself is worth a look.

Fukuoka Airport (☎international terminal 621-0303, domestic terminal 621-6059; ⊘6.20am-10.20pm; ℝFukuoka Airport) Information desks on the ground floor handle hotel reservations and car rentals.

JR Hakata Station (⊘8am-8pm) The tourist information desk (福岡市観光案内所) here has everything you need. Ask for the free *Fukuoka Welcome Card Guide Book* containing maps and discounts at participating hotels, attractions, shops and restaurants.

Rainbow Plaza (レインボープラザ; ☎733-2220; www.rainbowfia.or.jp; 8F, IMS Bldg, 1-7-11 Tenjin; ⊘10am-8pm, closed 3rd Tue most months; ℝTenjin) The Fukuoka International Association's Rainbow Plaza has bilingual staff, free internet and plenty of foreign-language resources.

Travel Agencies

HIS Travel (☎415-6121; 1st fl, 2-6-10 Hakata-ekimae; ⊘10am-6.30pm Mon-Fri, 11am-4.30pm Sat; ℝHakata) Discount international and domestic arrangements can be made at the Hakata branch of this international chain.

JR Kyūshū Travel Agency (☎431-6215; 1-1 Chuo-gai, Hakata-eki; ⊘10am-8pm Mon-Fri, to 6pm Sat & Sun; ℝHakata) Provides bookings and advice for travel within Kyūshū and Japan. Located within JR Hakata Station.

No 1 Travel (ナンバーワントラベル; ☎761-9203; www.no1-travel.com/fuk/index.html; 3rd fl, ACROS Fukuoka Bldg, 1-1-1 Tenjin; ⊘10am-6.30pm Mon-Fri, 11am-4.30pm Sat; ℝNakasu-Kawabata or Tenjin) For discount international airfares and reliable information in English.

❶ Getting There & Away

Air

Fukuoka Airport (☎international 621-0303, domestic 621-6059; www.fuk-ab.co.jp) is an international hub serving carriers from east and Southeast Asia, as well as many domestic routes including Tokyo (¥36,800, 1½ hours, from Haneda and Narita airports), Osaka (¥21,900, one hour) and Okinawa (Naha; from ¥27,500, 1½ hours).

Cut-rate carrier **Skymark** (☎736-3131, in Tokyo 03-3433-7026; www.skymark.co.jp/en) flies to Tokyo's Haneda Airport (from ¥16,800).

Boat

Ferries from Hakata connect to Okinawa and other islands off Kyūshū. **Beetle** (☎in Japan 092-281-2315, in Korea 051-465-6111; www.jrbeetle.co.jp/english) high-speed hydrofoils connect

Fukuoka with Busan in Korea (one way/round trip ¥13,000/24,000, three hours, at least four daily). The **Camellia line** (☑ in Japan 092-262-2323, in Korea 051-466-7799; www.camellia-line .co.jp, in Japanese & Korean) has a regular ferry service from Fukuoka to Busan (one way ¥9000, six hours, daily at noon). Both ships dock at Chūō Futō (Hakata Port Ferry Terminal) via bus 88 from JR Hakata Station (¥220), or bus 80 from Tenjin (Solaria Stage-mae; ¥180).

Bus

Long-distance buses (☑ English information 733-3333) depart from the Fukuoka Kōtsū Centre (福岡交通センター) next to JR Hakata Station (Hakata-gate) and also from the Tenjin bus centre. Destinations include Tokyo (¥15,000, 14½ hours), Osaka (from ¥7000, 9½ hours), Nagoya (¥10,500, 11 hours) and many towns in Kyūshū; ask about discounted round-trip fares.

Train

JR Hakata Station (☑ English information 471-8111, JR English info line 03-3423-0111) is the hub of travel in northern Kyūshū. *Shinkansen* services operate to/from Tokyo (¥22,520, five hours), Osaka (¥15,090, 2½ to three hours), Hiroshima (¥9100, 1½ hours), Kumamoto (¥5190, 50 minutes) and Kagoshima-Chūō (¥10,370, one hour and 40 minutes).

Within Kyūshū, the JR Nippō line runs through Beppu and Miyazaki; the Sasebo line runs from Saga to Sasebo; and the Nagasaki line runs to Nagasaki. You can also travel by subway and JR train to Karatsu and continue to Nagasaki by train.

ⓘ Getting Around

To/From the Airport

The subway takes just five minutes to reach JR Hakata Station (¥250) and 11 minutes to Tenjin (¥250). Shuttle buses connect domestic and international terminals.

Taxis cost around ¥1600 to Tenjin/Hakata.

ⓘ KYŪSHŪ SHINKANSEN

Hakata Station in Fukuoka used to be the western terminus of the *shinkansen* from Honshū, but as of March 2011 the completion of the Kyūshū *shinkansen* means that it's possible to travel more than 910km from Shin-Osaka in Osaka to Kagoshima-Chūō Station without changing trains, in a little over five hours. Between Hakata and Kagoshima-Chūō the journey takes just over 1½ hours. Other stops along the way include Kurume and Kumamoto.

Bus

City bus services operate from the Fukuoka Kōtsū Centre adjacent to JR Hakata Station and from the Nishitetsu Tenjin Bus Terminal (西鉄天神バスセンター). Many stop in front of the station (Hakata-guchi). Specially marked buses have a flat ¥100 rate for city-centre rides, or a one-day pass costs ¥600/1000 for one/two adults.

Train

Fukuoka has three subway lines (subway.city. fukuoka.lg.jp; ⊙5.30am-12.25am), of which visitors will find the Kūkō (Airport) line most useful, running from Fukuoka Airport to Meinohama Station via Hakata, Nakasu-Kawabata and Tenjin stations. Fares start at ¥200 (¥100 if going just one stop); a one-day pass costs adult/child ¥600/300.

Dazaifu　太宰府

☑ 092 / POP 70,245

Dazaifu, former governmental centre of Kyūshū and now home to Japan's newest national museum, has a beautiful cluster of temples and a famous shrine, making for a popular day trip from Fukuoka. The **tourist information office** (☑925-1880; ⊙9am-5.30pm) at Nishitetsu Dazaifu Station has helpful staff and an English-language map.

⊙ Sights

Kyūshū National Museum　MUSEUM
(九州国立博物館; www.kyuhaku.com; 4-7-2 Ishibashi, Dazaifu City; adult/student ¥420/210; ⊙9.30am-5pm, closed Mon) Built into the tranquil hills of Dazaifu and reached through a colour-shifting tunnel, this striking structure (built in 2005) resembles a massive space station for the arts. Highlights include Jōmon pottery, a fascinating Silk Road exhibit, stone carvings of AD 1st-century women with spears on horseback and a delicate 13th-century oil-spot *tenmoku* tea bowl. Self-guided audio tours and HD video theatre are free, and there's a wonderful 'please touch' section for the youngest visitors. The architect was Fukuoka's own Kikutake Kiyonori, who also built the Edo-Tokyo Museum (p81).

Tenman-gū　SHRINE
(天満宮; www.dazaifutenmangu.or.jp; 4-7-1 Saifu) Poet and scholar Sugawara-no-Michizane was a distinguished figure in the Kyoto court until he fell afoul of political intrigue and was exiled to distant Dazaifu, where he died two years later. Subsequent disasters that struck Kyoto were blamed on his unfair dismissal,

TACHIARAI

From 1919 to 1945, the isolated farm village of Tachiarai (大刀洗) hosted a training school for Japanese fighter pilots, including some on kamikaze suicide missions. Expanded in 2009, **Tachiarai Heiwa Kinenkan** (大刀洗平和記念館; Tachiari Peace Memorial Museum; admission ¥500; ⊙9.30am-5pm) shows the rigorous training these men endured. English signage is basic, but the artefacts are evocative (uniforms, medals, gold-plated sake cups etc). The centrepiece is a jet fighter shot down during the war and recovered from Hakata Bay in 1996. The museum also memorialises kamikaze pilots and townspeople who died during a USAF B-29 bombing on 27 March 1945.

The museum is across from Tachiarai Station. From Fukuoka, take the Nishitetsu line to Nishitetsu Ogōri (¥500, 30 minutes); from Dazaifu (¥330) it takes 25 minutes plus transfer time at Nishitetsu Futsukaichi. Then walk to Ogōri Station on the Amagi Railway for the trip to Tachiarai (¥280, 15 minutes). JR passengers can transfer to the Amagi Railway at Kiyama (¥330, 20 minutes).

and he became deified as Tenman Tenjin, god of culture and scholars. Among the countless visitors to the grand, sprawling Tenman-gū, his shrine and burial place, are students hoping to pass college entrance exams. The *hondō* (main hall) was rebuilt in 1591.

Behind the shrine is the **Kankō Historical Museum** (菅公歴史館; admission ¥200; ⊙9am-4.30pm Wed-Mon), with dioramas showing Tenjin's life (an English leaflet provides explanations). Across the grounds, the **Daizifu Tenman-gū Treasure House** (太宰府天満宮宝物殿; admission ¥300; ⊙9am-4.30pm, closed Mon) has artefacts from his life including some excellent swords.

Every second month the shrine hosts an *omoshiro-ichi* (market), selling treasures from antique kimonos to Mickey Mouse telephones. Dates can vary, so check with tourist information.

Kōmyōzen-ji
TEMPLE

(光明禅寺; admission ¥200; ⊙9am-4.30pm) Secreted away on the southern edge of Dazaifu, this small temple has an exquisite jewel of a Zen garden. It's a peaceful contrast to the crowds at the nearby shrine.

Kaidan-in
MONASTERY

(戒壇院) Across town, nestled among rice paddies and reachable by bus (¥100), Kaidan-in dates from 761 and was one of the most important Buddhist ordination monasteries in Japan.

Kanzeon-ji
TEMPLE

(観世音寺) Adjacent to the monastery, this temple dates from 746 but only the great bell, said to be Japan's oldest, remains from the original construction. Its **treasure hall**

(宝蔵; admission ¥500; ⊙9am-4.30pm) has an impressive collection of statuary, most of it wood, dating from the 10th to 12th centuries. Many of the items show Indian or Tibetan influence.

Dazaifu Exhibition Hall
MUSEUM

(大宰府展示館; admission ¥150; ⊙9am-4.30pm, closed Mon) Dazaifu Exhibition Hall displays finds from local archaeological excavations. Nearby are the **Tofurō ruins** (都府楼) of ancient government buildings.

Enoki-sha (榎社) is where Sugawara-no-Michizane died. His body was transported to Tenman-gū on the ox cart that appears in so many local depictions.

❶ Getting There & Around

The private Nishitetsu train line connects Nishitetsu Fukuoka (in Tenjin) with Dazaifu (¥390, 25 minutes). Change trains at Nishitetsu Futsukaichi Station. Bicycles can be rented (per three hours/day ¥300/500) at Nishitetsu Dazaifu Station.

Kurume
久留米

⚑0942 / POP 303,000

Kurume, south of Dazaifu, is sure to gain prominence as a stop on the new Kyūshū *shinkansen*. You don't even need to leave the station to purchase its most famous crafts: splash-dyed indigo textiles, papermaking, lacquerware and bamboo work are all for sale by the tourist information office. It's about 30 minutes on foot or a quick bus ride between the *shinkansen* station and the other main gateway, Nishitetsu Kurume Station (which is also closer to sights).

Narita-san (成田山; ⊙7am-5pm), a branch of the temple in Narita (see p160), is the town's biggest attraction. Its 62m-high statue of Kannon stands beside a miniaturised replica of Borobudur. Inside the statue you can climb up past Buddhist treasures and religious dioramas right into the divine forehead. Narita-san is about 30 minutes by bus from the town centre.

Between the two stations is **Teramachi** (Temple Town), where 17 temples, ancient to contemporary, make for a nice ramble.

Ishibashi Museum of Art (石橋美術館; www.ishibashi-museum.gr.jp; adult/concession ¥500/300; ⊙10am-5pm, closed Mon) boasts a private collection of Asian and Western art, particularly Nihonga (Japanese oil paintings) by Aoki Shigeru and Kishida Ryu. The collection was assembled by the founder of the Bridgestone Tyre Company (which has a plant nearby), who felt strongly that art should be accessible to everybody.

Kurume can be reached from Hakata by *shinkansen* (¥2630, 20 minutes) or on the JR Kagoshima line (¥720, 40 minutes). You can also take the Nishitetsu line from Nishitetsu Fukuoka Station in Tenjin to Nishitetsu Kurume Station (¥600, 40 minutes).

SAGA PREFECTURE

Occupying Kyūshū's northwestern corner, Saga-ken (佐賀県) is chiefly known for three towns: Karatsu, Imari and Arita. The towns were central to Japan's historic pottery trade. Karatsu is at the base of the scenic Higashi-Matsūra Peninsula, whose dramatic coastline was pounded into shape by the roiling Sea of Genkai.

Karatsu   唐津

☑0955 / POP 130,000

This world-renowned pottery town may not be as busy as it once was, but pottery fanatics will be in their element. Historically, Karatsu's Korean influences elevated the town's craft from useful ceramics to art. There are some historic buildings and a homey Shōwa-era town centre.

At JR Karatsu Station, the **tourist information office** (☑72-4963; ⊙9am-6pm) has a selection of English-language tourist maps and brochures, and some enthusiastic English-speaking staff who can book accommodation.

◉ Sights & Activities

Around town are **kilns and studios** where you can see local potters at work, and ceramic shops line the street between Karatsu Station and the town centre.

A **walking path** cuts through the pine trees planted behind the 5km-long Niji-no Matsubara Beach.

FREE **Nakazato Tarōemon**   ART GALLERY
(3-6-29 Chōda; ⊙9am-5.30pm) This kiln-gallery is dedicated to the life and work of the potter responsible for the revival of Karatsu ware. His work is in the inner gallery.

KYŪSHŪ POTTERY TOWNS

In mountainous Kyūshū many villages had difficulty growing rice and looked towards other industries to survive. Access to good clay, forests and streams made pottery-making a natural choice and a number of superb styles can be found here.

Karatsu, Arita and Imari are the major pottery towns of Saga-ken. From the early 17th century, pottery was produced in this area by captive Korean potters, experts who were zealously guarded so that neither artist nor the secrets of their craft could escape. When trade routes opened up to the west, potters in Japan began imitating the more highly decorated, Chinese-style ware popular in Europe. The pottery styles are often named after the town with the suffix -*yaki* (pottery) added to the town name.

» **Arita** Highly decorated porcelain, usually with squares of blue, red, green or gold.

» **Imari** Fine, white-and-blue porcelain, bursting into colours in the mid-Edo period.

» **Karatsu** Marked by subtle earthy tones, prized for its use in tea ceremony.

In southern Kyūshū, Kagoshima Prefecture is known for Satsuma-yaki (Satsuma is the feudal name for that region). Styles vary from crackled glazes to porcelains painted with gleaming gold, and rougher, more ponderous 'black Satsuma' ware.

FREE Karatsu Ware Federation Exhibition Hall
ART GALLERY

(2nd fl, Arpino Bldg; ⊘9am-6pm) Adjacent to Karatsu Station, this exhibition hall displays and sells (from ¥500) local potters' works and provides contact information.

Kyū-Takatori-tei
NOTABLE BUILDING

(5-40 Kita-jōnai; admission ¥500; ⊘9am-5pm Tue-Sun) Kyū-Takatori-tei is a fabulously restored house of a local trader, built in a mix of Japanese and Western styles with lantern-filled gardens, a Buddhist altar room, a wealth of paintings on cedar boards and an indoor Noh stage. An English audioguide rents for ¥300.

Karatsu-jō
CASTLE

(8-1 Higashi-jōnai; admission ¥400; ⊘9am-5pm) This reconstructed castle, picturesquely perched on a hill overlooking the sea, houses antique ceramics, samurai armour and archaeological displays.

Hikiyama Festival Float Exhibition Hall
MUSEUM

(6-33 Nishi-jōnai; admission ¥300; ⊘9am-5pm) Contains the 14 amazing floats used in the annual Karatsu Kunchi Matsuri. Floats include the Aka-jishi (Red Lion, constructed 1819), samurai helmets, and the auspicious phoenix and sea bream. There's good signage in English, and a video shows festival scenes. It's near scenic **Karatsu-jinja** (3-13 Minami-jōnai), the shrine which sponsors the festival.

✈ Festivals & Events

Doyō-yoichi
NIGHT MARKET

Held in the town centre over four consecutive Saturdays from late July.

Karatsu Kunchi Matsuri
TRADITIONAL

From 2 to 4 November, Karatsu comes to life in this spectacular festival, designated a festival of national cultural importance, dating from 1592. At the highlight of the celebrations, townsfolk carrying massive, exquisitely decorated *hikiyama* (floats) parade from Nishinohama beach into town.

🛏 Sleeping & Eating

TOP CHOICE Yoyōkaku
RYOKAN $$$

(☏72-7181; www.yoyokaku.com; 2-4-40 Higashi-Karatsu; per person incl 2 meals from ¥15,750; P@☏) In a word: gorgeous. Here are some more words: rambling, minimalist, woodwork, pine garden and Karatsu-yaki pottery

for your in-room seafood meals. A real getaway, yet under 10 minutes' walk from the castle. Can't stay here? Visit the on-site gallery of Nakazato family pottery.

Karatsu Dai-Ichi Hotel
HOTEL $$

(☏74-1000; www.kugimoto.co.jp/dai-ichi.info.htm; 488-1 Nishi-Teramachi; s/d/tw from ¥6100/10,000/11,100; P@) A sane choice about five minutes on foot from Karatsu Station. Rooms don't break any style barriers, but they're spotless and the staff are accommodating. Some singles are nonsmoking. The rate includes a simple Continental breakfast.

Kawashima Tōfu
TOFU $$

(☏72-2423; www.zarudoufu.co.jp, in Japanese; Kyōmachi 1775; set meals ¥1575-2675; ⊘8am-6.30pm, meal seatings at 8am, 10am & noon, kaiseki dinner 5.30-10pm) On the shopping street near the station, this renowned tofu shop has been in business since the Edo period and serves set meals (reservations required) around its 10-seat counter. *Zaru-dōfu,* its speciality, is scooped like ice cream and served on Karatsu-yaki plates. No time for a full meal? Try tofu soft cream for ¥200.

In the station are several quick, cheap and cheerful options for noodles, *gyōza* (dumplings) and the like.

ℹ Getting There & Around

From Fukuoka, take the Kūkō (Airport) subway line from Hakata or Tenjin to the end of the line at Meinohama, then change to the JR Chikuhi line to reach Karatsu (¥1110, 70 minutes). From Karatsu to Nagasaki (¥2420, 3½ hours) take the JR Karatsu line to Saga, and the JR Nagasaki line from there.

From Karatsu's **Ōtemachi bus centre** (☏73-7511), highway buses depart for Fukuoka (¥1000, 70 minutes) and Nagasaki (¥2400, two hours).

Tourists are able to borrow bicycles free from the **Arpino** (☏75-5155) building. For excursions around Saga-ken, **Eki-mae Rent-a-Car** is located in front of Karatsu Station, with half- and full-day rentals.

Imari
伊万里

☏0955 / POP 58,050

Imari is the name commonly associated with pottery from this area. Tourist brochures are available at **Imari City Information** (☏23-3479; ⊘9am-6pm) at Imari Station on the regional Matsūra Railway, across the street from JR Imari Station.

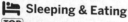

The pottery kilns are concentrated in Ōkawachiyama (大川内山), a 20-minute bus ride (¥150) from the station area. The 30 or so workshops make for a lovely ramble uphill alongside streams and a bridge covered with local shards. Arrive by midday to allow time for exploring and shopping. Buses stop near the bridge at the base of the hill, and there are several cafes throughout the village. Taxis between central Imari and Ōkawachiyama cost approximately ¥1700 each way.

At the bottom of the hill, **Kataoka Tsurutarō Kōgeikan** (片岡鶴太郎工芸館; admission ¥300) gallery is an austere structure dedicated to the intense work of potter-genius Sawada Chitōjin.

On a shopping street near the train station, **Akira Kurosawa Memorial Satellite Studio** (黒澤明記念館サテライトスタジオ; 358 Imari-machi; admission ¥500; ◷9am-5.30pm, to 7pm Sat, closed 2nd & 4th Mon) has little English labelling, but this shouldn't deter fans of one of cinema's greatest visionaries. Explore three floors of memorabilia (including an Oscar trophy, scripts and sketches and many posters of his films), and glimpse behind-the-scenes documentaries and rare footage. It was built in this place because Kurosawa fell in love with the light here while filming *Ran* in Fukuoka-ken. Our favourite part: the gift shop selling unique Kurosawa souvenirs. There's also a lunch and wine bar.

Imari is connected to Karatsu (¥630, 50 minutes) by the JR Chikuhi line, and also to Arita by the private Matsūra-tetsudō line (¥410, 25 minutes).

WORTH A TRIP

YOBUKO

The quaint, dwindling fishing port of Yobuko (呼子) has a wonderful **morning market** (◷7.30am-noon) for fish and produce. Local delicacies include squid sashimi and tempura. While it's easily done as a morning excursion from Karatsu (Shōwa bus; ¥730, 30 minutes), if you've fallen in love with the place there's a series of wooden ryokan lining a narrow lane alongside the waterfront (from around ¥9500 including meals). Nightly you can watch the flickering lights of the departing fishing boats heading out to sea, and ready yourself for the next morning's market.

Arita 有田

☏0955 / POP 21,390

Kaolin clay was discovered here in 1615 by Ri Sampei, a naturalised Korean potter, enabling the manufacture of fine porcelain in Japan for the first time. By the mid-17th century, the porcelain was being exported to Europe.

The town of Arita is a beautiful example of how tourism can support the preservation of history and culture. The staff at the tiny **tourist information desk** (☏42-4052; www.arita.or.jp/index_e.html; ◷9am-5pm) inside Arita Station can assist with maps, timetables and accommodation, predominantly small private *minshuku* (guesthouses).

The streets of Arita fill with vendors for the annual **pottery market**, held from 29 April to 5 May.

Between the station and Kyūshū Ceramic Museum is the **Yakimono Sanpo-michi** (Pottery Promenade), housing around 16 galleries. The tourist office has a map that's in Japanese but easy enough to follow.

Out of the town centre, two of Arita-yaki's prime practitioners have been at it for 14 generations. The **Imaemon Gallery** (今右衛門ギャラリー; ☏42-5550; admission ¥300; ◷9.30am-4.30pm, closed Mon) and **Kakiemon Kiln** (柿右衛門窯; ☏43-2267; admission free; ◷9am-5pm) both have museums in addition to sales shops. **Genemon Kiln** (源右衛門窯; ☏42-4164; admission free; ◷8am-5.30pm Mon-Sat) makes and sells more contemporary styles. These can be reached by a short taxi ride (about ¥1000), or infrequent community bus from the station.

Taxi or Arita bus (¥150, four daily) can also take you out to the **clay mines** (磁石場; *jisekiba*), from where you can walk back to the station in about an hour, via a route lined with numerous old houses with left-over pottery used in the bricks, as well as many galleries.

A short train ride east of Arita, **Takeo Onsen** (武雄温泉) is a modern hot-springs town with about a dozen onsen hotels. For a quick dip, the original **Takeo Onsen** (admission ¥400; ◷6.30am-midnight) has a 1300-year history and is said to have refreshed the armies of Toyotomi Hideyoshi. Its impressive lacquered Chinese-style entrance gate was built without nails, and the oldest existing bathing building (Moto-yu) is a wood-built hall from 1870. It's a 15-minute walk west of the station's north exit.

DON'T MISS

KYŪSHŪ CERAMIC MUSEUM

The best ceramics museum in the region, about five minutes on foot from Arita Station, is the large, hilltop **Kyūshū Ceramic Museum** (九州陶磁文化館; Toshaku Otsu; admission free; ⊙9am-5pm, closed Mon). The Shibata Collection comprehensively showcases the development and styles of Kyūshū's many ceramic arts, with excellent English signage.

The bold red and green **Takeo Onsen Youth Hostel** (武雄温泉ユースホステル; ☎0954-22-2490; fax 0954-20-1208; 16060 Nagashima; dm with breakfast member/nonmember ¥3300/3900) is comfortable and has hot-spring baths and dinner available for ¥1500 extra. Ring ahead to request a pick-up if you might miss the last bus to the hostel (¥250, 4pm).

The private Matsūra-tetsudō line connects Arita with Imari (¥410, 25 minutes). JR *tokkyū* trains between Hakata (¥2690, 80 minutes) and Sasebo (¥1050, 30 minutes) stop at Arita and Takeo Onsen. Takeo Onsen is also connected to Arita by local trains (¥270, 20 minutes). Community buses (¥150) cover most sights, but infrequent departures mean that you'll save time by taking taxis (about ¥1000 to most sights). At Arita Station, you can rent bicycles (¥300 per day).

NAGASAKI PREFECTURE

Nagasaki 長崎

☑095 / POP 443,400

How ironic it is that the name Nagasaki conjures up the tragic destruction of war. For much of its history the city of Nagasaki was Japan's only link to the outside world, and other parts of Nagasaki Prefecture (長崎県) served a similar role. A visit to the scenes of atomic devastation is a must, but beyond them you'll find that this one-of-a-kind, embracing city boasts a colourful trading history, alluring churches, shrines, temples and an East-meets-West culinary scene, prettily set within hills around a harbour. Schedule a few days here to meet the people and get a sense of Nagasaki's spirit.

History

Nagasaki Prefecture played a multilayered role in Japan's emergence as a modern nation. An off-course Chinese ship landed on southern Kagoshima-ken in 1543, with guns and Portuguese adventurers aboard, followed some six years later by the missionary St Francis Xavier in 1549, ushering in what became known as Japan's 'Christian Century' (1549–1650).

By 1570 Nagasaki was an active trading port, with Portuguese traders acting as intermediaries between Japan, China and Korea, and it quickly became a fashionable and wealthy city. In 1580 the *daimyō* (domain lord) Ōmura Sumitada, one of Francis Xavier's converts, briefly ceded Nagasaki to the Society of Jesuits.

By decade's end, however, the shōgun had come to see Christianity as a threat, reclaimed Nagasaki and expelled the Jesuits; 26 European and Japanese Christians were crucified here in 1597. Catholic Portuguese and Spanish traders were replaced with the Protestant Dutch, thought to be more interested in trade than religion, and Christianity was officially banned altogether in 1613. Following a peasant uprising at Shimabara (in southeastern Nagasaki Prefecture) in 1637–38, which was perceived as a Christian revolt, authorities went even further, forbidding all contact with foreigners, including travel outside Japan, which was the beginning of a period called *sakoku* (national seclusion).

The single exception to this closure was Dejima, a man-made island in Nagasaki harbour where Dutch traders lived under close scrutiny. Via this small outpost, a trickle of Western science and culture found its way into Japan. When Japan reopened its doors to the West in the 1850s, Nagasaki became once again a major economic force, particularly in shipbuilding, the industry that ultimately led to its tragic bombing on 9 August 1945.

⊙ Sights

Nagasaki's sights are scattered over a broad area, but it's feasible to walk from the Shianbashi nightlife and shopping district about 2km south of JR Nagasaki Station, through Shinchi Chinatown, all the way south to the Dutch slopes and Glover Garden. The atomic bomb hypocentre is in the suburb of Urakami, about 2.5km north of JR Nagasaki Station.

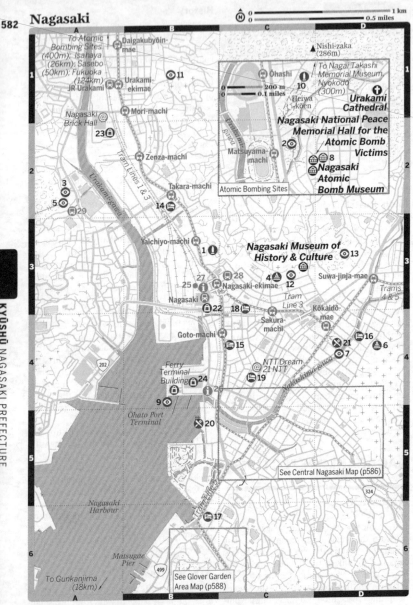

0 ———————————— 1 km
0 ———————————— 0.5 miles

Atomic Bombing Sites

200 m
0.1 miles

Urakami
Cathedral

Nagasaki National Peace
Memorial Hall for the
Atomic Bomb
Victims

Nagasaki
Atomic
Bomb Museum

URAKAMI (NORTHERN NAGASAKI)

Urakami, the hypocentre of the atomic explosion, is today a prosperous, peaceful suburb. While nuclear ruin seems comfortably far away seven decades later, many sights here keep the memory alive.

TOP CHOICE Nagasaki Atomic Bomb Museum

MUSEUM

(長崎原爆資料館; Map p582; www1.city.nagasaki.nagasaki.jp/peace/English.abm; 7-8 Hirano-machi; admission ¥200, audioguide ¥150; ⏰8.30am-5.30pm Sep-Apr, to 6.30pm May-Aug;

Nagasaki

🏠Matsuyama-machi) An essential Nagasaki experience, this sombre place recounts the city's destruction and loss of life through photos and artefacts, including mangled rocks, trees, furniture, pottery and clothing, first-hand accounts from survivors and stories of heroic relief efforts. Exhibits cover Japan's military prewar aggression and the postbombing struggle for nuclear disarmament, and conclude with a chilling illustration of which nations still bear nuclear arms.

FREE **Nagasaki National Peace Memorial Hall for the Atomic Bomb Victims**   MONUMENT
(国立長崎原爆死没者追悼平和祈念館; Map p582; www.peace-nagasaki.go.jp; 7-8 Hirano-machi; ⊙8.30am-5.30pm Sep-Apr, to 6.30pm May-Aug; 🏠Matsuyama-machi) Adjacent to the Atomic Bomb Museum and completed in 2003, this minimalist memorial is a profoundly moving place. It is best approached by quietly reading the carved inscriptions and walking around the sculpted water basin above before entering the hall below. Be prepared for tears.

FREE **Heiwa-kōen**   PARK
(平和公園; Peace Park; Map p582; 🏠Ōhashi) North of the hypocentre, the Peace Park is presided over by the 10-tonne bronze **Nagasaki Peace Statue** (平和祈念像), designed in 1955 by Kitamura Seibo, and includes the Peace Symbol Zone, an unusual sculpture garden with contributions from around the world. On 9 August, a rowdy antinuclear protest is held within earshot of the more respectful official memorial ceremony for those lost to the bomb.

FREE **Atomic Bomb Hypocentre Park**   PARK
(長崎爆心地公園; Map p582; 🏠Matsuyama-machi) The park has a smooth, black stone column marking the point above which the bomb exploded. Nearby are bomb-blasted relics, including a section of the wall of the Urakami Cathedral.

FREE **Urakami Cathedral**   CHURCH
(浦上天主堂; Map p582; 1-79 Motō-machi; ⊙9am-5pm, closed Mon) Once the largest church in Asia (1914), the cathedral took three

THE ATOMIC EXPLOSION

When USAF B-29 bomber *Bock's Car* set off from the Marianas to drop a second atomic bomb on Japan, the target was Kokura on Kyūshū's northeastern coast. Due to poor visibility, the crew diverted to the secondary target, Nagasaki. It was 9 August 1945.

The B-29 arrived over Nagasaki at 10.58am amid heavy cloud. When a momentary gap appeared and the Mitsubishi Arms Factory was sighted, the 4.57-tonne 'Fat Man' bomb, with an explosive power equivalent to 21.3 kilotonnes of TNT (almost twice that of Hiroshima's 'Little Boy'), was released over Nagasaki.

The bomb missed the arms factory, its intended target, and exploded at 11.02am, at an altitude of 500m almost directly above the largest Catholic church in Asia (Urakami Cathedral). In an instant, it annihilated the suburb of Urakami and 74,000 of Nagasaki's 240,000 people. Ground temperatures at the hypocentre were estimated between 3000 and 4000°C, and as high as 600°C 1.5km away. Everything within a 1km radius of the explosion was destroyed, and searing winds estimated at 170km/h (typhoons generally top out at 80km/h) swept down the valley of the Urakami-gawa towards the city centre. With able-bodied men at work or at war, most victims were women, children and senior citizens, as well as 13,000 conscripted Korean labourers and 200 allied POWs. Another 75,000 people were horribly injured (and it is estimated that as many people died as a result of the after-effects). After the resulting fires burned out, a third of the city was gone.

Yet the damage might have been even worse had the targeted arms factory been hit. Unlike in the flatlands of Hiroshima or the Nagasaki port itself, the hills around the river valley protected outlying suburbs from even greater damage.

decades to complete and three seconds to flatten. This smaller replacement cathedral was completed in 1959 on the ruins of the original. Walk around the side of the hill to see one of the buttresses where the original building fell after the blast.

Nagai Takashi Memorial Museum MUSEUM
(永井隆記念館; off Map p582; 22-6 Ueno-machi; admission ¥100; ◎9am-5pm) The courage and faith of one man in the face of overwhelming adversity is the subject of this small but quietly moving museum. Already suffering from leukaemia, Dr Nagai survived the atomic explosion but lost his wife to it. He immediately devoted himself to the treatment of bomb victims until his death in 1951. In his final days, he continued to write prolifically and secure donations for survivors and orphans, earning the nickname 'Saint of Nagasaki'. Ask to watch the video in English.

Next door is **Nyokodō** (如己堂), the simple hut from which Dr Nagai worked – its name comes from the biblical commandment 'love thy neighbour as thyself'.

FREE **Nagasaki City Museum of History & Folklore** MUSEUM
(長崎市歴史民俗資料館; Map p582; 7-8 Hirano-machi; ◎9am-5pm, closed Mon; ◎Matsuyama-machi) This old-fashioned case museum highlights the connections between Japa-

nese, Chinese, Dutch and Portuguese cultures here in Nagasaki, with antique items relating to daily life, plus a toy display. It's inside the Nagasaki Peace Hall building.

FREE **One-Pillar Torii** LANDMARK
(一本柱鳥居; Map p582; ◎Daigakubōyin-mae) The blast knocked down half of the stone entrance arch to the Sanno-jinja shrine, 800m southeast of the hypocentre, but the other pillar remains.

CENTRAL NAGASAKI

TOP
CHOICE **Dejima** HISTORICAL SITE
(出島) By 1641 the Tokugawa shōgunate had banished all foreigners from Japan, with one exception: Dejima, a fan-shaped, man-made island 560m in circumference (15,000 sq m), in Nagasaki harbour. From then until the 1850s, this small Dutch trading post was the sole sanctioned outside presence in Japan; about the only local contact for the Dutch segregated here was with trading partners and courtesans, and an annual official visit to Edo, which took 90 days!

These days the city has filled in around the island and you might walk right past it. Don't. Seventeen buildings, walls and structures (plus a miniature Dejima) have been painstakingly reconstructed based on pictoral representations into the **Dejima Museum** (出島資料館; Map p586; www1.city

.nagasaki.nagasaki.jp/dejima; 6-1 Dejima-machi; admission ¥500; ⊙8am-6pm; 🚃Dejima). Completed in 2006, the buildings here are as instructive inside as they are good-looking outside, with exhibits covering the spread of Western learning and culture, archaeological digs, and rooms combining Japanese tatami (woven floor matting) with Western wallpaper. There's excellent English signage.

🔝CHOICE Nagasaki Museum of History & Culture
MUSEUM

(長崎歴史文化博物館; Map p582; www.nmhc .jp; 1-1-1 Tateyama; admission ¥500; ⊙8.30am-7pm, closed 3rd Tue of month; 🚃Sakura-machi) This large, excellent museum opened in 2005 to focus on Nagasaki's proud history of international exchange. The main gallery is a fabulous reconstruction of a section of the Edo-period Nagasaki Magistrate's Office, which controlled trade and diplomacy. The free English-language audioguide is one of the best in the country.

Suwa-jinja
SHRINE

(諏訪神社; Map p582; 18-15 Kaminishiyama-machi; ⊙24hr; 🚃Suwa-jinja-mae) Situated on a forested hilltop and reached via multiple staircases, this enormous shrine was established in 1625. Around the grounds are statues of *komainu* (protective dogs), including the *kappa-komainu* (water-sprite dogs), which you pray to by dribbling water onto the plates on their heads. The *gankake komainu* (turntable dog) was often called on by prostitutes, who prayed that storms would arrive, forcing the sailors to stay at the port another day. Between 7 and 9 October each year, the shrine comes to life with the dragon dance of Kunchi Matsuri, Nagasaki's most important annual celebration.

Nagasaki Station Area
NEIGHBOURHOOD

The **26 Martyrs Memorial** (日本二十六聖人殉教地; Map p582) features reliefs commemorating the six Spanish and 20 Japanese crucified in 1597, when authorities cracked down on practising Christians. The youngest killed were boys aged 12 and 13. Behind the memorial is a simple Christianity-related **museum** (7-8 Nishizaka-machi; admission ¥250; 🚃JR Nagasaki).

Fukusai-ji Kannon (福済寺〈長崎観音〉; Nagasaki Universal Kannon Temple; Map p582; 2-56 Chikugo-machi; admission ¥200; ⊙8am-4pm; 🚃Sakura-machi) is in the form of a huge astral turtle carrying an 18m-high figure of the goddess Kannon. Inside, a Foucault

pendulum, demonstrating the rotation of the earth, hangs from the top. It's the third-largest such pendulum in the world, after those in St Petersburg and Paris. The original temple, built in 1628, was completely burnt by the A-bomb fire. The replacement was built in 1976. The temple bell tolls at 11.02am daily, the time of the explosion.

Nearby, the gardens of the temple **Shōfuku-ji** (聖福寺; Map p582; 3-77 Tamazono-machi; ⊙24hr; 🚃Sakura-machi) contain an arched stone gate dating from 1657. It's worth the significant uphill climb to reach the palmy inner court and main building, dating from 1715. Also note the interesting *onigawara* (ogre-covered wall) and sacred kiln used for the ceremonial burning of disused Buddhist scriptures.

Teramachi
NEIGHBOURHOOD

(寺町) Between the Shianbashi shopping and nightlife area and Nakashima-gawa (the smaller of the city's two rivers), the Teramachi district is anchored at either end by Nagasaki's two best-known temples.

Sōfuku-ji (崇福寺; Map p586; 7-5 Kajiya-machi; admission ¥300; ⊙8am-5pm; 🚃Shōkakuji-shita) was built in 1629 by Chinese monk Chaonian. Its red entrance gate (Daiippo-mon) exemplifies Ming-dynasty architecture. Inside the temple is a huge cauldron that was used to prepare food for famine victims in 1681, and a statue of Maso, goddess of the sea.

From here, it's a relaxing walk of about 1.2km to **Kōfuku-ji** (興福寺; Map p582; 4-32 Tera-machi; admission ¥300; ⊙8am-5pm; 🚃Kōkaidō-mae), along a side street lined with more temples, stone walls and shops selling Buddhist articles, crafts and dolls. The temple dates from the 1620s and is noted for the Ming architecture of the main hall. Like Sōfuku-ji, it is an Ōbaku Zen temple – and the oldest in Japan.

FREE Nakashima-gawa
PROMENADE

(中島川; 🚃Kōkaidō-mae or Nigiwai-bashi) Parallel to Teramachi, the Nakashima-gawa is crossed by a picturesque collection of 17th-century stone bridges. At one time, each bridge was the distinct entranceway to a separate temple. Best known is the double-arched **Megane-bashi** (めがね橋; Spectacles Bridge; Map p582), originally built in 1634 and so called because the reflection of the arches in the water looks like a pair of Meiji-era spectacles. Six of the 10 bridges, including Megane-bashi, were washed away by flooding in 1982 and restored using the recovered stones.

KYUSHU NAGASAKI

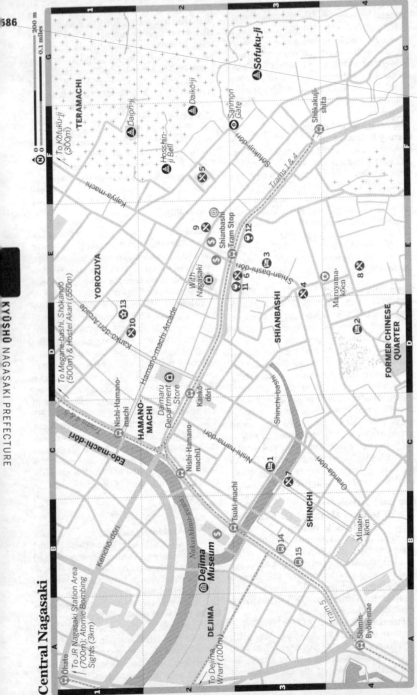

Central Nagasaki

586

N

0   200 m
0   0.1 miles

TERAMACHI

YOROZUYA

HAMANO-MACHI

SHIANBASHI

FORMER CHINESE QUARTER

SHINCHI

DEJIMA

Sōfuku-ji

Daikō-ji

Sanmon Gate

Shōkaku-ji-shita

Dajō-ji

Hosshin-ji Bell

Kaiya-machi

Shōkaku-ji-dōri

Trams 1 & 4

5

Shianbashi Tram Stop

9

12

With Nagasaki

3

Shian-bashi-dōri

11 6

4

8

Maruyama-kōen

13

10

Kankō-dōri Arcade

Hamano-machi Arcade

Daimaru Department Store

Kankō-dōri

Nishi-Hamano-machi

Nishi-Hamano-machi

Nishi-hama-dōri

Shinchi-bashi

Oranda-dōri

Minato-kōen

To Megane-bashi, Shōkandō (500m) & Hostel Akari (550m)

Edo-machi-dōri

Trams 4 & 5

Kenchō-dōri

Nakashima-gawa

Tsuki-machi

1

14

15

7

Dejima Museum

Tram 5

Shimin-Byōin-mae

Ohato

To JR Nagasaki Station Area (700m); Atomic Bombing Sights (3km)

To Dejima Wharf (100m)

Central Nagasaki

Shinchi Chinatown NEIGHBOURHOOD
(新地中華街; Map p586; 🚊Tsuki-machi) During Japan's long period of seclusion, Chinese traders were theoretically just as restricted as the Dutch, but in practice they were relatively free. Only a couple of buildings remain from the old area, but Nagasaki still has an energetic Chinese community, evident in the city's culture, architecture, festivals and cuisine. Visitors come from far and wide to eat here and shop for Chinese crafts and trinkets.

Inasa-yama Lookout LANDMARK
(稲佐山展望台) From the western side of the harbour, a **cable car** (長崎ロープウェイ; Map p582; return ¥1200; ⊘9am-10pm; 🚊Kōkaidō-mae) ascends every 20 minutes to the top of 333m-high Inasa-yama, offering superb views over Nagasaki, particularly at night. Buses 3 and 4 leave from outside JR Nagasaki Station going towards Shimo-Ōhashi; get off at the Ropeway-mae (ロープウェイ前) stop and walk up the stone steps through the grounds of **Fuchi-jinja** (淵神社).

Elsewhere on the mountainside is **Onsen Fukunoyu** (admission ¥800; ⊘9.30am-1am). In addition to the wet baths, try the *gaban-yoku* stone baths (additional ¥700), with temperatures from a balmy 38°C to the *are-you-nuts?* 70°C. There's a free shuttle from JR Nagasaki and Urakami stations (20 minutes, twice per hour).

SOUTHERN NAGASAKI

Glover Garden GARDEN
(グラバー園; Map p588; 🕿822-8223; www.glover-garden.jp; 8-1 Minami-yamatemachi; adult/student ¥600/300; ⊘8am-9.30pm 29 Apr–mid-Jul, to 6pm mid-Jul–28 Apr; 🚊Ōura Tenshudō-shita) Some former homes of the city's Meiji-period European residents have been reassembled in this hillside garden. Glover Garden is named after Thomas Glover (1838–1911), the Scottish merchant who built Japan's first railway, helped establish the shipbuilding industry and whose arms-importing operations influenced the course of the Meiji Restoration.

The best way to explore the garden is to take the moving walkways to the top of the hill then walk back down. The **Mitsubishi No 2 Dock building** (旧三菱第2ドックハウス) is highest, with panoramic views of the city and harbour from the 2nd floor. Next highest is **Walker House** (旧ウォーカー住宅), filled with artefacts donated by the families, followed by **Ringer House** (旧リンガー住宅), **Alt House** (旧オルト住宅) and finally **Glover House** (旧グラバー住宅). Halfway down is the **Madame Butterfly Statue** of Japanese opera singer Miura Tamaki, inspiration of the famous opera by Puccini – the story took place here in Nagasaki. Exit the garden through the **Nagasaki Traditional Performing Arts Museum** (長崎伝統芸能館), which has a display of dragons and floats used in Nagasaki's colourful Kunchi Matsuri.

Ōura Catholic Church CHURCH
(大浦天主堂; Map p588; 🕿823-2628; admission ¥300; ⊘8am-6pm; 🚊Ōura Tenshudō-shita) This hilltop church, Japan's oldest (1865) is dedicated to the 26 Christians who were crucified in Nagasaki in 1597. It's more like a museum than a place of worship, with an ornate Gothic altar and bishop's chair, and an oil painting of the 26 martyrs. To pray for free, use the regular church across the street.

Dutch Slopes HISTORICAL SITE
(オランダ坂; Oranda-zaka; Map p588; 🚊Ishibashi) The gently inclined flagstone streets

Glover Garden Area

known as the Dutch Slopes were once lined with wooden **Dutch houses**. Several buildings here have been beautifully restored and offer glimpses of Japan's early interest in the West. The quiet **Ko-shashin-shiryōkan** (古写真資料館; Museum of Old Photographs; Map p588) and **Maizō-shiryōkan** (埋蔵資料館; Museum of Unearthed Artefacts; Map p588; 6-25 Higashi-yamatemachi; combined admission ¥100; ◷9am-5pm, closed Mon) showcase the area's history (note that most signage is in Japanese).

Historical Museum of China MUSEUM
(中国歴代博物館; Map p588; ☎824-4022; 10-36 Ōuramachi; shrine & museum admission ¥600; ◷8.30am-5.30pm; ⓘIshibashi) This glossy museum of Chinese art spans jade artefacts and Neolithic archaeological finds to terracotta warriors and Qing-dynasty porcelain, much of it on loan from the Palace Museum in Beijing. There's also a large gift shop.

The jauntily painted **Kōshi-byō** (長崎孔子廟) shrine nearby claims to be the only Confucian shrine built by and for Chinese outside of China, and the statues of sages in its courtyard certainly make you feel like you've journeyed across the sea. The original 1893 building was destroyed by fire following the A-bomb explosion.

☞ Tours

One-hour **Nagasaki Harbour Cruises** (長崎港めぐりクルーズ; Map p582; ☎822-5002; Nagasaki Harbour Terminal Bldg; adult/child ¥1300/650) are a great way to glimpse picturesque Nagasaki. Check at the ferry terminal for up-to-date schedules.

✦ Festivals & Events

Peiron Dragon Boat Races   DRAGON BOATS
Colourful boat races were introduced by the Chinese in the mid-1600s, and held to appease the god of the sea. They still take place in Nagasaki Harbour in late July.

Shōrō-nagashi   TRADITIONAL
On 15 August lantern-lit floats are carried down to the harbour in honour of one's ancestors. The boats are hand-crafted from a variety of items (bamboo, wood, rice stems etc) and vary in size depending on the family or individual. Eventually they are carried out to sea and destroyed by the waves. The best viewpoint for the procession is at the Ōhato ferry terminal.

Kunchi Matsuri   TRADITIONAL
Held from 7 to 9 October, this energetic festival features Chinese dragons dancing all around the city but especially at Suwa-jinja (Map p582). The festival is marked by elaborate costumes, fireworks, cymbals and giant dragon puppets on poles.

🛏 Sleeping

For ease of transport and access to restaurants and nightlife, we recommend staying near JR Nagasaki Station or Shianbashi.

TOP CHOICE Sakamoto-ya
RYOKAN $$$

(料亭旅館坂本屋; Map p582; ☎826-8211; www .sakamotoya.co.jp, in Japanese; 2-13 Kanaya-machi; r per person with 2 meals from ¥15,750; ☒Ōhato or Gotō-machi) This magnificent old-school ryokan has been in business since 1894. Look for art-filled rooms, hallways lined with Arita-yaki pottery, postage-stamp-sized gardens, *kaiseki* meals (Japanese haute cuisine) and only 10 rooms for personal service.

Hostel Akari
HOSTEL $

(Map p582; ☎801-7900; www.nagasaki-hostel .com; 2-2 Kajiya-machi; dm/s from ¥2500/3900, d & tw from ¥5600; ☺reception 8am-8pm; ☒@☎; ☒Kōkaidō-mae) This commendably friendly 28-bed hostel sets the standard, with bright, clean Japanese-style rooms with Western-style bedding and bathrooms, uber-helpful staff and a dedicated crew of local volunteers who lead free walking tours around the city. It's by the lovely Nakashima-gawa.

Richmond Hotel Nagasaki Shianbashi
HOTEL $$

(リッチモンドホテル長崎思案橋; Map p586; ☎832-2525; www.richmondhotel.jp; 6-38 Motoshikkui-chō; s/d/tw from ¥8000/11,000/14,000; ☒@; ☒Shianbashi) You can't be closer to the heart of Shianbashi than here. Completed in 2007, rooms are ultra-modern with dark tones and flat-screen TVs. Deluxe rooms are large by Japanese standards and have feature walls. There's a terrific breakfast buffet including Nagasaki specialities.

Hotel Monterey Nagasaki
HOTEL $$

(ホテルモントレ長崎; Map p582; ☎827-7111; www.hotelmonterey.co.jp/nagasaki, in Japanese; 1-22 Ōura-machi; s/d from ¥12,000/16,500; ☒@)

At this Portuguese-themed hotel near the Dutch Slopes and Glover Garden, rooms are spacious and light filled, beds are comfy, and staff are courteous and used to the vagaries of foreign guests. Look for online discounts.

Nishiki-sō Bekkan
MINSHUKU $

(にしき荘別館; Map p586; ☎826-6371; 1-2-7 Nishikojima; r per person ¥4200-5250) It's easy to love this creaky inn perched on a crag and run by the kind and easy-going Fujita family, whose pride in their city and half-century-old home is evident. You'll feel like a guest in a Japanese house, but with the privacy of a hotel. There's a communal stone bath and laundry, or rooms with private facilities are available, and the delights of Shianbashi are on your doorstep.

Best Western Premier Hotel Nagasaki
HOTEL $$

(ベストウエスタンプレミアホテル長崎; Map p582; ☎821-1111; www.bestwestern.com/premier; 2-26 Takara-machi; s/d incl breakfast from ¥15,000/22,000; ℗☒@; ☒Takara-machi) Nagasaki's most extravagant hotel has a vast marble lobby, comfortably elegant rooms with marble bathrooms and panoramic views from the top-floor restaurant, where a Japanese–Western buffet breakfast is served.

Hotel Dormy Inn Nagasaki
HOTEL $

(Map p586; ☎820-5489; www.hotespa.net/hotels/nagasaki; 7-24 Dōza-machi; s/d from ¥4900/8000; ☒@; ☒Tsuki-machi) Adjacent to Chinatown, this spanking-new hotel would be worth it just for the location. Rooms are crisp and neat as a pin with quality mattresses, and there are large gender-separated common baths and saunas in addition to in-room facilities.

KYŪSHŪ NAGASAKI

WORTH A TRIP

GUNKANJIMA

Gunkanjima means 'warship island', a foreboding name that captures the eeriness of this abandoned cluster of buildings rising out of the Pacific. 'Warship' refers to its outline when viewed from afar, and not its purpose, which was harvesting coal from underground mines beginning in 1890. When supplies ran out, the island was abandoned in 1975 and remained so for years. Now visitors can take one-hour rambles around shell-shocked high-rises, concrete remnants of conveyor belts and impressive fortified walls that all look straight out of an apocalyptic manga.

Three-hour cruises (¥4300, including one hour on the island) are by reservation (conditions permitting), running twice daily from April to October, with fewer departures November to March. Contact **Nagasaki Harbour Cruises** (長崎港めぐりクルーズ; Map p582; ☎822-5002; Nagasaki Harbour Terminal Bldg).

Chisun Grand Nagasaki
HOTEL $$

(チサングランド長崎; Map p582; ☑826-1211; www.solarehotels.com/english; 5-35 Goto-machi; s/d/tw ¥12,000/16,000/18,000; ⊜@; ⋒JR Nagasaki) On the main drag, with sleek rooms with dark woods. Doubles are relatively large, and there's a coin laundry.

Nagasaki Ebisu Youth Hostel
HOSTEL $

(長崎ゑびすユースホステル; Map p582; ☑824-3823; www5a.biglobe.ne.jp/~urakami; 6-10 Ebisumachi; dm ¥2500; ⊜@; ⋒Goto-machi) This hidden yellow house offers a mix of Japanese and Western rooms, plus coupons for local restaurants and attractions. Look for signs near the Toyota dealer.

✗ Eating

Nagasaki is a culinary crossroads and one of Japan's most interesting dining scenes. *Champon* is a nationally famous local take on *rāmen* featuring squid, octopus, pork and vegetables in a white, salt-based broth. *Sara-udon* nests the same toppings in a thick sauce over crispy fried noodles. Chinese and Portuguese influences converge in *shippoku ryōri*, Nagasaki-style *kaiseki*. *Kakuni-manju* is a Chinese import, a slab of pork belly in a thick, sweet sauce, served in a steamed wheat bun and often found at street stalls.

Shikairō
CHINESE $

(四海楼; Map p588; ☑822-1296; 4-5 Matsugae-machi; champon or sara-udon ¥997; ⊙lunch & dinner; ⊜⋒; ⋒Oura-Tenshudō-shita) This huge, freestanding Chinese restaurant (look for the giant red pillars) near Glover Garden is credited as the creator of *champon* and has been in operation since 1899. There are dead-on harbour views and a small *champon* museum.

Yosso
JAPANESE $$

(吉宗; Map p586; ☑821-0001; 8-9 Hama-machi; set meals from ¥1260; ⊙11am-8pm, closed 2nd & 4th Tue; ⋒; ⋒Shianbashi) People have been coming to eat variations on the *chawan-mushi teishoku* (Japanese egg custard set meal, with *soboro* – chopped meat and julienned egg over rice) since 1866. Look for the traditional shopfront festooned with red lanterns.

Ryōtei Kagetsu
KAISEKI $$$

(史跡料亭花月; Map p586; www.ryoutei-kagetsu.co.jp, in Japanese; ☑822-0191; 2-1 Maruyama-machi; set meals lunch/dinner from ¥10,080/13,860; ⊙lunch & dinner, closed most Tue; ⋒Shianbashi) A

sky-high *shippoku* restaurant dating to 1642 when it was a high-class brothel. If you have Japanese skills or a chaperone, dining companions and a love of food, you might not flinch at the price.

TOP CHOICE Hamakatsu
KAISEKI $$

(Map p586; ☑826-8321; www.sippoku.jp, in Japanese; 6-50 Kajiya-machi; lunch/dinner menus from ¥1500/2940; ⊙lunch & dinner; ⋒; ⋒Shianbashi) Come here if you would like to experience *shippoku ryōri* and still afford your airfare home. Course menus are filling and varied (the Otakusa Shippoku is served on a dramatic round tray). In addition, there is a choice of either Japanese- or Western-style seating.

Kairaku-en
CHINESE $$

(会楽園; Map p586; ☑822-4261; 10-16 Shinchi-chō; dishes ¥700-1600; ⋒) This place has been serving southern Chinese cuisine since 1950, and there's a distinct possibility that some of the wonderful staff dressed in black with white aprons have been here ever since. For a splurge, try the Peking duck with miso (¥5000). It's just inside the Chinatown North gate.

Tsuru-chan
CAFE $

(Map p586; ☑824-2679; 2-47 Aburaya-machi; dishes ¥980-1180; ⊙9am-10pm; ⋒; ⋒Shianbashi) You might at first brush by this *kissaten* (coffee shop) that seems barely changed since the Shōwa era, but you'd miss Nagasaki's most famous *torokko rice*. This hearty local speciality typically features pork cutlet in hearty brown gravy over pasta and curry-flavoured rice. Creative recent twists include chicken, beef and even cream sauces.

Higashi-yamate Chikyū-kan
INTERNATIONAL $$

(東山手「地球館」; Map p588; ☑822-7966; www.h3.dion.ne.jp/~chikyu/e_frame.htm; 6-25 Higashiyamate-machi; ⊙cafe 10am-5pm Thu-Tue, World Foods Restaurant noon-3pm Fri-Sun) In the Dutch Slopes, this 'World Foods Restaurant' operates most Fridays through Sundays; a different chef comes to prepare an inexpensive meal from their home country. This little gem is what cultural exchange is all about.

Hōuntei
IZAKAYA $

(Map p586; ☑821-9333; 1-8 Motoshikkui-machi; dishes ¥360-520; ⊙5pm-midnight; ⋒; ⋒Shianbashi) Patrons have been ordering the *hito-kuchi gyōza* (one-bite *gyōza*; ¥360 for 10)

CASTELL-AHHHH!

Many visitors to Japan are surprised at Japanese bakers' mastery of Western-style pastries, all the more remarkable in that traditional homes don't have ovens. Nagasaki, naturally, is different, and the Portuguese-style sponge cake called *castella* has been popular here for four centuries. Japanese visitors who do not return from Nagasaki with a box of *castella* as an *o-miyage* (gift) will have some 'splainin' to do.

These yellow brick-shaped cakes are ubiquitous in Nagasaki, but two shops of note are **Fukusaya** (Map p586; www.castella.co.jp, in Japanese; 3-1 Funadaiku-machi; ⊘8.30am-8pm; Shianbashi), which has been making the cakes since 1624, and **Shōkandō** (Map p582; www.shokando.jp; ⊘9am-7pm; Kōkaidō-mae), across from Megane-bashi, which supplies *castella* to the Japanese imperial family.

at this rustic establishment since the 1970s. Also try *butaniratoji* (pork and shallots cooked omelette style; ¥520).

Mirai Cocowalk Nagasaki   FAST FOOD

(Map p582; Mori-machi) The Coco Walk shopping mall features dozens of restaurants on its 4th and 5th floors. **Aletta** (⌨801-5245; lunch/dinner ¥1580/1980; ⊘10am-11pm) is an airy buffet restaurant on the 4th floor, with a different national theme each month. On the 5th floor, **Big Man** (⌨865-8600; sandwiches ¥350-750; ⊘10am-9pm; ⊜⏧⏹) serves burgers that are popular in nearby Sasebo, where a US naval base has brought yet another cultural influence. The burgers have a Japanese twist, like bacon-egg burgers or Kyūshū's own *kurobuta* (black pork) sandwiches.

Other good places for restaurant browsing include the restaurant floors of the shopping mall **Amu Plaza** (アミュプラザ長崎; Map p582) and **Dejima Wharf** (長崎出島ワーフ; Map p582), a picturesque, harbourside collection of open-air restaurants (sushi to Italian), bars and galleries just west of Dejima.

🍷 Drinking & Entertainment

Nagasaki doesn't bustle after dark, but little nightspots punctuate the narrow lanes around Hamano-machi and Shianbashi.

Chotto-Ippai   BAR

(Map p586; 2-17 Motoshikkui-machi; ⊘6pm-3am, closed Sun) Otherwise known as Ken's bar, for the American owner who holds court in both English and prodigious Nagasaki dialect, this cheerful bar has big windows onto the narrow lane behind the main street, and a great selection of *shochu* (Japanese distilled spirit). Look for the US flag and the sign reading 'Kendall' in English.

Panic Paradise   BAR

(パニックパラダイス; Map p586; basement, 5-33 Yorozuya-machi; drinks from ¥600; ⊘9pm-late) Cool but friendly, this dark basement bar is a bit of a local icon, cluttered with rock memorabilia. There's a huge collection of tunes, cosy booths with dim lamps and the staff has pride in the environment.

Country Road   BAR

(カントリーロード; Map p586; 7-34 Maruyama-machi; ⊘6pm-midnight) This cosy family-run country-music bar oozes Americana with a Japanese twist. You'll feel welcome here and the Western bar snacks tempt. It's off the main street before the steps to Maruyama.

🔒 Shopping

Local crafts and products are sold around and opposite JR Nagasaki Station, as well as in shops along busy Hamano-machi shopping arcade near Shianbashi tram stop. Try to ignore tortoiseshell crafts: turtles actually need their shells.

For mall shopping, **Amu Plaza** (アミュプラザ長崎; Map p582) at the station is nice and easy, and you can't miss **Mirai Cocowalk Nagasaki** (みらい長崎ココウォーク; Map p582; www.cocowalk.jp, in Japanese; 1-55 Morimachi; ⊘10am-9pm; Mori-machi, JR Urakami), a massive shopping, dining and cinema complex with a Ferris wheel on the roof (¥500).

ℹ Information

Internet Access

Chikyū-shimin Hiroba (地球市民ひろば; ⌨842-3783; www1.city.nagasaki.nagasaki. jp/kokusai/exchange/plaza.html; 2nd fl, Nagasaki Brick Hall, 2-38 Morimachi; per hr ¥100; ⊘9am-8pm; Mori-machi) Also offers Japanese-language and other cultural classes; behind Mirai Cocowalk Nagasaki.

Cybac Café (サイバックカフェ; ☎818-8050; 3rd & 4th fl, Hashimoto Bldg, 2-46 Aburaya-chō; registration fee ¥300 then 1st 30/subsequent 15min ¥300/100; ◙Shianbashi) This enormous internet cafe has showers, darts, drinks and more.

Kinko's (キンコーズ; ☎818-2522; 1st fl, Amu Plaza, 1-1 Onoue-machi; per 10min ¥210; ◷8am-10pm Sat-Mon, 24hr Tue-Fri; ◙JR Nagasaki)

Money

In addition to postal and 7-Eleven ATMs, several branches of 18 Bank (十八銀行) handle foreign-currency exchange.

Tourist Information

Nagasaki Prefectural Convention and Visitors Bureau (Map p582; ☎828-7875; 8th fl, 14-10 Motofuna-machi; ◷9am-5.30pm, closed 27 Dec-3 Jan) Has detailed information on the city and prefecture.

Nagasaki Tourist Information Centre (長崎市総合観光案内所; Map p582; www.at-nagasaki .jp/foreign/english; ☎823-3631; 1st fl, JR Nagasaki Station; ◷8am-8pm) Can assist with finding accommodation and has brochures and maps in English.

Travel Agencies

JR Kyūshū Travel Agency (Map p582; ☎822-4813; JR Nagasaki Station; ◷10am-5.30pm) Handles domestic travel and hotel arrangements.

❶ Getting There & Away

Air

There are flights between Nagasaki and Tokyo (Haneda; ¥38,900), Osaka (Itami; ¥25,700), Okinawa (¥25,500) and Nagoya (¥31,900).

Boat

Ferries sail from a few places around Nagasaki, including Ōhato terminal, south of JR Nagasaki Station.

Bus

From the Kenei bus station opposite JR Nagasaki Station (Map p582), buses depart for Unzen (¥1900, 1¾ hours), Sasebo (¥1450, 1½ hours), Fukuoka (¥2500, 2¼ hours), Kumamoto (¥3600, 13¼ hours) and Beppu (¥4500, 3½ hours). Night buses for Osaka (¥11,000, 10 hours) leave from both the Kenei bus station and the Shinchi bus terminal (長崎新地バスターミナル; Map p586).

Train

JR lines from Nagasaki head for Sasebo (kaisoku; ¥1600, 1¾ hours) or Fukuoka (tokkyū; ¥4710, two hours). Kyūshū shinkansen trains do not stop at Nagasaki.

❶ Getting Around

To/From the Airport

Nagasaki's airport is located about 40km from the city. Airport buses (¥800, 45 minutes) operate from stand 4 of the Kenei bus terminal opposite JR Nagasaki Station (Map p582) and outside the Shinchi bus terminal (長崎新地バスターミナル; Map p586). A taxi to the airport costs about ¥9000.

Bicycle

Bicycles can be rented (40% discount for JR Pass holders) from **JR Nagasaki Station** (Map p582; ☎826-0480; per 2hr/day ¥500/1500) at the Eki Rent-a-Car. Some are even electric powered.

Bus

Buses cover a wider area than trams do, but they're less user-friendly for non-Japanese speakers.

Tram

The best way of getting around Nagasaki is by tram. There are four colour-coded routes numbered 1, 3, 4 and 5 (route 2 is for special events) and stops are signposted in English. It costs ¥120 to travel anywhere in town, but you can transfer for free at the Tsuki-machi (築町) stop only (ask for a noritsugi, or transfer pass), unless you have a ¥500 all-day pass for unlimited travel, available from tourist information centres and many hotels. Most trams stop running around 11.30pm.

Hirado-jima 平戸島

☎0950 / POP 36,000

This little island in Nagasaki-ken's northwest corner (closer to the pottery towns of Saga-ken than to Nagasaki City) played a big role in Japan's early opening to the West. Portuguese ships – and missionaries – landed here in 1550. In 1584 a trading post followed, and Hirado grew wealthy off trade as the entry point for Japan's first tobacco, bread and beer. The Dutch and British soon followed, and by 1618 the Japanese had to restore law and order on the island! There are many reminders of early Western involvement, particularly of kakure-Kurisutan (hidden Christians) who populated this region. It's also a popular beach getaway.

The **tourist information centre** (☎22-2015; ◷8am-5pm) located near the bus terminal has lots of English-language materials and can book accommodation. The main town, Hirado, is small enough to navigate on foot.

◉ Sights & Activities

Hirado-jō   CASTLE

(平戸城; ☏22-2201; 1458 Iwanoue-machi; admission ¥500; ☺8.30am-5.30pm) Hirado-jō presides over the town, with an enormous number of rebuilt structures. Inside you'll see traditional armour and clothing, and photos and models of old Hirado.

Matsūra Historical Museum   MUSEUM

(松浦史料博物館; ☏22-2236; www.matsura.or.jp; 12 Kagamigawa-chō; admission ¥500; ☺8am-5.30pm) Across the bay, the historical museum is housed in the stunning residence of the Matsūra clan, who ruled the island from the 11th to the 19th centuries. Among the treasures you'll find thatched-roof **Kanun-tei**, a *chanoyu* (tea ceremony) house for the unusual Chinshin-ryū warrior-style tea ceremony that is still practised on the island.

Ji-in to Kyōkai no Mieru Michi   STREET

Also in town is Ji-in to Kyōkai no Mieru Michi (Street for Viewing Temples and Churches), one of the most photogenic vantage points in all of Kyūshū. The Buddhist temples and large Christian church are testimony to the island's history.

Oranda Shōkan   NOTABLE BUILDING

Just across the road from the waterfront, this former Dutch trading house was being renovated as this book went to press and should be open by the time you read this. Shōgunal authorities took the Gregorian date on the front of the Dutch East India Company's building (1639) as proof of forbidden Christianity, later used in the justification to confine Dutch traders to Dejima in Nagasaki.

Cape Shijiki   BEACH

From Hirado, it's about a 40km (one-hour) drive to the island's southern tip at Cape Shijiki, from where there are views of the Gotō-rettō archipelago. En route, **Hotel Ranpū** (ホテル蘭風; ☏23-2111) rents sailboarding equipment.

Long **Neshiko Beach** on Hirado's lovely west coast is popular for swimming.

Hirado Christian Museum   MUSEUM

(平戸切支丹資料館; ☏28-0176; admission ¥200; ☺8am-5.30pm, closed Wed) Across the middle of the island, this museum displays items including a Maria-Kannon statue that the hidden Christians used in place of the Virgin Mary.

✦✦ Festivals & Events

Hirado's famous **Jangara Matsuri** folk festival, held on 18 August, is particularly colourful, reminiscent of Okinawa or Korea. Arrive in Hirado by late morning for the afternoon events. From 24 to 27 October, the **Okunchi Matsuri** has dragon and lion dancing at Kameoka-jinja.

⌇ Sleeping

Grass House Hirado-guchi Youth Hostel   HOSTEL $

(平戸ユースホステル・グラスハウス; ☏57-1443; 1502-1 Ōishiwaki-chō; dm ¥3360; ℙ@) In Hirado-guchi, the closest mainland town, is this unexpectedly awesome hostel with koi pond, hilltop water views, two lovely *rotemburo* (outdoor baths) and a sprawling grassy campground. There are private rooms (from ¥8400 per person including two meals) and a restaurant. Request pick-up from Tabira-Hirado-guchi Station.

❶ Getting There & Away

Hirado-jima is joined to Kyūshū by a mini Golden Gate–lookalike bridge from Hirado-guchi. The train station, Tabira-Hirado-guchi on the private Matsūra-Tetsudō line (to Imari ¥1090, 67 minutes; Sasebo ¥1190, 80 minutes), is Japan's westernmost, and local buses cross the bridge (¥260, 10 minutes). From Nagasaki, Hirado is best reached via Sasebo by JR/express bus (¥1600/1450, both 1½ hours), continuing to Hirado by bus (¥1300, 1¼ hours).

SHIMABARA PENINSULA

The hilly Shimabara Peninsula (島原半島) along the calm Ariake Sea is a popular route between Nagasaki and Kumamoto, via ferry from Shimabara.

The 1637–38 Shimabara Uprising led to the suppression of Christianity in Japan and the country's subsequent two centuries of seclusion from the West. Peasant rebels made their final stand against overwhelming odds (37,000 versus 120,000 people) and held out for 80 days before being slaughtered.

More recently, on 3 June 1991, the 1359m peak of **Unzen-dake** erupted after lying dormant for 199 years, taking the lives of 43 journalists and scientists. Over 12,000 people were evacuated from nearby villages before the lava flow reached the outskirts of Shimabara.

Unzen 雲仙

📞0957

In **Unzen-Amakusa National Park**, Japan's first, Unzen boasts dozens of onsen and woodsy walks through volcanic landscapes. Unzen village (population 1089) is easily explored in an afternoon, and once the day trippers clear out it's a peaceful night's stay in some great hot-spring accommodation. For town maps and accommodation bookings, consult **Unzen Tourist Association** (雲仙観光協会; 📞73-3434; 320 Unzen; ⊙9am-5pm).

⊙ Sights & Activities

Hot Springs

A path just outside the village winds through the bubbling *jigoku* (meaning 'hells'; boiling mineral hot springs). Unlike the touristy *jigoku* of Beppu (p625), these natural wonders are broken up only by stands selling *onsen tamago* (onsen-steamed hard-cooked eggs). A few centuries ago, these *jigoku* lived up to their name, when some 30 Christian martyrs were plunged alive into Oito Jigoku.

Onsen

Check at Unzen Tourist Association for which lodgings accept visitors during your visit. The following public facilities are open regularly.

Unzen Spa House   ONSEN
(雲仙スパハウス; 📞73-3131; admission ¥800; ⊙10am-6pm Mon-Fri, to 7pm Sat & Sun) This large bathing complex also has glass-blowing workshops (lessons ¥2000 to ¥3000 per 10 to 15 minutes).

Kojigoku   ONSEN
(小地獄温泉館; 500-1 Unzen; admission ¥400; ⊙9am-9pm) Super-rustic wooden public bath, a few minutes' drive or about 15 minutes on foot from the village centre.

Shin-yu   ONSEN
(新湯共同浴場; 320 Unzen; admission ¥100; ⊙9am-11pm, closed Wed) Simple *sentō* (public bath) style with lots of local colour.

Yunosato   ONSEN
(湯の里温泉; 303 Unzen; admission ¥100; ⊙9am-11pm, closed 10th & 20th each month) Also *sentō* style, known for its distinctive round stone bathtubs.

Hiking

From the town, popular walks to Kinugasa, Takaiwa-san and Yadake are all situated within the national park. The **Mt Unzen Visitors Centre** (雲仙お山の情報館; 📞73-3636; ⊙9am-7pm 20 Jul-Aug, to 5pm 1 Sep-19 Jul, closed Thu) has displays on volcanoes, flora and fauna, and information in English.

Nearby, via Nita Pass, is **Fugen-dake** (1359m), part of the Unzen-dake range. Its hiking trail has incredible views of the lava flow from the summit. A shared **Heisei Taxi** (📞73-2010; per person each way ¥430) ride takes you to the Nita-tōge parking area, starting point for the Fugen-dake walk. A **cable car** (ropeway; 📞73-3572; ticket each way ¥610; ⊙8.55am-5.23pm) gets you close to a shrine and the summit of **Myōken-dake** (1333m), from where the hike via **Kunimi-wakare** takes just under two hours return. Walk 3.5km back from the shrine to Nita via the village and valley of Azami-dani.

For a longer excursion (three hours), detour to **Kunimi-dake** (1347m) for a good glimpse of Japan's newest mountain, the smoking lava dome of **Heisei Shinzan** (1483m), created in November 1990, when Fugen-dake blew its stack.

🛏 Sleeping & Eating

Unzen has numerous hotels, *minshuku* and *ryokan,* with nightly rates from around ¥9500 including dinner and breakfast.

Kyūshū Hotel   HOTEL $$$
(九州ホテル; 📞73-3234; www.kyushuhtl.co.jp/language/en; r per person with 2 meals from ¥16,950; P ⊙ @) Unzen's *jigoku* make a dramatic backdrop for this five-storey, mid-century property, updated with plush fabrics and a splash of Zen. There's a variety of tempting room types (Japanese and Western, some with open-air baths and balconies), lovely indoor–outdoor common baths, East–West meals, and rates sometimes lower if you just walk in.

Unzen Kankō Hotel   HOTEL $$$
(雲仙観光ホテル; 📞73-3263; www.unzenkankohotel.com, in Japanese; s/d & tw from ¥13,860/23,300; P ⊙ @ 🛜) Designers of this grand 1936 edifice in stone and timber clearly had Yosemite in mind. A destination in itself, it has a charming library, woody billiard room, decadent onsen baths and large, ornate but not overdone rooms with clawfoot tubs. Dinners start at ¥9800.

Unzen Sky Hotel   HOTEL $
(雲仙スカイホテル; www.unzen-skyhotel.com, in Japanese; 📞73-3345; r per person with/without 2 meals from ¥8555/5400; P 🛜) Ignore the exterior and the lobby; the well-maintained rooms (mostly Japanese-style) are a great deal. The *rotemburo* is in an attractive garden.

Shirakumo-no-Ike Camping Ground
CAMPGROUND $

(白雲の池キャンプ場; ☎73-2642; campsites from ¥400; ⊘10 Jul-31 Aug) This picturesque summertime campsite next to Shirakumo Pond is about a 600m walk downhill from the post office, then a few hundred metres from the road. Tent hire is available (¥3000) or you may pitch your own tent (one/two persons ¥600/2000).

❶ Getting There & Away

Three buses daily run between Nagasaki and Unzen (¥1900, 100 minutes), or more frequently from Isahaya (¥1300, 80 minutes), with train connections to Nagasaki (¥450, 35 minutes) and Sasebo (for Hirado; ¥1250, 1¼ hours). More frequent buses link to Shimabara (¥730, 45 minutes).

Shimabara 島原
☎0957 / POP 48,815

This relaxed castle town (with ferry connections to Kumamoto) flows with springs which are so clear that the streets are lined with koi-filled waterways. The springs first appeared following the 1792 eruption of nearby Mt Unzen, and the town still vividly recalls the deadly 1991 eruption, commemorated with a harrowing museum. Other at-

tractions to note include the reconstructed Shimabara castle, a samurai street as well as a reclining Buddha. The **Tourist Information Office** (島原温泉観光協会; ☎62-3986; Shimokawashiri-machi; ⊘8.30am-5.30pm) is located inside the ferry-terminal bus station.

◉ Sights

Shimabara-jō
CASTLE

(島原城; ☎62-4766; ⊘9am-5pm) Built between 1618 and 1625, Shimabara Castle was ruled mostly by the Matsudaira Clan since the 1660s, played a part in the Shimabara Rebellion and was rebuilt in 1964. Amid carp ponds, tangled gardens, almost 4km of mossy walls, picturesque pines and staff dressed in period costumes, the grounds house four **museums** (combined admission adult/child ¥520/260; ⊘9am-5pm), most notably the main castle, displaying arms, armour and items relating to the Christian uprising; and **Seibō Kinenkan**, dedicated to the work of Kitamura Seibō, sculptor of the Nagasaki Peace Statue.

FREE **Samurai Houses** NOTABLE BUILDINGS

In the Teppō-machi area, northwest of the castle, are *bukeyashiki* (武家屋敷), or samurai houses, set along a pretty, 450m-long gravel road with a stream down the middle. Most of the houses are currently inhabited, but three are open to the public, and a free rest area serves tea.

FREE **Kōtō-ji** TEMPLE

In the cemetery of Kōtō-ji is the tranquil **Nehan-zō** (江東寺· ねはん像; Nirvana statue), dating from 1957. At 8.6m, it's the longest reclining Buddha in Japan.

Shimabara

Gamadas Dome Mt Unzen Disaster Memorial Hall
MUSEUM

(がまだすドーム雲仙岳災害記念館; www.ud mh.or.jp, in Japanese; 1-1 Heisei-chō; admission ¥1000; ⏰9am-6pm) About 3km south of the town centre, this excellent high-tech museum about the 1991 eruption and vulcanology in general is plonked eerily at the base of the lava flow. Get the free English audioguide, and visit the lifelike simulation theatre.

⛩ Festivals & Events

The town's **water festival** is held in early August.

🛏 Sleeping & Eating

Hotel & Spa Hanamizuki
HOTEL $$

(花みずき; ☎62-1000; 548 Nakamachi; s/tw ¥6090/10,290; P❄☀@) Near Shimabara Station, this bright 42-room tower has communal onsen baths, sauna and Japanese-style breakfast (¥840).

Shimabara Youth Hostel
HOSTEL $

(島原ユースホステル; ☎62-4451; 7938-3 Shimokawashiri-machi; dm HI member/nonmember ¥2950/3450; P❄) A short walk from Shimabara-Gaikō Station will lead you to what looks like a misplaced ski chalet. There are both bunk beds and futons.

Himematsu-ya
JAPANESE $

(姫松屋; ☎63-7272; 1-1208 Jōnai; meals from ¥750; ⏰10am-8pm; ▣) Serves Shimabara's best-known dish, *guzōni* (¥980), clear broth with *mochi* (pounded rice dumplings), seafood and vegetables. There are more standard Japanese *shokudō* (all-round restaurant) faves too. It's across from Shimabara-jō.

🍷 Drinking

There's a cluster of *izakaya* (pub-eateries) around the castle, but more unique to Shimabara are teahouses.

Shimeisō
TEAHOUSE

(四明荘; 2-125 Shinmachi; ⏰9am-5pm) The city-owned Shimeisō is a former villa on stilts over a spring-fed pond.

Shimabara Mizuyashiki
TEAHOUSE

(しまばら水屋敷; www.mizuyashiki.com, in Japanese; 513 Yorozumachi; tea & sweets from ¥525; ⏰11am-5pm) This delightful, Meiji-era teahouse features a lovely garden and obsessive collection of *maneki-neko* (lucky cat) figurines from all over Japan, some for sale.

ℹ Getting There & Around

JR trains from Nagasaki to Isahaya (*futsū/tokkyū* ¥450/750, 30/15 minutes) connect with hourly private Shimabara-tetsudō line trains to Shimabara/Shimabara-gaikō (¥1390/1470, one hour) for the castle/port.

Ferries to Kumamoto Port depart frequently from Shimabara Port (7am to 7pm), both fast **Ocean Arrow ferries** (adult/child ¥800/400, 30 minutes) and slower car ferries (adult/child ¥680/340, one hour). From Kumamoto Port, buses take you to the city (¥480, 30 minutes).

Local buses shuttle between Shimabara Station and the port (¥100). Bikes can also be rented at the ferry terminal and train station (per hour ¥150).

KUMAMOTO PREFECTURE

Kumamoto-ken (熊本県) is the crossroads of Kyūshū. Chief draws are the city of Kumamoto, which played a key role in Japanese history, and Aso-san, the gigantic and mysterious volcanic crater at the island's centre.

Kumamoto
熊本

☎096 / POP 730,000

Kumamoto is deeply proud of its castle and greatest landmark, Kumamoto-jō, and the city radiates around it both physically and spiritually. There's a tempting collection of restaurants, bars and shopping east of the castle. This new Kyūshū *shinkansen* stop is also the gateway to the Aso-san region, which is fortunate indeed since in summer Kumamoto is one of the warmest cities in Japan.

◉ Sights

Former Hosokawa Gyōbutei
NOTABLE BUILDING

(旧細川刑部邸; 3-1 Furukyō-machi; admission with/without castle ¥640/300; ⏰8.30am-5.30pm Apr-Oct, to 4.30pm Nov-Mar) North of the castle, down paths of immaculately raked gravel, is the large villa and garden built for the Hosokawa clan. Inside are displays of furniture, lacquer and art pieces.

FREE Chibajo Annexe
ART GALLERY

(熊本県立美術館分館; 2-18 Chibajō-machi; ⏰9.30am-6.30pm, closed Mon & 25 Dec-4 Jan) The Kumamoto Prefectural Museum of Art's postmodern Chibajo Annexe, built in

DON'T MISS

KUMAMOTO-JŌ

Dominating the skyline, Kumamoto's robust **castle** (熊本城; Hon-maru; admission ¥500; ⊙8.30am-5.30pm Apr-Oct, to 4.30pm Nov-Mar) is one of Japan's best. Although it's a reconstruction, it's unique in that the original building (built 1601–07 and seat of the powerful Hosokawa clan from 1632) was destroyed honourably, in a battle among Japanese, rather than dismantling by shōgunal or imperial edict, or WWII bombings. During the 1877 Satsuma Rebellion (see p689), rebels against the new imperial order held out for a 50-day siege before the castle was burned. Free tours are offered in English; call ☑322-5900 to check availability.

The castle's massive curved stone walls, 5.3km in circumference, are crammed with 13 photogenic buildings, turrets, keeps and the soaring black **Tenshūkaku** (main building), today a historical museum with 6th-storey lookouts. Next door, the 2008 reconstruction of the **Honmaru Palace** (Honmaru Goten) fairly gleams with fresh wood and gold leaf paintings, particularly in the Sho-kun-no-ma receiving room.

Nearby, the **Kumamoto Prefectural Museum of Art** (熊本県立美術館; 2 Ninomaru; admission ¥260; ⊙9.30am-4.30pm, closed Mon & 25 Dec-4 Jan) has ancient Buddhist sculptures and modern paintings.

1992 by the Spanish architects Elias Torres and José Antonio Martínez-Lapeña as part of the Artpolis urban reconstruction project, is recognised for its merit by architects worldwide.

Kumamoto Prefectural Traditional Crafts Centre
ART GALLERY
(熊本県伝統工芸館; 3-35 Chibajō-machi; admission ¥200; ⊙9am-5pm, closed Mon & 28 Dec-4 Jan) Has displays of local Higo inlay, Yamaga lanterns, porcelain and woodcarvings, many for sale in the excellent museum shop, which is free to enter.

The **Kumamoto Prefectural Products Centre** (Kumamoto-ken Bussankan; NTT Bldg, 3-1 Sakura-machi) near the Kōtsū bus centre also sells craft items (plus foods and shōchū liquor).

Suizenji-kōen
GARDEN
(水前寺公園; www.suizenji.or.jp, in Japanese; 8-1 Suizenji-kōen; admission ¥400; ⊙7.30am-6pm Mar-Nov, 8.30am-5pm Dec-Feb) Southeast of the city centre, this photogenic strolling garden around a lake represents the 53 stations of the Tōkaidō (the old road that linked Tokyo and Kyoto). The miniature Mt Fuji is instantly recognisable, though much of the rest of the analogy is often lost in translation.

The **Kokindenju-no-ma Teahouse** (tea & Hosokawa sweets ¥500-600) building was moved here from the Kyoto Imperial Palace in 1912 and now has serene views across the ornamental lake. Originally it was where the young emperor was tutored in poetry.

Honmyō-ji
TEMPLE
(本妙寺) On the grounds of this sprawling hillside temple complex northwest of the castle, over 150 steps lined with hundreds of lanterns lead to the mausoleum of **Katō Kiyomasa** (加藤清正公のお墓; 1562–1611), daimyō and Kumamoto castle's architect, often shown with a tall cone-shaped hat. The mausoleum was designed at the same height as the castle's tenshūkaku (central tower). A **treasure house** (宝物館; 4-13-20 Hanazono; admission ¥300; ⊙9am-5pm Sat & Sun) exhibits Kiyomasa's crown and other personal items.

Writers' Homes
HISTORICAL BUILDINGS
The one-time home of Irish-Greek immigrant **Lafcadio Hearn** (小泉八雲熊本旧居; 2-6 Ansei-machi; admission ¥200; ⊙9.30am-4.30pm, closed Mon & 29 Dec-3 Jan) in the city centre dates from 1877. Also known as Koizumi Yakumo, Hearn (1850–1904) became one of the foremost interpreters of Japanese culture to the outside world. Hearn also had a residence in Matsue (see p413).

Meiji-era novelist Natsume Sōseki (1867–1916) is honored at the **Sōseki Memorial Hall** (夏目漱石内坪井旧居; 4-22 Tsuboi-machi; admission ¥200; ⊙9.30am-4.30pm, closed Mon), which is about one minute's walk west of the river. Sōseki lived here as an English teacher for about four years.

Both houses include explanations in English.

Shimada Museum of Art
MUSEUM
(島田美術館; 4-5-28 Shimazaki; admission ¥700; ⊙10am-6pm Thu-Tue) Through the winding

KYŪSHŪ KUMAMOTO

Central Kumamoto

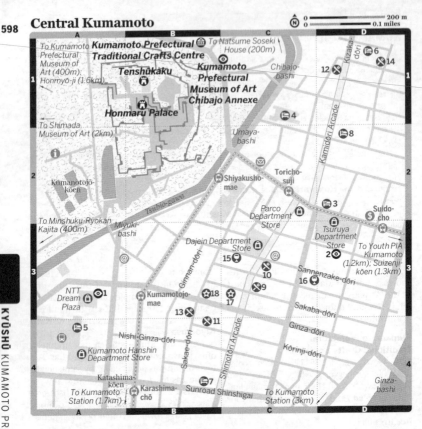

backstreets south of Honmyō-ji (about 20 minutes on foot), this quiet museum displays the calligraphy and scrolls of Miyamoto Musashi (1584–1645), samurai, artist and strategist. Current artists' work is on display in adjoining galleries.

✯✯ Festivals & Events

Takigi Nō TRADITIONAL
Traditional performances at Suizenji-kōen take place by torchlight on the first Saturday in August (from 6pm).

Hi-no-kuni Matsuri TRADITIONAL
Kumamoto lights up with fireworks and dancing for the Land of Fire Festival in mid-August.

Autumn Festival TRADITIONAL
From mid-October to early November, Kumamoto-jō stages its grand festival, including *taiko* drumming and cultural events.

🛏 Sleeping

Wasuki HOTEL $$
(☎352-5101; www.wasuki.jp, in Japanese; 7-35 Kamitōri-machi; s/d/tw from ¥8400/12,600/16,800; P@) A mid-20th-century building redone as Kumamoto Castle might have been, with fantastic results. There's a charcoal exterior, white plaster and dark beams, and atmospheric *tansu*-style furniture in the generously sized rooms, most with both tatami and hardwood floors. So what if the water pressure is sometimes a bit weak and the doorways are a bit low? It's well located for eating and nightlife, and there are common baths on the top floor (in addition to in-room facilities).

Kumamoto Hotel Castle HOTEL $$
(熊本ホテルキャッスル; ☎326-3311; www .hotel-castle.co.jp; 4-2 Jōtō-machi; s/d/tw from ¥10,280/19,630/18,480, Japanese-style r ¥34,650; P◉@) Overlooking the castle, this upmarket hotel has formal service, a beamed ceil-

Central Kumamoto

ing inspired by its namesake, and rooms with slick renovations. Make sure to request a castle-view room.

Kumamoto Kōtsū Centre Hotel   HOTEL $$

(熊本交通センターホテル; ☎326-8828; www .kyusanko.co.jp/hotel, in Japanese; 3-10 Sakurama-chi; s/tw from ¥7800/13,000; P🅿⊖@) In a prime location above the main bus terminal, this hotel in a refurbished 1960s building retains a mid-century Japanese vibe and has kind staff. Look for discounted rates online (if you can read Japanese) or by phone.

Youth PIA Kumamoto   HOSTEL $

(ユースピア熊本（県青年会館; Kumamoto-ken Seinen-kaikan; ☎381-6221; www.ks-kaikan .com; 3-17-15 Suizenji; dm HI member ¥3145,

nonmembers ¥3600-4800; @) Seven minutes' walk from JR Suizen-ji Station, this well-kept hostel has dorms and private rooms (Japanese and Western style) and an 11pm curfew. A simple restaurant serves *shokudō* standards.

Minshuku-Ryokan Kajita   MINSHUKU $

(民宿梶田; ☎/fax 353-1546; kajita@titan.ocn .ne.jp; 1-2-7 Shinmachi; s/d without bathroom ¥3800/7000; ⊖🎵) This 10-room, wood-built inn is clean, quiet and a stone's throw from the castle walls. Breakfast/dinner is available from ¥700/2000. From the main street, turn right where you see the orange brick building.

Richmond Hotel Kumamoto
Shinshigai   HOTEL $$$

(リッチモンドホテル熊本新市街; ☎312-3511; www.richmondhotel.jp; 6-16 Shinshigai; s/d/tw from ¥13,000/19,000/23,000; ⊖@) You can't beat the location or the standard of this crisp hotel in the heart of it all, with great-looking rooms in blonde woods, orange silks and chocolate browns, and excellent amenities. The breakfast (¥800) features local specialities. Look for special rates online.

Hotel Nikko Kumamoto   HOTEL $$$

(ホテル日航熊本; ☎211-1111; www.nikko-kuma moto.co.jp/english/en_index.html; 2-1 Kamidōri-chō; s/d/tw from ¥17,325/43,890/31,185; P🅿⊖@) Kumamoto's premier hotel has fine-grained woods, soothing marble, and spacious rooms with big bathrooms and views to the castle or Aso-san.

Maruko Hotel   RYOKAN $$

(丸小ホテル; ☎353-1241; www.maruko-hotel.jp , in Japanese; 11-10 Kamidōri-machi; per person with/without 2 meals from ¥12,600/6300) Kindly, old-school Japanese-style rooms and top-storey *o-furo* (common bath), just outside the covered arcade.

JR Kyūshū Hotel Kumamoto   HOTEL $$

(JR九州ホテル熊本; ☎354-8000; www.jrho telgroup.com/eng/hotel/eng150.htm; 3-15-15 Ka-suga; s/tw ¥6900/12,600; ⊖@) Conveniently located next to JR Kumamoto Station, this 150-room tower has a comfortably contemporary design.

🍴 Eating

From gourmet extravaganzas to fast food, the Kamidōri and Shimotōri arcades and surrounding lanes are happy grazing grounds.

Kumamoto's noodle dish of record is *taipien*, bean vermicelli soup with seafood and vegetables. The city is also famous for *karashi-renkon* (fried lotus root with mustard) and *Higo-gyū* (Higo beef); however, the most popular dish seems to be *basashi* (raw horsemeat). Other menus include whale meat (*kujira*; 鯨).

TOP CHOICE Kome no Kura
IZAKAYA **$$**

(212-5551; 2nd fl, 1-6-27 Shimotōri; dishes ¥450-950; ☉dinner; 🖬) This black-walled quietly chic *izakaya*, with cosy private booths and *hori-kotatsu* (well in the floor for your feet) seating, has a whole menu of Kumamoto specialities in addition to more standard fare. *Tsukune* (ground chicken) is served pressed around a bamboo pole. Look for 'dynamic kitchen' on its sign.

Kōran-tei
CHINESE **$$**

(紅蘭亭; 352-7177; 5-26 Ansei-machi; meals from ¥735; ☉lunch & dinner, 🖬) Above a Swiss pastry shop, this two-storey restaurant has an endless menu. Sit upstairs to enjoy the action on the arcade as you tuck into *taipien* (¥735), daily lunch specials (¥750) or a six-course feast for a mere ¥1575.

Yokobachi
IZAKAYA **$$**

(351-4581; 11-40 Kaminoura, Kamidōri; small plates ¥480-1200; ☉5pm-midnight) It's quiet on this backstreet, but energetic in Yokobachi's leafy courtyard and rangey suite of rooms around an open kitchen. Standout small plates include spicy *tebasaki* (chicken wings), an inventive Caesar salad with sweet potato and lotus root chips, delicately fried *mābō-nasu* (eggplant in spicy meat sauce) and, if you dare, *basashi* (¥1200). There are about a dozen *shōchū* liquors to choose from.

Ramen Komurasaki
RĀMEN **$**

(熊本ラーメンこむらさき; 325-8972; 8-16 Kamidōri; rāmen ¥550-1000; ☉lunch & dinner; 🖬) This popular and fast *rāmen* joint is opposite Higo Bank in the arcade. The signature dish is 'king *rāmen*' (¥560) in garlicky, cloudy Kumamoto-style *tonkotsu* (pork) broth with bamboo shoots, julienned mushrooms and *chashū* (roast pork) so lean you'd think it'd been working out.

Okonomiyaki Arashiyama
OKONOMIYAKI **$**

(お好み焼き嵐山; 355-2003; Sakai Bldg, 1-11-5 Shimotōri; okonomiyaki from ¥680; ☉6pm-3am, closed Sun) This tiny hole-in-the-wall has about 10 seats and no English is spoken, but the cool young chefs enthusiastically dish out *okonomiyaki* (savoury pancakes) and *yakisoba* (fried noodles).

Second Sight
INTERNATIONAL **$$**

(www.s-sight.com; 12-10 Hanahata-chō; per person around ¥2500; ☉11.30am-3am, to 2am Sun) Restaurants in this dining building and trendy date spot include Italian (Giardino), Chinese (Jang Jan Go, dinner only) and Swiss Konditorei bakery cafe.

🍷 Drinking

The laneways off Shimotōri Arcade and the hip Namikizaka-dōri area at the north end of Kamidōri Arcade are lively after dark.

Jeff's World Bar
BAR

(ジェフズワールドバー; 2nd fl, 1-4-3 Shimotōri) Predominantly *gaijin* expats and local Japanese frequent this sometimes friendly, sometimes sleazy 2nd-floor pub with satellite TV, sofas and a good selection of beers. There's dancing some weekends.

Good Time Charlie
BAR

(5th fl, 1-7-24 Shimotōri) Charlie Nagatani earned the rank of Kentucky Colonel for his contributions to the world of country music (he runs the Country Gold Festival near Asosan), and this bar is his home base. Look for live music, a tiny dance floor and thousands of pictures on the walls.

Days
BAR

(www.rockbar-days.com, in Japanese; 3rd fl SMILE Bldg, 1-7-7 Shimotōri; drinks around ¥600) It's Kumamoto's underground, three storeys up. An incredible cross-genre collection of CDs adorns the wall of this grungy rock bar. Dance if you have the space, or make friends at the bar or in comfy chairs.

Shark Attack
BAR

(シャークアタック; 8th fl, TM-11 Bldg, 6-3 Ansei-machi; drinks from ¥500; ☉closed Tue) The mood is mellow at this tiny surf-themed bar, with sandy floor, board decor, tiki lamps, and Japanese and expats happily mingling.

ℹ Information

Higo Bank (肥後銀行) handles currency exchange, and there are conveniently located postal ATMs. Visit www.kumamoto-icb.or.jp/english for city information.

Cybac Café (サイバックカフェ; 24-3189; www.cybac.com; 5th & 6th fl, Carino Shimotōri, 1-2 Ansei-machi; membership fee/per 15min ¥300/100; ☉24hr)

Kumamoto City International Centre (熊本市国際交流会館; ☎ 359-2020; 4-8 Hanabata-chō; ⊙ 9am-8pm Mon-Sat, to 7pm Sun & holidays) Has free 30-minute internet use, BBC news and English-language magazines on the 2nd floor.

Tourist information desk (熊本駅総合観光案内所) JR Kumamoto Station (☎ 352-3743; ⊙ 8.30am-7pm); Kumamoto Castle parking area (☎ 322-5060; ⊙ 9am-5pm) Has English-speaking assistants and accommodation listings.

❶ Getting There & Away

JR Kumamoto Station is an inconvenient few kilometres southwest of the centre (though an easy tram ride). It's a stop on the Kyūshū *shinkansen* with destinations including Kagoshima-Chūō (¥6760, 45 minutes), Fukuoka (Hakata Station; ¥4990, 40 minutes), Hiroshima (¥12,790, 1¾ hours) and Shin-Osaka (¥18,020, 3¼ hours). Slower, less expensive trains run on the JR Kagoshima line between Hakata and Kagoshima via Kumamoto. The JR Hōhi line goes to Beppu (*tokkyū*; ¥5130, three hours) via Aso. There are flights to Aso-Kumamoto Airport from Tokyo (from ¥30,600, 1½ hours) and Osaka (¥23,500, 1¼ hours).

Highway buses depart from the Kumamoto Kōtsū bus centre. Routes include Fukuoka (¥2000, two hours), Kagoshima (¥3650, 3½ hours), Nagasaki (¥3600, 3¼ hours) and Miyazaki (¥4500, three hours).

❶ Getting Around

To/From the Airport

Buses to and from the airport (¥670, 50 minutes) stop at the Kumamoto Kōtsū centre (熊本交通センター) and JR Kumamoto Station.

Bus

City buses reach beyond the Shiden tram service but are harder to manage without Japanese skills. One exception: the Castle Loop Bus (per ride/day pass ¥170/300) connects the bus centre with most sights in the castle area at least every half-hour, between 8.30am and 5pm daily.

Car & Motorcycle

Renting a car is recommended for trips to Aso and beyond, from about ¥5250 per 12 hours. Rental services line the street across from JR Kumamoto Station.

Tram

Kumamoto's tram service (Shiden) reaches the major sights for ¥150 per ride. One-/two-day passes (¥500/800) can be bought onboard, offer discount tickets to sights and can be used on city buses.

☑ 0967 / POP 30,000

Halfway between Kumamoto and Beppu lies the very beautiful Aso-san volcano caldera. It's the world's largest (128km in circumference), so big that it's hard at first to get a sense of its scale. Formed through a series of eruptions over the past 300,000 years, the current outer crater is about 90,000 years old and now accommodates towns, villages and trainlines.

Aso-san is still active, and the summit is frequently off-limits due to toxic gas emissions or wind conditions. You can check with the Tourist Information Centre or www.aso.ne.jp/~volcano/eng/for updates in English.

Best explored by car, the area offers some fabulous drives, diverse scenery and peaceful retreats. Routes 57, 265 and 325 make a circuit of the outer caldera, and the JR Hōhi line runs across the northern section. If you're driving, **Daikanbō Lookout** (大観峰) is one of the best places to take it all in, but it's often crowded with tour buses. **Shiroyama Tembōdai** on the Yamanami Hwy is a nice alternative. Aso is the main town, but Takamori, to the south, is more intimate and charming.

❂ Sights

Aso-gogaku   MOUNTAINS

(阿蘇五岳) The **Five Mountains of Aso** are the smaller mountains within the outer rim: Eboshi-dake (1337m), Kijima-dake (1321m), Naka-dake (1506m), Neko-dake (1408m), furthest east, and the highest, Taka-dake (1592m).

Naka-dake is the active volcano and has indeed been very active in recent years, with fatal eruptions occurring in 1958 and 1979, and other significant eruptions in 1989, 1990 and 1993.

If Naka-dake is behaving, a **cable car** (ropeway; one way/round trip ¥600/1000; ⊙ 9am-5pm) whisks you up to the summit in just four minutes, or it's ¥560 in tolls and parking if driving yourself. The cable car is 3km from the Aso Volcano Museum. From there, the walk to the top takes less than 30 minutes. The 100m-deep crater varies in width from 400m to 1100m, and there's a walk around the southern edge of the crater rim. Arrive early in the morning to glimpse a sea of clouds hovering inside the crater, with Kujū-san (1787m) on the horizon.

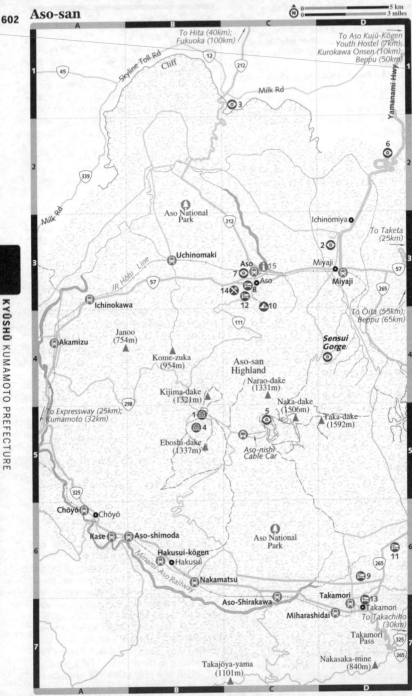

KYŪSHŪ KUMAMOTO PREFECTURE

0 ——— 5 km
0 ——— 3 miles

To Hita (40km);
Fukuoka (100km)

To Aso Kujū-Kōgen
Youth Hostel (7km);
Kurokawa Onsen (10km);
Beppu (50km)

Yamanami Hwy

Skyline Toll Rd
Cliff

Milk Rd

Milk Rd

Aso National
Park

Ichinomiya

To Taketa
(25km)

Uchinomaki

JR Hōhi Line

Aso
Aso

Miyaji
Miyaji

Ichinokawa

To Ōita (55km);
Beppu (65km)

Akamizu

Janoo
(754m)

Kome-zuka
(954m)

Aso-san
Highland

Narao-dake
(1331m)

Sensui
Gorge

Kijima-dake
(1321m)

Naka-dake
(1506m)

Taka-dake
(1592m)

To Expressway (25km);
Kumamoto (32km)

Eboshi-dake
(1337m)

Aso-nishi
Cable Car

Chōyō
Chōyō

Kase
Aso-shimoda

Aso National
Park

Hakusui-kōgen
Hakusui

Minami Aso Railway

Nakamatsu

Takamori
Takamori

Aso-Shirakawa

Miharashidai

To Takachiho
(30km)

Takamori
Pass

Takajōya-yama
(1101m)

Nakasaka-mine
(840m)

Aso-san

Aso Volcano Museum   MUSEUM
(阿蘇火山博物館; ☑34-2111; www.asomuse.jp, in Japanese; 1939-1 Akamizu; admission ¥840; ◎9am-5pm) This unique museum has a real-time video feed from a camera mounted inside the active crater wall, which you can direct from inside the museum. There are English-language brochures and a video presentation of Aso friends showing off.

Opposite the volcanic museum, **Kusasenri** (草千里) is a grassy meadow with two 'lakes' in the flattened crater of an ancient volcano. It's postcard-perfect on a clear day. Just off the road that runs from the museum to Aso town is the perfectly shaped cone of **Kome-zuka** (954m), another extinct volcano.

Aso-jinja   SHRINE
(阿蘇神社) Dedicated to the 12 gods of the mountain, this shrine is about a 300m walk north of JR Miyaji Station, and is one of only three shrines in Japan with its original gate. The drinking water here is so delicious that visitors fill canteens to take home.

☆ Activities

From the top of the cable-car run you can **walk** around the crater rim to the peak of

Naka-dake, on to the top of Taka-dake and then descend to Sensui Gorge (Sensui-kyō), which blooms with azaleas in mid-May, or to the road that runs between Taka-dake and Neko-dake. Either way will lead you to Miyaji, the next train station east of Aso. The direct descent to Sensui Gorge is steep, so it's easier to continue back from Taka-dake to the Naka-dake rim and then follow the old Aso-higashi cable-car route down to Sensui Gorge. Allow four to five hours from the Aso-nishi cable-car station (阿蘇西ロープウェイ乗り場) walking uphill to Sensui Gorge, then another 1½ hours for the descent.

Shorter walks include the easy ascent of Kijima-dake from the Aso Volcano Museum (阿蘇火山博物館), about 25 minutes to the top. You can then return to the museum or take the branch trail to the Naka-dake ropeway in about 30 minutes. You can also climb to the top of Eboshi-dake in about 50 minutes.

Yume-no-yu Onsen   ONSEN
(阿蘇坊中温泉夢の湯; 1538-3 Kurokawa; admission ¥400; ◎10am-10pm, closed occasional Mon) After a long hike, this welcoming onsen, just in front of JR Aso Station, has wonderful indoor and outdoor pools, a large sauna and private 'family' bath (¥1000 per hour).

☆ Festivals & Events

A spectacular fire festival, **Hi-furi Matsuri**, is held at Aso-jinja in mid-March.

🛌 Sleeping & Eating

Most accommodation is in Aso or Takamori. Away from the towns, restaurants and lodgings are scattered and hard to reach by public transport. Stocking up on snacks is suggested, and there's a cluster of eateries on Hwy 57 near JR Aso Station.

ASO TOWN

TOP CHOICE Shukubō Aso   RYOKAN $$
(☑34-0194; fax 34-1342; 1076 Kurokawa; r per person with/without 2 meals from ¥11,000/5000; ℗) This lovely rustic ryokan in a reconstructed 300-year-old samurai house has modern touches and a tree-lined setting, less than 500m from Aso Station. Rooms have private toilet and shared bath. It's near pretty Saigen-den-ji temple, which dates from AD 726.

Aso Base Backpackers   HOSTEL $
(☑34-0408; 1498 Kurokawa; www.aso-backpackers.com; d/s/tw without bathroom ¥2800/5500/6000; ℗@; ◎closed mid-Jan–mid-Feb) A quick walk

from JR Aso Station, this clean new hostel has English-friendly accommodation, warm staff and an excellent local map.

Bōchū Kyampu-jo
CAMPGROUND $

(阿蘇坊中キャンプ場; ☑34-0351; 1442-2 Kurokawa; campsites per person ¥310, plus per tent ¥310; ☺Jun-Sep) Easiest to reach by car, this sprawling campground off the highway en route to the mountain has a lovely position, good facilities and tent rentals (from ¥1500).

Sanzoku-Tabiji
JAPANESE $

(山賊旅路; ☑34-2011; 2127-1 Kurokawa; meals from ¥650-1500; ☺closed Wed; 🚻🚗🍴) Cute shop known for *dangojiru* (miso soup with thick-cut noodles) and *takana ryōri* (dishes using mustard greens). It's on Hwy 57, opposite the Villa Park Hotel, 10 minutes' walk from JR Aso Station.

TAKAMORI
Bluegrass
INN $

(ブルーグラス; ☑62-3366; www.aso-bluegrass .com, in Japanese; 2814 Takamori; r per person with/ without 2 meals ¥7000/3000; ℗) This cowboy ranch house and inn has attractive clean tatami rooms and a jacuzzi! The restaurant serves burgers, steaks and local cuisine (lunch and dinner from ¥1150, closed 1st and 3rd Wednesday of the month) from a picture menu. It's on Hwy 325, about a 20-minute hike from the station.

Kyūkamura Minami-Aso
HOTEL $$

(休暇村南阿蘇; ☑62-2111; www.qkamura.or.jp/ aso, in Japanese; 3219 Takamori, Takamori-machi; r per person with 2 meals from ¥9800; ℗🚲@🛜) This modern, national vacation village is beautifully maintained, and the views of the three main peaks are magnificent. Rates vary by facilities: Japanese or Western room, with or without bath etc, and all have access to onsen and *rotemburo*. It's easiest to reach by car, and crowded in July and August.

Takamori-Murataya Ryokan Youth Hostel
HOSTEL $

(ユースホステル村田家旅館; ☑62-0066; www13.ocn.ne.jp/~okuaso, in Japanese; 1672 Takamori; per person dm HI member/nonmember ¥2940/3540, ryokan with 2 meals ¥8000) This seven-room, 1930s hostel in central Takamori feels like you're in a private home. Ryokan rooms have more amenities, and all have shared facilities. It's about 800m from the station.

ℹ Information

Next to JR Aso Station, the helpful **Tourist Information Centre** (阿蘇駅インフォメーションセンター; ☑34-0751 or 35-5088; Michi-no-Eki Bldg, 1440-1 Kurokawa; ☺9am-6pm) offers free road and hiking maps and local information, and coin lockers. A postal ATM is 100m south, across Hwy 57.

ℹ Getting There & Around

Aso is on the JR Hōhi line between Kumamoto (*tokkyū*; ¥1680, 70 minutes) and Ōita (*tokkyū*; ¥2990, 1¾ hours). Some buses from Beppu (¥2950, three hours) continue to the Aso-nishi cable-car station (an extra ¥540).

For Takamori, transfer from the JR Hōhi line at Tateno (¥360, 30 minutes) to the scenic Minami-Aso private line, which terminates at Takamori (¥470, 30 minutes). Buses from Takamori continue southeast to Takachiho (¥1280, 70 minutes, three daily).

Buses operate approximately hourly from JR Aso Station via the volcano museum to Aso-nishi cable-car station (¥540, 40 minutes).

Rent bikes at JR Aso Station (two hours ¥300), or cars at **Eki Rent-a-Car** (駅レンタカー; ☑34-1001; www.ekiren.co.jp, in Japanese; from ¥6300), adjacent to the train station.

Kurokawa Onsen 黒川温泉
☎0967 / POP 500

Along a steep gorge about one hour northeast of Aso Town, tranquil Kurokawa Onsen is one of Japan's prettiest hot-spring villages. Safely secluded from the rest of the world, it's the perfect spot to experience a ryokan.

For day trippers, a *nyūtō tegata* (onsen passport; ¥1200) allows access to three baths of your choice from Kurokawa's 24 ryokan (open 8.30am to 9pm). Buy one at the **tourist information desk** (☑44-0076; Kurokawa-sakura-dōri; ☺9am-6pm), and ask which locations are open during your visit. Favourites include Yamamizuki, Kurokawa-sō and Shimmei-kan, with cave baths and riverside *rotemburo* (Kurokawa is especially famous for its *rotemburo*). Many places offer *konyoku* (mixed bathing).

🛏 Sleeping

Kurokawa's onsen ryokan aren't cheap, but this isn't an experience you'll have every day. English is spoken at the two recommended here, which can arrange pick-up from Kurokawa Onsen bus stop.

Sanga Ryokan
RYOKAN $$

(山河旅館; ☎44-0906; www.sanga-ryokan.com, in Japanese; r per person with 2 meals from ¥13,800; ℗) Deep in the gorge, about 1.5km from the town centre, several of the 15 deluxe rooms at this romantic ryokan have private onsen attached. Exquisite *kaiseki* meals, attention to detail and heartfelt service make this a place to experience the Japanese art of hospitality.

Okyakuya Ryokan
RYOKAN $$

(御客屋旅館; ☎44-0454; www.okyakuya.jp, in Japanese; r per person with 2 meals from ¥13,800; ℗) At Kurokawa Onsen's oldest ryokan (in its seventh generation of the same family), all 10 rooms have river views, plus sink and toilet, and share common onsen baths; the riverside *rotemburo* is worth it by itself.

Aso Kujū-Kōgen Youth Hostel
HOSTEL $

(阿蘇くじゅう高原ユースホステル; ☎44-0157; www.asokujuuyh.sakura.ne.jp; 6332 Ogunimachi Senohara; dm HI member/nonmember from ¥2000/2600) About 5km before Kurokawa Onsen, this friendly hostel has English information about hiking Kujū-san and other high peaks in the area, which can be viewed from the property; there are also a couple of log cabins. Breakfast and dinner (¥500 and ¥1000) are available.

Chaya-no-hara Campground
CAMPGROUND $

(茶屋の原キャンプ所; ☎44-0220; campsite per person from ¥600) A little further down the road towards the resort is this place, which is essentially a sloping lush green paddock with a truly wonderful outlook.

❶ Getting There & Away

Experiencing this area is most enjoyable by car, but there are four daily buses between JR Aso Station and Kurokawa Onsen (¥960, one hour). The last bus back to Aso departs at 5.55pm, to Kumamoto at 8.30pm (¥2000, 2½ hours) or Beppu at 7.14pm (¥2350, 2½ hours).

KAGOSHIMA PREFECTURE

Shaped like a southward-facing dragon with a pearl in its mouth, Kagoshima-ken (鹿児島県), Kyūshū's southernmost prefecture, nestled around Kinkō-wan, is one of Japan's most beautiful and relaxed. Kagoshima city lies in the shadow of the highly active Sakurajima volcano (the pearl), with the fertile coastal plains of the Satsuma Peninsula to the south. To the north is the striking Kirishima-Yaku National Park, with its own string of volcanoes and superb hiking.

Kagoshima 鹿児島
☑099 / POP 605,640

Japan's southernmost metropolis, sunny Kagoshima's backdrop is Sakurajima, a very much living volcano *just* across the bay. Unfazed, locals raise their umbrellas against the mountain's recurrent ablutions, when fine ash coats the landscape like snow and obscures the sun like fog – creepy, yet captivating. Kagoshima's position as terminus of the new Kyūshū *shinkansen* has added extra vitality to this city, already voted Japan's friendliest in national polls.

Kagoshima spreads north–south beside the bay and has two JR stations, the main one being Kagoshima-Chūō to the south. The centre of the action is about 1km north where the Tenmonkan-dōri shopping arcade crosses the tramlines.

History

For much of its history, present-day Kagoshima-ken was called the Satsuma region and ruled by the Shimazu clan for a remarkable 700 years. Its location helped Satsuma grow wealthy through trade, particularly with China. Contact was also made with Korea, whose pottery methods were influential in the creation of Satsuma-yaki. St Francis Xavier arrived here in 1549, making Kagoshima, like Nagasaki, one of Japan's earliest gateways to Christianity and the West.

When Japan opened to the word in the mid-19th century, Satsuma's government competed with the shōgunate, engaging in war with Britain and hosting a Satsuma pavilion – independent from the Japanese pavilion – at the 1867 Paris Expo. Satsuma's best known samurai, the complicated and (literally) towering figure of Saigō Takamori, played a key role in the Meiji Restoration (see p689). There's a **statue of Saigō Takamori** in central Kagoshima.

◉ Sights

Sengan-en (Iso-teien)
GARDEN

(仙巌園(磯庭園); ☎274-1551; 9700-1 Yoshinochō; admission with/without guided villa tour & tea ceremony ¥1500/1000; ⊘8.30am-5.15pm) Starting in 1658, the 19th Shimazu lord laid out this hilly, rambling bayside garden, incorporating

KYŪSHŪ KAGOSHIMA PREFECTURE

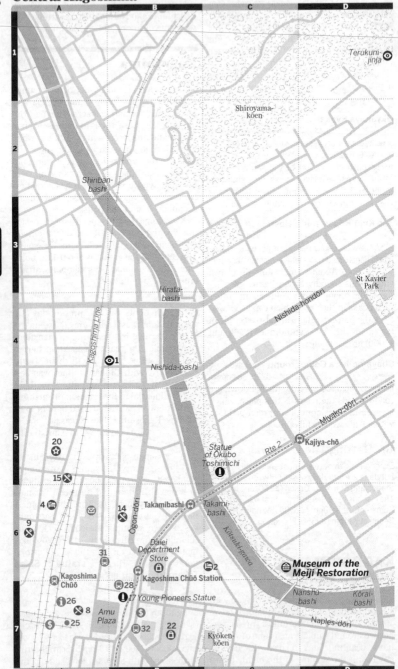

Terukuni-jinja

Shiroyama-kōen

Shinban-bashi

Hirata-bashi

Kagoshima Line

Nishida-hondōri

St Xavier Park

1

Nishida-bashi

Miyako-dōri

20

Statue of Ōkubo Toshimichi

Rte 2

Kajiya-chō

15

4

9

14

Takamibashi

Takami-bashi

Ōgon-dōri

Kōtsuki-gawa

Museum of the Meiji Restoration

31

Daiei Department Store

2

Kagoshima Chūō Station

Nanshū-bashi

Kōrai-bashi

Kagoshima Chūō

26

28

17 Young Pioneers Statue

8

Amu Plaza

Naples-dōri

25

32

22

Kyōken-kōen

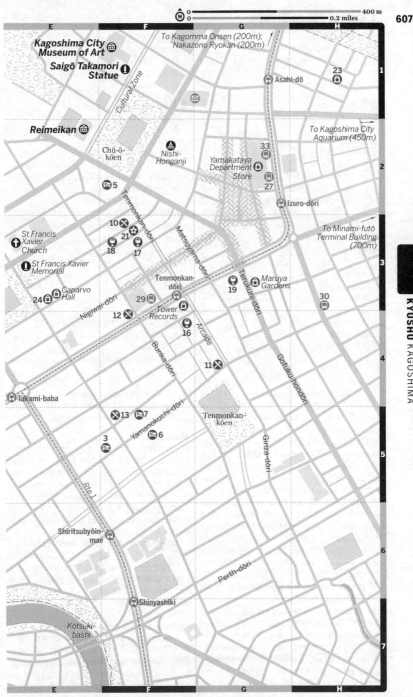

0 —————— 400 m
0 —————— 0.2 miles

Kagoshima City Museum of Art
Saigō Takamori Statue

To Kagomma Onsen (200m);
Nakazono Ryokan (200m)

Asahi-dō

23

Reimeikan

To Kagoshima City Aquarium (450m)

Chū-ō-kōen

Nishi-Honganji

Yamakataya Department Store

33

27

5

Izuro-dōri

St Francis Xavier Church

10

21

18

17

St Francis Xavier Memorial

To Minami-futō Terminal Building (700m)

24

Caparvo Hall

29

Tenmonkan-dōri

19

Maruya Gardens

30

Nigiwai-dōri

12

Tower Records

16

Bunka-dōri

Arcade

11

Takami-baba

13

7

Tenmonkan-kōen

3

Yamanokuchi-dōri

6

Ginza-dōri

Gotuku-hondōri

Rte 1

Shiritsubyōin-mae

Perth-dōri

KYŪSHŪ KAGOSHIMA

Shinyashiki

Kotsuki-bashi

E   F   G   H

Central Kagoshima

one of Japan's most impressive pieces of 'borrowed scenery': the fuming peak of Sakurajima. It was also a strategically important lookout for ships entering Kinkō-wan. Poetry parties took place along the stream in the **Kyokusui Garden** – participants had to compose a poem before the next cup of sake floated by. Allow at least 30 minutes for a leisurely stroll, more if you visit the **Shimazu-ke villa**, once a second home of the Shimazu clan. Kimono-clad women guide you through the villa, followed by traditional tea and sweet service. Other teashops around the garden sell *jambo-mochi* (pounded rice cakes on a stick, in soy and miso flavours).

The adjacent **Shōko Shūseikan** (尚古集成館; admission free with garden ticket; ⊙8.30am-5.15pm) museum once housed Japan's first factory (1850s). Exhibits relate to the Shimazu family and early Japanese industrial history, with over 10,000 items and precious heirlooms, including scrolls, military goods, Satsuma-yaki pottery, and Japan's earliest cannons, steam engines and cut glass.

Iso-teien is about 2km north of the city centre. Nearby is **Iso-hama**, the city's popular, kid-friendly swimming beach.

Museums
MUSEUMS

Reimeikan (黎明館; Kagoshima Prefectural Museum of Culture; admission ¥300; ⊙9am-5pm, closed Mon) has extensive displays on Satsuma history and ancient swordmaking. It's inside the site of Kagoshima's castle, Tsurumaru-jō (1602); the walls and moat are all that remain, and bullet holes in the stones are still visible.

Museum of the Meiji Restoration (維新ふるさと館; 23-1 Kaijiya-chō; admission ¥300; ⊙9.30am-6pm 15 Jul-31 Aug, to 5pm 1 Sep-14 Jul) has hourly performances by robotic Meiji-era reformers, including Saigō Takamori and Sakamoto Ryōma. Ask for headphones for English translation – otherwise, it's helpful to have a Japanese speaker in tow.

Kagoshima City Museum of Art (鹿児島市立美術館; 4-36 Shiroyama-chō; admission ¥200; ⊙9.30am-6pm, closed Mon) has a small, permanent collection of works by modern-day Kagoshima painters, as well as some

16th-century porcelains and woodblock prints, and a wonderful collection of Sakurajima paintings.

Kagoshima City Aquarium
AQUARIUM
(かごしま水族館; 3-1 Hon Minato Shinmachi; adult/child ¥1500/750; ⊙9am-5pm) Beautiful seascapes brim with your favourite marine life by the harbour, plus dolphin and otter shows. There's great English signage.

Onsen
HOT SPRINGS
Kagoshima boasts some 50 bathhouses, most recalling the humble yet atmospheric *sentō* of old. They include **Nishida Onsen** (西田温泉; 12-17 Takasu; admission ¥360; ⊙5.30am-10.30pm), about five minutes' walk from JR Kagoshima-Chūō Station, and **Kagomma Onsen** (かごつま温泉; 3-28 Yasuichō; admission ¥360; ⊙8am-midnight, closed 15th) near city hall.

SAKURAJIMA
This volcanic island is best enjoyed by car; the drive around takes a couple of hours, depending on stops. Cycling, while possible if you're fit, would take a full day, and if the volcano erupts you risk prolonged exposure to noxious air.

A drive along the tranquil north coast and then inland will lead you to **Yunohira Lookout**, for views of the mountain and back across the bay to central Kagoshima. On the east coast, the top of a once-3m-high **torii** emerges from the volcanic ash at Kurokami, the rest buried in the 1914 eruption.

Before you head off, stop first at the **Sakurajima visitors centre** (📞293-2443; ⊙9am-5pm), near the ferry terminal, with exhibits about the volcano including a model showing its growth. There's decent English signage.

Karasujima Observation Point
LANDMARK
South of the visitors centre is this observation point, where the 1914 lava flow engulfed a small island that had once been 500m offshore. There's now an *ashi-yu* (footbath), Japan's second longest.

Rotemburo Shrine
ONSEN
(admission ¥1050, rental locker & towel ¥410; ⊙8am-8pm, closed Mon & Thu morning) Going anticlockwise around the island, Furusato Kankō hotel has a waterside rotemburo-shrine that's accessible for onsen-only visitors, nestled among rocks at the foot of an impressively gnarled 210-year-old tree.

ISN'T IT RYŌMANTIC?

Saigō Takamori may be Kyūshū's most famous historical figure, but **Sakamoto Ryōma** (坂本龍馬; 1836–67) is the most beloved. In a 2009 survey of candidates in Japanese national elections, Ryōma was cited as the second most inspirational political figure, after Abraham Lincoln. A 2010 historical drama series on NHK TV, *Ryōmaden,* has increased his popularity among younger Japanese, as both rebel and romantic hero.

Born to a samurai family on Shikoku, Ryōma grew skillful at both swordsmanship and business. As Japan cracked open to the West with the arrival of the Black Ships in 1853, he became inspired by the American ideal that 'all men are created equal', and thus that Japan needed to end its feudal system. Unable to maintain his enthusiasm for the shōgunate, he quit his samurai post and became a *rōnin* (masterless samurai).

On the one hand, losing his patron left him poorer, but on the other hand he was free to live by his own principles. An apocryphal story has Ryōma going to assassinate an official of the Tokugawa regime, but after listening to the official and realising that they shared common goals, they instead became allies, working to bring change from within and without.

In 1864 Ryōma came to Kagoshima and used his negotiation skills to unite the mighty Satsuma and Chōshū clans (of present-day Kagoshima and Yamaguchi Prefectures, respectively) towards unseating the Tokugawa regime.

In 1866, while Ryōma was staying at a Kyoto inn, intruders came to assassinate him, and a bathing chambermaid sprang naked from her tub to warn him. He survived but was injured, and the maid, Oryo, and Ryōma soon married. At Saigō Takamori's invitation, they went to recuperate in the onsen of Satsuma, on what's said to be Japan's first honeymoon.

Although the Satsuma and Chōshū armies were successful, Ryōma did not live to see the Meiji Restoration. In 1867 assassins completed the job they had failed the year before, bringing to mind Ryōma's legendary saying, 'Even if you die in a ditch during battle, you should die moving forward'.

SAKURAJIMA STORY

Kagoshima residents speak reverently of Sakurajima's *nanatsu-no-iro* (seven colours) visible throughout the day on the surface of this volcanic island across Kinkō-wan. The city's iconic symbol, Sakurajima has been spewing an almost continuous stream of smoke and ash since 1955. In 2010 alone there were over 1000 eruptions, mostly innocuous. The most violent recent eruption was in 1914, when over three billion tonnes of lava swallowed numerous villages – over 1000 homes – and joined the island to the mainland to the southeast.

Despite its vocality, Sakurajima is currently friendly enough to get up fairly close. Among the volcano's three peaks, only Minami-dake (1040m) is active. Climbing the mountain is prohibited, but there are several lookout points with walkways across a small corner of the immense lava flow.

Where Sakurajima is not covered in deep volcanic ash or crumbling lava, there's exceptionally fertile soil, producing highly prized local produce like gigantic daikon (radishes) weighing up to 35kg and tiny *mikan* (oranges) only 3cm in diameter.

Guests wear *yukata* (bathing kimono) in the water, so that men and women can bathe together. There's a free shuttle service to and from the port, departing roughly every half-hour except during lunchtime and when the onsen is closed.

Arimura Lava Observatory
LANDMARK

Continuing along the south coast, Arimura Lava Observatory is one of the best places to observe the smoky Minami-dake and the lava flow.

🎇 Festivals & Events

Sogadon-no-Kasayaki
TRADITIONAL

One of Kagoshima's more unusual events is the Umbrella Burning Festival in late July. Boys burn umbrellas on the banks of Kōtsuki-gawa in honour of two brothers who used umbrellas as torches in one of Japan's oldest revenge stories.

Isle of Fire Festival
TRADITIONAL

Held in late July on Sakurajima.

Ohara Festival
DANCE

A festival featuring folk dancing in the streets on 3 November; visitors are invited to join in.

🛏 Sleeping

Kagoshima has plenty of good-value places to sleep. The station is a bit far from the action, so aim to stay towards Tenmonkan.

TOP CHOICE Onsen Hotel Nakahara Bessō
HOTEL $$

(温泉ホテル中原別荘; ☑225-2800; www.nakahara-bessou.co.jp, in Japanese; 15-19 Terukuni-chō; r per person with/without 2 meals from ¥12,600/8400;

P ⊖ @ �

; ℝTenmonkan-dōri) Just outside Tenmonkan and across from a park, this family-owned inn traces its history to 1904. Ignore its boxy exterior; inside are spacious Japanese-style rooms, a modern *rotemburo*, traditional artwork and a good *Satsuma-ryōri* restaurant.

Hotel Lexton
HOTEL $$

(ホテル・レクストン鹿児島; ☑222-0505; www.nisikawa.net/lexton/english; 4-20 Yamanokuchi-chō; s/d from ¥7900/12,800; P ⊖ @ �

; ℝTenmonkan-dōri) Popular with wedding parties, this smart 156-room hotel in Tenmonkan was recently refurbished to a minimalist design and with occasional Japanese touches like *ranma* (carved wooden panels). Decent-sized rooms encircle an open, light-filled atrium, and there is an onsen on-site.

Hotel Gasthof
HOTEL $

(ホテルガストフ; ☑252-1401; www.gasthof.jp, in Japanese; 7-1 Chūō-chō; s/d & tw/tr ¥5565/8900/12,600; ⊖@; ℝJR Kagoshima-chūō) Old-world Europe meets urban Japan at this unusual 48-room hotel, with good-sized rooms and chunky wooden furniture. Near the station and with triple and interconnecting rooms, it's a good choice for families.

Nakazono Ryokan
RYOKAN $

(中薗旅館; ☑226-5125; 1-18 Yasui-chō; s/d/tr without bathroom ¥4200/8400/11,970; ⊖@⦿; ℝShiyakusho-mae) Creaky, kindly and over half a century old, this friendly Japanese Inn member has been looking after Lonely Planet readers for years and will give you a taste of Kagoshima hospitality. Plus, it's filled with the personality of its keeper. Baths are down the hall.

Sun Days Inn Kagoshima
HOTEL $

(サンデイズイン鹿児島; ☎227-5151; www.sun daysinn.com, in Japanese; 9-8 Yamanokuchi-chō; s/tw ¥5400/8900; P🖷@🛜; 🚉Tenmonkan-dōri) Slick, modern and Euro styled, and offering excellent value. The rooms are compact, but the beds, showers and warm decor make up for it. Rates are cheaper booked online (in Japanese).

Plaza Hotel Tenmonkan
HOTEL $

(かごしまプラザホテル天文館; ☎222-3344; fax 222-9911; 7-8 Yamanokuchi-chō; s/d/ tw with breakfast from ¥5700/10,300/11,000; 🖷@; 🚉Tenmonkan-dōri) Rooms are small but bright in a nightlife-friendly location, and rates include a generous Japanese–Western breakfast buffet.

Kagoshima Little Asia Guesthouse
HOSTEL $

(鹿児島リトルアジア; ☎251-8166; www.chea photelasia.com; 2-20-8 Nishida; dm/s ¥1500/2500; 🖷@🛜; 🚉JR Kagoshima-Chūō) Good luck finding cheaper accommodation anywhere in Japan. This very basic but clean and super-friendly hostel is a stone's throw from the station.

SAKURAJIMA

The following properties are on Sakurajima, for a break from city life. There's also a simple campground opposite Sakurajima's visitors centre.

Rainbow Sakurajima Hotel
RYOKAN $$

(☎293-2323; www.rainbow-sakurajima.com, in Japanese; 1722-16 Yokoyama-chō; per person d & tw with 2 meals from ¥9285; P🖷) Adjacent to the ferry terminal, this light-filled property faces the puffing volcano in one direction, and central Kagoshima across the bay in the other. Most rooms are Japanese style. There's an onsen open to the public (¥300) from 8am to 8pm, and a bayside beer garden over summer.

Furusato Kankō Hotel
RYOKAN $$

(☎221-3111; www.furukan.co.jp, in Japanese; 1076-1 Furusato-chō; r per person with 2 meals from ¥13,800; P) This wonderful mid-century seaside ryokan is slowly being refurbished. All 38 rooms have private facilities and a water view, and some pricier new rooms have private earthenware *rotemburo* on the balcony. Meals emphasise local seafood.

Sakurajima Youth Hostel
HOSTEL $

(☎/fax 293-2150; 189 Yokoyama-chō; dm with/ without 2 meals ¥3870/2650; P🖷@) Less than

500m from the ferry terminal, this large, ageing but cheery hostel has dorm and Japanese bunk-bed rooms, plus onsen baths. Curfew is 10pm.

🍴 Eating

Kagoshima's regional cuisine, *Satsuma-ryōri*, is prized for dishes like *kurobuta* shabu-shabu (black pork hotpot), *tonkotsu* (pork ribs) seasoned with miso and black sugar, and *satsuma-age* (deep-fried fish cake).

JR Kagoshima-Chūō Station area and the backstreets of Tenmonkan abound with restaurants, and local friends will think you're really in the know if you venture into the narrow lanes of the Meizanbori neighbourhood southeast of City Hall, crammed with tiny, yet often chic, purveyors of everything from *yakitori* and curry rice to French and Spanish cuisine.

🔝 Kumasotei
SATSUMA RYŌRI $$

(☎222-6356; 6-10 Higashi-Sengoku-chō; set meals lunch/dinner from ¥1500/2800; ⊙lunch & dinner; ▣; 🚉Tenmonkan-dōri) This atmospheric, multistorey restaurant near central Tenmonkan covers all your *Satsuma-ryōri* needs: *Satsuma-age, tonkotsu, kurobuta* shabu-shabu, and lots of fresh fish and seafood.

Ajimori
JAPANESE $$

(☎224-7634; 13-21 Sennichi-chō; shabu-shabu courses from ¥4200; ⊙lunch & dinner; 🚉Tenmonkan-dōri) There's no English menu but all you really need to know is that this classy, multistorey shop claims to have invented *kurobuta* shabu-shabu. Set meals come with handmade udon noodles and side dishes depending on the price. There are also *tonkatsu* (deep-fried pork cutlet) meals (from ¥650 at lunchtime).

Tenmonkan Mujyaki
SWEETS $

(☎222-6904; 5-8 Sennichi-chō; large/small shirokuma ¥672/441; ⊙11am-10pm, from 10am Jul & Aug; 🚉Tenmonkan-dōri) Slake Kagoshima's steamy summers with highly refreshing *kakigori* (shaved ice with condensed milk, fruits and beans). Go for the *shirokuma,* with toppings arranged to look like its namesake polar bear. Look for the polar bear outside.

Izakaya Wakana
IZAKAYA $$

(吾愛人中央駅店; ☎286-1501; 2-21-21 Nishida-chō; dishes from ¥600; ⊙dinner; 🚉JR Kagoshima-Chūō) The Kagoshima-Chūō branch of this

Other Japanese regions are known for their fine sake, but the drink of choice throughout Kyūshū is *shōchū*, a strong distilled liquor (sometimes nicknamed Japanese vodka). Kagoshima-ken claims the highest consumption in Japan, which may well explain why everyone's so friendly! Each prefecture is known for its own particular variety. In Kumamoto, *shōchū* is usually made from rice; in Oita, it's barley, and in the south, it's *imo-jōchū* from sweet potatoes. Drink it straight, with soda or over ice, but the most traditional way is *oyu-wari*, with water heated in a stone pot over glowing coals, until you begin to glow yourself.

famous local eatery is a two-minute walk from the station's west exit. For tasting, try the *kushiage moriawase* (barbecue skewer selection; five pieces ¥650) or *miso oden moriawase* (hotpot selection; five pieces ¥700). Order off a picture menu, or sit and point from the counter. It's across from Tōyoko Inn.

Marutora Ikka   IZAKAYA $
(☑219-3948; 2nd fl, 14-17 Sennichi-chō; dishes from ¥300; ☺dinner, closed Mon; ☒Tenmonkan-dōri) This happy spot is festooned with an eclectic collection of Shōwa-period (1926–89) pop-culture memorabilia, where young Japanese come to hang out over a few rounds of beer and comfort food like bite-sized *hitokuchi-gyōza* (20 pieces for ¥750!). Look for the dark wooden street frontage and staircase leading upstairs.

Xiang Xiang   VIETNAMESE $
(香香; ☑255-0468; 1-11 Chūo-machi; dishes ¥400-1050; ☺lunch & dinner, closed Sun; 🖭; ☒JR Kagoshima-Chūō) A short walk from the station, this tidy restaurant serves aromatic Vietnamese cuisine. Some staff speak English. Look for the twin characters on the sign.

Tontoro   RĀMEN $
(豚とろ; rāmen dishes from ¥650; 🖭) Chūo-machi (☑258-9900; 3-3 Chūō-machi; ☺11am-1am; ☒JR Kagoshima-Chūō); Yamanokuchi (☑222-5857; 9-41 Yamanokuchi; ☺11am-3.30am; ☒Tenmonkan-dōri) The homey, bustling shop on Yamanoku-chi is a local institution for *rāmen* in thick *tonkotsu* pork broth. Look for the old house with the red awning. There's another, more polished branch near JR Kagoshima-Chūō Station.

Sunny Public Market   ITALIAN $
(サニー　パブリック　マーケット; ☑219-9550; 2nd fl, 1-30 Higashi-sengoku-chō; dishes from ¥850; ☺lunch & dinner; ☒Tenmonkan-dōri) This

bright, open Italian-style trattoria on Ten-monkan's main street specialises in pastas, pizzas and desserts for a youthful clientele. Lunch set meals (from ¥750) are a great deal including soup, salad, drink and dessert. All-you-can-eat and drink dinner buffet from ¥3000 (¥3500 includes alcohol).

Amu Plaza   FAST FOOD
(アミュプラザ鹿児島) Amu Plaza at JR Kagoshima-Chūō Station has good seated dining options on the upper floors and a variety of stalls, takeaway and fast food in the basement-level food court.

🍷 Drinking

Tenmonkan is where most of the action happens – shot bars, clubs and karaoke boxes. Most dance clubs don't get going until around 11pm and many bars have an admission charge (average ¥500 to ¥1000).

Kanezyō   BAR
(☑223-0487; 2nd fl, 7-20 Higashi-sengoku-chō; ☺closed Mon & Tue; ☒Tenmonkan-dōri) This arty-cool yet earnest bar with wood-beamed ceiling and concrete walls hung with Chinese textiles is a great place to sample *shochū* or sip teas from China and Taiwan.

Recife   BAR
(レシフェ; ☑258-9774; 2-1-5 Takashi; ☒JR Kagoshima-Chūō) Arty and cool, this mellow multipurpose bar-restaurant also has DJ decks and hosts occasional parties. It's popular with locals and expat groovers, and has Latin-American eats.

Big Ben   PUB
(Basement, 8-23 Sennichi-chō; ☒Tenmonkan-dōri) This basement meeting spot has dozens of beers from around the world, footy and memorabilia from around the world, and patrons – wait for it – from around the world. Vittles include *kurobuta* burgers and steamed mussels, alongside fish and chips.

Wine & Jazz Pannonica
BAR

(パノニカ; ☎216-3430; 2nd fl, 7-10 Higashi-sengoku-chō; ◷6pm-2am, closed Mon; ⒭Tenmonkan-dōri) The classy, jazzy, brick-walled *boîte* features live jazz most Fridays and Saturdays, and uses impressively perfect balls of ice in the cocktails.

Beer Reise
BAR

(ビアライゼ; ☎227-0088; Hirata Bldg, 9-10 Sennichi-chō; ◷6pm-1am; ⒭Tenmonkan-dōri) This cheery narrow bar has Guinness and Kilkenny, a variety of German and Belgian (including Hoegaarden) beers, and happy hour from 6pm to 7pm.

Salisbury Pub
BAR

(ソールズベリーパブ; ☎223-2389; 2nd fl, 1-5 Gofuku-chō; ◷6pm-3am, closed Tue; ⒭Tenmonkan-dōri) This classy, quiet bar appeals to a 30-something crowd and stocks a good selection of foreign beers and wines. Food is available, but the menu is in Japanese.

🔒 Shopping

Regional specialities include Satsuma Kiriko cut glass, Tsumugi silk, bamboo and wood products, and Satsuma-yaki pottery (most typically in austere black and white). Some are for sale at Sengan-en and the **Kagoshima Brand Shop** (鹿児島ブランドショップ; 1st fl, Sangyo Kaikan bldg, 9-1 Meizan-chō; ◷9am-5pm) in Tenmonkan. Pick up the English-language *Guidebook of Local Specialty Products* (free), including a detailed map.

Fun shopping experiences include the **Asa-ichi** (朝市; morning market; ◷6am-noon Mon-Sat) just south of JR Kagoshima-Chūō Station. At **Village Vanguard** (Caparvo Bldg, 3-41 Sennichi-chō; ◷11am-midnight), the sign may read 'bookshop' but it's crammed with all manner of lighthearted housewares and clothing.

ℹ Information

The English-language www.synapse.ne.jp/update has current arts and entertainment listings.

The central post office (鹿児島中央郵便局) near JR Kagoshima-Chūō Station has an ATM.

JR Kyūshū Travel Agency (☎253-2201; inside JR Kagoshima-Chūō Station; ◷10am-6pm) Can assist with domestic travel bookings.

Tourist information centre (鹿児島中央駅総合観光案内所; ☎253-2500; inside JR Kagoshima-Chūō Station; ◷8.30am-7pm) Has plenty of information in English and the handy *Kagoshima* visitor's guide.

ℹ Getting There & Away
Air

Kagoshima Airport has connections to Shanghai and Seoul, and convenient domestic flights include to Tokyo (¥39,000, 1½ hours), Osaka (¥26,800, one hour) and Okinawa (Naha; ¥26,300, 85 minutes).

Boat

Ferries depart from Minami-futō to Yakushima (jetfoil from ¥6500/11,600, three hours; regular ferry ¥4600, four hours). From Kagoshima Shin-kō (Kagoshima New Port), **Queen Coral Marix Line** (☎225-1551) has ferries to Naha (Okinawa) via the Amami archipelago (¥14,600, 25 hours).

Bus

Long-distance buses depart from the Express bus centre located opposite Amu Plaza. Highway bus stops are near Kagoshima-Chūō Station and Yamakataya department store in Tenmonkan.

Routes include Miyazaki (¥2700, 2¾ hours), Fukuoka (¥5300, 3¾ hours), Oita (¥5500, 5½ hours) and overnight to Osaka (¥12,000, 12 hours).

Train

JR Kagoshima-Chūō Station is the terminus of the Kyūshū *shinkansen,* with stops including Kumamoto (¥6760, 45 minutes), Hakata (¥10,170, 1¾ hours), Hiroshima (¥17,200, 2¼ hours) and Shin-Osaka (¥21,300, 4½ hours). Also stopping at Kagoshima Station, the JR Nippō line goes to Miyazaki (*tokkyū;* ¥3790, two hours) and Beppu (¥9460, five hours).

ℹ Getting Around
To/From the Airport

Express buses to Kagoshima Airport depart every 20 minutes from JR Kagoshima Chūō Station (鹿児島中央駅) and Tenmonkan (¥1200, 40 minutes).

Bicycle

Bikes can be rented (two hours/day ¥500/1500, discount for JR pass holders) at JR Kagoshima-Chūō Station and returned at participating hotels (¥300). Near the ferry on Sakurajima, **Sakurajima Renta Car** (☎293-2162) also rents bikes (one/two hours ¥300/600).

Boat

Frequent passenger and car ferries shuttle around the clock between Kagoshima and Sakurajima (¥150, 15 minutes). From central Kagoshima, the ferry terminal can be reached via City View Bus or any bus headed for Suizokukan-mae (aquarium).

Bus

Hop-on, hop-off City View Buses (¥180, every 30 minutes, 9am to 6.30pm) loop around the major sights. A one-day pass (¥600) is also valid on trams. Otherwise, trams are usually simpler than buses. Infrequent buses run on Sakurajima, from the ferry terminal past Furusato Onsen (¥290) to the Arimura Lava Observatory.

Car & Motorcycle

Many outlets around JR Kagoshima-Chūō Station rent cars for trips around the region. On Sakurajima, try **Sakurajima Rentacar** (☑293-2162; 2hr from ¥4500).

Tram

Trams are the easiest way around town. Route 1 starts from Kagoshima Station and goes through the centre into the suburbs. Route 2 diverges at Takami-baba (高見馬場) to JR Kagoshima-Chūō Station and terminates at Korimoto. Either pay the flat fare (¥160) or buy a one-day travel pass (¥600) from the tourist information centre or on board.

Kirishima-Yaku National Park 霧島屋久国立公園

This mountainous park straddling northern Kagoshima-ken and western Miyazaki-ken has excellent hikes of many lengths. If the peaks aren't being lashed by thunderstorms or shrouded in fog, common during the rainy season (mid-May through June), the vistas are superb. The area is known for its wild azaleas, hot springs and the 75m waterfall, **Senriga-taki**.

⊙ Sights

Kirishima-jingū   SHRINE
(霧島神宮; 2608-5 Kirishima-Taguchi; ⊙24hr) Picturesque, tangerine Kirishima-jingū has a good vantage point. Though it dates from the 6th century, the present shrine was built in 1715. It is dedicated to Ninigi-no-mikoto, who, according to *Kojiki* (a book compiled in 712), led the gods from the heavens to the Takachiho-no-mine summit. The shrine is accessible by bus (¥240, 15 minutes) from JR Kirishima-jingū Station.

🏃 Activities

Ebino Plateau Walks

The Ebino-kōgen circuit is a relaxed 4km stroll around a series of volcanic lakes – **Rokkannon Mi-ike** is intensely cyan in colour. Across the road from the lake, Fudō-ike, at the base of Karakuni-dake, is a steam-

ing *jigoku*. The stiffer climb to the 1700m summit of **Karakuni-dake** skirts the edge of the volcano's deep crater before arriving at the high point on the eastern side. The panoramic view southward is outstanding, taking in the perfectly circular caldera lake of Ōnami-ike, rounded **Shinmoe-dake** (which made headlines with a 26 January 2011 eruption that shut down rail and air traffic) and the perfect cone of **Takachiho-no-mine**. On a clear day, you can see Kagoshima and the smoking cone of Sakurajima. Naka-dake is another nice half-day walk, blooming with azaleas in May and June. Friendly wild deer roam freely through the town of **Ebino-kōgen** and are happy to be photographed.

Longer Walks

The long views across the lunar terrain of volcano summits are truly otherworldly. If you are in good shape and have six or seven hours, it's 15km from the summit of Karakuni-dake (1700m) via Shishiko-dake, Shinmoe-dake, Naka-dake and Takachiho-gawara to the summit of Takachiho-no-mine (1574m), another formidable volcano with a gaping crater. The hike goes above and below the treeline on a trail that can be muddy or dry, clear or foggy; some Kagoshima monks in training do this route daily!

Check bus schedules before setting out. It's a 7km walk down to the village shrine area, or a ¥1200 taxi ride. A taxi up to Ebino-kōgen is about ¥3750.

🛏 Sleeping & Eating

Most lodging is near Kirishima-jingū or in Ebino-kōgen village, with good accommodation options, but few eateries. Most village shops close by 5pm.

Kirishima Jingū-mae Youth Hostel   HOSTEL $
(霧島神宮前ユースホステル; ☑0995-57-1188; 2459-83 Kirishima-Taguchi; dm HI member/nonmember ¥3200/3800; ℗@) A few minutes from Kirishima-jingū, this neat, comfy youth hostel has Japanese rooms and mountain views from its onsen baths. Breakfast/dinner cost ¥500/1000. It also operates as a more expensive *minshuku*, with better meals and amenities.

Minshuku Kirishima-ji   MINSHUKU $
(民宿きりしま路; ☑0995-57-0272; 2459 Kirishima-Taguchi; r per person with/without 2 meals ¥7350/4500) This basic but friendly eight-room inn is close to the shrine, has forest

UENOHARA JŌMON-NO-MORI

Archaeology enthusiasts will want to detour to this **museum** (上野原縄文の森; 1-1 Ue-nohara Jōmon-no-mori, Kokubu, Kirishima-shi; admission ¥300; ◎9am-5pm, to 7pm Jul & Aug, closed Mon), on the site where the oldest authenticated Jōmon-era pottery shards were discovered during excavations for nearby office parks. Based on these findings, anthropologists began to conclude that the first humans may have come to Japan from the south rather than the north, via canoes or rafts along the Ryūkyū island chain. Look also for a re-created village of Jōmon-era dwellings, demonstrations, tools and artefacts. The museum can be reached by train from Kagoshima to Kokubu, from where six daily buses (¥400) run to the museum, or you can rent a car.

views out the windows and has been looking after Lonely Planet readers for years. Onsen baths are shared.

Ebino-kōgen Onsen Hotel HOTEL $$
(えびの高原荘温泉ホテル; ☎0984-33-0161; www.ebinokogenso.com; 1489 Ōaza Suenaga; r per person incl 2 meals with/without bathroom from ¥9800/8800; P☺@) The friendly front-desk staff of this large 'people's hotel' communicate well in English. The facilities are excellent, the location is superb and the restaurant makes tasty affordable meals. The lovely *rotemburo* is open to the public from 11.30am to 7.30pm (¥500). There's a shuttle bus to JR Kobayashi Station.

Ebino-kōgen Campground & Lodge CAMPGROUND $
(えびの高原キャンプ村; ☎0984-33-0800; 1470 Ōaza Suenaga; campsites/tent rental/lodge cabins per person from ¥800/1100/1130; P) A pretty stream runs through the middle of this delightful campground, 500m from the Eco-Museum Centre. Rates rise in July and August, and midwinter closing dates vary.

Takachiho-gawara camping ground CAMPGROUND $
(高千穂河原キャンプ場; ☎0995-57-0996; campsite ¥1100; ◎Jul & Aug, by reservation mid-Apr–Oct; P) Tent rental with blankets and cooking utensils for five people costs ¥2800.

❶ Information

Nature centres at each end of the volcano walk have bilingual maps and hiking information, and exhibits on local wildlife.

Ebino-kōgen Eco Museum Centre (えびの
エコミュージアムセンター; ☎0984-33-3002; ◎9am-5pm)

Takachiho-gawara Visitors Centre (高千
穂河原ビジターセンター; ☎0995-57-2505; ◎9am-5pm)

❶ Getting There & Away

The main train junctions are JR Kobayashi Station, northeast of Ebino Plateau, and Kirishima-jingū Station to the south, but a direct bus from Kagoshima to Ebino-kōgen (¥1570, 1¾ hours) is the best method of public transport. Schedules change often.

Satsuma Peninsula
薩摩半島

The peninsula south of Kagoshima city has fine rural scenery, samurai houses and a kamikaze museum in Chiran, and sand baths in Ibusuki. While buses operate to Chiran and trains to Ibusuki, renting a car from Kagoshima will save time and hassles. You'll also find wonderful views along Ibusuki Skyline Rd of Kinkō-wan and the main islands' southernmost mountains.

CHIRAN 知覧
☎0993 / POP 40,391 (MINAMI-KYŪSHŪ CITY)
A river runs through Chiran, 34km south of Kagoshima, parallel to a collection of restored samurai houses. On the town's edge is a fascinating memorial to WWII's kamikaze pilots.

Seven of the mid-Edo period residences along Chiran's 700m street of **samurai houses** (武家屋敷; 6198 Chiran-chō, Kōri; combined admission to all houses ¥500; ◎9am-5pm) have gardens open to the public, in which water is usually symbolised by sand, *shirasu* (volcanic ash) or gravel. Allow up to one leisurely hour to view them all.

Near the samurai street, **Taki-An** (高城庵; 6329 Chiran-chō, Kōri; soba ¥630; ◎10.30am-4.30am) is a restaurant in another traditional house where you can sit on tatami and admire the garden over a bowl of hot *soba* (¥630) or *Satsuma tonkotsu teishoku* (¥1575) and Chiran's famous green tea.

SATSUMA DENSHŌKAN

The new **Satsuma Denshōkan** (薩摩伝承館; www.satsuma-denshokan.com, in Japanese; 12131-4 Higashikata; admission ¥1500; ⊙9am-5pm) museum is the prefecture's – if not Kyūshū's – most striking, offering a history of the Satsuma region, plus jaw-dropping displays of Chinese ceramics and gleaming, golden Satsuma-yaki, in a temple-style building that seems to float on its own lake. There's an English-language audio guide. It's about 3.5km (taxi ¥1000, 10 minutes) from Ibusuki Station, on the grounds of the Hakusuikan onsen hotel.

Having tea in the English-style tearoom of **Chiran Eikoku-kan** (Tea World; ☑83-3963; 13746-4 Chiran-chō, tea from ¥530; ⊙10am-6pm, closed Tue) entitles you to take the tour of the tiny one-room collection of photos and memorabilia of the **Anglo-Satsuma Museum**, commemorating the 1862 war between Britain and Satsuma, which started when British visitors refused to bow to a samurai of the Shimazu clan. Eikoku-kan's Yumefuki loose tea, made with Chiran leaves, has won Britain's Great Taste Award for several years running.

Around 2km west of town, Chiran's air base was the point of departure for 1036 WWII kamikaze pilots *(tokkō),* the largest percentage in the Japanese military. On its former site, the large, thought-provoking **Kamikaze Peace Museum** (知覧特攻平和会館; ☑83-2525; 17881 Chiran-chō; admission ¥500; ⊙9am-5pm) presents aircraft, mementos and photographs of the fresh-faced young men selected for the Special Attack Corps. It's worth investing in the audioguide (¥100), which harrowingly tells individual pilots' stories.

Kagoshima Kōtsū (鹿児島交通) buses to Chiran (to samurai houses/Peace Museum; ¥890/930, 80/85 minutes, hourly) run from the Yamakataya bus centre (山形屋バスセンター) in Tenmonkan and JR Kagoshima-Chūō Station. From Chiran, infrequent buses run to Ibusuki (¥940, 70 minutes).

IBUSUKI   指宿
☑0993 / POP 44,200

In southeastern Satsuma Peninsula, around 50km from Kagoshima, the hot-spring resort of Ibusuki is quiet, particularly in the low season, and more especially after dark. Ibusuki Station is located about 1km from the beachfront and most accommodation, but the few eateries are near the station. The station **information desk** (☑22-2111; ⊙9am-6pm) has basic maps and can assist with directions.

◉ Sights & Activities

Ibusuki's *raison d'etre* is sand baths, in which onsen steam rises through natural sand, reputedly with blood-cleansing properties.

Ibusuki Sunamushi Kaikan
Saraku   SAND BATH
(いぶすき砂むし会館「砂楽; ☑23-3900; 5-25-18 Yunohama; admission ¥900; ⊙8.30am-9pm) On the beachfront, pay at the entrance, change into the provided *yukata* and wander down to the beach where women with shovels bury you in hot volcanic sand. Reactions range from panic to euphoria. It's said that 10 minutes will get rid impurities, but many stay longer. When you're through, head back up to soak in the onsen.

Yaji-ga-yu   PUBLIC BATH
(弥次ヶ湯; 1068 Jūchō; admission ¥270; ⊙7am-9pm, closed 2nd & 4th Thu) Loads of atmosphere in this historic wooden *sentō* (1892) away from the town centre, so old it has no showers; you wash by dipping buckets in the tub.

Yoshi-no-yu   PUBLIC BATH
(吉乃湯; 4-2-41 Yunohama; admission ¥300; ⊙2-9pm, closed Thu) Up-to-date *sentō* with a pretty *rotemburo* in a garden.

⌂ Sleeping & Eating
Hakusuikan   HOTEL $$$
(白水館; ☑22-3131; www.hakusuikan.co.jp/en; Chirin-no-Sato; per person with 2 meals from ¥15,900; P@☒) Visiting dignitaries might stay in one of the stratospheric-priced rooms in the sumptuous Rikyū wing, but we of more modest means can splurge on the less expensive of its 205 rooms. The opulent onsen/*rotemburo*/ sand baths are worth it. The Fenice de Acqua Pazza Italian restaurant in the Denshōkan building is as tasty as it is attractive.

Ryokan Ginshō   RYOKAN $$
(旅館吟松; ☑22-3231; www.ginsyou.co.jp, in Japanese; 5-26-27 Yunohama; r per person with 2 meals from ¥15,750; P@) The exquisite 2nd and

9th-floor *rotemburo* of this upscale beach-front ryokan have broad views and a lovely relaxation garden. Ocean-facing rooms start from ¥17,850 and rooms with baths on the balcony are available. There's an onsen vent right in your dinner table, as genteel servers cook *Satsuma-age* before your eyes.

Iwasaki Hotel   HOTEL $$
(いわさきホテル; ☑22-2131; http://ibusuki.iwa sakihotels.com/en; 3775 Jūni-chō; tw from ¥15,015; P ✜ ✖ ✿) Straight out of 1980s Hawaii, this kid-friendly pink tower has a putting green, onsen, pools, soccer fields and acres of land-scaped gardens. All rooms face the ocean and have balconies. Sand baths cost ¥1050. The beachfront summer beer garden is lots of fun.

Tsukimi-sō   RYOKAN $$
(月見荘; ☑22-4221; www.tsukimi.jp, in Japanese; 5-24-8 Yunohama; r per person with 2 meals from ¥12,750; P ✿) Rooms at this spotless, new seven-room ryokan across from the sand baths have private facilities, in addition to pretty indoor and outdoor baths and meals featuring *Satsuma-ryōri* like *tonkotsu* and sashimi. There's not much English spoken, but amenable staff make it work.

Tamaya Youth Hostel   HOSTEL $
(圭屋ユースホステル; ☑22-3553; 5-27-8 Yu nohama; dm with 2 meals/breakfast ¥4665/3720; ✜ @) This 25-room, three-storey hostel with both Japanese- and Western-style bedding is rather plain, but it's located diagonally across from the sand baths.

Aoba   IZAKAYA $
(青葉; ☑22-3356; 1-2-41 Minato; dishes from ¥480; ⊙lunch & dinner, closed Wed) Behind the yellow *noren* (door curtain) two-minutes' walk left of the station, this cheery shop serves satisfying *kurobuta roosukatsu* (black pork cutlet) *teishoku* (¥1320) or, if you dare, *Satsuma ji-dori sashimi* (raw sliced chicken, ¥780).

❶ Getting There & Away
Ibusuki is about 1¾ hours from Kagoshima by bus (¥930) or about half that by train (*kyūko/tokkyū* ¥970/2070, 55/50 minutes).

Around Satsuma Peninsula

Ikeda-kō is a volcanic caldera lake west of Ibusuki, inhabited by giant eels kept in tanks by the parking lot. South of the lake is **Cape Nagasaki-bana**, from where you can see off-shore islands on a clear day.

In a gorge near Ikeda-kō, **Tōsenkyō Sōmen Nagashi** (唐船峡そうめん流し; ☑32- 2143; 5967 Jūchō, Kaimon; sōmen ¥550; ⊙9.30am-5pm, later hr in summer) is a pilgrimage for many Japanese as the 1967 birthplace of *nagashi-sōmen* (flowing noodles). *Sōmen* (vermicelli) spin around a tank of swiftly flowing 13°C water at your table; catch the noodles with your chopsticks and dip in sauce to eat. Tonnes of fun, and ultrarefreshing on hot days. *Teishoku* (¥1300) come with *onigiri* (rice balls), miso soup and grilled *ayu* (trout).

The beautifully symmetrical 924m cone of **Kaimon-dake**, nicknamed 'Satsuma Fuji', dominates the skyline and can be climbed in two hours. An early start may reward you with views of Sakurajima, Cape Sata, and Yakushima and Tanegashima islands.

At the southwestern end of the peninsula is **Makurazaki**, a port famous for *katsuo* (bonito) and the terminus of the train line from Kagoshima. From here it's a gorgeous drive to **Bōnotsu**, a fishing village and great swimming beach that was an unofficial trading link with the outside world via Okinawa during Japan's two centuries of seclusion.

MIYAZAKI PREFECTURE

Miyazaki-ken (宮崎県) is best known for its palmy, balmy coastline from the city of Miyazaki southward. Surfing, fishing boats and picturesque coastal drives here may remind you of California or the Italian Riviera. At the prefecture's northern reaches (easier accessed from Kumamoto) is lovely Takachiho, mythical home of the sun goddess Amaterasu.

Although there are train and bus services, the most rewarding way to explore this diverse prefecture is by car.

Miyazaki   宮崎
☑0985 / POP 398,100
The prefectural capital makes a convenient base for forays around the region, with a friendly, low-key vibe and fun, unique restaurants and night spots in the Nishitachi nightlife district, about 700m from the station.

⊙ Sights
Miyazaki-jingū & Museum   SHRINE
(宮崎神宮・宮崎総合博物館; 2-4-1 Jingū) This shrine honours the Emperor Jimmu, the semimythical first emperor of Japan and founder of the Yamato court. Spectacular

600-year-old wisteria vines cover the thickly forested grounds. It's a 500m walk from Miyazaki-jingū Station (one stop, ¥160, from Miyazaki Station).

Just north of the shrine, **Miyazaki Prefectural Museum of Nature & History** (2-4-4 Jingū; admission free; ☉9am-4.30pm, closed Tue) exhibits items on local history, archaeology, festival artefacts and folkcrafts. Behind the museum, **Minka-en** (民家園; admission free) hosts four traditional-style Kyūshū farmhouses.

Heiwadai-kōen   PARK
(平和台公園; Peace Park) The park's centrepiece is a 37m-high tower constructed in 1940, a time when peace in Japan was about to disappear. **Haniwa Garden**, within the park, is dotted with reproductions of the clay *haniwa* (earthenware figures found in Kōfun-period tombs) that have been excavated from the Saitobaru burial mounds.

Heiwadai-kōen is about 1km north of Miyazaki-jingū. Frequent buses stop along Tachibana-dōri (¥290, 20 minutes).

Miyazaki Science Centre   MUSEUM
(宮崎科学技術館; 38-3 Miyawakichō; admission with/without sky show ¥730/520; ☉9am-4.30pm, closed Mon) Only steps away from Miyazaki Station, this interactive science museum boasts one of the world's largest planetariums; some shows also include English translations.

🎇 Festivals & Events

Yabusame   ARCHERY
You can witness samurai-style horseback archery at Miyazaki-jingū on 2 and 3 April.

Fireworks   FIREWORKS
Kyūshū's largest fireworks show lights up the summer sky over the Oyodo-gawa in early August.

Miyazaki

Erekocha Matsuri　　　　　TRADITIONAL
Miyazaki's newest festival with dancers and *taiko* drummers filling Tachibana-dōri in mid-August.

Miyazaki-jingū Grand Festival　TRADITIONAL
In late October, this festival brings in the autumn with horses and *mikoshi* being carried through the streets.

🛏 Sleeping

Hotel Route Inn　　　　　　HOTEL **$**
(ホテルルートイン宮崎; ☑61-1488; www.route -inn.co.jp/english; 4-1-27 Tachibana-dōri-nishi; s/d

with breakfast ¥5900/9500; 🅿🔄@) Across from the Nishitachi district, this 200-plus-room hotel is excellent value with a great breakfast buffet, spacious, decently appointed rooms, a granite lobby and common bath (in addition to private bathrooms).

Richmond Hotel Miyazaki Ekimae HOTEL **$$**
(リッチモンドホテル宮崎駅前; ☑60-0055; www.richmondhotel.jp; 2-2-3 Miyazaki-eki-higashi; s/d/tw with breakfast from ¥7000/9000/12,500; 🅿🔄@) Behind Miyazaki Station, this light-filled business hotel has clean, modern furnishings, larger-than-average rooms and a breakfast buffet including local specialities.

Sheraton Grande Ocean Resort　HOTEL **$$$**
(☑21-1133; www.starwoodhotels.com; Hamayama, Yamazaki-cho; d/tw from ¥22,880; 🅿🔄@🐾) Seriously good rates are often found online for this true five-star hotel with excellent leisure facilities. The 154m-high oceanfront tower adjoins the SeaGaia entertainment complex. Oversized rooms are well appointed, although internet access costs ¥1575. From Miyazaki take a bus for SeaGaia (25 minutes).

Miyazaki Kankō Hotel　　　　HOTEL **$$**
(宮崎観光ホテル; ☑27-1212; www.miyakan-h .com/english; 1-1-1 Matsuyama; s/d from ¥7700/ 15,120, Japanese-style r from ¥9075; 🅿🔄@) This hotel towers over the river with two buildings, the dowdier west wing and snappier east wing. Rooms are fittingly spacious and well furnished. There's an on-site onsen with *rotemburo*, plus a baby grand piano in the lobby.

Sunflower Miyazaki Youth Hostel HOSTEL **$**
(☑24-5785; 1-3-10 Asahi; dm ¥2900; 🔄@) Near the Prefectural office, this basic hostel doubles as a community centre during the day, so all guests must be out between 10am and 3pm. There's a giant kitchen, a restaurant downstairs and a nominal 10pm curfew.

Hotel Kensington　　　　　　HOTEL **$**
(ホテルケンジントン宮崎; ☑20-5500; www .kensington.jp, in Japanese; 3-4-4 Tachibanadōri-higashi; s/d ¥6600/11,500; 🅿🔄@🛜) Cheerful spot near Nishitachi, with a very British lobby (eg suit of armour) and a couple of rental bikes.

🍴 Eating

Miyazaki is famous for chicken *nanban* (sweet fried chicken with tartar sauce), refreshing *hiya-jiru* (cold summer soup

619

KYŪSHŪ MIYAZAKI

SATA-MISAKI

Collectors of 'mosts' will want to journey to the east side of Kinkō-wan to **Sata-misaki** (佐多岬), the southernmost cape of Japan's main islands, at the tip of the Ōsumi Peninsula and marked by Japan's oldest lighthouse. Glass-bottomed **Sata-Day-Go Boats** (☑0994-27-3355; 30min tours adult/child ¥2000/1000) offer day cruises to see coral, sea turtles, *fugu* (pufferfish), dolphins and even sharks. Cape Sata is best reached by car.

made from baked tofu, fish, miso paste and cucumbers, served over rice), *jidori* (local chicken) and *kama-age udon* (wheat noodles boiled in a cauldron). Snack foods include *nikumaki onigiri* (rice balls wrapped in marinated pork) and *chiizu manjū* (cream cheese-filled dumplings). Local produce includes mango and *yuzu* (citron), sometimes mixed with pepper for spicy *yuzu-kōshō* paste.

The Nishitachi neighbourhood is great for restaurant browsing. Also try the 8th-floor restaurants and basement marketplace at **Bon Belta** department store (ボンベルタ橘), or pick up a *shiitake ekiben* (mushroom boxed lunch) at Miyazaki Station.

Ogura Honten
JAPANESE $

(☑22-2296; 3-4-24 Tachibana-higashi; chicken nanban ¥980; ☉lunch & dinner Wed-Mon) Chicken *nanban* was invented here half a century ago, and crowds continue to flock to Ogura's red and white awning in the alley behind Yamakataya department store. For shorter queues, try the larger, kitsch-filled crosstown **branch** (☑23-5301; 2-2-23 Segashira; ☉11am-10pm; 🚻).

Maruman Honten
JAPANESE $$

(☑22-6068; 3-6-7 Tachibana-dōri-nishi; grilled chicken ¥1100; ☉dinner, closed Sun) This homey shop serves *jidori*, full of flavour but tougher and cooked rarer than you may be used to. The standard is *momoyaki* (grilled chicken leg), but *tataki* (seared; ¥600) and *sashimi* (what you think it is; ¥650) are also popular, and meals come with a light and delicious chicken broth. For more thorough cooking, say '*yoku yaite kudasai*'. Some English spoken. Look for the Kirin Classic Lager sign out the front.

Togakushi
NOODLES $

(☑24-6864; 7-10 Chūō-dōri; noodles ¥600-900; ☉6pm-2am) Workmanlike Togakushi has no English menu, but ordering is easy: delicate, thin *kama-age-udon* (¥600) in cloudy broth with your choice of *negi* (green onion), *tempura-ko* (tempura crispies) and refreshing *yuzu* (Japanese citron); dip noodles in tangy sauce. Look for the giant red lantern. It's what locals crave after a bender; during the day, there's another **branch** (1-3-3 Tachibana-nishi-dōri; ☉11am-7pm, closed Sun) near city hall.

Bosco
ITALIAN $$

(☑23-5462; 1st fl, 7-22 Chūōmachi; mains ¥950-1260; ☉5pm-midnight, closed alternate Sun & Mon) Just outside the covered arcade (look for the pink lit signs), this cosy trattoria has an open kitchen, two large tables and a long counter. *Ebi-abokado* spaghetti (with shrimp, avocado and clams) has legions of fans.

Okashi no Hidaka
SWEETS $

(☑25-5300; 2-7-25 Tachibana-nishi-dōri; nanjakō-daifuku ¥320; ☉9.30am-9.30pm) Peruse, if you will, the refrigerator case of luscious-looking Japanese and Western pastries, but order the giant *nanjakō-daifuku* (dumpling of sweet bean paste, strawberry, chestnut and cheese in a wrapper of airy *mochi*). Cheese *manju* (dumplings) are another signature taste of Miyazaki.

Izakaya Seoul
KOREAN $$

(韓国居酒屋ソウル; ☑29-8883; 1st fl, 7-26 Chūōmachi; most mains ¥1000-1200; ☉dinner; 🏮) This Korean restaurant does brisk business in barbecue, *bibimba* (rice hotpot) and *pajeon* (savoury pancakes).

Nikumaki Honpō
JAPANESE $

(☑20-2900; 3-8-7 Tachibana-nishi; nikumaki onigiri ¥300; ☉6pm-3am, from 11am Sat & Sun) Corner stand that invented *nikumaki onigiri*.

🍷 Drinking

Miyazaki also plays to the wee hours, especially in the summer, with hundreds of tiny bars. Most of the action is in Nishitachi.

The Bar
BAR

(www.thebarmiyazaki.com; 3rd fl, Paul Smith Bldg, 3-7-15 Tachibana-dōri-higashi; ☉8pm-3am) This hub of the expat community and its local friends draws a cheery mixed crowd who are proud of their city and keen to welcome visitors over a few cold beers. There's even a full-sized billiard table.

Planet Café
BAR

(プラネットカフェ; 8-25 Kamino-machi; ☺7pm-2am) This welcoming place is great for baseball or soccer on the telly and local *jidori* chicken washed down with a cold beer or any of 200 cocktails.

One Coin Bar
BAR

(ワンコインバー; 8-21 Chūō-dōri; ☺closed Tue) All drinks are ¥500 (one coin!) at this smart eight-stool hole-in-the-wall with a regular clientele who return for the conversation. The well-mannered 'master' speaks English and appreciates the custom of travellers.

Lifetime
BAR

(2nd fl, 2-3-8 Hiroshima; admission Fri ¥500; ☺11.45am-2pm & 5pm-12.30am, closed Sun) Modern jazz is alive and well in Miyazaki with near-nightly jams at this upstairs bistro-bar. Drinks start at ¥600, with coffee, snacks and steaks on the menu.

Suntory Shot Bar 4665
BAR

(サントリーショットバー4665; 1-12 Chūōdōri; ☺closed Mon) Drink a highball at nightfall at this subdued art deco–styled spot. The owner speaks some English.

Anbai
BAR

(3-1-24 Tachibana-dōri-nishi; ☺closed Sun) Located on Tachibana-dōri, just south of Janjanyokocho alley and UFJ Bank, this *izakaya* has more than 350 varieties of *shōchū*, Guinness on tap, and a selection of dishes to go with it.

Café Lanai
BAR

(カフェラナイ; ☎23-3412; 2-1-1 Shimizu; ☺6pm-midnight) This mellow establishment with an island-fever vibe plays surf videos above the full bar. Dishes (from ¥700) also have a tropical twist.

🛍 Shopping

Miyazaki Prefectural Products Promotion Exhibition Hall
JAPANESE CRAFTS

(みやざき物産館; 1-6 Miyata-chō; ☺9.30am-7pm Mon-Fri, 10am-6.30pm Sat & Sun) This place sells distinctively coloured, handwoven nubby silk *tetsumugi* textiles, clay *haniwa*, Takachiho *kagura* masks and a wall of *shōchū* liquors.

ℹ Information

Located inside JR Miyazaki Station, the helpful **tourist information centre** (宮崎市観光案内所; ☎22-6469; ☺9am-6.30pm) has maps of the city and its surroundings. There are international ATMs both at the station and at the central post office, five minutes' walk west along Takachiho-dōri. Opposite the post office, the **Miyazaki Prefectural International Plaza** (宮崎県国際交流協会; ☎32-8457; 8th fl, Carino Bldg; ☺10am-7pm Tue-Sat) has satellite TV as well as various foreign-language newspapers and magazines.

Near the station's west exit is the internet cafe **E-Planet** (2-12-20 Hiroshima; ☺24hr).

ℹ Getting There & Away

Air

Miyazaki is connected by air with Tokyo (ANA & JAL/Skynet ¥36,800/30,600, 1½ hours), Osaka (¥23,500, 1½ hours), Okinawa (¥25,500, 1½ hours) and Fukuoka (¥19,700, 50 minutes), plus a few flights weekly to Seoul and Taipei.

Boat

Miyakō Car Ferry (☎29-5566; 2nd-class bunks ¥11,700) links Miyazaki with Osaka; it's a 13-hour trip.

Bus

Routes include Kagoshima (¥2700, 2¾ hours), Kumamoto (¥4500, 3¼ hours), Nagasaki (¥6500, 5½ hours) and Fukuoka (¥3300, four hours). Phone the **bus centre** (☎53-1000).

Train

The JR Nippō line runs down to Kagoshima (*tokkyū*, ¥4090, two hours) and up to Beppu (*tokkyū*, ¥6070, 3¼ hours).

ℹ Getting Around

Miyazaki's airport is connected to the city centre by bus (¥430, 30 minutes) or train (¥340, 10 minutes) from JR Miyazaki Station. Most city bus services use the **Miyazaki Ekimae Bus Centre** (宮崎交通; ☎53-1000) opposite the station.

Car rental is the most convenient way to explore this coastal area. There are many agencies outside the station's west exit (12 hours from ¥4725).

ℹ VISIT MIYAZAKI BUS CARD

For budget travellers not in a hurry, this **bus pass** (¥1000 per day) is a fabulous deal, covering city and regional buses including to Aoshima and Nichinan Coast. Buy it at tourist counters and some hotels.

Aoshima & Kaeda
青島・加江田

📞0985

Aoshima is a tiny palm-covered island (1.5km in circumference), said to host some 200 species of flora and fringed by unique washboard rock formations. It's connected by a narrow bridge (cars are not permitted) to the mainland town of Aoshima. Beneath its touristy exterior, Aoshima is a relaxed, alternative community, great for surrendering to the summer heat and a good alternative to staying in central Miyazaki.

👁 Sights & Activities

On the island, photogenic **Aoshima-jinja** (青島神社) is reputedly good for matchmaking. Nearby is a **botanical garden** (青島熱帯植物園; admission ¥200) boasting 64 different species of fruit trees.

West of town, an 8km-long, well-maintained **hiking path** winds through **Kaeda Gorge** (加江田渓谷) following the Kaedagawa, a refreshingly clear stream filled with boulders and excellent swimming holes. Lush foliage includes banana palms and mountain cedars. Your own transport is helpful to get here; turn off Rte 220 onto prefectural road 339.

🎎 Festivals & Events

On the second Monday in January, loincloth-clad locals dive ceremoniously into the ocean at Aoshima-jinja. At the end of July there's more splashing as *mikoshi* are carried through the shallows to the shrine.

🛏 Sleeping & Eating

Log Cabin Rashinban RUSTIC $
(丸太小屋羅針盤; 📞65-0999; dm ¥3500; P🚗) If it's time for a tree change, head to this fascinating owner-builder chalet on the banks of a soothing stream. You'll need directions or a taxi from town if you don't have a rental car, at least for the first trip. When you get there, little English is spoken – but this distinctive accommodation in a tranquil setting is great if you want to get away, and even better if you're travelling with someone.

Hotel Grantia Aoshima Taiyokaku HOTEL $
(ホテルグランティアあおしま太陽閣; 📞65-1531; www.route-inn.co.jp/english; s/d from ¥5500/10,000; P🚗@) On the hillside midway between Aoshima and Kodomo-no-kuni

stations, this hot-spring property offers excellent value. Day use of onsen, *rotemburo* and *ganbanyoku* (stone bath) is from ¥650.

Aoshima Palm Beach Hotel HOTEL $$
(青島パームビーチホテル; 📞65-1555; www.palmbeach-h.com, in Japanese; 1-16-1 Aoshima; d from ¥13,400; P@🚗🛏) This shiny white, semicylindrical, beachfront tower with glass elevators has ocean-view rooms and onsen baths (day use ¥1000). The Japanese restaurant, **Shizuku** (set menus from ¥1500, kaiseki dinners from ¥3000), serves great tempura and sashimi straight from the waters.

Miyazaki Cocona Shirahama Drive-in Campsite CAMPGROUND $
(宮崎白浜オートキャンプ場ココナ; 📞65-2020; tent hire ¥1570, campsites from ¥2940, cabins for up to 4 people ¥9970; 🛏) Opposite Shirahama beach, this modern complex has plenty of room and some nice rustic cabins set back from the main area.

Sounders Lunch & Bar INTERNATIONAL $
(📞65-0767; 1-6-23 Aoshima; set meals from ¥650; ⏱lunch Sun & Mon, Wed-Fri, dinner Fri & Sat; 🛏🍴) A surf shack by the railroad tracks, serving spinach-and-bacon salads, *loco moco* (burger with fried egg, gravy and rice) bowls, and avocado-and-bacon burgers. It has a laid-back vibe and live music most weekends.

Tenkū Zeal ORGANIC $$
(天空ジール; 📞65-1508; 6411 Kaeda; buffet adult/child ¥1500/800; ⏱lunch Wed-Sun; 🍴) This wonderful hillside macrobiotic lunch spot with sunny alfresco dining offers a constantly changing menu from produce grown onsite. This is as delightfully hippie as it gets in Japan; some staff speak English, and the food couldn't be better for you.

ℹ Getting There & Around

Aoshima is on the JR Nichinan line from Miyazaki (¥360, 30 minutes). Buses from Miyazaki Station stop at Aoshima (¥700, 40 minutes, hourly) en route to Udo-jingū. It's about five minutes' walk to the island from the station.

Udo-jingū
鵜戸神宮

Reached via a coastal path, this brightly painted Shintō **shrine** (📞0987-29-1001; 3232 Ōaza Miyaura) occupies an open cavern overlooking unusual rock formations in the cove below. It's protocol to buy five *undama* (luck stones, ¥100), make a wish and try to hit the shallow depression on top of the turtle-shaped rock.

Wishes are usually related to marriage, childbirth and lactation, because the boulders in front of the cavern are said to represent Emperor Jimmu's grandmother's breasts.

Hourly buses from Aoshima (¥1020, 40 minutes) and Miyazaki (¥1470, 1½ hours) stop on the highway. From the bus stop, it's about a 700m walk to the shrine past interesting rock formations and picturesque fishing boats.

Obi 飫肥

In this quaint town nicknamed 'Little Kyoto', the wealthy Ito clan ruled from Obi castle for 14 generations beginning in 1587, somehow surviving the 'one kingdom, one castle' ruling in 1615.

Only the walls of the original **Obi-jō** (飫肥城; ☑0987-25-4533; combined admission ¥600; ☉9.30am-4.30pm) are intact, but the grounds have six important buildings, including the impressive, painstakingly reconstructed **Ōte-mon** gate and **Matsuo-no-maru**, the lord's private residence. The **museum** has a collection relating to the Ito clan's long rule over Obi. **Yōshōkan**, formerly the residence of the clan's chief retainer, stands just outside the castle entrance and has a large garden with Atago-san as 'borrowed scenery'.

Once you've seen these sights, rent bikes (¥300 for three hours) to explore the rest of the town, with some photogenic streetscapes, shrines and a historic shopping street; your admission ticket has a simple map.

By the castle, **Obiten** (☑0987-25-5717; tempura with udon ¥850) serves a local version of *Satsuma-age* (fried cakes of fish paste and vegetables, here called *tempura*).

The JR Nichinan line connects Obi with Miyazaki (*kaisoku*; ¥910, 65 minutes) via Aoshima. From Obi Station, it's a 10 minute walk to the castle. Buses from Miyazaki (¥2020, 2¼ hours, last return bus 3.40pm) stop below the castle entrance.

Nichinan-kaigan & Cape Toi 日南海岸・都井岬

The 50km stretch of coastal road from Aoshima to Cape Toi via the town of Nichinan is a rewarding drive, with views of the islands reminiscent of gumdrops and camels, along a palm-lined road coursing along seaside cliffs. At Cape Toi, a dramatic **fire festival** is held on the last weekend in September. The cape is also famed for herds of wild horses, which now seem rather friendly.

Just off the coast from the beach at **Ishinami-kaigan**, the tiny island of **Kō-jima** is home to a group of monkeys that apparently rinse their food in the ocean before eating, but they're a fickle bunch, and hard to spot.

To stay overnight in the area, head to **Koigaura Beach**, where the surf-*zoku* (tribe) hang out. It's about 5km from Cape Toi or 7km from Kōjima. The spartan, six-room **Minshuku Tanaka** (☑0987-76-2096; 2050-2 Ōaza; per person lodging/with 2 meals from ¥3150/5250) is your only lodging option.

Saitobaru 西都原

☑0983

North of Miyazaki, the **Saitobaru Burial Mounds Park** looks not unlike a golf course at first glance, but the hillocks you see dotting the several square kilometres of fields and forests are over 300 *kofun* (tumuli, or burial mounds). These mostly keyhole-shaped mounds, dating from AD 300 to 600, served much the same function as Egyptian pyramids for early Japanese nobility.

The large **Saitobaru Archaeological Museum** (西都原考古博物館; admission free; ☉10am-6pm, closed Mon) displays excavated items like Jōmon pottery, ancient swords, armour and *haniwa*. Rent the English audioguide (¥400); signage is in Japanese. A hall nearby is built around an excavation site.

Buses run frequently to Saitobaru from Miyakō City bus terminal (¥1040, one hour), but you'll need your own transport if you want to explore the tomb-strewn countryside. Saitobaru is not on the Visit Miyazaki Bus Card.

In the nearby town of Saito, drummers wear odd pole-like headgear for the unique **Usudaiko dance festival** in early September. A harvest festival lasts from 12 to 16 December, highlighted by **Shiromi Kagura** performances on the 14th and 15th.

Takachiho 高千穂

☑0982 / POP 14,000

In remote northern Miyazaki-ken, this pretty mountain town claims to be where Japan's sun goddess brought light back to the world. As if that weren't reason enough to visit, there's a deep and dramatic gorge through the town centre. **Takachiho Tourism Association** (高千穂町観光協会; ☑73-1213; 809-2 Mitai; ☉8.30am-5.30pm) is west of the bus centre.

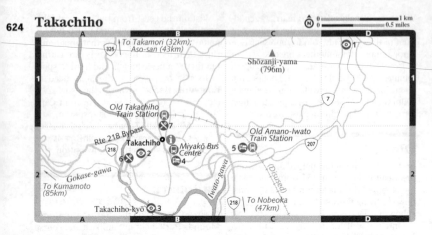

Takachiho

⊙ Sights

Ama-no-Iwato-jinja   SHRINE
(天岩戸神社; 1073-1 Iwato; ⊙24hr, office 8.30am-
5pm) One of Shintō's loveliest shrines honours the cave where Amaterasu hid. The
cave itself is off-limits, but Nishi Hongū (the
shrine's main building) sits right across the
river Iwato-gawa. If you have a Japanese
speaker, ask a staff member to show you the
viewpoint behind the *honden* (main hall).
Buses leave about hourly (¥300, 20 minutes)
from Takachiho's Miyakō bus centre.

A seven-minute walk beside a picturesque
stream takes you to **Ama-no-Yasukawara**,
a deep cave where tradition says that thousands of other deities discussed how to lure
Amaterasu from the cave. Modern-day visitors have left innumerable stacks of stones in
tribute, imparting a sort of Indy Jones feeling.

Higashi Hongū, across the river, marks
where Amaterasu lived after emerging from
hiding.

Takachiho-kyō   GORGE
(高千穂峡) Takachiho's magnificent gorge
with its waterfall, overhanging rocks and
sheer walls was formed over 120,000 years
ago by a double volcanic eruption. There's
a 1km-long nature trail above the gorge. Or
view it up close from a **rowboat** (☎73-1213;
per 30min ¥1500; ⊙8.30am-5pm), though during high season it can be as busy as rush
hour.

Takachiho-jinja   SHRINE
(高千穂神社) Takachiho-jinja, about 10 min-
utes' walk from the bus centre, is set in a
grove of cryptomeria pines.

🎎 Festivals & Events

Takachihō's artistic claim to fame is **kagura** (sacred dance). In May, September and
November (the dates change annually),
performances are held at Ama-no-Iwato-
jinja from 10am to 10pm, while hour-long
performances of **yokagura** (night-time kagura; tickets ¥500; ⊙8pm) take place nightly at
Takachiho-jinja.

There are also all-night performances
(satokagura) in farmhouses on 19 nights
from November to February. In all, 33 dances are performed from 6pm until 9am the
next morning. If you brave the cold until
morning, you'll be caught up in a wave of
excitement. Contact the tourist information
office for details.

🛏 Sleeping & Eating

Takachiho has about 30 hotels, ryokan,
minshuku and pensions, which all typically
book out during the autumn foliage season.

Folkcraft Ryokan Kaminoya
RYOKAN $$

(民芸旅館かみの家; ☎72-2111; www.kaminoya
.jp; 806-5 Mitai; r with/without 2 meals from
¥12,600/7350; P@) In central Takachiho, this
ryokan was beautifully renovated in 2010
and has folkcraft pieces strategically placed.
There's a *hinoki* (cypress) bath as well as in-
room facilities. Look for the woodwork and
whitewashed facade.

Takachiho Youth Hostel
HOSTEL $

(高千穂ユースホステル; ☎72-3021; 5899-2
Mitai, Takachiho; dm HI member/nonmember
¥2800/3400; P☺@) This large hostel is far
from the sights but clean, efficient and deep
in the woods. Rooms are Japanese style, and
breakfast/dinner (¥500/900) are available,
as are laundry machines and pick-up from
the bus centre.

Young Echō
CAFE $

(ヤングエコー; ☎72-3345; 2nd fl, 1444-1 Mitai;
dishes from ¥600; ☺lunch & dinner; @✍🗎) This
cheery cafe with a young clientele serves a
mix of Western and Japanese foods, includ-
ing a popular set menu of chicken *nanban*
(¥950). Veggie-friendly options are also
available, and some staff speak English. Fol-
low the signs for Takachiho Station (now
closed).

Chiho-no-ie
JAPANESE $

(千穂の家; ☎72-2115; 62-2 Ojimukoyama; meals
from ¥500; ☺lunch) At the base of the gorge,
this three-storey building serves seasonal
regional treats and *nagashi-sōmen* (¥600) –
have fun catching tasty noodles with your
chopsticks as they float by in halved bam-
boo rafts.

❶ Getting There & Around

Most visitors arrive in Takachiho by car from
Kumamoto or Aso-san. Two buses daily serve
Takachiho's Miyakō bus centre (宮交バスセ
ンター) from Kumamoto (¥2300, 2¾ hours)
via Takamori (¥1280, 1¼ hours). From the bus
centre it's walkable to the gorge and Takachiho-
jinja, but you'll need transport to reach other
sights.

Beppu
別府

☎0977 / POP 120,536

You don't have to look far in Beppu, in Ōita
Prefecture (大分県), to see the reason for its
popularity: steam rising from vents in the
earth means onsen bathing opportunities
galore. Beppu is at turns quaint, touristy,
modern, traditional, solid and rickety, but
the charm of this hospitable city grows on
visitors as sure as the waters are warm.

❂ Sights & Activities
Hot Springs

Beppu has two types of hot springs, collec-
tively pumping out more than 100 million
litres of hot water every day. *Jigoku* (hells)
are for looking at; onsen are for bathing.

Hells
HOT SPRINGS

(Map p626; each hell/combination ticket
¥400/2000; ☺8am-5pm) Beppu's most hyped
attraction is **jigoku meguri** (hell circuit),
where waters bubble forth from under-
ground with unusual results. Unlike Unzen
(p594), where the geothermal wonders are
unadorned, the circuit's eight stops have
become mini amusement parks, each with a
theme and some loaded with tourist kitsch;
consider yourself warned.

The hells are in two groups, six at **Kan-
nawa**, over 4km northwest of Beppu Sta-
tion, and two about 2.5km further north. In
the Kannawa group are steaming blue **Umi
Jigoku** (海地獄; Sea Hell), **Oni-bōzu Jigoku**
(Demon Monk Hell, where bubbling mud
looks like a monk's shaved head), **Shira-ike
Jigoku** (白池地獄; White Pond Hell) and
Kamado Jigoku (かまど地獄; Oven Hell,
named because it was once used for cook-
ing). At **Oni-yama Jigoku** (鬼山地獄; Dev-
il's Mountain Hell) and **Yama Jigoku** (山地
獄; Mountain Hell), a variety of animals are
kept in enclosures that look uncomfortably
small.

SUN GODDESS DISAPPEARS! WORLD GOES DARK!

According to Shintō legend, the sun goddess Amaterasu, angered by the misbehaviour
of her brother, exiled herself into a cave sealed by a boulder, plunging the world into dark-
ness. Alarmed, other gods gathered at another nearby cave to discuss how to get her
to re-emerge. Eventually the goddess Ama-no-Uzume performed a bawdy dance which
aroused Amaterasu's curiosity, and she emerged from the cave and light was restored to
earth. *Iwato kagura* dances performed in Takachiho today re-enact this story.

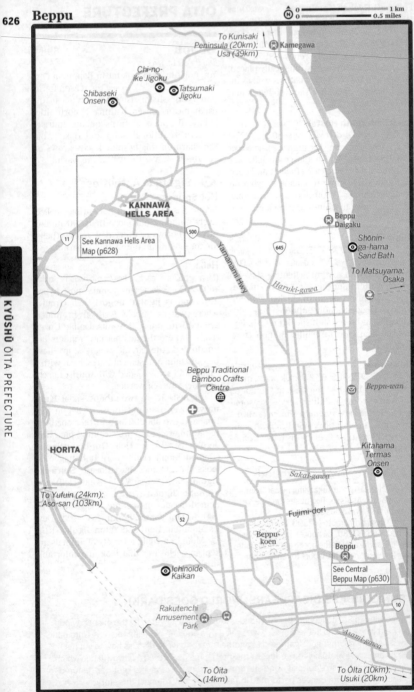

N
0 ———————————— 1 km
0 ———————————— 0.5 miles

To Kunisaki
Peninsula (20km);
Usa (39km)
Kamegawa

Chi-no-
ike Jigoku
Tatsumaki
Jigoku
Shibaseki
Onsen

KANNAWA
HELLS AREA

See Kannawa Hells Area
Map (p628)

11

500

Yamanami Hwy

645

Beppu
Daigaku

Shōnin-
ga-hama
Sand Bath

To Matsuyama;
Osaka

Haruki-gawa

Beppu Traditional
Bamboo Crafts
Centre

Beppu-wan

HORITA

Kitahama
Termas
Onsen

Sakai-gawa

To Yufuin (24km);
Aso-san (103km)

52

Fujimi-dori

Beppu-
kōen

Beppu

See Central
Beppu Map (p630)

10

Ichinoide
Kaikan

Rakutenchi
Amusement
Park

Asami-gawa

To Ōita
(14km)

To Ōita (10km);
Usuki (20km)

The smaller group of hells has **Chi-no-ike Jigoku** (血の池地獄; Blood Pool Hell), with its photogenic red water, and **Tatsu-maki Jigoku** (龍巻地獄; Tornado Hell), where a geyser shoots off about every 35 minutes.

Onsen

Beppu has eight onsen districts, **Beppu Hattō** (www.city.beppu.oita.jp/01onsen/english/index.html). Onsen aficionados spend their time in Beppu moving from one bath to another and consider at least three baths a day *de rigueur*; bathing costs from ¥100 to ¥1000. Bring your own soap, washcloth and towel, as some places don't rent them.

In central Beppu, the *very* hot **Take-gawara Onsen** (竹瓦温泉; Map p630; 16-23 Moto-machi; admission ¥100, sand bath ¥1000; ⊘6.30am-10.30pm, sand bath 8am-9.30pm) occupies a fabulous wooden building dating back to the Meiji era. Bathing is simple; scoop out water with a bucket, wash yourself, then soak. There's also a sand bath where a *yukata* is provided so you can lie in a shallow trench and get buried up to your neck in hot sand; arrive earlier for warmest sand. The simple half-timber building of **Ekimae Kōtō Onsen** (駅前高等温泉; Map p630; 13-14 Ekimae-machi; admission ¥300; ⊘24hr) is just a couple of minutes' walk from the station.

Downhill from Kannawa bus stop is **Kannawa Mushi-yu** (steam bath; Map p626; 1-gumi, Kannawa-kami; admission/yukata ¥500/210; ⊘6.30am-8pm), where wrapped in a *yukata* you steam at 65°C (ow!) on top of Japanese rush leaves. Nearby **Hyōtan Onsen** (ひょうたん温泉; Map p626; 159-2 Kannawa; admission/yukata ¥700/200, admission after 6pm ¥550; ⊘9am-1am) has multiple pools, *rotemburo*, sand baths and private baths.

Shibaseki Onsen (柴石温泉; Map p626; 4-kumi Noda; admission ¥210; ⊘7am-8pm, closed 2nd Wed of each month) is en route to the smaller pair of hells. You can rent a private *kazoku-buro* (family bath) for ¥1570 per hour.

Nearby, popular **Onsen Hoyōland** (温泉保養ランド; 5-1 Myōban; admission ¥1050; ⊘9am-8pm) has giant mud baths, plus open-air and mixed-gender bathing.

Between JR Beppu Station and the Kamegawa onsen area, **Shōnin-ga-hama sand bath** (上人ヶ浜; Map p626; admission ¥1000; ⊘8.30am-6pm Apr-Oct, 9am-5pm Nov-Mar) has a great beach location and some English-speaking staff.

For a seaside onsen experience, head to **Kitahama Termas Onsen** (北浜温泉テルマス; Map p626; admission ¥500; ⊘10am-8pm). You'll need a bathing suit, as the outside *rotemburo* mixes it up.

The owner of **Ichinoide Kaikan** (いちのいで会館; Map p626; 14-2 Uehara-machi; ⊘11am-5pm) loves onsen so much that he built three pool-sized *rotemb14ro* in his backyard. There are fabulous views over Beppu to the sea. The general deal is that you order a delicious *teishoku* (¥1300), prepared while you bathe. Ask for directions at Foreign Tourist Information Offices.

Other Sights
Beppu Traditional Bamboo
Crafts Centre   CRAFTS CENTRE
(別府市竹細工伝統産業会館; Map p626; 8-3 Higashi-sōen; admission ¥300; ⊘8.30am-5pm Tue-Sun) The hands-on crafts centre displays refined works from Edo-period masters as well as current examples of uses for this versatile material which grows copiously in this region. From Beppu Station, take bus 22 or 25 to Dentō Sangyō-kaikan-mae or bus 1 to Minami-haru (about 200m away). If you'd like to try your own hand (¥300), reservations are requested a couple days ahead.

Hihōkan Sex Museum   MUSEUM
(別府秘宝館; Map p626; 338-3 Kannawa; admission ¥700; ⊘9.30am-5pm) Among the Kannawa hells, this sex museum spans the lurid to the bawdy: erotic *ukiyo-e* (woodblock prints), natural and sculpted objects shaped like private parts, and a depiction of Snow White we frankly wish we hadn't seen.

Festivals & Events

Onsen Festival   ONSEN
Held during the first weekend in April.

Tanabata Matsuri   TRADITIONAL
In adjacent Ōita city, held over three days from the first Friday in August.

Sleeping

TOP CHOICE **Beppu Hotel Umine**   HOTEL $$$
(Map p630; ☎26-0002; www.umine.jp; 3-8-3 Kitahama; r per person with breakfast from ¥15,750; P❋@) In-room onsen baths with water views, gorgeous common baths, savvy contemporary design, excellent restaurants and oodles of personal service make this Beppu's top stay. Rates are expensive but cover your minibar bill, and drinks and snacks in the library lounge.

Kannawa Hells Area

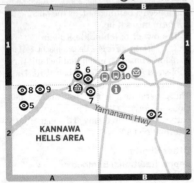

0 ————— 200 m
0 ————— 0.1 miles

Kannawa Hells Area

Yamada Bessou   RYOKAN **$**

(山田別荘; Map p630; ☎24-2121; http://yama dabessou.jp; 3-2-18 Kitahama; r per person with/without 2 meals from ¥10,650/5400; P@❀🐾) You could be stepping back in time at this sprawling family-run 1930s inn with wonderfully well-preserved rooms and fabulous art deco features and furnishings. The onsen and private *rotemburo* are so lovely you'll hardly mind that only a couple of its eight rooms have full bath and toilet.

Suginoi Hotel   HOTEL **$$$**

(杉乃井ホテル; ☎24-1141; www.suginoi-hotel .com/english; 1 Kankaiji; r per person with 2 meals from ¥15,900; P@❀) On a hillside above town, Suginoi offers the tiered rooftop Tanayu *rotemburo,* the Aqua Garden onsen swimming pool (combined day use ¥1300,

bathing suit required) and high standards indoors. Japanese-style rooms are more alluring than Western ones, but the 15 Ceada Floor rooms are slick and special.

Nogami Honkan Ryokan   RYOKAN **$**

(野上本館; Map p630; ☎22-1334; www.yukem uri.net; 1-12-1 Kitahama; r per person with/without breakfast ¥6000/5000; P@❀) In a classic, boxy 1950s building near Takegawara Onsen, most of the 25 rooms here don't have private bathrooms. Three small baths can be reserved for private use, and owner Ken is a knowledgeable and gracious host.

Kokage International Minshuku   MINSHUKU **$**

(国際民宿こかげ; Map p630; ☎23-1753; http:// ww6.tiki.ne.jp/~kokage; 8-9 Ekimae-chō; s/d ¥4350/7650; @❀) This cosy 10-room inn is old and friendly, chock-full of antiques and trinkets. There's a lovely stone onsen, and toast and coffee for breakfast. Rooms over the entrance are quietest.

Hotel Aile   BUSINESS HOTEL **$$**

(ホテル エール; Map p630; ☎21-7272; 2-14-35 Kitahama; s/d/tw ¥6240/9540/10,590; P❀@) A rooftop *rotemburo,* 10th-storey common baths with sweeping city views and spacious guest rooms make this an excellent midrange choice. Japanese breakfast includes *dango-jiru* (miso soup). Ignore the music-box soundtrack in the hallways.

Beppu Guest House   HOSTEL **$**

(別府ゲストハウス; Map p630; ☎76-7811; www .beppu-g-h.net; 1-12 Ekimae-chō; dm/s ¥1500/2500; P❀@❀) A jazz soundtrack courses through the big kitchen and living rooms of this arty-funky and welcoming hostel, a great place to hang out with fellow travellers. English-speaking staff can steer you to Beppu's bubbliest spots.

Spa Hostel Khaosan Beppu   HOSTEL **$**

(スパホステルカオサン別府はまゆう; Map p630; ☎23-3939; www.khaosan-beppu.com; 3-3-10 Kitahama; dm/s ¥2000/3000; P❀@❀) Beppu's newest backpackers is excellent value with clean, renovated rooms (mix of Japanese and Western styles) and hot-spring baths.

Hotel Arthur   HOTEL **$**

(ホテルアーサー; Map p630; ☎25-2611; 1-2-5 Kitahama; s/d from ¥5500/9500; P❀@) About five minutes on foot from the station, with onsen baths and sauna.

Hotel Seawave Beppu   BUSINESS HOTEL **$**

(ホテルシーウェーブ別府; Map p630; ☎27-

1311; www.coara.or.jp/seawave, in Japanese; 12-8 Ekimae-chō; s/tw/ste from ¥5800/8400/17,800; P⚼) Right across from the station.

🍴 Eating

Beppu is renowned for *toriten* (chicken tempura), freshwater fish, *Bungo-gyū* (local beef), *fugu* (pufferfish), wild mountain vegetables and *dango-jiru* (miso soup with thick-cut noodles). On the 1st floor of the You-Me Town shopping mall, English-friendly restaurants include conveyor-belt sushi, noodles and a buffet.

Toyotsune   JAPANESE $$
(とよ常; Map p630; ☎22-2083; mains ¥630-1260; 🍴) Main branch (☎22-3274; 2-13-11 Kitahama; ⏰lunch & dinner, closed Wed); Beppu Station (3-7 Ekimae-honmachi; ⏰lunch & dinner, closed Thu) Toyotsune nails the Beppu specialities: *toriten, Bungo-gyū* and lots of fresh fish, plus tempura. The main branch is on the corner behind Jolly Pasta, and the second branch is across from Beppu Station.

Ureshi-ya   SHOKUDŌ $
(うれしや; Map p630; ☎22-0767; 7-12 Ekimae-honmachi; dishes from ¥200-850; ⏰5pm-2am, closed Mon) You'll get your money's worth at this friendly and busy *shokudō* with *donburi* (dishes served over rice), sashimi, *oden* (hotpot), noodle dishes and more, displayed for you to choose.

Shinanoya   JAPANESE $
(off Map p630; ☎25-8728; 6-32 Nishi-noguchi; mains ¥600-1300; ⏰9am-9.30pm) A few minutes from the station's west exit and dating back to 1926, this kindly *kissaten* also serves a renowned *dango-jiru* loaded with veggies and best enjoyed while viewing the piney garden. It's the traditional building just before Family Mart.

Gyōza Kogetsu   GYŌZA $
(餃子湖月; Map p630; ☎21-8062; 3-7 Ekimae-honmachi; gyōza ¥600; ⏰2-9.30pm, closed Tue)

This seven-seat counter shop has only two things on the menu – generous plates of *gyōza* fried to a delicate crunch and bottles of beer – and a manic local following. It's in the tiny alley behind the covered arcade.

Fugu Matsu   FUGU $$$
(ふぐ松; Map p630; ☎21-1717; 3-6-14 Kitahama; fugu set meals from ¥7350; ⏰lunch & dinner; 🍴) This friendly shop is the place to try *fugu* in style (diehards love it).

Tomonaga Panya   BAKERY $
(友永パン屋; ☎23-0969; Chiyo-machi 2-29; pastries from ¥90; ⏰8.30am-5.30pm Mon-Sat) This charming, historic bakery has been in business since 1916, and people still queue for its ever-changing selection of oven-fresh breads and pastries. The *wanchan* (doggie) bun is filled with custard cream and uses raisins for the eyes and nose. Note: it closes when sold out.

Jin Robata & Beer Pub   IZAKAYA $
(ろばた仁; Map p630; ☎21-1768; 1-15-7 Kitahama; ⏰5pm-midnight) A flashing neon fish sign directs you to this welcoming, international pub. There's plenty of great food to go with your booze. Pick from the rows of fresh fish on display, then watch it being grilled behind the counter.

🍷 Drinking

Natsume Kissa   CAFE
(喫茶なつめ; Map p630; 1-4-23 Kitahama; ⏰10am-8.30pm, closed Wed) This retro snack and dessert spot in the covered arcade is best known for its own *onsen kōhī* (¥530), coffee made with hot-spring water. Look for the wooden barrel above the door.

World Sports Bar Small Eye   BAR
(ワールドスポーツバースモールアイ; Map p630; 1st fl, 1-10-12 Kitahama; drinks/snacks from ¥500/400; ⏰closed Thu) You'll find a good mix of young folk at this Yankee-styled bar with high ceilings, darts and beach umbrellas.

DON'T MISS

JIGOKU MUSHI KŌBŌ

Ingenious! Amid the hells of Kannawa, you can cook your own meal in onsen steam in this **'workshop'** (地獄蒸し工房; Hell Steaming Workshop; Map p626; ☎66-3775; 5-kumi Furomoto; dishes from ¥600-1300, steamers ¥500 per 30min; ⏰9am-9pm, closed 3rd Wed of month). Purchase ingredients on the spot (or bring your own), and steam them in *kama* (vats) roiling from the onsen below. It shares a building with the Foreign Tourist Information Office, so there's usually an English speaker on hand to help.

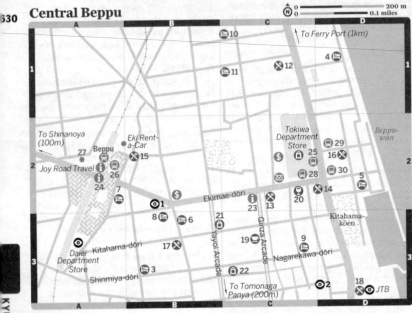

🛍 Shopping

For over a century, the must-have Beppu souvenir for Japanese holidaymakers was everyday-use bamboo products (such as baskets); nowadays the trend is towards art pieces. Shops in the city's central shopping arcades sell both, although many pieces are Chinese imports. Ask 'Nihon-sei des[u] ka?' (Is this made in Japan?) to check. Most of the wares at **Yamashō** (Map p630; 4-9 Kusunoki-machi) and **Chiku-en** (Map p630; 1-4-5 Kitahama) are local.

ℹ Information

Foreign Tourist Information Offices (別府外国人観光客内所; www.beppuftio.blogspot.com) Beppu International Plaza (別府外国人観光客内所; Map p630; ☎23-1119; cnr Ekimae-dōri & Ginza Arcade; ◷10am-5pm; @); Beppu Station (Map p630; ☎21-6220; 12-13 Ekimae-machi; ◷9am-5pm; Kannawa (Map p626; ☎66-3855; 5-kumi Furomoto; ◷9am-5pm; @) Well equipped with helpful bilingual volunteers and an arsenal of local information and advice.

International ATMs can be found at Beppu Station, Kitahama post office (別府北浜郵便局) and the nearby Cosmopia shopping centre. Ōita Bank (大分銀行) handles foreign-exchange services.

ℹ Getting There & Away

AIR Flights go to Ōita Airport from Tokyo Haneda (¥35,700, 1½ hours) and Osaka (¥19,300, one hour). Flights also operate to Seoul.

BOAT The **Ferry Sunflower Kansai Kisen** (☎22-1311) makes an overnight run between Beppu and Osaka and Kōbe (¥11,300, 11 hours), stopping at Matsuyama (4½ hours). The evening boat departs at 6.35pm to western Honshū and passes through the Inland Sea, arriving at 7.35am the next morning. For the port, take bus 20 or 26 from Beppu Station's west exit.

BUS There's a Kyūshū Odan bus to Aso Station (¥3500, 3¼ hours) and Kumamoto (¥6450, five hours).

TRAIN The JR Nippō line runs from Hakata (Fukuoka) to Beppu (tokkyū; ¥5550, two hours) and Miyazaki (¥6070, 3¼ hours). The JR Hōhi line connects Beppu with Kumamoto (¥5130, three hours) via Aso (¥3740, two hours).

ℹ Getting Around

To/From the Airport

Beppu Airport buses to Ōita Airport stop outside Tokiwa department store (¥1450, 45 minutes) and Beppu Station.

Bus

Kamenoi is the main bus company. An unlimited 'My Beppu Free' pass comes in two varieties: 'mini' (adult/student ¥900/700), which covers

KYŪSHŪ YUFUIN

Beppu city (and offers discounts), and the 'wide' (one/two days ¥1600/2400), which extends to Yufuin. Passes are available from Foreign Tourist Information Offices and some lodgings. From JR Beppu Station, buses 2, 5, 7, 41 and 43 go to Kannawa (15 to 25 minutes), and buses 16 and 26 serve Chi-no-ike and Tatsumaki *jigokus*.

Yufuin   由布院

☏ 0977 / POP 35,380

About 25km inland from Beppu, delightful Yufuin sits in a ring of mountains, with the twin peaks of Yufu-dake especially notable. The town lives for tourism and is a good place to see contemporary Japanese crafts; ceramics, clothing, woodworking and even interesting foods abound in its narrow lanes. However, Yufuin gets crowded on holidays and weekends. If staying overnight, arrive before dusk, when the day trippers leave and wealthier Japanese retreat to the sanctuary of their ryokan.

The **tourist Information office** (☏84-2446; ◎9am-7pm) inside the train station has some information in English, including a detailed walking map showing galleries, museums and onsen. There's a postal ATM next to the station.

As in Beppu, making a pilgrimage from one onsen to another is a popular activity. **Shitan-yu** (下ん湯; admission ¥200; ◎10am-9pm) is a thatched bathhouse on the northern shore of **Kinrin-ko** (Lake of Golden Fish Scales), a lake named by a Meiji-era philosopher and fed by a hot spring.

Double-peaked **Yufu-dake** (1584m) volcano overlooks Yufuin and takes about 90 minutes to climb. Some buses from Yufuin stop at the base of Yufu-dake, Yufu-tozanguchi (由布登山口; ¥360, 16 minutes).

🛏 Sleeping & Eating

Most patrons take their meals while relaxing in their inn, but there's a handful of eateries by the station.

Kamenoi Bessō   RYOKAN $$$
(亀の井別荘; ☏84-3166; www.kamenoi-bessou .jp; 2633-1 Kawakami; r per person with 2 meals from ¥35,000; ℗@) For the no-holds-barred Yufuin splurge, look no further. From Kinrin-kō, enter the *kayabuki* (thatched roof) gate down gravel paths to this campus of craftsman-style wooden buildings, encircling stone baths with peaked wooden roofs. Meals are sure to contain local specialities, and staff seem never to have heard

the concept 'no'. Choose from Japanese, Western and combination Japanese–Western-style guest rooms.

Yufuin Country Road Youth Hostel

HOSTEL $

(由布院カントリーロードユースホステ
ル; ☎84-3734; www4.ocn.ne.jp/yufuinyh, in Japanese; 441-29 Kawakami; dm member/nonmember ¥2835/3435; P ⊖ ◉ ☎) On a forested hillside overlooking the town and especially pretty at night, this first-rate 25-bed hostel has its own onsen and hospitable, English-speaking owners. It's possible they may pick you up from the station if you aren't in time for one of the infrequent buses (¥200). Two meals are available for an extra ¥1680.

Makiba-no-ie

RYOKAN $$

(牧場の家; ☎84-2138; 2870-1 Kawakami; r per person with 2 meals from ¥9600; P) Atmosphere aplenty in these thatched-roof huts with sink and toilet around a *rotemburo*. The antique-filled garden restaurant does chicken *jidori* and *Bungō-gyū teishoku* meals from ¥1600. Visitors can use the *rotemburo* for ¥500.

Izumi Soba

NOODLES $

(泉そば; ☎85-2283; 1599-1 Kawakami; soba from ¥1260; ⊙11am-5pm) There are less inexpensive *soba* shops in town, but at this classy little *soba* shop by Kinrin-ko you can watch the noodles being made in the window before you sit down. The basic is *seirō-soba* (on a bamboo mat); *oroshi-soba* comes topped with grated daikon.

Sugitaya

JAPANESE $$

(すぎた屋; ☎84-5644; ⊙lunch & dinner, closed Tue) Walk straight out of the station for 400m to this spot under a sign reading 'Tachibana'. Try the generous speciality, *toriten* (¥800) and *dangojiru teishoku* for ¥1200. Set meals are great value.

🛈 Getting There & Away

Trains connect Beppu with Yufuin (*futsū/tokkyū* ¥1080/2580, 1¼ hours/one hour) via Ōita.

Buses connect JR Beppu Station with Yufuin throughout the day (¥900, 50 minutes). Express buses serve Fukuoka (¥2800), Aso and Kumamoto.

Usuki 臼杵

☎0972 / POP 41,500

Just outside Usuki is a superb collection of thousand-year-old **Buddha images** (臼杵石仏; Fukata, Usuki; admission ¥530; ⊙6am-6pm,

---

MADE IN USA

In the early post-WWII era, when 'Made in Japan' was no recommendation at all, it's said that companies would register in the town of Usa, so they could proclaim their goods were 'Made in USA'.

---

to 7pm Apr-Oct), although some of the magic is lost in the tourist-trap ambience. Four clusters comprising 59 images lie in a series of niches in a ravine. Some are complete statues, whereas others have only the heads remaining.

Usuki has several temples and well-preserved traditional houses. On the last Saturday in August, the town hosts a **fire festival**, and other festivities are held throughout the year; ask for details at the **tourist information office** (☎64-7130; ⊙8.30am-5pm) adjacent to Usuki Station. There's free internet and some local history exhibits at the community centre **Sala de Usuki** (サーラデ臼杵; ☎64-7271).

Local restaurants boast the best *fugu* in Japan; expect to pay from about ¥8000 for a dinner set, including *sake*.

Usuki is 40km southeast of Beppu. Take the JR Nippō line to Usuki Station (*tokkyū/futsū* ¥1810/910, 45/60 minutes), most involving a change in Ōita. From here infrequent buses take 20 minutes to the Buddha images, or it's about ¥2000 by taxi or 30 minutes via free loaner bike.

Kunisaki Peninsula 国東半島

North of Beppu, the Kunisaki Peninsula bulges northeastward from the Kyūshū coast. The town of Bungo-takada is nicknamed 'Buddha's Village' and the region is noted for its early Buddhist influence, including some rock-carved images linked to the more famous ones at Usuki.

The 11th-century **Fuki-ji** (富貴寺; Tashibufuki, Bungo-takada; admission ¥200) in Bungo-takada is the oldest wooden structure in Kyūshū and one of the oldest wooden temples in Japan. Ōita Kōtsū buses from Usa Station go to Bungo-takada (¥810, 35 minutes); from there, it's a 10-minute taxi ride (around ¥1000).

In the centre of the peninsula, near the summit of Futago-san (721m), is **Futago-ji** (両子寺; 1548 Futago, Akimachi; admission ¥200;

⊙8am-5pm), founded in 718 and dedicated to Fudō-Myō-o, the ferocious, fire-enshrouded, sword-wielding deity, able to repel attacks while appearing calm. It's a lovely climb, especially in spring or autumn.

Nearby **Taizō-ji** (admission ¥200; ⊙8.30am-5pm) is known for its famously uneven stone stairs. Local legend says that they are so random and haphazard that the Oni (devils) must have created them in a single night, confirming that, even in mythology, it has always been hard to get good help.

Around 2km south of **Maki Ōdō Hall** are two Heian-period Buddha images carved into a cliff, a 6m figure of the Dainichi Buddha and an 8m figure of Fudō-Myō-o. Known as **Kumano Magaibutsu** (Tashibu Hirano, ⊙8.30am-5pm), these are the largest Buddhist images of this type in Japan.

The sprawling, wooded and water-crossed **Usa-jingū** (宇佐神社; 2859 Ōaza, Min-ami-Usa) shrine, the original of which dates back some 1200 years, is the chief shrine among some 40,000 in Japan dedicated to the warrior-god Hachiman. It's a 4km bus or taxi ride from Usa Station (get off at Usa-Hachiman-mae), on the JR Nippō line from Beppu.

Okinawa & the Southwest Islands

Best Places to Eat

» Yūnangi (p654)

» Paikaji (p654)

» Pōcha Tatsuya (p661)

Best Places to Stay

» Sankara Hotel & Spa (p640)

» Pricia Resort (p648)

» Yakushima Youth Hostel (p640)

Why Go?

Japan's Southwest Islands (南西諸島; Nansei-shotō) are *the other Japan:* a chain of semitropical, coral-fringed islands that feels more like Hawaii or Southeast Asia.

It's a nature lover's paradise: in the northern Kagoshima Prefecture lush primeval forests hide among the craggy peaks of Yakushima. The starfish-like Amami-Ōshima has fine beaches in its convoluted coastline, and tiny Yoron-tō is basically all beach, with an airport on top. Heading south, the first stop is Okinawa-hontō (沖縄本島), the bustling main island of Okinawa prefecture. Kerama Islands are tiny gems with white-sand beaches and crystal-clear waters. Miyako-jima boasts killer beaches, plenty of sugarcane fields and a laid-back scene. Yaeyama Islands have Japan's best coral reefs, subtropical jungles and mangrove swamps.

But spectacular nature is only part of it: the islands also boast a fascinating, peculiarly 'un-Japanese' culture. Indeed, Okinawa was a separate country for most of its history and the Ryūkyū cultural heart still beats in the Southwest Islands.

When to Go
Naha

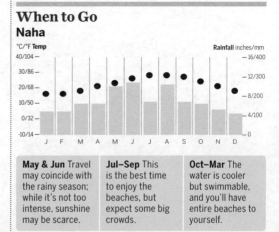

| **May & Jun** Travel may coincide with the rainy season; while it's not too intense, sunshine may be scarce. | **Jul–Sep** This is the best time to enjoy the beaches, but expect some big crowds. | **Oct–Mar** The water is cooler but swimmable, and you'll have entire beaches to yourself. |

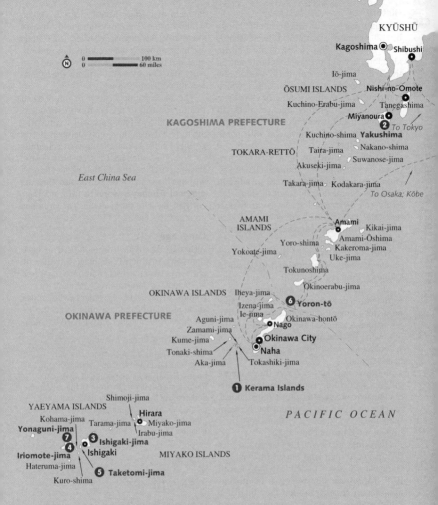

KYŪSHŪ

Kagoshima ● Shibushi

Iō-jima

ŌSUMI ISLANDS   Nishi-no-Omote

Kuchino-Erabu-jima   Tanegashima

KAGOSHIMA PREFECTURE   Miyanoura ● ❷ To Tokyo

Kuchino-shima   **Yakushima**

TOKARA-RETTŌ   Taira-jima   • Nakano-shima

Akuseki-jima   Suwanose-jima

East China Sea   Takara-jima   Kodakara-jima

To Osaka; Kōbe

AMAMI
ISLANDS   Amami   Kikai-jima

Yoro-shima   Amami-Ōshima

Yokoate-jima   Kakeroma-jima

Uke-jima

Tokunoshima

OKINAWA ISLANDS   Iheya-jima   Okinoerabu-jima

OKINAWA PREFECTURE   Izena-jima   ❻ **Yoron-tō**

Ie-jima   Okinawa-hontō

Aguni-jima   ● Nago

Zamami-jima   Okinawa City

Kume-jima   ● **Naha**

Tonaki-shima   Okinawa City

Aka-jima   Tokashiki-jima

❶ **Kerama Islands**

PACIFIC OCEAN

Shimoji-jima

YAEYAMA ISLANDS   **Hirara**

Kohama-jima   Tarama-jima   ● **Miyako-jima**

Yonaguni-jima ❼   Irabu-jima

❹ ❸ **Ishigaki-jima**

Iriomote-jima ● **Ishigaki**   MIYAKO ISLANDS

Hateruma-jima

❺ **Taketomi-jima**

Kuro-shima

Okinawa & the Southwest Islands Highlights

❶ Soak up the sun on one of the white-sand beaches of the **Kerama Islands** (p657)

❷ Hike into the mountainous heart of **Yakushima** (p637) to commune with ancient *yaku-sugi* trees

❸ Dive with playful mantas off **Ishigaki-jima** (p668)

❹ Explore the mangrove swamps, jungles and coral reefs of Japan's last frontier, **Iriomote-jima** (p668)

❺ Take a ferry to a simpler time on the 'living museum' island of **Taketomi-jima** (p670)

❻ Chill out on peaceful **Yoron-tō** (p647) and its blissful scenery of beaches and sugarcane

❼ Search the horizon for Taiwan from **Yonaguni-jima** (p671), Japan's westernmost island, and learn about its enormous moths

History

For centuries ruled by *aji* (local chieftains), in 1429 Okinawa and the Southwest Islands were united by Sho Hashi of the Chūzan kingdom, which led to the establishment of the Ryūkyū dynasty. During this period Sho Hashi increased contact with China, which contributed to the flourishing of Okinawan music, dance, literature and ceramics. In this 'Golden Era', weapons were prohibited, and the islands were rewarded with peace and tranquillity.

But the Ryūkyū kingdom was not prepared for war when the Shimazu clan of Satsuma (modern-day Kagoshima) invaded in 1609. The Shimazu conquered the kingdom easily and established severe controls over its trade. The islands were controlled with an iron fist, and taxed and exploited greedily for the next 250 years.

With the restoration of the Meiji emperor, the Ryūkyūs were annexed to Japan as Okinawa Prefecture in 1879. However, life hardly changed for the islanders as they were treated as foreign subjects by the Japanese government. Furthermore, the Meiji government stamped out local culture by outlawing the teaching of Ryūkyū history in schools, and establishing Japanese as the official language.

In the closing days of WWII, the Japanese military made a decision to use the islands of Okinawa as a shield against Allied forces. Sacrificing it cost the islanders dearly: more than 100,000 Okinawan civilians lost their lives in the Battle of Okinawa.

Following the war, the occupation of the Japanese mainland ended in 1952, but Okinawa remained under US control until 1972. Its return, however, was contingent upon Japan agreeing to allow the Americans to maintain bases on the islands and some 30,000 American military personnel remain there. For more information on the continuing occupation of Okinawa, see p657.

Climate

The Southwest Islands have a subtropical climate. With the exception of the peaks of Yakushima, which can be snowcapped between December and February, there's no real winter. You can comfortably travel the Southwest Islands any time of year, but swimming might be uncomfortable between late October and early May, unless you're the hardy sort.

The average daily temperature on Okinawa-hontō in December is 20°C, while in July it is 30°C. The islands of Kagoshima Prefecture average a few degrees cooler, while those of Yaeyama-shotō and Miyako-shotō are a few degrees warmer. The islands are most crowded during June, July and August and during the Golden Week holiday in early May. Outside of these times, the islands are often blissfully quiet.

The main thing to keep in mind when planning a trip to the Southwest Islands is the possibility of typhoons, which can strike anytime between June and October. If you go then, build flexibility into your schedule, as typhoons often cause transport delays. Ideally, purchase tickets that allow changes without incurring a fee. The **Japan Meteorological Agency's website** (www.jma.go.jp/en/typh) has the latest details on typhoons approaching Japan.

Language

Although the Ryūkyū islands used to have their own distinctive language, this has by and large disappeared. Standard Japanese is spoken by almost every resident of the islands. That said, travellers who speak some standard Japanese might find the local dialects and accent a little hard to catch.

ⓘ Getting There & Away

There are flights between major cities in mainland Japan and Amami-Ōshima, Okinawa-hontō (Naha), Miyako-jima and Ishigaki-jima. Kagoshima has flights to/from all these islands and many of the smaller islands as well. Other islands such as Yonaguni-jima, Kume-jima and Zamami-jima can be reached from Naha or Ishigaki.

ⓘ THE ALL-YOU-CAN-SAIL TICKET

Maruei Ferry/A Line (☑in Kagoshima 099-226-4141, in Tokyo 03-5643-6170; www.aline-ferry.com, in Japanese) sails from Kagoshima to Naha and offers a little-known but great deal in its *norihōdai kippu* (2nd-class sleeping rooms; ¥14,200), which lets you get on and off its south- or north-bound ferries freely within seven days; they stop at Amami-Ōshima, Tokunoshima, Okinoerabu-jima, Yoron-tō, and Motobu on Okinawa-hontō. There is more paperwork involved, as you have to get your pass stamped at each boarding, but the savings over individual 2nd-class trips is over ¥6000.

There are ferries between Tokyo, Osaka/Kōbe and Kagoshima to the islands of Amami-shotō and Okinawa-hontō, as well as plentiful ferries between Kagoshima and Yakushima and Tanegashima. Once you arrive in a port like Amami (previously called Naze) on Amami-Ōshima or Naha on Okinawa-hontō, there are local ferry services to nearby islands. However, you cannot reach Miyako-shotō or Yaeyama-shotō by ferry from mainland Japan or Okinawa-hontō.

If you are arriving in Japan by air, it is worth noting that JAL and ANA both offer 'visit Japan'-type airfares for domestic flights within Japan – as long as they are bought outside Japan in conjunction with a ticket to Japan. Such tickets, if used to Okinawa, are an incredible saving from standard domestic airfares bought within Japan.

❶ Getting Around

Aside from ferries, there are also reasonable air networks in Amami-shotō, Okinawa-shotō and Yaeyama-shotō, with airfields on most islands. While most islands have public bus networks, there are usually not more than a few buses per day on each route. We recommend bringing an International Driving Permit and renting a car or scooter, particularly on Yakushima, Ishigaki, Iriomote and Okinawa-hontō.

KAGOSHIMA PREFECTURE

The northern end of the Southwest Islands is part of Kagoshima Prefecture (鹿児島県; Kagoshima-ken), and contains three island groups (island groups are called 'shotō' or 'rettō' in Japanese). All are accessible by ferry or plane.

Northernmost is Ōsumi-shotō, which is home to the island of Yakushima, one of the most popular destinations in the Southwest Islands. Next is the Tokara-rettō, consisting of 12 rarely visited volcanic islets, which is one of the most remote destinations in the region. Southernmost is Amami-shotō, which is home to the population centre of Amami-Ōshima as well as several more picturesque islands. Located 380km south of Kyūshū, this group has a pronounced tropical feel.

Ōsumi Islands　大隈諸島

Ōsumi-shotō comprises the two main islands of Yakushima and Tanegashima and the seldom-visited triumvirate of islands known as Mishima-mura. The all-star attraction in the group is Yakushima, a virtual paradise for nature lovers that attracts large numbers of both domestic and international travellers. Tanegashima, which is famous as the home of Japan's space program, sees few foreign travellers, though it is a popular surfing destination for Japanese. Finally, the most commonly visited island in the Mishima-mura group is tiny Iō-jima, a rarely visited gem of a volcanic island with excellent onsen (hot springs).

YAKUSHIMA　屋久島
📞 0997 / POP 13,700

Designated a Unesco World Heritage Site in 1993, Yakushima is one of the most rewarding islands in the Southwest Islands. The craggy mountain peaks of the island's interior are home to the world-famous *yaku-sugi* (屋久杉; *Cryptomeria japonica*), ancient cedar trees that are said to have been the inspiration for some of the scenes in Miyazaki Hayao's animation classic *Princess Mononoke*.

Hiking among the high peaks and mossy forests is the main activity on Yakushima, but the island is also home to some excellent coastal onsen and a few sandy beaches.

Keep in mind that Yakushima is a place of extremes: the mountains wring every last drop of moisture from the passing clouds and the interior of the island is one of the wettest places in Japan. In the winter the peaks may be covered in snow, while the coast is still relatively balmy. Whatever you do, come prepared and don't set off on a hike without a good map and the proper gear. An International Driving Permit will also vastly increase your enjoyment here, as buses are few and far between.

◉ Sights

Yakushima's main port is Miyanoura (宮之浦), on the island's northeast coast. This is the most convenient place to be based, as most buses originate from here. From Miyanoura, a road runs around the perimeter of the island, passing through the secondary port of Anbō (安房) on the east coast, and then through the hot-springs town of Ono-aida (尾の間) in the south. Heading north from Miyanoura, the road takes you to the town of Nagata (永田), which has a brilliant stretch of white-sand beach.

Hirauchi Kaichū Onsen　ONSEN
(平内海中温泉; admission ¥100; ⊗24hr) Onsen lovers will be in heaven here. The outdoor baths are in the rocks by the sea and can only be entered at or close to low tide. You can walk to the baths from the Kaichū Onsen bus stop, but the next stop, Nishikaikon,

Yakushima

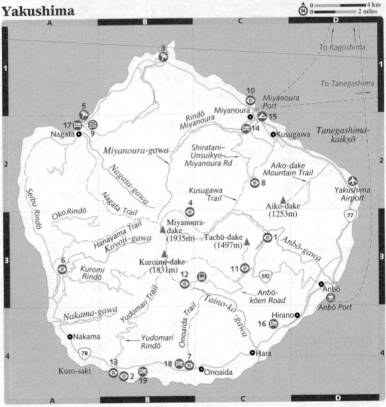

is actually closer. From Nishikaikon, walk downhill towards the sea for about 200m and take a right at the bottom of the hill. Note that this is a *konyoku* onsen (mixed bath), so if you're shy, you'll just have to wait until other bathers clear off, as swimsuits are not allowed.

Yudomari Onsen
ONSEN

(湯泊温泉; admission ¥100; ⊙24hr) About 600m west is another great seaside onsen that can be entered at any tide. Get off at the Yudomari bus stop and take the road opposite the post office in the direction of the sea. Once you enter the village, the way is marked. It's a 300m walk and you pass a great banyan tree en route.

Onoaida Onsen
ONSEN

(尾之間温泉; 136-2 Onoaida; admission ¥200; ⊙7am-9.30pm May-Oct, to 9pm Nov-Apr, from noon Mon) In the village of Onoaida is a rustic indoor bathhouse that is divided by gender.

Expect to rub shoulders with the village elders here. It's about 350m uphill from the Onoaida Onsen bus stop.

Yakushima Environment Culture Village Center
MUSEUM

(屋久島環境文化村センター; 891-4205; Miyanoura; admission & film ¥500; ⊙9am-5pm Tue-Sun Sep-Jun, daily Jul & Aug) In Miyanoura at the corner of the ferry-terminal road. It has exhibits about the island's natural environment and history, with limited English signage. It screens a large-format 25-minute film with English subtitles at 20 minutes past the hour.

Nagata Inaka-hama
BEACH

(長田いなか浜) On the island's northwest coast in the village of Nagata is a beautiful stretch of yellow sand where sea turtles lay their eggs from May to July. It's beside the Inaka-hama bus stop, served by Nagata-bound buses from Miyanoura.

Yakushima

Umigame-kan   MUSEUM
(うみがめ館; 489-8 Nagata; admission ¥200;
⊘9am-5pm, closed Tue) About midway along
Nagata Inaka-hama, along the main road, is
this place which has displays and information
about the turtles (mostly in Japanese).

Issō-kaisuiyokujō   BEACH
(一秦海水浴場) Another fine beach, lo-
cated on the north coast of the island,
about midway between Miyanoura and
Nagata. It's a short walk from the Yahazu
bus stop (served by any Nagata-bound bus
from Miyanoura).

Ōko-no-taki   WATERFALL
(大川の滝) On the west coast is Yakushi-
ma's highest waterfall at 88m. It's a
five-minute walk from Ōko-no-taki bus
stop, which is the last stop on some of
the buses running south and west from
Miyano-ura and Anbō (note that only two
buses a day run all the way out here).

🥾 Activities

Hiking is the best way to experience Yakushima's beauty. If you're planning anything
more than a short stroll around Yaku-sugi
Land, pick up a copy of the Japanese-language *Yama-to-Kougen-no-Chizu- Yakushima* (山と高原の地図屋久島; ¥840), available at major bookshops in Japan.

Even though trails can be very crowded
during holidays, be sure to alert someone at
your accommodation of your intended route
and fill in a *tōzan todokede* (route plan) at
the trailhead.

The most popular hike is to **Jōmon-sugi**
(縄文杉), a monster of a *yaku-sugi* estimated to be 3000 years old. There are two
ways to reach the tree: the 19.5km, eight-
to-10-hour round trip from the **Arakawa-
tozanguchi** (荒川登山口) trailhead (604m),
served by two daily buses to/from Miyanoura (¥1480 and ¥1700, two hours, March
to November); and the round trip from the
Shiratani-unsuikyō-tozanguchi (白谷
雲水峡登山口) trailhead (622m), served by
up to eight daily buses to/from Miyanoura
(¥530, 35 minutes, March to November).

The granddaddy of hikes here is the
day-long outing to the 1935m summit of
Miyanoura-dake, the highest point in
southern Japan. Fit climbers should allow
about seven hours return from **Yodogawa-
tozanguchi** (淀川登山口) trailhead (淀川登
山口;1370m). Yodogawa-tozanguchi is about
1.5km (about 30 minutes) beyond the Kigen-
sugi bus stop, served by two buses a day to/
from Anbō (¥910, one hour). The buses do
not give you sufficient time to complete the
round trip in a day – an early-morning taxi
from Miyanoura (around ¥11,000) gives you
time to make the second bus back to Anbō.

Finally, it's possible to make a traverse
of Miyanoura-dake with a stop at Jōmon
Sugi en route. Do not attempt this in a day;
you'll have to spend the night in one of the
yama-goya (mountain huts) above Jōmon
Sugi. Typical routes are between Yodogawa
and Arakawa or Yodogawa and Shiratani-
unsuikyō. A full traverse of the island is described in Lonely Planet's *Hiking in Japan*.

If you're feeling a little less adventurous,
consider a visit to **Yaku-sugi Land** (ヤクス
ギランド; admission ¥300; ⊘9am-5pm). This is
a great way to see some *yaku-sugi* without
a long trek into the forest. It offers shorter
hiking courses over wooden boardwalks,
and longer hikes deep into the ancient cedar
forest. There are four buses a day to/from
Anbō (¥720, 40 minutes).

🛏 Sleeping

The most convenient place to be based is
Miyanoura. You'll also find lodgings in larger
villages and several barebones *yama-goya* in
the mountains. In July and August and the
spring Golden Week holiday, it's best to try to
reserve ahead, since places fill up early.

SEA TURTLES

Loggerhead sea turtles and green sea turtles come ashore on the beaches of Yakushima to lay their eggs. Unfortunately, human activity can significantly interfere with the egg-laying process. Thus we recommend that you keep the following rules in mind when visiting the beaches of Yakushima (particularly those on the northwest coast):

» Never approach a sea turtle that has come ashore.

» Do not start fires on the beach as the light will confuse the chicks (who use moonlight to orient themselves). Likewise, do not shine torches (flashlights) or car headlights at or near the beach.

» Do not walk on the beach at night.

» Be extremely careful when you walk on the beach, as you might inadvertently step on a newly hatched turtle.

» If you want to observe the turtles, enquire at the **Umigame-kan** centre on Yakushima (p639).

TOP CHOICE Sankara Hotel & Spa
HOTEL $$$

(サンカラ; ☑47-3488; sakarahotel-spa.com; 553 Haginoue, Mugio; r per person with meals from ¥25,000; P@⊠) Overlooking Yakushima's southeast coast, this stunning collection of luxury villas blends ocean views with Balinese floral design elements and fine French and Yakushima cuisine. Add some Thai massage and it's pretty close to perfect. Staff can pick you up, but if you have transport, look for the English sign along the road between Hirano and Hara, and drive up into the hills.

MIYANOURA

Lodge Yaedake-sansō
RYOKAN $$

(ロッジ八重岳山荘; ☑42-1551; www17.ocn.ne.jp/~yakusima/lodge/index.html, in Japanese; Miyanoura; r per person with meals ¥7800; P) This secluded accommodation features Japanese-style rooms in rustic riverside cabins connected by wooden walkways. There are private baths where you can soak up the beauty of your surroundings and children will enjoy splashing in the river. The lodge is located inland upriver on the Miyanoura-gawa; staff can pick you up in Miyanoura. If it's full, it also runs the Yaedake Honkan minshuku in town (r per person with two meals ¥6300).

Miyanoura Portside Youth Hostel
HOSTEL $

(宮之浦ポートサイドユースホステル; ☑49-1316; www.yakushima-yh.net; 278-2 Miyanoura; dm ¥3800, HI member ¥3200; P@) About 10 minutes' walk from the pier in Miyanoura is this simple and clean youth hostel. The place doesn't offer meals, but there are several good restaurants close by. To get there from the pier, walk into the village, then follow the first main shoreline road on the left.

Seaside Hotel
HOTEL $$$

(シーサイドホテル屋久島; ☑42-0175; www.ssh-yakushima.co.jp, in Japanese; 1208-9 Miyanoura; r with 2 meals from ¥17,850; P@⊠) Overlooking the port in Miyanoura, this resort hotel has spacious Western-style rooms and some great ocean views. It's a three-minute walk from the Miyanoura ferry pier, on the right as you walk towards town.

Ocean View Campground
CAMPGROUND $

(オーシャンビューキャンプ場; Yakushima Youth Campground; ☑42-0091; campsite per person ¥840) This campground is pretty much just a field for tents and a couple of showers and bathrooms, with a bit of rocky beach down the hill. It's just west of the Eneos petrol station. There are a few other campgrounds on the island, including one in Anbō and another in Yahazu.

ONOAIDA

TOP CHOICE Yakushima Youth Hostel
HOSTEL $

(屋久島ユースホステル; ☑47-3751; www.yakushima-yh.net; 258-24 Hirauchi; dm with/without meals ¥4620/2940; P@) This well-run youth hostel is about 3km west of Onoaida. Accommodation is in Western-style dorms and the cypress wood tub in the new wing is great. Get off any southbound buses from Miyanoura at the Hirauchi-iriguchi bus stop and take the road towards the sea for about 200m.

Yakushima Iwasaki Hotel
HOTEL $$$

(屋久島いわさきホテル; ☑47-3888; http://yakushima.iwasakihotels.com; 1306 Onoaida; d from ¥25,410; P@🛜⊠) This luxury hotel commands an impressive view from its hilltop location above Onoaida. Spacious Western-style rooms have either ocean or mountain views. The hotel has its own onsen bath and meals are available in two restaurants. Southbound buses from Miyanoura stop right in front.

NAGATA

Sōyōtei
RYOKAN $$

(送陽邸; ☑45-2819; http://soyote.ftw.jp/u44579.html, in Japanese; Nagata-Inakahama; r per person with meals ¥13,650; ℗) On the northwest coast near Inaka-hama, this impressive guesthouse has a collection of semidetached units that boast private verandas and ocean views. There is an outdoor bath overlooking the sea, but it's not always open. It's very close to the Inaka-hama bus stop.

✕ Eating

There are a few restaurants in each of the island's villages, with the best selection in Miyanoura. If you're staying anywhere but Miyanoura, ask for the set two-meal plan at your lodgings. If you're going hiking, you can ask your lodging to prepare a *bentō* (boxed meal) the night before you set out.

If you need to stock up on supplies for camping or hiking, you'll find Yakuden supermarket on the main street in Miyanoura, just north of the entrance to the pier area.

Resutoran Yakushima
SHOKUDŌ $

(☑42-0091; Miyanoura; dishes ¥1000; ⊙9am-4.30pm) On the 2nd floor of the Yakushima Kankō Sentaa (look for the green, two-storey building on the main road, near the road to the pier), this simple restaurant serves a ¥520 morning set breakfast with eggs, toast and coffee and a tasty *tobi uo sashimi teishoku* (flying fish sashimi set meal; ¥980) for lunch. You can also access the internet on two Japanese laptops here.

ⓘ STAY DRY!

It rains *a lot* in Yakushima's interior. Be sure to be adequately prepared for hiking the rainforests. You may find yourself slogging through torrential rain for a whole day, so bring proper gear to protect yourself and whatever you're carrying. Mountain huts (*yama-goya*) have no staff, food or sleeping bags, so bring what you need. If you want to rent rainwear, Nakagawa Sports (ナカガワスポーツ ☑42-0341; rentals ¥1200) in Miyanoura can outfit you; it also has large sizes.

Ten Ten
SEAFOOD $$

(☑42-0689; Miyanoura; dishes ¥1000; ⊙5.30-10pm, closed irregularly) On the main road in the middle of Miyanoura, this friendly little *izakaya* (pub-eatery) serves a mouth-watering *yakizakana teishoku* (grilled fish set meal; ¥1000). It's a little hard to spot; you might have to ask a local to point it out.

Oshokuji-dokoro Shiosai
SEAFOOD $$

(☑42-2721; Miyanoura; dishes ¥1200; ⊙lunch, dinner, closed Thu) This fine restaurant offers a full range of Japanese standards like *sashimi teishoku* (sashimi full set; ¥1700) or the wonderful *ebi-furai teishoku* (fried shrimp full set; ¥1400). Look for the blue and whitish building and the automatic glass doors.

ⓘ Information

If you plan to get around the island by bus, we recommend buying a bus pass.

Tourist information centre (☑42-1019; ⊙8.30am-5pm) Miyanoura's ferry terminal has a useful information centre in the white building on your right as you emerge from the Toppy and Rocket ferry offices. It can help you find lodgings and answer all questions about the island.

Digiheal (per 15min ¥100; ⊙7am-5pm) On the 2nd floor of the same building there's a tiny internet cafe .

Tourist office (☑46-2333; ⊙9am-6pm) In Anbō there's a smaller tourist office on the main road just north of the river.

ⓘ Getting There & Away

AIR

JAC has flights between Kagoshima and Yakushima (¥13,900, 35 minutes, five daily). Yakushima's airport is on the northeastern coast between Miyanoura and Anbō. Hourly buses stop at the airport, though you can usually phone your accommodation for a pick-up or take a taxi.

BOAT

Three ferry services operate between Kagoshima and Yakushima, some of which stop at Tanegashima en route. **Kagoshima Shōsen/Toppy** (☑099-226-0128) and **Cosmo Line/Rocket** (☑099-223-1011) each run at least three hydrofoils a day between Kagoshima (leaving from the high-speed ferry terminal just to the south of Minamifutō pier) and Miyanoura (¥6500, one hour 50 minutes for direct sailings, two hours 50 minutes with a stop in Tanegashima). Kagoshima Shōsen/Toppy also has hydrofoil sailings between Kagoshima and Anbō Port on Yakushima.

The normal ferry *Yakushima 2* sails from Kagoshima's Minamifutō pier for Yakushima's Miyanoura port (one way/return ¥4600/7900, once daily). It leaves at 8.30am and takes four hours.

The *Hibiscus* also sails between Kagoshima and Yakushima, leaving at 6pm, stopping overnight in Tanegashima, and arriving at Miyanoura at 7am the following day (one way/return ¥3200/6400, once daily). Reservations aren't usually necessary for this ferry; it normally leaves from Kagoshima's Taniyama pier.

ⓘ Getting Around

Local buses travel the coastal road part way around Yakushima roughly every hour or two, though only a few head up into the interior. Buses are expensive and you'll save a lot of money by purchasing a *Furii Jōsha Kippu*, which is good for unlimited travel on island buses. One-/two-day passes cost ¥2000/3000 and are available at the Toppy Ferry Office in Miyanoura.

Hitching is also possible, but the best way to get around the island is to rent a car. **Toyota Rent-a-Car** (☑42-2000; up to 12hr from ¥5250; ⊗8am-8pm;) is located near the terminal in Miyanoura.

TANEGASHIMA   種子島
☑0997 / POP 35,000

A long narrow island about 20km northeast of Yakushima, Tanegashima is a laid-back destination popular with Japanese surfers and beach lovers. Home to Japan's Space Centre, Tanegashima was where firearms were first introduced to Japan by shipwrecked Portuguese in 1543. Good ferry connections make this island easy to pair with a trip to Yakushima. Unfortunately, the relative lack of buses makes it difficult to enjoy this island without a rental car or scooter, or, at least, a good touring bicycle.

The island's main port of **Nishi-no-Omote** (西の表) is located on the northwest coast of the island, while the airport is about halfway down the island near the west coast. The best beaches and most of the surfing breaks are on the east coast of the island, which is also home to an onsen.

There is a helpful **information office** (種子島観光案内所; ☑23-0111; ⊗8.30am-5.30pm) at the pier in Nishi-no-Omote, inside the Cosmo ferry office/waiting room.

⊙ Sights & Activities

Space Centre   MONUMENT
(種子島宇宙センター) Tanegashima's Space Centre, on the southeastern coast of the island, is a large parklike complex with rocket-launch facilities.

Space Technology Museum   MUSEUM
(宇宙科学技術館; Mazu, Kukinaga; ⊗9.30am-5pm, closed Mon, launch days) At the space centre, this place details the history of Japan's space program, with some English labels.

There are models of Japan's rockets and some of the satellites it has launched. The closest bus stop is Iwasaki Hotel, from where it's a 10-minute walk.

Takesaki-kaigan   BEACH
(竹崎海岸) Nearby to the Space Centre, this coastline is home to a beautiful stretch of white sand popular with surfers. The best spot to enjoy it is the beach in front of the Iwasaki Hotel (closest bus stop: Iwasaki Hotel), which has some impressive rock formations.

Nagahama-kaigan   BEACH
(長浜海岸) The west coast of Tanegashima is also home to a 12km stretch of beach that is equally popular with surfers.

Kumano-kaigan   BEACH
(熊野海岸) Further up the east coast, the Kumano-kaigan has a long beach.

Nakatanechō Onsen   ONSEN
(中種子町温泉保養センター; per person ¥300; ⊗11am-8pm Oct-Mar, to 9pm Apr-Sep, closed Thu) At the Kumano-kaigan. The closest bus stop Kumano-kaisuiyokujō.

Gun Museum   MUSEUM
(鉄砲館; 7585 Nishi-no-Omote; admission ¥420; ⊗8.30am-4.30pm) This museum has an excellent collection of antique firearms and cultural artefacts from Tanegashima. It's just north of Nagareboshi minshuku; the building looks like the stern of an old galleon.

🛏 Sleeping & Eating

Nagareboshi   MINSHUKU $
(流れ星; ☑23-0034; www.t-shootingstar.com; 7603-10 Nishi-no-Omote; r with/without breakfast ¥3000/2500; P@ⓢ) Run by a friendly, English-speaking woman, charming Nagareboshi has clean, renovated rooms and a laid-back vibe. Walk to the main road from the pier and take a right, then turn left at the post office and walk uphill, bearing right at the top of the steps. Look for the sign up on the slope, and walk up towards a temple; it's on the left.

Izakaya Minshuku Sangoshō   GUESTHOUSE $$
(居酒屋民宿珊瑚礁; ☑23-0005; www6.ocn.ne.jp/~sangosyo/top.html, in Japanese; 201 Nishi-no-Omote; r per person with 2 meals from ¥8400; Pⓢ) For something totally different, try this slice of Southeast Asia transported to Japan. It's a 'guesthouse-pub' with tonnes of cool features, including a brilliant rock-lined bathtub and a huge banyan tree out the front. Accommodation is in simple Japanese-style rooms. It's on the northwest coast, about five minutes' drive from Nishi-no-Omote.

GET AWAY FROM IT ALL

Depending on when you go, the more remote Southwest Islands can be havens of tranquility with few other travellers. But if you really want to escape, it's just a question of hopping on the right ferry. In Kagoshima Prefecture, **Iō-jima** (硫黄島) is a tiny bamboo-covered island with a smouldering volcano and two brilliant seaside onsen. **Mishima Sonei Ferry** (☑099-222-3141) sails there from Kagoshima. The city is also home to **Nakagawa Unyu** (☑099-222-2101), which plies the **Tokara-rettō** (トカラ列島), a chain of seven inhabited and five uninhabited islands between Yakushima and Amami-Ōshima that offer plenty of hiking, fishing and onsen. Even for the Japanese, they seem like the end of the world.

East Coast
BUNGALOWS $$

(イーストコースト; ☑25-0763; www.eastcoast.jp, in Japanese; Kanehama-kaigan, Anjō; bungalow for up to 3 people ¥10,500, per additional person ¥3150; **P**) This surf school-restaurant has two cosy bungalows for those who want to stay near the breaks. The owner is an English-speaking Japanese surfer. The bungalows can handle small groups and families, and have cooking facilities and bathrooms. As you might guess, it's on the east coast of the island.

Mauna Village
BUNGALOWS $$

(マウナヴィレッジ; ☑25-0811; www.mauna-village.com, in Japanese; 9668-40 Genna; r per person with 2 meals from ¥7140; **P**⚟) Also on the east coast of the island, this collection of cute, red-roofed cottages is popular with surfers and families. Some units have sea views and all have toilets, but bathing facilities are shared and meals are taken in a common dining room.

Dolphin
BAR $

(アースビレッジドルフィン; ☑23-0747; http://dolphin.uijin.com; 21 Higashi-chō, Nishi-no-Omote; dishes from ¥1000) This laid-back surf bar in Nishi-no-Omote has pizzas, pastas and taco rice dishes on offer, as well as funky grooves, comfy sofas and friendly conversation. It's a short walk south from the post office, on the left side of the street past a ramen shop. It also runs a **dormitory** (d with breakfast ¥2500) about 10 minutes' drive southeast of town.

Koryōri Shirō
SEAFOOD $$

(小料理しろう; ☑23-2117; 24-6 Higashi-chō, Nishi-no-Omote; dishes from ¥1000; ⏱5-11pm) Head to this friendly little *izakaya* in Nishi-no-Omote to sample tasty dishes like the *sashimi teishoku* (sashimi full set; ¥1200). There are plants out the front and blue-and-white *noren* (doorway curtains). It's a short walk from the Hotel New Tanegashima.

❶ Getting There & Away
Tanegashima has flights to/from Kagoshima (¥12,600, 30 minutes) on JAC.

There are also several daily high-speed ferries to/from Kagoshima and Yakushima; for details, see p641. Finally, **Kashō Kaiun** (☑099-261-7000) operates one normal ferry a day between Kagoshima and Tanegashima (¥3000, three hours and 40 minutes).

Amami Islands   奄美諸島

The southernmost island group in Kagoshima-ken is Amami-shotō. Amami-Ōshima, the largest and most popular island, lies at the northern end of the group. It serves as the main transport hub and boasts excellent beaches, as well as dense jungle. The other islands in the chain are dominated by sugarcane fields but also have some good beaches. Heading south, Tokunoshima is famous for its 'bovine sumo', Okinoerabu-jima has intriguing caves and tiny Yoron-tō is fringed with excellent beaches.

AMAMI-ŌSHIMA
奄美大島

☑0997 / POP 68,600

Amami-Ōshima is Japan's third-largest offshore island after Okinawa-hontō and Sado-ga-shima. With a mild subtropical climate year-round, the island is home to some unusual flora and fauna, including tree ferns and mangrove forests. The coastline of the island is incredibly convoluted – a succession of bays, points and inlets, punctuated by the occasional white-sand beach – making the island an interesting alternative to islands further south. Note that at the time of writing, landslides had damaged many roads and cut access to the island's interior.

⊙ Sights & Activities
Ōhama-Kaihin-kōen
BEACH

(大浜海浜公園) The closest beach to Amami, it's popular for swimming, snorkelling and

OKINAWA & THE SOUTHWEST ISLANDS KAGOSHIMA PREFECTURE

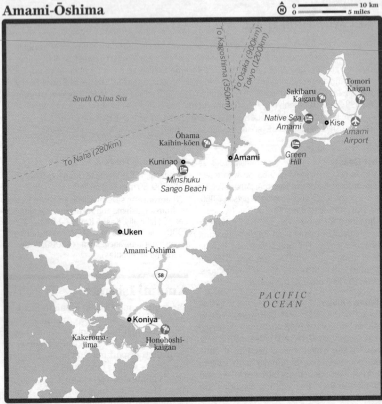

sea kayaking in summer. It can get crowded and it's not as nice as beaches further afield, but it's convenient. Take an Ōhama-bound bus from Amami and get off at the Ōhama stop (¥400).

Sakibaru Kaigan   BEACH
(崎原海岸) For a really stunning beach head here, about 4.5km down a point of land just north of Kise (about 20km northeast of Amami). Take a Sani-bound bus from Amami and get off at Kiseura (¥950), and then walk. If you're driving, it's marked in English off the main road (be prepared for *narrow* roads).

Tomori Kaigan   BEACH
(土盛海岸) It's easier to get to this beach, which also offers brilliant white sand and some great snorkelling with a channel leading outside the reef. It's about 3km north of the airport. Take a Sani-bound bus from Amami and get off at Tomori (¥1210).

Amami-Ōshima is great to explore by touring bike or rental car. The coastal route to **Uken** (宇検) on the west coast has some lovely stretches. Another option is Rte 58 south to **Koniya** (古仁屋), from where you can continue southwest to the **Honohoshi-kaigan** (ホノホシ海岸), a rocky beach with incredible coastal formations, or catch a ferry to **Kakeroma-jima** (加計呂麻島), a small island with a few shallow beaches.

🛏 Sleeping

Native Sea Amami   HOTEL $$$
(ネイティブシー奄美; ☎62-2385; www.native -sea.com, in Japanese; 835 Ashitoku, Tatsugō-chōs; per person with 2 meals from ¥15,750; P@) About 28km east of Amami (or 3km from the Akaogi bus stop), this dive centre-resort has nice accommodation in a room block perched on a promontory over a lovely bay. There is a nice shallow beach below the resort and the dining room and guest rooms have great views.

Minshuku Tatsuya Ryokan   MINSHUKU **$**
(民宿たつや旅館; ☎52-0260; www3.synapse.ne
.jp/tatsuya; 15-18 Irifune-chō; r per person ¥3000;
[P][@][🛜]) If you're looking for a bargain in
Amami, this foreigner-friendly ryokan has
simple but acceptable rooms and a kindly,
informative owner. It's roughly in the centre
of town, next to the Hotel New Amami.

Minshuku Sango Beach   MINSHUKU **$$**
(民宿さんごビーチ; ☎57-2580; 68 Kuninao;
per person with 2 meals from ¥6000; [P][@]) Overlooking a lovely sand beach, this laid-back
minshuku has a vaguely Southeast Asian
feeling. Guests sleep in six semidetached
units and meals are taken overlooking the
sea. Take a bus to Kuninao (¥800), walk to
the sea and look for the curving concrete
stairs out the front, or call ahead for pick-up.

Green Hill   GUESTHOUSE **$$**
(ペンショングリーンヒル; ☎62-5180; www
.greenhill-amami.com, in Japanese; Tebiro, Tatsugō-
chō; s per person with 2 meals from ¥8400; [P][@])
A favourite among Japanese surfers, convivial, rough-around-the-edges Green Hill has
ocean views, Japanese- and Western-style
rooms, some with lofts. It's about 30 minutes from the airport and a few minutes'
walk to the beach. Call ahead to ask for a
pickup.

🍴 Eating
Okonomiyaki Mangetsu   OKONOMIYAKI **$$**
(☎53-2052; 2-2-1F Irifune-chō; dishes ¥1000;
🕙11.30am-2.30am) Locals pile in for the excellent *okonomiyaki* (Japanese griddle-
fried cabbage and batter cakes with various
fillings) at this excellent Amami eatery. For
carnivores, we recommend the *kurobuta*
mix (pork-shrimp-squid mix; ¥1260), and
for veggies, we recommend the *isobecchi*
(*mochi* rice and nori seaweed; ¥750). There's
a picture menu.

ℹ Information
The main city and port, Amami (previously
called Naze; 名瀬), is on the north coast. The
island's tiny airport is 55 minutes away by bus
(¥1100, almost hourly, buses are timed to meet
flights) on the northeast coast. The best beaches are at the northeast end of the island.

Tourist information counter (☎63-2295;
🕙8.30am-6.45pm) In the airport arrivals hall;
can help with maps and bus schedules.

Amami Nangoku Travel Service (☎53-0085)
In the centre of Amami, across from the Amami
Sun Plaza Hotel; a useful travel agency that can
help with ferry and air bookings.

ℹ Getting There & Around
Amami-Ōshima has flights to/from Tokyo
(¥42,500, 2½ hours, one daily), Osaka
(¥33,200, one hour 45 minutes, one daily) and
Kagoshima (¥21,200, one hour, four daily) on
Japan Airlines (JAL) or JAC. RAC operates a
daily flight between Naha and Amami-Ōshima
(¥21,400, one hour). There are also flights
between Amami-Ōshima and the other islands
in the Amami group (see each island's Getting
There & Away section for details).

Maruei Ferry/A Line (☎in Kagoshima 099-
226-4141; www.aline-ferry.com, in Japanese)
Operates four or five ferries a month running
to/from Tokyo (¥19,500, 37 hours) and Osaka/
Kobe (¥14,700, 29 hours), as well as daily
ferries to/from Kagoshima (¥8800, 11 hours).
Most of these ferries continue on to Naha, so
you can travel in the reverse direction from
Naha to Amami-Ōshima as well.

Amami Kaiun (☎in Kagoshima 099-222-
2338) Also part of Maruei Ferry; operates five
ferries a week to/from Kagoshima (¥9200, 14
hours).

Amami-Ōshima has a good bus system, but you
will definitely appreciate a rental car if you have
an International Driving Permit. **Matsuda Renta
Car** (☎63-0240) on the main street in Amami
near the Amami Sun Plaza Hotel has subcom-
pacts from ¥4500. It also has a branch near the
airport.

SNAKES IN THE GRASS

Heard about the 'deadly' habu snakes? Perhaps it's a reflection of Japan's shortage of
real dangers, but you could get the impression that the poor habu, a species of pit viper,
is the world's most dangerous snake, and that there's one waiting behind every tree,
shrub and bush on the islands. They're hardly so prolific – the most likely place to see
one is at a mongoose-versus-habu fight put on for tourists, or floating in a jar of very
expensive (and slightly poisonous) sake.

Nevertheless, they are venomous! It's not a good idea to go barefoot when stomping
through the bushes, though you should stomp – the vibrations will scare any snakes
away. If you do get bitten, take it seriously and seek immediate medical advice as fatalities (though rare) can occur if antivenin is not administered.

OKINAWA & THE SOUTHWEST ISLANDS KAGOSHIMA PREFECTURE

TOKUNOSHIMA 徳之島
☎ 0997 / POP 25,500

Tokunoshima, the second-largest island in Amami-shotō, has some interesting coastal rock formations and a few good beaches. The island is famous for **tōgyū** (闘牛大会, bovine sumō), which has been practised on the island for more than 500 years. Attractions include decent diving and snorkelling and views that occasionally call to mind parts of Hawaii.

On the island's east coast is the main port of **Kametoku-shinkō** (亀徳新港) and the main town of **Kametsu** (亀津). Tokunoshima's airport is on its west coast, not far from the secondary port of **Hetono** (平土野). A small **tourist information office** (徳之島観光協会; ☎ 82-0575; ⏱ 9am-5.30pm Mon-Sat) at the ferry building has a detailed Japanese pamphlet and a simple English one about the island. It can help with accommodation, but book ahead.

◉ Sights & Activities

If the spectacle of bulls locking horns interests you (the animals are goaded on by human handlers), there are 13 official *tōgyu* (bovine sumo) venues on the island that stage tournaments. The three biggest fights are held in January, May and October – call the tourist office to confirm details.

Several good beaches are dotted around the coast, including the excellent **Aze Prince Beach** (畦プリンスビーチ), which is near the Aze/Fruits Garden bus stop on the northeast coast.

About 9km north of the airport at the northwestern tip of the island, **Mushirose** (ムシロ瀬) is an interesting collection of wave-smoothed rocks that would make a great picnic spot. On a point on the southwest coast of the island, the **Innojō-futa** (犬の門蓋) is a collection of bizarrely eroded upthrust coral that includes a formation that resembles a giant pair of spectacles. It's hard to find and poorly marked. Look for it on the coast about 10km south of the airport.

🛏 Sleeping

Kanami-sō MINSHUKU $$
(金見荘; ☎ 84-9027; kanamiso.cool.ne.jp, in Japanese; r per person with 2 meals from ¥7000; P @) In the village of Kanami at the very northeast tip of the island, this friendly divers' lodge has a great location overlooking a good snorkelling beach. Some of the upstairs rooms have sweeping views. The place specialises in *ise ebi ryōri* (Japanese lobster cuisine).

Cōpo Shichifukujin MINSHUKU $
(コーポ七福人; ☎ 82-2618; Kametsu; r per person ¥3000; P @) These slightly funky rooms in a converted apartment building have showers and kitchen facilities and are good for a cheap night in central Kametsu. The friendly owner also runs a pension just north of town, which has more spacious rooms.

Aze Campground CAMPGROUND
(畦キャンプ場; campsites free; P) This fine little campground at Aze Prince Beach has showers, nice grassy campsites and a trail down to its own private beach.

❶ Getting There & Around

Tokunoshima has flights to/from Kagoshima (JAL; ¥26,800, one hour, four daily) and Amami-Ōshima (JAC; ¥13,300, 35 minutes, two daily).

Tukunoshima is served by Maruei/A Line ferries, which run between Kagoshima (some originating in Honshu) and Naha, and Amami Kaiun ferries, which run between Kagoshima and Okinoerabu-shima. See p645 for details.

There are bus stations at both ports, and a decent bus system to all parts of the island, but you'll definitely appreciate the convenience of a car, scooter or touring bicycle. **Toyota Renta Car** (トヨタレンタカー; ☎ 85-5089) is right outside Kametoku-shinkō pier. There are also car-rental places near the pier.

OKINOERABU-JIMA 沖永良部島
☎ 0997 / POP 15,000

About 33km southwest of Tokunoshima, Okinoerabu is a sugarcane-covered island with some excellent beaches, interesting coastal formations and a brilliant limestone cave.

Wadomari (和泊), the island's main town, is decidedly retro. The airport is at the eastern tip of the island, with **Wadomari-kō** (和泊港), the main port and town, 6km away on the east coast. There is a small **tourist information booth** (☎ 92-2901; ⏱ 8.30am-5pm) at Wadomari port on the 2nd floor of the terminal building, which has maps of the island (the office is next to the ferry ticket window).

◉ Sights & Activities

There are excellent beaches all around the island. You'll also find several 'secret' little beaches off the coastal road between Fūcha and the airport.

The island's coast has many impressive geographical landforms. **Taminamisaki** (田皆崎), at the northwest tip of the island, has ancient coral that has been upthrust to form a 40m cliff. At the island's northeast tip, **Fūcha** (フーチャ) is a blowhole in the limestone rock, which shoots water 10m into the air on windy days.

Okidomari-kaigan
BEACH

(沖泊海岸) Backed by green cliffs, the white sand and offshore coral formations of this beach make it very worthwhile. At the northwest end, about 3km east of Tamina-misaki.

Shōryūdō
CAVE

(昇竜洞; Sumiyoshi, China-machi; admission ¥1000; ⊘8.30am-5pm) On the southwest slopes of Ōyama (the mountain at the west end of the island), you will find this brilliant limestone cave with 600m of walkways and illumination. Part of the cave was under renovation at the time of writing, but most is still walkable. It's a few kilometres inland from the southwest coastal road.

🛏 Sleeping & Eating

Business Hotel Ugurahama HOTEL $$
(ビジネスホテルうぐら浜; ☑92-2268; www .erabu.net/ugurahama, in Japanese; 6-1 Wadomari; r per person with/without meals from ¥6000/4300; P@) This friendly hotel has simple Japanese- and Western-style rooms. From the port, take a left on the main road and follow it over the bridge and through the town; look for the white building with a blue trim on your right.

Business Hotel Wadamari-kō HOTEL $
(ビジネスホテル和泊港; ☑92-1189; 512-32 Wadomari; s with breakfast ¥4000; P🤙) A few minutes' walk from the port, this simple, cheap hotel looks more like a private house, and has relatively modern rooms. It is on the left soon after exiting the pier area.

Okidomari Campground CAMPGROUND
(沖泊キャンプ場; campsites free; P) This excellent campground at Okidomari Kaigan beach has showers and large grassy areas with trees for shade.

Mouri Mouri IZAKAYA $$
(もおりもおり; ☑92-0538; 582 Wadomari; meals from ¥1500; ⊘dinner, closed Sun). Opposite the Kankō Hotel Azuma, this is a friendly place for dinner in Wadomari, with small dishes like *gō yā chanpuru* (bitter melon stir-fry; ¥500). See if you can break the local beer-chugging record, which stands at under three seconds. It's a little hard to spot: from the Menshiori Shopping Street (when coming from port), take the first right then the first left; it's across from the Hotel Azuma.

There are two minimarkets in town.

ℹ Getting There & Around
Okinoerabu has flights to/from Kagoshima (¥29,500, one hour 30 minutes, three daily), Amami-Ōshima (from ¥16,800, 35 minutes, one daily) and Yoron-tō (from ¥10,000, 25 minutes, one daily) on JAC.

Okinoerabu-shima is served by Maruei/A Line ferries, which run between Kagoshima (some originating in Honshu) and Naha, and Amami Kaiun ferries, which run between Kagoshima and Okinoerabu-shima. See the Amami-Ōshima section (p649) for details.

The island has a decent bus system, but you'll definitely welcome the convenience of a car, scooter or touring bicycle. You'll find **Toyota Renta Car** (トヨタレンタカー; ☑92-2100) right outside the airport.

YORON-TŌ
与論島

☑0997 / POP 5500

Fringed with picture-perfect white-sand beaches and extensive coral reefs, Yoron-tō is one of the most appealing islands in the Southwest Islands chain. A mere 5km across, tiny Yoron is the southernmost island in Kagoshima-ken. On a good day, Okinawa-hontō's northernmost point of Hedo-misaki is visible 23km to the southwest.

The harbour is next to the airport on the western tip of the island, while the main town of **Chabana** (茶花) is 1km to the east. Beside the city office in Chabana is the useful **tourist information office** (ヨロン島観光協会; ☑97-5151; 32-1 Chabana; ⊘8.30am-5.30pm), which provides maps, an English pamphlet and can make accommodation bookings.

⊙ Sights & Activities
On the eastern side of the island, Yoron's best beach is the popular **Oganeku-kaigan** (大金久海岸). About 500m offshore from Oganeku-kaigan is **Yurigahama** (百合ヶ浜), a stunning stretch of white sand that disappears completely at high tide. Boats (¥1000 return) putter back and forth, ferrying visitors out to it. Other good beaches include **Maehama-kaigan** (前浜海岸), on the southeast coast, and **Terasaki-kaigan** (寺崎海岸), on the northeast coast.

Yoron Minzoku-mura
MUSEUM

(与論民族村; 693 Higashi; admission ¥400; ⊘9am-6pm) At the island's southeastern tip, the excellent Yoron Minzoku-mura is a collection of traditional thatch-roof island dwellings and storehouses that contain exhibits on the island's culture and history. If

A FOOD LOVER'S GUIDE TO OKINAWA

Reflecting the islands' geographic and historical isolation, Okinawa's food shares little in common with that of mainland Japan. The cuisine originated in the splendour of the Ryūkyū court and from the humble lives of the impoverished islanders. Healthy eating is considered to be extremely important; indeed, islanders have long held that medicine and food are essentially the same. Today, the island's staple foods are pork, which is acidic and rich in protein, and *konbu* (a type of seaweed), which is alkaline and calorie-free.

Every part of the pig is eaten. *Mimigā* (ミミガー) is thinly sliced pig's ears marinated in vinegar, perfect with a cold glass of local Orion beer (オリオンビール) on a sweltering night in Naha. *Rafutē* (ラフテー) is pork stewed with ginger, brown sugar, rice wine and soy sauce until it falls apart. If you're looking for a bit of stamina, you should also try an inky black bowl of *ikasumi-jiru* (イカスミ汁), which is stewed pork in black squid ink. Finally, try the *inamudotchi* (イナムドチ), a hearty stew of pork, fish, mushrooms, potatoes and miso that is said to be reminiscent of eating wild boar.

While stewing is common, Okinawans prefer stir-frying, and refer to the technique as *champurū* (チャンプルー). Perhaps the best known stir-fry is *gōyāchampurū* (ゴーヤーチャンプルー), a mix of pork, bitter melon and the island's uniquely sturdy tofu, *shima-dōfu* (島豆腐). Occasionally, you'll come across an unusual tofu variant known as *tōfuyō* (豆腐䴕), which is sorely fermented, violently spicy and fluorescent pink – taste it with caution!

The ubiquitous *okinawa-soba* (沖縄そば) is udon (thick white noodles) served in a pork broth. The most common variants are *sōki-soba* (ソーキそば), which contains pork spare ribs; and *shima-tōgarashi* (島とうがらし; pickled hot peppers in sesame oil) and *yaeyama-soba* (八重山そば), which contains thin white noodles akin to *sōmen*.

Others dishes to look out for include *hirayāchi* (ヒラヤーチ), a thin pancake of egg, vegetables and meat similar to the mainland *okonomiyaki* (お好み焼き). *Yagi-jiru* (山羊汁; goat soup) is invigorating though slightly stinky. Finally, there's nothing quite like Blue Seal (ブルーシール) ice cream, an American favourite introduced here after WWII.

While travelling through the Southwest Islands, be sure to sample the local firewater, *awamori* (泡盛), which is distilled from rice and has an alcohol content of 30% to 60%. Although it's usually served *mizu-wari* (水割; diluted with water), this is seriously lethal stuff, especially the *habushu* (ハブ酒), which comes with a small snake in the bottle. If you're hitting the *awamori* hard, take our advice and cancel your plans for the next day (or two).

at all possible, bring along a Japanese speaker, as the owner is an incredible source of information on the island.

Southern Cross Center
MUSEUM

(サザンクロスセンター; 3313 Ricchō; admission ¥300; ⏰9am-5.30pm) A short walk from the Ishini (石仁) bus stop, 3km south of Chabana, is a lookout that serves as a museum of Yoron and Amami history and culture. Offering good views south to Okinawa, it celebrates the fact that Yoron-tō is the northernmost island in Japan from where the Southern Cross can be seen.

🛏 Sleeping & Eating

TOP CHOICE Pricia Resort
HOTEL $$

(プリシアリゾート; ☎97-5060; fax 97-4982; www.pricia.co.jp; 358-1 Ricchō; r per person with breakfast from ¥6900; P@☒) These relaxing white-washed cottages by the airport evoke Yoron's sister island Mykonos in Greece; the

place looks like a transplanted village. The best cottages are the beachfront 'B type' units. Breezy Western-style rooms and Jacuzzi baths are popular with holidaying US servicemen from Okinawa. Staff can organise windsurfing, snorkelling and banana boat rides.

Shiomi-sō
MINSHUKU $

(汐見荘; ☎97-2167; 2229-3 Chabana; r per person with meals from ¥5500; P@) This friendly and casual *minshuku* is popular with young people. Starting from Chabana harbour, take the main road north (uphill) out of town and look for it on the left after the turn; it looks like a private house. Staff will pick you up if you phone ahead.

Umi Café
CAFE $

(海カフェ; ☎97-4621; 2309 Chabana; meals from ¥800; ⏰11am-6pm, from 1pm Sat; 📶) This delightful terraced gallery-cafe with ocean views is something you'd expect to find perched on a Greek cliff; it's no surprise to find chicken gyros pitas on the menu, along with Greek coffee. Go to the village office at the top of the main drag, turn left and then right at the end of the street. Look for small signs along the road, or ask locals. The owner also runs a small hostel (dorm ¥1500).

Bar Natural Reef
BAR $

(ナチュラルリーフ; 16-1 Chabana; snacks from ¥600) This tiki bar on Chabana's main drag is the best watering hole on the island, with plenty of *yū sen*, a local *shōchū* made from sugarcane, to keep everyone happy. Owner Kowaguchi-san has lots of tips about the best spots on Yoron.

In addition, there are two minimarkets in the centre of Chabana.

❶ Getting There & Away

Yoron-tō has direct flights to/from Kagoshima (JAC; ¥31,000, one hour 20 minutes, one daily), Okinoerabu-shima (JAC; ¥1000, 40 minutes, one daily, with connections onward to Amami-Ōshima) and Naha (RAC; ¥14,200, 40 minutes, one daily).

Yoron-tō is served by Maruei/A Line ferries, which run between Kagoshima (some originating in Honshu) and Naha, and Amami Kaiun ferries, which run between Kagoshima and Okinoerabu-shima. See the Amami-Ōshima section (p649) for details.

Yoron-tō has a bus system, but you'll definitely appreciate the convenience of a car, scooter or touring bicycle. **Yoron-tō Kankō Rentacar** (ヨロン島観光レンタカー; ☑97-5075), located in Chabana, will meet car-rental clients at the airport.

OKINAWA PREFECTURE

POP 1.39 MILLION

Japan's southernmost prefecture, Okinawa Prefecture (沖縄県; Okinawa-ken) makes up the southern half of the Southwest Islands. The prefecture stretches from the southern islands in Kagoshima-ken to within 110km of Taiwan. Three island groups make up the prefecture. From north to south, they are Okinawa-shotō, Miyako-shotō and Yaeyama-shotō.

The northernmost island group is Okinawa-shotō, which contains Okinawa-hontō (meaning 'Okinawa Main Island' in Japanese), home to the prefectural capital, Naha. This is the prefecture's transport hub, easily accessed by flights and ferries to/from the mainland. Plentiful ferries run between Naha and Kerama-shotō, which lie about 30km west of Okinawa-hontō.

Located 300km southwest of Okinawa-hontō, Miyako-shotō is home to the popular beach destination of Miyako-jima. There is no ferry access to this group; you must arrive via flights from the mainland, Naha or Ishigaki.

Yaeyama-shotō, a further 100km southwest, includes the coral-fringed island of Ishigaki and the nearby jungle-clad Iriomote-jima. Like Miyako-shotō, you have to fly in.

Okinawa-hontō 沖縄本島
☑ 098

Okinawa-hontō is the largest island in the Southwest Islands, and the historical seat of power of the Ryūkyū dynasty. Although its cultural differences with mainland Japan were once evident in its architecture, almost all traces were completely obliterated in WWII. Fortunately, Allied bombing wasn't powerful enough to completely stamp out other remnants of Okinawan culture, and today the island is home to a unique culinary, artistic and musical tradition.

The island is also home to some excellent beaches, delicious food and friendly people, many of whom speak a little more English than their mainland counterparts. Of course, with US Air Force jets flying overhead from time to time, it's hard to forget the reality of the continuing American military presence on the island and the history behind that presence.

Prefectural capital Naha is a transportation hub for the other islands. War memorials are clustered in the south of the island, while there are some good beaches and other attractions on the Motobu peninsula. The north is relatively undeveloped.

It's worth noting that Okinawa-hontō has been somewhat overdeveloped for domestic tourism. If you seek Southeast Asian–style beaches and fewer big resorts, the majority of your time is best spent on Okinawa-ken's smaller islands.

NAHA 那覇
POP 315,000

Flattened during WWII, the prefectural capital of Naha is now a thriving urban centre. The city sports a convenient elevated monorail and a rapidly expanding skyline of modern high-rise apartments, as well as the inevitable traffic jams.

The city plays host to an interesting mix of young Japanese holidaymakers, American GIs looking for off-base fun and a growing number of foreign tourists. The action centres

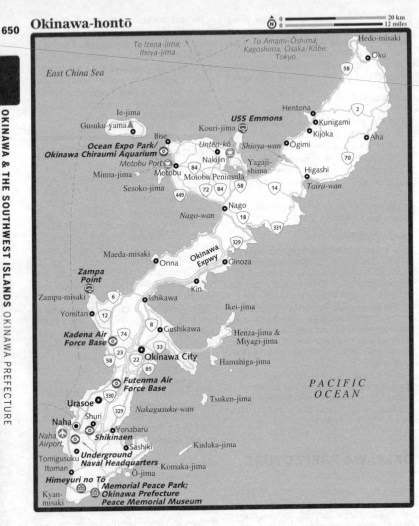

OKINAWA & THE SOUTHWEST ISLANDS OKINAWA PREFECTURE

on Kokusai-dōri (International Blvd), a colourful and energetic 2km main drag of hotels, restaurants, bars, clubs and just about every conceivable type of souvenir shop. And overlooking it all from a safe distance to the east is Shuri-jō, a wonderfully restored castle that was once the home of Ryūkyū royalty.

⊙ Sights & Activities

Naha is fairly easy to navigate, especially since the main sights and attractions are located in the city centre. The main drag is Kokusai-dōri, while the Tsuboya pottery area is to the southeast via a series of covered arcades. The Shuri district is located about 3km to the east of the city centre.

The city's main artery, **Kokusai-dōri** (国際通り), is a riot of neon, noise, souvenir shops, bustling restaurants and Japanese young things out strutting their stuff. It's a festival of tat and tackiness, but it's a good time if you're in the mood for it.

Many people prefer the atmosphere of the three shopping arcades that run south off Kokusai-dōri roughly opposite Mitsukoshi Department Store: **Ichibahon-dōri** (市場本道り), **Mutsumibashi-dōri** (むつみ橋通り) and **Heiwa-dōri** (平和通り).

Daichi Makishi Kōsetsu Ichiba
MARKET

(第一牧志公設市場; 2-10-1 Matsuo; ⏰10am-8pm) Our favourite stop in the arcade area is the covered food market just off Ichibahondōri, about 200m south of Kokusai-dōri. The colourful variety of fish and produce on offer here is amazing, and don't miss the wonderful local restaurants upstairs. Keep in mind, however, that this is a working market, so please don't get in the way of shopkeepers and consider buying something as a souvenir.

Tsuboya pottery area
NEIGHBOURHOOD

(壷屋) One of the best parts of Naha is this place, a centre of ceramic production from 1682, when Ryūkyū kilns were consolidated here by royal decree. Most shops sell all the popular Okinawan ceramics, including *shīsā* (lion-dog roof guardians) and containers for serving *awamori,* the local firewater. To get here from Kokusai-dōri, walk south through the Heiwa-dōri arcade for about 350m.

Tsuboya Pottery Museum
MUSEUM

(那覇市立壷屋焼物博物館; 1-9-32 Tsuboya; admission ¥315; ⏰10am-5.30pm, closed Mon) In Tsuboya, you will find the excellent Tsuboya Pottery Museum, which contains some fine examples of traditional Okinawan pottery. Here you can also inspect potters' wheels and inspect *arayachi* (unglazed) and *jōyachi* (glazed) pieces.

Tsuboya-yachimun-dōri
NEIGHBOURHOOD

(壷屋やちむん通り) The atmospheric Tsuboya-yachimun-dōri is lined with pottery shops. The lanes off the main street here contain some classic crumbling old Okinawan houses.

Okinawa Prefectural Museum
MUSEUM

(沖縄県立博物館; Omuromachi 3-1-1; admission ¥400; ⏰9am-5.30pm, closed Mon) Opened in 2007, this museum of Okinawa's history, culture and natural history is easily one of the best museums in Japan. Displays are well laid out, easy to understand and attractively presented. The art museum section holds interesting special exhibits with an emphasis on local artists. It's about 15 minutes' walk northwest of the Omuromachi monorail station.

Fukushū-en
GARDEN

(福州園; 2-29 Kume; admission free; ⏰9am-6pm Thu-Tue) Garden fans should take a stroll through Chinese-style Fukushū-en. All materials were brought from Fuzhou, Naha's sister city in China, including the pagoda that sits atop a small waterfall.

Shikina-en
GARDEN

(識名園; 421-7 Aza Māji; admission ¥400; ⏰9am-5pm, closed Wed) Around 4km east of the city centre is a Chinese-style garden containing stone bridges, a viewing pavilion and a villa that belonged to the Ryūkyū royal family. Despite its flawless appearance, everything was painstakingly rebuilt after WWII. To reach the garden, take bus 2, 3 or 5 to the Shikinaen-mae stop (¥220, 20 minutes).

Naha City Traditional Arts and Crafts Center
ART GALLERY

(那覇市伝統工芸館; 3-2-10 Makishi; admission ¥300; ⏰9am-6pm) Right on Kokusai-dōri, this place houses a collection of traditional Okinawan crafts. Staff members demonstrate glass-blowing, weaving and pottery-making in the workshops. Enter by 5.30pm.

SHURI DISTRICT
首里

The original capital of Okinawa, Shuri's temples, shrines, tombs and castle were all destroyed in WWII, but the castle and surrounding structures were rebuilt in 1992.

Shuri-jō
CASTLE

(首里城; admission ¥800; ⏰9am-5.30pm), The reconstructed castle sits atop a hilltop overlooking Naha's urban sprawl. It was originally built in the 14th century and served as the administrative centre and royal residence of the Ryūkyū kingdom until the 19th century.

Enter through the Kankai-mon (歓会門) and go up to the Hōshin-mon (奉神門), which forms the entryway to the inner sanctum of the castle, dominated by the impressive **Seiden** (正殿). Visitors can enter the Seiden, which has exhibits on the castle and the Okinawan royals. There is also a small collection of displays in the nearby Hokuden. To reach the complex, take the Yui-rail monorail to Shuri Station. Exit to the west, go down the steps, walk straight, cross one big street, then a smaller one and go right on the opposite side, then walk about 350m and look for the signs on the left.

Irino-Azana

(西のアザナ) While you're at the castle, visit the Irino-Azana, a viewpoint about 200m west of the Seiden that affords great views over Naha and as far as Kerama-shotō.

✦ Festivals & Events

Dragon-boat races
DRAGON BOATS

Held in early May, particularly in Itoman and Naha. These races *(hari)* are thought to bring luck and prosperity to fishermen.

Naha

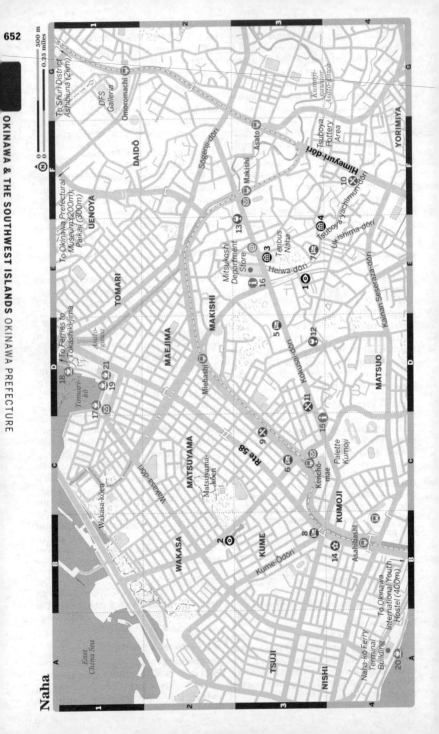

East China Sea

To Shuri District
Ashibiuna (2km)

DFS Galleria

Omoromachi

Kumoji-gawa

Asato-gawa

Sogenji-dori

Asato

Makishi

Tsuboya Pottery Area

Himeyuri-dori

10

Ukishima-dori

Tsuboya-yachimun-dori

4

13

Tenbus Naha

3

7

Heiwa-dori

16

1

Mitsukoshi Department Store

To Okinawa Prefectural Museum (200m)
Paikaji (300m)

5

12

Kokusai-dori

Miebashi

11

6

9

15

Palette Kumoji

Kenchō-mae

To Ferries to Tokashiki-jima

Asato-gawa

Tomari-kō

17

18

21

19

Wakasa-dōri

Matsuyama-kōen

Rte 58

Kume-Ōdori

2

8

14

Asahibashi

Kainan Seseraza-dōri

Naha-kō Ferry Terminal Building

To Okinawa International Youth Hostel (400m)

20

DAIDŌ

UENOYA

TOMARI

MAEJIMA

MAKISHI

MATSUO

YORIMIYA

MATSUYAMA

KUMOJI

KUME

WAKASA

TSUJI

NISHI

Wakasa-kōen

N

0   500 m
0   0.25 miles

Naha

Ryūkyū-no-Saiten   CULTURAL

Brings together more than a dozen festivals and special events celebrating Okinawan culture for three days at the end of October.

Naha Ōzunahiki   SPORTS

Takes place in Naha on Sunday around the national Sports Day Holiday in October, and features large teams that compete in the world's biggest tug of war, using a gigantic 1m-thick rope weighing over 40 tonnes.

🛏 Sleeping

Naha is the most convenient base for exploring Okinawa-hontō.

TOP CHOICE Hotel Sun Palace   HOTEL $$

(ホテルサンパレス球陽舘; ☑863-4181; www .palace-okinawa.com/sunpalace, in Japanese; 2-5-1 Kumoji; r per person with breakfast from ¥6500; P@) About 3 minutes' walk from Kokusai-dōri, the Sun Palace is a step up from a standard business hotel. The fairly spacious rooms have interesting design touches and some with balconies.

Stella Resort   GUESTHOUSE $

(ステラリゾート; ☑863-1330; www.stella-cg.com; 3-6-41 Makishi; dm ¥1500, r per person from ¥2500; P@🛜) Between Heiwa-dōri arcade and the Tsuboya pottery area, this refreshingly tropical guesthouse has private loft rooms, rooftop showers and an aquarium room for zoning out. Climb the stairs in the turquoise building next to the Okinawa Style Café.

Hotel JAL City Naha   HOTEL $$

(ホテルJALシティ那覇; ☑866-2580; http:// naha.jalcity.co.jp; 1-3-70 Makishi; s/d from ¥7900/12,000; P@) Right on Kokusai-dōri, the modern JAL City has 304 rooms, including smallish but swishy red-and-white ones on the Executive Floors. Staff here have very limited English, but service is excellent.

**Tōyoko Inn Naha
Asahibashi-eki-mae**   HOTEL $

(東横イン那覇旭橋駅前; ☑951-1045; www .toyoko-inn.com/e_hotel/00076/; 2-1-20 Kume; s/d from ¥4980/6980; P@) Just a short walk north of Kokusai-dōri, the Tōyoko is a good-value business hotel with small but serviceable rooms and useful features like free internet and breakfast. It's one of the better-value options in this price range.

**Okinawa International Youth
Hostel**   HOSTEL $

(沖縄国際ユースホステル; ☑857-0073; www .oiyh.org; 51 Ōnoyama; dm ¥3960, HI member ¥3360; P@) This excellent youth hostel is located in Ōnoyama-kōen, a five-minute walk from the Tsubogawa Station; turn left at the soccer pitch.

🍽 Eating & Drinking

Naha is the perfect spot to sample the full range of Okinawan cuisine. For descriptions of the Okinawan dishes mentioned in this section, see the box (p648).

DON'T MISS

THREE-STRING HARMONY

Stroll through any Okinawa town and before long you'll likely hear the tinkly sound of the *sanshin*, a banjo-like precursor to the ubiquitous *shamisen* that is played on Japan's main islands. Typically constructed of a wooden frame covered with python skin, the *sanshin* has a long lacquered neck, a bamboo bridge and three strings that are struck with a plectrum, often carved from the horn of a water buffalo.

Introduced from China in the 16th century, the *sanshin* was used for court music during the Ryukyu Kingdom and later prized by commoners for its soothing sound; in the devastation after WWII, *sanshin* made of tin cans and nylon string cheered the exhausted survivors. Today, you can hear folksongs featuring *sanshin* all over Japan. Musicians such as Takashi Hirayasu and Yoriko Ganeko have helped popularise the sound in and out of Japan so you can even find *sanshin* groups overseas.

Many restaurants in Naha feature *sanshin* players, but if you'd like a full-on *sanshin* folksong experience try Ganeko's **Utahime** (歌姫; ☎863-2425; 5-16 Higashi-machi; live show admission from ¥1000; ☉7pm-2am), where performers in dazzling kimono take the stage, singing and strumming their strings. From Asahibashi station, take Exit 3 and walk north along Route 58. You'll see it on your left, at the end of the third block, just before the overhead footbridge. Call ahead to reserve.

Yūnangi
TOP CHOICE — OKINAWAN **$$**

(ゆうなんぎい; ☎867-3765; 3-3-3 Kumoji; dishes ¥1200; ☉lunch, dinner, closed Sun) You'll be lucky to get a seat here, but if you do, you'll be treated to some of the best Okinawan food around, served in traditional but bustling surroundings. Try the *okinawa-soba* set (¥1400). Look for the wooden sign with white letters in Japanese and the plants.

Ashibiunā
OKINAWAN **$**

(あしびうなぁ; ☎884-0035; 12-13 Shuri-jō; dishes ¥900; ☉lunch, dinner) Perfect for lunch after touring Shuri-jō castle, Ashibiuna has a traditional ambiance and serves staple set meals like *gōyā-champurū* (bitter melon stir-fry; ¥840) and *okinawa-soba* (¥840) around a picturesque garden. Facing the entrance to the Kankai-mon gate, turn left and follow the road until just before the intersection. It will be on your right with a black and white sign and plants over the gate.

Paikaji
OKINAWAN **$$**

(ぱいかじ; ☎866-7977; 1-1-7 Uenoya; dishes ¥800; ☉dinner) In Omoromachi, this convivial traditional eatery has rocking *sanshin* minstrels, private rooms and an open kitchen bar. Okinawan eats include *tōfu-champurū* (tofu stir-fry; ¥500) and, for the adventurous, *yagi-sashi* (goat sashimi; ¥1250). From Exit 1 of Omoromachi Station, turn right and walk about six blocks (15 minutes) along the boulevard, past the Okinawa Prefectural Museum; it's the old-fashioned wooden building after Big Echo karaoke on the left.

Gen
YAKINIKU **$$**

(玄; ☎861-0429; 2-6-23 Kumoji; dishes ¥900; ☉lunch, dinner) This atmospheric *yakiniku* (grilled meat) place is one of our favourite places in Naha for a good meal. If you're a carnivore and want some excellent grilled meat washed down with great *awamori*, this is the place. Look for the English sign at the bottom of the steps. If you can't speak Japanese, ask your accommodation owner to call and order the *yakiniku* course (¥3500 per person) as it must be ordered in advance.

Uchina Chaya Buku Buku
CAFE **$**

(うちなー茶屋ぶくぶく; ☎861-2950; 1-28-3 Tsuboya; dishes ¥900; ☉10am-4.30pm, closed Sun, & Thu) This incredibly atmospheric teahouse near the east end of the Tsuboya pottery area is worth a special trip. It takes its name from the traditional frothy Okinawan tea served here: *buku buku cha*. It's up a small lane just north of Tsuboya-yachimun-dōri.

Daichi Makishi Kōsetsu Ichiba
MARKET **$**

(第一牧志公設市場; 2-10-1 Matsuo; meals from ¥800; ☉10am-8pm) We highly recommend a meal at one of the eateries on the 2nd floor of this food market. Just have a look at what the locals are eating and grab a seat.

Baobab
BAR

(バオバブ; 2-12-7 Matsuo; ☉Tues-Sat) Tucked away on Ukishima-dōri, Baobab is an eccentric ode to Africa, with booths sculpted out of mock tree trunks, African wines and beer, and original cocktails (¥750) on offer.

Rehab
BAR

(3-A Kakazu Bldg, 2-4-14 Makishi) This sleek international bar above Gera Gera internet cafe on Kokusai-dōri attracts a friendly, mixed crowd and has cosy nook seating, imported beer, and two-for-one drinks on Tuesdays.

❶ Information

Post offices are scattered around town, including the Miebashi post office (美栄橋郵便局), on the ground floor of the Palette Kumoji building, the Tomari-kō post office (泊ふ頭郵便局), in the Tomari port building, and the Kokusai-dōri post office (国際通り郵便局), around the corner from Makishi Station.

Gera Gera (ゲラゲラ; 2-4-14 Makishi; per hr ¥480; ⊙24hr) A convenient net cafe on Kokusai-dōri. It's just a little east of the Family Mart convenience store, on the 2nd floor.

Okinawa Tourist (沖縄ツーリスト; ☑862-1111; 1-2-3 Matsuo; ⊙9.30am-6.30pm, closed Sun) On Kokusai-dōri, a competent travel agency with English speakers who can help with all manner of ferry and flight bookings.

Tourist information counter (☑857-6884; 1F Arrivals Terminal, Naha International Airport; ⊙9am-9pm) At this helpful prefectural counter, we suggest picking up a copy of the *Naha City Guide Map* before heading into town. If you plan to explore outside Naha, also grab a copy of the *Okinawa Guide Map*.

Tourist information office (那覇市観光案内所; ☑868-4887; 2-1-4 Makishi; ⊙8.30am-8pm Mon-Fri, 10am-8pm Sat & Sun) The city office also has free maps. It's just off Kokusai-dōri (turn at Starbucks).

❶ Getting There & Away

AIR

Naha International Airport (OKA) has connections with Seoul, Taipei, Hong Kong and Shanghai. Connections with mainland Japan include Kagoshima (¥26,300, one hour 25 minutes), Hiroshima (¥32,000, two hours), Osaka (¥34,200, two hours 15 minutes), Nagoya (¥38,900, two hours 30 minutes) and Tokyo (¥40,900, two hours 45 minutes); significant discounts (*tabiwari* on All Nippon Airways and *sakitoku* on JAL) can sometimes be had if you purchase tickets a month in advance. Note that this is only a partial list; most large Japanese cities have flights.

Naha also has air connections with Kume-jima, Aka-jima, Miyako-jima, Ishigaki-jima and Yoron-tō, among other Southwest Islands. See the relevant sections for details.

BOAT

Naha has regular ferry connections with ports in Honshū (Tokyo and Osaka/Kōbe) and Kyūshū (Kagoshima).

Maruei Ferry/A Line (☑in Naha 861-1886, in Tokyo 03-5643-6170; www.aline-ferry.com, in Japanese) operates four or five ferries a month running to/from Tokyo (¥23,500, 47 hours) and Osaka/Kobe (¥18,800, 42 hours), as well as daily ferries to/from Kagoshima (¥14,200, 25 hours). Note that if you ask for a *norihōdai kippu* you can sail from Kagoshima to Naha and get on and off the ferries freely within seven days.

There are three ports in Naha, and this can be confusing: Kagoshima/Amami-shotō ferries operate from Naha-kō (Naha Port); Tokyo/Osaka/Kōbe ferries operate from Naha Shin-kō; and Kume-jima and Kerama-shotō ferries operate from Tomari-kō (Tomari Port).

Note that there is no ferry service to the Miyako-shotō or Yaeyama-shotō islands from Naha.

❶ Getting Around

The Yui-rail monorail runs from Naha International Airport in the south to Shuri in the north. Prices range from ¥200 to ¥290. Kenchō-mae Station is at the western end of Kokusai-dōri, while Makishi Station is at its eastern end.

Naha-kō is a 10-minute walk southwest from Asahibashi Station, while Tomari-kō is a similar distance north from Miebashi Station. Bus 101 from Naha bus terminal (那覇バスターミナル) heads further north to Naha Shin-kō (20 minutes, hourly).

When riding on local town buses, simply dump ¥200 into the slot next to the driver as you enter. For longer trips, take a ticket showing your starting point as you board and pay the appropriate fare as you disembark. Buses run from Naha to destinations all over the island.

A rental car makes everything easier when exploring Okinawa-hontō; there's a rental-car counter in the arrivals hall of Naha International Airport. Try **Matsuda Rentacar** (☑857-0802; 2-13-10 Akamine), which is near Akamine Station and has a courtesy bus to/from the airport.

SOUTHERN OKINAWA-HONTŌ
沖縄本島の南部

During the closing days of the Battle of Okinawa, the southern part of Okinawa-hontō served as one of the last holdouts of the Japanese military and an evacuation point for wounded Japanese soldiers. A visit to the area, a day or half-day trip from Naha, is highly recommended for those with an interest in wartime history.

Okinawa's most important war memorials are clustered in the **Memorial Peace Park** (平和祈念公園; ⊙dawn-dusk), located in the city of Itoman on the southern coast of the island. The centrepiece of the park is the **Okinawa Prefectural Peace Memorial**

Museum (沖縄県平和祈念資料館; 614-1 Mabuni, Itoman-shi; admission ¥300; ◌9am-5pm), which focuses on the suffering of the Okinawan people during the invasion of the island and under the subsequent American occupation. The main exhibits are on the 2nd floor. The museum strives to present a balanced picture of the Pacific War and the history that led to the invasion, but there is plenty here to stir debate. Outside the museum is the **Cornerstone of Peace** (◌dawn-dusk), which is inscribed with the names of everyone who died in the Battle of Okinawa.

To reach the park, take bus 89 from Naha bus terminal (那覇バスターミナル) to the Itoman bus terminal (¥500, one hour, every 20 minutes), then transfer to bus 82, which goes to Heiwa Kinen-kōen (¥400, 25 minutes, hourly).

An interesting stop en route to the Peace Park is the **Himeyuri no Tō** (ひめゆりの塔; Himeyuri Peace Museum; 671-1 Ihara, Itoman-shi; admission ¥300; ◌9am-5pm), located above a cave that served as an emergency field hospital during the closing days of the Battle of Okinawa. Here, 240 female high-school students were pressed into service as nurses for Japanese military wounded. As American forces closed in, the students were dismissed and the majority died. Bus 82 stops outside.

Directly south of Naha in Kaigungo-kōen is the **Former Japanese Navy Underground Headquarters** (旧海軍司令部壕; 236 Tomigusuku, Tomigusuku-shi; admission ¥420; ◌8.30am-5pm), where 4000 men committed suicide or were killed as the battle for Okinawa drew to its bloody conclusion. Only 250m of the tunnels are open, but you can wander through the maze of corridors, see the commander's final words on the wall of his room, and inspect the holes and scars in other walls from the grenade blasts that killed many of the men. To reach the site, take bus 33 or 46 from Naha bus terminal (那覇バスターミナル) to the Tomigusuku-kōen-mae stop (¥230, 20 minutes, hourly). From there it's a 10-minute walk – follow the English signs (the entrance is near the top of the hill).

MOTOBU PENINSULA　　　　本部半島

Jutting out to the northwest of Nago, the hilly peninsula of Motobu (Motobu-hontō) is home to some scenic vistas, islets and decent beaches, as well as an incredibly popular aquarium. Motobu peninsula is served by frequent loop lines from Nago – buses 66 and 65 respectively run anticlockwise and clockwise around the peninsula.

A couple of kilometres north of Motobu town is the **Ocean Expo Park** (海洋博公園), the centrepiece of which is the wonderful **Okinawa Chiraumi Aquarium** (沖縄美ら海水族館; 424 Ishikawa, Motobu-chō; admission adult/child ¥1800/600; ◌8.30am-5.30pm, later in summer, closed 1st Wed & Thu in Dec). The aquarium is built around the world's largest aquarium tank, which houses a fantastic variety of fish including whale sharks. Unfortunately, this place is on the checklist of every single tourist to the island, and it can be packed. From Nago, bus 70 runs directly to the park (¥800, 45 minutes). Both peninsula loop lines (buses 65 and 66) also stop outside.

About 1km north of the aquarium is the quaintly preserved village of **Bise** (備瀬), a leafy community of traditional Okinawan houses along a beach. An atmospheric lane lined with old garcinia trees (フクギ並木) is perfect for strolling, and a few shops sell seashell crafts. Near the lane's southern end, **Cahaya Bulan** (チャハヤブラン; ☏0980-51-7272; 429-1 Bise; ☏lunch, dinner; ☏) is a relaxing cafe with noodle dishes such as *ajian-soba* (Asian-style *soba;* ¥800) and a patio with views of Ie-jima. If you feel like overnighting, **Okinawa Motobu Guesthouse** (OKINAWA MOTOBU ゲストハウス; ☏090-9074-0328; www.geocities.jp/okinawa_motobu_guest_house, in Japanese; 571 Yamakawa; dm ¥2000; Ⓟ @) is a super-funky concrete box set amid sugarcane fields above the aquarium. The owner can pick you up from the Yamakawa bus stop.

If you're after natural attractions and have your own wheels, we recommend a drive out to **Kouri-jima** (古宇利島) via **Yagaji-shima** (屋我地島). The bridge between the two islands is surrounded by picturesque turquoise water, and there's a decent beach on either side of the road as you reach Kōri-jima. The bridge to Yagaji-shima starts just north of the Motobu peninsula off Rte 58.

NORTHERN OKINAWA-HONTŌ
沖縄本島の北部

The northern part of Okinawa-hontō is largely undeveloped and comparatively wild and rugged. Since there is limited public transport in the north, you will probably need a rental car. Rte 58 hugs the west coast all the way up to **Cape Hedo** (辺戸岬), which marks the northern end of Okinawa. The point is an incredibly scenic spot backed by hills, with rocks rising from the dense greenery. On a good day, Yoron-tō, the southernmost island in Amami-shotō, is easily seen only 23km to the northeast.

The US officially returned Okinawa to Japanese administration in 1972, but it negotiated a Status of Forces Agreement that guaranteed the Americans the right to use large tracts of Okinawan land for military bases, most of which are on Okinawa-hontō. These bases are home to approximately 24,000 American servicemen.

Although the bases support the Okinawa economy, they are a sore spot for islanders due in part to occasional crimes committed by American servicemen. Antibase feelings peaked in 1996, when three American servicemen abducted and raped a 12-year-old Okinawan girl. Similar incidents in recent years have perpetuated animosity. In April 2010, 90,000 protesters gathered to call for an end to the bases, the biggest such demonstrations in 15 years.

In 2010, then Prime Minister Yukio Hatoyama fell on his sword after breaking a promise to move Futenma air base off the island; he finally admitted it would stay. There are plans to move about 6000 servicemen to a base in Guam, but US military officials have said that this might not occur until as late as 2015.

Tourists to Okinawa are surprised to find that servicemen keep a relatively low profile. Unless one ventures to the areas north of Naha, it is possible to visit Okinawa without even noticing their presence – until another American fighter jet goes screaming overhead.

Islands Near Okinawa-hontō

If you've had enough of the crowds and resorts of Okinawa-hontō, hop on a ferry to one of the nearby islands. The best of the lot are the three main islands of Kerama-shotō, which lie a mere 30km offshore from Naha. These islands are among the most attractive in the entire Southwest Islands, with crystal-clear water and excellent white-sand beaches. A little further out is the rarely visited island of Kume-jima. For those with a sense of adventure, there are several other islands that we don't cover in this guide: Ie-jima, Iheya-jima, Izena-jima, Aguni-jima, Kita-daitō-jima and Tonaki-jima. A good source of information is Naha's Tourist Information Office (see p655).

KERAMA ISLANDS 慶良間諸島

The islands of Kerama-shotō are a world away from the hustle and bustle of Okinawa-hontō, though even these islands can get crowded during the summer holiday season. The three main islands here are Zamami-jima, Aka-jima and Tokashiki-jima. You can easily visit any of these as a day trip from Naha, but we recommend a few days in a *minshuku* on one of the islands to really savour the experience.

AKA-JIMA 阿嘉島
☑ 098 / POP 279

A mere 2km in diameter, tiny Aka-jima makes up for in beauty what it lacks in size. With some of the best beaches in the Kera-

mas and an extremely peaceful atmosphere, it's easy to get stuck here for several days. There's also some great snorkelling and diving nearby.

If you keep your eyes open around dusk you might spot a **Kerama deer** (慶良間シカ), descendants of deer that were brought by the Satsuma from Kagoshima when they conquered the Ryūkyūs in 1609. The deer are smaller and darker than their mainland cousins, and have been designated a National Treasure.

There are great beaches on every side of the island, but for sheer postcard-perfect beauty, it's hard to beat the 1km stretch of white sand on the northeast coast known as **Nishibama Beach** (ニシバマビーチ). This beach can be crowded in summer; if you want privacy, there are quieter beaches on the other sides of the island.

Dive shop-hotel **Marine House Seasir** (ペンションシーサー; ☑0120-10-2737; www .seasir.com, in Japanese; r per person with meals ¥7350) at the west end of the main village has good clean Western-style and Japanese rooms. Most of the guests are divers. It offers whale-watching tours (¥4800) from January to March.

Kawai Diving (☑987-2219; http://oki-zama mi.jp/~kawai/; 153 Aka; r per person with meals from ¥6510; P@), located along Maehama Beach on the south coast, has simple rooms and a family atmosphere. English-speaking staff are happy to tell guests about the island and take them diving (one/two dives ¥6300/10,500, equipment rental ¥1260 per piece).

Zamami Sonei Ferry (☏868-4567) has two or three fast ferries a day (¥3140, 50 minutes) and one regular ferry (¥2120, 1½ hours) to/from Naha's Tomari-kō. A motorboat also makes four trips a day between Aka-jima and Zamami-jima (¥300, 15 minutes).

Due to its small size, the best way to get around the island is on foot.

ZAMAMI-JIMA 座間味島
♪098 / POP 586

A stone's throw from Aka-jima, Zamami-jima is *slightly* more developed, but also has some great beaches and a few rocky vistas. It's got some brilliant offshore islands and great diving and snorkelling in the surrounding waters. There is a **tourist information office** (☏987-2277; ⊙9am-5pm) at the port.

Furuzamami Beach (古座間味ビーチ), approximately 1km southeast from the port (over the hill), is a stunning 700m stretch of white sand that is fronted by clear, shallow water and a bit of coral. The beach is well developed for day trippers, and has toilets, showers and food stalls. You can also rent snorkelling gear here (¥1000).

If you fancy a little solitude, you'll find picturesque empty beaches in several of the coves on the other sides of the island. The best beaches, however, are on **Gahi-jima** (嘉比島) and **Agenashiku-jima** (安慶名敷島), which are located about a kilometre south of the port. Ringed by delightful white-sand beaches, they are perfect for a half-day *Robinson Crusoe* experience. One boat operator who can take you to these islands and arrange snorkelling trips is **Zamami Tour Operation** (☏987-3586). The tourist information office can also help arrange boat tours (pickup/drop-off ¥1500 per person round trip).

Whale-watching is possible between the months of December and April. For more information, either enquire at the tourist information office or call the **Zamami-mura Whale-Watching Association** (座間味村ホエールウォッチング協会; ☏896-4141; tours ¥6000), which has one to two tours daily (two hours).

Zamami-jima makes a great day trip from Naha, but an overnight stay will be more relaxing. A good place to stay is **Joy Joy** (ジョイジョイ; ☏0120-10-2445; http://keramajoyjoy.com/index.html; 434-2 Zamami; r per person with breakfast from ¥5250) in the northwest corner of the village. Accommodation is in a variety of rooms that surround a small garden. This pension also runs a dive shop, with beach and sea dive tours from ¥4730.

Minshuku Summer House Yū Yū (民宿サマーハウス遊遊; ☏098-987-3055; www.yuyu-okinawa.jp/index.html, in Japanese; 130 Zamami; r per person with/without meals from ¥6000/3500) is a friendly *minshuku* that is just up the street from Joy Joy in the main village. Both places are an easy walk from the pier.

Zamami Sonei (☏868-4567) has two or three fast ferries a day (¥3140, 50 minutes) and one regular ferry (¥2120, two hours) to/from Naha's Tomari-kō. The ferries usually stop at Aka-jima en route from Naha to Zamami. A motorboat also makes four trips a day between Aka-jima and Zamami-jima (¥300, 15 minutes).

There are no buses or taxis on Zamami-jima, though nothing is too far away. Rental cars, scooters and bicycles are available near the pier.

TOKASHIKI-JIMA 渡嘉敷島
♪098 / POP 785

Tokashiki-jima, the largest island in Kerama-shotō, is a long, skinny, north–south island that has some great beaches. It's very popular with young Japanese holidaymakers, but is actually slightly less appealing than Aka-jima or Zamami-jima. Ferries arrive at the port of Tokashiki (渡嘉敷) on the east coast.

The island's most attractive beaches are **Tokashiku Beach** (とかしくビーチ) and **Aharen Beach** (阿波連ビーチ), both of which are located on the west coast. Both beaches are well developed for tourism, and have toilets, showers, food stalls and shops where you can rent snorkelling gear (¥1000).

You can easily visit Tokashiki as a day trip from Naha. If you prefer to spend the night, Aharen is the place to be. **Southern Cross** (サザンクロス; ☏987-2258; r per person with/without meals ¥7500/4000), a family-run inn with simple Western- and Japanese-style rooms, is practically on the beach. A little further back in the village you'll find **Kerama-sō** (けらま荘 ☏987-2125; r per person with/without meals ¥5775/3675), which is a slightly nicer *minshuku* with basic Japanese-style rooms and reasonable rates. Staff will pick you up at the pier if you can get someone to make a reservation in advance in Japanese.

Tokashiki Sonei (☏868-7541) operates one or two fast ferries a day (¥2430, 35 minutes) and one regular ferry (¥1620, one hour 10 minutes) from Naha's Tomari-kō.

The Southwest Islands have some excellent diving and an impressive variety of fish and coral species. There is also a healthy smattering of underwater wrecks, cavern systems and even the odd archaeological ruin.

Costs for diving in the Southwest Islands are higher than you might pay in Southeast Asia, but standards of equipment and guiding are fairly high. In order to dive around Okinawa and the Southwest Islands, you will need to be in possession of a valid diving certification. If you're renting equipment, you should know your weight in kilograms, your height in metres and your shoe size in centimetres.

Here are some English-speaking operators who welcome foreigners:

» **Ishigaki: Sea Friends** (☑0980-82-0863; sea-friends.net, in Japanese; 346 Ishigaki, Ishigaki-shi Aza; 1/2 dives ¥10,500/12,600, equipment rental ¥5250; ⊙8am-8pm)

» **Ishigaki: Umicoza** (☑0980-88-2434; www.umicoza.com/english; 827-15 Kabira, Ishigaki-shi; 1/2 dives ¥9450/12,600, equipment rental ¥5250; ⊙8am-6pm)

» **Okinawa Hontō: Piranha Divers** (☑080-4277-1155; www.piranha-divers.jp; 2288-75 Aza-Nakama, Onna; full-day dives from ¥17,000, equipment rental ¥5000)

» **Yonaguni: SaWest** (☑0980-87-2311; www.yonaguni.jp/sawes.htm; 59-6 Yonaguni; 1/2 dives ¥8000/12,000, equipment rental ¥5000; ⊙8am-6pm)

Buses run from Tokashiki Port to the beaches on the west coast. Bicycles, cars and scooters are available in Tokashiki Port. Try **Karyushi Rentasābisu** (☑987-3311) if you have an international license and want to rent a scooter.

KUME-JIMA
久米島

☑098 / POP 8713

The furthest flung of the outer islands, Kume-jima is a quiet island that sees fewer visitors than the Keramas. It's mostly flat and covered with sugarcane, with a few good beaches and the mother of all sandbars off its east coast.

The airport is at the western extreme of the island, while the main port of Kaneshiro (兼城) is on the southwest coast. There is a **tourist information office** (☑985-7115) at the airport that opens to meet incoming flights in summer.

The most popular beach on the island is **Ifu Beach** (イーフビーチ), on the east coast. *Ifu* means 'white' in the local Kume dialect, and not surprisingly, the beach is known for its powdery white sand. Another attractive beach is **Shinri-hama** (シンリ浜), on the west coast near the airport, which is known for its sunsets over the East China Sea.

Kume-jima's most famous attraction is **Hate-no-hama** (はての浜), a 7km sandbar that extends from the eastern point of the island, pointing back towards Okinawa-hontō. If you arrive by air, you can't miss this coral-fringed strip of white framed by the turquoise waters of the East China Sea. The best way to get there is on an excursion with **Hatenohama Kankō Service** (☑090-8292-8854), which runs a three-hour tour to the sandbar for ¥3500. If you book in advance, staff members can pick you up from your accommodation.

On tiny **Ōjima** (奥武島), which is connected to Kume-jima's east coast by a causeway, you'll find the intriguing **Tatami-ishi** (畳石), a natural formation of flat pentagonal rocks that covers the seashore.

Ifu Beach is the place to stay, and there are plenty of choices along the 1.5km waterfront. Our pick is **Minshuku Nankurunaisā** (民宿なんくるないさぁ; ☑985-7973; http://nankurunaisakume.ti-da.net, in Japanese; 160-68 Higa; r per person from ¥4000; P@), an excellent, friendly new *minshuku* set back just a bit from the beach. It's got Japanese- and Western-style rooms. For those with tents, there is a small campground on Ōjima, before the Tatami-ishi.

JTA and RAC operate five flights a day between Naha and Kume-jima (¥11,800, 35 minutes). JTA operates one daily flight from Tokyo to Kume-jima between June and September (¥46,700, 2½ hours). **Kume Shōsen** (☑098-868-2686) runs a daily ferry from Naha's Tomari-kō to/from Kume-jima (¥3000, three hours 15 minutes).

Kume-jima has an efficient bus system. **East Rentacar** (☑896-7766) has a counter at the airport.

Miyako Islands 宮古諸島

Located just north of the Tropic of Cancer, Miyako-shotō has some of the finest beaches in the Southwest Islands, and there is good diving and snorkelling in the waters offshore. It contains the main island of Miyako-jima, and the nearby islands of Ikema-jima, Irabu-jima, Shimoji-jima and Kurima-jima, as well as a scattering of tiny islets.

MIYAKO-JIMA 宮古島
♪0980 / POP 55,036

The main island in Miyako-shotō, Miyako-jima is a mostly flat expanse of sugarcane fringed by excellent beaches, with long fingers of land pointing out into the sea. Lying just offshore are four smaller islands, two of which are connected to the main island by bridges (another bridge is under construction that will allow road access to all the nearby islands).

Miyako-jima is a beach island and you can happily spend your days here hopping from one great beach to the next, with a spot of snorkelling at each one if you're so inclined. If you tire of that, a seaside drive to the various capes of the island is a great way to spend a few hours. And, finally, there are a few attractions in the main city of Hirara to keep you occupied on a rainy day.

⊙ Sights & Activities

Sunayama BEACH
(砂山ビーチ) Just 4km north of Hirara you will find this excellent little beach, which lies at the bottom of a large sand dune (hence the name 'Sand Mountain Beach'). A cool stone arch at one side of the beach provides a bit of shade.

Yonaha-Maehama BEACH
On the southwest coast, beautiful Yonaha-Maehama is a 6km stretch of white sand that attracts a lot of families and young folks due to its shallow waters. It's a lovely beach, but it can get crowded and the presence of the occasional jet-ski is a drawback. It's just before the Kurima-Ōhashi Bridge, on the north side.

Nagahama BEACH
(長浜) If you've had a look at the crowds at Yoneha-Maehama and decided you want something quieter, head across the Kurima-Ōhashi and drive to the northwest coast of **Kurima-jima** (来間島), where you will find the brilliant (and usually uncrowded) Nagahama.

Miyako Traditional Arts & Crafts Centre ART GALLERY
(Map p662; admission free; ⊙9am-6pm Mon-Sat) If you can pry yourself away from the beaches for a moment, there are a few sights in Hirara, including the Miyako Traditional Arts & Crafts Centre, which displays traditional island crafts – be sure to check out the *minsā* weaving looms on the 2nd floor. It's next to the small **Miyako-jinja** (宮古神社) and behind shops facing the Miyako Dai-ichi Hotel.

On the southeast corner of Miyako-jima are several attractions including **Boraga Beach** (保良川ビーチ), which is a popular spot for snorkelling and kayaking (with a hair-raisingly steep access road). Around the cape to the north, you'll find **Yoshino Beach** (吉野海岸) and **Aragusuku Beach** (新城海岸), two relatively shallow beaches with a lot of offshore coral (much of it dead).

If you've got a car, we recommend a drive out to the end of **Higashi Henna-zaki** (東平安名崎), a narrow finger of land that extends 2km into the Pacific Ocean. There are picnic tables, walking trails and a lighthouse at the point for you to explore.

Another good drive is across **Ikema-Ōhashi** (池間大橋) to **Ikema-jima** (池間島). The shallow turquoise water on either side of this 1.4km bridge is incredibly beautiful on a sunny day (just try to keep your eyes on the road). You'll find several **private pocket beaches** around the coast of Ikema-jima.

🛏 Sleeping

Most of the accommodation is located in the town of Hirara, but you'll also find places to stay closer to the beaches. There are free campgrounds at many beaches, including Yonaha-Maebama, Boraga and Aragusuku.

TOP CHOICE Raza Cosmica Tourist Home HOTEL $$
(ラザコスミカツーリストホーム; Map p661; ♪75-2020; www.raza-cosmica.com; 309-1 Hiraramaezato; r per person with breakfast from ¥8000; P) This charming South Asian–themed inn sits above a lovely secluded beach on Ikema-jima. Romantic Western-style rooms offer peace and quiet in truly lovely surroundings, which makes this the perfect destination for holidaying couples or honeymooners. Bathrooms are shared and children below 12 years of age are not permitted; owners ask that you reserve on their website. Look for the Shiva eyes on the door.

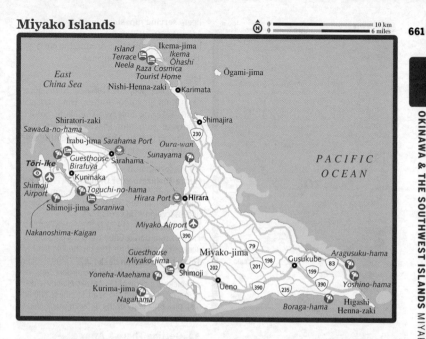

Island Terrace Neela
HOTEL $$$

(アイランドテラス・ニーラ; Map p661; ☑74-4678; www.neela.jp; 317-1 Hirara-maezato; for groups of 2, r per person with breakfast from ¥33,000; P@) Overlooking the same private beach as the Raza, this intimate high-end resort looks like a whitewashed Mediterranean resort airlifted to Japan. The private villas would make the perfect honeymoon destination.

Hiraraya
GUESTHOUSE $

(ひららや; Map p662; ☑75-3221; www.miyako -net.ne.jp/~hiraraya; 282 Higashi-nakasone; dm night/week ¥2000/12,000; r per person night/ week ¥3000/18,000; P@) Located in central Hirara just one block north of Miyako-jinja (look for the light blue curtain that says guesthouse), this laid-back spot is run by a charming couple who will do everything to make you feel at home. Accommodation is available in dorms with huge beds, and Japanese-style tatami rooms; there are special rates available for longer-term stays.

Guesthouse Miyako-jima
GUESTHOUSE $

(ゲストハウス宮古島; Map p661; ☑76-2330; www2.miyako-ma.jp/yonaha/index.html; 233 Yoneha; dm night/week ¥1800/11,200, r per person night/week ¥3500/21,000; P🛜) This bright and cheery guesthouse run by a kite-board-ing enthusiast has a scenic location near Yoneha-Maehama beach (与那覇前浜). Accommodation is in cosy Western-style dorms and private rooms with shared facilities, and there are special rates available for long-term stays. Guests can also borrow bicycles and, with an international license, scooters.

🍴 Eating & Drinking

There are eateries scattered here and there across the island, but you'll find the best selection in the town of Hirara.

TOP CHOICE Pōcha Tatsuya
IZAKAYA $$

(ぽうちゃたつや; off Map p662; ☑73-3931; 275 Nishizato; dishes ¥800; ⏰dinner, closed Tue) Just off McCrum-dōri, this hospitable izakaya serves delish local fare like *kobushime-ya-waraka-ni* (steamed cuttlefish; ¥730) and *sūchiki* (vinegared pork with bitter melon; ¥630). From McCrum, go past the National store on your left. Look for the green latticework over the windows and a seahorse curled around the sign above the door.

Chūzan
IZAKAYA $

(中山; Map p662; ☑73-1959; 108-10 Shimozato; dishes ¥800; ⏰4pm-midnight; 🅿) This popular *izakaya* is a great spot that offers a variety of locally caught seafood. You can't

Hirara

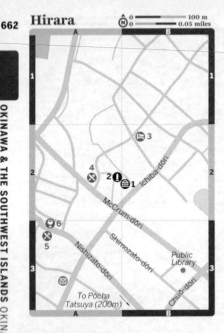

go wrong with the *sashimi-moriawase* (sashimi assortment; ¥1000), which washes down perfectly with a tall glass of *nama-biiru* (draught beer; ¥250). Service can be a little slow. Look for the green carpeted steps outside.

Koja Shokudō Honten   NOODLES $
(古謝食堂本店; Map p662; ☎72-2139; 165 Nishizato; dishes ¥700; ☉10am-8pm) One block northwest of the intersection between Ichiba-dōri and Nishizato-dōri, this nondescript noodle house is something of a local legend. For more than 50 years, Koja has been serving up steaming bowls of *sōki-soba* (¥650). It's across from a parking lot; look for the white tiles around the entryway. The owner speaks English.

Isla   BAR
(イスラ; Map p662; 172 Nishizato) Right across from Koja Shokudō Honten, Isla is a Caribbean watering hole with relaxing grooves, plenty of rum and snacks like Jamaican-style pizza (¥800). There are sometimes live bands on the small stage.

ℹ Information

Hirara-Nishizato Post Office (平良西里郵便局; Map p662; Ichiba-dōri; ☉9am-5pm, ATMs open longer, closed Sat & Sun) The ATMs here accept foreign ATM cards.

Public library (平良市立図書館; Map p662; cnr McCrum-dōri & Chūō-dōri) It's possible to access the internet for free on the 2nd floor.

Tourist information desk (☎72-0899; ☉9am-6pm) In the arrivals hall of the airport, you can pick up a copy of the *Miyako Island Guide Map*. Travellers who can read Japanese should also pick up a copy of the detailed *Guide Map Miyako*.

ℹ Getting There & Away

Miyako-jima has direct flights to/from Tokyo's Haneda Airport (JTA; ¥55,600, three hours and 20 minutes, one daily), Naha (JTA/ANA; ¥18,600, 50 minutes, 12 daily) and Ishigaki (JTA/RAC; ¥12,400, 20 minutes, four daily).

ℹ Getting Around

Miyako-jima has a limited bus network that operates from two bus stands in Hirara. Buses run between the airport and Hirara (¥270, 10 minutes). Buses also depart from Yachiyo bus terminal for Ikema-jima (¥500, 35 minutes), and from the Miyako Kyōei bus terminal, 700m east of town, to Yoshino/Bora (¥500, 50 minutes). Yet another line runs between Hirara and Yoneha/Kurima-jima (¥390, 30 minutes).

The island's flat terrain is perfectly suited to biking. If you want to move faster, there are rental-car counters at the airport and offices in Hirara.

IRABU-JIMA & SHIMOJI-JIMA   伊良部島・下地島

A 10-minute ferry ride from Hirara (Miyako-jima) brings you to Irabu-jima and Shimoji-jima, which are pleasantly rural islands covered with fields of sugar cane and linked by a series of bridges. Like Miyako, Irabu and Shimoji are a beach lover's paradise. The islands are best visited as a day trip from Hirara, though there are guesthouses and free campgrounds.

The best swimming beach is **Toguchi-no-hama** (渡口の浜) on Irabu-jima's west coast. Easily the best snorkelling beach is **Nakanoshima-kaigan** (中の島海岸), protected by a high-walled bay on the west coast of Shimoji-jima. Look for the sign reading 'Nakano Island The Beach'.

An interesting site to stroll is **Tōri-ike** (通り池), two seawater 'ponds' on the west coast of Shimoji-jima that are actually sinkholes in the coral that formed the island. It's near **Shimoji Airport**, used as a practise runway by Japanese airlines.

The chilled-out backpackers haven of **Guesthouse Birafuya** (びらふやー; ☎78-3380; www.birafuya.com, in Japanese; 1436-1 Irabu-sawada; dm/s/d ¥2000/3000/5000; closed Dec-Mar; P@) is a few blocks inland from Sawada-no-hama beach (佐和田の浜). Birafuya has a dorm and small Western-style rooms and is a great place to meet other travellers. If you phone ahead, staff will pick you up at the ferry terminal. Overlooking the south coast, **Soraniwa** (そらにわ ☎74-5528; www.soraniwa.org, in Japanese; 721-1 Irabu; d and tw from ¥10,500; ☺11.30am-10pm; P@) is a small but stylish cafe-hotel, with meals like *okinawa shioyaki-soba* (Okinawa-style salted fried *soba*; ¥780), sumptuous beds and a rooftop Jacuzzi.

Fast ferries (¥400, 15 minutes, 11 daily) and car ferries (¥350 per walking passenger, ¥2000 per car, 25 minutes, 13 daily) run between Hirara on Miyako-jima and Sarahama Port (佐良浜港) on Irabu-jima.

Yaeyama Islands 八重山諸島

At the far southwestern end of the Southwest Islands are the islands of Yaeyama-shotō, which include the main islands of Ishigaki-jima and Iriomote-jima as well as a spread of 17 isles. Located near the Tropic of Cancer, they are renowned for their lovely beaches, superb diving and lush landscapes.

Yaeyama-shotō is arguably the top destination in the Southwest Islands. It offers Japan's best snorkelling and diving, and some of Japan's last intact subtropical jungles and mangrove swamps (both on Iriomote-jima). Perhaps the best feature of the Yaeyamas is their variety and the ease with which you can explore them: plentiful ferry services run between Ishigaki City and nearby islands like Iriomote-jima and Taketomi-jima, and you can easily explore three or four islands in one trip.

Located 100km southwest of Miyako-jima, Ishigaki-jima is the most populated and developed island in Yaeyama-shotō. Ishigaki-jima has some excellent beaches around its coastline, and there are some brilliant diving and snorkelling spots offshore. The rugged geography of the island is also extremely attractive, both for long drives and day hikes, and there are times when you might think you're in Hawaii instead of southern Japan.

⊙ Sights & Activities

Ishigaki City (石垣市) occupies the southwestern corner of the island. You'll find most of the action in the two shopping arcades, which run parallel to the main street. The city is easily walkable, and can be explored in an hour or two.

A series of roads branch out from Ishigaki City and head along the coastline and into the interior. There are several settlements near the coast, though most of the interior is mountains and farmland.

Some of the best beaches on the island are found on the west coast. Before you hit the beaches though, you might want to spend a half-day exploring some of the city's sights.

The sea around Ishigaki-jima is famous among the Japanese diving community for its large schools of manta rays, particularly from June to October. The most popular place is **Manta Scramble**, off the coast of Kabira Ishizaki. Although it's likely that you'll be sharing with a fair number of dive boats, you're almost guaranteed to see a manta (or four). There are a number of dive shops on Ishigaki-jima.

Ishigaki City Yaeyama Museum MUSEUM
(石垣市立八重山博物館; Map p667; 4-1 Tonoshiro, Ishigaki City; admission ¥200; ☺9am-4.30pm, closed Mon) Located 100m southeast of the post office is this modest museum, which has exhibits on the culture and history of the island.

Miyara Dōnchi HISTORICAL BUILDING
(宮良殿内; Map p667; 178 Ōkawa, Ishigaki City; admission ¥200; ☺9am-5pm) The unique home of a Ryūkyū Kingdom official dating from 1819; walk north along Sanbashi-dōri until you see signs in English.

Tōrin-ji TEMPLE
(桃林寺; 285 Ishigaki, Ishigaki City; ☺9am-7pm) Founded in 1614, the Zen temple of Tōrin-ji, near the intersection of Shimin-kaikan-dōri and Rte 79, is home to the 18th-century

OKINAWA & THE SOUTHWEST ISLANDS OKINAWA PREFECTURE

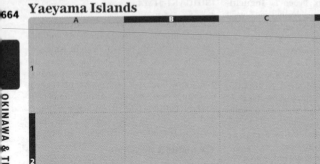

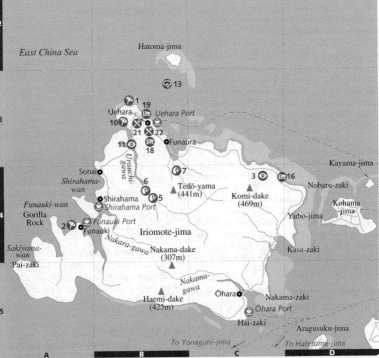

guardian statues of Deva kings. Adjacent to the temple is **Gongen-dō** (権現堂), a small shrine rebuilt after being destroyed by a tsunami in 1771.

Yonehara Beach BEACH
(米原ビーチ; Map p664) North of Ishigaki City along Rte 79 is Yonehara Beach, a nice sand beach with a good bit of reef offshore. You can rent snorkel gear (¥1000) at any of the shops along the main road.

Kabira-wan BEACH
(川平湾; Map p664) Just west of Yonehara is the equally famous Kabira-wan, a sheltered

bay with white-sand shores and a couple of interesting clumplike islands offshore. This is more of a wading beach than a swimming beach and it's usually busy with boat traffic, which detracts somewhat from its beauty.

Sukuji Beach BEACH
(底地ビーチ; Map p664) On the opposite side of the peninsula is a shallow beach that is good for families with children.

Sunset Beach BEACH
(サンセットビーチ; Map p664) At the north end of the island, on the west coast, you will

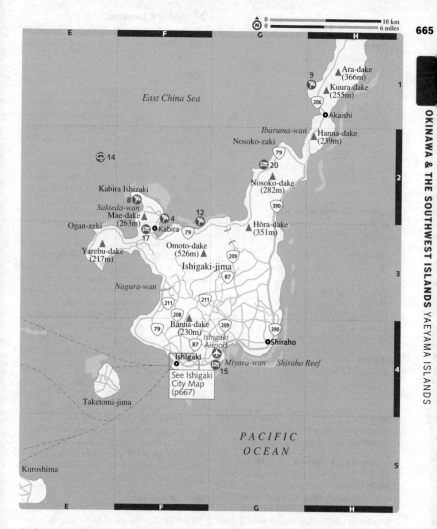

find another long strip of sand with a bit of offshore reef. As the name implies, this is a good spot to watch the sun set into the East China Sea.

🛌 Sleeping

Pension Yaima-biyōri GUESTHOUSE $
(ペンションやいま日和; Map p667; ☎88-5578; www.yaima-well.net/ybiyori/index.htm, in Japanese; 10-7 Miaski-chō; r per person from ¥2800; **P @**) Located two blocks north of the ferry and bus station, this welcoming pension offers simple but spacious Western- and Japanese-style rooms with shared facilities.

ANA Intercontinental Ishigaki
Resort HOTEL $$$
(ANAインターコンチネンタル石垣リゾート; off Map p667; ☎88-7111; www.ichotelsgroup .com; 354-1 Maesato; r from ¥16,800; **P @ ☎**) Right by the airport but not overwhelmed by plane noise, the Intercontinental has gorgeously refurbished rooms, free high-speed internet and large LCD TVs.

Iriwa GUESTHOUSE $
(イリワMap p664; ☎88-2563; iriwa.org; 599 Kabira; dm/r per person ¥2000/4500; **P @**) Just above Kabira-wan bay on the north coast, Iriwa is a comfortable guesthouse with

Yaeyama Islands

dorm beds and large private rooms. It's run by a young couple who like to share meals and snorkelling expeditions with guests.

Tsundara Beach Retreat APARTMENTS $$$
(つんだらビーチ・リトリート; Map p664; ☎090-7587-2029; tsundarabeach.com; 895-2 Nosoko; couples per person per night from ¥20,000; 🅿) This spacious beach house on the sparsely populated north coast comes with a huge bed, kitchen and a beautiful private beach (shared with the owners, who can organise ecotours such as **jungle zip-lining**). It's designed for vacationing couples.

Rakutenya GUESTHOUSE $
(楽天屋; Map p667; ☎83-8713; www3.big .or.jp/~erm8p3gi/english/english.html; 291 Ishigaki; r per person ¥3000; 🅿@🛜) This quaint guesthouse is two blocks north of the covered markets, and has attractive Western- and Japanese-style rooms in a rickety, old wooden house. The managers are a friendly Japanese couple who speak a little bit of English, and are a fantastic source of local information.

✕ Eating & Drinking

Ishigaki City has a good mix of boutique tourist restaurants, cheap but atmospheric local dives and boisterous watering holes.

TOP CHOICE Paikaji IZAKAYA $$
(南風; Map p667; ☎82-6027; 219 Ōkawa; dishes ¥700; ⏰5pm-midnight) No relation to Naha's Paikaji, this local favourite serves all the Okinawan and Yaeyama standards. Both the atmosphere and kitchen get top marks. Try the *ikasumi chahan* (squid ink fried rice; ¥650), the *gōya-champurū* (gōya stir-fry; ¥700) or the *sashimi moriawase* (sashimi assortment; ¥750/1300/1800 depending on size). There's no English sign or menu. Look for the traditional front, coral around the entryway and a red-and-white sign.

Eifuku Shokudō NOODLES $
(栄福食堂; Map p667; ☎82-5838; 274 Ōkawa; dishes ¥500; ⏰8.30am-12pm) This hole in the wall is plastered with write-ups from old editions of Lonely Planet. It's also a shrine to 1950s actor Akagi 'Tony' Kei-ichirō. Tony Soba, as it's known, is one of the cheapest places on the island for *yaeyama-soba* (thin noodles in broth; ¥300), though we recommend the stinky (but tasty) *yagi-soba* (goat *soba*; ¥500).

Asian Kitchen KAPI ASIAN $$
(アジアンキッチンカピ; Map p667; ☎82-2026; 199 Ōkawa; lunch/dinner ¥1000/3000; ⏰11.30am-3pm & 6.30-10pm, closed Thu; 🈺) Next door to Mori-no-Kokage (look for the English sign), this trendy Pan-Asian bistro is a good choice if your Japanese is limited. In addition to the local cuisine, KAPI also offers an impressive range of Asian favourites, from Korean-style hotpots to fiery Indonesian curries.

Mori-no-Kokage IZAKAYA $$
(森のこかげ居酒屋てぃんがーら; Map p667; ☎83-7933; 199 Ōkawa; ⏰5pm-midnight, closed Tue) This little *izakaya* has warmth and natural ambience. Local treats are *ishigaki-gyuu salada* (beef salad; from ¥1280) and the microbrew *ishigaki-shima-zake* (¥500). Look for the plants and tree trunks outside.

🔒 Shopping

A good place to shop for *omiyage* (souvenirs) is the main shopping arcade, which also has a public market.

Minsā Kōgeikan ART GALLERY
(みんさー工芸館; ☎82-3473; 909 Tonoshiro; ⏰9am-6pm) Also worth a look is the Minsā Kōgeikan, which is a weaving workshop and

Ishigaki City

(N) 0 —————— 400 m
0 —————— 0.2 miles

showroom with exhibits on Yaeyama-shotō textiles. The building is located between the city centre and the airport, and can be reached via the airport bus (tell the driver you want to stop here).

ℹ Information

Gera Gera (ゲラゲラ; 7-23 Misaki-chō; per hr ¥400; ⊙24hr) Internet access is available here.

Information counter (☎83-8384; airport; ⊙8.30am-9pm) Small but helpful.

Tourist information office (石垣市観光協会; ☎82-2809; 1st fl, Ishigaki-shi Shōkō Kaikan; ⊙8.30am-5.30pm Mon-Fri) Has a friendly English-speaking staff and simple English maps of the island. Japanese readers should pick up the *Ishigaki Town Guide* and the *Yaeyama Nabi*.

Yaeyama Post Office (八重山郵便局; Sanbashi-dōri; ⊙lobby 9am-7pm Mon-Fri, to 3pm Sat, ATM 8.45am-7pm Mon-Fri, 9am-7pm Sat, Sun & holidays) Has international ATMs.

ℹ Getting There & Away

AIR

Ishigaki-jima has direct flights to/from Tokyo's Haneda Airport (JTA; ¥59,000, 3½ hours, two daily), Osaka's Kansai International Airport (JTA; ¥48,400, two hours 50 minutes, one daily), Naha (JTA/ANA; ¥23,100, one hour, 20 daily), Miyako-jima (JTA/RAC; ¥11,900, 35 minutes, two daily) and Yonaguni-jima (JTA/RAC; ¥11,800, 30 minutes, two daily).

Ishigaki City

⊙ Sights
1 Ishigaki City Yaeyama Museum C3
2 Miyara Dōnchi C1
3 Tōrin-ji & Gongen-dō...........................B1

🛌 Sleeping
4 Pension Yaima-biyōri A2
5 Rakutenya C2

🍴 Eating
6 Asian Kitchen KAPI C2
7 Eifuku Shokudō B2
8 Paikaji B2

🍸 Drinking
9 Mori-no-Kokage C2

BOAT

Ishigaki-jima Rittō Ferry Terminal (石垣港離島ターミナル) serves islands including Iriomote-jima, Kohama-jima, Taketomi-jima and Hateruma-jima (see the relevant sections for details). Departures are frequent enough that you can usually just turn up in the morning and hop on the next ferry departing for your intended destination (except during the summer high season). The three main ferry operators are **Yaeyama Kankō Ferry** (☎82-5010), **Ishigaki Dream Kankō** (☎84-3178) and **Anei Kankō** (☎83-0055).

ⓘ Getting Around

The bus station is across the road from the ferry terminal in Ishigaki City. There are hourly buses to the airport (¥200, 20 minutes), as well as a few daily buses to Kabira-wan (¥700, 40 minutes), Yonehara Beach (¥800, one hour) and Shiraho (¥400, 30 minutes).

Rental cars, scooters and bicycles are readily available at shops throughout the city centre. If you're comfortable on a scooter, it's a scenic four-to five-hour cruise around the island, though you should plan for longer if you want to spend some time relaxing on the island's beaches. **Ishigaki Rentacar** (石垣島レンタカー; ☎82-8840) is located in the city centre and has reasonable rates.

IRIOMOTE-JIMA   西表島
☎0980 / POP 2279

Although it's just 20km west of Ishigaki-jima, Iriomote-jima could easily qualify as Japan's last frontier. Dense jungles and mangrove forest blanket more than 90% of the island, and it's fringed by some of the most beautiful coral reefs in all Japan. If you're super lucky, you may even spot one of the island's rare *yamaneko,* a nocturnal and rarely seen wildcat.

Several rivers penetrate far into the lush interior of the island and these can be explored by riverboat or kayak. Add to the mix sun-drenched beaches and spectacular diving and snorkelling, and it's easy to see why Iriomote-jima is one of the best destinations in Japan for nature lovers.

◉ Sights & Activities

The majority of the island's beaches are shallow due to the extensive coral reef that surrounds the island.

Tsuki-ga-hama   BEACH
(月ヶ浜; Moon Beach) The best swimming beach on the island is Tsuki-ga-hama, a crescent-shaped yellow-sand beach at the mouth of the Urauchi-gawa on the north coast.

Hoshisuna-no-hama   BEACH
(星砂の浜; Star Sand Beach) If you're looking to do a bit of snorkelling, head to this beach on the northwestern tip of the island. The beach is named after its star sand, which actually consists of the dried skeletons of tiny sea creatures. If you are a competent swimmer and the sea is calm, make your way with mask and snorkel to the outside of the reef – the coral and tropical fish here are spectacular.

Ida-no-hama   BEACH
(イダの浜) From **Shirahama** (白浜), at the western end of the north coast road, there are four daily boats to the isolated settlement of **Funauki** (船浮; ¥500). Once there, it's a mere 10-minute walk on to the absolutely gorgeous Ida-no-hama.

Iriomote Onsen   ONSEN
(西表島温泉; ☎85-5700; 243 Takana; admission ¥1500; ☺noon-10pm) Part of the Painu Maya Resort hotel, on the east coast of the island, Iriomote Onsen has indoor and outdoor baths. The grounds are attractively landscaped, and there are soothing views of the nearby forest. The onsen-hotel is easy to miss; it's off the main road about 20km north of Ōhara.

HIKING

Iriomote has some great hikes, but do not head off into the jungle interior without notifying police and hiring a guide: the trails in the interior are hard to follow – many people have gotten lost and required rescue. We suggest that you stick to well-marked tracks like the one listed here. If you're more ambitious, your accommodation can help arrange a guide (at least ¥20,000).

At the back of a mangrove-lined bay called Funaura-wan a few kilometres east of Uehara, you can make out a lovely waterfall plunging 55m down the cliffs. This is **Pinaisāra-no-taki** (ピナイサーラの滝), Okinawa's highest waterfall. When the tide is right, you can paddle a kayak across the shallow lagoon and then follow the Hinai-gawa river (on the left) to the base of the falls. The short Māre-gawa river (on the right) meets a trail where it narrows. This climbs to the top of the falls, from where there are superb views down to the coast. From the river, walk inland until you come to a pumping station, then turn around and take the right fork in the path. The walk takes less than two hours, and the river is great for a cooling dip.

Unfortunately, it is difficult to find a tour company that will rent you a kayak without requiring you to join a guided tour (half/full days cost about ¥5500/9000). If you have a foldable or inflatable kayak, we suggest bringing it. Otherwise, accommodation owners can arrange participation in a guided tour.

For another good hike, try the hikes along the Urauchi-gawa.

DIVING

Iriomote has some brilliant coral around its shores, much of which is accessible to proficient snorkellers. Most of the offshore dive sites around Iriomote are served by dive operators based on Ishigaki; see the box on p659 for details.

One spot worth noting is the unusual **Barasu-tō** (バラス島), between Iriomote-jima and Hatoma-jima, which is a small island formed entirely of bits of broken coral. In addition to the island itself, the reefs nearby are in quite good condition and make for good boat-based snorkelling on a calm day.

👉 Tours

Iriomote's number-one attraction is a boat trip up the **Urauchi-gawa** (浦内川), a winding brown river reminiscent of a tiny stretch of the Amazon. From the mouth of the river, **Urauchi-gawa Kankō** (☎85-6154) runs boat tours 8km up the river (round trip ¥1800, 30 minutes each way, multiple departures daily between 8.30am and 5pm). At the 8km point, the boat docks and you can walk a further 2km to the scenic waterfalls of **Mariyudō-no-taki** (マリユドゥの滝), from where another 200m brings you to the **Kambiray-no-taki** (カンビレーの滝). The walk from the dock to Kambiray-no-taki and back takes around two hours. Of course, you can just take the boat trip to the dock and back. The pier (浦川遊覧船乗り場) is about 6km west of Uehara.

From a pier on the south side of the river just east of the bridge in Ōhara, **Tōbū Kōtsū** (☎85-5304; ⊙8.30am-5.30pm) runs river cruises up Iriomote's second-largest river, the **Nakama-gawa** (仲間川). The one-hour tour (¥1500) passes through lush mangroves and thick vegetation.

If you're the independent type, you can rent kayaks and canoes (¥8000 per day) near both departure points for the river tours.

🛏 Sleeping

Iriomote-jima's accommodation is spread out around the island. Most places will send a car to pick you up from the ferry terminal if you let them know what time you will be arriving.

Eco Village Iriomote   HOTEL $$

(エコヴィレッジ西表; ☎85-5115; http://eco-village.jp, in Japanese; 280-36 Takana; r per person from ¥6000; Ⓟ@) This upscale resort on the northeast coast of the island is a good choice for those who want a bit more comfort. There are several types of rooms, from simple rooms in the main building to full-detached beachfront suites. There is an on-site restaurant.

Kanpira-sō   MINSHUKU $

(カンピラ荘; ☎85-6508; www.kanpira.com; 545 Uehara; r with/without meals from ¥4500/3000; Ⓟ) Two minutes' walk from the ferry landing in Uehara, hospitable Kanpira has basic

rooms and an informative manager who produces extraordinarily good, bilingual maps of the island. From the ferry, walk to the main road; you'll soon see it on the right.

Irumote-sō Youth Hostel   HOSTEL $

(いるもて荘; ☎85-6255; www.ishigaki.com/irumote, in Japanese; 870-95 Uehara; dm from ¥3600, HI member from ¥3300; Ⓟ@) Fairly close to Uehara port (上原港), this hillside hostel has comfortable dorms and simple Japanese-style private rooms (from ¥4600). Meals are served in the large communal dining room (breakfast/dinner ¥500/1200). We recommend calling for a pick-up before you arrive since it's hard to find.

🍴 Eating

With few restaurants on the island, most travellers prefer to take meals at their accommodation (or self-cater). However, if you want a meal out, we recommend the following.

Laugh La Garden   OKINAWAN $

(ラフラガーデン; ☎85-7088; 550-1 Uehara; dishes ¥900; ⊙lunch & dinner, closed Thu) Near the road from Uehara port and beside the petrol station, this relaxed cafe-restaurant has sets like *ishigakibuta-no-misokatsu teishoku* (miso-seasoned Ishigaki pork cutlets; ¥950) and oddities such as *inoshishi-sashimi* (wild boar sashimi; ¥600).

Shinpachi Shokudō   NOODLES $

(☎85-6078; 870 Uehara; dishes ¥700; ⊙lunch & dinner) Just 200m south of the port in Uehara, this no-frills noodle shop is the perfect spot for a hot bowl of *sōki-soba* (¥700) or a *gōya champuru* (¥800), washed down with a nice draught beer. Look for the blue front and the banners outside.

ℹ Getting There & Around

Iriomote-jima has a 58km-long perimeter road that runs about halfway around the coast. No roads run into the unspoiled interior. Boats from Ishigaki-jima either dock at Uehara on the north coast, which is closer to the main points of interest, or at the more populous Ōhara on the southeast coast.

Yaeyama Kankō Ferry (☎82-5010), **Ishigaki Dream Kankō** (☎84-3178) and **Anei Kankō** (☎83-0055) operate ferries between Ishigaki City (on Ishigaki-jima) and Iriomote-jima. Ferries from Ishigaki sail to/from two main ports on Iriomote: Uehara Port (上原港; ¥2000, 40 minutes, up to 20 daily), convenient for most destinations, and Ōhara Port (大原港; ¥1540, 35 minutes, up to 27 daily).

Six or nine buses daily run between Ōhara and Shirahama (¥1200, 1½ hours); raise your hand to get on anywhere. There's a 'free pass' for buses (one/three day passes ¥1000/1500) that also gives you 10% off attractions like the Urauchi-gawa river cruise.

If you have an International Driving Permit, try **Yamaneko Rentacar** (☑85-5111) or **McQueen** (☑090-9786-9280). Most of the island accommodation also rents bicycles to guests.

TAKETOMI-JIMA 竹富島
☑0980 / POP 347

A mere 15-minute boat ride from Ishigaki-jima, the tiny islet of Taketomi-jima is a living museum of Ryūkyū culture. Centred on a flower-bedecked village of traditional houses complete with red *kawara* (tiled) roofs, coral walls and *shiisa* statues, Taketomi is a breath of fresh air if you're suffering from an overdose of modern Japan.

In order to preserve the island's historical ambience, residents have joined together to ban some signs of modernism. The island is criss-crossed by crushed-coral roads and free of chain convenience stores.

While Taketomi is besieged by Japanese day trippers in the busy summer months, the island is blissfully quiet at night, even in summer. If you have the chance, it's worth spending a night here as Taketomi truly weaves its spell after the sun dips below the horizon.

⊙ Sights & Activities

There are a number of modest sights in Taketomi village, though it's best for simply wandering around and soaking up the ambience. Taketomi-jima also has some decent beaches. **Kondoi Beach** on the west coast offers the best swimming on the island. Just south is **Gaiji-hama**, which is the main *hoshi-suna* (star sand) hunting ground.

Nagomi-no-tō   MONUMENT
(admission free; ⊙24hr) Roughly in the centre of the village, the modest lookout tower of Nagomi-no-tō has good views over the red-tiled roofs of the pancake-flat island.

Nishitō Utaki   SHRINE
Near Nagomi-no-tō is a shrine dedicated to a 16th-century ruler of Yaeyama-shotō who was born on Taketomi-jima.

Kihōin Shūshūkan   MUSEUM
(☑85-2202; admission ¥300; ⊙9am-5pm) A private museum with a diverse collection of folk artefacts.

Taketomi Mingei-kan   ART GALLERY
(☑85-2302; admission free; ⊙9am-5pm) Where the island's woven *minsā* belts and other textiles are produced.

🛏 Sleeping & Eating

Many of the traditional houses around the island are Japanese-style ryokan serving traditional Okinawan cuisine. However, don't turn up on the last ferry expecting to find accommodation; Taketomi fills up quickly in the summer, so be sure to book ahead.

Takana Ryokan   HOSTEL $
(高那旅館; ☑85-2151; www.kit.hi-ho.ne.jp/haya saka-my, in Japanese; 499 Taketomi; dm with/without meals ¥4500/3100, r per person with meals from ¥8500) Opposite the tiny post office, Takana actually consists of a basic youth hostel and an attached upmarket ryokan. Basic Western-style dorms in the youth hostel are a great option if you're on a budget, though the Japanese-style tatami rooms in the ryokan are a bit more comfortable.

Ōhama-sō   MINSHUKU $$
(大浜荘; ☑85-2226; fax 85-2226; 501 Taketomi; r per person with/without meals ¥5500/3500) Also located beside the post office, this *minshuku* has a light and jovial atmosphere. Accommodation is in simple yet comfortable Japanese-style tatami rooms with shared facilities.

Soba Dokoro Takenoko   NOODLES $
(☑85-2251; 101-1 Taketomi; dishes ¥800; ⊙10.30am-4pm & 6.30-10pm) This tiny restaurant on the northwest side of the village (look for the blue banner and the umbrellas) serves up *sōki-soba* (¥800) and *yaki-soba* (fried *soba;* ¥800), and you can wash it all down with some Orion beer.

ⓘ Information

Ferries arrive at the small port (竹富東港) on the northeast corner of the island, while Taketomi village is located in the centre of the island. There's a small **information desk** (☑84-5633; ⊙7.30am-6pm) in the port building.

ⓘ Getting There & Around

Yaeyama Kankō Ferry (☑82-5010), **Ishigaki Dream Kankō** (☑84-3178) and **Anei Kankō** (☑83-0055) operate ferries between Ishigaki City (on Ishigaki-jima) and Taketomi-jima (¥580, 10 minutes, up to 45 daily).

Rental bicycles are great for exploring the crushed-coral roads. Since the island is only 3km long and 2km wide, it is easily explored on foot or by bicycle. **Maruhachi Rentals** (丸八レンタサイクル; ☑85-2260; bicycles per hr ¥300; ⊙8am-5.15pm) runs a free shuttle between its shop and the port. Another way to see the island is by taking a tour in a water buffalo cart. Two operators in the village offer 30-minute rides for ¥1200 per person.

HATERUMA-JIMA 波照間島
☎0980 / POP 546

Forty-five kilometres south of Iriomote-jima is the tiny islet of Hateruma-jima, Japan's southernmost inhabited island. Just 15km around, Hateruma-jima has a couple of nice beaches and a seriously laid-back vibe.

Ferries arrive at the small port on the northwest corner of the island, while Hateruma village is in the centre. Slightly larger than Taketomi-jima, Hateruma-jima is easily explored by bicycle or scooter. There's a small **information desk** (☎82-5445; ⏱8.30am-5pm, closed Sat, Sun & holidays) in the port building, and also in the airport, that can help you find accommodation on the island.

Just to the west of the port is **Nishihama** (ニシ浜), a perfect beach of snow-white sand with some good coral offshore. Here you will find free public showers, toilets and a campground. At the opposite southeast corner of the island, directly south of the airport, is the impressive **Takanasaki** (高那崎), a 1km-long cliff of Ryūkyū limestone that is pounded by the Pacific Ocean. At the western end of the cliffs is a small monument marking **Japan's southernmost point** (日本最南端の碑), which is an extremely popular photo spot for Japanese visitors.

There are several *minshuku* on the island, including **Minami** (美波; ☎85-8050; http://homepage2.nifty.com/minami85, in Japanese; 3138 Hateruma; r per person from ¥3000; P) east of the town centre. Accommodation is in simple, detached Japanese- and Western-style rooms close to sugar cane fields.

Another good choice is **Pension Sainantan** (ペンション最南端; ☎85-8686; www5.ocn.ne.jp/~besuma, in Japanese; 886-1 Hateruma; r per person from ¥8500; P@), which has both Japanese- and Western-style rooms, all with unit baths. This place is only three minutes' walk from Nishihama.

Anei Kankō (☎83-0055) and **Hateruma Kaiun** (☎82-7233) each have three ferries a day to Hateruma-jima from Ishigaki (¥3000 and ¥3050 respectively, one hour). There is no public transport on the island, but rental bicycles and scooters are readily available for hire.

YONAGUNI-JIMA 与那国島
☎0980 / POP 1627

About 125km west of Ishigaki and 110km east of Taiwan is the islet of Yonaguni-jima, Japan's westernmost inhabited island. Renowned for its strong sake, small horses and marlin fishing, the island is also home to the jumbo-sized Yonaguni atlas moth, the largest moth in the world.

However, most visitors come to see what lies beneath the waves here. In 1985, a diver discovered what appeared to be man-made 'ruins' off the south coast of the island. In addition, the waters off the west coast are frequented by large schools of hammerhead sharks. This makes the island perhaps the most famous single diving destination in Japan.

⊙ Sights

Just as Hateruma-jima has a monument to mark Japan's southernmost point, Yonaguni-jima has a rock to mark the country's **westernmost point** (日本最西端の碑) at **Irizaki** (西崎). If the weather is perfect, the mountains of Taiwan are visible far over the sea (this happens only about twice a year – so don't be disappointed if you can't make them out).

Yonaguni has an extremely rugged landscape, and the coastline is marked with great rock formations, much like those on the east coast of Taiwan. The most famous of these are **Tachigami-iwa** (立神岩), literally 'Standing-God Rock', **Gunkan-iwa** (軍艦岩) and **Sanninu-dai** (サンニヌ台), all of which are off the southeast coast. At the eastern tip of the island, Yonaguni horses graze in the pastures leading out to the lighthouse at **Agarizaki** (東崎).

Ayamihabiru-kan　　　　　MUSEUM
(アヤミハビル館; ☎87-2440; admission ¥500; ⏱10am-4pm Wed-Sun) Displays on Yonaguni's giant moths, which have a wingspan of 25cm to 30cm and are affectionately known as Yonaguni-san, can be seen here, about 1km south of Sonai.

Kokusen Awamori　　　　　BREWERY
(国選泡盛; ☎87-2315; ⏱8am-5pm) If you want to sample Hanazake, the island's infamous local brew, head to Kokusen Awamori, which is located in Sonai and offers free tastings and sales on-site.

⚓ Activities

Local divers have long known about the thrills that await at **Irizaki Point** (西崎ポイント), off the coast of Cape Irizaki. In the winter months, the waters here are frequented by large schools of hammerhead sharks.

Kaitei Iseki　　　　　DIVING
(海底遺跡; Underwater Ruins) Popular are the Kaitei Iseki, discovered by chance in 1985 by marine explorer Kihachirou Aratake. Some claim that these ruins, which look like

giant blocks or steps of a sunken pyramid, are the remains of a Pacific Atlantis, although there are equally compelling arguments that they are just the random result of geological processes. If you don't dive, **Jack's Dolphin glass-bottomed boat** (87-2311; per person ¥6000; ⊙sailings at 9am & noon) and **Mosura no Tamago** (もすらのたまご; 87-2115; per person ¥4000) do trips to the ruins, but don't expect to see too much if it's choppy.

There are numerous dive operators on the island. One shop with English-speaking guides is **SaWest** (87-2311; 59-6 Yonaguni; 1/2 dives ¥8000/12,000, equipment rental ¥5000; ⊙8am-6pm).

Ubudomai-hama
BEACH

(ウブドゥマイハマ) The best beach here is Ubudomai-hama, which is located at the east end of the island, shortly before Agarizaki (look out for the steep access road).

Marlin fishing
FISHING

In addition to diving, the seas off Yonaguni are also renowned for marlin, and the All-Japan Billfish Tournament is held here each year in June or July. If you're interested in trolling, boats in Kubura can be chartered from ¥55,000 a day – call the **Yonaguni Fishing Co-operative** (87-2803, in Japanese) for information.

🛏 Sleeping & Eating

Although there are several sleeping options around the island, it's best to phone ahead as Yonaguni is quite a distance to travel without a reservation.

There is a decent campground on the south coast near the village of Higawa, next to Kataburu Hama (a decent beach). If you want to self-cater, there are two simple supermarkets in the centre of Sonai.

The following places will pick you up at either the airport or the ferry terminal.

Ailand Resort
HOTEL $$$

(アイランドリゾート与那国; 87-2300; www.ailand-resort.co.jp/yonaguni, in Japanese; 4647-1 Yonaguni; tw per person with breakfast from ¥13,000; P@) This spiffy new hotel-resort is located on the north side of the island, between the airport and Sonai. It's got spacious, light, comfortable Western-style rooms and an on-site restaurant.

Minshuku Yoshimarusō
MINSHUKU $

(民宿よしまる荘; 87-2658; www.yonaguni yds.com, in Japanese; 3984-3 Yonaguni; dm/r per person with meals ¥5775/6825; 🕾) Near the ferry terminal in Kubura, Yoshimarusō is ideal for divers, as the friendly owners also operate the on-site Yonaguni Diving Service. Simple Japanese- and Western-style rooms with shared facilities have nice views of the nearby port, though the real appeal of this *minshuku* is the owners' local diving expertise. It's up the hill, overlooking the port.

Fujimi Ryokan
RYOKAN $

(ふじみ旅館; 87-2143; fax 87-2659; 71-1 Yonaguni; r per person with 2 meals from ¥6000) One block inland from the Hotel Irifune in Sonai, this basic ryokan is a good choice if you're looking for more traditional accommodation. It's roughly between the traffic light and the post office.

Dō-rai
IZAKAYA $$

(どぅーらい; 87-2909; 62 Yonaguni; dishes ¥8000; ⊙dinner, closed Sun) In the centre of Sonai is this delightful little Okinawan izakaya that serves local specialities like *ishigakigyū-sutēki* (Ishigaki-style steak; ¥1300) and *rafutē* (gingered, stewed pork; ¥700). It's about 100m southeast of the post office in Sonai. Look for the blue and white sign on the brick wall.

ℹ Information

The ferry port of Kubura (久部良) is at the island's western extreme. The main settlement is around the secondary port of Sonai (租内) on the north coast. In between, on the northwest coast, you'll find the airport.

There is an **information counter** (87-2402; ⊙8.30am-12pm, call after) in the airport, which can help you find accommodation. Even if you can't read Japanese, it's worth picking up a copy of the Japanese-language *Yonaguni-jima* map.

ℹ Getting There & Around

RAC has flights between Yonaguni and Naha (¥31,700, one hour 20 minutes, four daily). RAC or JTA operate flights between Yonaguni and Ishigaki-jima (¥11,800, 30 minutes, two daily).

Fukuyama Kaiun (82-4962) operates four ferries a week between Ishigaki-jima and Kubura Port on Yonaguni (¥3460, four hours 30 minutes).

There are public buses here, but they make only four trips around the island per day, so the best transport is rental car or scooter. **Yonaguni Honda** (87-2376) in central Sonai will send a car to meet you at the airport or the ferry terminal if you phone ahead. Another good car-rental operation that will also pick you up at the airport is **Ailand Rentacar** (87-2300).

Understand
Japan

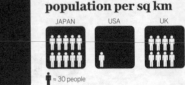

Japan Today

The year 2011 was indeed a terrible year for the Japanese, and it came hard on the heels of two pretty tough years by any standards, with the severe economic downturn brought on by the global financial crisis of 2008.

In March 2011, just as the plum trees had burst into bloom and the nation was gearing up for the annual orgy of *hanami* (cherry-blossom viewing) parties, the Great East Japan Earthquake struck off the northeast coast of Japan. The resulting tsunami (a word that, not coincidentally, happens to be Japanese) was of epic proportions: reaching almost 40m in height, it washed away entire villages along the east coast of Tōhoku (the northern part of the main island of Japan).

To add to the devastation, the tsunami also triggered a major crisis at a nuclear powerplant in Fukushima Prefecture, about 240km northeast of Tokyo. At press time, the Tokyo Electric Power Company (TEPCO), which operates the plants, working with the Japanese government, seemed to have brought that situation under control, but the entire nation was still jittery and wondering how long it would be before the power stations could be declared cooled, cleared and no longer a concern.

Even without a sluggish economy and a severe natural disaster, things were already pretty tough for the Japanese as they set out into the new millennium.

In September 2010 the Japanese Coast Guard took the crew of a Chinese trawler into custody after a collision near the disputed Senkaku Islands in the East China Sea. About a week later, the Japanese were forced to release the crew in the face of threats by the Chinese. If you listened closely, you could almost hear the nation letting out a resounding *'Ara!'* ('uh-oh!'). The reason is this: since the end of WWII, Japan has done little to cultivate warm relations with China (some would say they've even actively antagonised China) and has, instead, focused on its

» Population: 126.5 million (2011 estimate)

» GDP: US$4.4 trillion (purchasing power parity; 2010 estimate)

» GDP per capita: US$34,200 (2010 estimate)

» Inflation: -0.7% (2010 estimate)

Dos & Don'ts

» Do take off your shoes when entering a house, the inner hall of a temple, or any place where you step up onto tatami mats. Try to step out of your shoes right onto the tatami mats (ie don't take off your shoes a short distance away and walk over).

» Do learn a few Japanese pleasantries, but don't worry too much about communication difficulties – the Japanese don't expect you to speak their language, and they might know a bit of English.

» Don't get into a sento (public bath) or onsen (hot springs) bath tub before thoroughly rinsing your body.

» Do slurp when you eat noodles.

belief systems
(% of population)

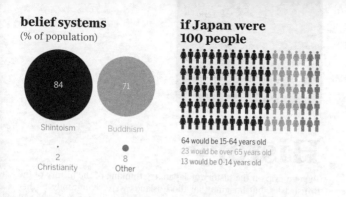

Shintoism **84**

Buddhism **71**

Christianity **2**

Other **8**

if Japan were 100 people

64 would be 15-64 years old
23 would be over 65 years old
13 would be 0-14 years old

alliances with Western nations. Now, with China rising fast (the nation overtook Japan as the world's second-largest economy in 2010), Japan faces a new and rather unsettling geopolitical situation.

Compounding the problems is the situation at home. The population of Japan fell by more than 100,000 people in 2010 and experts predict that – barring large-scale immigration, which most Japanese oppose – the population may shrink to 100 million people by 2050 (from its present level of 126.5 million). Don't think for a moment that the Japanese are unaware of this. Indeed, the words *shōshika* (declining birthrate) and *kōreika* (ageing population) find their way into every bathhouse, bar and cafe conversation.

Reading all this, you might think that the Japanese were down for the count. But here's the surprising part: that's not the case at all. As shown by the Japanese people's response to the earthquake and tsunami, when faced with a tough situation they band together, roll up their sleeves and get to work. Let's not forget that these are the same people who took a country that was little more than rubble in 1945 and turned it into one of the world's most advanced and efficient countries in just a few short decades.

But more than rebuilding, one senses that the crisis of 2011 will yield a variety of benefits for Japan, and the world as a whole. Nuclear power will come under some serious scrutiny (some countries may abandon it, while others will make their nuclear powerplants safer). Japan, already a leader in solar-energy technology, will surely explore other forms of alternative energy and energy conservation.

And perhaps best of all, in the days following the quake, the Japanese news showed rescue teams arriving from around the world, including China, and Japan deeply and sincerely felt the strength and warmth of the world's support. In a country where debts are scrupulously honoured, this can only bring Japan closer to the world, and the world closer to Japan.

» Number of onsen: more than 3000

» World's busiest station: Tokyo's Shinjuku Station, servicing 740,000 passengers a day

» Cruising speed of the *shinkansen* (bullet train): 300km/h

» Islands in the Japanese archipelago: approximately 3900

Top Books

The Thousand Autumns of Jacob de Zoet: A Novel A fascinating historical novel by David Mitchell that tells a story of a Dutchman living in Japan during the *sakkoku* (closed country) period.

Dogs and Demons: Tales from the Dark Side of Japan Alex Kerr reveals the hard truth about modern Japan. Read it on the plane – on the way home.

The Roads to Sata: A 2000-Mile Walk Through Japan Alan Booth's beautiful account of a walking journey through Japan.

History

To get a grip on the history of Japan, try thinking of the history of the British Isles, but imagine that those islands were significantly further from the mainland. While there has been contact between Japan and mainland Asia, separation from the mainland was crucial in allowing Japan to evolve into the unique country you find today.

Broadly speaking, Japan's history can be divided into five main periods: prehistory, which comes to an end in about 400 BC; pre-classical, from 400 BC until AD 710; classical, from 710 to 1185; medieval, from 1185 to 1600; and pre-modern to modern, from 1600 onward.

Ancient Japan: From Hunter-Gatherers to Divine Rule

Once upon a time, two deities, the male Izanagi and the female Izanami, came down from Takamagahara (The Plains of High Heaven) to a watery world in order to create land. Droplets from Izanagi's 'spear' solidified into the land now known as Japan. Izanami and Izanagi then populated the new land with gods. One of these was Japan's supreme deity, the Sun Goddess Amaterasu (Light of Heaven), whose great-great grandson Jimmu was to become the first emperor of Japan, reputedly in 660 BC.

Such is the seminal creation myth of Japan. More certainly, humans were present in Japan at least 200,000 years ago, though the earliest human remains go back only 30,000 years or so. Till around the end of the last ice age some 15,000 years ago Japan was linked to the continent by a number of land bridges – Siberia to the north, Korea to the west and probably present-day Taiwan to the south – so access was not difficult.

Amid undoubted diversity, the first recognisable culture to emerge was the neolithic Jōmon (named after a 'rope-mark' pottery style), from around 13,000 BC. The Jōmon were mostly hunter-gatherers, with a preference for coastal regions, though agriculture started to develop from

TIMELINE	c 13,000 BC	c 400 BC	3rd Century AD
	First evidence of the hunter-gatherer Jōmon, ancestors of the present-day Ainu of northern Japan, and producers of the world's earliest pottery vessels.	Yayoi people appear in southwest Japan (probably via Korea), practising wet rice farming and using metal tools. They also promote inter-regional trade and a sense of territoriality.	Queen Himiko reigns over Yamatai (Yamato) and is recognised by Chinese visitors as 'over-queen' of Japan, then comprising more than a hundred kingdoms. The Yamato clan's dominance continues hereafter.

around 4000 BC and this brought about greater stability in settlement and the emergence of larger tribal communities. The present-day indigenous Ainu people of northern Japan are of Jōmon descent.

From around 400 BC Japan was effectively invaded by waves of immigrants later known as Yayoi (from the site where their distinctive reddish wheel-thrown pottery was first found). They first arrived in the southwest, probably through the Korean Peninsula. Their exact origins are unknown, and may well be diverse, but they brought with them iron and bronze technology, and highly productive wet rice-farming techniques.

Opinion is divided as to the nature of Yayoi relations with the Jōmon, but the latter were gradually displaced and forced ever further north (although modern Japanese possess significant amounts of Jōmon DNA, indicating a certain amount of intermingling of the races). The Yayoi had spread to the middle of Honshū by the 1st century AD, but northern Honshū could still be considered 'Jōmon' till at least the 8th century.

Other consequences of the Yayoi advent included greater intertribal regional trade based on greater and more diverse production through new technologies, but at the same time increased rivalry between regional tribal groups, often over resources, and greater social stratification.

Yamato Clan

Agriculture-based fixed settlement led to the consolidation of territory and the establishment of boundaries. According to Chinese sources, by the end of the 1st century AD there were more than a hundred kingdoms in Japan, and by the middle of the 3rd century these were largely subject to an 'over-queen' named Himiko, whose own territory was known as Yamatai (later Yamato). The location of Yamatai is disputed, with some scholars favouring northwest Kyūshū, but most favour the Nara region. The Chinese treated Himiko as sovereign of all Japan – the name Yamato eventually being applied to Japan as a whole – and she for her part acknowledged through tribute her allegiance to the Chinese emperor.

On her death in 248 Himiko is said to have been buried – along with 100 sacrificed slaves – in a massive barrow-like tomb known as a *kofun*, indicative of the importance of status. Other dignitaries chose burial in similar tombs, and so from this point on, till the establishment of Nara as a capital in 710, Japan is usually referred to as being in the Kofun or Yamato period.

The period saw the confirmation of the Yamato as the dominant – indeed imperial – clan in Japan. Their consolidation of power often appears to have been by negotiation and alliance with (or incorporation of) powerful potential foes. This was a practice Japan was to continue through the ages where possible, though it was less accommodating in the case of perceived weaker foes.

Jōmon pottery vessels dating back some 15,000 years are the oldest known pottery vessels in the world.

THE JŌMON PEOPLE

HISTORY ANCIENT JAPAN: FROM HUNTER-GATHERERS TO DIVINE RULE

c 300	390–410	Mid-5th Century	Mid-6th Century
Suijin is the first verifiable emperor of Japan, possibly arriving as the leader of 'horse-riders' from Korea, and almost certainly affiliated with the Yamato clan.	Yamato forces sail to the Korean Peninsula in an attempt to intervene in an internal dispute there, but are defeated by the Koguryo dynasty.	Writing is introduced by scholars from the Korean kingdom of Paekche. Using Chinese characters to express spoken Japanese leads to an extremely complex writing system.	Scholars from Paekche introduce Buddhism, the texts of which are able to be read by a now literate elite, who use it to unify and control the nation.

PERIOD	DATE
Jōmon	c 13,000 BC–c 400 BC
Yayoi	c 400 BC–c AD 250
Kofun/Yamato	250–710
Nara	710–94
Heian	794–1185
Kamakura	1185–1333
Muromachi	1333–1568
Azuchi-Momoyama	1568–1600
Edo/Tokugawa	1600–1868
Meiji	1868–1912
Taishō	1912–26
Shōwa	1926–89
Heisei	1989–present

The first verifiable emperor was Suijin (died c 318), very likely of the Yamato clan, though some scholars think he may have been leader of a group of 'horse-riders' who are believed to have come into Japan around the start of the 4th century from the Korean Peninsula. The period also saw the adoption of writing, based on Chinese but first introduced by scholars from the Korean kingdom of Paekche in the mid-5th century. Scholars from Paekche also introduced Buddhism a century later.

Buddhism was promoted by the Yamato rulers as a means of unification and control of the land. Though Buddhism originated in India, it was seen by the Japanese as a Chinese religion, and as such was one of a number of 'things Chinese' that they adopted to achieve recognition – especially by China – as a civilised country. Through emulating powerful China, Japan hoped it too could become powerful.

In 604 the regent Prince Shōtoku (573–620) enacted a constitution of 17 articles, with a very Chinese and indeed Confucian flavour, esteeming harmony and hard work. Major Chinese-style reforms, such as centralisation of government, nationalisation and allocation of land, and law codes, followed some decades later in 645. To strengthen its regime, under Emperor Temmu (r 673–86) the imperial family initiated the compilation of historical works such as the *Kojiki* (Record of Old Things; 712)

Early 7th Century	710	712 & 720	740
Japan tries to emulate China, in 604 drawing up a basic constitution, and in 645 implementing major Chinese-style policies such as centralisation of government, nationalisation of land and codification of law.	Japan's first intended permanent capital is established at Nara, based on Chinese models. Japan is arguably a nation-state by this stage.	The imperial family traces its 'divine' origins, and hence legitimises its right to rule, through the compilation of two major historical works, *Kojiki* (712) and *Nihon Shoki* (720).	Construction begins on the vast Tōdai-ji temple complex in Nara, built, it's thought, to provide a focus for the nation and to ward off attacks of smallpox.

and *Nihon Shoki* (Record of Japan; 720), with the aim of legitimising their power-holding through claimed divine descent. It had the desired effect, and despite a number of perilous moments, Japan continues to have the longest unbroken monarchic line in the world.

Emulation of things Chinese was not indiscriminate. For example, in China Confucianism condoned the removal of an unvirtuous ruler felt to have lost the 'mandate of heaven', but this idea was not promoted in Japan. Nor was the Chinese practice of allowing achievement of high rank through examination, for the Japanese ruling class preferred birth over merit.

Though northern Japan might be excluded at this point, in terms of factors such as effective unification, centralised government, social stratification, systematic administration, external recognition, legitimisation of power, a written constitution and a legal code, Japan, with its estimated five million people, could be said to have formed a nation-state by the early 8th century.

The Age of Courtiers

In 710 an intended permanent capital was established at Nara (Heijō-kyō), built to a Chinese grid pattern. The influence of Buddhism in those days is still seen today in the Tōdai-ji, which houses a huge bronze Buddha and is the world's largest wooden building (and one of the oldest).

In 784 Emperor Kammu (r 781–806) decided to relocate the capital. His reasons are unclear but may have related to an inauspicious series of disasters following the move to Nara, including a massive smallpox epidemic of 735–7 that killed as many as one-third of the population. Presently, in 794, the capital was transferred to nearby Kyoto (Heian-kyō), newly built on a similar grid pattern. It was to remain Japan's capital for more than a thousand years – though not necessarily as the centre of actual power.

It was in Kyoto that, over the next few centuries, courtly life reached a pinnacle of refined artistic pursuits and etiquette, captured famously in the novel *The Tale of Genji,* written by the court-lady Murasaki Shikibu around 1004. It showed a world where courtiers indulged in divertissements such as guessing flowers by their scent, building extravagant follies and sparing no expense to indulge in the latest luxury. On the positive side, it was a world that encouraged aesthetic sensibilities, such as of *mono no aware* (the bitter-sweetness of things) and *okashisa* (pleasantly surprising incongruity), which were to endure right through to the present. But on the negative side, it was also a world increasingly estranged from the real one. Put bluntly, it lacked muscle. The effeteness of the court was exacerbated by the weakness of the emperors, manipulated over centuries by the intrigues of the notorious and politically powerful Fujiwara family.

The Tale of Genji, written by court lady Murasaki Shikibu around 1004, is widely believed to be the world's first novel.

» Tōdai-ji (p334), Nara

700s

The classical age of Japanese religious sculpture takes place, in which some of Japan's greatest works of Buddhist art are produced (some are still visible in and around Nara).

794

Following a series of misfortunes, including a terrible smallpox epidemic, while the capital is at Nara, Japan's formal capital is relocated to Heian (present-day Kyoto), and remains there for over a thousand years.

By contrast, while the major nobles immersed themselves in courtly pleasures and/or intrigues, out in the real world of the provinces powerful military forces were developing. They were typically led by minor nobles, often sent out on behalf of court-based major nobles to carry out 'tedious' local gubernatorial and administrative duties. Some were actually distant imperial family members, barred from succession claims – a practice known as 'dynastic shedding' – and often hostile to the court. Their retainers included skilled warriors known as samurai (literally 'retainer').

The two main 'shed' families were the Minamoto (also known as Genji) and the Taira (Heike), who were basically enemies. In 1156 they were employed to assist rival claimants to headship of the Fujiwara family, though these figures soon faded into the background, for it developed into a feud between the Minamoto and the Taira.

The Taira were to prevail, under Kiyomori (1118–81), who based himself in the capital and, over the next 20 years or so, fell prey to many of the vices that lurked there. In 1180, following a typical court practice, he enthroned his own two-year-old grandson, Antoku. However, a rival claimant requested the help of the Minamoto, who had regrouped under Yoritomo (1147–99) in Izu. Yoritomo was more than ready to agree.

Both Kiyomori and the claimant died very shortly afterwards, but Yoritomo, with his younger half-brother Yoshitsune (1159–89), continued the campaign against the Taira – a campaign interrupted by a pestilence during the early 1180s. By 1185 Kyoto had fallen and the Taira had been pursued to the western tip of Honshū. A naval battle ensued (at Dannoura), and the Minamoto were victorious. In a well-known tragic tale, Kiyomori's widow clasped her grandson Antoku (now aged seven), and leaped with him into the sea, rather than have him surrender. Minamoto Yoritomo was now the most powerful man in Japan, and was to usher in a martial age.

> In 1191, the Zen monk Eisai is said to have brought tea leaves to Japan from China, starting a tradition of tea drinking that continues to this day.

The Age of Warriors

Yoritomo did not seek to become emperor, but rather to have the new emperor confer legitimacy on him through the title of shōgun (generalissimo). This was granted in 1192. Similarly, he left many existing offices and institutions in place, though often modified. Nor did he set up his base at Kyoto but rather in his home territory of Kamakura. In theory he represented merely the military arm of the emperor's government, but in practice he was in charge of government in the broad sense. His 'shōgunate' was known in Japanese as the *bakufu*, meaning the tent headquarters of a field general, though it was far from temporary. As an institution, it was to last almost 700 years.

804	9th–12th Centuries	1156	1185
Kūkai (also known as Kōbō Daishi) travels to China and studies Buddhism, later founding Shingon (Esoteric) Buddhism in Japan and establishing the famous Kōya-san religious centre.	The court develops a high degree of cultural sophistication but becomes increasingly effete and removed from the real world. Actual power comes to lie with provincial military clans.	Two major 'dynastically shed' provincial families, the Taira and the Minamoto, are employed by rival court factions and engage in bitter warfare, with the Taira prevailing under Kiyomori.	The Taira are toppled by Minamoto Yoritomo, who becomes the most powerful man in the land and brings a certain unity to it. A suspicious man, he kills many of his own relatives.

The system of government now became feudal, centred on a lord-vassal system in which loyalty was a key value. It tended to be more personal and more 'familial' than medieval European feudalism, particularly in the extended *oya-ko* relationship ('parent-child', in practice 'father-son'). This 'familial hierarchy' was to become another enduring feature of Japan.

But 'families' – even actual blood families – were not always happy, and the more ruthless powerseekers would not hesitate to kill family members they saw as threats. Yoritomo himself, seemingly very suspicious by nature, killed off so many of his own family there were serious problems with the shōgunal succession upon his death in 1199 (following a fall from his horse in suspicious circumstances). One of those he had killed was his half-brother Yoshitsune, who earned an enduring place in Japanese literature and legend as the archetypical tragic hero.

Yoritomo's widow, Masako (1157–1225), was a formidable figure, arranging shōgunal regents and for much of her remaining life controlling the shōgunate. Having taken religious vows on her husband's death, she became known as the 'nun shōgun', and is one of the most powerful women in Japanese history. She was instrumental in ensuring that her own family, the Hōjō, replaced the Minamoto as shōguns. The Hōjō shōgunate continued to use Kamakura as the shōgunal base, and was to endure till the 1330s.

Mongol Threats

It was during their shōgunacy that the Mongols twice tried to invade, in 1274 and 1281. The Mongol empire was close to its peak at this time, under Kublai Khan (r 1260–94). After conquering Korea in 1259 he sent requests to Japan to submit to him, but these were ignored.

His expected first attack came in November 1274, allegedly with some 900 vessels carrying around 40,000 men – many of them reluctant Korean conscripts – though these figures may be exaggerated. They landed near Hakata in northwest Kyūshū and, despite spirited Japanese resistance, made progress inland. However, for unclear reasons, they presently retreated to their ships. Shortly afterwards a violent storm blew up and damaged around a third of the fleet, after which the remainder returned to Korea.

A more determined attempt was made seven years later, from China. Kublai ordered the construction of a huge fleet of allegedly 4400 warships to carry a massive force of 140,000 men – again, these are questionable figures. They landed once more in northwest Kyūshū, in August 1281, and again met spirited resistance, and had to retire to their vessels. Once again, the weather soon intervened – this time a typhoon – and half their vessels were destroyed, many of which were actually designed for

Top Historic Sites

» Nagasaki (Kyūshū)
» Asuka (Kansai)
» Nara (Kansai)
» Kyoto
» Tokyo

1192	1199	1200–50	1223
Yoritomo takes the title shōgun (generalissimo) from a largely puppet emperor and establishes the *bakufu* (shōgunate) in his home territory at Kamakura. This is the effective start of feudalism in Japan.	Upon Yoritomo's suspicious death his formidable wife, Masako – known as the 'nun shōgun' – becomes the most powerful figure in Japan, establishing her family, the Hōjō, as shōguns.	Hōnen and Shinran promote the 'Pure Land' schools of Buddhism in Japan, which remain the most popular sects of Buddhism in Japan today.	Dōgen, a monk, travels to China to study Chang Buddhism, and later returns to Japan to found the influential Sōtō school of Zen Buddhism.

river use: they lacked keels, and were unable to withstand rough conditions. The survivors went back to China, and there was to be no further Mongol attempt to invade Japan.

It was the typhoon of 1281 in particular that led to the idea of divine intervention to save Japan, with the coining of the term *kamikaze* (literally 'divine wind'). Later this came to be used of the Pacific War suicide pilots who, said to be infused with divine spirit, gave their lives in the cause of protecting Japan from invasion. It also led the Japanese to feel that their land was indeed the Land of the Gods.

Demise of the Hōjō Shōgunate

Despite the successful defence of Japan, the Hōjō shōgunate suffered. It was unable to make a number of promised payments to those involved in repelling the Mongols, which brought considerable dissatisfaction towards it, while the payments it did make severely depleted its finances.

It was also during the Hōjō shōgunacy that Zen Buddhism was brought from China. Its austerity and self-discipline appealed greatly to the warrior class, and it was also a factor in the appeal of aesthetic values such as *sabi* (elegant simplicity). More popular forms of Buddhism were the Jōdo (Pure Land) and Jōdo Shin (True Pure Land) sects, based on salvation through invocation of Amida Buddha.

Dissatisfaction towards the Hōjō shōgunate came to a head under the unusually assertive emperor Go-Daigo (1288–1339), who, after escaping from exile imposed by the Hōjō, started to muster anti-shōgunal support in western Honshū. In 1333 the shōgunate despatched troops to counter this, under one of its most promising generals, the young Ashikaga Takauji (1305–58). However, realising that between them he and Go-Daigo had considerable military strength, and also aware of the dissatisfaction towards the Hōjō, Takauji threw in his lot with the emperor and attacked the shōgunal offices in Kyoto. Others also soon rebelled against the shōgunate in Kamakura itself.

This was the end for the Hōjō shōgunate, but not for the shōgunal institution. Takauji wanted the title of shōgun for himself, but his ally Go-Daigo was reluctant to confer it, fearing it would weaken his own imperial power. A rift developed, and Go-Daigo sent forces to attack Takauji. However, Takauji emerged victorious, and turned on Kyoto, forcing Go-Daigo to flee into the hills of Yoshino some 100km south of the city, where he set up a court in exile. In Kyoto Takauji installed a puppet emperor from a rival line, who returned the favour by declaring him shōgun in 1338. Thus there were two courts in co-existence, which continued till 1392 when the 'southern court' (at Yoshino) was betrayed by Ashikaga Yoshimitsu (1358–1408), Takauji's grandson and third Ashikaga shōgun.

The kamikaze ('divine wind') of 1281 is said to have drowned 70,000 Mongol troops, which, if true, would make it the world's worst maritime disaster.

THE MONGOLS

13th Century
Zen Buddhism becomes established in Japan, especially among warriors. It also influences Japanese aesthetics. 'Mass-appeal' forms of Buddhism are also established.

1274 & 1281
Under Kublai Khan the Mongols twice attempt to invade Japan, but fail due to poor planning, spirited Japanese resistance and, in particular, destruction of their fleets by kamikaze typhoons.

» Daibutsu (Great Buddha; p157) at Kamakura

BOB CHARLTON / LONELY PLANET IMAGES ©

Warring States

Takauji set up his shōgunal base in Kyoto, at Muromachi, which gives its name to the period of the Ashikaga shōgunate. With a few exceptions such as Takauji himself and his grandson Yoshimitsu, who among other things had Kyoto's famous Kinkaku-ji (Golden Pavilion) built, and once declared himself 'King of Japan', the Ashikaga shōguns were relatively weak. In the absence of strong centralised government and control the country slipped increasingly into civil war as regional warlords – who

SAMURAI

The prime duty of a samurai, a member of the warrior class from around the 12th century onwards, was to give faithful service to his lord. In fact, the term 'samurai' is derived from a word meaning 'to serve'. Ideally, 'service' meant being prepared to give up one's life for one's lord, though there were many ranks of samurai and, at least in the early days, it was typically only the hereditary retainers who felt such commitment. At the other end of the ranks, samurai were in effect professional mercenaries who were by no means reliable and often defected if it was to their advantage.

The renowned samurai code, *bushidō* (way of the warrior), developed over the centuries but was not formally codified till the 17th century, by which time there were no real battles to fight. Ironically, the intention of the code appears to have been to show samurai as moral exemplars in order to counter criticism that they were parasitic. It was thus greatly idealised.

Core samurai ideals included *gaman* (endurance), *isshin* (whole-hearted commitment) and *makoto* (sincerity). Samurai were supposed to be men of Zen-like austerity who endured hardship without complaint. Chivalry among samurai was not so dominant as in Europe, and certainly not towards women, even though samurai were often highly educated and sometimes paralleled European knights.

Samurai who for one reason or another became lordless were known as *rōnin* (wanderers or masterless samurai); they acted more like brigands and were a serious social problem.

Samurai who fell from grace were generally required to commit ritual disembowelment (hara kiri or seppuku), meant to show the purity of the soul, which was believed to reside in the stomach.

The samurai's best-known weapon was the *katana* sword, though in earlier days the bow was also prominent. Arguably the world's finest swordsmen, samurai were formidable opponents in single combat. During modernisation in the late 19th century, the government – itself comprising samurai – realised that a conscript army was more efficient as a unified fighting force, and disestablished the samurai class. However, samurai ideals such as endurance and fighting to the death were revived through propaganda prior to the Pacific War, and underlay the determination of many Japanese soldiers.

1333	1338–92	1400s & 1500s	1543
General Ashikaga Takauji, initially in alliance with Emperor Go-Daigo, topples the increasingly unpopular Hōjō shōgunate. Ashikaga requests the title of shōgun, but Go-Daigo is reluctant and a rift develops.	Takauji installs a puppet emperor who names him shōgun (1338), establishing the Ashikaga shōgunate at Muromachi. Two rival emperors exist till Go-Daigo's line is betrayed by Takauji's grandson Yoshimitsu (1392).	Japan is in almost constant internal warfare, including the particularly fierce Ōnin War of 1467–77. The era (especially from the late 15th to late 16th centuries) is known as the Sengoku (Warring States) period.	Portuguese arrive (by chance) in Japan, the first Westerners, heralding the advent of firearms and Christianity. Firearms prove popular among warlords, while Christianity has a mixed reception.

came to be known as *daimyō* (regional lords) – vied with each other in seemingly interminable feuds and power struggles. Eventually, starting with the Ōnin War of 1467–77, the country entered a period of virtually constant civil war for the next hundred years, a time appropriately known as the Sengoku (Warring States) era.

Ironically perhaps, it was during the Muromachi period that a new flourishing of the arts took place, such as in the refined nō drama, ikebana (flower arranging) and *cha-no-yu* (tea ceremony). Key aesthetics were, in addition to the earlier-mentioned *sabi, yūgen* (elegant and tranquil otherworldliness, as seen in nō), *wabi* (subdued taste) and *kare* (severe and unadorned).

The later stages of the period also saw the first arrival of Europeans, specifically three Portuguese traders blown ashore on the island of Tanegashima, south of Kyūshū, in 1543. Presently other Europeans arrived, bringing with them two important items, Christianity and firearms. They found a land torn apart by warfare, ripe for conversion to Christianity – at least in the eyes of missionaries such as Francis Xavier, who arrived in 1549 – while the Japanese warlords were more interested in the worldly matter of guns.

> Books and films such as *Letters from Iwo Jima* and *Memoirs of a Geisha* help provide realistic historical context and an increased understanding of other eras and cultures.

Reunification

One of the most successful warlords to make use of firearms was Oda Nobunaga (1534–82), from what is now Aichi Prefecture. Though starting from a relatively minor power base, his skilled and ruthless generalship resulted in a series of victories over rivals. In 1568 he seized Kyoto in support of the shōgunal claim of one of the Ashikaga clan (Yoshiaki) and duly installed him, but then in 1573 he drove him out, and presently made his own base at Azuchi. Though he did not take the title of shōgun himself, Nobunaga was the supreme power in the land.

Noted for his brutality, he was not a man to cross. In particular he hated Buddhist priests, whom he saw as troublesome, and he tolerated Christianity as a counterbalance to them. His ego was massive, leading him to erect a temple where he could be worshipped, and to declare his birthday a national holiday. His stated aim was '*Tenka Fubu*' – 'A Unified Realm under Military Rule' – and he went some way to achieving this unification by policies such as strategic redistribution of territories among the *daimyō*, land surveys and standardisation of weights and measures.

In 1582 he was betrayed by one of his generals and forced to commit suicide. However, the work of continuing unification was carried on by another of his generals, Toyotomi Hideyoshi (1536–98), a foot soldier who had risen through the ranks to become Nobunaga's favourite. He too was an extraordinary figure. Small and simian in his features, he was

1568	1582	late 1500s	1592 & 1597–8
The warlord Oda Nobunaga seizes Kyoto and soon becomes the supreme power in the land, though he does not take the title of shōgun. He is noted for his massive ego and brutality.	Nobunaga is betrayed and forced to commit suicide. Power switches to one of his loyal generals, Toyotomi Hideyoshi, who becomes increasingly paranoid and anti-Christian. Hideyoshi takes the title of regent.	Sen-no-Rikyū lays down the form of the tea ceremony, the ritualised drinking of tea originally practised by nobility and later spreading to wealthy commoners.	Hideyoshi twice tries to conquer Korea as part of a plan to control Asia, the second attempt ending after his death in 1598. The invasions seriously damage relations between Japan and Korea.

nicknamed Saru-chan (Little Monkey) by Nobunaga, but his huge will for power belied his physical smallness. He disposed of potential rivals among Nobunaga's sons, took the title of regent, continued Nobunaga's policy of territorial redistribution and also insisted that *daimyō* should surrender their families to him as hostages to be kept in Kyoto – his base being at Momoyama. He also banned weapons for all classes except samurai.

Hideyoshi became increasingly paranoid, cruel and megalomaniacal in his later years. He would saw in half messengers who gave him bad news, and had young members of his own family executed for suspected plotting. He also issued the first expulsion order of Christians (1587), whom he suspected of being an advance guard for an invasion. This order was not necessarily enforced, but in 1597 he crucified 26 Christians, of whom nine were Europeans. His grand scheme for power included a pan-Asian conquest, and as a first step he attempted an invasion of Korea in 1592, which failed amid much bloodshed. He tried again in 1597, but the campaign was abandoned when Hideyoshi died of illness in 1598.

On his deathbed Hideyoshi entrusted the safeguarding of the country and the succession of his young son Hideyori (1593–1615), whom he had unexpectedly fathered late in life, to one of his ablest generals, Tokugawa Ieyasu (1542–1616). However, upon Hideyoshi's death Ieyasu betrayed that trust. In 1600, in the Battle of Sekigahara, he defeated those who were trying to protect Hideyori, and became effectively the overlord of Japan. In 1603 his power was legitimised when the emperor conferred on him the title of shōgun. His Kantō base, the once tiny fishing village of Edo – later to be renamed Tokyo – now became the real centre of power and government in Japan.

Through these three men, by fair means or more commonly foul, the country had been reunified within three decades.

Stability & Seclusion

Having secured power for the Tokugawa, Ieyasu and his successors were determined to retain it. Their basic strategy was of a linked two-fold nature: enforce the status quo and minimise potential for challenge. Orthodoxy and strict control were key elements.

Their policies included tight control over military families in particular, such as requiring authorisation for castle-building and marriages, continuing strategic redistribution (or confiscation) of territory, and, importantly, requiring *daimyō* and their retainers to spend every second year at Edo, with their families kept there permanently as hostages. In addition the shōgunate directly controlled ports, mines, major towns and other strategic areas. Movement was severely restricted by deliberate

The rickshaw was not developed until 1869, following the lifting of the Tokugawa ban on wheeled transport.

1600	1603	1638	1689–91
The warlord Tokugawa Ieyasu breaks his earlier promise to the dying Hideyoshi to protect his young son and heir Hideyori, and seizes power for himself at the Battle of Sekigahara.	Ieyasu becomes shōgun, leading to policies aimed at maintaining the status quo and minimising potential threats in order to retain power for the Tokugawa.	Japanese Christians are massacred by shōgunal forces in the Christian-led Shimabara Rebellion. Westerners are by now expelled, except for a small Protestant Dutch presence on a tiny island off Nagasaki.	Matsuo Bashō, the greatest name in haiku poetry, completes a journey around Japan which serves as the source of his most famous collection of poems: *The Narrow Road to the Deep North*.

destruction of many bridges, the implementation of checkpoints and requirements for written travel authority, the banning of wheeled transport, the strict monitoring of potentially ocean-going vessels, and the banning of overseas travel for Japanese and even the return of those already overseas. Social movement was also banned, with society divided into four main classes: in descending order *shi* (samurai), *nō* (farmers), *kō* (artisans) and *shō* (merchants). Detailed codes of conduct applied to each of these classes, including clothing, food and housing – right down to the siting of the toilet!

HIDDEN CHRISTIANS *ANDREW BENDER*

Japan's 'Christian Century' began in 1549 with the arrival of Portuguese missionaries on the island of Kyūshū. Within decades, hundreds of thousands of Japanese from peasants to *daimyō* (regional lords) were converted.

The rapid rise of Christian belief, as well as its association with trade, new Western weaponry and control of Japanese territory, came to be viewed as a threat by the *bakufu* (military government) under Toyotomi Hideyoshi. The 1587 expulsion of missionaries began an era of suppression of Christians. Christians estimated in the thousands were executed over the next six decades, of which the best known was the 1597 crucifixion of 26 Japanese and Spanish Franciscans in Nagasaki (see p585). Many thousands of Christian peasants rebelled in the 1637–38 Shimabara Rebellion, after which Christianity was outlawed completely.

Other persecution took the form of *fumi-e*, in which suspected Christians were forced to walk on images of Jesus. The Gregorian date on the front of the Dutch trading house on the island of Hirado was taken as proof of the Dutch traders' Christianity and used to justify their exile to Nagasaki's Dejima, ushering in over two centuries of *sakoku* (closure to the outside world).

Japanese Christians reacted by going undercover as *kakure Kirishitan* (hidden Christians). With no more priests, they worshipped in lay-led services, in secret rooms inside private homes. On the surface, worship resembled other Japanese religions, including the use of Shintō *kamidana* altars and Buddhist *butsudan* ancestor-worship chests in homes, and ceremonial rice and *sake*. But *kakure Kirishitan* also kept hanging scrolls of Jesus, Mary and saints as well as statues like the Maria-Kannon, depicting Mary in the form of the Buddhist deity of mercy holding an infant symbolising Jesus. The sounds of worship, too, mimicked Buddhist incantations. Scholars put the numbers of hidden Christians at about 150,000.

It was not until 1865, 12 years after the arrival of the Black Ships, that Japan had its first large-scale church again, Oura Cathedral in Nagasaki, and missionaries began to return to Japan with its reopening in 1868. The Meiji government officially declared freedom of religion in 1871. Today, estimates put the number of Japanese Christians at between one and two million (about 1% of the population).

1600s–1800s	**1701–03**	**mid- to late 1700s**	**1808**
The Tokugawa shōgunate is based at Edo (later renamed Tokyo). Life is tightly controlled, and the nation is shut off from most of the world. Nonetheless, 'Edo merchant culture' emerges.	The mass suicide of the Forty-Seven Rōnin after avenging their lord's death is seen by many as a model for samurai ethics, recently codified as *bushidō*.	Itō Jakuchū creates a flamboyant and seminaturalistic style of painting that shows hints of Western influence but retains a Japanese heart. To this day, Jakuchū remains one of Japan's most famous painters.	The British ship HMS *Phaeton* captures several Dutch personnel at the island of Dejima and demands supplies. The British obtain supplies and leave before Japanese reinforcements arrive to exact reprisals.

Christianity, though not greatly popular, threatened the authority of the shōgunate. Thus Christian missionaries were expelled in 1614. By 1638, following the bloody quelling of the Christian-led Shimabara Rebellion, which saw Christianity banned and Japanese Christians – probably several hundred thousand – forced into hiding, all Westerners except the Protestant Dutch were expelled. The shōgunate found Protestantism less threatening than Catholicism – among other things it knew the Vatican could muster one of the biggest military forces in the world – and would have been prepared to let the British too stay on if the Dutch, showing astute commercial one-upmanship, had not convinced it that Britain was a Catholic country. Nevertheless, the Dutch were confined geographically to a tiny trading base on the artificial island of Dejima, near Nagasaki, and numerically to just a few dozen men.

Thus Japan entered an era of *sakoku* (closure to the outside world) that was to last for more than two centuries. Within the isolated and severely prescribed world of Tokugawa Japan, breach of even a trivial law could mean execution. Even mere 'rude behaviour' was a capital offence, and the definition of this was 'acting in an unexpected manner'. Punishments could be cruel, such as crucifixion, and could be meted out collectively or by proxy, with for example a village headman being punished for the misdemeanour of a villager. Secret police were used to report on misdeeds.

As a result, people at large learned the importance of obedience to authority, of collective responsibility and of 'doing the right thing'. These are values still prominent in present-day Japan.

For all the constraints there was nevertheless a considerable dynamism to the period, especially among the merchants, who as the lowest class were often ignored by the authorities and thus had relative freedom. They prospered greatly from the services and goods required for the *daimyō* processions to and from Edo, entailing such expense that *daimyō* had to convert much of their domain's produce into cash. This boosted the economy in general.

A largely pleasure-oriented merchant culture thrived, and produced the popular kabuki drama, with its colour and stage effects. Other entertainments included *bunraku* (classic puppet theatre), haiku (17-syllable poems), popular novels and *ukiyo-e* (woodblock prints), often of female geisha, who came to the fore in this period. (Earlier geisha – meaning 'artistic person' – were male.)

Samurai, for their part, had no major military engagements. Well educated, most ended up fighting mere paper wars as administrators and managers. Ironically, it was during this period of relative inactivity that the renowned samurai code of *bushidō* was formalised. Though much of it was idealism, occasionally the code was put into practice, such as the

SAKOKU

The Thousand Autumns of Jacob de Zoet: A Novel, by David Mitchell, tells about the Dutch living on the island of Dejima during the period of *sakoku*.

1800–50		**Early to Mid-19th Century**
Ukiyo-e (pictures of the floating world), highly stylised woodblock prints depicting entertainment districts and landscapes, become popular, led by two great names, Hiroshige and Hokusai.		National isolation comes under threat from increasing numbers of foreign whalers and other vessels entering Japanese waters. Treatment of those attempting to land is harsh.

» Ukiyo-e at the Kyoto Handicraft Center (p295)

exemplary loyalty shown by the Forty-Seven Rōnin (Masterless Samurai) in 1701–3, who waited two years to avenge the unfair enforced suicide by seppuku of their lord, killing the man responsible, whereupon they in turn were all obliged to commit seppuku.

In more general terms, Confucianism was officially encouraged, with the apparent aim of reinforcing the idea of hierarchy and status quo – which unfortunately was not in the best interests of women – but at the same time it encouraged learning, and along with this, literacy. By the end of the period as many as 30% of the 30 million population were literate – far ahead of the Western norm at the time. In some opposition to the 'Chinese learning' represented by Confucianism, there was also a strong trend of nationalism, centred on Shintō and the ancient texts. This was unhelpful to the shōgunate as it tended to focus on the primacy of the emperor. Certainly, by the early to mid-19th century, there was considerable dissatisfaction towards the shōgunate, fanned also by corruption and incompetence among shōgunal officials.

> The Japanese religion of Shintō is one of the few religions in the world to have a female solar deity.

It is questionable how much longer the Tokugawa shōgunate and its secluded world could have continued, but as it happened, external forces were to hasten its demise.

Modernisation Through Westernisation

Since the start of the 19th century a number of Western vessels had appeared in Japanese waters. Any Westerners who landed, even through shipwreck, were almost always met with expulsion or even execution.

This was not acceptable to the Western powers, especially America, which was keen to expand its interests across the Pacific and had numerous whaling vessels in the northwest that needed regular provisioning. In 1853, and again the following year, US Commodore Matthew Perry steamed into Edo-wan with a show of gunships and demanded the opening of Japan for trade and provisioning. The shōgunate had little option but to accede to his demands, for it was no match for Perry's firepower. Presently an American consul arrived, and other Western powers followed suit. Humiliatingly, Japan was obliged to give 'most favoured nation' rights to all the powers, and lost control over its own tariffs.

Meiji Restoration

The humiliation of the shōgunate, the nation's supposed military protector, was capitalised upon by anti-shōgunal samurai in the outer domains of Satsuma (southern Kyūshū) and Chōshū (western Honshū) in particular. A movement arose to 'revere the emperor and expel the barbarians' *(sonnō jōi)*. However, after unsuccessful skirmishing with the Western powers, the reformers realised that expelling the barbarians was not feasible, but restoring the emperor was. Their coup, known as the Meiji

1853–4	1854–67	1867–8	1870s–Early 1890s
US Commodore Matthew Perry uses 'gunboat diplomacy' to force Japan to open up for trade and reprovisioning, bringing criticism by many Japanese towards the ineffective shōgunate.	Opposition to the shōgunate grows, led by samurai from the Satsuma and Chōshū domains. Initially hostile to foreigners, they soon come to realise Japan's defensive limitations.	The Meiji Restoration disestablishes the shōgunate and in theory restores imperial authority, but 15-year-old emperor Mutsuhito is a puppet, and oligarchs rule. Japan's capital moves to Edo, renamed Tokyo.	The oligarchs implement policies of modernisation and Westernisation, such as creating a conscript army (1873), disestablishing the samurai (1876) and adopting a constitution (1889).

(Enlightened Rule) Restoration, was put into effect in late 1867–early 1868, and the new teenage emperor Mutsuhito (1852–1912, later to be known as Meiji) found himself 'restored', following the convenient death of his stubborn father Kōmei (1831–67). After some initial resistance, the last shōgun, Yoshinobu (1837–1913), retired to Shizuoka to live out his numerous remaining years peacefully. The shōgunal base at Edo became the new imperial base, and was renamed Tokyo (Eastern Capital).

Mutsuhito did as he was told by those who had restored him, though they would claim that everything was done on his behalf and with his sanction. Basically, he was the classic legitimiser. His restorers – driven by both personal ambition and genuine concern for the nation – were

THE REAL LAST SAMURAI *ANDREW BENDER*

Saigō Takamori (1828–77) was a giant of a man for his day, at about 180cm (6ft) tall, with a broad build, square head and large eyes. His importance in Japanese history is just as big.

Born to a samurai family in Kagoshima, Kyūshū (then called Satsuma Province, in the southwestern corner of the main islands), Saigō was an ardent supporter of the emperor Meiji and field commander of the imperial army against the forces of the Tokugawa shōgunate. The quashing of a rebellion of Tokugawa loyalists at Ueno in Tokyo in 1868 cemented the Meiji Restoration.

But things did not turn out as he had hoped. The samurai system was abolished once Meiji ascended to the Chrysanthemum Throne, and by 1872 this system of professional warriors had given way to a Western model of military conscription. Saigō, by then part of the Meiji government, advocated invasion of Korea, and after this idea was rejected in 1873, he resigned and returned to Satsuma.

By 1874, small riots by former samurai had broken out around the country, put down by the new army. Other former samurai rallied around Saigō and urged him to lead a rebellion against the imperial forces. The 1877 siege of Kumamoto Castle lasted 54 days, with a reported force of 40,000 samurai and armed peasants arrayed against the imperial army. When the castle was incinerated and defeat became inevitable, it is said that Saigō retreated to Kagoshima and committed seppuku.

The Satsuma Rebellion, as it came to be called, soon gained the status of legend among common Japanese. Capitalising on this fame, the Meiji government posthumously pardoned Saigō and granted him full honours, and today he remains an exemplar of the samurai spirit. Statues of his image can be found most prominently in Kagoshima and walking his faithful dog in Tokyo's Ueno-kōen. His most famous maxim, *keiten aijin,* translates to 'Revere heaven, love humankind'.

Fans of the 2003 movie *The Last Samurai* may recognise elements of this story in Katsumoto, the character played by Watanabe Ken. However, there is no evidence that any Western soldier, such as the one played by Tom Cruise, had any role in these events in Saigō's life.

1894–5	**1902**	**1904–05**	**1910**
Japan starts a war with China, which at this stage is a weak nation and which Japan defeats in the Sino-Japanese War (1895). Japan gains Taiwan as a result, thereby starting its territorial expansion.	Japan signs the Anglo-Japanese Alliance, the first-ever equal alliance between a Western and a non-Western nation. This effectively means that Japan has succeeded in becoming a major power.	Japan is victorious in the Russo-Japanese War. Antipathy towards Russia had grown after the Sino-Japanese War, when Russia pressured Japan into renouncing Chinese territory that Russia itself then occupied.	Now free from any Russian threat, Japan formally annexes Korea, in which it had had an increasing interest since the 1870s. The international community makes no real protest.

largely leading Satsuma or Chōshū samurai in their early 30s, the most prominent of them being Itō Hirobumi (1841–1909), who was to become prime minister on no fewer than four occasions. Fortunately for Japan, they proved a very capable oligarchy.

Japan was also fortunate in that the Western powers were distracted by richer and easier pickings in China and elsewhere and did not seriously seek to occupy or colonise Japan, though Perry does seem to have entertained some such thoughts at one stage. Nevertheless, the fear of colonisation made the oligarchs act with great urgency. Far from being colonised, they themselves wanted to be colonisers, and make Japan a major power.

Westernisation

Under the banner of *fukoku kyōhei* (rich country, strong army), the young men who now controlled Japan decided on Westernisation as the best strategy – again showing the apparent Japanese preference for learning from a powerful potential foe. In fact, as another slogan, *oitsuke, oikose* (catch up, overtake), suggests, they even wanted to outdo their models. Missions were sent overseas to observe a whole range of Western institutions and practices, and Western specialists were brought to Japan to advise in areas from banking to transport to mining.

In the coming decades Japan was to Westernise quite substantially, not just in material terms such as telegraphs, railways and clothing, but also, based on selected models, in the establishment of a modern banking system and economy, a legal code, a constitution and Diet, elections and political parties, and a conscript army.

Existing institutions and practices were disestablished where necessary. *Daimyō* were 'persuaded' to give their domain land to the government in return for governorships or similar compensation, enabling the implementation of a prefectural system. The four-tier class system was scrapped, and people were now free to choose their occupation and place of residence. This included even the samurai class, phased out by 1876 to pave the way for a more efficient conscript army – though there was some armed resistance to this in 1877 under the Satsuma samurai (and oligarch) Saigō Takamori, who ended up committing seppuku when the resistance failed.

To help relations with the Western powers, the ban on Christianity was lifted, though few took advantage of it. Nevertheless numerous Western ideologies entered the country, one of the most popular being 'self-help' philosophy. This provided a guiding principle for a population newly liberated from a world in which everything had been prescribed for them. But at the same time, too much freedom could lead to an unhelpful type of individualism. The government quickly realised

The disorienting collapse of the regimented Tokugawa world produced a form of mass hysteria called *Ee Ja Nai Ka* (Who Cares?), with traumatised people dancing naked and giving away possessions.

The salaries of the foreign specialists invited to Japan in the Meiji period are believed to have amounted to 5% of all government expenditure during the period.

1912	1914–15	1920s	1923
Emperor Meiji (Mutsuhito) dies, having seen Japan rise from a remote pre-industrial nation to world-power status in just half a century. His mentally disabled son, Yoshihito, succeeds him.	Japan utilises the involvement of many Western countries in WWI in Europe to occupy German territory in the Pacific in 1914 (as Britain's ally) and in 1915 to present China with the 'Twenty-One Demands'.	Japan becomes increasingly disillusioned with much of the West, feeling unfairly treated, such as in the Washington Conference naval ratios (1921–2) and the USA's immigration policies in 1924.	The Great Kantō Earthquake strikes Japan near Tokyo, killing an estimated 100,000 to 140,000 people. Much of the destruction is caused by the fires that sweep Tokyo and Yokohama after the quake.

that nationalism could safely and usefully harness these new energies. People were encouraged to make a success of themselves and become strong, and in so doing show the world what a successful and strong nation Japan was. Through educational policies, supported by imperial pronouncements, young people were encouraged to become strong and work for the good of the family-nation.

The government was proactive in many other ways, such as taking responsibility for establishing major industries and then selling them off at bargain rates to chosen 'government-friendly' industrial entrepreneurs – a factor in the formation of huge industrial combines known as *zaibatsu*. The government's actions in this were not really democratic, but this was typical of the day. Another example is the 'transcendental cabinet' that was not responsible to the parliament but only to the emperor, who followed his advisers, who were members of the same cabinet! Meiji Japan was outwardly democratic but internally retained many authoritarian features.

The 'state-guided' economy was helped by a workforce that was well educated, obedient and numerous, and traditions of sophisticated commercial practices such as futures markets. In the early years Japan's main industry was textiles and its main export silk, but later in the Meiji period, with judicious financial support from the government, it moved increasingly into manufacturing and heavy industry, becoming a major world shipbuilder by the end of the period. Improvement in agricultural technology freed up surplus farming labour to move into these manufacturing sectors.

A key element of Japan's aim to become a world power with overseas territory was the military. Following Prussian (army) and British (navy) models, Japan soon built up a formidable military force. Using the same 'gunboat diplomacy' on Korea that Perry had used on the Japanese, in 1876 Japan was able to force on Korea an unequal treaty of its own and thereafter interfered increasingly in Korean politics. Using Chinese 'interference' in Korea as a justification, in 1894 Japan manufactured a war with China, a weak nation at this stage despite its massive size, and easily emerged victorious. As a result it gained Taiwan and the Liaotung Peninsula. Russia pressured Japan into renouncing the peninsula and then promptly occupied it itself, leading presently to the Russo-Japanese War of 1904–05, from which Japan again emerged victorious. One important benefit was Western recognition of its interests in Korea, which it proceeded to annex in 1910.

By the time of Mutsuhito's death in 1912, Japan was indeed recognised as a world power. In addition to its military victories and territorial acquisitions, in 1902 it had signed the Anglo-Japanese Alliance, the first ever equal alliance between a Western and a non-Western nation. The unequal treaties had also been rectified. Western-style structures were in place. The economy was world ranking. The Meiji period had been a truly extraordinary half-century of modernisation. But where to now?

The Coming of the Barbarians, by Pat Barr, is perhaps the most interesting account of the opening of Japan in the mid-19th century.

HISTORY MODERNISATION THROUGH WESTERNISATION

Japan was arguably the first Asian nation to defeat a Western nation in a military conflict (in the Russo-Japanese War of 1904–05).

1931	**1937**	**1941**	**1942**
Increasingly defiant of the West, Japan invades Manchuria on a pretext, and withdraws dramatically from the League of Nations after criticism from it. Japan's behaviour becomes more aggressive.	During its attempted occupation of China, Japan perpetrates an atrocity at Nanjing, torturing and killing tens of thousands of people, mostly innocent civilians.	Japan enters WWII by striking Pearl Harbor on 7 December, with no warning, destroying much of the USA's Pacific fleet and thereby bringing the USA into the war.	After early successes, Japan's expansion is thwarted at the Battle of Midway in June, with significant carrier loss. From this point on Japan is largely in retreat.

Growing Dissatisfaction with the West

Mutsuhito was succeeded by his son Yoshihito (Taishō), who suffered mental deterioration that in 1921 led to his own son Hirohito (1901–89) becoming regent.

On the one hand the Taishō period (Great Righteousness; 1912–26) saw continued democratisation, with a more liberal line, the extension of the right to vote and a stress on diplomacy. Until WWI Japan was able to benefit economically from the reduced presence of the Western powers, and also politically, for it was allied with Britain (though with little actual involvement) and was able to occupy German possessions in East Asia and the Pacific. On the other hand, using that same reduced Western presence, Japan aggressively sought in 1915 to gain effective control of China with its notorious 'Twenty-One Demands', which were eventually modified.

There was in Japan a growing sense of dissatisfaction towards the West, and a sense of unfair treatment. The Washington Conference of 1921–22 set naval ratios of three capital ships for Japan to five American and five British, which upset the Japanese despite being well ahead of France's 1.75. Around the same time a racial-equality clause that Japan proposed to the newly formed League of Nations was rejected. And in 1924 America introduced race-based immigration policies that effectively targeted Japanese.

This dissatisfaction was to intensify in the Shōwa period (Illustrious Peace), which started in 1926 with the death of Yoshihito and the formal accession of Hirohito. He was not a strong emperor, and was unable to curb the rising power of the military, who pointed to the growing gap between urban and rural living standards and accused politicians and big businessmen of corruption. The situation was not helped by repercussions from the Great Depression in the late 1920s. The ultimate cause of these troubles, in Japanese eyes, was the West, with its excessive individualism and liberalism. According to the militarists, Japan needed to look after its own interests, which in extended form meant a resource-rich, Japan-controlled Greater East Asian Co-Prosperity Sphere that even included Australia and New Zealand.

In 1931 Japan invaded Manchuria on a pretext, and presently set up a puppet government. When the League of Nations objected, Japan promptly left the league. It soon turned its attention to China, and in 1937 launched a brutal invasion that saw atrocities such as the infamous Nanjing Massacre of December that year. Casualty figures for Chinese civilians at Nanjing vary between 340,000 (some Chinese sources) and a 'mere' 20,000 (some Japanese sources). Many of the tortures, rapes and murders were filmed and are undeniable, but persistent (though not universal) Japanese attempts to downplay this and other massacres in Asia remain a stumbling block in Japan's relations with many Asian nations even today.

YAMATO DYNASTY

The Yamato dynasty is the longest unbroken monarchy in the world, and Hirohito's reign from 1926 to 1989 the longest of any monarch in Japan.

1945
After intensive firebombing of Tokyo in March, on 6 August Hiroshima becomes the victim of an atomic bombing, followed on 9 August by Nagasaki, leading Hirohito to announce surrender on 15 August.

1945–52
Japan undergoes US-led occupation and a rapid economic recovery follows. Hirohito is spared from prosecution as a war criminal, angering many American allies.

BRENT WINEBRENNER / LONELY PLANET IMAGES ©

» Peace Memorial Park, Hiroshima (p365)

WWII

Japan did not reject all Western nations, however, for it admired the new regimes in Germany and Italy, and in 1940 it entered into a tripartite pact with them. This gave it confidence to expand further in Southeast Asia, principally seeking oil, for which it was heavily dependent on American exports. However, the alliance was not to lead to much cooperation, and since Hitler was openly talking of the Japanese as *untermenschen* (lesser beings) and the 'Yellow Peril', Japan was never sure of Germany's commitment. The US was increasingly concerned at Japan's aggression and applied sanctions. Diplomacy failed, and war seemed inevitable.

So it was that the Japanese struck at Pearl Harbor on 7 December 1941, damaging much of the US' Pacific fleet and allegedly catching the US by surprise, though some scholars believe Roosevelt and others deliberately allowed the attack to happen in order to overcome isolationist sentiment and bring the US into the war against Germany. Whatever the reality, the US certainly underestimated Japan and its commitment, which led to widespread occupation of Pacific islands and parts of Asia. Most scholars agree that Japan never expected to beat the US but hoped to bring it to the negotiating table and emerge better off.

The tide started to turn against Japan from the battle of Midway in June 1942, which saw the destruction of much of its carrier fleet. Japan had over-extended itself, and over the next three years was subjected to an island-hopping counter-attack under General Douglas MacArthur. By mid-1945 the Japanese, ignoring the Potsdam Declaration calling for unconditional surrender, were preparing for a final Allied assault on their homelands. On 6 August the world's first atomic bomb was dropped on Hiroshima, with 90,000 civilian deaths. On 8 August, Russia, which Japan had hoped might mediate, declared war. On 9 August another atomic bomb was dropped, on Nagasaki, with another 50,000 deaths. The emperor formally announced surrender on 15 August. Hirohito probably knew what the bombs were, for Japanese scientists were working on their own atomic bomb, though their state of progress is unclear.

> Until it was occupied by the USA and other Allies following WWII, Japan (as a nation) had never been conquered or occupied by a foreign power.

The Modern Period

Japan's recovery from the war is now the stuff of legend. The American occupation officially ended in 1952, as the USA was engaged in yet another war, this time on the Korean Peninsula. Many historians, both Japanese and American, say that Japan's role as a forward base reignited the Japanese economy. Whatever the case, its growth from the 1950s onwards can only be termed miraculous – only in the late 1980s, with the bursting of the so-called Bubble Economy, did it finally come down to earth. For a discussion of recent Japanese history, see the Japan Today section (p674).

1954	1964	1972	2011
Godzilla makes his first appearance in an animated movie of the same name, directed by Honda Ishirō. The premise was that Godzilla was a monster somehow created by the atomic bombings of WWII.	Tokyo hosts the Summer Olympics, an event which, for many Japanese, marked Japan's full re-entry in the international community and the completion of its recovery from WWII.	The USA returns administrative control of Okinawa to Japan, while keeping many bases in place (a source of tension to this day).	On 11 March, the Great East Japan Earthquake strikes off the coast of northeast Japan (Tōhoku), generating a tsunami that kills thousands and setting off a crisis at a nuclear powerplant in Fukushima Prefecture.

The People of Japan

The uniqueness and peculiarity of the Japanese is a favourite topic of both Western observers and the Japanese themselves. It's worth starting any discussion about the people of Japan by noting that there is no such thing as 'the Japanese'. Rather, there are 127 million individuals in Japan with their own unique characters, interests and habits. And despite popular stereotypes to the contrary, the Japanese are as varied as any people on earth. Just as importantly, Japanese people have more in common with the rest of humanity than they have differences.

It is thought that modern Japanese result from the mixing of early Jōmon people, who walked over to Japan via land bridges formed during an ice age, and later Yayoi people, who arrived from the Korean Peninsula in boats.

Why then the pervasive images of the Japanese as inscrutable or even bizarre? These stereotypes are largely rooted in language: few Japanese are able to speak English as well as, say, your average Singaporean, Hong Kong Chinese or well-educated Indian, not to mention most Europeans. This difficulty with English is largely rooted in the country's appalling English-education system, and is compounded by a natural shyness, a perfectionist streak and the nature of the Japanese language itself, which contains fewer sounds than most other major languages (making pronunciation of other languages difficult). Thus, what appears to the casual observer to be a maddening inscrutability is more likely just an inability to communicate effectively. Outsiders who become fluent in Japanese discover a people whose thoughts and feelings are surprisingly – almost boringly – similar to those of folks in other developed nations.

All this said, the Japanese do have certain characteristics that reflect their unique history and interaction with their environment. First, Japan is an island nation. Second, until WWII, Japan was never conquered by an outside power, nor was it heavily influenced by Christian missionaries. Third, until the beginning of last century, the majority of Japanese lived in close-knit rural farming communities. Fourth, most of Japan is covered in steep mountains, so the few flat areas of the country are quite crowded – people literally live on top of each other. Finally, for almost all of its history, Japan has been a strictly hierarchical place, with something approximating a caste system during the Edo period.

All of this has produced a people who highly value group identity and social harmony – in a tightly packed city or small farming village, there simply isn't room for colourful individualism. One of the ways harmony is preserved is by forming consensus, and concealing personal opinions and true feelings. Thus, the free-flowing exchange of ideas, debates and even heated arguments that one expects in the West are far less common in Japan. This reticence about sharing innermost thoughts perhaps contributes to the Western image of the Japanese as mysterious.

Of course, there is a lot more to the typical Japanese character than just a tendency to prize social harmony. Any visitor to the country will soon discover a people who are remarkably conscientious, meticulous, industrious, honest and technically skilled. A touching shyness and sometimes almost painful self-consciousness are also undoubted features of many Japanese. These characteristics result in a society that is a joy for the traveller to experience.

And let us say that any visit to Japan is a good opportunity to explode the myths about Japan and the Japanese. While you may imagine a nation of suit-clad conformists or inscrutable automatons, a few rounds in a local *izakaya* (pub-eatery) will quickly put all of these notions to rest.

Lifestyle

The way most Japanese live today differs greatly from the way they lived before WWII. As the birth rate has dropped and labour demands have drawn more workers to cities, the population has become increasingly urban. At the same time, Japan continues to soak up influences from abroad and the traditional lifestyle of the country is quickly disappearing in the face of a dizzying onslaught of Western pop/material culture. These days, the average young Tokyoite has a lot more in common with her peers in Melbourne or London than she does with her grandmother back in her *furusato* (hometown).

JAPANESE ETIQUETTE

Many visitors to Japan worry about committing a dreadful breach of etiquette. Perhaps this is natural. After all, Japan is a relatively formal society with a complex system of manners and mores. And let's not even get into the language, which makes the *tu/vous* questions of French look like child's play. But here is something we cannot emphasise strongly enough: *relax*. No one expects you to know all the rules of polite Japanese behaviour and no one is watching you like a hawk, waiting for you to do something wrong. So, the first rule is this: just do what would be polite in your own country, and you won't go too far wrong. That said, there are a few things to keep in mind if you want to gain bonus points with the locals.

» **Use two hands** when giving your name card or receiving one. Ditto for presents or important documents. And when giving money, try to put it into an envelope.

» **Take off your shoes** if you find yourself stepping up onto tatami mats. And do it by stepping right out of the shoes onto the mats, not by taking them off a few blocks away and carrying them with you over to the shoe rack.

» **Temples are religious places** so don't enter the grounds or main halls dressed like you're out for a day at the beach, and talk quietly while in the main halls. Shrines tend to be a little more casual, but flip-flops and cut-off shorts aren't going to impress anyone with your fashion sense.

» **Keep language difficulties in mind when speaking** with the Japanese. Some people will try harder to understand what you are saying, but not everyone speaks or understands English at a high level. So go slowly, smile and use standard and, if necessary, simplified English when communicating with locals.

» **Don't expect too much flexibility** Not all restaurants are willing to alter dishes to suit dietary preferences or requirements, and not every ryokan has slippers or futons big enough to fit a foreigner. Keep in mind that, most of the time, they are doing their best to help you – at the same time, remember that few Japanese complain or ask for special services or changes in similar situations.

Needless to say, eating a meal, particularly at a fancy restaurant or at someone's house, involves some very particular etiquette. For details on this see the box, p704.

For more insights into the Japanese people, the following books are highly recommended:

» *The Chrysanthemum and the Sword* by Ruth Benedict is a groundbreaking work on the psychology of the Japanese.

» *A Japanese Mirror: Heroes and Villains of Japanese Culture* by Ian Buruma is a look into the Japanese psyche by one of the world's most astute commentators on Japan.

» *Wages of Guilt* by Ian Buruma is the most revealing study of Japanese postwar psychology.

» *The Anatomy of Dependence* by Takeo Doi, a Japanese psychologist, looks at the Japanese through the lens of '*amae*' (sometimes defined as the feeling a child has towards its parents).

In the City

The overwhelming majority of Japanese live in the bustling urban environments of major cities. These urbanites live famously hectic lives dominated by often gruelling work schedules and punctuated by lengthy commutes from city centres to more affordable outlying neighbourhoods and suburbs.

Until fairly recently, the nexus of all this activity was the Japanese corporation, which provided lifetime employment to the legions of blue-suited white-collar workers, almost all of them men, who lived, worked, drank, ate and slept in the service of the companies for which they toiled. These days, as the Japanese economy makes the transition from a manufacturing economy to a service economy, the old certainties are vanishing. On the way out are Japan's famous 'cradle to grave' employment and age-based promotion system. Now, the recent college graduate is just as likely to become a *furiitaa* (part-time worker) as he is to become a salaryman. Needless to say, all this has wide-ranging consequences for Japanese society.

Most families once comprised a father who was a salaryman, a mother who was a housewife, kids who studied dutifully in order to earn a place at one of Japan's elite universities, and an elderly in-law who had moved in. Although the days of this traditional model may not be completely over, it has been changing fast in recent years. As in Western countries, *tomobataraki* (both spouses working) is now increasingly common.

The kids in the family probably still study like mad: if they are in not yet in high school, they will be working towards gaining admission to a select high school by attending an after-school cram school, known as a *juku;* if they are already in high school, they will be attending a *juku* in hopes of passing university admission exams.

As for the mother- or father-in-law, who in the past would have expected to be taken care of by the eldest son in the family, they may have found that beliefs about filial loyalty have changed substantially since the 1980s, particularly in urban centres. Now, more and more Japanese families are sending elderly parents and in-laws to live out their 'golden years' in *rōjin hōmu* (literally 'old-folks homes').

In the Country

Only one in four Japanese live in the small farming and fishing villages that dot the mountains and cling to the rugged coasts. Mass postwar emigration from these rural enclaves has doubtless changed the weave of Japanese social fabric and the texture of its landscape, as the young continue their steady flight to the city, leaving untended rice fields to slide down the hills from neglect.

Most Japanese identify themselves as both Shintō and Buddhist, but many young Japanese get married in Christian ceremonies performed by foreign 'priests' (many of whom are not real Christian priests).

RELIGION

Today only 15% of farming households continue to make ends meet solely through agriculture, with most rural workers holding down two or three jobs. Though this lifestyle manages to make the incomes of some country dwellers higher than those of their urban counterparts, it also speaks clearly of the crisis that many rural communities are facing in their struggle to maintain the traditional way of life.

The salvation of traditional village life may well rely on the success of the 'I-turn' (moving from urban areas to rural villages) and 'U-turn' (moving from country to city, and back again) movements. Although not wildly successful, these movements have managed to attract young people who work at home, company workers who are willing to put in a number of hours on the train commuting to the nearest city, and retirees looking to spend their golden years among the thatched roofs and rice fields that symbolise a not-so-distant past.

Population

Japan has a population of approximately 127 million people (the ninth largest in the world) and, with 75% of it concentrated in urban centres, population density is extremely high. Areas such as the Tokyo–Kawasaki–Yokohama conurbation are so densely populated that they have almost ceased to be separate cities, running into each other and forming a vast coalescence that, if considered as a whole, would constitute the world's largest city.

One notable feature of Japan's population is its relative ethnic and cultural homogeneity. This is particularly striking for visitors from the USA, Australia and other multicultural nations. The main reason for this ethnic homogeneity lies in Japan's strict immigration laws, which have ensured that only a small number of foreigners settle in the country.

The largest non-Japanese group in the country is made up of 650,000 *zai-nichi kankoku-jin* (resident Koreans). For most outsiders, Koreans are an invisible minority. Indeed, even the Japanese themselves have no way of knowing that someone is of Korean descent if they adopt a Japanese name. Nevertheless, Japanese-born Koreans, who in some

MINORITY CULTURES

The Ainu, of whom there are roughly 24,000 living in Japan, are the indigenous people of Hokkaidō and, some would argue, the only people who can claim to be natives of Japan. Due to ongoing intermarriage and assimilation, almost all Ainu consider themselves bi-ethnic. Today, fewer than 200 people in Japan can claim both parents with exclusively Ainu descent.

The Burakumin are a largely invisible (to outsiders, at least) group of Japanese whose ancestors performed work that brought them into contact with the contamination of death – butchering, leatherworking and the disposing of corpses. The Burakumin were the outcasts in the social hierarchy (some would say caste system) that existed during the Edo period. While the Burakumin are racially the same as other Japanese, they have traditionally been treated like an inferior people by much of Japanese society. Estimates put the number of hereditary Burakumin in present-day Japan at anywhere between 890,000 and three million.

While discrimination against Burakumin is now technically against the law, there continues to be significant discrimination against Burakumin in such important aspects of Japanese social life as work and marriage. It is common knowledge, though rarely alluded to, that information about any given individual's possible Burakumin origin is available to anyone (generally employers and prospective fathers-in-law) who is prepared to make certain discreet investigations. Many Japanese consider this a very culturally sensitive issue and may prefer to avoid discussion of this topic with foreigners.

cases speak no language other than Japanese, were only recently released from the obligation to carry ID cards with their fingerprints at all times, and some still face discrimination in the workplace and other aspects of their daily lives.

Aside from Koreans, most foreigners in Japan are temporary workers from China, Southeast Asia, South America and Western countries. Indigenous groups such as the Ainu have been reduced to very small numbers, due to intermarriage with non-Ainu and government attempts to hasten assimilation of Ainu into general Japanese society. At present, Ainu are concentrated mostly in Hokkaidō, the northernmost of Japan's main islands.

The most notable feature of Japan's population is the fact that it is shrinking. Japan's astonishingly low birth rate of 1.3 births per woman is among the lowest in the developed world and Japan is rapidly becoming a nation of elderly citizens. The population began declining in 2007, and is predicted to reach 100 million in 2050 and 67 million in 2100. Needless to say, such demographic change will have a major influence on the economy in coming decades.

Most Japanese babies are born with a Mongolian spot *(mōkohan)* on their lower backs. This harmless birthmark is composed of melanin-containing cells and usually fades by the age of five. It's common in several Asian races and in Native Americans, raising interesting questions about the origins of the Japanese.

Women in Japan

Traditional Japanese society restricted the woman's role to the home, where as housekeeper she wielded considerable power, overseeing all financial matters, monitoring the children's education and, in some ways, acting as the head of the household. Even in the early Meiji period, however, the ideal was rarely matched by reality: labour shortfalls often resulted in women taking on factory work, and even before that women often worked side by side with men in the fields.

As might be expected, the contemporary situation is complex. There are, of course, those who stick to established roles. They tend to opt for shorter college courses, often at women's colleges, and see education as an asset in the marriage market. Once married, they leave the role of breadwinner to the husband.

Increasingly, however, Japanese women are choosing to forgo or delay marriage in favour of pursuing their own career ambitions. Of course, changing aspirations do not necessarily translate into changing realities, and Japanese women are still significantly underrepresented in upper management and political positions, and there is a disproportionately high number of females employed as OLs (office ladies). Part of the reason for this is the prevalence of gender discrimination in Japanese companies. Societal expectations, however, also play a role: Japanese women are often forced to choose between having a career and having a family. Not only do most companies refuse to hire women for career-track positions, many Japanese men are simply not interested in having a career woman as a spouse. This makes it very intimidating for a Japanese woman to step out of her traditional gender role and follow a career path.

Those women who do choose full-time work suffer from one of the worst gender wage gaps in the developed world: Japanese women earn only 66% of what Japanese men earn, compared to 76% in the USA, 83% in the UK and 85% in Australia (according to figures released by the respective governments). In politics, the situation is even worse: Japanese women hold only 10% of seats in the Diet, the nation's governing body.

Japanese Cuisine

Those familiar with Japanese cuisine *(nihon ryōri)* know that eating is half the fun of travelling in Japan. Even if you've already tried some of Japan's better-known specialities, you're likely to be surprised by how delicious the original is when served on its home turf. More importantly, the adventurous eater will be delighted to find that Japanese food is far more than just sushi, tempura or sukiyaki. Indeed, it is possible to spend a month in Japan and sample a different speciality restaurant every day.

With the exception of *shokudō* (all-round restaurants) and *izakaya* (pub-eateries), most Japanese restaurants concentrate on a speciality cuisine. In this chapter we discuss the main types of restaurants you are likely to encounter and we provide sample menus for each type. If you familiarise yourself with the main types of restaurants and what they serve, you'll be able to get the most out of Japan's incredible culinary scene.

Of course, you may baulk at charging into a restaurant where both the language and the menu are likely to be incomprehensible. Those timid of heart should take solace in the fact that the Japanese will go to extraordinary lengths to understand what you want and will help you to order. To assist you further, eating reviews in this book recommend specific dishes for restaurants in which no English menu is available. If there is an English menu, this is indicated in the review with the symbol 📖.

In this guide, restaurant listings are organised by price category, indicated by the symbols $ (budget), $$ (midrange) or $$$ (top end). Budget options cost ¥1000 or less; midrange meals cost between ¥1000 and ¥4000; and top-end meals will cost more than ¥4000.

The film *Tampopo* (Itami Jūzō, 1987) is essential preparation for a visit to Japan – especially if you intend to visit a *rāmen* shop while you're there! It's about two fellows who set out to help a *rāmen* shop owner improve her shop, with several food-related subplots woven in for good measure.

Restaurant Types & Sample Menus

Shokudō

A *shokudō* is the most common type of restaurant in Japan, and is usually found near train stations, tourist spots and just about any other place where people congregate. Easily distinguished by the presence of plastic food displays in the window, these inexpensive places usually serve a variety of *washoku* (Japanese dishes) and *yōshoku* (Western dishes).

At lunch, and sometimes dinner, the easiest meal to order at a *shokudō* is a *teishoku* (set-course meal), which is sometimes also called *ranchi setto* (lunch set) or *kōsu* (course). This usually includes a main dish of meat or fish, a bowl of rice, *misoshiru* (miso soup), shredded cabbage and some *tsukemono* (Japanese pickles). In addition, most *shokudō* serve a fairly standard selection of *donburi-mono* (rice dishes) and *menrui* (noodle dishes). When you order noodles, you can choose between *soba* and *udon,* both of which are served with a variety of toppings. If

RESTAURANT GUIDE

you're at a loss as to what to order, simply say '*kyō-no-ranchi*' (today's lunch) and they'll do the rest. Expect to spend from ¥600 to ¥1000 for a meal at a *shokudō*.

katsu-don	かつ丼	rice topped with a fried pork cutlet
oyako-don	親子丼	rice topped with egg and chicken
ten-don	天丼	rice topped with tempura prawns and vegetables

Izakaya

An *izakaya* is the Japanese equivalent of a pub-eatery. It's a good place to visit when you want a casual meal, a wide selection of food, a hearty atmosphere and, of course, plenty of beer and sake. When you enter an *izakaya*, you are given the choice of sitting around the counter, at a table or on a tatami floor. You usually order a bit at a time, choosing from a selection of typical Japanese foods, such as *yakitori* (p700), sashimi and grilled fish, as well as Japanese interpretations of Western foods like French fries and beef stew.

Izakaya can be identified by their rustic facades and the red lanterns outside their doors bearing the kanji for *izakaya* (居酒屋). Many also stack crates of beer and sake bottles outside. Since *izakaya* food is casual fare to go with drinking, it is usually fairly inexpensive. Depending on how much you drink, you can expect to get away with spending ¥2500 to ¥5000 per person. See also the box, p701.

agedashi-dōfu	揚げだし豆腐	deep-fried tofu in a *dashi* broth
hiyayakko	冷奴	a cold block of tofu with soy sauce and spring onions
jaga-batā	ジャガバター	baked potatoes with butter
niku-jaga	肉ジャガ	beef and potato stew
sashimi mori-awase	刺身盛り合わせ	a selection of sliced sashimi
shio-yaki-zakana	塩焼魚	a whole fish grilled with salt
yaki-onigiri	焼きおにぎり	a triangle of grilled rice with *yakitori* sauce

Yakitori

Yakitori (skewers of charcoal-grilled chicken and vegetables) is a popular after-work meal. *Yakitori* is not so much a full meal as an accompaniment for beer and sake. At a *yakitori-ya* (*yakitori* restaurant) you sit around a counter with the other patrons and watch the chef grill your selections over charcoal. The best way to eat here is to order several varieties, then order seconds of the ones you really like. Ordering in these places can be a little confusing since one serving often means two or three skewers (be careful – the price listed on the menu is usually that of a single skewer).

In summer, the beverage of choice at a *yakitori* restaurant is beer or cold sake, while in winter it's hot sake. A few drinks and enough skewers to fill you up should cost ¥3000 to ¥4000 per person. *Yakitori* restaurants are usually small places, often located near train stations, and are best identified by a red lantern outside and the smell of grilled chicken.

hasami/negima	はさみ/ねぎま	pieces of white meat alternating with leek
kawa	皮	chicken skin
piiman	ピーマン	small green capsicums (peppers)

What's What in Japanese Restaurants: A Guide to Ordering, Eating and Enjoying (Robb Satterwhite) is a brilliant guide to Japanese restaurants. With thorough explanations of the various types of dishes and sample menus, this is a must for those who really want to explore and enjoy what's on offer.

Ōta Kazuhiko is considered by many to be Japan's leading authority on *izakaya*, Japan's beloved pub-eateries. Ōta-san travels the length of Japan seeking out the best traditional *izakaya* and he has published his findings in more than a dozen books, including one titled *Ōta Kazuhiko no Izakaya Mishuran*, the 'Mishuran' in the title being a play on the famed Michelin restaurant guide series.

What is the definition of an izakaya? Simply put, an *izakaya* is a place where you can enjoy sake. More broadly, an *izakaya* is a place where you can enjoy sake and food. In addition, they are places that you can easily enter alone.

What is the history of the izakaya? Prior to the Meiji period, *saka-ya* (sake shops) would serve alcohol to customers who dropped by for a drink. The customers would stand around and drink their sake out of *masu* (square wooden boxes used to measure sake). Thus, these places were *tachi-nomiya* (stand-and-drink places). Later, some *saka-ya* turned the sake barrels into seats for their customers, so they could relax and enjoy their drink. Thus, they became '*izakaya*' (the 'i' here means 'to be' which, added to *saka-ya*, forms *izakaya*, or a *saka-ya* where you can stay and drink). Later on, some places started to serve snacks to go with the sake, and this evolved into proper food to go with the sake.

What role did izakaya play in Japanese society? *Izakaya* played an important role in Japanese society. Traditionally, after men finished work at a company, they would go together to an *izakaya*. The older members of the group, or the boss, would often pay for the younger workers. While they drank, they could talk freely about work and also about things outside work, like their personal lives and their past. The older guys would teach the young ones how to drink, how to order, and also about the ways of the world. Thus, the *izakaya* served as a place of human and social education, not just drinking places.

What should you order in an izakaya? First of all, don't rush. Just have a look around. Maybe start with some *ginjō-shu* (a high-grade sake). Have the first one cold. Then, consider having some hot sake. As for food, seafood is the way to go: sashimi, stewed fish, grilled fish or shellfish. You can also try some chicken dishes. Have a look at what the other customers are eating, or check out the specials board. If you can't speak or read Japanese, you can point at things or bring along a Japanese friend to help you order.

Where can you find good izakaya? Well, there are lots of chain *izakaya* near the train stations in most cities, but the best place to look for really good ones is in the old *hanka-gai* (entertainment district), which is usually not where the train station is. The best places have been run for generations by the same family, and the customers have also been coming for generations. So, the master might have watched his customers grow up. These are the places that take pride in their work and are the most reliable.

What is the best thing about izakaya? *Izakaya* are places where people show their true selves, their true hearts. The sake allows people to drop their pretensions and let their hair down. *Izakaya* are places where people show their individuality. They bind people together, whether strangers or friends. I think all countries have a place like this, but in Japan, if you want to see the way people really are, the *izakaya* is the place to go.

rebā	レバー	chicken livers
sasami	ささみ	skinless chicken-breast pieces
shiitake	しいたけ	Japanese mushrooms
tama-negi	玉ねぎ	round white onions
tebasaki	手羽先	chicken wings
tsukune	つくね	chicken meatballs
yaki-onigiri	焼きおにぎり	a triangle of grilled rice with *yakitori* sauce

When you enter a restaurant in Japan, you'll be greeted with a hearty '*irasshaimase*' (Welcome!). In all but the most casual places the waiter will next ask you '*nan-mei sama*' (How many people?). Answer with your fingers, which is what the Japanese do. You will then be led to a table, a place at the counter or a tatami room.

At this point you will be given an *o-shibori* (a hot towel), a cup of tea and a menu. The *o-shibori* is for wiping your hands and face. When you're done with it, just roll it up and leave it next to your place. Now comes the hard part: ordering. If you don't read Japanese, you can use the romanisations and translations in this book to help you, or direct the waiter's attention to the Japanese script. If this doesn't work, there are two phrases that may help: '*o-susume wa nan desu ka*' (What do you recommend?) and '*o-makase shimasu*' (Please decide for me).

When you've finished eating, you can signal for the bill by crossing one index finger over the other to form the sign of an 'x'. This is the standard sign for 'Bill, please'. You can also say '*o-kanjō kudasai*'. Remember there is no tipping in Japan and tea is free of charge. Usually you will be given a bill to take to the cashier at the front of the restaurant. Only the bigger and more international places take credit cards, so cash is always the surer option.

When leaving, it is polite to say to the restaurant staff '*gochisō-sama deshita*', which means 'It was a real feast'.

Sushi & Sashimi

Like *yakitori*, sushi is considered an accompaniment for beer and sake. Nonetheless, both Japanese and foreigners often make a meal of it, and it's one of the healthiest meals around. All proper sushi restaurants serve their fish over rice, in which case it's called sushi; without rice, it's called sashimi or *tsukuri* (or, politely, *o-tsukuri*).

There are two main types of sushi: *nigiri-zushi* (served on a small bed of rice – the most common variety) and *maki-zushi* (served in a seaweed roll).

Sushi is not difficult to order. If you sit at the counter of a sushi restaurant you will be able to simply point at what you want, as most of the selections are visible in a refrigerated glass case between you and the sushi chef. You can also order à la carte from the menu (see the following sample menu). When ordering, you usually order *ichi-nin mae* (one portion), which normally means two pieces of sushi. Be careful, since the price on the menu will be that of only one piece.

If ordering à la carte is too daunting, you can take care of your whole order with just one or two words by ordering *mori-awase,* an assortment plate of *nigiri-zushi.* These usually come in three grades: *futsū nigiri* (regular *nigiri*), *jō nigiri* (special *nigiri*) and *toku-jō nigiri* (extra-special *nigiri*). The difference is in the type of fish used. Most *mori-awase* contain six or seven pieces of sushi.

Be warned that meals in a good sushi restaurant can cost upwards of ¥10,000, while an average establishment can run from ¥3000 to ¥5000 per person. One way to sample the joy of sushi on the cheap is to try an automatic sushi place, usually called *kaiten-zushi,* where the sushi is served on a conveyor belt that runs along a counter. Here you simply reach up and grab whatever looks good to you (which certainly takes the pain out of ordering). You are charged by the number of plates of sushi that you have eaten. Plates are colour-coded by their price and the cost is written either somewhere on the plate itself or on a sign on the wall. You can usually fill yourself up in one of these places for ¥1000 to ¥2000 per person.

The Japanese Ministry of Agriculture created a team a few years ago to assess the quality of Japanese restaurants abroad. The so-called 'Sushi Police' are intended to put a stop to third-rate restaurants serving poor imitations of real Japanese food. Does this spell the end of the California roll?

Before eating the sushi, dip it very lightly in *shōyu* (soy sauce), which you pour from a small decanter into a low dish specially provided for the purpose. If you're not good at using *hashi* (chopsticks), don't worry – sushi is one of the few foods in Japan that is perfectly acceptable to eat with your hands. Slices of *gari* (pickled ginger) are served to refresh the palate. The beverage of choice with sushi is beer or sake (hot in winter, cold in summer), with a green tea at the end of the meal.

Note that most of the items on this sample sushi menu can be ordered as sashimi. Just add the words '*no o-tsukuri*' to get the sashimi version (*o-tsukuri* is the more common Japanese expression for sashimi). So, for example, if you wanted some tuna sashimi, you would order '*maguro no o-tsukuri*'. Note that you'll often be served a different soy sauce to accompany your sashimi; if you like wasabi with your sashimi, you can add some directly to the soy sauce and stir.

Randy Johnson's 'Sushi a la Carte' (www.ease.com/~randyj/rjsushi.htm) is a must for sushi lovers – it explains everything you need to know about ordering and enjoying sushi.

ama-ebi	甘海老	sweet shrimp
awabi	あわび	abalone
ebi	海老	prawn or shrimp
hamachi	はまち	yellowtail
ika	いか	squid
ikura	イクラ	salmon roe
kai-bashira	貝柱	scallop
kani	かに	crab
katsuo	かつお	bonito
maguro	まぐろ	tuna
tai	鯛	sea bream
tamago	たまご	sweetened egg
toro	とろ	the choice cut of fatty tuna belly
unagi	うなぎ	eel with a sweet sauce
uni	うに	sea-urchin roe

Sukiyaki & Shabu-shabu

Restaurants usually specialise in both of these dishes. Popular in the West, sukiyaki is a favourite of most foreign visitors to Japan. Sukiyaki consists of thin slices of beef cooked in a broth of *shōyu*, sugar and sake, and accompanied by a variety of vegetables and tofu. After cooking, all the ingredients are dipped in raw egg before being eaten. When made with high-quality beef, such as Kōbe beef, it is a sublime experience.

Shabu-shabu consists of thin slices of beef and vegetables cooked by swirling the ingredients in a light broth, then dipping them in a variety of special sesame-seed and citrus-based sauces. Both of these dishes are prepared in a pot over a fire at your private table. Don't fret about preparation – the waiter will usually help you get started, and keep a close watch as you proceed. The key is to go slow, add the ingredients a little at a time and savour the flavours.

Sukiyaki and *shabu-shabu* restaurants usually have traditional Japanese decor and sometimes a picture of a cow to help you identify them. Ordering is not difficult. Simply say 'sukiyaki' or '*shabu-shabu*' and indicate how many people are dining. Expect to pay from ¥3000 to ¥10,000 per person.

Tempura

Tempura consists of portions of fish, prawns and vegetables cooked in a light batter. When you sit down at a tempura restaurant, you will be given a small bowl of *ten-tsuyu* (a light brown sauce) and a plate of grated *daikon* (Japanese radish) to mix into the sauce. Dip each piece of tempura into this sauce before eating it. Tempura is best when it's hot, so don't wait too long – use the sauce to cool each piece and dig in.

While it's possible to order à la carte, most diners choose to order *teishoku*, which includes rice, *misoshiru* and *tsukemono*. Some tempura restaurants offer courses that include different numbers of tempura pieces.

Expect to pay between ¥2000 and ¥10,000 for a full tempura meal. Finding these restaurants is tricky as they have no distinctive facade or decor. If you look through the window, you'll see customers around the counter watching the chefs as they work over large woks filled with oil.

kaki age	かき揚げ	tempura with shredded vegetables or fish
shōjin age	精進揚げ	vegetarian tempura
tempura moria-wase	天ぷら盛り合わせ	a selection of tempura

Rāmen

The Japanese imported this dish from China and put their own spin on it to make what is one of the world's most delicious fast foods. *Rāmen* dishes are big bowls of noodles in a meat broth, served with a variety of toppings, such as sliced pork, bean sprouts and leeks.

More than five billion servings of instant *rāmen* are consumed each year in Japan.

In some restaurants, particularly in Kansai, you may be asked if you'd prefer *kotteri* (thick and fatty) or *assari* (thin and light) soup. Other than this, ordering is simple: just sidle up to the counter and say *'rāmen'*, or ask for any of the other choices usually on offer (a list follows). Expect to pay between ¥500 and ¥900 for a bowl. Since *rāmen* is derived from Chinese cuisine, some *rāmen* restaurants also serve *chāhan* or *yaki-meshi* (both dishes are fried rice), *gyōza* (dumplings) and *kara-age* (deep-fried chicken pieces).

EATING ETIQUETTE

When it comes to eating in Japan, there are quite a number of implicit rules, but they're fairly easy to remember. If you're worried about putting your foot in it, relax – the Japanese don't expect you to know what to do, and they are unlikely to be offended as long as you follow the standard rules of politeness from your own country. Here are a few major points to keep in mind:

» **Chopsticks in rice** Do not stick your *hashi* (chopsticks) upright in a bowl of rice. This is how rice is offered to the dead in Buddhist rituals. On a similar note, do not pass food from your chopsticks to the chopsticks of someone else. This is another funeral ritual.

» **Polite expressions** When eating with other people, especially when you're a guest, it is polite to say *'itadakimasu'* (literally 'I will receive') before digging in. This is as close as the Japanese come to saying grace. Similarly, at the end of the meal, you should thank your host by saying *'gochisō-sama deshita'*, which means 'It was a real feast'.

» **Kampai** It is bad form to fill your own glass. You should fill the glass of the person next to you and wait for them to reciprocate. Raise your glass a little off the table while it is being filled. Once everyone's glass has been filled, the usual starting signal is a chorus of *'kampai'*, which means 'Cheers!'.

» **Slurp** When you eat noodles in Japan, it's perfectly OK, even expected, to slurp them. In fact, one of the best ways to find *rāmen* (egg noodle) restaurants in Japan is to listen for the loud slurping sound that comes out of them!

Ramen restaurants are easily distinguished by their long counters lined with customers hunched over steaming bowls. You can sometimes hear a *rāmen* shop as you wander by – it's considered polite to slurp the noodles and aficionados claim that slurping brings out the full flavour of the broth.

chāshū-men	チャーシュ一麺	*rāmen* topped with slices of roasted pork
miso-rāmen	みそラーメン	*rāmen* with miso-flavoured broth
rāmen	ラーメン	soup and noodles with a sprinkling of meat and vegetables
wantan-men	ワンタン麺	*rāmen* with meat dumplings

Soba & Udon

Soba (thin brown buckwheat noodles) and *udon* (thick white wheat noodles) are Japan's answer to Chinese-style *rāmen*. Most Japanese noodle shops serve both *soba* and *udon* in a variety of ways.

Noodles are usually served in a bowl containing a light, bonito-flavoured broth, but you can also order them served cold and piled onto a bamboo screen along with a cold broth for dipping the noodles (this is called *zaru soba*). If you order *zaru soba*, you will additionally receive a small plate of wasabi and sliced spring onions – you put these into the cup of broth and then eat the noodles by dipping them into this mixture. When you have finished your noodles, the waiter will give you some hot broth to mix with the leftover sauce, which you drink like a kind of tea. As with *rāmen*, you should feel free to slurp as loudly as you please.

Soba and *udon* places are usually quite cheap (about ¥800 a dish), but some fancy places can be significantly more expensive (the decor is a good indication of the price).

The superb Tokyo Food Page (www. bento.com) offers explanations of Japanese dishes, great places to eat in Tokyo and much, much more.

kake soba/udon	かけそば/うどん	*soba/udon* noodles in broth
kitsune soba/udon	きつねそば/うどん	*soba/udon* noodles with fried tofu
tempura soba/udon	天ぷらそば/うどん	*soba/udon* noodles with tempura prawns
tsukimi soba/udon	月見そば/うどん	*soba/udon* noodles with raw egg

Unagi

Unagi (eel) is an expensive and popular delicacy in Japan. Even if you can't stand the creature when it's served in your home country – or if you've never tried it – you owe it to yourself to try *unagi* at least once while you're visiting Japan. *Unagi* is cooked over hot coals and brushed with a rich sauce of *shōyu* and sake. Full *unagi* dinners can be expensive, but many *unagi* restaurants also offer *unagi bentō* (boxed meals) and lunch sets for around ¥1500. Most *unagi* restaurants display plastic models of their sets in their front windows, and may have barrels of live eels to entice passers-by.

kabayaki	蒲焼き	skewers of grilled eel without rice
una-don	うな丼	grilled eel over a bowl of rice
unagi teishoku	うなぎ定食	full-set *unagi* meal with rice, grilled eel, eel-liver soup and pickles
unajū	うな重	grilled eel over a flat tray of rice

MUSHROOMS

The highly prized Japanese *matsutake* mushroom can sell for up to US$2000 per kilogram.

Tonkatsu

Tonkatsu is a deep-fried breaded pork cutlet that is served with a special sauce, usually as part of a set meal *(tonkatsu teishoku)*. *Tonkatsu* is served both at speciality restaurants and at *shokudō*. Naturally, the best *tonkatsu* is to be found at the speciality places, where a full set will cost ¥1500 to ¥2500. When ordering *tonkatsu*, you are able to choose between *rōsu* (a fatter cut of pork) and *hire* (a leaner cut).

hire katsu	ヒレかつ	tonkatsu fillet
tonkatsu teishoku	とんかつ定食	a set meal of tonkatsu, rice, misoshiru and shredded cabbage

Okonomiyaki

Sometimes described as Japanese pizza or pancake, the resemblance is in form only. Actually, *okonomiyaki* are various forms of batter and cabbage cakes cooked on a griddle.

At an *okonomiyaki* restaurant you sit around a *teppan* (iron hotplate), armed with a spatula and chopsticks to cook your choice of meat, seafood and vegetables in a cabbage and vegetable batter.

Some restaurants will do most of the cooking and bring the nearly finished product over to your hotplate for you to season with *katsuo bushi* (bonito flakes), *shōyu*, *ao-nori* (an ingredient similar to parsley), Japanese Worcestershire-style sauce and mayonnaise. Cheaper places, however, will simply hand you a bowl filled with the ingredients and expect you to cook it for yourself. If this happens, don't panic. First, mix the batter and filling thoroughly, then place it on the hotplate, flattening it into a pancake shape. After five minutes or so, use the spatula to flip it and cook for another five minutes. Then dig in.

Most *okonomiyaki* places also serve *yaki-soba* (fried noodles with meat and vegetables) and *yasai-itame* (stir-fried vegetables). All of this is washed down with mugs of draught beer.

One final word: don't worry too much about preparation of the food – as a foreigner you will be expected to be awkward, and the waiter will keep a sharp eye on you to make sure no real disasters occur.

gyū okonomiyaki	牛お好み焼き	beef okonomiyaki
ika okonomiyaki	いかお好み焼き	squid okonomiyaki
mikkusu	ミックスお好み焼き	mixed fillings of seafood, okonomiyaki meat and vegetables
modan-yaki	モダン焼き	okonomiyaki with yaki-soba and a fried egg
negi okonomiyaki	ネギお好み焼き	thin okonomiyaki with spring onions

Kaiseki

Kaiseki is the pinnacle of Japanese cuisine, where ingredients, preparation, setting and presentation come together to create a dining experience quite unlike any other. Born as an adjunct to the tea ceremony, *kaiseki* is a largely vegetarian affair (though fish is often served, meat never appears on the *kaiseki* menu). One usually eats *kaiseki* in the private room of a *ryōtei* (an especially elegant style of traditional restaurant), often overlooking a private, tranquil garden. The meal is served in several small courses, giving the diner an opportunity to admire the plates and bowls, which are carefully chosen to complement the food and season. Rice is eaten last (usually with an assortment of pickles) and the drink of choice is sake or beer.

All meals involving Kōbe beef should come with the following label: warning, consuming this beef will ruin your enjoyment of any other type of beef. We're not kidding, it's that good.

The first thing you should know about Kōbe beef is how to pronounce it: 'ko-bay' (rhymes with 'no way'). In Japanese, Kōbe beef is known as Kōbe-gyū. Second, Kōbe beef is actually just one regional variety of *wa-gyū* (literally 'Japanese beef'). *Wa-gyū* can be any of several breeds of cattle bred for the extreme fatty marbling of their meat (the most common breed is Japanese Black). Kōbe beef is simply *wa-gyū* raised in Hyogō-ken, the prefecture in which the city of Kōbe is located.

There are many urban legends about Kōbe beef – promulgated, we suppose, by the farmers who raise them, or simply imaginative individuals who ascribe to cows the lives they'd like to lead. It is commonly believed that Kōbe-beef cattle spend their days drinking beer and receiving regular massages. However, in all our days in Japan, we have never seen a single drunk cow or met a 'cow masseur'. More likely, the marbling pattern of the beef is the result of selective breeding and the cow's diet of alfalfa, corn, barley and wheat straw.

The best way to enjoy Kōbe beef, or any other type of *wa-gyū*, is cooked on a *teppan* (iron hotplate) at a *wa-gyū* specialist, and these restaurants are known as *teppan-yaki-ya*. In the West, a giant steak that hangs off the side of the plate is generally considered a good thing. But due to the intense richness (and price) of a good *wa-gyū* steak, it is usually consumed in relatively small portions – say, smaller than the size of your hand. The meat is usually seared quickly, then cooked to medium rare – cooking a piece of good *wa-gyū* to well done is something akin to making a tuna-fish sandwich from the best cut of *toro* (fatty tuna belly) sashimi.

Although Kōbe beef and *wa-gyū* are now all the rage in Western cities, like most Japanese food, the real thing consumed in Japan is far superior to what is available overseas. And – surprise, surprise – it can be cheaper to eat it in Japan than overseas. You can get a fine *wa-gyū* steak course at lunch for around ¥5000, and at dinner for around double that. Of course, the best place for Kōbe beef is – you got it – Kōbe. See p322 for some of our picks.

All this comes at a steep price – a good *kaiseki* dinner costs upwards of ¥10,000 per person. A cheaper way to sample the delights of *kaiseki* is to visit a *kaiseki* restaurant for lunch. Most places offer a boxed lunch containing a sampling of their dinner fare for around ¥2500.

You can enter *kaiseki* places at lunchtime without a reservation, but you should ask your hotel or ryokan to call ahead to make arrangements for dinner.

bentō	弁当	boxed meal, usually of rice, with a main dish and pickles or salad
kaiseki	懐石	traditional, Kyoto-style haute cuisine
matsu	松	extra-special course
take	竹	special course
ume	梅	regular course

The most important Shintō deity is Inari, the god of the rice harvest.

Sweets

Although most restaurants don't serve dessert (plates of sliced fruit are sometimes served at the end of a meal), there is no lack of sweets in Japan. Most Japanese sweets (known generically as *wagashi*) are sold in speciality stores for you to eat at home. Many of the more delicate-looking ones are made to balance the strong, bitter taste of the special *matcha* (powdered green tea) served during the tea ceremony.

JAPANESE CUISINE DRINKS

TASTY TRAVEL

There's one word every food lover should learn before coming to Japan: *meibutsu*. It means 'speciality', as in regional speciality, and despite its small size Japan has loads of them. In fact, it never hurts to simply ask for the *meibutsu* when you order at a restaurant or *izakaya* (pub-eatery). More often than not, you'll be served something memorable. Here are some of Japan's more famous local specialities.

» **Hiroshima** *kaki* (oysters); *Hiroshima-yaki,* which is Hiroshima-style *okonomiyaki* (batter and cabbage cakes cooked on a griddle)

» **Hokkaidō** *kani-ryōri* (crab cuisine); salmon

» **Kyoto** *kaiseki* (Japanese haute cuisine); *wagashi* (Japanese traditional sweets); *yuba* (the skim off the top of tofu, or soymilk skin); *Kyō-yasai* (Kyoto-style vegetables)

» **Kyūshū** *tonkotsu-rāmen* (pork-broth *rāmen*); *Satsuma-imo* (sweet potatoes)

» **Northern Honshū** *wanko-soba* (eat-till-you-burst *soba*); *jappa-jiru* (cod soup with Japanese radish and miso)

» **Okinawa** *gōya champurū* (bitter melon stir-fry); *sōki-soba* (rāmen with spare ribs); *mimiga* (pickled pigs' ears)

» **Osaka** *tako-yaki* (battered octopus pieces); *okonomiyaki*

» **Shikoku** *sansai* (wild mountain vegetables); *Sanuki-udon* (a type of wheat noodles); *katsuo tataki* (lightly seared bonito)

» **Tokyo** sushi

Some Westerners find Japanese sweets a little challenging, due to the liberal use of a sweet, red *azuki*-bean paste called *anko*. This unusual filling turns up in even the most innocuous-looking pastries. The next main ingredient is often pounded sticky rice *(mochi)*, which has a consistency that is unfamiliar to many Westerners.

With such a wide variety of sweets, it's impossible to list all the names. However, you'll probably find many variations on the *anko*-covered-by-*mochi* theme.

Okashi-ya (sweet shops) are easy to spot; they usually have open fronts with their wares laid out in wooden trays to entice passers-by. Buying sweets is simple – just point at what you want and indicate with your fingers how many you'd like.

The Tsukiji Fish Market in Tokyo is the world's largest. It handles 2246 tonnes of marine products a day (more than 450 kinds of fish!).

anko	あんこ	sweet paste or jam made from *azuki* beans
kashiwa-mochi	柏餅	pounded glutinous rice with a sweet filling, wrapped in an aromatic oak leaf
mochi	餅	pounded rice cakes made of glutinous rice
wagashi	和菓子	Japanese-style sweets
yōkan	ようかん	sweet red-bean jelly

Drinks

Drinking plays a big role in Japanese society, and there are few social occasions where beer or sake is not served. Alcohol (in this case sake) also plays a ceremonial role in various Shintō festivals and rites, including the marriage ceremony. As a visitor to Japan, you'll probably find yourself in lots of situations where you are invited to drink, and tipping back a few beers or glasses of sake is a great way to get to know the locals. However, if you don't drink alcohol, it's no big deal. Simply order *oolong cha* (oolong tea) in place of beer or sake. While some folks might put pressure on you to drink alcohol, you can diffuse this pressure by saying '*sake o nomimasen*' (I don't drink alcohol).

What you pay for your drink depends on where you drink and, in the case of hostess bars, with whom you drink. Hostess bars are the most expensive places to drink (up to ¥10,000 per drink), followed by upmarket traditional Japanese bars, hotel bars, beer halls and casual pubs. If you are not sure about a place, ask about prices and cover charges before sitting down. As a rule, if you are served a small snack (called *o-tsumami*, or 'charm') with your first round, you'll be paying a cover charge (usually a few hundred yen, but sometimes much more).

Izakaya (p700) and *yakitori-ya* (p700) are cheap places for beer, sake and food in a casual atmosphere resembling that of a pub. All Japanese cities, whether large or small, will have a few informal bars with reasonable prices. These are popular with young Japanese and resident *gaijin* (foreigners), who usually refer to such places as *gaijin* bars. In summer, many department stores and hotels in Japan's big cities open up beer gardens on the roof. Many of these places offer all-you-can-eat/drink specials for around ¥3000 per person.

The Insider's Guide to Sake (Philip Harper) offers a fine introduction to sake, including information on how to choose a good sake and the history of the drink.

SAKE

Beer

Introduced at the end of the 1800s, *biiru* (beer) is now the favourite tipple of the Japanese. The quality is generally excellent and the most popular type is light lager, although recently some breweries have been experimenting with darker brews. The major breweries are Kirin, Asahi, Sapporo and Suntory. Beer is dispensed everywhere, from vending machines to beer halls, and even in some temple lodgings. A standard can of beer from a vending machine is about ¥250, although some of the gigantic cans cost more than ¥1000. At bars, a beer starts at ¥500 and the price climbs upwards, depending on the establishment. *Nama biiru* (draught beer) is widely available, as are imported beers.

biiru	ビール	beer
biniru	瓶ビール	bottled beer
nama biiru	生ビール	draught beer

Shōchū

For those looking for a quick and cheap escape route from the sorrows of the world, *shōchū* is the answer. It's a distilled spirit made from a variety of raw materials, including potato (in which case it's called *imo-jōchū*) and barley (in which case it's called *mugi-jōchū*). It's quite strong, with an alcohol content of about 30%. In recent years it has been resurrected from its previous lowly status (it was used as a disinfectant in the Edo period) to become a trendy drink. You can drink it *oyu-wari* (with hot water) or *chūhai* (in a highball with soda and lemon). A 720mL bottle sells for about ¥600, which makes it a relatively cheap option compared with other spirits.

chūhai	チューハイ	shōchū with soda and lemon
oyu-wari	お湯割り	shōchū with hot water
shōchū	焼酎	distilled grain liquor

Nonalcoholic Drinks

Most of the drinks you're used to at home will be available in Japan, with a few colourfully named additions like Pocari Sweat and Calpis Water. One convenient aspect of Japan is the presence of drink-vending machines on virtually every street corner, and at ¥120, refreshment is rarely more than a few steps away.

Brewed from rice, sake has been enjoyed for centuries in Japan, and although it has been overtaken in terms of consumption by beer and *shōchū* (distilled grain liquor) in recent years, it is still regarded by most Japanese people as the national drink. Indeed, what we call 'sake' in the West is more commonly known as *nihonshu* in Japan: the 'drink of Japan'. Sake has traditionally been associated with Shintō and other traditional ceremonies, and you will still be able to see huge barrels of sake (known as *o-miki*) on display at almost every shrine you visit. Although consumption has been on the wane in recent years, it is generally agreed that the quality of sake available is better than ever, and many of the best have a complexity of flavours and aromas comparable to the fine wines and beers of Europe.

Not surprisingly, sake makes the perfect accompaniment to traditional Japanese food, and sake pubs (see *izakaya*, p700) generally also serve excellent seasonal fish and other foods to go with the booze. Sake is drunk chilled (*reishu*), at room temperature (*jō-on*), warmed (*nuru-kan*) or piping hot (*atsu-kan*), according to the season and personal preference. The top-drawer stuff is normally served well chilled. Sake is traditionally served in a ceramic jug known as a *tokkuri*, and poured into tiny cups known as *o-choko* or *sakazuki*. A traditional measure of sake is one *gō* (一合) – a little over 180mL, or 6 fluid oz. In speciality bars, you will have the option of ordering by the glass, which will often be filled to overflowing and brought to you in a wooden container to catch the overspill. If you're in company, the tradition is to pour for your neighbour first, then be waited on by them in turn.

Sake is always brewed during the winter, in the cold months that follow the rice harvest in September. The main ingredients of sake are rice and yeast, together with a benign mould known as *kōji* that helps to convert the starch in the rice into fermentable sugars. Sake is categorised by law into two main classes: *futsū-shu* (ordinary sake, which makes up the bulk of what is currently produced), and premium sake (known as *tokutei-meishōshu*), which is further classified by the extent to which the rice is refined before fermentation to remove proteins and oils that interfere with the flavour of the final product. This is generally shown on the label as the *seimai buai*, expressed as the percentage of the original size to which the grain is reduced by polishing before the brewing process starts. As a general rule, the lower this number, the better (or at least, the more expensive) the sake will be. Sake made from rice kernels with 40% to 50% of their original volume polished away is known as *ginjō*. Sake made from rice kernels with 50% or more of their original volume polished away is known as *dai-ginjō*. It is believed that sake made from the inner portion of the rice kernel is the smoothest and most delicious of all. Sake made only with rice and *kōji* (without the use of added alcohol) is known as *junmai-shu*, (pure rice) sake.

Coffee & Tea

Kōhii (coffee) served in a *kissaten* (coffee shop) tends to be expensive in Japan, costing between ¥350 and ¥500 a cup, with some places charging up to ¥1000. For a caffeine fix, a cheap alternative is one of the coffee-restaurant chains like Doutor or Pronto, or doughnut shops like Mr Donut (which offers free coffee refills). An even cheaper alternative than these is a can of coffee, hot or cold, purchased from a vending machine. Although unpleasantly sweet, at ¥120 the price is hard to beat.

In 1997 there were 44 cases of poisoning from eating improperly prepared *fugu* (globefish or pufferfish), resulting in three fatalities.

When ordering coffee at a coffee shop in Japan, you will be asked whether you would like it *hotto* (hot) or *aisu* (cold). Black tea also comes hot or cold, and served with *miruku* (milk) or *remon* (lemon). A good way to start a day of sightseeing in Japan is with a *mōningu setto* (morning set) of tea or coffee, toast and eggs, which generally costs around ¥400.

Sake is brewed in every prefecture in Japan – with the single exception of Kagoshima in southern Kyūshū, the traditional stronghold of the distilled drink known as *shōchū* (see p709) – and there are more than 1500 breweries in operation today. Niigata and other parts of Northern Honshū are particularly famous for the quality of their sake, with Hiroshima and Nada-ku (in Kōbe) also major centres of the brewing industry. Almost everywhere you go in Japan you will have an opportunity to drink sake brewed just a few kilometres from where you are staying. A foreign visitor who shows an interest in the *jizake* (local brew) is likely to be treated to enthusiastic recommendations and the kind of hospitality that has been known to lead to sore heads the next morning.

ama-kuchi	甘口	sweet flavour
ama-zake	甘酒	sweet sake served at winter festivals
dai-ginjō	大吟醸	sake made from rice kernels with 50% or more of their original volume polished away
futsū-shu	普通酒	ordinary sake
genshu	原酒	undiluted sake, often with an alcohol content close to 20%
ginjō	吟醸	sake made from rice kernels with 40% to 50% of their original volume polished away
jizake	地酒	'local sake', often from small, traditional breweries
junmai-shu	純米酒	'pure rice' sake, made from only rice, *kōji* and water
kara-kuchi	辛口	dry, sharp flavour
kōji	麹	the mould that helps to convert the starch in the rice into fermentable sugars
kura/saka-gura	蔵/酒蔵	sake brewery
nama-zake	生酒	fresh, unpasteurised sake
nigori-zake	濁り酒	milky-white 'cloudy sake', often rather sweet
nihonshu	日本酒	Japanese word for 'sake'
o-choko	お猪口	small cups traditionally used for sake
seimai buai	精米歩合	the percentage of the original size to which the grain is reduced by polishing before the brewing process starts
tokkuri	德利	traditional ceramic serving vessel
tokutei-meishōshu	特定名称酒	premium sake

American kōhii	アメリカンコーヒー	weak coffee
burendo kōhii	ブレンドコーヒー	blended coffee, fairly strong
kafe ore	カフェオレ	*cafe au lait*, hot or cold
kōcha	紅茶	black English tea
kōhii	コーヒー	regular coffee
orenji jūsu	オレンジジュース	orange juice

Japanese Tea

Unlike black tea, which Westerners are familiar with, most Japanese tea is green and contains a lot of vitamin C and caffeine. The powdered form used in the tea ceremony is called *matcha* and is drunk after being whipped into a frothy consistency. The more common form, a leafy green tea, is simply called *o-cha,* and is drunk after being steeped in a pot. In addition to green tea, you'll probably drink a lot of a brownish tea called *bancha,* which restaurants serve for free. In summer, a cold beverage called *mugicha* (roasted barley tea) is served in private homes.

bancha	番茶	ordinary-grade green tea, with a brownish colour
matcha	抹茶	powdered green tea used in the tea ceremony
mugicha	麦茶	roasted barley tea
o-cha	お茶	leafy green tea
sencha	煎茶	medium-grade green tea

Vegetarians & Vegans

Travellers who eat fish should have almost no trouble dining in Japan: almost all *shokudō, izakaya* and other common restaurants offer a set meal with fish as the main dish. Vegans and vegetarians who don't eat fish will have to get their protein from tofu and other bean products. Note that most *misoshiru* is made with *dashi* broth that contains fish, so if you want to avoid fish, you'll also have to avoid *misoshiru.*

Most big cities in Japan have vegetarian and/or organic restaurants which naturally serve a variety of choices that appeal to vegetarians and vegans. (See the Eating sections of the destination chapters for specific recommendations. Reviews that include the symbol ✍ throughout this guide indicate places with a good vegetarian selection.)

In the countryside, you'll have to do your best to find suitable items on the menu, or try to convey your dietary preferences to the restaurant staff. Note that many temples in Japan serve *shōjin-ryōri* (Buddhist vegetarian cuisine), which is made without meat, fish or dairy products. A good place to try this is Kōya-san (p350) in Kansai.

For some ways to express your dietary preferences to restaurant staff, see the Language chapter (p767).

Cooking Courses

If you enjoy the food in Japan, why not deepen your appreciation of Japanese cuisine by taking a cooking class? There are good cooking courses available in both Tokyo (p84) and Kyoto (p280). Market tours can be arranged through **Uzuki** (www.kyotouzuki.com; 3hr-class per person ¥4000) – reserve via the website, and you can learn how to cook typical Japanese dishes in a Kyoto home, or even request specific dishes, including Japanese sweets.

The average Japanese person consumes 58 kg of rice per year.

RICE

Arts & Architecture

Arts

Traditional Visual Art
Painting

From 794 to 1600, Japanese painting borrowed from Chinese and Western techniques and media, ultimately transforming them into its own aesthetic ends. By the beginning of the Edo period (1600–1868), which was marked by the enthusiastic patronage of a wide range of painting styles, Japanese art had come completely into its own. The Kanō school, initiated more than a century before the beginning of the Edo era, continued to be in demand for its depiction of subjects connected with Confucianism, mythical Chinese creatures or scenes from nature. The Tosa school, which followed the *yamato-e* style of painting (often used on scrolls during the Heian period, 794–1185), was also kept busy with commissions from the nobility, who were eager to see scenes re-created from classics of Japanese literature.

The Rimpa school (from 1600) not only absorbed the styles of painting that had preceded it, but progressed beyond well-worn conventions to produce a strikingly decorative and delicately shaded form of painting. The works of art produced by a trio of outstanding artists from this school – Tawaraya Sōtatsu, Hon'ami Kōetsu and Ogata Kōrin – rank among the finest of this period.

Calligraphy

Shodō (the way of writing) is one of Japan's most valued arts, cultivated by nobles, priests and samurai alike, and still studied by Japanese schoolchildren today as *shūji*. Like the characters of the Japanese script, the art of *shodō* was imported from China. In the Heian period, a fluid, cursive, distinctly Japanese style of *shodō* evolved that was called *wayō*, though the Chinese style remained popular in Japan among Zen priests and the literati for some time.

In both Chinese and Japanese *shodō* there are three important types. Most common is *kaisho* (block-style script). Due to its clarity this style is favoured in the media and in applications where readability is key. *Gyōsho* (running hand), is semicursive and often used in informal correspondence. *Sōsho* (grass hand) is a truly cursive style. *Sōsho* abbreviates and links the characters together to create a flowing, graceful effect.

Ukiyo-e (Woodblock Prints)

The term *ukiyo-e* means 'pictures of the floating world' and derives from a Buddhist metaphor for the transient world of fleeting pleasures. The

HIROSHIGE

Hiroshige, noted for many collections of *ukiyo-e* prints including *One Hundred Famous View of Edo*, was a firefighter by trade, though he later retired to become a Buddhist monk.

subjects chosen by artists for these woodblock prints were characters and scenes from the tawdry, vivacious 'floating world' of the entertainment quarters in Edo (latter-day Tokyo), Kyoto and Osaka.

The floating world, centred on pleasure districts, such as Edo's Yoshiwara, was a topsy-turvy kingdom, an inversion of the usual social hierarchies that were held in place by the power of the Tokugawa shōgunate. Here, money meant more than rank, while actors and artists were the arbiters of style, and prostitutes elevated their art to such a level that their accomplishments matched those of the women of noble families.

The vivid colours, novel composition and flowing lines of *ukiyo-e* caused great excitement in the West, sparking a vogue that one French art critic dubbed 'Japonisme'. *Ukiyo-e* became a key influence on Impressionists (for example, Toulouse-Lautrec, Manet and Degas) and post-Impressionists. Among the Japanese the prints were hardly given more than passing consideration – millions were produced annually in Edo. They were often thrown away or used as wrapping paper for pottery. For many years, the Japanese continued to be perplexed by the keen interest foreigners took in this art form, which they considered of ephemeral value.

Ceramics

Ceramics are Japan's oldest art form: Jōmon pottery, with its distinctive cordlike decorative patterns, has been dated back some 15,000 years. When the Jōmon people were displaced by the Yayoi people, starting around 400 BC, a more refined style of pottery appeared on the scene. While Jōmon pottery was an indigenous Japanese form, Yayoi pottery had clear Continental influences and techniques. Continental techniques and even artisans continued to dominate Japanese ceramic arts for the next millennia or more: around the 5th century AD Sue Ware pottery was introduced from Korea, and around the 7th century Tang Chinese pottery became influential.

WABI-SABI

No, it isn't the spicy green stuff you eat with your sushi; *wabi-sabi* is one of the fundamental visual principles that governs the traditional Japanese idea of beauty. It's a rather lofty concept – most scholars argue that it's undefinable using the English lexicon – but we're gonna take a stab at it anyway. The idea of *wabi-sabi* is an aesthetic that embraces the notion of ephemerality and imperfection as it relates to all facets of Japanese culture.

The term *wabi-sabi* comes from the Japanese *wabi* and (you guessed it) *sabi* – both with quite convoluted definitions. *Wabi* roughly means 'rustic' and connotes the loneliness of the wilderness, while *sabi* can be interpreted as 'weathered', 'waning' or 'altered with age' (so it's no surprise that the Japanese word for 'rust' is also *sabi*). Together the two words signify an object's natural imperfections that arise during its inception and the acknowledgement that the object will evolve as it confronts mortality.

This penchant for impermanence and incompleteness transcends Japanese visual culture from the fragrant cherry blossoms that bloom in spring, to the slightly asymmetric *Hagi-yaki* pottery, but is perhaps most palpable in landscape design and traditional architecture. Japanese teahouses are the paradigm of nuance, and reflect the *wabi-sabi* motifs with their natural construction materials, handmade ceramics and manicured gardens.

Although the origins of *wabi-sabi* can be traced back to ancient Buddhism, these aesthetic ideals are still present in modern Japan and can even be found throughout the imaginative cityscapes we see today.

In the medieval period Japan's great ceramic centre was Seto in Central Honshū. Here, starting in the 12th century, Japanese potters took Chinese forms and adapted them to Japanese tastes and needs to produce a truly distinctive pottery style known as Seto Ware. One Japanese term for pottery and porcelain, *setomono* (literally 'things from Seto'), clearly derives from this still-thriving ceramics centre.

Today, there are more than 100 pottery centres in Japan, with scores of artisans producing everything from exclusive tea utensils to souvenir folklore creatures. Department stores regularly organise exhibitions of ceramics and offer the chance to see some of this fine work up close.

Shikki (Lacquerware)

The Japanese have been using lacquer to protect and enhance the beauty of wood since the Jōmon period (13,000–400 BC). In the Meiji era (1868–1912), lacquerware became very popular abroad and it remains one of Japan's best-known products. Known in Japan as *shikki* or *nurimono*, lacquerware is made using the sap from the lacquer tree *(urushi)*, a close relative of poison oak. Raw lacquer is actually toxic and causes severe skin irritation in those who have not developed immunity. Once hardened, however, it becomes inert and extraordinarily durable.

The most common colour of lacquer is amber or brown, but additives have been used to produce black, violet, blue, yellow and even white lacquer. In the better pieces, multiple layers of lacquer are painstakingly applied and left to dry, and finally polished to a luxurious shine.

The screen paintings of Hasegawa Tohaku, created almost 400 years ago, are said to be the first examples of impressionist art.

Contemporary Visual Art

In the years that followed WWII, Japanese artists struggled with issues of identity. This was the generation that grappled with duelling philosophies: 'Japanese spirit, Japanese knowledge' versus 'Japanese spirit, Western knowledge'. This group was known for exploring whether Western artistic media and methods could convey the space, light, substance and shadows of the Japanese spirit, or if this essence could only truly be expressed through traditional Japanese artistic genres.

Today's emerging artists and movements have no such ambivalence. Gone is the anxiety about coopting, or being coopted by, Western philosophies and aesthetics; in its place is the insouciant celebration of the smooth, cool surface of the future articulated by fantastic colours and shapes. This exuberant, devil-may-care aesthetic is most notably represented by Takashi Murakami, whose work derives much of its energy from *otaku*, the geek culture which worships characters that figure prominently in manga, Japan's ubiquitous comic books (a good introduction to the art of manga is the Kyoto International Manga Museum; see p255). Murakami's spirited, prankish images and installations have become emblematic of the Japanese aesthetic known as *poku* (a concept that combines pop art with an *otaku* sensibility), and his *Super Flat Manifesto*, which declares that 'the world of the future might be like Japan is today – super flat', can be seen as a primer for contemporary Japanese pop aesthetics.

Beyond the pop scene, artists continue to create works whose textures and topics relay a world that is broader than the frames of a comic book. Three notable artists to look for are Yoshie Sakai, whose ethereal oil paintings, replete with pastel skies and deep waters, leave the viewer unsure whether they are floating or sinking; Noriko Ambe, whose sculptural works with paper can resemble sand dunes shifting in the Sahara, or your high-school biology textbook; and the indomitable Hisashi Tenmyouya, whose work chronicles the themes of contemporary Japanese life, echoing the flat surfaces and deep impressions of wood-block prints while singing a song of the street.

HASEGAWA TOHAKU

Traditional Theatre & Dance

Nō

Nō is a hypnotic dance-drama that reflects the minimalist aesthetics of Zen. The movement is glorious, the chorus and music sonorous, the expression subtle. A sparsely furnished cedar stage directs full attention to the performers, who include a chorus, drummers and a flautist. There are two principal characters: the *shite*, who is sometimes a living person but more often a demon, or a ghost whose soul cannot rest; and the *waki*, who leads the main character towards the play's climactic moment. Each nō school has its own repertoire, and the art form continues to evolve and develop.

The breathtakingly haunting masks of nō theatre always depict female or nonhuman characters; adult male characters are played without masks.

Kabuki

The first performances of kabuki were staged early in the 17th century by an all-female troupe. The performances were highly erotic and attracted enthusiastic support from the merchant class. In true bureaucratic fashion, Tokugawa officials feared for the people's morality and banned women from the stage in 1629. Since that time, kabuki has been performed exclusively by men, giving rise to the institution of *onnagata*, or *ōyama* – male actors who specialise in female roles.

Over the course of several centuries, kabuki has developed a repertoire that draws on popular themes, such as famous historical accounts and stories of love-suicide, while also borrowing copiously from nō, *kyōgen* (comic vignettes) and *bunraku* (classical puppet theatre). Most kabuki plays border on melodrama, although they vary in mood.

Formalised beauty and stylisation are the central aesthetic principles of kabuki; the acting is a combination of dancing and speaking in conventionalised intonation patterns, and each actor prepares for a role by studying and emulating the style perfected by his predecessors. Kabuki actors are born into the art form, and training begins in childhood. Today, they enjoy great social prestige and their activities on and off the stage attract as much interest as those of popular film and TV stars.

Tokyo's main kabuki venue, Kabuki-za, is closed for renovation until 2013. Shinbashi Enbujyō, in the Ginza area, is currently the main place to check out the traditional Japanese theatrics.

Bunraku

Japan's traditional puppet theatre developed at the same time as kabuki, when the *shamisen* (a three-stringed instrument resembling a lute or a banjo), imported from Okinawa, was combined with traditional puppetry techniques and *joruri* (narrative chanting). *Bunraku,* as it came to be known in the 19th century, addresses many of the same themes as kabuki; in fact many famous plays in the kabuki repertoire were originally written for puppet theatre. *Bunraku* involves large puppets – nearly two-thirds life-sized – manipulated by up to three black-robed puppeteers. The puppeteers do not speak; a seated narrator tells the story and provides character voices and emotions. One of the best places to see *bunraku* is at Osaka's National Bunraku Theatre (p316).

Rakugo

A traditional Japanese style of comic monologue, *rakugo* (literally 'dropped word') dates back to the Edo period. The performer, usually in kimono, sits on a square cushion on a stage. Props are limited to a fan and hand towel. The monologue begins with a *makura* (prologue), which is followed by the story itself and, finally, the *ochi* (punch line or 'drop', which is another pronunciation of the Chinese character for *raku* in *rakugo*). Many of the monologues in the traditional *rakugo* repertoire date back to the Edo and Meiji periods and, while well known, reflect a social milieu unknown to modern listeners. Accordingly, many practitioners today also write new monologues addressing issues relevant to contemporary life.

Manzai

Manzai is a comic dialogue, with its origins in the song-and-dance and comedy routines traditionally performed by itinerant entertainers. It is a highly fluid art that continues to draw large audiences to hear snappy duos exchange clever witticisms on up-to-the-minute themes from everyday life. Much of the humour derives from wordplay and double entendre. Needless to say, much of this will be lost on anyone but a truly fluent Japanese speaker. Still, if you'd like to see a performance, check journals like the *Japan Times, Metropolis* or the *Tokyo Journal* in Tokyo, or *Kansai Time Out* in Kansai, or ask at a local tourist information office.

Contemporary Theatre & Dance

Contemporary theatre and dance are alive and well in Japan, though you'll quickly notice that most major troupes are based in Tokyo (p106).

Underground Theatre

Theatre the world over spent the 1960s redefining itself, and it was no different in Japan. The *shōgekijō* movement, also called *angura* (underground), has given Japan many of its leading playwrights, directors and actors. It arose as a reaction to the realism and structure of *shingeki* (a 1920s movement that borrowed heavily from Western dramatic forms), and featured surrealistic plays that explored the relationship between human beings and the world. Like their counterparts in the West, these productions took place in any space available – in small theatres, tents, basements, open spaces and street corners.

The first generation of *shōgekijō* directors and writers often included speedy comedy, wordplay and images from popular culture in their works to highlight the lunacy of modern life. More recent *shōgekijō* productions have dealt with realistic and contemporary themes, such as modern Japanese history, war, environmental degradation and social oppression. Changing cultural perceptions have propelled the movement in new directions, notably towards socially and politically critical dramas.

Tokyo Art Beat (www.tokyoart beat.com) is a bilingual art and design guide, with a regularly updated list of events.

Butoh

In many ways, butoh is Japan's most accessible (there are no words except for the occasional grunt) and exciting dance form. It is also its newest dance form, dating only from 1959, when Hijikata Tatsumi (1928–86) gave the first butoh performance. Butoh was born out of a rejection of the excessive formalisation that characterises traditional forms of Japanese dance. It also stems from the desire to return to the ancient roots of the Japanese soul, and is therefore also a rejection of Western influences that flooded Japan in the postwar years.

Displays of butoh are best likened to performance-art happenings rather than traditional dance performances. During a butoh performance, one or more dancers use their naked or seminaked bodies to express the most elemental and intense human emotions. Nothing is sacred in butoh, and performances often deal with topics such as sexuality and death. For this reason, critics often describe butoh as scandalous, and butoh dancers delight in pushing the boundaries of what can be considered tasteful in artistic performance.

Butoh tends to be more underground than the more established forms of Japanese dance and it is, consequently, harder to catch a performance. The best way to see what's on while you're in town is to check the local English-language media (see p114 and p296), or to ask at a local tourist information office.

Literature

Interestingly, much of Japan's early literature was written by women. One reason for this was that men wrote in kanji (imported Chinese characters), while women wrote in hiragana (Japanese script). Thus, while the men were busy copying Chinese styles and texts, the women of the country were producing the first authentic Japanese literature. Among these early female authors is Murasaki Shikibu, who wrote Japan's first great novel, *Genji Monogatari* (The Tale of Genji). This detailed, lengthy tome documents the intrigues and romances of early Japanese court life, and although it is perhaps Japan's most important work of literature, its extreme length probably limits its appeal to all but the most ardent Japanophile or literature buff.

Most of Japan's important modern literature has been penned by authors who live in and write about cities. Though these works are sometimes celebratory, many also lament the loss of a traditional rural lifestyle that has given way to the pressures of a modern, industrialised society. *Kokoro,* the modern classic by Sōseki Natsume, outlines these rural–urban tensions, as does *Snow Country,* by Nobel laureate Kawabata Yasunari. These works touch upon the tensions between Japan's nostalgia for the past and its rush towards the future, between its rural heartland and its burgeoning cities.

Although Mishima Yukio is probably the most controversial of Japan's modern writers, and is considered unrepresentative of Japanese culture by many Japanese themselves, his work still makes for very interesting reading. *The Sailor Who Fell from Grace with the Sea* and *After the Banquet* are both compelling. For unsettling beauty, reach for the former; history buffs will want the latter tome, which was at the centre of a court case that became Japan's first privacy lawsuit.

Ōe Kenzaburo, Japan's second Nobel laureate, has produced some of Japan's most disturbing, energetic and enigmatic literature. *A Personal Matter* is the work for which he is most widely known. In this troubling novel, which echoes Ōe's frustrations at having a son with autism, a 27-year-old cram-school teacher's wife gives birth to a brain-damaged child. His life claustrophobic and his marriage failing, he dreams of escaping to Africa while planning the murder of his son.

Of course, not all Japanese fiction can be classified as literature in highbrow terms. Murakami Ryū's *Almost Transparent Blue* is strictly sex and drugs, and his ode to the narcissistic early 1990s, *Coin Locker Babies,* recounts the toxic lives of two boys who have been left to die in coin lockers by their mothers. Like Murakami Ryū, Banana Yoshimoto is known for her ability to convey the prevailing Zeitgeist in easily, um, digestible form. In her novel *Kitchen,* she relentlessly chronicles Tokyo's fast-food menus and '80s pop culture, though underlying the superficial digressions are hints of a darker and deeper world of death, loss and loneliness.

Japan's internationally most celebrated living novelist is Murakami Haruki, a former jazz-club owner gone literary. His most noted work, *Norwegian Wood,* set in the late '60s against the backdrop of student protests, is both a portrait of the artist as a young man (as recounted by a reminiscent narrator) and an ode to first loves. The book was adapted into a movie in December 2010 and stars Kikuchi Rinko (see the box, p68) as the ill-fated Naoko.

Music

Japan has a huge, shape-shifting music scene supported by a local market of audiophiles who are willing to try almost anything. International artists make a point of swinging through on global tours, and the local scene surfaces every night in one of thousands of live houses. The jazz

MURAKAMI
HARUKI

Popular writer Murakami Haruki attended Waseda University and worked in a record shop, much like the main character of his novel *Norwegian Wood* (1987).

scene is enormous, as are the followings for rock, house and electronica. More mainstream gleanings are the *aidoru,* idol singers whose popularity is generated largely through media appearances and is centred on a cute, girl-next-door image. Unless you're aged 15, this last option probably won't interest you.

These days, J-pop (Japan pop) is dominated by female vocalists who borrow heavily from American pop stars. The most famous of these is Utada Hikaru, whose great vocal range and English ability (she peppers her songs with English lyrics) make her a standout from the otherwise drab *aidoru* field.

AKB48 is one of the inexplicably popular crazes in Japan's current pop scene – the ever-expanding group is made up of over 50 teenage girls who perform in rotation at their purpose-built theatre in Akihabara.

ARTS & ARCHITECTURE ARTS

Cinema

Japan has a vibrant film industry and proud, critically acclaimed cinematic traditions. Renewed international attention since the mid-1990s has reinforced interest in domestic films, which account for an estimated 40% of box-office receipts, nearly double the level in most European countries. Of course, this includes not only artistically important works, but also films in the science-fiction, horror and 'monster-stomps-Tokyo' genres for which Japan is also known.

At first, Japanese films were merely cinematic versions of traditional theatrical performances, but in the 1920s Japanese directors starting producing films in two distinct genres: *jidaigeki* (period films) and new *gendaigeki* films, which dealt with modern themes. The more realistic storylines of the new films soon reflected back on the traditional films with the introduction of *shin jidaigeki* (new period films). During this era, samurai themes became an enduring staple of Japanese cinema.

The golden age of Japanese cinema arrived with the 1950s and began with the release in 1950 of Kurosawa Akira's *Rashōmon,* winner of the Golden Lion at the 1951 Venice International Film Festival and the Oscar for best foreign film. The increasing realism and high artistic standards of the period are evident in such landmark films as *Tōkyō Monogatari* (Tokyo Story; 1953) by the legendary Ōzu Yasujirō; Mizoguchi Kenji's classics *Ugetsu Monogatari* (Tales of Ugetsu; 1953) and *Saikaku Ichidai Onna* (The Life of Oharu; 1952); and Kurosawa's 1954 masterpiece *Shichinin no Samurai* (Seven Samurai). Annual attendance at the country's cinemas reached 1.1 billion in 1958, and Kyoto, with its large film studios, such as Shōchiku, Daiei and Tōei, and more than 60 cinemas, enjoyed a heyday as Japan's own Hollywood.

As it did elsewhere in the world, TV spurred a rapid drop in the number of cinema-goers in Japan in the high-growth decades of the 1960s and '70s. But despite falling attendance, Japanese cinema remained a major artistic force. These decades gave the world such landmark works as Ichikawa Kon's *Chushingura* (47 Samurai; 1962) and Kurosawa's *Yōjimbo* (1961).

The plots of most modern Japanese horror films can be traced back to the popular *kaidan* of the Edo and Meiji periods.

The decline in cinema-going continued through the 1980s, reinforced by the popularisation of videos, with annual attendance at cinemas bottoming out at just over 100 million. Yet Japan's cinema was far from dead: Kurosawa garnered acclaim worldwide for *Kagemusha* (1980), which shared the Palme d'Or at Cannes, and *Ran* (1985). Imamura Shōhei's heart-rending *Narayama Bushiko* (The Ballad of Narayama) won the Palme d'Or at Cannes in 1983. Itami Jūzō became perhaps the most widely known Japanese director outside Japan after Kurosawa, with such biting satires as *Osōshiki* (The Funeral; 1987), *Tampopo* (Dandelion; 1987) and *Marusa no Onna* (A Taxing Woman; 1987). Ōshima Nagisa, best known for controversial films such as *Ai no Corrida* (In the Realm of the Senses; 1976), scored a critical and popular success with *Senjo no Merry Christmas* (Merry Christmas, Mr Lawrence) in 1983.

In recent years, Japanese cinema has been enjoying something of a renaissance and foreign audiences and critics have taken note. In 1997 Japanese directors received top honours at two of the world's most prestigious film festivals: *Unagi* (Eel), Imamura Shōhei's black-humoured look at human nature's dark side, won the Palme d'Or at Cannes, making him the only Japanese director to win this award twice; and 'Beat' Takeshi Kitano took the Golden Lion in Venice for *Hana-bi,* a tale of life and death, and the violence and honour that links them. More recently, in 2009, Takita Yojiro's film *Okuribito* (Departures) won the Oscar for best foreign film.

Anime

The term anime, a contraction of the word 'animation', is used worldwide to refer to Japan's highly sophisticated animated films. Unlike its counterparts in other countries, anime occupies a position very near the forefront of the film industry in Japan. Anime films encompass all genres, from science fiction and action adventure to romance and historical drama.

MIYAZAKI HAYAO – THE KING OF ANIME

Miyazaki Hayao, Japan's most famous and critically acclaimed anime director, has given us some of the most memorable images ever to appear on the silver screen. Consider, for example, the island that floated through the sky in his 1986 classic *Laputa*. Or the magical train that travelled across the surface of an aquamarine sea in *Spirited Away* (2001). Or the psychedelic dreamworlds that waited outside the doors of *Howl's Moving Castle* (2004). Watching scenes like this, one can only conclude that Miyazaki is gifted with the ability to travel to the realm of pure imagination and smuggle images back to this world intact and undiluted.

Miyazaki Hayao was born in 1941 in wartime Tokyo. His father was the director of a firm that manufactured parts for the famous Japanese Zero fighter plane. This early exposure to flying machines made a deep impression on the young Miyazaki, and one of the hallmarks of his films is skies filled with the most whimsical flying machines imaginable: winged dirigibles, fantastic flying boats and the flying wings of *Nausicaa of the Valley of the Winds* (to see one is to want one).

In high school, Miyazaki saw one of Japan's first anime, *Hakujaden,* and resolved to become an animator himself. After graduating from university in 1963, he joined the powerful Tōei Animation company, where he worked on some of the studio's most famous releases. He left in 1971 to join A Pro studio, where he gained his first directorial experience, working on the now famous (in Japan, at least) *Lupin III* series as codirector. In 1979 he directed *The Castle of Cagliostro,* another *Lupin* film and his first solo directorial credit.

In 1984 Miyazaki wrote and directed *Nausicaa of the Valley of the Winds*. This film is considered by many critics to be the first true Miyazaki film, and it provides a brilliant taste of many of the themes that run through his later work. The film enjoyed critical and commercial success and established Miyazaki as a major force in the world of Japanese anime. Capitalising on this success, Miyazaki founded his own animation studio, Studio Ghibli, through which he has produced all his later works.

In 1988 Studio Ghibli released what many consider to be Miyazaki's masterwork: *My Neighbor Totoro*. Much simpler and less dense than many Miyazaki films, *Totoro* is the tale of a young girl who moves with her family to the Japanese countryside while her mother recuperates from an illness. While living in the country, she befriends a magical creature who lives in the base of a giant camphor tree and is lucky enough to catch a few rides on a roving cat bus (a vehicle of pure imagination if ever there was one). For anyone wishing to make an acquaintance with the world of Miyazaki, this is the perfect introduction.

Serious Miyazaki fans will want to make a pilgrimage to his Ghibli Museum (p73), located in the town of Mitaka, a short day trip out of Tokyo.

Anime targets all age and social groups. The films include deep explorations of philosophical questions and social issues, humorous entertainment and bizarre fantasies. They offer breathtakingly realistic visuals, exquisite attention to detail, complex and expressive characters, and elaborate plots. Leading directors and voice actors are accorded fame and respect, while characters become popular idols.

Some of the best-known anime include *Akira* (1988), Ōtomo Katsuhiro's psychedelic fantasy set in a future Tokyo inhabited by speed-popping biker gangs and psychic children. Ōtomo also worked on the interesting *Memories* (1995), a three-part anime that includes the mind-bending 'Magnetic Rose' sequence where deep-space garbage collectors happen upon a spaceship containing the memories of a mysterious woman. Finally, there is *Ghost in a Shell* (1995), an Ōishii Mamoru film with a sci-fi plot worthy of Philip K Dick – it involves cyborgs, hackers and the mother of all computer networks.

Of course, one name towers above all others in the world of anime: Miyazaki Hayao, who almost single-handedly brought anime to the attention of the general public in the West.

Architecture

Most Nihon neophytes liken their first glimpses of Japan to touching down on an alien world. The sounds are different, the smells are different, but it's the sights that truly transport visitors to another planet – a place where glances out of the bullet-train window reveal an awe-inducing alternative universe bubbling over with bright lights and geometric shapes. From the wooden temples hidden in a bamboo forest, to the urban frenzies of metal and glass, Japan offers the ultimate feast of architectural eye candy.

Traditional Architecture

Upon glimpsing the visual chaos of Japan's urban centres, it's hard to believe that once upon a time the local architectural aesthetic was governed by a preference for understated, back-to-nature design. Long before the Japanese borrowed and bested Western design motifs, the island nation honed its craft and style during two centuries of self-inflicted isolation when Tokugawa Ieyasu defeated the last of his enemies and secured total control for the Tokugawa shōgunate.

Japan's flamboyant temples are undoubtedly the best examples of the nation's early architectural abilities. Important religious complexes were usually quite large and featured a great hall surrounded by smaller buildings like pagodas – the ancient version of the skyscraper – and structures that served as quarters for devotees.

Equally impressive was the country's collection of feudal castles, although most of the bastions we see today are concrete replicas of the original wooden structures destroyed by war, fire or decay. Initially, the feudal castles were simple mountain forts that relied more on natural terrain than structural innovation when defending the keep from invaders. Castle construction boomed during the 16th and 17th centuries, each one more impressive than the next; however, most were later razed by Edo and Meiji governments. The main castles in Osaka (Osaka-jō; p304) and Nagoya (Nagoya-jō; p174) are quite impressive and boast interactive museum spaces, but the country's must-see castle is Himeji-jō (p325), also known as the 'white heron', after its stately white form.

Principally simple and refined, the typical house was also constructed using post-and-beam timber, with sliding panels of wood or rice paper (for warmer weather) making up the exterior walls. *Shōji* (moveable screens) would divide the interior rooms. In more densely populated areas, traditional housing took the form of *machiya* (traditional Japanese townhouse),

Several distinguished Japanese architects have won the Pritzker Prize, including Tange Kenzō, Maki Fumihiko, Andō Tadao, Sejima Kazuyo and Nishizawa Ryue.

Long before lasers, padlocks and klaxons hampered trespassers, Japanese feudal lords employed a much simpler method of safeguarding their castles from stealth, black-masked assassins. Charged with the difficult task of protecting their masters from things that go bump in the night, court architects devised a straightforward security system known as *uguisubari* (nightingale floors). These special floorboards were rigged together with nails that would scratch against their clamps making a warbling noise when walked upon. Weathered timber planks usually creak on their own, but these special contraptions would sing like a songbird as people moseyed on by. The creaking floors of Nijō-jō (p257) are an excellent example of this melodic security technique. Tiptoe across the squeaky planks and see how far you can get before the ground starts to sing.

usually built by merchants. Although most of the neat, narrow rows of these structures have been replaced with flashier modern dwellings, one can still stumble across *machiya* in Kyoto. The reasoning behind the gossamer construction of domestic dwellings was twofold: light materials were favourable during boiling summer months, and heavier building products were inadvisable due to the abundance of earthquakes.

The most distinctive type of Japanese farmhouse was the thatched-roofed *gasshō-zukuri*, so named for the shape of the rafters, which resemble a pair of palms pressed together in prayer. While these farmhouses appear cosy and romantic, they were often home for up to 40 people and the occasional farm animal. The dark floorboards, soot-covered ceilings and lack of windows starkly contrasted with the breezy merchant houses in more populated areas.

Early Modern Architecture

When the Tokugawa shōgunate lost control of the island nation, the Meiji Restoration (1868) opened Japan's doors once more and architectural influences began to change. Josiah Conder, a British architect, was invited to Tokyo to design many structures that embodied the pillars of Western architecture. Conder erected numerous buildings in Gothic, Renaissance, Moorish and Tudor styles, energising Tokyo's heterogeneous cityscape. Conder was trying to develop an adaptation of Western architecture that could be understood as uniquely Japanese, but the adaptation of so many Western styles exhibited the difficulty of choosing and propagating a Japanese architecture. The Meiji administration was not pleased. They sought a ubiquitous Western aesthetic rather than a garish mishmash of colonial styles. Offended that Conder tried to impose a synthetic 'Japanisation' of the Western style, the Meiji administration rescinded his contract.

Japan's newest contribution to superlative architecture is the Tokyo Sky Tree, which stands at 634m. It is officially the tallest tower in the world, though not the tallest structure.

This resistance to Western architecture continued until after WWI, when foreign architects such as Frank Lloyd Wright came to build the Imperial Hotel in Tokyo. Wright was careful to pay homage to local sensibilities when designing the Imperial's many elegant bridges and unique guest rooms (though he famously used modern, cubic forms to ornament the interiors of the hotel). The building was demolished in 1967 to make way for the current Imperial Hotel, which shows little of Wright's touch.

By the end of WWII, Tokyo was a veritable blank slate. The city barely had time to regain its footing in the aftermath of the Great Kantō Earthquake (1923) before being bombed beyond recognition by the Allied forces. The other major metropolises in Japan suffered a similar fate. Through both geological and political phenomena, most of the country had been washed clean of the traditional Tokugawa aesthetic that had sustained the island nation through 200 years of forced isolation.

When TV was introduced as a Western marvel, Japan built its first broadcasting tower in the heart of Tokyo, known as Tokyo Tower. They didn't, however, just build an ordinary beacon; engineers constructed a duplicate of Paris' Eiffel Tower. True to the latent Japanese desire for importation and improvement, the orange-and-white behemoth was built to stand at 333m – 13m higher than the icon of modernity in the City of Lights.

Contemporary Architecture

In 1964 all eyes were on Japan – the first time since WWII – for Tokyo's Summer Olympic Games. The newly founded Japanese government decided that the new Olympic centre would be built where the American occupation compound had once stood in Yoyogi, a southwestern district of the city. But choosing a site was the easy part. The Olympic planners were faced with the problems of identifying and exemplifying modern Japanese design. The architectural concept for the Olympics had to accomplish two things: first, it should demonstrate modernity through a unique architectural gesture, and second, it must reflect a distinctive sense of Japanese-ness. The Olympic complex would dictate the future language of Japanese design.

Capturing this inherent Japanese-ness and expressing it through architecture proved to be much more difficult than expected, even for native architects. A modern design by Japanese architect Tange Kenzō was ultimately chosen. Tange was a young architect whose ideas were highly influenced by the works of Le Corbusier, although the ideas did not feel reappropriated and improved. The designs for the two large stadiums were like swirling shells plucked from the depths of an alien ocean. The larger structure was shaped as though the hull of a majestic boat had

TOP FIVE WOODEN WONDERS

Although Japan is currently known for its eye-popping alien architecture – like the buzzing metallic haze depicted in Sofia Coppola's film *Lost In Translation* – it was the almighty tree that dominated the nation's traditional construction materials. The following structures are among Japan's finest flourishes of timber.

» **Hōryū-ji** (p340) Located in the ancient capital city of Nara, this temple complex is commonly believed to feature the two oldest wooden structures in the world: the pagoda (rising just over 32m) and the *kondō* (golden or main hall). Its full name, *Hōryū Gakumonji*, means 'Learning Temple of the Flourishing Law', a moniker chosen because the grounds were used for sermons and monastic practices.

» **Tōdai-ji** (p334) Tōdai-ji's original Daibutsu-den and giant bronze Buddha were constructed by more than two million people during the 8th century. The structure has been incinerated twice and the current incarnation dates back to 1709.

» **Chion-in** (p263) This stunning temple complex is the centre of the Jōdo shū, a sect of Pure Land Buddhism established by Hōnen, a Japanese monk who lived during the 12th century. Chion-in's main gate, known as San-mon, is the largest structure of its kind in all of Japan. Several structures in the precinct were incinerated in the 17th century, but were rebuilt by the Tokugawa shōgunate a few years later.

» **Kiyomizu-dera** (p262) One of the most beloved temples in Kyoto, this stunning sanctuary overlooks the city's sea of chestnut-coloured roofs from a privileged hillside position. The temple's pièce de résistance is the main hall with its signature verandah sitting atop a scaffolding-like structure.

» **Byōdō-in** (p275) Originally built as a country estate for the Fujiwara clan in 998, Byōdō-in was transformed into a temple a century later. The Amida-dō (Phoenix Hall; also known as Hōō-dō) is one of the most prized pieces of architecture from the Fujiwara period and is featured on the ¥10 coin. The Byōdō-in complex was duplicated on Hawai'i's island of O'ahu.

been flipped upside down. The gracious gestures of the design masked the sheer volume required to house thousands of spectators. Indeed, the entire world was captivated by these inspired designs. Tange went on to have a very successful career, and would later design the Tokyo Metropolitan Government Offices (1991; p71).

Also in the 1960s, architects such as Shinohara Kazuo, Kurokawa Kisho, Maki Fumihiko and Kikutake Kiyonori began a movement known as Metabolism, which promoted flexible spaces and functions instead of fixed forms in building. Shinohara came to design in a style he called Modern Next, incorporating both modern and postmodern ideas combined with Japanese influences. This style can be seen in his Centennial Hall at Tokyo Institute of Technology, an elegant and uplifting synthesis of clashing forms in a shiny metal cladding. Kurokawa's architecture blends Buddhist building traditions with modern influences, while Maki, the master of minimalism, pursued design in a modernist style while still emphasising the elements of nature – like the roof of his Tokyo Metropolitan Gymnasium (near Sendagaya Station), which takes on the form of a sleek metal insect. Another Maki design, the Spiral Building, built in Aoyama in 1985, is a favourite with Tokyo residents and its interior is also a treat.

Skip ahead a decade and Japan's second generation of architects began gaining recognition within the international architecture scene, including Andō Tadao, and Toyo Ito. This younger group continued to explore both modernism and postmodernism, while incorporating a renewed interest in Japan's architectural heritage.

In 2010, SANAA (helmed by Sejima Kazuyo and Nishizawa Ryue) won the prestigious Pritzker Prize for their unwavering dedication to creating luminous form-follows-function spaces. They have dozens of impressive projects under their belt, including the 21st Century Museum of Contemporary Art in Kanazawa, and the New Museum of Contemporary Art in New York City.

Traditional Japanese Accommodation

Let's face it: a hotel is a hotel wherever you go. And while some of Japan's hotels are very nice indeed, you're probably searching for something unique to the culture. If this is what you're after, you'll be pleased to learn that Japan is one of the last places in Asia where you can find truly authentic traditional accommodation: ryokan, *minshuku* and *shukubō*.

Ryokan

Simply put, ryokan are traditional Japanese inns. Ryokan are where Japanese travellers stayed before they had heard the word *hoteru* (hotel). They are Japanese-style accommodation with tatami-mat rooms and futons instead of beds. Most serve Japanese-style breakfast and dinner, as well. However, this simple explanation doesn't do justice to ryokan.

A high-end ryokan is the last word in relaxation. The buildings themselves set the tone: they employ traditional Japanese architecture in which the whole structure is organic, made entirely of natural materials such as wood, earth, paper, grass, bamboo and stone. Indeed, a good ryokan is an extension of the natural world. And nature comes into the ryokan in the form of the Japanese garden, which you can often see from the privacy of your room or even your bathtub.

But more than the building, the service is what sets ryokan apart from even the best hotels. At a good ryokan, you will be assigned a personal maid who sees to your every need. These ladies seem to have a sixth sense: as soon as you finish one course of your dinner, you hear a knock on the door and she brings the next course. Then, when you stroll down the hall to take a bath, she dashes into your room and lays out your futon.

Many ryokan in Japan pride themselves on serving *kaiseki ryōri* (Japanese haute cuisine), which rivals that served in the best restaurants. Staying at one of these so-called *ryōri* ryokan (cuisine ryokan) is like staying at a three-star 'residential restaurant', where you sleep in your own private dining room.

Another wonderful variety is the onsen ryokan: a ryokan with its own private hot-spring bath. These places were like luxury spas long before anyone had heard the word 'spa'. Some of the top places have rooms with private en suite onsen baths, usually built overlooking gardens. When you stay at an onsen ryokan, your day involves a gruelling cycle of bathe-nap-eat-repeat. A night at a good onsen ryokan is the perfect way to get over your jet lag when you arrive in the country or a special treat to round out the journey in Japan.

It is said that there are more than 80,000 ryokan in Japan, but that number decreases each year as modern Japanese find hotels to be more convenient.

Of course, it would be irresponsible to suggest that all ryokan fit this description. A lot of places that call themselves ryokan are really just hotels with Japanese-style rooms. Some places may not even serve dinner. That isn't to say they aren't comfortable: simple ryokan are often very friendly and relaxing and they may cost less than hotels in some places. But if you can do it, we strongly recommend staying in a high-end ryokan for at least one night of your trip.

Note that ryokan may not have en suite bathtubs or showers, and at some simple places even the toilet facilities are shared. If this is an issue, be sure to enquire when you make a reservation.

Staying in a Ryokan

Due to language difficulties and unfamiliarity, staying in a ryokan is not as straightforward as staying in a Western-style hotel. However, it's not exactly rocket science, and with a little education, it can be a breeze, even if you don't speak a word of Japanese. Note that much of what we say here will also apply to staying at a *minshuku*.

Here's the basic drill. When you arrive, leave your shoes in the *genkan* (entry area or foyer) and step up into the reception area. Here, you'll be asked to sign in. Next, you'll be shown around the place and then to your room, where you will be served a cup of tea. You'll find that there is no bedding to be seen in your room – your futon is in the closet and will be laid out later. You can leave your luggage anywhere except the *tokonoma* (sacred alcove) that will usually contain some flowers or a hanging scroll. If it's early enough, you can then go out to do some sightseeing.

When you return, you'll change into your *yukata* (lightweight Japanese robe) and will be served dinner in your room or in a dining room. After dinner, it's time for a bath. If it's a big place, you can generally bathe anytime in the evening until around 11pm. If it's a small place, you'll be given a time slot. While you're in the bath, some mysterious elves will go into your room and lay out your futon so that it's waiting for you when you return all toasty from the bath.

In the morning, you'll be served a Japanese-style breakfast (some places these days serve a simple Western-style breakfast for those who can't stomach rice and fish in the morning). You pay on check-out, which is usually around 11am.

Minshuku

A *minshuku* is usually a family-run private lodging, rather like a B&B in Europe or the USA. In some very simple *minshuku* you're really just staying with a Japanese family that has turned a few of the rooms in their house into guestrooms. Other places are purpose-built to serve as accommodation. In either case, the rooms will be Japanese style, with tatami mats and futons. Bathroom facilities are usually shared and meals are usually eaten in a common dining room. Unlike at a ryokan, in a *minshuku* you are usually expected to lay out and put away your bedding.

The average price per person per night, including two meals, is around ¥5500. *Minshuku* are a little hard to find on your own if you don't speak and read Japanese. And, needless to say, owners are less likely to speak English than at hotels or popular ryokan. The best way to find a *minshuku* is to ask at a local tourist information office, where they will usually call ahead and make all arrangements for you.

Shukubō

Staying in a *shukubō* (temple lodging) is one way to experience another facet of traditional Japan. Sometimes you are allocated a simple room in the temple precincts and left to your own devices. At other places, you

Best Ryokan in Japan

» Tawaraya (p283)

» Hiiragiya (p283)

» Kayōtei (p238)

» Nishimuraya Honkan (p361)

Staying at a *minshuku* can be like staying with your extended family over the holidays. If you've got a few boisterous relatives in the room next door, you'll probably hear what they're saying. Still, most guests are pretty good at observing quiet hours (midnight to 8am).

JAPANESE ACCOMMODATION MADE EASY

More than one foreign traveller has turned up unannounced in a ryokan or *minshuku* and been given a distinctly cold reception, then concluded that he has been the victim of discrimination. More than likely, he simply broke one of the main rules of Japanese accommodation: don't surprise them. With this in mind, here are a few tips to help you find a bed each night in Japan. Note that the following also goes for hotels, although these are generally a little more flexible than traditional accommodation.

» Reservations Make reservations whenever possible, even if it's just a quick call a few hours before arriving.

» Fax The Japanese are much more comfortable with written than spoken English. If you fax a room request with all your details, you will find a warm welcome. You can always follow it up with a phone call, once you're all on the same page.

» The baton pass Get your present accommodation to call ahead and reserve your next night's lodging. This will put everyone at ease – if you're acceptable at one place, you'll be just fine at another.

» Tourist information offices Even in the smallest hamlet or island in Japan, you'll find tourist information offices, usually right outside train stations or ferry terminals. These exist just to help travellers find accommodation (OK, they also give brilliant directions). They will recommend a place and call to see if a room is available, then they will tell you exactly how to get there. This is another form of introduction.

Lastly, there will be times when you just have to slide that door open and hope for the best. Even the surprise-averse Japanese have to resort to this desperate expedient from time to time. The secret here is to try to minimise the shock. Smile like you're there to sell them insurance, muster your best *konbanwa* ('good evening') and try to convince them that you actually prefer futons to beds, green tea to coffee, chopsticks to forks, and baths to showers.

may also be allowed to participate in prayers, services or meditation. At some temples *shōjin-ryōri* (Buddhist vegetarian cuisine) is served.

The tourist information centres in Tokyo and Kyoto produce leaflets on temple lodgings in their regions. Kōya-san (p349), a renowned religious centre, includes more than 50 *shukubō* and is one of the best places in Japan to try this type of accommodation. Some youth hostels in Japan are also located in temple grounds, which make them a form of *shukubō*.

Onsen

Japan is in hot water. Literally. The stuff percolates up out of the ground from one end of the country to the other. The Japanese word for a hot spring is 'onsen', and there are more than 3000 of them here, more than anywhere else on earth. So if your idea of relaxation involves soaking your bones in a tub of bubbling hot water, you've come to the right place.

With so many onsen, it's hardly surprising that they come in every size, shape and colour. There is an onsen on an artificial island in Tokyo Bay. There are onsen high up in the Japan Alps that you can only get to by walking for a full day over high mountain peaks. There are onsen bubbling up among the rocks on the coast that only exist when the tide is just right.

Some Japanese will tell you that the only distinctively Japanese aspect of their culture – that is, something that didn't ultimately originate in mainland Asia – is the bath. There are accounts of onsen bathing in Japan's earliest historical records, and it's pretty certain that the Japanese have been bathing in onsen as long as there have been Japanese.

Japan's Hidden Onsen by Robert Neff is a good guide to secluded onsen across the archipelago. It's a little out of date, but it still contains some fantastic finds.

Over the millennia, they have turned the simple act of bathing in an onsen into something like a religion. Today, the ultimate way to experience an onsen is to visit an onsen ryokan, a traditional Japanese inn with its own private hot-spring bath. At an onsen ryokan you spend all day enjoying the bath, relaxing in your room and eating sumptuous food.

Like many of the best things in life, some of the finest onsen in Japan are free. Just show up with a towel and your birthday suit, splash a little water on yourself and plunge in. No communication hassles, no expenses and no worries. And even if you must pay to enter, it's usually just a minor snip – averaging about ¥700 (US$6) per person.

Best Onsen Experiences

With so many onsen to choose from in Japan, it's a thankless task to pick favourites. And no matter how many onsen you try, there's always the suspicion that somewhere out there is the Holy Grail of onsen just waiting to be discovered. That said, we're going to go way out on a limb here and recommend a few of our favourites, broken up into categories to help you choose.

Urban Onsen
Ōedo Onsen Monogatari (Tokyo; p82) Located on the artificial island of Odaiba in Tokyo Bay, this giant super-onsen is modelled on an Edo-period town. There is a huge variety of tubs, including outdoor tubs, as well as restaurants, relaxation rooms and shops. You can easily spend a whole day here soaking away your cares.

Oceanside Onsen
Jinata Onsen (Shikine-jima, Izu-shotō; p164) The setting of this onsen couldn't be more dramatic: it's located in a rocky cleft in the seashore of lovely little Shikine-jima. The pools are formed by the seaside rocks and it's one of those onsen that only works when the tide is right. You can spend a few lovely hours here watching the Pacific rollers crashing on the rocks. There are two other excellent onsen on the island.

Riverside Onsen

Takaragawa Onsen (Gunma Prefecture, Central Honshū; p129) Japanese
onsen maniacs often pronounce Gunma-ken's onsen to be the best in the country.
Difficult for us to argue. 'Takaragawa' means 'treasure river', and its several slate-
floored pools sit along several hundred metres of riverbank. Most of the pools
are mixed bathing, with one ladies-only bath. The alkaline waters are said to cure
fatigue, nervous disorders and digestive troubles.

Onsen Town

Kinosaki (Kansai; p360) Kinosaki, on the Sea of Japan coast in northern Kansai,
is the quintessential onsen town. With seven public baths and dozens of onsen
ryokan, this is the place to sample the onsen ryokan experience. You can relax in
your accommodation taking the waters as it pleases you, and when you get tired of
your ryokan's bath, you can hit the streets in a *yukata* (light cotton robe) and *geta*
(wooden sandals) and visit the public baths.

Hidden Onsen

Lamp no Yado (Noto-hantō, Central Honshū; p237) Noto-hantō is about as far
as one can go in Central Honshū, and the seaside is about as far as one can go on
this peninsula. A country road takes you to a narrow 1km path, from where you
have to climb a switchback hill on foot. Sit in the *rotemburo* (outdoor bath) and
enjoy the Sea of Japan views through craggy rocks.

Semitropical Onsen

Urami-ga-taki Onsen (Hachijō-jima, Izu-shotō; p164) Even in a country of lovely
onsen, this is a real standout: the perfect little *rotemburo* located next to a waterfall
in lush semitropical jungle. It's what they're shooting for at all those resorts on Bali,
only this is the real thing. Sitting in the bath as the late-afternoon sunlight pierces
the ferns here is a magical experience. Did we mention that's it's free?

Onsen-Beach Combination

Shirahama (Wakayama Prefecture, Kansai; p351) There's something peculiarly
pleasing about dashing back and forth between the ocean and a natural hot-spring
bath – the contrast in temperature and texture is something we never tire of. At
Shirahama, a beach town in southern Kansai, there is a free onsen right on the
beach. And Sakino-yu Onsen here is just spectacular – you sit in the tubs and
watch the rollers from the Pacific break over the rocks just a few metres away.

Do-It-Yourself Onsen

Kawa-yu Onsen (Wakayama Prefecture, Kansai; p356) If you like doing things
your own way, you'll love this natural oddity of an onsen in southern Kansai. Here,
the onsen waters bubble up through the rocks of a riverbed. You choose a likely
spot and dig out a natural hotpot along the riverside and wait for it to fill with hot
water and – voila – your own private *rotemburo*. In the winter, it gets even better:
they use bulldozers to turn the entire river into a giant 1000-person onsen. It
doesn't hurt that the river water is a lovely translucent emerald colour.

Be warned: the
minerals in some
onsen can dis-
colour jewellery,
particularly silver.
But don't worry
too much if you
forget to take off
your wedding ring
before jumping
in the tub – after
a few hours, the
discolouration
usually fades.

TATTOO WARNING

Be warned that if you have any tattoos, you may not be allowed to enter Japanese
onsen, or *sentō* (public bath). The reason for this is that Japanese *yakuza* (gangsters)
almost always sport tattoos. Banning people with tattoos is an indirect way of banning
gangsters. Unfortunately, to avoid the appearance of unfairness (and because Japan
is a country where rules are rigorously adhered to), the no-tattoo rule also applies to
foreigners. If your tattoo is small enough to cover with some Band-Aids, cover it up and
you'll have no problem. Otherwise, ask the people at the front desk if you can go in despite your tattoos. The phrase to use is '*irezumi wa daijōbu desu ka*' (Are tattoos okay?).

ONSEN

JAPANESE	SCRIPT	ENGLISH
dansei-no-yu	男性の湯	male bath
josei-no-yu	女性の湯	female bath
kake-yu	かけ湯	rinsing one's body
kazoku-no-yu	家族の湯	family bath
konyoku	混浴	mixed bath
onna-yu	女湯	female bath (most commonly used)
otoko-yu	男湯	male bath (most commonly used)
yu	ゆ/湯	hot water
o-yu	お湯	hot water (polite)
rotemburo	露天風呂	outdoor bath
soto-yu	外湯	public bath
uchi-yu	内湯	private bath
yubune	湯船	bath tub

Onsen Ryokan
Nishimuraya Honkan (Kinosaki, Kansai; p361) If you want to sample the ultimate in top-end onsen ryokan, this is the place. With several fine indoor and outdoor baths and elegant rooms, your stay here will be a highlight of your trip to Japan, and will shed some light on why the Japanese consider an onsen vacation to be the utmost in relaxation.

Onsen Ski Town
Nozawa Onsen (Nagano Prefecture, Central Honshū; p212) What could be better than a day spent on the slopes, followed by a soak in a jacuzzi? Well, how about a day on the slopes followed by a soak in a real natural hot spring? This fine little ski town boasts some first-rate skiing, reliable snow, ripping alpine views and no fewer than 13 free onsen. Best of all, the onsen here are scalding hot, which is a nice contrast to the snow outside and it feels wonderful on tired skier's legs.

Onsen Etiquette
First: relax. That's what onsen are all about. You'll be relieved to hear that there really is nothing tricky about taking an onsen bath. If you remember just one basic point, you won't go too far wrong. This is the point: the water in the pools and tubs is for soaking in, not washing in, and it should only be entered after you've washed or rinsed your body.

I Love U Blog (http://kansaionsen.blogspot.com) is a useful source of information on Kansai onsen, with occasional reviews of onsen outside Kansai.

This is the drill: pay your entry fee, if there is one. Rent a hand towel if you don't have one. Take off your shoes and put them in the lockers or shelves provided. Find the correct changing room or bath for your gender (man: 男; woman: 女). Grab a basket, strip down and put your clothes in the basket. Put the basket in a locker and bring the hand towel in with you.

Once in the bathing area, find a place around the wall (if there is one) to put down your toiletries (if you have them), and wash your body or, at least, rinse your body. You'll note that some local men dispense with this step and just stride over to the tubs and grab a bucket (there are usually some around) and splash a few scoops over their 'wedding tackle'. Some miscreants can't even be bothered with this step and plunge right into the tubs unwashed and unrinsed. Frankly, we like to think that these people will be reincarnated into a world where there are only cold-water showers for their bathing needs.

Living Art of the Geisha

No other aspect of Japanese culture is as widely misunderstood as the geisha. First – and let's get this out of the way – geisha are not prostitutes. Nor is their virginity sold off to the highest bidder. Nor do they have to sleep with regular patrons. To put it simply, geisha are highly skilled entertainers who are paid to facilitate and liven up social occasions in Japan.

The origins of geisha are subject to some debate, but most historians believe that the institution of the geisha started in the Edo period (1600–1868). At this time, there were various types of prostitutes who served men in the pleasure quarters of the large cities. Some of these ladies became very accomplished in various arts and it is said that some pleasure houses even employed male performers to entertain customers. Some believe that these male entertainers were the first to be dubbed 'geisha', which means 'artistic person'.

Eventually, there arose a class of young ladies who specialised exclusively in entertainment and who did not engage in sexual relations with clients. These were the first true female geisha, and over the years they became prized for the accomplishments in a wide variety of Japanese arts.

Without a doubt, Kyoto is the capital of the geisha world. Confusingly, in Kyoto they are not called 'geisha'; rather, they are called *maiko* or *geiko*. A *maiko* is a girl between the ages of 15 and 20, who is in the process of training to become a fully fledged *geiko* (the Kyoto word for 'geisha'). During this five-year period, she lives in an *okiya* (geisha house) and studies traditional Japanese arts, including dance, singing, tea ceremony and *shamisen* (a three-stringed instrument). During this time, she will also start to entertain clients, usually in the company of a *geiko*, who acts like an older sister.

Due to the extensive training she receives, a *maiko* or *geiko* is like a living museum of Japanese traditional culture. In addition to her skills, the kimono she wears and the ornaments in her hair and on her *obi* (kimono sash) represent the highest achievements in Japanese arts. It's therefore hardly surprising that both Japanese and foreigners consider a meeting with a geisha to be a magical occurrence.

While young girls may have been sold into this world in times gone by, these days girls make the choice themselves, often after coming to Kyoto to see one of the city's famous geisha dances. The proprietor of the *okiya* will meet the girl and her parents to determine if the girl is serious and if her parents are willing to grant her permission to enter the world of the geisha (the *okiya* makes a considerable investment in terms of training and kimonos, so they are loathe to take girls who may quit).

Memoirs of a Geisha by Arthur Golden is an entertaining fictional account of the life of a Kyoto geisha.

There's no doubt that catching a glimpse of a geisha is a once-in-a-lifetime Japanese experience. Unfortunately, the sport of 'geisha-spotting' has really gotten out of hand in Kyoto's Gion district (the city's main geisha district). It's probably best to keep the following in mind if you join the ranks of geisha-spotters in Gion:

» The geisha you see in Gion are usually on the way to or from an appointment and cannot stop for photos or conversation.

» You shouldn't touch or grab a geisha, or physically block their progress.

» No one likes being mobbed by photographers or hounded as they walk down the street.

» If you really want to get close to a geisha, private tour agencies and high-end ryokan or hotels can arrange geisha entertainment.

» Finally, if you are intent on getting a few photos of geisha, you will find plenty of 'tourist geisha' in the streets of Higashiyama during the daytime. These are tourists who have paid to be made up as geisha. They look pretty much like the real thing and they are usually more than happy to pose for pictures.

Once a *maiko* completes her training and becomes a *geiko,* she is able to move out of the *okiya* and live on her own. At this point she is free to have a boyfriend, but if she gets married she has to leave the world of the geisha. It's very easy to spot the difference between a *maiko* and a *geiko: geiko* wear wigs with minimal ornamentation (usually just a wooden comb in the wig), while *maiko* wear their own hair in an elaborate hairstyle with many bright hair ornaments called *kanzashi.* Also, *maiko* wear elaborate long-sleeve kimonos, while *geiko* wear simpler kimonos with shorter sleeves.

Maiko and *geiko* entertain their clients in exclusive restaurants, banquet halls, 'teahouses' (more like exclusive traditional bars) and other venues. An evening of *maiko/geiko* entertainment usually starts with a *kaiseki* (Japanese haute cuisine) meal. While their customers eat, the *maiko/geiko* enter the room and introduce themselves in Kyoto dialect. They proceed to pour drinks and make witty banter with the guests. Sometimes they even play drinking games, and we can tell you from experience that it's hard to beat geisha at their own games! If it's a large party with a *jikata* (*shamisen* player), the girls may dance after dinner.

The best way to see geisha – a whole lot of geisha – is to attend one of Kyoto's spring or autumn geisha dances. For more information, see p293.

As you might guess, this sort of entertainment does not come cheap: a dinner with one *maiko* and one *geiko* and a *jikata* might cost about US$900, but it's definitely worth it for a once-in-a-lifetime experience. Let's face it: 'I had dinner with a geisha' is a pretty good entry in any 'been-there-done-that' contest.

It's impossible to arrange private geisha entertainment without an introduction from an established patron. However, these days geisha entertainment can be arranged through top-end hotels, ryokan and some private tour operators in Kyoto.

Knowledgeable sources estimate that there are perhaps 100 *maiko* and just over 100 *geiko* in Kyoto. Geisha can also be found in other parts of the country, most notably Tokyo. However, it is thought that there are less than 1000 geisha or *geiko* and *maiko* remaining in all of Japan.

Environment

Stretching from the tropics to the Sea of Okhotsk, the Japanese archipelago is a fantastically varied place. Few countries in the world enjoy such a richness of different climes and ecosystems, with everything from coral-reefed islands to snowcapped mountains. Unfortunately, this wonderful landscape is also one of the world's most crowded, and almost every inch of the Japanese mainland and coastline bears the imprint of human activity (see p734).

Although Japan's environment has been manipulated and degraded by human activity over the centuries, there are still pockets of real beauty left, some quite close to heavily populated urban areas. Indeed, there is decent hiking to be found in the mountains within two hours of Tokyo, an hour from Osaka and just a few minutes from central Kyoto.

Fortunately, environmental consciousness is on the rise in Japan, and more effort is being put into recycling, conservation and protection of natural areas. We can only hope that some of Japan's remaining areas of beauty will be preserved for future generations.

The Land

Japan is an island nation but it has not always been so. As recently as the end of the last ice age, around 10,000 years ago, the level of the sea rose enough to flood a land bridge that connected Japan to the Asian continent.

Today, Japan consists of a chain of islands that rides the back of a 3000km-long arc of mountains along the eastern rim of the continent. It stretches from around 25°N at the southern islands of Okinawa to 45°N at the northern end of Hokkaidō. Cities at comparable latitudes are Miami and Cairo in the south and Montreal and Milan in the north. Japan's total land area is 377,435 sq km, and more than 80% of it is mountainous.

Japan consists of some 3900 small islands along with its four major ones: Honshū (which is slightly larger than Britain), Hokkaidō, Kyūshū and Shikoku. Okinawa, the largest and most significant of Japan's many smaller islands, is situated about halfway along an archipelago that stretches from the western tip of Honshū almost all the way to Taiwan.

Japan has the dubious distinction of being one of the most seismically active regions of the world. In March 2011 the 9.0-magnitude Great East Japan Earthquake, one of the strongest in history, caused a tsunami that devastated coastal areas of northeast Honshū and killed thousands (for more on this earthquake, see the box on p435). Fortunately, most of the more than 1000 earthquakes which strike Japan every year are too weak to feel. Still, if you find yourself near a coastal area and you feel an earthquake, you should make for high ground immediately.

In 2005 the Japanese Ministry of the Environment launched the 'Cool Biz' campaign to cut CO_2 emissions. They encouraged 'casual Fridays' in offices and raising thermostats in summer (to use less air-con). After a year it was estimated that annual CO_2 emissions were reduced by over 1 million tonnes – but makers of neckties complained of a decline in sales.

Some Japanese households recycle their bathwater in their laundry machines. Hang-drying clothes in the sun is still favoured over dryers.

In addition to all this shaking, Japan is rich with volcanoes starting with the famous Mt Fuji. In February 2009 Mt Asama, northwest of Tokyo, sent smoke 2km into the air and scattered ash over the capital. Kyūshū, however, lays claim to being the most active volcano region in Japan and this is where most visitors will see volcanoes close up, including Aso-san (p601).

The Human Impact

Visitors to Japan are often shocked at the state of the Japanese landscape. It seems that no matter where you look, the hills, rivers, coastline and fields bear the unmistakable imprint of human activity. Indeed, it is only in the highest, most remote mountains that one finds nature untouched by human hands. Why is this?

Undoubtedly, population density is the crucial factor here. However, it is not just simple population pressure that accounts for Japan's scarred and battered landscape; misguided land-management policies and money-influenced politics also play a role.

> According to the *Japan Times*, some 5570km (nearly 50%) of Japan's coastline has been completely or substantially altered.

Almost 70% of Japan's total land area is forested. Of this area, almost 40% is planted (rather than natural) forest, most of it with uniform rows of conifers, known as *sugi* (cryptomeria). Even national forests are not exempt from tree farming, and these forests account for 33% of Japan's total lumber output. The end result of this widespread tree farming is a patchwork effect over most of Japan's mountains – monotonous stands of *sugi* interspersed with occasional swathes of bare, clear-cut hillside.

To make matters worse, the planting of monoculture forests and clear-cutting reduces the stability of mountain topsoil, resulting in frequent landslides. To combat this, land engineers erect concrete retaining walls over huge stretches of hillside, particularly along roads or near human habitations.

As if this weren't enough, it is estimated that only three of Japan's 30,000 rivers and streams are undammed. In addition to dams, concrete channels and embankments are built around even the most inaccessible mountain streams.

In Japan rural areas yield enormous power in national politics, as representation is determined more by area than by population. In order to insure the support of their constituencies, rural politicians have little choice but to lobby hard for government spending on public-work projects, as there is little other work available in these areas. Despite the

SUSTAINABLE TRAVEL IN JAPAN

As a traveller, you can minimise your impact on the Japanese environment in several ways.

Refuse packaging The Japanese are nuts about packaging – some would say overpackaging. The solution to this is simply to refuse excess packaging. At the cash register, you can say: *'Fukuro wa irimasen'* (I don't need a bag), or simply *'Kekkō desu'* (That's alright).

Carry your own chopsticks Say no to *waribashi* (disposable chopsticks) provided in restaurants. Either keep the first nice pair of *waribashi* that you are given, or visit a convenience store or ¥100 shop and ask for *my hashi* – lacquered, washable chopsticks with a carrying case.

Less tuna, please When you go to a sushi place, try to stay away from species of fish that are endangered, such as *maguro* (tuna) – including *toro* (fatty tuna belly). We know, this one hurts!

Use public transport Japan's public transport system is among the best in the world and using public transport is an environmental no brainer.

Hop on a bike Many of Japan's cities are perfect for cycling – join the legions of Japanese who commute on their *mama-charis* (shopping bikes).

negative effects this has on the Japanese landscape and economy, Japanese politicians seem unable to break this habit.

The upshot of all this is a landscape that looks, in many places, like a giant construction site. Perhaps the writer Alex Kerr put it best in his book *Lost Japan:* 'Japan has become a huge and terrifying machine, a Moloch tearing apart its own land with teeth of steel, and there is absolutely nothing anyone can do to stop it.' For the sake of the beauty that remains in Japan, let's hope he is wrong.

Wildlife

The latitudinal spread of Japan's islands makes for a wide diversity of flora and fauna. The Nansei and Ogasawara archipelagos in the far south are subtropical, and flora and fauna in this region are related to those found on the Malay peninsula. Mainland Japan (Honshū, Kyūshū and Shikoku), on the other hand, shows more similarities with Korea and China, while Hokkaidō shares some features with nearby Sakhalin Island (part of Russia).

Animals

Japan's land bridge to the Asian continent allowed the migration of animals from Korea and China. There are species that are unique to Japan, such as the Japanese giant salamander and the Japanese macaque. In addition, Nansei-shotō, which has been separated from the mainland for longer than the rest of Japan, has a few examples of fauna that are classified by experts as 'living fossils', such as the Iriomote cat.

Japan's largest carnivorous mammals are its bears. Two species are found in Japan – the *higuma* (brown bear) of Hokkaidō, and the *tsukinowaguma* (Asiatic brown bear) of Honshū, Shikoku and Kyūshū.

According to a 2009 report by the International Union for Conservation of Nature and Natural Resources (IUCN), there are 312 endangered animal species in Japan. Endangered species include the Iriomote cat, the Tsushima cat, Blakiston's fish owl and the Japanese river otter.

Plants

The flora of Japan today is not what the Japanese saw hundreds of years ago. This is not just because a lot of Japan's natural landscape has succumbed to modern urban culture, but also because much of Japan's flora is imported. It is thought that 200 to 500 plant species have been introduced to Japan since the Meiji period, mainly from Europe but also from North America.

A large portion of Japan was once heavily forested. The cool to temperate zones of Central and Northern Honshū and southern Hokkaidō were home to broadleaf mixed deciduous forests. These days, however, one is much more likely to see monotonous stands of *sugi* (cryptomeria; see p734).

Plums (early February–mid-March)

Whether white or pink, plums are the first sign that winter is loosening its grip.

Camellias (March & April)

Big, bold and coming in a variety of colours, these blossoms grace many fine gardens and temples in Japan and they often overlap nicely with the plums and cherries.

Cherries (mid-March–mid-April)

Who hasn't heard of Japan's famous cherry blossoms *(sakura)*? In a really good cherry-blossom year, whether you're in Tokyo, Nara, Kyoto or some other spot, it can seem like Mother Nature has forgotten all her modesty and decided to put on her best party dress and go mad. This is obviously the most popular time to visit Japan, but don't expect to have it all to yourself!

Azaleas (April & May)

Not headline grabbers like the cherries or plums, these flowering shrubs (some grow to tree size) can be magnificent. Hikers should keep an eye out for some of the great wild varieties that festoon the hills of Japan.

THE FUKUSHIMA NUCLEAR INCIDENT

When the Great East Japan Earthquake (see the box, p435) struck on 11 March 2011, it caused a tsunami that devastated coastal areas of northeast Honshū (the main island of Japan). This area is home to several of Japan's nuclear powerplants, most of which were unscathed. But the Fukushima One nuclear powerplant (Fukushima Dai-ichi), located about 240km northeast of Tokyo, suffered serious damage.

The tsunami easily breached the seawalls intended to protect the plant from such waves. At the time of the quake, three of the six nuclear reactors at the site were shut down for maintenance. The remaining three were automatically shut down ('scrammed') when the quake struck. However, even when scrammed, nuclear reactors and their spent fuel (stored in nearby pools) emit significant heat and require cooling. Fukushima One's emergency on-site generators were knocked out by the tsunami and backup battery power quickly ran out, resulting in a complete loss of cooling capability.

The three reactors that had been operating quickly started to overheat, along with the spent fuel rods stored at one of the nonoperational reactors. The Tokyo Electric Power Company (TEPCO), which operates the powerplants, and the Japanese government, suddenly faced a terrifying scenario: the possibility of a partial or complete meltdown at one or more nuclear reactors. The world watched with bated breath as the Japanese struggled to restore cooling to the plants. While doing so, there were several explosions and fires, but as this book went to press the Japanese government stated that the situation was under control and that cooling had been restored sufficiently to avoid a true disaster. Both TEPCO and the Japanese government have announced plans to try to contain the affected reactors and prevent leakage of radioactive materials into the environment.

Two words were on everyone's lips as the drama unfolded: 'meltdown' and 'Chernobyl'. While the incident at Fukushima One was serious by any standard, it is important to realise that it is radically different from what happened at Chernobyl. At Chernobyl, the reactor vessel was not surrounded by a containment vessel. When the reactor at Chernobyl underwent a power surge, the top blew off and the nuclear core exploded and burst into flames. This sent highly radioactive particles high into the atmosphere, leading to extremely potent nuclear fallout over parts of the Soviet Union and Europe.

The reactors at Fukushima One were designed quite differently from the Chernobyl reactor: each Fukushima reactor vessel is surrounded by a thick concrete containment vessel. While it is speculated that partial meltdowns may have occurred in one or more of the reactor vessels at Fukushima, and the reactor vessels may have been partially damaged, the nuclear cores were still largely contained within the concrete containment vessels. Though there is some evidence that the containment vessels at one or more of the reactors may have suffered slight damage (a crack or hole, according to the Japanese government), at press time there was no open-core/core-explosion situation like the one that happened at Chernobyl.

Radiation was released by the reactors and stored fuel rods at Fukushima One, mostly in the form of radioactive gases and water with isotopes of relatively short half-lives. At press time, the Japanese government had established a 20km-radius no-entry zone around the powerplant and extended it to include a few villages to the north of this zone. *The Japanese government states that areas outside this zone are safe for travel.* Furthermore, at press time Japanese government figures showed that radiation in Tokyo was back within the normal range for the time of year. Indeed, except for areas quite close to the plant, radiation levels all over the country were within normal annual ranges.

The government was also monitoring radiation levels in produce, livestock, dairy products and seafood in the area of the plants, and had prohibited sale of anything found to contain radiation exceeding common international limits.

Of course, the situation could change significantly by the time you are reading this book. Thus, we urge you to check your government's latest travel warnings before travelling, particularly to the northern Honshū region (see p748 for more details). Furthermore, internet searches will provide information on the current status of the reactors and the safety of travel in the area published by the Japanese government as well as a variety of third-party and independent sources, such as Greenpeace.

Fortunately, the sheer inaccessibility of much of Japan's mountainous topography has preserved some areas of great natural beauty – in particular the alpine regions of Central Honshū (p199), the lovely national parks of Hokkaidō (p462) and the semitropical island of Iriomote (p668).

According to a 2008 report in the *Proceedings of the Japan Academy,* there are 1690 endangered and threatened species of vascular plants in Japan. For more information, visit the website of the Biodiversity Center of Japan at www.biodic.go.jp/index_e.html.

National Parks

Japan has 29 *kokuritsu kōen* (national parks) and 56 *kokutei kōen* (quasi-national parks), ranging from the far south (Iriomote National Park; p668) to the northern tip of Hokkaidō (Rishiri-Rebun-Sarobetsu National Park; p498). Although national and quasi-national parks account for less than 1% of Japan's total land area, it is estimated that 14% of Japan's land is protected or managed for sustainable use.

Few of the parks have facilities that you might expect in national parks (ranger stations, campgrounds, educational facilities etc). More importantly, national park status doesn't necessarily mean that the area in question is free from residential, commercial or even urban development.

For descriptions of Japan's parks, see www.env.go.jp/en/np/index.html.

Environmental Issues

Japan has spent a lot of time in the spotlight recently due to environmental issues. In 2009 the film *The Cove* was released and quickly went on to win an Academy Award for best documentary feature. The film focuses on the annual capture and slaughter of dolphins in the town of Taiji (southern Kansai), where more than 1500 dolphins are killed or captured for sale to aquariums around the world. While the film received good reviews and was seen by millions around the world, few Japanese have seen it. Most of the cinema owners who considered screening the film gave up in the face of a campaign of intimidation by right-wing organisations (in the end only six cinemas in the whole country showed it). As for the Taiji fishermen themselves, they claim that they were lied to and misrepresented by the filmmakers.

The dolphin issue was brought to the fore again in 2010, when the government of Kyoto allowed Orix Corporation to start construction of an aquarium that would feature dolphin shows. Despite widespread opposition by Kyoto citizens who claim that the project is unsuitable for Kyoto (a landlocked city), construction continued at the time of writing.

Meanwhile, Japan remains under international criticism for continuing to hunt whales, despite a 1982 International Whaling Commission moratorium on commercial whaling. Japan claims that it is whaling for research purposes, but critics point out that killing more than 900 minke, 50 fin and 50 humpback whales per season is impossible to justify in the name of research. They also point out that the meat is widely sold as food in Japan (and is even served in some school cafeterias). In

Shinryoku (late April–May)

Only in Japan would they have a special word for that particularly fresh shade of green that typifies the new leaves of springtime: *shinryoku.* For about two or three weeks after budding, the broadleaved trees of Japan look absolutely magnificent. Photographers would call this 'oversaturation'.

Wisteria (May)

The purple blossoms from these vines decorate many temple gardens and mountainsides in Japan. When they're really working, the forest can seem more purple than green.

Autumn foliage (late October– early December)

For many Japanophiles, autumn is the best season to visit Japan. When the leaves of the maples, ginkos and other broadleaved trees turn colour, the effect is truly magical, and nothing suits a beautiful Japanese temple like a backdrop of crimson *momiji* (maple leaves).

January 2010 the issue came to a head in the Southern Ocean when the antiwhaling organisation Sea Shepherd's vessel *Ady Gil* was rammed and sunk by Japanese whalers, who then turned their water cannons on the stricken crew.

Unfortunately, the issues of whaling and dolphin hunting have become so politicised in Japan that meaningful dialogue is impossible. The domestic media seem to be so fearful of right-wing attacks that they cannot say anything critical about the practices, and most politicians and members of the public interpret any such criticism as 'Japan bashing'.

As if this weren't enough, Japan has also been criticised for its failure to join international efforts to protect the tuna, which many biologists say could be driven extinct if commercial fishing is not banned. In 2010 Japan fought hard against the ban on tuna fishing proposed by the Convention on International Trade in Endangered Species (CITES), and many observers say that Japan's opposition was instrumental in dooming the bill. Even if the bill had passed, Japan had long ago announced its intention not to comply.

Of course, the news is not all grim. In 2009 environmentalists were cheered by the results of the general election in which the Democratic Party of Japan (DOJ) took power from the Liberal Democratic Party of Japan (LDP). The DOJ had promised to end the sort of unrestrained public-works projects that have left Japan littered with what many consider needless dams, bridges, concrete retaining walls and other eyesores. Soon after taking power, the DOJ announced plans to cancel 48 large public-works projects. Unfortunately, they ran headlong into the power of the bureaucrats who are intimately tied to such projects, as well as the local communities that have become dependant on the so-called 'construction state'. At the time of writing, with DOJ leaders the target of one scandal probe after another, it was unclear whether they would actually be able to wean the country off the sort of public-works spending that has left a significant portion encased in concrete.

Twenty-five billion pairs of *waribashi* (disposable chopsticks) are used in Japan annually – equivalent to the timber needed to build 17,000 houses.

Under the 1997 Kyoto Protocol, Japan pledged to cut CO_2 emissions by 6% from 1990 levels, but emissions to 2007 rose by 8%. The government lets companies implement voluntary environmental action plans.

Survival Guide

Directory A–Z

Accommodation

Japan offers a wide range of accommodation, from cheap guesthouses to first-class hotels. In addition to the Western-style hotels, you'll also find distinctive Japanese-style places like ryokan and *minshuku*. We introduce ryokan, *minshuku* and *shukubō* in the Traditional Japanese Accommodation chapter (p725).

In this guide, accommodation listings are organised by price category, indicated by the symbols $ (budget), $$ (midrange) or $$$ (top end). Budget options cost ¥6000 or less; midrange rooms cost between ¥6000 and ¥15,000; and top-end rooms will cost more than ¥15,000 (per double). Room rates listed in this book include tax (ie the national 5% consumption tax is figured into the rates), but note that some hotels quote exclusive of taxes.

Of course, there are some regional and seasonal variations. Accommodation tends to be more expensive in big cities than in rural areas. Likewise, in resort areas like the Izu-hantō, accommodation

is more expensive during the warm months. In ski areas like Hakuba and Niseko, needless to say, accommodation prices go up in winter and down in summer.

Since airconditioning is ubiquitous in Japan (due to its hot summers), we only mention air-con in reviews when a place does *not* have it.

Reservations

It can be hard to find accommodation during high-season holiday periods (see p748). If you plan to be in Japan during these periods, you should make reservations as far in advance as possible.

Tourist information offices at main train stations can usually help with reservations, and are often open until about 6.30pm or later. Even if you are travelling by car, the train station is a good first stop in town for information, reservations and cheap car parking.

Making phone reservations in English is usually possible at larger hotels and foreigner-friendly ryokan. Providing you speak clearly and simply, there will usually be someone around who can get the gist of what you want.

Welcome Inn Reservation Center (WIRC), run by International Tourism Center of Japan (www.itcj.jp), operates five reservation counters in Japan as well as an online booking system. The free service includes hundreds of affordable hotels, *minshuku*, ryokan, capsule hotels and hostels in Japan. It operates counters in Tokyo (see p115), Kyoto (see p297), and at the main tourist information counters in Narita and Kansai Airports. You can also make reservations online through its website (which is also an excellent source of information on member hotels and inns).

Japanese Inn Group (www.jpinn.com) is a collection of foreigner-friendly ryokan and guesthouses. You can book member inns via its website or phone/fax. Pick up a copy of its excellent guide to member inns at major tourist information centres in Japan.

Camping

Camping is possible at official campgrounds across Japan, some of which are only open during the summer high season of July and August. Camping is also possible year-round (when conditions permit) at campgrounds in the mountains or around certain mountain huts (p742). 'Guerrilla' or unofficial camping is also possible in many parts of rural Japan, but we recommend

BOOK YOUR STAY ONLINE

For more reviews by Lonely Planet authors, check out hotels.lonelyplanet.com/Japan. You'll find independent reviews, as well as recommendations on the best places to stay. Best of all, you can book online.

PRACTICALITIES

» **Newspapers & Magazines** There are three main English-language daily newspapers in Japan: the *Japan Times, Daily Yomiuri* and *Asahi Shimbun/International Herald Tribune*. In the bigger cities, these are available at bookstores, convenience stores, train-station kiosks and some hotels. In the countryside, you may not be able to find them anywhere. Foreign magazines are available in major bookshops in the bigger cities.

» **Radio** Recent years have seen an increase in the number of stations aimed specifically at Japan's foreign population. InterFM (76.1FM; www.interfm.co.jp/) is a favourite of Tokyo's expat community, and the Kansai equivalent is FM Cocolo (76.5FM; www .cocolo.co.jp).

» **Electricity** The Japanese electric current is 100V AC. Tokyo and eastern Japan are on 50Hz, and western Japan, including Nagoya, Kyoto and Osaka, is on 60Hz. Most electrical items from other parts of the world will function on Japanese current. Japanese plugs are the flat two-pin type.

» **Video Systems** Japan uses the NTSC system.

» **Weights & Measures** Japan uses the international metric system.

---

asking a local person about acceptable areas before setting up your tent.

Cycling Terminals

Cycling terminals (*saikuringu tāminaru*) provide low-priced accommodation of the bunk-bed or tatami-mat variety and are usually found in scenic areas suited to cycling.

Cycling-terminal prices compare favourably with those of a youth hostel: at around ¥3000 per person per night, or ¥5000 including two meals.

Hostels

Japan has an extensive network of youth hostels, often located in areas of interest to travellers. The best source of information on youth hostels is the *Zenkoku Youth Hostel no Tabi* booklet, which is available for ¥1365 from **Japan Youth Hostels, Inc** (JYHA; ☑03-3288-1417; www .jyh.or.jp/english/index.html; 9th fl, Kanda Amerex Bldg, 3-1-16 Misaki-chō, Chiyoda-ku, Tokyo 100-0006). Many youth hostels in Japan sell this handbook.

The best way to find hostels is via the JYHA website, which has details in English on all member hostels, and allows online reservations.

Another option is the *Youth Hostel Map of Japan*, which has one-line entries on each hostel. It's available for free from Japan National Tourism Organization (JNTO) and travel information centres (TICs) in Japan.

MEMBERSHIP, PRICES & REGULATIONS

You can stay at youth hostels in Japan without being a member of either the JYHA or the International Youth Hostel Federation (IYHA). Sample hostel charges:

One-year membership ¥2500

One-night stay (dorm) ¥3000

One-night stay (private room) ¥4000

Breakfast ¥500

Dinner ¥900

Sheet rental ¥100

Hostellers are expected to check in between 3pm and 8pm to 9pm. There is usually a curfew of 10pm or 11pm. Checkout is usually before 10am and dormitories are closed between 10am and 3pm. Bath time is usually between 5pm and 9pm, dinner is between 6pm and 7.30pm, and breakfast is between 7am and 8am.

Hotels

You'll find a range of Western-style hotels in most Japanese cities and resort areas. So-called business hotels are efficient, utilitarian hotels that are geared to Japan's business travellers; while the rooms tend to be small, they are usually perfectly adequate for a night's stay. Luxury hotels are what you'd find anywhere else in the world. Sample hotel charges:

Single room in a business hotel ¥8000

Twin room in a business hotel ¥12,000

Single room in a luxury hotel ¥15,000

Twin room in a luxury hotel ¥20,000

Capsule in a capsule hotel ¥3800

Twin room in a 'love hotel' (overnight) ¥6500

In addition to the 5% consumption tax that is levied on all accommodation in Japan (see p740), you may have to pay an additional 10% or more as a service charge at luxury hotels.

CAPSULE HOTELS

One of Japan's most famous forms of accommodation is the *capseru hoteru*. As the name implies, the 'rooms' in a capsule hotel consist of banks of neat white capsules stacked in rows two or three high. The capsules are about the size of a spacious coffin. Inside is a bed, a TV, a reading light, a radio and an alarm clock. Personal belongings are kept in a locker room. Most capsule hotels have the added attraction of a sauna and a large communal bath.

Capsule hotels are common in major cities and often cater to workers who have partied too hard to make it home or have missed the last train. The majority of capsule hotels only accept male guests, but some also accept women.

LOVE HOTELS

As the name implies, love hotels are used by Japanese couples for discreet trysts. You can use them for this purpose as well, but they're also fine, if a little twee, for overnight accommodation.

To find a love hotel on the street, just look for flamboyant facades and signs clearly stating the rates. Love hotels are designed for maximum privacy: entrances and exits are kept separate; keys are provided through a small opening without contact between desk clerk and guest; and photos of the rooms are displayed to make the choice easy for the customer.

Most love hotels are comfortable with foreign guests, but travellers have reported being turned away at some places. Same-sex couples may have more trouble than heterosexual couples.

Kokumin-shukusha

Kokumin-shukusha (people's lodges) are government-supported institutions offering affordable accommodation in scenic areas. Private Japanese-style rooms are the norm, though some places offer Western-style rooms. Prices average ¥5500 to ¥6500 per person per night, including two meals.

Mountain Huts

Mountain huts (*yama-goya*) are common in many of Japan's hiking and mountain-climbing areas. While you'll occasionally find free emergency shelters, most huts are privately run and charge for accommodation. These places offer bed and board (two meals) at around ¥5000 to ¥8000 per person; if you prepare your own meal, that figure drops to ¥3000 to ¥5000 per person. It's best to call ahead to reserve a spot (contact numbers are available in Japanese hiking guides and maps, and in Lonely Planet's *Hiking in Japan*), but you won't be turned away if you show up without a reservation.

Rider Houses

Catering mainly to touring motorcyclists, rider houses (*raidā hausu*) provide extremely basic shared accommodation from around ¥1000 per night. You should bring your own sleeping bag or ask to rent bedding from the owner. For bathing facilities, you will often be directed to the local *sentō* (public bath).

Rider houses are most common in Hokkaidō, but you'll also find them in places like Kyūshū and Okinawa. If you can read some Japanese, spiral-bound *Touring Mapple* maps, published by Shobunsha and available in Japan, mark almost all of the rider houses in a specific region, as well as cheap places to eat along the way. Japanese readers will also find the **Rider House Database** (www.tabizanmai.net/rider/index_new.html, in Japanese) useful.

Toho

The **Toho network** (www.toho.net/eng.html) is a diverse collection of places that has banded loosely together to offer a more flexible alternative to youth hostels. Most of the network's 90 members are in Hokkaidō, although

there are a few scattered around Honshū and other islands further south. Prices average ¥4000 per person for dormitory-style accommodation, or ¥5000 with two meals. Private rooms are sometimes available for about ¥1000 extra.

Business Hours

Typical business hours:

Banks Open 9am to 3pm Monday to Friday.

Bars Open 6pm to midnight or later, closed one day per week.

Department stores Open 10am to 7pm, closed one or two days per month.

Offices Open 9am to 5pm or 6pm Monday to Friday.

Post offices Local open 9am to 5pm Monday to Friday; central open 9am to 7pm Monday to Friday and 9am to 3pm Saturday (in larger cities may have after-hours window open 24 hours a day, seven days a week).

Restaurants Open 11am to 2pm and 6pm to 11pm, closed one day per week.

Smaller shops Open 9am to 5pm, may be closed Sunday.

Customs Regulations

Customs allowances:

Alcohol Up to three 760cc bottles.

Gifts/souvenirs Up to ¥200,000 in total value.

Perfume Up to 2oz.

Tobacco products Up to 100 cigars or 400 cigarettes or 500g.

You must be over the age of 20 to qualify for these allowances. Customs officers will confiscate any pornographic materials in which pubic hair is visible.

There are no limits on the importation of foreign or Japanese currency. The

ADDRESSES IN JAPAN

In Japan, finding a place from its address can be difficult, even for locals. The problem is twofold: first, the address is usually given by an area rather than a street; and, second, the numbers are not necessarily consecutive, as prior to the mid-1950s numbers were assigned by date of construction.

To find an address, the usual process is to ask directions. Have your address handy. The numerous local police boxes are there largely for this purpose. Businesses often include a small map in their advertisements or on their business cards to show their location.

Most taxis and many rental cars now have satellite navigation systems, which make finding places a breeze, as long as you can program the address or phone number into the system. Needless to say, you'll have to be able to read Japanese to input the address, but phone numbers should be no problem.

export of foreign currency is also unlimited but there is a ¥5 million export limit for Japanese currency.

Visit **Japan Customs** (www.customs.go.jp/english/index.htm) for more information on Japan's customs regulations.

Discount Cards

Hostel Cards

See p741 about obtaining a youth hostel membership card.

Museum Discount Card

The **Grutt Pass** (www.museum.or.jp/grutto/english.html) is a useful ticket that allows free or discounted admission to almost 50 museums in the Tokyo area. For more information see the box, p59.

Senior Cards

Japan is an excellent place for senior travellers, with discounts available on entry fees to many temples, museums and cinemas. To qualify for widely available senior discounts, you have to be aged over 60 or 65, depending upon the place or company. In almost all cases a passport will be sufficient proof of age.

Japanese domestic airlines (JAS, JAL and ANA) offer senior discounts of about 25% on some flights. See their websites for details.

Electricity

100v/50hz/60hz

Embassies & Consulates

Australia Tokyo embassy (☎03-5232-4111; www.australia.or.jp/en/; 2-1-14 Mita, Minato-ku, Tokyo); Fukuoka consulate (☎092-734-5055; 7th fl, Tenjin Twin Bldg, 1-6-8 Tenjin, Chūō-ku, Fukuoka); Osaka consulate (☎06-6941-9271; 16th fl, Twin 21 MID Tower, 2-1-61 Shiromi, Chūō-ku, Osaka).

Canada Tokyo embassy (☎03-5412-6200; www.canadanet.or.jp/english.shtml; 7-3-38 Akasaka, Minato-ku, Tokyo); Nagoya consulate (☎052-972-0450; Nakatō Marunouchi Bldg, 6F, 3-17-6 Marunouchi, Naka-ku, Nagoya); Sapporo consulate (☎011-281-6565; Nikko Bldg, 5F, Kita 4 Nishi 4, Chūō-ku, Sapporo); Hiroshima consulate (☎082-246-0057; 4-33 Komachi, Naka-ku, Hiroshima).

France Tokyo embassy (☎03-5798-6000; www.ambafrance-jp.org; 4-11-44 Minami Azabu, Minato-ku, Tokyo); Osaka consulate (☎06-6131-5278; 6th fl, Dōjima East Bldg, 1-4-19 Dōjima hama, Kita-ku, Osaka).

Germany Tokyo embassy (☎03-5791-7700; www.tokyo.diplo.de/Vertretung/tokyo/de/Startseite.html; 4-5-10 Minami Azabu, Minato-ku, Tokyo); Osaka consulate (☎06-6440-5070; 35th fl, Umeda Sky Bldg Tower East, 1-1-88-3501 Ōyodonaka, Kita-ku, Osaka).

Ireland Tokyo embassy (☎03-3263-0695; www.irishembassy.jp; Ireland House, 2-10-7 Kōji-machi, Chiyoda-ku, Tokyo).

Netherlands Tokyo embassy (☎03-5776-5400; www.mfa.nl/tok-en/; 3-6-3 Shibakōen, Minato-ku, Tokyo); Osaka consulate (☎06-6944-7272; 33rd fl, Twin 21 MID Tower, 2-1-61 Shiromi, Chūō-ku, Osaka).

New Zealand Tokyo embassy (☎03-3467-2271; www.nzembassy.com/home.cfm?c=17; 20-40 Kamiyama-chō, Shibuya-ku, Tokyo); Osaka consulate (☎06-6373-4583; Umeda Centre Bldg, 2-4-12 Nakazaki-nishi Kita-ku, Osaka 530-8323).

Russia Tokyo embassy (☎03-3583-4445; www .rusconsul.jp; 2-1-1, Azabudai, Minato-ku); Sapporo consulate (☎011-561-3171~2; www .rusconsul.jp; 2-5 12-chōme Nishi, Minami 14-jo, Chūō-ku, Sapporo).

South Korea Tokyo embassy (☎03-3452-7611; http://jpn-tokyo.mofat.go.kr/jpn/index.jsp, in Japanese; 4-4-10 Yotsuya, Shinjuku-ku, Tokyo); Fukuoka consulate (☎092-771-0461; 1-1-3 Jigyōhama, Chūō-ku, Fukuoka).

UK Tokyo embassy (☎03-5211-1100; www.uknow.or.jp/index_e.htm; 1 Ichiban-chō, Chiyoda-ku, Tokyo); Osaka consulate (☎06-6120-5600; 19th fl, Epson Osaka Bldg, 3-5-1 Bakurōmachi, Chūō-ku, Osaka).

USA Tokyo embassy (☎03-3224-5000; http://japan.usembassy.gov/t-main.html; 1-10-5 Akasaka, Minato-ku, Tokyo); Fukuoka consulate (☎092-751-9331; 2-5-26 Ōhori, Chūō-ku, Fukuoka); Osaka consulate (☎06-6315-5900; 2-11-5 Nishitenma, Kita-ku, Osaka).

Gay & Lesbian Travellers

With the possible exception of Thailand, Japan is Asia's most enlightened nation with regard to the sexual preferences of foreigners. Shinjuku-nichōme in Tokyo is an established scene where English is spoken and meeting men is fairly straightforward.

In provincial areas there may be one so-called 'snack' bar, where gay men meet. Snack bars can be found in the central entertainment districts of towns and cities. They are usually small places capable of seating only a dozen or fewer customers. They may appear like hole-in-the-wall bars. Note that most snack bars cater to heterosexual customers. Gay-friendly snack bars are hard to locate without an inside connection.

The lesbian scene is growing but is still elusive for most non-Japanese-speaking foreigners. Outside Tokyo you may find it difficult to break into the local scene unless you spend considerable time in a place or have local contacts who can show you around.

Staying in hotels is simple as most have twin rooms, but love hotels are less accessible; if you know someone Japanese and can overcome the language barrier, a stay in a love hotel may be possible, but some are not particularly foreigner friendly (see p742).

Utopia (www.utopia-asia .com) is the site most commonly frequented by English-speaking gays and lesbians. For information about gay and lesbian venues in Tokyo, see the box, p86.

There are no legal restraints to same-sex sexual activities of either gender. Public displays of affection are not really done, whether the couple be same-sex or heterosexual, but they are not usually a problem in cities. In the countryside, they may raise some eyebrows, but that's probably all.

Health

Japan is an advanced country with high standards of hygiene and few endemic diseases. There are no special immunisations needed to visit and, other than bringing prescription medications from home, no special preparations to make. Hospitals and clinics can be found all over the archipelago, and only the smallest outer

---

MEDICAL CARE IN JAPAN

While the Japanese medical system is extensive and comprehensive, the level of care is very uneven. Here are some things to note if you need to seek medical attention:

» It is better to seek care at university hospitals or other large hospitals rather than clinics.

» Japanese doctors and hospitals are sometimes reluctant to treat foreigners. It helps to carry proof of insurance and be willing to show it. If a doctor or hospital seems reticent about giving care, you should insist on it (even though Japan has no Hippocratic oath, doctors can be told that they have to treat patients in need of care).

» Most hospitals and clinics have regular hours (usually in the mornings) when they will see patients.

» Hotels and ryokan that cater to foreigners will usually know the best hospitals in a particular area and will also know hospitals with English-speaking doctors.

» Most doctors speak some English. However, it helps to bring along a Japanese speaker if possible to help you explain your condition and to navigate the hospital.

Japan is one of the world's most technologically advanced countries, but if you're expecting to find free internet hot spots wherever you go, you're in for a surprise. Sure, wi-fi or mobile internet is everywhere, but most of it is available only to subscribers of various Japanese services, many of which are not easy for travellers to join (especially those who don't speak and read Japanese). **Freespot Map** (www.freespot.com/users/map_e.html) has a list of internet hot spots; it's not exhaustive and the maps are in Japanese, but it's quite useful. Failing that, here are some ways to get online:

» **FON Network** Virtually all Starbucks have FON wi-fi. Foneros (FON members) can connect for free; nonmembers can use Google services like Gmail for free. Other services must be paid for (credit-card payment is possible).

» **SIM cards** If you bring an internet device that takes a SIM card, you can buy B-Mobile data SIM cards from major electronics shops. These will usually allow unlimited internet use for a specific length of time (a month is common).

» **Boingo** Subscribers to Boingo's global plan (www.boingo.com) can use BB Mobile-point wi-fi at McDonald's restaurants.

» **Portable internet connections** You can rent data cards, USB dongles or pocket wi-fi devices from various phone-rental companies. The most user-friendly option with English service is provided by Rentafone Japan (www.rentafonejapan.com), which offers two types of pocket wi-fi from ¥3900 per week with unlimited use.

islands lack medical facilities. That said, there are some things to keep in mind, which we outline in the box above.

Insurance

A travel-insurance policy to cover theft, loss and medical problems is a good idea. Some policies will specifically exclude 'dangerous activities', which can include scuba diving, motorcycling and even trekking; if you plan to engage in such activities, you'll want a policy that covers them.

You may prefer a policy that pays doctors or hospitals directly rather than having you pay on the spot and claim later. If you have to claim later, make sure you keep all documentation. Some policies ask you to call (reverse charge) a centre in your home country where an immediate assessment of your problem is made. Check that the policy covers ambulances or an emergency flight home.

Be sure to bring your insurance card or other certificate of insurance to

Japan; Japanese hospitals have been known to refuse treatment to foreign patients with no proof of medical insurance.

Internet Access

Internet access in a nutshell:
» Current: 100V AC; 50Hz in east Japan, 60Hz in west Japan
» Plugs: flat two-pin type, identical to most ungrounded North American plugs
» Connections: LAN cable access more common than wi-fi
» Internet-cafe rates: ¥200 to ¥700 per hour

If you plan on bringing your laptop to Japan, make sure that it is compatible with the current and check to see if your plug will fit the wall sockets. Transformers and plug adaptors are readily available in electronics districts, such as Tokyo's Akihabara (p112), Osaka's Den Den Town (p316) or Kyoto's Teramachi-dōri (p294).

In this book, an internet symbol (@) indicates that the accommodation option

has at least one computer with internet for guests' use. We also note where wi-fi (📶) is available. Note that wi-fi is far less common in Japanese hotels than in their Western counterparts. About a third of hotels in Japan have free wi-fi; another third charge for wi-fi; and a third have no wi-fi at all.

It is much more common to find LAN cable internet access points in hotel rooms (the hotels can usually provide LAN cables, but you may want to bring your own to avoid having to ask for one everywhere you stay). These LAN connections usually work fine, but you may occasionally find it hard to log on due to software or hardware compatibility issues or configuration problems – the front-desk staff *may* be able to help.

You'll find internet cafes and other access points in most major Japanese cities. As a rule, internet connections are fast (DSL or ADSL) and reliable. Most accommodation options also have some way of getting online, with terminals in the lobby, wi-fi or LAN access.

Left Luggage

Only major train stations have left-luggage facilities, but almost all stations have coin-operated storage lockers (¥100 to ¥500 per day, depending on size). The lockers are rented until midnight (not for 24 hours). After that time you have to insert more money before your key will work. If your bag is simply too large to fit in the locker, ask someone 'tenimotsu azukai wa doko desu ka' (Where is the left-luggage office?).

Legal Matters

Japanese police have extraordinary powers. They can detain a suspect for up to three days without charging them; after this time a prosecutor can decide to extend this period for another 20 days. Police can also choose whether to allow a suspect to phone their embassy or lawyer, though if you find yourself in police custody you should insist that you will not cooperate in any way until allowed to make such a call. Your embassy is the first place you should call if given the chance.

Police will speak almost no English; insist that a tsūyakusha (interpreter) be summoned. Police are legally bound to provide one before proceeding with any questioning. Even if you do speak Japanese, it's best to deny it and stay with your native language.

If you have a problem, call the **Japan Helpline** (☏0120-46-1997), a nationwide emergency number that operates 24 hours a day, seven days a week.

Maps

If you'd like to buy a map of Japan before arriving, both Nelles and Periplus produce reasonable ones. If you want something more detailed,

wait until you get to Tokyo or Kyoto, where you'll find lots of detailed maps in both English and Japanese.

The JNTO's free *Tourist Map of Japan*, available at JNTO-operated tourist information centres inside the country and JNTO offices abroad, is a reasonable English-language map that is suitable for general route planning.

The *Japan Road Atlas* (Shobunsha) is a good choice for those planning to drive around the country; unfortunately, it's out of print (you might be able to find a copy online, but it won't be cheap). Those looking for something less bulky should pick up a copy of the *Bilingual Atlas of Japan* (Kodansha). Of course, if you can read a little Japanese, you'll do much better with one of the excellent *Super Mapple* road atlases published by Shobunsha.

Money

The currency in Japan is the yen (¥). The Japanese pronounce yen as 'en', with no 'y' sound. The kanji for yen is 円.

Yen denominations:

¥1 Coin; lightweight; silver colour.

¥5 Coin; bronze colour, hole in the middle, value in Chinese character.

¥10 Coin; copper colour.

¥50 Coin; silver colour, hole in the middle.

¥100 Coin; silver colour.

¥500 Coin; large with silver colour.

¥1000 Banknote.

¥2000 Banknote (rare).

¥5000 Banknote.

¥10,000 Banknote.

The Japanese postal system has recently linked its ATMs to the international Cirrus and Plus networks, and 7-Eleven convenience stores have followed suit, so getting money is no longer the issue it once was for travellers to Japan. Of course, it always makes sense to carry some foreign cash and some credit cards just to be on the safe side. For those who don't have credit cards, it would be a good idea to bring some travellers cheques as a back-up.

ATMs

Automated teller machines are almost as common as vending machines in Japan. Unfortunately, most of these do not accept foreign-issued cards. Even if they display Visa and MasterCard logos, most accept only Japan-issued versions of these cards.

Fortunately, Japanese postal ATMs accept cards that belong to the following

WARNING: JAPAN IS A CASH SOCIETY

Be warned that cold hard yen is the way to pay in Japan. While credit cards are becoming more common, cash is still much more widely used, and travellers cheques are rarely accepted. Do not assume that you can pay for things with a credit card; always carry sufficient cash. The only places where you can count on paying by credit card are department stores and large hotels.

For those without credit cards, it would be a good idea to bring some travellers cheques as a back-up. As in most other countries, the US dollar is still the currency of choice in terms of exchanging cash and cashing travellers cheques.

USING A JAPANESE POSTAL ATM

Postal ATMs are relatively easy to use. Here's the drill: press 'English Guide', select 'Withdrawal', then insert your card, press 'Visitor Withdrawal', input your pin number, then hit the button marked 'Kakunin' (確認), then enter the amount, hit 'Yen' and 'Confirm' and you should hear the delightful sound of bills being dispensed.

international networks: Visa, Plus, MasterCard, Maestro, Cirrus, American Express and Diners Club cards. Check the sticker(s) on the back of your card to see which network(s) your card belongs to. You'll find postal ATMs in almost all post offices, and you'll find post offices in even the smallest Japanese village.

Note that postal ATMs work with bank or cash cards – you cannot use credit cards, even with a pin number, in postal ATMs. That is to say, you cannot use postal ATMs to perform a cash advance.

Most postal ATMs are open 9am to 5pm on weekdays, 9am to noon on Saturday, and are closed on Sunday and holidays. Some postal ATMs in very large central post offices are open longer hours.

In addition to postal ATMs, you will find a few specialised international ATMs in big cities like Tokyo, Osaka and Kyoto, as well as major airports like Narita and Kansai International Airports.

International cards also work in the ATMs at **Citibank Japan** (www.citibank.co.jp/en/branch/index.html). Visit its site for a branch locator.

Finally, 7-Eleven convenience stores across Japan have linked their ATMs to international cash networks, and these often seem to accept cards that for one reason or other will not work with postal ATMs. They are also open 24 hours. So, if you can't find an open post office or your card won't work with postal ATMs, don't give up:

ask around for a 7-Eleven (pronounced like '*sebun erebun*' in Japanese).

Credit Cards

Except for making cash withdrawals at banks and ATMs, it is best not to rely on credit cards in Japan (see the box, p746). While department stores, top-end hotels and some large or fancy restaurants do accept cards, most businesses do not. Cash and carry is still very much the rule. If you do decide to bring a credit card, you'll find Visa the most useful, followed by MasterCard, Amex and Diners Club.

The main credit-card offices in Tokyo are:

Amex (☎0120-02-0120; 4-30-16 Ogikubo, Suginami-ku; ☺24hr)

MasterCard (☎03-5728-5200; 16th fl, Cerulean Tower, 26-1 Sakuragaoka-chō, Shibuya-ku)

Visa (☎03-5275-7604; 7th fl, Hitotsubashi Bldg, 2-6-3 Hitotsubashi, Chiyoda-ku)

Exchanging Money

You can change cash or travellers cheques at most banks, major post offices, discount ticket shops, some travel agents, some large hotels and most big department stores. Note that discount-ticket shops (known as *kakuyasu kippu uriba* in Japanese) often have the best rates. These can be found around major train stations. However, only US dollars and euros fetch decent exchange rates (see the box, p747).

International Transfers

To make an international transfer you'll have to find a Japanese bank associated with the bank transferring the money. Start by asking at the central branch of any major Japanese bank. If they don't have a relationship with your bank, they can usually refer you to a bank that does. Once you find a related bank, you'll have to give your home bank the exact details of where to send the money: the bank, branch and location. A credit-card cash advance is a worthwhile alternative.

Taxes

Japan has a 5% consumption tax (*shōhizei*). If you eat at expensive restaurants and stay in top-end accommodation, you will encounter a service charge that varies from 10% to 15%.

Tipping

There is little tipping in Japan. If you want to show your gratitude to someone, give them a gift rather than a tip. If you do choose to give someone (your maid at a ryokan, for instance) a cash gift, place the money in an envelope first.

CURRENCY WARNING

Exchange rates for the US dollar and euro are reasonable in Japan. All other currencies, including the Australian dollar and the currencies of nearby countries, fetch very poor exchange rates. If you want to bring cash to Japan, we suggest US dollars or euros. Or, if you must change other currencies into yen, we suggest doing so in your home country.

DIRECTORY A–Z

Post

The Japanese postal system is reliable, efficient and, for regular postcards and airmail letters, not markedly more expensive than in other developed countries.

Postal Rates

The airmail rate for postcards is ¥70 to any overseas destination; aerograms cost ¥90. Letters weighing less than 25g are ¥90 to other countries within Asia, ¥110 to North America, Europe or Oceania (including Australia and New Zealand), and ¥130 to Africa and South America. One peculiarity of the Japanese postal system is that you will be charged extra if your writing runs over onto the address side (the right side) of a postcard.

Sending & Receiving Mail

The symbol for post offices is a red T with a bar across the top on a white background (〒).

Mail can be sent to, from or within Japan when addressed in English (Roman script).

Although any post office will hold mail for collection, the poste-restante concept is not well known and can cause confusion in smaller places. It is probably better to have mail addressed to you at a larger central post office. Letters are usually only held for 30 days before being returned to sender. When enquiring about mail for collection ask for *kyokudome yūbin*. Such mail should be addressed as follows:

» Name
» Poste Restante
» Central Post Office
» Tokyo, JAPAN

Public Holidays

Japan has 15 national holidays. When a public holiday falls on a Sunday, the following Monday is taken as a holiday. If that Monday is already a holiday, the following day becomes a holiday as well. And if two weekdays (say, Tuesday and Thursday) are holidays, the day in between also becomes a holiday.

Japan's national holidays:

Ganjitsu (New Year's Day) 1 January

Seijin-no-hi (Coming-of-Age Day) Second Monday in January

Kenkoku Kinem-bi (National Foundation Day) 11 February

Shumbun-no-hi (spring equinox) 20 or 21 March

Shōwa-no-hi (Shōwa Emperor's Day) 29 April

Kempō Kinem-bi (Constitution Day) 3 May

Midori-no-hi (Green Day) 4 May

Kodomo-no-hi (Children's Day) 5 May

Umi-no-hi (Marine Day) Third Monday in July

Keirō-no-hi (Respect-for-the-Aged Day) Second Monday in September

Shūbun-no-hi (autumn equinox) 22 or 23 September

Taiiku-no-hi (Health-Sports Day) Second Monday in October

Bunka-no-hi (Culture Day) 3 November

Kinrō Kansha-no-hi (Labour Thanksgiving Day) 23 November

Tennō Tanjōbi (Emperor's Birthday) 23 December

You will find transport crowded and accommodation bookings hard to come by during the following high-season travel periods:

Shōgatsu (New Year) 31 December to 3 January

Golden Week 29 April to 5 May

O-Bon Mid-August

Safe Travel

The Great East Japan Earthquake of March 2011 and the following nuclear crisis (see the box, p736) made it unsafe to travel in certain parts of northeast Honshū (at press time, this was an area within 20km of the Fukushima One nuclear powerplant and some villages just to the north of this zone). Of course, the situation may change by the time you read this, so we strongly recommend that you check the latest situation online, eg your government's travel warnings. Here are a few resources:

Australian Department of Foreign Affairs (www.smart traveller.gov.au)

British Foreign Office (http://www.fco.gov.uk/en/travelling-and-living-overseas/travel-advice-by-country)

US State Department (http://travel.state.gov/travel/travel_1744.html)

If you find yourself near a coastal area and you feel an earthquake, make for high ground immediately.

Solo Travellers

Japan is an excellent place for solo travellers: it's safe, convenient and friendly. Almost all hotels have single rooms, and business-hotel singles can cost as little as ¥4000. Ryokan usually charge by the person, not the room, which keeps the price down for the solo. The only hitch is that some ryokan owners baulk at renting a room to a single traveller, when they might be able to rent it to two people instead.

Many restaurants have small tables or counters that are perfect perches for solo travellers. *Izakaya* (pub-eateries) are also generally welcoming to solo travellers, and you probably won't have to wait long before you're offered a drink and roped into a conversation, particularly if you sit at the counter. Finally, the 'gaijin bars' in the larger cities are generally friendly, convivial places; if you're after a travel partner or just an English-speaking conversation partner, you'll find these are good places to start.

Telephone

Japanese telephone codes consist of an area code plus the number. You do not dial the area code when making a call in that area. When dialling Japan from abroad, dial the country code, ☑81, followed by the area code (drop the '0') and the number. The most common toll-free prefixes are ☑0120, 0070, 0077, 0088 and 0800. Directory-assistance numbers:

Local directory assistance ☑104 (¥60 to ¥150 per call)
Local directory assistance in English ☑0120-36-4463 (from 9am to 5pm Monday to Friday)
International directory assistance ☑0057

International Calls

The best way to make an international phone call from Japan is to use a prepaid international phone card (see p749).

Paid overseas calls can be made from grey international ISDN phones. These are usually found in phone booths marked 'International & Domestic Card/Coin Phone'. Unfortunately, these are very rare; try looking in the lobbies of top-end hotels and at airports. Some new green phones found in phone booths also allow international calls. Calls are charged by the unit, each of which is six seconds, so if you don't have much to say you could phone home for just ¥100. Reverse-charge (collect) overseas calls can be made from any pay phone.

You can save money by dialling late at night. Economy rates are available from 11pm to 8am. Note that it is also cheaper to make domestic calls by dialling outside the standard hours.

Useful international numbers:
International operator-assisted calls ☑0051 (KDDI; operators speak English)
Direct-dial international numbers ☑KDDI 001 010, SoftBank Telecom 0041 010, NTT 0033 010

There's very little difference in the direct-dial rates. Dial one of the above numbers, then the international country code, the local code and the number.

PREPAID INTERNATIONAL PHONE CARDS

Because of the lack of pay phones from which you can make international phone calls in Japan, the easiest way to make a call is to buy a prepaid international phone card. Most convenience stores carry at least one of the following, which can be used with any regular pay phone:

» KDDI Superworld Card
» NTT Communications World Card
» SoftBank Telecom Comica Card

Local Calls

The Japanese public-telephone system is extremely reliable and efficient. Unfortunately, the number of pay phones is decreasing fast as more and more Japanese buy mobile phones. Local calls from pay phones cost ¥10 per minute; unused ¥10 coins are returned after the call is completed but no change is given on ¥100 coins.

In general it's much easier to buy a telephone card (terefon kādo) when you arrive rather than worry about always having coins on hand. Phone cards are sold in ¥500 and ¥1000 denominations (the latter earns you an extra ¥50 in calls) and can be used in most green or grey pay phones. Cards are available from vending machines (some of which

can be found in public phone booths) and convenience stores. They come in myriad designs and are also a collectable item.

Mobile Phones

Japan's mobile-phone networks use 3G (third generation) mobile-phone technology on a variety of frequencies. Thus, non-3G mobile phones cannot be used in Japan, which means that most foreign mobile phones will not work there. Furthermore, SIM cards are not commonly available. Thus, for most foreigners who want to use a mobile phone, the only solution is to rent one.

Several telecommunications companies specialise in short-term rentals; two are listed below.

Mobile Phone Japan (☑090-6660-7645; www.mobilephonejp.com) Basic rental from ¥2900 per week. Incoming calls, international or domestic, are free; outgoing domestic calls are ¥90 per minute (outgoing international calls vary according to country and time of day). Free delivery anywhere in Japan; free prepaid return envelope.

Rentafone Japan (☑0120-74-6487; www.rentafonejapan.com) Rental from ¥3900 per week. Free delivery to your accommodation. Domestic/overseas rates are ¥35/45 per minute.

Time

All of Japan is in the same time zone: nine hours ahead of Greenwich Mean Time (GMT). Sydney and Wellington are ahead of Japan (by one and three hours respectively), and most of the world's other big cities are behind: (New York by 14 hours, Los Angeles by 17 and London by nine). Japan does not have daylight savings time (also known as summer time).

Toilets

You will come across both Western-style toilets and Asian squat toilets. When you are compelled to squat, the correct position is facing the hood, away from the door. Take special care to ensure the contents of your pockets don't spill out! Toilet paper isn't always provided, so it is always a good idea to carry tissues with you. You may be given small packets of tissues on the street, which is a common form of advertising.

In many bathrooms, separate toilet slippers are sometimes provided – usually located just inside the toilet door. These are for use in the toilet only, so remember to change out of them when you leave.

It's quite common to see men urinating in public – the unspoken rule is that it's acceptable at night time if you happen to be drunk. Public toilets are free. The katakana for 'toilet' is トイレ, and the kanji is お手洗い. You'll often also see these kanji signs:

» Female 女
» Male 男

Tourist Information

You will find tourist information offices (kankō annai-sho; 観光案内所) in most cities and towns and even in some small villages. They are almost always located inside or in front of the main train station. The staff usually speaks some English, but don't count on it. English-language materials are usually available. Naturally, places that get a lot of foreign visitors are more likely to have English-speaking staff and English-language materials. Nonetheless, with a little patience and a smile you will usually be able to get the information you need from even the smallest local tourist information office.

The **Japan National Tourism Organization** (JNTO; www.japantravelinfo .com/top/index.php) is Japan's main English-language information service for foreign travellers. JNTO produces a great deal of useful literature, which is available from its overseas offices as well as its Tourist Information Center (p115) in Tokyo. Most of its publications are available in English and, in some cases, other European and Asian languages. The organisation's website is a very useful tool when planning your journey to Japan.

JNTO has a overseas offices in the following locations:

Australia (☎02-9279 2177; Ste 1, Level 4, 56 Clarence St, Sydney NSW 2000)

Canada (☎416-366 7140; Ste 306, 481 University Ave, Toronto, ON M5G 2E9)

France (☎01 42 96 20 29; 4 rue de Ventadour, 75001 Paris)

Germany (☎069-20353; Kaiserstrasse 11, 60311 Frankfurt am Main)

UK (☎020-7398-5670; 5th fl, 12/13 Nicholas Lane, London, EC4N 7BN)

USA Los Angeles (☎213-623 1952; Ste 302, 340 E 2nd St, Little Tokyo Plaza, Los Angeles, CA 90012); New York (☎212-757 5640; 19th fl, 11 West 42nd St, New York, NY 10036)

Tours

The following companies offer private tours of Japan:

All Japan Private Tours & Speciality Services (www .kyoto-tokyo-private-tours. com/) This company offers exclusive unique tours of Kyoto, Nara and Tokyo, as well as business coordination and related services.

Windows to Japan (www .windowstojapan.com/) Offers private and group tours of all parts of Japan.

Travellers with Disabilities

Japan gets mixed marks in terms of ease of travel for those with disabilities. On the plus side, many new buildings have access ramps, traffic lights have speakers playing melodies when it is safe to cross, train platforms have raised dots and lines to provide guidance for the visually impaired, and some ticket machines in Tokyo have Braille. Some attractions also offer free entry to disabled persons and one companion. On the negative side, many of Japan's cities are still rather difficult for disabled persons to negotiate, often due to the relative lack of normal sidewalks on narrow streets.

Train cars on most lines have areas set aside for people in wheelchairs. Those with other physical disabilities can use the seats near the train exits, called yūsen-zaseki. You will also find these seats near the front of buses; usually they're a different colour from the regular seats.

Useful organisations and services for travellers with disabilities:

Japanese Red Cross Language Service Volunteers (housii@tok-lanserv.jp; www.tok-lanserv.jp/index.html, in Japanese; c/o Volunteers Division, Japanese Red Cross Society, 1-1-3 Shiba Daimon, Minato-ku, Tokyo 105-8521) A useful resource for travellers with disabilities, but you may need to have a Japanese-speaking friend call to make enquiries. Also produces the following website.

Accessible Japan (http:// accessible.jp.org/tokyo/en/ index.html) The most comprehensive online guide to accessible Tokyo; also has some useful background information for travellers with disabilities.

Eagle Bus Company

(☎049-227-7611; www.new -wing.co.jp/english/english .html) Has lift-equipped buses and some English-speaking drivers who are also licensed caregivers. Offers tours of Tokyo and around for travellers with disabilities. The number of English-speaking driver-caregivers is limited, so reserve well in advance. Group bookings are possible. Also offers English-language tours of Kawagoe, a small town outside Tokyo, which is sometimes known as little Edo.

Visas

Generally, visitors who are not planning to engage in income-producing activities while in Japan are exempt from obtaining visas and will be issued a 90-day *tanki-taizai* (temporary-visitor) visa on arrival. Nationals of Australia, Canada, France, Germany, Ireland, Italy, the Netherlands, New Zealand, Spain, the UK and the USA are eligible for this visa.

Stays of up to six months are permitted for citizens of Austria, Germany, Ireland, Mexico, Switzerland and the UK. Citizens of these countries will almost always be given a 90-day temporary visitor visa upon arrival, which can usually be extended for another 90 days at immigration bureaux inside Japan (for details, see p751).

Japanese law requires that visitors entering on a temporary-visitor visa possess an ongoing air or sea ticket or evidence thereof. In practice, few travellers are asked to produce such documents, but it pays to be on the safe side.

For additional information on visas and regulations, contact your nearest Japanese embassy or consulate, or visit the website of the **Ministry of Foreign Affairs of Japan** (www.mofa.go.jp). Here you can find out about the different types of visas available,

read about working-holiday visas and find details on the Japan Exchange & Teaching (JET) program, which sponsors native English speakers to teach in the Japanese public school system.

Note that, on entering Japan, all short-term foreign visitors are photographed and fingerprinted.

Alien Registration Card

Anyone who stays for more than 90 days is required to obtain an Alien Registration Card (Gaikokujin Torokushō). This card can be obtained at the municipal office of the city, town or ward in which you're living or staying.

You must carry your card at all times as the police can stop you and ask to see it. If you don't have it, you may be taken back to the police station and will have to wait there until someone fetches the card for you. In practice, police almost never stop foreigners and ask to see their cards.

Visa Extensions

With the exception of those nationals whose countries have reciprocal visa exemptions and can stay for six months, the limit for most nationalities is 90 days or three months. To extend a temporary-visitor visa beyond the standard 90 days or three months, apply at the nearest immigration office. The **Japanese Immigration Bureau** (www.immi-moj.go.jp/ english/soshiki/index.html) site lists the offices in Japan. You must provide two copies of an Application for Extension of Stay (available at the immigration office), a letter stating the reasons for the extension, supporting documentation and your passport. There is a processing fee of ¥4000.

Many long-term visitors to Japan get around the extension problem by briefly leaving the country, usually going to South Korea. Be warned, though, that immigration

officials are wise to this practice and many 'tourist visa returnees' are turned back at the entry point.

Work Visas

Unless you are on a cultural visa and have been granted permission to work, or hold a working-holiday visa, you are not permitted to work without a proper work visa. If you have the proper paperwork and an employee willing to sponsor you, the process is straightforward, although it can be time-consuming.

Once you find an employer who is willing to sponsor you, it is necessary to obtain a Certificate of Eligibility from the nearest immigration office. The same office can then issue you your work visa, which is valid for one or three years. The whole procedure usually takes two to three months.

Working-Holiday Visas

Citizens of Australia, Canada, Denmark, France, Germany, Ireland, New Zealand, the Republic of Korea and the UK who are aged between 18 and 25 (the limit can be pushed up to 30 in some cases) can apply for a working-holiday visa. The program is also open to residents of Hong Kong and Taiwan.

This visa allows a six-month stay and two six-month extensions. It is designed to enable young people to travel extensively during their stay; although employment is supposed to be part-time or temporary, in practice many people work full time.

A working-holiday visa is much easier to obtain than a work visa and is popular with Japanese employers. Single applicants must have the equivalent of US$2000 of funds, a married couple must have US$3000 and all applicants must have an onward ticket from Japan. For details, enquire at the nearest Japanese embassy or consulate.

Volunteering

Japan doesn't have as many volunteer opportunities as some other Asian countries. However, there are positions out there for those who look. One of the most popular options is provided by **Willing Workers on Organic Farms Japan** (WWOOF Japan; www.wwoofjapan.com/main/index.php?lang=en; fax 011-780-4908; 6-7 3-chōme Honchō 2jō, Higashi-ku, Sapporo 065-0042). This organisation places volunteers on organic farms around the country and provides participants with a good look at Japanese rural life and the running of an organic farm. It's also a great chance to improve your Japanese-language skills.

Alternatively, you can look for volunteer opportunities once you arrive. There are occasional ads for volunteer positions in magazines like *Kansai Scene* in Kansai and the various English-language journals in the Tokyo area. Word of mouth is also a good way to search for jobs.

Hikers, for example, are sometimes offered short-term positions in Japan's mountain huts.

Women Travellers

Japan is a relatively safe country for women travellers, though perhaps not quite as safe as some might think. Crimes against women are generally believed to be widely underreported, especially by Japanese women. Foreign women are occasionally subjected to some forms of verbal harassment or prying questions. Physical attacks are very rare, but have occurred.

The best advice is to avoid being lulled into a false sense of security by Japan's image as one of the world's safest countries and to take the normal precautions you would in your home country. If a neighbourhood or establishment looks unsafe, then treat it that way. As long as you use your common sense, you will most likely find that Japan is a pleasant and rewarding place to travel as a woman.

Several train companies have recently introduced women-only cars to protect female passengers from *chikan* (men who feel up women and girls on packed trains). These cars are usually available during rush-hour periods on weekdays on busy urban lines. There are signs (usually in pink) on the platform indicating where you can board these cars, and the cars themselves are usually labelled in both Japanese and English (again, these are often marked in pink).

If you have a problem and you find the local police unhelpful, you can call the **Japan Helpline** (0120-46-1997), a nationwide emergency number that operates 24 hours a day, seven days a week.

Finally, an excellent resource available for any woman setting up in Japan is Caroline Pover's excellent book *Being A Broad in Japan*, which can be found in bookstores and can also be ordered from her website at www.being-a-broad.com.

TSUNAMI RELIEF

At the time of writing, relief efforts to help victims of the Great East Japan Earthquake (see the box, p435) were being conducted mostly by Japanese and some international rescue or military groups. A few Japanese and Japan-based foreigners were undertaking their own 'unofficial' relief efforts but, at press time, there were limited opportunities for foreign visitors to Japan to participate in relief efforts. This may well change by the time you read this, so those wishing to do actual relief work should make use of the internet to search for opportunities.

Organisations that are actively involved in the relief effort and accept donations include the following:

» **IDRO Japan** (www.idrojapan.org) This Kyoto-based charity has minimal overheads and works by bringing needed supplies directly to victims of the disaster. Longer-term, it aims to build small, expandable homes for people whose homes were washed away by the tsunami.

» **Oxfam Japan** (http://oxfam.jp/en/2011/03/emergency_appeal_for_earthquak.html) Oxfam Japan is working with local organisations to bring relief to tsunami victims.

» **Save the Children** (www.savethechildren.org/japanquake) This organisation is working specifically to help children in the affected areas.

» **Second Harvest** (www.2hj.org/index.php/eng_home) Originally organised to provide food to the hungry in Japan, Second Harvest has been actively involved in providing food to the disaster victims.

Work

Japan is an excellent and rewarding place to live and work and you'll find expats in all the major cities doing just that. Teaching English is still the most common job for Westerners, but bartending, hostessing, modelling and various writing-editorial jobs are also possible.

The key to success is doing your homework and presenting yourself properly. You will definitely need a sharp outfit for interviews, a stack of *meishi* (business cards) and the right attitude. If you don't have a university degree, you won't be eligible for most jobs that qualify you for a work visa. Any qualification, like an English-teaching certificate, will be a huge boost.

Finally, outside of the entertainment, construction and English-teaching industries, you can't expect a good job unless you speak good Japanese (any more than someone could expect a job in your home country without speaking the language of that country).

Bartending

Bartending does not qualify you for a work visa; most of the foreign bartenders in Japan are either working illegally or are on another kind of visa. Some bars in big Japanese cities hire foreign bartenders; most are strict about visas but others don't seem to care. The best places to look are 'gaijin bars', although a few Japanese-oriented places also employ foreign bartenders for 'ambience'. The pay is barely enough to survive on: usually about ¥1000 per hour. The great plus of working as a bartender (other than free drinks) is the chance to practise speaking Japanese.

English Teaching

Teaching English has always been the most popular job for native English speakers in Japan. A university degree is

an absolute essential as you cannot qualify for a work visa without one (be sure to bring the actual degree with you to Japan). Teaching qualifications and some teaching experience will be a huge plus when job hunting.

Consider lining up a job before you arrive. Some big schools, like AEON, now have recruitment programs in the USA and the UK. One downside to the big 'factory schools' that recruit overseas is that working conditions are often pretty dire compared with smaller schools that recruit within Japan.

Australians, New Zealanders, Canadians and British citizens, who can take advantage of the Japanese working-holiday visa (p751), are in a slightly better position. Schools are happier about taking on unqualified teachers if they don't have to bother with sponsoring a teacher for a work visa.

There is a definite hierarchy among English teachers and teaching positions. The bottom of the barrel are the big chain *eikaiwa* (private English-language schools), followed by small local *eikaiwa*, in-house company language schools and private lessons, with university positions and international-school positions being the most sought after. As you would expect, newcomers start at the lower rungs and work their way up the ladder.

ELT News (www.eltnews.com) is an excellent website with lots of information and want ads for English teachers in Japan.

GOVERNMENT SCHOOLS

The program run by **Japan Exchange & Teaching** (JET; www.jetprogramme.org) provides teaching-assistant positions for foreign teachers. The job operates on a yearly contract and must be organised in your home country. The program gets very good reports from many of its teachers.

Teachers employed by the JET program are known as Assistant Language Teachers (ALTs). Although you will have to apply in your home country in order to work as an ALT with JET, it's worth bearing in mind that many local governments in Japan are also employing ALTs for their schools. Such work can sometimes be arranged within Japan.

Visit the JET website or contact the nearest Japanese embassy or consulate for more details.

INTERNATIONAL SCHOOLS

Major cities with large foreign populations, such as Tokyo and Yokohama, have a number of international schools for the children of foreign residents. Work is available for qualified, Western-trained teachers in all disciplines; the schools will organise your visa.

PRIVATE SCHOOLS

Private language schools (*eikaiwa*) are the largest employers of foreign teachers and the best bet for job-hunting newcomers. The classifieds section of Monday's *Japan Times* is the best place to look. Some larger schools rely on direct enquiries from would-be teachers.

Tokyo is the easiest place to find teaching jobs; schools across Japan advertise or recruit in the capital. Heading straight to another of Japan's major population centres (say Osaka, Fukuoka, Hiroshima or Sapporo), where there are smaller numbers of competing foreigners, is also a good bet, but, as noted in this section, the hiring situation is tight these days and you cannot count on just showing up and finding work.

Proofreading, Editing & Writing

There is demand for skilled editors, copywriters, proofreaders and translators (Japanese to English and, less commonly, vice versa) in Japan. And with the advent of the internet, you don't even have to be based in Japan to do this work. Unfortunately, as with many things in Japan, introductions and connections play a huge role, and it's difficult to simply show up in Tokyo or plaster your resume online and wind up with a good job.

You'll need to be persistent and do some networking to make much in this field. Experience, advanced degrees and salesmanship will all come in handy. And even if you don't intend to work as a translator, some Japanese-language ability will be a huge plus, if only for communicating with potential employers and clients. If you think you've got what it takes, check the Monday edition of the *Japan Times* for openings.

For more information about proofreading and editing in Japan, visit the website for the **Society of Writers, Editors & Translators** (SWET; www.swet.jp). The website has a job-listings section that is useful for those seeking work in this field.

Ski Areas

Seasonal work is available at ski areas, and this is a popular option for Australian and Kiwi travellers who want to combine a trip to Japan, a little skiing and a chance to earn some money. A working-holiday visa (see p751) makes this easier, although occasionally people are offered jobs without visas. The jobs are typical ski-town jobs – ski-lift attendants, hotel workers, bartenders and, for those with the right skills (language and skiing), ski instructors. You won't earn much more than ¥1000 per hour unless you're an instructor, but you'll get lodging and lift tickets. All told, it's a fun way to spend a few months in Japan.

Transport

GETTING THERE & AWAY

Entering the Country

While most travellers to Japan fly via Tokyo, there are several other ways of getting into and out of the country. For a start, there are many other airports, which can make better entry points than Tokyo's somewhat inconvenient Narita International Airport. It's also possible to arrive by sea from South Korea, China and Russia.

Flights, tours and rail tickets can be booked online at lonelyplanet.com/bookings.

Passport

A passport is essential. If your passport is within a few months of expiry, get a new one now. For information on visas, see p751.

Air

There are flights to Japan from all over the world, usually to Tokyo, but also to a number of other airports. Although Tokyo may seem the obvious arrival and departure point,

for many visitors this may not be the case. For example, if you plan to explore western Japan or the Kansai region, it might be more convenient to fly into Kansai International Airport near Osaka.

Airports & Airlines

There are international airports situated on the main island of Honshū (Nagoya, Niigata, Osaka/Kansai, Haneda and Tokyo Narita), as well as on Kyūshū (Fukuoka, Kagoshima, Kumamoto and Nagasaki), Okinawa (Naha) and Hokkaidō (Sapporo):

» The majority of international flights to/from Tokyo use **Narita International Airport** (NRT; www.narita -airport.jp/en/), about an hour from Tokyo by express train (¥2940); it's cheaper and more convenient to fly via Haneda Airport if you can.

» Some international flights now go via **Tokyo International Airport** (HND; www .tokyo-airport-bldg.co.jp/en/), better known as **Haneda Airport**, about 30 minutes from Tokyo by monorail and thus more convenient than Narita. There's a new international terminal and runway; at the time of writing there were flights to/from 12 countries.

» All of Osaka's international flights go via **Kansai International Airport** (KIX; www .kansai-airport.or.jp/en/index. asp), which serves the key Kansai cities of Kyoto, Osaka, Nara and Kōbe.

» Near Nagoya, **Central Japan International Airport** (Centrair; NGO; www.centrair.jp) has international connections with 14 countries.

» Fukuoka, at the northern end of Kyūshū, is the main arrival point for western Japan. **Fukuoka International Airport** (FUK; www.fuk-ab .co.jp/english/frame_index .html), conveniently located near the city, has connections with nine countries, mostly in Asia.

» On Kyūshū, **Kagoshima Airport** (KOJ; www.koj-ab .co.jp/english/index.html) has flights to/from Shanghai and Seoul.

» Located on Okinawa-hontō (the main island of Okinawa), **Naha Airport** (OKA; www .naha-airport.co.jp, in Japanese) has flights to/from Hong Kong, Kaohsiung, Seoul, Shanghai, Taichung and Taipei.

» Central Honshū's **Niigata Airport** (KIJ; www.niigata -airport.gr.jp/?lang=en) has flights to/from Guam, Harbin, Khabarovsk, Seoul, Shanghai, Vladivostok and Xian.

» Kuyshū's **Kumamoto Airport** (KMJ; www.kmj-ab.co.jp/ eng/index.html) has flights to/ from Seoul.

» **Nagasaki Airport** (NGS; www.nabic.co.jp/english) has flights to/from Shanghai and Seoul.

» On Hokkaidō, **New Chitose Airport** (CTS; www .new-chitose-airport.jp/en/) has connections with 11 countries, mostly in Asia.

Tickets

Generally, high season for travel between Japan and Western countries is in late December (around Christmas and the New Year period) and late April to early

May (around Japan's Golden Week holiday), as well as July and August. If you must fly during these periods, book well in advance.

Land

Trans-Siberian Railway

The main option for the Trans-Siberian Railway is via China, ie on Chinese Trans-Mongolia or Russian Trans-Manchuria routes, followed by ferry to/from Japan via Tientsin, Qingdao and Shanghai. See p756 for info on ferry connections between Japan, Russia and China.

Sea

China

China Express Line (✆in Japan 078-321-5791, in China 022-2420-5777; www.celkobe .co.jp, in Japanese) Tienstin–Kōbe; 2nd class US$230, 48 hours. See p324.

Japan China International Ferry Company (✆in Japan 06-6536-6541, in China 021-6325-7642; www .shinganjin.com, in Japanese) Shanghai–Osaka/Kōbe; 2nd class US$200, 48 hours. See p318.

Orient Ferry Ltd (✆in Japan 083-232-6615, in China 0532-8387-1160; www.orientferry. co.jp, in Japanese) Qingdao–Shimonoseki; US$130, 28 hours. See p409.

Russia

Heartland Ferry (✆in Japan 011-233-8010, in Russia 7-4242-72-6889; www.heart landferry.jp/english/index. html) Korsakov (Sakhalin Island, Russia)–Wakkanai (Hokkaidō); US$250, 7½ hours, mid-May to late October. See p498.

South Korea

South Korea is the closest country to Japan and there are several ferry connections between them.

Beetle (✆in Japan 092-281-2315, in Korea 051-441-8200; www.jrbeetle.co.jp/english) Busan–Fukuoka; US$140, three hours. See p575.

Camellia Line (✆in Japan 092-262-2323, in Korea 051-466-7799; www.camellia-line .co.jp, in Japanese & Korean) Busan–Fukuoka; from US$95, six hours from Fukuoka to Busan, six to 10 hours from Busan to Fukuoka. See p575.

Kampu Ferry (✆in Japan 083-224-3000, in Korea 82-2-730-2137 or 463-3165(-8); www.kampuferry.co.jp, in Japanese) Busan–Shimonoseki; from US$85, 12 hours. See p409.

GETTING AROUND

Japan has one of the best public-transport systems in the world, which makes getting around the country an absolute breeze for travellers.

Air

Air services in Japan are extensive, reliable and safe. In many cases, flying is much faster than even *shinkansen* (bullet trains) and not that much more expensive. Flying is also an efficient way to travel from the main islands to the many small islands, particularly the Southwest Islands (the southern islands of Kagoshima and Okinawa Prefectures).

In most of Japan's major cities there are travel agencies where English is spoken. For an idea of the latest prices in Tokyo check the travel ads in the various local English-language publications, and in Kansai check *Kansai Scene*.

Airlines in Japan

Japan Airlines (JAL; ✆03-5460-0522, 0570-025-071; www.jal.co.jp/en) A major international carrier with an extensive domestic network.

All Nippon Airways (ANA; ✆0570-029-709, in Tokyo 03-6741-1120, in Osaka 06-7637-6679; www.ana.co.jp/eng) The other major Japanese international and domestic carrier.

Japan Trans Ocean Air (JTA; ✆03-5460-0522, 0570-025-071; www.jal.co.jp/ jta, in Japanese) A smaller domestic carrier that mostly services routes in the Southwest Islands.

Skymark Airlines (SKY; ✆050-3116-7370; www .skymark.co.jp/en) A recent start-up budget airline.

CLIMATE CHANGE & TRAVEL

Every form of transport that relies on carbon-based fuel generates CO_2, the main cause of human-induced climate change. Modern travel is dependent on aeroplanes, which might use less fuel per person than most cars but travel much greater distances. The altitude at which aircraft emit gases (including CO_2) and particles also contributes to their climate change impact. Many websites offer 'carbon calculators' that allow people to estimate the carbon emissions generated by their journey and, for those who wish to do so, to offset the impact of the greenhouse gases emitted with contributions to portfolios of climate-friendly initiatives throughout the world. Lonely Planet offsets the carbon footprint of all staff and author travel.

BAGGAGE FORWARDING

If you have too much luggage to carry comfortably or just can't be bothered, you can do what many Japanese travellers do: send it to your next stop by *takkyūbin* (express shipping companies). Prices are surprisingly reasonable and overnight service is the norm. Perhaps the most convenient service is Yamato Takkyūbin, which operates from most convenience stores. Simply pack your luggage and take it to the nearest convenience store; staff will help with the paperwork and arrange for pick-up. Note that you'll need the full address of your next destination in Japanese, along with the phone number of the place. Alternatively, ask the owner of your accommodation to come and pick it up (this is usually possible but might cost extra).

Shinchūō Kōku (☑ 0422-31-4191; www.central-air.co.jp, in Japanese) Has light-plane flights between Chōfu Airport, outside Tokyo, and the islands of the Izu Archipelago.

Tickets & Discounts

For domestic flights, return fares are usually around 10% cheaper than buying two one-way tickets. You can also get advance-purchase reductions: both ANA and JAL offer discounts of up to 50% if you purchase your ticket a month or more in advance, with smaller discounts for purchases made one to three weeks in advance. Seniors over 65 also qualify for discounts on most Japanese airlines, but these are sometimes only available if you fly on weekdays.

ANA also offers the Star Alliance Japan Airpass for foreign travellers on ANA or Star Alliance network airlines. Provided you reside outside Japan, purchase your tickets outside Japan and carry a valid international ticket on any airline, you can fly up to five times within 60 days on any ANA domestic route for only ¥11,550 per flight (a huge saving on some routes). Visit www.ana.co.jp/wws/us/e/travelservice/reservations/special/airpass.html for more details.

Bicycle

Japan is a good country for bicycle touring, and several thousand cyclists, both Japanese and foreign, traverse the country every year. Favourite bike-touring areas include Kyūshū, Shikoku, the Japan Alps (if you like steep hills!), the Noto Peninsula and Hokkaidō.

There's no point in fighting your way out of big cities by bicycle. Put your bike on the train or bus and get out to the country before you start pedalling. To take a bicycle on a train you may need to use a bicycle-carrying bag, available from good bicycle shops.

See p760 for information on road maps of Japan. In addition to the maps mentioned in that section, a useful series of maps is the *Touring Mapple* (Shōbunsha) series, which is aimed at motorcyclists but is also very useful for cyclists.

For more information on cycling in Japan, check out the excellent website of **KANcycling** (www.kancycling.com).

Hire

You will find bicycle-rental shops outside the train or bus stations in most of Japan's popular tourist areas, as well as near the ferry piers on many of the country's smaller islands. Typical charges are around ¥200/1000 per hour/day. Kyoto, for example, is ideally suited to bicycle exploration and there are plenty of cheap hire shops to choose from.

Note that the bicycles for rent are not usually performance vehicles. More commonly they're what the Japanese call *mama chari* (literally 'mama's bicycles'): one- or three-speed shopping bikes that are murder on hills of any size. They're also usually too small for anyone over 180cm in height.

Many youth hostels also have bicycles to rent – there's a symbol identifying them in the *Japan Youth Hostel Handbook*.

Purchase

In Japan, prices for used bikes range from a few thousand yen for an old shopping bike to several tens of thousands of yen for good mountain and road bikes. New bikes range from about ¥10,000 for a shopping bike to ¥100,000 for a flash mountain or road bike.

Touring cycles are available in Japan but prices tend to be significantly higher than you'd pay back home. If you're tall, you may not find any suitably sized bikes in stock. One solution for tall riders, or anyone who wants to save money, is to buy a used bike – in Tokyo, check the English-language publications; in Kansai, check *Kansai Scene* or visit the Kyoto International Community House (p297) and check the message board.

Boat

Japan is an island nation and there are a great many ferry services both between islands and between ports on the same island. Ferries can be an excellent way of

FERRY FARES & DURATIONS

HOKKAIDŌ–HONSHŪ	FARE (¥)	DURATION (HR)
Otaru–Maizuru	9000	21.5
Otaru–Niigata	6000	20
Tomakomai–Hachinohe	4500	8-9
Tomakomai–Ōarai	8500	19
FROM TOKYO	**FARE (¥)**	**DURATION (HR)**
Naha (Okinawa)	23,500	47-55
Shinmoji (Kitakyūshū)	14,470	35
Tokushima (Shikoku)	9750	18
FROM OSAKA/KŌBE	**FARE (¥)**	**DURATION (HR)**
Beppu (Kyūshū)	9000	12½
Miyazaki (Kyūshū)	10,000	12
Naha (Okinawa)	18,800	38
Shibushi (Kyūshū)	10,900	15
Shinmoji (Kitakyūshū)	6000	12½
KYŪSHŪ–OKINAWA	**FARE (¥)**	**DURATION (HR)**
Kagoshima–Naha	14,200	25

getting from one place to another and for seeing parts of Japan you might otherwise miss. Taking a ferry between Osaka (Honshū) and Beppu (Kyūshū), for example, is a good way of getting to Kyūshū and – if you choose the right departure time – seeing some of the Inland Sea on the way.

On overnight ferries, 2nd-class travel means sleeping in tatami-mat rooms where you simply unroll your futon on the floor and hope that your fellow passengers aren't too intent on knocking back the booze all night. In this basic class, fares are usually near equivalent land travel, but there are also more expensive private cabins. Bicycles can be brought along and most ferries also carry cars and motorcycles.

Information on ferry routes, schedules and fares is found in the JR Jikokuhyō (p765) and on information sheets from the Japan National Tourism Organization (JNTO; see p750). Some ferry services and their lowest one-way fares appear in the table, p758.

If you plan to explore Okinawa and the Southwest Islands by ferry, be sure to check out the 'all-you-can-sail' ticket offered by the Marui/A-Line ferry company. For details, see p636.

Bus

Japan has a comprehensive network of long-distance buses. These 'highway buses' are nowhere near as fast as the shinkansen but the fares are comparable with those of normal futsū (local) trains. For example, the trip between Tokyo and Kyoto takes just over 2½ hours by shinkansen and about eight hours by bus. Of course, there are many places in Japan where trains do not run and bus travel is the only public-transport option.

Bookings can be made through any travel agency in Japan or at the midori-no-madoguchi (green counters – look for the counter with the green band across the glass) in large Japan Rail (JR) stations. The Japan Rail Pass is valid on some highway buses, but in most cases the shinkansen would be far preferable (it's much faster and more comfortable).

Costs

Some typical long-distance fares and travel times out of Tokyo include the following (note that the cheapest fares on each route are shown).

DESTINA-TION	ONE WAY (¥)	DURA-TION (HR)
Aomori	8500	9½
Hakata	8000	14
Hiroshima	11,600	11½
Kōbe	8600	10
Kyoto	8100	8
Nagano	4000	4
Nagoya	5100	6
Nara	8400	9½
Osaka	8600	8

Night Services

Night buses are a good option for those on a tight budget without a Japan Rail Pass. They are relatively cheap, spacious (allowing room to stretch out and get some sleep) and they also save on a night's accommodation. They typically leave at around 10pm or 11pm and arrive the following day at around 6am or 7am.

Car & Motorcycle

Driving in Japan is quite feasible, even for just the mildly adventurous. The major roads are signposted in English; road rules are generally adhered to and driving is safer than in other Asian countries; and petrol, while expensive, is not prohibitively so. Indeed, in some areas of the country it can prove much more convenient than other forms of travel and, between a group of people, it can also prove quite economical.

In some parts of Japan (most notably Hokkaidō, the Noto Peninsula, some parts of Kyūshū and the Southwest Islands), driving is really the only efficient way to get around unless you have a good touring bicycle or fancy long waits for buses each time you need to make a move.

Automobile Associations

If you're a member of an automobile association in your home country, you're eligible for reciprocal rights with the **Japan Automobile Federation** (JAF; ☎03-6833-9000, 0570-00-2811; www.jaf.or.jp/e/index_e.htm; 2-2-17 Shiba, Minato-ku, Tokyo 105-0014). Its office is near Onarimon Station on the Tōei Mita line.

Driving Licence

Travellers from most nations are able to drive in Japan with an International Driving Permit backed up by their own regular licence. The International Driving Permit is issued by your national automobile association and costs around US$5 in most countries. Make sure it's endorsed for cars and motorcycles if you're licensed for both.

Travellers from Switzerland, France and Germany (and others whose countries are not signatories to the Geneva Convention of 1949 concerning international driving licences) are not allowed to drive in Japan on a regular International Driving Permit. Rather, travellers from these countries must have their own licence backed by an authorised translation of the same licence. These translations can be made by their country's embassy or consulate in Japan or by the JAF. If you are unsure which category your country falls into, contact the nearest JNTO office (p750) for more information.

Foreign licences and International Driving Permits are only valid in Japan for six months. If you are staying longer, you will have to get a Japanese licence from the local department of motor vehicles.

Expressways

The expressway system is fast, efficient and growing all the time. Tolls cost about ¥24.6 per kilometre. Tokyo to Kyoto, for example, will cost ¥10,050 in tolls.

There are good rest stops and service centres at regular intervals. A prepaid highway card, available from tollbooths or at the service areas, saves you having to carry so much cash and gives you a 4% to 8% discount in the larger card denominations. You can also pay tolls with most major credit cards. Exits are usually fairly well signposted in English, but make sure you know the name of your exit as it may not necessarily be the same as the city you're heading towards.

Fuel

You'll find *gasoreen sutando* (petrol stations) in almost every town and in service

---

BARGAIN BUSES

Japan Railways (JR) operates the largest network of highway buses in Japan, and we quote its prices for most long-distance bus routes in this guide. However, several budget bus companies have recently sprung up in Japan and these are gaining popularity with backpackers. One such company is **123Bus** (☎050-5805-0383 from outside Japan; http://willerexpress.com/bus/pc/3/top/). Some of its services include Tokyo–Osaka (from ¥3500), Tokyo–Nagoya (from ¥2800) and Tokyo-Hiroshima (from ¥6000). Booking is possible in English online. Check the website for the latest details and pick-up/drop-off points.

Another good deal is offered by a group of bus companies on Kyūshū, which have banded together to offer the **SUNQ Pass** (www.sunqpass.jp/english; 3/5 day ¥10,000/14,000, northern Kyūshū only ¥8000), which offers unlimited travel. Kyūshū buses reach many places trains don't.

DRIVING IN JAPAN

Unless you plan on driving in central Tokyo or Osaka or forget that the Japanese drive on the left, you should have no major problems driving in Japan. In fact, driving here is remarkably sane compared to many countries (perhaps because it's so difficult to pass the test). Still, there are a few peculiarities that are worth keeping in mind.

» **Turn signals** Some Japanese drivers have the annoying habit of turning on their turn signals only after they stop at a light or enter an intersection. This seems to defeat the purpose of a signal (ie to tell people *in advance* what you plan to do). This doesn't cause too many problems, but be ready for it.

» **Petrol stations** While self-serve petrol stations are becoming popular, full-service stations are still the rule. And in Japan, when they say 'full service', they really mean it. They'll empty your ashtray, take any garbage you have, wipe your windshield and then wave you back into traffic. And if you're wondering how to say 'fill 'er up' in Japanese, it's *'mantan'* (full tank).

» **Chains** If you drive in mountain areas in winter, you might be required to put chains on your car. If you rent a car in these areas, it will probably come equipped. Petrol stations in mountain areas will usually put the chains on for a charge (¥1000 to ¥2000). There may be police stops in these areas to make sure that cars have chains.

stations along the expressways. The cost of petrol per litre ranges from ¥137 to ¥139 for regular and ¥148 to ¥150 for high octane.

Hire

You'll usually find car-rental agencies clustered around train stations and ferry piers. Typical rates for a small car are ¥5000 to ¥7000 per day, with reductions for rentals of more than one day. On top of the rental charge, there's about a ¥1000-per-day insurance cost.

Communication can sometimes be a major problem when hiring a car. Some of the offices will have a rent-a-car phrasebook, with questions you might need to ask in English. Otherwise, just speak as slowly as possible and hope for the best. A good way to open the conversation is to say *'kokusai menkyō wo motteimasu'* (I have an international licence).

Toyota Rent-a-Car (☑ in Japan 0800-7000-111, outside Japan 81-3-5954-8020; http://rent.toyota.co.jp/en/index.html) has the largest rental network and has a very informative website which allows reservations from overseas.

Parking

In most big cities, free curbside parking spots are almost nonexistent, while in rural areas you'll be able to park your car just about anywhere you want. In the cities you'll find that you usually have to pay ¥200 per hour for metered street parking, or anywhere from ¥300 to ¥600 per hour for a spot in a multistorey car park. You'll find car parks around most department stores and near some train stations. Fortunately, most hotels have free parking for guests, as do some restaurants and almost all department stores.

Road Rules

Driving is on the left. There are no unusual rules or interpretations of them and most signposts follow international conventions. JAF (p759) has a *Rules of the Road* book available in English and five other languages for ¥1000.

Maps & Navigation

If you can find a used copy of the *Road Atlas Japan* (Shōbunsha), grab it. It's all in English (romaji) with enough names in kanji to make navigation possible even off the major roads.

Unfortunately, it's out of print and hard to find these days. If you're really intent on making your way through the back blocks, a Japanese map will prove useful even if your knowledge of kanji is nil. The best Japanese road atlases by far are the *Super Mapple* series (Shōbunsha), which are available in bookshops and some convenience stores.

There is a reasonable amount of signposting in romaji, so getting around isn't all that difficult, especially in developed areas. If you are attempting tricky navigation, use your maps imaginatively – watch out for the railway line, the rivers, the landmarks. They're all useful ways of locating yourself when you can't read the signs. A compass will also come in handy when navigating.

These days, many rental cars come equipped with satellite navigation systems, making navigation a snap, provided you can figure out how to work the system; ask the person at the rental agency to explain it and be sure to take notes or, if you're just going from point A to point B, have them set it for you. With most of these systems, you can input the phone number of your destination, which is easy, or its address, which is just about impossible if you don't read Japanese. Even without programming in your destination, with the device on the default 'genzai-chi' (present location) setting, you will find it very useful.

Motorcycles

For citizens of most countries, your overseas driving licence and an International Driving Permit are all you need to ride a motorcycle in Japan (see p759 for details on which nationalities require additional documentation). Crash helmets are compulsory. Touring equipment – panniers, carrier racks, straps and the like – is readily available from dealers.

Drivers in Japan tend to be relatively sane and safe, making Japan a good country for motorcycle touring.

HIRE & PURCHASE

Hiring a motorcycle for long-distance touring is not as easy as hiring a car, although small scooters are available in many places for local sightseeing.

Small motorcycles (those below 125cc) are banned from expressways and are generally not suitable for long-distance touring, but people have ridden from one end of Japan to the other on little 50cc scooters (taking the back roads, of course). An advantage of these bikes is that you can ride them with just a regular driving licence, so you won't need to get a motorcycle licence.

The best place to look for motorcycles in Japan is the Korin-chō motorcycle neighbourhood in Tokyo's Ueno district. There are over 20 motorcycle shops in the area and some employ foreign salespeople who speak both Japanese and English. For used bikes in Kansai check Kansai Scene, Kansai

Flea Market or the message board in the Kyoto International Community House (p297).

Hitching

Hitching is never entirely safe in any country in the world, and we don't recommend it. Travellers who decide to hitch should understand that they are taking a small but potentially serious risk. In particular, Japan is a dangerous place for solitary female hitchhikers; there have been cases of solitary female hitchers being attacked, molested and raped. People who do choose to hitch will be safer if they travel in pairs and let someone know where they are planning to go.

Provided you understand the risks and take appropriate precautions, Japan is known as a good country for hitchhiking. Many hitchhikers have tales of extraordinary kindness from motorists who have picked them up.

The rules for hitchhiking are similar to those anywhere else in the world. Dress neatly and look for a good place to hitch – expressway on-ramps and expressway service areas are probably your best bets.

Truck drivers are particularly good for long-distance travel as they often head out on the expressways at night. If a driver is exiting before your intended destination, try to get dropped off at one of the expressway service areas. The Service Area Parking Area (SAPA) guide maps are excellent for hitchhikers. They're available free from expressway service areas and show full details of each interchange (IC) and rest stop. These are important orientation points if you have a limited knowledge of Japanese.

For more on hitching in Japan, pick up a copy of the excellent Hitchhiker's Guide to Japan by Will Ferguson.

Local Transport

All the major cities offer a wide variety of public transport. In many cities you can get day passes for unlimited travel on bus, tram or subway systems. Such passes are usually called an ichi-nichi-jōsha-ken. If you're staying for an extended period in one city, commuter passes are available for regular travel.

Bus

Almost every Japanese city has an extensive bus service, but it's usually the most difficult public-transport system for foreign travellers to use. Destinations and stops are often written only in Japanese.

Fares are usually paid when you get off. In Tokyo and some other cities, there's a flat fare regardless of distance. In the other cities, you take a ticket (known as a seiri-ken) as you board that indicates the zone number at your starting point. When you get off, an electric sign at the front of the bus indicates the fare charged at that point for each starting zone number. You simply pay the driver the fare that matches your zone number (you put both the seiri-ken and the fare into the fare box). There is often a change machine near the front of the bus that can exchange ¥100 and ¥500 coins and ¥1000 notes.

Taxi

Taxis are convenient and can be found even in very small cities and on tiny islands; the train station is the best place to look. Fares are fairly uniform throughout the country. Flagfall (posted on the taxi windows) is ¥600 to ¥710 for the first 2km, after which it's around ¥100 for each 350m (approximately). There's also a time charge if the speed drops below 10km/h. A red light in the lower right corner of the windshield indicates if a taxi is free (it says 'vacant' in Japanese) – this can be difficult to spot during the day. At night, taxis usually have the light on their roof on when they're vacant and off when they're occupied, but there are regional variations.

Don't open the door when you get into the taxi; the driver does that with a remote release. The driver will also shut the door when you leave the taxi.

Communication can be a problem with taxi drivers, but perhaps not as much as you fear. If you can't tell the driver where you want to go, it's useful to have the name written down in Japanese. At hotel front desks there will usually be business cards complete with name and location, which can be used for just this purpose.

Tipping is not necessary. A 20% surcharge is added after 11pm or for taxis summoned by radio. There may also be an added charge if you arrange the taxi by phone or reserve the taxi. Finally, taxis can usually take up to four adult passengers (one person can sit in the front). Drivers are sometimes willing to bend the rules for small children.

Train & Subway

Several cities, especially Osaka and Tokyo, have mass-transit rail systems comprising a loop line around the city centre and radial lines into the central stations and the subway system. Subway systems operate in Fukuoka, Kōbe, Kyoto, Nagoya, Osaka, Sapporo, Tokyo and Yokohama. They are usually the fastest and most convenient way to get around the city.

For subways and local trains, you'll most likely have to buy your ticket from a machine. They're pretty easy to understand even if you can't read kanji as there is a diagram explaining the routes; from this you can find out what your fare should be. If you can't work the fare out, a solution is to buy a ticket

for the lowest fare. When you finish your trip, go to the fare-adjustment machine (*seisan-ki*) or the staffed counter before you reach the exit gate and pay the excess. JR train stations and most subway stations have posted above the platform not only their names in kanji and romaji but also the names of the preceding and following stations.

Tram

Many cities have tram lines, in particular, Nagasaki, Kumamoto and Kagoshima on Kyūshū; Kōchi and Matsuyama on Shikoku; and Hakodate on Hokkaidō. These are excellent ways of getting around as they combine many of the advantages of bus travel (good views of the passing parade) with those of subways (it's easy to work out where you're going). Fares work on similar systems to bus travel and there are also unlimited-travel day tickets.

Train

Japanese rail services are among the best in the world: they are fast, frequent, clean and comfortable. The 'national' railway is Japan Railways, commonly known as 'JR', which is actually a number of separate private rail systems providing one linked service.

The JR system covers the country from one end to the other and also provides local services around major cities like Tokyo and Osaka. JR also operates buses and ferries, and convenient ticketing can combine more than one form of transport.

In addition to JR services, there is a huge network of private railways. Each large city usually has at least one private train line that services that city and the surrounding area, or connects that city to nearby cities. These are often a bit cheaper than equivalent JR services.

Types of Trains

The slowest trains stopping at all stations are called *futsū* or *kaku-eki-teisha*. A step up from this is the *kyūkō* (ordinary express), which stops at only a limited number of stations. A variation on the *kyūkō* trains is the *kaisoku* (rapid) service (usually operating on JR lines). Finally, the fastest regular (non-*shinkansen*) trains are the *tokkyū* (limited-express) services, which are sometimes known as *shin-kaisoku* (again, usually operating on JR lines).

SHINKANSEN

The fastest and best-known services are JR's *shinkansen*, Japan's famed 'bullet trains'. *Shinkansen* lines operate on separate tracks from regular trains, and, in some places, the *shinkansen* station is a fair distance from the main JR station (as is the case in Osaka).

On most *shinkansen* routes, there are two or three types of service: faster express services stopping at a limited number of stations, and slower local services stopping at more stations. There is no difference in fare, except for the Green Car (1st-class) carriages, which cost slightly more.

Most *shinkansen* cars are nonsmoking but there are also a limited number of smoking cars on each train. There are reserved and unreserved cars on all trains. If you're travelling outside peak travel periods, you can usually just show up and expect to get a seat in an unreserved car. If you're travelling during a peak period, it is a good idea to stop at a JR station to make a reservation a few days prior to your departure.

For prices on specific *shinkansen* routes, see p763.

Classes

Most long-distance JR trains, including *shinkansen*, have regular and Green Car carriages. The seating is slightly more spacious in Green Car carriages (think of a typical business-class seat on an airplane). The Green Car carriages also tend to be quieter and less crowded. However, all Green Car seats are reserved, so if you've got a Green Japan Rail Pass, you'll have to reserve every trip in advance (with a regular pass you just go through the turnstiles and get on the next available train).

Costs

JR fares are calculated on the basis of *futsū-unchin* (basic fare), *tokkyū-ryōkin* (an express surcharge levied only on express services) and *shinkansen-ryōkin* (a special charge for *shinkansen* services). Note that if you buy a return ticket for a trip that is more than 600km each way, you qualify for a 10% discount on the return leg.

The following are some typical fares from Tokyo or Ueno (prices given for *shinkansen* are the total price of the ticket):

DESTINATION	BASIC (¥)	SHINKANSEN (¥)
Hakata	13,440	22,320
Hiroshima	11,340	18,550
Kyoto	7980	13,220
Morioka	8190	13,840
Nagoya	6090	10,580
Niigata	5460	10,270
Okayama	10,190	16,860
Shin–Osaka	8510	14,050
Shin–Shimonoseki	12,810	20,570

SURCHARGES

Fares for reserved seats are slightly higher (5% to 10%) during peak travel seasons (21 March to 5 April, 28 April to 6 May, 21 July to 31 August and 25 December to 10 January).

Further surcharges apply for overnight sleepers, and these vary with the berth type. Japan Rail Pass users must still pay the sleeper surcharge (for more on the Japan Rail Pass, see p763).

The Nozomi super express has higher surcharges than other *shinkansen* services and cannot be used with a Japan Rail Pass. As a guideline, the Nozomi surcharge for Tokyo–Kyoto is ¥300; for Tokyo–Hakata it's ¥600.

Passes & Discount Tickets

JAPAN RAIL PASS

The **Japan Rail Pass** (www.japanrailpass.net/eng/en001.html) is a must for anyone planning to do extensive train travel within Japan. Not only will it save you a lot of money, it will save you from having to fish for change each time you board a train.

The most important thing to note about the pass is this: *the Japan Rail Pass must be purchased outside Japan*. It is available to foreign tourists and Japanese overseas residents (but not foreign residents of Japan). The pass cannot be used for the super express Nozomi *shinkansen* service but is OK for everything else (including other *shinkansen* services). Children between the ages

TRAIN TERMINOLOGY

PRONUNCIATION	SCRIPT	ENGLISH
futsū	普通	local
green-sha	グリーン車	1st-class car
jiyū-seki	自由席	unreserved seat
kaisoku	快速	JR rapid or express
kaku-eki-teisha	各駅停車	local
katamichi	片道	one way
kin'en-sha	禁煙車	nonsmoking car
kitsuen-sha	喫煙車	smoking car
kyūkō	急行	ordinary express
ōfuku	往復	round trip
shin-kaisoku	新快速	JR special rapid train
shinkansen	新幹線	bullet train
shitei-seki	指定席	reserved seat
tokkyū	特急	limited express

of six and 11 qualify for child passes, while those aged under six ride for free. Japan Rail Pass costs are outlined in the following table.

DURA-TION	REGULAR (ADULT/ CHILD)	GREEN (ADULT/ CHILD)
7 day	¥28,300/ 14,150	¥37,800/ 18,900
14 day	¥45,100/ 22,550	¥61,200/ 30,600
21 day	¥57,700/ 28,850	¥79,600/ 39,800

Since a one-way reserved-seat Tokyo–Kyoto *shinkansen* ticket costs ¥13,220, you only have to travel Tokyo–Kyoto–Tokyo to make a seven-day pass come close to paying off. Note that the pass is valid only on JR services; you will still have to pay for private-train services.

In order to get a pass, you must first purchase an 'exchange order' outside Japan at a JAL or ANA office or a major travel agency. Once you arrive in Japan, you must bring this order to a JR Travel Service Centre (in most major JR stations and at Narita and Kansai International Airports). When you validate your pass, you'll have to show your passport.

The clock starts to tick on the pass as soon as you validate it. So don't validate it if you're just going into Tokyo or Kyoto and intend to hang around for a few days. Instead, validate when you leave those cities to explore the rest of the country.

For more information on the pass and overseas purchase locations, visit the Japan Rail Pass website.

JR EAST PASS
The **JR East Pass** (www .jreast.co.jp/e/eastpass/top. html) is a great deal for those who only want to travel in eastern Japan. The passes are good on all JR lines in eastern Japan (including Tōhoku, Yamagata,

Akita, Jōetsu and Nagano *shinkansen*, but not including the Tōkaidō *shinkansen*). This includes the area around Tokyo and everything north of Tokyo to the tip of Honshū but doesn't include Hokkaidō. In addition to the normal five- and 10-day passes, four-day 'flexible' passes allow travel on any four consecutive or nonconsecutive days within any one-month period. Pass costs are outlined in the following table.

DU-RA-TION	REGULAR (ADULT/ YOUTH/ CHILD)	GREEN (ADULT/ CHILD)
5 day	¥20,000/ 16,000/ 10,000	¥28,000/ 14,000
10 day	¥32,000/ 25,000/ 16,000	¥44,800/ 22,400
flex-ible 4 day	¥20,000/ 16,000/ 10,000	¥28,000/ 14,000

For normal passes, 'adult' means anyone over 26, 'youth' means anyone between 12 and 25, and 'child' means anyone between six and 11. Strangely, for the Green passes, there are only adult passes (anyone over 12) and child passes (anyone between six and 11).

As with the Japan Rail Pass, this can only be purchased outside Japan (in the same locations as the Japan Rail Pass) and can only be used by those with temporary visitor visas (you'll need to show your passport). See the preceding Japan Rail Pass section for more details on purchase places and validation procedures.

JR WEST SAN-YŌ AREA PASS
Similar to the JR East Pass, the **San-yō Area Pass** (www .westjr.co.jp/english/global. html) allows unlimited travel on the San-yō *shinkansen*

line (including the Nozomi super express) between Osaka and Hakata, as well as local trains running between the same cities. The pass is only good on consecutive days. Costs are outlined in the following table.

DURATION	REGULAR (ADULT/CHILD)
4 day	¥20,000/10,000
8 day	¥30,000/15,000

For this pass, 'child' means anyone between six and 11 (children aged under six travel free). The pass can be purchased both inside Japan (at major train stations, travel agencies and Kansai International Airport) and outside Japan (same locations as the Japan Rail Pass) but can only be used by those with a temporary visitor visa. The pass also entitles you to discounts at station rental-car agencies.

JR WEST KANSAI AREA PASS
A great deal for those who only want to explore the Kansai area, the **Kansai Area Pass** (www.westjr.co.jp/ english/global.html) covers unlimited travel on JR lines between most major Kansai cities, such as Himeji, Kōbe, Osaka, Kyoto and Nara. It also covers JR trains to/ from Kansai International Airport but does not cover any *shinkansen* lines. The pass also entitles holders to reserved seats at no extra charge (you'll have to reserve each trip before boarding the train). Passes are only good on consecutive days. Costs are outlined in the following table.

DURATION	REGULAR (ADULT/CHILD)
1 day	¥2000/1000
2 day	¥4000/2000
3 day	¥5000/2500
4 day	¥6000/3000

For these passes, 'child' means anyone between six and 11 (children aged under six travel free). The pass can be purchased at the same places as the San-yō Area Pass (both inside and outside Japan) and also entitles you to discounts at station car-hire offices. Like the San-yō Area Pass, this pass can only be used by those with a temporary visitor visa.

JR KYŪSHŪ RAIL PASS
JR Kyūshū (www.jrkyushu.co.jp/english/index.html) offers two passes: one that covers all JR lines in the northern part of Kyūshū and another that is good for all JR lines in Kyūshū (see the website for areas covered). Costs are outlined in the following table.

DURA-TION	ALL AREAS (ADULT/CHILD)	NORTHERN KYŪSHŪ (ADULT/CHILD)
3 day	¥13,000/6500	¥7000/3500
5 day	¥16,000/8000	N/A

For these passes, 'child' means anyone between six and 11 (those below six travel free). These passes can be purchased both inside Japan (at travel agencies in major train stations in Kyūshū) and outside Japan, at the same locations as the Japan Rail Pass. It can only be used by those on a temporary visitor visa. If you purchase an exchange order overseas, you can pick up your pass at major train stations in Kyūshū.

SEISHUN JŪHACHI KIPPU
If you don't have a Japan Rail Pass, one of the best deals going is a five-day **Seishun Jūhachi Kippu** (www.jreast.co.jp/e/pass/seishun18.html), literally a 'Youth 18 Ticket'. Despite its name, it can be used by anyone of any age.

Basically, for ¥11,500 you get five one-day tickets valid for travel anywhere in Japan on JR lines. The only catches are that you can't travel on *tokkyū* or *shinkansen* trains and each ticket must be used within 24 hours. However, even if you only have to make a return trip, say, between Tokyo and Kyoto, you'll be saving a lot of money. Seishun Jūhachi Kippu can be purchased at most JR stations in Japan. Sale and validity periods are outlined in the following table.

SEASON	SALES PERIOD	VALIDITY PERIOD
Spring	20 Feb–31 Mar	1 Mar–10 Apr
Summer	1 Jul–31 Aug	20 Jul–10 Sep
Winter	1 Dec–10 Jan	10 Dec–20 Jan

Note that these periods are subject to change. For more information, ask at any JR ticket window. If you don't want to buy the whole book of five tickets, you can sometimes purchase separate tickets at the discount-ticket shops around train stations.

KANSAI THRU PASS
See p303 for details on this pass, which allows unlimited travel on all non-JR private train lines and most bus lines in Kansai.

OTHER SPECIAL TICKETS & PASSES
There are a number of other special tickets, especially for travel in the Tokyo area. For more information on these passes, see the JR East website's **Fares & Passes** (www.jreast.co.jp/e/pass/index.html) section.

DISCOUNT-TICKET SHOPS
Discount-ticket shops are known as *kakuyasu-kippu-uriba* (格安切符売り場) or *kinken shoppu* (金券ショップ) in Japanese. These shops deal in discounted tickets for trains, buses, domestic plane flights, ferries, and a host of other things like cut-rate stamps and phone cards. You can typically save between 5% and 10% on *shinkansen* tickets. Discount-ticket agencies are found around train stations in medium and large cities – ask at your lodgings for the nearest one.

Schedules & Information
The most complete timetables can be found in the *JR Jikokuhyō* (Book of Timetables), which is available at all Japanese bookshops but is written in Japanese. JNTO, however, produces a handy English-language *Railway Timetable* booklet that explains a great deal about the services in Japan and gives timetables for the *shinkansen* services, JR *tokkyū* and major private lines. If your visit to Japan is a short one and you will not be straying far from the major tourist destinations, this booklet may well be all you need.

Major train stations all have information counters, and you can usually get your point across in simplified English.

If you need to know anything about JR, such as schedules, fares, fastest routes, lost baggage, discounts on rail travel, hotels and car hire, call the **JR East Infoline** (☎050-2016-1603; www.jreast.co.jp/e/info/index.html; ◷10am-6pm). Information is available in English, Korean and Chinese. More information can be found on the website. The website **Hyperdia** (www.hyperdia.com) is also a useful online source for schedules and is probably the most user-friendly English-language site.

Tickets & Reservations
Tickets for most journeys can be bought from train-station vending machines,

TRAIN RESERVATIONS FROM ABROAD

First, keep in mind that you do not usually have to make reservations in advance for train travel in Japan. The only times you should consider reserving in advance are Golden Week, Obon (mid-August) and New Year.

Unfortunately, it is not possible to make reservations for JR trains online in English. However, most travel agents who handle the Japan Rail Pass can also make train reservations and sell you tickets in advance, but they will charge a fairly hefty surcharge to do this. A list of travel agents can be found here: www.japanrailpass.net/eng/en001.html.

There's one more thing to keep in mind: if you've got a Japan Rail Pass, you will not be able to reserve travel through a travel agent outside Japan. The reason for this is that you must activate the pass in Japan and show the pass when you make reservations.

In all cases, if you're nervous about getting seats for your train travel in Japan, you can always walk into a JR office and book all your train travel immediately upon arrival or early in your stay (you can reserve travel up to a month in advance at JR ticket offices inside Japan).

ticket counters and reservation offices. For reservations of complicated tickets, larger train stations have *midori-no-madoguchi*. Major travel agencies in Japan also sell reserved-seat tickets, and you can buy *shinkansen* tickets through JAL offices overseas if you will be flying JAL to Japan.

On *futsū* services, there are no reserved seats. On the faster *tokkyū* and *shinkansen* services you can choose to travel reserved or unreserved. However, if you travel unreserved, there's always the risk of not getting a seat and having to stand, possibly for the entire trip. This is a particular danger at weekends, peak travel seasons and on holidays. Reserved-seat tickets can be bought any time from a month in advance to the day of departure.

Information and tickets can be obtained from travel agencies, of which there are a great number in Japan.

Nearly every train station of any size will have at least one travel agency in the station building to handle all sorts of bookings in addition to train services. Japan Travel Bureau (JTB) is the big daddy of Japanese travel agencies. However, for most train tickets and long-distance bus reservations, you don't need to go through a travel agency – just go to the ticket counters or *midori-no-madoguchi* of any major train station.

Language

Japanese is spoken by more than 125 million people. While it bears some resemblance to Altaic languages such as Mongolian and Turkish and has grammatical similarities to Korean, its origins are unclear. Chinese is responsible for the existence of many Sino-Japanese words in Japanese, and for the originally Chinese kanji characters which the Japanese use in combination with the home-grown hiragana and katakana scripts.

Three main dialect groups exist across Japan, but the standard language as spoken in Tokyo serves as the lingua franca. It's also the language used in this chapter, so you shouldn't have problems making yourself understood anywhere in the country.

Japanese pronunciation is easy to master for English speakers, as most of its sounds are also found in English. If you read our coloured pronunciation guides as if they were English, you'll be understood. It's important to make the distinction between short and long vowels, as vowel length can change the meaning of a word. The long vowels – shown in our pronunciation guides with a horizontal line on top of them (ā, ē, ī, ō, ū) – should be held twice as long as the short ones. It's also important to make the distinction between single and double consonants, as this can produce a difference in meaning. Pronounce the double consonants with a slight pause between them, eg sak·ka (writer).

Note also that the vowel sounds ai is pronounced as in 'aisle', air as in 'pair' and ow as in 'how'. As for the consonants, ts is pronounced as in 'hats', f sounds almost like 'fw' (with rounded lips), and r is halfway between 'r' and 'l'. All syllables in a word are pronounced fairly evenly in Japanese.

WANT MORE?

For in-depth language information and handy phrases, check out Lonely Planet's *Japanese Phrasebook*. You'll find it at **shop.lonelyplanet.com**, or you can buy Lonely Planet's iPhone phrasebooks at the Apple App Store.

BASICS

Japanese uses an array of registers of speech to reflect social and contextual hierarchy, but these can be simplified to the form most appropriate for the situation, which is what we've done in this language guide too.

Hello.	こんにちは。	kon·ni·chi·wa
Goodbye.	さようなら。	sa·yō·na·ra
Yes.	はい。	hai
No.	いいえ。	ī·e
Please.	ください。	ku·da·sai
Thank you.	ありがとう。	a·ri·ga·tō
Excuse me.	すみません。	su·mi·ma·sen
Sorry.	ごめんなさい。	go·men·na·sai

You're welcome.
どういたしまして。　dō i·ta·shi·mash·te

How are you?
お元気ですか？　o·gen·ki des ka

Fine. And you?
はい、元気です。　hai, gen·ki des
あなたは？　a·na·ta wa

What's your name?
お名前は何ですか？　o·na·ma·e wa nan des ka

My name is ...
私の名前は　wa·ta·shi no na·ma·e wa
…です。　... des

Do you speak English?
英語が話せますか？　ē·go ga ha·na·se·mas ka

I don't understand.
わかりません。　wa·ka·ri·ma·sen

ACCOMMODATION

Where's a ...?	…が ありますか?	... ga a·ri·mas ka
campsite	キャンプ場	kyam·pu·jō
guesthouse	民宿	min·shu·ku
hotel	ホテル	ho·te·ru
inn	旅館	ryo·kan
youth hostel	ユース ホステル	yū·su· ho·su·te·ru

Do you have a ... room?	…ルームは ありますか?	... rū·mu wa a·ri·mas ka
single	シングル	shin·gu·ru
double	ダブル	da·bu·ru

How much is it per ...?	…いくら ですか?	... i·ku·ra des ka
night	1泊	ip·pa·ku
person	1人	hi·to·ri

air-con	エアコン	air·kon
bathroom	風呂場	fu·ro·ba
window	窓	ma·do

DIRECTIONS

Where's the ...?
…はどこですか? … wa do·ko des ka

Can you show me (on the map)?
(地図で)教えて (chi·zu de) o·shi·e·te
くれませんか? ku·re·ma·sen ka

What's the address?
住所は何ですか? jū·sho wa nan des ka

Could you please write it down?
書いてくれませんか? kai·te ku·re·ma·sen ka

behind ...	…の後ろ	... no u·shi·ro
in front of ...	…の前	... no ma·e
near ...	…の近く	... no chi·ka·ku
next to ...	…のとなり	... no to·na·ri
opposite ...	…の 向かい側	... no mu·kai·ga·wa
straight ahead	この先	ko·no sa·ki

Turn ...	…まがって ください。	... ma·gat·te ku·da·sai
at the corner	その角を	so·no ka·do o
at the traffic lights	その信号を	so·no shin·gō o
left	左へ	hi·da·ri e
right	右へ	mi·gi e

KEY PATTERNS

To get by in Japanese, mix and match these simple patterns with words of your choice:

When's (the next bus)?
(次のバスは) (tsu·gi no bas wa)
何時ですか? nan·ji des ka

Where's (the station)?
(駅は)どこですか? (e·ki wa) do·ko des ka

Do you have (a map)?
(地図) (chi·zu)
がありますか? ga a·ri·mas ka

Is there (a toilet)?
(トイレ) (toy·re)
がありますか? ga a·ri·mas ka

I'd like (the menu).
(メニュー) (me·nyū)
をお願いします。 o o·ne·gai shi·mas

Can I (sit here)?
(ここに座って) (ko·ko ni su·wat·te)
もいいですか? mo ī des ka

I need (a can opener).
(缶切り) (kan·ki·ri)
が必要です。 ga hi·tsu·yō des

Do I need (a visa)?
(ビザ) (bi·za)
が必要ですか? ga hi·tsu·yō des ka

I have (a reservation).
(予約)があります。 (yo·ya·ku) ga a·ri·mas

I'm (a teacher).
私は(教師) wa·ta·shi wa (kyō·shi)
です。 des

EATING & DRINKING

I'd like to reserve a table for (two people).
(2人)の予約を (fu·ta·ri) no yo·ya·ku o
お願いします。 o·ne·gai shi·mas

What would you recommend?
なにが na·ni ga
おすすめですか? o·su·su·me des ka

What's in that dish?
あの料理に何 a·no ryō·ri ni na·ni
が入っていますか? ga hait·te i·mas ka

I don't eat (red meat).
(赤身の肉) (a·ka·mi no ni·ku)
は食べません。 wa ta·be·ma·sen

That was delicious!
おいしかった。 oy·shi·kat·ta

Cheers!
乾杯! kam·pai

Please bring the bill.
お勘定をください。 o·kan·jō o ku·da·sai

Signs

入口	**Entrance**
出口	**Exit**
営業中/開館	**Open**
閉店/閉館	**Closed**
インフォメーション	**Information**
危険	**Danger**
トイレ	**Toilets**
男	**Men**
女	**Women**

Key Words

appetisers	前菜	zen·sai
bottle	ビン	bin
bowl	ボール	bō·ru
breakfast	朝食	chō·sho·ku
cold	冷たい	tsu·me·ta·i
dinner	夕食	yū·sho·ku
fork	フォーク	fō·ku
glass	グラス	gu·ra·su
grocery	食料品	sho·ku·ryō·hin
hot (warm)	熱い	a·tsu·i
knife	ナイフ	nai·fu
lunch	昼食	chū·sho·ku
market	市場	i·chi·ba
menu	メニュー	me·nyū
plate	皿	sa·ra
spicy	スパイシー	spai·shī
spoon	スプーン	spūn
vegetarian	ベジタリアン	be·ji·ta·ri·an
with	いっしょに	is·sho ni
without	なしで	na·shi de

Meat & Fish

beef	牛肉	gyū·ni·ku
chicken	鶏肉	to·ri·ni·ku
duck	アヒル	a·hi·ru
eel	うなぎ	u·na·gi
fish	魚	sa·ka·na
lamb	子羊	ko·hi·tsu·ji
lobster	ロブスター	ro·bus·tā
meat	肉	ni·ku
pork	豚肉	bu·ta·ni·ku
prawn	エビ	e·bi
salmon	サケ	sa·ke
seafood	海産物	kai·sam·bu·tsu
shrimp	小エビ	ko·e·bi
tuna	マグロ	ma·gu·ro
turkey	七面鳥	shi·chi·men·chō
veal	子牛	ko·u·shi

Fruit & Vegetables

apple	りんご	rin·go
banana	バナナ	ba·na·na
beans	豆	ma·me
capsicum	ピーマン	pī·man
carrot	ニンジン	nin·jin
cherry	さくらんぼ	sa·ku·ram·bo
cucumber	キュウリ	kyū·ri
fruit	果物	ku·da·mo·no
grapes	ブドウ	bu·dō
lettuce	レタス	re·tas
nut	ナッツ	nat·tsu
orange	オレンジ	o·ren·ji
peach	桃	mo·mo
peas	豆	ma·me
pineapple	パイナップル	pai·nap·pu·ru
potato	ジャガイモ	ja·ga·i·mo
pumpkin	カボチャ	ka·bo·cha
spinach	ホウレンソウ	hō·ren·sō
strawberry	イチゴ	i·chi·go
tomato	トマト	to·ma·to
vegetables	野菜	ya·sai
watermelon	スイカ	su·i·ka

Other

bread	パン	pan
butter	バター	ba·tā
cheese	チーズ	chī·zu
chilli	唐辛子	tō·ga·ra·shi
egg	卵	ta·ma·go
honey	蜂蜜	ha·chi·mi·tsu
horseradish	わさび	wa·sa·bi
jam	ジャム	ja·mu
noodles	麺	men
pepper	コショウ	koshō
rice (cooked)	ごはん	go·han
salt	塩	shi·o
seaweed	のり	no·ri
soy sauce	しょう油	shō·yu
sugar	砂糖	sa·tō

Drinks

beer	ビール	bī·ru
coffee	コーヒー	kō·hī
(orange) juice	(オレンジ) ジュース	(o·ren·ji·) jū·su
lemonade	レモネード	re·mo·nē·do
milk	ミルク	mi·ru·ku
mineral water	ミネラル ウォーター	mi·ne·ra·ru· wō·tā
red wine	赤ワイン	a·ka wain
sake	酒	sa·ke
tea	紅茶	kō·cha
water	水	mi·zu
white wine	白ワイン	shi·ro wain
yogurt	ヨーグルト	yō·gu·ru·to

EMERGENCIES

Help!	たすけて!	tas·ke·te
Go away!	離れろ!	ha·na·re·ro
I'm lost.	迷いました。	ma·yoy·mash·ta

Call the police.
警察を呼んで。 kē·sa·tsu o yon·de

Call a doctor.
医者を呼んで。 i·sha o yon·de

Where are the toilets?
トイレはどこですか? toy·re wa do·ko des ka

I'm ill.
私は病気です。 wa·ta·shi wa byō·ki des

It hurts here.
ここが痛いです。 ko·ko ga i·tai des

I'm allergic to ...
私は… wa·ta·shi wa ...
アレルギーです。 a·re·ru·gī des

SHOPPING & SERVICES

I'd like to buy ...
…をください。 ... o ku·da·sai

I'm just looking.
見ているだけです。 mi·te i·ru da·ke des

Question Words		
How?	どのように?	do·no yō ni
What?	なに?	na·ni
When?	いつ?	i·tsu
Where?	どこ?	do·ko
Which?	どちら?	do·chi·ra
Who?	だれ?	da·re
Why?	なぜ?	na·ze

Can I look at it?
それを見ても so·re o mi·te mo
いいですか? ī des ka

How much is it?
いくらですか? i·ku·ra des ka

That's too expensive.
高すぎます。 ta·ka·su·gi·mas

Can you give me a discount?
ディスカウント dis·kown·to
できますか? de·ki·mas ka

There's a mistake in the bill.
請求書に間違いが sē·kyū·sho ni ma·chi·gai ga
あります。 a·ri·mas

ATM	ATM	ē·tī·e·mu
credit card	クレジット カード	ku·re·jit·to· kā·do
post office	郵便局	yū·bin·kyo·ku
public phone	公衆電話	kō·shū·den·wa
tourist office	観光案内所	kan·kō·an·nai·jo

TIME & DATES

What time is it?
何時ですか? nan·ji des ka

It's (10) o'clock.
(10)時です。 (jū)·ji des

Half past (10).
(10)時半です。 (jū)·ji han des

am	午前	go·zen
pm	午後	go·go
Monday	月曜日	ge·tsu·yō·bi
Tuesday	火曜日	ka·yō·bi
Wednesday	水曜日	su·i·yō·bi
Thursday	木曜日	mo·ku·yō·bi
Friday	金曜日	kin·yō·bi
Saturday	土曜日	do·yō·bi
Sunday	日曜日	ni·chi·yō·bi
January	1月	i·chi·ga·tsu
February	2月	ni·ga·tsu
March	3月	san·ga·tsu
April	4月	shi·ga·tsu
May	5月	go·ga·tsu
June	6月	ro·ku·ga·tsu
July	7月	shi·chi·ga·tsu
August	8月	ha·chi·ga·tsu
September	9月	ku·ga·tsu
October	10月	jū·ga·tsu
November	11月	jū·i·chi·ga·tsu
December	12月	jū·ni·ga·tsu

Numbers

1	一	i·chi
2	二	ni
3	三	san
4	四	shi/yon
5	五	go
6	六	ro·ku
7	七	shi·chi/na·na
8	八	ha·chi
9	九	ku/kyū
10	十	jū
20	二十	ni·jū
30	三十	san·jū
40	四十	yon·jū
50	五十	go·jū
60	六十	ro·ku·jū
70	七十	na·na·jū
80	八十	ha·chi·jū
90	九十	kyū·jū
100	百	hya·ku
1000	千	sen

TRANSPORT

Public Transport

boat	船	fu·ne
bus	バス	bas
metro	地下鉄	chi·ka·te·tsu
plane	飛行機	hi·kō·ki
train	電車	den·sha
tram	市電	shi·den

What time does it leave?
これは何時に
出ますか？
ko·re wa nan·ji ni
de·mas ka

What time does it get to (Nagoya)?
これは(名古屋)に
何時に着きますか？
ko·re wa (na·go·ya) ni
nan·ji ni tsu·ki·mas ka

Does it stop at (Yokohama)?
(横浜)に
停まりますか？
(yo·ko·ha·ma) ni
to·ma·ri·mas ka

Please tell me when we get to (Osaka).
(大阪)に着いたら
教えてください。
(ō·sa·ka) ni tsu·i·ta·ra
o·shi·e·te ku·da·sai

A ... ticket (to Tokyo).	(東京行き の) ... 切符。	(tō·kyō·yu·ki no) ... kip·pu
one-way	片道	ka·ta·mi·chi
return	往復	ō·fu·ku

When's the ... (bus)?	...(バス)は 何時ですか？	... (bas) wa nan·ji des ka
first	始発の	shi·ha·tsu no
last	最終の	sai·shū no
next	次の	tsu·gi no

I'd like a/an ... seat.	...席をお願い します。	...se·ki o o·ne·gai shi·mas
aisle	通路側	tsū·ro·ga·wa
window	窓側	ma·do·ga·wa

bus stop	バス停	bas·tē
cancelled	キャンセル	kyan·se·ru
delayed	遅れ	o·ku·re
ticket window	窓口	ma·do·gu·chi
timetable	時刻表	ji·ko·ku·hyō
train station	駅	e·ki

Driving & Cycling

I'd like to hire a ...	...を借りたい のですが。	... o ka·ri·tai no des ga
4WD	四駆	yon·ku
bicycle	自転車	ji·ten·sha
car	自動車	ji·dō·sha
motorbike	オートバイ	ō·to·bai

child seat	チャイル ドシート	chai·ru·do· shī·to
diesel	ディーゼル	dī·ze·ru
helmet	ヘルメット	he·ru·met·to
mechanic	機械工	ki·kai·kō
petrol	ガソリン	ga·so·rin
pump	ポンプ	pom·pu
service station	ガソリン スタンド	ga·so·rin· stan·do

Is this the road to (Sapporo)?
この道は(札幌)
まで行きますか？
ko·no mi·chi wa (sap·po·ro)
ma·de i·ki·mas ka

(How long) Can I park here?
(どのくらい)ここに
駐車できますか？
(do·no·ku·rai) ko·ko ni
chū·sha de·ki·mas ka

The car has broken down (at Minato-ku).
車が(港区
で)壊れました。
ku·ru·ma ga (mi·na·to·ku
de) ko·wa·re·mash·ta

I have a flat tyre.
パンクしました。
pan·ku shi·mash·ta

I've run out of petrol.
ガス欠です。
gas·ke·tsu des

For lists of culinary terms, see p699; for useful words when visiting an onsen, see the box, p730; and for train terminology, see p762.

Ainu – indigenous people of Hokkaidō and parts of Northern Honshū

Amaterasu – sun goddess and link to the imperial throne

ANA – All Nippon Airways

annai-sho – information office

asa-ichi – morning market

bama – beach; see also *hama*

bashō – *sumō* tournament

bonsai – the art of growing miniature trees by careful pruning of branches and roots

bugaku – dance piece played by court orchestra in ancient Japan

buke yashiki – *samurai* residence

bunraku – classical puppet theatre which uses huge puppets to portray dramas similar to *kabuki*

Burakumin – traditionally outcasts associated with lowly occupations such as leatherwork; literally 'village people'

bushidō – a set of values followed by the *samurai*; literally 'the way of the warrior'

butsudan – Buddhist altar in Japanese homes

chō – city area (in large cities) between a *ku* and a *chōme* in size; also a street

chōchin – paper lantern

chōme – city area of a few blocks

daibutsu – Great Buddha

daimyō – regional lord under the *shōgun*

daira – plain; see also *taira*

dake – peak; see also *take*

dani – valley; see also *tani*

danjiri – festival float

dera – temple; see also *tera*

dō – temple or hall of a temple

eki – train station

fu – prefecture; see also *ken*

fusuma – sliding screen door

futsū – local train; literally 'ordinary'

gaijin – foreigner; literally 'outside people'

gasoreen sutando – petrol station

gasshō-zukuri – an architectural style (usually thatch-roofed); literally 'hands in prayer'

gawa – river; see also *kawa*

geiko – the Kyoto word for *geisha*

geisha – woman versed in arts and drama who entertains guests; *not* a prostitute

gekijō – theatre

genkan – foyer area where shoes are removed or replaced when entering or leaving a building

geta – traditional wooden sandals

gū – shrine

gun – county

habu – a venomous snake found in Okinawa

haiku – 17-syllable poem

hama – beach; see also *bama*

hanami – blossom viewing (usually cherry blossoms)

haniwa – earthenware figure found in tombs of the Kōfun period

hantō – peninsula

hara – uncultivated field or plain

hari – dragon-boat race

hatsu-mōde – first shrine visit of the new year

henro – pilgrim on the Shikoku 88 Temple Circuit

Hikari – the second-fastest type of *shinkansen*

hiragana – phonetic syllabary used to write Japanese words

hondō – main route or main hall

honsen – main rail line

ichi-nichi-jōsha-ken – day pass for unlimited travel on bus, tram or subway systems

ikebana – art of flower arrangement

irezumi – a tattoo or the art of tattooing

irori – hearth or fireplace

izakaya – pub-style eatery

JAF – Japan Automobile Federation

JAL – Japan Airlines

ji – temple

jigoku – boiling mineral hot spring, which is definitely not for bathing in; literally 'hells'

jikokuhyō – timetable or book of timetables

jima – island; see also *shima*

jingū – shrine

jinja – shrine

jizō – small stone statue of the Buddhist protector of travellers and children

JNTO – Japan National Tourism Organization

jō – castle

JR – Japan Railways

JTB – Japan Travel Bureau

juku – after-school 'cram' school

JYHA – Japan Youth Hostel Association

kabuki – a form of Japanese theatre based on popular legends, characterised by elaborate costumes, stylised acting and the use of male actors for all roles

kaikan – hall or building

kaikyō – channel/strait

kaisoku – rapid train

kaisū-ken – a book of transport tickets

kami – Shintō gods; spirits of natural phenomena

kamikaze – typhoon that sunk Kublai Khan's 13th-century invasion fleet and the name adopted by suicide pilots in the waning days of WWII; literally 'divine wind'

kana – the two phonetic syllabaries, *hiragana* and *katakana*

kanji – Chinese ideographic script used for writing Japanese; literally 'Chinese script'

Kannon – Bodhisattva of Compassion (commonly referred to as the Buddhist Goddess of Mercy)

karaoke – bar where you sing along with taped music; literally 'empty orchestra'

katakana – phonetic syllabary used to write foreign words

katamichi – one-way transport ticket

katana – Japanese sword

kawa – river; see also *gawa*

ken – prefecture; see also *fu*

kendo – oldest martial art; literally 'the way of the sword'

ki – life force, will

kimono – brightly coloured, robe-like traditional outer garment

kin'en-sha – nonsmoking train carriage

kippu – ticket

kissaten – coffee shop

ko – lake

kō – port

kōban – police box

kōen – park

kōgen – high plain (in the mountains); plateau

kokumin-shukusha – people's lodge; an inexpensive form of accommodation

kokuritsu kōen – national park

kotatsu – heated table with a quilt or cover over it to keep the legs and lower body warm

koto – 13-stringed instrument derived from a Chinese zither that is played flat on the floor

ku – ward

kūkō – airport

kura – earth-walled storehouse

kyō – gorge

kyūkō – ordinary express train (faster than a *futsū*, only stopping at certain stations)

machi – city area (in large cities) between a *ku* and *chōme* in size; also street

machiya – traditional Japanese townhouse or merchant house

maiko – apprentice *geisha*

mama-san – woman who manages a bar or club

maneki-neko – beckoning or welcoming cat figure frequently seen in restaurants and bars; it's supposed to attract customers and trade

manga – Japanese comics

matsuri – festival

meishi – business card

midori-no-madoguchi – ticket counter in large Japan Rail stations, where you can make more complicated bookings (look for the green band across the glass)

mikoshi – portable shrine carried during festivals

minato – harbour

minshuku – the Japanese equivalent of a B&B; family-run budget accommodation

misaki – cape; see also *saki*

mon – gate

mura – village

N'EX – Narita Express

NHK – Nihon Hōsō Kyōkai (Japan Broadcasting Corporation)

Nihon – Japanese word for 'Japan'; literally 'source of the sun'; also *Nippon*

ningyō – Japanese doll

Nippon – see *Nihon*

nō – classical Japanese drama performed on a bare stage

noren – cloth hung as a sunshade, typically carrying the name of the shop or premises; indicates that a restaurant is open for business

norikae-ken – transfer ticket (trams and buses)

NTT – Nippon Telegraph & Telephone Corporation

o- – prefix used to show respect to anything it is applied to

ōfuku – return ticket

o-furo – traditional Japanese bath

OL – 'office lady'; female clerical worker; pronounced 'ō-eru'

onnagata – male actor playing a woman's role (usually in *kabuki*)

onsen – hot spring; mineral-spa area, usually with accommodation

oshibori – hot towel provided in restaurants

pachinko – popular vertical pinball game, played in *pachinko* parlours

rakugo – Japanese raconteur, stand-up comic

rettō – island group; see also *shotō*

Rinzai – school of Zen Buddhism which places an emphasis on *kōan* (riddles)

romaji – Japanese roman script

rōnin – student who must resit university entrance exam; literally 'masterless *samurai*', sometimes referred to as 'wanderer'

ropeway – Japanese word for a cable car, tramway or funicular railway

rotemburo – open-air or outdoor bath

ryokan – traditional Japanese inn

saki – cape; see also *misaki*

sakoku – Japan's period of national seclusion prior to the Meiji Restoration

sakura – cherry blossom

salaryman – male white-collar worker, usually in a large firm

sama – even more respectful suffix than *san*; used in instances such as *o-kyaku-sama* – the 'honoured guest'

samurai – warrior class

san – mountain; also suffix which shows respect to the person it is applied to

san-sō – mountain hut or cottage

sentō – public bath

seppuku – ritual suicide by disembowelment

shamisen – a three-stringed traditional Japanese instrument that resembles a banjo or lute

shi – city (used to distinguish cities from prefectures of the same name, eg Kyoto-shi)

shikki – lacquerware

shima – island; see also *jima*

shinkaisoku – express train or special rapid train (usually on JR lines)

shinkansen – superexpress train, known in the West as 'bullet train'

Shintō – the indigenous religion of Japan; literally 'the way of the gods'

shirabyōshi – traditional dancer

shitamachi – traditionally the low-lying, less affluent parts of Tokyo

shodō – Japanese calligraphy; literally the 'way of writing'

shōgekijō – small theatre

shōgi – a version of chess in which each player has 20 pieces and the object is to capture the opponent's king

shōgun – former military ruler of Japan

shōgunate – military government

shōji – sliding rice-paper screen

shōjin ryōri – Buddhist vegetarian meal (served at temple lodgings etc)

shokudō – all-round restaurant

shotō – archipelago or island group; see also *rettō*

Shugendō – offbeat Buddhist school, which incorporates ancient shamanistic rites, *Shintō* beliefs and ascetic Buddhist traditions

shūji – a lesser form of *shodō*; literally 'the practice of letters'

shukubō – temple lodging

soapland – Japanese euphemism for a bathhouse offering sexual services, eg massage parlour

Sōtō – a school of Zen Buddhism which places emphasis on *zazen*

sumi-e – black-ink brush painting

sumō – Japanese wrestling

tabi – split-toed Japanese socks used when wearing *geta*

taiko – drum

taira – plain; see also *daira*

taisha – great shrine

take – peak; see also *dake*

taki – waterfall

tani – valley; see also *dani*

tanuki – racoon or dog-like folklore character frequently represented in ceramic figures

tatami – tightly woven floor matting on which shoes are never worn; traditionally, room size is defined by the number of tatami mats

teien – garden

tera – temple; see also *dera*

to – metropolis, eg Tokyo-to

tō – island

tokkyū – limited express train; faster than a *kyūkō*

tokonoma – sacred alcove in a house in which flowers may be displayed or a scroll hung

torii – entrance gate to a Shintō shrine

tōsu – lavatory

uchiwa – paper fan

ukiyo-e – woodblock print; literally 'pictures of the floating world'

wa – harmony, team spirit; also the old *kanji* used to denote Japan, and still used in Chinese and Japanese as a prefix to indicate things of Japanese origin, eg *wafuku* (Japanese-style clothing)

wabi – enjoyment of peace and tranquillity

wan – bay

washi – Japanese handmade paper

yabusame – samurai-style horseback archery

yakimono – pottery or ceramic ware

yakuza – Japanese mafia

yama – mountain; see also *zan*

yamabushi – mountain priest (Shugendō Buddhism practitioner)

yama-goya – mountain hut

yamato – a term of much debated origins that refers to the Japanese world

yamato-e – traditional Japanese painting

yatai – festival float; hawker stall

yukata – light cotton summer *kimono*, worn for lounging or casual use; standard issue when staying at a *ryokan*

zaibatsu – industrial conglomerate; the term arose pre-WWII but the Japanese economy is still dominated by huge firms such as Mitsui, Marubeni and Mitsubishi, which are involved in many different industries

zaki – cape

zan – mountain; see also *yama*

zazen – seated meditation emphasised in the Sōtō school of Zen Buddhism

Zen – an offshoot of Buddhism, introduced to Japan in the 12th century from China, that emphasises a direct, intuitive approach to enlightenment rather than rational analysis

behind the scenes

SEND US YOUR FEEDBACK

We love to hear from travellers – your comments keep us on our toes and help make our books better. Our well-travelled team reads every word on what you loved or loathed about this book. Although we cannot reply individually to postal submissions, we always guarantee that your feedback goes straight to the appropriate authors, in time for the next edition. Each person who sends us information is thanked in the next edition – and the most useful submissions are rewarded with a free book.

Visit **lonelyplanet.com/contact** to submit your updates and suggestions or to ask for help. Our award-winning website also features inspirational travel stories, news and discussions.

Note: We may edit, reproduce and incorporate your comments in Lonely Planet products such as guidebooks, websites and digital products, so let us know if you don't want your comments reproduced or your name acknowledged. For a copy of our privacy policy visit lonelyplanet.com/privacy.

OUR READERS

Many thanks to the travellers who used the last edition and wrote to us with helpful hints, useful advice and interesting anecdotes:

Niall Aitcheson, Holly Allin, John Atwood, Matthieu Bajolet, Ursula Barth, Adrien Barton, Chan, Cheung, Christine Bennett, Kathleen Bourke, Paolo Calvino, Rita Cavanagh, Anna Chenery, Julian Chichester, Julie Cromwell, Justin Dabner, Daniele De Blasio, Sabiha Docrat, Hannah Doughty, Petra Ederer, Moritz Eppenstein, Alexander Fieger, Ross Findlay, Anthea Freshwater, Gary, Katrin Hamacher, John Haptas, Matthew Hayday, Eric Heintz, Boon Hian Tan, Keith Hockly, Thomas Hudson, Ken Kasischke, David Kerkhoff, Lisa Knights, Carsten Krebs, Suzie Lee, Jasmine Liddington, Markus Lindner, Ze'ev Lipan, Wai Lun Chiu, Anna Macpherson, Janet Malowany, Laurence Mann, Clare Marks, Melissa Mayer, Irene Mittrop, Ignacio Morejon, Hiroko Nakahara, Regina Neubauer, Adam Newman, Yusuke Nishizaki, Dan Nover, Matt Patrick, Serge Pavlov, Marion Penaud, Oded Perry, Cassandre Pignon, Kate Ponton, Maarten Pullen, Gal Rotholz, Stacey Ruel, Joy Sachie Mori, Elie Sasson, Marieke Scholing, Wanda Serkowska, Tiffanie Shakespeare, Rebecca Shields, Andrea Slovakova, Maria Sole Paroni, Pete Stockall, Kunihiko Taguchi, Kiminori Takahata, Bernd Talasch, Felix Timischl, Nick Tsurikov, Raymond Tung, Derek Uram, Matt Van Der Peet, Bart Verbauwhede, Cher Walk, Matthieu Walterspiler, Tay Wan Cheng, Sandi Watanabe, Wendy, Simon Wickens, John Woolsey, Brendan Zwanikken

AUTHOR THANKS
Chris Rowthorn

Thanks to Hiroe, SK, Ijuin Koko, Hagiwara Keiko, Ito Mie, Daniel Milne, Wes Lang, Justin Giffin, Michael Lambe and Paul Carty. Thanks also to the great team of *Japan 12* authors: Andrew Bender, Laura Crawford, Matt Firestone, Tim Hornyak, Rebecca Milner, Brandon Presser and Tom Spurling. Thanks also to Emily Wolman, Liz Heynes, Nora Gregory and David Connolly. I would also like to thank all the readers of Lonely Planet's books on Japan who emailed us with great tips!

Andrew Bender

Nick Szasz, Hoashi Chie, Tsuji Mitsuo, Inanami Noriko, Morita Mikiko, Uezono Tomohiro, Iwasaki Yuka, Kajiwara Akiko, Sakamoto Hisatoshi, Akagi Nozomu, Tagami Jun-ichi, Araki Masakazu, Hiranuma Hidetoshi, Steve Beimel, Nancy Craft, Kishikawa Shingo, Nanae, and in-house, Emily Wolman, Averil Robertson and Chris Rowthorn.

Laura Crawford

Big thanks go to the many locals who gave advice and suggestions throughout my travels. Special *arigatō* also to Masako Sugiyama, Yasuko Yamaoka and Keiko Hasegawa. Thanks to Cath Lanigan and Emily Wolman for the opportunity, Annelies Mertens for encouragement, Chris Rowthorn and Liz Heynes for support, Naoko Akamatsu for friendship, and to the hard-working *Japan* team at Lonely Planet, especially Brana Vladisavljevic and Csanad Csutoros. Finally, thanks to my fella (and sometime map reader) Amrit.

Matthew D Firestone

This book is dedicated to my mother, who has astounded my family with her optimism and resilience, and will no doubt be around for many more dedication pages to come. Your presence was missed at many a Mahjong game this past year, but there are still countless tiles left to play. I would also like to acknowledge my lovely wife Aki, without whom my wonderful life in Japan would not be possible. Finally, a special thanks to the entire Lonely Planet *Japan* team, particularly Chris, who has overseen this wonderful travel tome through so many editions.

Timothy Hornyak

A big *arigatō* to my colleagues Chris Rowthorn, Andy Bender, Emily Wolman, Brandon Presser, and other Lonely Planet staff, as well as Ari Taira, Mamiko Hokari, Kyoko Abe, Gary Wyckoff on Ishigaki-jima, Kowaguchi-san on Yoron-tō, Minshuku Sango Beach on Amami-Ōshima, Sachiko Nakamichi, Jiro Takeuchi, Yuka Tanaka and Hiroe Teramura. I'd also like to thank the staff of countless tourist offices, from the mountains of Central Honshū to the southern- and westernmost isles of the Southwest Islands – they made it all so much easier. My sincere gratitude as well to my family for their unflagging support, enthusiasm and patience.

Rebecca Milner

Thank you to my family for teaching me to travel well. To Chikara for everything, but especially for Mt Fuji. Thank you to Robin, Kazz, Yusuke, Kato-san and Watanabe-san for their input on the Mt Fuji section and to the following people for their time, support and company: Naomi, Jesse, Mark, Howard, Mike, Dex, Michelle, Yasuko-san, Pierre, Keita, Tatsuya, Carlos, Gideon, Baba-san, Teppō-san, Kogi-san, Eiko-baba, Ryō-san, the Lonely Planet *Japan* team and my wonderful, neglected friends.

Brandon Presser

First and foremost, I'd like to thank my dear friend Misa – I could not have done this without you! A very special thank you to Ariel, Makoto, Cécile, Naomi, Rinko, Marissa, Aiko, Taro, Richard, Jud, BAPE, the JNTO, and everyone else who took time out of their busy schedules to help me piece together my coverage. At Lonely Planet, thank you to Emily, captain Chris, Liz, Brana, Nora, and my fellow authors. And Joanne!

Tom Spurling

In Tokushima, thanks to Norman for showing me the way to Ingrid's, and Ten and Matt L for their goofy-footed expertise. Thanks to all at the Horseshoe Bar. In Ohkihama, thanks to Mitsu for the inspiration. To Paul at Chiiori, a very merry Xmas. Massive high-fives to Tom Lawler for enduring the trip. At Lonely Planet-land, thanks to Chris Rowthorn for the guiding light and Emily Wolman for the green light. Lastly, to Lucy and Oliver, so much love!

THIS BOOK

This 12th edition of Lonely Planet's *Japan* was researched and written by a team of stellar authors, led by Chris Rowthorn, who also coordinated and contributed to the 11th edition. This guidebook was commissioned in Lonely Planet's Oakland, USA, office and produced by the following:

Commissioning Editor
Emily K Wolman

Coordinating Editors
Branislava Vladisavljevic, Kate Whitfield

Coordinating Cartographer Csanad Csutoros

Coordinating Layout Designer Frank Deim

Managing Editors
Brigitte Ellemor, Liz Heynes, Annelies Mertens, Kirsten Rawlings

Managing Cartographers
David Connolly, Amanda Sierp

Managing Layout Designers Chris Girdler, Jane Hart

Assisting Editors Janet Austin, Sarah Koel, Alan Murphy, Kristin Odijk, Martine Power, Simon Williamson

Assisting Cartographers
Katalin Dadi-Racz, Marc Milinkovic

Cover Research Naomi Parker

Internal Image Research Sabrina Dalbesio

Thanks to Yvonne Bischofberger, Helen Christinis, Diana Duggan, Nora Gregory, Keiko Hagiwara, Yvonne Kirk, Lisa Knights, Anna Metcalfe, Susan Paterson, Raphael Richards, Averil Robertson, Juan Winata

ACKNOWLEDGMENTS

Climate map data adapted from Peel MC, Finlayson BL & McMahon TA (2007) 'Updated World Map of the Köppen-Geiger Climate Classification', *Hydrology and Earth System Sciences*, 11, 163344.

Cover photograph: Bridge crossing garden pond at New Otani Hotel, Chiyoda-Ku. Tokyo, Kanto, Japan, North-East Asia, Asia, John Sones/Lonely Planet Images.

Many of the images in this guide are available for licensing from Lonely Planet Images: www.lonelyplanetimages.com.

NOTES

index

000 Map pages
000 Photo pages

000 Map pages
000 Photo pages

how to use this book

These symbols will help you find the listings you want:

👁 Sights   🎊 Festivals & Events   ⭐ Entertainment

🏃 Activities   🛏 Sleeping   🛍 Shopping

🐟 Courses   🍴 Eating   ℹ️ Information/Transport

👉 Tours   🍷 Drinking

These symbols give you the vital information for each listing:

📱	Telephone Numbers	📶	Wi-Fi Access	🚌	Bus
⊙	Opening Hours	🏊	Swimming Pool	🚢	Ferry
Ⓟ	Parking	🍽	Vegetarian Selection	Ⓜ	Metro
🚭	Nonsmoking	📖	English-Language Menu	Ⓢ	Subway
❄	Air-Conditioning	👶	Family-Friendly	⊖	London Tube
@	Internet Access	🐾	Pet-Friendly	🚋	Tram
				🚆	Train

Reviews are organised by author preference.

Look out for these icons:

TOP CHOICE Our author's recommendation

FREE No payment required

🌿 A green or sustainable option

Our authors have nominated these places as demonstrating a strong commitment to sustainability – for example by supporting local communities and producers, operating in an environmentally friendly way, or supporting conservation projects.

Map Legend

Sights
- 🏖 Beach
- 🛕 Buddhist
- 🏰 Castle
- ✝ Christian
- 🕉 Hindu
- ☪ Islamic
- ✡ Jewish
- 🗿 Monument
- 🏛 Museum/Gallery
- ⛪ Ruin
- 🍇 Winery/Vineyard
- 🐾 Zoo
- ⊙ Other Sight

Activities, Courses & Tours
- 🤿 Diving/Snorkelling
- 🛶 Canoeing/Kayaking
- ⛷ Skiing
- 🏄 Surfing
- 🏊 Swimming/Pool
- 🚶 Walking
- 🏄 Windsurfing
- ⊙ Other Activity/Course/Tour

Sleeping
- 🛏 Sleeping
- ⛺ Camping

Eating
- 🍴 Eating

Drinking
- ☕ Drinking
- ☕ Cafe

Entertainment
- 🎭 Entertainment

Shopping
- 🛍 Shopping

Information
- 🏦 Bank
- 🏛 Embassy/Consulate
- ✚ Hospital/Medical
- @ Internet
- 👮 Police
- 📮 Post Office
- ☎ Telephone
- 🚻 Toilet
- ℹ Tourist Information
- • Other Information

Transport
- ✈ Airport
- ⊗ Border Crossing
- 🚌 Bus
- Cable Car/Funicular
- Cycling
- Ferry
- Ⓜ Metro
- Monorail
- Ⓟ Parking
- Petrol Station
- 🚕 Taxi
- Train/Railway
- Tram
- • Other Transport

Routes
- Tollway
- Freeway
- Primary
- Secondary
- Tertiary
- Lane
- Unsealed Road
- Plaza/Mall
- Steps
- Tunnel
- Pedestrian Overpass
- Walking Tour
- Walking Tour Detour
- Path

Geographic
- 🏠 Hut/Shelter
- 🔦 Lighthouse
- 👁 Lookout
- ▲ Mountain/Volcano
- 🌴 Oasis
- 🏞 Park
-)(Pass
- ⊙ Picnic Area
- 💧 Waterfall

Population
- 🔵 Capital (National)
- ◉ Capital (State/Province)
- 🔴 City/Large Town
- 🔸 Town/Village

Boundaries
- International
- State/Province
- Disputed
- Regional/Suburb
- Marine Park
- Cliff
- Wall

Hydrography
- River, Creek
- Intermittent River
- Swamp/Mangrove
- Reef
- Canal
- Water
- Dry/Salt/Intermittent Lake
- Glacier

Areas
- Beach/Desert
- + + + Cemetery (Christian)
- × × × Cemetery (Other)
- Park/Forest
- Sportsground
- Sight (Building)
- Top Sight (Building)

Matthew D Firestone

Northern Honshū; Sapporo & Hokkaidō; Skiing in Japan Matt is a trained anthropologist and epidemiologist who has authored more than two dozen guidebooks for Lonely Planet, and covered far-flung destinations from the Darién Gap to the Dead Sea. When he's not living the Tokyo high life with his wonderful wife or out in the field on assignment, he likes to spend his free time exploring the American West with his parents, or catching up with the in-laws on the foothills of Mt Fuji.

Timothy Hornyak

The Japan Alps & Central Honshū; Okinawa & the Southwest Islands A native of Montreal, Tim Hornyak moved to Japan in 1999 after watching Kurosawa's *Ran* too many times. Since then, he has written on Japanese culture, technology and history for CNET News, *Scientific American* and *Far Eastern Economic Review*. He has played bass in a rock band in Tokyo, lectured on Japanese robots at the Kennedy Center in Washington, and travelled to the heart of Hokkaidō to find the remains of a forgotten theme park called Canadian World. Tim is the author of *Loving the Machine: The Art and Science of Japanese Robots* and his favourite robot is Astro Boy, but he firmly believes that the greatest Japanese invention of all time is the onsen.

Rebecca Milner

Mt Fuji & Around Tokyo Rebecca first travelled 'around Tokyo' when she moved to the Japanese capital in 2002 from California. Since then, and in between long trips around Asia, she paid her dues teaching English, waiting tables and studying Japanese. These days she works as a freelance writer, publishing regularly on CNN Go, Tokyo Art Beat and in Tokyo's local *Metropolis* magazine. She is also currently working with a Japanese media team on a project documenting little-known regional cuisines, for which she has been travelling to villages from Hokkaidō to Okinawa. For this book, she found herself revisiting in almost uncanny chronological order the places that formed her first impression of Japan nine years ago. This is Rebecca's first Lonely Planet title.

Brandon Presser

Tokyo; Arts & Architecture Tokyo has held a special place in Brandon's heart for as long as he can remember. At Harvard University he wrote his thesis on the city's fascinating hybrid architecture and has since collaborated with many Japanese architects throughout his professional career. These days Brandon has joined the glamorous ranks of eternal nomadism – he travels the world, pen in hand – and has contributed to more than 20 Lonely Planet titles, from *Iceland* to *Thailand* and many lands in between.

Tom Spurling

Shikoku Tom Spurling has worked on Lonely Planet guides to Central America, Australia, Turkey and India. His first experience in Japan was a naked job interview in a sports club near Kōbe where his apartment overlooked the castle of the nationally televised TV series *The Samurai*. When not teaching English as a very foreign language, he's been humbled by plum wine–drunk kendo masters, explored the mossier side of Kansai's rock bars and gardens with a Zen Buddhist techno DJ and ashamedly travelled from Hokkaidō to Okinawa on a forged Japan Rail pass. For this edition, Tom discovered world-class surf beaches and a super orange vitamin drink. Unfortunately, by following the great Buddhist saint Kōbō Daishi's pilgrimage in the wrong direction around the island, he may have unwittingly released a powerful demon force.

OUR STORY

A beat-up old car, a few dollars in the pocket and a sense of adventure. In 1972 that's all Tony and Maureen Wheeler needed for the trip of a lifetime – across Europe and Asia overland to Australia. It took several months, and at the end – broke but inspired – they sat at their kitchen table writing and stapling together their first travel guide, *Across Asia on the Cheap*. Within a week they'd sold 1500 copies. Lonely Planet was born.

Today, Lonely Planet has offices in Melbourne, London and Oakland, with more than 600 staff and writers. We share Tony's belief that 'a great guidebook should do three things: inform, educate and amuse'.

OUR WRITERS

Chris Rowthorn

Coordinating Author; Kyoto; Kansai Born in England and raised in the USA, Chris has lived in Kyoto since 1992. Soon after his arrival in Kyoto, Chris started studying the Japanese language and culture. In 1995 he became a regional correspondent for the *Japan Times*. He joined Lonely Planet in 1996 and has worked on guides to Kyoto, Tokyo, Japan and hiking in Japan. When not on the road, he spends his time seeking out Kyoto's best restaurants, temples, hiking trails and gardens. Chris wrote a book in Japanese with professional guide Koko Ijuin, called *Pro ga Oshieru: Genba no Eigo Tsuyaku Gaido Skiru* (Pro English Guide Skills), for Japanese guides who want to explain the country to Western tourists. He conducts walking tours of Kyoto, Nara and Tokyo. For more on Chris, check out his website at www.chrisrowthorn.com.

Andrew Bender

Kyūshū France was closed, so after college Andy left his native New England for Japan. It ended up being a life-changing journey, as visits to Japan often are. He's since mastered chopsticks, the language, karaoke and taking his shoes off at the door. Now, from his home base in Los Angeles, he writes about Japan for the *Los Angeles Times*, *Forbes*, *Travel + Leisure* and inflight magazines, not to mention over a half-dozen Lonely Planet titles. In an effort towards ever greater trans-Pacific harmony, Andy also assists business with cross-cultural consulting and sometimes helps tour groups around Japan. Find out more at www.wheres-andy-now.com.

Laura Crawford

Hiroshima & Western Honshū English-born and Australian-raised, Laura first went to Japan after a last-minute undergraduate decision to major in Japanese led to university in Kansai. She later travelled up and down the country, set up home in Osaka for two years, returned to Oz to write a thesis on Japanese English, and eventually landed a job as an editor in Lonely Planet's Melbourne office. Her favourite on-the-road memory: walking through the predawn mist to take an onsen soak in Yunotsu.

OVER MORE
PAGE WRITERS

Published by Lonely Planet Publications Pty Ltd
ABN 36 005 607 983
12th edition – Sep 2011
ISBN 978 1 74179 805 0
© Lonely Planet 2011   Photographs © as indicated 2011
10 9 8 7 6 5 4 3 2 1
Printed in Singapore

Although the authors and Lonely Planet have taken all reasonable care in preparing this book, we make no warranty about the accuracy or completeness of its content and, to the maximum extent permitted, disclaim all liability arising from its use.